Contemporary Authors®

NEW REVISION SERIES

ISSN 0275-7176

Contemporary Authors®

A Bio-Bibliographical Guide to
Current Writers in Fiction, General Nonfiction,
Poetry, Journalism, Drama, Motion Pictures,
Television, and Other Fields

JAMES G. LESNIAK
Editor

NEW REVISION SERIES
volume 32

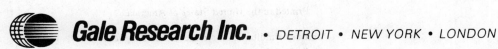 Gale Research Inc. • DETROIT • NEW YORK • LONDON

STAFF

James G. Lesniak, *Editor, New Revision Series*

Marilyn K. Basel, Kevin S. Hile, Sharon Malinowski, Michael E. Mueller, Kenneth R. Shepherd,
Diane Telgen, and Thomas Wiloch, *Associate Editors*

Elizabeth A. Des Chenes, Margaret Mazurkiewicz, Jani Prescott, Edward G. Scheff,
and Michaela Swart Wilson, *Assistant Editors*

Jean W. Ross and Walter W. Ross, *Interviewers*

Marian Gonsior, Anne Janette Johnson, Tom Kozikowski, Emily J. McMurray, Susan Salter,
Les Stone, and Louise Westling, *Contributing Editors*

Hal May, *Senior Editor, Contemporary Authors*

Victoria B. Cariappa, *Research Manager*
Mary Rose Bonk, *Research Supervisor*

Jane A. Cousins, Andrew Guy Malonis, and Norma Sawaya, *Editorial Associates*

Mike Avolio, Reginald A. Carlton, Shirley Gates, Sharon McGilvray,
and Tracey Head Turbett, *Editorial Assistants*

Special acknowledgment is due to members of the
Contemporary Authors Original Volumes staff who assisted in the preparation of this volume.

The paper used in this publication meets the minimum requirements
of American National Standard for Information Sciences—Permanence
Paper for Printed Library Materials, ANSI Z39.48-1984.

Library of Congress Catalog Card Number 81-640179
ISBN 0-8103-1986-1
ISSN 0275-7176

Printed in the United States of America.

Published simultaneously in the United Kingdom
by Gale Research International Limited
(An affiliated company of Gale Research Inc.)

Contents

Authors and Media People
Featured in This Volume...vii

Preface.. ix

Volume Update Chart... xiii

Author Listings...1

Indexing note: All *Contemporary Authors New Revision Series* entries are indexed in the *Contemporary Authors* cumulative index, which is published separately and distributed with even-numbered *Contemporary Authors* original volumes.

Authors and Media People
Featured in This Volume

Jean Anouilh (French playwright who died in 1987)—Anouilh, a popular playwright who won Tony Awards for *Thieves' Carnival* and *Becket,* presented a dim view of society through comic and tragic works that contrasted an idealistic individual with his or her corrupt surroundings.

Barbara Taylor Bradford (British novelist)—Author of such best-selling works as *A Woman of Substance* and *To Be the Best,* Bradford tells stories of wealth and intrigue that are popular for their strong female characters.

James L. Brooks (American screenwriter and director)—Known as the creator of television's "Mary Tyler Moore Show," "Taxi," and "Tracey Ullman Show," Brooks is now highly respected as a filmmaker due to his works *Broadcast News* and the Oscar-winning *Terms of Endearment.*

Luis Bunuel (Spanish screenwriter and director who died in 1983)—Bunuel was one of the world's most acclaimed filmmakers; movies such as *An Andalusian Dog, Nazarin,* and *Viridiana* shocked audiences with their surrealistic attacks on conventional morality and organized religion.

Ernesto Cardenal (Nicaraguan poet, priest and political activist)—In works such as *With Walker in Nicaragua and Other Early Poems, 1949-1954* and *Psalms of Struggle and Liberation,* Cardenal uses pre-Columbian native-American cultural values and Christian ideals in speaking for justice and self-determination.

Jimmy Carter (Thirty-ninth president of the United States)—Since leaving the White House in 1981, Carter—who writes all his material himself—has produced several books on subjects from Middle Eastern politics to retirement to fly fishing.

Robert Coles (American child psychiatrist and author)—Coles, who won a Pulitzer Prize for *Children of Crisis,* is noted for his humanistic, individualized approach to documenting the development of children under stress. (Entry contains interview.)

Jose Donoso (Chilean writer, journalist, and translator)—Donoso, one of Latin America's "Boom" writers, presents ominous, complex portraits of his native society through his many short stories and novels such as *The Obscene Bird of Night.*

Frances FitzGerald (American journalist and essayist)—Since winning a National Book Award and Pulitzer Prize for *Fire in the Lake,* her examination of the American presence in Vietnam, FitzGerald has focused on domestic issues in *America Revised* and *Cities on a Hill.* (Entry contains interview.)

Joseph Frank (American biographer and literary critic)—Frank's multi-volume biography *Dostoevsky,* which considers the author's cultural background and its effect on his fiction, is considered the definitive work on the Russian novelist. (Entry contains interview.)

Max Frisch (Swiss dramatist and novelist)—In novels such as *I'm Not Stiller* and plays such as *The Firebugs,* Frisch uses a sometimes surrealistic style to investigate the question of man's identity and the consequences of denying one's true self.

Carlos Fuentes (Mexican novelist, essayist, and playwright)—An influential literary critic as well as the author of noted novels *The Death of Artemio Cruz* and the best-selling *The Old Gringo,* Fuentes explores Mexican themes through his innovative narrative style.

Theodor Seuss Geisel (American author and illustrator of books for children)—Best known as Dr. Seuss to his many fans, the author of *The Cat in the Hat* broke new ground in children's literature with his whimsical illustrations and energetic verse.

Beth Henley (American playwright and screenwriter)—Henley, who won a Pulitzer Prize for *Crimes of the Heart,* features the concerns of young Southern women in plays that are praised for their ironic humor and memorable characters.

S. E. Hinton (American author of young adult fiction)—Published when she was just seventeen, Hinton's *The Outsiders* ushered in an era of realism in young adult fiction with its graphic portrayal of teenage class violence.

Elia Kazan (American stage and film director)—Kazan has earned Tonys and Oscars for his direction of such socially conscious works as *Death of a Salesman, Cat on a Hot Tin Roof, East of Eden,* and *On the Waterfront;* he has also written an autobiography, *A Life.*

Ursula K. Le Guin (American science-fiction writer)—Le Guin's science fiction novels feature thoughtful characters who challenge harsh and unyielding ideological structures. Winner of the Hugo and Nebula Awards for *The Left Hand of Darkness,* Le Guin earned the Hugo, Nebula, Jules Verne, and Jupiter Awards for *The Dispossessed: An Ambiguous Utopia.* (Entry contains interview.)

Stanislaw Lem (Polish science-fiction writer)—With over 20 million books in print, Lem is an internationally known writer of science fiction who often deals with human/alien or human/machine interactions. John Leonard of the *New York Times* describes him as "a Jorge Luis Borges for the space age," while Kurt Vonnegut, Jr., writing in the *Nation,* calls him "a master of utterly terminal pessimism."

Claude Levi-Strauss (French anthropologist)—One of the most distinguished anthropologists in the world today, Levi-Strauss is credited with founding structural anthropology, the study of the underlying patterns of thought in human activity. His books include *A World on the Wane* and *Introduction to a Science of Mythology.*

Ann M. Martin (American children's writer)—Martin is the author of the best-selling "Baby-sitters Club," a series of children's books featuring the adventures of teenaged girls and the children they babysit. (Entry contains interview.)

Kate Millett (American feminist)—Millett's book *Sexual Politics,* a 1970 bestseller, made her one of the leading spokespersons for the feminist movement. Later titles, including *Flying* and *The Basement,* explore the psycho-social dilemmas of sexual discrimination.

Octavio Paz (Mexican poet and essayist)—Winner of the 1990

Nobel Prize for Literature, Paz writes of his native Mexico but is interested in finding harmony in opposing forces from many cultural traditions. His books include *The Labyrinth of Solitude: Life and Thought in Mexico* and *The Monkey Grammarian.*

Anthony Powell (British novelist)—Author of "A Dance to the Music of Time," a twelve-volume series of novels tracing several generations of England's upper class, Powell is one of England's leading novelists. "Dance" is described by Naomi Bliven in the *New Yorker* as "one of the most important works of fiction since the Second World War." Named a Commander of the Order of the British Empire, Powell has also won the James Tait Black Memorial Prize, for the novel *At Lady Molly's,* and the T. S. Eliot Award for the body of his work.

Manuel Puig (Argentinian novelist who died in 1990)—Combining cinematic influences with the trappings of popular culture, Puig wrote ironic novels of Argentinian rural life. Among his best-known works are *Betrayed by Rita Hayworth* and *Kiss of the Spider Woman.*

Ruth Rendell (British mystery novelist)—Rendell's mystery novels featuring Chief Inspector Reginald Wexford of rural Sussex are noted for their deft plotting and likeable characters. Under the pseudonym Barbara Vine, she also writes psychological thrillers. Rendell has won two Edgar Allan Poe Awards, as well as three Gold Dagger Awards. (Entry contains interview.)

Steven Spielberg (American filmmaker)—Of the top twenty box office hits of all time, Spielberg has written, produced, or directed seven, including "Jaws," "Close Encounters of the Third Kind," "ET: The Extraterrestrial," and "The Color Purple." In 1987, Spielberg received the Irving J. Thalberg Award from the Academy of Motion Picture Arts and Sciences.

Allen Tate (American poet and critic who died in 1979)—Tate wrote of the American South and championed its agrarian, essentially conservative, values. A member of the Fugitives, a group of writers including Robert Penn Warren, John Crowe Ransom, and Merrill Moore, Tate emphasized the importance of Southern literature and had an enormous impact on criticism of the 1930s. He won the Bollingen Prize, the Academy of American Poets Award, and other prizes for his poetry.

Thomas Tryon (American actor and novelist)—After a successful acting career, including the title role in 1963's "The Cardinal," Tryon became a best-selling novelist with his first book, *The Other.* Subsequent novels include *Harvest Home, Crowned Heads,* and *All That Glitters.*

Eudora Welty (American short story writer, novelist, and memoirist)—Welty is noted for her stories of the American South and for her ability to honestly portray her characters' emotions. Winner of a Pulitzer Prize, two American Book Awards, and a National Book Critics Circle Award, Welty is considered one of America's most prominent writers of fiction. Her books include *The Ponder Heart, The Optimist's Daughter, The Collected Stories of Eudora Welty,* and *One Writer's Beginnings.*

George F. Will (American journalist and political commentator)—Winner of a Pulitzer Prize for distinguished commentary, Will is a conservative newspaper columnist and television commentator with an estimated audience of twenty million Americans. His books *The Pursuit of Happiness, and Other Sobering Thoughts* and *Statecraft as Soulcraft: What Government Does* explore the relationship between government and public morality.

Preface

The *Contemporary Authors New Revision Series* provides completely updated information on authors listed in earlier volumes of *Contemporary Authors (CA)*. Entries for active individual authors from *any* volume of *CA* may be included in a volume of the *New Revision Series*. The sketches appearing in *New Revision Series* Volume 32, for example, were selected from more than twenty previously published *CA* volumes.

As always, the most recent *Contemporary Authors* cumulative index continues to be the user's guide to the location of an individual author's listing.

Compilation Methods

The editors make every effort to secure information directly from the authors. Copies of all sketches in selected *CA* volumes published several years ago are routinely sent to the listees at their last-known addresses. Authors mark material to be deleted or changed and insert any new personal data, new affiliations, new writings, new work in progress, new sidelights, and new biographical/critical sources. All returns are assessed, more comprehensive research is done, if necessary, and those sketches requiring significant change are completely updated and published in the *New Revision Series*.

If, however, authors fail to reply or are now deceased, biographical dictionaries are checked for new information (a task made easier through the use of Gale's *Biography and Genealogy Master Index* and other Gale biographical indexes), as are bibliographical sources such as *Cumulative Book Index* and *The National Union Catalog*. Using data from such sources, revision editors select and revise nonrespondents' entries that need substantial updating. Sketches not personally reviewed by the biographees are marked with an asterisk (*) to indicate that these listings have been revised from secondary sources believed to be reliable, but they have not been personally reviewed for this edition by the authors sketched.

In addition, reviews and articles in major periodicals, lists of prestigious awards, and, particularly, requests from *CA* users are monitored so that writers on whom new information is in demand can be identified and revised listings prepared promptly.

Format

CA entries provide biographical and bibliographical information in an easy-to-use format. For example, individual paragraphs featuring such rubrics as "Addresses," "Career," and "Awards, Honors" ensure that a reader seeking specific information can quickly focus on the pertinent portion of an entry. In sketch sections headed "Writings," the title of each book, play, and other published or unpublished work appears on a separate line, clearly distinguishing one title from another. This same convenient bibliographical presentation is also featured in the "Biographical/Critical Sources" sections of sketches where individual book and periodical titles are listed on separate lines. *CA* readers can therefore quickly scan these often-lengthy bibliographies to find the titles they need.

Comprehensive Revision

All listings in this volume have been revised and/or augmented in various ways, though the amount and type of change vary with the author. In many instances, sketches are totally rewritten, and the resulting *New Revision Series* entries are often considerably longer than the authors' previous listings. Revised entries include additions of or changes in such information as degrees, mailing addresses, literary agents, career items, career-related and civic activities, memberships, awards, work in progress, and biographical/critical sources. They may also include extensive bibliographical additions and informative new sidelights.

Writers of Special Interest

CA's editors make every effort to include in each *New Revision Series* volume a substantial number of revised entries on active authors and media people of special interest to *CA*'s readers. Since the *New Revision Series* also includes sketches on noteworthy deceased writers, a significant amount of work on the part of *CA*'s editors goes into the revision of entries on important deceased authors. Some of the prominent writers, both living and deceased, whose sketches are contained in this volume are noted in the list on pages vii-viii headed Authors and Media People Featured in This Volume.

Exclusive Interviews

CA provides exclusive, primary information on certain authors in the form of interviews. Prepared specifically for *CA,* the never-before-published conversations presented in the section of the sketch headed "*CA* Interview" give users the opportunity to learn the authors' thoughts, in depth, about their craft. Subjects chosen for interviews are, the editors feel, authors who hold special interest for *CA*'s readers.

Authors and journalists in this volume whose sketches contain exclusive interviews are Robert Coles, Frances FitzGerald, Joseph Frank, Ward Just, Ursula K. Le Guin, Ann M. Martin, and Ruth Rendell.

Contemporary Authors Autobiography Series

Designed to complement the information in *CA* original and revision volumes, the *Contemporary Authors Autobiography Series* provides autobiographical essays written by important current authors. Each volume contains from twenty to thirty specially commissioned autobiographies and is illustrated with numerous personal photographs supplied by the authors. Common topics of discussion for these authors include their motivations for writing, the people and experiences that shaped their careers, the rewards they derive from their work, and their impressions of the current literary scene.

Autobiographies included in the series can be located through both the *CA* cumulative index and the *Contemporary Authors Autobiography Series* cumulative index, which lists not only personal names but also titles of works, geographical names, subjects, and schools of writing.

Contemporary Authors Bibliographical Series

The *Contemporary Authors Bibliographical Series* is a comprehensive survey of writings by and about the most important authors since World War II in the United States and abroad. Each volume concentrates on a specific genre and nationality and features approximately ten major writers. Series entries, which complement the information in other *CA* volumes, consist of three parts: a primary bibliography that lists works written by the author, a secondary bibliography that lists works about the author, and a bibliographical essay that thoroughly analyzes the merits and deficiencies of major critical and scholarly works.

These bibliographies can be located through both the *CA* cumulative index and the *Contemporary Authors Bibliographical Series* cumulative author index. A cumulative critic index, citing critics discussed in the bibliographical essays, also appears in each *Bibliographical Series* volume.

CA Numbering System

Occasionally questions arise about the *CA* numbering system. Despite numbers like "97-100" and "131," the entire *CA* series consists of only 105 physical volumes with the publication of *CA New Revision Series* Volume 32. The following information notes changes in the numbering system, as well as in cover design, to help users better understand the organization of the entire *CA* series.

CA First Revisions	• 1-4R through 41-44R (11 books) *Cover:* Brown with black and gold trim. There will be no further *First Revisions* because revised entries are now being handled exclusively through the more efficient *New Revision Series* mentioned below.
CA Original Volumes	• 45-48 through 97-100 (14 books) *Cover:* Brown with black and gold trim. • 101 through 131 (31 books) *Cover:* Blue and black with orange bands. The same as previous *CA* original volumes but with a new, simplified numbering system and new cover design.
CA New Revision Series	• *CANR*-1 through *CANR*-32 (32 books) *Cover:* Blue and black with green bands. Includes only sketches requiring extensive change; **sketches are taken from any previously published *CA* volume.**

CA **Permanent Series**	• *CAP*-1 and *CAP*-2 (2 books) *Cover:* Brown with red and gold trim. There will be no further *Permanent Series* volumes because revised entries are now being handled exclusively through the more efficient *New Revision Series* mentioned above.
CA **Autobiography Series**	• *CAAS*-1 through *CAAS*-12 (12 books) *Cover:* Blue and black with pink and purple bands. Presents specially commissioned autobiographies by leading contemporary writers to complement the information in *CA* original and revision volumes.
CA **Bibliographical Series**	• *CABS*-1 through *CABS*-3 (3 books) *Cover:* Blue and black with blue bands. Provides comprehensive bibliographical information on published works by and about major modern authors.

Retaining *CA* Volumes

As new volumes in the series are published, users often ask which *CA* volumes, if any, can be discarded. The Volume Update Chart on page xiii is designed to assist users in keeping their collections as complete as possible. All volumes in the left column of the chart should be retained to have the most complete, up-to-date coverage possible; volumes in the right column can be discarded if the appropriate replacements are held.

Cumulative Index Should Always Be Consulted

The key to locating an individual author's listing is the *CA* cumulative index, which is published separately and distributed with even-numbered original volumes. Since the *CA* cumulative index provides access to *all* entries in the *CA* series, the latest cumulative index should always be consulted to find the specific volume containing a listee's original or most recently revised sketch.

Those authors whose entries appear in the *New Revision Series* are listed in the *CA* cumulative index with the designation **CANR-** in front of the specific volume number. For the convenience of those who do not have *New Revision Series* volumes, the cumulative index also notes the specific earlier volumes of *CA* in which the sketch appeared. Below is a sample index citation for an author whose revised entry appears in a *New Revision Series* volume.

> Clavell, James (duMaresq) 1925- CANR-26
>   Earlier sketch in CA 25-28R
>   See also CLC 6, 25

For the most recent *CA* information on Clavell, users should refer to Volume 26 of the *New Revision Series*, as designated by "CANR-26"; if that volume is unavailable, refer to *CA* 25-28 First Revision, as indicated by "Earlier sketch in CA 25-28R," for his 1977 listing. (And if *CA* 25-28 First Revision is unavailable, refer to *CA* 25-28, published in 1971, for Clavell's original listing.)

Sketches not eligible for inclusion in a *New Revision Series* volume because the biographee or a revision editor has verified that no significant change is required will, of course, be available in previously published *CA* volumes. Users should always consult the most recent *CA* cumulative index to determine the location of these authors' entries.

For the convenience of *CA* users, the *CA* cumulative index also includes references to all entries in these related Gale literary series: *Authors and Artists for Young Adults, Authors in the News, Bestsellers, Black Writers, Children's Literature Review, Concise Dictionary of American Literary Biography, Contemporary Literary Criticism, Dictionary of Literary Biography, Short Story Criticism, Something About the Author, Something About the Author Autobiography Series, Twentieth-Century Literary Criticism,* and *Yesterday's Authors of Books For Children.*

Acknowledgments

The editors wish to thank Judith S. Baughman for her assistance with copyediting.

Suggestions Are Welcome

The editors welcome comments and suggestions from users on any aspect of the *CA* series. If readers would like to suggest authors whose *CA* entries should appear in future volumes of the *New Revision Series,* they are cordially invited to write: The Editors, *Contemporary Authors New Revision Series,* 835 Penobscot Bldg., Detroit, MI 48226-4094; or, call toll-free at 1-800-347-GALE.

Volume Update Chart

IF YOU HAVE:	YOU MAY DISCARD:
1-4 First Revision (1967)	1 (1962) 2 (1963) 3 (1963) 4 (1963)
5-8 First Revision (1969)	5-6 (1963) 7-8 (1963)

Both 9-12 First Revision (1974)
   AND *Contemporary Authors Permanent Series*,
   Volume 1 (1975)
	9-10 (1964)
	11-12 (1965)

Both 13-16 First Revision (1975)
   AND *Contemporary Authors Permanent Series*,
   Volumes 1 and 2 (1975, 1978)
	13-14 (1965)
	15-16 (1966)

Both 17-20 First Revision (1976)
   AND *Contemporary Authors Permanent Series*,
   Volumes 1 and 2 (1975, 1978)
	17-18 (1967)
	19-20 (1968)

Both 21-24 First Revision (1977)
   AND *Contemporary Authors Permanent Series*,
   Volumes 1 and 2 (1975, 1978)
	21-22 (1969)
	23-24 (1970)

Both 25-28 First Revision (1977)
   AND *Contemporary Authors Permanent Series*,
   Volume 2 (1978)
	25-28 (1971)

Both 29-32 First Revision (1978)
   AND *Contemporary Authors Permanent Series*,
   Volume 2 (1978)
	29-32 (1972)

Both 33-36 First Revision (1978)
   AND *Contemporary Authors Permanent Series*,
   Volume 2 (1978)
	33-36 (1973)

37-40 First Revision (1979)	37-40 (1973)
41-44 First Revision (1979)	41-44 (1974)
45-48 (1974) 49-52 (1975) ↓ ↓ 131 (1991)	NONE: These volumes will not be superseded by corresponding revised volumes. Individual entries from these and all other volumes appearing in the left column of this chart will be revised and included in the *New Revision Series*.
Volumes in the *Contemporary Authors New Revision Series*	NONE: The *New Revision Series* does not replace any single volume of *CA*. All volumes appearing in the left column of this chart must be retained to have information on all authors in the series.

* Indicates that a listing has been revised from secondary sources believed to be reliable
but has not been personally reviewed for this edition by the author sketched.

ACKOFF, Russell L(incoln) 1919-

PERSONAL: Born February 12, 1919, in Philadelphia, PA; son of Jack (a factory representative) and Fannie (Weitz) Ackoff; married Alexandra Makar, July 17, 1949 (died February, 1987) married Helen Marx, December 20, 1987; children: Alan Walter, Karen Beth, Karla Stephanie. *Education:* University of Pennsylvania, B. Architecture, 1941, Ph.D., 1947.

ADDRESSES: Office—Interact, 401 City Ave., Suite 525, Bala Cynwyd, PA 19004.

CAREER: Wayne University (now Wayne State University), Detroit, MI, assistant professor of philosophy and mathematics, 1947-51; Case Institute of Technology (now Case Western University), Cleveland, Ohio, associate professor, 1951-55, professor of operations research, 1955-64; University of Pennsylvania, Wharton School of Finance and Commerce, Philadelphia, professor of statistics and operations research, 1964-71, Daniel H. Silverberg Professor of Systems Sciences, 1971-84, Anheuser-Busch Professor of Management Science, 1984-86, chairman of department of statistics and operations research, 1964-66, director of Management Science Center, 1964-67, 1969-70, chairman, Graduate Program in Social Sciences and director of Busch Center; Institute for Interactive Management (Interact), Bala Cynwyd, PA, founder and chairman, 1986—. Anheuser-Busch Visiting Professor, Washington University, 1989-90; core faculty, Union Institute, 1989—. Advisory editor in management sciences, John Wiley & Sons, Inc., 1964—. Consultant to National Academy of Sciences, Scientific and Technical Research Council (Turkey), U.S. Bureau of the Census, and to prominent corporations. *Military service:* U.S. Army, 1942-46; became lieutenant.

MEMBER: Operations Research Society of America (charter member; former president), Institute of Management Sciences (charter member; former vice-president), American Statistical Association (fellow), Society for General Systems Research (former president), Operational Research Society (Great Britain), Operational Research Society of India, Sigma Xi, Tau Sigma Delta.

AWARDS, HONORS: D.Sc., University of Lancaster, 1967; silver medal from Operational Research Society, 1971; George E. Kimball medal from Operations Research Society of America, 1975.

WRITINGS:

(With C. W. Churchman and Murray Wax) *Measurement of Consumer Interest,* University of Pennsylvania Press, 1947.
(With Churchman) *Methods of Inquiry,* Educational Publishers, 1950.
The Design of Social Research, University of Chicago Press, 1953.
(With Churchman and E. L. Arnoff) *Introduction to Operations Research,* Wiley, 1957.
(With J. S. Minas and S. K. Gupta) *Scientific Method: Optimizing Applied Research Decisions,* Wiley, 1962.
(With B. H. P. Rivett) *A Manager's Guide to Operations Research,* Wiley, 1963.
(With M. W. Sasieni) *Fundamentals of Operations Research,* Wiley, 1968.
A Concept of Corporate Planning, Wiley, 1970.
The Management of Change and How It Changes Management, University of Lancaster, 1970.
(With F. E. Emery) *On Purposeful Systems,* Aldine-Atherton, 1972.
Redesigning the Future, Wiley, 1974.
(Editor and contributor) *Systems and Management Annual,* Petrocelli Books, 1974—.
(With T. A. Cowan and others) *Designing a National Scientific and Technological Communication System: The SCATT Report,* University of Pennsylvania Press, 1976.
The Art of Problem Solving, Wiley, 1978.
Creating the Corporate Future, Wiley, 1981.
(With Elsa Vergara, Finnel, and Gharajedaghi) *A Guide to Controlling Your Corporation's Future,* Wiley, 1984.
(With Paul Broholm and Roberts Snow) *Revitalizing Western Economies: A New Agenda for Business and Government,* Jossey-Bass, 1984.
(With Gharajedaghi) *A Prologue to National Development Planning,* Greenwood Press, 1986.

Contributor to numerous books, including J. F. McCloskey and F. N. Trefethen, editors, *Operations Research for Management,* John Hopkins Press, 1954; D. P. Eckman, editor, *Systems Research and Design,* Wiley, 1961; M. C. Youitzetal, editor, *Research Program Effectiveness,* Gordon & Breach, 1966; *The Place of Research in Social Choice,* Tavistock Institute of Human Relations, 1970; *Presidential Lectures, 1975-76,* University of Pennsylvania, 1976; Niels Bjorn-Andersen, editor, *The Human Side of Information Processing,* North-Holland, 1980. Also contributor to *American People's Encyclopedia, International Encyclopedia of the Social Sciences,* and *Encyclopaedia Britannica,* 15th edition, 1974. Contributor of more than a hundred scientific articles to proceedings and professional journals. Book review editor, *Philosophy of Science,* 1947-53; member of abstracting staff, *Biological Abstracts,* 1950-51; associate editor of *Operations Research,* 1953-65, and *Conflict Resolution,* 1964-70; editor, *Management Science,* 1965-70; member of advisory board, *Mathematical Spectrum,* 1968-80; member of editorial board, *Management Decision,* 1968-80.

WORK IN PROGRESS: Obstructions to Development: Irreverent Reflections, essays accompanied by Ackoff's fables.

*   *   *

ADAMS, Joanna Z.
    See KOCH, Joanne

*   *   *

ALEGRIA, Fernando 1918-

PERSONAL: Born September 26, 1918, in Santiago, Chile; son of Santiago Alegría Toro and Julia Alfaro; married Carmen Letona Melendez, January 29, 1943; children: Carmen, Daniel, Andres, Isabel. *Education:* Bowling Green State University, M.A., 1941; University of California, Berkeley, Ph.D., 1947.

ADDRESSES: Home—55 Arlmonte Dr., Berkeley, Calif. 94707. *Office*—Department of Spanish and Portuguese, Stanford University, Stanford, Calif. 94305.

CAREER: University of Chile, Santiago, Chile, professor of Spanish, 1939; Bowling Green State University, Bowling Green, Ohio, Extension Division, instructor in Spanish, 1940-41; University of California, Berkeley, instructor, 1947-49, assistant professor, 1949-55, associate professor, 1955-63, professor of Spanish and Portuguese, 1964-67; Stanford University, Stanford, Calif., professor of Spanish, 1967-87, professor of Portuguese, 1976-87, professor emeritus, 1987—. Consultant in Spanish American literature, UNESCO, 1968. Cultural attaché in Chilean Embassy, Washington, D.C.

MEMBER: Instituto Internacional de Literatura Iberoamericana, American Association of Teachers of Spanish, Sociedad de Escritores (Chile).

AWARDS, HONORS: Latin American Prize of Literature, 1943, for *Lautaro: Joven libertador de Arauco;* Guggenheim fellow, 1947-48; Premio Atenea and Premio Municipal (both Chile), for *Caballo de copas.*

WRITINGS:

Recabarren, Antares, 1938.
Ideas estéticas de la poesía moderna, Multitud, 1939.
Leyenda de la ciudad perdida, Zig-Zag, 1942.
Lautaro: Joven libertador de Arauco (juvenile fiction), Zig-Zag, 1943, 5th edition, 1965.
Ensayo sobre cinco temas de Tomás Mann, Funes, 1949.
Camaleón, Ediapsa, 1951.
La poesía chilena: Origenes y desarrollo del siglo XVI al XIX, University of California Press, 1954.
Walt Whitman en hispanoamérica, Studium, 1954.
El poeta que se volvió gusano, Cuadernos Americanos, 1956.
Caballo de copas, Zig-Zag, 1957, 2nd edition, 1961, reprinted, Casa de las Américas, 1981, translation by Carlos Lozano

published as *My Horse Gonzáles,* Casa de las Américas, 1964.
Breve historia de la novela hispanoamericana, Studium, 1959, 2nd edition published as *Historia de la novela hispanoamericana,* De Andrea, 1965, published as *Nueva historia de la novela hispanoamericana,* Ediciones del Norte, 1985.
El cataclismo (short stories), Nascimento, 1960.
Las noches del cazador, Zig-Zag, 1961.
Las fronteras del realismo: Literatura chilena del siglo XX, Zig-Zag, 1962, 2nd edition published as *La literatura chilena del siglo XX,* 1967.
(Editor) *Novelistas contemporaneos hispanoamericanos,* Heath, 1964.
Mañana los guerreros (novel), Zig-Zag, 1964.
Viva chile M!, Editorial Universitaria (Santiago), 1965.
(Editor and translator) Rene Marill, *Historia de la novela moderna,* Union Tipografica Editorial Hispano Americana, 1966.
Genio y figura de Gabriela Mistral, Editorial Universitaria de Buenos Aires, 1966.
La novela hispanoamericana, siglo XX, Centro Editor de America Latina, 1967.
(Translator with others) Nicanor Parra, *Poems and Antipoems,* edited by Miller Williams, New Directions, 1967.
Los días contados (novel), Siglo XXI, 1968.
Ten Pastoral Psalms (poetry; bilingual edition; English versions by Bernardo Garcia and Matthew Zion), Kayak, 1968.
Como un árbol rojo, Editora Santiago, 1968.
La maraton del palomo (short stories), Centro Editor de America Latina, 1968.
Los mejores cuentos de Fernando Alegría, edited with prologue by Alfonso Calderon, Zig-Zag, 1968.
La literatura chilena contemporánea, Centro Editor de America Latina, 1969.
Instructions for Undressing the Human Race/Instrucciones para desnudar a la raza humana (poem; bilingual edition; English version by Matthew Zion and Lennart Bruce), Kayak, 1969 (also see below).
Amerika (manifiestos de Vietnam), Editorial Universitaria, 1970.
(With others) *Literatura y praxis en América Latina,* Monte Avila Editores, 1974.
Retratos contemporaneos, Harcourt, 1979.
Coral de guerra, Nueva Imagen, 1979.
El paso de los gansos, Laia, 1980.
The Chilean Spring, translated by Stephen Fredman, Latin American Literary Review Press, 1980.
(Contributor of poetry) Moraima de Semprún Donahue, *Figuras y contrafiguras en la poesía de Fernando Alegría,* Latin American Literary Review Press, 1981.
(Author of prologue) Pablo Neruda, *Canto general,* 2nd edition, Biblioteca Ayacucho, 1981.
(Editor and contributor) *Chilean Writers in Exile: Eight Short Novels,* Crossing Press, 1982.
Una especie de memoria, Editorial Nueva Imagen, 1983.
Changing Centuries: Selected Poems of Fernando Alegría (includes selections from *Instrucciones para desnudar a la raza humana*), translated by Stephen Kessler, Latin American Literary Review Press, 1984, 2nd edition, 1988.
Los trapecios, Ediciones Agua Pesada, 1985.
The Funhouse, translated by Kessler, Arte Publica, 1986.

Also author of *La venganza del general, La prensa, Literatura y revolución,* 1970, and *Allende: Mi vecino, el presidente,* 1989, translation published as *Allende: My Neighbor, the President,* 1990.

SIDELIGHTS: "The most distinguished Chilean writer living in the United States," reports Victor Perera in the *Nation*, "is the critic and novelist Fernando Alegría, who was [former Chilean President] Allende's cultural attaché in Washington." Noted for his important critical works on Latin American literature, his poetry, and his novels, Alegría has been living in exile since a military junta overthrew Allende's government on September 11, 1973. *The Chilean Spring*, Alegría's fictionalized account of a young photographer's ordeal and death at the hands of the junta, is a "tribute to a modestly heroic photographer [that] becomes a poignant elegy to a nation whose future has been taken from it," declares *New York Times Book Review* contributor Jeffrey Burke. "That Mr. Alegría accomplishes so much so effectively in so few pages," Burke continues, "is a remarkable achievement."

BIOGRAPHICAL/CRITICAL SOURCES:

BOOKS

Epple, Juan Armando, *Nos reconoce el tiempo y silba su tonada* (interview), Ediciones LAR, 1987.

PERIODICALS

Books Abroad, winter, 1970.
Carleton Miscellany, Number 3, 1969.
Chicago Review, Number 1, 1968, January/February, 1971.
Nation, February 11, 1978.
New York Times Book Review, May 11, 1980.
Poetry, March, 1970.*

*   *   *

ALEGRIA, Ricardo E(nrique) 1921-

PERSONAL: Born April 14, 1921, in San Juan, P.R.; son of Jose S. and Celeste (Gallardo) Alegría; married Mela Pons (an artist), December 7, 1947; children: Ricardo, Jose Francisco. *Education:* University of Puerto Rico, B.A., 1943; University of Chicago, M.A., 1947; Harvard University, graduate study, 1953-55. *Religion:* Roman Catholic.

ADDRESSES: Home—San Jose 101, San Juan, P.R. 00901. *Office*—Department of History, University of Puerto Rico, Río Piedras, P.R. 00901.

CAREER: University of Puerto Rico, Río Piedras, associate professor of history, 1947-55, director of archaeological museum and research center, 1947-55; Instituto de Cultura Puertorriqueña (Institute of Puerto Rican Culture), San Juan, director, 1955-73; University of Puerto Rico, professor of anthropology and history, 1955—. Director, Office of Cultural Affairs, San Juan, 1973-76.

MEMBER: American Anthropological Association (fellow), Society for American Archaeology.

AWARDS, HONORS: Guggenheim Foundation fellow, 1953-55; Doctorate Honoris Causae, humanities, Catholic University (Puerto Rico), 1971; Doctorate Honoris Causae, law, New York University, 1971; National Trust for Historic Preservation award, 1973; Ph.D., University of Puerto Rico, 1974.

WRITINGS:

Historia de nuestros indios, illustrated by wife, Mela Pons de Alegría, Sección de Publicaciones e Impresos, Departamento de Instrucción (San Juan, Puerto Rico), 1950, 8th edition, Colección de Estudios Puertorriqueños (San Juan), 1972, translation by C. Virginia Matters published as *History of*

the Indians of Puerto Rico, Colección de Estudios Puertorriqueños, 1970, 3rd edition, 1974.
La fiesta de Santiago Apóstol en Loíza Aldea, prologue by Fernando Ortiz, Artes Gráficas (Madrid), 1954.
El Instituto de Cultura Puertorriqueña: Los primeros cinco años, 1955-1960, Instituto de Cultura Puertorriqueña (San Juan), 1960.
El tema del café en la literature puertorriqueña, Instituto de Cultura Puertorriqueña, 1965.
(With others) *Café*, Instituto de Cultura Puertorriqueña, 1967.
(Collector and editor) *Cuentos folklóricos de Puerto Rico*, Editorial El Ateneo (Buenos Aires), 1967.
(Selector and adaptor) *The Three Wishes: A Collection of Puerto Rican Folktales*, translated by Elizabeth Culbert, illustrated by Lorenzo Homar, Harcourt, 1968.
Descubrimiento, conquista y colonización de Puerto Rico, 1493-1599, Colección de Estudios Puertorriqueños, 1969, translation published as *Discovery, Conquest and Colonization of Puerto Rico, 1493-1599*, 1971.
El fuerte de San Jerónimo del Boquerón, Instituto de Cultura Puertorriqueña, 1969.
A History of Our Indians, Urban Media Materials, 1970.
Apuntes en torno a la mitología de los indios taínos de las Antillas Mayores y sus orígenes suramericanos, Centro de Estudios Avanzados de Puerto Rico y el Caribe, Museo del Hombre Dominicano (Santo Domingo, Dominican Republic), 1978.
Las primeras representaciones gráficas del indio americano, 1493-1523, Centro de Estudios Avanzados de Puerto Rico y el Caribe, Instituto de Cultura Puertorriqueña, 1978.
El Instituto de Cultural Puertorriqueña, 1955-1973: 18 años contribuyendo a fortalecer neustra conciencia nacional, Instituto de Cultura Puertorriqueña, 1978.
Fort of San Jeronimo Del Boqueron, Gordon Press, 1979.
Institute of Puerto Rican Culture, Gordon Press, 1979.
Utuado Ceremonial Park, Gordon Press, 1979.
Cristobal Colón el tesoro de los indios taínos de La Española, Fundación Garcia-Arevalo (Santo Domingo), 1980.
El uso de la incrustación en la escultura de los indios antillanos, Centro de Estudios Avanzados de Puerto Rico y el Caribe con la colaboración de la Fundación García Arévalo, 1981.
Las primeras noticias sobre los indios Caribes, Editorial Universidad de Puerto Rico, en colaboración con el Centro de Estudios Avanzados de Puerto Rico y el Caribe, 1981.
Ball Courts and Ceremonial Plazas in the West Indies, Yale University Publications in Anthropology, 1983.
(With Lucas Morán Arce and others) *Historia de Puerto Rico*, Librotex (San Juan), 1985, 2nd edition, 1986.

Also author of *Cacicazgo among the Aborigines of the West Indies*, 1947, and *La población aborigen antillana y su relación con otras áreas de América*, 1948. Contributor of articles on archaeology and folklore to journals in Puerto Rico, the United States, and Mexico, including *Revista del Instituto de Lutural Puertorriqueña*, *American Antiquity*, and *Revista Mexicana de Estudios Antropológicos*.

SIDELIGHTS: Ricardo E. Alegría is a noted Puerto Rican historian and anthropologist who, from 1955 through 1973, served as director of the prominent Instituto de Cultura Puertorriqueña (Institute of Puerto Rican Culture).

WORK IN PROGRESS: Writing on the folklore and history of Puerto Rico and on archaeology of the West Indies.

BIOGRAPHICAL/CRITICAL SOURCES:

PERIODICALS

Book World, August 17, 1969.
Horn Book, August, 1969.
New York Times Book Review, May 4, 1969.*

*   *   *

ALLEN, G(eorge) C(yril) 1900-1982

PERSONAL: Born June 28, 1900, in Kenilworth, England; died July 31, 1982 in Oxford, England; son of George Henry and Elizabeth (Sharman) Allen; married Eleanora Cameron Shanks, December 21, 1929 (died May, 1972). *Education:* University of Birmingham, B. Com., 1921, M. Com., 1922, Ph.D., 1928. *Religion:* Church of England. *Avocational interests:* Literature, especially English and French; water-color painting, gardening, mountain walking, traveling.

CAREER: Koto Shogyo Gakko, Nagoya, Japan, lecturer in economics, 1922-25; University of Birmingham, Birmingham, England, research fellow and lecturer in industrial economics, 1925-29; University College of Hull, England, professor of economics, 1929-33; University of Liverpool, Liverpool, England, Brunner Professor of Economy Science, 1933-47; University of London, London, England, professor of political economy, 1947-67, professor emeritus, 1967-82. Fellow, School of Oriental and African Studies, University of London, 1973-82, and St. Anthony's College, Oxford University, 1979-82. Temporary assistant secretary, Board of Trade, London, 1940-44; member of Price Regulation Committee, 1944-53; temporary counselor, British Foreign Office, 1945-46; member, United Kingdom Monopolies Commission, 1950-62; director, Anglo-Nippon Trust Ltd., 1965-68; member of Elstub Inquiry into aircraft industry, 1967-69. Trustee, Institute of Economic Affairs, 1972-82. *Military service:* Royal Air Force, 1918; became second lieutenant.

MEMBER: British Association for the Advancement of Science (president of economics section, 1950), Royal Economic Society (vice-president, 1933-63), British Academy (fellow, 1965-82), Japan Society (London), Political Economy Club, Reform Club.

AWARDS, HONORS: International Research Bureau of Harvard and Radcliffe Colleges grant to study in Japan, 1936; Commander of Order of British Empire, 1958; Order of the Rising Sun (third class), 1961; Japan Foundation Award, 1980, for contribution to the study of the Japanese economy.

WRITINGS:

Modern Japan and its Problems, Allen & Unwin, 1928.
The Industrial Development of Birmingham and the Black Country, Allen & Unwin, 1929, revised edition, 1966.
British Industries and Their Organisation, Longmans, Green, 1933, 5th edition, 1970.
Japan: The Hungry Guest, Allen & Unwin, 1938.
(With E. B. Schumpeter and others) *The Industrial Development of Japan and Manchukuo,* Macmillan, 1940.
Japanese Industry: Its Recent Development and Present Condition, Institute of Pacific Relations, 1940.
A Short Economic History of Modern Japan, Allen & Unwin, 1946, 4th edition, St. Martin's Press, 1981.
(With A. G. Donnithorne) *Western Enterprise in Far Eastern Economic Development,* Allen & Unwin, 1954.
(With Donnithorne) *Western Enterprise in Indonesia and Malaya: A Study in Economic Development,* Allen & Unwin, 1957, reprinted, Kelley (New York), 1968.
Japan's Economic Recovery, Oxford University Press, 1958.

The Structure of Industry in Britain, Longmans, Green, 1961, 3rd edition, 1970.
Japan's Economic Expansion, Oxford University Press, 1965.
Japan as a Market and Source of Supply, Pergamon, 1966.
Economic Fact and Fantasy, Institute of Economic Affairs, 1967.
Monopoly and Restrictive Practices, Allen & Unwin, 1968.
(With others) *Mergers, Take-overs, and the Structure of Industry: Ten Papers on Economics, Law, Rules,* Institute of Economic Affairs, 1973.
(With Chiaki Nishiyama) *The Price of Prosperity,* Institute of Economic Affairs, 1974.
The British Disease: A Short Essay on the Nature and Causes of the Nation's Lagging Wealth, Institute of Economic Affairs, 1976, 2nd edition, 1979.
How Japan Competes, Institute of Economic Affairs, 1978.
British Industry and Economic Policy, Macmillan, 1979.
Collected Papers, two volumes, Macmillan, 1979-80.
Japan's Economic Policy, Holmes & Meier, 1980.

Contributor to economic journals.

SIDELIGHTS: George Cyril Allen once told *CA:* "My appointment as a lecturer in Japan in 1922 greatly influenced my career and thought. My first important research into the changing structure of the British West Midlands (resulting in *The Industrial Development of Birmingham and the Black Country*) created an interest in industrial structure and development."

He continued, "From my earliest youth I was fond of history and literature and I enjoyed trying to write. Subsequently my study of economic affairs gave me something substantial to write about. So I can say that I have written books and articles chiefly because I enjoyed being so engaged. of course, I have hoped to make a contribution to knowledge and to affect policy, but the fact that most of my criticisms of British economic policy have had little effect does not dismay me.

"Some of my books have been suggested to me by publishers, editors, or colleagues; others were conceived in the course of my reflections on events or propositions. My books have been translated into French, Italian, Spanish, Potuguese, Polish, Japanese, Chinese, Persian, and various Indian languages.

"Initially I was influenced by my instructor, Sir William Ashley, and later by Professor Joesph Schumpeter's work. To my mind, British economics took a wrong turn both when it spurned institutional studies and also after the war, when the Keynesians diverted attention from the problems of supply and productive efficiency to the management of demand. I have little sympathy with the tendancy of economic theorists to soar into the outer ether of mathematical symbolism. Economists should concern themselves with the problems of the real world. As far as possible, they should address themselves, as Marshall and his predecessors did, to an audience of educated men and not to a small circle of specialists who tend to study what is intellectually interesting rather than what is practically important. The arrogance of many modern economists is disturbing. They seem unable to recognise the limitations of their subject as a guide to policy. Finally, the subject would be better served if young economists at least tried to write with clarity even if elegance is beyond them."

OBITUARIES:

PERIODICALS

Times (London), August 5, 1982.

ALLEN, Kenneth S. 1913-1981
(Avis Murton Carter, Alastair Scott)

PERSONAL: Born September 18, 1913, in Southend-on-Sea, Essex, England; died February 19, 1981; son of George Thomas (a builder) and Hannah Daisy (Sellar) Allen; married Avis Murton Carter, June 3, 1950; children: David Stuart, Alastair Scott, Fiona Margaret. *Education:* Attended Southend College of Art and St. Martin's School of Art. *Politics:* "Minimal." *Religion:* "Minimal."

ADDRESSES: Home and office—74 Eastbury Rd., Northwood, Middlesex HA6 3AR, England.

CAREER: Worked for advertising agencies in London, England, 1931-39; employed by Gaumont British Films Co., London, 1945-49; EMI Film and Theatre Corp., London, employed in public relations and publicity, 1954-72; full-time writer, 1972—. *Military service:* British Merchant Navy.

MEMBER: Film Publicity Guild, Association of Film and Television Technicians, Poetry Club (London), Variety Club.

WRITINGS:

Wings of Sail: The Story of British Ships in the Glorious Days of Sail (self-illustrated), John Crowther, 1944.
The A.B.C. of Stagecraft for Amateurs (self-illustrated), Stacy, 1945.
Mistress of the Seas: The Story of Britain's Steamships (self-illustrated), John Crowther, 1945.
The Silver Screen, John Gifford, 1948.
In the Beginning, Warne, 1948.
Sea Captains and Their Ships, illustrations by Peter M. Woods, Odhams, 1965.
(Editor) *Radiology in World War II,* Office of the Surgeon General, Department of the Army, 1966.
Crimson Harvest: The Story of the Bloodiest Massacre Britain Has Ever Known, R. Hale, 1966.
Exploring the Sea, illustrations by Wilfred Hardy, Odhams, 1966.
The World's Greatest Sea Disasters, Odhams, 1968.
Mighty Men of Valour: The Great Warriors and Battles of Biblical Times, Smythe, 1972.
The Vikings, Purnell, 1973.
A First Look at Transporting Goods (illustrations by G. Tuckwell), Hamlyn, 1973.
A First Look at Transporting People, illustrations by Tuckwell, F. Watts, 1973.
Big Guns of the Twentieth Century and Their Part in Great Battles, Firefly Books, 1976.
"That Bounty Bastard": The True Story of Captain William Bligh, R. Hale, 1976, St. Martin's, 1977.

JUVENILE

Soldiers in Battle, illustrations by James McIntyre, Odhams, 1966.
Sailors in Battle, illustrations by Martha Hart, Odhams, 1966.
Exploring the Cinema, illustrations by Jane Michaelis, Odhams, 1966.
The Story of London Town, illustrations by Janet Duchesne, Odhams, 1967.
Knights and Castles, Macdonald Educational, 1970.
Ships of Long Ago, Macdonald Educational, 1970.
Pirates and Buccaneers, Macdonald Educational, 1971.
Fighting Ships, illustrations by George Tuckwell, Purnell, 1971.
Fighting Men and Their Uniforms, Hamlyn, 1971.
One Day in Roman Britain, Tyndall, 1973.

Record Breakers, Purnell, 1973.
One Day in Tutankhamen's Egypt, Tyndall, 1973, Abelard, 1974.
(Under pseudonym Avis Murton Carter) *One Day with the Vikings,* Purnell, 1973, Abelard, 1974.
Wars of the Roses, Wayland, 1973.
Spotlight on the Wild West, illustrations by G. J. Galsworthy, Michael McGuinness, and Michael Shoebridge, Hamlyn, 1973.
The Story of Gunpowder, Wayland, 1973.
Battle of the Atlantic, Wayland, 1973.
One Day in Ancient Greece, Tyndall, 1974.
(Under pseudonym Alastair Scott) *One Day in Regency England,* 1974.
One Day in Ancient Rome, Tyndall, 1974.
(Under pseudonym Alastair Scott) *One Day in Victorian England,* Tyndall, 1974.
(Under pseudonym Avis Murton Carter) *One Day in Shakespeare's England,* Tyndall, 1973, Abelard, 1974.
Ships and Boats, illustrations by Jack Pelling, Collins, 1975.
(Editor) *Spy and Mystery Stories,* Octopus Books, 1978.
The Children's Book of Cars, Trains, Boats, and Planes, Mayflower Books, 1978.
Lawrence of Arabia, illustrations by Roy Schofield, Macdonald Educational, 1978.
What Animal Is That?, Octopus Books, 1978.
Great Warriors, Macdonald Educational, 1979.

OTHER

Also author of *The History of the Ship,* 1968, *Cowboys,* 1973, *The How Annual,* 1975, *The London Experience,* 1977, *Ships and Trains and Boats and Planes,* 1977, *One Thousand Great Events, One Day in Inca Peru,* and *Earthquakes and Volcanoes.* Author of radio series *Personal Appearance;* editor of cassette series *The Historymakers.* Contributor to *What Do You Know?: An Illustrated History of Aircraft,* 1972, *Question and Answer Book, Magpie Story Book, Great Disasters, One Hundred Great Adventures,* and *Fifty Great Journeys;* contributor to *International Encyclopedia of Aviation.*

WORK IN PROGRESS: A novel, with a film background.

SIDELIGHTS: In *That Bounty Bastard,* Kenneth S. Allen attempted to clear the reputation of the much-maligned Captain Bligh, commander of the Bounty. Despite the Hollywood image of Bligh as a power-mad tyrant, records state that after the Bounty mutiny a court martial cleared Bligh of wrongdoing, and that he went on to occupy other positions of authority, including the governorship of New South Wales, Australia. His next ship after the court martial included two former Bounty sailors, proving that his unpopularity was not universal. Allen quoted Bligh's gravestone, which states Bligh "first transplanted the bread fruit tree . . . to the West Indies . . . and died beloved, respected, and lamented." *New York Times Book Review* critic Doris Grumbach finds that with "taste, grace and admirable restraint that characterize[s] the whole biography, Allen pays no attention to Fletcher Christian and the other Bounty mutineers except to note their divergence from Bligh's path. . . . It is Bligh's book, and his mutinous crew sails off into seemingly deserved oblivion."

BIOGRAPHICAL/CRITICAL SOURCES:

BOOKS

Allen, Kenneth S., *That Bounty Bastard,* St. Martin's, 1977.

PERIODICALS

New York Times Book Review, May 22, 1977.*

ALLEN, Ronald Royce 1930-

PERSONAL: Born December 8, 1930, in Horicon, WI; son of Clayton Francis and Hazel Ann (Whipple) Allen; married Jo Anne Elizabeth Kuehl, February 2, 1957; children: John Jeffery, David Jennings. *Education:* Wisconsin State College at Eau Claire (now University of Wisconsin—Eau Claire), B.S., 1952; University of Wisconsin—Madison, M.S., 1957, Ph.D., 1960. *Politics:* Democrat. *Religion:* Methodist.

ADDRESSES: Home—1809 Peacock Ct., Sun Prairie, WI 53590. *Office*—Department of Communication Arts, University of Wisconsin—Madison, Madison, WI 53706.

CAREER: Amherst College, Amherst, MA, assistant professor of public speaking and chairman of department, 1960-63; University of Wisconsin—Madison, assistant professor, 1963-66, associate professor, 1966-69, professor of communication arts and curriculum and instruction, 1969—. *Military service:* U.S. Naval Reserve, active duty, 1952-56; became lieutenant.

MEMBER: Speech Communication Association (first vice-president, 1978; president, 1979), Wisconsin Speech Communication Association (president, 1968-69).

AWARDS, HONORS: Andrew T. Weaver Award, Wisconsin Speech Communication Association, 1978.

WRITINGS:

(With Sharol Parish and C. David Mortensen) *Communication: Interacting through Speech,* C. E. Merrill, 1974.
(With Kenneth L. Brown) *Developing Communication Competence in Children,* National Textbook Co., 1976.
(With Wil A. Linkugel and Richard L. Johannesen) *Contemporary American Speeches,* Kendall/Hunt, 1978, 6th edition, 1988.
(With Ray McKerrow) *The Pragmatics of Public Communication,* Kendall/Hunt, 1981, 3rd edition, 1985.
(With Brown and Joanne Yatvin) *Learning Language through Communication,* Wadsworth Publishing, 1986.
(With Theodore Rueter) *Teaching Assistant Strategies: An Introduction to College Teaching,* Kendall/Hunt, 1990.
(With S. Clay Wilmington and Jo Sprague) *Communication in the Secondary School: A Pedagogy,* 3rd edition, Gorsuch Scarisbrick, 1990.

SIDELIGHTS: Ronald Royce Allen told *CA,* "All my writings have been motivated by my interest in improving the quality of speaking and listening instruction in schools (kindergarten through twelve) and colleges."

*   *   *

ALURISTA
See URISTA, Alberto H.

*   *   *

AMES, Leslie
See ROSS, W(illiam) E(dward) D(aniel)

*   *   *

ANAND, Mulk Raj 1905-

PERSONAL: Born December 12, 1905, in Peshawar, India; son of Lal Chand (a coppersmith and soldier) and Ishwar (Kaur) Anand; married Kathleen Van Gelder (an actress), 1939 (di-

vorced, 1948); married Shirin Vajifdar (a classical dancer), 1949; children: one daughter. *Education:* University of Punjab, B.A. (with honors), 1924; University College, London, Ph.D., 1929; additional study at Cambridge University, 1929-30.

ADDRESSES: Home—Jassim House, 25 Cuffe Parade, Colaba, Bombay 400 005, India. *Office*—MARG Publications, Army & Navy Bldg., 148, Mahatma Gandhi Rd., Bombay 400 023, India.

CAREER: Novelist, essayist, and lecturer. Fought with Republicans in Spanish Civil War, 1937-38; helped found the Progressive Writer's Movement in India, 1938; lecturer in literature and philosophy at London County Council Adult Education Schools, and broadcaster and scriptwriter in films division for British Broadcasting Corp., 1939-45; lecturer at various Indian universities, 1948-63; Tagore Professor of Fine Arts at University of Punjab, 1963-66; visiting professor at Institute of Advanced Studies in Simla, 1967-68; president of Lokayata Trust (an organization developing community and cultural centers in India), 1970—. Editor, *MARG* (Indian art quarterly), Bombay, India, 1946—.

MEMBER: Indian National Academy of Letters (fellow), Indian National Academy of Art (fellow), Indian National Council of Arts, Sahitya Academy (fellow), Lalit Kala Academy (fellow).

AWARDS, HONORS: Leverhulme fellow, 1940-42; International Peace Prize, World Council of Peace, 1952, for promoting understanding among nations; Padma Bhusan award from the President of India, 1968; honorary doctorates from Indian universities in Delhi, Benares, Andhra, Patiala, and Shantiniketan.

WRITINGS:

Persian Painting, Faber, 1931.
The Golden Breath: Studies in Five Poets of the New India, Dutton, 1933.
The Hindu View of Art, Allen & Unwin, 1933, 2nd edition published as *The Hindu View of Art with an Introductory Essay on Art and Reality by Eric Gill,* Asia Publishing House, 1957, 3rd edition, Arnold Publishers (New Delhi), 1988.
Apology for Heroism: A Brief Autobiography of Ideas, Drummond, 1934, 2nd edition, Kutub-Popular (Bombay), 1947.
Letters on India, Transatlantic, 1942.
"India Speaks" (play), first produced in London at the Unity Theatre, 1943.
Homage to Tagore, Sangam (Lahore, India), 1946.
(With Krishna Hutheesing) *The Bride's Book of Beauty,* Kutub-Popular, 1947, published as *The Book of Indian Beauty,* Tuttle (Tokyo), 1981.
On Education, Hind Kitabs (Bombay), 1947.
The Story of India (juvenile history), Kutub-Popular, 1948.
The King-Emperor's English; or, The Role of the English Language in Free India, Hind Kitabs, 1948.
Lines Written to an Indian Air: Essays, Nalanda (Bombay), 1949.
The Indian Theatre, illustrated by Usha Rani, Dobson, 1950, Roy, 1951.
The Story of Man (juvenile natural history), Sikh (Amritsar, India), 1954.
The Dancing Foot, Publications Division, Indian Ministry of Information & Broadcasting (Delhi), 1957.
Kama Kala: Some Notes on the Philosophical Basis of Hindu Erotic Sculpture, Nagel, 1958, Lyle Stuart, 1962.
(Author of introduction and text) *India in Color,* McGraw, 1958.
(With Stella Kramrisch) *Homage to Khajuraho,* MARG Publications (Bombay), 1960, 2nd edition, 1962.

Is There a Contemporary Indian Civilisation?, Asia Publishing House, 1963.

The Third Eye: A Lecture on the Appreciation of Art, edited by Diwan Chand Sharma, privately printed for the University of Punjab, 1963.

(With Hebbar) *The Singing Line*, Western Printers & Publishers, 1964.

(With others) *Inde, Napal, Ceylan* (French guidebook), Editions Vilo (Paris), 1965.

The Story of Chacha Nehru (juvenile), Rajpal, 1965.

Bombay, MARG Publications, 1965.

Design for Living, MARG Publications, 1967.

The Volcano: Some Comments on the Development of Rabindranath Tagore's Aesthetic Theories and Art Practice, Maharaja Sayajirao University of Baroda, 1967.

The Humanism of M. K. Gandhi, Three Lectures, University of Punjab, 1967.

(With others) *Konorak*, MARG Publications, 1968.

Indian Ivories, MARG Publications, 1970.

(Author of text) *Ajanta*, photographs by R. R. Bhurdwaj, MARG Publications/McGraw, 1971.

Roots and Flowers: Two Lectures on the Metamorphosis of Technique and Content in the Indian-English Novel, Karnatak University (Dharwar), 1972.

Mora, National Book Trust (New Delhi), 1972.

Album of Indian Paintings, National Book Trust, 1973.

Author to Critic: The Letters of Mulk Raj Anand, edited by Saros Cowasjee, Writers Workshop (Calcutta), 1973.

Folk Tales of Punjab, Sterling (New Delhi), 1974.

Lepakshi, MARG Publications, c. 1977.

(With others) *Persian Painting, Fifteenth Century*, Arnold-Heinemann/MARG Publications (India), 1977.

Seven Little-Known Birds of the Inner Eye, Tuttle, 1978.

The Humanism of Jawaharlal Nehru, Visva-Bharati (Calcutta), 1978.

The Humanism of Rabindranath Tagore, Marathwada University (Aurangabad, India), 1979.

Album of Indian Paintings, Auromere, 1979.

Maya of Mohenjo-Daro (juvenile), 3rd edition, Auromere, 1980.

Conversations in Bloomsbury (reminiscences), Arnold-Heinemann, 1981.

Madhubani Painting, Publications Division, Ministry of Information and Broadcasting, 1984.

Ghandhian Thought and Indo-Anglican Novelists, Chanakya Publications (India), 1984.

Poet-Painter: Paintings by Rabindranath Tagore, Abhinav Publications (New Delhi), 1985.

Pilpali Sahab: The Story of a Childhood under the Raj (autobiography), Arnold-Heinemann, 1985.

Aesop's Fables, Apt Books, 1987.

NOVELS

Untouchable, preface by E. M. Forster, Wishart, 1935, Hutchinson, 1947, revised edition, Bodley Head, 1970, reprinted, Penguin, 1989.

The Coolie, Lawrence & Wishart, 1936, Liberty Press, 1952, new revised edition, Bodley Head, 1972.

Two Leaves and a Bud, Lawrence & Wishart, 1937, Liberty Press, 1954, Ind-US, 1979.

Lament on the Death of a Master of Arts, Naya Sansar (Lucknow, India), 1938.

The Village, J. Cape, 1939.

Across the Black Waters, J. Cape, 1940, Ind-US, 1980.

The Sword and the Sickle, J. Cape, 1942, Ind-US, 1984.

The Big Heart, Hutchinson, 1945, Ind-US, 1980.

Seven Summers: The Story of an Indian Childhood (first book of autobiographical septet, "Seven Ages of Man"), Hutchinson, 1951, Ind-US, 1973.

Private Life of an Indian Prince, Hutchinson, 1953, revised edition, Bodley Head, 1970.

The Old Woman and the Cow, Kutub-Popular, 1960, published as *Gauri*, Arnold-Heinemann, 1987.

The Road, Sterling, 1961, reprinted, 1989.

Death of a Hero: Epitaph for Maqbool Sherwani, Kutub-Popular, 1963, reprinted, Arnold-Heinemann, 1988.

Morning Face (second book of autobiographical septet, "Seven Ages of Man"), Kutub-Popular, 1968, Ind-US, 1976.

Confessions of a Lover (third book of autobiographical septet, "Seven Ages of Man"), Arnold-Heinemann, 1984.

The Bubble (fourth book of autobiographical septet, "Seven Ages of Man"), Arnold-Heinemann, 1984.

STORY COLLECTIONS

The Lost Child and Other Stories (also see below), J. A. Allen, 1934.

The Barber's Trade Union and Other Stories (includes the stories from *The Lost Child and Other Stories*), J. Cape, 1944, Ind-US, 1983.

Indian Fairy Tales: Retold, Kutub-Popular, 1946, 2nd edition, 1966.

The Tractor and the Corn Goddess and Other Stories, Thacker (Bombay), 1947, reprinted, Arnold-Heinemann, 1987.

Reflections on the Golden Bed and Other Stories, Current Book House (Bombay), 1954, reprinted, Arnold Publishers, 1984.

The Power of Darkness and Other Stories, Jaico (Bombay), 1959.

More Indian Fairy Tales, Kutub-Popular, 1961.

Lajwanti and Other Stories, Sterling, 1973.

Between Tears and Laughter, Sterling, 1973, Ind-US, 1974.

Selected Short Stories of Mulk Raj Anand, edited by M. K. Naik, Arnold-Heinemann, 1977.

EDITOR

Marx and Engels on India, Socialist Book Club (Allahabad, India), 1933.

(With Iqbal Singh) *Indian Short Stories*, New India (London), 1946.

Ananda Kentish Coomaraswamy, *Introduction to Indian Art*, Theosophical Publishing, 1956.

Annals of Childhood, Kranchalson (Agra, India), 1968.

Experiments: Contemporary Indian Short Stories, Kranchalson, 1968.

Grassroots (short stories), Kranchalson, 1968.

Contemporary World Sculpture, MARG Publications, 1968.

Homage to Jaipur, MARG Publications, 1977.

Homage to Amritsar, MARG Publications, 1977.

Tales from Tolstoy, Arnold-Heinemann, 1978.

Alampur, MARG Publications, 1978.

Homage to Kalamkari, MARG Publications, 1979.

Splendours of Kerala, MARG Publications, 1980.

Golden Goa, MARG Publications, 1980.

Splendours of the Vijayanagara, MARG Publications, 1980.

Treasures of Everyday Art, MARG Publications, 1981.

Maharaja Ranjit Singh as Patron of the Arts, MARG Publications, 1981, Humanities, 1982.

(With Lance Dane) *Kama Sutra of Vatsyayana* (from a translation by Richard Burton and F. F. Arbuthnot), Humanities, 1982.

(With S. Balu Rao) *Panorama: An Anthology of Modern Indian Short Stories*, Sterling, 1986.

(And author of background essay) *The Historic Trial of Mahatma Gandhi,* National Council of Educational Research and Training (New Delhi), 1987.

OTHER

Editor of numerous magazines and journals, 1930—.

WORK IN PROGRESS: The last three books of the septet, "Seven Ages of Man," tentatively titled *And So He Plays His Part, A World Too Wide,* and *Last Scene;* a Tagore lecture on Indian fiction, *A Novel Form in the Ocean of Story,* for Punjab University Publication Bureau; a third edition of *Apology for Heroism: A Brief Autobiography of Ideas,* for Arnold Publishers.

SIDELIGHTS: A champion of the underprivileged classes in India, Mulk Raj Anand attacks religious bigotry and established institutions in his numerous novels and short stories. His basic philosophy mixes humanism and socialism into the concept of "bhakti." Bhakti, explains Margaret Berry in her *Mulk Raj Anand: The Man and the Novelist,* is "the relation of personal, efficacious love between the members of the units of society—family, community, nation, or world. It is the maintenance of loving service which constitutes the 'wholeness' of Anand's ideal man. It is, indeed, . . . a new religion, i.e. a new value system supplanting 'superstitious' personal devotion to God by rational devotion to man."

As the author once told *CA:* "I believe in the only ism possible in our age—humanism. I feel that man can grow into the highest consciousness from insights into the nature of human experience derived through creative art and literature. The piling up of these insights may make a man survive at some level of the quality of life, in our tragic age. I believe in co-existence among human beings and co-discovery of cultures. I believe the world must end the arms race and get five percent disarmament to give resources for building basic plenty throughout the world by the year 2000. I believe, though man has fallen very low at various times in history, he is not so bad that he will not survive on this planet—as long as the earth does not grow cold. I always dream the earth is not flat, but round."

Anand's devotion to socialism and humanism has had a dual effect on his writing. According to Berry, the author's "humanism gives effective formal expression to the dignity of the individual person in the lowest ranks of society, struggling to realize his potential—though in doing so the author often forgets the dignity and the value of persons who are rich." Berry continues by saying Anand's humanism lends more artistry to the value of his works, while his belief in socialism tends to detract from their literary worth. "Anand is technically unable to cope with the dangers of 'writing for a cause,' " asserts Berry, and this results in a certain amount of stereotyping against such people as "Brahmans, schoolteachers, Capitalists, moneylenders, [and] landlords."

However, critics like Krishna Nandan Sinha note that Anand's integration of characterization with situation has improved over the years. In his *Mulk Raj Anand,* Sinha comments that "while the [author's] earlier novels show a sense of horror and disgust against social and economic ills, the novels of the middle period show a greater concern for and with the human heart. It is, however, in the later novels that a healthy synthesis of the social and personal concerns is achieved. Thus, the art of Anand gradually gains much in confidence. . . . While the later novels retain the passion for social justice, they sound greater emotional depths."

Anand's short stories suffer from problems similar to those in his novels, say several critics. M. K. Naik, for example, points out in his *Mulk Raj Anand* that "time and again, his compassion for the underdog bowls him over; his indignation at the injustice of traditional practices erupts into hysteria; and he can seldom resist the temptation to squeeze the last tear out of a pathetic situation." Nevertheless, Anand's short stories have many strengths as well. "His range is wider than that of Raja Rao," attests Naik, comparing Anand to other Indian authors, "and his work exhibits a greater variety of mood and tone and a greater complexity than R. K. Narayan's short stories evince." *World Literature Today* contributor Shyam M. Asnani adds that "Anand writes about Indians much as Chekhov writes about Russians, or Sean O'Faolain or Frank O'Connor about the Irish." "In the field of Indian writers of short stories," Asnani later concludes, "he is still matchless."

For his realistic portrayals of the social and economic problems suffered by Indians at the hands of the British, as well as those of other more affluent and powerful Indians, Anand is accepted by several critics as one of India's best writers. The value of his novels, concludes Berry, "is the witness they offer of India's agonizing attempt to break out of massive stagnation and create a society in which men and women are free and equal." Other virtues of the author's work, according to Berry, include Anand's portrayal "of the modern educated Indian's struggle to identify with himself and his country" and Anand's search for "a principle of unity," which the writer considers to be bhakti. Because of these strengths in his writings, critics like Sinha esteem Anand to be "the most authentic interpreter of responsible human experience *here* and *now*. His vision of the vast human concourse, his serene contemplation of characters and situations, his control of words and sentences, and, above all, his choice between alternatives make him perhaps the foremost and most significant novelist of today's India."

BIOGRAPHICAL/CRITICAL SOURCES:

BOOKS

Berry, Margaret, *Mulk Raj Anand: The Man and the Novelist,* Oriental Press, 1971.

Contemporary Literary Criticism, Volume 23, Gale, 1983.

Cowasjee, Saros, *So Many Freedoms: A Study of the Major Fiction of Mulk Raj Anand,* Oxford University Press (Delhi), 1977.

Fisher, Marlene, *Wisdom of the Heart,* Sterling, 1980.

Iyengar, K. R. Srinivasa, *Indian Writing in English,* Asia Publishing House, 1962.

Kaul, Premila, *The Novels of Mulk Raj Anand: A Thematic Study,* Sterling, 1983.

Lindsay, Jack, *The Lotus and the Elephant,* Kutub-Popular, 1954.

Naik, M. K., *Mulk Raj Anand,* Arnold-Heinemann, 1973.

Niven, Alastair, *The Yoke of Pity,* Arnold-Heinemann, 1978.

Riemenschneider, D., *The Ideal of Man in Anand's Novels,* Kutub-Popular, 1969.

Sinha, Krishna Nandan, *Mulk Raj Anand,* Twayne, 1972.

PERIODICALS

Contemporary Indian Literature, December, 1965.

Scrutiny, June, 1935.

World Literature Today, summer, 1978.

World Literature Written in English, November, 1975, spring, 1980.

—Sketch by Kevin S. Hile

ANAYA, Rudolfo A(lfonso) 1937-

PERSONAL: Born October 30, 1937, in Pastura, N.M.; son of Martín (a laborer) and Rafaelita (Mares) Anaya; married Patricia Lawless (a counselor), July 21, 1966. *Education:* Attended Browning Business School, 1956-58; University of New Mexico, B.A. (English), 1963, M.A. (English), 1968, M.A. (guidance and counseling), 1972.

ADDRESSES: Home—5324 Canada Vista N.W., Albuquerque, N.M. 87120. *Office*—Department of English, University of New Mexico, Albuquerque, N.M. 87131.

CAREER: Public school teacher in Albuquerque, N.M., 1963-70; University of Albuquerque, Albuquerque, N.M., director of counseling, 1971-73; University of New Mexico, Albuquerque, associate professor, 1974-88, professor of English, 1988—. Teacher, New Mexico Writers Workshop, summers, 1977-79. Lecturer, Universidad Anahuac, Mexico City, Mexico, summer, 1974; lecturer at other universities, including Yale University, University of Michigan, Michigan State University, University of California, Los Angeles, University of Indiana, and University of Texas at Houston. Board member, El Norte Publications/Academia; consultant.

MEMBER: Modern Language Association of America, American Association of University Professors, National Council of Teachers of English, Trinity Forum, Coordinating Council of Literary Magazines (vice president, 1974-80), Rio Grande Writers Association (founder and first president), La Academia Society, La Compañía de Teatro de Albuquerque, Multi-Ethnic Literary Association (New York, N.Y.), Before Columbus Foundation (Berkeley, Calif.), Santa Fe Writers Co-op, Sigma Delta Pi (honorary member).

AWARDS, HONORS: Premio Quinto Sol literary award, 1971, for *Bless Me, Ultima;* University of New Mexico Mesa Chicana literary award, 1977; City of Los Angeles award, 1977; New Mexico Governor's Public Service Award, 1978 and 1980; National Chicano Council on Higher Education fellowship, 1978-79; National Endowment for the Arts fellowships, 1979, 1980; Before Columbus American Book Award, Before Columbus Foundation, 1980, for *Tortuga;* New Mexico Governor's Award for Excellence and Achievement in Literature, 1980; literature award, Delta Kappa Gamma (New Mexico chapter), 1981; D.H.L., University of Albuquerque, 1981; Corporation for Public Broadcasting script development award, 1982, for "Rosa Linda"; Award for Achievement in Chicano Literature, Hispanic Caucus of Teachers of English, 1983; Kellogg Foundation fellowship, 1983-85; D.H.L., Marycrest College, 1984; Mexican Medal of Friendship, Mexican Consulate of Albuquerque, N.M., 1986.

WRITINGS:

Bless Me, Ultima (novel; also see below), Tonatiuh International, 1972.

Heart of Aztlán (novel), Editorial Justa, 1976.

Bilingualism: Promise for Tomorrow (screenplay), Bilingual Educational Services, 1976.

(Editor with Jim Fisher, and contributor) *Voices from the Rio Grande,* Rio Grande Writers Association Press, 1976.

(Contributor) Charlotte I. Lee and Frank Galati, editors, *Oral Interpretations,* 5th edition, Houghton, 1977.

(Contributor) *New Voices 4 in Literature, Language and Composition,* Ginn, 1978.

(Author of introduction) Sabine Ulibarri, *Mi abuela fumaba puros,* Tonatiuh International, 1978.

(Contributor) *Anuario de letras chicanas,* Editorial Justa, 1979.

(Contributor) *Grito del sol,* Quinto Sol Publications, 1979.

Tortuga (novel), Editorial Justa, 1979.

"The Season of La Llorona" (one-act play), first produced in Albuquerque, N.M., at El Teatro de la Compañia de Albuquerque, October 14, 1979.

(Translator) *Cuentos: Tales from the Hispanic Southwest, Based on Stories Originally Collected by Juan B. Rael,* edited by José Griego y Maestas, Museum of New Mexico Press, 1980.

(Editor with Antonio Márquez) *Cuentos Chicanos: A Short Story Anthology,* University of New Mexico Press, 1980.

(Editor with Simon J. Ortiz) *A Ceremony of Brotherhood, 1680-1980,* Academia Press, 1981.

The Silence of the Llano (short stories), Tonatiuh/Quinto Sol International, 1982.

The Legend of La Llorona (novel), Tonatiuh/Quinto Sol International, 1984.

The Adventures of Juan Chicaspatas (epic poem), Arte Publico, 1985.

A Chicano in China (nonfiction), University of New Mexico Press, 1986.

The Farolitos of Christmas: A New Mexican Christmas Story (juvenile), New Mexico Magazine, 1987.

Lord of the Dawn: The Legend of Quetzacoatl, University of New Mexico Press, 1987.

(Editor) *Voces: An Anthology of Nuevo Mexicano Writers,* University of New Mexico Press, 1987.

"Who Killed Don José" (play), first produced in Albuquerque, N.M., at La Compañía Menval High School Theatre, July, 1987.

"The Farolitos of Christmas" (play), first produced in Albuquerque, N.M., at La Compañía Menval High School Theatre, December, 1987.

Selected from "Bless Me, Ultima," Literary Volumes of New York City, 1989.

(Editor with Francisco Lomelí) *Aztlán: Essays on the Chicano Homeland,* El Norte, 1989.

(Editor) *Tierra: Contemporary Fiction of New Mexico* (short story collection), Cinco Puntos, 1989.

Author of unproduced play "Rosa Linda," for the Corporation for Public Broadcasting; author of unpublished and unproduced dramas for the Visions Project, KCET-TV (Los Angeles). Contributor of short stories, articles, essays, and reviews to periodicals in the United States and abroad, including *La Luz, Bilingual Review-Revista Bilingüe, New Mexico Magazine, La Confluencia, Contact II, Before Columbus Review, L'Umano Avventura, 2 Plus 2,* and *Literatura Uchioba;* contributor to *Albuquerque News.* Editor, *Blue Mesa Review;* associate editor, *American Book Review,* 1980-85, and *Escolios;* regional editor, *Viaztlán: International Chicano Journal of Arts and Letters;* member of advisory board, *Puerto Del Sol Literary Magazine.* Anaya's manuscript collection is available at the Zimmerman Museum, University of New Mexico, Albuquerque.

SIDELIGHTS: Best known for his first novel, *Bless Me, Ultima,* Rudolfo A. Anaya's writing stems from his New Mexican background and his fascination with the oral tradition of Spanish *cuentos* (stories). The mystical nature of these folk tales has had a significant influence on his novels, which portray the experiences of Hispanics in the American Southwest. But the novelist's books are also about faith and the loss of faith. As Anaya explains in his *Contemporary Authors Autobiography Series* entry, his education at the University of New Mexico caused him to question his religious beliefs, and this, in turn, led him to write poetry and prose in order to "fill the void." "I lost faith in my

God," Anaya writes, "and if there was no God there was no meaning, no secure road to salvation. . . . The depth of loss one feels is linked to one's salvation. That may be why I write. It is easier to ascribe those times and their bittersweet emotions to my characters."

Bless Me, Ultima, "a unique American novel that deserves to be better known," in *Revista Chicano-Riqueña* contributor Vernon Lattin's opinion, leans heavily on Anaya's background in folklore in its depiction of the war between the evil Tenorio Trementina and the benevolent *curandera* (healer) Ultima. Several critics, such as *Latin American Literary Review*'s Daniel Testa, have praised Anaya's use of old Spanish-American tales in his book. "What seems to be quite extraordinary," avers Testa, ". . . is the variety of materials in Anaya's work. He intersperses the legendary, folkloric, stylized, or allegorized material with the detailed descriptions that help to create a density of realistic portrayal."

The novel is also a *bildungsroman* about a young boy, named Antonio, who grows up in a small village in New Mexico around the time of World War II. Most of Antonio's maturation is linked with a struggle with his religious faith and his trouble in choosing between the nomadic way of life of his father's family, and the agricultural lifestyle of his mother's. Reviewers of *Bless Me, Ultima* have lauded Anaya for his depiction of these dilemmas in the life of a young Mexican-American. For example, in *Chicano Perspectives in Literature: A Critical and Annotated Bibliography,* authors Francisco A. Lomelí and Donaldo W. Urioste call this work "an unforgettable novel . . . already becoming a classic for its uniqueness in story, narrative technique and structure." And *America* contributor Scott Wood remarks: "Anaya offers a valuable gift to the American scene, a scene which often seems as spiritually barren as some parched plateau in New Mexico."

Anaya's next novel, *Heart of Aztlán,* is a more political work about a family that moves from a rural community to the city; but as with its predecessor, Anaya mixes in some mystical elements along with the book's social concern for the Chicano worker in capitalist America. Reception of this second book has been somewhat less enthusiastic than it was for *Bless Me, Ultima.* Marvin A. Lewis observes in *Revista Chicano-Requeña* that "on the surface, the outcome [of *Heart of Aztlán*] is a shallow, romantic, adolescent novel which nearly overshadows the treatment of adult problems. The novel does have redeeming qualities, however, in its treatment of the urban experience and the problems inherent therein, as well as in its attempt to define the mythic dimension of the Chicano experience." Similarly, *World Literature Today* critic Charles R. Larson feels that *Heart of Aztlán,* along with *Bless Me, Ultima,* "provide[s] us with a vivid sense of Chicano Life since World War II."

Tortuga, Anaya's third novel, continues in the mythical vein of the author's other works. The novel concerns a young boy who must undergo therapy for his paralysis and wear a body cast, hence his nickname "Tortuga," which means turtle. "Tortuga," however, also "refers . . . to the 'magic mountain' (with a nod here to Thomas Mann) that towers over the hospital for paralytic children," according to Angelo Restivo in *Fiction International.* While staying at the Crippled Children and Orphans Hospital, Tortuga becomes more spiritually and psychologically mature, and the novel ends when he returns home after his year-long ordeal. As with the novelist's other books, *Tortuga* is a story about growing up; indeed, *Bless Me, Ultima, Heart of Aztlán,* and *Tortuga* form a loosely-tied trilogy that depicts the Hispanic experience in America over a period of several decades. As the author

once told *CA,* these novels "are a definite trilogy in my mind. They are not only about growing up in New Mexico, they are about life."

All of Anaya's novels attempt to find the answers to life's questions, doing so from the perspective of his own personal cultural background. "If we as Chicanos do have a distinctive perspective on life," he tells John David Bruce-Novoa in *Chicano Authors: Inquiry by Interview,* "I believe that perspective will be defined when we challenge the very basic questions which mankind has always asked itself: What is my relationship to the universe, the cosmos? Who am I and why am I here? If there is a Godhead, what is its nature and function? What is the nature of mankind?" These questions echo the doubts that the author has had all his life, and that he links closely to American mythology. Anaya explains to Bruce-Novoa, "All literature, and certainly Chicano literature, reflects, in its more formal aspects, the mythos of the people, and the writings speak to the underlying philosophical assumptions which form the particular world view of culture. . . . In a real sense, the mythologies of the Americas are the only mythologies of all of us, whether we are newly arrived or whether we have been here for centuries. The land and the people force this mythology on us. I gladly accept it; many or most of the American newcomers have resisted it."

BIOGRAPHICAL/CRITICAL SOURCES:

BOOKS

Bruce-Novoa, John David, *Chicano Authors: Inquiry by Interview,* University of Texas Press, 1980.
Contemporary Authors Autobiography Series, Volume 4, Gale, 1986.
Contemporary Literary Criticism, Volume 23, Gale, 1983.
Dictionary of Literary Biography, Volume 82: *Chicano Writers, First Series,* Gale, 1989.
Lomelí, Francisco A. and Donaldo W. Urioste, *Chicano Perspectives in Literature: A Critical and Annotated Bibliography,* Pajarito, 1976.

PERIODICALS

America, January 27, 1973.
American Book Review, March-April, 1979.
Fiction International, Number 12, 1980.
La Luz, May, 1973.
Latin American Literary Review, spring-summer, 1978.
Revista Chicano-Riqueña, spring, 1978, summer, 1981.
University of Albuquerque Alumni Magazine, January, 1973.
University of New Mexico Alumni Magazine, January, 1973.
World Literature Today, spring, 1979.

—*Sketch by Kevin S. Hile*

*   *   *

ANDERSON, Robert (Woodruff) 1917-

PERSONAL: Born April 28, 1917, in New York, N.Y., son of James Hewston (a businessman) and Myra Esther (a teacher; maiden name, Grigg) Anderson; married Phyllis Stohl (a teacher, producer, and literary agent), June 24, 1940 (died, 1956); married Teresa Wright (an actress), December 11, 1959 (divorced, 1978). *Education:* Harvard University, A.B. (magna cum laude), 1939, M.A., 1940; attended Dramatic Workshop, New School for Social Research.

ADDRESSES: Home—Transylvania Rd., Roxbury, Conn. 06783. *Agent*—Mitch Douglas, International Creative Management, 40 West 57th St., New York, N.Y. 10019.

CAREER: Writer, 1946—. South Shore Players, Cohasset, Mass., actor, summers, 1937-38; Harvard University, Cambridge, Mass., assistant in English, 1939-42; Erskine School, Boston, Mass., teacher, 1941; American Theatre Wing, New York City, teacher of playwriting, 1946-50; Playwrights Producing Co., New York City, producer, partner, and member, 1953-60; Actor's Studio, New York City, teacher of playwriting, 1955-56. Faculty member, Salzburg Seminar in American Studies, 1968; writer in residence, University of North Carolina, Chapel Hill, 1969; instructor, Iowa Writers' Workshop, University of Iowa, Iowa City, 1976. President, New Dramatist Committee, 1955-56; member of board of governors, American Playwrights Theatre, 1963-79; former chairman, Harvard Board of Overseers' Committee to Visit the Performing Arts. *Military service:* U.S. Naval Reserve, 1942-46; became lieutenant senior grade; received Bronze Star.

MEMBER: Dramatists Guild (president, 1970-73; member of council), Dramatists Guild Fund (member of board of directors), Authors League of America (member of council, 1965—; vice-president, 1980—), Authors League Fund (member of board of directors), Harvard Club.

AWARDS, HONORS: First prize, Army-Navy Playwriting Contest for Servicemen Overseas, 1945, for "Come Marching Home"; National Theatre Conference fellowship, 1945, for "Come Marching Home," "Boy Grown Tall," and "The Tailored Heart"; Rockefeller fellowship, 1946; *Variety*/New York Drama Critics Poll Award, 1954, for "Tea and Sympathy"; Writers Guild of America award for best drama adapted from another medium, 1971, for "I Never Sang for My Father"; elected to Theatre Hall of Fame, 1980; Academy of Motion Picture Arts and Sciences Award nominations for "The Nun's Story" and "I Never Sang for My Father"; Writers Guild of America nominations for "The Nun's Story," "The Sand Pebbles," and "The Patricia Neal Story"; lifetime achievement award, William Inge Festival.

WRITINGS:

After (novel), Random House, 1973.
Getting up and Going Home (novel), Simon & Schuster, 1978.
(Co-author and editor with John Leggett and John Malcolm Brinnin) *Elements of Literature* (textbook anthology), six volumes, Holt, 1988.

PLAYS

"Hour Town" (musical comedy), first produced in Cambridge, Mass., at Harvard University, December, 1938.
"Come Marching Home," first produced in Iowa City at State University of Iowa, 1945, produced in New York City at Blackfriars Guild, May 18, 1946.
"The Eden Rose," first produced in Ridgefield, Conn., at Theatre Workshop, July 27, 1949.
"Dance Me a Song," first produced on Broadway at Royale Theatre, January 20, 1950.
"Love Revisited," first produced at the Westport Country Playhouse, June 25, 1951.
Tea and Sympathy (three-act; also see below; first produced on Broadway at Ethel Barrymore Theatre, September 30, 1953), Random House, 1954.
All Summer Long (two-act; adapted from the novel, *A Wreath and a Curse,* by Donald Wetzel; first produced in Washington, D.C., at Arena State, January 13, 1953; produced on Broadway at Coronet Theatre, September 23, 1954), Samuel French, 1955.

Silent Night, Lonely Night (two-act; first produced on Broadway at Morosco Theatre, December 4, 1959), Random House, 1960.
The Days Between (two-act; first produced in Dallas, Tex., 1965; produced by American Playwrights Theatre on a national tour, 1965-66; produced Off-Broadway, 1976), Random House, 1965, revised edition, Samuel French, 1969.
You Know I Can't Hear You When the Water's Running (four one-acts; first produced on Broadway at Ambassador Theatre, March 13, 1967), Random House, 1967.
I Never Sang for My Father (two-act; also see below; first produced on Broadway at Longacre Theatre, January 25, 1968; produced on the Public Broadcasting Service [PBS-TV] for "American Playhouse," 1988), Random House, 1968, screenplay edition, New American Library, 1970.
Solitaire/Double Solitaire (two one-acts; also see below; first produced in New Haven, Conn., at Long Wharf Theatre, February 11, 1971; produced on Broadway at John Golden Theatre, September 30, 1971), Random House, 1972.
"Free and Clear," first produced at Long Wharf Theatre, February, 1983.

FILM SCREENPLAY ADAPTATIONS

"Tea and Sympathy" (based on the author's play of the same title), Metro-Goldwyn-Mayer Co. (MGM), 1956.
"Until They Sail" (based on the novel, *Return to Paradise,* by James A. Michener), MGM, 1956.
"The Nun's Story" (based on the novel of the same title by Kathryn Hulme), Warner Brothers, 1959.
"The Sand Pebbles" (based on the novel of the same title by Richard McKenna), Twentieth Century-Fox, 1965.
"I Never Sang for My Father" (based on the author's play of the same title), Columbia, 1970.

TELEVISION SCREENPLAYS

"Double Solitaire" (adapted from the author's play of the same title), PBS-TV, 1972.
"The Patricia Neal Story," Columbia Broadcasting System (CBS-TV), 1981.

Also author of "The Old Lady Shows Her Medals" (based on the play by J. M. Barrie), first produced December 19, 1956, "Rise up and Walk," "Still Life," "Biography," and "At Midnight on the Thirty-first of March."

OTHER

Author of unproduced plays "Boy Grown Tall," 1945, and "The Tailored Heart," 1945. Author of radio play adaptations, including Maxwell Anderson's "Valley Forge," Robert Sherwood's "The Petrified Forest," and Elmer Rice's "Dream Girl"; author of adaptations for Theatre Guild radio programs, including "David Copperfield," "The Glass Menagerie," "A Farewell to Arms," "The Scarlet Pimpernel," "Arrowsmith," "Trilby," "Summer and Smoke," "Goodbye, Mr. Chips," "Oliver Twist," and "Vanity Fair."

WORK IN PROGRESS: "The Kissing Was Always the Best," a full-length play; "The Last Act Is a Solo," a one-act play; a two hour movie for CBS-TV.

SIDELIGHTS: Robert Anderson "is the dramatist of loneliness, of one person reaching out to another (sometimes *any* other) for warmth and reassurance," writes Michael Witkoski in the *Dictionary of Literary Biography.* "He has followed this need as it affects people in youth, the middle years, and old age. His favorite theme is marriage." Anderson's plays, the majority of which have been produced on Broadway, have progressed over the years from the idealism of his early works to the more ambiguous conclusions of later productions. Witkoski attributes much of this change to the death of the playwright's first wife, Phyllis Stohl, in 1956. "After 1956," remarks Witkoski, "the transitory nature of human happiness and relationships is sounded more often and more deeply by Anderson. The human need for love and affection is measured against those forces which place limitations on love: time, death, the stale familiarity of married life. Increasingly in Anderson's dramas his characters struggle against these forces to maintain the vitality of their loves and relationships."

Of all Anderson's works, one of his earliest plays, *Tea and Sympathy,* remains the title with which he is most often associated today. A number of critics have praised the stylistic skill of *Tea and Sympathy,* including Eric Bentley, who states in his *The Dramatic Event: An American Chronicle* that Anderson's play "is a highly superior specimen of the theatre of 'realist' escape. Superior in craftsmanship, superior in its isolation, combination, and manipulation of the relevant impulses and motifs." *Commonweal* critic Richard Hayes similarly notes that *Tea and Sympathy* "is entrenched in that plenitude and elegance of craft of which the American stage is sometimes capable." But these reviewers and others have also discovered several flaws in the play that concern a tendency toward oversimplifying characters and situations.

The plot of *Tea and Sympathy* involves a young boy named Tom Lee who is falsely accused of being a homosexual and is shunned by his fellow students at a New England prep school. The housemaster's wife, however, shows Tom sympathy and kindness, and, in her effort to restore the boy's self-confidence, goes to bed with him to alleviate any doubts he might have about his sexuality. Although Witkoski recognizes that this conclusion represents only part of the "more encompassing need for communication and companionship" that Anderson attempts to convey, and praises Anderson for being "realistic enough to concede that such relationships, particularly between men and women, generally involve sex," other critics are more skeptical about the author's denouement. "Is a single sexual act," Hayes wonders, ". . .so therapeutic? Will it unravel so tangled and branching a history of inferiority [in Tom]?" Harold Clurman echoes this doubt in a *Nation* review, in which he remarks that the "theme, characterization, and story development" of *Tea and Sympathy* is "primitive"; but he adds that "this is no adverse comment on it. It is the work of a young playwright . . . whose approach is honorable, craftsmanlike and humane."

Just as *Tea and Sympathy* is about a sensitive boy surrounded by a cruel, insensitive world, Anderson's next play, *All Summer Long,* concerns the need for adolescents to be heard. In this case, the self-involved members of one family are too involved with their own lives to listen to their children, who are the only ones who realize that their house's foundation is being eroded away by a nearby river. Because Anderson once again deals more sympathetically with his young protagonists than with the adult characters of the play, some critics have objected to what *New Yorker* contributor Wolcott Gibbs perceives to be "the author's tendency to identify himself with children in a children's world, to see life sheerly as a war between passionate young innocence and tarnished adult experience, [which] keeps his work from being really very stimulating to the mature." But Witkoski points out that this theme "is not strictly predicated on mere age: Anderson is more interested in the vitality of spirit than he is in years. Quite often the theme is the conflict between reason and feeling, and Anderson clearly favors youth and passion over rationality associated with age and experience."

What has excited critics most about *All Summer Long,* however, is the author's skill at adaptation. The play was taken from Donald Wetzel's novel, *A Wreath and a Curse,* but Anderson adds his own touches to the stage version. According to Witkoski, "most reviewers were impressed by Anderson's formidable ability in establishing his own atmosphere." "It would have been difficult to find a more intelligent and sensitive playwright for the assignment of dramatizing Donald Wetzel's" novel, remarks John Gassner in his book, *Theatre at the Crossroads: Plays and Playwrights of the Mid-Century American Stage.* Witkoski attributes Anderson's skill at adaptation to the years he spent from 1948-53 rewriting plays and novels for radio and television. "During these years," Witkoski remarks, "Anderson learned how to work quickly and competently, how to compress a conflict into its most economical form. His own plays reveal a beneficial effect in the absence of unnecessary characters and in the deft narration of past or offstage actions."

Another even more significant influence on Anderson's writing, though, was the death of his first wife from cancer in 1956, an experience that is the basis for his 1973 novel *After.* Anderson's first play to be produced after this tragedy was the deeply introspective *Silent Night, Lonely Night,* the plot of which consists almost entirely of a man and a woman discussing marriage, love, and adultery. The characters in this play are two people who meet by chance at an inn on Christmas Eve. Both have unhappy marriages and find solace in each other's company; but, unlike *Tea and Sympathy,* the sexual encounter at the play's end provides no therapeutic value. Their problems remain unresolved. This type of ambiguous ending is characteristic of Anderson's later plays about marriage and relationships, such as *The Days Between,* in which a married couple fails to be convinced that they will be able to reaffirm their marriage vows. The conclusions of these later plays illustrate the playwright's departure from the happy endings of earlier works like "Love Revisited."

Because *Silent Night, Lonely Night* involves so much dialogue and offers little plot action, a number of reviewers have felt that it suffers from being too undramatic. "The sad, short, tender relationship between the pair," says Richard Watts, Jr., in the *New York Post,* ". . .is presented with delicacy and sympathy, but the monotony does creep in." Writing a play with so little action was a move that, indeed, involved some risk, as Anderson himself realizes. In a *Theatre Arts* article he states: "Somehow [*Silent Night, Lonely Night*] seems to many a static play in which two people sat around talking about their lives; whereas I meant it as a fairly dramatic play in which the 'lives' were only important so far as they bore on the immediate developing situation between the two people on stage."

But the nature of Anderson's work has sometimes caused critics to chastise him for being overly melodramatic, while simultaneously imbuing a "general mildness of action and characterization," as Gassner calls it. "The 'melodrama of sentiment,'" observes Witkoski, "is an ever-present danger for a writer such as Anderson who has chosen to explore human relationships, especially to those that do not necessarily lend themselves to overtly dramatic representation, and that often must be explored solely through dialogue." *I Never Sang for My Father,* one of Anderson's more successful plays, suffers in this respect, as Clive Barnes comments in a *New York Times* article quoted by Witkoski: "The poignancy of the situation, real enough and believable in all conscience, is constantly betrayed by the over-obviousness and sentimentality of the writing, and by a lack of genuine dramatic focus." Despite this objection, several reviewers have been touched by the playwright's portrayal of a strained relationship between a father and son. David Richard, for example, says in a *Washington Post* article that Anderson's work "goes right to your heart and breaks it" and that the author weaves his story with "humble eloquence and rare sensitivity."

Another extremely popular play of Anderson's is his light-hearted *You Know I Can't Hear You When the Water's Running.* Still exploring the relationships between married couples, as in *Silent Night, Lonely Night* and *The Days Between,* three of the four skits which comprise the play involve marriages, while in the opening act a playwright attempts to convince his producer to allow an actor to appear on stage in the nude. This opening, which sets the tone for the remaining skits, "is not only remarkably hilarious but has a good deal of shrewd comment to make on matters concerned with the state of the contemporary theater," remarks Watts in a *New York Post* review. Two other skits maintain this humorous look at love and sex, but one section, entitled "I'll Be Home for Christmas," ends on a serious note with, as Witkoski describes it, "a husband and wife comment[ing] obliquely and hesitantly on the meaning of sex, love, and the tenuous hold people have on one another."

Solitaire/Double Solitaire is another kind of departure for Anderson as he ventures into the genre of science fiction in the first part of the play. A number of reviewers have expressed dissatisfaction with the playwright's story of a future dystopian society in *Solitaire,* noting its resemblances to George Orwell's *1984* and Aldous Huxley's *Brave New World.* "The idea is hardly original and Mr. Anderson does little that is original with it," complains *America* contributor Catherine Hughes. The playwright explained to *CA,* however, that "most people missed the theme of these plays. *Solitaire* was about the loneliness of being alone. *Double Solitaire* was about the loneliness of marriage." Critics were kinder to *Double Solitaire,* though, evaluating it on its own merits irrespective of its complementary work. "While the play explores the conflict between Barbara and Charley," attests *The Strands Entwined* author Samuel J. Bernstein, ". . .it ultimately succeeds in putting all marriages on trial. In so doing, the play makes one of the most tortured, honest, and sensitive explorations of marriage in American theatre." Like such works as *Silent Night, Lonely Night* and *I Never Sang for My Father,* Witkoski observes that *Double Solitaire* "ends on a highly unresolved note. . . . It is an ending completely removed from that of the earlier plays, such as 'Love Revisited' and *The Days Between,* where couples use sex as a means to rekindle their marriage. Perhaps in the intervening years," Witkoski speculates, "Anderson had cause to question the revitalizing effects of sex; more likely, he realized that the endings of his earlier plays were too tidy, too obvious to be convincing."

Since *Solitaire/Double Solitaire,* Anderson has leaned away from play writing and has concentrated on screenplays for television; but it is not true, Anderson told *CA,* "that I have turned away from the theatre for the movies. I think, rather, the theatre has turned away from me." The author has also published two novels, *After* and *Getting up and Going Home,* that dwell on the familiar theme of marriage. However, Anderson admits that "the novel is not his medium," according to *Akron Beacon Journal* contributor Mike Clary; and in a *Los Angeles Times* interview with Dan Sullivan, the author reveals that he still prefers writing stage productions over screenplays, despite his success with the latter. "From the writer's point of view," the dramatist asserts, "movies and television are a medium of the approximate" when compared to plays. Therefore, it is for the stage that the author prefers to write, believing that it is through this medium that he can best express himself. "Most plays do not come from an 'idea' or a gimmick," writes Anderson in *Theatre Arts,* "but rather grow out of the essence of the writer, what he is, feels, thinks,

believes and experiences." "The mission of the playwright," he adds in a later *Theatre Arts* article, ". . .is to look in his heart and write: to write whatever concerns him at the moment; to write with passion and conviction." It is this attitude that is revealed in Anderson's plays and has, as Gassner declares, "secured his sensitivity a place in the popular American theatre."

MEDIA ADAPTATIONS: All Summer Long was produced for television in 1955; a television screenplay adaptation of *Silent Night, Lonely Night,* by John Vlahos, was produced by Universal and broadcast on NBC-TV, December 16, 1969; the rights to *After* have been bought for a film production.

BIOGRAPHICAL/CRITICAL SOURCES:

BOOKS

Adler, Thomas, *Robert Anderson,* Twayne, 1978.
Bentley, Eric, *The Dramatic Event: An American Chronicle,* Horizon Press, 1954.
Bentley, Eric, *What Is Theatre? A Query in Chronicle Form,* Horizon Press, 1956.
Bernstein, Samuel J., *The Strands Entwined,* Northeastern University Press, 1980.
Contemporary Literary Criticism, Volume 23, Gale, 1983.
Dictionary of Literary Biography, Volume 7: *Twentieth-Century American Dramatists,* Gale, 1981.
Gassner, John, *Theatre at the Crossroads: Plays and Playwrights of the Mid-Century American Stage,* Holt, 1960.
Lewis, Allan, *American Plays and Playwrights of the Contemporary Theatre,* Crown, 1970.

PERIODICALS

Akron Beacon Journal, October 27, 1974.
America, October 23, 1971.
American Drama since 1945, 1988.
Commonweal, October 30, 1953, April 28, 1967.
Hudson Review, summer, 1968.
Los Angeles Times, December 6, 1987.
Nation, October 17, 1953, April 3, 1967.
National Observer, March 20, 1967, February 5, 1968.
Newsweek, March 27, 1967, February 5, 1968.
New Yorker, October 2, 1954, February 3, 1968.
New York Post, December 4, 1959, March 14, 1967.
New York Times, March 14, 1967, November 23, 1969.
Punch, July 3, 1968.
Saturday Review, February 10, 1968.
Theatre Arts, January, 1954, March, 1958, December, 1961.
Time, February 2, 1968.
Variety, December 18, 1968.
Washington Post, February 7, 1968, June 12, 1978, September 4, 1987.
Writer, September, 1970.

—Sketch by Kevin S. Hile

*   *   *

ANOUILH, Jean (Marie Lucien Pierre) 1910-1987

PERSONAL: Surname pronounced "Ahn-wee"; born June 23, 1910, in Bordeaux, France; died of a heart attack October 3, 1987, in Lausanne, Switzerland; son of Francois (a tailor) and Marie-Magdeleine (a pianist; maiden name, Soulue) Anouilh; married first wife, Monelle Valentin (divorced); married second wife, Nicole Lancon, July 30, 1953; children: (first marriage) Catherine; (second marriage) Caroline, Nicolas, Marie-

Colombe. *Education:* College Chaptal, baccalaureate; Sorbonne, University of Paris, law student, 1931-32.

ADDRESSES: Home—7 rue Saint-James, 92200 Neuilly-sur-Seine, France.

CAREER: Writer, 1929-87. Advertising copy writer, author of publicity scripts and comic gags for films, 1929-32; secretary to theatrical company Comedie des Champs-Elysees, Paris, 1931-32. Also directed several films in France. *Military service:* Served in French Army during 1930s.

AWARDS, HONORS: Grand Prix du Cinema Francais, 1949, for film "Monsieur Vincent"; Antoinette Perry ("Tony") Award and citation from the cultural division of the French Embassy, both 1955, both for *Thieves' Carnival* (New York production); New York Drama Critics Circle Award for best foreign play of 1956-57, for *Waltz of the Toreadors;* Prix Dominique for the direction of film "Madame M.," 1959; *Evening Standard* newspaper drama award and Antoinette Perry Award for best foreign play of the year, both 1961, both for *Becket; or, The Honor of God; Evening Standard* newspaper drama award for best play of the year, 1963, for *Poor Bitos;* first prize for best play of the year, Syndicate of French Drama Critics, 1970, for *Cher Antoine; ou, l'amour rate* and *Les poissons rouges; ou, mon pere, ce heros;* Paris Critics Prize, 1971, for *Ne reveillez pas madame.*

WRITINGS:

PLAYS

(With Jean Aurenche) *Humulus le muet,* Editions Francaises Nouvelles, c. 1929.

"L'hermine," first produced in Paris at Theatre de l'Oeuvre, 1932.

"Mandarine," first produced in Paris at Theatre de l'Athenee, 1933.

"Y'avait un prisonnier" (title means "There Was a Prisoner"), first produced in Paris at Theatre des Ambassadeurs, 1935.

"Le voyageur sans bagage" (first produced in Paris at Theatre des Mathurins, 1937; English translation by Lucienne Hill produced in New York at ANTA Theatre, 1964; also see below), translation by John Whiting published as *Traveller without Luggage,* Methuen, 1959.

La sauvage (first produced in Paris at Theatre des Mathurins, 1938), translation by Hill published as *Restless Heart,* Methuen, 1957.

Le bal des voleurs (first produced in Paris at Theatre des Arts, 1938; produced in New York at Theatre des Quatre Saisons, 1938; English version produced as *Thieve's Carnival* in New York at Cherry Lane Theatre, 1955), Editions Francaises Nouvelles, 1945, translation by Hill published as *Thieves' Carnival,* Samuel French, 1952.

Rendez-vous de Senlis (first produced in Paris at Theatre de l'Atelier, 1938; produced as *Dinner with the Family,* in New York at Gramercy Arts Theatre, 1961; also see below), Editions de la Table Ronde, 1958, translation by Edwin O. Marsh published as *Dinner with the Family,* Methuen, 1958.

Leocadia (first produced at Theatre de l'Atelier, 1939; produced as *Time Remembered,* in New York at Morosco Theater, 1957; also see below), Appleton, 1965, translation by Patricia Moyes published as *Time Remembered,* Methuen, 1955.

Eurydice (first produced at Theatre de l'Atelier, 1941; produced in English in Hollywood at Coronet Theatre, 1948; also see below), annotation by Rambert George, Bordas, 1968, translation by Kitty Black published as *Point of Departure,* Samuel French, 1951, second English translation published as *Legend of Lovers,* Coward, 1952.

Antigone (first produced at Theatre de l'Atelier, 1944; produced in English in New York at Cort Theatre, 1946; also see below), Editions de la Table Ronde, 1946, translation by Lewis Galantiere, Random House, 1946; excerpts published as *Antigone: Extraits,* Bordas, 1968.

"Romeo et Jeannette" (also see below), first produced at Theatre de l'Atelier, 1946, translation by Miriam John produced as "Jeannette," in New York at Maidman Playhouse, 1960.

L'invitation au chateau (first produced at Theatre de l'Atelier, 1947; produced as *Ring around the Moon,* in New York at Martin Beck Theatre, 1950), Editions de la Table Ronde, 1948, translation by Christopher Fry published as *Ring around the Moon,* Oxford University Press, 1950.

"Episode de la vie d'un auteur" (one-act; also see below), first produced in Paris at Comedie des Champs-Elysees, 1948; translation produced as "Episode in the Life of an Author" in Buffalo, N.Y., at Studio Arena Theatre, September, 1969.

Ardele; ou, la Marguerite (first produced with *Episode de la vie d'un auteur,* at Comedie des Champs-Elysees, 1948; produced as "Cry of the Peacock," in New York at Mansfield Theatre, 1950), Editions de la Table Ronde, 1949, translation by Hill published as *Ardele,* Methuen, 1951.

Cecile; ou, l'ecole des peres (first produced at Comedie des Champs-Elysees, 1949; also see below), Editions de la Table Ronde, 1954.

La repetition; ou, l'amour puni (first produced in Paris at Theatre Marigny, 1950; produced in New York at Ziegfeld Theatre, 1952), La Palatine (Geneva), 1950, critical edition, Bordas, 1970, translation by Pamela Hansford Johnson and Black published as *The Rehearsal,* Coward, 1961.

Colombe (first produced at Theatre de l'Atelier, 1951; adaptation by Denis Cannan produced in New York at Longacre Theatre, 1954), Livre de Poche, 1963, translation by Cannan published as *Colombe,* Coward, 1954.

Monsieur Vincent (dialogue), Beyerische Schuelbuch-Verlag, 1951.

La valse des toreadors (English translation produced in New York at Coronet Theatre, 1957), Editions de la Table Ronde, 1952, translation by Hill published as *The Waltz of the Toreadors,* Elek, 1956, Coward, 1957.

L'alouette (first produced in Paris at Theatre Montparnasse, 1953; adaptation by Lillian Hellman produces as "The Lark" in New York at Longacre Theatre, 1955), Editions de la Table Ronde, 1953, translation by Christopher Fry published as *The Lark,* Methuen, 1955.

Medee (first produced at Theatre de l'Atelier, 1953; also see below), Editions de la Table Ronde, 1953.

Ornifle; ou, le courant d'air (first produced at Comedie des Champs-Elysees, 1955), Editions de la Table Ronde, 1955, translation by Hill published as *Ornifle: A Play,* Hill & Wang, 1970.

Pauvre Bitos; ou, le diner de tetes (first produced at Theatre Montparnasse, 1956; produced in English in New York at Classic Stage Repertory, 1969), Editions de la Table Ronde, 1958, translation by Hill published as *Poor Bitos,* Coward, 1964.

L'hurluberlu; ou, le reactionnaire amoureux (first produced at Comedie des Champs-Elysees, 1959; produced in English in New York at ANTA Theatre, 1959), Editions de la Table Ronde, 1959, translation by Hill published as *The Fighting Cock,* Coward, 1960.

Becket; ou, l'honneur de Dieu (first produced in Paris at Theatre Montparnasse-Gaston Baty, 1959; produced as "Becket," in New York at St. James Theatre, 1960), Editions de la

Table Ronde, 1959, translation by Hill published as *Becket; or, The Honor of God,* Coward, 1960.

Madame de . . . (produced with "Traveller without Luggage" in London at Arts Theatre, 1959), translation by John Whiting, Samuel French, c. 1959.

"La petite Moliere," first produced in France at Festival of Bordeaux, 1960.

La grotte (first produced at Theatre Montparnasse, 1961; produced in English in Cincinnati at Playhouse in the Park, June, 1967), Editions de la Table Ronde, 1961, translation by Hill published as *The Cavern,* Hill & Wang, 1966.

La foire d'empoigne (first produced in Paris, 1962), Editions de la Table Ronde, 1961.

"L'orchestre," first produced in Paris, 1962; produced in English in Buffalo, at Studio Arena Theatre, September, 1969.

Fables, Editions de la Table Ronde, 1962.

Le boulanger, la boulangere et le petit mitron (first produced at Comedie des Champs-Elysees, November 13, 1968; English translation by Hill produced in Newcastle, England, at University Theatre, fall, 1972), Editions de la Table Ronde, 1969.

Cher Antoine; ou, l'amour rate (first produced at Comedie des Champs-Elysees, October 1, 1969; produced in English in Cambridge, Mass., at Loeb Drama Center of Harvard University, July 20, 1973), Editions de la Table Ronde, 1969, translation by Hill published as *Dear Antoine; or, The Love That Failed,* Hill & Wang, 1971.

"Le Theatre; ou, la vie comme elle est," first produced at Comedie des Champs-Elysees, c. 1970.

Ne reveillez pas madame (first produced at Comedie des Champs-Elysees, October 21, 1970), Editions de la Table Ronde, 1970.

Les poissons rouges; ou, mon pere, ce heros (first produced at Theatre de l'Oeuvre, c. 1970), Editions de la Table Ronde, 1970.

Tu etais si gentil quand tu etais petit (first produced at Theatre Antoine, January 18, 1972), Editions de la Table Ronde, 1972.

Le directeur de l'opera, Editions de la Table Ronde, 1972.

Monsieur Barnette, avec l'orchestre, Schoenhof, 1975.

L'arrestation: piece en deux parties, Editions de la Table Ronde, 1975, translation by Hill published as *The Arrest: A Drama in Two Acts,* Samuel French, 1978.

Le scenario, Schoenhof, 1976.

Chers Zoiseaux, Schoenhof, 1977.

La culotte, Editions de la Table Ronde, 1978.

"Number One," produced in English in London at Queen's Theatre, April 24, 1984.

Also author of plays published in French periodicals, including "Attile le magnifique," 1930, "Le petit bonheur," 1935, "L'incertain," 1938, "Oreste," 1945, "Jezebel," 1946, and "Le songe du critique," 1961.

TRANSLATOR

(And editor) William Shakespeare, *Trois comedies* (contains *As You Like It, Winter's Tale, and Twelfth Night*), Editions de la Table Ronde, 1952.

(With wife, Nicole Anouilh) Graham Greene, *L'amant complaisant* (translation of *The Complacent Lover*) Laffont, 1962.

Shakespeare, "Richard III," performed at Theatre Montparnasse, 1964.

OMNIBUS VOLUMES IN FRENCH

Pieces roses: Le bal des voleurs, Le rendez-vous de Senlis, Leocadia, Editions Balzac, 1942, 2nd edition, with addition of *Humulus le muet,* Editions de la Table Ronde, 1958.

Pieces noires: L'hermine, La sauvage, Le voyageur sans bagage, Eurydice, Editions Balzac, 1942.

Nouvelles pieces noires: Jezebel, Antigone, Romeo et Jeannette, [et] Medee, Editions de la Table Ronde, 1946.

Antigone [et] Medee, Le Club Francais du Livre, 1948.

Pieces brillantes: L'invitation au chateau, Colombe, La repetition; ou, l'amour puni, [et] Cecile; ou, l'ecole des peres, Editions de la Table Ronde, 1951.

Deux pieces brillantes: L'invitation au chateau [et] La repetition; ou, l'amour puni, Le Club Francais du Livre, 1953.

La sauvage [et] Le bal des voleurs, Colmann-Levy, 1955.

Antigone [et] L'alouette, Livre Club de Libraire, 1956.

Pieces grincantes (includes *Ardele; ou, la Marguerite, La valse des toreadors, Ornifle; ou, le courant d'air,* and *Pauvre Bitos; ou, le diner de tetes*), Editions de la Table Ronde, 1956.

Une piece rose, deux pieces noires (includes *Le bal des voleurs, La sauvage,* and *Eurydice*), Club des Libraires de France, 1956.

Le rendez-vous de Senlis [et] Leocadia, Editions de la Table Ronde, 1958.

Le voyageur sans bagage [et] Le bal des voleurs, Editions de la Table Ronde, 1958.

Antigone, Becket, [et] Cecile, Editions de la Table Ronde, 1959.

La sauvage [et] L'invitation au chateau, Editions de la Table Ronde, 1960.

Pieces costumees (includes *L'alouette, Becket; ou, l'honneur de Dieu,* and *La foire d'empoigne*), Editions de la Table Ronde, 1960.

Theatre complet, six volumes, Editions de la Table Ronde, 1961-63.

Deux pieces roses: Le bal des voleurs [et] Le rendezvous de Senlis, Le Club Francais du Livre, 1963.

Ardele; ou, la Marguerite suivi de La valse des toreadors, Editions de la Table Ronde, 1970.

Nouvelles pieces grincantes (contains *L'hurluberlu; ou, le reactionnaire amoreux, La grotte, L'orchestre, Le boulanger, la boulangere, et le petit mitron,* and *Les poissons rouges; ou, mon pere, ce heros*), Editions de la Table Ronde, 1970.

Eurydice, suivi de Romeo et Jeannette, Editions de la Table Ronde, 1971.

Pieces baroques (includes *Cher Antoine, Ne reveillez pas madame, Le directeur de l'opera*), French & European, 1974.

Pieces secrets (includes *Tu etais si gentil quand tu etais petit, L'arrestation,* and *Le scenario*), French & European, 1977.

Also author of *La repetition; ou, L'amour puni, Leocadia [et] Eurydice,* Club des Amis.

OMNIBUS VOLUMES IN ENGLISH

Antigone [and] Eurydice, Methuen, 1951.

. . . Plays, three volumes, Hill & Wang, Volume 1: *Five Plays* (contains *Antigone, Eurydice, The Ermine, The Rehearsal,* and *Romeo and Jeannette*), 1958, Volume 2: *Five Plays* (contains *Restless Heart, Time Remembered, Ardele, Mademoiselle Colombe,* and *The Lark*), 1959, Volume 3: *Seven Plays* (contains *Thieves' Carnival, Medea, Cecile; or, The School for Fathers, Traveler without Luggage, The Orchestra, Episode in the Life of an Author,* and *Catch as Catch Can*), 1967.

Ardele [and] Colombe, Methuen, 1959.

Leocadia [and] Humulus le muet, Harrap, 1961.

Ardele [and] Pauvre Bitos, Dell, 1965.

The Collected Plays, Methuen, Volume 1 (contains *The Ermine, Thieves' Carnival, Restless Heart, Traveller without Luggage,* and *Dinner with the Family*), 1966, Volume 2 (contains *Time Remembered, Point of Departure, Antigone, Romeo and Jeannette,* and *Medea*), 1967.

FILMS

(With Aurenche) "Le voyageur sans bagage," 1943, released in U.S. as "Identity Unknown," Republic, 1945.

(With J. Bernard-Luc) "Monsieur Vincent," released in U.S. by Lopert, 1949.

"The End of Belle," released in U.S. as "The Passion of Slow Fire," Trans-Lux Distributing, 1962.

Also author of screenplays (with Jean Aurenche) "Les degourdis de la onzieme," 1936, (with Aurenche) "Vous n'avez rien a declarer," 1937, (with J. Duvivier and G. Morgan) "Anna Karenina," 1947, (with Bernard-Luc) "Pattes Blanches," 1948, "Un caprice de Caroline cherie," 1950, (with Monelle Valentin) "Deux sous de violettes," 1951, "Le rideau rouge (ce soir on joue Macbeth)," 1952, "Le chevalier de la nuit," 1953, "Waterloo," c. 1969, "La grain de beaute," c. 1969, and "Time for Loving," 1972.

OTHER

(With Pierre Imbourg and Andre Warnod) *Michel-Marie Poulain,* Braun, 1953.

(With Georges Neveux) *Le loup* (ballet), score by Henri Dutilleux, Editions Ricordi, 1953.

(With Leon Thoorens and others) *Le dossier Moliere,* Gerard, 1964.

Also author of ballet "Les demoiselles de la nuit," score by Jean-Rene Francaix, 1948. Contributor to anthologies, including *Contemporary Drama,* Scribner, 1956; *One-Act: Eleven Short Plays of the Modern Theatre,* Grove, 1961; *Joan of Arc: Fact, Legend, and Literature,* Harcourt, 1964; and *Masterpieces of Modern French Theatre,* Macmillan, 1967.

SIDELIGHTS: The late Jean Anouilh was ranked among France's most successful popular playwrights for more than forty years. One of several theatrical craftsmen whose work marked an exceptionally rich era in French theatre, Anouilh authored numerous dramas that have been performed all over the world. His plays often feature moral heroes, forced to desperate confrontations with "a world fueled by cowardice, revenge and hatred," to quote *Washington Post* contributor Richard Pearson. This expressed horror at mankind's predicament led Anouilh to pen many grim dramas (he called them "black plays" and "grating plays"), but it also spawned humorous pieces that have been compared to the works of Moliere. In *Jean Anouilh: Stages in Rebellion,* B. A. Lenski wrote: "For thirty years, through bedroom as well as metaphysical farces, Anouilh has been providing us with his orchestration of the eternal debate between the body and the soul. . . . [His] voice rises in indignation before certain historical crimes and yet always remains stylized, elegant and perfectly allied to the action on the stage." Sylvie Drake put it more succinctly in the *Los Angeles Times.* Anouilh, Drake concluded, "was a man of ideas who skillfully disguised them as entertainments."

Anouilh held strong views on the purpose of the theatre. He saw drama as a temporary escape from awareness of the inevitability of death, and he therefore strove to make his work highly theatrical. A London *Times* reviewer found Anouilh's plays "compellingly watchable," with "dialogue which could be spoken easily and effectively on stage." *Nation* correspondent Harold Clurman also observed that the playwright desired "to do little more than purvey material for enjoyable theatregoing. But that is only a disguise: Anouilh [possessed] an artistic individuality, deep-rooted in his personality and in the nature of the French nation." Lenski wrote that Anouilh was "the type of playwright who [poured] all his life into his plays, crying, laughing, vituperating, battling,

confessing. . . . Such theatre often exhibits cheap sentimentality, is talkative, abounds in locker-room jokes, relies on vaudeville gimmicks—yet in so doing it is only true to life." The effect of such entertainment, concluded Jack Kroll in *Newsweek,* is "like a child being held by a sage and cynical uncle who talks seductively of the bittersweet pleasure-pains of life."

Anouilh enjoyed grouping his plays in categories. He did it, he said, to satisfy the public's need for classifications—but it also helped to organize his prolific oeuvre. His categories included *pieces noires* (black plays), *pieces roses* (rosy plays), *nouvelles pieces noires* (new black plays), *pieces brillantes* (brilliant plays), *pieces grincantes* (grating plays), *pieces costumees* (costume plays), and *pieces baroques* (baroque plays). *Jean Anouilh* author Alba Della Fazia wrote: "In plays classified as 'black,' 'pink,' 'brilliant,' 'jarring,' and 'costumed,' Anouilh treats an assortment of themes that range from the soul of man to the world of men, from the heroism of the individual to the mediocrity of the masses. Some of the plays are heavy and dismal, some are light and fanciful, but all reveal the author's profound and often painful insight into the human condition."

The *pieces noires* and the *pieces roses* are similar in content—both are concerned with man's survival in an inhospitable environment. In the *pieces noires,* society triumphs over the hero's ideals, forcing the hero to seek a tragic form of escape. Lenski observed that the central characters in the *pieces noires* "are deaf to arguments in favor of a humble sort of happiness. They want all or nothing at all, and the lower they stand, the greater their claims on the Ideal, the louder their plea for help." In the *pieces roses,* the hero escapes not through death but through fantasy, illusion, and changing personality. In *The World of Jean Anouilh,* author Leonard Cabell Pronko contended that although the characters of the *pieces roses* are unheroic in their compromise with happiness, "they at least possess the noble desire for the purity of life that dares to be what it is without excuses. But they are satisfied with a happiness that Anouilh later satirizes as illusory and unworthwhile." In his book entitled *Jean Anouilh,* Lewis W. Falb concluded: "Anouilh may choose to present his observations in the guise of amusing fables, but one must not be deceived by their often pleasing surfaces; the vision underlying them is brutal and unpleasant. . . . But in his theatre, even at his most misanthropic, Anouilh offers a glimpse of an ideal, which, although faint or parodied, is not forgotten."

Over time Anouilh gradually became more grim in his theatrical treatments of his fellow men. Harold Hobson noted in *Drama* magazine that these *pieces gricantes* "certainly caused audiences and critics to say that Anouilh was a man who hated life itself." *New York Times* contributor Gerald Jonas described these "grating plays" as productions in which "moments of realism, even tragedy, alternate with moments of corrosive humor. In such plays, judgments about events on the stage and the motivations of the principals must be constantly revised in the light of new revelations. Anyone in the audience who does not feel a certain discomfort as the evening progresses is probably not paying attention." Pronko claimed that the picture "is one of compromise, and the outlook seems more pessimistic than ever. We can find no hole in the fabric of an absurd universe through which to bring in some meaning." Della Fazia, too, stated that the effect of the plays "is 'jarring' because two irreconcilables—comedy and tragedy—clash on a battlefield strewn with the castoff armor of humanity's defense mechanisms."

In his *The Theatre of Jean Anouilh,* H. G. McIntyre wrote: "It is hardly an exaggeration to say that there is only one central theme running through the whole of Anouilh's work—the eternal and universal conflict between idealism and reality. All his other themes are related to this, either as expressions of the idealistic rejection of life or as explorations of the various obstacles to idealism and self-realization in an imperfect world." Lenski felt that Anouilh judged reality "from the height of the ideal and inevitably, seen from high up, the world seems a very sad place to live. At the same time, in showing reality in black coloring, Anouilh places the ideal into proper perspective." According to Joseph Chiari in *The Contemporary French Theatre: The Flight from Naturalism,* the pessimism of Anouilh is "the revolt of a sensitive being appalled and wounded by the cruelty of life and expressing man's despair at never being able to know his true self or to meet another self in a state of purity. . . . His heroes and heroines are alone, and when they hope to escape from their loneliness through another they generally realize that there is no escape, that life soils everything and that unless they choose to live a lie, death is the only solution—or failing death, the acceptance of suffering as a refining fire which will consume the dross into the ashes of a life devoted to an ideal."

This tendency to champion nonconformity gave Anouilh's work a political edge, especially during the Second World War. During the Nazi occupation of France, Anouilh produced the play *Antigone,* a reworking of the classical story of a young woman who dies because she defies the state. With *Antigone,* Bryan Appleyard wrote in the London *Times,* Anouilh "confronted the ironic contrast between the life of the imagination and the life of the world." Resistance critics hailed the work as a position statement, but Nazi collaborators also praised it for the pragmatic, reasoned arguments it offered in favor of capitulation. A *Times* contributor claimed, however, that *Antigone* "remains the quintessential French play of the 1940s. It combines moving if ambiguous references to the politics of the Resistance with a metaphysical despair that went straight to many an adolescent heart." After the war, Anouilh continued to pen dramas about martyrs; his best-known plays include *Becket; or, The Honor of God,* the story of an English archbishop murdered for his steadfast adherence to the church, and *The Lark,* a treatment of the life of Joan of Arc. Pronko noted that these works show a conflict between "the hero's or the heroine's aspirations and the world of compromise that they must face and in contact with which they would become sullied. . . . Contrasted to them are the mediocre who consent to play the game, and who seek happiness by hiding the truth of life's absurdity from themselves."

Anouilh died of a heart attack at the age of 77. Ironically, given his predilection for viewing himself as an entertainer, he was eulogized as a playwright of ideas. Pronko called Anouilh "a writer who [was] bound to the cause of man's freedom." Likewise, Falb praised the author for his "rich statement of a personal vision, a lucid yet entertaining exploration of themes that involve the anxieties and preoccupations of contemporary audiences." Still, Chiari maintained that it was "human reality and not systems or concepts which Anouilh [was] after, and that is why his characters, full of human contradictions, are emotionally alive. It is in fact not what they think, but above all what they feel which is the main factor." In comedies that force audiences to laugh uncomfortably at their own absurdities, and in tragedies that highlight the venality of life, Anouilh strove to reveal his deepest torments. In the process, to quote Bettina L. Knapp in *Books Abroad,* he "has given the world some very great plays." As Harold Hobson put it, "Jean Anouilh, savage and ferocious at the crucifixion of humanity's highest values, was the greatest dramatist of our time."

MEDIA ADAPTATIONS: L'alouette was adapted for television and presented as "The Lark," in the "Hallmark Hall of Fame" series, 1956-57; *Madame de . . .* was filmed in 1959; *Leocadia* was adapted for television and presented by Compass Productions as "Time Remembered" for the "Hallmark Hall of Fame" series, 1961; *La valse des toreadors* was filmed with the title "Waltz of the Toreadors," Continental Distributing, 1962; *Becket; ou, l'honneur de Dieu* was filmed with the title "Becket," Paramount Pictures, 1963; the film "Monsoon," United Artists, 1963, was based on *Romeo et Jeannette; Colombe* was produced as an opera at Opera Comique, Paris, c. 1970; *Traveller without Luggage* was adapted for NET Playhouse in 1971; *Antigone* was produced in English for "Playhouse New York," Public Broadcasting System, 1972.

BIOGRAPHICAL/CRITICAL SOURCES:

BOOKS

Archer, Marguerite, *Jean Anouilh,* Columbia University Press, 1971.

Bogard, Travis and William I. Oliver, editors, *Modern Drama: Essays in Criticism,* Oxford University Press, 1965.

Brustein, Robert, *Seasons of Discontent: Dramatic Opinions, 1959-1965,* Simon & Schuster, 1965.

Chiari, Joseph, *The Contemporary French Theatre: The Flight from Naturalism,* Gordian Press, 1970.

Chiari, Joseph, *Landmarks of Contemporary Drama,* Herbert Jenkins, 1965.

Cole, Toby, editor, *Playwrights on Playwrighting,* Hill & Wang, 1961.

Contemporary Literary Criticism, Gale, Volume 1, 1973, Volume 3, 1975, Volume 8, 1978, Volume 13, 1980, Volume 40, 1986, Volume 50, 1988.

Curtis, Anthony, *New Developments in the French Theatre: A Critical Introduction to the Plays of Jean-Paul Sartre, Simone de Beauvoir, Albert Camus and Jean Anouilh,* Curtain Press, 1948.

Della Fazia, Alba M., *Jean Anouilh,* Twayne, 1969.

de Luppe, Robert, *Jean Anouilh,* Editions Universitaires, 1959.

Falb, Lewis W., *Jean Anouilh,* Ungar, 1977.

Fowlie, Wallace, *Dionysus in Paris: A Guide to Contemporary French Theater,* World, 1960.

Gassner, John, *Theatre at the Crossroads: Plays and Playwrights of the Mid-Century American Stage,* Holt, 1960.

Gassner, John, *Dramatic Soundings: Evaluations and Retractions Culled from 30 Years of Drama Criticism,* Crown, 1968.

Grossvogel, David I., *The Self-Conscious Stage in Modern French Drama,* Columbia University Press, 1958.

Harvey, John, *Anouilh: A Study in Theatrics,* Yale University Press, 1964.

Jolivet, Phillippe, *Le Theatre de Jean Anouilh,* Michel Brient, 1963.

Kelly, K. W., *Jean Anouilh: An Annotated Bibliography,* Scarecrow, 1973.

Lenski, B. A., *Jean Anouilh: Stages in Rebellion,* Humanities Press, 1975.

Marsh, E. O., *Jean Anouilh,* British Book Centre, 1953.

McIntyre, H. G., *The Theatre of Jean Anouilh,* Barnes & Noble, 1981.

Picon, Gaetan, *Contemporary French Literature: 1945 and After,* Ungar, 1974.

Pronko, Leonard Cabell, *The World of Jean Anouilh,* University of California Press, 1961.

Smith, H. A., *Contemporary Theater,* Arnold, 1962.

Thody, P. M. W., *Anouilh,* Oliver & Boyd, 1968.

PERIODICALS

Books Abroad, autumn, 1976.
College English, March, 1955.
Nation, October 8, 1973.
New Republic, February 11, 1957.
Newsweek, September 24, 1973.
New York Times, November 7, 1979, October 13, 1985, October 17, 1985, May 29, 1989.
Plays and Players, April, 1974.
Romance Notes, fall, 1978.
Times (London), April 23, 1984.
Yale French Studies, winter, 1954-55.

OBITUARIES:

PERIODICALS

Chicago Tribune, October 6, 1987.
Drama, 1st quarter, 1988.
Los Angeles Times, October 7, 1987.
New York Times, October 5, 1987.
Times (London), October 5, 1987.
Village Voice, October 20, 1987.
Washington Post, October 5, 1987.*

—Sketch by Anne Janette Johnson

* * *

ARMOUR, Richard (Willard) 1906-1989

PERSONAL: Born July 15, 1906, in San Pedro, Calif.; died of complications resulting from Parkinson's disease, February 28, 1989, in Claremont, Calif.; son of Harry Willard (a drugstore owner) and Sue (Wheelock) Armour; married Kathleen Fauntleroy Stevens, December 25, 1932; children: Geoffrey Stevens, Karin Elizabeth Ries. Education: Pomona College, B.A., 1927; Harvard University, M.A., 1928, Ph.D., 1933. Politics: Independent. Religion: Protestant.

ADDRESSES: Home—894 West Harrison Ave., Claremont, Calif. 91711.

CAREER: University of Texas, Main University (now University of Texas at Austin), instructor in English, 1928-29; Northwestern University, Evanston, Ill., instructor in English, 1930-31; College of the Ozarks, Clarksville, Ark., professor of English, 1932-33; University of Freiburg, Germany, American lecturer, 1933-34; Wells College, Aurora, N.Y., professor of English, 1934-44; Scripps College, Claremont, Calif., professor of English, 1945-63, dean of the faculty, 1961-63; Claremont Graduate School, Claremont, professor of English, 1945-63, dean and professor emeritus, 1966-89. Carnegie Visiting Professor, University of Hawaii, 1957; Chancellor's Lecturer, California State University and Colleges, 1964-89; author of the year, Stanford University, 1965; writer in residence, University of Redlands, 1974; visiting professor, Whittier College, 1975. Trustee, Claremont Men's College, 1968-89. Lecturer at colleges and universities throughout the United States; U.S. State Department lecturer in Europe and Asia, 1964-70. Military service: U.S. Army, Antiaircraft Artillery, member of general staff of War Department, 1942-46, 1950; became colonel; received Legion of Merit with oak leaf cluster.

MEMBER: PEN, California Writers Guild, Modern Language Association of America, American Association of University Professors, Sunset Club.

AWARDS, HONORS: Harvard research scholar at John Forster Library, Victoria and Albert Museum, London, 1931; Ford Foundation faculty fellow, Paris, 1954; Litt.D., College of the Ozarks, 1944, Pomona College, 1972; L.H.D., Whittier College, 1968, Southern California College of Optometry, 1972; LL.D., College of Idaho, 1969, Claremont Men's College, 1974; second prize for educational film, American Film Festival, 1971, for "On Your Marks"; Author of the Year awards from Los Angeles Public Library Association, 1975, and PEN, 1979.

WRITINGS:

Barry Cornwall: A Biography of Bryan Waller Procter, Meador, 1935.
The Literary Recollections of Barry Cornwall, Meador, 1936.
(Editor with Raymond F. Howes) Coleridge the Talker: A Series of Contemporary Descriptions and Comments, Cornell University Press, 1940, new edition, Johnson Reprint, 1969.
(Editor) Young Voices: A Book of Wells College Verse, Wells College Press, 1941.
Yours for the Asking: A Book of Light Verse, Humphries, 1942.
(With Bown Adams) To These Dark Steps (play), New York Institute for the Education of the Blind, 1943.
Privates' Lives, Humphries, 1943.
Golf Bawls, Humphries, 1946.
Leading with My Left, Beechurst, 1946.
Writing Light Verse, Writer, Inc., 1947, 3rd edition published as Writing Light Verse and Prose Humor, 1971.
For Partly Proud Parents: Light Verse about Children, Harper, 1950.
Light Armour: Playful Poems on Practically Everything, McGraw, 1954.
Nights with Armour: Lighthearted Light Verse, McGraw, 1958.
The Medical Muse, McGraw, 1963.
An Armoury of Light Verse, International Pocket Library, 1964.
Punctured Poems: Famous First and Infamous Second Lines, Prentice-Hall, 1966, new edition, with Eric Gurney, published as Richard Armour's Punctured Poems: Famous First and Infamous Second Lines, Woodbridge, 1982.
On Your Marks: A Package of Punctuation, McGraw, 1969.
All in Sport, McGraw, 1972.
The Spouse in the House, McGraw, 1975.
Educated Guesses: Light-Serious Suggestions for Parents and Teachers, Woodbridge, 1983.

PROSE HUMOR AND SATIRE

It All Started with Columbus: Being an Unexpurgated, Unabridged, and Unlikely History of the United States from Christopher Columbus to the Present for Those Who, Having Perused a Volume of History in School, Swore They Would Never Read Another, McGraw, 1953, 2nd revision published as It All Would Have Startled Columbus: A Further Mangling of American History That Started with It All Started with Columbus, 1976.
It All Started with Europa: Being an Undigested History of Europe from Prehistoric Man to the Present, Proving That We Remember Best Whatever Is Least Important, McGraw, 1955.
It All Started with Eve: Being a Brief Account of Certain Famous Women, Each of Them Richly Endowed with Some Quality That Drives Men Mad, Omitting No Impertinent and Unbelievable Fact, and Based upon a Stupendous Amount of Firsthand and Secondhand Research, Some of It in Books, McGraw, 1956, large print edition, 1976.
Twisted Tales from Shakespeare: In Which Shakespeare's Best-Known Plays Are Presented in a New Light, the Old Light Having Blown a Fuse, together with Introductions, Questions, Appendices, and Other Critical Apparatus Intended to

Contribute to a Clearer Misunderstanding of the Subject, McGraw, 1957.

It All Started with Marx: A Brief and Objective History of Russian Communism, the Objective Being to Leave Not One Stone, but Many, Unturned, to State the Theories of Marx So Clearly That They Can Almost Be Understood, and to Show How These Theories and Many Old Friends Were Carried Out by Lenin, Trotsky, Stalin, Malenkov, Khrushchev, and Others, McGraw, 1958.

Drug Store Days: My Youth among the Pills and Potions, McGraw, 1959 (published in England as *Pills, Potions and Granny,* Hammond, 1959).

The Classics Reclassified: In Which Certain Famous Books Are Not So Much Digested as Indigested, Together with Mercifully Brief Biographies of Their Authors, a Few Unnecessary Footnotes, and Questions Which It Might Be Helpful Not to Answer, McGraw, 1960.

A Safari into Satire, California Library Association, 1961.

Golf Is a Four-Letter Word: The Intimate Confessions of a Hooked Slicer, McGraw, 1962.

Armour's Almanac; or, Around the Year in 365 Days, McGraw, 1962.

Through Darkest Adolescence: With Tongue in Cheek and Pen in Checkbook, McGraw, 1963.

American Lit Relit: A Short History of American Literature for Long-Suffering Students, for Teachers Who Manage to Keep One Chapter Ahead of the Class, and for All Those Who, No Longer Being in School, Can Happily Sink Back into Illiteracy, McGraw, 1964.

Going around in Academic Circles: A Low View of Higher Education, McGraw, 1965.

It All Started with Hippocrates: A Mercifully Brief History of Medicine, McGraw, 1966.

It All Started with Stones and Clubs: Being a Short History of War and Weaponry from Earliest Times to the Present, Noting the Gratifying Progress Made by Man since His First Crude, Small-Scale Efforts to Do Away with Those Who Disagreed with Him, McGraw, 1967.

A Satirist Looks at the World, Graduate School of Business Administration, University of Michigan, 1967.

My Life with Women: Confessions of a Domesticated Male, McGraw, 1968.

A Diabolical Dictionary of Education, McGraw, 1969.

English Lit Relit: A Short History of English Literature from the Precursors (Before Swearing) to the Pre-Raphaelites and a Little After, Intended to Help Students See the Thing Through, or See through the Thing, and Omitting Nothing Unimportant, McGraw, 1969.

A Short History of Sex, McGraw, 1970.

Out of My Mind, McGraw, 1972.

It All Started with Freshman English: A Survival Kit for Students and Teachers of English and a Relaxed Review for Those Who Are Happily Past It All, McGraw, 1973.

The Academic Bestiary, Morrow, 1974.

Going Like Sixty: A Lighthearted Look at the Later Years, McGraw, 1974, large print edition, G. K. Hall, 1974.

The Happy Bookers: A Playful History of Librarians and Their World from the Stone Age to the Distant Future, McGraw, 1976.

It All Started with Nudes: An Artful History of Art, McGraw, 1977.

Anyone for Insomnia? A Playful Look at Sleeplessness by a Bleary-Eyed Insomniac, Woodbridge, 1982.

FOR CHILDREN

The Year Santa Went Modern, McGraw, 1964.

Our Presidents, Norton, 1964, reprinted, Woodbridge, 1983.

The Adventures of Egbert the Easter Egg, McGraw, 1965.

Animals on the Ceiling, McGraw, 1966.

A Dozen Dinosaurs, McGraw, 1967.

Odd Old Mammals: Animals after the Dinosaurs, McGraw, 1968.

All Sizes and Shapes of Monkeys and Apes, McGraw, 1970.

Who's in Holes?, McGraw, 1971.

The Strange Dreams of Rover Jones, McGraw, 1973.

Sea Full of Whales, McGraw, 1974.

Strange Monsters of the Sea, McGraw, 1979.

Insects All around Us, McGraw, 1981.

Have You Ever Wished You Were Something Else?, Childrens Press, 1983.

Contributor of more than 6000 pieces of light verse and prose to over two hundred magazines in America and England; author of weekly feature in *Family Weekly* (Sunday supplement to 350 newspapers). Member of editorial board, *Writer;* department editor, *Quote.*

SIDELIGHTS: Richard Armour told *CA:* "Perhaps because I took a Ph.D. in English philology at Harvard, studying ten dead or deadly languages, I am fascinated by words. Dictionaries surround me while I write, and I call my place of work my wordshop. I envy Wordsworth his name, the perfect name for a writer. Always, when I look up a word, I check not only the spelling and pronunciation but the etymology. It helps in the precise use of a word to know something about its source and its earlier meanings. If I were marooned on a desert island and could have but one book with me, it would be a dictionary. Of course I should like to have a Bible with me also, for respectability if I should have visitors.

"I dislike the word pun, it is so ugly and abrupt. Moreover, as you know, a bad pun is a pun made by someone else. I prefer the more descriptive word, wordplay. This is the word used in other languages, as in the German *Wortspiel* and the French *jeu de mots.* In some of my books there is much wordplay, perhaps too much. But in others, such as *Drug Store Days,* my favorite of my books, there is none at all.

"This suggests that I write in many styles. I hope I do. I try not to get into a rut. I write light verse, which I think of as poetry written in the spirit of play and with emphasis on technique, and I write playful prose. All of my dozen or so books for young readers are written in verse, whether I am writing about the Presidents of the United States (in *Our Presidents* I used many different verse forms, trying to match my subject) or about dinosaurs or whales or whatever. Young people like rhymes and meters, but at some point—by their teachers or their peers, or by being asked to read poetry that is too obscure—they turn against poetry of any kind. One of my missions is to lead readers back to poetry by means of light verse. Too many close a book when they see that the words don't come out even at the right margin of the page.

"I am always encouraging students to write for their school paper or yearbook or whatever allows them to see their work in print. I wish I had started earlier, but in college I wrote for the campus paper, the literary magazine, the humor magazine, and the yearbook. A number of times I have judged writing contests, and I have been amazed and pleased at how well students in elementary school, junior high school, and high school can write.

They have the imagination if they have not as yet the vocabulary and technique for writing.

"My own start at published writing was in 1937. I sent one piece of light verse to *The New Yorker* and one to *The Saturday Evening Post*—and sold them both. It was a little like making two holes-in-one on a golfer's first round. Had both pieces been returned to me, I might have stopped writing, thinking I couldn't write well enough or editors didn't like me. But after making those two sales I was stuck for life. Stuck to my typewriter, that is.

"I started with light verse, but my books of prose humor and satire outnumber the books of light verse three to one. I continue to write both: prose when I have longer stretches of time and light verse when I have what would otherwise be a few idle moments. And of course I carry with me at all times a pen and a notebook for jotting down ideas or lines. As the years go by, I forget more and more rapidly. . . .

"I make a distinction between humor and satire, both of which I write. They are alike in that they are both based on the sudden recognition of incongruity or absurdity. But they differ in purpose. The purpose of humor is to relax and entertain. The purpose of satire is to debunk, deflate, point out a wrong. An example of humor is a collection of my light verse such as *Light Armour*. An example of satire is my *It All Started with Stones and Clubs*, applying irony and understatement to the history of war and weaponry. My model was Swift's *A Modest Proposal*. This may be hard to believe, but the book is recommended reading in the first year at West Point and was purchased by every Army library in the world, some 4,500.

"Mention was made of Swift. I greatly admire Swift's works, and if I were thirty years younger and had thirty times the talent, I would like to undertake a new *Gulliver's Travels*, satirizing the absurdities of my time as Swift satirized his. But of course Swift's satire is still applicable to our own day. That timelessness is one of the marks of greatness. You will find it also in Mark Twain's *Huckleberry Finn*, one of my favorite books, and Voltaire's *Candide*. Imitation is not only the sincerest form of flattery but probably the best way to learn the art or skill of writing. Remember Robert Louis Stevenson's remark about how he played the sedulous ape to many writers.

"In any kind of writing it is important to catch the reader as soon as possible. S. J. Perelman is a master at writing a first paragraph that causes the reader to read on. I once had the privilege of knowing Catherine Drinker Bowen, not a humorist but a writer whose books were invariably best sellers. She told me she had a little sign on her desk that she read whenever she looked up from her work. The sign asked a simple but important question: Will the reader turn the page?

"My greatest usefulness, I suppose, is to bring lightness as well as enlightenment into the classroom. My most numerous readers are junior high school, high school, and college students. One thing that keeps me going is their letters, in which they thank me for taking the dullness out of study, [and] making learning fun."

MEDIA ADAPTATIONS: On Your Marks was made into an animated film in 1971; *Going around in Academic Circles* was made into a musical in 1976.

BIOGRAPHICAL/CRITICAL SOURCES:

BOOKS

Allen, Everett S., *Famous American Humorous Poets,* Dodd, Mead, 1968.
Elliot, Jeffrey M., *Literary Voices #1,* Borgo Press, 1980.

PERIODICALS

Atlantic Monthly, December, 1964.
Best Sellers, November 15, 1965, May 15, 1969, January 15, 1970, September 11, 1973.
Book Week, December 13, 1964, May 16, 1965.
Book World, December 24, 1967, October 19, 1978.
Chicago Sunday Tribune, May 24, 1953, October 14, 1956.
Christian Science Monitor, September 22, 1955, May 5, 1966.
Nation, March 16, 1970.
New York Herald Tribune, August 9, 1953, September 4, 1955.
New York Times, May 17, 1953, October 9, 1955, November 18, 1965.
New York Times Book Review, December 6, 1964, May 22, 1966.
San Francisco Chronicle, May 18, 1953, September 6, 1955, October 4, 1956.
Saturday Review, December 3, 1955, December 18, 1965, November 9, 1968, April 18, 1970.
Springfield Republican, October 14, 1956.
Times Literary Supplement, October 16, 1960.

OBITUARIES:

PERIODICALS

Los Angeles Times, March 1, 1989.
New York Times, March 2, 1989.
Washington Post, March 2, 1989.
Writer, June, 1989.*

*   *   *

ARNOSKY, James Edward 1946-
(Jim Arnosky)

PERSONAL: Born September 1, 1946, in New York City; son of Edward J. (a draftsman) and Marie (Telesco) Arnosky; married Deanna L. Eshleman, August 6, 1966; children: Michelle L., Amber L. *Education:* Attended high school in Pennsylvania. *Avocational interests:* Leisurely walking, growing food, fishing, flytying, training his team of Newfoundland dogs, watching wildlife, "thinking, listening, worrying, and smiling."

ADDRESSES: Home—South Ryegate, VT 05069.

CAREER: Draftsman in Philadelphia, PA, 1964; Braceland Brothers (printers), Philadelphia, art trainee, 1965-66, creative artist, 1968-72; free-lance illustrator and writer, 1972—. *Military service:* U.S. Navy, 1966-68.

AWARDS, HONORS: Outstanding Science Book Award, American Association of Science Teachers, 1978, for *Possum Baby;* Christopher Award, 1984, for *Drawing from Nature;* Nonfiction Award, *Washington Post*/Children's Book Guild, 1988.

WRITINGS:

UNDER NAME JIM ARNOSKY; SELF-ILLUSTRATED CHILDREN'S BOOKS

I Was Born in a Tree and Raised by Bees, Putnam, 1977.
Outdoors on Foot, Coward, 1977.
Nathaniel, Addison-Wesley, 1978.
Crinkleroot's Animal Tracks and Wildlife Signs, Putnam, 1979.
A Kettle of Hawks, Coward, 1979.

Mudtime and More Nathaniel Stories, Addison-Wesley, 1979.
Drawing from Nature, Lothrop, 1982.
Freshwater Fish and Fishing, Four Winds, 1982.
Mouse Numbers and Letters, Harcourt, 1982.
Secrets of a Wildlife Watcher, Lothrop, 1983.
Mouse Writing, Harcourt, 1983.
Drawing Life in Motion, Lothrop, 1984.
Watching Foxes, Lothrop, 1984.
Deer at the Brook, Lothrop, 1986.
Flies in the Water, Fish in the Air: A Personal Introduction to Fly Fishing, Lothrop, 1986.
Raccoons and Ripe Corn, Lothrop, 1987.
Sketching Outdoors in Spring, Lothrop, 1987.
Sketching Outdoors in Summer, Lothrop, 1988.
Sketching Outdoors in Autumn, Lothrop, 1988.
Sketching Outdoors in Winter, Lothrop, 1988.
Gray Boy, Lothrop, 1988.
Come Out, Muskrats, Lothrop, 1989.
In the Forest, edited by Dorothy Briley, Lothrop, 1989.

UNDER NAME JIM ARNOSKY; ILLUSTRATOR

Melvin Berger and Gilda Berger, *Fitting In: Animals in Their Habitats,* Coward, 1976.
Miska Miles, *Swim, Little Duck,* Atlantic Monthly Press, 1976.
Miles, *Chicken Forgets,* Atlantic Monthly Press, 1976.
Miles, *Small Rabbit,* Atlantic Monthly Press, 1977.
Marcel Sislowitz, *Look: How Your Eyes See,* Coward, 1977.
Berniece Freschet, *Porcupine Baby,* Putnam, 1978.
Freschet, *Possum Baby,* Putnam, 1978.
Kaye Starbird, *Covered Bridge House,* Four Winds, 1979.
Freschet, *Moose Baby,* Putnam, 1979.
Eloise Jarvis McGraw, *Joel and the Magic Merlini,* Knopf, 1979.
Betty Boegehold, *Bear Underground,* Doubleday, 1980.
Margaret Bartlett and Preston Bassett, *Raindrop Stories,* Four Winds, 1980.

SIDELIGHTS: Jim Arnosky's children's books have elicited praise for their competent integration of enlightening, factual detail and attractive drawings. "*Secrets of a Wildlife Watcher . . .* is more than just a collection of useful hints and attractive illustrations," writes Francja C. Bryant in a review of Arnosky's 1983 book for *Christian Science Monitor,* "It is an ardent attempt to nourish a child's interest in the world around him." Norma Bagnell, in *Appraisal: Children's Science Books,* holds similar acclaim for Arnosky's *Freshwater Fish and Fishing:* "It is . . . an information book for young children that not only presents facts accurately but also uses our language with skill and appreciation." She adds: "His black and white illustrations are integrated skillfully into the text so that instructions are easy to follow and techniques are made clear."

With more than twenty self-illustrated books to his credit, Arnosky has established himself as a consistent producer of quality children's literature. Becoming an author/illustrator of children's books, however, was not necessarily by design, says Arnosky. He told *CA:* "I had no formal art training but learned a great deal about drawing from my dad who is a skillful patent draftsman. With this training at home I began working in the art field as a trainee. . . . It wasn't until I had been on my own freelancing in illustration for nearly five years that I was introduced to the writing end of books. . . . Like solid, well-written poetry, writing for children emphasizes structure and the need for every word to count."

The discretion he considers necessary for children's writing seems rooted in the way Arnosky gathers his subject matter—with the keen observational eye of a naturalist. Reviewing *Secrets of a Wildlife Watcher* for *Appraisal: Children's Science Books,* Douglas B. Sands writes, "When we have a skilled artist imbued with a naturalist's discerning eye, the result is a rare book— enjoyable from cover to cover by any lover of the out-of-doors. Jim Arnosky's notes on nature are accurate, lacking the flaws so common in many so-called nature books. Here is a writer who obviously knows and understands his natural surroundings." Arnosky's knowledge of nature, however, is not merely the product of detached research. He told *CA:* "I have always had a deep connection with the natural world and find its rhythm close to my own. I think of myself as an artist/naturalist. Most of my close friends are working naturalists, teachers, writers, photographers, farmers, and woodsmen. For four and a half years my wife, my two daughters, and I lived in a tiny cabin at the base of Hawk Mountain in Pennsylvania. There I matured as a writer and illustrator of natural subjects. . . . We have made our home in the hills of northern Vermont because its natural pace of life fits our needs best as a family and mine as a writer and illustrator."

BIOGRAPHICAL/CRITICAL SOURCES:

BOOKS

Children's Literature Review, Volume 15, Gale, 1988.

PERIODICALS

Appraisal: Children's Science Books, fall, 1982; winter, 1984.
Christian Science Monitor, April 6, 1984.*

*   *   *

ARNOSKY, Jim
    See ARNOSKY, James Edward

*   *   *

ARTS, Herwig (W. J.) 1935-

PERSONAL: Born April 7, 1935, in Antwerp, Belgium; son of Joseph (a lawyer and professor of law) and Maria (Dekkers) Arts. *Education:* University of Louvain, Lic. Class. Philology, 1958, L.Th., 1967; University of Munich, L.Ph., 1961; University of Edinburgh, Compl. lic. Div., 1968; University of Strasbourg, Th.D., 1970. *Religion:* Roman Catholic.

ADDRESSES: Home and office—Prinsstraat 13, 2000 Antwerp, Belgium.

CAREER: Entered Society of Jesus (Jesuits), 1953; ordained Roman Catholic priest, 1967; University of Antwerp, Antwerp, Belgium, professor of philosophical anthropology and religion, 1970—. Visiting professor at St. Teresa College, Winona, Minn., 1973, 1975, and 1977, Catholic University of America, 1980-81, and St. John's University, Collegeville, Minn., 1984, 1986, 1988, and 1989. *Military service:* Belgian Army, 1957-58.

AWARDS, HONORS: Literary Prize, Province of Antwerp, 1984, for *Het Ongeloof gewogen: Over Onzekerheid en Atheisme.*

WRITINGS:

Moltmann et Tillich: Les Fondements de l'esperance chretienne, Duculot, 1973.
Met heel uw Ziel: Over de christelijke Godservaring, Patmos, 1978, translation by Helen Rolfson published as *With Your Whole Soul: On the Christian Experience of God,* Paulist Press, 1983.
Het Ongeloof gewogen: Over Onzekerheid en Atheisme (title means "Faith and Unbelief: About Uncertainty and Atheism"), Nederlandsche Boekhandel, 1982.

Waarom moeten mensen lijden? (title means "Why Do People Have to Suffer?"), Davidsfonds (Leuven), 1985.

Een kluizenaar in New York: De spiritualiteit van Dag Hammarskjoeld (title means "A Hermit in New York: The Spirituality of Dag Hammarskjoeld"), Uitgeverij Pelckmans (Antwerp), 1987.

Waarom nog huwen? Een antropologische en christelijke benadering (title means "Why Still Marry? An Anthropological and Christian Perspective on the Meaning of Modern Marriage"), Uitgeverij Pelckmans, 1988.

De lange weg naar binnen (title means "The Long Journey Inwards"), Davidsfonds, 1990.

WORK IN PROGRESS: A book on the psychological and Christian meaning of "friendship."

* * *

ASLET, Clive (William) 1955-

PERSONAL: Born February 15, 1955, in London, England; son of Kenneth and Monica Aslet; married Naomi Roth, 1980. *Education:* Attended King's College School, Wimbledon; Peterhouse College, Cambridge, M.A., 1977. *Avocational interests:* opera, writing, travel, living in London.

ADDRESSES: Home—Flat 5, 19 Gloucester St., London SW1V 2DB, England. *Office—Country Life,* King's Reach Tower, Stamford St., London SE1 9LS, England. *Agent*—Andrew Best, Curtis Brown, 162-68 Regent St., London W1R 5TA, England.

CAREER: Country Life (magazine), London, England, senior architectural writer, 1977-84, architectural editor, 1984—. Member of National Arts Collection Fund.

MEMBER: National Union of Journalists, Victorian Society, Thirties Society (honorary secretary, 1979-87), Garrick Club.

WRITINGS:

The Last Country Houses, Yale University Press, 1982.
(With Alan Powers) *The National Trust Book of the English House,* Viking, 1985.
Quinlan Terry: The Revival of Architecture, Viking, 1986.
The American Country House, Yale University Press, 1990.

SIDELIGHTS: In *The Last Country Houses* Clive Aslet, a writer for England's *Country Life* magazine, examines the English country houses built during the Edwardian and post-World War I eras. No longer supported by agricultural rent, these country homes were financed by industrial and commercial fortunes and had little relationship to the countryside that surrounded them. Aslet provides "a witty and entertaining history and analysis, both social and architectural," noted a *New York Times* reviewer, "of dozens of those millionaires' palaces, mock castles, fanciful weekend retreats and grand cottages."

Times Literary Supplement critic Andrew Saint called *The Last Country Houses* "arresting, handsome, and stylish," adding: "The book is also very fluently written. Aslet has inherited from the [Mark] Girouard tradition a keen eye for the telling quotation or apt social detail, so that the reader bounces along, beguiled without seeming effort even into such technical matters as drains and domestic appliances. . . . By talking about fashion, entertainment, technology, transport, gardening and 'the servant question' he is able to convey more about these houses and their life than he would do by analysing their formal features." The *New York Times* critic concurred: "Technical excellence aside, the casual reader can browse happily in the gossip about the famous, titled or merely rich who built these mansions and why."

BIOGRAPHICAL/CRITICAL SOURCES:

PERIODICALS

Los Angeles Times Book Review, November 17, 1985.
New York Times, November 25, 1982.
Times Literary Supplement, November 26, 1982; November 8, 1985; February 13, 1987.
Washington Post Book World, November 28, 1982.

* * *

ASTURIAS, Miguel Angel 1899-1974

PERSONAL: Surname pronounced "As-*too*-ree-ahs"; born October 19, 1899, in Guatemala City, Guatemala; stripped of Guatemalan citizenship and forced into exile in Argentina, 1954; Guatemalan citizenship restored, 1966; died June 9, 1974, in Madrid, Spain; son of Ernesto (a supreme court magistrate, later an importer) and María (Rosales) Asturias; married Clemencia Amado; married second wife, Blanca Mora y Araujo; children: Rodrigo, Miguel Angel. *Education:* Universidad de San Carlos de Guatemale, Doctor of Laws, 1923; attended the Sorbonne, University of Paris, 1923-28.

CAREER: Diplomat and writer. Left Guatemala for political reasons, 1923; European correspondent for Central American and Mexican newspapers, 1923-32; returned to Guatemala, 1933; founded and worked as broadcaster for radio program "El Diario del Aire" and worked as a journalist, c. 1933-42; elected deputy to Guatemalan national congress, 1942; member of Guatemalan diplomatic service, 1945-54, cultural attaché to Mexico, 1946-47, and to Argentina, 1947-51, minister-counselor to Argentina, 1951-52, diplomat in Paris, 1952-53, ambassador to El Salvador, 1953-54; correspondent for Venezuelan newspaper *El Nacional* and adviser to Editorial Losada publishers in Argentina, 1954-62; member of cultural exchange program Columbianum in Italy, 1962; Guatemalan ambassador to France, 1966-70. Co-founder of Universidad Popular de Guatemala (a free evening college), 1921, and of Associacion de Estudiantes Universitarios (Unionist party group).

MEMBER: International PEN.

AWARDS, HONORS: Premio Galvez for dissertation, and Chavez Prize, both 1923; Prix Sylla Monsegur, 1931, for *Leyendas de Guatemala;* Prix du Meilleur Roman Etranger, 1952, for *El señor presidente;* International Lenin Peace Prize from U.S.S.R., 1966, for *Viento fuerte, El papa verde,* and *Los ojos de los enterrados;* Nobel Prize for literature from Swedish Academy, 1967.

WRITINGS:

POETRY

Rayito de estrella (title means "Little Starbeam"), privately printed, 1925.
Emulo lipolidón, Typografía América (Guatemala), 1935.
Anoche, 10 de marzo de 1543, Ediciones del Aire (Guatemala), 1943.
Poesía sien de alondra, preface by Alfonso Reyes, Argos (Buenos Aires), 1949.
Ejercicios poéticos en forma de soneto sobre temas de Horacio, Botella al Mar (Buenos Aires), 1951.
Bolívar, El Salvador (San Salvador), 1955.
Nombre custodio, e imagen pasajera, La Habana, 1959.
Clarivigilia primaveral (anthology), Losada (Buenos Aires), 1965.

Also author of *Fantomina,* 1935, *Sonetos,* 1936, *Alclasán,* 1939, *Fantomina,* 1940, and *Con el rehen en los dientes,* 1946.

NOVELS

El señor presidente, Costa-Amic (Mexico), 1946, critical edition, Editions Klincksieck (Paris), 1978, translation by Frances Partridge published as *The President,* Gollancz, 1963, published as *El Señor Presidente,* Atheneum, 1964 (also see below).

Hombres de maíz, Losada, 1949, reprinted, 1968, translation by Gerald Martin published as *Men of Maize,* Delacorte, 1975.

Viento fuerte (first volume in "Banana Trilogy"), Ministerio de Educacion Pública (Guatemala), 1950, translation by Darwin Flakoll and Claribel Alegria published as *The Cyclone,* Owen, 1967, translation by Gregory Rabassa published as *Strong Wind,* Delacorte, 1968.

El papa verde (second volume in "Banana Trilogy"), Losada, 1954, reprinted, 1973, translation by Rabassa published as *The Green Pope,* Delacorte, 1971.

Los ojos de los enterrados (third volume in "Banana Trilogy"), Losada, 1960, translation by Rabassa published as *The Eyes of the Interred,* Delacorte, 1973.

Mulata de tal, Losada, 1963, translation by Rabassa published as *Mulata,* Delacorte, 1967 (published in England as *The Mulatta and Mr. Fly,* Owen, 1967).

PLAYS

Soluna: Comedia prodigiosa en do jornados y un final, Ediciones Losange (Buenos Aires), 1955 (also see below).

La audiencia de los confines: Cronica en tres andanzas, Ariadna (Buenos Aires), 1957 (also see below).

Teatro: Chantaje, Dique seco, Soluna, La audiencia de los confines (collected plays), Losada, 1964.

OTHER

(Translator with J. M. González de Mendoza) *Anales de los xahil de los indios cakchiqueles,* c. 1925, 2nd edition, Tipografía Nacional, 1967.

(Translator from the French with González de Mendoza) Georges Raynaud, *Los dioses, los héroes y los hombres de Guatemala antigua, o, el libro del consejo, Popol-vuh de los indios quichés,* Paris-America (Paris), 1927, 2nd edition published as *Popul-vuh, o librio del consejo de los indios quichés,* Losada, 1969.

La arquitectura de la vida nueva (lectures; title means "The Building of a New Life"), Goubaud, 1928.

Leyendas de Guatemala (collection of Indian tales), preface by Paul Valéry, Ediciones Oriente (Madrid), 1930, reprinted, Losada, 1957 (also see below).

Weekend en Guatemala (short stories), Goyanarte (Buenos Aires), 1956.

(Editor) *Poesía precolombina* (collection of Aztec and Mayan poetry), Fabril (Buenos Aires), 1960.

(With Jean Mazon and F. Diez de Medina) *Bolivia: An Undiscovered Land,* translated by Frances Hogarth-Gaute, Harrap, 1961.

El alhajadito (poem and children's stories), Goyanarte, 1961, translation by Martin Shuttleworth published as *The Bejeweled Boy,* Doubleday, 1971 (also see below).

(Editor) *Páginas de Rubén Darío,* Universitaria de Buenos Aires, 1963.

Rumania, su nueva imagen, Universidad Veracruzanna, 1964.

Juan Girador, Centre de Recherches de l'Institut d'Etudes Hispaniques, 1964.

El espejo de Lida Sal, Siglo Veintiuno Editores (Mexico), 1967.

(Translator from the Rumanian) *Antologia de la prosa rumana,* Losada, 1967.

Latinoamérica y otros ensayos, Guadiana de Publicaciones (Madrid), 1968.

(With Pablo Neruda) *Comiendo en Hungría* (poems and sketches), Lumen (Barcelona), 1969, translation by Barna Balogh revised by Mary Arias and published as *Sentimental Journey around the Hungarian Cuisine,* Corvina (Budapest), 1969.

Maladrón: Epopeya de los Andes verdes, Losada, 1969.

Hector Poleo, Villand & Golanis (Paris), 1969.

The Talking Machine (juvenile), translated by Beverly Koch, Doubleday, 1971.

Viernes de dolores, Losada, 1972.

América: Fábula de fábulas y otros ensayos (essays), compiled with preface by Richard J. Callan, Monte Avila (Caracas), 1972.

Sociología guatemalteca: El problema social del indio, (dual language edition, including original Spanish text followed by English text titled *Guatemalan Sociology: The Social Problem of the Indian*), English translation by Maureen Ahern, introduction by Callan, Arizona State University Center for Latin American Studies, 1977.

Tres de cuatro soles, preface by Marcel Bataillon, introduction and notes by Dorita Nouhaud, Fondo de Cultura Ecomómica (Madrid), 1977.

Sinceridades (essays), edited by Epaminondas Quintana, Académica Centroamericana (Guatemala), 1980.

El hombre que lo tenia todo, todo, todo, illustrations by Jacqueline Duheme, Bruguera (Barcelona), 1981.

Viajes, ensayos y fantasias (selected articles), Losada, 1981.

Founder of periodical *Tiempos Nuevos,* 1923; contributor to periodicals.

Work collected in omnibus volumes, including *Obras escogidas,* Aguilar (Madrid), 1955; *Obras completas,* three volumes, Aguilar, 1967; *Antologia de Miguel Angel Asturias,* edited by Pablo Palomina, Costa-Amic, 1968; *Miguel Angel Asturias: Samblanza papa el estudio de su vida y obra, con una seleccion de poemas y prosas,* Cultural Centroamericana Libreria Proa (Guatemala), 1968; *El Problema social del indio y ostro testos,* edited by Claude Couffon, Centre de Recherches de l'Institut d'Etudes Hispaniques, 1971; *Novelas y cuentos de juventud,* edited by Couffon, Centre de Recherches de l'Institut d'Etudes Hispaniques, 1971; *Mi mejor obra,* Orgainzación Editorial Novaro (Mexico), 1973, reissued as *Lo mejor de mi obra,* 1974; *Tres obras* (includes *Leyendas de Guatemala, El alhajadito,* and *El señor presidente*), introduction by Arturo Uslar Pietri, notes by Giuseppe Bellini, Biblioteca Ayacucho (Caracas), 1977.

SIDELIGHTS: Guatemalan statesman and Nobel laureate Miguel Angel Asturias is best known for the novels *El señor presidente,* about a Latin American dictator, and *Hombres de maíz,* about the conflicts between Guatemalan native Indians and land-exploiting farmers, as well as for a trilogy of novels about the Latin American banana industry. His writing—an extensive canon of fiction, essays, and poetry—often blends Indian myth and folklore with surrealism and satiric social commentary, and is considered to evidence his compassion for those unable to escape political or economic domination. "My work," Asturias promised when he accepted the 1967 Nobel Prize for literature, "will continue to reflect the voice of the peoples, gathering their myths and popular beliefs and at the same time seeking to give birth to a universal consciousness of Latin American problems."

Asturias was born in 1899 in Guatemala City, Guatemala, just one year after the country succumbed to the dictatorship of Manuel Estrada Cabrera. Asturias's father, a supreme court magistrate, lost his position in 1903, when he refused to convict students who protested against Estrada Cabrera's totalitarian regime. Consequently, Asturias's family was forced to leave the city for a rural area in Guatemala, where the young Asturias's interest in his country's Indian and peasant customs perhaps originated. Although his family returned to Guatemala City four years later, Asturias had nonetheless suffered the first of the many personal disruptions that autocracy and political unrest would cause throughout his career.

After attending secondary school, Asturias entered the Universidad de San Carlos to study law. As a college student, he was politically active, participating in demonstrations that helped to depose Estrada Cabrera and then serving as court secretary at the dictator's trial. Asturias also helped to found both a student association of Guatemala's Unionist party and the Universidad Popular de Guatemala, an organization that provided free evening instruction for the country's poor. In 1923, as the military gained strength and Guatemala's political climate worsened, Asturias took his law degree and shortly thereafter founded the weekly newspaper *Tiempos Nuevos,* in which he and several others began publishing articles decrying the new militarist government. Asturias fled the country the same year, his own life in danger after a colleague on the paper's writing staff was assaulted.

Asturias lived for the next five months in London, spending much of his time learning about Mayan Indian culture at the British Museum. He moved then to Paris, where he supported himself for several years as European correspondent for Mexican and Central American newspapers while he studied ancient Central American Indian civilizations at the Sorbonne. There he completed a dissertation on Mayan religion and translated sacred Indian texts, including the *Popol-vuh* and the *Anales de los xahil.*

In Paris Asturias also began his literary career. Associating with such avant-garde French poets as André Breton and Paul Valéry, Asturias was introduced to the techniques and themes of the surrealist literary movement, which would become important elements of his writing style. In 1925 Asturias privately published *Rayito de estrella,* a book of poetry, and later, his *Leyendas de Guatemala,* a critically acclaimed collection of Indian stories and legends recalled from childhood, garnered him the 1931 Prix Sylla Monsegur.

Asturias returned to Guatemala in 1933 after further travel in Europe and the Middle East. He spent the next ten years working as a journalist and poet while Guatemala operated under the military dictatorship of Jorge Ubico Casteñeda. He also founded and worked as a broadcaster for the radio program "El Diario del Aire," and between 1935 and 1940, he published several more volumes of poetry, including *Emulo lipolidón, Sonetos, Alclasán,* and *Fantomina.* Asturias first entered politics in 1942 with his election as deputy to the Guatemalan national congress. Three years later, after the fall of the Casteñeda regime and the installation of the new president, Juan José Arévalo, Asturias joined the Guatemalan diplomatic service. The more liberal policies of the new government proved important for the author, both politically and artistically. Under Arévalo's rule, Asturias served in several ambassadorial posts in Mexico and Argentina from the early 1940s until 1952. In addition, the more tolerant atmosphere made it possible for Asturias to publish his first novel, *El señor presidente,* in 1946.

Asturias began writing *El señor presidente* while he was a law student at San Carlos University. Based on his own and others' memories of the Estrada Cabrera administration, the novel was first conceived as a short story about a ruthless dictator—reportedly Estrada Cabrera himself—and his schemes to dispose of a political adversary in an unnamed Latin American country usually identified as Guatemala. Asturias had developed the story through numerous revisions into a novel and completed it in the early 1930s, when publication of the book under Ubico Casteñeda's rule would have been too dangerous.

Translated as *The President* in 1968, *El señor presidente* was acclaimed for portraying both totalitarian government and its damaging psychological effects. Drawing from his experiences as a journalist writing under repressive conditions, Asturias employed such literary devices as satire to convey the government's transgressions and used surrealistic dream sequences to demonstrate the police state's impact on the individual psyche. Asturias also made use of colloquial Latin American dialogue to render realistically the varying perspectives of the country's social classes. Asturias's stance against all forms of injustice in Guatemala caused critics to view the author as a compassionate spokesman for the oppressed. "Asturias . . . does not see the drama of his people from the outside, as a dilettante, . . . but from the inside, as a participant," noted *Les Temps Modernes* contributor Manuel Tuñón de Lara, for example. And a *Times Literary Supplement* review, also commenting on Asturias's success in portraying the country's unique political circumstances, asserted that *El señor presidente* presents "Latin American problems according to their merits and not according to preconceived stereotypes."

Proclaimed by *Los Angeles Times Book Review* contributor Eduardo Geleano as "the best novel about dictators ever written in Latin America," *El señor presidente* especially elicited praise for its representation of severe political repression. Critics expressing this view included T. B. Irving, who wrote in the *Inter-American Review of Bibliography* that Asturias "has achieved in a splendid manner a grotesque and almost asphyxiating conception of the total state." "Asturias leaves no doubt about what it is like to be tortured, or what it is like to work for a man who is both omnipotent and depraved," applauded the *Times Literary Supplement* reviewer. "When the reader puts down the novel," Irving remarked, "he does so with a feeling of compassion and, at the same time, relief that he has not had to live through similar circumstances."

Three years after the publication of *El señor presidente,* while serving as Guatemalan cultural attaché in Buenos Aires, Argentina, Asturias completed and published *Hombres de Maíz,* the first of his novels explicitly to evoke the mythology of his country's ancient past. Translated as *Men of Maize* in 1975, the book abandons *El señor presidente*'s satiric approach for a poetic, surrealistic treatment of the struggle between the Guatemalan *indigenista,* or highland Indians, and the *ladinos,* peasants who, much like their conquering Spanish ancestors, attempt to usurp Indian territory in order to raise commercial corn crops. The story unfolds from the point of view of the *indigenista,* whose ancient beliefs teach that the first human was made from corn and that the grain is therefore sacred and must be grown only for tribal use. When their resistance leader, Gaspar Ilóm, is assassinated, the Indians place a curse on their enemies, beginning a series of events that becomes part of the Indian mythological heritage. According to Joseph Sommers in the *Journal of Inter-American Studies,* "the reader sees briefly . . . the concrete situation which gives rise to myth. Then . . . he witnesses the formation of legends, as the novel traces their spread and elaboration into full-fledged folklore."

While *Men of Maize* was coolly received at the time of its publication in 1949, many critics have come to view the work as Asturias's masterpiece—his most successful integration of the social and the artistic. Reviewers especially admired the author's portrayal of the contrasting *indigenista* and *ladino* conceptions of the world. "At one level," noted *Washington Post Book World* reviewer Patrick Breslin, the book is "symbolic of the Spanish conquest itself. The social and economic order violently introduced by the Spanish four and a half centuries ago is still tenuous, not only in the highlands of Guatemala, but throughout the Andes of South America as well." Other readers, such as Sommers, who criticized what he saw as the author's "baroque profusion of imagery" and frequent use of "expressive but difficult localism," praised Asturias's surrealistic combination of myth and reality as an original and insightful portrait of Indian attitudes. *Men of Maize*, Sommers explained, "transcends the former stereotype of superficial realism and frequently elementary social protest."

During his diplomatic assignments in Argentina, Asturias also worked on what has come to be known to English-speaking readers as his "Banana Trilogy"—three novels about the Latin American banana industry. Consisting of *Viento fuerte, El papa verde,* and *Los ojos de los enterrados,* the trilogy focuses on the conflicts between the labor force in an unidentified country (taken again by critics to be Guatemala), and Tropical Banana, Inc., a North American conglomerate commonly accepted as a portrait of the real-life United Fruit Company. *Viento fuerte,* translated as *The Strong Wind,* relates the attempts of the main character, former Tropical Banana official Lester Mead, to bring about cooperation between the native growers and the company by urging fairness over profit. *El papa verde,* the second volume of the trilogy translated as *The Green Pope,* depicts Mead's continued and ultimately unsuccessful efforts to convince the head of Tropical Banana—the "Green Pope"—to offer banana growers a stable market and fairer prices for their crops. The final novel, *Los ojos de los enterrados,* translated as *The Eyes of the Interred,* deals with the spread of the banana industry's turmoil into the political arena through a general strike that helps depose the country's president. Although the "Banana Trilogy" was not as critically acclaimed as either *El señor presidente* or *Hombres de maíz,* it earned Asturias the International Lenin Peace Prize from the Soviet Union, who honored the works' stance against capitalist imperialism.

Working for the government of Arévalo's successor Jacobo Arbenz Guzmán in 1953, Asturias was sent as Guatemalan ambassador to El Salvador to try to prevent El Salvadorean rebels from invading Guatemala. Although he had enlisted the El Salvadorean government's aid, the rebels, with backing from the United States, nonetheless invaded Guatemala and overthrew Arbenz Guzmán. Because of his support for the defeated leader, Asturias was stripped of his citizenship and exiled in 1954. Asturias later incorporated details from these El Salvadorean events in his 1956 collection of stories titled *Weekend en Guatemala.*

Asturias lived in exile, working in Argentina as a journalist for the Caracas, Venezuela, newspaper *El Nacional* until 1962, when he traveled to Italy as part of a cultural exchange program. During this period he continued to write, completing scholarly studies and publishing lectures, children's stories, and another novel, *Mulata de tal.* Asturias did not recover his Guatemalan citizenship until the election of president César Méndes Montenegro's moderate government in 1966, when he accepted a job as French ambassador, the position in which he remained until 1970. Throughout his life of service and exile, Asturias remained committed to exposing through his writing the injustice and op-

pression plaguing his fellow Guatemalans. For his efforts, he was awarded the 1967 Nobel Prize for literature. "Latin American literature is still a literature of combat," Asturias once declared, as quoted by Robert G. Mead, Jr., in the *Saturday Review.* "The novel is the only means I have of making the needs and aspirations of my people known to the world."

MEDIA ADAPTATIONS: El señor presidente was made into a film of the same title by Imago Producciones, Argentina.

BIOGRAPHICAL/CRITICAL SOURCES:

BOOKS

Anderson-Imbert, Enrique, *Spanish American Literature: A History,* translation by John V. Falconiere, Wayne State University Press, 1963.

Callan, Richard, *Miguel Angel Asturias,* Twayne, 1970.

Contemporary Literary Criticism, Gale, Volume 3, 1975, Volume 8, 1978, Volume 13, 1980.

Dardon, Hugo Cerezo, editor, *Coloquio con Miguel Angel Asturias,* Universitario, 1968.

Miquel Angel Asturias en la literatura, Istmo (Guatemala), 1969.

Meyer, Doris, *Lives on the Line: The Testimony of Contemporary Latin American Authors,* University of California Press, 1988.

PERIODICALS

Inter-American Review of Bibliography, April-June, 1965.

Journal of Inter-American Studies, April, 1964.

Les Temps Modernes, November, 1954.

Los Angeles Times Book Review, May 28, 1989.

New Statesman, October 25, 1963, September 29, 1967, April 22, 1988.

New York Review of Books, May 22, 1969.

New York Times, October 20, 1967, January 2, 1971, June 10, 1974.

New York Times Book Review, November 19, 1967, January 26, 1979.

Saturday Review, January 25, 1969.

Times Literary Supplement, October 18, 1963, September 28, 1967, November 19, 1971.

Washington Post Book World, August 17, 1975.

OBITUARIES:

PERIODICALS

Newsweek, June 24, 1974.

New York Times, June 10, 1974.

Time, June 24, 1974.

Washington Post, June 10, 1974.*

—Sketch by Emily J. McMurray

*   *   *

ATIL, Esin   1938-

PERSONAL: Born June 11, 1938, in Istanbul, Turkey; married Taskin Atil. *Education:* American College for Girls, Istanbul, B.A., 1956; Western College for Women, B.A., 1958; University of Michigan, M.A., 1960, Ph.D., 1969.

ADDRESSES: Office—Arthur M. Sackler Gallery and Freer Gallery of Art, Smithsonian Institution, Washington, DC 20024.

CAREER: Tippetts-Abbott-McCarthy-Stratton, New York, NY, research librarian, 1961-63; Queens College of the City University of New York, Flushing, NY, curator, 1963-66; Smithsonian Institution, Washington, DC, Freer Gallery of Art, curator of Islamic art, 1970-85, Arthur M. Sackler Gallery and Freer Gallery of Art, head of exhibition programs and collection management, 1987-89, historian of Islamic art, 1989—. Guest curator, National Gallery of Art, Washington DC, 1985-87. Has organized numerous exhibitions, 1971—. Member of translations panel in near eastern languages, National Endowment for the Humanities, 1978; member of master jury, Aga Khan Award for Architecture, 1989—. Lecturer at colleges, universities, and museums, 1972—; conference organizer, 1974—.

MEMBER: Asia Society (member of advisory council, 1975—), Middle East Studies Association (member of board of directors, 1976-78), American Council of Learned Societies (member of advisory committee of Islamic Teaching Materials Project, 1977-80), Smithsonian Institution (member of steering committee of Office of Academic Studies, 1977-79; member of foreign currency advisory council, 1977-79), Institute of Turkish Studies (associate member of advisory board, 1983-85), Royal Society for Asian Affairs (honorary secretary), American Turkish Association of Washington, DC (member of board of directors, 1971-78).

AWARDS, HONORS: Smithsonian Institution, Mamluk Art Research grant, Foreign Currency Program, 1977-81, Mamluk Art Research assistant grant, Scholarly Studies Program, 1980-81; Fulbright Islamic Civilization Research Award, 1982-83, for Ottoman art research; Grand Award for Culture and Art, Republic of Turkey, 1987; Medal of Honor, Assembly of Turkish American Associations, 1987; honorary doctorate, Bosporus University, Istanbul, and Karadeniz University, Trabzon, Turkey, both 1987; TUTAV Award for Outstanding Achievement in the Arts, Foundation for Turkish Culture (Turkey), 1988.

WRITINGS:

Exhibition of Twenty-Five Hundred Years of Persian Art, Freer Gallery of Art, 1971.
Ceramics from the World of Islam, Freer Gallery of Art, 1973.
Turkish Art of the Ottoman Period, Freer Gallery of Art, 1973.
(Translator) *Turkish Miniature Painting,* [Istanbul], 1974.
Art of the Arab World, Freer Gallery of Art, 1975.
(With John A. Pope and Josephine Knapp) *Oriental Ceramics, the World's Greatest Collections: Freer Gallery of Art,* [Tokyo], 1975.
The Brush of the Masters: Drawings from Iran and India, Freer Gallery of Art, 1978.
(Editor and translator) *Islamic Miniature Painting: Topkapi Palace Museum,* [Istanbul], 1979.
(Editor and contributor) *Turkish Art,* Abrams and Smithsonian Institution Press, 1980.
Renaissance of Islam: Art of the Mamluks, Smithsonian Institution Press, 1981.
Kalila wa Dimna: Fables from a Fourteenth-Century Arabic Manuscript, Smithsonian Institution Press, 1981.
(Editor and translator) *Anatolian Civilizations: Seljuk and Ottoman Art,* [Istanbul], 1983.
(With W. T. Chase and Paul Jett) *Islamic Metalwork in the Freer Gallery of Art,* Freer Gallery of Art, 1985.
(Contributor) *Ceramic Art of the World,* Volume 21: *Islamic Pottery,* [Tokyo], 1985.
Suleymanname: The Illustrated History of Suleyman, Abrams and National Gallery of Art, 1986.
The Age of Sultan Suleyman the Magnificent, Abrams and National Gallery of Art, 1987.
(Contributor) *Dictionary of Art,* [London], 1987.

(Editor) *Islamic Art and Patronage: Selections from the Kuwait National Museum,* Smithsonian Institution Press, 1990.

Also author of exhibition brochure, *Traditional Architecture of Saudi Arabia,* for Smithsonian Institution, 1984, and of introduction to the catalogue of an exhibition held at King Faisal Center, Riyadh, *The Unity of Islamic Art,* London, 1984. Also author of several films and audio-visual programs. Contributor to numerous periodicals, including *Turkey Today, Washington Post, New York Times, Smithsonian, Arts and the Islamic World, Sanat Tarihi Arastirmalari,* and *Pegasus.* Member of editorial board, *Ars Orientalis,* 1970-85, *Muqarnas,* 1981—, and *Bulletin of the Asia Institute,* 1982—; member of advisory board, *Middle East Annual,* 1981—.

BIOGRAPHICAL/CRITICAL SOURCES:

PERIODICALS

New Republic, November 29, 1980.

*   *   *

AVALLE-ARCE, Juan Bautista de 1927-
(Luis Galvez de Montalvo, Gabriel Goyeneche)

PERSONAL: Surname is pronounced "Ah-*vah*-yay Ar-say"; born May 13, 1927, in Buenos Aires, Argentina; came to U.S., 1948; son of Juan Bautista (a senator) and Maria (Martina) Avalle-Arce; married Constance M. Marginot, August 20, 1956 (died, 1969); married Diane Janet Pamp (a writer), August 29, 1969; children: (first marriage) Juan Bautista Alejandro Guadalupe III, Maria Martina, Alejandro Alcantara; (second marriage) Maria la Real Alejandra, Fadrique Martin Manuel. *Education:* Attended Colegio Nacional de Buenos Aires, 1941-47, and Universidad de Buenos Aires, 1942-47; Harvard University, A.B., 1951, M.A., 1952, Ph.D., 1955; Ohio State University, postdoctoral fellow, 1958-59. *Politics:* Carlist. *Religion:* Catholic.

ADDRESSES: Home—"Etxeberria," 4640 Oak View Rd., Santa Yuez, Calif. 93460. *Office*—Department of Spanish, University of California, Santa Barbara, Santa Barbara, Calif. 93106.

CAREER: Ohio State University, Columbus, assistant professor, 1955-57, associate professor of Romance languages, 1957-61, acting chairman of department, 1960; Smith College, Northampton, Mass., professor of Spanish, 1961-65, Sophia Smith Professor of Hispanic Studies, 1965-69, chairman of department, 1966-69, director of graduate studies, 1961-69; University of North Carolina at Chapel Hill, William Rand Kenan, Jr. Professor of Spanish, 1969-84; University of California, Santa Barbara, professor, 1984—. Visiting scholar in the humanities at University of Bridgeport, 1968, University at Georgia, 1972, University of Virginia, 1976, Universidad de Salamanca, Universidad de Cádiz, Universidad de Alicante, and Fundacion Juan March (Madrid). Lecturer at various universities in the U.S., Asia, and Europe. Member of editorial board of Tamesis Books. Consultant for several university presses, including those of Princeton University, University of Texas, and University of California. Member of national board of advisors, Instituto Cultural Hispanico; member of advisory board, Bryn Mawr College. Cultural correspondent, Radio Nacional de España, Euskadiko Erradio (Basque Government Radio).

MEMBER: Instituto Internacional de Literatura Iberoamericana, Academia Argentina de Letras, Hispanic Society of America, Modern Humanities Research Association, Renaissance Society of America, Council of Graduate Schools, Academy of Literary Stories (founding member), Real Sociedad Vascongada de

Amigos del Pais, Asociacion Internacional de Hispanistas (founding member), Sociedad de Bibliofilos Espanoles, Centro de Estudios Jacobeos (Santiago), Centre d'Etudes Superieures de Civilisation Medievale (Universite de Poitiers), Cervantes Society of America (president, 1980), Society of Spanish and Spanish Americans (honorary fellow).

AWARDS, HONORS: Premio Literario del Centro Gallego, 1948, for "Rosalia de Castro: A Critical Study"; Susan Anthony Potter Literary Prize, Harvard University, 1951, for "The Poetry of Jorge de Montemayor"; grants from American Philosophical Society, 1958 and 1963, American Council of Learned Societies, 1962 and 1967-68, and National Endowment for the Humanities, 1967-68 and 1978-80; Guggenheim fellow, 1960-61; Bonsoms Medal from the government of Spain, 1962, for critical works on Cervantes; Diploma of Merit, Universita delle Arte (Italy); Medal *au merit*, Kyoto University for Foreign Affairs (Japan); created Marqués de la Lealtad for Teutonic Order of the Levant Trust.

WRITINGS:

Conocimiento y vida en Cervantes, Imprenta Universitaria (Buenos Aires), 1959.

La novela pastoril española, Revista de Occidente (Madrid), 1959.

Deslindes cervantinos, Edhigar (Madrid), 1961.

El Inca Garcilaso en sus comentarios, Gredos (Madrid), 1963, 2nd edition, 1970.

Bernal Frances y su romance, Imprenta Universitaria (Barcelona), 1966.

Don Juan Valera: Morsamor, Labor (Barcelona) 1970.

Temas hispanicos medievales, Gredos, 1972.

(Editor with E. C. Riley) *Suma cervantina,* Longwood Publishing, 1973.

El cronista Pedro de Escavias: Una vida del siglo XV, University of North Carolina Press, 1974.

Neuvos deslinoes cervantinos, [Barcelona], 1975.

Las memorias de Gonzalo Fernandez de Ouieda, two volumes, University of North Carolina Press, 1975.

Don Quijote como forma de vida, [Madrid], 1976.

(Editor) *Don Quijote de la Mancha,* two volumes, [Madrid], 1983.

(Editor) Lope de Vega, *Las hazañes del segundo David,* [Madrid], 1984.

(Editor) Garcia Rodriguez de Montalvo, *Amadis de Gaula,* two volumes, [Barcelona], 1984.

La Galatea de Cervantes: Cuatrocientos años despoés, Juan de la Cuesta, 1985.

Lecturas, Scripta Humanistica, 1987.

OTHER

(Author of prologue and notes) Miguel de Cervantes Saavedra, *La Galatea,* two volumes, Espasa-Calpe (Madrid), 1961, 2nd edition, 1968.

(Author of prologue and notes) Gonzalo Fernandez de Oviedo, *El sumario de historia natural,* Anaya (Madrid), 1962.

(Author of introduction and notes) Miguel de Cervantes Saavedra, *Three Exemplary Novels: El licenciado vidriera, El casamiento enganoso, El coloquio de los perros,* Dell, 1964.

(Contributor) German Bleiberg and E. L. Fox, editors, *Spanish Thought and Letters in the Twentieth Century,* Vanderbilt University Press, 1966.

(Contributor) A. N. Zahareas, editor, *Ramon del Valle-Inclan: A Critical Appraisal of His Life and Works,* Las Americas, 1968.

(Editor and author of introduction and notes) Miguel de Cervantes Saavedra, *Los trabajos de Persiles y Sigismunda,* Castalia (Madrid), 1969.

(Editor and author of introduction and notes) Miguel de Cervantes Saavedra, *Ocho entremeses,* Prentice-Hall, 1970.

(Author of prologue and notes) Lope de Vega, *El peregrino,* Castalia, 1972.

Also author, under pseudonym Luis Galvez de Montalvo, of "The Poetry of Jorge de Montemayor"; author, under pseudonym Gabriel Goyeneche, of several lyric poems. Contributor of more than 250 articles, essays, and poems to numerous periodicals and journals, including *Hispanic Review, Romance Philology, Bulletin of Hispanic Studies, Hispanofila, Insula, Boletin de Ia Real Academia Española, Cuadernos Hispanoamericanos, Romance Notes,* and *Filologia.* Editor, *Studies in the Romance Languages and Literatures;* contributing editor, *McGraw-Hill Encyclopedia of World Biography* and *Diccionario Enciclopedico Salvat Universal.* Member of editorial board, *Hispanic Review, Crítica Hispánica, Anales Cervantinos, Anales Galdosianos, Romance Monographs,* and *Romance Notes.*

WORK IN PROGRESS: Don Fadrique Enriquez: *Vida y obras.*

SIDELIGHTS: Juan Bautista de Avalle-Arce told *CA* he "cannot remember having had an interest other than books (except horses); probably reading Don Quixote at age 7-8 got me as affected by literature as he was. The traditional values and way of life are vital to me. Being Baifitt Grand Cross of the Sovereign Military Teutonic Order of the Levant and its Grand Prior is proof." Avalle-Arce has traveled extensively in the Americas, Europe, Asia, and Africa, and knows Basque, French, Italian, Portuguese, German, Guarani, Latin, Greek, and Arabic in addition to his native Spanish.

AVOCATIONAL INTERESTS: Fox-hunting, polo, breaking and training hunting horses, cooking, wine tasting.

B

BAIRD, Nancy Disher 1935-

PERSONAL: Born April 30, 1935, in Cincinnati, OH; daughter of I. Clinton (a consulting engineer) and Whitlock (a professor of home economics; maiden name, Fennell) Disher; married Thomas L. Baird (a physician), June 21, 1958; children: Alice Whitlock, Mary Nell. *Education:* University of Kentucky, B.A., 1957; Western Kentucky University, M.A., 1972, Ed.S., 1975. *Religion:* Episcopalian.

ADDRESSES: Home—1913 Nashville Rd., Bowling Green, KY 42101. *Office*—Kentucky Library, Western Kentucky University, Bowling Green, KY 42101.

CAREER: High school history teacher in Cincinnati, OH, 1957-58; history teacher at preparatory school in New Orleans, LA, 1958-59; Western Kentucky University, Bowling Green, part-time instructor in history, 1974-75, special collections librarian at Kentucky Library, 1975—.

MEMBER: Southern Historical Association, Kentucky Historical Society, Phi Alpha Theta, Phi Kappa Phi, Filson Club.

WRITINGS:

David Wendel Yandell: Physician of Old Louisville, University Press of Kentucky, 1978.
Luke Pryor Blackburn: Physician, Governor, Reformer, University Press of Kentucky, 1979.
Tradition and Progress: A History of Hummel Industries, Inc., privately printed, 1981.
(With Carol Crowe-Carraco) *The Kentucky Story: A Teacher's Guide,* Kentucky Educational Television (Lexington), 1983.
(With Crowe-Carraco and Michael L. Morse) *Bowling Green: A Pictorial History,* Donning, 1983.
Hand-Me-Down History: A Teacher's Guide, Bowling Green, 1987.
(With Crowe-Carraco) *Kentucky Story,* Allyn & Bacon, 1989.
Pioneer Life in South Central Kentucky: A Teacher's Guide, Bowling Green, 1989.

Contributor to history journals.

WORK IN PROGRESS: A history of the U.S.O.

BALFORT, Neil
See FANTHORPE, R(obert) Lionel

*   *   *

BANKS, James A(lbert) 1941-

PERSONAL: Born September 24, 1941, in Marianna, AR; son of Matthew (a farmer) and Lula (Holt) Banks; married Cherry A. McGee (a counselor and an author), February 15, 1969; children: Angela Marie, Patricia Ann. *Education:* Chicago City Junior College, A.A., 1963; Chicago State College (now Chicago State University), B.Ed., 1964; Michigan State University, M.A., 1967, Ph.D., 1969. *Religion:* Methodist.

ADDRESSES: Home—1333 Northwest 200th St., Seattle, WA 98177. *Office*— 122 Miller Hall-DQ-12, University of Washington, Seattle, WA 98195.

CAREER: Teacher in Joliet, IL 1965, and in Chicago, IL 1965-66; University of Washington, Seattle, assistant professor, 1969-71, associate professor, 1971-73, professor of education, beginning 1973, chairman of curriculum and instruction, 1982-87. Visiting professor of education at University of Michigan, 1975, and University of Guam, 1979; distinguished scholar lecturer, Kent State University, 1978, University of Arizona, 1979, Indiana University, 1983, Humboldt State University, 1989, University of North Carolina, Chapel Hill, 1989; eminent scholar lecturer, Virginia State University, 1981; visiting lecturer, British Academy, 1983; distinguished visiting lecturer, California State University, Fullerton, 1989; Harry F. and Alva K. Ganders Memorial Fund Distinguished Lecturer, Syracuse University, 1989.

MEMBER: Association for Supervision and Curriculum Development (member of board of directors, 1976-79), National Advisory Council on Ethnic Heritage Studies, 1975-79, Social Science Education Consortium (member of board of directors, 1976-79), National Council for the Social Studies (member of board of directors, 1973-74 and 1980-85; chairperson of task force on Ethnic Studies Curriculum Guidelines, 1975-76; vice-president, 1980; president-elect, 1981; president, 1982).

AWARDS, HONORS: National Defense Education Act fellowship, U.S. Office of Education, 1966; Spencer fellowship, National Academy of Education, 1973; "Outstanding Young Man", Washington State Jaycees, 1975; Rockefeller Foundation research fellowship, 1980; Kellogg Foundation national fellowship, 1980-83; distinguished lecturer for 1982, Association of Teacher Educators; Distinguished Scholar/Researcher on Minority Education, American Educational Research Association, 1986.

WRITINGS:

(With wife, Cherry A. McGee Banks) *March toward Freedom: A History of Black Americans,* Fearon, 1970, revised edition, 1978.

Teaching the Black Experience: Methods and Materials, Fearon, 1970.

Ethnic Studies in the Social Context (monograph), National Urban League, 1972.

(With Ambrose A. Clegg, Jr.) *Teaching Strategies for the Social Studies,* Addison-Wesley, 1973, 4th edition, Longman, 1990.

Teaching Strategies for Ethnic Studies, Allyn & Bacon, 1975, 4th edition, 1987.

(With Carlos E. Cortes, Geneva Gay, Ricardo L. Garcia and Anna S. Ochoa) *Curriculum Guidelines for Multiethnic Education,* National Council for the Social Studies, 1976.

Multiethnic Education: Practices and Promises, Phi Delta Kappa Educational Foundation, 1977.

Multiethnic Education: Theory and Practice, Allyn & Bacon, 1981, 2nd edition, 1988.

(With Sam L. Sebesta) *We Americans: Our History and People,* two volumes, Allyn & Bacon, 1982.

EDITOR

(With William W. Joyce) *Teaching the Language Arts to Culturally Different Children,* Addison-Wesley, 1971.

(With Joyce) *Teaching Social Studies to Culturally Different Children,* Addison-Wesley, 1971.

(With Jean D. Grambs) *Black Self-Concept: Implications for Education and Social Science,* McGraw, 1972.

Teaching Ethnic Studies: Concepts and Strategies, National Council for the Social Studies, 1973.

Education in the Eighties: Multiethnic Education, National Education Association, 1981.

(And contributor with James Lynch) *Multicultural Education in Western Societies,* Holt, 1986.

(And contributor with Cherry Banks) *Multicultural Education: Issues and Perspectives,* Allyn and Bacon, 1989.

CONTRIBUTOR

Contributor to numerous books on education, including *The Humanities in Precollegiate Education,* 1984, *Social Issues and Education: Challenge and Responsibility,* 1987, *Cultural and Ethnic Factors in Learning and Motivation: Implications for Education,* 1988, *Black Adolescents,* 1989, *Handbook for Research on Teacher Education,* and *Handbook for Research on Social Studies Teaching and Learning.* Also contributor to *International Encyclopedia of Education,* Vol. 6 and Vol. 9, 1985. Contributor of over ninety book reviews and articles to professional journals, including *Educational Leadership, Social Studies, New Era, Educational Review,* and *Journal of Negro Education.* Guest editor, *Phi Delta Kappan,* January, 1972, and April, 1983, and *Social Education,* October, 1982. Member of editorial boards, *Interracial Books for Children Bulletin, Journal of Negro Education,* and *Multicultural Leader.* Principal consultant, *Preparation in the Social Studies,* 1986; general consultant, *A World of Difference,* 1986.

WORK IN PROGRESS: Teaching Strategies for Ethnic Studies, 5th edition, for Allyn and Bacon; "History of Multicultural and Minority Education," in *Encyclopedia of Educational Research,* 6th edition, for Macmillan; a chapter on the relationship between multicultural and anti-racist education for *Education for Cultural Diversity: Convergence and Divergence,* for Falmer Press; "Multicultural Education and Student Empowerment," in *Empowerment through Multicultural Education,* for State University of New York Press; a videotape series on multicultural education; research on the knowledge base of multicultural teaching.

*   *   *

BARBER, Benjamin R. 1939-

PERSONAL: Born August 2, 1939, in New York, NY; children: Jeremy, Rebecca. *Education:* Albert Schweitzer College, Churwalden, Switzerland, Certificate, 1956; London School of Economics and Political Science, ceritificate, 1959; Grinnell College, B.A. (with honors), 1960; Harvard University, A.M., 1963, Ph.D., 1966.

ADDRESSES: Agent—Charlotte Sheedy Literary Agency, Inc., 145 West 86th St., New York, NY 10024. *Office*—Department of Physical Science, Rutgers University, New Brunswick, NJ 08903.

CAREER: Albert Schweitzer College, Churwalden, Switzerland, lecturer in politics and ethics, 1963-65; University of Pennsylvania, Philadelphia, assistant professor of political science, 1966-69; Rutgers University, New Brunswick, NJ, assistant professor, 1969-70, associate professor, 1971-75, professor of political science, 1975—; currently Walt Whitman Professor of Political Science and Director, Whitman Center for the Culture and Politics of Democracy. Visiting assistant professor, Haverford College, 1968; visiting associate professor, Hunter College of the City University of New York, 1970; senior Fulbright-Hays research scholar, Essex University, 1976-77; visiting fellow, New York Institute for the Humanities, 1980-81; guest lecturer at Yale Drama School and Hopkins Center, Dartmouth College; visiting professor, Princeton University, 1986-87.

MEMBER: American Political Science Association (co-chairperson of program committee, 1975-76), Conference for the Study of Political Thought (chairman, 1983-84), Authors Guild, Authors League of America, American Society of Composers, Authors and Publishers, American Society for Political and legal Philosophy, Academy of Political Science, International Political Science Association, Caucus for a New Political Science, Dramatists Guild.

AWARDS, HONORS: Rutgers University Research Council grant, 1972-73; Guggenheim fellowship, and American Council of Learned Societies fellowships, 1980-81 and 1984-85; honorary doctor of laws, Grinnell College, 1986.

WRITINGS:

(With C. J. Friedrich and M. Curtis) *Totalitarianism in Perspective: Three Views,* Praeger, 1969.

Superman and Common Men: Freedom, Anarchy and the Revolution, Praeger, 1971.

The Death of Communal Liberty: A History of Freedom in a Swiss Mountain Canton, Princeton University Press, 1974.

Liberating Feminism, Continuum Books, 1975.

Marriage Voices (novel), Simon & Schuster, 1981.

The Artist and Political Vision, Transaction Books, 1982.

Strong Democracy: Participatory Politics for a New Age, University of California Press, 1984.

The Conquest of Politics, Princeton University Press, 1988.

(With Patrick Watson) *The Struggle for Democracy,* Lester & Orpen Dennys/CBC Enterprises, 1988.

PLAYS

The People's Heart, produced Off-Off Broadway at Theatre 3, November, 1969.

Delly's Oracle, produced at Berkshire Theatre Festival, October, 1970.

Fightsong (musical), produced in New York at Gene Frankel Theatre, 1975.

(With Martin Best) *Journeys: A Musical Myth,* produced in Hanover, NH at Hopkins Center, 1975.

Making Kaspar, produced in New York City, 1983.

Also author of *The Bust, Doors,* and *Winning,* all produced in New York at Equity Showcase, and of *Home On the River* (opera music theatre). Author, with Patrick Watson, of "The Struggle for Democracy" television series, CBC/ITV, Anglo-Canadian co-production, 1989.

CONTRIBUTOR

R. Goldwin, editor, *Political Parties in the Eighties,* American Enterprise Institute, 1980.

F. Bauman, editor, *Democratic Capitalism,* University of Virginia Press, 1986.

T. Cronin, editor, *Essays in Honor of James MacGregor Burns,* Prentice-Hall, 1988.

S. B. Thurow, *To Secure These Rights: First Principles of the Constitution,* University Press of America, 1988.

Contributor to about twenty other books on sociology. Contributor of articles to *Atlantic, New York Times, Newsday, New Republic, London Review of Books, Harper's, Progressive,* and other periodicals. Editor, *Political Theory: An International Journal of Political Philosophy,* 1974-84.

MEDIA ADAPTATIONS: Journeys: A Musical Myth was recorded by E.M.I. Records as *Knight on the Road.*

BIOGRAPHICAL/CRITICAL SOURCES:

BOOKS

Murchland, B., editor, *Voices in America: Bicentennial Conversation,* Prakken Publications, 1986.

PERIODICALS

New York Times Book Review, December 18, 1988.
Times Literary Supplement, September 23, 1988.
U.S. News and World Report, February 9, 1975; July 7, 1975.
Village Voice, December 11, 1969.

*   *   *

BARBER, Richard (William) 1941-

PERSONAL: Born October 30, 1941, in Dunmow, Essex, England; married Helen Tolson, 1970; children: Humphrey, Elaine. *Education:* Corpus Christi College, Cambridge, M.A., 1967, Ph.D., 1982.

ADDRESSES: Home—Stangrove Hall, Alderton, Woodbridge, England.

CAREER: Writer and publisher. Founder, Boydell Press, 1969.

MEMBER: Royal Society of Literature (fellow), Royal Historical Society (fellow), Society of Antiquaries (fellow).

AWARDS, HONORS: Somerset Maugham Award, Society of Authors, 1971, for *The Knight and Chivalry; Times Educational*

Supplement Junior Information Book Award, 1979, for *Tournaments.*

WRITINGS:

Arthur of Albion: An Introduction to the Arthurian Literature and Legends of England, Barnes & Noble, 1961, 2nd revised and extended edition published as *King Arthur in Legend and History,* Cardinal Publications, 1973, 3rd revised and extended edition published as *King Arthur: Hero and Legend,* St. Martin's, 1986.

Henry Plantagenet: A Biography, Barrie & Rockliff, 1964, Roy, 1967.

(With Francis E. Camps) *The Investigation of Murder,* M. Joseph, 1966.

Knighthood and Chivalry, Scribner, 1970, revised edition, Cardinal Publications, 1974 (published in England as *The Knight and Chivalry,* Longmans, Green, 1970, revised edition, Boydell Press, 1974).

Samuel Pepys Esq., University of California Press, 1970.

(Translator with E. C. Elstob) *Russian Folktales,* Bell, 1971.

(With Anne Riches) *A Dictionary of Fabulous Beasts,* Macmillan, 1971, Walker & Co., 1972.

The Figure of Arthur, Longman, 1972, Rowan & Littlefield, 1973.

Cooking and Recipes from Rome to the Renaissance, Lane, 1974.

(Editor) John Aubrey, *Brief Lives,* Folio, 1975, revised and enlarged edition, Boydell Press, 1982.

A Strong Land and a Sturdy: England in the Middle Ages (juvenile), Seabury, 1976.

Edward, Prince of Wales and Aquitaine: A Biography of the Black Prince, Longwood, 1976.

The Companion Guide to South West France: Bordeaux and the Dordogne, Collins, 1977.

Tournaments (juvenile), Kestrel, 1978.

(Editor) *The Life and Campaigns of the Black Prince,* Folio, 1978.

The Devil's Crown: Henry II, Richard I, John, BBC Publications, 1978.

A Companion to World Mythology, Kestrel, 1979, Delacorte, 1980.

(Editor) *The Arthurian Legends: An Illustrated History,* Littlefield, 1979.

Living Legends, BBC Publications, 1980.

The Reign of Chivalry, St. Martin's, 1980.

(Editor) *The Pastons: A Family in the Wars of the Roses,* Folio, 1981.

(Editor) *The Penguin Guide to Medieval Europe,* Penguin, 1984.

The Worlds of John Aubrey, Folio, 1986.

(With Juliet Barker) *Tournaments,* Weidenfeld & Nicolson, 1989.

Editor, *Arthurian Literature* (annual volume on Arthurian studies), 1981—.

SIDELIGHTS: In several volumes, scholar Richard Barber has explored the various myths and truths surrounding medieval history, in particular that of the celebrated King Arthur. His *Arthur of Albion,* a review of Arthurian legends, was published by the time he was twenty, and since then the author has undertaken two major revisions of the work. In his most recent version, 1986's *King Arthur: Hero and Legend,* Barber "spices up the usual procession of romances and evidences (of the elusive 'real' Arthur) with generally solid perspective and occasionally pointy opinions," Terry Atkinson summarizes in the *Los Angeles Times Book Review.* As Toronto *Globe and Mail* contributor James P. Carley explains, *King Arthur* is "deceptively straightforward in narrative: Barber so smoothly negotiates his way through the labyrinth of Arthurian theses and counter-theses that many of the controversies seem never to have existed." The critic adds that "nobody will be shocked by what Barber says, but all his readers will be charmed and stimulated by how he says it. It is only after finishing the book that one realizes what a fine and learned synthesis the urbane prose and elegant illustrations provide." Barber performs a similar uncovering in *The Knight and Chivalry,* showing "how, century by century, Christianity and heresy and technology transformed a barbarian war party into a social elite whose military skills became less important than its genealogy and elegance," as a *New Yorker* critic describes. The result, states Vincent Cronin in *Book World,* is "a useful, well-documented book about what knights actually did and what writers liked to think they did."

BIOGRAPHICAL/CRITICAL SOURCES:

PERIODICALS

Book World, December 27, 1970.
Globe and Mail (Toronto), February 21, 1987.
Los Angeles Times Book Review, March 8, 1987.
New Yorker, December 26, 1970.
Times Literary Supplement, April 16, 1971.

* * *

BARKER, A(nthony) W(ilhelm) 1930-

PERSONAL: Born January 24, 1930, in Sydney, Australia; son of Annesley Michael and Greta (Mueller) Barker; married Joyce Sawyer, February 19, 1955; children: Simon, Sarah. *Education:* Educated in Sydney, Australia.

ADDRESSES: Home—18 Captain Strom Pl., Dundas, New South Wales, Australia.

CAREER: Sydney Morning Herald, Sydney, Australia, proofreader, 1954-66; Angus & Robertson (publishers), Sydney, editor, 1966-73; free-lance editor and writer, 1973-88; Mead & Beckett (publishers), Sydney, senior editor, 1988—. Musician.

MEMBER: Australian Society of Authors, Library Society.

WRITINGS:

(Editor with R. G. Howarth) *Letters of Norman Lindsay,* Angus & Robertson, 1979.
(And editor) *Dear Robertson: Letters to an Australian Publisher,* Angus & Robertson, 1982.
When Was That?: Chronology of Australia, John Ferguson, 1988.
(Compiler) *Illustrated Treasury of Australian Epic Journeys,* Macmillan (Australia), 1990.

Also contributor to *Australian Dictionary of Biography.* Contributor of reviews and articles to periodicals, including *Nation Review, Reader's Digest,* and *Sydney Morning Herald.*

WORK IN PROGRESS: A biography of bookseller and publisher George Robertson.

SIDELIGHTS: In the late nineteenth century, Scottish-born George Robertson bought half a share in a small Sydney, Australia, bookshop owned by David Angus. Angus and Robertson became the city's first major publishing house, with Robertson encouraging such writers as Banjo Paterson, Henry Lawson, and C. J. Dennis. Robertson was also responsible for the publishing of such Australian classics as *The Magic Pudding* and *Snugglepot and Cuddlepie.* In *Dear Robertson: Letters to an Australian Publisher,* A. W. Barker provides readers with a collection of let-

ters both to and from Robertson. "Barker is a polished and unobtrusive master of ceremonies," observes critic Craig Munro in *Australian Literary Studies,* "whose commentaries provide a fluent narrative which never threatens to overwhelm the letters and yet amplifies them with historical and biographical background."

In the *Sydney Morning Herald,* reviewer Belinda Henwood labels Barker as "one of those people who should be declared a national treasure," in reference to his *When Was That?: Chronology of Australia.* She describes this "thoroughly researched" volume as a "godsend." She recommends that "if you are at all interested in Australian history reference books this is definitely one to add to the collection."

Barker told *CA:* "Although I have always been fascinated by words in themselves, as well as by the challenge of putting the right ones in the right order, my first published writings were produced out of necessity. I wrote my first article—for the *Times of India* in 1953—after arriving in Bombay, broke, in a 1936 London taxi in which I had traveled overland from England. I began writing reviews of jazz concerts some years later in order to get free tickets. (I started out as a jazz musician—not a lucrative occupation, especially when one is not particularly good at it.)

"My first book—a collection of letters by the Australian artist and novelist Norman Lindsay—was passed on to me when the original editor died suddenly; I had just resigned from the editorial department of the publisher to become a free-lance editor/writer/musician. By now the disease had taken hold, and subsequent books have been of my own choice. My motivating factor is simply to write a book that I would like to read or to have as a reference."

BIOGRAPHICAL/CRITICAL SOURCES:

PERIODICALS

Australian Book Review, July, 1983.
Australian Literary Studies, October, 1983.
Bulletin (Sydney, Australia), December 14, 1982.
Sydney Morning Herald, October 1, 1988.
Times Literary Supplement, October 7, 1983.

* * *

BARKER, Dennis (Malcolm) 1929-

PERSONAL: Born June 21, 1929, in Lowestoft, Suffolk, England; son of George Walter (a company director) and Gertrude Edith (Seeley) Barker; married Sarah Katherine Alwyn. *Education:* Attended grammar schools in High Wycombe and Lowestoft, England.

ADDRESSES: Home—London, England. *Office*—*Guardian,* 119 Farringdon Rd., London E.C.1, England. *Agent*—David Higham Associates, 5-8 Lower John St., Golden Sq., London W.1, England.

CAREER: Suffolk Chronicle and Mercury, Ipswich, Suffolk, England, reporter, 1947-48; *East Anglian Daily Times,* Ipswich, reporter, feature writer, and theater critic, 1948-58; *Express and Star,* Wolverhampton, Staffordshire, England, estates and property editor, theater critic, and columnist, 1958-63; *Guardian,* London, England, reporter on Midlands staff, Birmingham, 1963-67, reporter, columnist, media correspondent, and feature writer on London staff, 1967—.

MEMBER: National Union of Journalists (chairman of Home Counties district council, 1956-57), Newspaper Press Fund (life member), Society of Authors, Broadcasting Press Guild, Writers Guild of Great Britain.

WRITINGS:

Candidate of Promise (novel), Collins, 1969.

The Scandalisers (novel), Weidenfeld & Nicolson, 1974.

Soldiering On: An Unofficial Portrait of the British Army (first book in "The People of the Forces Trilogy"), Andre Deutsch, 1981.

One Man's Estate: The Preservation of an English Inheritance, Andre Deutsch, 1983.

Parian Ware, Shire Publications, 1985.

Ruling the Waves: An Unofficial Portrait of the Royal Navy (second book in "The People of the Forces" trilogy), Viking, 1986.

Winston Three Three Three (novel), Grafton, 1987.

Guarding the Skies: An Unofficial Portrait of the Royal Air Force (third book in "The People of the Forces" trilogy), Viking, 1989.

Fresh Start, Rosters, 1990.

Also author of screenplay draft of *Candidate of Promise* for Associated British Productions. Also contributor of scripts and short stories to British Broadcasting Corp. programs. Editorial director and contributor, *East Anglian Architecture and Building Review,* 1955-58.

SIDELIGHTS: Dennis Barker told *CA:* "[I] believe that laughter can lead to serious truths, solemnity to trifling humbug. I believe that that applies in life and in writing: as much to my novels as to my (I hope) essentially human view of the modern British Army, Royal Army, and Royal Air Force, or the great estate of a modern English lord struggling against economic and social pressures to keep his home."

(Field Marshal Lord) Michael Carver described Barker's book *Soldiering On: An Unofficial Portrait of the British Army* in the London *Times* as "a first-class bit of public relations for the Army. Both he and the Army's PR branch, who helped and encouraged him, have earned the Army's gratitude. It is a sympathetic picture that he paints, which should remove many misconceptions about what the Army is like today, based on stories, some true, some exaggerated, of what it was like some time ago."

Barker's *Guarding the Skies* prompted John Ellis to note in the *Guardian* that "interviews with serving personnel are the main research tool and are quoted to good purpose, giving one a real feeling for the RAF as a functioning organism." David Moreau observed in the *Sunday Times* that *Guarding the Skies* contains "some fine anecdotes. . . . The result is an exciting and detailed portrait of the life, hardware and often grisly living conditions that RAF personnel accept uncomplainingly."

AVOCATIONAL INTERESTS: Painting, sailing, walking, reading, talking, music, cinema.

BIOGRAPHICAL/CRITICAL SOURCES:

PERIODICALS

Daily Telegraph (London), September 26, 1986.

Guardian (London), December 7, 1989.

Sunday Times (London), September 3, 1989.

Times (London), November 29, 1981.

* * *

BARON, Othello
See FANTHORPE, R(obert) Lionel

BARRIO, Raymond 1921-

PERSONAL: Born August 27, 1921, in West Orange, NJ; son of Saturnino and Angelita (Santos) Barrio; married Yolanda Sánchez Ocio, February 2, 1957; children: Angelita, Gabriel, Raymond, Jr., Andrea, Margarita. *Education:* Attended University of Southern California, 1941-43, and Yale University, 1943-44; University of California, Berkeley, B.A., 1947; Art Center College of Los Angeles, B.P.A., 1952. *Politics:* Humanist. *Religion:* Humanist.

ADDRESSES: P.O. Box 1076, Guerneville, CA 95446.

CAREER: Taught art at Los Angeles county adult education schools in Burbank, CA, and at Ventura College, Ventura, CA; art instructor at colleges and universities in California, including University of California, Santa Barbara, 1963-65, West Valley College, Saratoga, 1969-72, De Anza College, Cupertino, 1972, Skyline College, San Bruno, 1972, Foothill College, Los Altos Hills, 1975-77, and Sonoma State University, Rohnert Park, 1985-86; writer. Owner and operator of Ventura Press. Art work has been displayed in more than eighty national exhibitions. *Military service:* U.S. Army, 1943-46; served in Europe.

AWARDS, HONORS: Creative Arts Institute faculty grant from University of California, 1964-65.

WRITINGS:

The Big Picture (art manual), self-illustrated, Ventura, 1967, published as *Experiments in Modern Art,* Sterling, 1968.

Art: Seen (drawings and commentary), self-illustrated, Ventura, 1968.

The Plum Plum Pickers (novel), self-illustrated, Ventura, 1969, 2nd edition, Bilingual Review/Press, 1984.

Selections From Walden, self-illustrated, Ventura, 1970.

Prism: Essays in Art, self-illustrated, Ventura, 1970.

The Fisherman's Dwarf (juvenile), self-illustrated, Ventura, 1970.

Mexico's Art and Chicano Artists, self-illustrated, Ventura, 1975.

The Devil's Apple Corps: A Trauma in Four Acts, self-illustrated, Ventura, 1976.

Political Portfolio (commentary), Ventura, 1985.

Carib Blue (novel), Ventura, 1990.

Contributor to anthologies. Contributor of weekly column "Barrio's Political Estuary" to local and national periodicals. Contributor of articles to art magazines and fiction to literary quarterlies.

SIDELIGHTS: When Raymond Barrio's novel *The Plum Plum Pickers* was turned down by every publishing house to which he offered it, he published it himself. In less than two years the "social proletarian" novel, as Adorna Walia calls it in *Bilingual Journal,* was an underground classic and had sold more than ten thousand copies. At that point Harper & Row publishers took another look at Barrio's story of a Chicano migrant family and published it. Since then *The Plum Plum Pickers* has sold twenty-two thousand copies and has been included in numerous high school and college level anthologies. Barrio repurchased the rights to the book in 1976.

Examining the lives of Manuel Gutiérrez, his family, and other migrant workers in *The Plum Plum Pickers,* Barrio gives the reader "a study of the persistent exploitation of the stoop-workers, the migrant laborers in Santa Clara County," writes Walia. "Barrio has an unusually good understanding," continues the reviewer, "of the psychology of groveling foremen and managers who maintain their positions by oppressing those below them. He skillfully employs irony when he writes of the 'clear' consciences of Anglo executives and growers who sleep peacefully unaware of the misery of the migrants in their orchards because they leave the most sordid tasks to their Mexican overseers." Linda Gray in the *Penninsula Bulletin* comments that Barrio, "with uncompromising clarity, opens up the lives that are lived almost on the subterranean level."

In *The Plum Plum Pickers* Barrio details the frustration the migrant worker feels: "The competition was not between pickers and growers, . . . it was between pickers. . . . Between the poor and the hungry, the desperate and the hunted, the slave and the slave, slob against slob, the depraved and himself. You were your own terrible boss. That was the cleverest part of the whole thing. The picker his own bone picker, his own willing built-in slave driver. Pick fast, pick hard, pick furious, pick, pick, pick. They didn't need straw bosses studying your neck to see if you kept bobbing up and down to keep your picking pace up. Like the barn-stupid chicken, you drove yourself to do it."

More than an examination of migrant life, *The Plum Plum Pickers* is an indictment of the economic system that perpetuates the exploitation of the migrants, the Chicanos, and the illegal aliens who are often recruited to do the picking. "*The Plum Plum Pickers* is both an ode to and a denunciation of California and the United States—an ode because California has some of the most fertile land in the world, and a denunciation because of the labor exploitation by the agricombines which perpetuate the migrant slavery," states Walia. "Everyone gets rich from the fertile lands of California except the pickers. The corporation heads view the migrants as refuse." However, Gray notes, despite *The Plum Plum Picker's* strong indictment of the way in which migrant workers are treated and "although deep with sadness, the book avoids moroseness through its fine satire of the local growers and politicians. A meeting of 'socially-conscious' corporation wives and a governor being dubbed 'Howlin' Mad' are good examples."

Barrio is also praised for his skillful prose in *The Plum Plum Pickers*. "Barrio's language is lyrical, a stream of consciousness that gathers poetic momentum through use of newscopy, graffiti, and excerpts from a government pamphlet of 'How to Pick Canning Tomatoes,' " says Gray. Walia considers "the dialogues that imitate the speech of the migrant workers [to be] particularly effective, because of their black humor. As his workers speak, they often garble their words, and their malapropisms are humorous in an ironic way. Through dialogue, Barrio reveals the twisted thinking of landowners and company owners; their rationalizations and self-justifications. He apes the language of American politicians exposing them in all their hypocrisy."

As evidenced in *The Plum Plum Pickers*, Barrio is concerned with inequalities he perceives in a capitalist system. He told *CA*: "Our modern America is suffering from a hideous disease called superaffluence. Mechanization, specialization, and modern technology are all linked together, eroding and destroying America's fine moral spirit. American multinational corporations conspire to drain all the resources they can rob from Third World countries, causing their misery, underdevelopment, and famine.

"Young writers coming through our schools see the tremendous production of great blockbuster million-dollar best-sellers. Some use up great amounts of energy trying to figure out how to jump aboard that luscious circus wagon. It can be done, by a very few, but the price is devastating—the destruction of one's very soul.

"Young writers are the key to humanity's survival. As a lifelong teacher, artist, and writer, I do my best to persuade young people coming up to ignore the siren ululations of the money merchant

and to learn to listen to their own private drummer. To thine own self be true. Integrity above all. The most ignorant rural dweller can possess more integrity than the head of a great corporation—and often does. Therein lies the hope a young person needs to carry out his dreams, visions, ideals, and mission.

"To the question, 'What do you hope to achieve through the books you write?,' my answer is: the salvation of humanity. Nothing less. I would hope that that would serve as a role model for the idealistic young."

The Plum Plum Pickers has been translated into German.

BIOGRAPHICAL/CRITICAL SOURCES:

BOOKS

Barrio, Raymond, *The Plum Plum Pickers*, Ventura, 1969.

PERIODICALS

Bilingual Journal, fall, 1982.
Penninsula Bulletin, December 11, 1976.
Top of the News, January, 1969.

* * *

BARTON, Erle
See FANTHORPE, R(obert) Lionel

* * *

BARTON, Lee
See FANTHORPE, R(obert) Lionel

* * *

BATES, Betty
See BATES, Elizabeth

* * *

BATES, Elizabeth 1921-
(Betty Bates)

PERSONAL: Born October 5, 1921, in Evanston, IL; daughter of Alexander Willett (a civil engineer) and Elizabeth (a teacher; maiden name, Bragdon) Moseley; married Edwin R. Bates (a lawyer), September 3, 1947; children: Thomas, Daniel, Lawrence, Sarah. *Education:* Attended National Park College, 1939-40, Beloit College, 1940-41, and Katherine Gibbs Secretarial School, 1941-42.

ADDRESSES: Home—5 Milburn Park, Evanston, IL 60201.

CAREER: Writer of children's books. Worked as a secretary, 1942-48. Former member of Evanston board of directors of Rehabilitation Institute of Chicago.

MEMBER: Children's Reading Round Table (Chicago), Off-Campus Writers Workshop (Winnetka, IL), Garden Club of Evanston.

AWARDS, HONORS: Carl Sandburg Award, 1985, for *Thatcher Payne-in-the-Neck.*

WRITINGS:

JUVENILES UNDER NAME BETTY BATES

Bugs in Your Ears (Junior Literary Guild selection), Holiday House, 1977.
The Ups and Downs of Jorie Jenkins (Junior Literary Guild selection), Holiday House, 1978.

My Mom, the Money Nut, Holiday House, 1979.
Love Is Like Peanuts, Holiday House, 1980.
Picking Up the Pieces, Holiday House, 1981.
It Must Have Been the Fish Sticks, Holiday House, 1982.
That's What T.J. Says, Holiday House, 1982.
Call Me Friday the Thirteenth, Holiday House, 1983.
Herbert and Hortense, illustrations by John Wallner, Albert Whitman, 1984.
Say Cheese (Junior Literary Guild selection), Holiday House, 1984.
Thatcher Payne-in-the-Neck, Holiday House, 1985.
The Great Male Conspiracy, Holiday House, 1986.
Ask Me Tomorrow, Holiday House, 1987.
Tough Beans, Holiday House, 1988.
Hey There, Owlface, Holiday House, 1991.

SIDELIGHTS: Elizabeth Bates, known to readers as Betty Bates, told *CA:* "I often wonder if my love of writing didn't come because of my soft voice. All my life I've had trouble getting people to listen to me, so instead of shouting I began to work at expressing myself on paper. My teachers encouraged me, and when I was seven I made the children's page of the local news magazine.

"I don't believe people if they say a person doesn't remember the pain of childhood. I remember mine too well. I remember the joys too. Maybe that's why I tend to get caught up in the turmoil of today's young people and adapt chunks of my life, and my children's, into my contemporary fiction. I feel too that young people need to know that humor is vital. My book *Tough Beans,* dealing with Nat Berger, a nine-year-old juvenile diabetic, had to include plenty of that.

"My young-adult book *Ask Me Tomorrow* has roots stretching back over a hundred years, when a Bates ancestor, a young woman, came from an apple farm in Maine to teach in Illinois. After she married, she and her husband traveled back to the farm and built a cottage there, where they spent time in the summers. To this day the Bates family follows their example. The farm is still in the hands of the original family, having been passed along from generation to generation for nearly two hundred years. My grandchildren treasure the farm's beauty and respect the care and appreciation of family roots that have kept it prospering over the years. *Ask Me Tomorrow* is the story of a fifteen-year-old Page Truitt, who lives on such a farm and comes to sense its worth and beauty as we do. The book's characters, my affectionate creations, have traits of those on the real-life farm, and many of its incidents actually took place."

BIOGRAPHICAL/CRITICAL SOURCES:

PERIODICALS

Booklist, February 1, 1986.
Diabetes Forecast, 1989.

*   *   *

BAUMAN, Clarence 1928-

PERSONAL: Born May 19, 1928, in Mennon, Saskatchewan, Canada; son of Alexander (a teacher) and Elizabeth (Quiring) Bauman; married Alice Margaret Nikkel, August 27, 1954. *Education:* University of British Columbia, B.A., 1951; Goshen Biblical Seminary, graduate study, 1951-52; Fuller Theological Seminary, B.D., 1954; Theologische Hochschule Bethel bei Bielefeld, graduate study, 1955-56; University of Bonn, Dr.Theol., 1961; University of Edinburgh, Ph.D., 1975. *Religion:* Mennonite.

ADDRESSES: Office—Department of Theology and Ethics, Mennonite Biblical Seminaries, 3003 Benham Ave., Elkhart, IN 46517.

CAREER: High school biology and religion teacher in Clearbrook, British Columbia, 1954-55; Associated Mennonite Biblical Seminaries, Elkhart, IN, assistant professor, 1962-64, associate professor, 1964-68, professor of theology, ethics, and New Testament, 1968—. Mennonite Brethren Seminary, lecturer, 1964; Ecumenical Institute of Advanced Theological Studies, Jerusalem, Israel, resident scholar, 1976-77.

MEMBER: American Theological Society, Society of Biblical Literature, Mennonite Historical Society, American Society of Christian Ethics, Chicago Society of Biblical Literature.

AWARDS, HONORS: World Council of Churches scholarship, 1955; American Association of Theological Schools Faculty fellowship, 1967-69.

WRITINGS:

Gewaltlosigkeit im Taeufertum: Eine Untersuchung zur theologischen Ethik des oberdeutschen Taeufertums der Reformationszeit (title means "Nonviolence in Anabaptism: An Examination in Theological Ethics of the Anabaptists of the Reformation in Southern Germany and Austria"), E. J. Brill (Leiden), 1968.
The Sermon on the Mount: The Modern Quest for Its Meaning, Mercer University Press, 1985.

Contributor to books, including *The Church in Mission,* Mennonite Brethren, 1967; *Die Mennoniten,* Evangelisches Verlagswerk (Stuttgart), 1969. Contributor to periodicals, including *Mennonite Quarterly Review.*

WORK IN PROGRESS: The Spiritual Legacy of Hans Denck, a translation and critical edition of his works; *On the Meaning of Life: An Anthology of Theological Reflection.*

*   *   *

BAYM, Nina 1936-

PERSONAL: Born June 14, 1936, in Princeton, NJ; daughter of Leo and Frances (Levinson) Zippin; married Gordon Baym, June, 1958 (marriage ended); married Jack Stillinger, May 21, 1971; children: Nancy, Geoffrey. *Education:* Cornell University, B.A., 1957; Harvard University, M.A., 1958, Ph.D., 1963.

ADDRESSES: Home—Urbana, IL. *Office*—Department of English, University of Illinois at Urbana-Champaign, 608 South Wright St., Urbana, IL 61801.

CAREER: University of Illinois at Urbana-Champaign, Urbana, instructor, 1963-67, assistant professor, 1967-69, associate professor, 1969-72, professor of English, 1972—, director of School of Humanities, 1976-87, associate at the Center for Advanced Studies, 1989-90, Liberal Arts and Sciences Jubilee Professor, 1989—.

MEMBER: Modern Language Association of America (member of executive committee; chairman of American literature section, 1984), American Studies Association (member of national council, 1982-84), American Association of University Women (fellow), Organization of American Historians, Nathaniel Hawthorne Association, Robert Frost Society.

AWARDS, HONORS: Guggenheim fellowship, 1975-76; National Endowment for the Humanities fellowship, 1982-83; named University of Illinois Senior University Scholar, 1985.

WRITINGS:

The Shape of Hawthorne's Career, Cornell University Press, 1976.

Women's Fiction: A Guide to Novels by and about Women in America, 1820-1870, Cornell University Press, 1978.

(Editor) Kate Chopin, *The Awakening and Other Stories,* Random House, 1981.

(Editor) Nathaniel Hawthorne, *The Scarlet Letter,* Penguin, 1982.

Novels, Readers, and Reviewers: Responses to Fiction in Antebellum America, Cornell University Press, 1984.

(Co-editor) *Norton Anthology of American Literature,* 3rd edition, Norton, 1989.

(Editor) Maria Susanna Cummins, *The Lamplighter,* Rutgers University Press, 1988.

(Co-editor) *Columbia Literary History of the United States,* Columbia University Press, 1988.

Contributor of articles and reviews to literature journals and literary magazines, including *American Literary History, American Quarterly, American Literature, New England Quarterly, Studies in Modern Fiction, Studies in Short Fiction, Nineteenth-Century Fiction, PMLA,* and *JEGP;* contributor to *New York Times Book Review* and *New York Newsday.* Member of editorial board, *American Quarterly, American Literature, New England Quarterly, Tulsa Studies in Women's Literature, Legacy: A Newsletter of Nineteenth-Century American Women Authors,* and *Studies in American Fiction.*

SIDELIGHTS: Nina Baym once told *CA:* "I became interested in Hawthorne because of the disparity between the clear functional centrality of the heroine of *The Scarlet Letter* and the negative criticism of her character in scholarship at the time; I felt Hawthorne viewed her as a heroine, not a sinner. Interested in women in literature, I found it reasonable to extend my interest from major (male) authors to minor (female) authors. From there, it became reasonable to consider the matter of major and/ versus minor authors, the contexts of authorship, the constitution of the canon, and other matters concerning the way in which we make our literary choices and, having made them, justify them. I find this subject particularly germane to fiction, where storytelling is the essence of the form but where literary choices are seldom validated by discussions of the writer's skill at telling a story or the interest of the story he or she tells."

BIOGRAPHICAL/CRITICAL SOURCES:

PERIODICALS

South Atlantic Quarterly, winter, 1968.

*   *   *

BEALER, George Persson 1944-

PERSONAL: Born September 20, 1944, in Detroit, MI; son of Irving Willis (a space engineer) and Elizabeth (a teacher; maiden name, Persson) Bealer. *Education:* University of California, Berkeley, A.B., 1966, Ph.D., 1973.

ADDRESSES: Office—Department of Philosophy, University of Colorado, Boulder, CO 80309.

CAREER: University of California, Berkeley, instructor in philosophy, 1973-74; University of California, Santa Barbara, lecturer in philosophy, 1974-75; Reed College, Portland, OR, assistant professor, 1975-80, associate professor, 1980-85, professor of philosophy, 1985-89; University of Colorado at Boulder, professor of philosophy, 1989—. University of Michigan, visiting associate professor of philosophy, 1983; Graduate School and University Center of the City University of New York, visiting professor of philosophy, 1986; University of Tuebingen, visiting professor of philosophy, 1987-88; University of Padua, visiting professor of philosophy, 1989. Affiliated with Mellon Foundation interdisciplinary seminar on history and philosophy of science, 1978-79, and on sociobiology, 1980-81.

MEMBER: American Philosophical Association, Philosophy of Science Association, Association for Symbolic Logic, Society for Philosophy and Psychology, Phi Beta Kappa.

AWARDS, HONORS: Kraft Prize, University of California, Berkeley, 1964; fellowships from Ford Foundation, 1967-73, National Endowment for the Humanities, 1977-78, 1984-85, Mellon Foundation, 1979, 1987, 1988, and American Council of Learned Societies, 1981-82.

WRITINGS:

Quality and Concept, Oxford University Press, 1982.
The Philosophical Limits of Science, Oxford University Press, in press.

Contributor to books, *Mass Terms: Some Philosophical Problems,* edited by Jeffry Pelletier, D. Reidel, 1979; *Handbook for Philosophical Logic,* edited by Dov Gabbay and Hans Gunther, D. Reidel, 1985; also contributor of articles to philosophy journals, including *Journal of Symbolic Logic, Linguistics and Philosophy, Synthese, Journal of Philosophy, American Philosophical Quarterly, Philosophical Review, Midwest Studies in Philosophy,* and *Philosophical Perspectives.* Reviewer for *Mathematical Reviews.*

WORK IN PROGRESS: Articles, including "Three Arguments for Dualism"; "An Argument for the Existence of Universals"; "Why Computers Cannot Think"; and "The Incoherence of Empiricism"; a book, *Property Theory.*

*   *   *

BEARD, Helen 1931-

PERSONAL: Born March 20, 1931, in Mudgee, Australia; daughter of Norman Charles (an electrical technician) and Elsie (a confectionist; maiden name, Stewart) Winter; married Clifford Beard (a minister), September 1, 1952; children: Sharon Beard Stawarski, Ruth Beard Milne, Rebecca Beard Milne, Phillip, John. *Education:* Sydney Nursing School, nurses aide diploma, 1949; Crusade Theological College, diploma, 1962.

ADDRESSES: Home—10 Nentura St., Highbury SA, 5089 Australia. *Office*—198 North East Rd., Vale Park, 5081 Australia. *Agent*—OSFO International Gospel Centre, Box 707572, Tulsa, OK 94170.

CAREER: Ordained Christian Revival Crusade minister, 1965; Sunraysia School of Evangelism, Mildura, Victoria, Australia, founder and principal, 1965-67; Christian Centre, Mildura, founder and pastor, 1965-71; itinerant minister in the United States and Canada, 1971-74; Idaho Falls Christian Centre, Idaho Falls, ID, associate minister, 1974-76; international itinerant minister, 1976-83; Idaho Falls Christian Centre, associate minister of Charisma Christian Fellowship Christian Revival Crusade, 1984-86; International Gospel Centre, Tulsa, OK, associate pastor, 1988—. President, International Women's Ministries, 1986—.

WRITINGS:

Love and You, Crusade Publications, 1963.
The Release of the Inner Man, Crusade Publications, 1963.

School of Praise, Engage Publishing, 1979.
Royal Ambassadors, Christian Printers, 1979.
Women in Ministry Today, Logos International, 1980.
Ministry Gifts and Prophets Today, Engage Publishing, 1985.
Woman of Wisdom, Early Bird Publishing, 1990.
A Woman's Full Redemption, Early Bird Publishing, 1990.

Contributor to periodicals.

WORK IN PROGRESS: Man's Great Redemption Power, Men with a Mission, and *Biblical Complimentary Equality for Men and Women,* all for Early Bird Publishing.

SIDELIGHTS: Helen Beard told *CA:* "As a minister of the gospel, I have a responsibility and compassion toward bringing a biblical knowledge into people's lives, to encourage their faith, to bring balance into their lives, and to give answers to large and real problems. I want to bring God into the hearts of mankind as a living person to know and to love. It is my deep conviction that wisdom is the way of peace, prosperity, and happiness. The wisdom is to be found in the knowledge and experience of the Bible.

"I believe my books will help women to find acceptance in ministry—still a largely male-dominated sphere. I also hope my books will help people build the kind of positive self-image necessary for facing problems. This is done by pointing out biblical examples of women used in ministry, by encouraging men and women to be themselves, and by valuing women, family relationships, and creativity in different areas of work and thought.

"My book *Women in Ministry Today* is totally revolutionary in comparison to the usual religious beliefs concerning women. It is based on biblical truth and asserts the scriptural right of women to minister today with dignity and worth.

She adds: "It is my deep conviction that it is time for the value of motherhood and fatherhood to be established in complimentary and equal positions in the Christian Church today rather than fatherhood being everything and motherhood having little value or position. I am most convinced the most powerful forces created by God is redeemed motherhood and fatherhood potential standing side by side, and it is time for these two dynamic powers to be revealed to the world as God first intended. These redeemed mighty potentials will change the world and made it a better place."

*   *   *

BEATY, Shirley MacLean
See MacLAINE, Shirley

*   *   *

BELL, Colin (John) 1938-

PERSONAL: Born April 1, 1938, in London, England; son of Alexander John (an antique dealer) and Regina (Knott) Bell; married Rose Thomson (an archaeologist), July 22, 1961; children: Rachel, Catherine, Alexander, Georgina. *Education:* King's College, Cambridge, B.A., 1959. *Religion:* Church of Scotland.

ADDRESSES: Home—7 Water St., Chesterton, Cambridge, England. *Agent*—Deborah Rogers Ltd., 49 Blenheim Crescent, London W11 2EF, England.

CAREER: Writer. *Scotsman,* Edinburgh, Scotland, reporter, 1960-61; *Scene,* London, England, managing editor, 1963; *Lon-*

don Life, London, assistant editor, 1965-66. Visiting lecturer, Morley College, London, 1965-67, and King's College, Cambridge, 1968-71.

MEMBER: National Union of Journalists.

WRITINGS:

(Editor) *Boswell's Johnson,* Albany Books, 1969.
(With wife, Rose Bell) *City Fathers: History of Town Planning in Britain,* Barrie & Rockliffe, 1969, published as *City Fathers: Town Planning in Britain from Roman Times to 1900,* Praeger, 1970.
Middle Class Families: Social and Geographical Mobility, Humanities, 1969.
Making a Start in Life, Heron Books, 1970.
(With Howard Newby) *Community Studies: An Introduction to the Sociology of the Local Community,* Allen & Unwin, 1971, Praeger, 1972, 3rd edition, Allen & Unwin, 1979.
(Editor with Newby) *The Sociology of Community: A Selection of Readings,* Frank Cass & Co., 1974.
(Editor and author of introduction) *"The Times" Reports National Government, 1931: Extracts from "The Times,"* Times Books, 1975.
(Editor with Newby) *Doing Sociological Research,* Free Press, 1977.
(Editor with Helen Roberts) *Social Researching: Politics, Problems, Practice,* Routledge & Kegan Paul, 1984.

Also author of *Bless General Wade,* 1975. Frequent contributor to *Sunday Times, Daily Telegraph, Guardian, Daily Mirror, Reader's Digest, Radio Times, New Statesman,* and other publications.

WORK IN PROGRESS: A biography of King William IV of England; a study of industrialization of the United Kingdom and Europe.*

*   *   *

BELL, Thornton
See FANTHORPE, R(obert) Lionel

*   *   *

BENDER, Louis W. 1927-

PERSONAL: Born February 8, 1927, in Graceham, MD; son of Elmer D. (a minister) and Mildred L. (Walters) Bender; married Elizabeth N.; children: James Perry, Paul Douglas. *Education:* Moravian College, B.A., 1950; Lehigh University, M.A., 1952, Ed.D., 1965; additional graduate study at Temple University and New York University, 1953-56. *Religion:* Presbyterian.

ADDRESSES: Home—4325 Jackson View Dr., Tallahassee, FL 32303. *Office*— Department of Higher Education, Florida State University, Tallahassee, FL 32306.

CAREER: English teacher and counselor in Quakertown, PA, 1951-54; director of guidance in grades kindergarten through twelve, Westwood, NJ, 1954-57; high school and junior high school dean of boys, Scarsdale, NY, 1957-61; Washington Irving High School, Tarrytown, NY, principal, 1961-62; Bucks County public schools, PA, assistant county superintendent, 1962-65; Pennsylvania Department of Education, Harrisburg, PA, director of bureau of community colleges, 1965-68, acting assistant commissioner for higher education, 1968-69, assistant commissioner, 1969-70; Florida State University, Tallahassee, professor of higher education, 1970—, director of Institute for Studies in

Higher Education, 1980-83; director, Center for State and Regional Leadership of Higher Education. Evening and summer session instructor, Fairleigh Dickinson University, 1954-60; visiting professor at numerous universities, including Lehigh University, 1964, Syracuse University, 1969, University of Lima, 1981, Virginia Polytechnic Institute and State University, 1983. National lecturer, Nova University, 1972-78. Member of advisory board, E.R.I.C. Clearing House for Higher Education, 1975-78; consultant for media systems, Harcourt Brace Jovanovich, Inc., 1976; consultant to numerous educational groups; doctoral program evaluator, Fairleigh Dickinson University, 1983, State University of New York at Buffalo, 1979, and North Texas State University and the University of Houston, 1989. *Military service:* U.S. Army, 1945-47.

MEMBER: National Council of State Directors of Community Junior Colleges (life member; secretary-treasurer, 1967-68; chairman, 1968-69), Council of Colleges and Universities (president, 1975-76), National Council for Resource Development (member of executive committee, 1989-90), American Association of School Administrators, National Education Association, Council of Educational Facility Planners, American Association of Community and Junior Colleges (member of board of directors, 1986-89; member of executive committee, 1988-89), Alumni Association of Moravian College (president, 1965), Phi Delta Kappa.

AWARDS, HONORS: Pennsylvania governor's awards for excellence, 1967, 1968; Distinguished Service Award, Council of University and College Professors of the American Association of Community/Junior Colleges, 1985; Distinguished Research Award, American Association of Community and Junior Colleges Council of University and College Professors, 1988; Special Recognition Award, National Council for Resource Development of the American Association of Community/Junior Colleges, 1989.

WRITINGS:

(With James L. Wattenbarger and Norman C. Harris) *A Plan for Community College Education in West Virginia,* West Virginia Board of Regents, 1971.

(With Richard C. Richardson, Jr. and Clyde E. Blocker) *Governance of the Two-Year College,* Prentice-Hall, 1972.

Improving Statewide Planning, Jossey-Bass, 1974.

(With Blocker and S. V. Martorana) *The Political Terrain of American Post-Secondary Education,* Nova University Press, 1975.

Federal Regulation and Higher Education, American Association for Higher Education, 1977.

(With Benjamin Wygal) *Relating to the Public: Challenge of the Community College,* Jossey-Bass, 1978.

(With Lora P. Conrad) *Computers and the Small College: A National Study,* Florida State University, Institute for Higher Education, 1982.

(With Joan Edwards) *Women and Community College Foundations: Status, Myths and Insights,* Florida State University, Institute for Higher Education, 1983.

(With Conrad) *Word Processing and Microcomputers in Small Two-Year Colleges: A National Study,* Florida State University, Institute for Higher Education, 1983.

(Contributor) Kenneth Young, editor, *Understanding Accreditation,* Jossey-Bass, 1983.

(With Richardson) *Students in Urban Settings: Achieving the Baccalaureate Degree* (research report), George Washington University, 1985.

(With Richardson) *Helping Minorities Achieve Degrees: The Urban Connection* (report), Arizona State University, National Center for Postsecondary Governance and Finance, 1986.

(With Howard L. Simmons and Carmen L. Myers) *Involvement and Empowerment of Minorities and Women in the Accrediting Process: Report of a National Study,* Florida State University State and Regional Higher Education Center, 1986.

(With Thomas A. Henry) *Computer and Information Applications in Two-Year College Collective Bargaining,* Florida State University State and Regional Higher Education Center, 1987.

(With Richardson) *Urban Community College Students: An Autobiographic Profile,* Florida State University State and Regional Higher Education Center, 1987.

Emerging Land Use Practices in Two-Year Colleges: A Report of a National Survey of Land Use Practices of Community, Junior and Technical Colleges, Florida State University, Institute for Studies in Higher Education, 1987.

(With Richardson) *Fostering Minority Access and Achievement in Higher Education,* Jossey-Bass, 1987.

Also author of education monographs and studies. Contributor to *Proceedings of the National Seminar for State Directors of Community Junior Colleges,* Ohio State University, 1972, and *Proceedings of an Annual Workshop of The Southeastern Community College Leadership Program,* Florida State University, 1976. Contributor to journals, including *College Review, American Association of Community/Junior Colleges Journal, Community Services Catalyst,* and *Community College Review.* Member of editorial board, *Community College Review,* 1986—; member of editorial review board, *E.R.I.C. Clearinghouse for Junior Colleges,* 1986—.

WORK IN PROGRESS: A national study of state level policies on articulation/transfer between two year to four year institutions, for the board of directors of the American Association of Community/Junior Colleges.

*   *   *

BENSON, Lyman (David) 1909-

PERSONAL: Born May 4, 1909, in Kelseyville, CA; son of Charles A. (a horticulturist) and Cora (a teacher; maiden name, West) Benson; married Evelyn Linderholm, August 16, 1931; children: David, Robert Leland. *Education:* Stanford University, A.B., 1930, M.A., 1931, Ph.D., 1939. *Religion:* Protestant.

ADDRESSES: Home—The Sequoias, 501 Portola Rd., Box 8011, Portola Valley, CA 94025. *Office*—Department of Botany, Pomona College, Claremont, CA 91711.

CAREER: Bakersfield Junior College (now Bakersfield College), Bakersfield, CA, instructor in botany and zoology, 1931-38; University of Arizona, Tucson, instructor, 1938-40, assistant professor of botany, 1940-44, assistant botanist at Agricultural Experiment Station, 1938-44; Pomona College, Claremont, CA, associate professor, 1944-49, professor of botany, 1949-74, Wig Distinguished Professor, 1963, 1974, professor emeritus, 1974—, chairman of Department of Botany, 1944-73, director of herbarium, 1944-74; Claremont Graduate School, Claremont, associate professor, 1944-49, professor, 1949-74.

MEMBER: International Organization for Succulent Plant Study, International Association for Plant Taxonomy, American Association for the Advancement of Science (fellow; member of council, 1948), Cactus and Succulent Society of America (fellow;

president, 1956, 1957), American Society of Plant Taxonomists (president, 1960), Society for the Study of Evolution, American Institute of Biological Sciences, American Fern Society, Botanical Society of America (president of Pacific section, 1947), Association for Tropical Biology, Western Society of Naturalists (president, 1955), California Academy of Sciences (fellow), Southern California Botanists (president, 1949-50), Torrey Botanical Club, Phi Beta Kappa, Sigma Xi.

AWARDS, HONORS: Greater Linnaeus Medal from Swedish Royal Academy of Sciences, 1952; National Science Foundation grants, 1956-59, 1959-64, 1965-67; merit award from Botanical Society of America, 1978.

WRITINGS:

The Native Cacti of California, Stanford University Press, 1940, 3rd edition, 1969.
The Cacti of Arizona, University of Arizona, 1940, 3rd edition, University of Arizona Press, 1969.
(With Robert A. Darrow) *A Manual of Southwestern Desert Trees and Shrubs,* University of Arizona, 1945, 2nd edition published as *The Trees and Shrubs of the Southwestern Deserts,* University of Arizona Press, 1954, 3rd edition, 1981.
Plant Classification, Heath, 1957, 2nd edition, 1979.
Plant Taxonomy: Methods and Principles, Ronald, 1962.
The Cacti of the United States and Canada, Stanford University Press, 1982.

Contributor to numerous books, including L. R. Abrams, editor, *Illustrated Flora of the Pacific States,* Volume II, Stanford University Press, 1944; Thomas H. Kearney and Robert H. Peebles, editors, *Arizona Flora,* University of California, 1951, 2nd edition, 1960; and Donovan S. Correll and Marshall C. Johnston, editors, *Manual of the Vascular Plants of Texas,* Texas Research Foundation, 1970. Also contributor to reference works, including *Encyclopaedia Britannica* and *Encyclopedia Americana,* and to *Proceedings of the California Academy of Sciences.* Contributor of about sixty-five articles to professional journals, including *American Midland Naturalist, American Journal of Botany, Cactus and Succulent Journal, Annals of the Missouri Botanical Garden,* and *Bulletin of the Torrey Botanical Club.*

WORK IN PROGRESS: Evolution of the North American Floras, Interpreted in the Light of Geological History; Evolution of the Plant Kingdom, a general textbook.

SIDELIGHTS: Lyman Benson wrote *CA:* "A technical monograph does not have to be as dry as the dust in the attic. Catching human interest lies in recreating the imagination and insight that started the research in the first place. Any investigation captures the research worker because he likes problems, but he must figure out why each problem interests him and present this simply and clearly to others. Thus, a monograph shorn of unnecessarily technical language, presented in a clear style, and well illustrated becomes understandable. It is not just in sheep's clothing; it is no longer a fearsome thing."

*   *   *

BENY, Roloff
  See BENY, Wilfred Roy

*   *   *

BENY, Wilfred Roy 1924-1984
  (Roloff Beny)

PERSONAL: Born January 7, 1924, in Medicine Hat, Alberta, Canada; died of a heart attack March 16 (one source says March

15), 1984, in Rome, Italy; cremated in Rome with ashes buried in Medicine Hat, Alberta, Canada; son of Charles John Francis and Rosalie Melina (Roloff) Beny; unmarried. *Education:* Banff School of Fine Arts, student, 1939; Trinity College, University of Toronto, B.A. and B.F.A., 1945; University of Iowa, M.A. and M.F.A., 1947; further study at Columbia University and New York University Insitute of Fine Arts, 1947-48, and in Europe, 1948-49, 1951-52. *Religion:* Anglican.

ADDRESSES: Home and studio—Lungotevere Ripa 3-B, Rome, Italy; and 432 13th St. S., Lethbridge, Alberta, Canada.

CAREER: Artist and photographer. His first public showing was a watercolor accepted for exhibition by Manitoba Society of Artists when he was fifteen, and two years later the first of his twenty-five one-man shows was staged in Toronto; has prepared ten major public photographic exhibits since 1962, including "Image Canada," a collection of thirty-eight murals commissioned for the Federal Pavilion at Expo '67. Work exhibited in one-man shows in New York, Paris, and London, and the principal cities of Canada and Italy; paintings and graphic art in the permanent collections of National Gallery of Canada, Fogg Museum of Boston, Yale University Museum, Brooklyn Museum, New York Museum of Modern Art, New York Public Library, Wesleyan University, Bezalel Museum (Jerusalem), in galleries, in museums in Italy and London, and private collections; works represented in numerous national exhibitions, such as Art Institute of Chicago, Library of Congress, Dallas Museum of Fine Art) and Canadian National Exhibition, Toronto. Prepared the photographic exhibits, "A Time of Gods," shown in Rome and Toronto, 1962; "Metaphysical Monuments," in Rome and Toronto; "Pleasure of Photography," in London, England, and throughout Canada, 1966; "Sculpture of the Renaissance," by National Film Board of Canada, 1967; "The Renaissance," 1968; "In the Cloister of San Francesco," Sorrento, Italy, 1974; "La Perse-Pont de Turquoise at La Maison de l'Iran," Paris, 1977; "Patterns of Persia," Tehran, 1978; "Roloff Beny in Italy and Canada," Palazzo dell'Esposizioni, Rome, 1980; "Churches of Rome," Royal Institute of British Architects, 1981; the "Image Canada" touring exhibit, Ankara, Bonn, Rabat, and Athens, 1981-82; the "Odyssey: Mirror of the Mediterranean" touring exhibit, 1982; an exhibition about the restoration of Colonna Antonina in Rome's Piazza Colonna, 1983. "A Visual Odyssey, 1958-68," a ten-year retrospective, was exhibited at the Gallery of Modern Art, New York, and in 1973 was acquired for the permanent art collection of the University of Calgary. A special exhibition of Roloff Beny's books was held at Canada House, New Delhi, India, 1971, to commemorate Canada's Flag Day.

MEMBER: Royal Canadian Academy (life member).

AWARDS, HONORS: Guggenheim fellowship for printmaking and painting, 1953; Silver Medallion, International Prize for Design at Leipzig Book Fair, 1959, for *The Thrones of Earth and Heaven* and 1962, for *A Time of Gods; Terre des Dieux* (French edition of *A Time of Gods*) was selected as one of the fifty great books of 1965 by Comite des Arts Graphiques Francais; Centennial Medal from Government of Canada, 1967; elected Knight of Mark Twain, 1967, for outstanding contribution to history in *To Every Thing There Is a Season,* which was one of the books chosen by the Canadian Government for presentation to heads of state invited to Canada's Centennial celebration; Canada Council Visual Arts Award, 1968; Gold Medal, International Book Fair at Leipzig, 1968, for *Japan in Color;* Silver Eagle, International Book Fair (Nice, France), 1969; LL.D., University of Lethbridge, 1972; Officer of the Order of Canada, 1972; Special Award for Excellence, Stuttgart Book-Week, 1976, and Charles Blanc medallion, Academie francaise, 1977, for the French edition of *Persia, La Perse—Pont de Turquoise;* first prize, Lithoprinters of Great Britain for Overall Excellence, and *Nebiolo* Award for Presswork, 1978, for *Iran;* Bronze Medal, Leipzig International Book Fair, 1982, for *Odyssey.*

WRITINGS:

ALL SELF-DESIGNED PHOTOGRAPHIC BOOKS, EXCEPT AS NOTED

An Aegean Note Book (collection of lithographs), Thames & Hudson, 1950.

(Text by Bernard Berenson; commentaries by Jean Cocteau and others) *The Thrones of Earth and Heaven,* Abrams, 1958.

A Time of Gods: A Photographer in the Wake of Odysseus, Viking, 1962.

(Text by Rose Macaulay) *Pleasure of Ruins,* Time-Life Books, 1964, revised edition published as *Roloff Beny Interprets in Photographs Pleasure of Ruins by Rose Macaulay* (Book-of-the-Month Club selection), Harper, 1977.

To Every Thing There Is a Season: Roloff Beny in Canada, edited by Milton Wilson, Thames & Hudson, 1967.

(Text by Anthony Thwaite) *Japan in Color,* McGraw, 1967.

(With Aubrey Menen) *India* (Book-of-the-Month Club selection), McGraw, 1969.

(Text by John Lindsay Opie) *Island Ceylon,* Thames & Hudson, 1971.

(Text by Anthony Thwaite and Peter Porter; epilogue by Gore Vidal) *Roloff Beny in Italy* (Book-of-the-Month Club selection), Harper, 1974.

Persia: Bridge of Turquoise, New York Graphic Society, 1975.

Iran: Elements of Destiny, McClelland & Stewart, 1978.

(With Peter Gunn) *The Churches of Rome,* Simon & Schuster, 1981.

Odyssey: Mirror of the Mediterranean, Thames & Hudson, 1981.

(With Arianna Stassinopoulos) *The Gods of Greece,* Abrams, 1983.

Rajasthan, Land of Kings, Vendome Press (New York), 1984.

The Romance of Architecture, Abrams, 1985.

(With Pamela Sanders) *Iceland,* McClelland & Stewart, 1985.

OTHER

Produced a series of posters for Alitalia (Italy's international airline). Articles and photographs represented in Canadian, American, English, and continental publications, including *Catelaine, Harper's Bazaar, Canadian Art, Mayfair, Sunday Times* (London), *Vogue, Queen,* a special Italian edition of *La Revue des Voyages,* and many others.

WORK IN PROGRESS: A book of 100 poems by Desmond O'Grady inspired by 100 photographs by Beny; major works on Egypt and Great Britain; *World of Nature; The Visual Journals of Roloff Beny,* Volume 1: *A Private View,* Volume 2: *Dreams in Architecture,* Volume 3: *Pavilions of Nature.*

SIDELIGHTS: The excellence of Roloff Beny's artistry in painting and photography has won many major awards and is appreciated around the world. A *New York Times* reviewer said of "A Visual Odyssey, 1958-68": "No individual photographer has ever had this kind of space to work with in any gallery or museum in this city, if not the country." There have been foreign editions of Beny's first three photographic books; *A Time of Gods* and *Pleasure of Ruins* have been published in eight languages. *To Every Thing There Is a Season,* a Centennial book about Canada, hit the top spot on that nation's list of best sellers. Beny said that his study of etching and graphic art (largely at the Univer-

sity of Iowa) provided the link between his painting, photography, and book design. A painter who photographed scenes he intended to paint, Beny became enchanted with the photographic process and dedicated himself to it. His work attracted commissions from the governments of India and Ceylon, and the Imperial Court of Persia.

BIOGRAPHICAL/CRITICAL SOURCES:

PERIODICALS

New York Times, September 29, 1968.

OBITUARIES:

PERIODICALS

Chicago Tribune, March 20, 1984.
Globe & Mail (Toronto), March 17, 1984.
New York Times, March 17, 1984.
Times (London), March 23, 1984.

*   *   *

BERGAUST, Erik   1925-1978

PERSONAL: Born March 23, 1925, in Baerum, Oslo, Norway; immigrated to the United States, 1949, naturalized, 1956; died of cancer March 1, 1978, in McLean, VA; married Jean Cameron Somers, January 13, 1951; children: Christine C., Erik R., Paul R., Jane. *Education:* Frogner Gymnasium, B.S., 1943; attended Oslo Handelgymnasium, 1944.

ADDRESSES: Home—Falls Church, VA.

CAREER: Author, editor, publisher. Editor and publisher of numerous publications concerning air and sea exploration, 1946-78; manager of airplane and helicopter services, 1948-52; free-lance aviation writer, 1949-52; North Springs Inc., president, 1962-64. Conducted a weekly radio program, "Washington Radio Features" and was associated with the Voice of America. President's Committee on Scientists and Engineers, member of information advisory group, 1957; Republican Advisory Committee on Space and Aerospace, chairman, 1962-78. *Military service:* Served with the Norwegian Resistance Movement, 1943, and Norwegian Exile Army, 1944-45.

MEMBER: National Press Club, Authors League of America, Authors Guild, Environmental Writers Association of America (member of board of directors, 1972-78), Aviation and Space Writers Association, National Space Club (founder; president, 1957-59), American Helicopter Society, American Military Engineers, American Rocket Society, Convertible Aircraft Pioneers, Norsk Astronautisk Forening, Mason.

WRITINGS:

(With Gunnar Oxaal) *Reisen til Manen Blir Alvor,* Fabritius, 1952.

(With Bernt Balchen) *The Next Fifty Years of Flight,* Harper, 1954.

(With William Beller) *Satellite!,* Hanover House, 1956.

(With Seabrook Hull) *Rocket to the Moon,* Van Nostrand, 1958.

Reaching for the Stars, Doubleday, 1960.

(With Thorstein Thelle) *Romfartens ABC,* P. F. Steensballes Boghandels, 1961.

Rocket City: U.S.A., Macmillan, 1963.

The Next Fifty Years in Space, Macmillan, 1964.

(With Thelle) *Havforsking,* B. H. Reenskaug, 1970.

National Outdoorsmen's Encyclopedia, Remington and Ross, 1973.

Wernher von Braun: The Authoritative and Definitive Biographical Profile of the Father of Modern Space Flight, National Space Institute, 1976.

PUBLISHED BY PUTNAM

Rockets and Missiles, 1957.
Rockets around the World, 1958.
Rockets of the Navy, 1959.
Satellites and Space Probes, 1959.
First Men in Space, 1960.
Rockets of the Air Force, 1960.
Rockets of the Army, 1960.
Birth of a Rocket, 1961.
Rocket Aircraft: U.S.A., 1961.
Rockets to the Moon, 1961.
Rockets to the Planets, 1961.
(With William O. Foss) *Coast Guard in Action,* 1962.
(With Foss) *Helicopters in Action,* 1962.
Our New Navy, 1962.
Rocket Power, 1962.
Saturn Story, 1962.
Space Stations, 1962.
(With Foss) *The Marine Corps in Action,* 1965.
(With Foss) *Skin Divers in Action,* 1965.
(Editor) *Illustrated Space Encyclopedia,* 1965, revised edition published as *The New Illustrated Space Encyclopedia,* 1971.
Rockets of the Armed Forces, 1966.
Aircraft Carriers in Action, 1968.
Mars: Planet for Conquest, 1968.
Murder on Pad 34, 1968.
(With Foss) *Oceanographers in Action,* 1968.
Convertiplanes in Action: The VTOL Success Story, 1969.
The Russians in Space, 1969.
(Editor) *The Illustrated Nuclear Encyclopedia,* 1971.
The Next Fifty Years on the Moon, 1974.
Rescue in Space: Lifeboats for Astronauts and Cosmonauts, 1974.
Colonizing the Planets, 1975.
Colonizing the Sea, 1976.
Colonizing Space, 1978.

SIDELIGHTS: Already a successful aviation editor for Norway's largest newspaper, Erik Bergaust immigrated to the United States at the age of twenty-four and soon entered the publishing industry. He became founder and editor of numerous periodicals on rocketry and air and sea exploration, including *Missiles and Rockets,* America's first magazine devoted entirely to rocketry and space science. At twenty-seven he began a successful book-writing career that includes two biographies on noted space pioneer Wernher von Braun and *Murder on Pad 34,* a critical account of the 1967 Apollo spacecraft accident that took the lives of three astronauts. Erik Bergaust's aptitude in rocketry prompted his appointment to several government advisory committees on space safety as well as the position of consultant to a number of aerospace companies and NASA.

BIOGRAPHICAL/CRITICAL SOURCES:

PERIODICALS

Book World, July 14, 1968.
New York Times Book Review, November 3, 1968.

OBITUARIES:

PERIODICALS

Washington Post, March 4, 1978.*

BERGER, Michael L(ouis) 1943-

PERSONAL: Surname is pronounced *Ber*-jer; born February 11, 1943, in Boston, MA; son of Clarence Quinn (an educational consultant) and Ethel J. (a social worker; maiden name, Goldberg) Berger; married Linda A. Cannizzo (a speech clinician), October 9, 1976. *Education:* Harvard University, B.A., 1965; Yale University, M.A.T., 1966; Columbia University, Ed.D., 1972. *Avocational interests:* Collecting various artifacts of Americana, gardening.

ADDRESSES: Home—10 Esperanza Dr., Lexington Park, MD 20653. *Office*—Division of Human Development, St. Mary's College of Maryland, St. Mary's City, MD 20686.

CAREER: High school social studies teacher in Englewood, NJ, 1966-69; Marymount College, Tarrytown, NY, instructor in education, 1971-72; Fordham University, New York City, assistant professor of education, 1972-77, director of Rose Hill Program, 1975-77; St. Mary's College of Maryland, St. Mary's City, associate professor, 1977-82, professor of education, 1982—, director of teacher education, 1977-84, head of Division of Human Development, 1984—.

Universidade de Aveiro, Fulbright senior lecturer/research scholar, 1983; Universidade de Lisboa, Galouste Gulbenkian Lecturer, 1983. New York State Council on Social Education, president, 1973-74, member of executive committee, 1974-77; New York State Council for the Social Studies, member of board of directors, 1974-76; National Association of State Directors of Teacher Education and Certification accreditation visits, team leader (chairman), 1977, 1979; Maryland Association of Small Teacher Education Programs, coordinator, 1978-81; Maryland State Board of Education, member and chairperson of subcommittee on new areas of certification, professional standards, and teacher education advisory board, 1978-81; Maryland State Board for Higher Education, member of advisory group, statewide review of education programs, 1979-81, member of advisory task force on higher education and the public schools, 1984-85; National Humanities Alliance, representative for Society for the History of Technology, 1985—, American Council on Education, discussion leader for Workshop on Chairing the Academic Department, 1986. Presentation of papers to organizations, including U.S. Department of Agriculture, National Council for Geographic Education, and Detroit Historical Society.

MEMBER: American Association for Higher Education, American Educational Studies Association, American Historical Association, Fulbright Alumni Association, National Council for the Social Studies, Authors League of America, Authors Guild, Society for the History of Technology, History of Education Society, History of Science Society, Society of Automotive Historians, Antique Automobile Club of America, Phi Delta Kappa (former faculty sponsor).

AWARDS, HONORS: Grants from Fordham University, 1974, Center for Global Community Education, 1976, 1977, St. Mary's College of Maryland, 1982, Education for Economic Security Act, 1986, 1987, GTE Foundation, 1989, and Jewish Chautauqua Society, 1989, 1990; Certificate of Merit, Phi Delta Kappa, 1976, 1977; Thomas McKean Memorial Cup, Antique Automobile Club of America, 1980, for significant contributions to automotive history.

WRITINGS:

Violence in the Schools: Causes and Remedies, Phi Delta Kappa Educational Foundation, 1974.

The Public Education System, F. Watts, 1977.

Firearms in American History, F. Watts, 1979.

The Devil Wagon in God's Country: The Automobile and Social Change in Rural America, 1893-1929, Archon Books, 1979.

An Album of Aircraft Testing, F. Watts, 1981.

The Automobile: A Reference Guide, Greenwood Press, in press.

Also author of scripts for three media programs. Contributor of chapters to books, including *The American People,* edited by P. R. Baker and W. H. Hall, Sadlier-Oxford, 1977; *The Growth of a Nation,* with teacher's guide, edited by Baker and Hall, Sadlier-Oxford, 1977; and *The Automobile and American Culture,* edited by L. Goldstein and D. Lewis, University of Michigan Press, 1983. Contributor of approximately forty articles and reviews to professional journals and popular magazines, including *Road & Track, Education Week, Michigan Quarterly Review, Antiques Journal, Hadassah Magazine,* and *Maine Life.* Book review editor, *Social Science Record,* 1974-78.

WORK IN PROGRESS: Research in the areas of automotive history and environmental psychology, concerning the impact of technology on society and human behavior; also, research on instructional design and evaluation in relation to curriculum materials development.

SIDELIGHTS: Michael L. Berger told *CA:* "*The Automobile: A Reference Guide* will be the first major attempt to list and describe the impact of the automobile on American history and life. This will be accomplished through a series of bibliographical essays, each devoted to one specific area of the car's influence. As such, it hopefully will prove a powerful reference tool for students of automotive history and will indirectly contribute to additional work in a field that has been somewhat neglected given the pervasiveness of the car in twentieth-century American life.

"Despite an increasing list of credits, I continue to be in sympathy with an observation made, I believe, by Dorothy Parker: 'I do not enjoy writing, but I like having written.'"

*   *   *

BERNHARD, Thomas 1931-1989

PERSONAL: Born September 11, 1931, in Heerland, Holland; emigrated to Austria; died c. February 12 (exact date unknown), 1989, in Gmunden, Austria, of apparent heart failure; grandson of Johannes Freumbichler (a carpenter). *Education:* Studied music in Vienna and Salzburg.

ADDRESSES: Office—c/o Alfred A. Knopf, Inc., 201 East 50th St., New York, N.Y. 10022.

CAREER: Novelist, dramatist, poet, and journalist. Also worked as a court reporter, critic, and librarian.

AWARDS, HONORS: Bremen Prize, 1965; Austrian State Prize for Literature, 1967; Wildgans Prize, 1968; George Buechner Prize from German Academy of Language and Literature, 1970; Grillparzer Prize, 1971; Seguier Prize, 1974.

WRITINGS:

IN ENGLISH

Vestoerung (novel; title means "Perturbation"), Insel, 1967, translation by Richard Wilson and Clara Wilson published as *Gargoyles,* Knopf, 1970, University of Chicago Press, 1986.

Das Kalkwerk (novel), Suhrkamp, 1970, translation by Sophie Wilkins published as *The Lime Works,* Random House, 1973, University of Chicago Press, 1986.

Die Macht der Gewohnheit: Komoedie (play; also see below; first produced in Salzburg, 1974), Suhrkamp, 1974, translation by Neville Plaice and Stephen Plaice published as *The Force of Habit: A Comedy,* (produced in London, 1976), Heinemann Educational, 1976, text edition published as *Die Salzburger Stucke* (title means "National Theatre Plays: The Force of Habit, a Comedy.")

Der Praesident, Suhrkamp, 1975, translation by Gitta Honegger published in *The President and Eve of Retirement: Two Plays,* Performing Arts Journal, 1982.

Korrektur (novel), Suhrkamp, 1975, translation by Wilkins published as *Correction,* Knopf, 1979.

Vor dem Ruhestand (play; title means "Before Retirement"; first produced in Bochom, 1980; English version produced as "Eve of Retirement" in Minneapolis, 1982), Suhrkamp, 1979, translation by Honegger published in *The President and Eve of Retirement: Two Plays,* Performing Arts Journal, 1982.

Beton, Suhrkamp, 1983, translation by David McLintock published as *Concrete,* Knopf, 1984.

Gathering Evidence: A Memoir, translation by McLintock, Knopf, 1986.

Wittgenstein's Neffe: Eine Freundschaft (autobiographical; title means "Wittgenstein's Nephew: A Friendship"), 1983, translation by McLintock published as *Wittgenstein's Nephew: A Novel,* Knopf, 1989.

Holzfaellen, Suhrkamp, 1984, translation by McLintock published as *The Woodcutters,* Knopf, 1988.

OTHER

Auf der Erde und in der Hoelle (poetry; title means "On Earth and in Hell"), Mueller (Salzburg), 1957.

Unter dem Eisen des Mondes (poetry; title means "Under the Iron of the Moon"), Kipenheuer & Witsch, 1958.

In hora mortis (poetry; title means "In the Hour of Death"), Mueller, 1958.

Die Rosen der Einoede: fuenf Saetze fuer Ballet, Stimmen und Orchester, S. Fischer, 1959.

Frost (novel), Insel, 1963.

Amras (prose), Suhrkamp, 1967.

Prosa, Suhrkamp, 1967.

Ungemach (prose; title means "Trouble"), Suhrkamp, 1968.

Watten: ein Nachlass (prose; title means "Mudflats"), Suhrkamp, 1969.

Ereignisse (title means "Events"), Literarisches Colloquium, 1969.

An der Baumgrenze (novel; title means "At the Timberline"), illustrations by Anton Lehmden, Residenz, 1969.

Ein Fest fuer Boris (play; title means "A Party for Boris"; produced in Hamburg, Germany, 1970), Suhrkamp, 1970.

"Der Berg," published in *Literatur und Kritik,* Number 5, June, 1970.

Gehen, Suhrkamp, 1970.

Midland in Stilfs: Drei Erzaelungen, Suhrkamp, 1970.

Der Italiener (screenplay; title means "The Italian"), Residenz, 1971.

Der Ignorant und der Wahnsinnige (play; first produced in Salzburg, Austria, at Salzburg Festival, 1972; title means "The Ignoramus and the Madman"), Suhrkamp, 1972.

Der Kulterer (screenplay), Residenz, 1974.

Die Jagdgesellschaft (play; title means "The Hunting Party"; first produced in Vienna, 1974), Suhrkamp, 1974.

Die Salzburger Stuecke (also includes *Die Macht der Gewohnheit*), Suhrkamp, 1975.

Die Ursache: Eine Andeutung (autobiographical stories; title means "The Cause"; also see below), Residenz, 1975.

Der Wetterfleck, illustrations by Otto F. Best, Reclam, 1976.

Der Beruehmten (play; title means "The Famous"; first produced at the Burgtheater in Vienna, Austria, 1988), Suhrkamp, 1976.

Der Keller: Eine Entziehung (autobiographical; sequel to *Die Ursache;* title means "The Basement"), Residenz, 1976.

"Heldenplatz" (play; title means "Heroes' Square"), first produced in Vienna, 1976.

Minetti: ein Portrait des Kuenstlers als alter Mann (a play; first produced in Stuttgart, 1976), photographs by Digne Meller Marcovicz, Suhrkamp, 1977.

Immanuel Kant (comedy; first produced in Stuttgart, 1978), Suhrkamp, 1978.

Ja, Suhrkamp, 1978.

Der Atem: Eine Entscheidung (autobiographical; sequel to *Der Keller;* title means "The Breath"), Residenz, 1978.

Die Erzaelungen, edited by Ulrich Greiner, Suhrkamp, 1979.

Der Weltverbesserer (play; title means "Worldimprover"; first produced in Bochum, 1980), Suhrkamp, 1979.

Der Stimmenimitator (title means "The Voice-Mime"), Suhrkamp, 1980.

Die Billigesser, Suhrkamp, 1980.

Ueber allen Gipfeln ist Ruh: Ein deutscher Dichtertag um 1980 (play), Suhrkamp, 1981.

Die Kaelte: Eine Isolation (autobiographical; sequel to *Der Atem;* title means "The Cold"), Residenz, 1981.

Am Ziel (play), Suhrkamp, 1981.

Ave Vergil (poems), Suhrkamp, 1981.

Ein Kind (autobiographical; sequel to *Die Kaelte;* title means "A Child"), Residenz, 1982.

Die Untergeher, Suhrkamp, 1983.

Der Schein truegt, Suhrkamp, 1983.

Die Stuecke, 1969-1981, Suhrkamp, 1983.

Der Theatermacher, Suhrkamp, 1984.

Ausloeschung, Suhrkamp, 1986.

Elisabeth II, Suhrkamp, 1987.

Der deutsche Mittagstisch, Suhrkamp, 1988.

Also author of *Die heiligen drei Koenige von St. Vitus* (title means "The Three Wise Men of St. Vitus"), 1955, *Der Schweinehueter* (title means "The Swineherd"), 1956, and *Die Jause* (title means "The Afternoon Snack"), 1965.

SIDELIGHTS: Austrian playwright Thomas Bernhard's pessimistic view of human nature was ever-present in his controversial plays and novels. His works often presented the faults of his culture in a critical light such that he gained a reputation as German literature's most melancholy and bitter writer. Like the works of Mark Twain, Bernhard's later plays were indictments of a culture in decline. His 1984 novel *Holzfaellen (The Woodcutters)* was seized by the police because it was thought that it drew an unflattering portrait of a famous Viennese personage. His play "Heldenplatz" ("Heroes' Square"), forthright in its charges that anti-Semitism is widespread in Austria, angered his audiences and the Austrian government, who began to discuss whether or not such work should be censored. Considered by some to be unimportant due to the views he expressed, he was esteemed by others as "one of the greatest writers of the century," noted a writer for the London *Times.*

Bernhard's novel *Vestoerung,* translated as *Gargoyles,* revealed Bernhard's belief in the hopelessness of the human condition. In the story, "the patients are the gargoyles of the title and their peculiar arrangements could be well skipped were it not for the brilliance, erudition, and suggestiveness with which Bernhard writes about them," commented a critic in *Antioch Review.* The book was not widely read in the United States, but was very popular in Europe.

Grotesque figures that depict Bernhard's view of human nature appeared often in his other works, as well. The works unanimously stress that man is motivated primarily by madness and disease, noted Martin Esslin in *Modern Drama.* "Life itself is a disease only curable by death. Cripples and madmen merely exhibit, more plainly and therefore perhaps more frankly, what all men suffer from beneath the surface. And even 'genius is a disease,' as the doctor asserts in *The Ignoramus and the Madman,*" Esslin maintained. In *German Life and Letters,* D. A. Craig observed that "the introspective sickness of many of [Bernhard's] characters indirectly represented the troubles besetting the Austrian people in the wake of two world wars.

Many of Bernhard's characters are diseased or disabled. The ringmaster of the circus in *Die Macht der Gewohnheit (The Force of Habit)* has a wooden leg; the narrator of *Korrektur (Correction),* an idealistic scientist, has a psychotic hatred, and commits suicide. In *Ein Fest fuer Boris,* thirteen legless guests attend a party hosted by a wealthy woman who also has no legs. The woman, misnamed the "Gute" or "Good," is married to Boris, also legless, who dies while pounding on a drum; because the guests are absorbed in sharing their morbid experiences and dreams with one another, they don't notice the death until the end of the party. "Taken as a whole, the meaning of the play is opaque," wrote a *Books Abroad* reviewer. "Still it communicates messages typical of Thomas Bernhard: life is insufferable, a stifling routine in which human relations are based on mutual hatred and intimidation; social injustice prevails."

Death and disease had always been Bernhard's major concerns. Bernhard's father died just a few years before he himself contracted a lung disease and entered a tuberculosis sanatorium. His mother and grandfather died within the next two years. During these years Bernhard composed his first poems, plays, and short fiction. *Partisan Review* contributor Betty Falkenberg generalized, "All Bernhard's books, all his plays, are really about one thing: death. Death in death, death in life, the futility of all human contact or attempts at understanding, the senselessness of all existence and the cruelty of creating new life, the stupidity of all human beings, the futility of all systems, political or religious, both encompassing as they do the same corruption and stupidity to be found everywhere else." This focus on death paradoxically led his more sensitive characters to an appreciation of the value of commitment; explains Falkenberg, "If there is one thing that can bind people together . . . it can only be the awareness of the total hopelessness of all human endeavor in the light of the fact of death."

Though Bernhard's works express the same themes, they do so by means of a variety of unusual techniques. For example, the novel *Das Kalkwerk (The Lime Works)* is narrated by a life-insurance salesman who weaves the story from rumors about a frustrated Austrian writer who has blasted his crippled wife in the head with a shot from her own rifle. "The book is a jungle of meaning, the opposite of simplistic allegory, and a major achievement because of this. . . . *The Lime Works* invites comparison with the run-on novels of Beckett," a *New Republic* reviewer wrote. Ronald De Feo concluded in *National Review* that in this book Bernhard had again demonstrated that he was "one of the most substantive and intense" among German writers.

Bernhard's facility with a variety of techniques brought him the ongoing appreciation of writers and critics. Between 1960 and 1980, he won a number of literary prizes, including the Austrian

State Prize for Literature in 1967. American critics valued the masterful style in which he couched his social criticism. Of *The Woodcutters,* a novel in which the narrator deflates the pretentiousness of local artists, *New York Times Book Review* contributor Mark Anderson commented, "What raises this denunciation of Austria's cultural parochialism above the level of mere satire is Mr. Bernhard's supremely ironic tone of voice and musical sensibility. The narrator's own credibility is constantly undermined by the anxious excessiveness of his attacks, which one gradually comes to see as being aimed as much at himself and his own fear of death as at the guests."

In *The Woodcutters,* a dinner party for artists and intellectuals is the springboard from which the narrator, a vituperative artist largely isolated from the others, berates them in a manner that begins to sound unsound. Part of the attraction for readers is the question of the narrator's reliability as he recounts observations based on thirty years experience with the aristocrats of culture. In this novel, said *Chicago Tribune* writer Joseph Coates, Bernhard "comes close to the novelist's ideal of making every gesture meaningful, bathing it in a garish light from the past whose quality of illumination we can never entirely trust." Richard Eder of the *Los Angeles Times* praised the novel's finish, in which the narrator demonstrates that he practices the same kind of pretention that so offends him in the others. Though the reviewer would have liked to see the revelation come sooner, "it is an abrupt reversal, and startlingly effective," he remarked.

Critics also admired Bernhard's mature prose for achieving its effects in the same way that music does. Coates explained that all Bernhard's work shows his training in music. "His books embody such musical values as counterpoint, fugue, leit-motif and harmony, and in at least two of them a play-within-the-novel obliquely reflects on the action." For these reasons and more, *The Woodcutters,* said Martin Seymour-Smith in a *Washington Post Book World* review, is a representative work that can well serve as an "introduction to Bernhard's work as a whole. Apart from perfectly illustrating his shrewdness, disgruntlement and acute awareness, *Woodcutters* is very funny." The novel's success firmly established Bernhard's reputation as a world class novelist to the extent that in the year before his death, some critics regarded the playwright as a candidate for the Nobel Prize.

Bernhard's depiction of the least admirable facets of human nature endeared him to some readers and enraged others. Some critics pointed out that one need not share Bernhard's views to appreciate his mastery of dramatic and novelistic techniques. Speaking of the later plays which had sharpened into "savage aggression against the public itself," Esslin remarked that what makes the playwright's misanthropic works notable is "the artistry with which these impulses are hammered into shape. Bernhard's theatre is essentially a *mannerist* theatre. If his characters are puppets, all the greater the skill with which they perform their intricate dance; if his subject-matter is venom and derision, all the more admirable the perfection of the language in which the venom is spat out, the intricacy of the pattern it creates."

BIOGRAPHICAL/CRITICAL SOURCES:

BOOKS

Arnold, Heinz Ludwig, editor, *Bernhard,* Boorberg, 1974.
Bernhard, Thomas, *Der Ignorant und der Wahnsinnige,* Suhrkamp, 1972.
Bernhard, Thomas, *Die Ursache: Eine Andeutung,* Residenz, 1975.
Bernhard, Thomas, *Der Keller: Eine Entziehung,* Residenz, 1976.
Bernhard, Thomas, *Der Atem: Eine Entscheidung,* Residenz, 1978.
Bernhard, Thomas, *Die Kaelte: Eine Isolation,* Residenz, 1981.
Bernhard, Thomas, *Ein Kind,* Residenz, 1982.
Bernhard, Thomas, *Wittgenstein's Neffe: Eine Freundschaft,* Suhrkamp, 1983.
Bernhard, Thomas, *Gathering Evidence: A Memoir,* translation by David McLintock, Knopf, 1986.
Botond, Anneliese, editor, *Ueber Bernhard,* Suhrkamp, 1970.
Calandra, Denis, *New German Dramatists,* Macmillan, 1983.
Contemporary Literary Criticism, Gale, Volume 3, 1975, Volume 32, 1985.
Dittmar, Jens, *Bernhard Wergeschichte,* Suhrkamp, 1981.
Sorg, Bernard, *Bernhard,* Beck, 1977.

PERIODICALS

Antioch Review, fall, 1970.
Booklist, February 15, 1971; July 15, 1975.
Book World, January 3, 1971.
Chicago Tribune, February 24, 1989.
German Life and Letters, July, 1972.
Globe and Mail (Toronto), August 18, 1984.
Los Angeles Times, January 20, 1988.
Modern Austrian Literature, Number 11, 1978; Number 12, 1979.
Modern Drama, January, 1981.
National Review, February 1, 1974.
New Republic, December, 1973.
New York Times Book Review, July 1, 1984; February 19, 1989.
Partisan Review, Volume 47, number 2, 1980.
Saturday Review, October 31, 1970.
Times Literary Supplement, February 12, 1971; September 29, 1972; February 13, 1976; June 11, 1976.
Tribune Books (Chicago), January 31, 1988.
Washington Post Book World, April 17, 1988; February 19, 1989; March 5, 1989.
World Literature Today, summer, 1977; winter, 1978.

OBITUARIES:

PERIODICALS

Chicago Tribune, February 17, 1989.
Los Angeles Times, February 17, 1989.
New York Times, February 17, 1989.
New York Times Book Review, February 14, 1989.
Times (London), February 17, 1989.
Washington Post, February 21, 1989.*

*   *   *

BERTRAM, Noel
   See FANTHORPE, R(obert) Lionel

*   *   *

BIAGI, Shirley 1944-

PERSONAL: Born June 21, 1944, in San Francisco, CA; daughter of Herbert H. and Gerbina Mary (Biagi) Rickey; married Victor J. Biondi (a broadcast lobbyist), 1964; children: Paul and Tom (twins), David. *Education:* California State University, Sacramento, B.A., 1967, M.A., 1975.

ADDRESSES: Office—California State University, 6000 J St., SSC-308, Sacramento, CA 95819.

CAREER: California Journal, Sacramento, assistant editor, 1970-72; California State University, Sacramento, lecturer,

1972-75, associate professor, 1975-80, professor of journalism, 1980—. Poynter Institute Faculty, 1989.

MEMBER: Association for Journalism and Mass Communication, American Journalism Historians Association.

AWARDS, HONORS: Literary merit award, Sacramento Regional Arts Council, 1974; Distinguished Teaching Award, Poynter Institute for Media Studies, 1983.

WRITINGS:

How to Write and Sell Magazine Articles, Prentice-Hall, 1981.
A Writer's Guide to Word Processors, Prentice-Hall, 1984.
Interviews That Work: A Practical Guide for Journalists, Wadsworth, 1985.
Newstalk I, Wadsworth, 1987.
Newstalk II, Wadsworth, 1987.
Media/Impact, Wadsworth, 1988.
Media/Reader, Wadsworth, 1989.

Contributor of articles to *Parade, Writer's Digest, Family Circle, Christian Science Monitor,* and *Antioch Review.*

WORK IN PROGRESS: Interviews with pioneering women journalists for Washington Press Club Foundation Oral History Project; *Yesterday's Parade: A History of Mass Media,* expected publication 1992.

SIDELIGHTS: Shirley Biagi told *CA:* "I'm fascinated with today's journalists and how they work. *Interviews That Work: A Practical Guide for Journalists* took me from New Orleans to New York and Vancouver to Hawaii to interview famous and not-so-famous reporters who write our history every day. What a wonderful occupation—writing. It's one of the few jobs I know where you can go to work down the hall at home in your pajamas."

*   *   *

BIEGEL, Paul 1925-

PERSONAL: Born March 25, 1925, in Bussum, Netherlands; son of Herman (a merchant) and Madeleine (Povel) Biegel; married Marijke Straeter (a social worker), September 10, 1960; children: Leonie, Arthur. *Education:* Attended University of Amsterdam.

ADDRESSES: Home—Keizersgracht 227, Amsterdam, Netherlands.

CAREER: De Radiobode (radio weekly), Amsterdam, Netherlands, editor, 1948-65; Koevesdi (press agency), Amsterdam, editor, 1965-67; Ploegsma (publishing firm), Amsterdam, editor, 1967-69; free-lance writer, 1969—. Text writer for "Marten Toonder Comics." Advisor to Van Holkema en Warendorf (publishing firm), Bussum, Netherlands, 1969—.

MEMBER: Dutch Society of Writers (V.V.L.), Dutch Society of Literature.

AWARDS, HONORS: Best Children's Book of the Year Award, Collective Promotion of Dutch Books (CPNB), 1965, for *Het sleutelkruid;* award from Children's Jury of Amsterdam, 1970, for *De tuinen van Dorr;* Golden Pencil Award, CPNB, 1972, for *De kleine kapitein;* Silver Pencil Award, CPNB, 1972, for *De twaalf rovers,* 1974, for *Het olifantenfeest,* 1982, for *Haas, eerst boek: Voorjaar,* and 1988, for *De Rode Prinses;* prize from Jan Campert Foundation, 1973, for *De twaalf rovers;* State prize, 1973, for complete works.

WRITINGS:

IN ENGLISH TRANSLATION; ORIGINALLY PUBLISHED IN HAARLEM, HOLLAND

Het sleutelkruid, 1964, translation by Gillian Hume and the author published as *The King of the Copper Mountains,* F. Watts, 1969.
Ik wou dat ik anders was, 1967, translation by Hume and the author published as *The Seven-Times Search,* Dent, 1971.
De tuinen van Dorr, 1969, translation by Hume and the author published as *The Gardens of Dorr,* Dent, 1975.
De twaalf rovers, 1971, translation by Patricia Crampton published as *The Twelve Robbers,* Dent, 1974, Puffin, 1977.
De kleine kapitein, 1971, translation by Crampton published as *The Little Captain,* Dent, 1971.
Het olifantenfeest, 1973, translation by Crampton published as *The Elephant Party,* Puffin, 1977.
De kleine kapitein in het land van waan en wijs, 1973, translation by Crampton published as *The Little Captain and the Seven Towers,* Dent, 1973.
Het stenen beeld, 1974, translation by Crampton published as *Far Beyond and Back Again,* Dent, 1977.
De kleine kapitein en de schat van schrik en vreze, 1975, translation by Crampton published as *The Little Captain and the Pirate Treasure,* Dent, 1980.
Het spiegelkasteel, 1976, translation by Crampton published as *The Looking-Glass Castle,* Blackie & Son, 1979.
De dwergjes van Tuil, 1977, translation by Crampton published as *The Dwarfs of Nosegay,* Blackie & Son, 1978.
De rover Hoepsika, 1977, translation by Crampton published as *The Robber Hopsika,* Dent, 1978.
Twaalf sloeg de klok, 1974, translation by Crampton published as *The Clock Struck Twelve,* Glover & Blair, 1979.
De brieven van de generaal, 1977, translation by Crampton published as *Letters from the General,* Dent, 1979.
De toverhoed, 1979, translation by Crampton published as *The Tin Can Beast and Other Stories,* Glover & Blair, 1980.
De vloek van Woestewolf, 1974, translation by Crampton published as *The Curse of the Werewolf,* Blackie & Son, 1981.
Virgilius van Tuil, 1978, translation by Crampton published as *The Fattest Dwarf of Nosegay,* Blackie & Son, 1980.
Virgilius van Tuil op zoek naar een taart, 1979, translation by Crampton published as *Virgil Nosegay and the Cake Hunt,* Blackie & Son, 1981.
Virgilius van Tuil overwintert bij de mensen, 1982, translation by Crampton published as *Virgil Nosegay and the Wellington Boots,* Blackie & Son, 1984.
Jiri, 1981, translation by Crampton published as *Crocodile Man,* Dent, 1982.

IN DUTCH; PUBLISHED IN HAARLEM, HOLLAND

De gouden gitaar (title means "The Golden Guitar"), 1962.
Het grote boek (title means "The Great Book"), 1962.
De kukelhaan (title means "Crow Cockerel"), 1964.
Het lapjesbeest (title means "Patch-Animal"), 1964.
Kinderverhalen (title means "Children's Stories"), 1966.
De rattenvanger van Hameln (title means "The Pied Piper of Hamlin"), 1967.
De zeven fabels uit Ubim (title means "The Seven Fables from Ubim"), 1970.
Sebastiaan Slorp, 1971.
Reinaart de vos (title means "Reynard the Fox"), 1972.
Virgilius van Tuil en de rijke oom uit Zweden (title means "Virgil Nosegay and the Rich Uncle from Sweden"), 1980.

Haas, eerste boek: Voorjaar (title means "Hare, First Book: Spring"), 1981.
Haas, tweede boek: Zomer (title means "Hare, Second Book: Summer"), 1982.
Haas, derde boek: Najaar (title means "Hare, Third Book: Autumn"), 1982.
Tante Mathilde en de sterren van de Grote Beer (title means "Aunt Mathilda and the Stars of Big Dipper"), 1984.
De zwarte weduwe (title means "The Black Widow"), 1984.
Japie (title means "Little Jacob"), three volumes, 1985.
Van de Oude Dame en de Muis (title means "The Old Lady and the Mouse"), 1985.
De Rode Prinses (title means "The Red Princess"), 1987.
Beer in het Verkeer (title means "Teddybear in Traffic"), 1989.
Het Eiland Daarginds (title means "The Island Yonder"), 1989.

OTHER WRITINGS

Wie je droomt ben je zelf (title means "You Are the Ones You Dream Of "), Collective Promotion of Dutch Books (CPNB), 1977.

OTHER

Also author of television series, "De vloek van Woestewolf," based on his book of the same title.

WORK IN PROGRESS: Juttertje Tim (title means "Little Beachcomber Tim").

SIDELIGHTS: Paul Biegel told *CA:* "I was born in an estate-like home with a huge garden, two parents, two brothers, six sisters, a German maid, a gardener, and a dog. I remember a lot, but I am convinced it is the memories without words, of the years before a child has words to [his] disposition (Adam before he named the things of paradise) that the source of any one's creative urge lies. And the writer, for the rest of his life, tries in vain to find words for it."

A *Times Literary Supplement* critic describes Biegel's award-winning *The Little Captain* as "a story told with extreme art, especially in the light yet memorable opening." Cara Changeau asserts, also in the *Times Literary Supplement,* that *The Curse of the Werewolf* possesses "a strong story line using time-honoured features with a judicious mix of the suitably sinister and downright comic."

BIOGRAPHICAL/CRITICAL SOURCES:

PERIODICALS

Times Literary Supplement, April 28; 1972, March 27, 1981.

* * *

BLACK, Maggie
   See BLACK, Margaret K(atherine)

* * *

BLACK, Margaret K(atherine) 1921-
   (Maggie Black, M. K. Howorth)

PERSONAL: Born September 22, 1921, in London, England; daughter of Humphrey Noel (a civil servant) and Gladys (Lewis) Howorth; married Robert Alastair Lucien Black (a university teacher), May 15, 1943 (deceased); children: Andrew Ian, Christopher James Robert. *Education:* Attended University of the Witwatersrand and the Sorbonne, University of Paris. *Religion:* Agnostic.

ADDRESSES: Home—167 Putney Bridge Rd., London SW15, England.

MEMBER: Authors Lending and Copyright Society, Society of Authors.

WRITINGS:

Three Brothers: Two Young Explorers, Acorn Press, 1945.
Three Brothers and a Lady, Acorn Press, 1947.
The Magic Way Readers, three books, A.P.B. Bookstore (Johannesburg), 1950.
The Mabunga Family, Institute of Race Relations, 1954.
The City Built on Gold, Longmans, Green, 1957.
(With others) *Happy Trek Readers,* five books, Longmans, Green, 1957.
A South African Holiday, Longmans, Green, 1958.
(Editor with Lionel T. Bennett) *The Golden Journey: Anthologies of English Poetry for High Schools,* three books, A.P.B. Bookstore, 1959.
New Adventure Stories: Johannesburg, Longmans, Green, 1961.
(With Molly Brearley) *Honey Family,* three books, Educational Supply Association (London), 1961.
No Room for Tourists (nonfiction), preface by Angus Wilson, Secker & Warburg, 1965.

UNDER NAME MAGGIE BLACK

Waste Not, Eat Well, M. Joseph, 1976.
Meat Preserving at Home, E.P. Publishing, 1976.
One Hundred Ways with Cheese, Charles Letts, 1976.
A Heritage of British Cooking, Charles Letts, 1977.
Georgian Meals and Menus, Kingsmead Reprints, 1977.
Homemade Butter, Cheese, and Yoghurt, E.P. Publishing, 1977.
Cheesecakes, Ward, Lock, 1980.
(With Pat Howard) *Eating Naturally: Recipes for Food with Fibre,* Faber, 1980.
(Translator) Louisette Bertholle, *French Cooking for All,* Weidenfeld & Nicolson, 1982.
The Wholesome Food Cookbook, David & Charles, 1982.
Barbecue with an International Flavour, Foulsham, 1983.
Food and Cooking in Medieval Britain, English Heritage, 1985.
Food and Cooking in Nineteenth-Century Britain, English Heritage, 1985.
Calendar of Feasts, WI Books, 1985.
Food Smoking at Home, David & Charles, 1985.
Book of Soups and Starters, WI Books, 1986.
Vegetarian Meals in Minutes, Foulsham, 1986.
Healthy Eating on a Low Budget, Blandford Press, 1986.
Book of Vegetables and Salads, WI Books, 1987.
New Vegetarian Barbecue, Foulsham, 1988.

EDITOR UNDER NAME MAGGIE BLACK OF "MRS. BEETON'S" SERIES; ALL BY ISABELLA MARY BEETON; ALL PUBLISHED BY BOBBS-MERRILL

Mrs. Beeton's Favorite Cakes and Breads, 1977.
Mrs. Beeton's Favorite Sweet Dishes, 1977.
Mrs. Beeton's Favorite Recipes, 1977.
Mrs. Beeton's Poultry and Game, 1977.
(With Susan Dixon) *Mrs. Beeton's Cookery and Household Management,* 1980.

OTHER

Also author of *Paxton and Whitfield Cheese Book,* 1989; also author of revision of *T. I. New World Complete Cookery,* 1989; also author of *The Bennet Readers,* "The Kindly Islands" (play), and of radio plays for children. Also editor of *The New Barbecue Cookbook,* in the "Mrs. Beeton's" series. Contributor of articles to periodicals, including *History Today* and *Herbalist.*

WORK IN PROGRESS: Research work for *RHS Dictionary of Gardening; Day School: The World of Pepys and Evelyn; Weald and Downland Open Air Museum: Medieval Cookbook.*

*   *   *

BLACKWOOD, Caroline 1931-

PERSONAL: Born Lady Caroline Hamilton-Temple-Blackwood, July 16, 1931, in Northern Ireland; daughter of the Marquis and Marchioness of Dufferin and Ava; married Lucien Freud (a painter; divorced); married Israel Citkovitz (a pianist; divorced); married Robert Lowell (a poet), 1972 (died September 12, 1977); children: (with Citkovitz) three daughters (one deceased); (with Lowell) Robert Sheridan.

ADDRESSES: Home—Redcliffe Square, London, England. *Office*—c/o Heinemann Ltd., 10 Upper Grosvenor St., London W1X 9PA, England.

CAREER: Essayist, short-story writer, and novelist.

WRITINGS:

For All That I Found There (short stories and nonfiction), Duckworth, 1973, Braziller, 1974.
The Stepdaughter (novel), Duckworth, 1976, Scribner, 1977.
Great Granny Webster (novel), Duckworth, 1977, Scribner, 1978.
(With Anna Haycraft) *Darling, You Shouldn't Have Gone to So Much Trouble* (cookbook), Cape, 1980.
The Fate of Mary Rose (novel), Summit, 1981.
Goodnight Sweet Ladies (short stories), Heinemann, 1983.
Corrigan (novel), Heinemann, 1984, Viking, 1985.
On the Perimeter (nonfiction), Heinemann, 1984, Penguin, 1985.
In the Pink: Caroline Blackwood on Hunting (nonfiction), Bloomsbury, 1987.

SIDELIGHTS: Well known in England as a novelist and nonfiction writer, Caroline Blackwood evokes unusual praise from a variety of critics. As Priscilla Martin notes in a *Dictionary of Literary Biography* article on the author, "Her material is anguish, dementia, and despair—injuries of all kinds, insanity, rape, murder, internecine marriages, a disastrous face-lift, suicidal isolation. Her distinctive power is to direct an unflinching gaze at the intolerable and convey it in elegant, witty, and dispassionate prose." Such subject matter seems initially unlikely for a woman born Lady Caroline Hamilton-Temple-Blackwood, heiress to an Irish peerage, as well as a descendent of the eighteenth-century dramatist Richard Brinsley Sheridan. "She grew up in the beautiful, crumbling, leaky ancestral mansion, Clandeboye, in County Down, the basis for the white elephant of a stately home in [Blackwood's novel] *Great Granny Webster*," adds Martin. Educated in boarding schools, Blackwood nonetheless learned enough about life to produce a first collection, *For All That I Found There*, that reflects on her youth around Ulster, Northern Ireland, where "the troubles" plagued others. This book "is odd because it's split into three parts: Fiction, Fact, and Ulster," reports *London Magazine* writer Digby Durrant. "But it's not the hopscotch this makes it sound. In fact, this curious dividing . . . is revealing. For the excellent short story writer she is turns into an equally excellent journalist with such smoothness there seems little difference."

With *The Stepdaughter* Blackwood moves into the kind of psychological drama that characterizes the best of her style. The anti-heroine of this first novel has been abandoned by her husband in Manhattan and left with "his grotesquely fat child bloated by rejection and a magnificent apartment with dizzy views through plexiglass," as Duncan Fallowell describes it in a *Spectator* review. There is also a howling infant, the product of their marriage, who is being cared-for by an unhappy *au pair*. The stepmother, known only as "K," fumes constantly and quietly through letters as she plots a way out of her unhappy lot. "Like all [Blackwood's] novels, *The Stepdaughter* can be seen as a modern variation on an established form," notes Martin. "It is a miniature epistolary novel whose arena is . . . the conscience of a threatened and isolated woman." With its "unblinking view of man's selfishness and woman's dependence *The Stepdaughter* is a notable contribution to the women's movement," finds *Encounter* reviewer James Price. "It is also, I should hazard, a philosophical and religious novel. It begins with a cry of pain, which can be seen to be a philosophical position. It ends with a sense of loss, which can be seen to be a religious one. It is an unusual and affecting experience."

The title character of Blackwood's second novel, *Great Granny Webster*, "is enormously wealthy [but] stingy with a vengeance," as Carol Greenberg Felsenthal puts it in *Chicago Tribune Book World*. Granny is "nearly as old-fashioned as she is stingy, but there is absolutely nothing charming or even eccentric about her aversion to modern conveniences," writes Felsenthal, who adds that "no matter what the season, her manor is cold and damp." Since Granny outlives all her friends and enemies, her eventual death is noted only by her great-granddaughter (the book's narrator) and Richards, her "trampled maid," as described by *New York Review of Books* critic Karl Miller. As Granny's history unfolds, it becomes apparent that "the women of the dynasty have been inclined to go mad," Miller offers. The critic goes on to say that in England, where *Great Granny Webster* was first published, "the tale has gone down well [since there] the appetite for the eccentricities and sufferings of the privileged never sleeps. But there is another reason for its doing well, which has to do with the appetite of its writer. Without being, in any extensive way, artless or careless, it reads like a long and colorful letter, and has the force of an eager unburdening."

Among Blackwood's other novels, *Corrigan* gained favorable notices as a gothic satire in the author's tradition. It centers on the unlikely romance between Devina, a widow wasting away from ennui, and Corrigan, the wheelchair-bound man who rejuvenates her. "Meanwhile, Devina's daughter, Nadine, discovers that she loathes her journalist husband, madly envies her mother, and feels savage ill will toward Corrigan," Laurie Stone observes in a *Village Voice* column. "What Nadine discovers about the mysterious Corrigan and his complex relationship with her mother at the end of her life provides a denouement filled with surprises and irony," *New York Times Book Review* writer Carolyn Gaiser explains. To this reviewer, the author's "sly wit and her affection for her characters brings a glow to these pages, a sunniness that manages to be believable without ever becoming sentimental. [Blackwood] has written a charming tour de force."

Departing from fiction, Blackwood has co-written a cookbook with the arresting title *Darling, You Shouldn't Have Gone to So Much Trouble*, as well as an examination of the British passion for fox hunting and its equally passionate anti-hunting foes. *In the Pink: Caroline Blackwood on Hunting* didn't garner the praise that Blackwood's novels have—"It cannot be said that Lady Caroline knows much about the vast and boring literature on this touchy subject," finds *Spectator* critic Raymond Carr—but the author continues to be cherished in England as a stringent social critic.

BIOGRAPHICAL/CRITICAL SOURCES:

BOOKS

Contemporary Literary Criticism, Gale, Volume 6, 1976, Volume 9, 1978.
Dictionary of Literary Biography, Volume 14: *British Novelists since 1960,* Gale, 1983.

PERIODICALS

Chicago Tribune Book World, September 10, 1978.
Encounter, September, 1976.
London Magazine, October/November, 1974.
Los Angeles Times Book Review, July 28, 1985.
New Statesman, November 30, 1973, June 4, 1976.
New York Review of Books, September 15, 1977, November 9, 1978.
New York Times Book Review, July 26, 1981, July 14, 1985, December 1, 1985.
Spectator, June 5, 1976, September 17, 1977, December 13, 1980, March 7, 1981, October 15, 1983, October 10, 1987.
Times Literary Supplement, April 5, 1974, September 2, 1977, November 14, 1980, February 27, 1981, September 21, 1984, October 19, 1984, September 25, 1987.
Village Voice, June 25, 1985.
Washington Post Book World, June 2, 1974, October 16, 1977, July 10, 1981, June 30, 1985.*

—*Sketch by Susan Salter*

* * *

BLINDER, Alan S(tuart) 1945-

PERSONAL: Born October 14, 1945, in Brooklyn, NY; children: two sons. *Education:* Princeton University, A.B. (summa cum laude), 1967; London School of Economics and Political Science, London, M.Sc., 1968; Massachusetts Institute of Technology, Ph.D., 1971.

ADDRESSES: Home—218 Cherry Hill Rd., Princeton, NJ 08540. *Office*—Department of Economics, 110 Dickinson Hall, Princeton University, Princeton, NJ 08544-1017.

CAREER: Rider College, Trenton, NJ, instructor in finance, 1968-69; Boston State College, Boston, MA, instructor in economics, 1969; Princeton University, Princeton, NJ, assistant professor, 1971-76, associate professor, 1976-79, professor of economics, 1979—, Gordon S. Rentschler Memorial Professor of Economics, 1982—. Visiting professor at Institute for Advanced Studies, Vienna, Austria, 1982; fellow at Institute for Advanced Studies, Hebrew University of Jerusalem, 1976-77. Research associate of National Bureau of Economic Research, 1978—. Deputy assistant director of Fiscal Analysis Division at Congressional Budget Office, 1975; chairman of economic policy committee of National Policy Exchange, 1981-85; Brookings Panel on Economic Activity, member, 1981, senior adviser, 1982—. Consultant to Council of Economic Advisers and Board of Governors of Federal Reserve System.

MEMBER: American Economic Association, Econometric Society (fellow).

AWARDS, HONORS: W. S. Woytinsky Award, University of Michigan, 1981.

WRITINGS:

Toward an Economic Theory of Income Distribution, M.I.T. Press, 1974.

(Editor with Philip Friedman, and contributor) *Natural Resources, Uncertainty, and General Equilibrium Systems: Essays in Memory of Rafael Lusky,* Academic Press, 1977.
(With William J. Baumol) *Economics: Principles and Policy,* Harcourt, 1979, 4th edition, 1988.
Economic Policy and the Great Stagflation, Academic Press, 1979.
Hard Heads, Soft Hearts: Tough-Minded Economics for a Just Society, Addison-Wesley, 1987.
Economic Opinion, Harcourt, 1989.

CONTRIBUTOR

T. M. Havrilesky and J. T. Boorman, editors, *Current Issues in Monetary Theory and Policy,* AMH Publishing, 1976.
K. Brunner and A. H. Meltzer, editors, *Stabilization of the Domestic and International Economy,* Volume 5, Elsevier, 1977.
M. S. Feldstein, editor, *The American Economy in Transition,* University of Chicago Press, 1980.
Stanley Fischer, editor, *Rational Expectations and Economic Policy,* University of Chicago Press, 1980.
Laurence H. Meyer, editor, *The Supply-Side Effects of Economic Policy,* Kluwer-Nijhoff, 1981.
M. June Flanders and Assaf Razin, editors, *Development in an Inflationary World,* Academic Press, 1981.
G. Feiwel, editor, *Samuelson and Neoclassical Economics,* Kluwer-Nijhoff, 1982.
Saving and Government Policy, Federal Reserve Bank of Boston, 1983.
R. Hemming and F. Modigliani, editors, *The Determinants of National Savings and Wealth,* International Economic Association, 1983.
Meyer, editor, *The Economic Consequences of Government Deficits,* Center for the Study of American Business, 1983.
Monetary Policy Issues in the 1980s, Federal Reserve Bank of Kansas City, 1983.

OTHER

Author of monthly column in *Boston Globe,* 1981-85, and *Business Week,* 1985—; columnist for *Washington Post,* 1982—. Contributor of about fifty articles to economics journals. Associate editor, *Journal of Public Economics,* 1982—; member of board of editors, *Journal of Economic Literature,* 1981—; member of editorial board, *Journal of Monetary Economics,* 1981—.

WORK IN PROGRESS: Research on game theory, the new econometrics, private and public pensions, and inventories.

BIOGRAPHICAL/CRITICAL SOURCES:

PERIODICALS

New York Times Book Review, October 25, 1987.
Globe and Mail, January 16, 1988.

* * *

BLOUET, Brian Walter 1936-

PERSONAL: Born January 1, 1936, in Darlington, England; came to the United States, 1969; son of Raymond Walter and Marjorie (Gargett) Blouet; married Olwyn Mary Salt (a historian), July 30, 1970; children: Andrew Paul, Helen Clare, Amy Elizabeth. *Education:* University of Hull, B.A., 1960, Ph.D., 1964.

ADDRESSES: Office—Department of Government, College of William and Mary, Williamsburg, VA 23185.

CAREER: University of Sheffield, Sheffield, England, assistant lecturer, 1964-66, lecturer in geography, 1966-69; University of Nebraska, Lincoln, associate professor, 1969-75, professor of geography, 1975-82, head of department, 1976-81, director of Center for Great Plains Studies, 1979-82; Texas A & M University, College Station, professor of geography and head of department, 1983-89; College of William and Mary, Williamsburg, VA, Fred Huby Professor of Geography and International Education, 1989—. *Military service:* Royal Air Force, 1955-57.

MEMBER: Association of American Geographers, Center for Great Plains Studies (fellow), Royal Geographical Society (fellow), Institute of British Geographers.

WRITINGS:

The Story of Malta, Faber, 1967, 3rd edition, 1976.
(Editor with Merlin P. Lawson) *Images of the Plains,* University of Nebraska Press, 1975.
(Editor with Fred Luebke) *The Great Plains: Environment and Culture,* University of Nebraska Press, 1979.
Malta: A Short History, Progress Press, 1981.
The Origins of Academic Geography in the United States, Shoe String, 1981.
(Editor with wife, Olwyn M. Blouet) *Latin America: An Introductory Survey,* Wiley, 1981.
(With R. H. Stoddard and D. J. Wishart) *Human Geography: People, Places, and Cultures,* Prentice-Hall, 1986, 2nd edition, 1989.
Halford Mackinder: A Biography, Texas A & M University Press, 1987.

WORK IN PROGRESS: A new enlarged edition of *Latin America,* for Wiley, expected publication 1992; *Western Geostrategic Thought 1890-1990s.*

SIDELIGHTS: Speaking of his appointment as Huby Professor at the College of William and Mary, Brian Walter Blouet told *CA:* "The intention of the College was to establish a program in Geography and reach out into the school districts to improve the teaching of geographic perspectives. From the start the Education Program at the National Geographic Society supported the efforts to improve geography teaching in Virginia."

BIOGRAPHICAL/CRITICAL SOURCES:

PERIODICALS

Times Literary Supplement, December 21, 1967.

*   *   *

BOK, Sissela Ann 1934-

PERSONAL: Born December 2, 1934, in Stockholm, Sweden; naturalized U.S. citizen, 1959; daughter of Gunnar (an economist) and Alva (a diplomat; maiden name, Reimer) Myrdal; married Derek Bok (a university president), May 7, 1955; children: Hilary Margaret, Victoria, Tomas Jeremy. *Education:* Attended Sorbonne, University of Paris, 1953-55, and Harvard University, 1961-62; George Washington University, A.B., 1957, M.A., 1958; Harvard University, Ph.D., 1970.

ADDRESSES: Home—33 Elmwood Ave., Cambridge, MA 02138.

CAREER: Simmons College, Boston, MA, lecturer in philosophy, 1971-72; Harvard University, Cambridge, MA, fellow of Interfaculty Program in Medical Ethics, 1972-73, Harvard-M.I.T. Division of Health Sciences and Technology, lecturer in medical ethics, 1975-80, lecturer in university core curriculum,

1982-84, visiting professor, 1986; Brandeis University, associate professor, 1985-89, professor of philosophy, 1989—. Co-director of project on teaching ethics, 1977-79, and of project on applied and professional ethics, 1980-83, both sponsored by Carnegie Corp. Has served on numerous committees and advisory boards concerned with medical ethics, including Massachusetts Task Force to Develop Regulations for Psychosurgery, 1973-74; Committee on Clinical Investigation, Children's Hospital (Boston), 1974-77; Amnesty International Medical Committee, 1975—; Ethics Advisory Board, U.S. Department of Health, Education, and Welfare, 1977-80; Committee on Philosophy and Medicine, American Philosophical Association, 1980—; Melcher Book Award Committee, 1986-89; Pulitzer Prize Board, 1988—; and American Philosophical Association and Soviet Academy of Sciences exchange on nuclear weapons policy, 1989.

MEMBER: American Philosophical Association (comittee on philosophy and medicine), Hastings Institute of Society, Ethics and the Life Sciences (fellow; member of board of directors, 1976—), Institute for Philosophy and Religion, Boston University (advisory board, 1986—), Cultural Survival (advisory board, 1986—), Phi Beta Kappa.

AWARDS, HONORS: Recipient of George Orwell Award from National Council of Teachers of English, 1978, and Frederic G. Melcher Book Award from Unitarian Universalist Association, 1978, both for *Lying: Moral Choice in Public and Private Life;* Abram L. Sachar Silver Medallion, Brandeis University National Women's Committee, 1985; LL.D., Mount Holyoke College, 1985; honorary doctor of humane letters, George Washington University, 1986, and Clark University, 1988.

WRITINGS:

(Editor with John A. Behnke) *The Dilemmas of Euthanasia,* Anchor Press, 1975.
Lying: Moral Choice in Public and Private Life, Pantheon, 1978.
(Editor with Daniel Callahan) *Ethics Teaching in Higher Education* (monograph), Plenum, 1980.
Secrets: On the Ethics of Concealment and Revelation, Pantheon, 1983.
Alva: Ett kvinnoliv (biography of Alva Myrdal, written in Swedish), Bonniers Foerlag (Stockholm, Sweden), 1987.
A Strategy for Peace: Human Values, Pantheon, 1989.

Contributor of articles to periodicals, including *Critique, Bio-Science, Scientific American, Ethics,* and *The Hastings Center Report.* Member of editorial board, *Ethics,* 1980-85; member of advisory board, *Encyclopedia of Bio-Ethics,* 1974—; contributing editor, *Literature and Medicine,* 1980—; member of editorial board, *Criminal Justice Ethics,* 1980—; member of nominating board, *The Philosopher's Annual,* 1985-89; member of editorial board, *Public Affairs Quarterly,* 1986-89; member, board of consulting editors, *Encyclopedia of Ethics,* 1986—.

SIDELIGHTS: In *Lying: Moral Choice in Public and Private Life,* Sissela Bok analyzes the problem of lying in America's professional institutions as well as among people from every walk of life. Though Bok points out the harm of lying, she differs with other philosophers in her assertion that sometimes lying may be justified. In an interview with *U.S. News & World Report,* she stated: "In special situations, lying can be justifiable—as in crises that are clear-cut and life-threatening. . . . Avoiding harm in these circumstances overrides the principle of veracity." For example, she cites that police may sometimes have to lie to a criminal to secure the release of people being held hostage. Other issues Bok deals with include "white lies," and using silence and subject-changing as means to avoid lying.

The book was praised by J. M. Cameron of *New York Review of Books*, who stated, "It is pleasant to find a work of such analytical power devoted to a set of severely practical problems and to find it so well written." He also commented favorably on her incorporation of "the entire philosophical tradition," specifically mentioning her inclusion, at the end of the book, of quotations from such famous philosophers as St. Augustine, St. Thomas Aquinas, Immanuel Kant, and Henry Sidgwick. She was further credited by *Nation* with having "written subtly and convincingly about lying."

In *Secrets: On the Ethics of Concealment and Revelation,* a sequel to *Lying,* Bok addresses the timely concern of many over the increased secrecy in government and other major institutions, specifically the medical and legal professions and media. Commenting in an article for the *New York Times,* she referred to her worry about "the effort by government and the American Bar Association to increase secrecy." And in an interview with *U.S. News & World Report,* she pointed to President Reagan's order making polygraph tests mandatory for federal employees dealing with classified information as an example of this trend toward greater secrecy. She cautioned, "We have been for the world a beacon of open government, and we have to be very careful not to squander that leadership." According to Richard Sennett of the *New York Times Book Review,* "Bok has written a subtle and often eloquent book about conundrums of secrecy." He added, "*Secrets* is a distinguished and necessary book."

A Strategy for Peace: Human Values and the Threat of War appeals for a new approach to internal and foreign relations based on morality. The preservation of national governments may depend on their willingness to take "steps toward a secure and lasting peace that are practical, nonutopian, and in keeping with widely shared human values," Bok declares. She reasons that growing interdependence between nations makes it imperative to maintain good relations by adhering to basic ethical standards. Building on the foundations of Kant's ethics—commitment to nonviolence, truthfulness, fulfillment of promises, and open communications—Bok argues that "their opposites—violence, deceit, breaches of trust, and excessive secrecy—doom a nation's foreign (and domestic) relations from the outset," reports Rushworth M. Kidder in the *Christian Science Monitor.* Furthermore, Kidder points out, "To her credit, [Bok] takes up the next and much harder part of the journey: defending her conclusions against hard-hitting objections. . . . She raises and refutes—quite pointedly, and often brilliantly—a whole array of arguments purporting to show that ethics and foreign policy don't mix."

New York Times Book Review contributor Daniel Schorr comments, "It is refreshing, if not customary, to see the issue of international conflict addressed in unashamedly moral terms. Who is to say whether 'moral constraints' represent a more naive approach to the threat of war than pragmatic hostility? In any event," he says, citing Soviet withdrawl from Afghanistan and the reduction of its forces in Europe, "it appears that since Mrs. Bok formulated her 'strategy,' some of her hopes for easing distrust have begun to be realized."

BIOGRAPHICAL/CRITICAL SOURCES:

PERIODICALS

Christian Science Monitor, February 17, 1989.
Columbia Journalism Review, March/April, 1983.
Commentary, October, 1978.
Commonweal, September 15, 1978.
Critic, September, 1978.
Los Angeles Times Book Review, October 16, 1983; March 12, 1989.
Nation, April 2, 1983.
New Republic, May 6, 1978; February 21, 1983.
New Statesman, January 19, 1979.
Newsweek, April 17, 1978; March 21, 1983.
New York Review of Books, June 1, 1978; March 31, 1983.
New York Times, March 6, 1983.
New York Times Book Review, June 25, 1978; June 8, 1980; February 20, 1983; March 19, 1989.
Times Literary Supplement, August 11, 1978; April 6, 1984.
U.S. News & World Report, March 31, 1980; April 18, 1983.
Washington Post Magazine, April 17, 1983.

*   *   *

BOLTON, Elizabeth
See St. JOHN, Nicole

*   *   *

BOROWITZ, Albert (Ira) 1930-

PERSONAL: Born June 27, 1930, in Chicago, IL; son of David (a business executive and book collector) and Anne (Wolkenstein) Borowitz; married Helen Osterman (an art historian), July 29, 1950; children: Peter Leonard, Joan, Andrew Seth. *Education:* Harvard University, B.A., 1951, M.A., 1953, J.D., 1956.

ADDRESSES: Home—2561 Coventry Rd., Shaker Heights, OH 44120. *Office*—Jones, Day, Reavis & Pogue, North Point, 901 East Lakeside Ave., Cleveland, OH 44114.

CAREER: Hahn, Loeser, Freedheim, Dean & Wellman, Cleveland, OH, associate, 1956-62, partner, 1956-83; Jones, Day, Reavis & Pogue, Cleveland, partner, 1983-90, of counsel, 1991—.

MEMBER: American Bar Association, American Law Institute, Great Lakes Theatre Festival (former vice-president), Ohio State Bar Association, Bar Association of Greater Cleveland (member of board of directors, 1976-79), Friends of the Cleveland Public Library (former member of board of trustees), Union Club, Rowfant Club.

WRITINGS:

Fiction in Communist China, M.I.T. Press, 1955.
Innocence and Arsenic: Studies in Crime and Literature (essays), Harper, 1977.
The Woman Who Murdered Black Satin: The Bermondsey Horror, Ohio State University Press, 1981.
A Gallery of Sinister Perspectives: Ten Crimes and a Scandal (essays), Kent State University Press, 1982.
The Jack the Ripper Walking Tour Murder, St. Martin's, 1986.
The Thurtell-Hunt Murder Case: Dark Mirror to Regency England, Louisiana State University Press, 1987.
This Club Frowns on Murder, St. Martin's, 1990.

Contributor of articles of *Opera News, American Scholar, Nineteenth-Century French Studies, Cleveland Magazine,* and *American Bar Association Journal.*

WORK IN PROGRESS: With wife, Helen O. Borowitz, *Pawnshop and Palaces; The Fall and Rise of the Campana Art Museum.*

SIDELIGHTS: Albert Borowitz told *CA:* "My special interest is the study of criminal cases that have directly involved writers and artist, either as murderers, victims, witnesses, or spectators, or that have inspired significant works of art or literature."

"Since 1986, I have also embarked on a series of crime novels featuring Paul Prye, crime historian, and his wife Alice, an art historian."

In the preface to his collection of essays on crime, *Innocence and Arsenic: Studies in Crime and Literature,* Borowitz writes: "I am drawn to works based on actual criminal experience because of the intriguing ambiguity of real crimes. There is uncertainty often as to guilt or innocence, and uncertainty oftener as to the motivations of the criminal and other participants in the drama. The appeal of such literature seems to me to be just the opposite of that of the classic detective story, where all doubts and suspense are finally resolved by the ingenious detective and the evil are firmly separated from the innocent. The ambiguity of historical crime is closer to the state of constant suspense in which we live. In the detective novel the puzzle is solved at the end, but in the study of crime, as in life, the puzzle goes on forever. In the title of my collection, I adopt a famous phrase from the work of the great nineteenth-century Swedish novelist C. J. L. Almqvist. The full quotation is: 'Two things are white: innocence and arsenic.' There can be no better statement of the ambiguity of criminal conduct, or any other human conduct, for that matter."

BIOGRAPHICAL/CRITICAL SOURCES:

BOOKS

Borowitz, Albert, *Innocence and Arsenic: Studies in Crime and Literature,* Harper, 1977.

PERIODICALS

Times Literary Supplement, November 20, 1981.

* * *

BOWLES, Edmund A(ddison) 1925-

PERSONAL: Born March 24, 1925, in Cambridge, Mass.; son of Edward L. (a consulting engineer) and Lois (Wuerpel) Bowles; married Marianne von Recklinghausen (an artist), June 4, 1952; children: Margaret Anne (Mrs. Richard Galen Price), David Addison. *Education:* Swarthmore College, B.A., 1949; Berkshire Music Center, Diploma, 1949; Yale University, Ph.D., 1956. *Politics:* None. *Religion:* None.

ADDRESSES: Home—5 Sage Court, White Plains, N.Y. 10605.

CAREER: Massachusetts Institute of Technology, Cambridge, instructor in humanities department, 1951-55; Bell Telephone Laboratories, Murray Hill, N.J., staff member of publications department, 1955-59; IBM Corp., New York, N.Y., assistant manager of department of arts and sciences, 1959-66, manager of professional activities in department of university relations, Armonk, N.Y., 1964-67, senior program administrator in humanities, libraries, museums, public sector industry marketing, Washington, D.C., 1968-78, senior program administrator, sales promotion, marketing communications, White Plains, N.Y., 1978-88. Baroque timpanist for Ars Musica, Ann Arbor, Mich., Carolina Consort, Winston-Salem, N.C., Genesee Baroque Ensemble, Ithaca, N.Y., and Smithsonian Chamber Players, Washington, D.C. Vice president, Westchester Symphony Orchestra, 1963-64; member of board of directors, Clarion Concerts and Music for Westchester, 1964-65; associate director, Dupont Circle Consortium, 1971-75; president, Northern Virginia Youth Symphony, 1974-76. Consultant to New York Pro Musica Antiqua, 1959-62, and Library-Museum of the Performing Arts at Lincoln Center, 1964-65. Lecturer in Europe on library automation, 1970, 1971; lecturer sponsored by town of Greenburgh, N.Y., and Westchester Community College, 1981, 1989; partici-

pant in Speakers in the Humanities program, New York Council for the Arts, 1990—; lecturer at various museums and universities. *Military service:* U.S. Army, 1943-46; became staff sergeant. U.S. Army Reserve, 1950-70; retired as major.

MEMBER: International Musicological Society, American Musicological Society (council member, 1966-70), American Musical Instrument Society (vice president, 1982-86), American Association for Information Science (liaison representative from Music Library Association, 1970-75), Music Library Association (member of U.S. RILM office oversight committee), Mediaeval Academy of America, Fellowship of Makers and Researchers of Ancient Instruments (London; fellow), Cosmos Club (Washington, D.C.).

AWARDS, HONORS: American Council of Learned Societies grant, 1964-65; National Endowment for the Humanities grant, 1971, 1972; Andrew W. Mellon Foundation grant, 1980.

WRITINGS:

(Contributor) Jan LaRue, editor, *Aspects of Medieval and Renaissance Music. A Birthday Offering to Gustave Reese,* Norton, 1966.
(Editor) *Computers in Humanistic Research: Readings and Perspectives,* Prentice-Hall, 1967.
(Contributor) Harry B. Lincoln, editor, *Music and the Computer: Composition and Research,* Cornell University Press, 1968.
Musikleben im 15. Jahrhundert, Deutsche Verlag fuer Musik, 1977.
La Pratique Musical au Moyen-Age/Musical Performance in the Late Middle Ages (bilingual text), Minkoff, 1983.
(Contributor) Allan W. Atlas, editor, *Music in the Classic Period: Essays in Honor of Barry S. Brook,* Pendragon Press, 1985.
Musical Ensembles in Festival Books, 1500-1800: An Iconographical and Documentary Survey, Volume 1, UMI Research Press, 1988.
The Timpani: A History in Pictures and Documents, Fritz Knuf, 1990.

Contributor of articles to *The New Grove Dictionary of Music and Musicians, The New Grove Dictionary of Musical Instruments, The New Grove Dictionary of American Music, Dictionary of the Middle Ages, The New Harvard Dictionary of Music, Encyclopedia Britannica,* and the Garland encyclopedias of keyboard and percussion instruments; contributor of about fifty articles and reviews to computer journals and music journals in the United States and Europe.

WORK IN PROGRESS: Selected Timpani Parts: An Historical Survey for Teachers and Students; Musical Ensembles in Festival Books, 1500-1800, Volume 2.

* * *

BRABEC, Barbara 1937-

PERSONAL: Born March 5, 1937, in Buckley, IL; daughter of William J. (a farmer and businessman) and Marcella E. (a nurse; maiden name, Williams) Schaumburg; married Harry J. Brabec (a musician and craft show producer), August, 1961. *Education:* Attended American Conservatory of Music, Chicago, IL, 1956-60. *Avocational interests:* Reading, music, ethnic cooking.

ADDRESSES: Office—Barbara Brabec Productions, P.O. Box 2137, Naperville, IL 60567.

CAREER: Pennsylvania Railroad, Chicago, IL, teletype operator, 1955-56; Kaiser Aluminum Co., Chicago, secretary,

1956-60; free-lance musical entertainer for clubs and organizations in Chicago area, 1960-61; Harding Restaurant Co., Chicago, executive secretary, 1961-62; Investment Guide Advertising, Inc., Chicago, administrative assistant, 1962-65; designer-craftsman and free-lance secretary, 1965-70; *Artisan Crafts* magazine, Reeds Spring, MO, editor, co-publisher, and co-owner, 1971-76; writer and secretarial assistant to husband's craft show productions, 1977-79; Countryside Books, Barrington, IL, 1979-81, began as publisher's assistant, became publisher and general manager; free-lance writer and publisher of newsletter, 1981-83; Barbara Brabec Productions (writing/publishing/mail order business), Naperville, IL, owner, 1984——.

WRITINGS:

(Editor) *Guide to the Craft World,* privately printed, 1974, revised edition, 1975.
Creative Cash: How to Sell Your Crafts, Needlework, Designs, and Know-How, Countryside Books, 1979, 5th revised edition, Barbara Brabec Productions, 1990.
Homemade Money: The Definitive Guide to Success in a Home Business, Betterway, 1984, revised 3rd edition, 1989.
Crafts Marketing Success Secrets, Barbara Brabec Productions, 1986, revised edition, 1988.
Help for Your Growing Homebased Business, Barbara Brabec Productions, 1987, revised edition, 1989.

Also author of *The Handcrafts Business,* 1981. Contributor to other books, including *National Directory of Shops and Galleries,* Writer's Digest, 1982; *The Complete Guide to Writing Nonfiction,* Writer's Digest, 1983; *Women Working Home,* WWH Press, 1983. Author of columns "Selling What You Make," for *Crafts,* 1979——, and "The Crafts Spotlight," for *Creative Crafts,* 1979-82. Editor and publisher, *Craftspirit '76* and *National Home Business Report,* 1981——.

WORK IN PROGRESS: Several books.

SIDELIGHTS: In a letter to *CA,* Barbara Brabec once commented: "I literally fell into writing in 1971 when my intense interest in crafts led my husband to suggest that we ought to publish a crafts marketing magazine for people like me. 'But I'm not a writer,' I said. 'Try,' he replied.

"Although I edited our magazine for five years and wrote much of the material in it, I did not think of myself as a writer until 1976, when a book publisher asked me to write a crafts marketing guide for homemakers. 'Just string all your articles together, and you'll have a book,' he told me.

"Of course, there was much more to writing *Creative Cash* than this! Although I now accept the fact that I had been a writer all my life (having always been an avid letter writer and journal-keeper), I also realized I knew absolutely nothing about the *craft* of writing. Since I wanted to be a *good* writer, I began a period of intense study that has never ended, and that, in fact, actually served as the springboard for what is now a full-time, homebased writing/publishing/mail order business.

"As I began to write *Creative Cash,* I also began to read books and magazines on how to be a good writer. I soon found myself writing a chapter . . . reading a book . . . then cringing as I realized I had just written something ghastly! Then I'd go back and rewrite that chapter, read another book, and rewrite some more. By the time I finished my book, I knew quite a bit about the craft of writing. My effort paid off.

"To date, some 75,000 copies of *Creative Cash* have been sold, and it is recognized as a 'bible' in its field. When my publisher elected to let this book go out of print in mid-1984, I published the third edition myself. Now that I've published one book, I figure I might as well publish a few more, and I now have several books in progress.

"Meanwhile, my second book, *Homemade Money,* published in 1984, is finding its market. Recommended by the U.S. Small Business Administration, it is now being used as a textbook in college courses on small businesses, and has been called one of the best books in its field.

"While trade reviews are nice, they can't compare to letters full of praise from satisfied individuals who are benefitting from the words you've written. It's extremely satisfying to know that you're able to communicate so well with thousands of people you've never met, and it's this knowledge that will keep me writing as long as I live."

BIOGRAPHICAL/CRITICAL SOURCES:

PERIODICALS

Interweave 65, winter, 1979-80.
Library Journal, October, 1979.
Nutshell News, November/December, 1979.
Publishers Weekly, May 18, 1984.

*   *   *

BRADFORD, Barbara Taylor   1933-

PERSONAL: Born May 10, 1933, in Leeds, Yorkshire, England; came to the United States, 1963; daughter of Winston (an industrial engineer) and Freda (a children's nurse; maiden name Walker) Taylor; married Robert Bradford (a producer), 1963.

CAREER: Yorkshire Evening Post, Yorkshire, England, reporter, 1949-51, women's editor, 1951-53; *Women's Own,* London, England, fashion editor, 1953-54; *London Evening News,* London, columnist, 1955-57; *Woman,* London, features editor, 1962-64; National Design Center, New York, N.Y., editor, 1964-65; *Newsday,* Long Island, N.Y., syndicated columnist, 1966——; writer. Also served as feature writer for *Today* magazine and executive editor of the *London American.*

WRITINGS:

NONFICTION

(Editor) *Children's Stories of the Bible from the Old Testament,* Lion Press, c. 1966.
(Editor) *Children's Stories of Jesus from the New Testament,* Lion Press, c. 1966.
(Editor) Samuel Nisenson, *The Dictionary of One Thousand and One Famous People,* Lion Press, 1966.
A Garland of Children's Verse, Lion Press, 1968.
The Complete Encyclopedia of Homemaking Ideas, Meredith Press, 1968.
How to Be the Perfect Wife: Etiquette to Please Him, Essandess, 1969.
How to Be the Perfect Wife: Entertaining to Please Him, Essandess, 1969.
How to Be the Perfect Wife: Fashions That Please Him, Essandess, c. 1970.
Easy Steps to Successful Decorating, Simon & Schuster, 1971.
How to Solve Your Decorating Problems, Simon & Schuster, 1976.
Decorating Ideas for Casual Living, Simon & Schuster, c. 1977.
Making Space Grow, Simon & Schuster, 1979.

Luxury Designs for Apartment Living, Doubleday, 1981.

FICTION

A Woman of Substance (alternate selection of Doubleday Book
    Club and Literary Guild), Doubleday, 1979.
Voice of the Heart, Doubleday, 1983.
Hold the Dream (also see below), Doubleday, 1985.
Act of Will, Doubleday, 1986.
To Be the Best, Doubleday, 1988.
The Women in His Life, Grafton, 1990.

OTHER

Also author of "Hold the Dream," a television miniseries adaptation of her novel, 1986. Editor-in-chief, "Guide to Home Decorating Ideas," 1966—.

SIDELIGHTS: Barbara Taylor Bradford has earned a wide
readership with her lengthy novels of wealth, intrigue, and love.
Bradford's fiction has sold by the millions in paperback, and two
of her books, *A Woman of Substance* and *Hold the Dream,* have
been adapted as television miniseries. A former journalist specializing in home decorating, Bradford expresses great satisfaction over the lucrative turn her writing career has taken since
1980. "If anyone asks me whether I like being a popular writer,"
she told the *New York Times,* "I ask them whether they think
I'd rather be an unpopular writer."

Bradford grew up in northern England, an imaginative youngster who had read all the works of Charles Dickens and the
Bronte sisters by the time she was twelve. While still a pre-teen
she sold her first story, for ten shillings and sixpence, to a British
children's magazine. Bradford was determined to become a
writer, so at sixteen she abandoned her formal schooling to work
as a typist at the *Yorkshire Evening Post.* Within two years she
was promoted to editor of the paper's women's page, and two
years after that—at the tender age of twenty—she went to London as fashion editor of *Women's Own* magazine. She subsequently worked for a number of London periodicals, including
Today magazine, the *London Evening News,* and the *London
American.*

In 1963 Bradford married and moved to the United States,
where she continued her career as a journalist. Through the aegis
of *Newsday,* she became author of a syndicated column, "Designing Women," that covered lifestyle and interior decorating
topics. Bradford also wrote several books on interior design, including *How To Solve Your Decorating Problems, Decorating
Ideas for Casual Living,* and *Luxury Designs for Apartment Living.* As a sideline she began experimenting with fiction; she abandoned four novels before beginning *A Woman of Substance* in the
late 1970s.

A Woman of Substance sold an impressive 45,000 copies in hard
cover, but it was the paperback edition that broke records. In soft
cover, *A Woman of Substance* stayed on the bestseller lists for
more than forty weeks; eventually its sales totalled some three
million copies. The book begins the saga of Emma Harte, a
Yorkshire woman who rises from obscurity to found a retail empire and to enact revenge on the nobleman who seduced and
abandoned her. In the *New York Times* Bradford characterized
Emma as "a powerful woman who started with nothing but acquired dignity and polish." Bradford added that she strove to
make Emma—and her other female characters as well—"tough
but not hard."

Hold the Dream and *To Be the Best* continue the chronicle of the
Harte family, centering on Emma's shrewd and beautiful granddaughter, Paula McGill O'Neill. Those and Bradford's other

bestsellers present "indomitable women who valiantly struggle
with adversity, and with their own implacable natures," to quote
a *Los Angeles Times Book Review* contributor. Bradford does not
consider her works romances, but *Los Angeles Times Book Review* correspondent Judith Moore feels that the author "makes
tasteful, intelligent use of the romance genre." Moore continues:
"In [Bradford's] hands this maligned category takes on plausibility and a heft more than the book's weight." Moore also suggests
that Bradford's characters reveal a 1980s brand of emotional
complexity. Her heroes, writes Moore, "reflect the changes in relations between men and women. They encourage women's careers. They cook dinner and clean up the mess. . . . The heroines are also new . . . more autonomous, as motivated by work
as by love."

Bradford herself seems highly motivated by the work ethic. Her
writing days begin at six in the morning and can last ten to twelve
hours—she adapted her novel *Hold the Dream* for television in
just five weeks. Bradford told *Writer's Digest* that she derives
great satisfaction from the hard work she does for months at a
time. "I *need* it," she said. "If I didn't write fiction, they'd take
me away in a straitjacket, because I have all this . . . *stuff* going
on in my head. I have to get it out . . . . I enjoy writing." Reflecting on her status in the literary community, Bradford told
the *New York Times:* "I'm a commercial writer—a storyteller.
I suppose I will always write about strong women. I don't mean
hard women, though. I mean women of substance."

MEDIA ADAPTATIONS: A Woman of Substance was filmed for
television as a six-part miniseries. *Hold the Dream* was filmed for
television as a four-hour miniseries.

BIOGRAPHICAL/CRITICAL SOURCES:

PERIODICALS

Atlanta Journal, June 8, 1979.
Columbus Dispatch, July 8, 1979.
Daily Messenger, June 11, 1979.
Detroit News, May 19, 1985.
Globe and Mail (Toronto), November 3, 1984.
Los Angeles Times Book Review, March 20, 1983; August 10,
    1986; June 19, 1988.
Naples Daily News, July 29, 1979.
New York Times, November 10, 1981; October 26, 1986.
New York Times Book Review, September 9, 1979; April 24,
    1983; June 9, 1985; July 20, 1986; July 31, 1988.
People, June 13, 1983.
St. Louis Post-Dispatch, June 24, 1979.
Washington Post, June 12, 1979; May 17, 1985.
Washington Post Book World, April 3, 1983; July 6, 1986.
Writer, March, 1986.
Writer's Digest, June, 1987.*

—*Sketch by Anne Janette Johnson*

*   *   *

BRETT, Leo
    See FANTHORPE, R(obert) Lionel

*   *   *

BRIDGE, Raymond   1943-

PERSONAL: Born February 5, 1943, in Princeton, NJ; son of
Herbert Sage (a physicist) and Jeanne (Hall) Bridge; married
Madeleyne Claire DeSimone (an office manager), March 17,
1961; children: Diane Michelle, Cynthia Jeanne. *Education:* At-

tended California Institute of Technology, 1959-62, and University of California, 1963-65. *Politics:* "Civil libertarian-conservationist-populist." *Avocational interests:* History, philosophy.

ADDRESSES: Home and office—435 South 38th St., Boulder, CO 80303.

CAREER: KPFA-FM Radio, Berkeley, CA, non-commercial radio journalist, 1964-69; writer, 1973—. Director of Boulder Mountaineering School, 1974-76. Has also worked as a photographer and as a political campaign manager.

MEMBER: Authors Guild, Authors League of America, Sierra Club (member of Indian Peaks group executive committee, 1973-75), American Canoe Association, American Whitewater Affiliation, Colorado Mountain Club (member of Boulder group executive council, 1974-76), Colorado Open Space Council (member of board of directors, 1975-76), Colorado Whitewater Association.

WRITINGS:

The Complete Snow Camper's Guide, Scribner, 1973, new edition published as *The New Complete Snow Camper's Guide,* 1981.
America's Backpacking Book, Scribner, 1973, revised edition, 1981.
Freewheeling: The Bicycle Camping Book, Stackpole, 1974.
Tourguide to the Rocky Mountain Wilderness, Stackpole, 1975, 2nd edition, Pruett, 1980.
The Camper's Guide to Alaska, the Yukon, and Northern British Columbia, Scribner, 1976.
Climbing: A Guide to Mountaineering, Scribner, 1976.
The Runner's Book, Scribner, 1978.
The Complete Canoeist's Guide, Scribner, 1978.
The Complete Guide to Kayaking, Scribner, 1978.
High Peaks and Clear Roads: A Safe and Easy Guide to Outdoor Skills, Prentice-Hall, 1978.
Bike Touring: The Sierra Club Guide to Outings on Wheels, illustrated by John Lencicki, Sierra Books, 1979.
Running through the Wall: A Guide for the Serious Runner, Dial, 1980.
Running without Pain: A Guide to the Prevention and Treatment of Running Injuries, illustrated by Lencicki, Dial, 1980.

WORK IN PROGRESS: Research for books on the Alaskan pipeline, the history of mountaineering, and the relation of memory patterns to thought processes.

SIDELIGHTS: Raymond Bridge once told *CA:* "I am an active climber, kayaker, canoeist, and runner, and in my outdoor books I try to reflect personal experience and to communicate my strong conservationist position. I have led and participated in mountaineering expeditions, and I am particularly fond of the wilderness regions of northwestern Canada and Alaska. I believe that it is man's and woman's responsibility to husband the resources of the race and of the Earth, rather than unthinkingly exploiting them for the gain of a few, and to the detriment of the less fortunate, of future generations, and of other species of life."

BIOGRAPHICAL/CRITICAL SOURCES:

PERIODICALS

Washington Post Book World, September 9, 1979.*

BRODY, J(acob) J(erome) 1929-

PERSONAL: Born April 24, 1929, in Brooklyn, NY; son of Aladar (in business) and Esther (Kraiman) Brody; married Jean Lindsey, February 13, 1956; children: Jefferson Lindsey, Jonathan Edward, Allison Janet. *Education:* Cooper Union for the Advancement of Science and Art, Certificate in Fine Arts, 1950; University of New Mexico, B.A., 1956, M.A., 1964, Ph.D., 1970.

ADDRESSES: Home—Star Rt., Box 929, Sandia Park, NM 87047.

CAREER: Everhart Museum, Scranton, PA, curator of art, 1957-58; Isaac Delgado Museum of Art, New Orleans, LA, curator of collections, 1958-60; Museum of International Folk Art, Santa Fe, NM, curator of exhibits, 1961-62; University of New Mexico, Albuquerque, Maxwell Museum of Anthropology, curator of exhibits, 1962-67, curator of museum, 1968-71, director of museum, 1976-84, assistant professor, 1965-71, associate professor, 1971-80, professor of anthropology and art, 1980-89, professor emeritus, 1989—; School of American Research, Santa Fe, research associate, 1989—. Has organized numerous major exhibitions on American Indians and their pottery and artifacts, 1976—. Delivered Bandelier Lecture, Archaeological Society of New Mexico, 1983. Grant proposal reviewer for several government agencies. Member of numerous advisory boards, including Florence Hawley Ellis Museum of Anthropology, 1977-82, 1989—, Human Systems Research, Inc., 1977-88, Mimbres Foundation, 1977-84, New Mexico Museum of Natural History, 1980-84, and Wheelwright Museum of the American Indian, 1989—. Member of museum panel of National Endowment for the Humanities; member of Albuquerque Fine Arts Board, 1970-74; past member of New Mexico state paleontology task force. Consultant to numerous museums and organizations, 1976—, including California Academy of Natural Sciences, 1979, 1981, Museum of the American Indian, 1982, and American Federation of Arts, 1981-83. *Military service:* U.S. Army, 1952-54.

MEMBER: Society for American Archaeology, American Association of Museums, Council for Museum Anthropology, Native American Arts Studies Association, American Rock Art Research Association, Council for Museum Anthropology, New Mexico Museums Association, New Mexico Archaeological Society (member of board of trustees).

AWARDS, HONORS: Nonfiction award, Border-Regional Library Association, 1971, for *Indian Painters and White Patrons;* art book award, Border-Regional Library Association, and Governor's Award of Honor, New Mexico Cultural Properties Review Committee, both 1978, both for *Mimbres Painted Pottery;* National Endowment for the Humanities fellow at School of American Research, 1980-81.

WRITINGS:

Indian Painters and White Patrons, University of New Mexico Press, 1971.
Between Traditions: Navajo Weavings, 1880-1920, Museum of Art, University of Iowa, 1976.
Mimbres Painted Pottery, University of New Mexico Press, 1977.
The Chaco Phenomenon, Maxwell Museum of Anthropology, University of New Mexico, 1983.
(With Sallie Wagner and Beatien Yazz) *Yazz: Navajo Painter,* Northland Press, 1983.
(With Stephen LeBlanc and Catherine Scott) *Mimbres Pottery: Ancient Art of the American Southwest,* Hudson Hills Press, 1983.

(Author of introduction) J. Walter Fewkes, *The Mimbres: Art and Archaeology,* Avanyu Publishing (Albuquerque, NM), 1989.

Anasazi and Pueblo Painting of the Southwest, School of American Research (Santa Fe, NM) and University of New Mexico Press, 1990.

The Anasazi: Ancient People of the American Southwest, JACA Books, 1990.

CONTRIBUTOR

Explorations 1977, School of American Research, 1977.

(Contributor) Nelson H. H. Graburn, editor, *Ethnic and Tourist Arts,* University of California Press, 1977.

(Contributor) Carroll Riley, editor, *Across the Chichimec Sea,* Southern Illinois University Press, 1978.

(Contributor) Alfonso Ortiz, editor, *Handbook of North American Indians,* Volume 9, Smithsonian Institution, 1979.

(Contributor) *Papers in Honor of Helen Blumenschein,* New Mexico Archaeological Society, 1979.

(Contributor) Dorothy Washburn, editor, *Hopi Kachina: Spirit of Life,* California Academy of Sciences, 1980.

(Contributor) Washburn, editor, *Catalog of the Elkus Collection,* California Academy of Sciences, 1984.

(Contributor) David Grant Noble, editor, *New Light on Chaco Canyon,* School of American Research Press, 1984.

(Contributor) *Native American Artists,* Fort Wayne Museum of Art, 1987.

(Contributor) *Anasazi and Pueblo Indian Pottery,* University Museum, University of Pennsylvania (Philadelphia, PA), 1990.

OTHER

Also author, with Anita Thacher, of film "Painted Earth: Mimbres Painted Pottery," Program for Art on Film, Metropolitan Museum of Art and Getty Foundation. Also contributor to special publications of the Texas Tech University Museum, 1977, and to the New Mexico Archaeological Society, 1980; also contributor to *Proceedings* of 38th International Congress of Americanists. Contributor to periodicals, including *Antiques, Studio Potter,* and *New Mexico Magazine.* Member of editorial board, *American Indian Arts Magazine,* 1974—, *Journal of Anthropological Research,* 1984—, and *New Mexico Studies in the Fine Arts,* 1986-87.

SIDELIGHTS: J. J. Brody told *CA:* "I am interested in understanding how art works as an integrative social force and, therefore, in the art of small and isolated societies. I want to consider the methodological problems of studying history in the absence of written documentation. I am concerned about the interactions that occur between the makers and the users of art and how the need for art to be communicatively successful requires artists to conform to the rules of performance. I am interested in how those rules can become creatively liberating, rather than restrictive. Finally, I am most interested in the phenomenon of post-Bohemian alienation of artists in modern society and how this historical accident has negatively affected artists and art users by stressing idiosyncracy and novelty at the expense of communicative form and content."

BIOGRAPHICAL/CRITICAL SOURCES:

PERIODICALS

Archaeology, July-August, 1983.
Los Angeles Times Book Review, September 1, 1985.
Times Literary Supplement, July 27, 1984.

BRONNER, Stephen Eric 1949-

PERSONAL: Born August 19, 1949, in New York, NY; son of Harry and Edith (Kirchheimer) Bronner. *Education:* City College of the City University of New York, B.A., 1971; University of California, Berkeley, M.A., 1972, Ph.D., 1975.

ADDRESSES: Home—200 Cabrini Blvd., New York, NY 10033. *Office*—Department of Political Science, Rutgers University, New Brunswick, NJ 08903. *Agent*—Lois de la Haba Associates, 142 Bank St., New York, NY 10014.

CAREER: Rutgers University, New Brunswick, NJ, assistant professor, 1976-83, associate professor, 1983-89, professor of political science, 1990—.

MEMBER: American Political Science Association.

AWARDS, HONORS: Fulbright fellowship, 1973, for study in Tuebingen, West Germany.

WRITINGS:

A Beggar's Tales (novel), Pella Publishing, 1978.

(Editor, translator, and author of introduction) *The Letters of Rosa Luxemburg,* Westview, 1978.

A Revolutionary for Our Times: Rosa Luxemburg, Pluto Publishing, 1981, 2nd edition published as *Rosa Luxemburg: A Revolutionary for Our Times,* Columbia University Press, 1987.

(Editor with Douglas Kellner) *Passion and Rebellion: The Expressionist Heritage,* Bergin & Garvey, 1983, 2nd edition, Columbia University Press, 1988.

(Editor and author of introduction) *Socialism in History: The Political Essays of Henry Pachter,* Columbia University Press, 1984.

Leon Blum, Chelsea House, 1987.

(Editor with Kellner) *Critical Theory and Society: A Reader,* Routledge & Kegan Paul and Chapman & Hall, 1989.

Socialism Unbound, Routledge & Kegan Paul, 1990.

Contributor of articles to periodicals, including *Politics and Society, Review of Politics, Social Research, Salmagundi, Enclitic, Minnesota Review,* and *Political Theory.*

SIDELIGHTS: "Whatever the personal and philosophical changes that I have undergone," Stephen Eric Bronner told *CA,* "it is still an aspect of the 1960s which has fundamentally shaped my intellectual and political project. In essence, this involves the recognition that a basic connection between politics and culture exists, and that it must be addressed in a critical fashion.

"It was this insight that influenced my early choice of political aesthetics as the topic of inquiry for my early articles and my first novel. *A Beggar's Tales* has not received a great deal of notice, despite that fact that Charles Webel, writing for *Telos,* pointed out that its 'provocative' prose, its critical ideas, and its 'creativity . . . merit attention.' The novel grew out of the collapse of the old movement as it recognized and sought to discuss the motivations and the need for a new one. In the novel this was done by creating a 'pessimistic superstructure on a utopian base' through a broken-down narrator who cannot act, but rather lives only through the fictional stories that he tells in a shabby cafe. Politically influenced by the works of Sartre, Brecht, Walter Benjamin, and Ernst Bloch, the novel's literary use of the *recit* form derives from Benjamin Constant, Gide, and Camus.

"My concern with Marxian and critical thought must also be seen as a response to the collapse of the student movement. This concern was spurred on by the noted socialist, historian, and essayist, Henry Pachter, whom I met while a student at the City

College of New York. My views also reflect the influence of the great maverick, Marxist philosopher Ernst Bloch, with whom I studied at the University of Tuebingen.

"My own political position is in sharp contrast to the reformism of Western social democracy and the orthodoxy of Soviet or Chinese Communism. The great socialist, activist, and theorist Rosa Luxemburg also stands apart from both these camps and, in my opinion, her work constitutes a beginning for any revitalization of *socialist* thought. *A Revolutionary for Our Times* is an attempt to show the relevance of her thought for contemporary socialist politics.

"Thus, reappropriating the socialist tradition for the political demands of the present becomes a dominant theme within my work. This theme is continued in *Socialism Unbound*, which deals with the failures, consequences, and possibilities of traditional socialist thinkers and movements in the light of contemporary events."

BIOGRAPHICAL/CRITICAL SOURCES:

PERIODICALS

New German Critique, spring/summer, 1982.
New Political Science, summer/autumn, 1982.
Print Collector's Newsletter, November, 1983, December, 1983.
Salmagundi, winter, 1980, spring, 1980.
Telos, autumn, 1980, winter, 1981-82.
Village Voice Literary Supplement, November, 1984.

* * *

BROOKS, James L. 1940-

PERSONAL: Born May 9, 1940, in Brooklyn, N.Y.; son of Edward M. and Dorothy Helen (Sheinheit) Brooks; married Marianne Catherine Morrissey, July 7, 1964 (divorced, 1971); married Holly Beth Holmberg, July 23, 1978; children: (first marriage) Amy Lorraine. *Education:* Attended New York University, 1958-60.

ADDRESSES: Home—1890 Westridge, Los Angeles, Calif. 90049. *Office*—Paramount Studios, 5451 Marathon, Hollywood, Calif. 90038.

CAREER: Writer, producer, and director. Columbia Broadcasting System (CBS) News, New York, N.Y., reporter and writer, 1964-66; Wolper Productions, Los Angeles, Calif., writer and producer of documentaries, 1966-67; American Broadcasting Co. (ABC), Los Angeles, Calif., executive story editor and creator of television series "Room 222," 1968-69; CBS, Studio City, Calif., executive producer and creator of television series "The Mary Tyler Moore Show," 1970-77; also producer and writer on various television series and films, including "Thursday's Game," "Cindy" (musical), "Rhoda," "The New Lorenzo Music Show," "Friends and Lovers," "Lou Grant," "Taxi," "The Associates," "Broadcast News," and "The Tracey Ullman Show."

MEMBER: Writers Guild, Television Academy of Arts and Sciences.

AWARDS, HONORS: Oscar awards for best film and best adapted screenplay, American Academy of Motion Picture Arts and Sciences, 1984, Golden Globe award, and New York Film Critics Circle award, all for "Terms of Endearment"; Oscar nominations for best picture and best original screenplay, American Academy of Motion Picture Arts and Sciences, 1987, and best picture and best original screenplay, New York Film Critics Circle, for "Broadcast News"; recipient of several Emmy

Awards from the National Academy of Television Arts and Sciences, for "Room 222," "The Mary Tyler Moore Show," "Lou Grant," "Taxi," "Cindy," and "The Tracey Ullman Show"; Golden Globe Award from Hollywood Foreign Press Corps, for "Rhoda."

WRITINGS:

SCREENPLAYS

(And co-producer) "Starting Over," Paramount, 1979.
(And co-producer and director) "Terms of Endearment" (based on the novel by Larry McMurtry), Paramount, 1983.
(And producer and director) "Perfect," 1985.
(And producer and director) "Broadcast News," Twentieth Century-Fox, 1987.

SIDELIGHTS: "With his long jaw, black mustache and heavy beard," writes Aljean Harmetz in a *New York Times* profile, James L. Brooks "might be Mephistopheles as a stand-up comic. The comedy that gushes out like water from a lawn sprinkler has no edge of nastiness. It is sweet and cheerful and aimed at no one but himself." Indeed, Brooks, a screenwriter/producer/director of just a few years' seasoning, has made a name for himself as one of Hollywood's fastest-rising talents. Though he was well-known as the television writer who created, among other series, "The Mary Tyler Moore Show" and "Taxi," Brooks still found himself, in the early 1980s, with an adaptation of a Larry McMurtry novel, an idea for directing it, and no encouragement from the studio brass. "Not commercial," "too downbeat," and "Who would be interested in the problems of this mother and daughter?" were, according to Harmetz's article, just some of the rejection remarks Brooks got when he was trying to pitch "Terms of Endearment." Finally, Brooks was signed by Paramount, and "Terms of Endearment," starring Shirley MacLaine, Jack Nicholson, and Debra Winger, eventually opened in 1983. The reaction seemed instantaneous, with critics and public alike responding to the bittersweet comedy of family loyalty and romantic infidelity. Among the many gifted artists involved in the movie, Brooks was singled out for particular praise—even in the touchy subject of handling the concept of death in what ostensibly appears to be a comedy.

"In adapting [McMurtry's] entertaining and affecting but dramatically diffuse novel, Brooks has contrived to finesse most of the structural defects built into its rambling, episodic nature," notes *Washington Post* critic Gary Arnold. "His touch is so pleasant and the cast so skillful and enjoyable that it may seem immaterial to ask yourself if this narrative is really *getting someplace,* rather than passing the time agreeably." Continues Arnold: "When a decisive crisis [in the film] occurs, Brooks takes even more impressive advantage of the novel's belated, arguably underhanded resort to incurable illness as a cure-all for plot drift. Spectators who feel resentful about the way the movie activates and exploits its concluding, heartbreaking twist of fate will probably be in a clear minority, but it will be difficult for the rest of us to deny that they have a legitimate esthetic complaint."

"Let's get one thing straight immediately: ['Terms of Endearment'] is not a perfect movie," says Vincent Canby in a *New York Times* article. "This comedy . . . sort of meanders around a plot that covers approximately 30 years. It contains one more fatal illness than you may want to witness, and every now and then Mr. Brooks's sit-com background . . . is apparent in the film's inability to resist a fast response that may not be entirely in character with the person responding." "All of this, however, is beside the point," Canby goes on to say. "[This work] must be one of the most engaging films of the year, to be cherished as much for the low-pressure way in which it operates . . . as for the fact that it contains what are possibly the best performances ever given by Shirley MacLaine and Jack Nicholson." "Terms of Endearment" went on to capture three major Academy Awards, including best picture and best adapted screenplay for Brooks, and left film fans wondering what the writer/director's next effort would produce.

After what is commonly acknowledged as a false start, the 1985 aerobics-love story "Perfect," Brooks came back with an original screenplay culled from his own past as a writer in a television newsroom (the same fertile ground that provided seven seasons' worth of plot for Brooks's "The Mary Tyler Moore Show"). "Broadcast News," released in 1987, presents the traditional love triangle—between Jane, a savvy network-news producer, Aaron, a brilliant but uncharismatic reporter, and Tom, an attractive if less than gifted news anchorman—that evolves into a love quadrangle, as careerism takes as important a part in the character's lives as romance does. "The story unfolds as a series of 'days in the life of' a network news bureau, and a cautionary tale it is," remarks Sheila Benson in the *Los Angeles Times*. "Brooks is understandably distressed at the state of the news we're getting, in bright, flashy, easily digested 'bites,' a USA Today, 'Entertainment Tonight' version of the news."

"Broadcast News" is "funny, it's intelligent, and it's aimed at the upscale, but what will sell it . . . is that it's all about Washington Media Folk, the people America loves to hate and who, it might be speculated, love to hate themselves," according to *Washington Post* reviewer Tom Shales. To *Chicago Tribune* writer Dave Kehr, "though Brooks begins with a slightly sitcom-like sense of narrowly defined, single-trait characters—there's the dumb one, the smart one and the compulsive one—he builds on the archetypes to create remarkably full, complex figures, in whom strengths and weaknesses, generous impulses and selfish interests exist side by side." Benson feels that "Brooks' talent for observation and for truthful, careful writing borders on the eerie. He's captured these young people and their pressure-cooker jobs exactly—their banter, their rationalizations, the balance of their lives between work and whatever comes a close second. . . . [Brooks] has seen that a playful sort of ego-speak guards their vulnerability, and he understands that there is a distinct pragmatism to his whiz kids. But he likes them. And there's no way in the world that we won't either."

In *Washington Post* critic Hal Hinson's opinion, "Broadcast News" "never comes close to being a great, penetrating work about television news. It's not a scathing satire like 'Network,' nor is it to broadcast journalism what 'All the President's Men' was to print. But Brooks' ambitions for [this movie] appear to have been far less exalted. [He instead has crafted] a teasing, affectionately critical satire of his former profession. In the process, he's created a spunky romantic comedy with some of the snappiest lines heard onscreen in a long while." Members of the Motion Picture Academy agreed with these assessments, nominating Brooks for the best original screenplay and best picture Oscars.

For all his success, the writer/director is also known as a stern perfectionist, "feverishly obsessed and, once or twice, almost sadistic," as Harmetz describes, pointing to the filming of a scene in "Terms of Endearment" in which, in order to get the properly pained expression from Shirley MacLaine, "Brooks arranged for a prop man to create a noise he knew was physically painful to MacLaine—the sound of a wet finger rubbing the rim of a glass." But the filmmaker's friends find Brooks an engaging eccentric. "He's a thin guy who complains about his weight, a young guy

who says he has one foot in the grave," fellow screenwriter Jerry Belson tells Harmetz. According to Belson, Brooks's early-morning phone conversations focus on his two favorite topics. "On a good day it's age. On a bad day it's death."

BIOGRAPHICAL/CRITICAL SOURCES:

PERIODICALS

Chicago Tribune, April 8, 1984, December 16, 1987, January 3, 1988.
Los Angeles Times, November 23, 1983, December 16, 1987, December 20, 1987, January 11, 1988.
New York Times, November 20, 1983, November 23, 1983, December 4, 1983, December 20, 1987, January 7, 1988.
New York Times Magazine, April 8, 1984.
Washington Post, October 5, 1979, November 23, 1983, December 13, 1987, December 25, 1987.*

—Sketch by Susan Salter

* * *

BROWN, David E(arl) 1938-

PERSONAL: Born January 26, 1938, in Neenah, WI; son of Harold Valentine (an electrotyper) and Gladys (Blaney) Brown; married Louella Bailey (a certified public accountant), December 18, 1965; children: Elaine. *Education:* San Jose State College (now University), B.A., 1961.

ADDRESSES: Home—3118 West McLellan Blvd., Phoenix, AZ 85017. *Office*—Arizona Game and Fish Department, 2222 West Greenway Rd., Phoenix, AZ 85023.

CAREER: Arizona Game and Fish Department, wildlife manager in Gila Bend, 1961-62, in Casa Grande, 1962, and in Tucson, 1962-68, small game biologist in Phoenix, 1968-79, big game management supervisor in Phoenix, 1980-83, game management supervisor in Phoenix, 1983-88, regional supervisor in Kingman, 1984; writer, 1989—. Member of faculty at Arizona State University, 1981-82. *Military service:* Army National Guard, 1955-63.

MEMBER: Wildlife Society (president of Arizona chapter, 1977), Arizona-Nevada Academy of Sciences (fellow), Arizona Wildlife Federation, Desert Bighorn Sheep Society.

AWARDS, HONORS: Wildlife Conservationist of the Year, Arizona Wildlife Federation, 1973; Shikar Safari Award, Safari International, 1974; Biologist of the Year, New Mexico-Arizona Section of Wildlife Society, 1975; Southwest Book Award, Border Regional Library Association, 1984, for *The Wolf in the Southwest;* McCullough Award, Arizona Wildlife Federation, 1989.

WRITINGS:

(Editor with N. B. Carmony) G. P. Davis, *Man and Wildlife in Arizona,* Arizona Game and Fish Department, 1982.
(Editor) *The Biotic Communities of the Southwest,* Desert Plants, 1983.
(Editor with Carmony) *Tales from Tiburon,* Southwest Natural History Association, 1983.
(Editor) *The Wolf in the Southwest,* University of Arizona Press, 1983.
Arizona's Tree Squirrels, Arizona Game and Fish Department, 1984.
Wetlands and Waterfowl in Arizona, University of Arizona Press, 1985.
The Grizzly in the Southwest, University of Oklahoma Press, 1985.

(Editor with Carmony) *The Log of the Panthon,* Pruett, 1987.
(Editor with J. A. Murray) *The Last Grizzly and Other South-western Bear Stories,* University of Arizona Press, 1988.
Arizona Game Birds, University of Arizona Press, 1989.
(Editor with Carmony) *Aldo Leopold in the Wilderness,* Stackpole, 1990.

Contributor to wildlife and natural history journals.

WORK IN PROGRESS: Editing, with N. B. Carmony, *Cazadores in Mexico.*

SIDELIGHTS: David E. Brown told *CA:* "As a working field biologist in the Southwest for more than twenty years, I have had the opportunity to observe wildlife and those who work with wildlife. My educational background has given me a historical perspective that compels me to record outstanding events in the biological world. This and scientific curiosity have guided my efforts.

"Most of my career has been spent conducting and coordinating game studies and formulating hunt regulations. My hobbies have been wildlife and natural history inquiry coupled with hunting. The evolutionary adaptations and natural controls of wildlife never cease to interest me. This has led me to a general optimism for wildlife's future, provided that the animals are given time to adapt."

*   *   *

BROWN, Judith M(argaret) 1944-

PERSONAL: Born July 9, 1944, in India; daughter of Wilfred George (a parson) and Joan Margaret (Adams) Brown; married Peter James Diggle, July 21, 1984; children: James Wilfred Lachlan Diggle. *Education:* Girton College, Cambridge, M.A. (with honors), 1965, Ph.D., 1968.

ADDRESSES: Home—Oxford, England. *Office*—Balliol College, Oxford University, Oxford OX1 3BJ, England.

CAREER: Cambridge University, Girton College, Cambridge, England, research fellow, official fellow in history, and director of studies in history, 1968-71; University of Manchester, Manchester, England, lecturer, beginning 1971, senior lecturer in history, 1982-90, advisor in the central academic advisory service, 1978-90; Oxford University, Balliol College, Beit Professor of Commonwealth History, 1990—. Lecturer on Hinduism in Northern Ordination Course, 1982.

MEMBER: Royal Historical Society (fellow).

WRITINGS:

Gandhi's Rise to Power: Indian Politics, 1918-1922, Cambridge University Press, 1972.
Gandhi and Civil Disobedience: The Mahatma in Indian Politics, 1928-1934, Cambridge University Press, 1977.
Men and Gods in a Changing World: Some Themes in the 20th Century Experience of Hindus and Christians, SCM Press (London), 1980.
Modern India: The Origins of an Asian Democracy, Oxford University Press, 1984.
Gandhi: Prisoner of Hope, Yale University Press, 1989.

Contributor to texts, including *The Making of Politicians: Studies from Africa and Asia,* 1976, *Leadership in South Asia,* 1977, and *Congress and Indian Nationalism,* 1988; contributor to *Dictionary of Christian Spirituality,* 1983, *The Cambridge Encyclopedia of India,* 1989, and *Encyclopedia of Asian History,*

Scribner. Member of editorial advisory panel on politics and current affairs, *The Modern Churchman.*

WORK IN PROGRESS: A study of Jawaharlal Nehru, for Longman.

SIDELIGHTS: Focusing on the country of her birth and its most famous modern leader, Judith M. Brown's books "are very useful not only for scholars of India and of [Mohandas] Gandhi, but also for handy references for anyone generally knowledgable in these crucial periods (and apparently inexhaustible subjects) who may want to check out specific details," A. M. Davidon comments in a *New Republic* review of *Gandhi and Civil Disobedience: The Mahatma in Indian Politics, 1928-34.* Brown deftly manages a great number of sources, as *Times Literary Supplement* contributor Ainslie Embree remarks; the result is "a work that will enhance Brown's reputation as one of the most interesting of the scholars now interpreting recent Indian history." "Seeping through all the tightly-packed data," concludes Davidon, "are delicately tentative, objectively formulated expressions of Brown's sensibility and sympathies which raise the narrative above a dry tedious history to a cautiously positive assessment of this ungainly little man of mammoth spiritual proportions."

Because Gandhi's life "was a vast and varicolored mix of service, spirituality, idealism, politics and nonviolent force that puts him well beyond the breadth of ordinary biography," Colman McCarthy asserts in *Washington Post Book World,* in *Gandhi: Prisoner of Hope* Brown "offers what she calls modestly 'a study and interpretation' of Gandhi. The modesty is appreciated but not necessary," the critic continues, for Brown "has written commandingly and refreshingly of a man whom dozens of writers . . . have gone at." Bhikhu Parekh similarly praises the author's "four-dimensional" approach, writing in the *New Statesman and Society* that *Gandhi* "is a fairly comprehensive book that does justice to the complexity of Gandhi's life and thought. . . . [Brown] has an intuitive feel for the man and grasps him as a whole, using his personal and political life to illuminate each other."

In addition, Parekh finds "valuable chapters" born of the new material Brown has brought to her work; *Newsweek* critic Jim Miller likewise states that the author "paints a compelling portrait of an elusive personality" due to her "drawing on a wealth of new sources." Radhakrishnan Nayar, however, faults Brown for not resolving Gandhi's two contrasting roles as political strategist and as proponent of modest economic reform; "yet if Brown's overall assessment of Gandhi's role does not convince, there is no doubt that this a valuable work," the critic admits in the *Times Literary Supplement,* "with thought-provoking descriptions of every phase of Gandhi's career. It is a lucidly written analysis and summary of Gandhi's political and social reform activities," the critic continues, "which takes account of documentary sources and relevant studies published since the last major scholarly biography [in 1958]." Despite the limitations "inevitable in such a wide-ranging book," Parekh concludes, "this is the best biography of Gandhi so far and deserves to be read by everyone interested in him and in modern India."

BIOGRAPHICAL/CRITICAL SOURCES:

PERIODICALS

New Republic, July 9-16, 1977.
New Statesman and Society, November 3, 1989.
Newsweek, March 12, 1990.
Times Literary Supplement, August 5, 1977; August 2, 1985; June 8-14, 1990.
Washington Post Book World, January 7, 1990.

BRUCE-NOVOA
See BRUCE-NOVOA, Juan D.

*   *   *

BRUCE-NOVOA, John David
See BRUCE-NOVOA, Juan D.

*   *   *

BRUCE-NOVOA, Juan D. 1944-
(Bruce-Novoa, John David Bruce-Novoa)

PERSONAL: Born June 20, 1944, in San José, Costa Rica; immigrated to the United States, 1945, naturalized U.S. citizen; son of James H. Bruce (a coffee importer) and Dolores Novoa; married, 1969; children: one. *Education:* Regis College, Denver, Colo., B.A. (cum laude), 1966; University of Colorado, Boulder, M.A., 1968, Ph.D., 1974.

ADDRESSES: Home—535 Inwood Dr., Santa Barbara, Calif. 93111. *Office*—Department of Foreign Languages, Trinity University, 715 Stadium Dr., San Antonio, Tex. 78284.

CAREER: University of Colorado, Boulder, instructor in Spanish, 1967-72, Denver, instructor in Spanish, 1972-74; Yale University, New Haven, Conn., former assistant professor of Spanish, beginning 1974, director of undergraduate studies in Latin American studies; University of California, Santa Barbara, instructor and associate director of Center for Chicano Studies, 1983-85; Trinity University, San Antonio, Tex., member of foreign language department, 1985—. Mexican prose annotator for Library of Congress, 1977—. Member, Movimiento Estudiantil Chicano de Aztlán.

MEMBER: Modern Language Association of America, American Association of Teachers of Spanish and Portuguese, Popular Culture Association.

AWARDS, HONORS: Fellow of National Chicano Committee for Higher Education, 1978; Fullbright scholarship, 1983.

WRITINGS:

(Contributor) Felipe Ortego and David Conde, editors, *The Chicano Literary World—1974,* New Mexico Highlands University, 1975.
Inocencia perversa/Perverse Innocence (poem), Baleen Press, 1976.
(Author of afterword) Juan García Ponce, *Entry Into Matter: Modern Literature and Reality,* Applied Literature Press, 1976.
Canto al pueblo: An Anthology of Experiences II, edited by Leonardo Carrillo and others, Penca (San Antonio, Tex.), 1978.
Chicano Authors: Inquiry by Interviews, University of Texas Press, 1980.
Chicano Poetry: A Response to Chaos, University of Texas Press, 1982.
La literatura chicana a través de sus autores, Siglo Veintiuno Editores, 1983.

Work represented in anthologies, including *Christmas Anthology,* edited by Teresinha Pereira, Backstage Book Stores, 1975, and *El quetzal emplumece,* edited by Carmela Montalvo, Mexican American Cultural Center (San Antonio), 1976. Contributor of articles, poems, and stories to literature and ethnic studies journals and literary magazines, including *Mango, Riversedge, Puerto del Sol,* and *Xalman.* Editor of *La Luz* and *South Western Literature.*

SIDELIGHTS: Poet and short story writer Juan D. Bruce-Novoa asserted in *The Chicano Literary World—1974* that "no one would deny the predominance of the Mexican and the American influences [on Chicano literature]; yet, we are neither, as we are not Mexican-American. I propose that we are the space (not the hyphen) between the two, the intercultural nothing of that space. . . . Chicano art is the space created by the tensions of all its particular manifestations. It is the nothing of that continuous space where all possibilities are simultaneously possible and all achieved products are simultaneously in relationship, creating one unit. We may concentrate on one, but it is only a particular surface leading to the space of all: the impersonal, continuous nothing." Because of this belief, "Bruce-Novoa's poetry is not Chicano poetry in the sense that there are no social concerns, no specific Chicano themes or brown consciousness," according to *Revista Chicano-Riqueña* contributor Arthur Ramírez. As for his prose, Juanita Luna Lawhn explains in the *Dictionary of Literary Biography* that the author "develops a thesis that Chicano literature should not be limited to its own social or ethnic space, but that it should have an intertextual dialogue with all literatures."

Bruce-Novoa's manuscript collection is kept at the Nettie Lee Benson Collection, Latin American Collection, University of Texas at Austin.

BIOGRAPHICAL/CRITICAL SOURCES:

BOOKS

Dictionary of Literary Biography, Volume 82: *Chicano Writers,* Gale, 1989.
Ortego, Felipe, and David Conde, editors, *The Chicano Literary World—1974,* New Mexico Highland University, 1975.

PERIODICALS

Revista Chicano-Riqueña, fall, 1977.
World Literature Today, spring, 1981, spring, 1983.*

*   *   *

BUNUEL, Luis 1900-1983

PERSONAL: Born February 22, 1900, in Calanda, Spain; died of cirrhosis of the liver, July 29, 1983, in Mexico City, Mexico; son of Leonardo (a landowner) and María (Portoles) Buñuel; married Jeanne Rucar, 1934; children: Rafael, Juan Luis. *Education:* Attended University of Madrid, 1920-23, and Academie du Cinema, 1925.

ADDRESSES: Office—Greenwich Film Production, 72 Avenue des Champs-Elysees 75008, Paris, France.

CAREER: Writer, producer, and director of motion pictures. Director of motion pictures in Mexico, including "Las hurdes" (documentary; released in the U.S. as "Land Without Bread"), 1932, "Gran casino," 1947, "El gran calavera" (released in the U.S. as "The Great Madcap"), 1949, "Susana" (also released in the U.S. as "The Devil and the Flesh"), 1951, "La hija del engaño" (released in the U.S. as "Daughter of Deceit"), 1951, "Una mujer sin amor," 1951, "La ilusión viaja en tranvía" (released in the U.S. as "Illusion Travels by Streetcar"), 1953. Worked as actor and assistant to Jean Epstein on "Mauprat," 1926, "La sirene du tropiques," 1927, and "The Fall of the House of Usher," 1928; language dubber for Warner Bros., in Paris, France, 1932-34, and Spain, 1935; executive producer in Spain, 1935-36; technical adviser for Metro-Goldwyn-Mayer in Hollywood, Calif., on uncompleted motion picture, "Cargo of Innocence," 1938; assistant on anti-Nazi film projects for Museum of Modern Art in New York, N.Y., 1940; filmmaker for U.S. Army, 1940-43; language dubber for Warner Bros., in Hollywood, 1944-46.

AWARDS, HONORS: Best director award from Cannes Film Festival and International Critics' Prize, both 1951, both for "Los olvidados"; best avant-garde film award from Cannes Film Festival, 1952, for "Subida al cielo"; special international jury prize from Cannes Film Festival, 1958, for "Nazarín"; *hors concours* recognition from Cannes Film Festival, 1960, for "The Young One"; Golden Palm from Cannes Film Festival, 1961, for "Viridiana"; Golden Lion of St. Mark from Venice Film Festival, 1967, for "Belle de jour"; Order of the Yugoslav Flag, 1971: Academy Award for best foreign language film from Academy of Motion Picture Arts and Sciences, 1972, for "Le Charm discret de la bourgeoisie"; and other film awards.

WRITINGS:

SCREENPLAYS IN ENGLISH; AND DIRECTOR

(With Julio Alejandro) *Viridiana* (produced in Spain by Gustavo Alatriste and Uninci Films 59, 1961; also see below), Interspectacles, 1962.

(With Alejandro) *El angel exterminador* (title means "The Exterminating Angel"; produced in Mexico by Uninci Films 59, 1962; also see below), Ayma, 1964.

(With Alejandro) *Nazarín* (produced in Mexico by Manuel Barbachano Ponce, 1958; adapted from the novel by Benito Pérez Galdós; also see below), Belgium Ministre de l'Education National et de la Culture, Service Cinematographique, 1967.

(With Salvador Dali) *L'Age d'or* [and] *Un Chien andalou* (title of former means "The Golden Age," produced in France by Vicomte de Noailles, 1930; title of latter means "An Andalusian Dog," co-produced in France with Dali, 1928), translated by Marianne Alexandre from the unpublished French manuscripts, Simon & Schuster, 1968.

(With Alejandro) *Three Screenplays: Viridiana, The Exterminating Angel, Simon of the Desert* (latter by Buñuel only, produced in Mexico as "Simón del desierto" by Gustavo Alatriste, 1965; also see above), Orion Press, 1970.

(With Jean-Claude Carriere) *Belle de jour* (produced in France by Paris Film Production, 1966; adapted from the novel by Joseph Kessel, translated by Robert Adkinson from the unpublished French manuscript, Simon & Schuster, 1971.

(With Alejandro) *Tristana* (produced in Spain by Epoch Film, Talia Film, Selentia Cinematográfica, and Les Films Corona, 1970; adapted from the novel by Pérez Galdós), translated by Nicholas Fry from the unpublished French manuscript, Simon & Schuster, 1971.

(With Alejandro and Luis Alcoriza) *The Exterminating Angel, Nazarín, and Las Olvidados* (latter co-written with Alcoriza, produced in Mexico by Ultramar Films, 1950; also see above), translated by Fry from the unpublished French translations of the Spanish manuscripts, Simon & Schuster, 1972.

UNTRANSLATED WORKS; AND DIRECTOR

Un Chien andalou (poems and stories), [Spain], c. 1927.

(With Alcoriza) *Los náufragos de la calle de la providencia,* [Mexico], 1958.

(With Carriere) *Le Journal d'une femme de chambre* (screenplay; produced in France by Speva-Filmalliance-Filmsonor-Dear, 1964; released in U.S. as "The Diary of a Chambermaid"; adapted from the novel by Octave Mirbeau), Seuil, 1971.

(With Carriere) *El discreto encanto de la burguesía* (screenplay; produced in France as "Le Charme discret de la bourgeoisie" by Greenwich Productions, 1972; released in U.S. as "The Discreet Charm of the Bourgeoisie"), Ayme, 1973.

(With Carriere) *El fantasma de la liberte* (screenplay; produced in France as "Le Fantome de la liberté" by Greenwich Productions, 1974; released in U.S. as "The Phantom of Liberty"), Ayma, 1975.

UNPUBLISHED SCREENPLAYS IN ENGLISH; AND DIRECTOR

(With Philip Roll) "Robinson Crusoe" (adapted from the novel by Daniel Defoe), Ultramar Films, 1954.

(With H. B. Addis) "The Young One" (adapted from Peter Matthiesen's novel *Travellin' Man*), Producciones Olmeca, 1960.

UNPUBLISHED SCREENPLAYS IN SPANISH; AND DIRECTOR

(With Alcoriza) "El Bruto," International Cinematográfica, 1952.

(With Alcoriza) "El" (also released in U.S. as "This Strange Passion"; adapted from a novel by Mercedes Pinto), Nacional Film, 1952.

"Cumbres borrascosas" (also released as "Abismos de pasión"; adapted from the novel *Wuthering Heights,* by Emily Bronte), Tepeyac, 1953.

(With Alcoriza) "El río y la muerte" (adapted from the novel by Miguel Alvarez Acosta), Clasa Films Mundiales, 1954.

(With Eduardo Ugarte) "Ensayo de un crimen" (released in U.S. as "The Criminal Life of Archibaldo de la Cruz"; adapted from a story by Rodolfo Usigli), Alianza Cinematográfica, 1955.

(With Alcoriza, Louis Sapin, and Charles Dorat) "La Fievre monte a El Pao" (title means "Fever Mounts in El Paso"; adapted from the novel by Henri Castillou), C.I.C.C., Cite Films, Indus Films, Terra Films, Cormoran Films, and Cinematográfica Filmex, 1959.

UNPUBLISHED SCREENPLAYS IN FRENCH; AND DIRECTOR

(With Jean Ferry) "Cela s'appelle l'aurore" (title means "It's Called the Dawn"; adapted from the novel by Emmanuel Robles), Les Films Marceau and Laetitia Film, 1955.

(With Alcoriza, Raymond Queneau, and Gabriel Arout) "La Mort en ce jardin" (title means "Death in This Garden"), Dismage and Teperac, 1956.

(With Carriere) "La Voie lacteé" (released in U.S. as "The Milky Way"), Greenwich Film Productions and Medusa, 1969.

(With Carriere) "Cet obscur objet du desir" (released in U.S. as "That Obscure Object of Desire"; suggested from the novel, *La Femme et le pantin,* by Pierre Louys), Serge Silberman, 1977.

OTHER

My Last Sigh (autobiography), translated by Abigail Israel, Knopf, 1983.

SIDELIGHTS: Luis Buñuel once told an interviewer, "I'm . . . an atheist, thank God." The comment is an apt example of both Buñuel's obsession and disdain for religion as well as his desire to elicit doubletakes from his audience. In his films, Buñuel welds his love-hate attitude towards religion with an ability to jar audiences, especially those from the upper class, into realizing that the world is not entirely safe or predictable. His first film, "An Andalusian Dog," shocked audiences with its opening depiction of a woman's eye being sliced with a straight razor. Buñuel called it "a desperate appeal to violence and crime." But in a career that spans more than fifty years, he has tempered his disposition to violence by directing his talents towards indictments of the bourgeoisie and the Church. He has persisted in his efforts to eliminate complacency and expose the corruption inherent in social convention. "The final sense of my films is this: to repeat, over and over again, in case anyone forgets it or believes the contrary, that we do not live in the best of all possible worlds," he contends.

Buñuel first became interested in art as a student of entomology in Madrid where he met such artists as José Ortega y Gasset, Federico García Lorca, and Salvador Dali. Buñuel and Dali became close friends and began attending films together. After the two established Spain's first film club, however, Buñuel moved to Paris and enrolled in the Academie du Cinema. He subsequently obtained an apprenticeship with filmmaker Jean Epstein on two motion pictures, "Mauprat" and "The Fall of the House of Usher." Through Epstein, Buñuel befriended several artists involved in surrealism, including spokesman Andre Breton and painters such as Pablo Picasso, Max Ernst, Giorgio de Chirico, and Joan Miró. The group met informally in cafes throughout Paris, and their discussions helped Buñuel develop his own philosophy of art.

Inspired by the surrealists, Buñuel rushed back to Spain to fetch Dali. Together they returned to Paris and began work on a film scenario. The two agreed early in the venture to avoid conventional narrative techniques. Instead, they decided to use symbols and images from dreams to create a "poetic" effect similar to that being achieved on canvas by Breton, Ernst, and other surrealists. Their efforts resulted in "An Andalusian Dog," a silent, twenty-five-minute film that defied interpretation. It alternately shocked, humored, and confused the audience with a barrage of bizarre images: a character with ants emerging from a hole in his hand; another man hauling a piano weighted by the bodies of two dead horses; and an androgynous bicyclist who, upon toppling over on a curb, leaves only a single, severed hand at the site of his accident. Buñuel, expecting a violent reaction from the opening-night audience, had smuggled rocks into the theatre for his own protection. To his surprise, though, the crowd erupted into applause following the showing.

Throughout the following weeks, Buñuel and Dali were confronted with numerous interpretations of their film, all of which they denied. "The plot is the result of CONSCIOUS *psychic automatism,*" Buñuel insisted, "and, to that extent, it does not attempt to recount a dream, although it profits by a mechanism analogous to that of dreams." He explained that he and Dali selected the images at random, deliberately discarding anything that could be construed as relevant to a logical storyline. "The motivation of the images was . . . purely irrational," claimed Buñuel. "They are mysterious and inexplicable to the two collaborators as to the spectator. NOTHING, in the film, SYMBOLIZES ANYTHING."

Embarrassed by the enthusiastic reception accorded "An Andalusian Dog" by the bourgeoisie they had sought to offend, Buñuel and Dali began work on a second film, "The Golden Age," to rectify the situation. Their collaboration was short-lived, however, for Buñuel, upon discovering that Dali had fallen in love with their producer's wife, accused her of disrupting the filmmakers' relationship and tried to strangle her on the first day of shooting. Outraged, Dali stormed from the set and never returned.

"The Golden Age," as completed by Buñuel, proved quite different from its predecessor. Buñuel abandoned the random imagery of "An Andalusian Dog" in favor of a fairly coherent, though extremely disturbing, narrative. The film chronicles the efforts of two lovers to reunite despite the bourgeoisie's attempts to keep them apart. In the first scene, Buñuel compares the bourgeoisie to the scorpion and cuts from a glimpse of the latter to the lovers coupling in the sand. They are suddenly separated by celebrants attending an inaugural address who claim that the couple's moans are annoying the speaker. The film then proceeds to follow the protagonist in his quest for his lover. He encounters characters who reveal the hypocrisy and ennui that symbolize, for Buñuel, the decadence of bourgeois life. When the lovers are finally reunited, the film accelerates into a series of surrealist images depicting age and death. The film ends with Christ escorting fellow revelers from the Marquis de Sade's castle, where they've just participated in an orgy.

Despite the overt and deliberately offensive depiction of social values as practiced by hypocritical bourgeoisie, "The Golden Age" was shown without incident at its premier. On the second night, however, fights broke out in the audience and viewers hurled inkwells at the screen. After the showing, audience members vented their anger by destroying paintings by Dali, Ernst, and Miró on display in the theatre lobby. For Buñuel, who had considered himself an outsider among his surrealist contemporaries after the bourgeoisie's approval of "An Andalusian Dog," "The Golden Age" was an immense triumph.

"The Golden Age" was shown for two months before French censors yielded to public pressure and banned it. Buñuel became the target of right-wing critics eager to preserve the social status quo. Richard-Pierre Bodin wrote: "A film called *L'Age d'Or*—in which I defy any qualified authority to detect the slightest artistic merit—multiplies (in public showings!) its crop of utterly obscene, repugnant, and tawdry episodes. Country, family, religion are dragged through the mire. All those who saved the grandeur of France, all those who have faith in the future of a race which has enlightened the whole world, all those Frenchmen who have been chosen to protect you against the poison of rotten entertainment, now ask what you think of the job our censorship is doing."

In the wake of this violent reaction, numerous other writers rose to Buñuel's defense. His most celebrated supporter, Henry Miller, wrote, "They have called Buñuel everything—traitor, anarchist, pervert, defamer, iconoclast. But lunatic they have not called him. True, it is lunacy he portrays in his film, but it is not of his making. This stinking chaos which for a brief hour or so is amalgamated under his magic wand, this is the lunacy of man's achievements after ten thousand years of civilization."

Although it elicited dramatic responses from viewers, "The Golden Age" was relatively ignored by film scholars until the 1960s, when Buñuel's rejuvenated career sparked a renewed interest in his early works. Its stature then rose to that of classics such as "Potemkin" and "Citizen Kane," and Carlos Fuentes hailed it as "the greatest of the surrealist films and one of the most personal and original works in the history of the cinema."

While the controversy over "The Golden Age" raged in Paris, Buñuel was in Hollywood studying sequences from American films. He was drawn to the film capital by Metro-Goldwyn-Mayer (MGM) with the understanding that he would be permitted to make a film for the studio. The opportunity, however, never arose, and Buñuel returned to Spain in 1932.

His next film, "Land Without Bread," revealed few of the surrealist elements that characterized his previous films. In detailing the plight of an impoverished Spanish village, he replaced surrealism with realism. Buñuel called it "a simple documentary" and declared: "I didn't invent anything. Pierre Unik wrote a scientific, statistical text. We merely wished to show the most abject region of Spain."

"Land Without Bread" was Buñuel's only film during the next fifteen years. After the political uprising in Spain, he obtained work dubbing dialogue for Warner Brothers in Paris and then returned to Hollywood to work for MGM on a project that was eventually abandoned. In 1940, he was hired by the Museum of Modern Art. One of his tasks there was to re-edit footage from the pro-Nazi films of Leni Riefenstahl for use as American propaganda. But as Buñuel recalled: "Riefenstahl's images were so damned good and impressive . . . that the effect would be the contrary of what we were aiming at. . . . Audiences would be overpowered and come out feeling that German might was irresistible." The project was terminated at President Roosevelt's request.

He left the museum soon afterwards when Dali, in *The Secret Life of Salvador Dali,* revealed that Buñuel was both anti-Catholic and a member of the French Communist party. Buñuel later told Carlos Fuentes that he "resigned . . . to avoid embarrassing my good friends [at the museum]." He also recalled his final meeting with Dali. "I had decided to give him a good beating," he claimed. "But when I saw him walk down the lobby, I felt a surge of sympathy for the man, too many fond memories came back, our youth. . . . So I just called him a son of a bitch and told him our friendship was over. He looked nonplused and said, 'Luis, you understand that my remarks were not intended to hurt you, but to publicize myself.' I've never seen him since."

During the mid-1940s Buñuel resumed his work with Warner Brothers. He developed a number of film projects, including one with Man Ray, but was unable to finance them. In 1947 he moved from California to Mexico to begin work on an adaptation of García Lorca's "The House of Bernarda Alba." That project also failed to develop into a film, but that same year Buñuel was hired by a Mexican producer to work in that country as a director.

He directed several films that were essentially showcases for popular actors. In the midst of these mediocre ventures, however, Buñuel made "Los olvidados," an intense and graphic depiction of slum life in Mexico City. The film is often gruesome in its action, for in proposing that life is essentially a struggle, Buñuel unflinchingly presented torture, rape, and incest. Many critics, including Andre Bazin, defended Buñuel's grim portrayal as part of his surrealist heritage. "It is not possible to avoid touching on the surrealism in Buñuel's films," wrote Bazin in a review of "Los olvidados." "He is . . . one of the rare valuable representatives of this mode. . . . His surrealism is a part of the rich and fortunate influence of a totally Spanish tradition. . . . It reflects a tragic sense of life, which these painters expressed through the ultimate human degradations. . . . But their cruelty, too, served only as a measure of their trust in mankind itself, and in their art."

Buñuel followed "Los olvidados" with several more entertaining films, including "The Devil and the Flesh" and "The Daughter of Deceit." When an interviewer remarked to Buñuel during the 1960s that many of his early films in Mexico were rather mediocre, Buñuel responded that even his less-ambitious works reflected his philosophy. "I have made several frankly bad pictures," he confessed, "but not once did I compromise my moral code. . . . My bad films were always decent. I am against conventional morality."

Throughout the 1950s Buñuel was saddled with miniscule budgets and often untrained actors. He nevertheless produced sev-

eral films that rank among his finest works. In 1952 he made "El," the story of an obsessively jealous bourgeois poet. The following year he directed "Illusion Travels by Streetcar." This film begins with two trolley operators refusing to scrap their dilapidated car. They take the car on an unscheduled run but are unable to convince passengers that they are taking a "joy ride." Soon the car is overrun with characters, each of whom insists on paying fare. The conductor refuses to accept their money, however, for fear that he will be accused of robbery. This conflict results in a parody of freedom as the right to pay for that which is free. As Jean Delmas noted: "All the riders insist on paying, each for his own personal reason, and each resents the fact that in the society they live in, nothing can be free without being suspect. At this level, comedy becomes philosophy."

Buñuel's next film was an adaptation of Emily Bronte's *Wuthering Heights,* a novel that was particularly prized by his surrealist clan during the 1920s. Unfortunately, the small budget and inconsistent casting undermined the eerie romanticism Buñuel was attempting to evoke. He later dismissed it as "a bad film."

Buñuel fared much better with his next effort, an adaptation of Daniel Defoe's *Robinson Crusoe.* Supplied with American actors and financial backing, he managed to sustain a sense of isolation throughout Crusoe's solitary life on the island while at the same time delving into his subconscious and his past. A particularly memorable scene occurs when the exasperated Crusoe shouts God's name from the mountain top, but hears only his own voice echoing in response. Emilio García Riera called this film "a great triumph" for Buñuel. "One could say that the character of Robinson has been created especially for Buñuel," he observed. "For it is precisely through exceptional characters, alienated by circumstance from the elemental norms of common sense and customary morality, that Buñuel often penetrates into the mysterious, and therefore poetical, regions of the human being."

In 1955, Buñuel explored the relationship between sex and death in "The Criminal Life of Archibaldo Cruz." Cruz possesses a magic box that, when touched, causes the death of anyone he wishes. As a child, his first target is his wet-nurse. Later, he instigates the deaths of a number of people who are subjects in his sexual fantasies. He becomes guilt ridden and confesses to the police, but is released when it becomes impossible to prove that his victims perished through his actions. When he finally attempts to actually murder a woman, he is foiled by a bizarre mishap. He then falls in love with the woman and marries her. "The one point which makes it outstanding is the portrait of the central figure Buñuel offers us," contended Riera. "This central character is really an assassin who wishes and enjoys the death of his fellow beings and who, nevertheless, is quite innocent before the eyes of society; innocent to such a point that when the film ends, he is moving toward the enjoyment of a happy and peaceful future."

Three years later Buñuel made "Nazarín," which many critics consider one of his finest achievements. It details a priest's struggle to live a Christ-like existence. After suffering excommunication for sheltering a whore, Nazarín wanders about the Mexican countryside and unintentionally causes many catastrophes. As Louis Seguin explained, Buñuel "gives rein fully to his unfrocked priest in the certainty that, rejected by the Church, but always inhabited by a desperate love of God and men, he can only do what he does: sow fire and murder in his wake." Despite constant failure, though, Nazarín persists in his efforts to lead a Christian life. "What counts for Buñuel is that Nazarín applies to his own life the perception enunciated by Jesus," wrote Joan Mellen, "and like Jesus he is a man willing to stand up to the repressive ruling order." Buñuel contended: "If Christ were to return, they'd crucify him again. It is possible to be *relatively* Christian, but the *absolutely* pure, the absolutely innocent man—he's bound to fail. . . . I am sure that if Christ came back, the Church, the powerful churchmen, would condemn Him again."

By film's end, Nazarín has rejected the Church and turned against it. Disillusioned, he is offered a pineapple by a sympathetic woman, and the look on his face reveals that he has found a new faith: in humanity. Penelope Gilliatt wrote, "When Nazarín, the failed Christ figure, is on the road and is offered a pineapple, symbol of help and charity, one feels a flash of hope for loosening of human bondage." By putting his faith in humanity, according to Gavin Lambert, Nazarín "finds a reality with which to replace an illusion, and the film itself goes beyond protest to reach affirmation." Ado Kyrou came to a similar conclusion, finding "Nazarín" not merely a renunciation of Christianity but also a celebration of humanity. "This film places love and its Christian caricature in confrontation," wrote Kyrou. "Buñuel contrasts those who love with a man who adores a nonexistent being. 'Love your neighbor,' says the man of the Christian myth. 'Love women and your companions,' says Buñuel. The first precept leads to ideological wails, to resignation; the second, to love and rebellion." Kyrou concluded by calling the film one "charged with dynamite, hope, love and certainty—a film addressed to mankind."

Buñuel returned to Spain in 1961 to direct "Viridiana," his first film in that country since "Las hurdes." Ranked by many critics as one of his finest films, "Viridiana" is a variation on the faith-in-humanity theme of "Nazarín." A devout woman, Viridiana is duped by her bizarre uncle into believing that she has lost her virginity on the eve of her entry into the convent. Though she plans to leave her uncle's estate immediately, she suddenly becomes its owner when her uncle commits suicide. She decides to accept her new role and converts the home into a haven for beggars and cripples. But the vagrants simply exploit Viridiana's Christian charity without embracing Christian tenets. While Viridiana is away one evening, the ingrates stage a raucous banquet and orgy. When she returns to find the house in shambles and the beggars either drunk, sleeping, or fighting, several of them overpower her and rape her. The film ends with Viridiana joining a card game as her belongings, including a cross, nails, and a crown of thorns, burn outside.

Because Buñuel submitted "Viridiana" to Spanish censors in sections, they never perceived the anti-Christian emphasis. When it was shown in Cannes at the film festival, it was a huge success and was awarded the Golden Palm. But Spanish officials responded with outrage to the film's content. The film was banned and its censors fired from their positions. Even the pope condemned it. Buñuel, however, was baffled by the criticism. "It was not my intention to blaspheme," he responded, "but of course Pope John XXIII knows more than I do about these things." He also addressed charges that he had seemed to make a film that justified maliciousness. "I am also reproached for my cruelty," he said. "Where is it in the film? The novice proves her humanity. The old man, a complicated human being, is capable of kindness towards human beings and towards a lowly bee whose life he doesn't hesitate to rescue." Regarding Viridiana's transformation, he added: "I don't see why people complain. My heroine is more of a virgin at the denouement than she was at the start." Perhaps David Robinson summed up Buñuel's attitude best when he wrote, "The film's total effect is invigorating rather than depressing because Buñuel values them all alike as men, and likes them all because they are funny and human."

Despite critical acclaim, "Viridiana" was also banned in France, and Buñuel once again found himself amid controversy. His reaction was to return to Mexico to make another film, "The Exterminating Angel." It concerns a group of bourgeois Mexicans who meet together after attending an opera and find themselves unable to leave the premises. The doors of the home are open; the guests simply cannot leave. No explanation is given. What results, however, is a complete breakdown in the social order cherished by the bourgeois. Hunger and thirst become the primary motivation for the characters' actions, and tension becomes violence. "Coarseness, violence and filth have become our inseparable companions," Buñuel commented. "Death is better than this abject promiscuity." But the trapped figures in "The Exterminating Angel" do not die. They finally escape from the house and flee to a church. But as Buñuel exposes the restrictions imposed by class society as affectations and mannerisms, which conceal the animal-like will to survive that makes all people equal, he similarly indicts organized religion. At film's end, the bourgeois characters discover themselves unable to leave the church. "The implication," declared Randall Conrad, "is that to be free they will now have to kill their host, God."

Buñuel traveled to France for his next film, "The Diary of a Chambermaid." The film details the encounters of Celestine, a chambermaid, with a variety of characters, including Monteil, her employer, who enjoys seducing the chambermaids and firing his rifle; Madame Monteil, a compulsive hygienic who abstains from sex because of the pain it causes her; Captain Mauger, a soldier living with his common-law wife, Rose, whom he eventually evicts in order to pursue Celestine; and Joseph, the coachman whom Celestine loves but whom she nonetheless turns in to the police for having murdered a young girl. Throughout the film, Celestine uses her charms to the best advantage, encouraging Monteil, Captain Mauger, and Joseph with their romantic notions. Ultimately, as Peter Harcourt noted, she makes the wrong decision. "She sits on her bed, impatient with Mauger's unctuousness," he wrote, "biting her little finger as she recognizes her fate." He added that "there is no sense of divine retribution. The dice have simply rolled the wrong way." The film concludes with Joseph in a cafe watching a Fascist rally. Having been found not guilty by the court, he is now a supporter of the Fascists in Paris. Tom Milne called the last scene "a brilliantly ominous evocation, not only of the imminent rise of Hitler, but of the reverberations which still smolder under the surface today." Similarly, Conrad summarized "The Diary of a Chambermaid" as "Buñuel's strongest politically," and acknowledged it as "a global expression of the pessimism which is after all inherent in Buñuel's vision."

Buñuel returned to Mexico for "Simon of the Desert." The film is based loosely on the life of St. Simon Stylites, a preacher who spoke from a small platform overlooking the desert. More brutally funny than his previous efforts, "Simon of the Desert" reveals the uselessness of Christianity in a world that prizes love over abstract faith, action over prayer. In one scene, Simon performs a miracle, restoring an amputee's hands. The onlookers judge Simon's deed as unimpressive. The former amputee immediately uses his restored limbs to strike his child. Eventually, Simon accompanies Satan, who, as an alluring woman, had previously tempted him, to a bar filled with frenzied teenage dancers. Simon is confronted with the failure of his own actions and preachings to deter humanity from sin.

When Buñuel finally settled in France in 1966, he focused his attentions on the destructiveness of social conventions. In "Belle de jour," he depicts Severin, a woman whose Catholic beliefs were so deeply ingrained that she was incapable of consummating her marriage. She resorts instead to fantasies in which she is degraded by her husband and coachmen. Finally, she decides to overcome her guilt-produced fears by working during the day as a prostitute for an affluent madam. She soon learns, however, that the sex her clients desire involves the enactment of their fantasies. When she does enjoy what appears to be a sexually satisfying relationship, it is with a gangster who follows her home. Fearing that her husband will discover everything, she urges the visitor to leave. The film ends with the gangster shooting her husband before being killed by the police. The husband survives, though blinded and paralyzed. He has learned of his wife's actions from a friend who discovered her at the brothel. Severin assures him that she no longer has any sexual fantasies, at which point he rises from his wheelchair and suggests they take a vacation. Severin then gazes out the window and hears the coachmen's bells that signify a resumption of the fantasies.

With the enormous critical acclaim that was accorded "Belle de jour," Buñuel finally began to receive recognition as one of the world's greatest filmmakers. He began a series of collaborations with producer Serge Silberman and fellow screenwriter Jean-Claude Carriere. In 1969, Buñuel directed "The Milky Way," in which he traced the history of Christianity through the adventures of two travelers. Throughout the film, Buñuel tests the validity of Christian dogma. Oswaldo Capriles called the film "a single-minded, coherent compendium of the devastating reasons for opposing religion as an historical phenomenon, as rational thought, and as providing transcendence."

Buñuel's next film, "Tristana," is a reworking of the sexual repression theme of "Belle de jour." Tristana is a woman totally deprived of freedom by her guardian, Don Lope. An aristocratic lecher, Don Lope adheres to a double standard that permits him the sexual license he paranoically denies Tristana. "The only way to keep a woman honest," Don Lope insists, "is to break her leg and keep her home." Tristana rebels against her mentor by eloping with a young artist. She returns within two years, however, unmarried and disease-stricken. Because of her affliction, her leg is amputated. She takes to teasing a mute lad. As Joan Mellen noted, "Tristana is a woman whose sexuality has been perverted by a fear of seduction by an older, forbidding father figure, and who can now respond only to the brutal and the perverse." In the end, Tristana finally rids herself of Don Lope by opening the bedroom window for the now sickly guardian and allowing the cold air to cause a fatal heart attack.

There is little sense of victory in Don Lope's death. As Buñuel implies in film after film, the parasitic Christian customs and social conventions he exposes are too deeply ingrained in society to become vulnerable to his cinematic assaults. Mellen wrote that "Buñuel has relentlessly and brilliantly exposed the destruction of the individual by a corrupt, hypocritical moral code which makes no pretense of improving a society in which class animosities are deepening and brutality is growing." For Buñuel, true freedom involves the choice of the individual to separate from society. This is a choice society guarantees, but, by its parasitic nature, cannot grant. "Group solidarity was a tremendous thing among the surrealists," Buñuel related. "Breton would call us in to sit in judgment if we deviated from the group morality. I learned then that being free is not doing whatever you want, but acting in solidarity with friends you love and respect. But then, by choosing a certain morality, you are not really free at all. Only crypto-Fascists pretend they are ideologically free. Surrealism taught me that man is never free yet fights for what he can never be. That is tragic."

The notion of freedom as a destructive and deceiving element in society is embellished in Buñuel's next two films "The Discreet Charm of the Bourgeoisie" and "The Phantom of Liberty." In the former, several bourgeois characters find themselves unable to finish their extravagant meals. Buñuel's contention seems to be that the bourgeoisie's wealth affords them no greater escape from a repressive society. Raymond Durgnat declared that "Buñuel has selected only those meals whose bill of fare—or circumstances, or relationships with dream, love, or business— illustrates how a round of dinner parties can do as little to preserve their participants from the emptiness which society has sowed within their hearts as communing with nature could do to redeem the Victorian middle class from its materialism."

In "The Phantom of Liberty," Buñuel begins with a reenactment of the action depicted in Francisco Goya's painting, "The Third of May," as a firing squad executes a group of enemy soldiers. But whereas Goya's work is a passionate plea for peace, Buñuel's film exposes the absurdness of that plea. "Down with freedom!" shout the executioners' targets. "Long live the chains!" Throughout the remainder of the film, Buñuel reveals how society's faith in Christianity and social conventions perpetuates an order that often spawns absurd and criminal actions. In the final sequence, police charge a group of protesters who shout the same epithets as the victims in the initial sequence. For Buñuel, history's lessons are useless: by denying the past and perpetuating a social order that promotes destruction, humanity imprisons itself.

Buñuel's last film during the 1970s, "That Obscure Object of Desire," is a variation on the theme previously explored in both "The Exterminating Angel" and "The Discreet Charm of the Bourgeoisie." In this film, the object of desire is the virginity of Conchita, a young Spanish woman being pursued by Mathieu, a French businessman. For Mathieu, Conchita's sexual cooperation is always on the verge of acquisition. He tries to use his powers as her employer for seductive purposes, but she quits her job. When Mathieu tries to bribe Conchita's mother into delivering her to him, Conchita becomes incensed and leaves the city. Eventually, Mathieu and Conchita live together, but she continues to withhold herself from him. She then convinces him to give her a home of her own. After doing so, she insults him by feigning sexual intercourse with another man while Mathieu watches through an iron gate. Conchita returns to Mathieu's home the next day, though, and reveals that what he witnessed the previous night was only a simulation. Mathieu then beats her. The film ends with Mathieu and Conchita apparently reconciled, strolling arm-in-arm through a shopping district when a bomb planted by terrorists detonates and kills them.

"That Obscure Object of Desire" is one of Buñuel's many subtle exposes of the bourgeois mentality. Mathieu is not concerned with Conchita, except as a vehicle through which he can prove his power over women. Neither is Mathieu interested in the terrorists whose actions serve as a background to the film. Conchita, however, is as much to blame for her predicament as Mathieu. She teases Mathieu and manipulates his desire in order to further her own material worth. For her, the terrorists are simply another instrument she can use in her relationship with Mathieu. Ultimately, both Mathieu and Conchita fall victim to the terrorists who refuse to accept the parasitic social order maintained by the couple.

Since the mid-1960s, Buñuel has refused to acknowledge any long-range filmmaking projects. He seems content simply listening to classical music and studying insects. "I like idleness," he told an interviewer. "I enjoy my days without doing anything.

I am never bored." But he also laments the silence that has existed between Dali and himself since 1930. "I do hope I can invite him to drink a glass of champagne before we both die." In 1975 he finally convinced himself to hang a portrait Dali had painted during the 1920s. "Thirty-five years is too long for a fight."

Buñuel's feelings towards the cinema have also changed during his fifty years as a filmmaker. In 1953 he contended that "in the hands of a free spirit, the cinema is a magnificent and dangerous weapon." But in 1974, with the release of "The Phantom of Liberty," he reiterated Breton's last words to him and acknowledged that "it is no longer possible to scandalize people as we did in 1930." Buñuel also mentioned that he hopes the cinema will "give us the ease of a quest for pleasure and inquiry which isn't followed by the pounding hooves of guilt." He told Gilliatt, "It's guilt we must escape from, not God."

AVOCATIONAL INTERESTS: Classical music, entomology.

BIOGRAPHICAL/CRITICAL SOURCES:

BOOKS

Contemporary Literary Criticism, Volume 16, Gale, 1981.
Durgnat, Raymond, *Luis Buñuel,* University of California Press, 1967, revised edition, 1978.
Francisco Aranda, J., *Luis Buñuel: A Critical Biography,* translated by David Robinson, Da Capo Press, 1976.
Gould, Michael, *Surrealism in Cinema,* A. S. Barnes, 1976.
Harcourt, Peter, *Six European Directors,* Viking, 1972.
Kyrou, Ado, *Buñuel: An Introduction,* Simon & Schuster, 1963.
Matthews, J. H., *Surrealism in Film,* University of Michigan Press, 1971.
Mellen, Joan, editor, *The World of Luis Buñuel,* Oxford University Press, 1978.
Miller, Henry, *The Cosmological Eye,* New Directions, 1939.
Rebolledo, Carlos, *Luis Buñuel,* Editions Universitaires, 1964.
Stauffacher, Frank, *Art in Cinema,* Arno, 1968.

PERIODICALS

American Scholar, summer, 1973.
Cineaste, Volume VII, number 3, 1976.
Etudes Cinematographiques, spring, 1963.
Film Comment, May-June, 1975.
Film Culture, summer, 1960, spring, 1962, summer, 1966.
Film Quarterly, spring, 1960, spring, 1967, winter, 1970-71, summer, 1975.
Jeune Cinema, February, 1966.
Le Figaro, December 7, 1930.
Los Angeles Times, November 2, 1983, November 18, 1983.
New Yorker, December 5, 1977.
New York Times, November 3, 1972, February 25, 1973, October 16, 1977, June 10, 1979, September 28, 1983, December 27, 1983.
New York Times Magazine, March 1, 1973.
Positif, March, 1961, July, 1962.
Show, April, 1970.
Sight and Sound, January-March, 1954, summer, 1962, autumn, 1964.
Society, July-August, 1973.
Times (London), January 26, 1984.
Village Voice, May 2, 1968, May 9, 1968, May 5, 1980.
Washington Post, November 5, 1983.
Yale French Studies, summer, 1956.

OBITUARIES:

PERIODICALS

Chicago Tribune, July 31, 1983.
Detroit News, July 31, 1983.
Los Angeles Times, July 30, 1983.
Newsweek, August 8, 1983.
New York Times, July 31, 1983.
Time, August 8, 1983.
Times (London), August 1, 1983.
Washington Post, August 1, 1983.*

*   *   *

BURMAN, Ben Lucien   1896-1984

PERSONAL: Born December 12, 1896, in Covington, Ky.; died following a stroke (one source says from a cerebral hemorrhage), November 12, 1984, in New York, N.Y.; son of Sam and Minna B. Burman; married Alice Caddy (an illustrator), September 19, 1927 (died August 3, 1977). *Education:* Harvard University, A.B., 1920.

CAREER: Author. Reporter, *Boston Herald,* 1920; assistant city editor, *Cincinnati Times Star,* 1921; special writer, *New York Sunday World,* 1922; staff contributor, Newspaper Enterprise Association (Scripps-Howard), 1927; war correspondent in Africa and Middle East, 1941. *Military service:* U.S. Army, Field Artillery, World War I; severely wounded at Soissons, France, July, 1918.

MEMBER: Authors League of America (former member of board of directors), PEN (former member of board of directors), Overseas Press Club, Dutch Treat Club, Saville Club (London), Players Club.

AWARDS, HONORS: A river light was named in Burman's honor in 1937 by the Lighthouse Service of the U.S. Coast Guard; Southern Authors Prize for the most distinguished Southern book of the year, 1938, for *Blow for a Landing;* Thomas Jefferson Memorial Prize, 1945, for *Rooster Crows for Day;* French Legion of Honor for wartime reporting from Africa, 1947; German Young People's Book Festival prize, and New York Public Library citation as favorite American book of the year for young people, both for *High Water at Catfish Bend;* Dutch Treat Club's Gold Medal, 1969, for "distinguished service to American literature"; Donald T. Wright Marine Award, University of Illinois, 1975; named honorary citizen of New Orleans and Natchez, La., 1979; named honorary ambassador of St. Louis, 1979; October 8, 1983, designated Ben Lucien Burman Day by states of Kentucky and Louisiana; town of Port Hudson, La., designated Catfish Bend by governor of Louisiana.

WRITINGS:

Mississippi, illustrated by wife, Alice Caddy, Cosmopolitan Book Corp., 1929.
Then There's Cripple Creek, Butterworth, 1930.
Steamboat 'round the Bend, illustrated by Caddy, Farrar & Rinehart, 1933.
Blow for a Landing, Houghton, 1938.
Big River to Cross: Mississippi Life Today, illustrated by Caddy, John Day, 1940.
Miracle on the Congo: Report from the Free French Front, John Day, 1942.
Rooster Crows for Day, illustrated by Caddy, Dutton, 1945.
Everywhere I Roam, illustrated by Caddy, Doubleday, 1949.
Children of Noah: Glimpses of Unknown America, illustrated by Caddy, Messner, 1951.

The Four Lives of Mundy Tolliver, Messner, 1953.

It's a Big Country: America off the Highways, illustrated by Caddy, Reynal, 1956.

The Street of the Laughing Camel, illustrated by Caddy, McGraw, 1959.

It's a Big Continent, illustrated by Caddy, McGraw, 1961.

The Generals Wear Cork Hats: An Amazing Adventure That Made World History, illustrated by Caddy, Taplinger, 1963.

The Sign of the Praying Tiger, illustrated by Caddy, New American Library, 1966.

Look Down That Winding River: An Informal Profile of the Mississippi, illustrated by Caddy, Taplinger, 1973.

"CATFISH BEND" JUVENILE NOVELS; ILLUSTRATED BY WIFE, ALICE CADDY

High Water at Catfish Bend (also see below), Messner, 1952, reprinted, Avon, 1981.

Seven Stars for Catfish Bend (also see below), Funk, 1956, reprinted, Avon, 1981.

The Owl Hoots Twice at Catfish Bend (also see below), Taplinger, 1961, reprinted, Avon, 1981.

Three from Catfish Bend (includes *High Water at Catfish Bend, Seven Stars for Catfish Bend,* and *The Owl Hoots Twice at Catfish Bend*), Taplinger, 1967.

Blow a Wild Bugle for Catfish Bend, Taplinger, 1967.

High Treason at Catfish Bend, Vanguard Press, 1977.

The Strange Invasion of Catfish Bend, Vanguard Press, 1980.

Thunderbolt at Catfish Bend, Wieser & Wieser, 1984.

OTHER

"Steamboat 'round the Bend: Songs and Stories of the Mississippi" (sound recording), Folkway Records, 1956.

Regular contributor to *Reader's Digest* and *Saturday Review.*

SIDELIGHTS: Many of Ben Lucien Burman's tales drew on his rich heritage of river life. Born in the small town of Covington, Kentucky, on the banks of the Ohio River, Burman began writing in grade school; after graduation he worked as a reporter in Cincinnati, New York, and Boston before turning to fiction to support himself and his wife, Alice Caddy, the talented artist who illustrated many of his books. During the Second World War, Burman traveled to Africa to report on the Free French forces gathered under the command of General Charles De Gaulle in the Congo basin—experiences he later used in the novel *Rooster Crows for Day,* and retold in the books *Miracle on the Congo: Report from the Free French Front,* and *The Generals Wear Cork Hats: An Amazing Adventure That Made World History.*

Using the settings of the South he remembered from his childhood and which he encountered in his travels, Burman produced well-loved novels of quiet country folk, such as *Steamboat 'round the Bend, Blow for a Landing,* and *The Four Lives of Mundy Tolliver.* Writing about *Blow for a Landing,* the story of Willow Joe, a music-making river man on the lower Mississippi, a *Christian Science Monitor* contributor declared: "To read [the book] is to feel the hot sun on your back, to hear the mellow chime of an engine bell, the gentle, rhythmic sighing of twin stacks, the roar of whistle which reverberates miles in the gullied hills."

Burman's homespun, gentle humor and emphasis on river locales, especially the Mississippi and the quaint people who inhabit its shores, led some critics to compare his work to that of Mark Twain. Writing about Burman's book *It's a Big Country: America off the Highways,* a nonfictional account of the author's journeys, *San Francisco Chronicle* contributor William Hogan

stated: "Mr. Burman gets around with the enthusiasm of a latter-day Huck Finn, and puts down what he observes with grace and sly humor. For all the diesel motors in the Gulf Coast bayous, for all the navigational aids in the upper Missouri, the author's country seems strangely untouched by the Twentieth Century. Mark Twain might recognize it; the inhabitants of motels along routes quite near Mr. Burman's places might not." Burman explained to the *New Orleans Star* that "Twain used exaggeration and I like to needle. I see myself as a genial cynic or a cynical optimist." "I've given up on the human race," the author concluded, "but I love them."

Among Burman's best known works were the series of novels he wrote about the animal residents of Catfish Bend, Louisiana. Described by L. R. Markey in *Library Journal* as "a kind of Mississippi River 'Wind in the Willows,'" the Catfish Bend stories relate the adventures of "Doc" Raccoon, the narrator of the tales, Judge Black, the vegetarian blacksnake, J. C. Hunter, the sporty fox, a rabbit, and a bullfrog, who band together during a flood and sign an agreement to live peacefully with each other. The books proved very popular with both children and adults; since the publication of *High Water at Catfish Bend* in 1952, reported Tom Valeo of the *Arlington Heights Herald,* the books "have sold more than 1.25 million copies in numerous languages, including Thai, Burmese and Urdu."

"The novelist," Burman told *CA,* "is a curious cud-chewing animal, unlike the rarest found in any zoo. One moment he must have an ear and skin sensitive as the needle of some super-scientific instrument to record the impulses of his fellows; the next, when others would change or misinterpret his writing, he must possess ears of stone and an elephant's skin.

"Perhaps first of all he must have the eyes of the dragonfly, who, I have heard it said, can see in a thousand directions. Without this power to stand watch upon humanity as it goes its way in folly or wisdom, there is nothing. All is without depth, without universality. For the thousand-eyed novelist, the materials of drama are everywhere. But he must not be like the American tourists I have seen so often cruising in state to Casablanca or Algiers, who stop always in the same fashionable hotels and play bridge each night with the same dull companions, then return home thinking they know North Africa. The pursuit of true knowledge requires discomfort. I think it would be very difficult to be a snob and a good novelist. A bus is closer to the people of a country than a train; a buggy or a horse is closer than a bus. Walking is the closest of all. Out of the mosquito bites, the fleas, the hard beds in a tourist court, and all the varied accidents of the road, there gradually emerges a picture of a region, and an understanding of its inhabitants' philosophy.

"The novelist is a creature of many moods and professions, a jack of every trade. With his characters he must be at once doctor, priest, and devil's advocate. He is comedian, tragedian, villain, clown. He must know when to make his audience laugh and when to make it mourn; he must know when the play is ended and it is the hour to go home. As he writes and observes he cannot help but become a philosopher, with his own interpretation of the absurd but ever-fascinating pageant that is the human comedy. He need not hope to alter the universe. But he can hold a mirror up to life, so that men may study their reflections and laugh at their childish vanities. The mirror he uses may be of many sorts. His hope can be only one—to make the reflection true."

MEDIA ADAPTATIONS: Mississippi was filmed by Universal in 1929 under the title "Heaven on Earth." *Steamboat 'round the Bend* was filmed by Twentieth-Century Fox in 1935, and starred

Will Rogers; it was one of his last pictures. Film rights to many of the Catfish Bend stories have been sold to Walt Disney Productions. *High Water at Catfish Bend* was chosen by the puppeteer Lou Bunin for his first full-length motion picture since "Alice in Wonderland." The Selchow & Righter Company, makers of "Scrabble," have released the "Catfish Bend Storybook Game."

BIOGRAPHICAL/CRITICAL SOURCES:

PERIODICALS

Books, April 17, 1938.
Christian Science Monitor, April 7, 1938.
Library Journal, May 15, 1956.
Miami Herald, May 25, 1958.
New Orleans States, May 31, 1980.
New York Herald Tribune Book Review, May 11, 1952, November 2, 1955.
New York Times, November 1, 1953.
New York Times Book Review, May 13, 1973.
San Francisco Chronicle, November 8, 1956.
Weekly Book Review, August 26, 1945.

OBITUARIES:

PERIODICALS

Arlington Heights Herald, November 17, 1984.
Chicago Tribune, November 14, 1984.
Los Angeles Times, November 15, 1984.
New York Times, November 13, 1984.
Publishers Weekly, November 30, 1984.*

*   *   *

BUSH, William (Shirley, Jr.)   1929-

PERSONAL: Born July 21, 1929, in Plant City, FL; son of William Shirley (an auto dealer) and Vera (Crews) Bush; married Mary Sutcliffe (a French teacher), April 2, 1959; children: Anastasia, James, John, Andrew. *Education:* Stetson University, A.B., 1950; University of South Dakota, M.A., 1953; Universite de Paris, docteur de l'universite, 1959. *Religion:* Greek Orthodox.

ADDRESSES: Home—81 Wychwood Park, London, Ontario, Canada N6G 1R4. *Office*—Department of French, University of Western Ontario, London, Ontario, Canada N6A 3K7.

CAREER: Duke University, Durham, NC, instructor, 1959-62, assistant professor, 1962-65, associate professor of Romance lan-

guages, 1965-66; University of Western Ontario, London, associate professor of Romance languages, 1966-67, professor of French, 1967—.

MEMBER: American Maritain Association, American Weil Society, Amitie Charles Peguy, Fellowship of S. Alban and S. Sergius (president, 1967-69; secretary, 1971-72, 1973-77).

AWARDS, HONORS: Fulbright award, 1956-57, 1957-58; Duke University summer fellowship, 1963, 1966; Canada Council leave fellowship, 1972-73, 1979-80, 1986-87; Canada Council research grant, 1983-84, for *The Evolution of Bernanos' Creative Vision.*

WRITINGS:

Souffrance et expiation dans la pensee de Bernanos, Lettres Modernes (Paris), 1962.
L'Angoisse du mystere, Minard (Paris), 1966.
Georges Bernanos, Twayne, 1970.
(Editor) *Regards sur Baudelaire,* Lettres Modernes, 1974.
Genese et structures d'"Un Mauvais Reve," Lettres Modernes, 1982.
(Author of preface, notes, and new text conforming to original manuscript) Georges Bernanos, *Sous le soleil de Satan,* Plon (Paris), 1982.
(Author of preface) Michel Bernanos, *Ils ont dechire Son image . . . : Conte fantastique,* Pensee Universelle (Paris), 1982.
(Author of preface) M. Bernanos, *Au-devant de Vous: Poemes,* Cahiers Bleus (Troyes-en-Champagne), 1984.
Bernanos' "Dialogues des Carmelites": Fact and Fiction, Carmel de Compiegne, 1985.
(Contributor) *Dictionary of Literary Biography,* Volume 78: *American Short-Story Writers, 1880-1910,* Gale, 1988.
Genese et structures de "Sous le soleil de Satan," Lettres Modernes, 1988.

Also contributor to *A Critical Bibliography of French Literature, Understanding Maritain,* 1987, and *Jacques Maritain: The Man and His Metaphysics,* 1988. Contributor of articles to *Etudes Bernanosiennes, Prism,* and *Concern.* Member of editorial advisory council, *Twentieth-Century Studies.*

WORK IN PROGRESS: The Seventh Summer, a novel; *Morality and Poetic Structure: Essay on "Les Fleurs du mal"; The Evolution of Bernarnos' Creative Vision; Genese et structures de "Dialogues des Carmelites"; Genese et structures de "Journal d'un cure de campagne"; To Quell the Terror,* an historical account of the guillotining of the sixteen Carmelites of Compiegne in 1794.

C

CADE, Alexander
    See METHOLD, Kenneth (Walter)

*   *   *

CANDELARIA, Nash 1928-

PERSONAL: Born May 7, 1928, in Los Angeles, Calif.; son of Ignacio N. (a railway mail clerk) and Flora (Rivera) Candelaria; married Doranne Godwin (a fashion designer), November 27, 1955; children: David, Alex. *Education:* University of California, Los Angeles, B.S., 1948. *Politics:* "I usually seem to vote for the person who doesn't get elected." *Religion:* "Non-church-going monotheistic and cultural Christian."

ADDRESSES: Home and office—1295 Wilson St., Palo Alto, Calif. 94301.

CAREER: Don Baxter, Inc. (pharmaceutical firm), Glendale, Calif., chemist, 1948-52; *Atomics International,* Downey, Calif., technical editor, 1953-54; Beckman Instruments, Fullerton, Calif., promotion supervisor, 1954-59; Northrup-Nortronics, Anaheim, Calif., in marketing communications, 1959-65; Hixon & Jorgensen Advertising, Los Angeles, Calif., account executive, 1965-67; Varian Associates, Inc. (in scientific instruments), Palo Alto, Calif., advertising manager, 1967-82; freelance writer, 1982-85; Daisy Systems Corp., Mountain View, Calif., marketing writer, 1985-87; Hewlett-Packard Co., Palo Alto, Calif., marketing writer, 1987—. *Military service:* U.S. Air Force, 1952-53; became second lieutenant.

AWARDS, HONORS: Not by the Sword was a finalist in the Western Writers of America Spur Award competition, 1982, and received the Before Columbus Foundation American Book Award, 1983.

WRITINGS:

Memories of the Alhambra (novel), Cíbola Press, 1977.
(Contributor) Gary D. Keller and Francisco Jiménez, editors, *Hispanics in the United States: An Anthology of Creative Literature,* Bilingual Press, Volume 1, 1980, Volume 2, 1982.
Not by the Sword (novel), Bilingual Press, 1982.
(Contributor) Nicholas Kanellos, editor, *A Decade of Hispanic Literature: An Anniversary Anthology,* Arte Público, 1982.
Inheritance of Strangers (novel), Bilingual Press, 1984.
The Day the Cisco Kid Shot John Wayne (short stories), Bilingual Press, 1988.

Contributor of short stories to *Bilingual Review;* contributor to *Science.* Editor, *VIA.*

WORK IN PROGRESS: Leonor Park, a novel about land, greed, and sibling rivalry in the U.S. Hispanic southwest of the 1920s.

SIDELIGHTS: Nash Candelaria writes: "*Memories of the Alhambra* is about the Chicano heritage myth of being descendants of conquistadors, the unsolvable dilemma of Hispanics from the state of New Mexico who acknowledge their European heritage and may not accept their American Indian heritage. . . . *Not by the Sword* is a look at the Mexican War (1846-48) from the point-of-view of New Mexicans, who became Americans by conquest. *Inheritance of Strangers,* a sequel to *Not by the Sword,* looks at the aftermath of the Mexican War forty years later, and the problems of assimilation; it focuses on the futility of revenge and the difficulty of forgiveness by a conquered people. *The Day the Cisco Kid Shot John Wayne* is a collection of twelve stories that give insight into and understanding of the Hispanic experience in the United States and its interface with the dominant Anglo culture.

"I am a descendant of one of the founding families of Albuquerque, New Mexico, and an ancestor, Juan, authored a history of New Mexico in 1776. Although I was born in California, I consider myself a New Mexican by heritage and sympathy. My writing is primarily about Hispanic Americans, trying, through fiction, to present some of their stories to a wider audience that may only be aware of them as a 'silent minority.' "

AVOCATIONAL INTERESTS: The arts and family, reading, and the stock market.

BIOGRAPHICAL/CRITICAL SOURCES:

BOOKS

Meier, Matt S., *Mexican American Biographies: A Historical Dictionary, 1836-1987,* Greenwood Press, 1988.

PERIODICALS

Best Sellers, August, 1977, May, 1983.
Carta Abierta, Number 9, 1977.
De Colores, Nos. 1 and 2, 1980.
New Mexico Magazine, September, 1977.
Western American Literature, Volume 34, number 2, 1978, Spring, 1984.

CARDENAL (MARTINEZ), Ernesto 1925-

PERSONAL: Born January 20, 1925, in Granada, Nicaragua; son of Rodolfo and Esmerelda (Martínez) Cardenal. *Education:* Attended University of Mexico, 1944-48, and Columbia University, 1948-49. *Politics:* "Christian-Marxist."

ADDRESSES: Home—Carretera a Masaya Km. 9 1/2, Apt. A-252, Managua, Nicaragua.

CAREER: Ordained Roman Catholic priest, 1965. Poet, and author; formerly Minister of Culture in Nicaragua.

AWARDS, HONORS: Christopher Book Award, 1972, for *The Psalms of Struggle and Liberation;* Premio de la Paz grant, Libreros de la República Federal de Alemania, 1980.

WRITINGS:

Ansias lengua de la poesía nueva nicaragüense (poems), [Nicaragua], 1948.

Gethsemani, Ky. (poems), Ecuador 0H0'0', 1960, 2nd edition, with foreword by Thomas Merton, Ediciones La Tertulia (Medellin, Colombia), 1965.

Epigramas: Poemas, Universidad Nacional Autónoma de Mexico, 1961.

Hora 0 (poems), Revista Mexicano de Literatura, 1960.

(Translator and editor at large with Jorge Montoya Toro) *Literatura indígena americana: Antología,* Editorial Universidad de Antioquia (Medellín), 1964.

(Translator with José Coronel Urtecho) *Antología de la poesía norteamericana,* Aguilar (Madrid), 1963, Alianza (Madrid), 1979.

Oración por Marilyn Monroe, y otros poemas, Ediciones La Tertulia, 1965, reprinted, Editorial Nueva Nicaragua-Ediciones Monimbó, 1985, translation by Robert Pring-Mill published as *Marilyn Monroe and Other Poems,* Search Press, 1975.

El estrecho dudoso (poems), Ediciones Cultura Hispanica (Madrid), 1966, Editorial Nueva Nicaragua-Ediciones Monimbó, 1985.

Antología de Ernesto Cardenal (poems), Editora Santiago (Santiago, Chile), 1967.

Poemas de Ernesto Cardenal, Casa de las Américas (Havana), 1967.

Mayapan (poem), Editorial Alemana (Managua, Nicaragua), 1968.

Salmos (poems), Institución Gran Duque de Alba (Avila, Spain), 1967, Ediciones El Pez y la Serpiente (Managua, Nicaragua), 1975, translation by Emile G. McAnany published as *The Psalms of Struggle and Liberation,* Herder & Herder, 1971, translation from the sixth edition of 1974 by Thomas Blackburn and others published as *Psalms,* Crossroad Publishing, 1981.

Homenaje a los indios americanos (poems), Universidad Nacional Autónoma de Nicaragua, 1969, Laia (Madrid), 1983, translation by Carlos Altschul and Monique Altschul published as *Homage to the American Indians,* Johns Hopkins University Press, 1974.

Vida en el amor (meditations; with foreword by Thomas Merton), Lohlé (Buenos Aires), 1970, translation by Kurt Reinhardt published as *To Live is to Love,* Herder & Herder, 1972 (published in England as *Love,* Search Press, 1974), translation by Dinah Livingstone published as *Love,* Crossroad Publishing, 1981.

La hora cero y otros poemas, Ediciones Saturno, 1971, translation by Paul W. Borgeson and Jonathan Cohen published as

Zero Hour and Other Documentary Poems, edited by Donald D. Walsh, New Directions, 1980.

Antología: Ernesto Cardenal, edited by Pablo Antonio Cuadra, Lohlé, 1971, 2nd edition, Universidad Centroamericana, 1975.

Poemas, Editorial Leibres de Sinera, 1971.

Poemas reunidos, 1949-1969, Dirección de Cultura, Universidad de Carabobo, 1972.

(And translator) *Epigramas* (with translations from Catullus and Martial), Lohlé, 1972.

En Cuba, Lohlé, 1972, translation published as *In Cuba,* New Directions, 1974.

Canto nacional, Siglo Veintiuno (Mexico), 1973.

Oráculo sobre Managua, Lohlé, 1973.

(Compiler and author of introduction) *Poesía nicaragüense,* Casa de las Américas, 1973, 4th edition, Editorial Nueva Nicaragua, 1981.

Cardenal en Valencia, Ediciones de la Dirección de Cultura, Universidad de Carabobo (Venezuela), 1974.

El Evangelio en Solentiname (also see below), Ediciones Sigueme, 1975, Editorial Nueva Nicaragua-Ediciones Monimbó, 1983, translation by Donald D. Walsh published as *The Gospel in Solentiname,* Orbis Books, 1976 (published in England as *Love in Practice: The Gospel in Solentiname,* Search Press, 1977), reprinted in four volumes, Orbis Books, 1982.

Poesía escogida, Barral Editores, 1975.

La santidad de la revolución (title means "The Sanctity of the Revolution"), Ediciones Sigueme, 1976.

Poesía cubana de la revolución, Extemporáneos, 1976.

Apocalypse, and Other Poems, translation by Thomas Merton, Kenneth Rexroth, Mireya Jaimes-Freyre, and others, New Directions, 1977.

Antología, Laia (Barcelona, Spain), 1978.

Epigramas, Tusquets (Barcelona), 1978.

Catulo-Marcial en versión de Ernesto Cardenal, Laia, 1978.

Canto a un país que nace, Universidad Autónoma de Puebla, 1978.

In der Nacht Leuchten die W⅜i‡er: Gedichte, Aufbau-Verlag, 1979.

Antología de poesía primitiva, Alianza, 1979.

Nueva antología poética, Siglo Veintiuno, 1979.

La paz mundial y la Revolución de Nicaragua, Ministerio de Cultura, 1981.

Tocar el cielo, Lóguez, 1981.

(With Richard Cross) *Nicaraugua: La Guerra de liberación — der Befreiungskrieg,* Ministerio de Cultura de Nicaragua, c. 1982.

Los campesinos de Solentiname pintan el Evangelio, Monimbó, c.1982.

(Translator from the German) Ursula Schulz, *Tu paz es mi paz,* Editorial Nueva Nicaragua-Ediciones Monimbó, 1982.

(Contributor) *Entrüstet Euch!: Für Frieden und vöerverstandigung; Katholiken gegen Faschismus und Krieg* (essays on nuclear disarmament), R⅜i‡Ôrberg, 1982. *La democratización de la cultura,* Ministerio de Cultura, 1982.

Nostalgia del futuro: Pintura y buena noticia en Solentiname, Editorial Nueva Nicaragua, 1982.

Evangelio, pueblo, y arte (selections from *El Evangelio en Solentiname*), Lóguez, 1983.

Waslala: Poems, translated by Fidel López-Criado and R. A. Kerr, Chase Avenue Press, 1983.

Antología: Ernesto Cardenal, Editorial Nueva Nicaragua-Ediciones Monimbó, 1983.

Poesía de la nueva Nicaragua, Siglo Veintiuno, 1983.

The Gospel in Art by the Peasants of Solentiname (translated from *Bauern von Solentiname malen des Evangelium,* selections from *El Evangelio en Solentiname*), edited by Philip and Sally Sharper, Orbis Books, 1984.

(Contributor) Teófilo Cabestrero, *Ministros de Dios, ministros del pueblo: Testimonio de tres sacerdotes en el Gobierno Revolucionario de Nicaragua, Ernesto Cardenal, Fernando Cardenal, Miguel d'Escoto,* Ministerio de Cultura, 1985.

Vuelos de Victoria, Visor (Madrid), 1984, Editorial Universitaria, (León, Nicaragua), 1987, translation by Marc Zimmerman published as *Flights of Victory: Songs in Celebration of the Nicaraguan Revolution,* Orbis Books, 1985.

Quetzalcóatl, Editorial Nueva Nicaragua-Ediciones Monimbó, 1985.

Nuevo cielo y tierra nueva, Editorial Nueva Nicaragua-Ediciones Monimbó, 1985.

With Walker in Nicaragua and Other Early Poems, 1949-1954, translated by Cohen, Wesleyan University Press, 1985.

(Compiler and author of introduction) *Antología: Azarias H. Pallais,* Nueva Nicaragua, 1986.

From Nicaragua with Love: Poems 1979-1986, translated by Cohen, City Lights Press, 1986.

Contributor to *Cristianismo y revolución,* Editorialal 1 Quetzal (Buenos Aires), and *La Batalla de Nicaragua,* Bruguera Mexicana de Ediciones (Mexico).

SIDELIGHTS: Ernesto Cardenal is a major poet of the Spanish language well-known in the United States as a spokesman for justice and self-determination in Latin America. Cardenal, who recognizes that poetry and art are closely tied to politics, used his poetry to protest the encroachments of outsiders in Nicaragua and supported the revolution that overthrew Somoza in 1979. Once the cultural minister of his homeland, Cardenal spends much of his time as "a kind of international ambassador," notes Richard Elman in the *Nation.*

Victor M. Valle, writing in the *Los Angeles Times Calendar,* cites Cardenal's statement, "There has been a great cultural rebirth in Nicaragua since the triumph of the revolution. A saving of all of our culture, that which represents our national identity, especially our folklore." Literacy and poetry workshops established throughout the "nation of poets," as it has been known since the early twentieth century, are well-attended by people whose concerns had been previously unheard. Most workshops are led by government-paid instructors in cultural centers, while others convene in police stations, army barracks, and workplaces such as sugar mills, Valle reports. In these sessions, Romantic and Modern poetry is considered below standard; Cardenal also denigrates socialist realism, which he says "comes from the Stalinist times that required that art be purely political propaganda." The "greatest virtue" of Cardenal's own poems, says a *Times Literary Supplement* reviewer, "is the indirectness of Cardenal's social criticism, which keeps stridency consistently at bay." In addition, says the reviewer, Cardenal's poems "are memorable and important both for their innovations in technique and for their attitudes." In this way they are like the works of Ezra Pound, whose aesthetic standards Cardenal promotes.

Review contributor Isabel Fraire demonstrates that there are many similarities between Cardenal's poetry and Pound's. Like Pound, Cardenal borrows the short, epigrammatic form from the masters of Latin poetry Catullus and Martial, whose works he has translated. Cardenal also borrows the canto form invented by Pound to bring "history into poetry" in a manner that preserves the flavor of the original sources—a technique Pablo Neruda employed with success. Cardenal's use of the canto form

"is much more *cantabile*" than Pound's *Cantos,* says Fraire. "We get passages of a sustained, descriptive lyricism . . . where the intense beauty and harmony of nature or of a certain social order or life style are presented." Pound and Cardenal develop similar themes: "the corrupting effect of moneymaking as the overriding value in a society; the importance of precision and truthfulness in language; the degradation of human values in the world which surrounds us; [and] the search through the past (or, in Cardenal's poetry, in more 'primitive' societies, a kind of contemporary past) for better world-models." Fraire also points out an important difference between the two: "Cardenal is rooted in a wider cultural conscience. Where Pound seems to spring up disconnected from his own contemporary cultural scene and to be working against it, Cardenal is born into a ready-made cultural context and shared political conscience. Cardenal's past is common to all Latin Americans. His present is likewise common to all Latin Americans. He speaks to those who are ready and willing to hear him and are likely to agree on a great many points."

Cardenal's early lyrics express feelings of love, social criticism, political passion, and the quest for a transcendent spiritual life. Following his conversion to Christianity in 1956, Cardenal studied to become a priest in Gethsemani, Kentucky, with Thomas Merton, the scholar, poet, and Trappist monk. While studying with Merton, Cardenal committed himself to the practice of nonviolence. He was not allowed to write secular poetry during this period, but kept notes in a journal that later became the poems in *Gethsemani, Ky.* and the spiritual diary in prose, *Vida en el amor.* Cardenal's stay in Kentucky was troubled by illness; he finished his studies in Cuernevaca, Mexico, where he was ordained in 1965. While there, he wrote *El estrecho dudoso* and other epic poems that discuss Central America's history.

Poems collected in *With Walker in Nicaragua and Other Early Poems, 1949-1954* look at the history of Nicaragua which touches upon the poet's ancestry. During the 1800s, the William Walker expedition from the United States tried to make Nicaragua subservient to the Southern Confederacy. According to legend, a defector from that expedition married into Cardenal's family line. Incorporating details from Ephraim George Squier's chronicles of that period, Cardenal's poem "With Walker in Nicaragua" "is tender toward the invaders without being sentimental," Elman observes. "This is political poetry not because it has a particular rhetorical stance but because it evokes the distant as well as the more recent historical roots of the conflict in Central America," Harris Schiff relates in the *American Book Review.* The poet identifies with a survivor of the ill-fated expedition in order to express the contrast between the violent attitudes of the outsiders and the beauty of the tropical land they hoped to conquer. "The theme of the gringo in a strange land," as Elman puts it, an essentially political topic, is developed frequently in Cardenal's work.

Later poems become increasingly explicit regarding Cardenal's political sympathies. "Zero Hour," for example, is his "single greatest historical poem about gringoism, a patriotic epic of sorts," says Elman. The poem's subject is the assassination of revolutionary leader César Augusto Sandino, who used guerilla tactics against the United States Marines to force them to leave Nicaragua in 1933. "It's a poem of heroic evocation in which the death of a hero is also seen as the rebirth of nationhood: when the hero dies, green herbs rise where he has fallen. It makes innovative use of English and Spanglais and is therefore hard to translate, but . . . it is very much a work of national consciousness and unique poetic expression," Elman relates.

Moving further back in time to reclaim a common heritage for his countrymen, Cardenal recaptures the quality of pre-Columbian life in *Homage to the American Indians.* These descriptions of Mayan, Incan and Nahuatl ways of life present their attractiveness in comparison to the social organization of the present. In these well-crafted and musical poems written at the end of the 1960s, the poet praises "a way of life which celebrates peace above war and spiritual strength above personal wealth. One has a strong sense when reading Cardenal that he is using the American Indian as a vehicle to celebrate those values which are most important to him as a well-educated Trappist monk who has dedicated himself to a life of spiritual retreat," F. Whitney Jones remarks in the *Southern Humanities Review.* That the poems are didactic in no way impedes their effectiveness, say reviewers, who credit the power of the verses to Cardenal's mastery of poetic technique.

The use of Biblical rhetoric and prosody energizes much of Cardenal's poetry. *El estrecho dudoso,* like the Bible, "seeks to convince men that history contains lessons which have a transcendent significance," James J. Alstrum maintains in *Journal of Spanish Studies: Twentieth Century.* Poems in *Salmos,* written in the 1960s, translated and published as *The Psalms of Struggle,* echo the forms and the content of the Old Testament psalms. Cardenal's psalms are updated to speak to the concerns of the oppressed in the twentieth century. "The vocabulary is contemporary but the . . . sheer wonder at the workings of the world, is biblical," Jack Riemer observes in *Commonweal.* "Equally memorable are those Psalms in which Cardenal expresses his horror at the cruelty and the brutality of human life. His anguished outcries over the rapaciousness of the greedy and the viciousness of the dictators are the work of a man who has lived through some of the atrocities of this century."

As the conflict between the Nicaraguan people and the Somoza government escalated, Cardenal became convinced that without violence, the revolution would not succeed. "In 1970 he visited Cuba and experienced what he described as 'a second conversion' which led him to formulate his own philosophy of Christian Marxism. In 1977 the younger Somoza destroyed the community at Solentiname and Cardenal became the field chaplain for the Sandinista National Liberation Front," reports Robert Hass in the *Washington Post Book World.* Poems Cardenal wrote during that "very difficult time in his country"—collected in *Zero Hour and Other Documentary Poems*—are less successful than the earlier and later work, says Hass, since "there is a tendency in them to make of the revolution a symbol that answers all questions." Some reviewers have found the resulting combination of Biblical rhetoric and Marxist revolutionary zeal intimidating. For example, Jascha Kessler, speaking on KUSC-FM radio in Los Angeles, California in 1981, commented, "It is clearly handy to be a trained priest, and to have available for one's poetry the voices of Amos, Isaiah, Hosea and Jeremiah, and to mix prophetic vision with the perspectives of violent revolutionary Marxist ideology. It makes for an incendiary brew indeed. It is not nice; it is not civilized; it is not humane or sceptical or reasonable. But it is all part of the terrible heritage of Central Latin America." Also commenting on *Zero Hour and Other Documentary Poems, American Book Review* contributor Harold Jaffe suggests, "Although the manifest reality of Cardenal's Central America is grim, it's future—which to Cardenal is as 'real' as its present—appears eminently hopeful. Furious or revolted as Cardenal is over this or that dreadful inequity, he never loses hope. His love, his faith in the disadvantaged, his great good humor, his enduring belief that communism and Christ's communion

are at root the same—these extraordinary convictions resound throughout the volume."

"Though Cardenal sees no opposition between Marxism and the radical gospel, neither is he a Moscow-line communist," Mary Anne Rygiel explains in *Southern Humanities Review.* Rygiel cites the poem "Las tortugas" (title means "The Turtles") to demonstrate that Cardenal's reference to "communism" as the order of nature might better be understood as "communalism," a social organization of harmonious interdependence founded on spiritual unity. The poet-priest's social vision stems from his understanding of "the kingdom of God," Lawrence Ferlinghetti notes in *Seven Days in Nicaragua Libre.* "And with [Cardenal's] vision of a primitive Christianity, it was logical for him to add that in his view the Revolution would not have succeeded until there were no more masters and no more slaves. 'The Gospels,' he said, 'foresee a classless society. They foresee also *the withering away of the state*' [Ferlinghetti's emphasis]."

In the 1980s, Pope John Paul II reprimanded Cardenal for promoting a liberation theology that the prelate found divergent from Roman Catholicism. Alstrum notes, however, that *El estrecho dudoso* "reaffirms the Judeo-Christian belief that there is an inexorable progression of historical events which point toward the ultimate consummation of the Divine Word. Cardenal himself views his poetry as merely the medium for his hopeful message of the transformation of the old order into a new and more just society in which the utopian dreams and Christian values of men . . . can finally be realized." Cardenal founded the Christian commune Solentiname on an island in Lake Nicaragua near the Costa Rican border to put that dream into practice.

Some critics feel that the political nature of Cardenal's poetry precludes its appreciation by a sophisticated literary audience. Reviewers responded to the 1966 volume *El estrecho dudoso,* for example, as an attack on the Somoza dynasty while neglecting "the intricate artistry with which Cardenal has intertwined the past and present through myth and history while employing both modern and narrative techniques in his poem," asserts Alstrum. Others point out that Cardenal's work gains importance to the extent that it provides valuable insights into the thinking of his countrymen. Cardenal's poetry, which he read to audiences in the United States during the seventies, was perhaps more informative and accessible than other reports from that region, Kessler concluded in 1981, soon after Nicaraguan revolutionaries ousted the Somoza regime. "It may well be that Cardenal's poems offer us a very clear entrance into the mentality of the men we are facing in the . . . bloody guerilla warfare of Central America," Kessler suggested. More recently, a *New Pages* reviewer comments, "We can learn some contemporary history, [and] discover the feelings and thoughts of the people who were involved in Nicaragua's revolution by reading Cardenal's poems. And once we know what the revolution 'felt' like, we'll be a lot smarter, I believe, than most . . . who . . . make pronouncements about Nicaragua's threat to the free world."

BIOGRAPHICAL/CRITICAL SOURCES:

BOOKS

Bhalla, Alok, *Latin American Writers: A Bibliography with Critical Biographical Introductions,* Envoy Press, 1987.
Brotherston, Gordon, *Latin American Poetry: Origins and Presence,* Cambridge University Press, 1975.
Cardenal, Ernesto, *Zero Hour and Other Documentary Poems,* edited by Donald D. Walsh, New Directions, 1980.
Contemporary Literary Criticism, Volume 31, Gale, 1985.

Ferlinghetti, Lawrence, *Seven Days in Nicaragua Libre,* City Lights Books, 1984.

PERIODICALS

America, November 6, 1976.
American Book Review, summer, 1978, January, 1982, January-February, 1982, September, 1985.
Commonweal, September 17, 1971.
Journal of Spanish Studies: Twentieth Century, spring & fall, 1980.
Los Angeles Times Calendar, January 8, 1984.
Nation, March 30, 1985.
New Leader, May 4, 1981.
New Pages, Volume 10, 1986.
New Republic, October 19, 1974, April 9, 1977.
Parnassus, spring-summer, 1976.
Review, fall, 1976.
Southern Humanities Review, winter, 1976, winter, 1988.
Times Literary Supplement, July 12, 1974, August 6, 1976.
Voice Literary Supplement, September, 1982.
Washington Post Book World, June 23, 1985.
World Literature Today, spring, 1983.

OTHER

Kessler, Jascha, "Ernesto Cardenal: 'Zero Hour and other Documentary Poems'" (radio broadcast), KUSC-FM, Los Angeles, Calif., April 15, 1981.

　　　　　　　　　　　—Sketch by Marilyn K. Basel

* * *

CARTER, Avis Murton
See ALLEN, Kenneth S.

* * *

CARTER, James Earl, Jr. 1924-
(Jimmy Carter)

PERSONAL: Born October 1, 1924, in Archery, Ga.; son of James Earl (a grocer, farm machinery salesman, and politician) and Lillian (a nurse; maiden name, Gordy) Carter; married Rosalynn Smith, July 7, 1946; children: John William, James Earl III, Donnel Jeffery, Amy Lynn. *Education:* Attended Georgia Southwestern College, 1941-42, and Georgia Institute of Technology, 1942-43; U.S. Naval Academy, B.S., 1946; Union College, Schenectady, N.Y., graduate study, 1952. *Politics:* Democrat. *Religion:* Baptist.

ADDRESSES: Home—One Woodland Dr., Plains, Ga. 31780. *Office*—The Carter Center, One Copenhill, Atlanta, Ga. 30307.

CAREER: Farmer, owner, and chief executive of general purpose seed and farm supply firm, 1953-62, 1966-70; State Government, Atlanta, Ga., state senator, 1963-67, governor of Georgia, 1971-75; chairman of Democratic National Committee, 1972-74; United States Government, Washington, D.C., thirty-ninth president of the United States, 1977-81; engaged in farming, diplomacy, public service, and writing, 1981—; Emory University, Atlanta, distinguished professor, 1982—; Carter Center, Atlanta, founder, 1982, chairman of board of trustees, 1986—; Carter-Menhil Human Rights Foundation, Atlanta, president, 1986—.

Member, Sumter County School Board, 1955-62 (chairman, 1960-62), Americus and Sumter County Hospital Authority,

1956-70, Georgia Crop Improvement Association, 1957-63 (president, 1961), and Sumter County Library Board, 1962. President, Plains Development Corp., 1963, and Sumter Redevelopment Corp., 1963; member of executive board, West Central Georgia Planning and Development Commission (now Middle Flint Area Planning and Development Commission), 1964-69 (chairman, 1964). President, Georgia Planning Association, 1968; state chairman, March of Dimes, 1968-70; district governor, Lions Club, 1968-69. Member of board of directors, Habitat for Humanity, 1984-87. Deacon and Sunday School teacher, Baptist Church, Plains, Ga. *Military service:* U.S. Navy, 1947-53; became lieutenant commander.

AWARDS, HONORS: Gold medal from International Institute for Human Rights, 1979; International Mediation Medal from American Arbitration Association, 1979; Harry S. Truman Public Service Award, 1981; Ansel Adams Conservation Award from Wilderness Society, 1982; distinguished service award from Southern Baptist Convention, 1982; Human Rights Award from International League for Human Rights, 1983; Albert Schweitzer Prize for humanitarianism, 1987. Honorary doctorates from Morris Brown College, 1972, University of Notre Dame, 1977, Georgia Institute of Technology and Emory University, both 1979, Weizmann Institute of Science, 1980, Kwansei Gakuim University (Japan) and Georgia Southwestern College, both 1981, Tel Aviv University, 1983, New York Law School, Connecticut State University, and Bates College, all 1985, Centre College and Creighton University, both 1987.

WRITINGS:

UNDER NAME JIMMY CARTER

Why Not the Best? (autobiography), Broadman, 1975.
Addresses of Jimmy Carter, Governor of Georgia, 1971-75, edited by Frank Daniel, Georgia Department of Archives and History, 1975.
"I'll Never Lie to You": Jimmy Carter in His own Words, edited by Robert L. Turner, Ballantine, 1976.
The Wit and Wisdom of Jimmy Carter, edited by Bill Adler, Citadel Press, 1977.
A Government as Good as Its People, Simon & Schuster, 1977.
Carter on the Arts, ACA, 1977.
Letters to the Honorable William Prescott, Gordon Press, 1977.
Jimmy Carter, 1977, two volumes, U.S. Government Printing Office, 1977-78.
The Spiritual Journey of Jimmy Carter, in His Own Words, edited by Wesley G. Pippert, Macmillan, 1978.
Keeping Faith: Memoirs of a President, Bantam, 1983.
Negotiation: The Alternative to Hostility, Mercer University Press, 1984.
The Blood of Abraham: Insights into the Middle East, Houghton, 1985.
(With wife, Rosalynn Carter) *Everything To Gain: Making the Most of the Rest of Your Life,* Random House, 1987.
An Outdoor Journal: Adventures and Reflections, Bantam, 1988.

SIDELIGHTS: Jimmy Carter's singular career has led him from a peanut farm outside Plains, Georgia, to the White House in Washington, D.C., and then back again to Plains. The thirty-ninth president of the United States, Carter took office in 1977 and was defeated by Republican Ronald Reagan in 1981. Since his "retirement," Carter has written a number of books on subjects as varied as Middle East politics and fly fishing; he has also made the news for his participation in humanitarian causes, diplomatic missions, and human rights advocacy.

Most former presidents in the modern era have written memoirs after retiring from politics. Critics feel that what distinguishes Carter's from the rest is his authentic voice. As *Washington Post Book World* correspondent Edwin M. Yoder puts it, "no ghostwriter has haunted this house." Arthur Schlesinger, Jr. describes Carter's style in a *New York Times Book Review* piece. Schlesinger writes: "Carter's tone is direct, colloquial, engaging, often flat but sometimes oddly moving. His faith in work, discipline, education, character recalls an older and better America. He speaks without embarrassment about deeply personal things— trust, truth, the family, love and, when pressed, the Almighty. He rarely goes in for rhetorical pretense or flourish. It is the tone of a plain, homespun American talking seriously to his neighbors or his Sunday School class."

James Earl Carter, Jr. was born and raised in rural Georgia near the tiny town of Plains. His parents were strict Baptists who expected their children to work hard on the farm and in the general store they owned. As a youth Carter showed an aptitude for school work. His love of reading and his Baptist upbringing combined to make him a polite, conscientious student; he graduated at sixteen. After high school Carter attended Georgia Southwestern College and the Georgia Institute of Technology, each for a year. Then he was admitted to the United States Naval Academy at Annapolis. He graduated in the top ten percent of his class in 1946.

Carter expected to spend his whole career in the Navy after his success in Annapolis. In 1951 he was assigned to the nascent nuclear submarine program based in Schenectady, New York. There he was a senior officer on the precommissioning crew of the *Sea Wolf,* the second atomic submarine built in the United States. Carter spent two years studying nuclear physics and supervising the *Sea Wolf.* Then his father died, and he decided to return to Plains to run the family business. The Carter finances were in disarray when he took over, but soon they rebounded when Carter expanded his seed and fertilizer business and opened shelling and warehouse services for his fellow peanut growers. By 1956 Carter was a thriving businessman who was beginning to take steps toward a career in public service.

Carter moved slowly but steadily through the ranks of Georgia Democratic politics. He was somewhat hampered in the late 1950s by his open stand in favor of civil rights legislation for minorities. Carter was elected to the state senate in 1963; he served until 1967, when he was defeated in a primary election for governor. That defeat—once described by Carter as the low point in his life—sparked a "born again" religious experience. With new confidence born of his Christian faith, Carter returned to the political arena. He was elected governor of Georgia in 1970.

The Carter governorship of Georgia saw the employment of women and blacks in record numbers; it was also responsible for streamlining state agencies, opening day care and drug abuse rehabilitation centers, and monitoring the budget on a line-item basis. Concurrent with his governorship, Carter served as the national campaign committee chairman for the Democratic National Committee. In 1974 he announced his intention to run for the presidency of the United States.

Carter and his wife Rosalynn mounted a rigorous campaign for the 1976 nomination, travelling across America and speaking as many as six different places in a day. Carter also released an autobiography, *Why Not the Best?,* that described his youth on the farm, his ideals, and his inspirations. *New Republic* contributor John Seeyle has called *Why Not the Best?* "a classic of its kind, . . . a mixture of the heroic with the pastoral mode that is endemic to the mythic layer of the American identity." Seeyle

adds that the work is "essential to an understanding of the meaning of Carter himself, as Jimmy Who? becomes Jimmy What Next?" In the *New York Times Book Review,* William V. Shannon suggests that candidate Carter's autobiography "is a skillful, simply-written blend of personal history, social description and political philosophy that makes fascinating reading." More than one critic has observed that the judicious publication of *Why Not the Best?* helped secure Carter's nomination as the Democratic candidate for president.

The Carter administration took power at a time when scandal had eroded public faith in the presidency. Carter helped to restore the presidential image, but he found himself burdened with rising inflation, high unemployment, and acts of hostility toward Americans abroad, especially in Iran. In the *New York Review of Books,* Nicholas von Hoffman also contends that Carter was "an alien and slightly distasteful figure to the prominent members of his party in Congress," rendering the president "the man running alone, the nude candidate." The last year of his presidency was especially difficult as Carter faced a hostage crisis in Iran that was only resolved the day his successor was sworn in. Still, writes William Shawcross in the *Spectator,* "there was a lot of solid achievement to the Carter years. . . . Carter made human rights for a time a central issue of much of American policy. This commitment, casually derided in drawing rooms of the West, was of immeasurable but immense importance to hundreds of thousands of people all over the world who languished under the neglect which Carter's predecessors and his successor[s] have displayed."

The most noticeable success of the Carter years was the landmark peace treaty between Egypt and Israel, drawn up at Camp David after days of delicate negotiation. A good portion of Carter's 1983 book *Keeping Faith: The Memoirs of a President* deals with the talks that brought an end to the hostilities between Egypt and Israel. That accomplishment helped give Carter "the world's best credentials as a Middle East peacemaker," to quote Stephen S. Rosenfeld in the *Washington Post Book World.* Since leaving the White House, Carter has continued—as a concerned private citizen—to work for peace in that region. In 1985 he published *The Blood of Abraham: Insights into the Middle East,* an account of his interviews with the area's rulers in the 1980s. *Los Angeles Times Book Review* contributor Marvin Seid notes that Carter's views on the Middle East "are shaped by compassion for all those, past and present, who have suffered in this cockpit of religious and nationalistic antagonisms."

Needless to say, Carter and his wife Rosalynn struggled with the sudden transition from public to private life. Both were able, however, to find meaningful goals and projects with which to fill their days. Carter continued his campaign for human rights and founded the Carter Center at Emory University in Atlanta. He also engaged in his favorite outdoor activities, hunting and fishing. In 1987, the two Carters published *Everything To Gain: Making the Most of the Rest of Your Life,* a tandem memoir and self-help book designed for those entering retirement. *New York Times Book Review* correspondent Letty Cottin Pogrebin calls the work "an inspiring account of the creation of a meaningful life—at home and in the larger world—by people who take their principles seriously enough to act on them. Basically, what the Carters decided to do with the rest of their lives was to focus on three personal and political ideals: promoting good health, fulfilling oneself, helping others." The critic concludes: "These are decent human beings. They do good things not because of a photo opportunity but because they believe one person can make a difference."

As a retired president, Carter still wields considerable influence in the political arena. His views are sought on developments in the Middle East, and he has made a number of trips to Central America as an observer. Carter told the *Chicago Tribune:* "Even though I'm out of office, I have access to nearly any leader in the world. I can bring together people who are experts on a specific subject, experts on starvation, on better ways to immunize children, on ways to alleviate human rights suffering. And I can invite political leaders who have the authority to do something about it." Carter offered his personal philosophy in a *Washington Post* profile. "No matter where you live in this nation and no matter what your level of income might be," he said, "you can always find things to do that are productive, helpful to others, challenging, interesting and to some degree adventurous." He concluded: "The second half [of life] can be the best half. And it can also prove that when you think you are making a sacrifice for the benefit of others, that can turn out to be the greatest advantage and most enjoyable experience of your own life."

BIOGRAPHICAL/CRITICAL SOURCES:

BOOKS

Allen, Gary, *Jimmy Carter—Jimmy Carter,* Seventy Six, 1976.
Carter, Jimmy, *Why Not the Best?,* Broadman, 1975.
Carter, Jimmy, *I'll Never Lie to You: Jimmy Carter in His Own Words,* edited by Robert Turner, Ballantine, 1976.
Carter, Jimmy, *Keeping Faith: Memoirs of a President,* Bantam, 1983.
Slosser, Bob and Howard Norton, *The Miracle of Jimmy Carter,* Logos, 1976.
Wheeler, Leslie, *Jimmy Who?,* Barron's, 1976.

PERIODICALS

Chicago Tribune, March 31, 1985, April 28, 1985, June 12, 1987.
Contemporary Review, September, 1985.
Globe & Mail (Toronto), July 13, 1985.
Harper's, August, 1979.
Los Angeles Times, May 20, 1987, October 14, 1987.
Los Angeles Times Book Review, November 7, 1982, April 7, 1985, August 14, 1988, September 11, 1988.
New Republic, September 11, 1976, June 16, 1979, December 6, 1982.
New Yorker, January 17, 1983, May 20, 1985.
New York Review of Books, August 5, 1976, August 4, 1977, December 16, 1982.
New York Times, June 1, 1982, November 3, 1982, April 18, 1985, December 10, 1985.
New York Times Book Review, June 6, 1976, June 5, 1977, November 7, 1982, April 28, 1985, May 31, 1987, July 3, 1988.
Spectator, January 1, 1983, August 3, 1985.
Time, June 15, 1987.
Times (London), February 6, 1987.
Times Literary Supplement, February 14, 1986.
Village Voice, July 12, 1976.
Washington Post, November 11, 1982, June 2, 1987, June 3, 1987.
Washington Post Book World, October 31, 1982, March 31, 1985, June 5, 1988.*

—*Sketch by Anne Janette Johnson*

*   *   *

CARTER, Jimmy
    See CARTER, James Earl, Jr.

CARTER, Marilyn
    See ROSS, W(illiam) E(dward) D(aniel)

*   *   *

CASTANEDA, Carlos   1931(?)-

PERSONAL: Author gives birthdate and place as December 25, 1931, in Sao Paulo, Brazil; cites Castaneda as an adopted surname. Immigration records list name as Carlos César Aranha Castaneda, birthdate as December 25, 1925, and place as Cajamarca, Peru; son of C. N. and Susana (Aranha) Castaneda; came to United States in 1951. Other sources list birthdate from 1925 to late 1930s. *Education:* University of California, Los Angeles, B.A., 1962, M.A., 1964, Ph.D., 1970.

ADDRESSES: Home—308 Westwood Plaza, B101, Los Angeles, Calif. 90024. *Office*—c/o Simon & Schuster, Inc., 1230 Avenue of the Americas, New York, N.Y. 10020. *Agent*—Ned Brown, 407 North Maple Dr., Beverly Hills, Calif. 90210.

CAREER: Anthropologist.

WRITINGS:

The Teachings of Don Juan: A Yaqui Way of Knowledge, University of California Press, 1968.
A Separate Reality: Further Conversations with Don Juan, Simon & Schuster, 1971.
Journey to Ixtlan: The Lessons of Don Juan, Simon & Schuster, 1972.
Tales of Power, Simon & Schuster, 1974.
Trilogy (three volumes), Simon & Schuster, 1974.
Don Juan Quartet (boxed set; includes *The Teachings of Don Juan: A Yaqui Way of Knowledge, A Separate Reality: Further Conversations with Don Juan, Journey to Ixtlan: The Lessons of Don Juan,* and *Tales of Power*), Simon & Schuster, 1975.
The Second Ring of Power, Simon & Schuster, 1977.
The Eagle's Gift, Simon & Schuster, 1981.
The Fire from Within, Simon & Schuster, 1984.
The Power of Silence: Further Lessons of Don Juan, Simon & Schuster, 1987.

SIDELIGHTS: Carlos Castaneda's recorded experiences as an apprentice to Don Juan, a Yaqui Indian *brujo,* or sorcerer, are detailed in his many books, all of which deal with becoming a Yaqui "man of knowledge." According to Castaneda, Don Juan sensed in the younger man "the possibility of a disciple and proceeded to introduce him, by way of rigorous curriculum, into realms of esoteric experience which clash disconcertingly with our prevailing scientific conception of reality," writes *Nation* contributor Theodore Roszak in a review of the author's first book, *The Teachings of Don Juan: A Yaqui Way of Knowledge.* The world through which Don Juan wished to lead Castaneda initially included using hallucinogenic drugs in order to attain certain experiences, although as the books progress, other means are used to reach different levels of consciousness.

A Separate Reality: Further Conversations with Don Juan records Castaneda's subsequent visits with Don Juan and his continuing visits to other phases of the intangible world. *Natural History* contributors William and Claudia Madsen feel the book's strength lies in its presentation of sorcery: "In his haunting story, [Castaneda] draws you into the weird world of witches—a world you will never be able to explain or forget. . . . Castaneda's work is unique because it reveals an inside view of how witchcraft works." However, *New York Times Book Review* contributor William Irwin Thompson thinks that by concentrating on the narrative instead of striving for an anthropological report, Castaneda's style becomes more readable. Throughout his books, the author shows himself as an occasional bungler and reports his teacher's often harsh criticism of his mistakes. Thompson notes this and remarks that Castaneda "can parody himself and mock his own ignorance without ever tilting the balance away from Don Juan toward himself. The tone is . . . perfect for the book."

Journey to Ixtlan: The Lessons of Don Juan concentrates on how a sorcerer becomes a "man of power" through "seeing" instead of using the ordinary means of perception, "looking." In *Book World*, Barry Corbet notes: "*Ixtlan* marks an enormous change in Castaneda. . . . His reporting is warm, human and perceptive. The extraordinary thing is that the book represents very little new teaching from don Juan, but is the result of Castaneda's new ability to discern the best of the earlier teachings. This is a book of rejects, all the field notes he previously considered irrelevant. And it is this material which makes *Ixtlan* such staggeringly beautiful reading. . . . *Journey to Ixtlan* is one of the important statements of our time." A *Times Literary Supplement* contributor, however, feels that Castaneda has drawn too close to his subject, and has "rejected the objective and scientific approach to [his] subject-matter in favour of an extravagant empathy with the human object of [his] studies." While a *Time* contributor, like many other critics, finds Don Juan himself puzzling, he appreciates the *Journey to Ixtlan*: "Indeed, though [Don Juan] is an enigma wrapped in mystery wrapped in a tortilla, [Castaneda's books are] beautifully lucid. [His] story unfolds with a narrative power unmatched in other anthropological studies. . . . In detail, it is as thoroughly articulated a world as, say, Faulkner's Yoknapatawpha County. In all the books, but especially in *Journey to Ixtlan*, Castaneda makes the reader experience the pressure of mysterious winds and the shiver of leaves at twilight, the hunter's peculiar alertness to sound and smell."

Tales of Power continues with Castaneda's mysterious experiences, although this book centers more on the pupil's dealings with the unseen than with the lessons of his master. Michael Mason, however, writes in the *New Statesman* that Castaneda's ideas may not be as unusual as they seem: "Ideas from European existentialism pervade the book more than Castaneda's admirers might care to recognise," Mason claims. He adds: "*Tales of Power* is not a work of mysticism." Mason also voices an objection to seeing Castaneda as a student of Yaqui spiritism: "The awkwardness arises of how Castaneda can be achieving enlightenment if he is such a spiritual clodhopper." *New York Times Book Review* contributor Elsa First finds the tale more convincing, however: "This is a splendid book, for all that it may seem ungainly, at times ponderous, at others overwrought. . . . [*Tales of Power*] could well be read as a farcical picaresque epic of altered states of consciousness. . . . One of the finest things in [*Tales of Power*], however stylized or fictional it may be, is the convincing portrait of a spiritual teacher working away at his student's tendency to 'indulge' in self-dramatization and self-pity."

Despite the factual presentation of Castaneda's books, many critics have debated whether Don Juan really exists. *New York Times Book Review* Paul Riesman sees them as scholarly works: "Taken together—and they should be read in the order they were written—[Carlos Castaneda's books] form a work which is among the best that the science of anthropology has produced." In another *New York Times Book Review* article, however, Joyce Carol Oates states another view: "I realize that everyone accepts them as anthropological studies, yet they seem to me remarkable

works of art, on the Hesse-like theme of a young man's initiation into 'another way' of reality." And Dudley Young, also writing in the *New York Times Book Review*, questions Don Juan's credibility: "Since we are given virtually no information about the Don's credentials as a sorcerer (or indeed about his family or friends) it is very difficult to decide whether his symbology has genuine ethnic roots in Yaqui culture, whether he is just a more or less harmless crank, or whether he was seeking a corrupting kind of power over his disciple. . . . But Mr. Castaneda nowhere considers this possibility." Other reviewers, however, have dismissed the question of Don Juan's origins as irrelevant. According to *Washington Post* contributor Joseph McLellan: "The material in Castaneda's books is probably rooted in some sort of objective or hallucinatory experience—not cynically invented. If he had made it all up, as some observers have suggested, he could surely have produced something more interesting and coherent; something in which he is not seen so constantly as a dimwitted blunderer. Seen in context with other mystical writings, Castaneda's work seems less eccentric and its authenticity seems less dubious. . . . But by the same token, his work becomes less interesting—simply an exotic variant on fairly well-known themes."

Other critics have voiced different objections to Castaneda's writings. Weston LaBarre, in *Seeing Castaneda: Reactions to the "Don Juan" Writings of Carlos Castaneda*, questions the disciple's memory: "The long disquisition of Don Juan and the detailing of each confused emotional reaction of the author, . . . imply either total recall, novelistic talent, or a tape recorder." And in *Horizon*, Richard de Mille brings up what he considers important inconsistencies: "First, the so-called field reports contradict each other. Carlos meets a certain witch named La Catalina for the first time in 1962 and *again* for the first time in 1965. . . . A second kind of proof arises from absence of convincing detail and presence of implausible detail. . . . A third kind of proof is found in [Don] Juan's teachings, which combine American Indian folklore, oriental mysticism, and European philosophy. Indignantly dismissing such a proof, [Don] Juan's followers declare that enlightened minds think alike in all times and places, but there is more to the proof than similar ideas; there are similar words." But according to Joshua Gilder in his *Saturday Review* article on *The Eagle's Gift*: "It isn't necessary to believe to get swept up in Castaneda's other-worldly narrative; like myth it works a strange and beautiful magic beyond the realm of belief. . . . Sometimes, admittedly, one gets the impression of a con artist simply glorifying in the game—even so, it is a con touched by genius."

BIOGRAPHICAL/CRITICAL SOURCES:

BOOKS

Contemporary Literary Criticism, Volume 12, Gale, 1980.
LaBarre, Weston, *Seeing Castaneda: Reactions to the "Don Juan" Writings of Carlos Castaneda*, edited by Daniel C. Noel, Putnam, 1976.

PERIODICALS

American Anthropologist, Volume 71, number 2, 1969.
Book World, October 22, 1972, November 17, 1974.
Horizon, April, 1979.
Nation, February 10, 1969.
Natural History, June, 1971.
New Statesman, June 27, 1975.
New York Times Book Review, September 29, 1968, February 13, 1972, October 22, 1972, November 26, 1972, October 27, 1974, January 22, 1978.

Psychology Today, December, 1977.
Saturday Review, May, 1981.
Time, November 6, 1972, March 5, 1973.
Times Literary Supplement, June 15, 1973.
Washington Post, December 18, 1987.*

　　　　　　　　　　　—*Sketch by Jani Prescott*

* * *

CASTLE, Anthony (Percy) 1938-
(Tony Castle; Paul Frost, a pseudonym)

PERSONAL: Born May 24, 1938, in Dover, England; son of Percy and May Castle; married Elizabeth Ann Herrington; children: Helena, Louise, Angela, Thomas. *Education:* Attended St. John's Seminary, Surrey, England, 1957-63; received B.Ed. from Coloma College. *Religion:* Roman Catholic.

ADDRESSES: Home—36 St. John's Rd., Great Wakering, Southend-on-Sea, Essex SS3 0AL, England. *Agent*—Edward England, 12 Highlands Close, Crowborough, Sussex, England.

CAREER: Ordained Roman Catholic priest, 1963; released from obligations of priesthood, 1975. Pastor of Roman Catholic churches in London, England, 1963-65, and in Abbeywood and Thamesmead, England, 1965-72; teacher of religious education and department head at Roman Catholic senior high school in London, 1971-73; Sandown Court Secondary School, Tunbridge Wells, England, youth tutor, 1973-76; free-lance publishing consultant, specializing in religious education and theology, 1976-85; St. Bernard's High School, Westcliff, England, head of theology department, 1985—. National Association of Youth Clubs, religious adviser, 1969-71.

WRITINGS:

UNDER NAME TONY CASTLE

Tuesday Again (teacher's resource book), Mayhew-McCrimmon, 1977.
Quotes and Anecdotes, Kevin Mayhew, 1979.
Assemble Together (teacher's resource book), Geoffrey Chapman, 1981.
Through the Year with Pope John Paul, Crossroads, 1982.
New Book of Christian Quotations, Crossroads, 1982.
Let's Celebrate, Hodder & Stoughton, 1984.
Hodder Book of Famous Prayers, Hodder & Stoughton, 1985.
More Quotes and Anecdotes, Fowler Wright, 1985.
Hodder Book of Famous Christians, Hodder & Stoughton, 1988.
Lives of Famous Christians, Servant Books, 1989.
Quotations for All Occasions, Marshall Pickering, 1989.
Gateway to the Trinity, St. Paul Publications, 1989.
Assembly Praise, Collins, 1990.

OTHER

(Under pseudonym Paul Frost) *Good Heavens,* Kevin Mayhew, 1980.

Past editor of *Christian Celebration.*

WORK IN PROGRESS: A novel.

SIDELIGHTS: Anthony Castle told *CA:* "All my books have been written or compiled to meet what I could see as a need. For example, there was a need for good, relevant resource books for teachers taking school assembly—an English phenomenon. The 1944 and 1988 Education Acts direct that every school, state and religious, shall assemble the students for an act of worship each day. So, *Tuesday Again, Assemble Together,* and *Assembly Praise*

are prepared service activities for schools, including full resource sections. *Quotes and Anecdotes* is a collection of materials to help preachers prepare sermons and teachers to prepare for school assembly.

"*Through the Year with Pope John Paul II* provides a reading for each day of the year and introduces the reader to the thoughts and interests of the pope, and my recent book, *Let's Celebrate,* is a tool for use in the home. I feel that family life needs all the support it can get, and this book provides practical suggestions for celebrating the church's year with the family. The novel I am currently working on will, I hope, give the ordinary person an insight into the daily life of a Catholic priest, with all its ups and downs. In a nutshell, everything I have written stems from my pastoral experience and concern."

* * *

CASTLE, Tony
See CASTLE, Anthony (Percy)

* * *

CATALA, Rafael 1942-

PERSONAL: Born September 26, 1942, in Las Tunas, Cuba; came to United States in 1961; son of Rafael Enrique (a businessman) and Caridad (Gallardo) Catalá. *Education:* New York University, B.A., 1970, M.A.; 1972, Ph.D., 1982.

ADDRESSES: Home—c/o P.O. Box 450, Corrales, N.M. 87048.

CAREER: Poet, editor, and educator. Lafayette College, Easton, Pa., instructor of languages, 1977-79; writer, 1979-84; Seton Hall University, South Orange, N.J., assistant professor of modern languages, 1983-84; Lafayette College, Cintas fellow, 1984-85, assistant professor, 1985-87; full-time writer, 1987—. Director of Racata Literary Workshop, City University of New York, spring, 1983.

MEMBER: International Institute of Ibero-American Literature, Society for Literature and Science, American Association of Teachers of Spanish and Portuguese, Modern Language Association of America, Pacific Coast Council of Latin American Studies, North East Modern Language Association.

AWARDS, HONORS: Penfield fellowship from New York University, 1974-75.

WRITINGS:

Caminos/Roads (bilingual edition with English translation by Nancy Sebastiani), Hispanic Press, 1972.
Círcula cuadrado, Anaya-Las Américas, 1974.
(Co-author) *Ojo sencillo/Triqui-traque,* Editorial Cartago, 1975, revised edition, Prisma, 1984.
(With Luis Jiménez, Gladys Zaldivar, Concepción Alzola, Arthur Natella) *Cinco aproximaciones a la narrativa hispanoamericana contemporánea,* Playor, 1977.
(With others) *Estudios de Historia, Literatura y Arte Hispánicos,* Ediciones Insula, 1977.
(Contributor) *Azor en vuelo,* Volume 5, Rondas, 1981.
Copulantes, Luna Caeez Caliente, 1981, 2nd edition, Prisma, 1983.
(Contributor) *Hispanics in the United States: An Anthology of Creative Literature,* Bilingual Press Review, 1982.
(Contributor) *Literatures in Transition: The Many Voices of the Caribbean Area,* Ediciones Hispamérica-Montclair State College, 1982.
(Editor with Robertoluis Lugo) *Soles emellis,* Prisma, 1983.

(Contributor) *Esta urticante pasión de la pimienta,* Prisma, 1983.

(Contributor) *Los Paraguas Amarillos,* Ediciones del Norte, 1983.

Cienciapoesía, Prisma, 1986.

Para una lectura americana del barroco mexicano: Sor Juana Inén de la Cruz y Sigüenza-y-Góngora, Institute of Ideologies and Literature, University of Minnesota, 1987.

Letters to a Student: Preparation for the Experience, Corrales Infinite Way Study Group, 1988.

(Contributor) *Poetas Cubanos en Nueva York,* Betania, 1988.

(Contributor) *El Jardín También es Nuestro,* SLUSA Press, 1988.

Sufficient Unto Itself Is the Day, Corrales Infinite Way Study Group, 1989.

Editor of "Index of American Periodical Verse" series, Scarecrow, 1981—. Work featured on videotape "First Symposium on New Tendencies in Latin American Literature," produced by Adelphi University, 1983. Contributor of poetry and essays to numerous periodicals, including *Norte, Lyra, Educacción, El Diario, Boreal, Septagon, New York Times, Publication of the Society for Literature and Science, Revista Iberamericana,* and *Catalyst.* Editor, *Románica,* 1973-75 and *Ometeca,* 1988—. Associate editor of *Cuadernos de Poética,* 1987—.

WORK IN PROGRESS: Cienciapoesía II; Towards a Theoretical Construct of Science and Poetry: A Unified View.

SIDELIGHTS: Rafael Catalá told *CA:* "For me writing is an act of listening, as if I were an instrument of a universal text that is unfolding. I am a tool through which this text comes forth into expression.

"Writing is my work. It requires some studying. I think I'll always be a student. Learning is fun and it's beautiful; what thrills me about learning is that everything is connected, whether it's math, science, literature, art or physics. Writing is learning to listen to what is inside me. To me inside and outside are one and the same.

"Writing is work, and real work is play. I believe that I am at play most of the time not only when writing or studying but when gardening, cycling, teaching or hiking."

In his book, *Cienciapoesía,* Catalá introduces the concept of sciencepoetry—the process of unifying or linking the humanities and science. Catalá explains in an article for the *Publication of the Society for Literature and Science:* "Science and the humanities, as the expression of human consciousness, are one. In order to have a balanced world view, both must be taken into account as a reasoning and as an intuitive process. In order to do this, we must learn to discern the commonality of principles that unifies both sub-systems of thought. I have named this process *cienciapoesía* (sciencepoetry—one word). It is the process where the sciences and the humanities, recognizing each other as one, meet in men and women as one body."

BIOGRAPHICAL/CRITICAL SOURCES:

PERIODICALS

Publication of the Society for Literature and Science, March, 1987.

*   *   *

CATANESE, Anthony James (Jr.) 1942-

PERSONAL: Born October 18, 1942, in New Brunswick, NJ; son of Anthony James, Sr. (an engineer), and Josephine (Barone) Catanese; married Sara Phillips, October 23, 1968; children: Mark Anthony, Mark Alexander, Michael Scott. *Education:* Rutgers University, B.A., 1963; Rider College, certificate in real estate, 1963; University of Washington, certificate in Computer Applications to Urban Analysis, 1964; New York University, M.U.P., 1965; University of Wisconsin, Ph.D., 1969.

ADDRESSES: Office—Florida Atlantic University, Boca Raton, FL 33431.

CAREER: Rutgers University, New Brunswick, NJ, began as assistant, became director of Rutgers Planning Service and Campus Planning Office, 1961-62; Middlesex County Planning Board, New Brunswick, planning assistant, 1962-63, senior planner, 1964-66; New Jersey Department of Conservation and Economic Development, Division of State and Regional Planning, Trenton, NJ, senior planner, 1963-64; Georgia Institute of Technology, School of Architecture, Atlanta, GA, assistant professor, 1967-68, associate professor of city planning and director of Urban Systems Simulation Laboratory, 1968-73; University of Miami, Coral Gables, FL, James A. Ryder Professor, 1973-77; University of Wisconsin—Milwaukee, dean of School of Architecture and Urban Planning, 1975-82; provost, Pratt Institute, 1982-84; Georgia Institute of Technology, Center for Planning and Development, director, 1984-86; University of Florida, Gainesville, dean of College of Architecture, 1986-90; Florida Atlantic University, Boca Raton, president, 1990—.

President, A. J. Catanese & Associates, Atlanta, 1967—; vice-president for management, MRC Realty Joint Venture, 1968—; executive vice-president, PP&C Properties, 1970—. Lecturer on state planning at New York University, 1964; visiting lecturer at Clark College, 1968; visiting professor of urban and regional studies, Virginia Polytechnic Institute, 1969. Member of New York University Planners Organization, Organization of Rutgers Planning, and University of Wisconsin Planning Club. State planning consultant, Wisconsin Department of Resource Development, Madison, 1966-67.

MEMBER: International Platform Association, American Academy of Political and Social Sciences, American Association of University Professors, American Institute of Planners, American Institute of Urban and Regional Affairs, American Society of Planning Officials, Association for Computing Machinery, Association of Collegiate Schools of Planning, National Association of Housing and Redevelopment Officials, National Urban Coalition, Urban America, Inc., Urban and Regional Information Systems Association, Regional Science Association, National Geographic Society, Association of Wisconsin Planners, Georgia Planning Association, Regional Plan Association (New York-New Jersey-Connecticut region), City Planners Section, Georgia Municipal Association, Wisconsin Alumni Union.

AWARDS, HONORS: American Institute of Planners, Contributions to the Profession Award, 1973, service award, 1974, 1978; Citizen of the Year, Walnut Area Improvement Council, 1981; named to American Heritage Hall of Fame, 1981; Man of the Year, Pompeii Club, 1982; distinguished service award, Wisconsin Society of Architects, 1982; Research Client Award, *Progressive Architecture,* 1983; distinguished service award, Wisconsin Planning Association, 1983.

WRITINGS:

(With others) *Plan for Manasquan, New Jersey,* Rutgers University, 1963.

The Alternatives of the Horizon Planning Concept, New Jersey Division of State and Regional Planning, 1964.

A Statewide Planning Analysis of Utility Services in New Jersey, New Jersey Division of State and Regional Planning, 1964.

The Residential Development of New Jersey: A Regional Approach, New Jersey Division of State and Regional Planning, 1964.

(With Alan Walter Steiss) *Commercial Land Use in New Jersey,* New Jersey Division of State and Regional Planning, 1964.

(With others) *The Stottsburg Plan: A Model of Growth and Factors Affecting Development,* Graduate School of Public Administration, New York University, 1965.

(Editor) *The Myths and Realities of the Image of Greenwich Village: A Workshop Model of a Planning Process,* Graduate School of Public Administration, New York University, 1966.

Data Processing for State Planning, Wisconsin Department of Resource Development, 1967.

The Economy of Northwestern Wisconsin, Wisconsin Department of Resource Development, 1967.

(With others) *Wisconsin Development Plan,* Wisconsin Department of Resource Development, 1967.

(Editor with John L. Gann and Leo Jakobson) *Explorations into Urban Functions, Spatial Organization, and Environmental Form,* University of Wisconsin Board of Regents, 1967.

(With Richard G. Poirier) *Planning for Recreation: A Methodology for Functional Planning,* Department of Planning and Economic Development (Honolulu), 1968.

(With others) *A Survey of Student Planning Organizations,* American Institute of Planners, 1968.

Comprehensive Plan for Cordele, Georgia, Keck & Wood, 1969.

Alpharetta Plans for the Future, Keck & Wood, 1969.

Systemic Planning: An Annotated Bibliography and Literature Guide, Council of Planning Librarians (Monticello), 1969.

(With Roger J. Budke) *Urban Transportation: Problems and Potentials,* Atlanta Chamber of Commerce, Leadership Development Foundation, 1969.

(With others) *An Information System for Fulton County, Georgia,* Fulton County Manager's Office, 1969.

(With James B. Grant and Edward N. Kashuba) *Application of Computer Graphics to Urban and Regional Planning,* School of Architecture, Georgia Institute of Technology, 1969.

Scientific Methods of Urban Analysis, University of Illinois Press, 1970.

(With Steiss) *Systemic Planning: Essays on Theory and Application,* Heath, 1970.

Structural and Socioeconomic Factors of Commuting, Clearinghouse for Federal Scientific and Technical Reports, 1971.

(Editor) *New Perspectives on Transportation Research,* Heath, 1972.

Planners and Local Politics: Impossible Dreams, Sage Publications, 1974, published as *Impossible Dreams: Planners and Local Politics,* Sagemark, 1977.

Urban Transportation in South Florida, University of Miami, 1974.

(With others) *Hawaii State Growth Policies Plan: 1974-1984,* State of Hawaii, 1974.

(With Steiss) *Managing Hawaii's Coast,* State of Hawaii, 1976.

(Editor with P. Farmer) *Personality, Politics, and Planning: How City Planners Work,* Sage Publications, 1978.

(With E. Alexander and D. Sawicki) *Urban Planning: Guide to Information,* Gale, 1978.

(With James C. Snyder) *Federal-State Institutions for Cooperative Planning and Management,* Federal-State Land Use Planning Commission for Alaska, 1979.

(Editor with Snyder) *Introduction to Urban Planning,* McGraw, 1979.

(Editor with Snyder) *Introduction to Architecture,* McGraw, 1979.

The Politics of Planning and Development, Sage Publications, 1984.

Urban Planning, McGraw, 1986.

CONTRIBUTOR

Michael Sumichrast, editor, *What's Ahead in 1966?,* National Association of Homebuilders, 1965.

Proceedings of Midwest Seminar on Urban and Regional Research, University of Wisconsin Board of Regents, 1967.

The Recreation Element of the General Plan Revision Program: State of Hawaii, Donald Wolbrink & Associates (Honolulu), 1967.

Handerworterbuch der Raumforshung and Raumordnung, Gebruder Janecks Verlag, 1970.

James J. Murray, editor, *Urban and Regional Ground Transportation,* High Speed Ground Transportation Journal, Inc., 1973.

H. Patton and R. H. Slavin, editors, *State Issues,* Council of State Governments, 1973.

(With Howard Harrenstien) *Proceedings of Governor's Conference on Development of Mass Transit Statewide,* Hawaii Department of Transportation, 1974.

T. R. Kitsos, editor, *Land Use in Colorado: The Planning Thicket,* University of Colorado, 1974.

(With D. Hinds and B. O'Neil) M. Golden and R. Schumacher, editors, *Proceedings of the Institute of Management Science,* TIMS, 1975.

(With Hinds and O'Neil) S. Elmagraby, editor, *Handbook of Operations Research,* Van Nostrand, 1978.

Naomi W. Lede, editor, *Strengthening Organizational Capabilities for Transportation Management,* Government Printing Office, 1978.

I. Stollman and others, editors, *The Practice of Local Government,* International City Management Association, 1980.

Snyder, editor, *Architectural Research,* Van Nostrand, 1984.

OTHER

Contributor of articles to periodicals, including *Jersey Plans, New Jersey Economic Review, Journal of Housing, Les annales de l'economie collective,* and *Traffic Quarterly.*

WORK IN PROGRESS: A book on the future of cities.

*   *   *

CELA, Camilo Jose 1916-
(Matilde Verdu)

PERSONAL: Surname pronounced *Say*-lah; born May 11, 1916, in Iria Flavia, La Coruña, Spain; son of Camilo (a customs official and part-time writer) and Camila Enmanuela (Trulock Bertorini) Cela; married María del Rosario Conde Picavea, March 12, 1944 (marriage ended); children: Camilo José. *Education:* Attended University of Madrid, 1933-36, and 1939-43.

ADDRESSES: Home—Finca el Espinar, Carretera de Fontanar, Apartado 333, Guadalajara, Spain.

CAREER: Writer; publisher of *Papeles de Son Armadans* (literary monthly), 1956-79. Lecturer in England, France, Latin America, Belgium, Sweden, Italy, and the United States. *Military service:* Served in Spanish Nationalist Army during Spanish Civil War, 1936-39; became corporal.

MEMBER: Real Academia Española, Premio Nacional de Literatura, Premio Príncipe de Asturias, Real Academia Gallega, Hispanic Society of America, American Association of Teachers of Spanish and Portuguese (honorary fellow, 1966—).

AWARDS, HONORS: Premio de la crítica, 1955, for *Historias de Venezuela: La Catira;* Spanish National Prize for Literature, 1984, for *Mazurca para dos muertos;* honorary doctorates from Syracuse University, 1964, University of Birmingham, 1976, University of Santiago de Compostela, 1979, University of Palma de Mallorca, 1979, John F. Kennedy University (Buenos Aires), and Interamericana University (Puerto Rico).

WRITINGS:

IN ENGLISH TRANSLATION

La familia de Pascual Duarte (novel), Aldecoa (Madrid), 1942, reprinted, Destino (Barcelona), 1982, translation by John Marks published as *Pascual Duarte's Family,* Eyre & Spottiswoode, 1946, translation by Anthony Kerrigan published as *The Family of Pascual Duarte,* Little, Brown, 1964, reprinted, 1990, Spanish/English version by Herma Briffault published as *Pascual Duarte and His Family,* Las Américas Publishing, 1965.

Pabellón de reposo (novel; first published serially in *El Español,* March 13 to August 21, 1943), illustrations by Suárez de Arbol, Afrodisio Aguado (Madrid), 1943, reprinted, Destino, 1977, Spanish/English version by Briffault published as *Rest Home,* Las Américas Publishing, 1961.

Las botas de siete leguas: Viaje a la Alcarría, con los versos de su cancionero, cada uno en su debido lugar (travel; also see below), Revista de Occidente, 1948, reprinted, Destino, 1982, published as *Viaje a la Alcarría,* Papeles de Son Armadans, 1958, reprinted, 1976, translation by Frances M. López-Morillos published as *Journey to the Alcarría,* University of Wisconsin Press, 1964, reprinted, Atlantic Monthly Press, 1990.

Caminos inciertos: La colmena (novel), Emecé (Buenos Aires), 1951, published as *La colmena,* Noguer (Barcelona), 1955, reprinted, Castalia (Madrid), 1984, translation by I. M. Cohen and Arturo Barea published as *The Hive,* Farrar, Straus, 1953, reprinted, 1990.

Mrs. Caldwell habla con su hijo (novel), Destino, 1953, reprinted, 1979, translation by Jerome S. Bernstein published as *Mrs. Caldwell Speaks to Her Son,* Cornell University Press, 1968.

Also author of *Avila* (travel), 1952, revised edition, 1968, translation by John Forrester published under same title, 1956.

NOVELS

Nuevas andanzas y desventuras de Lazarillo de Tormes, y siete apuntes carpetovetónicos (title means "New Wanderings and Misfortunes of Lazarillo de Tormes"; first published serially in *Juventud,* July 4 to October 18, 1944), La Nave (Madrid), 1944, reprinted, Noguer, 1975.

Santa Balbina 37: Gas en cada piso (novella; title means "Santa Balbina 37, Gas in Every Flat"; also see below), Mirto y Laurel (Melilla, Morocco), 1952, 2nd edition, 1977.

Timoteo, el incomprendido (novella; title means "Misunderstood Timothy"; also see below), Rollán (Madrid), 1952.

Café de artistas (novella; also see below), Tecnos (Madrid), 1953.

Historias de Venezuela: La catira (title means "Stories of Venezuela: The Blonde"), illustrations by Ricardo Arenys, Noguer, 1955, published as *La catira,* 1966.

Tobogán de hambrientos (title means "Toboggan of Hungry People"), illustrations by Lorenzo Goñi, Noguer, 1962.

Vísperas, festividad y octava de San Camilo del año 1936 en Madrid (title means "Eve, Feast and Octave of San Camilo's Day, 1936, in Madrid"), Alfaguara, 1969, Noguer, 1981.

Oficio de tinieblas 5; o, Novela de tesis escrita para ser cantada por un coro de enfermos (title means "Ministry of Darkness 5; or, Novel with a Thesis Written to Be Sung by a Chorus of Sick People"), Noguer, 1973.

Mazurca para dos muertos (title means "Mazurka for Two Bad People"), Ediciones del Norte (Hanover, N.H.), 1983.

Cristo versus Arizona (title means "Christ versus Arizona"), Seix Barral (Barcelona), 1988.

STORIES

Esas nubes que pasan (title means "The Passing Clouds"; also see below), Afrodisio Aguado, 1945, reprinted, Espasa-Calpe (Madrid), 1976.

El bonito crimen del carabinero, y otras invenciones (stories; title means "The Neat Crime of the Carabiniere and Other Tales"; one chapter first published in *Arriba,* April 25, 1946; also see below), José Janés (Barcelona), 1947, published as *El bonito crimen del carabinero,* Picazo, 1972.

Baraja de invenciones (title means "Pack of Tales"; also see below), Castalia (Valencia), 1953.

Historias de España: Los ciegos, los tontos, illustrations by Manuel Mampaso, Arión (Madrid), 1958, new enlarged edition published in four volumes as *A la pata de palo* (title means "The Man with the Wooden Leg"), illustrations by Goñi, Alfaguara, Volume 1: *Historias de España* (title means "Stories of Spain"), 1965, Volume 2: *La familia del Héroe; o, Discurso histórico de los últimos restos; ejercicios para una sola mano,* 1965, Volume 3: *El ciudadano Iscariote Reclús* (title means "Citizen Iscariote Reclús"), 1965, Volume 4: *Viaje a U.S.A.* (title means "Trip to the U.S.A."), 1967, published in one volume as *El tacatá oxidado: Florilegio de carpetovetonismos y otras lindezas,* Noguer, 1973.

Los viejos amigos, two volumes, illustrations by José María Prim, Noguer, 1960-61, 3rd edition, 1981.

Gavilla de fábulas sin amor (title means "A Bundle of Loveless Fables"), illustrations by Pablo Picasso, Papeles de Son Armadans (Palma de Mallorca), 1962, reprinted, 1979.

Once cuentos de fútbol, illustrations by Pepe, Nacional (Madrid), 1963.

Toreo de sálon: Farsa con acompañamiento de clamor y murga, photographs by Oriol Maspons and Julio Ubiña, Editorial Lumen (Barcelona), 1963, reprinted, 1984.

Izas, rabizas y colipoterras: Drama con acompañamiento de cachondeo y dolor de corazón, photographs by Juan Colom, Editorial Lumen, 1964, reprinted, 1984.

Nuevas escenas matritenses (title means "New Scenes of Madrid"), seven volumes, photographs by Enrique Palazuela, Alfaguara, 1965-66, published in one volume as *Fotografías al minuto,* Organización Sala (Madrid), 1972.

La bandada de palomas (juvenile), illustrations by José Correas Flores, Labor, 1969.

Cuentos para leer después del baño, La Gaya Ciencia (Barcelona), 1974.

Rol de cornudos, Noguer, 1976.

El espejo y otros cuentos, Espasa-Calpe, 1981.

TRAVEL

Del Miño al Bidasoa: Notas de un vagabundaje (title means "From the Mino to the Bidasoa: Notes of a Vagabondage"), Noguer, 1952, reprinted, 1981.

Vagabundo por Castilla (title means "Vagabond in Castile"), Seix Barral, 1955.

Judíos, moros y cristianos: Notas de un vagabundaje por Avila, Segovia y sus tierras (title means "Jews, Moors, and Christians: Notes of a Vagabondage through Avila, Segovia, and Their Surroundings"), Destino, 1956, reprinted, 1979.

Primer viaje andaluz: Notas de un vagabundaje por Jaén, Córdoba, Sevilla, Huelva y sus tierras (title means "First Andalusian Trip: Notes on a Vagabondage through Jaen, Cordoba, Seville, Huelva, and Their Surroundings"), illustrations by José Hurtuna, Noguer, 1959, reprinted, 1979.

Cuaderno del Guadarrama (title means "Guadarrama Notebook"), illustrations by Eduardo Vicente, Arión, 1959.

Páginas de geografía errabunda (title means "Pages of Wandering Geography"), Alfaguara, 1965.

Viaje al Pirineo de Lérida: Notas de un paseo a pie por el Pallars Sobirá, el Valle de Arán y el Condado de Ribagorza, Alfaguara, 1965.

Madrid, illustrations by Juan Esplandíu, Alfaguara, 1966.

Calidoscopio callejero, marítimo y campestre de C.J.C. para el reino y ultramar, Alfaguara, 1966.

La Mancha en el corazón y en los ojos, EDISVEN (Barcelona), 1971.

Balada del vagabundo sin suerte y otros papeles volanderos, Espasa-Calpe, 1973.

Madrid, color y siluta, illustrations by Estrada Vilarrasa, AUSA (Sabadell, Spain), 1985.

Nuevo viaje a la Alcarría, three volumes, Información y Revistas (Madrid), 1986.

Also author of *Barcelona*, 1970.

OMNIBUS VOLUMES

El molino de viento, y otras novelas cortas (title means "The Windmill and Other Short Novels"; contains *El molino de viento, Timoteo, el incomprendido* [also see below], *Café de artistas* [also see below], and *Santa Balbina 37: Gas en cada piso*), illustrations by Goñi, Noguer, 1956, reprinted, 1977.

Mis páginas preferidas (selections), Gredos (Madrid), 1956.

Nuevo retablo de don Cristobita: Invenciones, figuraciones y alucinaciones (stories; contains *Esas nubes que pasan, El bonito crimen del carabinero*, and part of *Baraja de invenciones*), Destino, 1957, reprinted, 1980.

Obra completa (title means "Complete Works"), fourteen volumes, Destino, 1962-83.

Las compañías convenientes y otros figimientos y cegueras (stories; title means "Suitable Companions and Other Deceits and Obfuscations"), Destino, 1963, reprinted, 1981.

Café de artistas y otros cuentos, Salvat/Alianza, 1969.

Timoteo el incomprendido y otros papeles ibéricos, Magisterio Español, 1970.

Obras selectas (includes *La familia de Pascual Duarte, Viaje a la Alcarría, La colmena, Mrs. Caldwell habla con su hijo, Iazas, rabizas y colipoterras*, and *El carro de heno; o, El inventor de la guillotina*), Alfaguara, 1971.

Prosa, edited by Jacinto-Luis Guereña with notes and commentaries, Narcea (Madrid), 1974.

Café de artistas y otros papeles volanderos, Alce (Madrid), 1978.

Also author of *Antología*, 1968.

OTHER

Mesa revuelta (essays) Ediciones de los Estudiantes Españoles, 1945, new and expanded edition (includes text of *Ensueños y figuraciones*), Taurus (Madrid), 1957.

Pisando la dudosa luz del día: Poemas de una adolescencia cruel (poems; title means "Treading the Uncertain Light of Day"), Zodíaco (Barcelona), 1945, new corrected and expanded edition, Papales de Son Armadans, 1963.

(Under pseudonym Matilde Verdu) *San Juan de la Cruz,* [Madrid], 1948.

El gallego y su cuadrilla y otros apuntes carpetovetónicos (title means "The Galician and His Troupe and Other Carpeto-Vettonian Notes"), Ricardo Aguilera (Madrid), 1949, 3rd edition corrected and enlarged, Destino, 1967.

Ensueños y figuraciones, Ediciones G.P., 1954.

La rueda de los ocios (title means "The Wheel of Idle Moments"), Mateu (Barcelona), 1957, reprinted, Alfaguara, 1972.

La obra literaria del pintor Solana: Discurso leído ante la Real Academia Española el día 26 de mayo de 1957 en su recepción pública por el Excmo. Sr. D. Camilo José Cela y contestación del Excmo. Sr. D. Gregorio Marañón, Papeles de Son Armadans (Madrid), 1957, reprinted, 1972.

Cajón de sastre (articles) Cid (Madrid), 1957, reprinted, Alfaguara, 1970.

Recuerdo de don Pío Baroja (title means "Remembrance of Pío Baroja"), illustrations by Eduardo Vicente, De Andrea (Mexico City), 1958.

La cucaña: Memorias (memoirs) Destino, 1959, portion printed as *La rosa*, Destino, 1979.

(Editor) *Homenaje y recuerdo a Gregorio Marañón (1887-1960)*, Papeles de Son Armadans, 1961.

Cuatro figuras del 98: Unamuno, Valle Inclán, Baroja, Azorín, y otros retratos ensayos españoles, Aedos (Barcelona), 1961.

El solitario: Los sueños de Quesada (title means "The Solitary One"), illustrations by Rafael Zabaleta, Papeles de Son Armadans, 1963.

Garito de hospicianos; o, Guirigay de imposturas y bambollas (articles; title means "Poorhouse Inmates; or, Jargon Frauds and Sham"), Noguer, 1963, reprinted, Plaza & Janés, 1986.

(Author of prologue) Tono y Rafael Florez, *Memorias de mi: Novela*, Biblioteca ca Nueva, 1966.

(With Cesáreo Rodríguez Aguilera) *Xam* (illustrated art commentary), Daedalus (Palma de Mallorca), 1966.

Diccionario secreto (title means "Secret Dictionary"), Alfaguara, Volume 1, 1968, Volume 2, 1972.

María Sabina (dramatic poem; also see below), Papeles de Son Armadans, 1967, 2nd edition bound with *El carro de heno; o, El inventor de la guillotina* (play; also see below), Alfaguara, 1970.

Poesía y cancioneros, [Madrid], 1968.

Homenaje al Bosco, I: El carro de heno; o, El inventor de la guillotina, Papeles de Son Armadans, 1969.

Al servicio de algo, Alfaguara, 1969.

La bola del mundo: Escenas cotidianas, Organización Sala (Madrid), 1972.

A vueltas con España, Seminarios y Ediciones (Madrid), 1973.

Cristina Mallo (monograph), Theo (Madrid), 1973.

Diccionari manual castellá-catalá, catalá-castellá, Bibliograf (Barcelona), 1974.

Enciclopedia de erotismo (title means "Encyclopedia of Eroticism"), D. L. Sedmay (Madrid), 1977.

(Adaptor) Fernando de Rojas, *La Celestina puesta respetuosamente en castellano moderno por Camilo José Cela quien añadio muy poco y quitó aún menos* (title means "La Celestina Put Respectfully into Modern Castilian by Camilo Jose Cela Who Added a Little and Took Out Even Less"), Destino, 1979.

Los sueños vanos, los ángeles curiosos, Argos Vergara (Barcelona), 1979.

Los vasos comunicantes, Bruguera (Barcelona), 1981.

Las compañías convenientes y otros figimientos y cegueras, Destino, 1981.

Vuelta de hoja, Destino, 1981.

Album de taller (art commentary), Ambit (Barcelona), 1981.

(Editor and author of prologue) Miguel de Cervantes Saavedra, *El Quijote,* Ediciones Rembrandt (Alicante, Spain), 1981.

El juego de los tres madroños, Destino, 1983.

El asno de Buridán (articles), El País (Madrid), 1986.

Also author of *San Camilo,* 1936, reprinted, 1969, *La bandada de palmoas,* 1969, and, with Alfonso Canales, *Crónica del cipote de Archidona* (first published as *La insólita y gloriosa hazaña del cipote de Archidona),* 1977. Author of poems "Himno a la muerte" (title means "Hymn to Death"), 1938, and *Dos romances de ciego,* 1966.

SIDELIGHTS: While not widely known in the United States, 1989 Nobel laureate Camilo José Cela has played a pivotal role in twentieth-century Spanish literature. Upon awarding the prize to Cela, the Swedish Academy praised the author "for a rich and intensive prose, which with restrained compassion forms a challenging vision of man's vulnerability," relates Sheila Rule for the *New York Times.* In the same article, Rule reports Julio Ortego's statement that "Cela represents the searching for a better literature from the Franco years, through the democratic experiments and into European Spain. At the same time, he remained very Spanish, keeping the cultural traditions of Spanish art and literature in his writing. He didn't follow a European literature, but developed his own style, and so, in his way, symbolized Spain's going through a long period of adjustment." Throughout the Franco regime, Cela suffered from heavy governmental censorship. Many of his books were banned outright or later removed from the shelves: the second edition of *Pascual Duarte* was seized; the censor found it "nauseating," and *The Hive* was initially published in South America. D. W. McPheeters maintains in *Camilo José Cela* that, in spite of such opposition, Cela "has always had the courage to express himself frankly, even forthrightly, . . . which has led to problems with an overly squeamish censorship."

Cela's stylistic development has moved from the more traditional *Pascual Duarte* to the innovative fiction of his later novels. McPheeters sees Cela as "dedicated to a constant trying of various forms . . . of fiction in a search for the one that best suits him and . . . what he has to say concerning the human situation. He [is] an outspoken critic of traditional forms of the novel and the restrictions which [some] would impose upon the creative artist." Cela's first novel, *The Family of Pascual Duarte,* has been called the most widely read Spanish novel since *Don Quixote.* It was published in the early 1940s, a time when "the Spanish novel . . . had virtually ceased to exist as a worthy genre," attests McPheeters. "Almost single-handedly, Cela [gave the genre] new life and international significance." Many critics have noted that Cela's national prominence and international fame is a result of the popularity of *The Family of Pascual Duarte* and a later novel, *The Hive.* McPheeters agrees, stating that while *Pascual Duarte,* Cela's first novel, "secured a wide foreign acceptance," *The Hive* "assured his place as one of Europe's outstanding novelists."

Pascual Duarte relates the life of a convicted murderer awaiting execution. It is introduced as a prison letter to an old family friend, but the reader soon becomes immersed in a first-person narrative. Pascual responds to a life of poverty and frustration through killing: his dog, his horse, his wife's lover, and finally, his mother, fall victim to his rage. "A deceptive objectivity masks the presentation of cruel and monstrous scenes, including murder and matricide," *Michigan Quarterly Review* contributor Francis Donahue describes. "In a taut style, with emotion carefully reined, Cela evokes an atmosphere of extreme brutality, one which a nation suffering from the after-effects of a brutal civil war could readily understand and believe." But some reviewers find such intense scenes hinder any identification with the main character. "Pascual Duarte speaks of suffering and ferocity so appalling as to be almost beyond the reach of our sympathy. They stun even more than they horrify," resolves *Saturday Review* contributor Emile Capouya. However, Pierre Courtines in *America* insists that the book is worth the reader's effort: "The dialogues between Cela's leading characters are rapid and dramatic, and his language is rich in imagery that reveals many popular traditions. Cela has combined realism with poetry, and his novel expresses the 'tragic sense of life,' so much a part of the Spanish character."

Some critics, as I. S. Bernstein states in his introduction to *Mrs. Caldwell Speaks to Her Son,* credit Cela with the invention of "tremendismo," a type of fiction which dwells on the darker side of life—the distasteful, the grotesque and the vulgar. Although in his prologue to the Spanish version of *Mrs. Caldwell Speaks to Her Son,* Cela denies this paternity, tremendista elements are abundant in *Pascual Duarte.* As an example of tremendismo, McPheeters translates a portion of the struggle in which Pascual kills his mother: "I was able to bury the blade in her throat. . . . Blood squirted out in a torrent and struck me in the face. It was warm like a belly and tasted the same as the blood of a lamb." Other gruesome incidents fill the pages of the novel; in one scene Pascual's retarded brother's ears are eaten off by a pig. This type of detail—meant to shock the placid reader—is present in a lesser degree or non-existent in some of Cela's novels, but even so, a *Times Literary Supplement* critic calls Cela's works "perversely restricted to a pathology of human decay and loneliness." His *Mazurca para dos muertos,* for example, concludes with a six-page postmortem examination of a cadaver. Even Cela's nonfiction works such as *Enciclopedia de eroticismo* (the title means "Encyclopedia of Eroticism") and *Diccionario secreto,* which contains definitions of vulgar words, are written in defiance of Spain's traditionalist moral code.

The Hive led critics to compare Cela with John Dos Passos, particularly to Dos Passos's novel *Manhattan Transfer,* which characterizes frenetic Manhattan life. Comparisons between the two novels are based on the large number of characters introduced in both works and by the novelists' similarly cinematographic styles. In both novels, the shifting time sequence is similar to the filmmaker's flashback. But while David W. Foster concedes in *Forms in the Work of Camilo José Cela* that an analogy can be made between the two techniques, he notes: "Cela's perspective goes much beyond that of the camera in what it is able to record. It is, in effect, all inclusive, omniscient, and omnipresent."

The Hive is frequently seen as Cela's greatest work. In *Books Abroad,* Jacob Ornstein and James Y. Causey note that "Spanish criticism has been almost unanimous in acclaiming this novel as Cela's masterpiece, both for its vigorous simplicity and for the author's artistry in evoking the atmosphere of Madrid during the final days of World War II and the years immediately following." *The Hive*'s publication was typical of Cela's struggle with the censors, as it was banned in Spain and printed in Buenos Aires in 1952; William D. Montalbano reports in the *Los Angeles Times* that Cela autographed copies "a bitter chronicle of a bitter time." *Nation* contributor Maxwell Geismar finds *The Hive* "suffused with anger and bitterness at society in Madrid." The novel portrays the lives of 346 characters during three days in Madrid in the winter of 1943, when the city was facing intense hardship. Although only forty-eight of *The Hive*'s characters play a significant role in the plot, their appearances and disappearances are more important than the story itself. As Foster notes, "[*The Hive*] is one continuous interplay of people. Although chronology is fragmented, the novel is able to develop a world based upon the activities of individuals." And a *Times Literary Supplement* contributor finds that "in spite of the author's literary theories which confuse the reader with an enormous gallery of characters presented in very short passages, *The Hive* is a work of art of great power."

While *The Hive,* as Foster remarks, "has stood as a sort of beacon for Cela's fiction, the one novel to which most critics turn with . . . admiration," Cela has continued producing innovative and award-winning novels. The author "has chosen," Foster points out, "to make his career one of a complete reexamination and reconsideration of the novel as an art form." Foster classifies most of Cela's novels since *Mrs. Caldwell Speaks to Her Son* as experimental. Among the characteristics most prominent in Cela's later work are the decreasing emphasis plot—the sequence of cause and effect is discarded—and an increasing emphasis on artificial patternings of events. Some of his more original novels besides *Mrs. Caldwell* include *Tobogán de hambrientos, Vísperas, festividad y octava de San Camilo del año 1936 en Madrid* (usually referred to as *San Camilo, 1936*), and *Oficio de tinieblas 5*. However, McPheeters believes that these later works may be less accessible to the general reader. He mentions that *Pascual Duarte* and *The Hive* "continue to influence contemporary Spanish writers, but certain innovations in his other works may not gain rapid acceptance."

Mrs. Caldwell contains excerpts from the letters of a mentally disturbed woman to her dead son. McPheeters finds that *Mrs. Caldwell* "is about as much an antinovel as has yet been conceived in Spain." The theme is incest, one ideally suited to Cela's fiction because of its shock value. The form is equally unexpected: although only slightly longer than two hundred pages, it contains two hundred and twelve chapters. There is no connection between the chapters (except for chapters fourteen and sixty) and no reason for ending the novel other than the illegibility of the last of the "Letters from the Royal Hospital for the Insane."

The form and content of *Tobogán de hambrientos, San Camilo, 1936,* and *Oficio de tinieblas 5* are also out of the ordinary. *Oficio de tinieblas,* for example, has no capital letters, while *San Camilo, 1936* has no paragraphs. *Tobogán de hambrientos,* Foster notes, "employs many of the devices of the new novel, especially in its use of pattern and in the rejection of chronology, definable plot, and unified points of view." The book is divided into two hundred units. These two hundred are in turn divided in half and labeled in ascending, then, at the half-way point, in descending numerical order. Each narrative unit presents a new individual or group of individuals and the characters from the first half of the book reappear in the corresponding chapters of the second half.

Except for the epilogue, *San Camilo, 1936* is a young student's continuous stream of consciousness. Again, in content and form the book is far removed from the traditional novel. The book's opening chapter, for instance, includes a list of Madrid's brothels, complete with addresses and names of proprietresses. A *Times Literary Supplement* reviewer remarks on the novel's unusual style: "[Cela] reinforces his . . . contempt for petit-

bourgeois credulity by quoting an enormous variety of patent medicine advertisements, [and] making astonishingly free with his sexual and other carnal references, indeed, the language of [the book] is scabrous." While noting Cela's emphasis on "the erotic, obscene and scatological" in *San Camilo, 1936, Hispania* contributor Robert Louis Sheehan also observes the "stylistic innovations" present in the novel, including "the rhythmic reiteration of names, clauses, [and] phrases," the "use of one-paragraph chapters, run-on sentences, and frequent use of commas in place of periods."

Today the name of Camilo José Cela is associated with the rebirth of the Spanish novel, and with experimentation in its form and content. *Pascual Duarte* is credited with starting a new school of Spanish literature, while *The Hive* brought a new cinematographic technique to literature, which Margaret E. W. Jones in *The Contemporary Spanish Novel, 1939-1975* believes "suggested new possibilities in [the] elasticity of novelistic form." Jones also confirms the author's sense of exploration, and claims that "Cela has consistently been at the forefront of new movements in the contemporary novel since the 1940s." And Cela himself sums up his feelings on his favorite genre in the dedication to *Journey to the Alcarría*—which Jones quotes—"Anything goes in the novel, as long as it's told with common sense."

MEDIA ADAPTATIONS: The Hive was filmed by director Mario Camus; *The Family of Pascual Duarte* was filmed by director Ricardo Franco.

AVOCATIONAL INTERESTS: Collecting wine bottles, stamps, and literary myths.

BIOGRAPHICAL/CRITICAL SOURCES:

BOOKS

Cela, Camilo José, *Caminos inciertos: La colmena,* Noguer, 1955.
Cela, Camilo José, *Mrs. Caldwell Speaks to Her Son,* translated and with introduction by J. S. Bernstein, Cornell University Press, 1968.
Chandler, Richard E. and Kessel Schwartz, *A New History of Spanish Literature,* Louisiana State University Press, 1961.
Contemporary Authors Autobiography Series, Volume 10, Gale, 1989.
Contemporary Literary Criticism, Gale, Volume 4, 1975, Volume 13, 1980.
Foster, David W., *Forms in the Work of Camilo José Cela,* University of Missouri Press, 1967.
Ilie, Paul, *La novelística de Camilo José Cela,* Gredos, 1963.
Jones, Margaret E. W., *The Contemporary Spanish Novel, 1939-1975,* Twayne, 1985.
Kirsner, Robert, *The Novels and Travels of Camilo José Cela,* University of North Carolina Press, 1964.
McPheeters, D. W., *Camilo José Cela,* Twayne, 1969.

PERIODICALS

America, November 7, 1964.
Books Abroad, spring, 1953, winter, 1971.
Christian Science Monitor, January 14, 1965.
Hispania, March, 1965, March, 1966, September, 1966, September, 1967, May, 1972.
Los Angeles Times, November 2, 1989.
Michigan Quarterly Review, summer, 1969.
Nation, November 14, 1953.
New Statesman, February 19, 1965.
New Yorker, January 30, 1965.

New York Times, October 20, 1989.
New York Times Book Review, May 26, 1968.
Observer, February 14, 1965.
Saturday Review, November 23, 1964.
Spectator, February 19, 1965.
Times Literary Supplement, February 2, 1965, February 25, 1965, May 27, 1965, November 11, 1965, February 12, 1970, April 2, 1970, November 5, 1971, February 11, 1972.
Washington Post, October 20, 1989.
World Literature Today, autumn, 1977, summer, 1982, autumn, 1984.

*   *   *

CHAMBERS, Catherine E.
See St. JOHN, Nicole

*   *   *

CHAMBERS, Kate
See St. JOHN, Nicole

*   *   *

CHAR, Rene(-Emile) 1907-1988

PERSONAL: Born June 14, 1907, in L'Isle-sur-Sorgue, Vaucluse, France; died, February 19, 1988, in the military hospital Val-de-Grace, Paris, France; buried in L'Isle-sur-Sorgue; son of Emile (an industrialist) and Marie-Therese-Armande (Rouget) Char; married Georgette Goldstein, 1933 (divorced, 1949). *Education:* Baccalaureate degree from Lycee d'Avignon; attended Ecole de Commerce a Marseille, 1925. *Religion:* No religious convictions.

*ADDRESSES:*c/o Editions Gallimard, 5 rue Sebastien Bottin, 75007, Paris, France.

CAREER: Poet. Sojourn in Tunisia, 1924; first went to Paris in 1929, where he met Louis Aragon, Paul Eluard, and Andre Breton; was a companion of the Surrealists, 1930-34, during the second period of the movement; in L'Isle-sur-Sorgue in 1940 the Vichy police searched his home, leading to his denunciation as a communist as a result of his association with Surrealists before the war; between 1940 and 1945, he was regional head of a partisan group in the Alpes-de-Provence for the Armee Secrete, working for the Resistance in France and North Africa, using the name Capitain Alexandre; in 1944, he was wounded by the Germans; a month later he was ordered to Algiers on an advisory mission to Supreme Allied Headquarters. *Military service:* French Artillery, Nimes, 1927-28; served again, 1939-40, in Alsace.

MEMBER: Academie de Baviere (Germany), Modern Language Association of America (honorary fellow).

AWARDS, HONORS: Prix des Critiques, 1966, for *Retour amont. Military*— Chevalier de la Legion d'Honneur; Medaille de la Resistance; Croix de Guerre.

WRITINGS:

Les Cloches sur le coeur, Le Rouge et le noir, 1928.
Arsenal, Meridiens (Nimes), 1929, new edition published as *De la Main a la main,* 1930.
(With Andre Breton and Paul Eluard) *Ralentir travaux,* Editions Surrealistes, 1930, reprinted, J. Corti, 1968.
Le Tombeau des secrets, [Nimes], 1930.
Artine, Editions Surrealistes, 1930, new edition published as *Artine et autres poemes,* Tchou, 1967.

L'Action de la justice est eteinte, Editions Surrealistes, 1931.
Le Marteau sans maitre (also see below), Editions Surrealistes, 1934.
Dependence de l'adieu, G.L.M., 1936.
Moulin premiere (also see below), G.L.M., 1936.
Placard pour un chemin des ecoliers (also see below), G.L.M., 1937.
Dehors la nuit est gouvernee (also see below), G.L.M., 1938.
Seuls demeurent, Gallimard, 1945.
Le Marteau sans maitre [and] *Moulin premier, 1927-1935,* J. Corti, 1945, reprinted, 1963.
Feuillets d'Hypnos (war journal), Gallimard, 1946, translation by Cid Corman published as *Leaves of Hypnos,* Grossman, 1973.
Le Poeme pulverise (also see below), Fontaine, 1947.
Fureur et Mystere, Gallimard, 1948, new edition, 1962.
Fete des arbres et du chasseur, G.L.M., 1948.
Dehors la nuit est gouvernee [and] *Placard pour un chemin des ecoliers,* G.L.M., 1949.
Claire: Theatre de verdure, Gallimard, 1949.
Le Soleil des eaux, etchings by Georges Braque, H. Matarasso, 1949, new edition, Gallimard, 1951.
Les Matinaux, Gallimard, 1950, new edition, 1962.
Art bref [and] *Premieres alluvions,* G.L.M., 1950.
Quatre fascinants: La Minutieuse, S.N. (Paris), 1951.
A une serenite crispee, Gallimard, 1951.
Poemes, wood-cuts by Nicolas de Stael, S.N., 1951.
La Paroi et la prairie, G.L.M., 1952.
Lettera amorosa, Gallimard, 1953, 2nd edition, 1962, lithographs by Braque, E. Engelberts (Geneva), 1963.
Arriere-histoire du "Poeme pulverise" (the 19 texts of *Le Poeme pulverise* with the author's comments on each), lithographs by de Stael, J. Hugues, 1953, 2nd edition, 1972.
Choix de poemes, Brigadas Liricas (Mendoza, Argentina), 1953.
Le Rempart de brindilles, etchings by Wifredo Lam, L. Broder, 1953.
A la sante du serpent, G.L.M., 1954.
Le Deuil des Nevons, etchings by Louis Fernandez, Le Cormier (Brussels), 1954.
Recherche de la base et du sommet [and] *Pauvrete et privilege* (also see below), Gallimard, 1955, new edition, 1965.
Poemes des deux annees, 1953-1954, G.L.M., 1955.
Chanson des etages, P.A.B. (Ales), 1955.
La Bibliotheque est en feu (also see below), etchings by Braque, L. Broder, 1956.
Hypnos Waking (poems and prose), selected and translated by Jackson Mathews, with the collaboration of William Carlos Williams, Richard Wilbur, William Jay Smith, Barbara Howes, W. S. Merwin, and James Wright, Random House, 1956.
Pour nous, Rimbaud, G.L.M., 1956.
En trente-trois morceaux (aphorisms), G.L.M., 1956, reprinted, 1970.
Jeanne qu'on brula verte, illustration by Braque, P.A.B., 1956.
La Bibliotheque est en feu, et autres poemes, G.L.M., 1957.
L'Abominable homme des neiges, Librairie L.D.F. (Cairo), 1957.
L'Une et l'autre, P.A.B., 1957.
De moment en moment, engravings by Joan Miro, P.A.B., 1957.
Les Compagnons dans le jardin, engravings by Zao Wou-Ki, L. Broder, 1957.
Poemes et prose choisis, Gallimard, 1957.
Elisabeth, petite fille, P.A.B., 1958.
Sur la poesie, G.L.M., 1958, new edition, 1967.
Cinq poesies en hommage a Georges Braque, lithographs by Braque, S.N. (Geneva), 1958.

L'Escalier de Flore, engravings by Pablo Picasso, P.A.B., 1958.

La Faux relevee, P.A.B., 1959.

Nous avons (prose poem), engravings by Miro, L. Broder, 1959.

Pourquoi la journee vole, engraving by Picasso, P.A.B., 1960.

Le Rebanque, P.A.B., 1960.

Anthologie, G.L.M., 1960, new edition published as *Anthologie, 1934-1969,* 1970.

Les Dentelles de Montmirail, P.A.B., 1960.

L'Allegresse, engraving by Madeleine Grenier, P.A.B., 1960.

(With Paul Eluard) *Deux poemes,* J. Hugues, 1960.

L'Inclemence lointaine, engravings by Vieira da Silva, P. Beres, 1961.

L'Issue, P.A.B., 1961.

La Montee de la nuit, P.A.B., 1961.

La Parole en archipel, Gallimard, 1962.

Deux Poemes, engraving by da Silva, P.A.B., 1963.

Poemes et prose choisis, Gallimard, 1963.

Impressions anciennes, G.L.M., 1964.

Commune presence, Gallimard, 1964.

L'An 1964, P.A.B., 1964.

L'Age cassant, J. Corti, 1965.

Flux de l'aimant, 2nd edition, G. P. Tarn (Veilhes), 1965.

La Provence, point Omega, [Paris], 1965.

(With Albert Camus) *La Posterite du soleil,* E. Engelberts, 1965.

Retour amont, illustrations by Alberto Giacometti, G.L.M., 1966.

Le Terme epars, Imprimerie Union, 1966.

Trois coups sous les arbres: Theatre saisonnier (collection of six plays), Gallimard, 1967.

Dans la pluie giboyeuse, Gallimard, 1968.

(With Martin Heidegger and others) *L'Endurance de la pensee: Pour Saleur Jean Beaufret,* Plon, 1968.

(With Andre Frenaud and others) *Bazaine,* Maeght, 1968.

Le Chien de coeur, G.L.M., 1969.

L'Effroi, la joie, Au vent d'Arles (Saint-Paul), 1969.

Le Nu perdu, Gallimard, 1971.

La Nuit talismanique, A. Skira (Geneva), 1972.

Picasso sous les ventes Etesiens, French & European, 1973.

Se recontrer paysage avec Joseph Sema, French & European, 1974.

Aromates Chasseurs, Gallimard, 1975.

Poems of Rene Char, translated with notes by Mary Ann Caws and Jonathan Griffin, Princeton University Press, 1976.

Recherche de la Base et du Sommet, Schoenhof, 1977.

Chants de la Balandrane: Poemes, Gallimard, 1977.

Le Nu perdu et autres poemes, Gallimard, 1978.

Fenetres dormantes et porte sur le toit, Gallimard, 1979.

Oeuvres completes, Gallimard, 1983.

No Seige Is Absolute, translation by Frank Wright, Lost Roads, 1983.

Eloge d'une soupconnee, Gallimard, 1990.

CONTRIBUTOR

Violette nozieres, N. Flamel (Brussels), 1933.

Reves d'encre, J. Corti, 1945.

Les Miroirs profonds, Editions Pierre a Feu, 1947.

Cinq parmi d'autres, Editions de Minuit, 1947.

A Braque, P.A.B., 1955.

Le Ruisseau de ble, P.A.B., 1960.

Poetes, Peintres, Sculpteurs, Maeght, 1960.

Un Jour entier, P.A.B., 1960.

25 octobre 1961, P.A.B., 1961.

13 mai 1962, P.A.B., 1962.

20 avril 1963, P.A.B., 1963.

OTHER

Also translator from the English of Tiggie Ghika's *Le Bleu de l'aile,* Cahiers d'Art, 1948, Theodore Roethke's "Le Reveil," and "Les Orchidees," published in *Preuves,* June, 1959, and (with Tina Jolas) *La Planche de vivre,* poems from the English, Italian, Spanish, and Russian, Gallimard, 1981. Author of numerous prefaces, forewords, introductions, and catalogs, and of Surrealism tracts (1930-34). Also author of numerous pamphlets and leaflets, some decorated with his own engravings. Contributor to *Le Revue Nouvelle, Sagesse, La Revolution Surrealiste, L'Impossible, Cahiers d'Art, Les Lettres Francaises, Les Quatre Vents, Fontaine, Cahiers du Sud, Combat, Mercure de France, Botteghe Oscure, Le Figaro Litteraire, Le Journal des Poetes, Temoins, Carrefour, Action, Realities Secretes, Poetry* (Chicago), *Miscellaneous Man, Western Review, Quarterly Review of Literature, Chelsea, Tiger's Eye, Minnesota Review,* and other publications.

SIDELIGHTS: In 1952 France's most prominent novelist, the late Albert Camus, wrote: "I consider Rene Char to be our greatest living poet, and *Fureur et Mystere* to be the most astonishing product of French poetry since *Les Illuminations* and *Alcools.*" Gabriel Bounoure notes a typical reaction to Char's work: "I remember when I first read Char's poetry I was drawn by its evident greatness, repelled by the asperities, the challenge, and the seismic violence of its inner meaning. . . . Nothing more salutary had appeared since Nietzsche. Cruel and devouring, this work, enclosing us like a single diamond, yet with all the sting of immense spaces of air. Char's universe is the kingdom of the open air." Camus called this poetry "strange and rigorous," emanating from "a poet of all time who speaks for our time in particular."

In the early thirties Char became involved with Surrealism (an artistic style that uses surprising, fantastical imagery) and though he broke with the movement shortly thereafter, the novelty of his imagery and his liberated imagination remain. He was his own master; Camus wrote: "No doubt he did take part in Surrealism, but rather as an ally than as an adherent, and just long enough to discover that he could walk alone with more conviction." Gaetan Picon added: "Char's work is great, in so far as it both confirms and transcends Surrealism, both fulfills and exposes the poetry of today, inherits the past and opens up the future."

Many of Char's poems are aphoristic—stabbing distillations of language. Emile Snyder writes: "A poem by Rene Char is an act of violence within which serenity awaits the end of violence." The concentrated lucidity he attains is, in Char's words "the wound closest to the sun," and, he might have added, closest to the essence of poetry, so simple that it is most commonly considered difficult. Camus remarked that this poetry "carries daytime and night on the same impulse. . . . And so, when Char's poetry appears to be obscure, it is because a furious condensation of imagery, an intensification of light removes it from that degree of abstract transparency which we all too often demand only because it makes no demands on us."

"A poem," wrote Char, "is the fulfillment of a desire which remains desire . . . [,] that instant when beauty, after keeping us waiting a long time, rises out of common things, passes across our radiant field, binds everything that can be bound, lights up everything that needs lighting in our bundle of shadows." His position is one of total involvement and his themes are great and often difficult. Rene Menard observes that "all the poetry of Char seems to me the writing of a presence who wishes himself just, at every instant in his relations with the world. . . . Char does not believe that man or his destiny are absurd. On the contrary, the circumstances of earth, if men would not ruin them by stupidity, blindness, or cruelty, would be a magnificent, an inexhaustible theater for them. . . . Man could be a great 'accompanist' of life. In order to understand and animate that alliance, he has at his disposal Poetry."

Char's concern was with human experience and with beauty amid struggle and chaos. He said: "Nothing obsesses me but life." And, "In our darkness, there is no one place for beauty. The whole place is for beauty." Ralph J. Mills, Jr., notes Char's concern with the primacy of the poet: "In a world 'faced with the destroyed god,' as he believes, the solitary figure of the poet is transformed into the last priest, the final proprietor of value." Char believed that "to every collapse of the proofs, the poet replies with a salvo of futurity." And, though he called himself a humanist, the meaning of the poem, James Wright observes, "is not to be found in a prose commentary. It is somehow to be found in the lightning's weeping face."

His language, most frequently compared to fireworks, is "a contained violence," according to Picon, and bears "the tranquil solidity of a mine which the slightest nudge will detonate." He has "surprised the secret of atomic energy in language," identifying "poetry with the word." He sought in language "cruel tools," and Picon believes this language is lethal, "possessing something of the feeling of weapons set beneath a glass case." Menard believes it to be a language "unique in present-day Letters. It is neither prose nor poem. . . . Char appears to me the first writer of that future in which, as Being is to be known directly without the cheats of myths and theologies, language will be truly, in the image of Heidegger, 'the house of Being' and will reflect its unity." When obscurity arises in Char's work, it is due, writes Wallace Fowlie in *A Guide to Contemporary French Literature*, to his "seeking essentially to transcribe the subconscious." Beyond this, he sought to transcribe with beauty, reinstating, writes Picon, "the language which all modern poetry from Rimbaud to Surrealism has constantly tended to disqualify," namely beautiful language. "Char demands not only that language be effective, but that it have beauty."

Char's philosophical master was Heraclitus whom he called that "vision of a solar eagle" reconciling opposites. Char believed that "the poem is always married to someone," and the technique of his poetry can be expressed in the Heraclitian saying, "The Lord whose oracle is at Delphi neither expresses nor conceals, but indicates." "I am torn," writes Char, "by all the fragments there are." Yet his mind could "polarize the most neutral objects," writes Bounoure. His inspiration was ancient. Camus noted Char's right to "lay claim to the tragic optimism of pre-Socratic Greece. From Empedocles to Nietzsche, a secret had been passed on from summit to summit, an austere and rare tradition which Char has revived after prolonged eclipse. . . . What he has called 'Wisdom, her eyes filled with tears,' is brought to life again, on the very heights of our disasters."

Translations of Char's poems have appeared in Germany, Italy, Spain, South America, Poland, Sweden, U.S.S.R., Yugoslavia, Japan, and other countries.

BIOGRAPHICAL/CRITICAL SOURCES:

BOOKS

Benoit, P. A., *Bibliographie des oeuvres de Rene Char de 1928 a 1963*, Demi-Jour, 1964.
Berger, Pierre, *Rene Char*, Segher, 1951.
Caws, Mary Ann, *The Presence of Rene Char*, Princeton University Press, 1976.
Caws, *Rene Char*, Twayne, 1977.
Contemporary Literary Criticism, Gale, Volume 9, 1981, Volume 11, 1982, Volume 14, 1983, Volume 55, 1989.
Fowlie, Wallace, *A Guide to Contemporary French Literature*, Meridian Books, 1957.
Lawler, James R., *Rene Char, The Myth and the Poetry*, Princeton University Press, 1978.
Mounin, Georges, *Avez-vous la Char?*, Gallimard, 1946.
Piore, Nancy Kline, *Lightning, The Poetry of Rene Char*, Northeastern University Press, Boston, 1981.
Rau, Greta, *Rene Char ou la Poesie accrue*, Corti, 1957.
Rene Char's Poetry, Editions de Luca (Italy), 1956.

PERIODICALS

Chicago Review, autumn, 1961.
The Fifties, third issue, 1959.
L'Arc, Number 22 (special Char issue), 1963.
L'Herne, Number 18 (special Char issue), 1971.
Liberte, July, 1968.
Times Literary Supplement, October 14, 1983.
Western Review, autumn, 1953.
World Literature Today, summer (special Char issue), 1977.

OBITUARIES:

PERIODICALS

Chicago Tribune, February 21, 1988.
Los Angeles Times, February 21, 1988.
New York Times, February 21, 1988.
Times (London), February 22, 1988.*

*   *   *

CHASE, Otta Louise 1909-1987

PERSONAL: Born July 8, 1909, in Salem, Mass.; died November 22, 1987, in South Waterford, Me.; daughter of Benjamin Franklin (a handyman) and Rita Townes (Young) Graffam; married Hunter Ellsworth Chase, February 17, 1929; children: Donald Clayton, Nancy Lee (deceased), Charles Frederick (deceased). *Education:* Attended high school in Massachusetts. *Politics:* Democrat. *Religion:* Protestant.

ADDRESSES: Home and office—Route 93, Sweden, Me. *Mailing address*—R.R. 2, Box 645, South Waterford, Me. 04081

CAREER: Boston Edison Co., Boston, Mass., dictaphone operator, 1927-29; Town of Sweden, Me., treasurer, 1957-58, clerk, 1959-87, registrar of voters, 1968-87, medical officer, 1970-75. *Wartime service:* Aircraft spotter instructor during World War II.

MEMBER: National League of American Pen Women, American Poetry League, Poetry Society of America, Gold Star Mothers of America, Poetry Fellowship of Maine (treasurer, 1964, 1965; corresponding secretary, 1966-70; member of board of review, 1971-87), Poetry Society of New Hampshire (charter member), Massachusetts State Poetry Society (associate member), Kentucky State Poetry Society, Pennsylvania Poetry Society, Florida State Poetry Society, California Federation of Chaparral Poets (associate member), Maine City and Town Clerks Association.

AWARDS, HONORS: Freedoms Foundation George Washington Honor Medal Award, 1963 and 1967, for poetry, 1965, for letter to editor; Poetry Society of New Hampshire first prize, 1969, 1973; California Federation of Chaparral Poets first prize, 1971; Kentucky State Poetry Society first prize, 1973, 1975; National Federation of State Poetry Societies award, 1973, for "The Connecticut Darn Man"; Driftwood E first prize, 1974; Oklahoma State Poetry Society first prize, 1974, for "Only in Oklahoma"; National League of American Pen Women (Cedar Rapids-Waterloo branch) award for serious poetry, 1974, for "Primer"; chosen one of the Golden Poets of 1985, *World of Poetry.*

WRITINGS:

November Violets (poems), Golden Quill, 1973.
Tender Vines (poems), Golden Quill, 1986.

Poems represented in anthologies, including *Selected Poems of the Florida State Poetry Society,* edited by Frances Clark Handler, Florida State Poetry Society, 1967-70; *Dr. Etta Josephean Murfey Memorial Book,* Florida State Poetry Society, 1968; *Alabama Sampler,* Alabama State Poetry Society, 1969-73; *Golden Quill Anthologies,* edited by Clarence E. Farrar, Golden Quill, 1969-71; *Golden Harvest,* Young Publications, 1971; *Variation in Mulberry,* edited by Lawrence Wiggin, Poetry Society of New Hampshire, 1971; *Rock Ledge and Apple Blossoms,* edited by Ina Ladd Brown, Poetry Fellowship of Maine, 1971; *International Who's Who in Poetry Anthology,* edited by Ernest Kay, Rowman, 1972. Contributor to State of Maine Writers Conference chapbooks, numbers 4-21. Contributor of poems to newspapers, including *Boston Globe, Manchester Union Leader, Nantucket Mirror and Enquirer,* and *Bridgton News;* and to periodicals, including *American Legion Magazine* and *Bittersweet.*

WORK IN PROGRESS: Poetry.

SIDELIGHTS: "I have been writing ever since I was in grade school," Otta Louise Chase told *CA.* "My first 'serial' novel was a thriller entitled *The Silver Rose,* patterned after the old-time weekly serials in the movies. I still have a copy typed by my aunt.

"Since I mainly write poetry I hope that some of my work will comfort or touch the lives of others in some constructive way, and selfishly, I hope to leave something worthwhile behind me."

Chase later noted: "When I began to try to be recognized, I thought I wrote 'deathless' literature. I attended the State of Maine Writers Conference and Kitty Parsons Recchia, Sue McConkey and Raymond C. Swain evidently saw something worthy in my work and took me under their tutelage and helped me attain whatever small measure of achievement that has come to me. . . .

"Since I am mainly a traditionalist in writing, I must confess that much of what is published as poetry escapes my comprehension. At the risk of offending some editors, I do not think *they* understand half of what they publish."

AVOCATIONAL INTERESTS: Watching and feeding wild birds, button collecting, corresponding with people in foreign lands.

[sketch reviewed by daughter-in-law, Marion J. Chase]

*   *   *

CHAVEZ, Angelico
   See CHAVEZ, Manuel

*   *   *

CHAVEZ, Fray Angelico
   See CHAVEZ, Manuel

CHAVEZ, Manuel   1910-
   (Angelico Chavez, Fray Angelico Chavez)

PERSONAL: Name in religion, Fray Angélico Chávez; born April 10, 1910, in Wagon Mound, N.M.; son of Fabián (a carpenter) and Nicolasa (a teacher; maiden name, Roybal) Chávez. *Education:* Attended Franciscan seminaries in Cincinnati, Ohio, and Detroit, Mich.

CAREER: Entered Franciscan religious order, 1929; ordained Roman Catholic priest, 1937; missionary among Pueblo Indians in New Mexico, 1937-72; laicized, 1972; writer, 1972—. Lecturer at University of Albuquerque, 1972-74. Member of board of regents of Museum of New Mexico, 1946-57. *Military service:* U.S. Army, Infantry, chaplain, 1943-46 and 1951-52; served in Pacific theater and Germany; became major.

AWARDS, HONORS: Catholic Poetry Award from Catholic Poetry Society of New York, 1948, for body of lyric poetry; award from National Council of Christians and Jews, 1963; literary award from governor of New Mexico, 1976, for body of literature. Honorary degrees from University of New Mexico, 1947 and 1974, University of Albuquerque, 1963, and Southern University of New Mexico, 1975.

WRITINGS:

UNDER NAME ANGELICO CHAVEZ, EXCEPT AS NOTED

(Under name Fray Angélico Chávez) *Clothed with the Sun* (poems), Rydal, 1939.
(Under name Fray Angélico Chávez; and illustrator) *New Mexico Triptych* (short stories), St. Anthony Guild Press, 1940, reprinted under name Angélico Chávez, Gannon, 1976.
Seraphic Days: Franciscan Thoughts and Affections on the Principal Feasts of Our Lord and Our Lady and All the Saints of the Three Orders of the Seraph of Assisi (meditations), edited by Sebastian Erbacher, Duns Scotus College, 1940.
Eleven Lady-Lyrics, and Other Poems, St. Anthony Guild Press, 1945.
The Single Rose (poems), Los Santos Bookshop, 1948.
Our Lady of the Conquest (nonfiction), Historical Society of New Mexico, 1948.
La Conquistadora: The Autobiography of an Ancient Statue (nonfiction), St. Anthony Guild Press, 1954, reprinted, Sunstone Press, 1983.
Origins of New Mexico Families in the Spanish Colonial Period (nonfiction), Historical Society of New Mexico, 1954, reprinted, Gannon, 1982.
(With E. B. Adams) *The Missions of New Mexico, 1776,* University of New Mexico Press, 1956.
Archives of the Archdiocese of Santa Fe, Academy of American Franciscan History, 1957.
From an Altar Screen; El retablo: Tales From New Mexico (short stories), Farrar, Straus, 1957, published as *When the Santos Talked: A Retable of New Mexico Tales,* Gannon, 1977.
The Virgin of Port Lligat (poems), Academy Library Guild, 1959.
(And illustrator) *The Lady from Toledo* (historical novel), Academy Guild Press, 1960.
Coronado's Friars: The Franciscans in the Coronado Expedition (nonfiction), Academy of American Franciscan History, 1968.
Selected Poems, with an Apologia, Press of the Territorian, 1969.
(Editor and translator) *The Oroz Codex; or, Relation of the Description of the Holy Gospel Province in New Spain, and the Lives of the Founders and Other Note-Worthy Men of Said*

Province Composed by Fray Pedro Oroz, 1584-1586, Academy of American Franciscan History, 1972.
The Song of Francis, Northland Press, 1973 (published in England under name Fray Angélico Chávez as *The Song of St. Francis,* Sheldon Press, 1978).
My Penitente Land: Reflections on Spanish New Mexico, University of New Mexico Press, 1974, 2nd edition, Gannon, 1979.
The Lord and New Mexico, Archdiocese of Santa Fe, 1975.
(Translator) *The Domínguez-Escalante Expedition, 1776,* Brigham Young University Press, 1976.
But Time and Chance: The Story of Padre Martínez of Taos, 1793-1867 (nonfiction), Sunstone Press, 1981.
Tres Macho, He Said: Padre Gallegos, New Mexico's First Congressman, Gannon, 1985.
(Under name Fray Angélico Chávez) *The Short Stories of Fray Angélico Chávez,* University of New Mexico Press, 1987.

Work represented in *Best Poems,* J. Cape, 1938, 1940, and 1941. Contributor of articles, poems, and reviews to history and literary journals.

WORK IN PROGRESS: Books on southwestern history.

SIDELIGHTS: Manuel Chávez told *CA:* "I have loved English literature since childhood. I started publishing poetry and prose in my teens. I left the Franciscan order and active priesthood at age sixty-two, obviously not for wine, women, and song at that age, but because of having outgrown former ideals. I started a new life, as happy as the first, with no regrets for the past."

BIOGRAPHICAL/CRITICAL SOURCES:

BOOKS

Dictionary of Literary Biography, Volume 82: *Chicano Writers, First Series,* Gale, 1989.*

*   *   *

CHRISTOPHER, Beth
See STEINKE, Ann E(lizabeth)

*   *   *

CLARK, Stephen R(ichard) L(yster) 1945-

PERSONAL: Born October 30, 1945, in Luton, England; son of David Allen Richard (a teacher of engineering) and Kathleen (Finney) Clark; married Edith Gillian Metford (a researcher), July 1, 1972; children: Samuel, Dorothea, Verity. *Education:* Oxford University, B.A., 1968, M.A. and D.Phil., both 1973. *Politics:* Libertarian. *Religion:* Episcopalian.

ADDRESSES: Home—1 Arnside Rd., Oxton, Birkenhead, Merseyside L43 2JU, England.

CAREER: University of Liverpool, Liverpool, England, professor of philosophy, 1984—.

MEMBER: Aristotelian Society, Vegan Society, Scottish Society for the Prevention of Vivisection.

WRITINGS:

Aristotle's Man, Oxford University Press, 1975.
The Moral Status of Animals, Oxford University Press, 1977.
The Nature of the Beast: Are Animals Moral?, Oxford University Press, 1982.
(Contributor) R. Elliot and A. Gare, editors, *Environmental Philosophy,* University of Queensland Press, 1983.
From Athens to Jerusalem, Oxford University Press, 1984.

The Mysteries of Religion, Blackwells, 1986.
Civil Peace and Sacred Order, Oxford University Press, 1989.
Neo-Platonic Psychology and Metaphysics, Oxford University Press, in press.

SIDELIGHTS: Stephen R. L. Clark's books admonish members of the philosophical and scientific community to reevaluate some of the cherished notions of various disciplines, particularly as they relate to the humane treatment of animals. Of his *The Nature of the Beast: Are Animals Moral?,* Brigid Brophy writes in the *Times Literary Supplement,* "The burden of this book is to dissuade scientists, and in particular ecologists and sociobiologists, from the notion that they are doing something scientific when, discounting the awareness that goes with perceptions, they try to adopt 'aseptic' attitudes and vocabulary in their accounts of animals' behaviour. . . . What in effect Clark presents is a well-documented survey of present ethological thought in which he points to the places where muddled concepts or concepts adopted without recognition of their implications are making a nonsense of science. . . . Clark's exercise is of practical and moral, as well as academic, value."

Clark also applies himself to the philosophical grounds for morality among human beings. In *From Athens to Jerusalem: The Love of Wisdom and the Love of God,* "Clark's main argument against embracing scepticism," writes *Times Literary Supplement* contributor D. Z. Phillips, "is his inviatation to the sceptic to note that, in all human activities, justifications must come to an end somewhere. We act without further reasons. Clark, however, wants us to call such bed-rock responses 'acting on faith.' If this lack of further grounds is true of basic responses, whether religious or not, why should all such responses be called faith, or compared to a religious faith which would naturally belong only to some of the responses? . . . Here, belief appears to be a presupposition entailed by our basic responses, whereas, in fact, it is those basic responses which are the conditions of concept-formation where our beliefs are concerned."

Clark writes: "I would want my philosophical studies to help clear away the prejudices and rationalizations which prevent affectionate understanding (and decent treatment) of our fellow-creatures of our own and other species; also to clear away such intellectual and emotional errors as hinder religious devotion. I am opposed to meatfarming, vivisection, and obedience to any authority not ordained of God. I am fond of cats, children, gadgets, and old roses."

BIOGRAPHICAL/CRITICAL SOURCES:

PERIODICALS

Nature, November 11, 1982.
Times Literary Supplement, January 25, 1985; October 15, 1982; June 12, 1987.

*   *   *

CLARKE, Austin C(hesterfield) 1934-

PERSONAL: Born July 26, 1934, in Barbados, West Indies; son of Kenneth Trothan (an artist) and Gladys Clarke; children: Janice, Loretta. *Education:* Harrison College, Barbados, West Indies, Oxford and Cambridge Higher certificate, 1950; additional study at University of Toronto.

ADDRESSES: Agent—Harold Ober Associates, 40 East 49th St., New York, NY 10017.

CAREER: Canadian Broadcasting Corp., Toronto, Ontario, producer and free-lance broadcaster, beginning 1963; Brandeis

University, Waltham, MA, Jacob Ziskind Professor of Literature, 1968-69; Williams College, Williamstown, MA, Margaret Bundy Scott Professor of Literature, 1971-72; Barbados Embassy, Washington, DC, cultural and press attache, 1974-75; currently affiliated with Caribbean Broadcasting Corp., St. Michael, Barbados. Visiting professor of Afro-American literature and creative writing, Yale University, 1968-71. Member of Board of trustees, Rhode Island School of Design, Providence, 1970-75; member, Immigrations and Refugees Board of Canada, 1989.

MEMBER: Writers Guild, Canadian Union of Writers, Yale Club (New Haven).

AWARDS, HONORS: Canada Council senior arts fellowships, 1968, 1970, 1974; University of Western Ontario President's medal for best story, 1965; Belmont Short Story Award, for "Four Stations in His Circle"; Casa de las Americas Literary Prize, 1980.

WRITINGS:

NOVELS

The Survivors of the Crossing, McClelland & Stewart, 1964.
Amongst Thistles and Thorns, McClelland & Stewart, 1965.
The Meeting Point, Macmillan, 1967.
Storm of Fortune, Little, Brown, 1973.
The Bigger Light, Little, Brown, 1975.
The Prime Minister, General Publishing, 1977.
Growing Up Stupid Under the Union Jack (autobiographical novel), McClelland & Stewart, 1980.
Proud Empires, Viking, 1986.

SHORT STORIES

When He Was Free and Young He Used to Wear Silks, Anansi, 1971, Little, Brown, 1974.
Nine Men Who Laughed, Penguin, 1986.

Author of *Short Stories of Austin Clark,* 1984.

OTHER

Also author of "myths and memories," "African Literature," and other filmscripts for Educational Television (ETV), Toronto, 1968—.

WORK IN PROGRESS: A study of the symbolism in Richard Wright's story, "the Man Who Lived Underground"; research concerning the position of black women in the Black American Revolution.

SIDELIGHTS: Austin C. Clarke's childhood in colonial Barbados and his experiences as a black immigrant to Canada have provided him with the background for most of his fiction. His writing is almost exclusively concerned with the cultural contradictions that arise when blacks struggle for success in a predominantly white society. Clarke's "one very great gift," in the words of a *New Yorker* critic, is the ability to see "unerringly into his characters' hearts," and this ability is what makes his stories memorable. Martin Levin writes in the *New York Times Book Review,* "Mr. Clarke is plugged into the fixations, hopes, loves and dreams of his characters. He converts them into stories that are charged with life."

Clarke's autobiographical novel, *Growing Up Stupid Under the Union Jack,* is an example of the author's typical theme and style. The narrator, Tom, is a young man from a poor Barbadan village. Everyone in the village is proud that Tom is able to attend the Combermere School, for it is run by a "real, true-true Englishman"—an ex-British army officer who calls his students

"boy" and "darky" and who flogs them publicly. The students eagerly imitate this headmaster's morals and manners, for to them, he represents "Mother England"; they are unaware that in England he would be looked down upon as a mere working-class soldier. The book is "a personal, captivating, provoking, and often humorous record of ignorance, inhumanity and lowly existence under colonial imperialism in World War II Barbados. . . . With its major emphasis on education and childhood, *Growing Up Stupid Under the Union Jack* continues to draw attention to one of the chief preoccupations of the anti-colonial Anglo-Caribbean novel," writes Robert P. Smith in *World Literature Today.* The theme is well rendered in what Darryl Pinckney calls in the *New York Review of Books* Clarke's "tender, funny, unpolemical style."

Clarke's best known work is a trilogy detailing the lives of the Barbadan blacks who immigrate to Toronto hoping to better their lot. In these novels, *The Meeting point, Storm of Fortune,* and *The Bigger Light,* "it is as if the flat characters of a Dickensian world have come into their own at last, playing their tragicomic roles in a manner which owes much to Clarke's extraordinary facility with the Barbadian dialect," writes Diane Bessai in *Canadian Literature.* Bessai also expresses eagerness for Clarke to "continue to create his Brueghel-like canvasses with their rich and contrasting detail and mood." "The sense of defeat among the poor islanders is enlivened by the humour of the characters and their glowing fantasies about the presumed wealth of relatives and friends who make it big in the fatlands of the United States or Canada," writes John Ayre in *Saturday Night.*

The first two novels dwell mostly on Bernice Leach, a live-in maid at a wealthy Toronto home, and her small circle of fellow immigrants. Martin Levin writes in the *New York Times Book Review:* "Mr. Clarke is masterful at delineating the oppressive insecurities of Bernice and her friends, and the claustrophobic atmosphere that envelops such a mini-minority" as the Caribbean blacks in Toronto. The third novel, *The Bigger Light,* explores the life of Boysie, the most successful of this immigrant group, and his wife, Dots. Boysie has at last realized the dream that compelled him to leave Barbados; he owns a prosperous business and his own home. However, in the process of realizing his goals, he has become alienated from his wife and his community. Now he searches for a greater meaning to his life—a "bigger light." "*The Bigger Light* is a painful book to read," writes David Rosenthal in the *Nation.* It is "a story of two people with many things to say and no one to say them to, who hate themselves and bitterly resent the society around them. . . . Certain African novelists have also dealt with the isolation of self-made blacks, but none with Clarke's bleak intensity." A *New Yorker* writer praises the book further, citing Clarke's strong writing skill as the element that lifts the book beyond social comment: "the universal longings or ordinary human beings are depicted with a simplicity and power that make us grateful for all three volumes of this long and honest record."

BIOGRAPHICAL/CRITICAL SOURCES:

BOOKS

Brown, Lloyd, *El Dorado and Paradise; A Critical Study of the Works of Austin Clarke,* Center for Social and Humanistic Studies, University of Western Ontario, 1989.
Contemporary Literary Criticism, Volume 8, Gale, 1978.

PERIODICALS

Canadian Literature, summer, 1974.
Listener, June 15, 1978.
Nation, November 1, 1975.

New Yorker, February 24, 1975.
New York Review of Books, May 27, 1982.
New York Times Book Review, April 9, 1972; December 9, 1973; February 16, 1975.
Saturday Night, October, 1971; June, 1975.
World Literature Today, winter, 1982.

*   *   *

CLARKE-STEWART, K(athleen) Alison 1943-

PERSONAL: Born September 25, 1943, in Summerland, British Columbia, Canada; came to the United States in 1966; daughter of William Clarke (a teacher) and Maebelle (McIntosh) Wilkin; divorced; children: Christopher. *Education:* University of British Columbia, B.A., 1965, M.A., 1967; Yale University, Ph.D., 1972.

ADDRESSES: Home—2125 Temple Hills Dr., Laguna Beach, CA 92651. *Office*—Department of Social Ecology, University of California, Irvine, CA 92717.

CAREER: Yale University, New Haven, CT, research associate, 1971-73; University of Chicago, Chicago, IL, assistant professor, 1974-79, associate professor of education and human development, 1979-83, director of early childhood education program, 1974-76; University of California, Irvine, professor of social ecology, 1983—.

MEMBER: Society for Research in Child Development, American Psychological Association, National Association for the Education of Young Children.

WRITINGS:

(With Greta Fein) *Daycare in Context,* Wiley, 1972.
Childcare in the Family, Academic Press, 1977.
(Editor with Joseph Glick) *The Development of Social Understanding,* Gardner Press, 1978.
Daycare, Harvard University Press, 1982.
(With Joanne Koch) *Children: Development through Adolescence,* Wiley, 1983.
(With Susan Friedman) *Development: Infancy through Adolescence,* Wiley, 1987.
(With Friedman and Marion Perlmutter) *Lifelong Human Development,* Wiley, 1989.

Contributor to psychology and education journals.

WORK IN PROGRESS: Research on the effects of divorce and various custodial arrangements on children and families; research on children's eyewitness testimony; research on infant daycare.

SIDELIGHTS: K. Alison Clarke-Stewart told *CA:* "My writing has focused on aspects of child development for both scholarly and lay audiences, although every now and then I think my place in life's soap opera would make more interesting reading (and writing). In my work I try to address issues that are of real and practical concern to parents and those who work with children, as well as being of some academic interest. It is important to me to bridge the gap between ivory tower and real world."

*   *   *

COFER, Judith Ortiz 1952-

PERSONAL: Born February 24, 1952, in Hormigueros, P.R.; immigrated to United States, 1956; daughter of J. M. (in U.S. Navy) and Fanny (Morot) Ortiz; married Charles John Cofer (in business), November 13, 1971; children: Tanya. *Education:* Augusta College, B.A., 1974; Florida Atlantic University, M.A., 1977; attended Oxford University, 1977.

ADDRESSES: P.O. Box 938, Louisville, Ga. 30434. *Office*— Mercer University College, Forsyth, Ga. 31029. *Agent*— Berenice Hoffman Literary Agency, 215 West 75th St., New York, N.Y. 10023.

CAREER: Bilingual teacher at public schools in Palm Beach County, Fla., 1974-75; Broward Community College, Fort Lauderdale, Fla., adjunct instructor in English, 1978-80, instructor in Spanish, 1979; University of Miami, Coral Gables, Fla., lecturer in English, 1980-84; University of Georgia, Athens, instructor in English, 1984-87, Georgia Center for Continuing Education, instructor in English, 1987-88; Macon College, instructor in English, 1988-89; Mercer University College, Forsyth, Ga., special programs coordinator, 1990. Adjunct instructor at Palm Beach Junior College, 1978-80. Conducts poetry workshops and gives poetry readings. Member of regular staff of International Conference on the Fantastic in Literature, 1979-82; member of literature panel of Fine Arts Council of Florida, 1982; member of administrative staff of Bread Loaf Writers' Conference, 1983 and 1984.

MEMBER: Poetry Society of America, Poets and Writers, Associated Writing Programs.

AWARDS, HONORS: Scholar of English Speaking Union at Oxford University, 1977; fellow of Fine Arts Council of Florida, 1980; Bread Loaf Writers' Conference, scholar, 1981, John Atherton Scholar in Poetry, 1982; grant from Witter Bynner Foundation for Poetry, 1988, for *Letters From a Caribbean Island;* National Endowment for the Arts fellowship in poetry, 1989.

WRITINGS:

Latin Women Pray (chapbook), Florida Arts Gazette Press, 1980.
The Native Dancer (chapbook), Pteranodon Press, 1981.
Among the Ancestors (chapbook), Louisville News Press, 1981.
"Latin Women Pray" (three-act play), first produced in Atlanta at Georgia State University, June, 1984.
Peregrina (poems), Riverstone Press, 1986.
Terms of Survival (poems), Arte Público, 1987.
(Contributor) *Triple Crown: Chicano, Puerto Rican and Cuban American Poetry* (trilogy; contains Cofer's poetry collection *Reaching for the Mainland*), Bilingual Press, 1987.
The Line of the Sun (novel), University of Georgia Press, 1989.
Silent Dancing (personal essays), Arte Público, 1990.

Also author of the poetry collection *Letters From a Caribbean Island.* Work represented in anthologies, including *Hispanics in the U.S.,* Bilingual Review/Press, 1982; *Latina Writers; Revista Chicano-Riqueña;* and *Heath Anthology of Modern American Literature.* Contributor of poems to magazines, including *Southern Humanities Review, Poem, Prairie Schooner, Apalachee Quarterly, Kansas Quarterly,* and *Kalliope.* Poetry editor of *Florida Arts Gazette,* 1978-81; member of editorial board of *Waves.*

SIDELIGHTS: An accomplished author of several books of poetry in the early 1980s, Judith Ortiz Cofer garnered praise for the poetic quality of her first novel, *The Line of the Sun,* published in 1989. Writing in the *New York Times Book Review,* Roberto Márquez commended the "vigorous elegance" of the novel's language and called Cofer "a prose writer of evocatively lyrical authority, a novelist of historical compass and sensitivity." The first half of *Line of the Sun* depicts the poor village of Salud, Puerto Rico, and introduces the characters Rafael Vivente and his wild brother-in-law, Guzmán. *Los Angeles Times Book Review* contributor Sonja Bolle noted that the author's eye for detail "brings alive the stifling and magical world of village life." The second part of the novel follows Rafael to Paterson, New Jersey, where his daughter Marisol, the story's narrator, grows up. Marisol's father encourages her to become wholly American, but her mother advises her to adopt the customs and values of Puerto Rico. Marisol learns about her heritage mainly through the stories told by her family, which often focus on her Uncle Guzmán, the "demon child"; his arrival at her New Jersey home helps Marisol to balance the American and Puerto Rican aspects of her identity. Though Márquez criticized parts of the plot as contrived, he proclaimed Cofer as "a writer of authentic gifts, with a genuine and important story to tell."

Cofer told *CA:* "The 'infinite variety' and power of language interest me. I never cease to experiment with it. As a native Puerto Rican, my first language was Spanish. It was a challenge, not only to learn English, but to master it enough to teach it and— the ultimate goal—to write poetry in it.

"My family is one of the main topics of my poetry; the ones left behind on the island of Puerto Rico, and the ones who came to the United States. In tracing their lives, I discover more about mine. The place of birth itself becomes a metaphor for the things we all must leave behind; the assimilation of a new culture is the coming into maturity by accepting the terms necessary for survival. My poetry is a study of this process of change, assimilation, and transformation."

BIOGRAPHICAL/CRITICAL SOURCES:

PERIODICALS

Los Angeles Times Book Review, August 6, 1989.
New York Times Book Review, September 24, 1989.

*　　*　　*

COHN, Ruby 1922-

PERSONAL: Born August 13, 1922, in Columbia, OH. *Education:* Hunter College (now of the City University of New York), B.A., 1942; University of Paris, D.Univ., 1952; Washington University, St. Louis, MO, Ph.D., 1960.

ADDRESSES: Office—Department of Dramatic Art, University of California, Davis, CA 95616.

CAREER: University of California, lecturer in English, 1960-61; San Francisco State College, San Francisco, CA, 1961-70, began as assistant professor, became associate professor and professor of English and world literature; California Institute of the Arts, Valencia, fellow, 1970-72; University of California, Davis, professor of comparative drama, 1972—.

MEMBER: Modern Language Association of America, American Comparative Literature Association.

AWARDS, HONORS: Guggenheim fellow, 1965-66.

WRITINGS:

Samuel Beckett: The Comic Gamut, Rutgers University Press, 1962.
(Editor) *Moonlight Monologues,* Macmillan, 1963.
A Casebook on Waiting for Godot, Grove, 1967.
Edward Albee (pamphlet), University of Minnesota Press, 1969.
(Editor) *Classics for Contemporaries,* Indiana University Press, 1969.
Currents in Contemporary Drama, Indiana University Press, 1969.

Dialogue in American Drama, Indiana University Press, 1971.
Back to Beckett, Princeton University Press, 1973.
Modern Shakespeare Offshoots, Princeton University Press, 1976.
Just Play: The Theater of Samuel Beckett, Princeton University Press, 1979.
New American Dramatists, 1960-1980, Grove, 1982.
(Editor) *Disjecta: Miscellaneous Writings and a Dramatic Fragment,* John Calder, 1983, Grove, 1984.
From Desire to Godot: Pocket Theater of Post-War Paris, University of California Press, 1987.
Samuel Beckett, Macmillan, 1987.

BIOGRAPHICAL/CRITICAL SOURCES:

PERIODICALS

Books, autumn, 1970.
Times Literary Supplement, November 7, 1980; December 3, 1982; February 10, 1984.

*　　*　　*

COLES, Robert (Martin) 1929-

PERSONAL: Born October 12, 1929, in Boston, MA; son of Philip Winston (an engineer) and Sandra (Young) Coles; married Jane Hallowell (a teacher), July 4, 1960; children: Robert Emmet, Daniel Agee, Michael Hallowell. *Education:* Harvard University, A.B., 1950; Columbia University, M.D., 1954. *Politics:* Independent. *Religion:* Episcopalian. *Avocational interests:* Tennis, skiing.

ADDRESSES: Home—P.O. Box 674, Concord, MA 01742. *Office*—Harvard University Health Services, 75 Mt. Auburn St., Cambridge, MA 02138.

CAREER: University of Chicago clinics, Chicago, IL, intern, 1954-55; Massachusetts General Hospital, Boston, resident in psychiatry, 1955-56; McLean Hospital, Belmont, MA, resident in psychiatry, 1956-57; Judge Baker Guidance Center— Children's Hospital, Roxbury, MA, resident, 1957-58, fellow in child psychiatry, 1960-61; Massachusetts General Hospital, Boston, member of psychiatric staff, 1960-62; Harvard University Medical School, Cambridge, MA, clinical assistant in psychiatry, 1960-62, research psychiatrist, 1963—, lecturer in general education, 1966—, professor of psychiatry and medical humanities, 1978—. Writer, 1966—.

Member of alcoholism clinic staff, Massachusetts General Hospital, 1957-58; supervisor in children's unit, Metropolitan State Hospital, Boston, 1957-58; psychiatric consultant, Lancaster Industrial School for Girls, Lancaster, MA, 1960-62; research psychiatrist, Southern Regional Council, Atlanta, GA, 1961-63. Consultant to Ford Foundation, Southern Regional Council, and Appalachian Volunteers. Member of board of trustees, Robert F. Kennedy Memorial. Member of board of Field Foundation, Institute of Current World Affairs, Reading is Fundamental, American Freedom from Hunger Foundation, National Rural Housing Coalition, Twentieth Century Fund, National Sharecroppers Fund, Lyndhurst Foundation, and National Advisory Committee on Farm Labor. *Military service:* U.S. Air Force, 1958-60; chief of neuropsychiatric service, Keesler Air Force Base, Biloxi, Miss.

MEMBER: American Psychiatric Association, American Orthopsychiatric Association, Group for the Advancement of Psychiatry, American Academy of Arts and Sciences (fellow), Phi Beta Kappa, Harvard Club (New York and Boston).

AWARDS, HONORS: Atlantic grant, 1965, in support of work on *Children of Crisis;* National Educational Television award, 1966, for individual contribution to outstanding programming; Family Life Book Award from Child Study Association of America, Ralph Waldo Emerson Award from Phi Beta Kappa, Anisfeld-Wolf Award in Race Relations from *Saturday Review,* Four Freedoms Award from B'nai B'rith, and *Parents' Magazine* medal, all 1968, all for *Children of Crisis;* Hofheimer Prize for research from American Psychiatric Association, 1968; Pulitzer Prize, 1973, for Volumes II and III of *Children of Crisis;* McAlpin Award from National Association of Mental Health, 1973; MacArthur Foundation fellowship, 1981-86; Sarah Josepha Hale Award from Friends of the Richard Library, Newport, NH, 1986; Robert F. Kennedy Book Award honorable mention citation, 1987, for *The Political Life of Children.*

WRITINGS:

Children of Crisis, Little, Brown, Volume 1: *A Study in Courage and Fear,* 1967, Volume 2: *Migrants, Sharecroppers, Mountaineers,* 1971, Volume 3: *The South Goes North,* 1971, Volume 4: *Eskimos, Chicanos, Indians,* 1978, Volume 5: *Privileged Ones: The Well-Off and the Rich in America,* 1978.
Dead End School, illustrated by Norman Rockwell, Little, Brown, 1968.
Still Hungry in America, with introduction by Edward M. Kennedy, World Publishing, 1969.
The Grass Pipe (juvenile), Little, Brown, 1969.
The Image Is You, Houghton, 1969.
(With Maria W. Piers) *The Wages of Neglect,* Quadrangle, 1969.
Uprooted Children: The Early Lives of Migrant Farmers (Horace Mann lecture, 1969), University of Pittsburgh Press, 1970.
(With Joseph H. Brenner and Dermot Meagher) *Drugs and Youth: Medical, Psychiatric, and Legal Facts,* Liveright, 1970.
Erik H. Erikson: The Growth of His Work, Little, Brown, 1970, reprinted, Da Capo, 1987.
The Middle Americans (photographs by Jon Erikson), Little, Brown, 1971.
(With Daniel Berrigan) *The Geography of Faith,* Beacon Press, 1971.
Saving Face, Little, Brown, 1972.
(Editor with Jerome Kagan) *Twelve to Sixteen: Early Adolescence* (essays), Norton, 1972.
Farewell to the South, Little, Brown, 1972.
A Spectacle unto World, Viking, 1973.
Riding Free, Atlantic-Little, Brown, 1973.
The Old Ones of New Mexico, University of New Mexico Press, 1973, reprinted, Harcourt, 1984.
Doris Ulmann: The Darkness and the Light, Aperture, 1974.
The Buses Roll, Norton, 1974.
Irony in the Mind's Life: Essays on Novels by James Agee, Elizabeth Bowen and George Eliot, University of Virginia Press, 1974.
Headsparks, Little, Brown, 1975.
William Carlos Williams: The Knack of Survival in America, Rutgers University Press, 1975.
Mind's Fate: Ways of Seeing Psychiatry and Psychoanalysis, Little, Brown, 1975.
A Festering Sweetness: Poems of American People, University of Pittsburgh Press, 1978.
(With wife, Jane Hallowell Coles) *Women of Crisis,* Delacorte, Volume 1: *Lives of Struggle and Hope,* 1978, Volume 2: *Lives of Work and Dreams,* 1980.
The Last and First Eskimos, New York Graphic Society, 1978.

Walker Percy: An American Search, Atlantic-Little, Brown, 1978.
Flannery O'Conner's South, Louisiana State University Press, 1980.
Dorothea Lange: Photographs of a Lifetime, Aperture, 1982.
(Editor) William Carlos Williams, *The Doctor Stories,* New Directions, 1984.
(With Geoffrey Stokes) *Sex & the American Teenager,* Harper, 1985.
The Moral Life of Children, Atlantic Monthly Press, 1986.
The Political Life of Children, Atlantic Monthly Press, 1986.
Simone Weil: A Modern Pilgrimage, Addison-Wesley, 1987.
Dorothy Day: A Radical Devotion, Addison-Wesley, 1987.
Harvard Diary: Reflection on the Sacred & the Secular, Crossroad, 1988.
The Red Wheelbarrow: Selected Literary Essays, University of Iowa Press, 1988.
Times of Surrender: Selected Essays, University of Iowa Press, 1988.
Learning by Example: Stories and the Moral Imagination, Houghton, 1989.
Rumors of Separate Worlds (poems), University of Iowa Press, 1989.
The Spiritual Life of Children, Houghton, 1990.

CONTRIBUTOR

Charles Rolo, editor, *Psychiatry in American Life,* Little, Brown, 1963.
Erik H. Erikson, editor, *Youth: Change and Challenge,* Basic Books, 1963.
Talcott Parsons and Kenneth Clark, editors, *The Negro American,* Houghton, 1966.
Jules Masserman, editor, *Science and Psychoanalysis,* Volume 9, Grune, 1966.
James L. Sundquist, *On Fighting Poverty,* Basic Books, 1969.
Philip Kelley and Ronald Hudson, editors, *Diary by E. B. B: The Unpublished Diary of Elizabeth Barrett Browning, 1831-1832,* Ohio University Press, 1969.
John H. Fandberg, editor, *Introduction to the Behavioral Sciences,* Holt, 1969.
Ross Spears and Jude Cassidy, *Agee: His Life Remembered,* Holt, 1985.
Helen Levitt, *In the Street: Chalk Drawings and Messages, New York City, 1938-1948,* Duke University Press, 1987.

AUTHOR OF INTRODUCTION

Barbara Field Bensiger, *The Prison of My Mind,* Walker & Co., 1969.
What Is a City?: A Multi-Media Guide on Urban Living, Boston Public Library, 1969.
A Letter to a Teacher, Random House, 1970.
Susan Sheehan, *Is There No Place on Earth for Me?,* Random House, 1983.

OTHER

Contributor to numerous periodicals and professional journals, including *Atlantic Monthly, New Yorker, New Republic, New York Review of Books, Book Week, Partisan Review, Harper's, Saturday Review, New York Times Book Review, Yale Review, American Journal of Psychiatry,* and *Commonweal.* Contributing editor, *New Republic,* 1966—; member of editorial board, *American Scholar,* 1968—, *Contemporary Psychoanalysis,* 1969-70, and *Child Psychiatry and Human Development,* 1969—.

SIDELIGHTS: Robert Coles has spent his professional life exploring and illuminating the inner world of children. His numerous works on child psychology include the Pulitzer Prize-winning series *Children in Crisis,* a study of childhood development under stressful circumstances. Coles was trained as a psychiatrist, but he tempers his scientific conclusions with humanism, recognizing and celebrating the individual within the group or the trend. As Jonathan Kellerman puts it in the *Los Angeles Times Book Review,* the author "has seemingly ignored the delineation between the academic and the popular, producing books that are scholarly, yet accessible, writing with warmth, clarity and grace that set him apart in a field notorious for jargon-laden puffery."

A native of the Boston area, Coles attended college at Harvard University. As an undergraduate he came under the influence of several notable scholars, chief among them physician-poet William Carlos Williams. The association with Williams proved momentous for Coles—the young student decided to go to medical school and take training as a doctor, just as Williams had. Coles received his medical education at Columbia University, specializing in child psychiatry, and the studies he undertook in the early 1960s began to reflect his thorough grounding in literature and the humanities. *New York Times Book Review* correspondent Helen Bevington writes that Coles "reminds one of Williams, with the same moral imagination, the kindness and compassion—though without the truculent manner, the toughness, the profanity, the anger, the scorn of intellectuals that marked the man he came to revere." Bevington continues: "The main lesson Williams the doctor taught [Coles] was always to listen to his patient, not only listen to his story but confide to him one's own, since only through stories can one person fully enter another's life. Slowly . . . Dr. Coles learned to let the patient be the teacher, without hurrying to a diagnosis."

Coles's monumental *Children of Crisis* series evolved from events the author witnessed in the deep South during the first tense moments of integration in the early 1960s. He was astounded by the courage some black children showed as they entered integrated schools through crowds of jeering, hostile adults. Volume I of *Children in Crisis, A Study in Courage and Fear,* documents the feelings of these black youngsters as they face threats and insults. The work was hailed as a sensitive portrayal of the effects of discrimination on its youngest victims. Coles followed this study with similar ones on migrant workers, Eskimos and Indians, Appalachian children, and children of the wealthy. "What I do," he told an audience in Chicago, "is listen to children and try to make sense of the various contradictions and inconsistencies, the struggles for coherence."

As an author, Coles departs from standard academic practice by allowing his subjects to tell their own stories and by listening to them over many years as their circumstances change. In the *New York Times Book Review,* Neil Postman remarks that Coles "is to the stories that children have to tell what Homer was to the tale of the Trojan War. . . . He is at his best when he is listening to children talk, recording their talk and then transforming their talk into a kind of narrative poetry." Coles's books, Postman adds, are "a major contribution to our understanding of how children become socialized. . . . But these books, like the 'Iliad,' are not about conclusions. They are about the myths, prejudices, worries and observations from which children generate their opinions and loyalties."

Coles's work on the *Children of Crisis* series and other studies in child psychology earned him a prestigious MacArthur fellowship in 1981. The fellowship provided a monthly stipend that allowed Coles to undertake his research on an international basis. In 1986 he released two books, *The Political Life of Children* and *The Moral Life of Children,* that drew on interviews in South Africa, Brazil, Northern Ireland, Poland, Southeast Asia, Nicaragua, French-speaking Canada, and a number of American locales. In her review of both works, *Washington Post Book World* contributor Katherine Paterson writes: "Children tend not to say what we want to hear when we want to hear it, but, to the patient, perceptive adult who takes them seriously, their words are eloquent, disturbing, transforming. Most of us are not good listeners, but the moral and political life of our nation would take a giant leap forward if we were to pay close attention to this man who is."

The MacArthur fellowship also allowed Coles to pursue other interests, including biographies of Dorothy Day and Simone Weil, essays, book reviews, lectures, and literary criticism. In the *Times Literary Supplement,* Iain Bamforth commends Coles for his "conviction that appreciation of literature is a useful adjunct to the study of medicine." Coles, adds the critic, "lends a cautionary voice to what is otherwise understated or overlooked in a profession which tends, like many others, to talk only to itself." *National Review* contributor Thomas Molnar likewise concludes that in his essays Coles "leaves the reader with the impression of a decent and religious man with common-sensical views."

Coles is professor of psychiatry and medical humanities at Harvard University. His curriculum includes literature classes for students of medicine, law, and architecture. In fact, writes Fitzhugh Mullan in the *Washington Post Book World,* the most consistent theme in Coles's work "is the importance of the humanities in our lives." The reviewer continues: "It is literature in all its forms, the interview, the child's story, the poem and the novel—that preoccupies Coles [because] . . . it is the humanities that recognize the individual and resist the tendency toward the average that is celebrated by statisticians." Kellerman concludes that in his own writings, Coles has blended scientific inquiry and literary form to great effect. Kellerman calls the author "a master chronicler, providing few answers but asking his questions so eloquently that his writings emerge as classic portrayals of social upheaval and its effect upon the young."

CA INTERVIEW

CA interviewed Robert Coles by telephone on June 17, 1989, at his home in Concord, Massachusetts.

CA: Before you began writing about and through the voices of children in the 1960s, you were a child psychiatrist. Before that, you gave pediatric medicine a try. Can you say where your concern for children came from, and when you knew you wanted to work with them?

COLES: I think it's fair to say that I decided to become a doctor because I became very much involved with William Carlos Williams. I wrote my thesis on the first two books of *Paterson,* and what started out as a college student's intellectual interest became a very important element in my entire life. I got to meet Dr. Williams and he was very kind to me, and very stimulating and provocative to know as a person. That relationship began to shape my professional life. Before I met him, I had thought of becoming a high school English teacher or perhaps studying some combination of literature and religion, because I had been very much influenced also in college by Perry Miller, who taught English and American literature at Harvard College and was my tutor and my thesis supervisor.

It was because of Dr. Williams that I began to think of medicine. He had taken training in pediatrics himself and has written about some of his work with children in the "Doctor Stories," which I eventually pulled together; they were published in 1984. Those are the lines of my interest: getting acquainted with a particular writer who also happened to be a pediatrician and an old-fashioned general practitioner, and becoming so involved with him that my own interests began to echo his.

As a psychiatrist and a psychoanalyst I suppose I must have had some earlier interest in children; probably that comes from my own life and its particular struggles and aspirations and conflicts. But to my conscious knowledge I had no great interest in either medicine or pediatrics until I met Dr. Williams and had an opportunity to see him with his patients in the last years of his practice, and to learn from him how much medicine can give both moral and intellectual shape to a particular life. He's constantly alive in my mind; I have pictures of him that I continue to look at, and I think of him so often when I'm with children, remembering the way he was with them. When I lecture on him to my Harvard College students, I try not only to give them some intellectual information, but to convey to them what kind of a person he was and even to show them how he practiced. Oftentimes he would plunk himself down on the floor with kids; he'd pull out candy bars and talk with them and learn from them in a certain way that even now strikes me as remarkable.

CA: You're best known for the Children of Crisis *series that began with the publication of* Study in Courage and Fear *in 1967. One of your first challenges in that work was getting children and their families to trust you enough to talk to you. How much methodology did you have at the start for the talks and for the later handling and shaping of your material?*

COLES: To tell you the truth, none. I'm not a great one for the word *methodology.* What I really had was a desire to get to know these children and their parents. I also had by my side a wife who is a high school English teacher and who comes from an old New England abolitionist family; I think her determination and her insistence that this work be done were the enabling factors. And her bravery—I would use that word, because at times this was not easy work to do in the violence of the early 1960s in the South. I think too that her personality made the work possible. She was the one who got along with those mothers in a way that gave them some sense of trust in us, and it was her ability to approach the children as a warm and spirited and affectionate human being that enabled me to get out of my professional shell. By that time I had learned to be a physician and pediatrician and child psychiatrist; I was pretty uptight and austere, loaded down in my head with social science and psychiatric jargon and with notions of how a doctor ought to be that were not going to be very helpful in the kind of work we were doing. I think the whole effort would have fallen flat on its face if my wife hadn't taken on as a project to wean me away from a certain kind of professional decorum, if not arrogance. I'm not going to say she's totally weaned me away from it; I'm afraid arrogance is part of all too many of our lives. But certainly she got me to relax and take off my necktie and sit on the floor with people, to eat with them and watch television with them and become part of their lives.

There is a picture of me with Ruby Bridges that my wife took with her Brownie camera when we started this work almost thirty years ago. Ruby is one of the first children I met—a six-year-old black child who was a mentor of mine and whose story I'm always telling. The picture shows me sitting with Ruby in the first weeks of our acquaintance, and in that sweltering, humid New Orleans weather, I'm wearing a jacket and a tie. It took a month or two to get me away from that, and a year or two to get me away from it in a more fundamental psychological way. If I were to try to get intellectual about this, I would say that I was moving away from a strictly psychoanalytic methodology to a more phenomenological one in which I was simply trying to be amidst events and let them in their own ways teach me and perhaps give me a kind of language for apprehending them. But this is getting pretty heavy!

CA: But relevant, because that last statement tells so much about what's given in the books: not a clinical treatment, but a presentation of what people were living through and how they talked about it.

COLES: Exactly. And in a sense, I think what I slowly began to learn was that my task was to be a mediator of sorts between two worlds—a translator, I've been called, correctly, and also maybe a storyteller. Instead of being the social science theorist or the psychoanalytic clinician, I think I became the one who listens to what is happening in the lives of people, listens to their stories as they're told, and then relates those stories to others as best he can as a writer. That requires a whole shift in one's sense of one's occupation. It hasn't been totally possible for me to make that shift; I teach at a medical school as well as a college, and I still work as a child psychiatrist and as a physician. But the primary intent of the *Children of Crisis* series—and of the two recent books that I consider part of that series, *The Moral Life of Children* and *The Political Life of Children*—is to convey to the ordinary reader some sense of the way children think and feel by conveying the stories they have to tell.

There again the methodology was deeply informed by my wife, who teaches English to high-schoolers, and by a novelist I met when I was working in Georgia, Margaret Long, who at the time was working for the Southern Regional Council, a group of white and black Southerners trying to change things in the region in the difficult period of the fifties, sixties, and seventies. Maggie Long, who had written several novels and was also a journalist, kept on pushing me to talk about these children in a way that a novelist would—to tell their stories rather than try to extricate from their lives certain information which would then be tucked into large-scale theoretical formulations. She taught me to approach lives as a listener does, and then as a storyteller does, rather than as "material" for social science generalizations.

CA: You've said previously that at least one medical colleague made the criticism that children don't talk the way you have them speaking in your books. Would you comment on your philosophy and your practice in reproducing their speech?

COLES: I've tried to pull together what I've heard so that what I present to the reader is a significant or interesting story. When you start seeing children and talking to them, even for several hours, they aren't going to say things the way I have them speaking in my books. But I listen to particular children sometimes for as long as five or six years, to the recurrent themes and topics that they bring up; and I keep recording, either with a tape recorder or in notes, what they have to say. Then my job becomes one of pulling together many conversations and remarks into a rather limited presentation in the pages of what becomes a book. It's a distillation and a condensation, a "reading" of a particular life through an examination of the spoken words—and of the pictures drawn or painted.

This is why, when I take on a project such as learning about how children develop their moral values, or learning, as I'm now doing, what their religious and spiritual lives are like, I can start at the beginning of a decade and only finish at the end of the decade. Some people read a particular section of the *Children of Crisis* series and say, "Well, I never heard a child talk like that." Of course children don't generally talk like that—although, if you listen to them over the years, you'll hear them say those words and come up with those thoughts. And if you pull together remarks that people have made over time, you can get a more rounded, dramatic, and convincing statement of what they have to say than if you listen to them only once or twice. This principle applies to novels and short stories too. People don't always talk in real life the way they talk in fiction. What a novelist does is try to highlight a certain moment. That's what I try to do too, so I pick those remarks of the children that I think are most convincing, or illustrative of certain themes, or dramatic or provocative.

CA: The voices have a great dignity that I like to think truly reflects the children.

COLES: That's what I try to do. It's an interaction between them and me, and I think I'm looking for that "dignity" in them and trying to evoke it. I'm trying to be as suggestive as I can in the selections I come up with so that the reader can glimpse something about some kind of essence in a particular child, something of a quintessential psychological and moral and even spiritual "reality" in that child.

CA: In The Call of Stories *you wrote about the value of books, stories, in all aspects of life. You've taken a responsibility for promoting your views by teaching "Literature and Medicine" in the Harvard Medical School and other courses in other professional curricula. What sort of effects have you seen on students of these courses?*

COLES: I'm hardly an objective person to answer that, but my feeling is that those novels and short stories and poems that I teach really reach the students in a way that I find very satisfying and at times even awe-inspiring. They are touched by what the writers have had to say, and touched in such a way that their lives, so they report to me, are at times changed or influenced. It's a great and lovely privilege to be able to go to medical students or law students or business students or undergraduates with William Carlos Williams's poetry, Tolstoy's stories, or Raymond Carver's or Tillie Olsen's or Flannery O'Connor's, and to teach them not so much analytically or with an emphasis on some of the abstract qualities that literary critics want to emphasize, but as stories, as moral moments conveyed through the suggestive power of language. After all, we are the creature on this planet who wants to make sense of life. We are the creature who tells stories and craves stories. I don't in any way dispute the value of teaching such classics as *Middlemarch* or *Anna Karenina* through an analysis of symbols or choice of language, or through the historical approach, to connect those particular novels to other novels as part of a literary and intellectual tradition. But I'd also like to say that those stories can have a tremendous moral and emotional impact on readers, and it's wonderful to connect readers to them who are college students or students in professional schools.

I teach an undergraduate course called "A Literature of Social Reflection," in which I use novelists and short story writers and poets, and a course in Harvard Medical School doing the same. I teach a course at Harvard Law School called "Dickens and the Law," because the law figures prominently in several of his novels; we read them and think about what Dickens is telling us

about the moral opportunities and hazards that particular profession offers its practitioners. In Harvard Business School I've taught a course in which we use F. Scott Fitzgerald, John Cheever, Walker Percy, Saul Bellow, and William Carlos Williams and his *Stecher Trilogy,* the three novels that he wrote to portray the rise of an immigrant family to wealth and position. We use those novels as a means of getting students to stop and think about this life.

CA: Blacks have without question made real political and social gains since the 1950s, but there seems to be a great deal of tension now between the races on an everyday level, at least here in the South. Do you see such tension, and, if so, do you have any feelings about its causes?

COLES: I agree, although I think the tensions are now worse in the North than in the South. The South has always been known for those tensions between the races, but it's interesting that blacks are now voting with their feet, so to speak: more of them return to the South than leave it. That's been going on for several years. Yes, I think the tensions persist, but they're a bit different from when I began recording them in the South in the sixties and in the North in the seventies, which is what I tried to do during those two decades. The blacks now can vote and go to movies and restaurants on an equal basis, and I think the present tensions are a result of their struggles for that ultimate access of economic and social equality, or at least economic and social opportunity of a kind that wasn't possible for them even in their dreams in the fifties and early sixties. The struggles now are a continuation of old struggles, but at a different level, with different goals in mind.

We have to have a little historical perspective on this. It was only twenty-five years ago, just a generation ago, that blacks were struggling very, very hard to get the vote, and twenty-five years ago when blacks were few and far between in our Northern colleges and universities and utterly segregated from our intellectual and social life in the North, never mind the South. What we're seeing now is the increased presence of blacks in our intellectual and social and political life, and their equality there is only to be attained, it seems, with continued struggles. But I don't think I'm just becoming an old Tory when I say that things really have changed a lot in this country, and for the better; and I think the country ought to be proud of that despite the tensions which persist. The tensions are evidence of continued progress, in my mind.

On the other hand, one has to say that in some of our cities there are ghettos which present to the people in them and to all of us a major social problem and, I would say, a major moral problem, because many of the families in those urban regions are disorganized and adrift and cut off from so much that the nation can offer. I see those problems not only as economic problems, and as racial problems to a certain extent, but as moral problems and family problems of a deep and disturbing nature. I think the children in such neighborhoods are in desperate need not only of the social and economic and political supports that many of their advocates insist upon, but of a moral and spiritual life that they don't have now, that is the only thing that can help give them a certain kind of strength they otherwise will lack.

CA: From your observation of young people today, what do you consider their biggest obstacles to growing up whole?

COLES: What I was just talking about: moral and spiritual gaps in their lives, a kind of emptiness that is all too sad to behold.

And what I've said about the ghettos, by the way, I wouldn't want to completely disconnect in significance from some of the middle-class neighborhoods of this country. I have come to know in the course of my work many young people growing up in very affluent white neighborhoods who are struggling with their own kinds of moral and spiritual problems. They don't know what they believe in; they don't know what they want to do in life; they are all too vulnerable to their own self-centeredness and greed and indifference to others. In that sense I very much go along with what the historian and social critic Christopher Lasch tried to say when he wrote *The Culture of Narcissism,* that there is a kind of crass egoism and materialism that too many of us in the higher realms of the society are susceptible to. And our children, of course, pick up on that and are influenced by it.

People like me in child and adolescent psychiatry are kept all too busy in this country, and what's asked of us, I don't think we have to offer. What's asked of us is a kind of moral leadership that we are not the ones to offer. We're trying to help people who have certain family and personal difficulties in a secular society which has turned significantly away from religious and spiritual life, a society whose politics has become so degraded and whose business and academic and even religious life has become so injured by scandals in recent years that it's very hard for people to find the kind of moral guidance they want, and often they turn to doctors.

CA: And it's hard for parents under the best of conditions to instill values in their children—and to make them stick through the teen years.

COLES: It's very hard, but one of the tasks of parents of teenagers—and I speak as a father whose youngest one has just gone off to college, so I'm a recent survivor—is to stand up for certain values with one's teen-age children, even at the risk of some pain and tension. You hope the tension will ease, and you hope that in a way they want and need for you to stand up for these matters, that they need the "resistance" they get from parents, even when they say they don't.

CA: In the early days you often described yourself as an agnostic, but you've come more and more to talk about religion in a personal sense, about God, about grace. Would you comment on your current religious beliefs and how they've evolved?

COLES: When I described myself as an agnostic, I was referring to the fact that I was brought up in the secular, agnostic world of contemporary psychoanalytic psychiatry and liberal politics, which was the world that I was deeply immersed in when I was a young doctor and when I started this work in the civil rights movement in the early sixties. But there's been a part of me that has always been involved in religion. After all, I was studying it in college with Perry Miller, whose work included the study of the Puritan divines of New England. I've always been very much interested in religious matters. When I was in college, I used to go to church even though I didn't much believe then in what I was hearing. When I was in medical school, I was a member of a Bible study group—and there were only three of us in the whole school who were! I used to sneak off to Union Theological Seminary and take courses. And, very important, I worked in the Catholic Worker Hospitality House that Dorothy Day had set up years before I came to it. I got to know her and she was a very important figure in my personal life, my religious and spiritual life. We became good friends, and eventually I would write about her and what I think her ideas mean for all of us.

As I've gotten older, those religious thoughts have been a very important part of my life, and they've influenced the writers I choose to stay close to. I don't think it's any accident that I've been so involved with Flannery O'Connor's work, and Walker Percy's, and that I've kept teaching Georges Bernanos's *The Diary of a Country Priest* to students who might not otherwise have come in contact with such work. There is a desire in some way in all of the writing and reading and teaching I do to connect with writers who have been religiously introspective, whether it be Tolstoy and Dostoevski or contemporary American writers such as Flannery O'Connor and Walker Percy—or even, in his own way, John Cheever.

When our children were younger, my wife and I used to go to an Episcopal church here in Concord every Sunday, and the children went to Sunday School. Every once in a while I get disenchanted with formal religion, particularly when I hear the ministers trying to tell the congregation how important Freud is. A couple of years ago I had a terrible moment in church. I went on Good Friday; I like to go on Good Friday and sit there from twelve to three. In the midst of that time, of all times, the minister was talking about the importance of psychoanalysis for our understanding not only of the mind but of religion. I just got up and walked out; I thought, This is another nail in the body of Jesus. It was a terrible moment. I'm very distrustful of the spurious efforts to find credibility for religion in contemporary psychology. It's a very sad and, my mother would say, disedifying effort.

CA: You've approached fiction from every other angle, surely. Have you been tempted to write it?

COLES: If only I could! I did write five children's books in conjunction with my own children's growing up, and they had a modest success among those who buy children's books. I wish I could write fiction; I would do it. But I don't seem to be able to. I very much need to know particular people and then describe what I've learned from them. That's my vocation, and I've been helped in it by reading the stories of others who can construct characters through their imaginative life. I think in a sense I'm following their lead and learning from them as I do my work in the so-called everyday world.

BIOGRAPHICAL/CRITICAL SOURCES:

PERIODICALS

American Spectator, March, 1989.
Chicago Tribune, April 24, 1979; May 13, 1986; March 24, 1989.
Chicago Tribune Book World, November 9, 1980; December 1, 1985.
Christian Science Monitor, May 2, 1968.
Library Journal, January 1, 1972; March 1, 1978.
Los Angeles Times, June 20, 1985.
Los Angeles Times Book Review, February 9, 1986; September 13, 1987.
National Review, June 2, 1989.
New York Review of Books, March 9, 1972.
New York Times, January 10, 1979; October 20, 1984.
New York Times Book Review, June 11, 1978; January 19, 1986; September 6, 1987; December 25, 1988; February 26, 1989.
Saturday Review, November 21, 1970.
Time, February 14, 1972; July 15, 1974; March 17, 1986.
Times Literary Supplement, November 21, 1980; July 7, 1989.
Village Voice, August 27, 1985.
Washington Post, June 4, 1985.

Washington Post Book World, June 29, 1980; February 2, 1986; May 8, 1988.

—*Sketch by Anne Janette Johnson*
—*Interview by Jean W. Ross*

* * *

COLORADO (CAPELLA), Antonio J(ulio) 1903-

PERSONAL: Born February 13, 1903, in San Juan, Puerto Rico; son of Rafael Colorado D'Assoy (a photographer) and Lorenza Capella Martínez; married Isabel Laguna Matienzo (a social worker), 1938; children: Antonio, Isabelita, Rafael. *Education:* University of Puerto Rico, B.A., 1932; Clark University, M.A., 1933; Universidad Central, Madrid, Spain, Ph.D., 1934. *Politics:* Popular Democratic Party. *Religion:* Roman Catholic.

ADDRESSES: Home—821 Vesta St., Río Piedras, Puerto Rico 00923.

CAREER: Writer, U.S. Department of State, 1942-43; University of Puerto Rico, Río Piedras Campus, professor and dean of faculty of social science, 1943-46, director of university press, 1946-48; Department of Education of Puerto Rico, Río Piedras, director of department of press, 1948-55; president, Labor Relations Board of Puerto Rico, 1962-69. Writer, translator, and literary critic.

MEMBER: Academia Puertorriqueña de la Lengua Española (treasurer), Academia de Artes y Ciencias (Puerto Rican branch), Ateneo Puertorriqueño, Fundación Puertorriqueña de las Humanidades (member of board of directors), Quinto Centenario del Descubrimiento de Puerto Rico.

WRITINGS:

(Collaborator) *New World Guides to Latin American Republics,* Duell, Sloan & Pearce, 1943.
Puerto Rico y tú; libro de estudios sociales para la escuela elemental, Prentice-Hall, 1948.
Noticia y pulso del movimiento político puertorriqueño (bound with *Noticia acerca del pensamiento político de Puerto Rico* by Lidio Cruz Monclova), Orion, 1955.
Luis Palés Matos, el hombre y el poeta, Rodadero, 1964.
The First Book of Puerto Rico, Watts, 1964, 3rd edition, 1978.
Puerto Rico: La tierra y otros ensayos, Editorial Cordillera, 1972.

TRANSLATOR

Breve historia de los Estados Unidos, Ginn & Co., 1953.
La canción verde, Troutman, 1956.
Nuestro mundo a través de las edades, Prentice-Hall, 1959.
La política puertorriqueña y el nuevo trato, University of Puerto Rico Press, 1960, translation published as *Puerto Rican Politics and the New Deal,* 1976.
América de todos, Rand McNally, 1963.
El árbol de la violeta, Troutman, 1964.

OTHER

Also author of *Haití Intervenido,* 1934. Editor, *Diario de Puerto Rico,* 1948-50. Contributor to *Asomante, Puerto Rico Ilustrado, El Mundo, El Imparcial, La Torre,* and other periodicals.

WORK IN PROGRESS: Semblanzas; Ensayos y conferencias; Crítica literaria; Campañas políticas.

SIDELIGHTS: Antonio J. Colorado told *CA* that he is interested in journalism, labor relations, political science, and sociology. He has traveled through Central and northern South America, Spain, France, Santo Domingo, the Caribbean Islands, Cuba, the United States, and Canada.

* * *

COOK, Thomas H. 1947-

PERSONAL: Born September 19, 1947, in Ft. Payne, AL; on of Virgil Richard (in management) and Myrick (a Secretary; maiden name, Harper) Cook; married Susan Terner (a writer for radio), March 17, 1978; children: Justine Ariel. *Education:* Georgia State College, B.A., 1969; Hunter College, City University of New York, M.A., 1972; Columbia University, M.Phil., 1976.

ADDRESSES: Home—New York, NY. *Agent*—Tim Seldes, Russell & Volkening, 50 West 29th St., New York, NY 10017.

CAREER: U.S. Industrial Chemicals, New York City, advertising executive, 1970-72; Association for Help of Retarded Adults, New York City, clerk and typist, 1973-75; Dekalb Community College, Clarkston, GA, teacher in English and history, 1978-81; full-time writer, 1981—.

MEMBER: Authors Guild.

AWARDS, HONORS: Edgar Allan Poe Award nomination from Mystery Writers of America, 1981, for *Blood Innocents,* and 1988, for *Sacrificial Ground.*

WRITINGS:

NOVELS

Blood Innocents, Playboy Press, 1980.
The Orchids, Houghton, 1982.
Tabernacle, Houghton, 1983.
Elena, Houghton, 1986.
Sacrificial Ground, Putnam, 1988.
Flesh and Blood, Putnam, 1989.
Streets of Fire, Putnam, 1989.
Night Secrets, Putnam, 1990.

OTHER

Contributing editor and book review editor of *Atlanta* magazine, 1978-82.

SIDELIGHTS: Thomas H. Cook told *CA:* "I began my first novel when I was ten years old, but published my first when I was thirty-two. This was *Blood Innocents,* a book I wrote while pursuing my doctoral dissertation from Columbia University. I was living in Atlanta at the time, writing about Big Jim Folsom, the rather radical Alabama governor who dominated state politics for a few years after World War II. Since *Blood Innocents* was actually published, to my surprise, I decided to begin another novel and forget about the dissertation. Eventually *The Orchids* came out of that effort.

"*Blood Innocents* was a police procedural set in New York City, with emphasis on strong characterizations in both the major character, Detective John Rardon, and the minor ones. I had never read a mystery or police procedural before I wrote the book. Essentially it is about the capacity of a man to hold to his goodness while pursuing a rather squalid labor/police work. It was well-reviewed, although not very widely because it was a paperback original.

"*The Orchids* deals in part with the Holocaust, with memory, with relentless intellectual honesty, and with the power of reflection to redeem, however belatedly, a terrible life. It is narrated in both first and third person, although the voice of the novel is that of Peter Langhof, a former Nazi war criminal now living in an unnamed South American republic.

"My scheme, if I may call it that, is to write solid and artistically sound police procedurals like *Blood Innocents* and *Tabernacle* in order to buy the time needed to write such literary efforts as *The Orchids* and *Elena.* I have no income outside my writing.

"In my literary novels I would like to help bring back what I think of as the 'meditative novel,' that is, the work with a quiet, reasoned, and highly reflective voice. I prefer novels that depart somewhat from strictly linear forms of action and narrative as well as works that have taken on greater themes, rather than yet more books about middle-class or academic angst or restrictively autobiographical works, those that never venture beyond the usually rather limited experience of the novelist. In *The Orchids,* for example, I tried to render the density and precision of the German language into English, and to create a narrative voice that could convey the horrors of Langhof's experience without resorting to sensationalism of any kind. In *Elena* the narrative voice is that of a brother talking of his sister's life, a method by which not only a woman's life can be portrayed, but that of a man as well, so that the two genuinely merge into a single narrative tone."

The Orchids has been warmly received by critics such as S. L. Stebel, who, in a *Los Angeles Herald Examiner* review, found that Cook's use of "language is meticulous, imbued with the kind of image and metaphor present in our very best poetry, and the story is told in a measured tone that borders on the reverential, appropriate to the anguish inherent in the subject matter." In the *Atlanta Journal* critic Michele Ross recommended Cook's work, writing: " 'The Orchids' is so beautifully written, so brimming with intelligence and thought that I found myself stopping over and again to wonder at a phrase or repeat a passage." "A book like this is more rare than an orchid," Ross declared.

Writing in the *Jerusalem Post,* Esther Hecht also praised *The Orchids.* "[It] is an excellent novel both because of and despite the fact that it deals with the Holocaust. Through convincing characterizations and natural dialogue, and without falling back on the rhetoric of evil, the book confronts the gravest ethical questions posed by the Holocaust. At the same time it transcends the historical event, by presenting as universal and enduring the human qualities that lead to damnation and salvation." And in *Literary Boston* Lee Grove deemed *The Orchids* "a Holocaust novel that will blow you away." "Cook wants you to be both comfortable and uncomfortable—and he succeeds, perfectly. You'll feel as cozy as a razor blade in a Halloween apple. You'll see just how easy it is for a brilliant, powerful, sensitive intellect to go bad, to weld itself to corruption. This novel, however, will never go bad and is anything but corrupt."

BIOGRAPHICAL/CRITICAL SOURCES:

PERIODICALS

Atlanta Journal, October 17, 1982.
Jerusalem Post, March 11, 1983.
Literary Boston, December, 1982.
Los Angeles Herald Examiner, February 13, 1983.
Minneapolis Star & Tribune, September 19, 1982.
New York Times Book Review, October 31, 1982.
Washington Post Book World, November 6, 1983; February 2, 1986.

COPLIN, William D(avid) 1939-

PERSONAL: Surname rhymes with "*rope*-in"; born September 22, 1939, in Baltimore, MD; son of Isidor (a salesman) and Dubbie (Lebowitz) Coplin; married Merry Roseman, September 2, 1963 (divorced May, 1976); married Vickie J. Bradley, July, 1977; children: Britt, Deborah, Laura, Richard. *Education:* Johns Hopkins University, B.A., 1960; American University, M.A., 1962, Ph.D, 1964; post-doctoral study at the University of Michigan, 1968-69.

ADDRESSES: Office—Public Affairs and Citizenship Program, 105 Maxwell Hall, Maxwell School of Citizenship and Public Affairs, Syracuse University, Syracuse, NY 13210.

CAREER: Instructor in political science at Howard University and American University, both Washington, DC, 1962-64; Wayne State University, Detroit, MI, assistant professor, 1964-67, associate professor of political science, 1967-69; Syracuse University, Syracuse, NY, 1969-72, began as assistant professor, became professor of political science, 1972—, director of International Relations Program, 1970-75, director of Public Affairs and Citizenship Program of Maxwell School of Citizenship and Public Affairs, 1975—. Lecturer, Foreign Service Institute, 1973-75. Member of executive committee of Consortium for International Studies Education, 1972-77. Director of Political Risk Services, Frost and Sullivan, Inc., 1979—. Consultant to various organizations, including the Industrial College of the Armed Forces, 1967-69, the Department of State External Research Bureau, 1972, and the Presidential Commission to Study the Organization of the Government for the Conduct of Foreign Policy, 1975-76.

MEMBER: International Studies Association (chairman of Education Commission, 1971-75), Association of Political Risk Analysts (member of board of directors, 1980—), American Political Science Association (chairman of international relations panels, 1974), American Society of International Law (member of executive council, 1975-77), Social Science Education Consortium.

AWARDS, HONORS: Faculty fellowships from the National Science Foundation, 1968-69, and the New York State Assembly Internship Program, 1977-78; Alumni Award, American University, 1982; Undergraduate Teaching Award for Excellence, College of Arts and Sciences, Syracuse University, 1986-87; ACCORD Annual Community Service Award, 1986-87.

WRITINGS:

The Functions of International Law, Rand McNally, 1966.
Introduction to International Politics: A Theoretical Overview, Markham, 1971, 3rd edition, Prentice-Hall, 1980.
PS-6: Introduction to the Analysis of Public Policy from a Problem Solving Perspective, Policy Studies Associates, 1973.
(With others) *A Description of the PRINCE Model,* Learning Resources in International Relations, 1974.
(With others) *American Foreign Policy,* Duxbury, 1974.
An Introduction to the Analysis of Public Policy Issues from a Problem-Solving Perspective, Learning Resources in International Studies, 1975.

WITH MICHAEL K. O'LEARY

(And Stephen L. Mills) *Participant's Guide to PRINCE: Concepts, Environments, and Procedures,* International Relations Program, Syracuse University, 1971.
(And Mills) *Everyman's PRINCE: A Guide to Understanding Political Problems,* Duxbury, 1972, 2nd edition, 1976.

(And Mills) *PRINCE-DOWN Student Manual: A Gaming Approach to the Study of Policy Issues,* International Relations Program, Syracuse University, 1973.

Quantitative Techniques in Foreign Policy Forecasting and Analysis, Praeger, 1975.

(And Robert F. Rich) *Toward the Improvement of Foreign Service Reporting,* U.S. Government Printing Office, 1975.

PS-17: Introduction to the Analysis of Public Policy, Policy Studies Associates, 1978.

Basic Policy Study Skills, Policy Studies Associates, 1981.

Political Risks in Thirty Countries: A Euromoney Report, Euromoney Publications, 1981.

Turkey: The Problems of Transition, Euromoney Publications, 1982.

Political Risk from Territorial Disputes: A Global Survey, Frost and Sullivan, 1983.

(And Carol Gould) *Power Persuasion: A Sure-Fire System for Getting Ahead in Business,* Addison-Wesley, 1985.

Effective Participation in Government: A Guide to Policy Skills, Policy Studies Associates, 1987.

Public Policy Skills, Policy Studies Associates, 1988.

OTHER

(Editor) *Simulation in the Study of Politics,* Markham, 1968.

(Editor with Charles W. Kegley, Jr.) *A Multi-Method Introduction to International Politics: Readings in Observation, Explanation, and Prescription,* Markham, 1971, 2nd edition published as *Analyzing International Relations: A Multi-Method Introduction,* Praeger, 1975.

(Editor) *Teaching Policy Studies: What and How,* Lexington Books, 1978.

Contributor to numerous books, including *The United Nations Syndrome,* edited by Michael Barkun and Robert W. Gregg, Van Nostrand, 1968; (with Michael K. O'Leary) *Political Risks in International Business,* edited by Thomas L. Brewer, Praeger, 1985; and, with O'Leary, *Assessing Corporate Political Risk,* edited by David M. Raddock, Rowman & Littlefield, 1986. Also author, with Leonard Stitleman, of exercises for the "American Government Simulation" series, and of teaching materials for *Learning Packages in International Relations.* Author of student manual and editor of test item catalogue for "Mentorex for American Politics." Contributor of articles to professional journals. Member of editorial board of *Simulation and Games,* 1971-75; editor of *Policy Studies Journal,* 1981-84, and, with O'Leary, *Political Risk Letter,* 1979—.

Power Persuasion: A Sure-Fire System for Getting Ahead in Business has been translated into Japanese, German, Swedish, and Spanish.

SIDELIGHTS: William D. Coplin told *CA:* "All of my writing, except for a few esoteric [pieces] required to gain promotion and tenure, has been to achieve one purpose: assist the individual to understand and deal with the political, social, and economic conditions he or she faces. If the social sciences have any value at all, it is in providing tools for analysis; and if these tools are any good, it is in helping people make better decisions. I take as a matter of faith that people can improve their understanding and control the social world by thinking more systematically and clearly. With this goal, there has been no need to pretend, as many of my colleges in the social sciences have, that my writing transmits scientific knowledge or, as is usually the case, discusses how I have searched for the elusive knowledge through massive computer data sets or the ideas of great thinkers. My writing works if it helps the student, the businessman, the civil servant, and the citizen cope."

CORNGOLD, Stanley Alan 1934-

PERSONAL: Born June 11, 1934, in Brooklyn, NY; son of Herman and Estelle (Bramson) Corngold; married Marie Josephine Brettle, July 26, 1961 (divorced, 1969); children: Isabel Anna. *Education:* Columbia University, A.B. (with honors), 1957; additional study at University of London, 1957-58, and Columbia University, 1958-59; Cornell University, M.A., 1963, Ph.D., 1969; University of Basel, additional study, 1965-66.

ADDRESSES: Home—20 Erdman Ave., Princeton, NJ 08540-3908. *Office*—Department of Germanic Languages and Literatures, Princeton University, Princeton, NJ 08544-5264.

CAREER: University of Maryland, European Division, Heidelberg, Germany, instructor in English, 1959-62; Princeton University, Princeton, NJ, assistant professor, 1966-72, associate professor, 1972-81, associate professor, 1979-81, professor of German and comparative literature, 1981—. Visiting professor, Bryn Mawr University, 1983-84. *Military service:* U.S. Naval Reserve, 1951-55; U.S. Army, 1955-57.

MEMBER: PEN (1970—), Academy of Literary Studies (1983—), Nietzsche Society of North America, Goethe Society of North America, Kafka Society of North America (member of executive board; vice president, 1985-86; president, 1987-88), Modern Language Association of America, Phi Beta Kappa.

AWARDS, HONORS: American Council of Learned Societies fellowship, 1965; grants-in-aid for research, Princeton Univerity, 1967, 1972; National Endowment for the Humanities junior fellowship, 1973; Guggenheim fellowship, 1977; Academy of Literary Studies award, 1983; Fulbright research fellow, University of Freiburg, 1986-87.

WRITINGS:

(Editor, and author of introduction, notes, and vocabulary) *"Ausgewaehlte Prosa" by Max Frisch,* Harcourt, 1968.

The Commentators' Despair: The Interpretation of Franz Kafka's "Metamorphosis," National University Publications, 1973.

(Editor with Michael Curschmann and Theodore Ziolkowski) *Aspekte der Goethezeit,* Vandenhoeck & Ruprecht, 1977.

The Fate of the Self: German Writers and French Theory, Columbia University Press, 1986.

Franz Kafka: The Necessity of Form, Cornell University Press, 1989.

(With Irene Giersling) *Borrowed Lives,* State University of New York Press, 1991.

Literary Tensions (essays), University of Nebraska Press, 1991.

TRANSLATOR

(And editor, and author of introduction, notes, and critical apparatus) Franz Kafka, *The Metamorphosis,* Bantam, 1972.

Translations represented in Willis Barnstone, editor, *Modern European Poetry,* Bantam, 1966; Gunnar Kaldewey, *German Romantics,* [Hamburg, Germany], 1979; *Norton Anthology of World Masterpieces,* Volume 2 (translation of Kafka's *Die Verwandlung*), Norton, 1985; *Writing Networks, 1800-1900,* Stanford University Press, 1989; *Franz Kafka: An Anthology of Criticism,* Pantheon, 1990; and *The Complete Works of W.H. Auden,* Princeton University Press, 1991. Translator of a Hartmut Binder essay printed in *Journal of the Kafka Society of America.*

CONTRIBUTOR

Willis Barnstone, editor, *Modern European Poetry,* Bantam, 1966.

R. G. Collins and Kenneth McRobbie, editor, *New Views of the European Novel,* University of Manitoba Press, 1972.

(And editor with Richard Ludwig) *Thomas Mann, 1875-1975,* Princeton University Press, 1975.

James Rolleston, editor, *Twentieth-Century Interpretations of "The Trial,"* Prentice-Hall, 1976.

Angel Flores, editor, *The Problem of "The Judgment": Eleven Approaches to Kafka's Story,* Gordian Press, 1977.

Flores, editor, *The Kafka Debate: New Perspectives for Our Time,* Gordian Press, 1977.

Maria Luise Caputo-Mayr, editor, *Franz Kafka Ein Symposium,* Agora Verlag, 1978.

William Spanos, editor, *Martin Heidegger and the Question of Literature: Toward a Post-modern Literary Hermeneutics,* Indiana University Press, 1979.

(With Howard Stern) *Yearbook of Comparative and General Literature,* University of Indiana, 1980.

Jonathan Arac and others, editors, *The Yale Critics: Deconstruction in America,* University of Minnesota Press, 1983.

Rodolfo E. Modern, editor, *Franz Kafka: Homenaje en su centenario (1833-1924),* [Buenos Aires], 1983.

Tak-Wai Wong and M. A. Abbas, editors, *Rewriting Literary History,* Hong Kong University Press, 1984.

Johnathan Hall and Abbas, editors, *Literature and Anthropology,* Hong Kong University Press, 1986.

Alan Udoff, editor, *Kafka and the Contemporary Critical Performance: Centenary Readings,* University of Indiana Press, 1987.

Moshe Lazar and Ronald Gottesman, editors, *The Dove and the Mole: Kafka's Journey into Darkness and Creativity,* Udena, 1987.

Volker Duerr and others, editors, *Nietzsche: Literature and Values,* University of Wisconsin Press, 1988.

Clayton Koelb, editor, *The Comparative Perspective on Literature: Approaches to Theory and Practice,* Cornell University Press, 1988.

Also contributor to *(Dis)Continuities: Essays on Paul de Man, Franz Kafka: An Anthology of Criticism, America: Visions and Revisions, Critical Narratology: Essays in Honor of Dorrit Cohn, Hegel and Hoelderlin,* and *Deconstruction: Pro and Contra.* Contributor to professional journals, including *European Judaism, Critical Inquiry, Literary Review, Newsletter of the Kafka Society of America,* and *Modern Language Studies.* Co-editor, *Journal of the Kafka Society of America,* 1987-88.

WORK IN PROGRESS: Babble: An Essay on the Romantic Quest (chapters on *Les confessions, Faust, Dan Juan, La charteuse de Parme, Pere Goriot, L'Education sentimentale, Notes from Underground, The Genealogy of Morals,* and *Doktor Faustus*).

BIOGRAPHICAL/CRITICAL SOURCES:

BOOKS

O'Hara, Daniel, *The Romance of Interpretation: Visionary Criticism from Pater to de Man,* Columbia University Press, 1985.

Sievers, Tobin, *The Romantic Fantastic,* Cornell University Press, in press.

*   *   *

CORTAZAR, Julio   1914-1984
(Julio Denis)

PERSONAL: Born August 26, 1914, in Brussels, Belgium; held dual citizenship in Argentina and (beginning 1981) France; died of a heart attack February 12, 1984, in Paris, France; son of Julio José and María Herminia (Descotte) Cortázar; married former spouse Aurora Bernárdez, August 23, 1953. *Education:* Received degrees in teaching and public translating; attended Buenos Aires University.

CAREER: Writer. High school teacher in Bolívar and Chivilcoy, both in Argentina, 1937-44; teacher of French literature, University of Cuyo, Mendoza, Argentina, 1944-45; manager, Argentine Publishing Association (Cámara Argentina del Libro), Buenos Aires, Argentina, 1946-48; public translator in Argentina, 1948-51; free-lance translator for UNESCO, Paris, France, 1952-84. Member of jury, Casa de las Américas Award.

AWARDS, HONORS: Prix Médicis, 1974, for *Libro de Manuel;* Rubén Darío Order of Cultural Independence awarded by Government of Nicaragua, 1983.

WRITINGS:

FICTION

Bestiario (stories; title means "Bestiary"; also see below), Sudamericana (Buenos Aires), 1951, reprinted, 1983.

Final del juego (stories; also see below), Los Presentes (Mexico), 1956, expanded edition, Sudamericana, 1964, reprinted, 1983.

Las armas secretas (stories; title means "The Secret Weapons"; also see below), Sudamericana, 1959, reprinted, Cátedra (Madrid), 1983.

Los premios (novel), Sudamericana, 1960, reprinted, Ediciones B, 1987, translation by Elaine Kerrigan published as *The Winners,* Pantheon, 1965, reprinted, 1984.

Historias de cronopios y de famas, Minotauro (Buenos Aires), 1962, reprinted, Alfaguara, 1984, translation by Paul Blackburn published as *Cronopios and Famas,* Pantheon, 1969.

Rayuela (novel), Sudamericana, 1963, reprinted, 1984, translation by Gregory Rabassa published as *Hopscotch,* Pantheon, 1966, reprinted, 1987.

Cuentos (collection), Casa de las Américas (Havana), 1964.

Todos los fuegos el fuego (stories), Sudamericana, 1966, reprinted, 1981, translation by Suzanne Jill Levine published as *All Fires the Fire, and Other Stories,* Pantheon, 1973, reprinted, 1988.

La vuelta al día en ochenta mundos (essays, poetry, and stories), Siglo Veintiuno (Mexico), 1967, reprinted, 1984, translation by Thomas Christensen published as *Around the Day in Eighty Worlds,* North Point Press, 1986.

El perseguidor y otros cuentos (stories), Centro Editor para América Latina (Buenos Aires), 1967, reprinted, Bruguera, 1983.

End of the Game, and Other Stories, translated by Blackburn (includes stories from *Final del juego, Bestiario,* and *Las armas secretas*), Pantheon, 1967, published as *Blow-Up, and Other Stories,* Collier, 1968, reprinted, Pantheon, 1985.

Ceremonias (collection), Seix Barral, 1968, reprinted, 1983.

62: Modelo para armar (novel), Sudamericana, 1968, translation by Rabassa published as *62: A Model Kit,* Pantheon, 1972.

Ultimo round (essays, poetry, and stories; title means "Last Round"), Siglo Veintiuno, 1969, reprinted, 1984.

Relatos (collection), Sudamericana, 1970.

La isla a mediodía y otros relatos (contains twelve previously published stories), Salvat, 1971.

Libro de Manuel (novel), Sudamericana, 1973, translation by Rabassa published as *A Manual for Manuel,* Pantheon, 1978.

Octaedro (stories; title means "Octahedron"; also see below), Sudamericana, 1974.

Antología (collection), La Librería, 1975.

Fantomas contra los vampiros multinacionales (title means "Fantomas Takes on the Multinational Vampires"), Excelsior (Mexico), 1975.

Los relatos (collection), four volumes, Alianza, 1976-1985.

Alguien que anda por ahí y otros relatos (stories), Alfaguara (Madrid), 1977, translation by Rabassa published as *A Change of Light, and Other Stories* (includes *Octaedro;* also see below), Knopf, 1980.

Territorios, Siglo Veintiuno, 1978.

Un tal Lucas, Alfaguara, 1979, translation by Rabassa published as *A Certain Lucas,* Knopf, 1984.

Queremos tanto a Glenda, Alfaguara, 1980, translation by Rabassa published as *We Love Glenda So Much, and Other Tales* (also see below), Knopf, 1983.

Deshoras (short stories), Alfaguara, 1982.

We Love Glenda So Much [and] *A Change of Light,* Vintage, 1984.

TRANSLATOR

Alfred Stern, *Filosofía de la risa y del llanto,* Imán (Buenos Aires), 1950.

Lord Houghton, *Vida y cartas de John Keats,* Imán, 1955.

Marguerite Yourcenar, *Memorias de Adriano,* Sudamericana, 1955.

Edgar Allan Poe, *Obras en prosa,* two volumes, Revista de Occidente, 1956.

Poe, *Cuentos,* Editorial Nacional de Cuba, 1963.

Poe, *Aventuras de Arthur Gordon Pym,* Instituto del Libro (Havana), 1968.

Poe, *Eureka,* Alianza (Madrid), 1972.

Daniel Defoe, *Robinson Crusoe,* Bruguera, 1981.

Also translator of works by G. K. Chesterton, Andre Gide, and Jean Giono, published in Argentina between 1948 and 1951.

OTHER

(Under pseudonym Julio Denís) *Presencia* (poems; title means "Presence"), El Bibliófilo (Buenos Aires), 1938.

Los reyes (play; title means "The Monarchs"), Gulab y Aldabahor (Buenos Aires), 1949, reprinted, Alfaguara, 1982.

(Contributor) *Buenos Aires de la fundación a la angustia,* Ediciones de la Flor (Buenos Aires), 1967.

(With others) *Cuba por argentinos,* Merlín (Buenos Aires), 1968.

Buenos Aires, Buenos Aires (includes French and English translations), Sudamericana, 1968.

Viaje alrededor de una mesa (title means "Trip around a Table"), Cuadernos de Rayuela (Buenos Aires), 1970.

(With Oscar Collazos and Mario Vargas Llosa) *Literatura en la revolución y revolución en la literatura,* Siglo Veintiuno, 1970.

(Contributor) *Literatura y arte nuevo en Cuba,* Estela (Barcelona), 1971.

Pameos y meopas (poetry), Editorial Libre de Sivera (Barcelona), 1971.

Prosa del observatorio, Lumen (Barcelona), 1972.

La casilla de los Morelli (essays), edited by José Julio Ortega, Tusquets, 1973.

Convergencias, divergencias, incidencias, edited by Ortega, Tusquets, 1973.

(Author of text) *Humanario,* La Azotea (Buenos Aires), 1976.

(Author of text) *Paris: Ritmos de una ciudad,* Edhasa (Barcelona), 1981.

Paris: The Essence of an Image, Norton, 1981.

(With Carol Dunlop) *Los autonautas de la cosmopista,* Muchnik (Buenos Aires), 1983.

Nicaragua tan violentamente dulce (essays), Nueva Nicaragua, 1983.

Argentina: Años de almabradas culturales (essays), edited by Saúl Yurkiévich, Muchnik, 1984.

Nada a pehuajó: Un acto; Adiós, Robinson (plays), Katún, 1984.

Salvo el crepúsculo (poems), Nueva Imagen, 1984.

Textos políticos, Plaza y Janés, 1985.

Divertimento, Sudamericana/Planeta, 1986.

El examen, Sudamericana/Planeta, 1986.

Nicaraguan Sketches, Norton, 1989.

Contributor to numerous periodicals, including *Revista Iberoamericana, Cuadernos Hispanoamericanos, Books Abroad,* and *Casa de las Américas.*

SIDELIGHTS: Argentine author Julio Cortázar was "one of the world's greatest writers," according to novelist Stephen Dobyns. "His range of styles," Dobyns wrote in the *Washington Post Book World,* "his ability to paint a scene, his humor, his endlessly peculiar mind makes many of his stories wonderful. His novel *Hopscotch* is considered one of the best novels written by a South American."

A popular as well as a critical success, *Hopscotch* not only established Cortázar's reputation as a novelist of international merit but also, according to David W. Foster in *Currents in the Contemporary Argentine Novel,* prompted wider acceptance in the United States of novels written by other Latin Americans. For this reason many critics, such as Jaime Alazraki in *The Final Island,* viewed the book as "a turning point for Latin American literature." A *Times Literary Supplement* reviewer, for example, called *Hopscotch* "the first great novel of Spanish America."

Still other critics, including novelists José Donoso and C. D. B. Bryan, saw the novel in the context of world literature. Donoso, in his *The Boom in Spanish American Literature: A Personal History,* claimed that *Hopscotch* "humanized the novel." Cortázar was a writer, Donoso continued, "who [dared] to be discursive and whose pages [were] sprinkled with names of musicians, painters, art galleries, . . . movie directors[, and] all this had an undisguised place within his novel, something which I would never have dared to presume to be right for the Latin American novel, since it was fine for [German novelist] Thomas Mann but not for us." In the *New York Times Book Review,* Bryan stated: "I think *Hopscotch* is the most magnificent book I have ever read. No novel has so satisfactorily and completely and beautifully explored man's compulsion to explore life, to search for its meaning, to challenge its mysteries. Nor has any novel in recent memory lavished such love and attention upon the full spectrum of the writer's craft."

Cortázar attempted to perfect his craft by constant experimentation. In his longer fiction he pursued, as Leo Bersani observed in the *New York Times Book Review,* both "subversion and renewal of novelistic form." This subversion and renewal was of such importance to Cortázar that often the form of his novels overshadowed the action that they described. Through the form of his fiction Cortázar invited the reader to participate in the writer's craft and to share in the creation of the novel.

Hopscotch is one such novel. In *Into the Mainstream: Conversations with Latin-America Writers,* Luis Harss and Barbara Dohmann wrote that *Hopscotch* "is the first Latin American novel which takes itself as its own central topic or, in other words, is essentially about the writing of itself. It lives in constant metamorphoses, as an unfinished process that invents itself as it goes, involving the reader in such a way to make him part of the creative impulse." Thus, *Hopscotch* begins with a "Table of Instructions" that tells the reader that there are at least two ways to read the novel. The first is reading chapters one to fifty-six in numerical order. When the reader finishes chapter fifty-six he can, according to the instructions, stop reading and "ignore what follows [nearly one hundred more short chapters] with a clean conscience." The other way of reading suggested by the instructions is to start with chapter seventy-two and then skip from chapter to chapter (hence, the title of the book), following the sequence indicated at the end of each chapter by a number which tells the reader which chapter is next. Read the second way, the reader finds that chapter 131 refers him to chapter fifty-eight, and chapter fifty-eight to chapter 131, so that he is confronted with a novel that has no end. With his "Table of Instructions" Cortázar forces the reader to write the novel while he is reading it.

Cortázar's other experimental works include *62: A Model Kit* (considered a sequel to *Hopscotch*), *A Manual for Manuel, Ultimo round* ("Last Round"), and *Fantomas contra los vampiros multinacionales* ("Fantomas Takes on the Multinational Vampires"). *62: A Model Kit* is based on chapter sixty-two of *Hopscotch* in which a character, Morelli, expresses his desire to write a new type of novel. "If I were to write this book," Morelli states, "standard behavior would be inexplicable by means of current instrumental psychology. Everything would be a kind of disquiet, a continuous uprooting, a territory where psychological causality would yield disconcertedly."

In *62: A Model Kit* Cortázar attempted to put these ideas into action. Time and space have no meaning in the novel: although it takes place in Paris, London, and Vienna, the characters move and interact as if they are in one single space. The characters themselves are sketchily presented in fragments that must be assembled by the readers; chapters are replaced by short scenes separated by blank spaces on the pages of the novel. Cortázar noted in the book's introduction that once again the reader must help create the novel: "The reader's option, his personal montage of the elements in the tale, will in each case be the book he has chosen to read."

A Manual for Manuel continues in the experimental vein. Megan Marshall described the book in *New Republic* as "a novel that merges story and history, a supposed scrapbook of news clippings, journal entries, diagrams, transcripts of conversations, and much more." The book, about the kidnapping of a Latin American diplomat by a group of guerillas in Paris, is told from the double perspective of an unnamed member of the group, who takes notes on the plans for the kidnapping, and a nonmember of the group, Andres, who reads the notes. Periodically, these two narrations are interrupted by the inclusion of English-, French-, and Spanish-language texts reproduced in the pages of the novel. These texts, actual articles collected by Cortázar from various sources, form part of a scrapbook being assembled for Manuel, the child of two of the members of the group. On one page, for example, Cortázar reprinted a statistical table originally published in 1969 by the U.S. Department of Defense that shows how many Latin Americans have received military training in the United States. The reader reads about the compilation of the scrapbook for Manuel, while at the same time reading the scrapbook and reacting to the historical truth it contains.

Other such experimentation is found in *Ultimo round,* a collection of essays, stories, and poetry. William L. Siemens noted in the *International Fiction Review* that this book, like *Hopscotch* and *62: A Model Kit,* "is a good example of audience-participation art." In *Ultimo round,* he declared, "it is impossible for the reader to proceed in a conventional manner. Upon opening the book the reader notes that there are two sets of pages

within the binding, and he must immediately decide which of them to read first, and even whether he will go through by reading the top and then the bottom of page one, and so on."

Cortázar's brief narrative *Fantomas contra los vampiros multinacionales* is yet another experiment with new forms of fiction. It presents, in comic book form, the story of a "superhero," Fantomas, who gathers together "the greatest contemporary writers" to fight the destructive powers of the multinational corporations. Chilean Octavio Paz, Italian Alberto Moravia, and American Susan Sontag, along with Cortázar himself, appear as characters in the comic book. Although short, the work embodies several constants in Cortázar's fiction: the comic (the comic book form itself), the interplay of fantasy and reality (the appearance of historical figures in a fictional work), and a commitment to social activism (the portrayal of the writer as a politically involved individual). These three elements, together with Cortázar's experiments with the novelistic form, are the basic components of his fiction.

Cortázar explained how these elements function together in his essay "Algunos aspectos del cuento" ("Some Aspects of the Story"), which Alazraki quoted in *The Final Island.* His work, Cortázar claimed, was "an alternative to that false realism which assumed that everything can be neatly described as was upheld by the philosophic and scientific optimism of the eighteenth century, that is, within a world ruled more or less harmoniously by a system of laws, of principles, of causal relations, of well defined psychologies, of well mapped geographies. . . . In my case, the suspicion of another order, more secret and less communicable [was one of the principles guiding] my personal search for a literature beyond overly naive forms of realism." Whatever the method, whether new narrative forms, unexpected humor, incursions into fantasy, or pleas for a more humane society, Cortázar strove to shake the reader out of traditional ways of thinking and seeing the world and to replace them with new and more viable models. Dobyn explained in the *Washington Post Book World,* "Cortázar wants to jolt people out of their self-complacency, to make them doubt their own definition of the world."

Cortázar's last full-length work of fiction, *A Certain Lucas,* for example, "is a kind of sampler of narrative ideas, a playful anthology of form, including everything from parables to parodies, folk tales to metafictions," as Robert Coover describes it in the *New York Times Book Review.* Including chapters with such titles as "Lucas, His Shopping," "Lucas, His Battles with the Hydra," and "Lucas, His Pianists," the book "builds a portrait, montage-like, through a succession of short sketches (humorous set-pieces, really) full of outrageous inventions, leaping and dream-like associations and funny turns of phrase," states *Los Angeles Times Book Review* critic Charles Champlin. "Lucas is not Cortázar," Dobyns suggests in the *Washington Post Book World,* "but occasionally he seems to stand for him and so the book takes on an autobiographical quality as we read about Lucas' friends, his struggles with himself, his dreams, his tastes, his view of writing." The result, writes Champlin, might appear to be "no more than a series of extravagant jokes, [and] it would be an exceptional passing entertainment but no more than that. Yet under the cover of raillery, self-indicting foolishness and extremely tall tales," the critic continues, "Cortázar is discovered to be a thoughtful, deep-feeling man, impassioned, sentimental, angry, complicated, a philosopher exploring appearances vs. realities is the way of philosophers ever." "What we see in Lucas and in much of Cortázar's work is a fierce love of this earth, despite the awfulness, and a fierce respect for life's ridiculousness," concludes Dobyns. "And in the midst of this ridiculousness,

Cortázar dances . . . and that dance comforts and eases our own course through the world."

This ridiculousness, or humor, in Cortázar's work often derived from what a *Time* reviewer referred to as the author's "ability to present common objects from strange perspectives as if he had just invented them." Cortázar, declared Tom Bishop in *Saturday Review,* was "an intellectual humorist. . . . [He had] a rare gift for isolating the absurd in everyday life [and] for depicting the foibles in human behavior with an unerring thrust that [was] satiric yet compassionate."

Hopscotch is filled with humorous elements, some of which Saúl Yurkiévich listed in *The Final Island.* He included "references to the ridiculous, . . . recourse to the outlandish, . . . absurd associations, . . . juxtaposition of the majestic with the popular or vulgar," as well as "puns, . . . [and] polyglot insults." *New York Times* writer John Leonard called absurdity "obligatory" in a work by Cortázar and gave examples of the absurd found in *A Manual for Manuel,* such as "a turquoise penguin [is] flown by jet to Argentina; the stealing of 9,000 wigs . . . and obsessive puns." In an interview with Evelyn Picon Garfield, quoted in *Books Abroad,* Cortázar called *Cronopios and Famas* his "most playful book." It is, he continued, "really a game, a very fascinating game, lots of fun, almost like a tennis match."

This book of short, story-like narratives deals with two groups of creatures described by Arthur Curley in *Library Journal* as the "warm life-loving cronopios and practical, conventional famas . . . imaginary but typical personages between whom communication is usually impossible and always ridiculous." One portion of the book, called "The Instruction Manual," contains detailed explanations of various everyday activities, including how to climb stairs, how to wind a clock, and how to cry. In order to cry correctly, the author suggested thinking of a duck covered with ants. With these satiric instructions Cortázar, according to Paul West in *Book World,* "cleanses the doors of perception and mounts a subtle, bland assault on the mental rigidities we hold most dear." By forcing us to think about everyday occurrences in a new way, Cortázar, Malva E. Filer noted in *Books Abroad,* "expresses his rebellion against objects and persons that make up our everyday life and the mechanical ways by which we relate to them." Filer continued: "In Cortázar's fictional world [a] routine life is the great scandal against which every individual must rebel with all his strength. And if he is not willing to do so, extraordinary elements are usually summoned to force him out of this despicable and abject comfort."

These "extraordinary elements" enter into the lives of Cortázar's characters in the form of fantastic episodes which interrupt their otherwise normal existences. Alexander Coleman observed in *Cinco maestros: Cuentos modernos de Hispanoamérica* ("Five Masters: Modern Spanish-American Stories"): "Cortázar's stories start in a disarmingly conversational way, with plenty of local touches. But something always seems to go awry just when we least expect it." "Axolotl," a short story described by novelist Joyce Carol Oates in the *New York Times Book Review* as her favorite Cortázar tale, begins innocently: a man describes his trips to the Parisian botanical gardens to watch a certain type of salamander called an axolotl. But the serenity ends when the narrator admits, "Now I am an axolotl." In another story, a woman has a dream about a beggar who lives in Budapest (a city the woman has never visited). The woman ends up actually going to Budapest where she finds herself walking across a bridge as the beggar woman from her dream approaches from the opposite side. The two women embrace in the middle of the bridge and the first woman is transformed into the beggar woman—she can

feel the snow seeping through the holes in her shoes—while she sees her former self walk away. In yet another story, a motorcyclist is involved in a minor traffic accident and suddenly finds himself thrown back in time where he becomes the victim of Aztec ritual sacrifice. Daniel Stern noted in *Nation* that with these stories and others like them "it is as if Cortázar is showing us that it is essential for us to reimagine the reality in which we live and which we can no longer take for granted."

Although during the last years of his life Cortázar was so involved with political activism that Jason Weiss described him in the *Los Angeles Times* as a writer with hardly any time to write, the Argentine had early in his career been criticized "for his apparent indifference to the brutish situation" of his fellow Latin Americans, according to Leonard. Evidence of his growing political preoccupation is found in his later stories and novels. Leonard observed, for instance, that *A Manual for Manuel* "is a primer on the necessity of revolutionary action," and William Kennedy in the *Washington Post Book World* noted that the newspaper clippings included in the novel "touch[ed] the open nerve of political oppression in Latin America." Many of the narratives in *A Change of Light, and Other Stories* are also politically oriented. Oates described the impact of one story in the *New York Times Book Review.* In "Apocalypse at Solentiname," a photographer develops his vacation photographs of happy, smiling people only to discover pictures of people being tortured. Oates commented, "The narrator . . . contemplates in despair the impotence of art to deal with in any significant way, the 'life of permanent uncertainty . . . [in] almost all of Latin America, a life surrounded by fear and death.' "

Cortázar's fictional world, according to Alazraki in *The Final Island,* "represents a challenge to culture." This challenge is embedded in the author's belief in a reality that reaches beyond our everyday existence. Alazraki noted that Cortázar once declared, "Our daily reality masks a second reality which is neither mysterious nor theological, but profoundly human. Yet, due to a long series of mistakes, it has remained concealed under a reality prefabricated by many centuries of culture, a culture in which there are great achievements but also profound aberrations, profound distortions." Bryan further explained these ideas in the *New York Times Book Review:* Cortázar's "surrealistic treatment of the most pedestrian acts suggest[ed] that one way to combat alienation is to return to the original receptiveness of childhood, to recapture this original innocence, by returning to the concept of life as a game."

Cortázar confronted his reader with unexpected forms, with humor, fantasy, and unseemly reality in order to challenge him to live a more meaningful life. He summarized his theory of fiction (and of life) in an essay, "The Present State of Fiction in Latin America," which appeared in *Books Abroad.* The Argentine concluded: "The fantastic is something that one must never say good-bye to lightly. The man of the future . . . will have to find the bases of a reality which is truly his and, at the same time, maintain the capacity of dreaming and playing which I have tried to show you . . . , since it is through those doors that the Other, the fantastic dimension, and the unexpected will always slip, as will all that will save us from that obedient robot into which so many technocrats would like to convert us and which we will not accept—ever."

MEDIA ADAPTATIONS: The story "Las babas del diablo," from the collection *Las armas secretas* was the basis for Michaelangelo Antonioni's 1966 film "Blow Up."

AVOCATIONAL INTERESTS: Jazz, movies.

BIOGRAPHICAL/CRITICAL SOURCES:

BOOKS

Alazraki, Jaime and Ivar Ivask, editors, *The Final Island: The Fiction of Julio Cortázar,* University of Oklahoma Press, 1978.

Boldy, Steven, *The Novels of Cortázar,* Cambridge University Press, 1980.

Coleman, Alexander, editor, *Cinco maestros: Cuentos modernos de Hispanoamérica,* Harcourt, Brace & World, 1969.

Contemporary Literary Criticism, Gale, Volume 2, 1974, Volume 3, 1975, Volume 5, 1976, Volume 10, 1979, Volume 13, 1980, Volume 15, 1980, Volume 33, 1985, Volume 34, 1985.

Donoso, José, *Historia personal del "boom,"* Anagrama (Barcelona), 1972, translation by Gregory Kolovakos published as *The Boom in Spanish American Literature: A Personal History,* Columbia University Press, 1977.

Foster, David W., *Currents in the Contemporary Argentine Novel,* University of Missouri Press, 1975.

Garfield, Evelyn Picon, *Julio Cortázar,* Ungar, 1975.

Garfield, Evelyn Picon, *Cortázar por Cortázar* (interviews), Universidad Veracruzana, 1981.

Giacoman, Helmy F., editor, *Homenaje a Julio Cortázar,* Anaya, 1972.

Harss, Luis and Barbara Dohmann, *Into the Mainstream: Conversations with Latin-American Writers,* Harper, 1967.

Prego, Omar, *La fascinación de las palabras* (interviews), Muchnik, 1985.

Vásquez Amaral, José, *The Contemporary Latin American Narrative,* Las Américas, 1970.

PERIODICALS

America, April 17, 1965, July 9, 1966, December 22, 1973.
Atlantic, June, 1969, October, 1973.
Books Abroad, fall, 1965, winter, 1968, summer, 1969, winter, 1970, summer, 1976.
Book World, August 17, 1969.
Casa de las Américas, numbers 15-16, 1962.
Chicago Tribune, September 24, 1978.
Chicago Tribune Book World, November 16, 1980, May 8, 1983.
Christian Science Monitor, August 15, 1967, July 3, 1969, December 4, 1978.
Commentary, October, 1966.
El País, April 19, 1981.
Hispania, December, 1973.
Hudson Review, spring, 1974.
International Fiction Review, January, 1974, January, 1975.
Library Journal, July, 1967, September, 1969, September 15, 1980.
Listener, December 20, 1979.
Los Angeles Times, August 28, 1983.
Los Angeles Times Book Review, December 28, 1980, June 12, 1983, May 27, 1984.
Nation, September 18, 1967.
National Review, July 25, 1967.
New Republic, April 23, 1966, July 15, 1967, October 21, 1978, October 25, 1980.
New Yorker, May 18, 1965, February 25, 1974.
New York Review of Books, March 25, 1965, April 28, 1966, April 19, 1973, October 12, 1978.
New York Times, November 13, 1978, March 24, 1983.
New York Times Book Review, March 21, 1965, April 10, 1966, June 15, 1969, November 26, 1972, September 9, 1973, November 19, 1978, November 9, 1980, March 4, 1984, May 20, 1984.

Novel: A Forum on Fiction, fall, 1967.
Review of Contemporary Fiction (special Cortázar issue), fall, 1983.
Revista Iberoamericana, July-December, 1973.
Saturday Review, March 27, 1965, April 9, 1966, July 22, 1967, September 27, 1969.
Time, April 29, 1966, June 13, 1969, October 1, 1973.
Times Literary Supplement, October 12, 1973, December 7, 1979.
Virginia Quarterly Review, spring, 1973.
Washington Post Book World, November 18, 1973, November 5, 1978, November 23, 1980, May 1, 1983, June 24, 1984.
World Literature Today, winter, 1977, winter, 1980.

OBITUARIES:

PERIODICALS

Chicago Tribune, February 14, 1984.
Globe and Mail (Toronto), February 18, 1984.
Los Angeles Times, February 14, 1984.
New York Times, February 13, 1984.
Times (London), February 14, 1984.
Voice Literary Supplement, March, 1984.
Washington Post, February 13, 1984.

*   *   *

CORWIN, Judith H(offman) 1946-

PERSONAL: Born November 14, 1946, in New York, NY; daughter of Harry (an investor) and Mary (Pastor) Hoffman; married Jules Arthur Corwin (a United Nations official), October 4, 1969; children: Oliver Jamie. *Education:* Pratt Institute, B.F.A., 1969.

ADDRESSES: Home and office—333 East 30th St., New York, NY 10016.

CAREER: Western Publishing Co., New York City, member of Experimental Toy Division, 1969; Cherry & Shackleford Design, New York City, design assistant, 1969-70; Parks, Recreation, and Cultural Affairs Administration, New York City, graphic designer, 1970-71; free-lance writer and illustrator, with exhibitions of her work, 1971—. Guest editor of *Mademoiselle,* summer, 1969.

AWARDS, HONORS: Design award from Keuffel & Esser, 1969, for optics and metrology log; awards from Children's Book Fair, Bologna, Italy, 1976, for "Satina Susanah," and 1980, for "If I Could Be Very, Very Small."

WRITINGS:

SELF-ILLUSTRATED CHILDREN'S BOOK

Words, Words, Words, Platt, 1976.
Sleepytime, Grosset, 1978.
Applique, Dover, 1979.
Creative Collage, McKay, 1980.
Christmas Fun, Messner, 1982.
Valentine Fun, Messner, 1983.
Halloween Fun, Messner, 1983.
Thanksgiving Fun, Messner, 1984.
Easter Fun, Messner, 1984.
Cookie Book, Messner, 1985.
Patriotic Fun, Messner, 1985.
Birthday Fun, Messner, 1986.
Jewish Holiday Fun, Messner, 1987.
Papercrafts, F. Watts, 1988.

"COLONIAL AMERICAN CRAFTS" SERIES

The Home, F. Watts, 1989.
The Village, F. Watts, 1989.
The School, F. Watts, 1989.

OTHER

Illustrator of children's books, including *Red Light Says Stop,* by Barbara Rinkoff, 1974; *666 Jellybeans,* by Malcolm Weiss, 1975; and *Weaving,* by Alice Gilbreath, 1976.

SIDELIGHTS: Judith H. Corwin told *CA:* "I am mainly an illustrator and graphic designer. I have done a lot of magazine and advertising illustration, and I have worked for the United Nations and the City of New York. Although my books are for all age groups, the vitality and imagination of children especially inspire me.

"Creating books for children is a special pleasure for me. Children have such a wonderful, curious nature. Almost everything interests them if presented in a fun way. Once you capture their imagination they aren't afraid to explore new things.

"Childhood, such a temporary part of our lives, is a transition that must be fully appreciated. A child's imagination is a special gift, one that plays an important part in the developing years. It's a time to feel free, to explore, to experiment, and to dream. As an artist my imagination is an integral part of myself and my work. I can let my imagination run free and color a funny looking creature pink or make a chair fly.

"I like to think my work has an honest approach and the fresh vitality to which a child can respond. Children delight in the natural world, and in my writing I try to see the world through a child's eyes—to respond to and at the same time encourage a wonder at the things around us. There are so many wonderful and beautiful things in our world all waiting to be captured on paper. I try to make children look at something ordinary in a different and fun way—to take a second look at things and imagine the possibilities."

BIOGRAPHICAL/CRITICAL SOURCES:

PERIODICALS

Print, November-December, 1973.

*　　*　　*

COURTNEY, Nicholas (Piers) 1944-
(Davina Hanmer)

PERSONAL: Born December 20, 1944, in Berkshire, England; son of Frederick Harold Deming and Sybil (an artist; maiden name, Leigh-Pemberton) Courtney; married Vanessa Sylvia Hardwicke (a television assistant producer), October 30, 1980. *Education:* Attended Nautical College, Berkshire, England; Royal Agricultural College, ARICS, 1966. *Religion:* Church of England.

ADDRESSES: Home—9 Kempson Rd., London SW6 4PX, England.

CAREER: Estate manager to Col. C. G. Lancaster, Kelmarsh Hall, Northampton, England, 1966-69; Island of Mustique, St. Vincent, West Indies, general manager, 1970-77; writer, 1980—. *Military service:* British Territorial Army, Glosters, 1964-66; became second lieutenant.

MEMBER: International PEN, Royal Institution of Chartered Surveyors (associate member).

WRITINGS:

The Self-Catering Holiday Guide to Shopping and Cooking in Europe, Hutchinson, 1980.
The Tiger: Symbol of Freedom, Quartet Books, 1981.
Diana, Princess of Wales, Rainbird Publishing Group, 1982.
Royal Children, Dent, 1982.
Sporting Royals, Hutchinson, 1983.
Prince Andrew, Macdonald & Co., 1983.
The Very Best of British, Collins, 1984.
The Queen Mother, Rainbird Publishing Group, 1984.
(Under pseudonym Davina Hanmer) *Diana, the Princess of Fashion,* Holt, 1984.
Princess Anne, Weidenfeld & Nicolson, 1986.
In Society, Pavilion Books, 1986.
The Luxury Shopping Guide to London, Weiden feld & Nicolson, 1987.
Sisters-in-Law: How Princess Diana and Sarah Ferguson Changed the Face of Royalty, Weidenfeld & Nicolson, 1988.
The Stratford Kingshall, Bachman & Turner, 1989.
The Mall, Bachman & Turner, 1989.
The Windsor Castle Kingshall, Bachman & Turner, 1989.

SIDELIGHTS: Nicholas Courtney told *CA:* "I feel that, with a drawerful of unpublishable manuscripts and even more synopses, I was an overnight success after five years. The first book is always the most rewarding, *The Self-Catering Holiday Guide to Shopping and Cooking in Europe,* a primer to what you find in the shops and markets of Europe—how to buy and how to cook it—was a great indulgence of travel and research. Passionately keen about the tiger and what it stands for, I then wrote *The Tiger: Symbol of Freedom.* This unique work coordinated many areas of research and presented a whole new, and after a recent fossil find, a now-accepted theory on the evolution of the tiger.

"It is too easy to become typecast in all of the arts. When an author becomes typecast, in my case with writing about the Royal Family, the financial rewards may be great but the originality and challenge are gone. Social history and biography are now replacing the Royal Family for my future works."

BIOGRAPHICAL/CRITICAL SOURCES:

PERIODICALS

Washington Post, December 13, 1987.

*　　*　　*

CRISPIN, A(nn) C(arol) 1950-

PERSONAL: Born April 5, 1950, in Stamford, CT; daughter of George Arthur (a maritime management specialist) and Hope (a teacher; maiden name, Hooker) Tickell; married Randy Lee Crispin (a pharmacist), May 19, 1973; children: Jason Paul. *Education:* University of Maryland, B.A., 1972. *Politics:* Liberal. *Religion:* "Universal."

ADDRESSES: Home—Hughesville, MD. *Agent*—Merrilee Heifetz, Writer's House, Inc., 21 West 26th St., New York, NY 10010.

CAREER: Worked variously as a customer service representative, receptionist, technical librarian, and typist, 1972-74; U.S. Census Bureau, Suitland, MD, computer programmer, training specialist, and technical writer, 1974-83; writer, 1983—. Also worked as a horseback riding teacher, horse trainer, writing instructor, and swimming instructor. Steward of local union of American Federation of Government Employees.

MEMBER: Science Fiction Writers of America.

WRITINGS:

SCIENCE FICTION NOVELS

Yesterday's Son, Pocket Books, 1983.
V, Pinnacle Books, 1984.
(With Weinstein) *V: East Coast Crisis,* Pinnacle Books, 1984.
(With Andre Norton) *Gryphon's Eyrie,* Tor Books, 1984.
Sylvester (movie novelization), Tor Books, 1985.
(With Deborah A. Marshall) *V: Death Tide,* Pinnacle Books, 1985.
Time for Yesterday, Pocket Books, 1988.
Starbridge (first book in "Starbridge" series), Ace Books, 1989.
The Eyes of the Beholders, Pocket Books, 1990.
Silent Dances (second book in "Starbridge" series), Ace Books, 1990.

OTHER

Also contributor to anthologies, including *Magic in Ithkar,* edited by Robert Adams and Norton, Volume 3, Tor Books, 1986; and *Tales of the Witch World,* edited by Norton, Tor Books, Volume 1, 1987, Volume 3, 1990. Two of Crispin's novels have been released on audio cassette by Simon & Shuster AudioWorks, *Yesterday's Son,* 1988, and *Time for Yesterday,* 1989.

WORK IN PROGRESS: *Songsmith,* a "Witch World" collaboration with Andre Norton; *Shadow World, Serpent's Gift,* and *Silent Songs,* the last three titles in the "Starbridge" series.

SIDELIGHTS: A. C. Crispin has been writing science fiction/fantasy full time for the past few years. Crispin told *CA:* "I am . . . fulfilling a dream I've envisioned ever since high school. Writing is for me mostly storytelling, and there is dignity in writing for entertainment, as long as the story told is an honest one, truly felt and experienced by the writer. I hope to advance my craft until I can make writing for entertainment and writing for emotional and cerebral effect one and the same.

"I am especially thrilled that professional writing contacts put me in touch with Andre Norton. We began corresponding long before the publication of *Yesterday's Son.* Ms. Norton has always been one of my favorite writers, and, as one of the first women to 'break into' the male-dominated science fiction field, she has also been a personal hero and an inspiration to me. The chance to collaborate with her is literally the chance of a lifetime. I have learned a great deal from her experience in crafting a story.

"In my writing, I get many ideas from visual images: mismatched words, pictures, and, often, dreams. *Gryphon's Eyrie* came about from a dream I had about Ms. Norton's characters in *The Crystal Gryphon* and *Gryphon in Glory.*

"The stories I tell in my books are *stories*—my realizations of theme, personal insight, symbolism, etc., come about much later, usually after the first draft has been completed. My most recurrent theme is 'be yourself—but don't stop trying to be a better person.' This may sound like Pollyanna in today's world, but I consider myself an optimist, if a somewhat cynical one."

BIOGRAPHICAL/CRITICAL SOURCES:

PERIODICALS

Baltimore Sun, September 1, 1983.
Chattanooga News-Free Press, September 11, 1983.
Dragon, January, 1990.
Locus, October, 1989.
Maryland Independent, July 27, 1983.
Minneapolis Star Tribune, July 16, 1989.
Washington Post, August 21, 1983.

CROZIER, Lorna 1948-

PERSONAL: Born in 1948, in Swift Current, Saskatchewan, Canada; daughter of Emerson and Peggy Crozier. *Education:* University of Saskatchewan, B.A., 1969; University of Alberta, M.A., 1980.

ADDRESSES: *Home*—812 14th St. E., Saskatoon, Saskatchewan, Canada M4C 3M1.

CAREER: High school English teacher in Swift Current, Saskatchewan, 1970-77; Cypress Hills Community College, Swift Current, writer-in-residence, 1980-81; Saskatchewan Department of Culture and Recreation, Regina, director of communications, 1981-83; Regina Public Library, Regina, writer-in-residence, 1983-84; University of Saskatchewan, Saskatoon, special lecturer, 1986—; University of Toronto, Toronto, Ontario, writer-in-residence, 1988-89.

MEMBER: League of Canadian Poets, Saskatchewan Writers' Guild (vice-president, 1977-79), Saskatchewan Artists' Colony (committee president, 1982-84).

AWARDS, HONORS: Poetry prize, Saskatchewan Department of Culture and Youth, 1978, for *Crow's Black Joy;* poetry manuscript prize, Saskatchewan Writers' Guild, 1983, for *The Weather,* and 1985, for *The Garden Going on without Us;* nomination for Governor General's Award for Poetry, 1985, for *The Garden Going on without Us,* and 1988, for *Angels of Flesh, Angels of Silence;* first prize for poetry, Canadian Broadcasting Corp. (CBC), 1987; second prize, *Prism International* poetry competition, 1987, for "Fear of Snakes"; Nellie Award for best public radio program, 1988, for "Chile."

WRITINGS:

Inside Is the Sky (poetry), Thistledown Press, 1975.
Crow's Black Joy (poetry), NeWest Press, 1978.
(With Patrick Lane) *No Longer Two People* (poetry), Turnstone Press, 1979.
Humans and Other Beasts (poetry), Turnstone Press, 1980.
The Weather (poetry), Coteau, 1983.
(Co-author) "If We Call This the Girlie Show, Will You Find It Offensive?" (three-act play), first produced in Regina, Saskatchewan, at Globe Theatre, January, 1984.
The Garden Going on without Us (poetry), McClelland & Stewart, 1985.
Angels of Flesh, Angels of Silence (poetry), McClelland & Stewart, 1988.

CONTRIBUTOR TO ANTHOLOGIES

Full Moon, Quadrant, 1984.
Anything Is Possible, Mosaic, 1984.
Canadian Poetry Now, House of Anansi, 1984.
Ride off Any Horizon, NeWest, 1984.
Dennis Lee, editor, *The New Canadian Poets,* McClelland & Stewart, 1985.

OTHER

Also author of "Chile" (radio program), broadcast on CBC-Radio. Contributor of poems and reviews to periodicals, including *Quarry* and *Saturday Night.* Poetry editor, *NeWest Review.*

WORK IN PROGRESS: A collection of poetry, *Dictionary of Symbols.*

SIDELIGHTS: Lorna Crozier told *CA:* "The most important influence on my writing was *As for Me and My House,* by Sinclair Ross. It was the first book I read that was set in the landscape where I grew up, the southwest corner of Saskatchewan. It made me realize that someone from my area could actually be a writer and, in some ways, it gave me the courage to try.

"The landscape of southwestern Saskatchewan has definitely influenced by writing. I've tried to thread the wind and sky into my poems, to make them breathe the way the prairie does. But the influence of place goes beyond the recurrence of images particular to a certain landscape. The mutability and the extremes of the natural world in Saskatchewan have given rise to my sense of the fragility of happiness, love, and life itself. Our hold on things and on each other is so tenuous. My poems, I think, express the fearful hope I feel for the human—for our capability to return to love through pain and for our journey towards that sense of unity with all things, with the mule deer I startled from feeding in the coulee yesterday, and with the mute explosions of lichens on the stones in my grandfather's pasture. If the magic that is poetry can't lead us to that oneness, then I hope it at least can make us feel less alone.

"Along with the impetus to write about the people and landscape that were mine by birth and inclination came the influence of writers like Rainer Maria Rilke and Pablo Neruda. They made me try to stretch to the limits of my imagination and beyond, to get in touch with the interior landscape of the soul."

BIOGRAPHICAL/CRITICAL SOURCES:

PERIODICALS

Globe and Mail (Toronto), March 31, 1990.

*   *   *

CRUZ, Victor Hernandez   1949-

PERSONAL: Born February 6, 1949, in Aguas Buenas, P.R.; son of Severo and Rosa Cruz; children: Ajani. *Education:* Attended high school in New York, NY.

ADDRESSES: P.O. Box 40148, San Francisco, CA 94140.

CAREER: Poet. Guest lecturer at University of California, Berkeley, 1969; San Francisco State University, San Francisco, CA, instructor, beginning 1973.

AWARDS, HONORS: Creative Artists public service award, 1974, for *Tropicalization.*

WRITINGS:

Papa Got His Gun!, and Other Poems, Calle Once Publications, 1966.
Doing Poetry, Other Ways, 1968.
Snaps (poems), Random House, 1969.
(Editor with Herbert Kohl) *Stuff: A Collection of Poems, Visions, and Imaginative Happenings from Young Writers in Schools—Open and Closed,* Collins & World, 1970.
Mainland (poems), Random House, 1973.

Tropicalization (poems and prose), Reed, Canon, 1976.
The Low Writings, Lee/Lucas Press, 1980.
By Lingual Wholes, Momo's, 1982.
Rhythm, Content and Flavor: New and Selected Poems, Arte Público, 1989.

Work has been included in anthologies, including *An Anthology of Afro-American Writing,* Morrow, 1968, and *Giant Talk: An Anthology of Third World Writings,* Random House, 1975. Contributor to *Evergreen Review, New York Review of Books, Ramparts, Down Here,* and *Revista del Instituto de Estudios Puertorriqueños.* Former editor, *Umbra.*

WORK IN PROGRESS: A novel, for Random House.

SIDELIGHTS: Victor Hernández Cruz wrote: "My family life was full of music, guitars and conga drums, maracas and songs. My mother sang songs. Even when it was five below zero in New York she sang warm tropical ballads." He continued: "My work is on the border of a new language, because I create out of a consciousness steeped in two of the important world languages, Spanish and English. A piece written totally in English could have a Spanish spirit. Another strong concern in my work is the difference between a tropical village, such as Aguas Buenas, Puerto Rico, where I was born, and an immensity such as New York City, where I was raised. I compare smells and sounds, I explore the differences, I write from the center of a culture which is not on its native soil, a culture in flight, living half the time on memories, becoming something totally new and unique, while at the same time it helps to shape and inform the new environment. I write about the city with an agonizing memory of a lush tropical silence. This contrast between landscape and language creates an intensity in my work."

In a *New York Times Book Review* of *By Lingual Wholes,* Richard Elman remarks: "Cruz writes poems about his native Puerto Rico and elsewhere which often speak to us with a forked tongue, sometimes in a highly literate Spanglish. . . . He's a funny, hard-edged poet, declining always into mother wit and pathos: 'So you see, all life is a holy hole. Bet hard on that.'" And Nancy Sullivan reflects in *Poetry* magazine: "Cruz allows the staccato crackle of English half-learned, so characteristic of his people, to enrich the poems through its touching dictional inadequacy. If poetry is arching toward the condition of silence as John Cage and Susan Sontag suggest, perhaps this mode of inarticulateness is a bend on the curve. . . . I think that Cruz is writing necessary poems in a period when many poems seem unnecessary."

BIOGRAPHICAL/CRITICAL SOURCES:

PERIODICALS

New York Times Book Review, September 18, 1983.
Poetry, May, 1970.*

D

DACEY, Philip 1939-

PERSONAL: Born May 9, 1939, in St. Louis, MO; son of Joseph and Teresa (McGinn) Dacey; married Florence Chard, May 25, 1963 (divorced, 1986); children: Emmet Joseph, Fay Pauline Teresa, Austin Warren. *Education:* St. Louis University, B.A., 1961; Stanford University, M.A., 1967; University of Iowa, M.F.A., 1970.

ADDRESSES: *Home*—Route 1, Box 32, Lynd, MN 56157. *Office*—English Department, Southwest State University, Marshall, MN 56258.

CAREER: Peace Corps, Eastern Nigeria, volunteer, 1963-65; Miles College, Birmingham, AL, instructor, 1966; University of Missouri—St. Louis, instructor in English, 1967-68; Southwest State University, Marshall, MN, 1970—, began as assistant professor, currently professor of English and coordinator of creative writing. Wichita State University, Distinguished Poet in Residence, 1985; Fulbright Lecturer in creative writing to Yugoslavia, 1988. Readings given in more than a third of the United States and in Mexico, Ireland, and Yugoslavia.

AWARDS, HONORS: Yankee Poetry Prize, 1968; Poet and Critic Prize, 1969; Borestone Mountain Poetry Award, 1974; Discovery Award, 1974; first prize, G. M. Hopkins Memorial Sonnet Competition, 1977; first prize in poetry, *Praire Schooner,* 1977; Pushcart Prize, 1977, 1982; first prize in poetry, *Kansas Quarterly,* 1980. Fellowships from the National Endowment for the Arts, 1975, 1980, Minnesota State Arts Council, 1975, 1983, Bush Foundation, 1977, and The Loft, A Place For Writing and Literature, 1984.

WRITINGS:

POETRY

The Beast with Two Backs (pamphlet), Gunrunner Press, 1969.
(Editor with Gerald Knoll) *I Love You All Day: It Is That Simple* (anthology), Abbey Press, 1970.
Fish, Sweet Giraffe, The Lion, Snake, and Owl (pamphlet), Back Door Press, 1970.
Four Nudes (pamphlet), Morgan Press, 1971.
How I Escaped from the Labyrinth and Other Poems, Carnegie-Mellon University Press, 1977.
The Condom Poems, Ox Head Press, 1979.
The Boy under the Bed, Johns Hopkins University Press, 1981.

Gerard Manley Hopkins Meets Walt Whitman in Heaven and Other Poems, Penmaen Press, 1982.
Fives, Spoon River Poetry Press, 1984.
(Editor with David Jauss) *Strong Measures: Contemporary American Poetry in Traditional Forms,* Harper, 1985.
The Man with Red Suspenders, Milkweed Editions, 1986.
The Condom Poems II, Spoon River Poetry Press, 1989.

Contributor of poems to more than fifty anthologies, including *American Poetry Anthology,* edited by D. Halpern, Avon, 1975; *Heartland II: Poets of the Midwest,* edited by L. Stryk, Northern Illinois University Press, 1975; *Ardis Anthology of New American Poetry,* edited by D. Rigsbee, Ardis, 1977; *A Geography of Poets,* edited by Field, Bantam, 1979; *Walt Whitman,* edited by Perlman, Holy Cow, 1981; *Beowulf to Beatles and Beyond,* edited by Pichaske, Macmillan, 1981; *Leaving the Bough,* edited by Gaess, International Publishers Co., 1982; *Knock at a Star: A Child's Introduction to Poetry,* edited by Kennedy, Little, Brown, 1982; *Poetspeak,* edited by Janeczko, Bradbury, 1983; and *Vital Signs: Contemporary American Poetry from the University Presses,* edited by Wallace, University of Wisconsin Press, 1989. Contributor of poems to more than one hundred fifty periodicals, including *Antaeus, Esquire, New York Quarterly, Poetry Northwest, Nation, Paris Review, American Review, Partisan Review, Hudson Review,* and *Shenandoah.*

OTHER

Contributor of more than twenty articles, essays, and reviews to periodicals and books. Editor, *Crazy Horse,* 1971-76; contributing editor, *Pushcart Prize: Best of the Small Presses,* 1983—.

MEDIA ADAPTATIONS: The poem "The Birthday" was set to music by David Sampson for soprano, harp, oboe, and cello, and performed at the Carnegie-Mellon Institute, spring, 1982.

WORK IN PROGRESS: Two books of poetry, *Night Shift at the Crucifix Factory* and *Cycle for Yugoslavia.*

SIDELIGHTS: Witty verse and an unmistakably upbeat style characterize the poetry of Philip Dacey. However, his early work attracted critical attention for what some reviewers considered his tonal inconsistency. Peter Stitt, for example, in a critique of *How I Escaped from the Labyrinth and Other Poems* for *Ohio Review,* termed the book "[a work of a] relatively scattered nature" and insisted that "a poet who adopts too many voices is a poet with no voice of his or her own." Barry Wallenstein, however, found Dacey's variety enlightening; in a review of Dacey's second volume of poems for *American Book Review* he wrote, "In *The Boy under the Bed* . . . we have a true voice that sings in various tones. . . . [Dacey's] adventurous imagination informs the whole."

Despite this early debate on his poetic voice Dacey's positive outlook has persisted since his first volume was published. "*How I Escaped from the Labyrinth* is an accomplished first book, pulsing with love and affirmation, acceptance and celebration," wrote Ronald Wallace in *Chowder Review.* "Dacey's voice is healing and compassionate." Vernon Young found Dacey equally upbeat in *The Boy under the Bed,* noting in a review for *Parnassus: Poetry in Review,* "I can think of no other contemporary poet who believes that almost everything is for the best in this best of possible worlds. Dacey writes as if he believed so." In a *Tar River Poetry* review of Dacey's more recent book, *The Man with Red Suspenders,* Dabney Stuart elaborated on Dacey's ability to impress upon his readers the inspirational attitude with which he approaches writing: "[Much] of Dacey's work in this book (as well as his others) incorporates . . . spiritual agency as a given in the world he creates. It is this . . . that makes effective his joining of usually disparate circumstances and categories."

Philip Dacey told *CA:* "Poetry came into my life uninvited, in my late twenties, at a time when I was stalled, directionless. I had always wanted to be a novelist; poetry interested me minimally at best. It came bubbling up like a spring, continued, grew, and transformed my life, giving it shape and meaning. I am grateful to poetry for doing so and have tried to serve it faithfully for the last twenty-five or so years. I do not believe in writers' block; I believe that if one wants to write one can and does, although there is no guarantee as to the lasting quality of the work one chooses to do on a regular basis.

"As I write this I am 50; that is not young but Thomas Hardy did not start publishing poetry—for which he is now considered as English master poet—until he was 55. Thus I hope to have at least another twenty-five years in which to write; the first twenty-five years should act as a good running start for the second twenty-five. I have always been a college teacher but have managed to take many leaves of absence over the years; I intend now to shift the balance even more toward the leaves and become something approaching a part-time teacher, even if it means some financial squeezing. The first fifty years of my life have been a bit of a shakedown cruise; poetry has come through it all in a central place and I want now to renew and even strengthen my commitment to the art."

BIOGRAPHICAL/CRITICAL SOURCES:

BOOKS

Contemporary Literary Criticism, Volume 51, Gale, 1989.
Contemporary Poets, 4th edition, St. James Press/St. Martin's, 1988.

PERIODICALS

American Book Review, Volume 4, number 6, 1982.
Chowder Review, number 9, 1977.
Great River Review, fall, 1977.
Minnesota Daily, August 8, 1977.
Ohio Review, Volume 19, number 2, 1978.
Parnassus: Poetry in Review, Volume 9, number 2, 1981.
Poet Lore, winter, 1981-82.
Shenandoah, winter, 1971.
Tar River Poetry, spring, 1979; spring, 1987.

DAHL, Roald 1916-

PERSONAL: Given name is pronounced "Roo-aal"; born September 13, 1916, in Llandaff, South Wales; son of Harald (a shipbroker, painter, and horticulturist) and Sofie (Hesselberg) Dahl; married Patricia Neal (an actress), July 2, 1953 (divorced, 1983); married Felicity Ann Crosland, 1983; children: (first marriage) Olivia (deceased), Tessa, Theo, Ophelia, Lucy. *Education:* Graduate of British public schools, 1932.

ADDRESSES: Home—Gipsy House, Great Missenden, Buckinghamshire HP16 0PB, England. *Agent*—Watkins Loomis Agency, 150 East 35th St., New York, N.Y. 10016.

CAREER: Shell Oil Co., London, England, member of eastern staff, 1933-37, member of staff in Dar-es-Salaam, Tanzania, 1937-39; writer. *Military service:* Royal Air Force, fighter pilot, 1939-45; became wing commander.

AWARDS, HONORS: Edgar Award, Mystery Writers of America, 1954, 1959, and 1980; Whitbread Award, 1983, for *The Witches;* World Fantasy Convention Lifetime Achievement Award, and Federation of Children's Book Groups Award, both 1983.

WRITINGS:

Sometime Never: A Fable for Supermen (novel), Scribner, 1948.
My Uncle Oswald (novel), M. Joseph, 1979, Knopf, 1980.
Going Solo (autobiography), Farrar, Straus, 1986.
Esio Trot, J. Cape, 1990.

FOR JUVENILES

The Gremlins, Random House, 1943.
James and the Giant Peach (also see below), Knopf, 1961.
Charlie and the Chocolate Factory (also see below), Knopf, 1964, revised edition, 1973.
The Magic Finger, Harper, 1966.
Fantastic Mr. Fox (also see below), Knopf, 1970.
Charlie and The Great Glass Elevator: The Further Adventures of Charlie Bucket and Willy Wonka, Chocolate-Maker Extraordinary, Knopf, 1972.
Danny: The Champion of the World, Knopf, 1975 (collected with *James and the Giant Peach* and *Fantastic Mr. Fox,* Bantam, 1983).
The Enormous Crocodile, Knopf, 1976.
The Wonderful Story of Henry Sugar and Six More, Knopf, 1977.
Complete Adventures of Charlie and Mr. Willy Wonka, Allen & Unwin, 1978.
The Twits, J. Cape, 1980, Knopf, 1981.
George's Marvellous Medicine, J. Cape, 1981.
Roald Dahl's Revolting Rhymes, Knopf, 1982.
The BFG, Farrar, Straus, 1982.
Dirty Beasts, Farrar, Straus, 1983.
The Witches, Farrar, Straus, 1984.
Boy: Tales of Childhood, Farrar, Straus, 1984.
The Giraffe and Pelly and Me, Farrar, Straus, 1985.
Matilda, Viking Kestrel, 1989.
Rhyme Stew (comic verse), Viking Kestrel, 1989.

SHORT STORY COLLECTIONS

Over to You: Ten Stories of Flyers and Flying, Reynal, 1946.
Someone Like You (Book-of-the-Month Club alternate selection; also see below), Knopf, 1953, revised edition, M. Joseph, 1961.
Kiss, Kiss (also see below), Knopf, 1960.

Twenty-Nine Kisses (contains contents of *Someone Like You* and *Kiss, Kiss*), M. Joseph, 1969.
Selected Stories, Random House, 1970.
Switch Bitch, Knopf, 1974.
The Best of Roald Dahl, Random House, 1978.
Tales of the Unexpected, Vintage, 1979.
Taste and Other Tales, Longman, 1979.
More Tales of the Unexpected, Penguin, 1980.
Roald Dahl's Book of Ghost Stories, Farrar, Straus, 1983.
The Roald Dahl Omnibus, Hippocrene Books, 1987.
Ah, Sweet Mystery of Life, Viking Kestrel, 1989.

SCREENPLAYS

"You Only Live Twice," United Artists, 1967.
(With Ken Hughes) "Chitty Chitty Bang Bang," United Artists, 1968.
"The Night-digger" (based on "Nest in a Falling Tree," by Joy Crowley), Metro-Goldwyn-Mayer, 1970.
"Willy Wonka and the Chocolate Factory" (based on *Charlie and the Chocolate Factory*), Paramount, 1971.

Also author of screenplays "Oh Death, Where Is Thy Sting-a Ling-a-Ling?," United Artists, and "The Lightning Bug" and "The Road Builder."

OTHER

Author of stage play "The Honeys," produced in New York, N.Y., 1955. Contributor to anthologies and to periodicals including *Harper's, Atlantic, Esquire,* and *Saturday Evening Post.*

SIDELIGHTS: "Roald Dahl is certainly one of the more difficult authors to categorise, not only because he writes for all ages from infancy upwards, but also because his work reflects several contrasting moods and a willingness to experiment with literary methods," observes Alasdair Campbell in an issue of *School Librarian.* Other critics have no problem pegging Dahl as engagingly cynical, as purposely outrageous, as rampantly hilarious. Best known for his children's books, the Welsh native began writing after leaving the RAF where, as a fighter pilot, he had crashed a plane "at 200 mph, bashing his head off the reflector sight and flattening his nose," as *Times* writer Peter Lennon relates. "Having until then produced only dogged schoolboy letters, [Dahl's] first letter home from hospital was brilliant. He was a writer. A squashed one, but a writer."

Soon afterward Dahl began publishing short stories, poems and novels, most with a bizarre bent to them, at least one provoking a great deal of controversy. This was the 1964 novel *Charlie and the Chocolate Factory.* Perhaps Dahl's best known work, this morality tale finds young Charlie Bucket one of five lucky children chosen to tour the legendary top-secret chocolate factory belonging to the reclusive Willy Wonka. The controversy began when critics and readers took umbrage with the author's depiction of a group of characters called the Oompa-Loompas, who work in the factory. Described by Dahl in the story as a tribe of "miniature pygmies" from "the very deepest and darkest part of the African jungle where no white man has ever been before," the Oompa-Loompas are also depicted as unthinking, unfeeling creatures who live only to serve. "It seems to me that the West has been treated to 'dark Africa' too many times and that it is racism to perpetuate the myth and image of darkness," notes Lois Kalb Bouchard in an article printed in the volume *The Black American in Books for Children: Readings in Racism.* "The children who find the golden admission tickets are never designated white in words, but the Oompa-Loompas are designated Black, and the illustrations show white children . . . ," concludes Bouchard. "I suspect, also, that in our cultural con-

text of racism, the small size of the Black characters becomes a symbol of their implied inadequacies."

But racism isn't the book's only shortcoming, according to Myra Pollack Sadker and David Miller Sadker in their study *Now upon a Time: A Contemporary View of Children's Literature.* "Were there greater sensitivity to mistreatment and misrepresentation of the elderly, [the novel] would have received criticism as an 'ageist' book as well," they write. "At the book's conclusion Charlie arrives home in triumph in a glass elevator piloted by Willy Wonka himself. When the bedridden grandparents learn that they are to live out the rest of their days in the chocolate factory, they refuse to go and scream that they would rather die in their beds. Willy Wonka and Charlie, taking no notice whatsoever of their protests and screams, simply push the old people, beds and all, into the glass elevator. The message with which we close the book is that the needs and desires and opinions of old people are totally irrelevant and inconsequential."

Not every critic objected to *Charlie and the Chocolate Factory.* *New York Times Book Review* writer Aileen Pippen called the book "a Dickensian delight, and [the factory], with its laughing, singing, tiny Oompa-Loompa workers, is sheer joy." And according to J. S. Jenkins in *Children's Book News,* "Roald Dahl has a rare and rich gift. . . . Children laugh and gasp at his splendid fantasies—the waterfalls of chocolate, the everlasting gobstoppers, the chewing-gum machines. All words and sounds are grist to his mill, and the mixture of elan and nicety with which he uses them gives a zest to his writing which is all too seldom found in children's books." Nevertheless, in a revised edition of *Charlie and the Chocolate Factory,* released in 1973 to coincide with a movie-musical version of the story, the Oompa-Loompas are rewritten as raceless gnomes who serve as a Greek chorus as well as factory workers.

Dahl brought out a sequel, *Charlie and the Great Glass Elevator: The Further Adventures of Charlie Bucket and Willy Wonka, Chocolate-Maker Extraordinary,* in 1972. In a *New York Times Book Review* article, Julia Whedon notes that this work features all of the original *Charlie* cast with new supporting players, including "a President of the United States whose Nanny is Vice President (and still pushes him around). He poses knock-knock jokes to other heads of state when he's playing around with his red telephone and has a childish Cabinet (the Chief Spy wears a false mustache, the Chief Financial Adviser 'balances' the budget—on the top of his head). In short, like the first 'Charlie,' this one strikes me as a very easy fantasy, not very intensively developed. It's almost funny, almost suspenseful, only coyly screwball."

More recently, the author has begun to produce autobiographical stories. In *Boy: Tales of Childhood,* a 1985 release, Dahl "explains in the introduction that he is not writing a boring history of his life, but about those things—comic, painful, unpleasant— that he has never been able to forget," according to *New York Times Book Review* critic Hazel Rochman. "There were vacations in Norway [Dahl's parentage is Norwegian], feasts and mischief in his close, large, wealthy and almost entirely female family. . . . But from age of 9 to 18 he endured the harsh rigor of select English boys' boarding schools, where, as in Dickens's novels of childhood, grotesque adults wielded savage power over the helpless and innocent students." In his memoirs, Rochman concludes, Dahl "is in quiet control, chatting to his readers, explaining a few historical differences, illustrating each incident with scraps of his weekly letters home. . . . The tension between this casual commonsense tone and the lurking demonic terror gives these tales their power."

Dahl followed *Boy* with *Going Solo,* which chronicles the author's tour of duty in the RAF, and spares no detail in relating the horrors of war. "He is a natural story-teller," says *Times Literary Supplement* critic of Dahl, "and *Going Solo* describes without either false modesty or conceit some remarkable exploits. If this book were fiction . . . one might suspect that the writer was laying it on a bit, but one trusts Dahl from the outset." In *Time* reviewer R. Z. Sheppard's view, Dahl "tells of his wartime adventures with an ordinariness of tone that contrasts with the ghastliness of his experiences. This, of course, is the preferred method for a successful horror story. *Going Solo* is much more: a brief, masterly remembrance of the gifts of youth and good luck."

The author has long acknowledged his bizarre reputation as a children's fantasist, but admits he cannot directly trace the beginnings of these tendencies. "I don't know where my ideas come from," Dahl tells Lennon in the *Times* interview. "Perhaps my Norwegian background is an influence. Plots just wander into my head. They are like dreams, one is terrified of losing them. Once I stopped the car and got out and wrote a word or two on the dust of the [trunk] lid so I wouldn't forget an idea."

MEDIA ADAPTATIONS: Charlie and the Chocolate Factory was adapted for the stage by Richard R. George, and published by Penguin Books in 1983; *The Witches* was filmed in 1990.

BIOGRAPHICAL/CRITICAL SOURCES:

BOOKS

Children's Literature Review, Volume 7, Gale, 1984.
Contemporary Literary Criticism, Gale, Volume 1, 1973, Volume 6, 1976, Volume 18, 1981.
Dahl, Roald, *Charlie and the Chocolate Factory,* Knopf, 1964, revised edition, 1973.
Dahl, Roald, *Boy: Tales of Childhood,* Farrar, Straus, 1985.
Dahl, Roald, *Going Solo,* Farrar, Straus, 1986.
McCann, Donnarae, and Gloria Woodard, editors, *The Black American in Books for Children: Readings in Racism,* Scarecrow, 1972.
Sadker, Mara Pollak, and David Miller Sadker, *Now upon a Time: A Contemporary View of Children's Literature,* Harper, 1977.

PERIODICALS

Chicago Tribune, October 21, 1986.
Chicago Tribune Book World, August 10, 1980, May 17, 1981.
Children's Book News, March-April, 1968.
Children's Literature in Education, summer, 1976.
Horn Book, December, 1972, February, 1973, April, 1973, June, 1973.
New Republic, October 19, 1974, April 19, 1980.
New York Review of Books, December 17, 1970, December 14, 1972.
New York Times Book Review, October 25, 1964, September 17, 1972, October 26, 1975, March 29, 1981, January 9, 1983, January 20, 1985, October 12, 1986, January 15, 1989.
Saturday Review, March 10, 1973.
School Librarian, June, 1981.
Times (London), December 22, 1983.
Times Literary Supplement, June 15, 1973, December 5, 1975, July 23, 1982, November 30, 1984, September 12, 1986.
Washington Post, October 8, 1986.
Washington Post Book World, November 13, 1978, May 8, 1983, January 13, 1985.

—*Sketch by Susan Salter*

* * *

DANA, Rose
   See ROSS, W(illiam) E(dward) D(aniel)

* * *

DAVEY, Frank(land Wilmot) 1940-

PERSONAL: Born April 19, 1940, in Vancouver, British Columbia, Canada; married Helen Simmons, 1962 (divorced, 1969); married Linda Jane McCartney, 1969; children: (second marriage) Michael Gareth, Sara Geneve. *Education:* University of British Columbia, B.A. (with honors), 1961, M.A., 1963; University of Southern California, Los Angeles, Ph.D., 1968.

ADDRESSES: Office—334 Stong, North York College, York University, Ontario, Canada M3J 1P4.

CAREER: Royal Roads Military College, Victoria, British Columbia, lecturer, 1963-66, assistant professor, 1967-69; Sir George Williams University, Montreal, Quebec, writer-in-residence, 1969-70; York University, Toronto, Ontario, assistant professor, 1970-72, associate professor, 1972-80, professor, 1980—, co-ordinator, Program in Creative Writing, 1976-79, chairman of English department, 1985—. Member of editorial board, Coach House Press, 1975—.

AWARDS, HONORS: Macmillan prize for poetry, 1962; Canada Council fellowships, 1966 and 1974; Humanities Research Council of Canada subvention, 1980; Social Sciences and Humanities Research Council of Canada leave fellowship, 1981.

WRITINGS:

POETRY

D-Day and After, Rattlesnake Press for Tishbooks, 1962.
City of the Gulls and Sea, privately printed, 1964.
Bridge Force, Contact Press, 1965.
The Scarred Hull, Imago, 1966.
Four Myths from Sam Perry, Talonbooks, 1969.
King of Swords, Talonbooks, 1972.
L'An Tretiesme: Selected Poems, 1961-70, Vancouver Community Press, 1972.
Arcana, Coach House Press, 1973.
The Clallam; or, Old Glory in Juan de Fuca, Talonbooks, 1973.
War Poems, Coach House Press, 1979.
The Arches: Selected Poems, edited by and with introduction by bp Nichol, Talonbooks, 1981.
Capitalistic Affection, Coach House Press, 1982.
Edward & Patricia, Coach House Press, 1984.
The Louis Riel Organ and Piano Company, Turnstone Press, 1985.
The Abbotsford Guide to India, Press Porcepic, 1986.
Postcard Translations, Underwhich Editions, 1988.

CRITICISM

(Contributor) Louis Dudek and M. Gnarowski, editors, *The Making of Modern Poetry in Canada,* Ryerson Press, 1967.
Five Readings of Olson's "Maximus", Beaver/Kosmos, 1970.
Earle Birney, Copp Clark, 1971.
From There to Here: A Guide to English-Canadian Literature since 1960, Press Porcepic, 1974.
(Contributor) C. H. Gervais, editor, *The Writing Life,* Black Moss Press, 1976.
(Contributor) Richard Kostelanetz, editor, *The Younger Critics of North America,* Margins, 1977.
Louis Dudek and Raymond Souster, Douglas and McIntyre, 1981.

(Contributor) Jeffrey Heath, editor, *Profiles in Canadian Literature,* Dundurn Press, 1981.
Surviving the Paraphrase: Essays in Canadian Literature, Turnstone Press, 1982.
(Contributor) William Toye, editor, *The Oxford Companion to Canadian Literature,* Oxford University Press, 1983.
(Contributor) Douglas Daymond and L. Monkman, editor, *Towards a Canadian Literature,* Borealis Press, 1985.

EDITOR

Tish, Volumes 1-19, Talonbooks, 1975.
Wyndham Lewis, *Mrs. Duke's Million,* Coach House Press, 1977.
Margaret Atwood: A Feminist Poetics, Talonbooks, 1984.
Judith Fitzgerald, *Given Names: New and Selected Poems, 1972-85,* Black Moss Press, 1985.
Reading Canadian Reading, Turnstone Press, 1988.

OTHER

Works represented in many anthologies, including *Black Mountain College: A Book of Documents,* M.I.T. Press, 1969; *How Do I Love Thee: Sixty Poets of Canada (and Quebec) Select and Introduce Their Favourite Poems from Their Own Work,* edited by Robert Columbo, Hurtig, 1970; *The Long Poem Anthology,* Edited by Michael Ondaatje, Coach House Press, 1979; and *The New Oxford Book of Canadian Verse,* edited by Margaret Atwood, Oxford University Press, 1982. Contributor of articles to *Canadian Literature, Studies in Canadian Literature, Alphabet, Open Letter, Line,* and *Boundary 2.* Co-founder and editor of *Tish,* 1962-63; founder and editor of *Open Letter,* 1965—, and of *Swift Current* (computer database of manuscripts and criticism accessed by telephone), 1984—.

WORK IN PROGRESS: Research on the evolution of the Canadian short story; long poem, "The Abbotsford Guide to Culture"; research on the politics of Canadian fiction.

SIDELIGHTS: Frankland Wilmot Davey is one of the members of what critic Jack David has termed Canada's "brave new wave" of poets. Together with students of the Black Mountain school of poetry and other poets affiliated with the Vancouver literary journal *Tish,* Davey has created a movement identified by that publication's name. Writing in David's book, *Brave New Wave,* contributor Douglas Barbour observes that "Davey's learning, his ability to amass and use a vast and scholarly range of allusions, finds expression in a personal and often deeply moving poetry. . . . It is their idiomatic strength that makes these poems [in *Kings of Swords, Arcana,* and *Weeds*] so immediately accessible to the reader, forging emotional connections that will not be denied." Writing in *The Arches,* bp Nicol suggests, "Davey would be rid of all . . . easily assumed 'traditions.' He constantly draws us back to the present fact of the world we live in. And as much as the beauty of his language moves us, . . . he constantly reminds us that we live in this present world, with all our strengths and weaknesses."

As the title of *Bridge Force* suggests, Davey's poetry establishes a field in which the poet can venture out into his natural landscape and at the same time allow that outer world to connect with his inner life. Critics note movement in both directions in Davey's poems. For example, Peter and Meredith Quartermain comment in *Dictionary of Literary Biography,* "The voice in both [*The Clallam; or, Old Glory in Juan de Fuca* and *King of Swords*] is the voice of the articulate more-or-less helpless man caught up in a world of attutudes, dreams, preconceptions, chivalries, expectations, desires, hungers, and roles over which he has no control and of which he wants no part. In both poems a hard, stark,

and highly crafted language and syntax explore a landscape (geographical, cultural, or psychic) to make discoveries about the self and one's own losses in the world in which one lives." Because they look at man's relationship to his environment, the poems have a narrative range. "Davey is a superb storyteller," Quartermain observes.

Davey is also noted for his literary criticism, most of which focuses on Canadian poets. A *Choice* reviewer calls Davey's study of poet Earl Birney "a balanced and informative study" and a *Times Literary Supplement* critic says that "anybody who wishes to examine particular aspects of Birney's career will find Professor Davey's book the best place to start from." Davey's essays in *Reading Canadian Reading* promote criticism highly attuned to the political content of individual works of literature.

Commenting on his own work, Davey told *CA:* "Writing is a guerilla act. Writers participate in the struggles within their societies to assert meaning and value. Since my first books, I've been engaged in doing violence to hegemonous literatures and their languages, simultaneously forcing a way into print for particular kinds of Canadian writing and forcing the 'in-print' world into a less centralized and more inclusive shape. The writing I value unmasks conventions, traditions, mythologies, all things that argue a static or valorized shape in experience, even the conventions one inevitably establishes in one's own texts. In Canada, various oppressive formations continue: European conventions that have been superimposed on the landscape, Ontario cultural reflexes that the province's media dominance has projected nationally, U.S. economic and lifestyle myths that spill continually across its borders, recurrent combinations of paranoia and sentimentality about both French and English languages.

"Criticism specifically is an act of contestation and violence, and concerns the construction of new textual and cultural readings and the dis-education of readers from conditioned expectations. Thus my various writings on Canadian literature, critical theory, technology, prosody; also my editorial work with magazines and publishing houses—publishing as exemplary reading activity."

BIOGRAPHICAL/CRITICAL SOURCES:

BOOKS

David, Jack, editor, *Brave New Wave,* Black Moss Press, 1978.
Dictionary of Literary Biography, Volume 53: *Canadian Writers since 1960, First Series,* Gale, 1986.
Kieth, W. S., *Canadian Book Review Annual,* 1984.
Nicol, bp, *The Arches,* Talonbooks, 1981.

PERIODICALS

American Book Review, May-June, 1988.
Canadian Forum, March, 1965; March, 1966; September, 1967; May, 1972; September, 1973; February, 1975.
Choice, October, 1972.
Globe and Mail (Toronto), April 13, 1985.
Open Letter, spring, 1979.
Poetry, April, 1966; November, 1966; volume 111, 1968.
Prairie Fire, winter, 1989.
Punch, May 19, 1965.
Saturday Night, June, 1972.
Times Literary Supplement, October 26, 1973; May 14, 1976.
University of Toronto Quarterly, fall, 1986.

*   *   *

DAVIAU, Donald G(eorge) 1927-

PERSONAL: Born September 30, 1927, in West Medway, MA; son of George (a spinner) and Jennie (Burbank) Daviau; married

Patricia Edith Mara (a teacher), August 20, 1950; children: Katherine Ann, Robert Laurence, Thomas George, Julie Marie. *Education:* Clark University, B.A., 1950; University of California, Berkeley, M.A., 1952, Ph.D., 1955; attended University of Vienna, 1953-54. *Politics:* Independent. *Religion:* Congregationalist.

ADDRESSES: Home—184 Nisbet Way, Riverside, CA 92507. *Office*—Department of Literatures and Languages, University of California, Riverside, CA 92521.

CAREER: University of California, Riverside, instructor, 1955-56, assistant professor, 1957-63, associate professor, 1964-70, professor of German, 1971—, head of department of German and Russian, 1969-75, head of department of literatures and languages, 1985-89. *Military service:* U.S. Naval Reserve, active duty, 1945-46.

MEMBER: International Arthur Schnitzler Research Association (president, 1978—), Modern Language Association of America, American Association of Teachers of German, American Council for the Study of Austrian Literature (president, 1981—), Society for Exile Studies, Robert Musil Gesellschaft, Western Association of German Studies, Austrian PEN.

AWARDS, HONORS: Fulbright scholarship for study in Vienna, 1953-54; Ehrenkreuz fuer Wissenschaft und Kunst, Government of Austria, 1977.

WRITINGS:

(Editor with Jorun B. Johns) *The Correspondence of Arthur Schnitzler and Raoul Auernheimer: With Raoul Auernheimer's Aphorisms,* University of North Carolina Press, 1972.

(Translator) Reinhard Urbach, *Arthur Schnitzler,* Ungar, 1973.

(With George J. Buelow) *The "Ariadne auf Naxos" of Hugo von Hofmannsthal and Richard Strauss,* University of North Carolina Press, 1975.

(Editor) *The Letters of Arthur Schnitzler to Hermann Bahr,* University of North Carolina Press, 1978.

(Editor with Ludwig M. Fischer) *Das Exilerlebnis,* Camden House, 1982.

(Editor with Johns and Jeffrey B. Berlin) *The Correspondence of Stefan Zweig with Raoul Auernheimer and Richard Beer-Hofmann,* Camden House, 1983.

Hermann Bahr: Der Mann von Uebermorgen, Oesterreichischer Bundesverlag, 1984.

(Editor) *Stefan Zweig/Paul Zech: Briefwechsel 1908-1942,* Greifenverlag, 1984.

Hermann Bahr, Twayne, 1985.

(Editor with Fischer) *Exilliteratur: Wirkung und Wertung,* Camden House, 1985.

(Editor and contributor) *The Major Figures of Contemporary Austrian Literature,* Peter Lang, 1987.

(Editor and contributor) *The Major Figures of Modern Austrian Literature,* Ariadne, 1988.

(Contributor with James Hardin) *Dictionary of Literary Biography,* Gale, Volume 81: *Austrian Figure Writers, 1875-1913,* 1989, Volume 85: *Austrian Fiction Writers after 1914,* 1989.

CONTRIBUTOR

W. Fleischmann, editor, *Encyclopedia of World Literature in the Twentieth Century,* Ungar, 1967.

O. Hietsch, editor, *Oesterreich und die angelsaechsische Welt II,* [Vienna], 1968.

(With Johns) John M. Spalek and Joseph Strelka, editors, *Deutsch Exilliteratur seit 1933,* Teil I, Francke Verlag, 1976.

Murray H. Sherman, editor, *Psychoanalysis and Old Vienna: Freud, Schnitzler, Kraus,* Human Sciences, 1978.

Wolfgang Paulsen, *Oesterreichische Gegenwart, Die moderne Literatur und ihr Verhaeltnis zur Tradition,* Francke Verlag, 1980.

Nachlab und Editionsprobleme bei modernen Schriftstellern, Peter Lang, 1981.

Deutsche Exilliteratur der Nachkriegszeit, Peter Lang, 1981.

Hans Schulte, *The Turn of the Century: German Literature and Art 1890-1915,* Bouvier Verlag, 1981.

Oesterreich in amerikanischer Sicht, Austrian Institute, 1981, 4th edition, 1988.

Encyclopedia of Twentieth-Century Literature, Ungar, 1981.

The World of Yesterday's Humanist Today, State University of New York Press, 1983.

P.O. Tax and Richard Lawson, editors, *Arthur Schnitzler and His Age,* Bouvier Verlag, 1984.

Alfred Pithertschatscher, editor, *Thomas Bernhard,* Adalbert Stifter Institut (Linz, Austria), 1985.

Helmut F. Pfanner, editor, *Kulturelle Wechselbeziehungen im Exil: Exile across Cultures,* Bouvier Verlag, 1986.

Jerry Glenn, editor, *Exile and Enlightenment,* Wayne State University Press, 1987.

Heinz Kindermann and Margaret Dietrich, editors, *Der Herr aus Linz Hermann Bahr Symposium,* Bruckner Haus, 1987.

Margarita Pazi, editor, *Max Brod: Untersuchungen zu Max Brods literarischen und philosophischen Schriften,* Peter Lang, 1988.

Karl Konrad Pohlheim, editor, *Sinn und Symbol,* Peter Lang, 1989.

OTHER

Contributor to periodicals, including *German Life and Letters.* Editor, *Modern Austrian Literature,* 1971—, and *Studies in Austrian Literature, Culture, and Thought,* 1988—.

WORK IN PROGRESS: Editing *Der Briefwechsel zwischen Stefan Zweig und Felix Braun,* with Johns; a critical biography of German writer Paul Zech; translating Zech's *Deutschland, dein Taenzer ist der Tod.*

*   *   *

DAVIS, Dorothy Salisbury   1916-

PERSONAL: Born April 26, 1916, in Chicago, IL; daughter of Alfred Joseph (a farmer) and Margaret Jane (Greer) Salisbury; married Harry Davis (an actor), April 25, 1946. *Education:* Barat College, A.B., 1938. *Politics:* Democrat.

ADDRESSES: Home—Palisades, NY 10964. *Agent*—McIntosh & Otis, Inc., 310 Madison Ave., New York, NY 10017.

CAREER: Writer. Swift & Co., Chicago, IL, research librarian and editor of *The Merchandiser,* 1940-46. Member of board of directors, Palisades Free Library, 1967-71. Honorary member of board of directors, Rockland County Center for the Arts, 1987—.

MEMBER: International Crime Writers Association, Author's Guild, Mystery Writers of America (president, 1955-56; executive vice president, 1977-78; member of board of directors), Sisters in Crime (founding director), Adam's Roundtable.

AWARDS, HONORS: Grandmaster Award for lifetime achievement, Mystery Writers of America, 1985, and International

Crime Writers Association, Boucheron XX, 1989; five nominations for best mystery novel of the year, two nominations for best mystery short story.

WRITINGS:

The Judas Cat, Scribner, 1949.
The Clay Hand, Scribner, 1950.
A Gentle Murderer, Scribner, 1951.
A Town of Masks, Scribner, 1952.
Men of No Property, Scribner, 1956.
Death of an Old Sinner, Scribner, 1957.
A Gentleman Called, Scribner, 1958.
(Editor) *A Choice of Murders,* Scribner, 1958.
Old Sinners Never Die, Scribner, 1959.
The Evening of the Good Samaritan, Scribner, 1961.
Black Sheep, White Lamb, Scribner, 1963.
The Pale Betrayer, Scribner, 1965.
Enemy and Brother, Scribner, 1966.
(With Jerome Ross) *God Speed the Night,* Scribner, 1968.
Where the Dark Streets Go, Scribner, 1969.
(Editor) *Crime Without Murder,* Scribner, 1970.
Shock Wave, Scribner, 1972.
The Little Brothers, Scribner, 1973.
A Death in the Life, Scribner, 1976.
Scarlet Night, Scribner, 1980.
Lullaby of Murder, Scribner, 1984.
Tales for a Stormy Night: Collected Crime Stories, Countryman Press, 1984.
The Habit of Fear, Scribner, 1987.

Contributor to anthologies, including *Mirror, Mirror, Fatal Mirror,* edited by Hans S. Santesson, Doubleday, 1973, and *When Last Seen,* edited by Arthur Maling, Harper, 1977. Also contributor to numerous periodicals, including *Ellery Queen's Mystery Magazine* and *Modern Maturity.*

MEDIA ADAPTATIONS: Film rights to *God Speed the Night* were sold to Herb Alpert in 1968; *Where the Dark Streets Go* was filmed for CBS-TV as *Broken Vows* in 1986.

SIDELIGHTS: "The work of Dorothy Salisbury Davis indicates her keen perception as a student of human nature," asserts Geoffrey Sadler in *Twentieth-Century Romance and Gothic Writers.* He continues: "Davis's explorations of the criminal mind are far from morbid. Rather she seeks for the minor flaws of character, the unforeseen shifts of circumstance, that lead certain human beings to break the confines of the law." Davis de-emphasizes violence in her work, concentrating instead on thematic, character, and plot development. She established her reputation as a suspense author with *A Gentle Murderer,* the story of an unlikely killer and the priest who attempts to track him down. Edward D. Hoch of *Twentieth-Century Crime and Mystery Writers* notes that "the insight into the characters of these two men raises the book far above the level of the usual suspense novel."

A critic for the *New York Times Book Review* observes that Davis "has a cultured style, handles dialogue with a sure ear, and understands people better than most of her colleagues." Davis' ability to create a diversity of well-rounded characters and intricate plots makes it difficult to categorize her work. Her stories take place in venues both large and small, populated by priests, blackmailers, fortune-tellers, spinsters, generals, shopkeepers, and police. Unlike many mystery authors, Davis has few "stock" series characters. Those she does have—Julie Hayes, Detective Marks, Mrs. Norris and Jasper Tully—are noted as much for their idiosyncrasies as their detecting abilities.

In Davis novels, the line separating hunter and prey is often tenuous, creating an interesting ambiguity with regard to what is right and wrong. This thematic construction is indicative of what Davis perceives as the nature of the mystery medium. Dorothy Salisbury Davis once told *CA:* "I believe the mystery [form] in which I have worked largely, to be a medium highly reflective of its time, morals, social attitudes." Davis has sometimes been at odds, however, with her mystery-writing persona. In an interview with *Publishers Weekly,* she stated: "I'm not ashamed of being a mystery writer, although I would like to have succeeded as a mainstream novelist. Any art is contrived; the degree of artistry lies in how you conceal that contrivance. You are guaranteed to have to write in a bizarre fashion for mysteries. Something violent has to happen, something that is not expected, something that is showy. Being bizarre means color, too, and I like that."

BIOGRAPHICAL/CRITICAL SOURCES:

BOOKS

Twentieth-Century Crime and Mystery Writers, St. James/St. Martin's, 1985.
Twentieth-Century Romance and Gothic Writers, Gale/Macmillan, 1982.

PERIODICALS

Back Stage, September 15, 1968; November 9, 1968.
Chicago Tribune Book World, July 8, 1984.
National Observer, January 5, 1970; July 15, 1972.
Newsday, December 12, 1970.
New York Times Book Review, July 22, 1972; July 30, 1972; August 29, 1976; May 31, 1981; November 2, 1986.
Publisher's Weekly, June 13, 1980.
Saturday Review, September 9, 1972.
Show Business, July 5, 1969; July 11, 1970.
Spectator, November 3, 1967.
Times Literary Supplement, February 23, 1967; August 14, 1970.
Variety, June 11, 1969; July 1, 1970.

*   *   *

DEACON, Richard
  See McCORMICK, (George) Donald (King)

*   *   *

DELIBES, Miguel
  See DELIBES SETIEN, Miguel

*   *   *

DELIBES SETIEN, Miguel 1920-
  (Miguel Delibes)

PERSONAL: Born October 17, 1920, in Valladolid, Spain; son of Adolfo (a professor) and María (Setien) Delibes; married Angeles de Castro Ruiz, April 23, 1946 (died November, 1974); children: Miguel, Angeles, Germán, Elisa, Juan, Adolfo, Camino. *Education:* Hermanos Doctrina Cristiana, Bachillerato; Universidad de Valladolid, Doctor en Derecho (law), 1944; attended Escuela Altos Estudios Mercantiles, and Escuela Periodismo. *Religion:* Roman Catholic.

ADDRESSES: Home—Dos de Mayo 10, Valladolid, Spain. *Agent*—Ediciones Destino, Consejo de Ciento 425, Barcelona 9, Spain.

CAREER: Novelist and writer. Teacher of mercantile law, University de Valladolid, Valladolid, Spain. Director, El Norte de

Castilla, Valladolid. Visiting professor, University of Maryland, 1964. *Military service:* Spanish Navy, 1938-39.

MEMBER: Real Academia Española, Hispanic Society.

AWARDS, HONORS: Nadal Prize, 1947, for *La sombra del ciprés es alargada;* Ministry of Information Cervantes Prize (Spanish national prize for literature), 1955, for *Diario de un cazador;* Critics Prize (Spain), 1963; Asturias Prize, 1982.

WRITINGS:

UNDER NAME MIGUEL DELIBES; NOVELS, EXCEPT AS INDICATED

La sombra del ciprés es alagarda (also see below; title means "The Cypress's Shadow is Long"), Ediciones Destino, 1948, reprinted, 1979.

Aún es de día, Ediciones Destino, 1949, 2nd edition, 1962, reprinted, 1982.

El camino (also see below; title means "The Road"), Ediciones Destino, 1950, reprinted, 1984, self-illustrated edition, Holt, 1960, translation by Brita Haycraft published as *The Path,* John Day, 1961.

Mi idolatrado hijo Sisí (also see below), Ediciones Destino, 1953, reprinted, 1980.

El loco (novella; also see below), Editorial Tecnos, 1953.

La partida (fiction; includes "La Partida," "El refugio," "Una peseta para el tranvía," "El manguero," "El campeonato," "El traslado," "El primer pitillo," "La contradicción," "En una noche así," and "La conferencia"), L. de Caralt, 1954, 2nd edition, Alianza Editorial, 1969, reprinted, 1982.

Diario de un cazador, Ediciones Destino, 1955, reprinted, 1980.

Siestas con viento sur (novellas; includes "La mortaja," "El loco," "Los nogales," and "Los railes"), Ediciones Destino, 1957, 2nd edition, 1967.

Diario de un emigrante, Ediciones Destino, 1958, reprinted, 1977.

La hoja roja, Ediciones Destino, 1959, 3rd edition, 1975.

Las ratas, Ediciones Destino, 1962, 7th edition, 1971, Harrap, 1969.

Obra completa (includes "Prólogo," "La sombra de ciprés es alargada," "El camino," and "Mi idolatrado hijo Sisí"), Part 1, Ediciones Destino, 1964.

Cinco horas con Mario, Ediciones Destino, 1966, 9th edition, 1975, translation by Frances M. López-Morillas published as *Five Hours with Mario,* Columbia University Press, 1989.

La Mortaja (novellas; also see above; includes "La mortaja," "El amor propio de Juanito Osuna," "El patio de vecindad," "El sol," "La fé," "El conejo," "La perra," and "Navidad sin ambiente"), Alianza Editorial, 1969, 2nd edition, 1974.

Parábola del náufrago, Ediciones Destino, 1969, 3rd edition, 1971, translation by López-Morillas published as *The Hedge,* Columbia University Press, 1983.

Mi mundo y el mundo: Selección antológica de obras del autor, para niños de 11 a 14 años, Miñon, 1970.

Smoke on the Ground, translation by Alfred Johnson, Doubleday, 1972.

El príncipe destronado, Ediciones Destino, 1973, reprinted, 1982.

Las guerras de nuestros antepasados, Ediciones Destino, 1974, 5th edition, 1979.

El disputado voto del señor Cayo, Ediciones Destino, 1978.

Los santos inocentes, Planeta, 1981.

Tres pájaros de cuenta, Miñon, 1982.

Cartas de amor de un sexagenario voluptuoso, Ediciones Destino, 1983.

El tesoro, Ediciones Destino, 1985.

377A, madera de héroe, Ediciones Destino, 1987.

NONFICTION

Un novelista descubre América, Editora Nacional, 1956.

La barbería: Portada de Coll, G. P. Ediciones , 1957.

Castilla, Editorial Lumen, 1960, published as *Viejas historias de Castilla la Vieja,* Ediciones Destino, 1964, 3rd edition, 1974, Alianza Editorial, 1982.

Por esos mundos: Sudamérica con escala en las Canarias, Ediciones Destino, 1971, 2nd edition, 1972.

La caza de la perdiz roja, Editorial Lumen, 1963, 2nd edition, 1975.

Europa: Parada y fonda, Ediciones Cid, 1963, reprinted, Plaza & Janés, 1981.

El libro de la caza menor, Ediciones Destino, 1964, 3rd edition, 1973.

USA y yo, Ediciones Destino, 1966, Odyssey, 1970.

Vivir al día (also see below), Ediciones Destino, 1968, 2nd edition, 1975.

(Contributor) Susanne Filkau, editor, *Historias de la guerra civil,* Edition Langewiesche-Brandt, 1968.

La primavera de Praga, Alianza Editorial, 1968.

Con la escopeta al hombro (also see below), Ediciones Destino, 1970, 2nd edition, 1971.

Un año de mi vida (also see below), Ediciones Destino, 1972.

La caza en España, Alianza Editorial, 1972.

Castilla en mi obra, Editorial Magistero Español, 1972.

S.O.S.: El sentido del progreso desde mi obra, Ediciones Destino, 1975.

Aventuras, venturas, y desventuras de un cazador a rabo, Ediciones Destino, 1976.

Mis amigas las truchas, Ediciones Destino, 1977.

Castilla, lo castellano y los castellanos, Editorial Planeta, 1979.

Las perdices del domingo, 2nd edition, Ediciones Destino, 1981.

Dos viajes en automóvil: Suecia y Paises Bajos, Plaza & Janés, 1982.

El otro fútbol, Ediciones Destino, 1982.

La censura de prensa en los años 40, y otros ensayos, Ambito, 1985.

Castilla habla, Ediciones Destino, 1986.

OTHER

César Alonso de los Ríos, *Conversaciones con Delibes,* Emesa (Madrid), 1971.

Javier Goñi, *Cinco horas con Miguel Delibes,* Anjana, 1985.

Also author of another volume of *Obra completa,* which includes "Vivir al día," "Con la escopeta al hombro," and "Un año de mi vida," for Ediciones Destino. Author of television plays *Tierras de Valladolid,* 1966, *La mortaja,* and *Castilla, esta es mi tierra,* 1983.

SIDELIGHTS: Miguel Delibes Setien is considered one of Spain's most important novelists; his work is distinguished by its stark realism, rural subject matter, and well-developed characters. Ronald Schwartz explains in *Spain's New Wave Novelists: 1950-1974,* "Delibes has been always considered a major novelist whose career is constantly developing, growing in quantity and quality, and becoming more prestigious because of his consistent use of Realism and his attachment to rural themes, which display a variety of character types. . . . Critics acknowledge his skepticism, pessimism, reactionary vision of nature, his love for the man of instinct, of nature in contrast to a 'civilized' product, in short, his negative view of progress and 'civilization,' his black humor and cold intellectualism."

A recurrent theme in fiction by Delibes is the message that technological and social changes brought about during the twentieth century have resulted in the alienation and repression of the individual. As they find their places in the world of business, many of his characters feel isolated. This is perhaps best seen in *The Hedge,* a novel in which a sensitive clerk degenerates into a fearful person who will do almost anything—even resort to violence—to maintain his sense of material security. At first, "Jacinto is scared of losing his job, of having children and having to raise them to be either victims or executioners in a pitiless society," Toby Talbot relates in the *New York Times Book Review.* Sent by an authoritarian official to be rehabilitated after questioning the difference between zero and the letter "O" in the documents he transcribes, Jacinto notices that a thick hedge separates him from the rest of the world. The hedge depicts "the encroachment of an Orwellian state," Talbot explains, and Jacinto's degeneration shows that the end result of the encroachment is "the dehumanization of man, victimized by his own progress, specialization and conformity. And along with it comes the disintegration of thought and language," two activities eventually dominated and regulated by the state.

Five Hours with Mario, a novel regarded as a masterpiece by some critics, also shows the human fight for liberty and dignity against oppressive forces. The narrator Carmen's husband has just died and we listen as she critically reviews their life together. Reduced to poverty for daring to confront the repressive authorities, her husband had failed to improve her material standard of living. While berating him, she exhibits her own failure to live up to her stated ideals. Delibes thus criticizes many aspects of traditional and modern life in Spain. In addition, the novel "addresses lost words, last words and listening—important issues in a country that is now free to examine its conscience and its recent history," *New York Times Book Review* critic Arthur J. Sabatini comments.

The realism and themes of nature in Delibes Setien's work have been widely praised. Schwartz believes that the author demonstrates "an enormous capacity to capture within his writings the essence of nature by means of his starkly Realist style." In the *New York Times Book Review,* Martin Levin contrasts the "charming and nostalgic" view of nature rendered by "Anglo-Saxon novels" to the harsh atmosphere of *Smoke on the Ground.* "The land is wretchedly poor," he writes, "the climate is harsh, and the atmosphere has a haunting, 19th-century bleakness, although it is set in the age of moon missions." Schwartz believes that with the "harmonious" combination of "humor, tenderness, nature and tragedy" evident in Delibes Setien's later work, he is "reviving the theme of nature as a literary element indispensable to the human condition and portraying this harmony through his extremely personal style."

MEDIA ADAPTATIONS: Some of Delibes Setien's works have been adapted for Spanish television. Feature-length film adaptations of his work include "Retrato de familia," based on his novel *Mi idolatrado hijo Sisí,* filmed in 1975, "La guerra de papa," produced in 1978, and based on the novel *El príncipe destronada,* and "The Holy Innocents," directed by Mario Camus. *Cinco horas con Mario* has also been filmed.

BIOGRAPHICAL/CRITICAL SOURCES:

BOOKS

Alonso de los Ríos, César, *Conversaciones con Delibes,* Emesa (Madrid), 1971.
Contemporary Literary Criticism, Gale, Volume 8, 1978, Volume 18, 1981.
Díaz, Janet W., *Delibes,* Twayne, 1971.
Estudios sobre Delibes, Universidad Complutense, 1983.

Gullón, Agnes, *La novela experimental de Delibes,* Taurus, 1981.
Schwartz, Ronald, *Spain's New Wave Novelists: 1950-1974,* Scarecrow Press, 1976.
Umbral, Francisco, *Delibes,* Emesa, 1970.

PERIODICALS

Antioch Review, June, 1973.
Booklist, February 15, 1971.
Hispania, December 1971, December, 1972, March, 1974, May, 1974, May, 1976.
New York Times Book Review, August 20, 1972, December 11, 1983, January 22, 1989.
Times Literary Supplement, April 20, 1967, June 11, 1970.
World Literature Today, summer, 1977.

* * *

DEMPSTER, Barry 1952-

PERSONAL: Born January 17, 1952, in Toronto, Ontario, Canada; son of A. E. and Helen (Robinette) Dempster; married Karen Ruttan (a writer and artist), September 26, 1981. *Education:* Centennial College, child care degree, 1974. *Religion:* Christian.

ADDRESSES: Home—65 Woodrow Ave., Toronto, Ontario, Canada M4C 1G6.

CAREER: Toronto Children's Aid Society, Toronto, Ontario, child care worker, 1971-73; child care worker in private group homes in Toronto, 1971-75; Lakeshore Psychiatric Hospital, Toronto, child therapist, 1974-75; Queen Street Mental Health Center, Toronto, member of emergency room team, 1980—.

MEMBER: League of Canadian Poets.

AWARDS, HONORS: Governor General's Award finalist, 1982, for *Fables for Isolated Men.*

WRITINGS:

(Editor) *Tributaries: Writer to Writer* (poetry), Mosaic Press/ Valley Editions, 1978.
Fables for Isolated Men (poetry), Guernica Editions, 1982.
Globe Doubts (poetry), Quarry Press, 1983.
Real Places and Imaginary Men (stories), Oberon Press, 1984.
David and the Daydreams (for children), Guernica Editions, 1984.
Writing Home (novel), Oberon Press, 1989.
Positions to Pray In (poetry), Guernica Editions, 1989.
The Unavoidable Man (poetry), Quarry Press, 1990.

Work represented in anthologies, including *Third Impressions,* edited by John Metcalf, Oberon Press, 1982; *Canadian Poetry Now: Twenty Poets of the Eighties,* House of Anansi, 1984; *And Other Travels,* Moonstone Press, 1988; and *Christian Poetry in Canada,* ECW Press, 1989. Contributor of more than one hundred fifty poems to magazines. Review editor of *Poetry Canada* and *Poetry Canada Chronicle.*

WORK IN PROGRESS: The Greedy Gifts, a children's novel; a manuscript of poetry based on the life of D. H. Lawrence, to be published in 1991; rewrite of a second novel; a third novel.

SIDELIGHTS: Barry Dempster told *CA:* "Fiction and poetry, in their web of moments, are large enough to contain ideals and faith. One moment, like one strand of hair or one kiss, is enough evidence through which an entire life can be glimpsed. And when that moment is linked with another and then another, even if only an hour is created, a life will step from the shadows like an actor from behind a curtain and there will be both time and vision in which that life will most certainly reveal itself.

"Focus on one or two people sitting in a garden, in a corner by the roses, or dancing in the middle of moonlight; moments pass, if they are talking they will glide from subject to subject or else to different levels of the same theme, if they are moving they will use a muscle here, a muscle there—they will change each moment, yet remain intricately the same. Fiction or poetry are the moods, the atmospheres.

"Say the story or poem is about a man who is attending a garden party, a man who off in his own corner is considering suicide, then it does not matter how many guests are laughing or having a wonderful time, whether the moon be full, whether there be a woman with the man who loves him . . . they will all, the fun folk, the miraculous moon, the warm woman, be seen in relation to the man and his mood of death. Fiction and poetry have the uncanny ability, while using everyday perceptions, to show us the mood and character of another human being. We are given the privilege of walking into the mind of a perfect stranger, the opportunity to study the landscape. The writer is the tour guide at the gates of the human heart. The moon will never be the same again."

* * *

DENIS, Julio
    See CORTAZAR, Julio

* * *

DERRICOTTE, Toi 1941-

PERSONAL: Name is pronounced Toy *Dare*-i-cot; born April 12, 1941, in Detroit, MI; daughter of Benjamin Sweeney Webster (a mortician and salesperson) and Antonia Webster Cyrus (a systems analyst; maiden name, Banquet); married Clarence Reese (an artist), July 5, 1960 (divorced, 1964); married Clarence Bruce Derricotte (a banking consultant), December 29, 1967; children: (first marriage) Anthony. *Education:* Wayne State University, B.A., 1965; New York University, M.A., 1984. *Politics:* "Anti-Nuke." *Religion:* Roman Catholic. *Avocational interests:* Cooking, "sharing good meals with good friends."

ADDRESSES: Home and office—7958 Inverness Ridge Rd., Potomac, MD 20854.

CAREER: Manpower Program, Detroit, MI, teacher, 1964-66; Farand School, Detroit, teacher of the mentally and emotionally retarded, 1966-68; Jefferson School, Teaneck, NJ, remedial reading teacher, 1969-70; New Jersey State Council on the Arts, poet-in-residence for Poet-in-the-Schools program, 1974—, master teacher, 1984—; Old Dominion University, Norfolk, VA, associate professor of creative writing and minority literature, 1988—. Guest poet and lecturer at numerous colleges and universities; featured poet in readings at more than one hundred theatres, museums, bookstores, and libraries. Panelist for Massachusetts Artists Foundation fellowship program, 1983. Educational consultant, Columbia University, 1979-82.

MEMBER: PEN, Poetry Society of America.

AWARDS, HONORS: Pen and Brush Award, New School for Social Research, 1973, for untitled poetry manuscript; first prize, Academy of American Poets, 1974, for "Unburying the Bird," and 1978, for excerpts from *Natural Birth;* fellowships from MacDowell Colony, 1982, New Jersey State Council on the Arts,

1983, and New York University's graduate English creative writing program, 1984; creative writing fellowship in poetry, National Endowment for the Arts, 1985, 1990; Lucille Medmick Memorial Award, Poetry Society of America, 1985; Arts Council fellowship, State of Maryland, 1987.

WRITINGS:

POETRY

The Empress of the Death House, Lotus Press, 1978.
Natural Birth, Crossing Press, 1983.
Books of Poetry Captivity, University of Pittsburgh Press, 1989.

CONTRIBUTOR TO ANTHOLOGIES

Lyn Lifshin, editor, *Ariadne's Thread: A Collection of Contemporary Women's Journals,* Harper, 1982.
Jane Cooper and others, editors, *Extended Outlooks: The Iowa Review Collection of Contemporary Women Writers,* Macmillan, 1982.
Barbara Smith, editor, *Home Girls: A Black Feminist Anthology,* Persephone, 1982.

OTHER

Also contributor to Louise Simpson, editor, *An Introduction to Poetry, Waltzing on the Water,* Dell, and Marge Piercy, editor, *Early Ripening.* Contributor of poems to numerous periodicals, including *Iowa Review, Poetry Northwest, American Poetry Review, Bread Loaf Quarterly, Massachusetts Review, Ploughshares,* and *Feminist Studies.* Member of editorial staff, *New York Quarterly,* 1973-77.

WORK IN PROGRESS: A volume of poetry and prose, *The Black Notebooks,* detailing the author's "experience being a member of one of the first black families to live in Upper Montclair, New Jersey"; another book of poetry.

SIDELIGHTS: Toi Derricotte told *CA:* "To some extent, my style of writing has always been 'confessional.' In Catholic school we learned that by confessing our sins, admitting faults and weaknesses, we were forgiven, made 'whole' and acceptable, put back into the state of grace. In my writing, truthtelling as a way to self-integrity operates as a strong impulse.

"As a black woman, I have used the confessional mode as a way of self-examination. I have been consistently confused about my 'sins,' unsure of which faults were in me and which faults were the results of others' projections. Truthtelling in my art is also a way to separate my 'self' from what I have been taught to believe about my 'self,' the degrading stereotypes of black females in our society.

"My fears of death were prominent in my early poems. In my first book, *The Empress of the Death House,* that theme persists and is embodied in 'The Grandmother Poems,' a group of poems about my early experiences at my grandparents' funeral home in Detroit. In my second book, *Natural Birth,* I am concerned again with the same themes—death, birth, and transcendence. I begin in this book to 'confess' my sexual experience, to confront my ambivalence as a mother, and, therefore, to examine the nature of love. In new manuscripts I write about our family's experiences as one of the first black families in Upper Montclair, of my problems at being unrecognized because of my light complexion, and my love and rage toward my neighbors."

BIOGRAPHICAL/CRITICAL SOURCES:

PERIODICALS

American Book Review, summer, 1979.

Black American Literature Forum, winter, 1983.
Hudson Review, winter, 1983-84.
lammos little review, winter, 1984.
13th Moon, Volume 7, numbers 1-2, 1983.
Womanews, July-August, 1983.

*   *   *

DOBYNS, Henry F(armer) 1925-

PERSONAL: Born July 3, 1925, in Tucson, AZ; son of Henry Farmer (a printer) and Susie Kell (Comstock) Dobyns; married Zipporah Pottenger, 1948 (divorced, 1958); married Cara E. Richards, 1958 (divorced, 1968); married Mary Faith Patterson, August 3, 1968 (divorced, 1984); children: (first marriage) Henry Farmer III, William C., Martha S., Mark McC.; (second marriage) York H. *Education:* University of Arizona, B.A., 1949, M.A., 1956; Cornell University, Ph.D., 1960.

ADDRESSES: c/o Newberry Library, 60 West Walton St., Chicago, IL 60610.

CAREER: Arizona State Museum, Tucson, AZ, research associate, 1950-51, 1958-59; Cornell University, Ithaca, NY, research associate of department of sociology and anthropology, 1959-63, lecturer and senior research associate of department of anthropology, 1963-66, coordinator of Cornell project in Lima, Peru, 1960-62; University of Kentucky, Lexington, professor of anthropology and chairman of department, 1966-70; Prescott College, Prescott, AZ, professor of anthropology, 1970-73; University of Wisconsin—Parkside, visiting professor of anthropology, 1974-75 and 1983-84. Visiting professor of anthropology, University of Florida, 1977-79; adjunct professor of anthropology, University of Oklahoma, 1989—. Director, Native American Historic Demography Project, Newberry Library, 1981-84. Democratic precinct chairman, Fayette County, KY. Has conducted research among Indians in the United States, Bolivia, Peru, Ecuador, Colombia, and Venezuela. Consulting editor, Center for Anthropological Studies. *Military service:* U.S. Army, 1942-43.

MEMBER: American Association for the Advancement of Science (fellow), American Anthropological Association (fellow), Society for Applied Anthropology (fellow), American Society for Ethnohistory (secretary-treasurer, 1968-70; president, 1976-77), Arizona Academy of Science (honorary fellow), Arizona Historical Society.

AWARDS, HONORS: Malinowski Award from Society for Applied Anthropology, 1951, for article, "Blunders with Bolsas"; National Science Foundation fellow, 1956-57; Social Science Research Council fellow, 1959; co-winner of Anisfield-Wolf award of Saturday Review, 1968, for "The American Indian Today"; Stoner Award, Arizona Archaeological and Historical Society, 1990.

WRITINGS:

Papagos in the Cotton Fields, 1950, [Tucson], 1951.
(Editor) *Hepah, California! The Journal of Cave Johnson Couts from Monterey, Nuevo Leon, Mexico, to Los Angeles, California, during the Years 1848-1849,* Arizona Pioneers' Historical Society, 1961.
(Editor with Mario C. Vazquez, and contributor) *Migracion e integracion en el Peru,* Editorial Estudios Andinos, 1963.
The Social Matrix of Peruvian Indigenous Communities, Department of Anthropology, Cornell University, 1964.
(With Paul L. Doughty and Allan R. Holmberg) *Measurement of Peace Corps Program Impact in the Peruvian Andes: Final Report,* Department of Anthropology, Cornell University, 1965.
(With Holmberg, Morris E. Opler, and Lauriston Sharp) *Recommendations for Future Research on the Processes of Cultural Change,* Department of Anthropology, Cornell University, 1966.
(With Holmberg, Opler, and Sharp) *Some Principles of Cultural Change,* Department of Anthropology, Cornell University, 1967.
(With Holmberg, Opler, and Sharp) *Strategic Intervention in the Cultural Change Process,* Department of Anthropology, Cornell University, 1967.
(With Holmberg, Opler, and Sharp) *Methods for Analyzing Cultural Change,* Department of Anthropology, Cornell University, 1967.
(With Susan C. Bourque, Leslie A. Brownrigg, and Eileen A. Maynard) *Factions and Faenas: The Developmental Potential of Checras District, Peru,* Department of Anthropology, Cornell University, 1967.
(With Robert C. Euler) *The Ghost Dance of 1889 among the Pai Indians of Northwestern Arizona,* Prescott College Press, 1967.
(With Earl W. Morris, Brownrigg, and Bourque) *Coming down the Mountain: The Social Worlds of Mayobamba,* Department of Anthropology, Cornell University, 1968.
Comunidades campesinas del Peru, Editorial Estudios Andinos, 1970.
(With Euler) *Wauba Yuma's People: The Comparative Socio-Political Structure of the Pai Indians of Arizona,* Prescott College Press, 1970.
(With Euler) *The Havasupai People,* [Phoenix], 1971.
(With Euler) *The Hopi People,* [Phoenix], 1971.
(Editor with Doughty and Harold D. Lasswell) *Peasants, Power, and Applied Social Change: Vicos as a Model,* Sage Publications, 1971.
(With Euler) *The Navajo People,* [Phoenix], 1972.
The Papago People, [Phoenix], 1972.
The Mescalero Apache People, [Phoenix], 1973.
Prehistoric Indian Occupation within the Eastern Area of the Yuman Complex: A Study in Applied Archaeology, Garland Publishing, 1975.
Native American Historical Demography: A Critical Bibliography, Indiana University Press, 1976.
Spanish Colonial Tucson: A Demographic History, University of Arizona Press, 1976.
(With Doughty) *Peru: A Cultural History,* Oxford University Press, 1976.
Indians of the Southwest: A Critical Bibliography, Indiana University Press, 1980.
(Editor) *Spanish Colonial Frontier Research,* University of New Mexico Press, 1980.
From Fire to Flood: Historical Human Destruction of Sonoran Desert Riverine Oases, Ballena, 1981.
Their Number Become Thinned: Native America Population Dynamics in Eastern North America, University of Tennessee Press, 1983.
The Pima-Maricopa, Chelsea House, 1989.

CONTRIBUTOR

Lyle W. Shannon, editor, *Underdeveloped Areas,* Harper, 1957.
R. E. Bolton, editor, *Case Studies to Accompany Getting Agriculture Moving,* Agricultural Development Council, 1967.
Stuart Levine and Nancy O. Lurie, editors, *The American Indian Today,* Everett Edwards, 1968.

K. R. Anschell, R. H. Brannon, and E. D. Smith, editors, *Agricultural Cooperatives and Markets in Developing Countries,* Praeger, 1969.

Virgil J. Vogel, editor, *This Country Was Ours: A Documentary History of the American Indian,* Harper, 1972.

Deward E. Walker, Jr., editor, *The Emergent Native Americans,* Little, Brown, 1972.

Also author with Euler of *The Walapai People,* 1976, and *Navajo Indians,* 1977. Author of series of monographs dealing with Pima-Maricopa Indian military power and water rights. Contributor of more than one hundred articles and reviews to *Saturday Review, Arizona Quarterly, Andean Air Mail and Peruvian Times,* and to history and anthropology journals. Scientific editor, "Indian Tribal" series, 1971-77.

SIDELIGHTS: Henry F. Dobyns wrote *CA:* "Having begun writing seriously on a small town weekly newspaper, I strive when writing books to communicate clearly with a general readership even when discussing technical subjects. Most of my books describe dimensions of the historic experience of native American peoples in the United States and Peru."

*   *   *

DOCKRELL, William Bryan   1929-

PERSONAL: Born January 12, 1929, in Manchester, England; son of James (an electrical engineer) and Elizabeth (Slater) Dockrell; married Ann Cirillo (a psychologist), June 12, 1954; children: Julia, Helen, Richard, Catherine, Martin, Mark. *Education:* University of Manchester, B. A., 1950; University of Edinburgh, M.Ed., 1952; University of Chicago, Ph.D., 1963.

ADDRESSES: Home—The Coachhouse, Inveresk, Musselburgh, Midlothian EH21 7TN, Scotland. *Office*—School of Education, University of Newcastle upon Tyne, Saint Thomas Street, Newcastle upon Tyne NE1 7RU, England.

CAREER: Education Authority, Manchester, England, psychologist, 1955-58; University of Alberta, Edmonton, assistant professor of educational psychology, 1958-67; Ontario Institute for Studies in Education, Toronto, professor of special education, 1967-71; Scottish Council for Research in Education, Edinburgh, Scotland, director, 1971-87; University of Newcastle upon Tyne, Newcastle upon Tyne, England, visiting professor, 1987—. *Military service:* British Army, 1956-57.

MEMBER: American Psychological Association, American Educational Research Association, British Psychological Association.

AWARDS, HONORS: Senior Imperial Relations fellow, London, 1966-67; fellow, Educational Institute of Scotland, 1980.

WRITINGS:

(Editor) *On Intelligence,* Methuen, 1971.

(With P. M. Broadfoot) *Pupils in Profile,* Hodder & Stoughton, 1977.

(Editor with W. Dunn and A. Milne) *Special Education in Scotland,* Scottish Council for Research in Education, 1978.

(Editor with D. Hamilton) *Rethinking Educational Research,* Hodder & Stoughton, 1980.

(With H. D. Black) *Diagnostic Assessment in Secondary Schools,* Scottish Council for Research in Education, 1982.

An Attitude of Mind, Scottish Council for Research in Education, 1984.

(With Black) *Criterion Referenced Assessment in the Classroom,* Scottish Council for Research in Education, 1984.

(Editor with Black) *New Developments in Educational Assessment,* Scottish Academic Press, 1988.

Achievement, Assessment and Reporting, Scottish Council for Research in Education, 1989.

*   *   *

DOIG, Jameson W.   1933-

PERSONAL: Born June 12, 1933, in Oakland, CA; son of James Rufus and Mary (Jameson) Doig; married Joan Nishimoto, October 8, 1955; children: Rachel, Stephen, Sarah. *Education:* Dartmouth College, B.A., 1954; Princeton University, M.P.A., 1958, M.A., 1959, Ph.D., 1961.

ADDRESSES: Home—122 Moore St., Princeton, NJ 08540. *Office*—Woodrow Wilson School of Public and International Affairs, Princeton University, Princeton, NJ 08544.

CAREER: Brookings Institution, Washington, D.C., research assistant and research associate, 1959-61; Princeton University, Princeton, NJ, assistant professor, 1961-67, associate professor, 1967-70, professor of politics and public affairs in department of politics and at Woodrow Wilson School of Public and International Affairs, 1970—, director of research program in criminal justice, 1973—. Visiting professor, John Jay College of Criminal Justice of the City University of New York, 1967-68, 1970-72. Committee chairman, New Jersey Governor's Council Against Crime, 1967-70; member of Correctional Master Plan Policy Council, 1974-77, and Advisory Council on Corrections, 1977-82 (both New Jersey). Member of Supreme Court task forces on probation and on minority concerns, 1981-82, 1985-90. Consultant to Fels Fund, 1966-68, New Jersey Department of Community Affairs, 1969-70, Guggenheim Foundation, 1970—, Center for Administrative Justice, 1972-77, governor of New Jersey on revision of parole statutes, 1975-77, and Police Foundation, 1977-78. *Military service:* U.S. Navy, 1954-56; became lieutenant junior grade.

MEMBER: American Political Science Association, American Society for Public Administration (member of executive committee of criminal justice section, 1977-81), American Correctional Association, American Society of Criminology, Society for the History of Technology, Policy Studies Organization.

WRITINGS:

(With Dean E. Mann) *The Assistant Secretaries,* Brookings Institution, 1965.

Metropolitan Transportation Politics and the New York Region, Columbia University Press, 1966.

(With David T. Stanley and Mann) *Men Who Govern,* Brookings Institution, 1967.

(With M. N. Danielson) *New York: The Politics of Urban Regional Development,* University of California Press, 1982.

(Editor and contributor) *Criminal Corrections: Ideals and Realities,* Lexington-Heath, 1983.

(Co-editor and contributor) *Leadership and Innovation: A Biographical Perspective on Entrepreneurs,* Johns Hopkins University Press, 1987, 2nd edition, 1990.

(Co-editor and contributor) *Combating Corruption/Encouraging Ethics,* American Society for Public Administration, 1990.

Contributor to numerous books, including Duane Lockard, editor, *Governing the States and Localities,* Macmillan, 1969; S. M. Davidson and P. E. Peterson, editors, *Urban Politics and Public Policy,* Praeger, 1973; G. Frederickson and C. Wise, editors, *Public Administration and Public Policy,* Lexington-Heath, 1977; J. Rabin and J. Bowman, editors, *Politics and Administra-*

tion: Woodrow Wilson and American Public Administration, Dekker, 1984; and J. P. Krieg, editor, *Robert Moses,* Greenwood Press, 1989. Also contributor of reviews and articles to *American Political Science Review, Political Science Quarterly, Public Policy, Urban Studies, Education and Urban Sociology, Public Administration Review, Criminal Justice Ethics,* and to numerous other journals of political affairs.

WORK IN PROGRESS: The role of government in urban development; police behavior; research on organizational crime and corruption.

SIDELIGHTS: In *Leadership and Innovation: A Biographical Perspective on Entrepreneurs* Jameson W. Doig and his co-editor compiled the biographies of thirteen public leaders who over the years successfully employed an entrepreneurial style in organizing and running an assortment of organizations. "To explore the proposition that leaders can 'make a difference,' Doig and Hargrove have assembled excellent short biographies of 13 such individuals," writes a reviewer for *Choice.* "In a brief introductory chapter, the editors identify some of the strategies and factors that contributed to or inhibited there leaders' success."

John N. Ingham remarks in the *Journal of American History* "the chapters on rhetorical leaders . . . were fascinating, and the chapter on Adm. Hyman Rickover by Eugene Lewis was absolutely superb. The essays all demonstrated what the editors had promised: that those administrators had indeed made a difference."

BIOGRAPHICAL/CRITICAL SOURCES:

PERIODICALS

Choice, July/August, 1988.
Journal of American History, December, 1988.

*   *   *

DONOSO (YANEZ), Jose   1924-

PERSONAL: Born October 5, 1924, in Santiago, Chile; son of José Donoso (a physician) and Alicia Yáñez; married María del Pilar Serrano (a translator), 1961. *Education:* Attended University of Chile, beginning in 1947; Princeton University, A.B., 1951.

ADDRESSES: Home—Santiago, Chile.

CAREER: Writer, journalist, and translator. Shepherd in southern Chile, 1945-46; dockhand in Buenos Aires, Argentina, c. 1946; Kent School, Santiago, Chile, English teacher, c. 1953; Catholic University of Chile, Santiago, professor of conversational English, beginning in 1954; worked in Buenos Aires, 1958-60; *Ercilla* (weekly newsmagazine), Santiago, journalist with assignments in Europe, beginning in 1960, editor and literary critic, beginning in 1962; University of Chile, Santiago, lecturer at school of journalism, beginning in 1962; *Siempre* (periodical), Mexico City, Mexico, literary critic, 1965; University of Iowa, Dubuque, teacher of writing and modern Spanish American literature at Writers' Workshop, 1965-67; Colorado State University, Fort Collins, teacher, 1969.

AWARDS, HONORS: Santiago Municipal Short Story Prize, 1955, for *Veraneo y otros cuentos;* Chile-Italia Prize for journalism, 1960; William Faulkner Foundation Prize, 1962, for *Coronación;* Guggenheim awards, 1968 and 1973; Critics Award for best novel in Spanish, 1979, for *Casa de campo.*

WRITINGS:

Veraneo y otros cuentos (title means "Summertime and Other Stories"), privately printed (Santiago, Chile), 1955.
Dos cuentos (title means "Two Stories"), Guardia Vieja, 1956.
Coronación (novel), Nascimento, 1957, Seix Barral, 1981, translation by Jocasta Goodwin published as *Coronation,* Knopf, 1965.
El charleston (short stories; title means "The Charleston"), Nascimento, 1960.
Los mejores cuentos de José Donoso (short stories; title means "The Best Stories of José Donoso"), Zig-Zag, 1965.
Este domingo (novel), Zig-Zag, 1965, translation by Lorraine O'Grady Freeman published as *This Sunday,* Knopf, 1967.
El lugar sin límites (novella; title means "The Place Without Limits"), J. Moritz (Mexico), 1966, translation by Suzanne Jill Levine and Hallie D. Taylor published as *Hell Has No Limits* in *Triple Cross,* Dutton, 1972.
(Editor with William A. Henkin and others) *The Tri-Quarterly Anthology of Contemporary Latin American Literature,* Dutton, 1969.
El obsceno párajo de la noche (novel), Seix Barral, 1970, translation by Hardie St. Martin and Leonard Mades published as *The Obscene Bird of Night,* Knopf, 1973.
Cuentos (title means "Stories"), Seix Barral, 1971, translation by Andrée Conrad published as *Charleston and Other Stories,* David Godine, 1977.
Historia personal del "boom" (memoir), Anagrama (Barcelona), 1972, translation by Gregory Kolovakos published as *The Boom in Spanish American Literature: A Personal History,* Columbia University Press, 1977.
Tres novelitas burguesas (title means "Three Bourgeois Novellas"), Seix Barral, 1973, translation by Andrée Conrad published as *Sacred Families: Three Novellas,* Knopf, 1977.
Casa de campo (novel), Seix Barral, 1978, translation by David Pritchard and Suzanne Jill Levine published as *A House in the Country,* Knopf, 1984.
El jardín de al lado (novel; title means "The Garden Next Door"), Seix Barral, 1981.
La misteriosa desparición de la Marquesita de Loria (novel; title means "The Mysterious Disappearance of the Young Marchioness of Loria"), Seix Barral, 1981.
Poemas de un novelista (poems), Ganymedes (Santiago), 1981.
Cuatro para Delfina (novellas; title means "Four for Delfina"), Seix Barral, 1982.
La desesperanza (novel; title means "Despair"), Seix Barral, 1986, translation by Alfred MacAdam published as *Curfew,* Weidenfeld & Nicolson, 1988.
(Contributor) Doris Meyer, editor, *Lives on the Line: The Testimony of Contemporary Latin American Authors,* University of California Press, 1988.

Translator into Spanish of numerous works, including *The Life of Sir Arthur Conan Doyle* by John Dickson Carr and *Last Tales* by Isak Dinesen, and, with wife, María del Pilar Serrano, of *The Scarlet Letter* by Nathaniel Hawthorne and *Les Personnages* by Françoise Malet-Joris. Contributor of articles and short stories to periodicals, including *Américas, mss.* (Princeton University), and *Review.*

WORK IN PROGRESS: A work set in the coal-mining community of Chile, excerpted in *Review,* January-June, 1988, under the title "The Fish in the Window."

SIDELIGHTS: "I fear simplification more than anything," said Chilean novelist José Donoso in *Partisan Review.* Donoso's novels, noted for their complexity and insistent pessimism, seem to embody his observation that life, society, and writing are each an "adventure into [a] mad, dark thing." Donoso has often been ranked among the finest Latin American authors of the twentieth century; he has been hailed as a master by Mexican novelist Carlos Fuentes and Spanish filmmaker Luis Buñuel, two of his most renowned contemporaries. "He is an extraordinarily sophisticated writer," wrote Newsweek's Walter Clemons, "in perfect control of time dissolves, contradictory voices, gritty realism and hallucinatory fugues."

Observers suggest that Donoso's concern with the complexity of life is particularly appropriate to the situation in his homeland. Chile, which appeared to be a moderate, stable democracy for most of the twentieth century, erupted in violent political conflict in the 1970s. The country lurched abruptly from the Marxist government of Salvador Allende to the brutal conservative dictatorship of General Augusto Pinochet. From the time his first novels appeared in the 1950s, Donoso was praised for his sense of the strained relations between rich and poor that underlay Chilean society. The author is reluctant, however, to be viewed as a social commentator: he seems determined, in both his life and his work, to avoid the didacticism he has seen in politics. "Ideologies and cosmogonies are alien to me," he stated in Lives on the Line. "Their life is too short and they are too soon proved wrong, their place immediately taken by another explanation of the world." Accordingly, as Donoso observed in Review, "I'm not interested in the novels of ideas. . . . If I write a novel, it won't be to express an idea I saw in an essay."

Writers of the Chilean left, Donoso suggested, have repeatedly challenged his political standoffishness; sometimes, he observed in Nation, he has been "denounced . . . as decadent bourgeois." But Donoso's many admirers suggest that his pessimistic outlook, even his refusal to offer a solution to the problems that he surveys in his work, reflects an acute awareness of the breadth and depth of human suffering. As Z. Nelly Martínez explained in Books Abroad: "Beyond the social reality and its multiple stratification, Donoso probes into life's duality of good and evil, order and chaos, life and death, and examines man's inability to reconcile both sides of existence. Therein lies the tragedy; for, despite man's effort to build an illusion of order, life's anarchy eventually overcomes him." In much of the author's work, as Martínez observed, "madness, abdication to chaos, becomes the only alternative." Against such all-encompassing pain, Donoso seems to offer hope primarily in the form of intellectual understanding. "Kicking people in the shins gets you nowhere," he said in the New York Times Book Review. "Understanding gets you much farther."

Donoso was born into a family that kept a tenuous foothold in Chile's respectable upper middle class. His father "was a young physician more addicted to horse racing and to playing cards than to his profession," the author recalled in Review. His mother, who "somehow coped," came from "the ne'er-do-well branch of a nouveau riche family." The father used family connections to get a newspaper job, but he was fired; thereafter he became house physician to three decrepit great-aunts whose fortunes he hoped to inherit. When the aunts died, the Donosos inherited nothing. But soon they were sheltering other relatives, including an irresponsible uncle and Donoso's grandmother, who lived with the family for ten years while slowly succumbing to insanity. "The gradual process of [my grandmother's] deterioration, intertwined with lightning flashes of memory and family lore . . . is one of the episodes that has most marked my life," Donoso declared, "not because I loved this old woman but because her madness brought the ironies of family life and the horrors of aging and dying so cruelly into focus." He became a high-

school truant and then a dropout, associating with bums and spending a year as a shepherd in the remote grasslands of southern Chile. In his early twenties he returned home and resumed his education, rejecting the traditional careers open to "an upper middle-class boy" by becoming an undergraduate English major.

Donoso describes his literary development in the memoir Historia personal del "boom" (The Boom in Spanish American Literature: A Personal History). The book introduces readers to one of the most renowned periods in Spanish American Literature—the "Boom," a flowering of literary activity during the 1960s—by showing its relationship to Donoso's own life. As an aspiring author in the 1950s, Donoso relates in his memoir, he shared with other young writers throughout Latin America the sense of being "asphyxiated" by the provincial cultural environment of his native land. Great authors of the past such as Mexico's Manuel Azuela, who saw the novel as a practical way to discuss contemporary social problems, seemed to members of Donoso's generation like "statues in a park." The earnest, simple style that such "grandfathers" had made popular seemed to rob the novel of creativity and expressiveness. The region's publishers, too poor to take risks on new talent, preferred to reprint literary classics and popular foreign works; accordingly, Donoso and his peers had difficulty getting published, often had to sell copies of their books on their own, and found it difficult to obtain each others' work in print. For role models, Donoso declares, writers of his generation looked beyond the Hispanic world. Some authors he mentions, including William Faulkner and Henry James, were subtle stylists who experimented with the conventions of the novel, showing, for instance, how a character's point of view could affect their perception of reality. Others, including Franz Kafka and Albert Camus, were critics of human nature who seemed to have little hope of reform: their works showed isolated individuals grappling with an uncaring and fundamentally absurd society. By the late 1950s and early 1960s, Donoso began to see such innovative writing in novels by his peers, notably Cuba's Alejo Carpentier and Mexico's Carlos Fuentes. Such works, Donoso recalls, were "a spur to my envy, to my need to emulate," and they confirmed his sense that "the baroque, the distorted, the excessive could all increase the possibilities of the novel."

In his first novel, Coronación (Coronation), Donoso combined traditional realism with the more complex personal vision that would emerge in his later works. The book's main character is an affluent old woman who lives with her servants in a mansion; her vivid delusions and curses frighten her grandson, a repressed middle-aged bachelor. The old woman, Donoso admitted, is a portrait of his insane grandmother, and some relatives were indignant at the resemblance. Reviewers in Chile praised Coronation as a realistic depiction of that country's society, especially, recalled Donoso in The Boom, "the decadence of the upper class." Wishing to transcend realism, Donoso found such praise frustrating. The resolution of the novel, he suggested, was designed to challenge traditional literary style. The book's climax largely abandons the restraints of realism by dwelling on madness and the grotesque. The old woman, costumed and crowned by her maids during a drunken prank, dies convinced she has already gone to heaven. The grandson, confronting his mortality and his unfulfilling life, concludes that God himself must have been mad to create such a world and then follows his grandmother into insanity. Coronation brought Donoso an international reputation and won the 1962 William Faulkner Foundation Prize, established in Faulkner's will to encourage the translation of outstanding Latin American fiction into English.

Donoso's second novel, *Este domingo* (*This Sunday*), with its themes of upper-class decay and incipient chaos, has often been likened to *Coronation*. Many reviewers considered the later work a significant advance for Donoso, showing greater subtlety, impact, and stylistic sophistication. "As Donoso sees it," wrote Alexander Coleman in the *New York Times Book Review,* "the rich are different because they cannot live without the underworld of the poor to exploit and command." Don Alvaro is an affluent, middle-aged professional who has grown up weak and ineffective, but has kept a sense of virility by making a chambermaid his mistress. His wife Chepa, who has an obsessive need to minister to others, becomes the domineering patroness to a paroled murderer still drawn toward a life of crime. The novel's climax occurs when Chepa, unhappy with the parolee's conduct, seeks him out in the slum where he lives; she is hounded by poor neighborhood children and collapses on a trash heap. Throughout the book Donoso experiments with differing points of view, showing parts of the story through the eyes of its obsessive participants, and part through the eyes of a young relative of Alvaro, too naive to understand the underlying brutality of the world around him. Noting Donoso's "cool and biting intelligence," Coleman praised the author's "perfect balance between compulsion and control as he exorcises his infernally driven characters."

Donoso delved much further into obsession and fantasy with his novella *El lugar sin límites* (*Hell Has No Limits*), written at about the same time as *This Sunday*. The work is set in an isolated small town owned by Don Alejo, a powerful, all-knowing, selfish aristocrat whom many reviewers saw as the satirical embodiment of an unfeeling God. The main character is Manuela, whose delusions about being a lithe, young female dancer are lavishly echoed by the story's narration; in fact, however, Manuela is an aging male transvestite who works as a dancer in his daughter's bordello and uses fantasy to transcend his absurd existence. The story culminates in violence when Pancho, a virile male truckdriver attracted to Manuela, lashes out against his own underlying homosexuality by savagely assaulting the transvestite. Biographer George McMurray considered *Hell Has No Limits* a powerful comment on the futility of human aspirations, so pessimistic as to approach nihilism. The author's intentions, McMurray explained, "are to undermine traditional values, reveal the bankruptcy of reason, and jar the reader onto new levels of awareness by exposing the other side of reality." McMurray found the story one of Donoso's most accomplished works.

During the 1960s Donoso moved beyond the intellectual confines of Chile to become part of a growing international community of Latin American writers—major figures of the Boom—who knew each other as friends and colleagues and shared moral support, ideas, and interesting books. At a 1962 conference of such writers he became close friends with Carlos Fuentes; after attending another conference in Mexico two years later, Donoso began more than a dozen years of voluntary exile from his homeland. He wrote *Hell Has No Limits* while renting a house from Fuentes in Mexico, taught for two years at the University of Iowa's prestigious Writers Workshop, then settled in Spain. Meanwhile he went through numerous drafts of a novel far more lengthy, intricate, and allusive than his previous efforts. Its title came from a letter that young Henry James received from his father Henry Sr., warning about life's underlying chaos. "Life is no farce," the letter advised: "the natural inheritance of everyone who is capable of spiritual life is an unsubdued forest where the wolf howls and the obscene bird of night chatters."

When *El obsceno párajo de la noche* (*The Obscene Bird of Night*) finally emerged in 1970, reviewers found it both masterful and indescribable—"How do you review a dream?" asked Wolfgang Luchtig in *Books Abroad.* The novel is narrated by Humberto, an unsuccessful writer who becomes the retainer to a decaying aristocratic family and the tutor of their only son and heir. The child, monstrously deformed, is seen by his father as an emblem of chaos and is surrounded by freaks so that he will seem "normal." Eventually Humberto apparently flees to one of the family's charitable ventures—a decrepit convent that houses some of society's castoff women, ranging from the elderly to young orphans. Throughout the novel past and present are confusingly intermingled, and characters undergo bizarre transformations, sometimes melting into one another. Humberto appears as a deaf-mute servant in the convent; is apparently transformed into a baby by the old women, who often seem to be witches; and is finally sealed in a bundle of rags and thrown onto a fire, where he turns to ashes as the book ends.

Observers such as McMurray suggest that the novel should not be viewed as a "story" in the conventional sense, but as an outpouring of the deranged mind of its narrator, Humberto. According to such a view, Humberto is a schizophrenic, driven mad, perhaps, by his lack of success; his narration is disordered because he freely mixes reality with his fantasies, fears, and resentments of the world. Humberto's many transformations reflect his disintegrating personality, as he picks up and discards various identities in an effort to define himself; his bizarre demise, in which he is cut off from the world and then destroyed, represents the madman's final withdrawal from reality. In *Review* Donoso said that while the narrator is hardly autobiographical in a literal sense, "he is the autobiography of my fears, of my fantasies"; interestingly, the author finished his book while recovering from an episode of near-madness, brought on by a traumatic ulcer operation and the administration of pain-killing drugs. "Basically I don't know what my novel is about," Donoso also observed. "It's something that has happened to me rather than something I've written." "Donoso does not offer us . . . a novel simply to read," explained *Review*'s John J. Hassett, "but one to experience in which we are continuously called upon to give the text some order by discovering its unities and its repetitions." Many commentators ranked *The Obscene Bird of Night* among the best novels of the Boom era, which ended in the early 1970s; Donoso was favorably compared with Gabriel García Márquez, a Boom author who eventually won the Nobel Prize.

Until the 1980s Donoso continued to reside primarily in Spain. After he finished *The Obscene Bird of Night,* his writing began to change: his style became less hallucinatory and his narratives were less concerned with the Chilean aristocracy. Some of his work was set in Spain, including *Tres novelitas burguesas* (*Sacred Families*), novellas that portray that country's upper middle class with a blend of fantasy and social satire, and *El jardín de al lado* ("The Garden Next Door"), which features a novelist-in-exile who is haunted by his past. Throughout his years in Spain, Donoso reported in *Lives on the Line,* he found it impossible to cut his emotional ties to Chile. He did not feel nostalgia, he continued, but rather "the *guilt of absence*" or the "guilt of not being connected with action." His dilemma was heightened because he remained abroad by choice while Pinochet established his dictatorship. "All of us who lived abroad during that period who didn't have to," he explained in *Vogue,* "have a terrible feeling of guilt" because "we didn't share in the history of Chile during a very important time."

In the mid-1970s Donoso resolved to discuss Chile's turmoil in a novel, which became *Casa de campo* (*A House in the Country*). Aware that he was cut off from the daily life of Chileans—including the way they spoke—he wrote about them indirectly, creating what reviewers called a political allegory. Once more

Donoso set his book in an aristocratic household. When the estate's owners leave on an excursion, their children (perhaps representing the middle class) and exploited Indians from the surrounding area (perhaps the working class) take over and wreak havoc. They are led by an aristocratic uncle (Salvador Allende?) who may be insane or may be the victim of injustice at the hands of his relatives. When the owners return, they use servants to ruthlessly re-establish order and then proclaim—despite all the bitterness they have engendered—that nothing has changed since they first left. Though some reviewers faulted the novel for being too intellectual and emotionally detached, others found it highly relevant and involving. "The combination of literary grace, political urgency and a fierce and untethered imagination," wrote Charles Champlin in the *Los Angeles Times Book Review*, "give Donoso and 'A House in the Country' the power of an aimed projectile."

By the mid-1980s Donoso had resettled in Chile, and in 1986 he produced a more direct study of life under Pinochet in the novel *La desesperanza* (*Curfew*). Though the book describes both Pinochet's torturers and the dispossessed poor, its principal focus is the country's well-educated, dispirited political left. The two main characters—a onetime revolutionary and a political folksinger who fled to Paris—share deep feelings of guilt because they were not punished as much by the regime as were other leftists. Their old comrades, meanwhile, seem paralyzed by infighting, didacticism, and bitterness. The book was highly praised by prominent American critics and, notably, by Jacobo Timerman, an Argentine journalist respected worldwide as an eloquent victim of political oppression. "Donoso is a moderate who has written a revolutionary novel," Timerman observed in *Vogue;* in *New Yorker* he wrote that "it is a relief, finally, to read a work of Chilean literature in which none of the characters are above history or appear to dominate it." *Curfew,* reviewers suggested, displays the deep personal flaws of leftists and rightists alike: by avoiding simple conclusions, the novel makes plain that Chile abounds in uncertainty and despair. In contrast to its reception abroad, *Curfew* was viewed rather coolly by many Chilean intellectuals. "The book doesn't flag-wave" or "present an alternative," Donoso explained in *Vogue,* and "people would respect me much more if it did." However, he observed, "I'm not a crusader. I'm not a hero. I'm just a man who is very hurt, and who wants change."

BIOGRAPHICAL/CRITICAL SOURCES:

BOOKS

Contemporary Literary Criticism, Gale, Volume 4, 1975, Volume 8, 1978, Volume 11, 1979, Volume 32, 1985.

Donoso, José, *The Boom in Spanish American Literature: A Personal History,* Columbia University Press, 1977.

Forster, Merlin H., editor, *Tradition and Renewal: Essays on Twentieth-Century Latin American Literature and Culture,* University of Illinois Press, 1975.

MacAdam, Alfred J., *Modern Latin American Narratives: The Dreams of Reason,* University of Chicago Press, 1977.

McMurray, George R., *José Donoso,* Twayne, 1979.

Meyer, Doris, editor, *Lives on the Line: The Testimony of Contemporary Latin American Authors,* University of California Press, 1988.

Schwartz, Ronald, *Nomads, Exiles, and Emigres: The Rebirth of the Latin American Narrative, 1960-80,* Scarecrow Press, 1980.

PERIODICALS

Américas, June 9, 1984, November/December, 1987.

Book Forum, summer, 1977.
Books Abroad, winter, 1968, winter, 1972, spring, 1972, spring, 1975.
Christian Science Monitor, June 27, 1973, June 2, 1988.
Commonweal, September 21, 1973, May 18, 1984.
Contemporary Literature, Volume 28, number 4, 1987.
Essays in Literature, spring, 1975.
Hispania, May, 1972.
Hudson Review, winter, 1978, winter, 1989.
Journal of Spanish Studies: Twentieth Century, winter, 1973.
Los Angeles Times Book Review, February 5, 1984, May 15, 1988.
Modern Fiction Studies, winter, 1978.
Nation, March 11, 1968, June 11, 1973, February 11, 1978.
New Leader, October 1, 1973.
New Statesman, June 18, 1965, March 1, 1974.
Newsweek, June 4, 1973.
New Yorker, June 16, 1973, April 30, 1984, November 2, 1987, June 13, 1988.
New York Review of Books, April 19, 1973, December 13, 1973, August 4, 1977, July 18, 1985.
New York Times Book Review, March 14, 1965, November 26, 1967, December 24, 1972, June 17, 1973, June 26, 1977, February 26, 1984, May 29, 1988.
Partisan Review, fall, 1974, number 1, 1982, number 2, 1986.
PMLA, January, 1978.
Punch, April 18, 1984.
Review, fall, 1973, January-May, 1984.
Revista de Estudios Hispánicos, January, 1975.
Saturday Review, March 13, 1965, December 9, 1967, January 23, 1971, July 9, 1977.
Spectator, June 18, 1965.
Studies in Short Fiction, winter, 1971.
Symposium, summer, 1976.
Time, April 23, 1965, July 30, 1973, June 27, 1977, February 20, 1984.
Times Literary Supplement, July 1, 1965, October 12, 1967, February 22, 1968, July 2, 1971, February 10, 1978, April 6, 1984.
Village Voice, March 27, 1984.
Vogue, May, 1988.
Washington Post Book World, May 27, 1973, August 14, 1977, February 26, 1984, May 22, 1988.
World Literature Today, autumn, 1977, spring, 1981, summer, 1982, winter, 1983.*

—*Sketch by Thomas Kozikowski*

*   *   *

DORSET, Ruth
    See ROSS, W(illiam) E(dward) D(aniel)

*   *   *

DROIT, Michel (Arnould Arthur) 1923-

PERSONAL: Born January 23, 1923, in Vincennes, France; son of Jean (an artist) and Suzanne (Plisson) Droit; married Janine Bazin, January 20, 1947; children: Corinne, Eric. *Education:* University of Paris, Faculte des Lettres, Licence es Lettres, 1944; Ecole Libre des Sciences Politiques, diploma, 1944. *Avocational interests:* Travel, big game hunting (has hunted professionally in the Central African Republic), skin-diving, judo, karate, jazz music, collecting paintings and exotic objects.

ADDRESSES: Home—76 rue Spontini, 75116 Paris, France.

CAREER: War correspondent with French Army and U.S. Army, 1944-45; reporter for newspapers, radio, and television in Paris, France, 1944-56; foreign affairs commentator for French television, 1956-60; editor-in-chief of television news service "Tribunes et debats," Radio Diffusion-Television Francaise, 1960-61; *Le Figaro litteraire,* Paris, editor-in-chief, 1961-71; *Le Figaro,* Paris, editorialist, 1971—. Producer of television programs "A propos," 1962-74, "Ces Annees la," 1975, and "Cela s'appelait l'Empire," 1980. Advisory editor, La Librairie Plon.

MEMBER: International PEN, Academie Francaise, Association des Grands Reporters Francais, Societe des Auteurs Dramatiques, Maison de la Chasse et de la Nature, Comite Francais des Grandes Chasses, Association des Chasseurs Professionels d'Afrique Francophone.

AWARDS, HONORS: Prix Max Barthou, 1955, for *Plus rien au monde;* Prix Carlos de Lazerme, 1961, and Grand Prix Rhodanian de Litterature, both for *La Camargue;* Grand Prix du Roman de l'Academie Francaise, 1964, for *Le Retour;* Prix Edmond-Michelet, 1972, for filmscript of documentary "Un Francais libre"; Prix Malherbe, 1975, for *La Coupe est pleine;* Officier de la Legion d'Honneure; Croix de Guerre; Medaille Militaire; Officier de l'Ordre National du Merite.

WRITINGS:

De Lattre, Marechal de France, P. Horay, 1952.
Jours et nuits d'Amerique, Nizet, 1952.
Andre Maurois, Editions Universitaires, 1953, 2nd edition, 1958.
Plus rien au monde (novel), Ferenczi, 1954, published as *L'Ecorche,* Julliard, 1968.
Visas pour l'Amerique du Sud, Gallimard, 1956.
Pueblo (novel), Julliard, 1957, translation by Edward Hyams published under same title, Eyre & Spottiswoode, 1959.
J'ai vu vivre le japon, Fayard, 1958.
Panoramas mexicains, Fayard, 1960.
La Camargue, Arthaud, 1961, translation by Ernest Heimann and Adair Heimann published as *Camargue,* Rand McNally, 1963.
(Editor) *Michel Droit presente le Japon vu par Michel Hetier,* G. Victor, 1964.
Le Retour (novel), Julliard, 1964, translation by Olwyn Hughes published as *The Return,* Deutsch, 1966.
Le Temps des hommes, Julliard, Volume 1: *Les Compagnons de la foret noire* (novel), 1966, Volume 2: *l'Orient perdu* (nonfiction), 1969, Volume 3: *La Ville blanche,* 1973, Volume 4: *La Mort du connetable,* 1976.
A propos, R. Solar, 1967.
Hambourg, P. Cailler, 1970.
L'Homme du destin: Charles de Gaulle, Larrieu-Bonnel, 1972, Volume 1: *La Resistance,* Volume 2: *La Liberation,* Volume 3: *Le Retour,* Volume 4: *L'Achevement,* Volume 5: *Documents et archives.*
(Author of introduction) *Vingt et quatrieme salon de dessin et de la peinture a l'eau: Grand Palais des Champs-Elysees, du 17 mai au 16 juin 1974* (exhibition catalog), Imprimerie Municipale (Paris), 1974.
La Coupe est pleine, Editions France-Empire, 1975.
(Author of introduction) *Michel Ciry,* Ides et Calendes, 1977.
Les Feux du crepuscule: Journal, 1968-1969-1970, Plon, 1977.
Les Clartes du jour: Journal, 1963-1964-1965, Plon, 1978.
Les Lueurs de l'aube: Journal, 1958-1959-1960, Plon,, 1981.
Une fois la nuit venue: Journal, 1972-1973-1974, Plon, 1984.
La Riviere de la guerre (novel), Julliard, 1985.
Lettre ouverte a ceux qui en ont plus qu'assez du socialisme (pamphlet), Albin Michel, 1985.

Le Fils unique (reminiscences), Plon, 1988.

Also author of a collection of short stories, *La Fille de l'ancre bleue;* author radio and television scripts, including "Les Roses de september" (adapted from the work of Andre Maurois), "Les Pelouses de Bagatelle" (adapted from the work of Pulman), and "De tres chers amis" (adapted from the work of R. Rose); author of a documentary film script on the life of Charles de Gaulle, "Un Francais libre."

WORK IN PROGRESS: Novels and memoirs.

SIDELIGHTS: Michel Droit is the only journalist to have interviewed Charles de Gaulle on television. His conversations with the late French general and president occurred in December, 1965, June, 1968, and April, 1969.

BIOGRAPHICAL/CRITICAL SOURCES:

PERIODICALS

Times Literary Supplement, April 14, 1966.*

* * *

DRYDEN, Pamela
See St. JOHN, Nicole

* * *

DUGAN, Michael (Gray) 1947-

PERSONAL: Born October 9, 1947, in Melbourne, Australia; son of Dennis Lloyd (a journalist) and June (Wilkinson) Dugan. *Education:* Educated in Melbourne, Australia.

ADDRESSES: Home—2/192 Union Rd., Surrey Hills, Victoria, Australia 3127.

CAREER: Writer. The Little Bookroom, Melbourne, Australia, bookseller's assistant, 1966; F. W. Cheshire, Melbourne, bookseller's assistant, 1967; Oldmeadow Booksellers, Heidelberg, bookseller and buyer, 1968-71. Consultant to Oldmeadow Booksellers, Jacaranda Press, and Penguin Books.

MEMBER: International PEN, Fellowship of Australian Writers, Australian Society of Authors, Victorian Fellowship of Australian Writers (committee member, 1970—), Children's Book Council of Victoria (vice president, 1977—; committee member, 1977-81), Melbourne Cricket Club, RACV.

AWARDS, HONORS: Commendation, Australian Visual Arts Foundation, 1975; finalist, Book of the Year, Children's Book Council of Australia, 1987.

WRITINGS:

JUVENILE

Travel and Transport, Oxford University Press, 1968.
Weekend, Macmillan, 1976.
Mountain Easter, Macmillan, 1976.
My Old Dad, Longmans-Cheshire, 1976.
The Race, Macmillan, 1976.
The Golden Ghost, Macmillan, 1976.
True Ghosts, Macmillan, 1977.
Goal, Macmillan, 1978.
Hostage, Hodder & Stoughton, 1978.
Dingo Boy (novel), Penguin, 1980.
The Great Overland Riverboat Race (novel), Penguin, 1982.
Race for Treasure, Thomas Nelson, 1982.
Growing Up in the Goldrush (biography), Kangaroo, 1983.
Melissa's Ghost (novel), J. M. Dent, 1986.

Growing Up in the Bush (biography), Kangaroo, 1986.
Teacher's Secret (novel), Penguin, 1987.
The Elephant Who Came to Stay, Rigby Educational, 1987.
Wombats Don't Have Christmas, Century Hutchinson, 1987.
It's Just a Trick, Rigby Educational, 1988.
The Hijacked Bathtub (short stories), Georgian House, 1988.
Leaving Home (nonfiction), Penguin, 1989.
Finding a Job (nonfiction), Penguin, 1989.
Should We Tell? (novel), Houghton, 1990.

Also author of series "Australian Fact Finders" (thirty-two titles), 1978-81, "Famous Australians" (sixteen titles), 1980-81, and "People in Australia" (sixteen titles), 1983-85, and author of five titles for "Southern Cross" series, 1987, all published by Macmillan; author of eight young adult titles in various series for Macmillan, Cheshire-Ginn, and Hodder. Book reviewer for *Age* and *Reading Time.* Editor of *Puffinalion: Australian Puffin Club Magazine,* 1977-81.

POEMS

Stones, The Hand Press, 1970.
Missing People, Sweeney Reed, 1970.
Returning from the Prophet, Contempa, 1972.
(Editor) *The Drunken Tram* (anthology), Stockland, 1972.
Clouds, Outback Press, 1975.
Nonsense Places (juvenile), Collins, 1976.
(Co-editor) *Neon Signs to the Mutes,* Broken Hill Proprietary/Fellowship of Australian Writers, 1978.
(Co-editor) *Messages in a Bottle,* Broken Hill Proprietary/Fellowship of Australian Writers, 1978.
(Co-editor) *Of Human Beings and Chestnut Trees,* Broken Hill Proprietary/Fellowship of Australian Writers, 1979.
Nonsense Numbers (juvenile), Thomas Nelson, 1980.
Billy (juvenile), Penguin, 1981.
(Co-editor) *Time and Change,* Heinemann Educational, 1981.
Flock's Socks and Other Shocks (juvenile), Penguin, 1988.
The Worst Dream of All (juvenile), Collins/Ingram, 1989.

Also editor and publisher of quarterly poetry journal, *Crosscurrents,* 1968.

PICTURE BOOKS

Dragon's Breath, Gryphon, 1978.
A House for Wombats, Century Hutchinson, 1985.
A Night for Frights, Century Hutchinson, 1988.
The Wombats' Party, Random Century, 1990.
Bathing Buster, Random Century, 1990.

JUVENILE; CONTRIBUTOR

(And compiler) *Stuff and Nonsense* (verse anthology), Collins, 1974.
(And editor) *The Puffin Fun Book* (anthology), Penguin, 1980.
(And compiler) *More Stuff and Nonsense* (verse), Collins, 1980.
(And editor) *Australian Children's Authors Wallcharts* (poster set), Macmillan, 1981.
(And editor) *The Moving Skull* (anthology), Hodder & Stoughton, 1981.
(And compiler) *Ten Times Funny* (verse), Houghton, 1990.

OTHER

(Editor with John Jenkins) *The Outback Reader* (prose), Outback Press, 1975.
Publishing Your Poems (handbook), Second Back Row Press, 1978.
(Compiler) *The Early Dreaming* (biographies), Jacaranda-Wiley, 1980.

(Co-editor) *The Hat Trick* (short stories), Broken Hill Proprietary/Fellowship of Australian Writers, 1981.
(With Josef Szwarc) *"There Goes the Neighborhood!": Australia's Migrant Experience* (history), Macmillan, 1984.
The Maltese Connection (social history), Macmillan, 1988.

Also author of other works on Australian immigration. Editor, *Australian School Librarian,* 1968-69, and *Australian Library News,* 1973-74; founding co-editor of annual directory, *Bookmark,* 1973; publications editor, Australian Institute of Multicultural Affairs, 1983-86; publisher with others of literary magazine, *Overland,* 1988—. Contributor to *Bulletin, Age, Nation Review,* and to ABC radio; occasional contributor to papers and journals.

WORK IN PROGRESS: Various books.

SIDELIGHTS: Michael Dugan once wrote *CA:* "My best memories of childhood are of my first eight years which were spent in the country near Melbourne. When my family moved to the suburbs of Melbourne, I took some time to adjust to the change, and it was during this period that I began to write, mainly poems and stories about the country and about my teddy bears and other toys. My first book was published when I was twenty.

"My father was a journalist and my mother wrote occasional articles and poems, so it was not surprising that I grew up wanting to be a writer. My most successful books for children have been collections of nonsense poetry and children's novels such as *Dingo Boy* and *Melissa's Ghost.*

"I live and write in a flat near Melbourne, and often I escape to the country or the coast for a few days. I have long been interested in how Australian society has grown and changed with the waves of different immigrant groups in this country and this has been the subject of my more recent non-children's books, such as *'There Goes the Neighborhood!'* and *The Maltese Connection.*"

*   *   *

DUNLOP, Eileen (Rhona)   1938-

PERSONAL: Born October 13, 1938, in Scotland; daughter of James and Grace (Love) Dunlop; married Antony Kamm (an editor and writer), October 27, 1979. *Education:* Moray House College of Edinburgh, teacher's diploma, 1959. *Religion:* Presbyterian. *Avocational interests:* Reading, going to the theater, gardening.

ADDRESSES: Home—46 Tarmangie Dr., Dollar, Clackmannanshire FK14 7BP, Scotland.

CAREER: Eastfield Primary School, Penicuik, Scotland, assistant mistress, 1959-62; Abercromby Primary School, Tullibody, Scotland, assistant mistress, 1962-64; Sunnyside School, Alloa, Scotland, assistant mistress, 1964-70, assistant headmistress, 1970-79; Dollar Academy, Dollar, Scotland, headmistress of preparatory school, 1980—.

MEMBER: International PEN (Scottish Centre.)

WRITINGS:

FOR CHILDREN

Robinsheugh, Oxford University Press, 1975, published as *Elizabeth Elizabeth,* Holt, 1976.
A Flute in Mayferry Street, Oxford University Press, 1976, published as *The House on Mayferry Street,* Holt, 1977.
Fox Farm, Oxford University Press, 1978, Holt, 1979.
The Maze Stone, Oxford University Press, 1982, Coward, McCann & Geohegan, 1983.

Clementina, Oxford University Press, 1985.
The House on the Hill, Oxford University Press, 1987.
The Valley of Deer, Oxford University Press, 1989.
The Chip Shop Ghost, Blackie & Son, 1991.
Finn's Island, Blackie & Son, 1991.

WITH HUSBAND, ANTONY KAMM

Edinburgh, Cambridge University Press, 1982.
The Story of Glasgow, Drew Publishing, 1983.
Kings and Queens of Scotland, Drew Publishing, 1984.
Scottish Heroes and Heroines of Long Ago, Drew Publishing, 1984.
A Book of Old Edinburgh, Macdonald Publishers, 1984.
Traditional Scottish Rhymes, Drew Publishing, 1984.
Scottish Homes through the Ages, Drew Publishing, 1985.

SIDELIGHTS: Eileen Dunlop writes: "In my writing I have tried to place my characters in settings which are meaningful to me, where I have myself been aware of the 'spirit of place.' I like to imagine the working of that spirit on the minds and hearts of my characters—the effect of the past on the present. Although I have travelled in Europe, moving from place to place does not mean much to me; I am concerned with 'rootedness,' with the continuity of human experience, and the power of the historical imagination."

BIOGRAPHICAL/CRITICAL SOURCES:

PERIODICALS

Times Literary Supplement, November 8, 1985; May 15, 1987; May 19-25, 1989.

*   *   *

DWYER, John C.   1930-

PERSONAL: Born February 10, 1930, in New York, NY; son of Charles A. (a college professor) and Marion (a nurse; maiden name, Young) Dwyer; married Odile Kencker (a teacher), March 26, 1971. *Education:* Loyola University of Chicago, A.B., 1958; Georgetown University, S.T.L., 1961; University of Tuebingen, Ph.D., 1970. *Politics:* Republican. *Religion:* Roman Catholic.

ADDRESSES: Home—2050 Donald Dr., Moraga, CA 94556. *Office*—Department of Religious Studies, St. Mary's College of California, Moraga, CA 94575.

CAREER: Member of Society of Jesus (Jesuits), 1949-70; civilian chaplain with U.S. Army in Europe, 1963-70; University of Tuebingen, Tuebingen, West Germany, research assistant, 1968-71; St. Mary's College of California, Moraga, professor of religious studies, 1971—. Teacher educator in Roman Catholic diocese of Sacramento, California.

WRITINGS:

Son of Man and Son of God: A New Language for Faith, Paulist Press, 1983.
Church History: Twenty Centuries of Catholic Christianity, Paulist Press, 1985.
Foundations of Christian Ethics, Paulist Press, 1987.
Human Sexuality: A Christian View, Sheed & Ward, 1988.
The Word Was Made Flesh: An Introduction to the Theology of the New Testament, Sheed & Ward, 1989.

WORK IN PROGRESS: The Lost Gospel of Paul.

SIDELIGHTS: John C. Dwyer told *CA:* "My feeling is that the 'old language' used by religious faith is simply no longer understood by most people and has lost its power to mediate the encounter with God. However, I believe that a new language can be constructed on the basis of an understanding of the New Testament."

Dwyer's languages include Latin, Greek, German, French, Hebrew, Italian, Dutch, and Russian. He works with computers and teaches others how to use word-processing equipment.

E

ECHEGARAY (y EIZAGUIRRE), Jose (Maria
  Waldo) 1832-1916
  (Jorge Hayaseca y Eizaguirre)

PERSONAL: Born in 1832 in Madrid, Spain; died in 1916 in Madrid, Spain.

CAREER: Spanish mathematician, engineer, statesman, and playwright. Worked as a professor of hydraulics, School of Civil Engineering, Madrid, Spain; held several government posts during the Spanish revolutionary period, 1868-1874; lived briefly as an exile in Paris, France; returned to Spain in 1874. Former Minister of Finance for Spain; founder of the Bank of Spain.

AWARDS, HONORS: Elected to Royal Spanish Academy, 1894; recipient, with Frédéric Mistral, of the Nobel Prize for literature, 1904.

WRITINGS:

PLAYS

(Under pseudonym Jorge Hayaseca y Eizaguirre) *El libro talonario* (also see below; one-act), [Spain], 1874, 3rd edition, José Rodríguez (Madrid), 1881, microcard edition, Falls City Press (Louisville, Ky.), 1968.

La esposa del vengador (also see below; three-act; title means "The Wife of the Avenger"), José Rodríguez, 1874.

En el puño de la espada (also see below; three-act), [Madrid], 1875, 3rd edition, José Rodríguez, 1876, microcard edition, Falls City Microcards (Louisville, Ky.), 1960.

O locura ó santidad (also see below; three-act; title means "Folly or Saintliness"; first produced at Teatro Español, January 22, 1877), Imprento de J. M. Ducazcal (Madrid), 1877, translation by Ruth Lansing published as *Madman or Saint,* R. G. Badger (Boston), 1912.

El gladiator de Ravena: Imitación de las últimas escenas de la tragedia alemana de Federico Halm (Munch de Bellinghaussen), T. Fortanet (Madrid), 1877, microcard edition, Falls City Press, 1968.

Como empieza y come acaba (three-act), T. Fortanet, 1877, microcard edition, Falls City Press, 1968.

Ni la paciencia de Job (three-act), José Rodríguez, 1879, microcard edition, Falls City Microcards, 1959.

Mar sin orillas (three-act), José Rodríguez, 1880, microcard edition, Falls City Microcards, 1960.

La muerte en los labios (also see below; three-act; first produced at Teatro Español, November 30, 1880), José Rodríguez, 1880, 9th edition, Sucesores de Rodríguez y Odriózola, 1897, microcard edition, Falls City Microcards, 1959.

El gran galeoto (also see below; three-act; produced in the United States as *The World and His Wife;* produced in England as *Calumny*), [Spain], 1881, edited with introduction, notes, and vocabulary by Aurelio M. Espinosa, C. A. Koehler & Co. (Boston), 1903, translation by Hannah Lynch published as *The Great Galeoto: A Play in Three Acts,* introduction by Elizabeth R. Hunt, Doubleday, 1914, new and revised edition, Knopf, 1918, reprinted, Las Américas (New York), 1964.

Haroldo el Normado (three-act), José Rodríguez, 1881, microcard edition, Falls City Press, 1970.

Conflicto entre dos deberes (three-act), Cosme Rodríguez (Madrid), 1883, microcard edition, Falls City Press, 1968.

Correr en pos de un ideal (three-act), Cosme Rodríguez, 1883, microcard edition, Falls City Press, 1968.

En el pilar y en la cruz (three-act), Cosme Rodríguez, 1883, microcard edition, Falls City Press, 1968.

Un milagro en Egipto (three-act), Cosme Rodríguez, 1883, microcard edition, Falls City Press, 1968.

La peste de Otranto (three-act), José Rodríguez, 1884, microcard edition, Falls City Microcards, 1960.

Piensa mal . . . ¿y acertarás? (also see below), first produced in Spain, February 5, 1884.

Obras dramáticas escogidas (contains *La esposa del vengador, En el puño de la espada, O locura ó santidad, En el seno de la muerte, La muerte en los labios,* and *El gran galeoto*), 12 volumes, Imprento de Tello (Madrid), 1884-1905.

Mancha que limpia (also see below; four-act), [Spain], 1885, José Rodríguez, 1895, microcard edition, Falls City Press, 1968.

Vida alegre y muerte triste (three-act), José Rodríguez, 1885.

Dos fanatismos (three-act), José Rodríguez, 1887, reprinted on microcards, Falls City Microcards, 1959.

Manantial que no se agota (three-act), José Rodríguez, 1889, microcard edition, Fall City Press, 1968.

Los rigidos (three-act), José Rodríguez, 1889, microcard edition, Falls City Press, 1970.

Siempre en ridículo, [Spain], 1890, translation by T. Walter Gilkyson published as *Always Ridiculous: A Drama in Three Acts,* R. G. Badger, 1916.

Un crítico incipiente: Capricho en tres actos y en prosa sobre crítica dramática, José Rodríguez, 1891, microcard edition, Falls City Microcards, 1960.

Irene de Otranto (three-act opera), music by Emilio Serrano, José Rodríguez, 1891, microcard edition, Falls City Press, 1968.

El hijo de Don Juan, [Spain], 1892, translation by James Graham published as *The Son of Don Juan: An Original Drama in Three Acts; Inspired by the Reading of Ibsen's Work Entitled "Gengangere,"* Roberts Brothers (Boston), 1895, reprinted, Little, Brown, 1918.

Mariana: An Original Drama in Three Acts and an Epilogue, [Spain], 1892, translated by Graham, Roberts Brothers, 1895.

A la orilla del mar (three-act; first performed in Spain at Teatro de la Comedia, December 12, 1893), R. Velasco, 1903.

The Great Galeoto; Folly or Saintliness: Two Plays, translated by Hannay Lynch, L. Wolffe & Co. (Boston), 1895, reprinted, Fertig, 1989.

El estigma (three-act), E. Odriózola (Madrid), 1896.

El prólogo de un drama (also see below; one-act), E. Odriózola, 1896, microcard edition, Falls City Press, 1970.

El poder de la impotencia (three-act), José Rodríguez, 1897, edited with introduction, notes, and vocabulary by Aurelio M. Espinosa, Schoenhof (Boston), 1906.

La duda (also see below), [Spain], 1898.

El loco dios (four-act; title means "The Insane Gods"), [Spain], 1900, translation by Hunt published in *Poet Lore* as *The Madman Divine (El loco dios),* 1908.

Sic vos non vobis; ó, La última limosna (also see below; three-act), R. Velasco (Madrid), 1905, microcard edition, Falls City Press, 1970.

A fuerza de arrastrarse (also see below), [Spain], 1905.

Silencio de muerte (three-act), R. Velasco, 1906, microcard edition, Falls City Press, 1970.

El preferido y los cenicientos, [Spain], 1908.

Tierra baja (three-act), R. Velasco, 1909, microcard edition, Falls City Press, 1968.

El primer acto de un drama (continuation of *El prólogo de un drama*), R. Velasco, 1914, microcard edition, Falls City Press, 1970.

La rencorosa (three-act), R. Velasco, 1915, microcard edition, Falls City Press, 1970.

Lo sublime en lo vulgar (three-act), R. Velasco, 1918, microcard edition, Falls City Press, 1970.

Teatro escogido (contains *El libro talonario, La última noche, En el puño de la espada, O locura ó santidad, En el seno de la muerte, La muerte en los labios, El gran galeoto, Piensa mal . . . ¿y acertarás?, De mala raza, Sic vos non vobis: o, La última limosna, Mancha que limpia, La duda,* and *A fuerza de arrastrarse*), introduction by Amando Lázaro Ros, Aguilar (Madrid), 1955.

Also author of *La realidad y el delirio.*

OTHER

Teoría matemática de la luz, Imprenta de la Viuda de Agualo (Madrid), 1871.

Disertaciones matemáticas sobre la cuadratura del círculo, el método de Wantzel, y la división de la circunferencia en partes iguales (mathematics), Imprento de la Viuda é Hijo de D. E. Aguado (Madrid), 1887.

Algunas reflexiones generales sobre la crítica y el arte literario [Spain], 1894.

Discursos leídos ante la Real Academia Española (lectures), Imprenta de los Hijos de J. A. García (Madrid), 1894.

Discurso leído en la Universidad central en la solemne inauguración del curso académico de 1905 á 1906 (mathematical physics), Colonial (Madrid), 1905.

Cuentos (short stories), [Spain], 1912.

(Translator of Spanish text) Angel Guimerá, *Marta of the Lowlands (Terra baixa)* (also see below), English text translation by Wallace Gillpatrick, introduction by John Garrett Underhill, Doubleday, 1914.

Recuerdos (autobiography), three volumes, Ruiz Hermanos (Madrid), 1917.

(Translator) Guimerá, *Tierra baja* (three-act play; translation of *Terra baixa*), illustrated by Mauricio de Vassal, Orbis (Barcelona), 1930.

SIDELIGHTS: Regarded as an important link in the history of Spanish drama, the plays of José Echegaray recall the romantic style of the nineteenth century, while also foreshadowing the socially conscious plays of the twentieth. Writing both romantic and naturalistic plays, the author drew large audiences during the three decades that followed his first popular work, *La esposa del vengador* ("The Wife of the Avenger"). Critics, however, felt that Echegaray's romances were too melodramatic and that his naturalistic plays were too contrived and suffered from lack of characterization. Consequently, some reviewers objected to the Nobel Prize committee's decision to honor the playwright in 1904. Frank W. Chandler summarized Echegaray this way in his *Modern Continental Playwrights:* Echegaray "delights to portray high-strung characters, intense hysterical souls, driven by passion or idea. He shows the individual struggling with himself or against social institutions. He loves the moral, the heroic, the perfervid. He is a natural rhetorician, less poetic than theatric. At his worst, Echegaray sinks to the level of extravagant melodrama; at his best, he rises to the heights with such original creations as *Folly or Saintliness* and *The Great Galeoto.*"

Part of Echegaray's success, according to Nora Archibald Smith in *Poet Lore,* may be attributed to his entering "upon the dramatic arena at a critical time, when the political disorder and disturbance which followed the revolution of 1868 were paralleled by similar disorder and disturbance upon the stage." Spanish drama had begun to seek its own individuality after a period when it followed the style of the French classicists and needed a playwright to spearhead this change. Echegaray's first works, such as *La esposa del vengador,* were romances in the same vein as *Romeo and Juliet.* Later, with the rise in popularity of dramas about social issues, the playwright also began to address this concern; but "he did so without in any way forsaking the Romantic tradition," noted E. Allison Peers in his *A History of the Romantic Movement in Spain.*

A major influence of Echegaray's social dramas was Norwegian playwright Henrik Ibsen, a point that was readily acknowledged by Echegaray and even noted directly in his play *The Son of Don Juan: An Original Drama in Three Acts; Inspired by the Readings of Ibsen's Work Entitled "Gengangere."* But although both *The Son of Don Juan* and Ibsen's "Gengangere" ("Ghosts") are studies of a character's decline into madness and contain other similarities in plot and dialogue, a number of critics argued that they are indeed completely different works. Bernard Shaw pointed out in a *Saturday Review* article that the cause of insanity in Ibsen's play is due to outside pressures of society beyond the protagonist's control, while in *The Son of Don Juan* Echegaray places all the blame on the main character himself. "Indeed," noted Shaw, "had Echegaray adapted Ibsen's moral to the conditions of domestic life and public opinion in Spain, the process would have destroyed all the superficial resemblances to

'Ghosts' which has led some critics hastily to describe Echegaray's play as a wholesale plagiarism."

Other Echegaray plays, such as *El loco dios* ("The Insane Gods"), also reveal the playwright's debt to Ibsen. As *Sewanee Review* contributor Ruth Lee Kennedy warned, however, not all resemblances in the author's plays are attributable to Ibsen's influence. In Echegaray's *Piensa mal . . . ¿y acertarás?*, for example, the "symbolic story of a wounded bird . . . immediately recalls the use of the wild duck in Ibsen's drama of that name." But *Piensa mal* was staged in early 1884, three years before Echegaray could have read Ibsen's *The Wild Duck*.

Besides *The Son of Don Juan*, other well-known Echegaray plays include *O locura ó santidad* ("Folly or Saintiness") and *El gran galeoto* ("The Great Galeoto"), which are "undoubtedly two of Echegaray's best," in *Academy* critic Wentworth Webster's opinion. Both plays are about the destructive powers of public opinion. In *The Great Galeoto*, the author begins with the story of Francesca and Paolo from Dante's *Inferno*, and adds a twist in which the couple's pure love is destroyed by slanderous rumors. In a similar manner, Lorenzo, the protagonist in "Folly or Saintliness" is declared insane by those who cannot understand his high moral principles. Critics like Webster considered the first acts in "Folly or Saintliness" "excellent," but the critic felt the story's resolution suffers when Lorenzo's fate is decided by the destruction of an important document that would vindicate him. "And thus, instead of the solution of the moral problem being laid before us, we have only the more commonplace result, that the world's sentence . . . on a man's sanity may depend on a mere accident."

When considering the lasting relevance of Echegaray's plays, some critics regarded his works as dated. Others, though, took more into consideration the time period in which he wrote. "To get any evaluation of the works of the Spaniard," remarked Kennedy, "his drama should be compared with what was being written in England, France, Italy, and Germany from 1874 to 1884. . . . [By] 1881 Echegaray had written both *O locura ó santidad* and *El gran galeoto*, dramas that certainly, from the standpoint of technique, bear comparison with anything written during that decade." Echegaray "is usually classified as a neo-romanticist," Wilma Newberry summarized in *PMLA*, "he is accused of being too melodramatic . . . [and] is called anachronistic and is criticised for blocking the Spanish realist movement." But, Newberry proposed, "Echegaray's true position in the procession of dramatists who have made important contributions to the history of ideas should be reevaluated. Although some aspects of his work may seem anachronistic at the end of the nineteenth century, in many ways he looks forward to the twentieth century, while often drawing inspiration from the great literature of the past."

BIOGRAPHICAL/CRITICAL SOURCES:

BOOKS

Chandler, Frank W., *Modern Continental Playwrights*, Harper, 1931.

Echegaray, José, *The Great Galeoto: A Play in Three Acts*, Doubleday, 1914.

Echegaray, José, *The Son of Don Juan: An Original Drama in Three Acts; Inspired by the Reading of Ibsen's Work Entitled "Gengangere,"* Little, Brown, 1918.

Jameson, Storm, *Modern Drama in Europe*, Collins, 1920.

Peers, E. Allison, *A History of the Romantic Movement in Spain*, Volume 2, Cambridge University Press, 1940.

Shaw, Donald L., *The Nineteenth Century*, Barnes & Noble, 1972.

Twentieth Century Literary Criticism, Volume 4, Gale, 1981.

PERIODICALS

Academy, November 2, 1895.
PMLA, March, 1966.
Poet Lore, May-June, 1909.
Saturday Review, April 27, 1895, June 1, 1901.
Sewanee Review, October-December, 1926.*

—*Sketch by Kevin S. Hile*

*　　*　　*

EDWARDS, Blake 1922-

PERSONAL: Born July 26, 1922, in Tulsa, Okla.; married first wife, Patricia, 1953 (divorced, 1967); married Julie Andrews (an actress and entertainer), November 12, 1969; children: (first marriage) one son and one daughter; (second marriage) adopted two Vietnamese orphans. *Military service:* U.S. Coast Guard.

ADDRESSES: Office—Blake Edwards Entertainment, 9336 West Washington Blvd., Culver City, Calif. 90230. *Agent*—c/o Triad Artists, 10100 Santa Monica Boulevard, 16th Floor, Los Angeles, Calif. 90067.

CAREER: Screenwriter and producer; director of films including "Breakfast at Tiffany's" and "Days of Wine and Roses"; also creator/writer of television series "Hey Mulligan," 1954-55, "Peter Gunn," 1958-60, "Mr. Lucky," 1959-60, and "Dante's Inferno," 1960-61. Producer of several television specials. Chairman of Blake Edwards Company (entertainment production company), Culver City, Calif.

MEMBER: Directors Guild of America, Writers Guild of America.

AWARDS, HONORS: Writers Guild Award nomination (with Arthur Carter and Jed Harris), 1957, for "Operation Mad Ball," 1962 (with Larry Gelbart), for "The Notorious Landlady," 1964 (with Maurice Richlin), for "The Pink Panther," and 1965 (with Arthur Ross), for "The Great Race"; Academy Award nomination for best adapted screenplay, 1982, for "Victor/Victoria," and 1983 (with Geoffrey Edwards and Milton Wexler), for "The Man Who Loved Women"; recipient of Lifetime Creative Achievement Award from American Comedy Awards, 1988.

WRITINGS:

SCREENPLAYS

(With John C. Champion) "Panhandle," Allied Artists, 1948.
(With Champion) "Stampede" (adapted from the novel by Edward B. Mann), Allied Artists, 1949.
(With Richard Quine) "Sound Off," Columbia, 1952.
(With Quine) "Rainbow 'round My Shoulder," Columbia, 1952.
(With Quine and Robert Wells) "All Ashore," Columbia, 1953.
(With Quine) "Cruisin' down the River," Columbia, 1953.
"Drive a Crooked Road," Columbia, 1954.
(Author of screen story) "The Atomic Kid," Republic, 1954.
(With Quine) "My Sister Eileen" (adapted from the earlier film of the same title, the play by Joseph Fields and Jerome Chodorov, and stories by Ruth McKenney), Columbia, 1955.
(With Quine, and director) "Bring Your Smile Along," Columbia, 1955.
(With Quine, and director) "He Laughed Last," Columbia, 1956.
(And director) "Mister Cory" (adapted from a story by Leo Rosten), Universal, 1957.

(With Arthur Carter and Jed Harris) "Operation Mad Ball" (adapted from the play by Carter), Columbia, 1957.

(And director) "This Happy Feeling" (adapted from the play "For Love or Money" by F. Hugh Herbert), Universal, 1958.

(And director) "The Perfect Furlough," Universal, 1958.

(Author of screen story, with Owen Crump) "The Couch," Warner Bros., 1962.

(With Larry Gelbart) "The Notorious Landlady" (adapted from the short story "Notorious Tenant" by Margery Sharp), Columbia, 1962.

(With Maurice Richlin, and director) "The Pink Panther," United Artists, 1964.

(With William Peter Blatty, and director) "A Shot in the Dark" (adapted form the play by Harry Kurnitz), United Artists, 1964.

(With Richlin) "Soldier in the Rain" (adapted from the novel by William Golden), Allied Artists, 1964.

(With Arthur Ross, and director) "The Great Race," Warner Bros., 1965.

(Author of screen story, with Richlin, and director) "What Did You Do in the War, Daddy?," United Artists, 1966.

(With Blatty, and director) "Gunn," Paramount, 1967.

(With Tom Waldman and Frank Waldman, and director) "The Party," United Artists, 1968.

(With Blatty, and director) "Darling Lili," Paramount, 1969.

(And producer/director) "Wild Rovers," Metro-Goldwyn-Mayer, 1972.

(Adaptor, and producer/director) "The Tamarind Seed," AVCO-Embassy, 1974.

(With Frank Waldman, and producer/director) "The Return of the Pink Panther," United Artists, 1975.

(With Waldman, and producer/director) "The Pink Panther Strikes Again," United Artists, 1976.

(With Waldman and Ron Clark, and producer/director) "Revenge of the Pink Panther," United Artists, 1978.

(And co-producer/director) "10," Warner Bros., 1979.

(And co-producer/director) "S.O.B.," Paramount, 1981.

(And co-producer/director) "The Trail of the Pink Panther," Metro-Goldwyn-Mayer/United Artists, 1982.

(And co-producer and director) "Victor/Victoria," Metro-Goldwyn-Mayer/United Artists, 1982.

(With Geoffrey Edwards and Milton Wexler, and co-producer/director) "The Man Who Loved Women" (adapted from the French film by Francois Truffaut), Columbia, 1983.

(And co-producer/director) "Curse of the Pink Panther," Metro-Goldwyn-Mayer/United Artists, 1983.

(Co-author under name Sam O. Brown) "City Heat," Warner Bros., 1984.

(And director) "A Fine Mess," Columbia, 1986.

(With Wexler, and director) "That's Life," Columbia, 1986.

(And director) "Blind Date," Tri-Star, 1987.

(And director) "Sunset," Tri-Star, 1988.

(And director) "Justin Case," Walt Disney Television, 1988.

(And director) "Peter Gunn," New World Television, 1989.

(And director) "Skin Deep," Twentieth Century-Fox, 1989.

SIDELIGHTS: "With a career that spans [several decades] and is surely one of the most checkered in Hollywood history," notes *New York Times* critic Janet Maslin, Blake Edwards "has yet to establish anything like a loyal following. And for good reason: no Edwards film, however entertaining, has ever failed to make its audience wince here and there, with the wrong actor, the wrong song, the too-garish setting or the too-dumb gag." The writer/producer/director is perhaps best known for the highly popular "Pink Panther" films, a series of no-holds-barred farces

centering on the cases of the quintessentially inept Inspector Clouseau. But Edwards' career didn't begin with slapstick comedies. Among his early films, two—"Breakfast at Tiffany's" and "Days of Wine and Roses"—were well-received as, respectively, a sophisticated character comedy and an insightful social drama. The "Pink Panther" movies helped cement his reputation as a viable creator of commercial, if not critical, hits. In the late 1960s, though, Edwards wrote and directed a legendary flop, the musical "Darling Lili," starring his wife, actress-singer Julie Andrews. As *New York Times* writer Susan Christian describes it, the "Darling Lili" debacle "was a sort of the 'Heaven's Gate' of its day that sank at the box office along with the $16 million invested in it. . . . [That movie] and the 10-year slump in Mr. Edwards's career that followed it would become fodder for 'S.O.B.,' his scathing satire on Hollywood."

Artistic recuperation for Edwards came in the form of a perfect "10"—the title of his comeback film, released in 1979; its popularity with moviegoers reestablished Edwards as a Hollywood influence. In "10," Dudley Moore plays George, a successful California songwriter who, though romantically involved with a famous singer, played by Andrews, finds himself obsessed with a mysterious blonde, played by Bo Derek, whom he first espies as she is en route to her wedding. His relentless pursuit of this "10" results in the kind of slapstick viewers enjoyed in the "Pink Panther" series.

"In Mr. Edwards's comic world, noses are meant to be stung, heads to have hangovers, and beautiful women to be pursued at any cost," notes *New York Times* reviewer Vincent Canby. The critic also finds that the theme of "10" is in George's "desperate efforts to come to terms with life in Southern California even though he knows he's inadequate. Everywhere he goes he sees youth, beauty and health. He drives casually down a street and feels assaulted by the sight of joggers. Nobody seems to drive anymore. They don't even walk. Everybody runs. It's as if their lives were on fire." Less impressed with "10" is Gary Arnold of the *Washington Post*. In his view, the film's premise buckles under its director's sense of judgement. "Edwards seems to take two dumb steps for every smart one," Arnold writes. "The prevailing Southern California ambience is very promising: warm and luxurious, a potentially disarming setting for haywire upper middle-class behavior. . . . [But Edwards] can't seem to resist the most miserable sight gags that occur to him—at the wedding George is bitten on the nose by a bee; at the dentist's he suffers, at home he keeps clunking his head and falling into the pool. Nor can [Edwards] perceive when he's destroying a truly funny situation with an offensive aside."

Though "10" and "S.O.B." aren't exactly documentaries, Blake acknowledges that both comedies feature scenes inspired from his life. "The scene in '10' with Dudley Moore hopping like crazy across the hot sand actually occurred to me in Mexico," Edwards tells Chris Peachment in a London *Times* interview. "I burned my feet before I discovered the method of throwing down towels in advance." And as for "S.O.B.," in Peachment's words "a withering stream of sniper fire at the more venal aspects of Hollywood," Edwards acknowledges: "I was certainly getting back at some of the producers of my life, although I was a good deal less scathing than I could have been. The only way I got to make it was because of the huge success of *10,* and even then they tried to sabotage it. I like to think it may become a cult film."

"It's difficult to remember a film as mean-spirited as 'S.O.B.,'" says Canby in his *New York Times* article, "that also was so consistently funny." In Edwards' version of a show biz fable, washed-up filmmaker Felix Farmer, played by Richard Mulligan, driven to suicidal impulses by the disastrous box-office of his "family film," desperately decides to reshoot scenes of its wholesome star (and Felix's wife), Sally Miles, played by Andrews, and turn the feature into a soft-core porn epic. Indeed, much of the publicity surrounding "S.O.B." centered on the fact that Andrews herself went topless for the film, an image that certainly differs from the former Mary Poppins. "Because the film is an all-out farce," Canby remarks, "everything in 'S.O.B.' is exaggerated, souped up and bent gloriously out of shape," adding that as a writer/director, Edwards "is rotten to everyone, including his beleaguered, studio-oppressed Felix Farmer, who seems no less opportunistic and a good deal crazier than his oppressors."

Following "S.O.B.," Edwards embarked on what became another great success, the comedy-with-music "Victor/Victoria." Based on an early German film, the movie follows the story of a down-and-out soprano in 1930s Paris. Victoria nearly starves to death before she meets Toddy, a homosexual playboy who convinces her to disguise herself as "Victor," a female impersonator par excellence. The Victor ruse works; Victoria and Toddy become wealthy and famous. Then American mobster King Marchand enters the picture. He finds himself strangely attracted to "Victoria," Victor's "alter ego." The real Victoria, of course, can reveal neither her true identity nor her true feelings for King.

With an all-star cast (Andrews in the title roles, Robert Preston as Toddy, and James Garner as King Marchand) and lush production values, "Victor/Victoria" became a box-office hit and brought an Academy Award nomination for best adapted screenplay for writer/director Edwards. A *New York Times* reviewer explains the way Edwards has conceptualized farce: "It's Peter Sellers' Inspector Clouseau, in one of his 'Pink Panther' films, being blessedly unaware that the putty nose by which he's disguised himself is melting over his upper lip. It's Dudley Moore, in '10,' hiding in a large floral display in a church during a wedding ceremony, being stung by a bee. . . . In 'Victor/Victoria' it's men dressed like women, women dressed like men, mistaken identities, barroom brawls, assignations interrupted, stools that collapse on cue, a thumb caught in a closet door and, later, the same thumb, wrapped in a large bandage, slammed with a hammer. It's also about an innocence that no one within the farce would ever for a minute recognize. The characters in 'Victor/Victoria' don't have time for such analyses—they're too busy working on schemes that will inevitably go wildly, unexpectedly wrong."

In 1986 Edwards created "That's Life," his most autobiographical film to date, and the second film co-written with his psychoanalyst, Milton Wexler. Though the protagonist, Harvey Fairchild, is an architect, not a film director, he is faced with many of the family problems suffered by Edwards and his audience. Fairchild's wife is ridden with illness-inspired anxiety, his children are more self-centered than he'd like, and Harvey himself is a hypochondriac. Though "That's Life" "fails to convince," says *Chicago Tribune* critic Dave Kehr, nevertheless "it is possible to salvage something from it. Throughout his 40-year career as a filmmaker, Edwards has described a world defined by unremitting cruelty and cold treachery. The one way his characters learn to survive in this hostile universe is by adopting an artificial pattern of behavior—a *shtick*—that acts as a barrier between the outside world and their private vulnerabilities. Life, Edwards insists, is not simply lived, but *performed*—hence his attraction to characters whose work requires them to adopt false identities."

"When Director Edwards is at his best, there is something bracing and, these days, unique about his comedy," suggests *Time*'s Richard Schickel. "He is uninterested in sentimentalizing characters like Harvey and not much interested in seeing them rescued from the consequences of their passionate irrationality. He really wants to save the world by showing just how stupid some of its creatures can be. He may go about his task with cool and stylish professionalism, but he stokes a crusader's fire beneath his admirably calculated wit." "The ups and downs of [Edwards'] career have less to do with his critical standing," finds Peachment in his article, "and more with the vagaries of the box office and the usual stupidities of the money men in Hollywood." As the director tells Peachment: "If I had continued to make box office hits then I could have been an axe-murderer or a child-molester and there would still have been a place for me in Hollywood. But I had been too much of a rebel, and an outspoken one too, and when I fell the first time my enemies, who were legion, were waiting in the wings to take my head off. I like the old Chinese proverb: If you wait long enough by the river then the bodies of your enemies will float by. That used to console me through the dark patches. And then one day I realized that downstream from me there was this whole gang of people I'd been rude to, all waiting for me to float by."

BIOGRAPHICAL/CRITICAL SOURCES:

PERIODICALS

Chicago Tribune, April 2, 1982, December 16, 1983, September 26, 1986.
Chicago Tribune Book World, September 21, 1986.
Los Angeles Times, December 16, 1983, December 20, 1984, September 26, 1986, July 12, 1987, April 29, 1988, July 26, 1988.
New York Times, October 5, 1979, October 18, 1979, July 1, 1981, March 19, 1982, April 4, 1982, December 12, 1983, September 21, 1986, September 26, 1986, September 28, 1986, May 3, 1987, April 29, 1988, May 8, 1988, May 15, 1988.
Time, September 29, 1986.
Times (London), December 20, 1982.
Washington Post, October 5, 1979, December 21, 1983, December 21, 1984, October 10, 1986, April 29, 1988, March 3, 1989.

—*Sketch by Susan Salter*

*   *   *

EHRLICH, Amy 1942-

PERSONAL: Born July 24, 1942, in New York, NY; daughter of Max (an author) and Doris (a travel agent; maiden name, Rubenstein) Ehrlich; married Henry Ingraham (a college professor), June 22, 1985; children: Joss Williams. *Education:* Attended Bennington College, 1960-62, 1963-65.

ADDRESSES: Home—Box 73, RFD 3, St. Johnsbury, VT 05819. *Agent*—Sheldon Fogelman, 10 East 40th St., New York, NY 10016.

CAREER: Early jobs for short periods included teacher in day care center, fabric colorist, and hospital receptionist; *Family Circle* magazine, New York City, roving editor, 1976-77; Delacorte Press, New York City, senior editor, 1977-78; Dial Books for Young Readers, New York City, senior editor, 1978-82, executive editor, 1982-84.

AWARDS, HONORS: "Best Book of the Year" list, *School Library Journal,* 1972, and *New York Times,* 1972, both for *Zeek*

Silver Moon; Reviewer's Choice, *Booklist,* 1979, for *Thumbelina;* "Best Book of the Year" list, *School Library Journal,* 1981, and Reviewer's Choice, *Booklist,* 1981, both for *Leo, Zack, and Emmie.*

WRITINGS:

FOR YOUNG PEOPLE

Zeek Silver Moon, Dial, 1972.
(Adaptor for young readers) Dee Brown, *Wounded Knee: An Indian History of the American West* (originally published as *Bury My Heart at Wounded Knee),* Holt, 1974.
The Everyday Train, Dial, 1977.
(Adaptor) Hans Christian Andersen, *Thumbelina,* Dial, 1979.
(Adaptor) Andersen, *The Wild Swans,* Dial, 1981.
Leo, Zack, and Emmie, Dial, 1981.
Annie and the Kidnappers, Random House, 1982.
Annie Finds a Home, Random House, 1982.
Annie: The Storybook Based on the Movie, Random House, 1982.
(Adaptor) Andersen, *The Snow Queen,* Dial, 1982.
(Adaptor) *Cinderella,* Dial, 1985.
(Editor) *The Random House Book of Fairy Tales,* Random House, 1985.
(Adaptor) *The Ewoks and the Lost Children,* Random House, 1985.
(Adaptor) *Bunnies All Day Long,* Dial, 1985.
(Adaptor) *Bunnies and Their Grandma,* Dial, 1985.
(Adaptor) *Bunnies On Their Own,* Dial, 1986.
(Adaptor) *Bunnies at Christmastime,* Dial, 1986.
Leo, Zack, and Emmie Together Again, Dial, 1987.
Buck-Buck the Chicken, Random House, 1987.
Emma's New Pony, Random House, 1988.
Where It Stops, Nobody Knows (novel), Dial, 1988.
(Adaptor) *Pome and Peel,* Dial, 1989.
The Story of Hanukkah, Dial, 1989.
(Adaptor) *Rapunzel,* Dial, 1989.
Lucy's Winter Tale, Dial, in press.
Maggie and Silky, Penguin Books, in press.
The Dark Card (novel), Penguin Books, in press.

WORK IN PROGRESS: A picture book to be illustrated by Steven Kellogg, for Dial.

SIDELIGHTS: Amy Ehrlich told CA: "As a child, I was an avid reader. Books were my escape, a private world that I could retreat to. But I also learned history, geography, psychology, and ethics from the experiences of characters in fiction. When I work on my books, I go back into my own childhood and try to recreate the vividness of life to me at that time. And now that I have my own child, I see it all over again through his eyes. As he's gotten older, my books have too. In my novel *Where It Stops, Nobody Knows,* my heroine was 13. In my new novel *The Dark Card,* my heroine is 17. And, I've just finished my first short story for adults. An adult novel seems inevitable."

She continues: "Basically I do feel that the best book (at least for children) is the most readable and entertaining book. The writer's job as far as I am concerned is first and foremost to tell a good story about characters that readers will care about," adding, "Good editing is terribly important for writers. And a good editor must know when to come forward and when to let the writer do it his or her way. I really do know what good editing is, and I really know I need it. A good editor is as valuable as the financial terms of a contract or the promotion budget for a book—much *more* valuable, come to think about it."

BIOGRAPHICAL/CRITICAL SOURCES:

PERIODICALS

Chicago Tribune, May 5, 1985.
Publishers Weekly, February 28, 1977.

*   *   *

EISENHOWER, John S(heldon) D(oud) 1922-

PERSONAL: Born August 3, 1922, in Denver, Colo.; son of Dwight David (General of the Army and 34th president of the United States) and Mamie Geneva (Doud) Eisenhower; married Barbara Jean Thomas, June 10, 1947 (divorced, 1986); children: Dwight David II, Barbara Anne, Susan Elaine, Mary Jean. *Education:* U.S. Military Academy, B.A., 1944; Columbia University, M.A., 1950; U.S. Army Command and General Staff College, graduate, 1955. *Politics:* Republican.

ADDRESSES: Home—P.O. Box 278, Kimberton, Pa. 19442.

CAREER: U.S. Army, cadet, 1941-44, regular officer, 1944-63 (resigned commission as lieutenant colonel, 1963), reserve officer, 1963—, with present rank of brigadier general; spent 1965-69 writing his book on World War II; U.S. Ambassador to Belgium, Brussels, 1969-71. Served with First U.S. Army, Europe, World War II, later with Army of Occupation in Europe, 1945-47; instructor in English at U.S. Military Academy, West Point, N.Y., 1948-51; battalion and division officer in Korea, 1952-53; member of War Plans Division, Army General Staff, Washington, D.C., 1958-61; researched and did editorial work for his father's memoirs, *The White House Years,* in Gettysburg, Pa., 1961-64. Chairman, Pennsylvania Citizens for Nixon, 1968, Interagency Classification Review Committee, 1972-73, and President's Advisory Committee on Refugees, 1975—. Trustee of Eisenhower College, Seneca Falls, N.Y., and of Eisenhower fellowships.

MEMBER: Seabrook Island Ocean Club (S.C.).

AWARDS, HONORS: Military—Legion of Merit; Bronze Star; Combat Infantryman's Badge; Belgium Order of the Crown Grand Cross. Civilian—L.H.D., Northwood Institute, 1970; Chungmu Distinguished Service medal.

WRITINGS:

The Bitter Woods: A Comprehensive Study of the War in Europe, Putnam, 1969.
Strictly Personal (memoir), Doubleday, 1974.
Allies: Pearl Harbor to D-Day, Doubleday, 1982.
So Far from God: The U.S. War with Mexico, 1846-48, Random House, 1989.

WORK IN PROGRESS: A study of the Mexican-American War, 1846-1848, entitled *Gringo.*

SIDELIGHTS: Reviewing John S. D. Eisenhower's *The Bitter Woods: A Comprehensive Study of the War in Europe* in the *Saturday Review,* Robert Leckie declares the author a "top-flight military historian." Drawing on personal experience as well as German and American sources, Eisenhower chronicles the events leading up to and following the Battle of the Bulge, Adolf Hitler's last great attempt to turn the course of the war in Germany's favor. According to Leckie, "few writers on either side of the conflict are better qualified to tell this story. Himself a staff officer of that First Army agent against whose units the attack was launched, son of the Supreme Commander, who met in the Bulge the crisis of both his 'crusade' and his career, John Eisenhower reveals in this study not only his intimacy with the members of the Allied High Command but great diligence in consulting German archives and interviewing those German officers who are still living. [This work] may stand as the definitive account of the critical battle of the European Theater."

Gordon A. Craig, however, writing in the *New York Times Book Review,* feels that the book "suffers in comparison with previous books on the subject. . . . It is too long; the author is slow in getting down to his subject; he is, particularly in the early pages, repetitive." Despite these criticisms, Craig credits Eisenhower with reconstructing "a complex series of events that involved simultaneous attacks by six German corps along a 70-mile front with a clarity and attention to detail that are a tribute both to his hard and careful work in the sources and to his personal examination of the terrain. He has made the battle his own—and, particularly when he is dealing with small-unit actions, his account conveys an excitement that is hard to resist." "With an amazing . . . grasp of detail," says Charles Poore in the *New York Times,* "[Eisenhower] tells us what was happening everywhere, at almost every level, within the German as well as the Allied lines. In short, he has bitten off an awful lot, and he chews it into the suburbs of infinity."

Eisenhower's more recent work *Allies: Pearl Harbor to D-Day* is based on a manuscript given the author by his father, Dwight D. Eisenhower, before the latter's death. The work examines, in the words of a critic for the *New York Times Book Review,* "the personalities who shaped the Allied cause during World War II," including such figures as Churchill, Stalin, Marshall, and de Gaulle. "John Eisenhower," the critic asserts, "has expanded [his father's] monograph into a lengthy, satisfying history that is at once colorful and clear."

Eisenhower told *CA:* "I write principally for selfish reasons; I feel better when I have a continuing outlet for expressing ideas. Aside from the occasional book introduction and book review, I write generally on subjects unfamiliar to me. This *The Bitter Woods* (1969) pertained to the Battle of the Bulge in the Ardennes, December, 1944, a battle I read about while back in the States. *Allies* (1982) dealt with the Mediterranean Theater of War, World War II; I was a cadet when those events were transpiring.

"I am not a scholar nor am I much of an original researcher. I use academic format only to verify facts that are the products of other people's ideas or are highly controversial. My objective is to put in simple, readable form those periods of history that are on the record but written in dull form. I try to popularize aspects of history that Americans should have some knowledge of but usually do not. The Mexican War fits handily in that category."

He added, "Like many other writers, I would like to try something else, in my case, to branch out from the military. I am afraid, however, that I am confined to nonfiction." While reading nonfiction about General Winfield Scott's involvement in the Mexican War, Eisenhower found his next book idea. *So Far From God: The U.S. War with Mexico, 1846-48,* is a major work about the war that "dismembered the huge if lightly populated Mexican Empire and increased the size of the United States by nearly 50 percent," a conflict that "was as controversial in its day as the Vietnam War has been in ours," Michael Kilian comments in the *Detroit Free Press.* The title comes from Mexican president Porfirio Diaz's lament, "Alas, poor Mexico! So far from God and so close to the United States!"

Critics remark that *So Far From God* is an important book for a number of reasons. Robert W. Johannsen writes in Chicago's *Tribune Books,* "Graphically and suspensefully, Eisenhower re-

counts the long and arduous marches, the tactical maneuvers, the epic engagements . . . and the desperate, hard-fought battles in the Valley of Mexico. It was, Eisenhower points out, a dirty war, costly to both sides. Using the letters and diaries of the soldiers themselves, he has captured the participants' suffering." Furthermore, "the story of this 'dirty little war' is splendidly narrated by Gen. John Eisenhower. . . . Not only do his background and special expertise provide graphic and detailed descriptions of the battles themselves, but he offers insightful portraits of the many colorful personalities who crowd the pages of this book," Robert V. Remini observes in the *Washington Post Book World.* The author excels, says Remini, "in explaining American success despite the interferences from Washington, the lack of resources, the danger of disease and the vast distances involved in transporting thousands of men to the war zone."

In addition, "Mr. Eisenhower wants his subject to receive its due. He believes the Mexican War is too often treated by historians as simply a rehearsal for the later and far greater Civil War," reports *New York Times Book Review* contributor Stephen W. Sears. "He gives little space to the dissent the war generated back home, instead commending his readers to John H. Schroeder's 'Mr. Polk's War: American Opposition and Dissent, 1846-1848,' and leaves unrecorded the impact of the war on American society, which is better found in Robert W. Johannsen's 'To the Halls of Montezumas: The Mexican War in the American Imagination.' What interests Mr. Eisenhower is command—how it was exercised in this war, who succeeded and who failed and why. On that subject he writes briskly and authoritatively, and his judgments are worth reading," adds Sears.

So Far From God puts the Mexican War into a new light. Often considered a scarcely justifiable act of military aggression, the conquering of the territory that is now comprises the southwestern states was a key to the United States's survival, Eisenhower maintains. European powers were eyeing Mexico's northern regions and were aware of its military weakness. "For Americans the thought of a hostile, European-controlled monarchy on the southern border of their democratic experiment was frightening indeed," Johannsen relates. Therefore, Eisenhower reasons, Americans can be proud of the conquest and the volunteers who fought in it. *Los Angeles Times Book Review* contributor Ferol Egan concludes, "For those who want to grasp the military and political causes of this invasion of our neighbor south of the border, Eisenhower's history is an excellent source."

AVOCATIONAL INTERESTS: Airplane piloting.

BIOGRAPHICAL/CRITICAL SOURCES:

PERIODICALS

Chicago Tribune, April 6, 1989.
Detroit Free Press, April 19, 1989.
Los Angeles Times Book Review, June 25, 1989.
New York Times, January 23, 1969, April 5, 1989.
New York Times Book Review, February 9, 1969, October 24, 1982, April 2, 1989.
Philadelphia Inquirer, April 6, 1975.
Saturday Review, January 25, 1969.
Times Literary Supplement, January 15, 1970.
Tribune Books (Chicago), April 9, 1989.
Washington Post Book World, March 26, 1989.

*   *   *

EMMERSON, Donald K(enneth) 1940-

PERSONAL: Born June 10, 1940, in Tokyo, Japan; son of John Kenneth (a writer and diplomat) and Dorothy (McLaughlin)

Emmerson; married Carolyn Holm (a teacher), December 27, 1965; children: Kirsten Holm, Katrina Louise. *Education:* Princeton University, B.A., 1961; Yale University, M.A., 1966, Ph.D., 1972.

ADDRESSES: Office—Department of Political Science, University of Wisconsin, North Hall, Madison, WI 53706.

CAREER: University of Wisconsin—Madison, instructor, 1970-72, assistant professor, 1972-76, associate professor, 1976-81, professor of political science, 1981—, director of Southeast Asian Studies Center, 1985-87. Visiting fellow at Australian National University, 1975, Hoover Institution on War, Revolution, and Peace, 1981-83, Woodrow Wilson Center for International Scholars, 1985, Monterey Institute of International Studies, 1988, Institute for Advanced Study, 1988-89; faculty associate, Universities Field Staff International, 1981-84. Has lectured in France, Indonesia, Japan, the Philippines, Singapore, Thailand, Vietnam, West Germany, and throughout the United States; has conducted field research in East and Southeast Asia. Member of advisory board, Woodrow Wilson Center for International Scholars, 1981-84, Association for Asian Studies, 1981-86, Social Science Research Council, 1986-88, Asia Society, 1982—, Pacific Basin Institute, 1987—. Consultant with Aspen Institute for Humanistic Studies, Ford Foundation, Luce Foundation, Mihaly International, TransCentury Foundation, United States Agency for International Development, Wells Fargo Bank, and World Bank.

MEMBER: Amnesty International, American Political Science Association, Association for Asian Studies.

AWARDS, HONORS: Has received grants from American Council of Learned Societies, Ford Foundation, Fulbright-Hays, National Endowment for the Humanities, and Social Science Research Council; award for excellence in teaching, University of Wisconsin—Madison, 1985.

WRITINGS:

(Editor and contributor) *Students and Politics in Developing Nations,* Praeger, 1968.
(Contributor) R. William Liddle, editor, *Political Participation in Modern Indonesia,* Yale University Press, 1973.
(Contributor) W. Howard Wriggins and James F. Guyot, editors, *Population, Politics, and the Future of Southern Asia,* Columbia University Press, 1973.
The Bureaucracy in Indonesia, Center for International Studies, Massachusetts Institute of Technology, 1974.
Indonesia's Elite: Political Culture and Cultural Politics, Cornell University Press, 1976.
Rethinking Artisanal Fisheries Development: Western Concepts, Asian Experiences, World Bank, 1980.
Pacific Optimism, Universities Field Staff International, 1982.
(Contributor) Benedict Anderson and Audrey Kahin, editors, *Interpreting Indonesian Politics,* Cornell Modern Indonesia Project, 1983.
(Contributor) Ronald Morse, editor, *Southeast Asian Studies,* Woodrow Wilson Center for International Scholars, 1984.
(Contributor) Karl Jackson and Hadi Soesartro, editors, *Economic and Political Stability in Southeast Asia,* Institute of East Asian Studies, University of California, Berkeley, 1984.
The "Stable" War: Cambodia and the Great Powers, Center for International Policy, 1985.
(Contributor) Jackson and Sukhumband Paribatra, editors, *ASEAN in Regional and Global Context,* Institute of East Asian Studies, University of California, Berkeley, 1986.

(Contributor) Robert Scalapino and others, editors, *Asian Political Institutionalization,* Institute of East Asian Studies, University of California, Berkeley, 1986.
(Contributor) Hans Indorf and E. W. Porta, Jr., editors, *ASEAN,* Woodrow Wilson Center for International Scholars, 1988.
(Contributor) J. Soedjati Djiwandono and Yong Mun Cheong, editors, *Soldiers and Stability in Southeast Asia,* Institute of Southeast Asian Studies, 1988.
ASEAN under Pressure, Asia Society, 1988.

Contributor to world and Asian affairs journals and newspapers, including *Christian Science Monitor, Japan Times, Los Angeles Times,* and *New York Times.*

WORK IN PROGRESS: A book, tentatively entitled *Apocalypse Postponed: Reconsidering Indonesia.*

SIDELIGHTS: Donald K. Emmerson told *CA:* "Growing up in the Foreign Service means changing countries every two years. So much of my life has been spent overseas and on the move that living in any one place now seems unnatural. My background probably also accounts for my anthropological bent.

"In my pantheon, empathy is a prime god. I enjoy meeting strangers and trying to understand their ways of seeing and doing. I am amazed and grateful that scholar-authors actually get paid for what amounts to intellectual fun. The cup of my luck runneth over."

AVOCATIONAL INTERESTS: California beach-jogging, Balinese sunset-watching, "the company of my family."

BIOGRAPHICAL/CRITICAL SOURCES:

BOOKS

Smith, Walter Bedell, *My Three Years in Moscow,* Lippincott, 1949.

PERIODICALS

Foreign Service Journal, November, 1955; August, 1960.

*   *   *

ENDERS, Richard
    See FENSTER, Robert

*   *   *

ERB, Peter C.   1943-

PERSONAL: Born April 22, 1943, in Tavistock, Ontario, Canada; son of Lloyd and Mildred Erb; married Elizabeth J. Schiedel; children: Catharine E., Suzanne M. *Education:* Pontifical Institute of Medieval Studies, M.S.L., 1970; University of Toronto, Ph.D., 1976.

ADDRESSES: Home—106 Allen St. W., Waterloo, Ontario, Canada N2L 1E7. *Office*—Wilfrid Laurier University, Waterloo, Ontario, Canada N2L 3C5.

CAREER: Wilfrid Laurier University, Waterloo, Ontario, professor of English and of religion and culture, 1970—. Associate director of Schwenkfelder Library, Pennsburg, PA, 1974—; managing editor of *Studies in Religion/Sciences Religieuses,* 1980-84.

WRITINGS:

(Editor and translator) Jacob Boehme, *The Way to Christ,* Paulist Press, 1978.
Schwenkfeld in His Reformation Setting, [Pennsburg, PA], 1978.

The Spiritual Diary of Christopher Wiegner, [Pennsburg], 1978.

(Editor and translator) Johann Arndt, *True Christianity,* Paulist Press, 1979.

(Editor and translator) *The Pietists: Selected Writings,* Paulist Press, 1983.

(Translator) Horst Weigelt, *The Schwenkfelders in Silesia,* Schwenkfelder Library (Pennsburg), 1985.

(Editor and translator) *Johann Conrad Beissel and the Ephrata Community,* Edwin Mellen Press, 1985.

(Editor) *Schwenkfelders and Early Schwenkfeldianism,* Schwenkfelder Library, 1986.

(Editor) *Schwenkfelders in America,* Schwenkfelder Library, 1987.

(Translator with Simone Nieuwoldt) Andre Seguenny, *The Christology of Caspar Schwenckfeld: Spirit and Flesh in the Process of Life Transformation,* Edwin Mellen Press, 1987.

Pietists, Protestants, and Mysticism: The Use of Late Medieval Spiritual Texts in the Work of Gottfried Arnold (1666-1714), Scarecrow Press, 1989.

Contributor to *Bibliotheca Dissidentium,* Koerner Verlag (Baden-Baden), 1985; *Visions and Realities,* edited by Harry Loewen and Al Reimer, Hyperion Press, 1985; *Protestant Spirituality,* edited by F. Senn, Paulist Press, 1986.

WORK IN PROGRESS: Studies in nineteenth-century Roman Catholic theology.

* * *

ERLANGER, Ellen (Louise) 1950-

PERSONAL: Born November 14, 1950, in Canton, OH; daughter of Robert H. (a retailer) and Rose (a volunteer worker; maiden name, Marx) Erlanger. *Education:* University of Michigan, B.A. (with highest honors), 1972, M.A. (with highest honors), 1976; graduate study at Ohio State University, Indiana University, and University of Akron. *Avocational interests:* Golf, reading, tennis, water sports, politics, art, music, film, theater, astronomy.

ADDRESSES: Home—1930 Concord Rd., Columbus, OH 43212. *Office*—Upper Arlington City School District, 1950 North Mallway, Columbus, OH 43221.

CAREER: High school history teacher in Ann Arbor, MI, 1972, and Canton, OH, 1972-75; director of education at synagogue in Canton, 1976-77; Jones Junior High School, Upper Arlington, OH, history teacher and head of social studies department, 1977-79; Upper Arlington City School District, Columbus, OH, career education program specialist, 1979-82, director of career education, 1982—. Has also worked as a camp director.

MEMBER: American Association for Career Education, National Anorexic Aid Society (member of executive board), Golf Writers Association of America, Career Education Association of Ohio, Phi Beta Kappa, Phi Delta Kappa, Alpha Epsilon Phi (former vice-president).

WRITINGS:

America Is (juvenile), C. E. Merrill, 1979.

You Are Always My Friend (poetry anthology), Blue Mountain Press, 1981.

Jane Fonda: More Than a Movie Star, Lerner, 1984.

Isaac Asimov: Scientist and Storyteller, Lerner, 1986.

Eating Disorders, Lerner, 1988.

Contributor to poetry anthology, *Have a Wonderful Day, Friend,* 1981, and to education, juvenile, golf, and general interest magazines, including *Seventeen, Senior Scholastic,* and *Golf for Women.*

WORK IN PROGRESS: Poetry; song lyrics; golf articles; possible further juvenile biography works.

SIDELIGHTS: Ellen Erlanger commented to *CA:* "I have enjoyed writing since my adolescent years, but began taking freelancing quite seriously about twelve years ago. When I began teaching junior high school American history, I recognized a need for more lively resource books about prominent Americans. Jane Fonda was a unique and exciting subject for me. My success in completing and marketing my first three books has given me great encouragement and satisfaction. Selling some of my poetry and several of my golf articles has also inspired me to continue writing for a variety of markets. I hope to find musicians to work with so that I can become a song lyricist as well as a poet, biographer, and golf writer.

"Why do I write? Because I feel that thoughtful, creative communication shows the beauty of human capability—and because its fun! Where my poetry is concerned, I'm very gratified when I capture an image or feeling that has meaning for others. And in regard to my juvenile biographies, my goal is to portray positive role models for young people in the most accurate, interesting way possible."

* * *

EVANS, Lawrence Watt 1954-
(Lawrence Watt-Evans)

PERSONAL: Born July 26, 1954, in Arlington, Mass.; son of Gordon Goodwin (a professor of chemistry) and Doletha (a secretary; maiden name, Watt) Evans; married Julie Frances McKenna (a systems engineer), August 30, 1977; children: Kyrith Amanda, Julian Samuel Goodwin. *Education:* Attended Princeton University, 1972-74 and 1975-77. *Politics:* "Erratic." *Religion:* Atheist.

ADDRESSES: Home—5 Solitaire Court, Gaithersburg, Md. 20878. *Agent*—Russell Galen, Scott Meredith Literary Agency, 845 Third Ave., New York, N.Y. 10022.

CAREER: Purity Save-Mor supermarket, Bedford, Mass., sacker, 1971; Griffith Ladder, Bedford, worker, 1973; Arby's, Pittsburgh, Pa., counterman and cook, 1974; Student Hoagie Agency, Princeton, N.J., occasional salesman, 1974-76; Mellon Institute of Science, Pittsburgh, bottle washer, 1976; writer, 1977—.

MEMBER: Science Fiction Writers of America, Horror Writers of America, Mystery Writers of America, National Space Society, Space Studies Institute.

AWARDS, HONORS: Hugo Award from World Science Fiction Society, Nebula Award nomination from Science Fiction Writers of America, and reader's poll award from *Isaac Asimov's Science Fiction Magazine,* all for best short story, 1988, for "Why I Left Harry's All-Night Hamburgers"; reader's poll award for best short story from *Isaac Asimov's Science Fiction Magazine,* 1990, for "Windwagon Smith and the Martians."

WRITINGS:

UNDER NAME LAWRENCE WATT-EVANS

The Lure of the Basilisk (Volume 1 of "Lords of Dus" series), Del Rey, 1980.

The Seven Altars of Dusarra (Volume 2 of "Lords of Dus" series), Del Rey, 1981.

The Cyborg and the Sorcerers (Volume 1 of "War Surplus" series), Del Rey, 1982.

The Sword of Bheleu (Volume 3 of "Lords of Dus" series), Del Rey, 1983.

The Book of Silence (Volume 4 of "Lords of Dus" series), Del Rey, 1984.

The Chromosomal Code, Avon, 1984.

The Misenchanted Sword ("Legend of Ethshar" series), Del Rey, 1985.

Shining Steel, Avon, 1986.

With a Single Spell ("Legend of Ethshar" series), Del Rey, 1987.

The Wizard and the War Machine (Volume 2 of "War Surplus" series), Del Rey, 1987.

Denner's Wreck, Avon, 1988.

Nightside City, Del Rey, 1989.

The Unwilling Warlord ("Legend of Ethshar" series), Del Rey, 1989.

The Nightmare People, New American Library, 1990.

(Editor and contributor) *Newer York* (anthology), New American Library, 1990.

Author of column "Rayguns, Elves, and Skin-Tight Suits" for *Comics Buyer's Guide,* 1983-87, and of comic book scripts and stories for Marvel Comics and Eclipse Comics. Work represented in anthologies, including *One Hundred Great Fantasy Short Short Stories,* edited by Isaac Asimov, Terry Carr, and Martin H. Greenberg, Doubleday, 1984; and *"Why I Left Harry's All-Night Hamburgers" and Other Stories from Isaac Asimov's Science Fiction Magazine,* edited by Sheila Williams and Charles Ardai, Delacorte, 1990. Contributor of short stories, articles, poems, and reviews to periodicals, including *Amazing,* Louisville *Courier-Journal, Bedford Patriot, Dragon, Late Knocking, Movie Collector's World, Sagebrush Journal, Space Gamer,* and *Starlog.*

WORK IN PROGRESS: A fantasy novel, *The Blood of a Dragon,* in the "Legend of Ethshar" series.

SIDELIGHTS: Lawrence Watt Evans told *CA:* "I write for a living because I'm not qualified for anything else, and because it's fun. I can't abide getting up in the morning to go to work for someone else. I write fantasy and science fiction because it's what I most enjoy reading. I collect comic books, with roughly eight thousand on hand (I've cut back drastically), because they're more fun than any other collectible I know of, and I write about them to defray the cost of collecting. I have no overblown ideas about 'art,' though I try to do the best I can and give value for my money."

EVANS, Robert L(eonard) 1917-

PERSONAL: Born May 30, 1917, in Duluth, MN; son of John Leonard (a banker) and Amy (Magnusson) Evans; married Frances Bentley, December 21, 1941 (died, 1955); married Elsie Hardy (a teacher), January 11, 1957; children: Amy Elizabeth Evans Levin, Thomas Randall, Julia May (Mrs. Russell Stickle). *Education:* Attended Duluth Junior College, 1934-36; University of Minnesota, B.Chem., 1938, M.S., 1939, Ph.D., 1951.

ADDRESSES: Home—2500 St. Anthony Blvd., Minneapolis, MN 55418. *Office*—Department of Physiology, University of Minnesota, Minneapolis, MN 55455.

CAREER: U.S. Bureau of Mines, Salt Lake City, UT, associate metallurgist, 1940-44; Allegheny Ballistics Laboratory, Cumberland, MD, research associate, 1944-45; University of Minnesota, Minneapolis, instructor in mathematics and mechanics, 1945-54, assistant professor of physiology, 1954-63, associate professor of biometry and mathematical biology, 1963-70, lecturer in physiology, 1970—.

MEMBER: American Association for the Advancement of Science, American Chemical Society, Wilderness Society, Nature Conservancy, Minnesota Academy of Science (president, 1962-63), Sigma Xi, Unitarian.

AWARDS, HONORS: Rockefeller Foundation grant, 1954-59; United States Public Health Service grants, 1958-68, 1966-69.

WRITINGS:

The Fall and Rise of Man, If . . . , Lund Press, 1973.

(Editor with LaVeta Randall) *Cimarron Family Legends,* Evans Publications, Volume 1, 1978, Volume 2, 1979.

(Editor) Helen H. Colgan, and others, *Eight Writers Seeking Readers,* Robert L. Evans, 1985.

(Editor) *Automotive Engine Alternatives,* Plenum, 1987.

Contributor of mathematics, chemistry, and biomedical research articles to scientific journals.

WORK IN PROGRESS: Human Biology Quantitated. *

*   *   *

EWING, Frederick R.
See STURGEON, Theodore (Hamilton)

F

FANE, Bron
See FANTHORPE, R(obert) Lionel

* * *

FANTHORPE, R(obert) Lionel 1935-
(Neil Balfort, Othello Baron, Erle Barton, Lee Barton, Thornton Bell, Noel Bertram, Leo Brett, Bron Fane, Phil Hobel, Mel Jay, Marston Johns, Victor La Salle, Oban Lerteth, Robert Lionel, John E. Muller, Elton T. Neef, Peter O'Flinn, Peter O'Flynn, Lionel Roberts, Rene Rolant, Deutero Spartacus, Robin Tate, Neil Thanet, Trebor Thorpe, Trevor Thorpe, Pel Torro, Olaf Trent, Karl Zeigfreid)

PERSONAL: Born February 9, 1935, in Dereham, England; son of Robert (a shop owner) and Greta Christine (a teacher; maiden name, Garbutt) Fanthorpe; married Patricia Alice Tooke (a writer), September 7, 1957; children: Stephanie Dawn Patricia, Fiona Mary Patricia Alcibiadette. *Education:* Norwich Teachers Training College, certificate, 1963; Open University, B.A., 1974, graduate study, 1980. *Politics:* "Last of Cromwell's Puritan Ironsides; strong on helping the poor and on law and order." *Religion:* "Enthusiastic Evangelical Christian, saved by the Lord Jesus Christ."

ADDRESSES: Home—Rivendell, 48 Claude Rd., Roath, Cardiff CF2 3QA, Wales.

CAREER: Worked as a machine operator, farm worker, driver, warehouseman, journalist, salesman, storekeeper, and yard foreman during the 1950s; secondary school teacher in Dereham, England, 1958-61 and 1963-67; Gamlingay Village College, Gamlingay, England, tutor, 1967-69; Phoenix Timber Co., Rainham, England, industrial training officer, 1969-72; Hellesdon High School, Hellesdon, England, head of English department, 1972, second master, beginning 1973, deputy head, 1978-79; Glyn Derw High School, Cardiff, Wales, headmaster, 1979-89; currently Anglican priest serving the church in Wales. Former extra-mural tutor, Cambridge University; examiner for Certificate of Secondary Education in English. *Military service:* British Army Cadet Force Officer, 1967-69; became first lieutenant.

MEMBER: British Institute of Management, Mensa, College of Preceptors, Judo Club.

AWARDS, HONORS: East of England Judo Championship silver medal, novices' section, Kyu grades, 1977; brown belt, B.J.A., 1978.

WRITINGS:

The Waiting World, Badger Books, 1958.
Alien from the Stars, Badger Books, 1959.
Hyperspace, Badger Books, 1959.
Space-Borne, Badger Books, 1959.
Fiends, Badger Books, 1959.
Doomed World, Badger Books, 1960.
Satellite, Badger Books, 1960.
Asteroid Man, Badger Books, 1960.
Out of the Darkness, Badger Books, 1960.
Hand of Doom, Badger Books, 1960.
Flame Mass, Badger Books, 1961.
The Golden Chalice, Badger Books, 1961.
Space Fury, Badger Books, 1962, Vega Books, 1963.
Negative Minus, Badger Books, 1963.
Neuron World, Badger Books, 1965.
The Triple Man, Badger Books, 1965.
The Unconfined, Badger Books, 1966.
The Watching World, Badger Books, 1966.
(With W. H. Farrer) *Spencer's Metric and Decimal Guide,* John Spencer, 1970.
(With wife, Patricia Alice Fanthorpe) *Spencer's Metric Conversion Tables,* John Spencer, 1970.
(With P. A. Fanthorpe) *Spencer's Office Guide,* John Spencer, 1971.
(With P. A. Fanthorpe) *Spencer's Metric and Decimal Companion,* John Spencer, 1971.
(With P. A. Fanthorpe) *Spencer's Decimal Payroll Tables,* John Spencer, 1971.
(With P. A. Fanthorpe) *The Black Lion,* Greystoke Mobray, 1979.
(With P. A. Fanthorpe) *The Holy Grail Revealed,* Newcastle, 1982.
God in All Things, Bishopsgate Press, 1987.
Thoughts and Prayers for Troubled Times, Bishopsgate Press, 1989.
The Story of St. Francis, Bishopsgate Press, 1989.

UNDER PSEUDONYM LEO BRETT

Exit Humanity, Badger Books, 1960.

The Microscopic Ones, Badger Books, 1960.
Faceless Planet, Badger Books, 1960.
March of the Robots, Badger Books, 1961.
Mind Force, Badger Books, 1961.
Black Infinity, Badger Books, 1961.
Nightmare, Badger Books, 1962.
Face in the Night, Badger Books, 1962.
The Immortals, Badger Books, 1962.
They Never Came Back, Badger Books, 1962.
The Forbidden, Badger Books, 1963.
From Realms Beyond, Badger Books, 1963.
The Alien Ones, Badger Books, 1963.
Power Sphere, Badger Books, 1963.

UNDER PSEUDONYM BRON FANE

Juggernaut, Badger Books, 1960, published as *Blue Juggernaut,* Arcadia House, 1965.
Last Man on Earth, Badger Books, 1960.
Rodent Mutation, Badger Books, 1961.
The Intruders, Badger Books, 1963.
Somewhere out There, Badger Books, 1963.
Softly by Moonlight, Badger Books, 1963.
Unknown Destiny, Badger Books, 1964.
Nemesis, Badger Books, 1964.
Suspension, Badger Books, 1964.
The Macabre Ones, Badger Books, 1964.
U.F.O. 517, Badger Books, 1966.

UNDER PSEUDONYM JOHN E. MULLER

The Ultimate Man, Badger Books, 1961.
The Uninvited, Badger Books, 1961.
Crimson Planet, Badger Books, 1961.
The Venus Venture, Badger Books, 1961, published under pseudonym Marston Johns, Arcadia House, 1965.
Forbidden Planet, Badger Books, 1961.
Return of Zeus, Badger Books, 1962.
Perilous Galaxy, Badger Books, 1962.
Uranium 235, Badger Books, 1962.
The Man Who Conquered Time, Badger Books, 1962.
Orbit One, Badger Books, 1962, published under pseudonym Mel Jay, Arcadia House, 1966.
The Eye of Karnak, Badger Books, 1962.
Micro Infinity, Badger Books, 1962.
Beyond Time, Badger Books, 1962, published under pseudonym Marston Johns, Arcadia House, 1966.
Infinity Machine, Badger Books, 1962.
The Day the World Died, Badger Books, 1962.
Vengeance of Siva, Badger Books, 1962.
The X-Machine, Badger Books, 1962.
Reactor XK9, Badger Books, 1963.
Special Mission, Badger Books, 1963.
Dark Continuum, Badger Books, 1964.
Mark of the Beast, Badger Books, 1964.
The Negative Ones, Badger Books, 1965.
The Exorcists, Badger Books, 1965.
The Man from Beyond, Badger Books, 1965.
Beyond the Void, Badger Books, 1965.
Spectre of Darkness, Badger Books, 1965.
Out of the Night, Badger Books, 1965.
Phenomena X, Badger Books, 1966.
Survival Project, Badger Books, 1966.

UNDER PSEUDONYM LIONEL ROBERTS

Dawn of the Mutants, Badger Books, 1959.

Time Echo, 1959, published under pseudonym Robert Lionel, Arcadia House, 1964.
Cyclops in the Sky, Badger Books, 1960.
The In-World, Badger Books, 1960.
The Face of X, Badger Books, 1960, published under pseudonym Robert Lionel, Arcadia House, 1965.
The Last Valkyrie, Badger Books, 1961.
The Synthetic Ones, Badger Books, 1961.
Flame Goddess, Badger Books, 1961.

UNDER PSEUDONYM PEL TORRO

Frozen Planet, Badger Books, 1960.
World of the Gods, Badger Books, 1960.
The Phantom Ones, Badger Books, 1961.
Legion of the Lost, Badger Books, 1962.
The Strange Ones, Badger Books, 1963.
Galaxy 666, Badger Books, 1963.
Formula 29X, Badger Books, 1963, published as *Beyond the Barrier of Space,* Tower Books, 1969.
Through the Barrier, Badger Books, 1963.
The Timeless Ones, Badger Books, 1963.
The Last Astronaut, Badger Books, 1963.
The Face of Fear, Badger Books, 1963.
The Return, Badger Books, 1964, published as *Exiled in Space,* Arcadia House, 1968.
Space No Barrier, Badger Books, 1964, published as *Man of Metal,* Lenox Hill, 1970.
Force 97X, Badger Books, 1965.

UNDER PSEUDONYM KARL ZEIGFREID

Walk through To-Morrow, Badger Books, 1962.
Android, Badger Books, 1962.
Gods of Darkness, Badger Books, 1962.
Atomic Nemesis, Badger Books, 1962.
Zero Minus X, Badger Books, 1962.
Escape to Infinity, Badger Books, 1963.
Radar Alert, Badger Books, 1963.
World of Tomorrow, Badger Books, 1963, published as *World of the Future,* Arcadia House, 1968.
The World That Never Was, Badger Books, 1963.
Projection Infinity, Badger Books, 1964.
No Way Back, Badger Books, 1964.
Barrier 346, Badger Books, 1965.
The Girl from Tomorrow, Badger Books, 1965.

OTHER

(Under pseudonym Victor La Salle) *Menace from Mercury,* John Spencer, 1954.
(Under pseudonym Trebor Thorpe) *Five Faces of Fear,* Badger Books, 1960.
(Under pseudonym Trebor Thorpe) *Lightning World,* Badger Books, 1960.
(Under pseudonym Lee Barton) *The Unseen,* Badger Books, 1963.
(Under pseudonym Neil Thanet) *Beyond the Veil,* Badger Books, 1964.
(Under pseudonym Neil Thanet) *The Man Who Came Back,* Badger Books, 1964.
(Under pseudonym Thornton Bell) *Space Trap,* Badger Books, 1964.
(Under pseudonym Thornton Bell) *Chaos,* Badger Books, 1964.
(Under pseudonym Erle Barton) *The Planet Seekers,* Vega Books, 1964.
(Under pseudonym Lee Barton) *The Shadow Man,* Badger Books, 1966.

Also author of "Supernatural Stories" monographs. Contributor to periodicals under pseudonyms, including Neil Balfort, Othello Baron, Noel Bertram, Phil Hobel, Oban Lerteth, Elton T. Neef, Peter O'Flinn, Peter O'Flynn, Rene Rolant, Deutero Spartacus, Robin Tate, Trevor Thorpe, and Olaf Trent.

WORK IN PROGRESS: The First Christmas, Birds and Animals of the Bible, Thoughts and Prayers for Special Occasions, and *The Story of Joseph,* all for Bishopsgate Press; *The Oak Island Treasure Mystery; Damascus Road,* a musical on the life of Saint Paul; *Sonnets from the Scriptures; Fanthorpe's Hammer, or Macabbacus Was Right!,* a collection of controversial Christian essays; *The Golden Tiger* and *Zotala the Priest,* parts two and three of the Derl Wothor trilogy, of which *The Black Lion* was part one, both with wife Patricia Alice Fanthorpe.

SIDELIGHTS: "I started writing when I was sixteen, having read and enjoyed most of the fantasy and science fiction I could get hold of at school," R. Lionel Fanthorpe told *CA.* "This was a mixture of Wells, Verne, Poe, etc., plus the odd paperback by authors whose names didn't register at the time. I have always had a poor memory for authors and titles, but I can recall the plot and characters of a story I've enjoyed for years afterwards."

Fanthorpe, who wrote nearly one hundred sixty books from 1957 to 1966, recalled the beginnings of his writing career: "In those days my mother ran a small shorthand and typing school from the front room of our house, and she did all the typing for me. Demand grew over the years. I married Patricia in 1957 and she shared the typing. Demand went on growing. At its peak we were being asked to produce a book a week, or almost a book in a weekend. Communications would arrive from Spencers to the effect that the printer was waiting, could I hurry up. Patricia's sister got called into the typing team. I bought tape recorders and dictated material as fast as I could, despatching reels to the various typists, proofreading the typescripts and sending the manuscripts to Spencers by express mail. They never sent proofs and on some occasions what came out of the printer's end bore only coincidental resemblance to what I'd sent in."

The author explained that his numerous pseudonyms were requested by his publishers, and he created them by using anagrams of his name. "I tried to give my pen-names an international flavour, but it was in the Milligan and Sellers vein. My international authors were music hall caricatures; my Scotsmen said, 'Och aye, the noo,' as a condition of their very existence; my Welshman came out of the infinite, terminated every utterance with, 'Look you, Dai Bach,' and usually worked in coal mines near nonconformist chapels. My French author, Rene Rolant, invariably pronounced *th* as *z* and darkly hinted of his past as a *souteneur* and resistance hero. My all-American boy was Elton T. Neef, known for some obscure reason as the Manhattan Magus, who was a faint shadow of John Wayne mixed with Damon Runyon and Mark Twain. The more blatantly unbelievable it all became, the more stories they bought. Like an impoverished latter-day Sheridan I tried giving characters names that went with their temperaments. He had Mrs. Malaprop and Sir Lucius O'Trigger. I had a gigantic security man with a sloping forehead and a love of fighting. I called him Slam Croberg and featured him in *Android.* It was Kingsley Amis's misfortune to review this for the *Observer* and his delicate artistic soul never fully recovered from the trauma."

Addressing himself to the question why an author writes as he does at a particular period in his life, Fanthorpe added: "I am conscious that some experiences have coloured my thinking and led me to emphasize certain characters, lifestyles and philosophies at different stages of my writing. At sixteen and seventeen I was an enthusiastic Christian, a left-wing socialist and an ardent pacifist. In my twenties I was less committed to religion and my political enthusiasm waned. In my thirties I left the church and stopped renewing my subscriptions to the Labour Party. In my forties, I was a vaguely theistic humanist, and sufficient of a Conservative to use my car to convey Conservative voters to the polling station to oblige a friend. I shall be fifty-five by the time this is printed: I praise and thank God for salvation in Jesus Christ. I'm an enthusiastic evangelical Christian and an ordained Anglican priest. I believe that writing should say something as well as telling a story: I want all my future writing to say something worthwhile about the Lord Jesus Christ and the new life He offers us."

*   *   *

FARKAS, Emil 1946-

PERSONAL: Born April 20, 1946, in Hungary; immigrated to the United States, 1965; naturalized U.S. citizen, 1975; son of Albert and Antonia Farkas; married Marika Komlos. *Education:* San Fernando Valley State College, B.A., 1970. *Religion:* Jewish.

ADDRESSES: Office—Creative Action, Inc., 9085 Santa Monica Blvd., Los Angeles, CA 90069. *Agent*—Aaron M. Priest Literary Agency, 565 Fifth Ave., New York, NY 10017.

CAREER: Beverly Hills Karate Academy, Beverly Hills, CA, chief instructor, 1970—; Creative Action, Inc., Los Angeles, CA, president and partner, 1974—. National Self-Defense Institute, president, 1976—. Free-lance writer, 1970—. Part-time high school teacher of self-defense; University of California, Los Angeles, part-time instructor. Maccabee Games for Israel (Karate division), co-chairman. Technical adviser and fight coordinator for films and television series, including "Mannix," "S.W.A.T.," "Killer Elite," "Easy Rider," "That Man Bolt," "Ginger," and "Mod Squad."

MEMBER: Screen Actors Guild.

AWARDS, HONORS: Has won black belt competitions in Judo and Karate in the United States and Europe.

WRITINGS:

The Martial Arts Catalogue, Simon & Schuster, 1977.
(With Margaret Leeds) *Fight Back: A Woman's Guide to Self-Defense,* Holt, 1977.
(Editor with Stuart Sobel) Benny Urquidez, *Training and Fighting Skills,* Unique Publications, 1981.
(With John Corcoran) *Martial Arts: Traditions, History, People,* Smith Publications, 1983.
The Overlook Martial Arts Dictionary, Overlook Press, 1985.

Author of film scripts "Anatomy of Revenge" and "Project: Silent Night." Author of column "Western Wrap Up" in *Official Karate.*

WORK IN PROGRESS: Self-Defense for Senior Citizens.

SIDELIGHTS: Emil Farkas once told *CA:* "The need for self-defense training in today's society is as vital as knowing how to drive a car safely. The skills we possess may not guarantee against accidents, but they can greatly reduce the chance of suffering personal injury or property damage.

"I advocate that every woman learn practical self-defense skills that are easily applied," Farkas continued. "The key, I feel, is anticipation and prevention. A person can learn to become aware, to watch for warning signals that violent behavior is imminent. Being aware enables one to avoid situations which could result in confrontation; for example, when boarding a bus one assumes a greater risk if she or he takes a window seat in the rear instead of sitting near the operator and close to other passengers. In short, I feel the best defense is to learn how to avoid danger, but to have the tools to fight back with if it becomes necessary."

BIOGRAPHICAL/CRITICAL SOURCES:

PERIODICALS

Black Belt, December, 1976.
Fighting Stars, December, 1973.
Inside Kung-Fu, January, 1975.
Karate Illustrated, November, 1973.
Official Karate, autumn, 1976.*

* * *

FENSTER, Robert 1946-
(Richard Enders)

PERSONAL: Born January 9, 1946, in Brooklyn, NY; son of Hy (in sales) and Lillian (a dance teacher; maiden name, Shapiro) Fenster; married Anne Bothwell; children: B.J. (son), Nicholas. *Education:* Attended San Francisco State College (now University), 1966-70.

ADDRESSES: Home—210 East Cactus Wren Dr., Phoenix, AZ 85020. *Office*— *Arizona Republic,* 120 East Van Buren St., Phoenix, AZ 85004. *Agent*—Connie Clausen, 250 East 87th St., New York, NY 10028.

CAREER: Has worked as a bartender, karate instructor, and confidential investigator. Free-lance writer, 1975—; *Palo Alto Weekly,* Palo Alto, CA, copy editor and movie critic, 1980-88; *Arizona Republic,* Phoenix, film critic, 1989—.

WRITINGS:

Literally Amazing Puzzles, Half Court Press, 1979.
Shakespeare Games, Crown, 1982.
(Under pseudonym Richard Enders) *Slow Twitch* (novel), Simon & Shuster, 1982.
(Under pseudonym Richard Enders) *Tight Squeeze* (novel), Simon & Shuster, 1982.
The Last Page (novel), Perseverance Press, 1989.
Out of Character (play), Theaterworks, 1989.

Contributing editor to *Confuserworld,* a newspaper parody, 1983, and to numerous periodicals.

WORK IN PROGRESS: Heroes, a novel; *The Almighty Account,* a play.

SIDELIGHTS: Robert Fenster told *CA:* "I took four years off from writing to work for an ad agency as a copywriter. As few ad people will admit, the emphasis in that profession is on the first part of the word, not the second. But it did teach me what work was like, and I didn't like it.

"Now that I've returned to my joyous profession as a film critic/editor/novelist/playwright, I'm much happier making a living from play, although it does provide us with more opportunities to examine the nuances of rice and macaroni than seem absolutely necessary.

"The best part about writing is when the little-voice-in-the-head tells me a great line, and I get the same kick out of it that readers will once it's printed.

"I still think writing should do for the mind what roller coasters, love, and loss of love do for the body.

"As for being a film critic, the great thing about it is when I get home from work and my wife asks, 'Did you have a hard day at the office?' and I say, 'Yeah, I had to see *two* movies today.' As a writer, talking to people about movies eventually gives you a chance to talk about nearly everything in the world."

* * *

FEUER, Avrohom Chaim 1946-

PERSONAL: Born May 23, 1946, in Brooklyn, NY; son of Sol and Recha Feuer; married Luba Rachel Gifter; children: five sons. *Education:* Attended Telshe Yeshiva, 1962-67, and Telshe Post-Graduate Institute for Talmudic Scholarship, 1967-79; Telshe Rabbinical College, Rabbi, 1969.

ADDRESSES: Home—4480 North Jefferson Ave., Miami Beach, FL 33140. *Office*—Congregation Ohr Chaim, 317 West 47th St., Miami Beach, FL 33140.

CAREER: Ordained rabbi, 1969; teacher at Jewish high school, Cleveland, OH, 1969-74; *Rosh Mesivta* and dean of Jewish high school, Miami, FL, 1979-80; Congregation Ohr Chaim, Miami Beach, FL, rabbi, 1980—. Lecturer at Yavne Teacher's Seminary for Women and Teacher's Institute of Telshe, both 1972-79; assistant professor in Talmud at Telshe Rabbinical College, 1972-79. Founder and director of intensive Torah study program at Camp Agudah of Toronto, 1970; scholar-in-residence at Sephardic Jewish Community of Deal, NJ, 1980, and Torah Retreat for the South, Gatlinburg, TN, 1983; member of Camp Kol Torah of Cleveland, 1971-78, and Camp Agudah of New York, 1982-83.

MEMBER: Institute for Advanced Halachic Research (founding fellow).

AWARDS, HONORS: Award from the Memorial Foundation for Jewish Studies, 1976, for unpublished manuscript "David and Absalom: A Study of Youth in Revolt"; Beren Award from Institute for Advanced Halachic Research, 1977-79.

WRITINGS:

(Translator) *Tehillim: Psalms,* five volumes, Artscroll Mesorah Press, 1977-82.
Tashlich, Artscroll Mesorah Press, 1979.
The Ten Commandments, Artscroll Mesorah Press, 1980.
The Light of Life, Newcastle, 1986.
A Letter for the Ages, Artscroll Mesorah Press, 1989.

Also author of *In God We Trust: The Jewish Concept of Money and Economics.* Author of "Parents and Children" and "Masters and Disciples," both published in *Jewish Parent.* Contributor to magazines, including *Jewish Light* and *Jewish Press.* Producer and editor, Mishna Yomit Torah Tape Library, 1975-79.

WORK IN PROGRESS: Prayer from the Heart, a book about how to communicate intimately with God during prayer.

SIDELIGHTS: Avrohom Chaim Feuer told *CA:* "The purpose of all my writing is to intensify the awareness of God's presence and control of our lives and of world history. I hope to be able to demonstrate that the Almighty loves us more than we can ever imagine and that he is always looking out for our best interests. What a wonderful world we live in—so chock full of endless opportunities to know Him!"

* * *

FINLER, Joel W(aldo) 1938-

PERSONAL: Born July 1, 1938, in New York, NY; son of Bennett (an economist) and Matilda (Hay) Finler. *Education:* Oberlin College, B.A. (cum laude), 1959; additional study at University College, London, and Slade School of Fine Art.

ADDRESSES: Home—7A Belsize Sq., London NW3 4HT, England.

CAREER: U.S. Department of Agriculture, Washington, DC, economist, 1957-63; Bath Academy of Art, Corsham, England, and Maidstone College of Art, Maidstone, England, lecturer in cinema history, 1964-68; writer, 1967—.

MEMBER: British Film Institute.

AWARDS, HONORS: Henry J. Haskell graduate fellowship, 1968-69; book award for outstanding film book of the year, British Film Institute, 1989, for *The Hollywood Story.*

WRITINGS:

Stroheim, Studio Vista, 1967, University of California Press, 1968.
(Co-editor and author of introduction) Jean Renoir, *The Rules of the Game,* Simon & Schuster, 1970.
(Editor and author of introduction) Eric von Stroheim, *Greed,* Simon & Schuster, 1972.
(Contributor) *Masterworks of the French Cinema,* Harper, 1974.
All-Time Movie Favorites, Longmeadow Press, 1976.
(Co-author) *Anatomy of the Movies,* Macmillan, 1981.
(Co-author) *Movie Mastermind,* McGraw, 1984.
(Co-author) *The Movie Stars Story,* Octopus Books, 1984.
The Movie Directors Story, Crescent Books, 1985.
All-Time Box Office Hits, Gallery Books, 1985.
The Hollywood Story, Crown, 1988.

WORK IN PROGRESS: The Story of the Movies in Color.

SIDELIGHTS: Joel W. Finler told *CA:* "Putting my career into perspective I recognize the extent to which my own career as a writer was related to the general cultural climate of the early sixties when the cinema (along with rock music) acquired a new 'respectability.' A large number of American universities began or expanded their departments of film. Around 1963 I recognized that it would be possible to make a viable career out of writing and lecturing on film, drawing on my own wide interests in the visual arts along with music, literature, and the social sciences. Probably typical of the period was my initial attraction to the serious ('art house') films of foreign directors like Godard, Antonioni, and Renoir, and to classic silent directors like D. W. Griffith and Stroheim (although, as a film critic, I also reviewed some of the more 'commercial' releases and was particularly interested in the work of the underground filmmakers).

"However, during more recent years I've come to value more highly the contribution of the American cinema, both the Hollywood of the thirties and forties and the work of that new generation of young directors brought up on the cinema, like myself, who emerged during the sixties, including Francis Ford Coppola, Brian de Palma, Martin Scorsese, Steven Spielberg, and others, testifying to the continuing vigor of the American cinema. It appears unfortunate to me that even with the fading of the French and Italian 'new wave,' many serious film-goers, particularly in the United States, still tend to be more interested in foreign films than in the new American cinema.

"In spite of the boom in film book publishing during the past ten years, the vast riches of the American cinema have only just begin to be explored in depth. They offer a challenge to the film historian unmatched by the films of any other country. The studio system, for example, provides a fascinating continuity of production for a period of forty-odd years and reflects a real and

continuing commitment to filmmaking which produced a fair number of bad films, but a surprisingly large number of good ones while preserving a remarkably high standard overall. Thus, my current book in progress, *The Story of the Movies in Color,* in spite of its popular-sounding title, represents a serious attempt to reassess the development of the American cinema during the years 1935-55 when color was first introduced and developed side-by-side with black-and-white for a period of twenty years. The phenomenon of the color film provides a new perspective for examining Hollywood at its peak and then in decline. This work has developed from my . . . [earlier] book on Hollywood, *All-Time Movie Favorites,* which represented a first step in this new direction, and I similarly plan to illustrate the book from my own extensive collection of thirty-five millimeter color film frames, stills, and posters."

* * *

FitzGERALD, Frances 1940-

PERSONAL: Born October 21, 1940, in New York, NY; daughter of Desmond FitzGerald (a former deputy director of the CIA) and Marietta Endicott (an urban planner; maiden name, Peabody) Tree. *Education:* Radcliffe College, B.A. (magna cum laude), 1962.

ADDRESSES: Agent—Robert Lescher, 67 Irving Place, New York, NY 10003.

CAREER: Congress for Cultural Freedom, Paris, France, writer, 1962-64; free-lance journalist and nonfiction writer, 1964—. Visiting professor and lecturer at numerous universities, including University of California at Berkeley and Lynchburg College.

AWARDS, HONORS: Overseas Press Club award, 1967, for best interpretation of foreign affairs; American Academy of Arts and Letters and National Institute for Arts and Letters Award, National Book Award, Pulitzer Prize, Front Page Award, Christopher Book Award, *Washington Monthly* Political Book Award, Sidney Hillman Award, and Bancroft Prize, all 1973, all for *Fire in the Lake: The Vietnamese and Americans in Vietnam;* Overseas Press Club award, 1974, for interpretation of events in Iran; American Book Award nomination, 1980, for *America Revised: History Schoolbooks in the Twentieth Century* (nomination declined); English Speaking Union award for *Cities on a Hill.*

WRITINGS:

Fire in the Lake: The Vietnamese and Americans in Vietnam (excerpts first published in the *New Yorker,* 1972), Atlantic/Little, Brown, 1972, revised edition, 1973.
America Revised: History Schoolbooks in the Twentieth Century (excerpts first published in the *New Yorker*), Atlantic/Little, Brown, 1979.
Cities on a Hill: A Journey through Contemporary American Cultures (excerpts first published in the *New Yorker*), Simon & Schuster, 1986.

Contributor to *Atlantic, New Yorker, New York Review of Books, New York Times Magazine, Village Voice,* and other periodicals.

MEDIA ADAPTATIONS: A documentary about FitzGerald and her family entitled "The Female Line" was televised on the Public Broadcasting Service in 1980.

SIDELIGHTS: Frances FitzGerald is a journalist and essayist whose prize-winning works explore issues crucial to modern American life. FitzGerald's first full-length work, *Fire in the Lake: The Vietnamese and Americans in Vietnam,* won an array of awards—including the Pulitzer Prize and the National Book Award—for its penetrating analysis of the American presence in Southeast Asia. Since then FitzGerald has been considered an expert reporter on foreign policy as well as an astute observer of the nation's domestic situation. Her subsequent books—also well-received critically—include *America Revised: History Schoolbooks in the Twentieth Century* and *Cities on a Hill: A Journey through Contemporary American Cultures.*

FitzGerald grew up in an atmosphere of high achievement. Her father, Desmond FitzGerald, was a Wall Street attorney who eventually became a deputy director of the Central Intelligence Agency. Her mother was a descendent of prominent Bostonians who became an urban planner and an associate of Adlai Stevenson at the United Nations. Raised in comfortable homes in Manhattan and the English countryside, FitzGerald herself experienced a "terror of mediocrity" that led her to excel in her pursuits. Through her parents she met many important international figures, including Winston Churchill; Adlai Stevenson took her to visit Albert Schweitzer in Africa when she was only sixteen.

FitzGerald was an avid reader and horseback rider who graduated at the top of her class at the Foxcroft preparatory school in Virginia. She then attended Radcliffe College, where she majored in Middle Eastern history and contemplated various careers, especially law and journalism. After graduating *magna cum laude* in 1962 she made her final decision—she would become a writer. Through a friend of her mother's, FitzGerald secured employment in Paris with the Congress of Cultural Freedom, a publisher and support group for non-Communist European intellectuals. In her spare time FitzGerald began to work on a novel, but she found the experience frustrating. She gravitated back to nonfiction, and after returning to New York in 1964, began to publish articles regularly in the *New York Herald Tribune, Vogue,* and the *Village Voice.*

The Vietnam War was escalating rapidly when FitzGerald made her first trip to Saigon in 1966. The author has since admitted that she was "very naive" about the circumstances surrounding the civil war in Vietnam; at any rate, she came to the country unfettered by strong opinions for or against American intervention. What began as a short visit to research several brief articles became a stay of over a year as FitzGerald tried to penetrate the politics behind the conflict. One of the first American journalists to confront the war from the perspective of the South Vietnamese people, she used her fluency in French to interview everyone from Saigon bureaucrats to besieged villagers. A fellow correspondent told *Esquire* magazine that FitzGerald "was able to understand better than any of us why the American government was doomed to fail" in its attempt to oust the communist guerrillas.

FitzGerald's writings on the Vietnam conflict first appeared in the *New Yorker* magazine as a series of essays. Then, with the help of French anthropologist Paul Mus, she compiled her observations and conclusions in *Fire in the Lake,* published in 1972. The work offered a full-scale analysis of Vietnamese culture and demonstrated how Vietnamese traditions and ideas conflicted with American notions of progress, urbanization, and relocation. Her reasoned approach notwithstanding, FitzGerald offered a strong indictment of American actions in the region, finding fault with the havoc wreaked on the local society in the name of global strategy. *Fire in the Lake* went into a second printing within days of its release and won numerous prestigious literary prizes. *Publishers Weekly* correspondent Michael Mok declares that the book managed "to get under the skin of this ugly war

which has left so many Americans feeling bewildered and morally bankrupt."

Her reputation established, FitzGerald spent much of the 1970s reporting stories from politically-sensitive locales such as North Vietnam, Iran, and Cuba. She was one of the first analysts to detect the narrow base of support for the Shah of Iran and to suggest that the leader would be ousted. Her second book-length work did not concern foreign policy, however, but concentrated on a sensitive domestic issue—the presentation of world history in the schoolbooks read by American students. FitzGerald's 1979 book *America Revised* "documents the extent to which the shifting values of each generation—or, lately, each four or five years—have reshaped the stress laid by textbooks on presidents, immigrants, blacks, battles, women, Indians, large political movements, banjo-playing, the concept of the nation as a melting-pot, the notion of the nation as a set of ramekins, and so on," to quote Richard Eder in the *New York Times.* Eder adds: "The quick changes in our textbooks seem to [FitzGerald] to be opportunism, an abandoning of the teaching function in favor of short-order political cookery."

Like *Fire in the Lake, America Revised* has garnered a number of favorable reviews for its careful research and trenchant conclusions. *American Heritage* contributor Bernard Weisberger praised FitzGerald for producing a work of "cultural anatomy—the careful dissection of the webs of habit and belief that hold a people together," adding that the book itself is "an X-ray of American culture that is not to be missed by anyone seriously interested in our national future or our past." Likewise, historian C. Vann Woodward writes in the *New York Review of Books* that FitzGerald "leaves her target riddled with direct hits." Woodward concludes: "No serious explanation of the stunted and abused plight of historical teaching and learning in American schools can afford to overlook the insights of [FitzGerald's] *America Revised.* She has used her sources with telling effect and left us the wiser for her efforts."

Cities on a Hill, published in 1986, concerns four utopian communities in different parts of the United States—the neighborhood of homosexuals around Castro Street in San Francisco, the membership of the Thomas Road Baptist Church in Lynchburg, Virginia, the retirement community of Sun City, Florida, and the commune Rajneeshpuram in rural Oregon. FitzGerald explored all of these special communities and was struck by the similarities between them. Her observations are recorded in the book in "even-handed description, often vivid and anecdotal," to quote Carl N. Degler in the *New York Times Book Review.* *New York Times* columnist Michiko Kakutani similarly praises *Cities on a Hill* for its unbiased approach to minority segments of American culture. "If Ms. FitzGerald approaches these communities with the watchful eye of an anthropologist, . . . she also writes with lucid sympathy for her subjects," Kakutani notes. "There is nothing judgmental about her accounts; rather, she attempts to understand the ideals of each community, the motivations and dreams that brought individual members into their folds."

FitzGerald is described in the *New York Times Book Review* as "a literary wanderer, roaming from subject to subject writing articles and hoping her peripatetic ways will lead her to a book." In addition to her journalistic career, the author teaches occasional classes at universities; she also takes an active role in the New York literary scene. *Newsweek* correspondent Jim Miller concludes that FitzGerald's various case studies "are never less than fascinating," adding: "She is a wonderful reporter and writer, with an eye for the telling detail."

CA INTERVIEW

CA interviewed Frances FitzGerald by telephone on August 11, 1989, while she was at her summer place in Maine.

CA: Fire in the Lake, which won a Pulitzer, a National Book Award, and the Bancroft Prize, was very influential in turning American opinion against the Vietnam War. When you first went to Vietnam, in February 1966, how much of a feeling did you have for the situation there and how you would approach it as a writer?

FITZGERALD: I had almost none. I'd just been doing journalism for a couple of years; I'd never been to Asia; I'd never been to a war. I had professors, one of whom actually had been there, who thought our involvement in Vietnam probably wasn't a good idea, but I hadn't any very fixed opinions. The war was just building up, and whatever I came up with really came from my experience there.

CA: You noted in Fire in the Lake *that "by the beginning of 1966 some five hundred journalists were accredited with MACV [Military Assistance Command, Vietnam]." Was there general acceptance among them of American policy there?*

FITZGERALD: I wouldn't say there was general acceptance. I think a lot of them were quite skeptical, but in the beginning they tended to be skeptical about means, not about ends. I think as time went on they grew much more skeptical about whether the war could be won and whether it was even a good idea; that process was taking place then. At the end of 1966 there were two important pieces written about the stalemate in Vietnam, R. W. Apple's piece for the *New York Times* and Ward Just's piece for the *Washington Post*.

CA: You didn't follow the rest of the war correspondents but rather began making contact with government officials and others who could give you more perspective on the situation. How did you know you didn't want to do the more usual sort of reporting that was being done?

FITZGERALD: From the time when I went to Laos, earlier (which led to the first piece I ever wrote on Asia, for the *Village Voice*), I thought to myself, Here's this American war being fought in a place that no one understands at all. When I got to Saigon the Buddhist crisis was going on. There were demonstrations in the streets daily. The government fell in half: the part that was in central Vietnam was refusing to answer the telephone. The cobbled-together junta led by Nguyen Cao Ky was in desperate straits, but for reasons that nobody—certainly nobody in the American Embassy—understood. I thought, It looks like there are two entirely separate enterprises going on here, the Vietnamese one and the American. Because of the rotation system, there were very few journalists around at that point who had any experience of the past. Those people who had been there in 1963 or '64 had left by that time and there was a whole new generation of war correspondents as well as embassy officials. The United States was going to war, but in what country?

CA: You told Robert Friedman for Esquire *in 1980 that you thought you'd do an article or two to pay for the trip to Vietnam and then come home; but "once I got there," you said, "I couldn't leave." Besides your growing interest in the political situation, did you feel a strong attraction to the country and the people?*

FITZGERALD: Absolutely, yes. Like so many Americans arriving in Asia for the first time, I was fascinated and awed. The Vietnamese are tough-minded and sophisticated. Not easy to get to know—especially at that time—but charming. And formidable.

CA: Have the Eastern religions and philosophies that constituted a large part of your study of the Vietnamese culture remained with you to some degree in a personal way?

FITZGERALD: Not in a religious sense. I cannot be said to have turned Buddhist. But the study of Buddhism has been important to me intellectually speaking. It is a different way of looking at the world, and one I find sympathetic.

CA: Do you think the general public consciousness regarding intervention in other countries has been much changed by our experience in Vietnam? Have we learned any lessons?

FITZGERALD: Yes, absolutely. You just have to look at what happened in Central America. Goodness knows it's not a parallel situation, but the parallel was announced by Secretary Weinberger early on in the Reagan administration when he said no American troops would be sent to Central America except on certain conditions—the conditions being that the U.S. public support the war and that there be some assurance of winning. The Pentagon had clearly learned to ask these questions from the experience of Vietnam. And of course the U.S. public always opposed sending American troops to Central America.

CA: How well do you think the growing body of fiction and movies on Vietnam portrays the American experience there, if you've been able to keep up with it?

FITZGERALD: I've read a number of novels, and certainly I've seen most of the major movies that have come out. The view tends to be rather limited, I think. In fact, at this point there seems to be only one story, which is that of the young, college-educated soldier, a draftee, who arrives in Vietnam and goes on horrendous long, hot walks in the sun and his buddies are shot all around him and he witnesses some kind of atrocity against a Vietnamese civilian and he courageously protests. It's astonishing how many times the story is told in novels and films, in slightly different ways. Of course it contains the classic stories of male bonding and growing up. And of course most of the writers were GIs who saw little more of Vietnam—or the war—than that in their one-year tours. All the same, it is surprising that there have not been more ambitious attempts to understand the war than that. There is nothing to compare with the French novels about Vietnam or the American novels about World War II. Perhaps Graham Greene's *Quiet American* and Joseph Heller's *Catch-22* said it all before the war began.

CA: Have you been back to Vietnam since the war ended?

FITZGERALD: No, I haven't. But I will go, one of these days soon.

CA: In America Revised *you analyzed America's history textbooks and showed how they have been shaped by political viewpoints and special interests, particularly since the 1960s. What attracted you to the subject?*

FITZGERALD: It's very difficult for a single journalist to figure out what is on the mind of this country. It seemed to me that one of the ways to do it was to look at history textbooks as a version of popular culture. It could have been rock lyrics, except textbooks address certain issues that rock lyrics don't. Who we are as a society is a question never permanently settled in this country. I was reading those textbooks mainly to find out how the popular view had changed over the decades. But then it turned out that the American educational establishment had a great deal to do with the form of these textbooks—if not their political content. So I ended by writing about the cycles in American pedagogical thinking as well.

CA: What response did America Revised *bring from educators?*

FITZGERALD: It was widely discussed, and I spoke at conventions of educators on both the university level and the secondary level, and also at meetings of publishers. I think their self-consciousness about what goes into textbooks was growing at that time. It's not a subject that makes anyone very happy, because there's extremely little that you can do about it, whether you're a publisher or a teacher. It's very hard to find a lever for reform. So I would never have anything very programmatic to tell them. What I did say was that the academic community ought to pay more attention to the content of the texts. At that point it had virtually abdicated in favor of the various popular pressure groups. It's a thing that goes in cycles. I think academics have taken on much more responsibility for those textbooks since then—which is not to say that things have totally changed, but just that the cycle has moved along. If my book contributed to that, I'm pleased.

CA: In Cities on a Hill *you examined four cultures: the gay community of San Francisco known as the Castro; Jerry Falwell's church in Lynchburg, Virginia; Sun City Center, a Florida retirement community; and the New Age religious community in Rajneeshpuram, Oregon. To what extent were you welcomed as an observer to each community?*

FITZGERALD: I was welcomed in all of them. Groups like that consider that they have found a new way, and consider that what they are doing is important and ought to be emulated; therefore they are interested in the press—and not just the press, but all outsiders who come in and want to find out what's going on.

CA: Was there much effort to shape your thinking?

FITZGERALD: Obviously there was, because most of the people I came in contact with had a very definite point of view and they were anxious to convince me of it. Virtually all of them were boosters of their particular way of life. But of course how they chose to present themselves was as interesting as anything else.

CA: It was mentioned in articles about you in 1979 and 1980 that you were working on a book about homosexuality. Did Cities on a Hill, *which contains a section on the homosexual Castro community of San Francisco, evolve from the idea for the book on homosexuality?*

FITZGERALD: For a while I thought about doing a book of intellectual history a la Foucault. But I am not an historian, and I soon realized that this particular project was impossibly difficult. Then, after I had written my first short piece on the Castro and was pondering the matter, I stumbled upon Jerry Falwell's church and became fascinated by that. Then I began to look at these two experiences and to realize that there was a book to be written about visionary American communities.

CA: You majored in Middle Eastern history at Radcliffe, I've read. Has that background been particularly helpful to you in writing about other cultures?

FITZGERALD: It certainly has. That's what really attracted me to Middle Eastern history in the first place, the big question of how you talk about another culture, how you deal with it. It's not quite an anthropological approach, but it's certainly one of comparative institutions and intellectual traditions and so on.

CA: It seems impossible to talk with you without asking the old question about the influence of your parents, Marietta Tree and Desmond FitzGerald, on your career.

FITZGERALD: My mother and my father were both involved in international affairs. My mother was at the United Nations for a time, my father at the CIA. My father was particularly involved with Asia and indeed with Vietnam for a period of time. Both believed strongly in the importance of public service; and both were very much engaged with the big issues. So what else could I do?

CA: You're said to be quite a voracious reader of all kinds of books. Is there anything you've been reading recently that you find especially exciting?

FITZGERALD: I do an awful lot of reading for work these days. I'm now working my way through twenty-seven volumes of depositions from the Iran-Contra Committee. So this summer has been rather light on outside reading.

CA: No Gothic romances?

FITZGERALD: No, I'm sorry to say. In general I just have to watch it, because if I get into a novel or a history, that's what I will be doing all day long.

CA: Will you be doing some major writing, then, about the Iran-Contra affair?

FITZGERALD: I just did a piece on the Oliver North trial for the *New Yorker,* and I may write some more about the whole affair.

CA: Is there another big book in the works?

FITZGERALD: I hope so, but it's too early to talk about it.

CA: You tried fiction just out of college and decided that it wasn't what you wanted to do. Have you had any second thoughts on that, any urge to try again?

FITZGERALD: No. I find life is more surprising than anything one could possibly make up. Then, too, reporting on it is an exercise in a lot of those things that I always thought fiction alone would demand. There's always something new to struggle with or to strive for in the writing of a page.

BIOGRAPHICAL/CRITICAL SOURCES:

PERIODICALS

Esquire, July, 1980.
Globe and Mail (Toronto), February 7, 1987.
Guardian, November 8, 1972.
New Republic, October 20, 1986.
Newsweek, August 7, 1972; November 3, 1986.
New York Post, July 21, 1972.
New York Review of Books, December 20, 1979.
New York Times, October 21, 1979; October 8, 1986.
New York Times Book Review, October 12, 1986.
People, September 15, 1980.

Time, August 28, 1972.
Vogue, January, 1973.
Washington Post, August 29, 1972.
Washington Post Book World, September 28, 1986.

—Sketch by Anne Janette Johnson

—Interview by Jean W. Ross

* * *

FITZGERALD, Judith 1952-

PERSONAL: Born November 11, 1952, in Toronto, Ontario, Canada. *Education:* York University, B.A. (with honors), 1976, M.A., 1977; attended University of Toronto, 1978-83. *Politics:* New Democrat. *Avocational interests:* Music, film.

ADDRESSES: Home—C-6 Pinewood Ave., Toronto, Ontario, Canada M6C 2V1; and Box 160, Station L, Toronto, Ontario, Canada M6E 4Y5.

CAREER: University of Toronto, Toronto, Ontario, lecturer in modern American and Canadian literature, 1978-81; Laurentian University of Sudbury, Sudbury, Ontario, assistant professor of Canadian literature, creative writing, and linguistics, 1981-83; free-lance writer, 1983-88.

AWARDS, HONORS: Grants from Ontario Arts Council, 1973-78, 1980-82, Canada Council, 1974-78, 1983-84, 1988-89, and Toronto Arts Council; Fiona Mee Literary Journalism award, 1983; Writer's Choice award, 1986.

WRITINGS:

POETRY

City Park, Northern Concept, 1972.
Victory, Coach House Press, 1975.
Lacerating Heartwood, Coach House Press, 1977.
Easy Over, Black Moss, 1981.
Split/Levels, Coach House Press, 1983.
The Syntax of Things, Prototype Press, 1984.
Beneath the Skin of Paradise: The Piaf Poems, Black Moss, 1984.
Heart Attacks, privately printed, 1984.
Given Names: New and Selected Poems, 1972-85, edited by Frank Davey, Black Moss, 1985.
My Orange Gorange (children's poetry), Black Moss, 1985.
Whale Waddleby (children's poetry), Black Moss, 1986.
Diary of Desire, Black Moss, 1987.
Rapturous Chronicles, Mercury Press, 1991.
Ultimate Midnight, Black Moss, 1991.

EDITOR

Un Dozen: Thirteen Canadian Poets, Black Moss, 1982.
SP/Elles: Poetry by Canadian Women, Black Moss, 1986.
First Person Plural, Black Moss, 1988.

OTHER

Journal Entries (prose), Dreadnaught Press, 1975.

Contributor to numerous periodicals, including *Nebula, West Coast Review, Island, Dialogue, Canadian Forum, Canadian Literature, Waves,* and *Books in Canada.* Assistant editor, *English Quarterly,* Toronto, Ontario, 1976-77. Entertainment critic, *Globe and Mail,* Toronto, Ontario, 1983.

WORK IN PROGRESS: Rapturous Chronicles: Book Two; [I/D]entographic; It's All in Your Head: The Complete Thyroid Book; Wiggity Boggs.

SIDELIGHTS: Judith Fitzgerald told *CA:* "My main inspiration and impetus for writing comes from language itself. I am always attempting to approximate the chaos of existence. I write because it is one of the few moral decisions available to individuals during these desolate times. It is a decision of conscience, to be, to do, to make, to continue. My major area of vocational interest is teaching creative writing and literary criticism."

BIOGRAPHICAL/CRITICAL SOURCES:

PERIODICALS

Books in Canada, October, 1983.
Globe and Mail (Toronto), July 9, 1983; November 16, 1985; February 14, 1987; January 2, 1988.
Quill and Quire, July, 1982; September, 1983.
Toronto Star, August 6, 1983.
Windsor Star, July 23, 1983.

* * *

FLIER, Michael S(tephen) 1941-

PERSONAL: Born April 20, 1941, in Los Angeles, CA; son of Albert Alfred (a clockshop owner) and Bonnie Flier. *Education:* University of California, Berkeley, A.B., 1962, M.A., 1964, Ph.D., 1968.

ADDRESSES: Office—Department of Slavic Languages and Literatures, 405 Hilgard Ave., University of California, Los Angeles, CA 90024.

CAREER: University of California, Los Angeles, assistant professor, 1968-73, associate professor, 1973-79, professor of Slavic languages and literatures, 1979—, chairman of department, 1978-84, 1987-89. Visiting acting assistant professor, University of California, Berkeley, summer, 1968; visiting professor, Columbia University, fall, 1988, and Harvard University, fall, 1989.

MEMBER: Linguistic Society of America, American Association of Teachers of Slavic and East European Languages, American Association for the Advancement of Slavic Studies, American Association for Ukrainian Studies, Early Slavic Studies Association, College Art Association, Western Slavic Association.

AWARDS, HONORS: Inter-University grant, 1966-67, for study in Russia; International Research and Exchanges Board fellowship, 1971, for study in Russia and Czechoslovakia, and 1978, for research in Russia, Belorussia, and the Ukraine; Summer College Institute fellowship, College of Letters and Science, University of California, Los Angeles, 1984; study grant, Kennan Institute for Advanced Russian Studies, 1985, for research at the Library of Congress; President's Fellowship in the Humanities, University of California, 1990.

WRITINGS:

(Editor) *Slavic Forum: Essays in Slavic Linguistics and Literature,* Mouton, 1974.
Aspects of Nominal Determination in Old Church Slavic, Mouton, 1974.
Say It in Russian, Dover, 1982.
(Editor and contributor) *American Contributions to the Ninth International Congress of Slavists, Kiev, September, 1983,* Volume I: *Linguistics,* Slavica, 1983.
(Editor with Henrik Birnbaum) *Medieval Russian Culture,* University of California Press, 1984.
(Editor with Simon Karlinsky) *Language, Literature, Linguistics: In Honor of Francis J. Whitfield on His Seventieth Birthday, March 25, 1986,* Berkeley Slavic Specialties, 1987.

CONTRIBUTOR

Dean S. Worth, editor, *The Slavic Word,* Mouton, 1972.

Demetrius J. Koubourlis, editor, *Topics in Slavic Phonology,* Slavica, 1974.

L'ubomir Durovic and others, editors, *Studia Linguistica Alexandro Vasilii filio Issatschenko Collegis et Amicis oblata,* De Ridder (Paris), 1977.

Richard D. Brecht and Dan E. Davidson, editors, *Soviet-American Russian Language Contributions,* G & G Press, 1978.

Birnbaum and others, editors, *American Contributions to the Eighth International Congress of Slavists,* Slavica, 1978.

Kenneth E. Naylor and others, editors, *Slavic Linguistics and Poetics: Studies for Edward Stankiewicz on His Sixtieth Birthday, 17 November, 1980,* Slavica, 1982.

Vladimir Markov and Worth, editors, *From Los Angeles to Kiev,* Slavica, 1983.

Alexander Schenker, editor, *American Contributions to the Tenth International Congress of Slavists, Sofia, September, 1988,* Volume I: *Linguistics,* Slavica, 1988.

Boris Gasparov and Robert P. Hughes, editors, *The Role of Christianity in the History of Russian Culture,* University of California Press, 1990.

Also contributor to *Phonology in the 1970s,* edited by D. L. Goyvaerts. Contributor of articles and reviews to numerous periodicals, including *International Journal of Slavic Linguistics and Poetics, Russian Linguistics, Slavic and East European Journal, Journal of Linguistics, Canadian-American Slavic Studies, Language,* and *Wiener Slawistischer Almanach.*

*   *   *

FLORES, Angel   1900-

PERSONAL: Born October 2, 1900, in Barceloneta, P.R.; son of Nepomuceno (in business) and Paula (a teacher; maiden name, Rodríguez) Flores; married Kate Mann (a writer), 1936; children: Ralph, Juan, Barbara Flores Dederick. *Education:* New York University, A.B., 1923; Lafayette College, A.M., 1925; Cornell University, Ph.D., 1947.

ADDRESSES: Home—P.O. Box 4833, Albuquerque, N.M. 87196.

CAREER: Union College, Schenectady, N.Y., instructor in Spanish, 1924-25; Rutgers University, New Brunswick, N.J., instructor in Spanish language and literature, 1925-29; editor of *Alhambra,* 1929-30; Cornell University, Ithaca, N.Y., instructor in Spanish, 1930-33; editor of *Literary World,* 1934-45; Queens College of the City University of New York, Flushing, N.Y., assistant professor, 1945-47, associate professor, 1948-52, professor of romance languages and comparative literature, 1952-70, professor emeritus, 1970—. Visiting professor at University of Wisconsin (now University of Wisconsin—Madison), 1953-54; professor at Graduate Center of the City University of New York, 1968-70. Editor of Dragon Press, 1931-33. Member of Pan American Union's Division of Intellectual Cooperation, 1941-45.

MEMBER: Instituto Internacional de Literatura Iberoamericana.

WRITINGS:

IN ENGLISH

Spanish Literature in English Translation, H. W. Wilson, 1926.

Lope de Vega: Monster of Nature, Brentano's, 1930, re-printed, Kennikat, 1969.

(With M. J. Benardete) *Cervantes across the Centuries: A Quadricentennial Volume,* Dryden, 1947, reprinted, Gordian, 1969.

Masterpieces of the Spanish Golden Age, Rinehart, 1957.

The Medieval Age, Dell, 1963.

The Literature of Spanish America, five volumes, Las Américas, 1966-69.

Ibsen: Four Essays, Haskell Booksellers, 1970.

(With Helene M. Anderson) *Masterpieces of Spanish American Literature,* two volumes, Macmillan, 1972.

A Bibliography of Spanish-American Writers, 1609-1974, Gordian, 1975.

A Kafka Bibliography, 1908-1976, Gordian, 1976.

The Problem of "The Judgment": Eleven Approaches to Kafka's Story, Gordian, 1977.

EDITOR; IN ENGLISH

(With Benardete) *The Anatomy of Don Quixote,* Dragon Press, 1932.

(With Dudley Poore) *Fiesta in November: Stories From Latin America,* Houghton, 1942.

The Kafka Problem: An Anthology of Criticism about Franz Kafka, New Directions, 1946, revised edition, Gordian, 1975.

Spanish Writers in Exile, Bern Porter, 1947, reprinted, 1977.

Great Spanish Stories, Modern Library, 1956.

An Anthology of French Poetry from Nerval to Valery, Doubleday, 1958.

(With Homer Swander) *Franz Kafka Today,* University of Wisconsin Press, 1958, revised edition, Gordian, 1977.

Nineteenth-Century German Tales, Doubleday, 1959.

Spanish Stories (in Spanish and English), Bantam, 1960, 8th edition, 1979.

An Anthology of German Poetry from Hoelderlin to Rilke, Doubleday, 1960.

An Anthology of Spanish Poetry from Garcilaso to García Lorca, Doubleday, 1961.

Great Spanish Short Stories, Dell, 1962.

Spanish Drama, Bantam, 1962.

An Anthology of Medieval Lyrics, Modern Library, 1962.

Giacomo Leopardi, *Leopardi: Poems and Prose,* Greenwood Press, 1966, reprinted, 1987.

The Kafka Debate: New Perspectives for Our Times, Gordian, 1977.

Explain to Me Some Stories of Kafka, Gordian, 1983.

(With wife, Kate Flores) *The Defiant Muse: Hispanic Feminist Poems from the Middle Ages to the Present,* Feminist Press, 1986.

TRANSLATOR INTO ENGLISH

José E. Rodó, *The Motives of Proteus,* Brentano's, 1928.

Ramón Gómez de la Serna, *Movieland,* Macaulay, 1930.

Miguel de Unamuno, *Three Exemplary Novels and a Prologue,* A. & C. Boni, 1930, reprinted, Grove Press, 1987.

Miguel A. Menéndez, *Nayar,* Farrar & Rinehart, 1942.

German Arciniegas, *Germans in the Conquest of America,* Macmillan, 1943.

Benjamin Subercaseaux, *Chile: A Geographic Extravaganza,* Macmillan, 1943, reprinted, Haffner, 1971.

Pablo Neruda, *Selected Poems,* privately printed, 1944.

Neruda, *Residence on Earth and Other Poems,* New Directions, 1946.

Neruda, *Tres cantos materiales: Three Material Songs,* East River Editions, 1948.

Jaime Sabartes, *Picasso: An Intimate Portrait*, Prentice-Hall, 1948.

Humberto Díaz Casanueva, *Requiem*, Grupo Fuego, 1958.

(With Esther S. Dillon) Baldomero Lillo, *The Devil's Pit*, UNESCO Collection of Representative Works, 1959.

Esteban Echeverría, *The Slaughter House*, Las Américas, 1959.

Neruda, *Nocturnal Collection: A Poem*, [Madison, Wis.], 1966.

IN SPANISH

(Translator) T. S. Eliot, *Tierra baldia* (title means "The Waste Land"), Editorial Cervantes, 1930, reprinted, Ocnos, 1973.

(With Alberto Vásquez) *Paisaje y hombres de América*, Dryden, 1947.

Historia y antología del cuento y la novela en Hispanoamérica, Las Américas, 1959.

First Spanish Reader, Bantam, 1964.

La literatura de España, Las Américas, 1970.

Aproximaciones a César Vallejo (title means "Approaches to César Vallejo"), two volumes, Las Américas, 1971.

Aproximaciones a Octavio Paz (title means "Approaches to Octavio Paz"), Mortiz, 1974.

Aproximaciones a Pablo Neruda (title means "Approaches to Pablo Neruda"), Ocnos, 1974.

Orígenes del cuento hispanoamericana (title means "Origins of the Spanish-American Short Story"), Premi, 1979.

Selecciones españolas (title means "Spanish Selections"), Macmillan, 1979.

Realismo mágico (title means "Magical Realism"), Premi, 1981.

César Vallejo (biography), Premi, 1981.

Narrativa hispanoamericana: Historia y antología (title means "Spanish-American Fiction: History and Anthology"), Siglo XXI, 1981.

Expliquémonos a Kafka, Siglo XXI, 1983.

El realismo mágico en el cuento hispanoamericano, Premi, 1985.

Nuevas aproximaciones a Pablo Neruda, Fondo de Cultura Económica, 1987.

Also author of volumes devoted to Jorge Luis Borges and other Hispanic writers.

BIOGRAPHICAL/CRITICAL SOURCES:

PERIODICALS

New York Times Book Review, May 3, 1987.*

*   *   *

FLORIT (y SANCHEZ de FUENTES), Eugenio 1903-

PERSONAL: Born October 15, 1903, in Madrid, Spain; immigrated to Cuba, 1918; immigrated to the United States, 1940; naturalized U.S. citizen, 1960; son of Ricardo (a law clerk) and María (a poet; maiden name, Sanchez de Fuentes) Florit. *Education:* Instituto La Habana, B.A., 1922; University of Havana, LL.D., 1926.

CAREER: Official in Cuban Exterior Ministry, 1927-40; Cuban Consular Service, New York City, consular official, 1940-45; Columbia University, New York City, instructor, 1942-45, professor at Barnard College, 1945-69, professor emeritus of Spanish, 1969—. Writer of poetry, essays, and literary criticism. Taught at Spanish summer school of Middlebury College, 1944-64.

MEMBER: Academia Norteamericana de la Lengua Española, Real Academia de la Lengua (correspondent member), Academia Chilena de la Lengua (correspondent member), Modern Language Association of America, Hispanic Society of America, Association of Professors of Spanish and Portuguese, Cruzada Educativa Cubana.

AWARDS, HONORS: Received medal from La Salle College, 1963, for distinguished contributions to Christian writing, scholarship, and research; Mitre Medal from Hispanic Society of America, 1969; Prize of Literature from Institute of Puerto Rico, 1972; award from Spanish Literary Society, Southern Connecticut College, 1978; Guadalupe Medal from St. John's University.

WRITINGS:

IN ENGLISH

(Editor) *Invitation to Spanish Poetry*, Dover, 1965.

(Editor and translator) *Spanish Poetry: A Selection from the Cantar de Mío Cid to Miguel Hernández*, Dover, 1971.

(Editor and translator) William D. Servodidio, *The Quest for Harmony*, Society of Spanish and Spanish-American Studies, 1979.

POETRY; IN SPANISH

Treinta y dos poemas breves (title means "Thirty-two Short Poems"), [Havana], 1927.

Trópico (title means "Tropic"), Revista de Avance, 1930.

Doble acento (title means "Double Accent"), Ucacia, 1937.

Reino (title means "Kingdom"), Ucar, García, 1938.

Cuatro poemas de Eugenio Florit (title means "Four Poems by Eugenio Florit"), Ucar, García, 1940.

Poema mío: poesía completa (title means "My Poem: Complete Poetry"), Letras de México, 1947.

(Editor and translator) *Antología de la poesía norteamericana contemporánea* (title means "Anthology of Contemporary North American Poetry"), Unión Panamericana, 1955.

Asonante final, y otros poemas (title means "Last Assonant, and Other Poems"), Orígenes, 1955.

Alfonso Reyes: la poesía (title means "The Poetry of Alfonso Reyes"), Hispanic Institute in the United States, 1956.

Antología poética (1930-1955) (title means "An Anthology of My Poems, 1930-1955"), prologue by Andrés Iduarte, Instituto Internacional de Literatura Ibero-Americana, 1956.

(Editor with Enrique Anderson Imbert) *Literatura hispanoamericana: antología e introducción histórica* (title means "Spanish-American Literature: Anthology and Historical Introduction"), Holt, 1960.

Siete poemas (title means "Seven Poems"), Cuadernos Julio Herrera y Reissig, 1960.

Tres autos religiosos (title means "Three Religious Short Plays"), Palma de Mallorca, 1960.

(With Beatrice P. Patt) *Retratos de Hispanoamérica* (title means "Portraits of Spanish America"), Holt, 1962.

(Editor) *Cien de las mejores poesías españolas* (title means "One Hundred of the Best Spanish Poems"), Las Américas, 1965.

Hábito de esperanza: poemas, 1936-1964 (title means "A Cloak of Hope, 1936-1964"), Insula, 1965.

(Editor) *José Martí: Versos*, Las Américas, 1965.

(Editor and author of introduction and notes) Federico García Lorca, *Obras escogidas* (title means "Selected Works"), Dell, 1965.

Concordancias de la obra poética de Eugenio Florit (title means "Concordances of the Poetical Works of Eugenio Florit"), edited by Alice M. Pollin, New York University Press, 1967.

(Compiler with José Olivio Jiménez) *La poesía hispanoamericana desde el modernismo* (title means "Spanish American

Poetry Since Modernism"), Appleton-Century-Crofts, 1968.

Antología penúltima (title means "Penultimate Anthology"), prologue by José Olivio Jiménez, Plenitude, 1970.

(Editor) *Antología poética (1898-1953)* (title means "An Anthology of Poems (1898-1953)"), Biblioteca Nueva, 1971.

De tiempo y agonía (title means "Of Time and Agony"), introduction by Amelia Agostini de del Río, Roberto Esquenazi-Mayo, and Jiménez, Revista de Occidente, 1974.

Versos pequeños (1938-1975) (title means "Short Poems (1938-1975)"), El Marco, 1979.

Obras completas, edited by Luis González-del-Valle and Roberto Esquenazi-Mayo, Society of Spanish and Spanish-American Studies, Volume 1, 1982, Volume 2, 1983, Volume 3, 1983, Volume 4, in press.

Castillo interior y otros versos, Universal, 1987.

A pesar de todo, Universal, 1987.

Tercero sueño y otros versos, Universal, 1989.

OTHER

Poesía casi siempre: ensayos literarios (title means "Mostly Poetry: Literary Essays"), Mensaje, 1978.

Poesía en José Martí, Juan Ramon Jiménez, Alfonso Reyes, Federico García Lorca y Pablo Neruda: cinco ensayos (title means "The Poetry of José Martí, Juan Ramon Jiménez, Alfonso Reyes, Federico García Lorca, and Pablo Neruda: Five Essays"), Universal, 1978.

Also author of literary criticism, essays, and reviews to scholarly journals. Editor of *Revista Hispánica Moderna,* 1960-69.

AVOCATIONAL INTERESTS: Music, painting.

BIOGRAPHICAL/CRITICAL SOURCES:

BOOKS

Burnshaw, Stanley, *The Poem Itself,* Holt, 1960.

Florit, Eugenio, *Antología penúltima,* prologue by José Olivio Jiménez, Plenitude, 1970.

PERIODICALS

Hispania, May, 1969, May, 1972, September, 1972.

*   *   *

FOREMAN, Richard 1937-

PERSONAL: Born June 10, 1937, in New York, N.Y.; son of Albert (an attorney) and Claire (Levine) Foreman; married Amy Taubin, 1961 (divorced, 1972). *Education:* Brown University, B.A. (magna cum laude), 1959; Yale University, M.F.A., 1962. *Religion:* Jewish.

ADDRESSES: Home and office—152 Wooster St., New York, N.Y. 10012. *Agent*—Artservices, 463 West St., New York, N.Y. 10014.

CAREER: Actors Studio, New York City, member of playwrights' unit, 1962-68; Ontological-Hysteric Theater, New York City, founder and director, 1968—. Artistic director in Paris, France, 1973-85; director in residence, New York Shakespeare Festival, New York City, 1975-76; director of "Three-Penny Opera" at Lincoln Center, 1976, Molier's "Don Juan" in Minneapolis at Guthrie Theater, 1981, Strauss's "Die Fledermaus," at the Paris Opera, 1983, and over forty other plays and operas. Member of theater division panel, National Endowment for the Arts, 1976-79; member of board of directors, Anthology Film Archives, 1976-84.

MEMBER: Dramatists Guild, Authors League of America, PEN, Society of Stage Directors.

AWARDS, HONORS: Obie Award, *Village Voice,* 1970, for "Elephant Steps," 1973, for work with Ontological-Hysteric Theater, 1976, for "Rhoda in Potatoland (Her Fall-Starts)," 1986, for directing "Largo Desolator," 1987, for "The Cure" and "Film Is Evil: Radio Is Good," and 1988, for lifetime achievement; Creative Artists Public Service fellowship, New York State Arts Council, 1971; Guggenheim play-writing fellowship, 1972, 1975; Rockefeller Foundation grant, 1974.

WRITINGS:

Plays and Manifestos of Richard Foreman, New York University Press, 1976.

Reverberation Machines: Later Plays and Essays, Station Hill, 1985.

PLAYS; AND DIRECTOR

"Angelface," first produced in New York at Cinematheque, April, 1968.

"Elephant Steps," music by Stanley Silverman, first produced in Lenox, Mass., at Tanglewood, July, 1968.

"Ida-Eyed," first produced in New York at New Dramatists Workshop, May, 1969.

"Total Recall (Sophia-(Wisdom): Part II)," first produced at Cinematheque, December, 1970.

"Dream Tantras for Western Massachusetts," first produced in Lenox, Mass., at Lenox Arts Center, August, 1971.

"Hotel China," first produced at Cinematheque, December, 1971.

"Evidence," first produced in New York at Theatre for the New City, April, 1972.

"Dr. Selavy's Magic Theatre," music by Silverman, first produced at Lenox Arts Center, July, 1972.

"Sophia-(Wisdom): Part III—The Cliffs," first produced at Cinematheque, December, 1972.

"Particle Theory," first produced at Theatre for the New City, April, 1973.

"Daily Life," first produced (in part) in New York at Cubiculo Theatre, May, 1973.

"Classical Therapy; or, A Week under the Influence," first produced in Paris at Festival d'Automne, September, 1973.

"Vertical Mobility (Sophia-(Wisdom): Part IV)," and "Pain(t)," both first produced in New York at Ontological-Hysteric Theatre, April, 1974.

"Sophia-(Wisdom): Part I," first produced at Theatre for the New City, November, 1974.

"Hotels for Criminals," first produced in New York at Exchange Theatre, January, 1975.

"Pandering to the Masses: A Misrepresentation," first produced at Ontological-Hysteric Theatre, January, 1975.

"Thinking (One Kind)," first produced in San Diego, Calif., at University of California, March, 1975.

"Out of the Body Travel," first produced in New London, Conn., at American Dance Festival, July, 1975.

"Rhoda in Potatoland (Her Fall-Starts)," first produced at Ontological-Hysteric Theatre, December, 1975.

"Livre des splendeurs," first produced at Festival d'Automne, October, 1976.

"Book of Splendours: Part II (Book of Levers) Action at a Distance," first produced in New York, January, 1977.

"Blv'd de Paris: I've Got the Shakes," first produced in New York, December, 1977.

"Madness and Tranquillity (My Head Was a Sledgehammer)," first produced in New York, January, 1979.

"Luogo + Bersaglio" (title means "Place plus Target"), first produced in Rome at Teatro di Roma, December, 1979.

"Penguin Touquet," first produced in New York at New York Public Theater, January, 1981.

"Cafe amerique," first produced in France, October, 1981.

"Egyptology (My Head Was a Sledgehammer)," first produced in New York at The Other Stage, May, 1983.

"Miss Universal Happiness," first produced Off-Broadway at the Performing Garage, May, 1985.

"Africanis-Instructus," music by Silverman, first produced at Ontological-Hysteric Theater, January, 1986.

"The Cure," produced at the Performing Garage, May, 1986.

"Film Is Evil: Radio Is Good," first produced Off-Broadway, 1986.

"Symphony of Rats," first produced Off-Broadway, January, 1988.

"What Did He See?," first produced at the New York Public Theater, October, 1988.

"Lava," first produced Off-Broadway, December, 1989.

Also author of unproduced and unpublished plays, including "Rhoda—Returning," 1969, "Maudlin Notations," 1970, "Forest: Depth," 1970, "Two Vacations," 1970, "Holy Moly," 1970, "Lines of Vision," 1970, "Op/Ra: An Isomorphic Representation of the Gradual Dismemberment from Within of Western Art in Which a New Unity That of Consciousness Itself Emerges," 1972, "Africa," 1972, "the Rem(ark)able Cabin-Cruiser: Depth," 1972, "Inspirational Analysis," 1973, "Walled Garden (language)," 1973, "Life of the Bee (I've Goet der Shakes)," 1973, "Seance," 1975, "End of a Beautiful Friendship," 1975, and "Radiant City," 1975.

OTHER

"Real Magic in New York" (concert), first produced at Cinamatheque, May, 1970.

"City Archives" (video play), Walker Art Center, 1977.

(And director) "Strong Medicine" (screenplay), music by Silverman, Ontological-Hysteric Theater, 1978.

(And director) "Madame Adare" (opera), music by Silverman, first produced in New York at Lincoln Center, October, 1980.

SIDELIGHTS: "I have always conceived of my theater as being a kind of mental and intellectual sensory gym . . . where I would work out the kinks of my perceptual apparatus," says avant-garde playwright and director Richard Foreman in a *New York Times* interview with Diane Solway. "I'm interested in trying to find ways to make physical the various abstractions that one's imagination spins and projects. If a painter is trying to paint 'treeness,' what he paints may not look like a tree, because he's trying to embody the kind of energy that gives birth to a tree. I'm trying to do something similar in the theater." Because of Foreman's efforts to capture his own personal vision on the stage, his plays may at first seem confusing to audiences unfamiliar with his work. Dropping all the usual conventions of plot, setting, characterization, and dialogue, the playwright recreates for the stage his thought processes about death, the search for identity, and the struggle for order in a world ruled by randomness. Despite the abstruseness of his work, *New York Times* critic Don Shewey asserts that "Mr. Foreman's plays are not meant to be obscure. His peculiar staging techniques represent in specific physical terms the philosophical and extremely personal themes that run through his plays." Shewey later notes that "the very strangeness of the work, the fact that it doesn't look like any other kind of theater, often makes it entertaining, comical, and surprisingly moving."

Foreman considers the works of Gertrude Stein and Bertold Brecht to have been an early influence on him, but what really affected his concept of what theater should be were the underground films of the 1960s, especially those made by Jack Smith, Jonas Mekas, and Yvonne Rainer. In order to duplicate the artistic freedom of these filmmakers for the stage, Foreman founded the Ontological-Hysteric Theater company in New York City in 1968. The name of the troupe initially discouraged people from attending the playwright's first plays, but the few critics who did see Foreman's work were fascinated, albeit confused. "I can't explain this work . . . because I don't know what the hell was going on," writes Harold C. Schonberg in a *New York Times* review of "Elephant Steps." "But I know one thing. Nobody was bored. . . . [In] its crazy way 'Elephant Steps' keeps moving along, and the electricism, the wonderful irreverence of the music, provides a perfect commentary. In this work, surrealism lives." "Elephant Steps" won Foreman his first Obie Award. He would later earn two more for "Rhoda in Potatoland (Her Fall-Starts)" and "Film Is Evil: Radio Is Good," as well as one for his work for the Ontological-Hysteric Theater.

Other plays that have garnered critical praise for Foreman include "Dream Tantras for Western Massachusetts," "Dr. Selavey's Magic Theater," and "Hotels for Criminals." As in his other works, these plays employ such techniques as bizarre, seemingly incongruous stage props, sudden electronic noises that interrupt the soundtrack, and ever-changing sets with sliding panels and the playwright's trademark framework of strings. Another now familiar element in Foreman's plays is the character of Rhoda, the author's "archetypal heroine" who is typically "an innocent entrapped by the decadent," according to *New York Times* contributor Mel Gussow. Through the character of Rhoda and others like her, Foreman provides himself with a voice for his thoughts. In this way, explains Shewey, "the actors do not so much play characters as embody states of mind."

Recently, however, Foreman's plays have become less intellectual and more emotional. A major reason for this evolution is the playwright's relationship with Kate Manheim, who has played Rhoda and other major Foreman characters in many of his works. Manheim, a German actress who immigrated to the United States in the early 1970s, is a fan of old television shows such as "I Love Lucy" and "The Honeymooners," and she felt some of this type of levity would be good for Foreman's plays. After acting in Foreman's plays for a number of years, doing "everything I was told," as she tells *Drama Review* interviewer Richard Schechner, she began to suggest changes in Foreman's plays such as adding more humor and increasing the pace of action.

Manheim's influence is readily apparent in "Film Is Evil: Radio Is Good." Foreman tells Schechner in the same *Drama Review* issue that "a good 30 percent of the play was added [in rehearsal], mostly because [of] Kate." This was an unprecedented move for the director, who before "Film Is Evil" always exercised absolute control over the dialogue and action of his plays. Reviews of the play were very positive, and *Downtown* critic David Kaufman feels that "Film Is Evil" "suggests that some artistic growth is taking place for the first time in years." It "is a departure for Foreman and an event in his career," Kaufman later adds, ". . . because for the first time he seems willing to make a statement beyond demonstrating that incoherence is the best we can hope for. The statement is the equivalent of the moral that is encapsulated in the title." *Christian Science Monitor* reviewer David Sterritt also believes that "Film Is Evil" shows Foreman "at his most complex and provocative, and also at his most obsessive."

Another recent influence on the playwright has been his age. "I've been purposely trying to make some connection with something as my death approaches," he tells Shewey, "and I think it's racing toward me. I've done the work of learning the grammar, and I want to show people that it's not just a perverse, irrelevant, dadaistic grammar, but a language that can speak clearly about all the things that touch us most profoundly." Despite his continuing "enigmatic quest for self-definition" that Gussow still observes as a presence in Foreman's 1989 play "Lava," it has never been the author's goal to frustrate and confound his audience. Foreman tells Solway: "People think, 'Oh, my God, we're going to see a Foreman play; it's going to be hard to understand, and we'd better sit there thinking all night.' That's not what I want at all. I want people to have fun, because I certainly have fun playing with implications and residues of ideas and all the stuff that's in the air."

BIOGRAPHICAL/CRITICAL SOURCES:

BOOKS

Contemporary Literary Criticism, Volume 50, Gale, 1987.

PERIODICALS

Christian Science Monitor, June 1, 1987.
Downtown, May 20, 1987.
Drama Review, winter, 1987.
New York Native, June 16, 1986.
New York Post, May 6, 1987.
New York Times, April 25, 1970, February 2, 1981, November 25, 1981, May 15, 1983, May 18, 1983, May 30, 1985, January 3, 1986, January 26, 1986, May 28, 1986, May 5, 1987, January 3, 1988, January 12, 1988, October 19, 1988, December 13, 1989.
Soho Arts Weekly, June 18, 1986.
Villager, June 5, 1986.
Village Voice, June 3, 1986.

—Sketch by Kevin S. Hile

*   *   *

FORREST, Gary Gran 1943-

PERSONAL: Born December 1, 1943, in New Castle, PA; son of Granville H. (a teacher) and Florence (Cox) Forrest; married Sandra Della-Giustina (a teacher), December 28, 1974; children: Sarah Ellen, Allison Giustina. *Education:* Westminster College, Fulton, MO, B.A., 1965; University of Missouri, Columbia, M.Ed., 1967; University of North Dakota, Grand Forks, Ed.D., 1970; Columbia Pacific University, San Raphael, CA, Ph.D., 1984. *Politics:* Republican. *Religion:* Methodist.

ADDRESSES: Home—935 War Eagle Dr. N., Colorado Springs, CO 80919. *Office*—Psychotherapy Associates, 3208 North Academy Blvd., Suite 160, Colorado Springs, CO 80917.

CAREER: Hot Springs Rehabilitation Research and Training Center, Hot Springs, AR, intern, 1966-67; Northeast Mental Health and Retardation Center, Grand Forks, ND, staff psychologist, 1967-69; U.S. Army Alcohol and Drug Rehabilitation Center, Department of Psychiatry, 1970-76, clinical director at Fort Gordon, GA, 1970-73, clinical director at Fort Carson, CO, 1973-76; Psychotherapy Associates, Colorado Springs, CO, clinical psychologist and executive director, 1976—. Augusta Mental Health Center, staff psychologist, 1973; part-time private practice of clinical psychology in Colorado Springs, 1973-76; Institute for Addictive Behavioral Change, executive director, 1976—. Pastoral Counseling Center of Augusta, GA, consul-

tant, 1973; Alcohol Services Division of Pikes Peak Mental Health Center, consultant, 1982—; national and international consultant on alcoholism. University of Northern Colorado, visiting professor of psychology, counseling, and guidance, 1973—; University of Denver doctoral program in counseling psychology, part-time faculty member, 1976—.

Guest appearances on radio and television, including Cable News Network (CNN-TV), Voice of America Radio, and American Broadcasting Co. (ABC-TV) show "Good Morning America." Speaker at workshops and seminars on alcoholism. Member of advisory boards of Salvation Army, 1976-77, Penrose Community Hospital, 1980-82, and Menninger Foundation, 1983—. *Military Service:* U.S. Army, 1970-72, served as clinical psychologist at Fort Gordon, GA; became first lieutenant; received Distinguished Service Medal.

MEMBER: International Academy of Behavioral Medicine, Counseling, and Psychotherapy (diplomate, division of psychotherapy), American Psychological Association, American Association for Counseling and Development, Council for the National Register of Health Service Providers in Psychology, National Council on Alcoholism (member of board of directors, 1975), Association for the Advancement of Psychology, Colorado Psychological Association, Phi Delta Kappa.

WRITINGS:

The Diagnosis and Treatment of Alcoholism, C. C Thomas, 1975, revised 2nd edition, 1978.
How to Live with a Problem Drinker and Survive, Atheneum, 1980.
Confrontation in Psychotherapy with the Alcoholic, Learning Publications, 1982.
Alcoholism and Human Sexuality, C. C Thomas, 1983.
How to Cope with a Teenage Drinker: New Alternatives and Hope for Parents and Families, Atheneum, 1983.
Alcoholism, Narcissism, and Psychopathology, C. C. Thomas, 1983.
Intensive Psychotherapy of Alcoholism, C. C Thomas, 1984.
(Editor with Thomas E. Bratter) *Current Management of Alcoholism and Substance Abuse,* Free Press, 1985.
Guidelines for Responsible Drinking, C. C Thomas, 1989.
(With Robert Gordon) *Substance Abuse, Homicide, and Violent Behavior,* Gardner Press, 1990.
Psychotherapy and Assessment of Substance Abusers, Addicts, and Psychopaths, Edgehill Publications, 1990.

Contributor to professional journals and newspapers, including *Family and Community Health, St. Louis Globe Democrat, Journal of Counseling Psychology, Georgia Journal of Dentistry, Atlanta Constitution, Nashville Tennessean,* and *USA Today.*

SIDELIGHTS: Gary Gran Forrest told *CA:* "I wrote my first book, *The Diagnosis and Treatment of Alcoholism,* during the middle 1970's while I was the clinical director of two comprehensive military alcohol and drug rehabilitation centers. I felt a profound need to share my clinical work and experiences with alcoholics with other psychologists and behavioral scientists. There were so few books available on the subject then." Reviewing the book for *Personnel and Guidance Journal,* Hugh C. Banks noted that the author relied heavily on his own clinical experience and commented, "Of particular value is the illuminating discussion on treatment strategies in which Forrest carefully welds practical treatment problems with underlying theory."

Forrest has written several other books for his colleagues, but he has also addressed the nonprofessional audience. He wrote *How to Live with a Problem Drinker and Survive* and *How to Cope with a Teenage Drinker* to help the families of alcoholics. In these guides Forrest provides a general understanding of the problem of alcoholism and its effects on the drinker. He suggests specific behavior modification techniques for the family to use in dealing with the alcoholic.

Forrest added: "My involvement in the alcoholism/addiction field occurred as a result of chance. However, once I became involved in the field I realized that it was for life. The addictions-treatment profession is exciting, challenging, difficult, and new. My books represent an attempt to contribute to our collective understanding of the various dimensions of addictive behavior and the successful treatment of the addictions. Writing is also a therapeutic, creative process for me. My writing enables me to transcend the 'grind' of clinical psychotherapeutic work and experience the many rewards of simply writing!"

BIOGRAPHICAL/CRITICAL SOURCES:

PERIODICALS

Personnel and Guidance Journal, April, 1977.

* * *

FOSTER, Lynn 1952-

PERSONAL: Born November 10, 1952, in Chicago, IL; daughter of James T. (a custodial engineer) and Janet (a keypunch operator; maiden name, Burkwest) Foster; married James B. Dinkins, May 17, 1975. *Education:* University of Illinois at Urbana-Champaign, A.B., 1973, M.S., 1975; Southern Illinois University at Carbondale, J.D., 1982.

ADDRESSES: Home—305 North Schiller, Little Rock, AR 72205. *Office*— University of Arkansas, Little Rock/Pulaski County Law Library, 400 West Markham, Little Rock, AR 72201.

CAREER: University of Illinois at Urbana-Champaign, instructor, 1975-78, assistant professor of library administration, 1978-79, assistant law librarian, 1975-79; University of Idaho, Moscow, assistant professor of library administration and associate law librarian, 1981-82; Southern Illinois University, Carbondale, assistant professor of library administration and assistant law librarian, 1982-1983; Ohio Northern University, Ada, associate professor of law and director of Law Library, 1983-1986; University of Arkansas, Little Rock, associate professor of law and director of the law library, 1986—.

MEMBER: American Association of Law Libraries, American Bar Association.

AWARDS, HONORS: Joseph L. Andrews Bibliographic Award, American Association of Law Libraries, 1982, for *Subject Compilations of State Laws.*

WRITINGS:

(With Carol Boast) *Subject Compilations of State Laws: Research Guide and Annotated Bibliography,* Greenwood Press, 1981.
(With Elizabeth Kelly) *Legal Research Exercises,* West Publishing, 1983, 3rd edition (with Nancy Johnson), 1989.
Arkansas Legal Bibliography: Documents and Selected Commercial Titles, American Association of Law Libraries, 1988.

Contributor to library journals.

SIDELIGHTS: Lynn Foster told *CA:* "In the academic world, librarians are hard to categorize for purposes of personnel classification. They have advanced degrees (are they faculty?) but don't teach (are they staff? or 'academic professionals'?). Some institutions view librarians as faculty, encouraging them to obtain doctoral degrees and requiring them to publish. This approach has its drawbacks. It's difficult to work an eight-hour day and publish copiously in addition. Librarians tend to view patrons as obstacles to writing. Some of the writing produced is mere 'make work.' On the other hand, I don't know whether I would have started writing had I not been forced to. No part of the writing process came easily to me, and at first I had a hard time generating ideas. However, I've certainly benefitted from the mental discipline it imposes."

* * *

FOXX, Jack
See PRONZINI, Bill

* * *

FRANK, Joseph (Nathaniel) 1918-

PERSONAL: Born October 6, 1918, in New York, N.Y.; son of William S. and Jennie (Garlick) Frank; married Marguerite J. Straus, May 11, 1953; children: Claudine, Isabelle. *Education:* Attended New York University, 1937-38, University of Wisconsin—Madison, 1941-42, and University of Paris, 1950-51; University of Chicago, Ph.D., 1960.

ADDRESSES: Office—Department of Slavic Languages and Literature, Stanford University, Stanford, Calif. 94305; Department of Comparative Literature, Princeton University, 326 E. Pyne St., Princeton, N.J. 08544.

CAREER: Bureau of National Affairs, Washington, D.C., editor, 1942-50; American Embassy, Paris, France, special researcher, 1951-52; Princeton University, Princeton, N.J., Christian Gauss Lecturer, 1954-55, lecturer in English, 1955-56; University of Minnesota, Minneapolis, assistant professor of English, 1958-61; Rutgers University, New Brunswick, N.J., 1961-66, began as associate professor, became professor of comparative literature; Princeton University, professor of comparative literature, 1966-84, professor of Slavic studies, 1966-68, director of Christian Gauss Seminars in Criticism, 1966-84, professor emeritus, 1984—; Stanford University, professor of Slavic studies and literature, 1984-88, professor emeritus, 1988—. Visiting professor at Harvard University, 1965.

MEMBER: Modern Language Association of America, American Association for the Advancement of Slavic Studies, American Academy of Arts and Sciences (fellow).

AWARDS, HONORS: Fulbright scholar in Paris, 1950-51; Rockefeller fellow, 1952-53; Rockefeller and University of Chicago fellow, 1953-54; Guggenheim fellow, 1956-57; National Institute of Arts and Letters award, 1958; grants from American Council of Learned Societies, 1961-62, 1964-65, 1967-68, 1970-71, Bollingen Foundation, 1962, and Rockefeller Foundation, 1979-80; National Endowment for the Arts Award, 1967, for article "N. G. Chernyshevsky: A Russian Utopia"; James Russell Lowell Prize from Modern Language Association of America, and Christian Gauss Award from Phi Beta Kappa, both 1977, both for *Dostoevsky: The Seeds of Revolt, 1821-1849;* Rockefeller fellow, 1983-84; Guggenheim fellowship, 1983; National Book Critics Circle Award in biography, 1984, for *Dostoevsky: The Years of Ordeal, 1850-1859;* National Book Critics Circle Award nomination for biography, 1987, for *Dostoevsky: The Stir of Liberation.*

WRITINGS:

The Widening Gyre: Crisis and Mastery in Modern Literature, Rutgers University Press, 1963.

(Editor) R. P. Blackmur, *A Primer of Ignorance,* Harcourt, 1967.

(Author of introduction) Paul Valery, *Masters and Friends* (essays), Princeton University Press, 1968.

(Author of introduction) Erich Kahler, *The Inward Turn of Narrative,* Princeton University Press, 1973.

Dostoevsky, Princeton University Press, Volume 1: *The Seeds of Revolt, 1821-1849,* 1976, Volume 2: *The Years of Ordeal, 1850-59,* 1983, Volume 3: *The Stir of Liberation, 1860-1865,* 1986.

(Editor with David I. Goldstein) *Selected Letters of Fyodor Dostoyevsky,* Rutgers University Press, 1987.

(Author of preface) Kahler, *The Tower and the Abyss,* Transaction Publishers, 1989.

Through the Russian Prism, Princeton University Press, 1990.

CONTRIBUTOR

Mark Schorer and others, editors, *Criticism: The Foundations of Modern Literary Judgment,* Harcourt, 1948.

R. W. Stallman, editor, *Critiques and Essays in Criticism, 1920-1948,* Ronald Press, 1949.

John W. Aldridge, editor, *Critiques and Essays on Modern Fiction,* Ronald Press, 1952.

The Arts in Mid-Century, Horizon Press, 1954.

R. W. B. Lewis, editor, *Malraux: A Collection of Critical Essays,* Prentice-Hall, 1964.

James M. McCrimmon and others, editors, *From Source to Statement,* Houghton, 1968.

American Literary Anthology, Volume 2, Random House, 1968.

Robert Louis Jackson, editor, *Twentieth-Century Interpretations of "Crime and Punishment": A Collection of Critical Essays,* Prentice-Hall, 1973.

OTHER

Contributor of translations, articles, and reviews to periodicals, including *Times Literary Supplement, Encounter, Dissent, Critical Inquiry, Sewanee Review, Partisan Review, New Republic, Slavic Review, New York Review of Books, American Political Science Review, American Scholar, New York Review,* and *Chronicle of Higher Education.*

WORK IN PROGRESS: The fourth and fifth volumes of *Dostoevsky.*

SIDELIGHTS: In the mid-1950s, Joseph Frank was invited to give a series of lectures at Princeton University on existential themes in modern literature. He decided Fyodor Dostoevsky's *Notes from Underground* would be a good place to begin his survey, since the Underground Man was a precursor of the isolated, sometimes criminally antisocial hero found in the works of Albert Camus and Jean-Paul Sartre. The more Frank read of Dostoevsky, however, the more his interest shifted from existentialism *per se* to the author who penned such towering achievements as *Crime and Punishment* and *The Brothers Karamazov.* For more than twenty years Frank has combined his talents as literary critic, cultural historian, and linguist to gather material for a study of the Russian novelist. The resulting multivolume work, *Dostoevsky,* "is clearly on the way toward [becoming] one of the great literary biographies of the age," according to Irving Howe in the *New York Times Book Review.* In another *New York Times Book Review* piece, Morris Dickstein calls *Dostoevsky* "a masterful work of cultural biography, which explores the writer's Russian milieu in a way that's never been attempted in English. In-

deed, it may be the most ambitious book on Dostoevsky undertaken in any language."

Prior to beginning his award-winning work on Dostoevsky, Frank was a literary critic and professor of comparative literature. He has therefore brought the perspective of an intellectual historian to his biographical works, seeking "to reground Dostoevsky in the contemporary world that furnished the terms and issues for his astonishing creations," to quote *New Republic* contributor Donald Fanger. Fanger adds: "Frank's ultimate aim remains to interpret Dostoevsky's art, but he understands that art means more than text. Origin, analogue, function, implication: these are all matters of importance, and Frank pursues them by first establishing the contexts out of which the texts emerged. He considers by turns the personal, the familial, the cultural, literary, social and political. The result—in contrast to the fashionable sophistication of the "deconstructionists"—is a massive historical *reconstruction,* sensible and persuasive."

Such an approach has necessitated thorough work with primary sources, so Frank learned Russian to facilitate his research and interpretations. Dickstein maintains that through his studies Frank has come to see the Russian author "as a writer who brought into sharp focus all the cultural tensions of his age." Paul Roazen elaborates in the *Virginia Quarterly Review.* "Frank treats Dostoevsky's creations as a genius's synthesis of the major themes of his times," writes Roazen. "Dostoevsky's stories are examined as personal expressions, but Frank sees him as oriented more than most by issues outside himself. Frank is fascinated by Dostoevsky in the context of 19th-century Russian culture, and his notable achievement is to present Dostoevsky in the milieu of his society. . . . Frank has sought to re-create an alien period of a great writer, and in that way to expand our horizons of the humanly possible. The result is intellectual history at its best."

Each volume of *Dostoevsky* has been nominated for some of the book industry's most prestigious prizes. Reviewers too have found much to praise in the works. In the *New York Review of Books,* for instance, V. S. Pritchett calls *Dostoevsky* "a work of detection and collation at its scrupulous best. Every detail is considered; evidence is weighed and fortunately the author has a pleasant and lucid style, unleadened by the fashionable vice of fact-fetishism." *Los Angeles Times Book Review* correspondent Edward Condren notes that the work proceeds "from the soundest theory of biography we have, benefits from Frank's extraordinary scholarly mind, and best of all, weaves some fascinating theories to account for heretofore inexplicable shifts in Dostoevsky's beliefs and attitudes." The critic concludes: "Frank [takes] care to make neither the literature explain the life, nor the life the literature. Rather he maintains his scholarly equilibrium by keeping a steady eye on the interrelationship of the two." Fanger deems *Dostoevsky* "a major contribution to Russian cultural history, whose very virtues make it resistant to summary."

Its scholarly aims notwithstanding, *Dostoevsky* does not neglect the interests of the general reader. Howe claims: "Mr. Frank's distinction as a biographer lies not so much in his scholarly investigations as in the justness and comprehensiveness of his portrait. For the general reader, what will matter most is the skill with which Mr. Frank has fused biography, literary criticism and cultural history to place [Dostoevsky] squarely in the mid-19th century Russian setting." According to Adam Gussow in the *Saturday Review,* Frank "is chiefly concerned with tracing the lineaments of Dostoevsky's restless and tortured soul. He knows how to tell a good story, too, which makes this painstaking study anything but an ordeal for the reader." Roazen likewise commends Frank, noting that the author "has not sought to invent a new Dostoevsky, at odds with the responses of intelligent readers over the past century. Rather we find Dostoevsky more present and critically alive than ever before."

Dostoevsky was originally conceived as a single volume work. Five volumes are now planned, each covering a seminal period in the novelist's life. *Washington Post Book World* contributor Paul F. Cardaci writes: "Joseph Frank's masterful study seems destined to replace all earlier biographies of Dostoevsky, because it treats him first as a novelist, not as a member of the Russian intelligentsia who happened to write novels, and because it is both thorough in its research and objective in its findings. Moreover, it provides the American reader with a thorough, helpful introduction to the complex, often stormy, cultural and social history of the time." *New Yorker* essayist George Steiner calls *Dostoevsky* "an absolutely indispensable piece of literary and social investigation," adding: ". . . In its scale and scholarly care, Frank's study . . . has no rival throughout the extensive critical and biographical literature on Dostoevsky." Fanger concludes: "Any future writing on Dostoevsky will clearly have to take account of Frank's unrivalled and henceforth fundamental work—a biography both of Dostoevsky and of his writing. . . . The book as a whole demonstrates . . . high sensitivity to literary values, . . . scrupulous historical scholarship, and . . . sane lucidity of judgment. Frank has set a standard that no single book on the subject in any language can match, or is likely to for a long time to come."

CA INTERVIEW

CA interviewed Joseph Frank by telephone on June 29, 1989, in Stanford, California.

CA: For the past twenty years or so you've been working primarily on Dostoevsky, but you were first known as a literary critic and the writer of the essays collected in The Widening Gyre: Crisis and Mastery in Modern Literature. *Both the epigraph and name for that book come from a quotation from William Butler Yeats's "The Second Coming": "Turning and turning in the widening gyre/The falcon cannot hear the falconer." Does that idea stay with you?*

FRANK: Yes. This is one of the problems of modern culture as a whole, and I think since then it's become a major theme in literature and in the culture in general, in philosophy as well as in the arts. I was concerned with it then and I still am, although I don't have much time to work on it. The fact is that right now I'm beginning to collect material for another volume of essays. I have a volume of Russian essays coming out in January 1990, and I'm now collecting a lot of the other material I wrote over the years, some things as far back as the fifties. I want to reprint my original essay, "Spatial Form in Modern Literature," published first in the *Sewanee Review* in 1945, along with several other essays on the same issues which I wrote about thirty years later. I'd like to bring all that out as a new volume of essays, for which I don't yet have a title.

CA: In "Spatial Form in Modern Literature," which appears as the first essay in The Widening Gyre, *you say that such writers as James Joyce, T. S. Eliot, Ezra Pound, Marcel Proust, and Djuna Barnes should be read "spatially in a moment of time, rather than as a sequence." Since readers normally read sequentially, doesn't this pose a serious problem?*

FRANK: I think the way in which they write and the organization which they give to their own works in a sense force a reader

to read in that way without paying too much attention to the time nature of language, which works as a sequence. In reading these writers, you see that they themselves break up language in such a way that the reader has to make connections between all kinds of things which are disconnected in the works and which don't follow in any kind of linear order. I think the reason that essay had such an effect is that a lot of people who read it and who had been baffled as to how to make sense out of works of that kind suddenly saw that they had to read them in a different way, and that, if they read them in this way, they could obtain a certain kind of coherence from them which they hadn't had in their earlier contact.

CA: Then a reader almost has to be trained to read in a new way?

FRANK: In a way, I think, contemporary literature has retrained all the generations of readers who read it. And if you read some of the accounts of the early reception of those works, you see all the complaints about incoherence and incomprehensibility. These gradually vanished as readers learned how to read these writers. I gave in "Spatial Form" a kind of formula for what had to be done on the part of the reader by returning to the classic issues that were raised in Gotthold Lessing's *Laocoon*. I'm now collecting material on that; I'm now going back and looking at some of these problems again. There is a considerable literature which has accumulated around my own essay!

CA: Yes. In fact, almost thirty years after that essay was first published, you replied to your critics in the September 1973 issue of Critical Inquiry. *One of the points you made in "Spatial Form" is that cultures undergo alternations between naturalistic art and non-naturalistic art. Do you suppose in the next fifty years or so we'll shift back to naturalism?*

FRANK: It's hard to say. I was using there the conceptions of the German art historian Wilhelm Worringer, who writes about huge expanses of time and the relation between Egyptian art and Greek art and so forth. Shifts of this kind required hundreds and hundreds of years, if not longer. However, everything is speeded up in modernity, so it may take much less time. I think there is a return in the plastic arts to a certain kind of naturalism, or at least of figuration, and I would say that some of the elements of what's called post-modernism would seem to go along those lines. However, I wouldn't like to make any predictions.

CA: How did you happen to run across Worringer?

FRANK: He's very important in the development of English literature. Around the time of the First World War he was read by T. E. Hulme, who translated some of his essays and wrote about him. This work was then picked up by Eliot and Pound and by Herbert Read later on. Worringer definitely was an influence of some importance on the whole evolution of Anglo-American writing around the time of the first war. His name was around in a lot of the writings of the people I was reading as I was growing up.

CA: Back in the 1950s and '60s you were concerned with existentialism. It seems now to be fading in interest among philosophers.

FRANK: That's true at least of existentialism as a coherent movement, which existed in the West largely as a result of Sartre's influence. However, one must look at the influence of Nietzsche and Heidegger, as well as Kierkegaard, whose work had a great impact on Heidegger. I would say that even though a lot of contemporary European thinkers have rejected existentialism or stopped using the term as some kind of slogan, actually all the existential themes and the work of the fathers of existentialism as a way of thought are very much alive in the current scene. The issues it raised are still there and are extremely important, even though the people who tackle them will do it in rather a different way.

CA: Much of your earlier writing was about Western European and American writers, and then your interest began to shift to Eastern Europe and Russia. What brought about the change?

FRANK: That's very much related to my interest in existentialism. I had always read Russian literature, like everybody else, but I was not a specialist in it and I didn't know Russian. Dostoevsky's work is the precursor of literary existentialism to a large extent; it was looked on in that way in the writings of the French existentialists. I started reading him seriously out of my interest in the existentialist interpretation. Then I began to realize all the limitations of that interpretation, became interested in Russian culture, and started to analyze how the problems in the works of Dostoevsky arose out of the issues in Russian culture. All those issues are existential; however, I began to be interested in the special coloring and the special ways in which they arose in Russian culture. I think Russian culture of the mid- and late nineteenth-century is an important precursor of the existential issues which arise in modern culture.

CA: You were beginning this work, I believe, when you delivered the Christian Gauss Lectures at Princeton in the mid-1950s.

FRANK: Exactly. I gave the Gauss Lectures on existentialism, beginning with Dostoevsky's *Notes from Underground*. It was that which got me started on my work on Dostoevsky. I began to wonder about the problems in that work, and I was led on and on and on.

CA: In the preface to the first volume of your Dostoevsky biography, Dostoevsky: The Seeds of Revolt, 1821-1849, *you say that your work is not a conventional biography since you have proceeded from the author's works to his life rather than the reverse. Do you think that approach should be the general rule for literary biographers?*

FRANK: That's a complicated issue. I think the real reason, after all, that we're interested in the life of a writer—aside from curiosity about people in general—is that he was a writer. If we don't learn anything about the books from the account of his life, then I don't much see the point.

CA: Then a biography becomes merely anecdotal?

FRANK: It becomes anecdotal, or it becomes a psychological study which could as well be done of any other kind of individual. So it seems to me that in the case of the life of a great writer, the focus ought to be on those elements in the life which help to illuminate the work itself. Or it ought to be on those elements in the whole cultural context that do so. And I think this (the social-cultural context) is much more important in the case of Russian culture and the works of Dostoevsky than the facts of his personal life. In my work on Dostoevsky I've been concerned with the interaction of the personal, the social-cultural, and the literary, and I've attempted to combine all of those in the books with the aim of illuminating Dostoevsky's work in this way.

CA: When you came to the second volume of the biography, Dostoevsky: The Years of Ordeal, 1850-1859, *did you find this approach somewhat difficult to follow since your subject was in prison and not so involved in literary activity?*

FRANK: He was involved in literary activity to a certain extent, and I used as much of that as I was able to. Although I wasn't writing primarily about books themselves, still I attempted to analyze all the events of this period of his life in relation to how he would later use the experience in his books. My eye was always on how this was going to operate in the literary context. There were complaints on the part of some critics that I wasn't giving enough attention to his private life or I was underplaying certain elements of his romantic life. I would agree with them. That was my intent. I wanted to focus on the other aspects of his life, which seemed to me more pertinent for what would later enter into his important novels.

CA: As you've continued to write your biography, have you found that you've had to change some of your original ideas about your approach?

FRANK: Not fundamentally, but each of the books has posed different issues and I have had to concern myself with things I hadn't thought about in advance. From that point of view, I would say that each of the works has involved some shift. On the other hand, I wouldn't say that there was a fundamental change in my own point of view. As I've gone along, of course, I have learned all kinds of things I wasn't aware of in the beginning. One of the most important is that Dostoevsky had rather been given a raw deal as a personality. Even though he wasn't a more likeable man, it seemed to me as I read through the source material that he was really a more decent one than I would have thought from reading the earlier works about him. However, I don't argue the point; this is not my focus anyway. Although I attempt to work this into my approach, it's not at all a major issue in anything I write about him.

CA: I've read that in fact you've already written the complete biography. Is that true?

FRANK: I have a sketch of the whole work, yes. I began to write it as a work in one volume; I hadn't thought I would embark on a large work of the kind I'm writing. So I do have a sketch of the whole thing in outline, much smaller than what it will become later on.

CA: When you made the shift from English and American literature to Russian, was there any feeling on the part of the Slavists that you were encroaching on their territory?

FRANK: Not at all. As a matter of fact, they have been wonderful; they haven't resented anything at all that I have done. I learned Russian so that I could use all the material available. All of them have been immensely helpful and even have been grateful for all the work I have done. In the reception of the work, of course, there are people who don't agree with me. However, I've been handled with great respect. I don't have any complaints—quite the opposite; I was amazed at how helpful everybody was and how much I was encouraged to continue my work.

CA: You've relied heavily on the Constance Garnett translations of Dostoevsky's work. Has that been a surprise to a lot of people?

FRANK: I don't know; it may have. The fact is, there are no translations which are really perfect. Over and over again I use two or three of them and I've been doing it lately on material I'm working on now. And once again I find that Constance Garnett seems to be a lot closer to the original than some of the other translators who read better, if you will, who read more smoothly, and yet who, to achieve that smoothness, have taken more liberties and caused the exact meaning, so far as one can establish it, to be lost. I want certain kinds of nuances in my quotations which are very close to the original, and often Garnett comes closest of all to what I think is the meaning of the text. This is confirmed over and over again. On the other hand, she edits occasionally, she leaves things out, so you have to read her carefully also.

CA: And of course you can make your own translations.

FRANK: Yes, but I like to base my quotes on standard versions. I often combine a few of them as I go along, but Garnett is the basis of all the quotes I have of material that she has translated.

CA: I heard the biographer Ernest J. Simmons speak some years ago, and after the lecture I asked him what writer the Russians revered more than any other. With almost no hesitation he said, "Pushkin."

FRANK: I would certainly agree with him.

CA: What do the Russians think of Dostoevsky?

FRANK: Everybody has read him, there's no doubt about that. For one thing, he's taught in the high schools, so anybody who goes to school has some contact with his work. There are a lot of people who don't like his work or who think he's exaggerated and melodramatic. On the other hand, there are an awful lot of people who admire him enormously. I don't think it's possible to answer that question with some overall statement. But his works are published in huge editions in the Soviet Union, and everybody reads him.

CA: Wasn't he very much in disfavor, though, at one time?

FRANK: He was, for quite a while after the Revolution. I've stated over and over again in some of the other writings of mine about him that he is the greatest opponent of the intellectual underpinnings of the present regime, the Bolshevist regime. He was the opponent in his lifetime of the men who were the fathers of Soviet culture, which has very little to do with Marxism in the Western sense. He was their enemy, except in his early writings, when he was definitely under Socialist influence.

CA: Three volumes of the Dostoevsky biography are now out. How long do you think it will be before the next one appears?

FRANK: I wish I could answer that! I've been working on the fourth, and I've been having a lot of problems with it. It's been held up for quite a while. For one thing, I left Princeton and came to Stanford, and that involved rethinking the courses I was teaching; that absorbed a lot of my time and I wasn't able to work on the biography as intensively as I had in my last years at Princeton, where everything was routine, in a way. Also, going to a new job and all the rest, even at my age, involves all kinds of problems that take extra time you don't have to worry about in a familiar routine. I think this has stopped some of the work on the book. But I hope to get it on the rails again. I've written about a quarter of it, I would say, and I hope to continue from here on out.

CA: So you're at Stanford on a permanent basis now?

FRANK: Yes. I'm retired from Princeton and I'm on the faculty at Stanford. I spend the fall in Princeton and come here in the early winter. It's very nice. Next year my wife and I (she also teaches) will be taking the whole year off, so I won't be coming here at all; I'll be going to Europe in mid-year. After that, it will depend on how things are. I'm now officially retired from Stanford too, at the age of seventy. However, I've been asked to continue here at my convenience, and I'd like to keep my hand in a little bit, so I will be doing some teaching and I can work on my writing. That's what I hope to do in the future.

BIOGRAPHICAL/CRITICAL SOURCES:

PERIODICALS

Commentary, March, 1977.
Commonweal, May 13, 1977.
Critical Inquiry, September, 1973.
Hudson Review, spring, 1985.
Los Angeles Times Book Review, May 20, 1984, May 31, 1987.
New Republic, November 20, 1976.
New Statesman, April 13, 1984.
Newsweek, January 23, 1984.
New Yorker, September 12, 1977.
New York Review of Books, November 11, 1976, September 25, 1986.
New York Times Book Review, November 21, 1976, January 1, 1984, August 31, 1986.
Philosophy and Literature, fall, 1984.
Saturday Review, January-February, 1984.
Sewanee Review, April, 1985, April, 1988.
Time, January 30, 1984.
Times (London), April 12, 1984.
Times Literary Supplement, September 30, 1977, October 30-November 5, 1987.
Virginia Quarterly Review, autumn, 1977.
Washington Post Book World, January 2, 1977, November 16, 1986.

—*Sketch by Anne Janette Johnson*

—*Interview by Walter W. Ross*

*   *   *

FRASER, Stewart Erskine   1929-

PERSONAL: Born January 7, 1929, in Tianjin, China; children: five. *Education:* University of Melbourne, B.Com., 1951, B.Ed., 1959; Oxford University, B.A., 1955, M.A., 1959; Stanford University, M.A., 1956; University of Colorado, Ed.D., 1961; University of London, Ph.D., 1970.

ADDRESSES: Office—Centre for International Comparative Education, School of Education, La Trobe University, Bundoora, Victoria, Australia 3095.

CAREER: Research officer, Australia Department of Defense, 1950-55; Englehart High School, Ontario, teacher of social studies, 1955-56; research officer, Australia Department of Defense, 1956-57; University of Melbourne, Melbourne, Australia, senior tutor in political science, 1958-60; Harvard University, Cambridge, Mass., assistant director of international office, 1961-62; George Peabody College for Teachers of Vanderbilt University, Nashville, Tenn., professor of international and comparative education, 1962-75, director of International Center, 1963-75; La Trobe University, Bundoora, Victoria, Australia, professor of education, 1975—.

MEMBER: National Education Association, National Association for Foreign Students Affairs, Comparative Education Society, Phi Delta Kappa, Kappa Delta Pi.

WRITINGS:

(Editor) *Jullien's Plan for Comparative Education, 1816-1817,* Teachers College Press, 1964.

(Editor) *Chinese Communist Education: Records of the First Decade,* Vanderbilt University Press, 1965.

Pacific Lands and Antarctica, Prentice-Hall, 1965.

(Editor) *Governmental Policy and International Education,* Wiley, 1965.

(Editor) Birdsey Northrop, *The Evils of a Foreign Education; or Birdsey Northrop on Education Abroad, 1873,* Peabody International Center, 1966.

Research in International Education, 1966-67, Institute of International Education, 1967.

(Compiler and editor with William W. Brickman) *A History of International and Comparative Education: Nineteenth-Century Documents,* Scott, Foresman, 1968.

(With Bragi S. Josephson) *Education in Iceland,* Peabody International Center, 1968.

(Editor and compiler) *American Education in Foreign Perspectives: Twentieth-Century Essays,* Wiley, 1969.

(Editor) *International Education: Understandings and Misunderstandings,* Peabody International Center, 1969.

(Editor and compiler) *Education and Communism in China: An Anthology of Commentary and Documents,* International Studies Group (Hong Kong), 1969.

A Study on North Korean Education under Communism since 1945, two volumes, Peabody International Center, 1969.

(Editor) *Ludvig Holberg's Memoirs: A Danish Eighteenth-Century Contribution to International Understanding,* two volumes, E. J. Brill, 1970.

British Commentary on American Education: A Select and Annotated Bibliography, the Nineteenth and Twentieth Centuries, London University Institute of Education, 1970.

Sex, Schools and Society: International Perspectives, Aurora Publishers, 1972.

(With Hsu Kuang-ung) *Chinese Education and Society: A Bibliographic Guide; the Cultural Revolution and Its Aftermath,* International Arts and Sciences Press, 1972.

(With others) *North Korean Education and Society: A Select and Partially Annotated Bibliography Pertaining to the Democratic People's Republic of Korea,* London University Institute of Education, 1972.

(With Barbara J. Fraser) *Scandinavian Education: A Bibliography of English-Language Materials,* International Arts and Science Press, 1973.

A Glimpse of China through Poster Art, Aurora Publishers, 1973.

(Co-author) *Taxonomical Guide to International Educational Objectives,* Phi Delta Kappa, 1973.

One Hundred Great Chinese Posters, Images Graphiques, 1976.

(With B. J. Fraser) *Population, Education and Children's Futures: Austral-Asian Perspectives,* Kyung Hee University Press, 1983.

China: Population, Education, and People, La Trobe University, 1987.

The Quality of Life of the World's Children: Pacific Rim Perspectives, La Trobe University, 1988.

Also author with B. J. Fraser of *The Story of Where Babies Come From,* 1988.

*   *   *

FRAZIER, Claude A(lbee) 1920-

PERSONAL: Born April 15, 1920, in Knoxville, Tenn.; son of Claude (a physician) and Nina (Toney) Frazier; married Karen

Bryson, August 31, 1957. *Education:* West Virginia Institute of Technology, B.S. (cum laude); Medical College of Virginia, M.D. *Religion:* Baptist.

ADDRESSES: Home—347 Vanderbilt Rd., Asheville, N.C. 28801. *Office*—4C Doctors Park, Asheville, N.C. 28801.

CAREER: Licensed to practice medicine in North Carolina; internship at Medical College of Virginia, Richmond; residency at Johns Hopkins University, Baltimore, Md.; residency in pediatrics at Children's Hospital, Washington, D.C.; now in private practice in Asheville, N.C.; Memorial Mission Hospital, Asheville, staff member, 1971—; St. Joseph's Memorial Hospital, Asheville, currently staff member. Regional consultant, Children's Asthma Hospital and Research Institute. Diplomate, American Board of Allergy and Immunology. Host of weekly television Sunday school program on WSPA-TV, Spartanburg, S.C., and of weekly radio program, "Teachers' Tips" on WMIT and WFGW radio, Black Mountain, N.C. Member of advisory board, *Today's Child.*

MEMBER: International Association of Allergology (fellow), American College of Allergists (fellow), American Academy of Allergy (fellow), American College of Chest Physicians, American Academy of Pediatrics (fellow), American Medical Writers Association.

AWARDS, HONORS: Hal M. Davison Memorial Award, Southeastern Allergy Association, 1964; West Virginia Institute of Technology alumnus of the year award, 1970; American Medical Association award for continuing studies to physicians, 1970; numerous awards for scientific exhibits.

WRITINGS:

Insect Allergy: Allergic and Toxic Reactions to Insects and Other Arthropods, Warren H. Green, 1969, 2nd edition, 1987.

Devotionals by a Physician, C. C Thomas, 1970.

Surgery and the Allergic Patient, C. C Thomas, 1971.

Through the Bible with a Physician, C. C Thomas, 1971.

Parents' Guide to Allergy in Children, Doubleday, 1973.

Coping with Food Allergy: Symptoms and Treatment, Quadrangle, 1974, revised edition, Times Books, 1985.

Psychosomatic Aspects of Allergy, Van Nostrand, 1977.

Sniff, Sniff, Al-er-gee (juvenile), illustrated by Paul H. Carlson, Johnny Reads, 1978.

Coping and Living with Allergies: A Complete Guide to Help Allergy Patients of All Ages, Prentice-Hall, 1980.

(With F. K. Brown) *Insects and Allergy and What to Do about Them,* University of Oklahoma Press, 1980.

EDITOR

Should Doctors Play God?, Broadman, 1971.

What Did the Bible Mean?, Broadman, 1971.

Notable Personalities and Their Faith, Independence Press, 1972.

Should Preachers Play God?, Independence Press, 1973.

Games Doctors Play, C. C Thomas, 1973.

Dentistry and the Allergic Patient, C. C Thomas, 1973.

Is It Moral to Modify Man?, C. C Thomas, 1973.

Faith Healing: Finger of God? or, Scientific Curiosity?, Thomas Nelson, 1973.

Doctor's Guide to Better Tennis and Health, Crowell, 1974.

Current Therapy of Allergy, Medical Examination Publishing, 1974, 2nd edition, 1978.

Mastering the Art of Winning Tennis, Pagurian, 1974.

Politics and Religion Can Mix!, Broadman, 1974.

Healing and Religious Faith, United Church Press, 1974.

What Faith Has Meant To Me, Westminster Press, 1975.

Self Assessment of Current Knowledge in Allergy, Medical Examination Publishing, 1976, reprinted as *Self-assessment of Current Knowledge in Allergy and Clinical Immunology*, 1981.

Occupational Asthma, Van Nostrand, 1980.

OTHER

Contributor to *Current Therapy*, edited by Howard F. Conn, Saunders; *Allergy and Immunology, Current Diagnosis*, edited by Howard F. Conn and Rex B. Conn, Jr., Saunders; *Current Pediatric Therapy*, edited by Sydney S. Gellis, and B. M. Kagan, Saunders; contributor to numerous other medical books. Writer of weekly Sunday school lessons for *Asheville Citizen and Times, Ironton Tribune*, and *Biblical Recorder*. Contributor to religious and medical publications. Guest editor, *CUTIS*, July, 1968, and *Clinical Symposia*, July-September, 1968; editor, *Bi-annual Review of Allergy*, 1979-80, and *Annual Review of Allergy;* religious books editor, *Asheville Citizen and Times;* member of editorial board, *Clinical Toxology;* former editor of allergy section, *Southern Medical Journal.*

* * *

FREDE, Richard 1934-
(Jocko Frederics, Macdowell Frederics, Oliver McNab)

PERSONAL: Born March 20, 1934, in Albany, NY; son of Henry (a manufacturer) and Helene (an advertising writer; maiden name, Spooner) Frede; married Judy Zwerdling, April, 1964 (divorced, 1966); married Barbara Trautenberg, April 16, 1967 (divorced, 1979); children: Michael Ari, Benjamin Dov. *Education:* Yale University, B.A., 1955. *Avocational interests:* Politics, tennis, skiing, flying, painting, music, cooking.

ADDRESSES: Home and office—58 Concord St., Peterborough, NH 03458. *Agent*—Henry Dunow, Curtis Brown Ltd., 10 Astor Pl., New York, NY 10003.

CAREER: Writer, photographer, sculptor. Writer for *Sports Illustrated*, New York City, 1955-56.

MEMBER: PEN, Authors Guild, Dramatists Guild.

AWARDS, HONORS: Recipient of six MacDowell Colony fellowships, 1956-61.

WRITINGS:

Entry E (novel), Random House, 1958.
The Interns (novel), Random House, 1960.
(Under pseudonym Jocko Frederics) *Every Body's Ready to Die* (novel), Holt, 1966, also published as *Ready to Die.*
The Secret Circus (novel), Random House, 1967.
Coming-Out Party (novel), Random House, 1969.
(Under pseudonym Macdowell Frederics) *Emergency Procedure*, Coward-McCann, 1970.
(Under pseudonym Macdowell Frederics) *Black Work*, Crowell, 1976.
(Contributor) *Graven Images* (includes novella "Oh Lovelee Appearance of the Lass from the North Countree"), Nelson, 1977.
The Pilots (novel), Random House, 1977.
(Under pseudonym Oliver McNab) *Horror Story*, Houghton, 1979.
The Nurses (novel), Houghton, 1985.

Also author of four unproduced screenplays. Contributor of poetry and short stories to *Harper's, McCall's, Ramparts, Gallery,*

American Pen, Short Story International, Fantasy and Science Fiction, and *American Scholar;* contributor of articles to *Publishers Weekly, New York Times Book Review, Country Journal,* and other periodicals.

MEDIA ADAPTATIONS: The Interns was made into two movies, *The Interns,* 1962, and *The New Interns,* 1964, and into a television series, airing 1971-72.

SIDELIGHTS: Since the appearance of his first novel in 1958, Richard Frede has been noted for the precision and perception he brings to his characters. In *Entry E,* for instance, the story of a college undergraduate's moral struggle, "the character analysis, the language and the conversational interchanges between the characters, catch the flavor of the modern collegian . . . so sharply that you gasp at the accuracy and insight," C. E. Kilpatrick asserts in *Library Journal. Nation* contributor Richard Schickel, although he faults Frede for "overreaching his technical competence," likewise states that the novel "is the best fictional statement so far on the plight of the . . . [silent] generation." " 'Entry E' is a pretty convincing study of a type not easy for me to understand, the young man without commitments," Granville Hicks remarks in *Saturday Review.* "It is also a disturbing portrayal of college life. . . . Frede seems to me to have made significant contribution to the genre."

Similarly, in two novels about the medical profession, *The Interns* and *The Nurses,* Frede presents a realistic portrait of the individuals involved in saving lives. *The Interns,* writes F. G. Slaughter in the *New York Times Book Review,* "pictures a cross-section of medical life which, if not exactly typical, is still sharply revealing." Patricia Seidenbaum, in her *Los Angeles Times Book Review* critique of *The Nurses,* also observes that "Frede's ability to describe both the hospital work and the people doing it is remarkably on target." While she criticizes the book for approaching "soap opera" at times, Seidenbaum nevertheless states that "the [medical] situations are real, accurate and dramatic." "[Frede] succeeds notably in lifting the individual stories out of the ferment of the highly populated hospital background," Rose Feld comments in her *New York Herald Tribune Book Review* article on *The Interns.* While novels about doctors "are always fascinating," the critic concludes, "this one is particularly so by virtue of its breadth and depth of content."

BIOGRAPHICAL/CRITICAL SOURCES:

PERIODICALS

Book Week, July 2, 1967.
Library Journal, July, 1958.
Los Angeles Times Book Review, December 1, 1985.
Nation, June 28, 1958.
New York Herald Tribune Book Review, June 15, 1958; May 1, 1960.
New York Times Book Review, April 17, 1960; July 25, 1976.
Saturday Review, May 24, 1958.

* * *

FREDERICS, Jocko
See FREDE, Richard

* * *

FREDERICS, Macdowell
See FREDE, Richard

FRIESEN, Patrick 1945-

PERSONAL: Born July 5, 1945, in Steinbach, Manitoba, Canada; son of Franz (a carpenter), and Margaret (Sawatzky) Friesen; married Carol Ann Greenaway (a librarian), May 9, 1970; children: Marijke, Nikolaus. *Education:* University of Manitoba, B.A. (with honors), 1969.

ADDRESSES: Home—Winnipeg, Manitoba, Canada.

CAREER: Teacher at public schools in Selkirk, Manitoba, 1972-78; Manitoba Educational Television, producer/director, 1979—. Writer, 1958—.

MEMBER: League of Canadian Poets (member of executive committee, 1980—), Playwrights Union of Canada, Manitoba Writers Guild (president, 1981-83), Manitoba Association of Playwrights.

AWARDS, HONORS: Grants from Manitoba Arts Council, 1978, 1983; award from Manitoba Branch of American Federation of Television and Radio Artists for best long radio documentary, 1981, for "Who Is George Forest?"; award of merit from AMTEC, 1983, for "Esther Warkov: A Spy in the House"; also recipient of other film and radio awards.

WRITINGS:

POEMS

the lands i am, Turnstone Press, 1976.
bluebottle, Turnstone Press, 1978.
The Shunning (also see below), Turnstone Press, 1980.
Unearthly Horses, Turnstone Press, 1984.
Flicker and Hawk, Turnstone Press, 1987.

FILM SCRIPTS

"Impressions," Manitoba Department of Education, 1979.
"Don Proch: The Works," Manitoba Department of Education, 1984.

Also producer of the film *Ester Warkov: A Spy in the House,* producer, director, and writer of the film *Don Proch: The Spirit of Assesippi,* producer and director of the film *Patrick Lane,* director of the film *A Ritual of Horses,* and director of other films, videos, and radio programs.

OTHER

"The Shunning" (play based on *The Shunning;* first produced at Prairie Theatre Exchange, October, 1985), published in *New Works* (anthology), Playwrights Union of Canada, 1987.
(With choreographer Stephanie Ballard) "Anna," produced at the Gas Station Theatre in Winnipeg, Manitoba, in June, 1987.
(With others) "Noah," produced at the Main/Access Gallery, Winnipeg, in fall, 1987.

Also author of "Who Is George Forest?", first broadcast by Canadian Broadcasting Corp. (CBC), of "Esther Warkov: A Spy in the House," and of numerous radio programs. Poetry editor of *Contemporary Verse II,* 1979. *Border Crossings,* poetry editor, 1985-87, member of editorial board, 1986-87.

SIDELIGHTS: Patrick Friesen commented: "It seems to me that all writers probably write out of the need to tell their individual stories, even if the stories have been told before. No two stories are identical. By story, I mean literally stories, ideas, desires, the process of a life, or the moments of silence in the process. While one poet writes his way to Lhasa, the next may be writing his way out of Seven Persons, Canada. A writer writes

from his own biography. His foundation is what he knows. Anything can be built on this base, in any style, with any spelling of words. As long as the whole business comes out of what the writer is and knows. As long as the writer moves toward what he doesn't know, which may be something he once knew.

"A writer must write for people. It is important that a writer not slavishly shape his work on some perceived expectations of readers, but it is equally important that, through his words, he make and maintain contact with readers. He must not write for critics, though in fact critics can sometimes help a writer.

"My own circumstances were not unique, though not everyone shares them. I was born to Mennonite parents in a small Mennonite town. Right there is half the story of my life: the conflict of rejecting what the parents believe yet not the parents themselves; of discovering that not everything in their beliefs should be rejected; of finding a place to stand, a ground that is mine, not what I have been given as inheritance; of recognizing the poet in me who cannot accept or reject any beliefs or thoughts or ideas based on where on the popularity spectrum they happen to sit at any given time. I am not a Mennonite poet, rather a poet of Mennonite background.

"*The Shunning* was a explicit exploration of that Mennonite background, particularly of the violence inherent in the Mennonite doctrine of the excommunication and shunning of members who do not conform closely enough to accepted faith and/or practice. This may be a paradox in a religious group founded on, among other things, nonresistance and nonviolence. *The Shunning* also tried to explore the biblical injunction, 'to be in this world, not of this world.'

"*Unearthly Horses* was attempted as a bridge over the space between the personal and public history. It is also a reminiscence about my father, a look at what our relationship was/wasn't, and how it was partly defined by outside authority. The book begins to sing of eternity behind the glass."

Friesen added: "I have an interest in films and have directed one film on Canadian artist Don Proch, and another on poet Patrick Lane. I produced a film on Esther Warkov, Canadian painter, and I have produced, directed, and written numerous radio programs."

*   *   *

FRISCH, Max (Rudolf) 1911-

PERSONAL: Born May 15, 1911, in Zurich-Hottingen, Switzerland; son of Franz Bruno (an architect) and Lina (Wildermuth) Frisch; married Gertrud Anna Constance von Meyenburg, July 30, 1942 (divorced, 1959); married Marianne Oellers, December, 1968 (divorced); children: (first marriage) Ursula, Hans Peter, Charlotte. *Education:* Attended University of Zurich, 1931-33; Federal Institute of Technology, Zurich, diploma in architecture, 1940.

ADDRESSES: Home—CH-6611 Berzona Tessin, Switzerland.

CAREER: Free-lance journalist for various Swiss and German newspapers, including *Neue Zuercher Zeitung* and *Frankfurter Zeitung,* beginning 1933; architect in Zurich, Switzerland, 1945-55; full-time writer, 1955—. *Military service:* Swiss Army, 1939-45, served as cannoneer and later as border guard on the Austrian and Italian frontiers.

MEMBER: Deutsche Akademie fuer Sprache und Dichtung, Akademie der Kuenste, PEN, American Academy and Institute of Arts and Letters (honorary member), American Academy of Arts and Sciences (honorary member), Comunita degli Scrittori.

AWARDS, HONORS: Conrad Ferdinand Meyer Prize, 1938; Rockefeller Foundation grant for drama, 1951; Georg Buechner Prize, German Academy of Language and Poetry, 1958; Literature Prize of the City of Zurich, 1958; Literature Prize of Northrhine-Westphalia, 1963; Prize of the City of Jerusalem, 1965; Grand Prize, Swiss Schiller Foundation, 1974; Peace Prize, German Book Trade, 1976; Commandeur de l'Ordre des Arts et des Lettres, 1985; Common Wealth Award, Modern Language Association of America, 1986; International Neustadt Prize for Literature, University of Oklahoma, 1987. Has received honorary doctorates from the City University of New York, 1982, Bard College, Philipps University, Marburg, West Germany, and Technische Universitaet, Berlin.

WRITINGS:

NOVELS

Juerg Reinhart: Eine sommerliche Schicksalsfahrt, Deutsche Verlags-Anstalt, 1934, revised edition published as *J'adore ce qui me brule; oder, Die Schwierigen: Roman,* Atlantis (Zurich), 1943, 2nd revised edition published as *Die Schwierigen; oder, J'adore ce qui me brule,* Atlantis, 1957.

Antwort aus der Stille: Eine Erzaehlung aus den Bergen (title means "Answer Out of the Silence: A Tale from the Mountains"), Deutsche Verlags-Anstalt, 1937.

Bin; oder, Die Reise nach Peking, (title means "Am; or, the Trip to Peking"), Atlantis, 1945.

Stiller: Roman, Suhrkamp (Frankfurt on the Main), 1954, translation by Michael Bullock published as *I'm Not Stiller,* Abelard, 1958.

Homo Faber: Ein Bericht, Suhrkamp, 1957, translation by Bullock published as *Homo Faber: A Report,* Abelard, 1959.

Meine Name sei Gantenbein, Suhrkamp, 1964, translation by Bullock published as *A Wilderness of Mirrors,* Methuen, 1965, Random House, 1966.

Montauk: Eine Erzaehlung, Suhrkamp, 1975, translation by Geoffrey Skelton published as *Montauk,* Harcourt, 1976.

Der Mensch erscheint im Holozaen: Eine Erzaehlung, Suhrkamp, 1979, translation by Skelton published as *Man in the Holocene: A Story,* Harcourt, 1980.

Blaubart: Eine Erzaehlung, Suhrkamp, 1982, translation by Skelton published as *Bluebeard,* Harcourt, 1984.

PLAYS

Nun singen sie wieder: Versuch eines Requiems (two-act; title means "Now They Sing Again: An Attempt at a Requiem"; first produced in Zurich at the Schauspielhaus, March 29, 1945), Schwabe (Switzerland), 1946, translation by David Lommen published as "Now They Sing Again" in *Contemporary German Theatre,* edited by Michael Roloff, Avon, 1972.

Santa Cruz: Eine Romanz (five-act; first produced at the Schauspielhaus, March 7, 1946), Suhrkamp, 1946.

Die chinesische Mauer: Eine Farce (also see below; first produced at the Schauspielhaus, October 10, 1946), Schwabe, 1947, 2nd revised edition, 1972, translation by James L. Rosenberg published as *The Chinese Wall,* Hill & Wang, 1961.

Als der Kriege zu Ende war: Schauspiel (also see below; title means "When the War Was Over"; first produced at the Schauspielhaus, January 8, 1948), Schwabe, 1949, edited by Stuart Friebert, Dodd, 1967.

Graf Oederland: Ein Spiel in Zehn Bildern (also see below; title means "Count Oederland: A Play in Ten Scenes"; first pro-

duced at the Schauspielhaus, February 10, 1951; produced in Washington, D.C., at Arena Stage as "A Public Prosecutor Is Sick of It All," 1973), Suhrkamp, 1951, revised edition published as *Graf Oederland: Eine Moritat in zwoelf Bildern,* Suhrkamp, 1963, edited by George Salamon, Harcourt, 1966.

Don Juan; oder, die Liebe zur Geometrie: Eine Komoedie in fuenf Akten (also see below; title means "Don Juan; or, The Love of Geometry: A Comedy in Five Acts"; first produced at the Schauspielhaus, May 5, 1953), Suhrkamp, 1953.

Rip van Winkle: Hoerspiel (radio play; first produced in Germany, 1953), Reclam (Stuttgart), 1969.

Herr Biedermann und die Brandstifter: Hoerspiel (also see below; radio play; first produced in Germany, 1953; first stage adaptation produced as *Biedermann und die Brandstifter: Eine Lehrstueck ohne Lehre, mit einem Nachspiel* at the Schauspielhaus, March 29, 1958; produced in London as *The Fire Raisers,* 1961; produced at the Maidman Playhouse as *The Firebugs,* February, 1963), Suhrkamp, 1958, translation by Bullock published as *The Fire Raisers: A Morality without Moral, with an Afterpiece,* Methuen, 1962, translation by Mordecai Gorelick published as *The Firebugs: A Learning Play without a Lesson,* Hill & Wang, 1963.

Die grosse Wut des Philipp Hotz (also see below; one-act; first produced at the Schauspielhaus, March 29, 1958; produced at the Barbizon-Plaza Theatre as "The Great Fury of Philipp Hotz," November, 1969), translation published as "Philipp Hotz's Fury" in *Esquire,* October, 1962.

Andorra: Stueck in zwoelf Bildern (also see below; one-act radio play; first broadcast in West Germany, 1959; stage adaptation first produced at the Schauspielhaus, November 2, 1961; produced on Broadway at the Biltmore Theatre, February 9, 1963), Suhrkamp, 1962, translation by Bullock published as *Andorra: A Play in Twelve Scenes,* Hill & Wang, 1964.

Three Plays (contains "The Fire Raisers," "Count Oederland," and "Andorra"), translation by Bullock, Methuen, 1962.

Zurich-Transit: Skizze eines Films (television play; first produced on German television, January, 1966), Suhrkamp, 1966.

Biografie: Ein Spiel (also see below; two-act; first produced at the Schauspielhaus, February 1, 1968), Suhrkamp, 1967, revised edition, 1968, translation by Bullock published as *Biography: A Game,* Hill & Wang, 1969.

Three Plays (contains "Don Juan; or, the Love of Geometry," "The Great Rage of Philipp Hotz," and "When the War Was Over"), translation by J. L. Rosenberg, Hill & Wang, 1967.

Four Plays: The Great Wall of China, Don Juan; or, the Love of Geometry, Philipp Hotz's Fury, Biography: a Game, translation by Bullock, Methuen (London), 1969.

Triptychon: Drei szenische Bilder, Suhrkamp, 1978, translation by Skelton published as *Triptych: Three Scenic Panels,* Harcourt, 1981.

Also author of plays "Stahl" (title means "Steel"), 1927, and "Judith," 1948, and "Herr Quixote," a radio play, 1955.

OTHER

Geschrieben im Grenzdienst 1939, [Germany], 1940.

Blaetter aus dem Brotsack (diary; title means "Pages from the Knapsack"), Atlantis (Zurich), 1940, reprinted, 1969.

Marion und die Marionetten: Ein Fragment, Gryff-Presse (Basel, Switzerland), 1946.

Das Tagebuch mit Marion (title means "Diary with Marion"), Atlantis, 1947, revised and expanded version published as

Tagebuch, 1946-1949, Droemer Knaur (Munich), 1950, translation by Skelton published as *Sketchbook, 1946-49,* Harcourt, 1977.

(Author of annotations) Robert S. Gessner, *Sieben Lithographien,* Huerlimann (Zurich), 1952.

(With Lucius Burckhardt and Markus Kutter) *Achtung, die Schweiz: Ein Gespraech ueber unsere Lage und ein Vorschlag zur Tat,* Handschin (Basel), 1956.

(Author of foreword) Markus Kutter and Lucius Burckhardt, *Wir selber bauen unsere Stadt: Ein Hinweis auf die Moeglichkeiten staatlicher Baupolitik,* Handschin (Basel), 1956.

(With Burckhardt and Kutter) *Die Neue Stadt: Beitraege zur Diskussion,* Handschin, 1956.

(Author of afterword) Bertold Brecht, *Drei Gedichten,* [Zurich], 1959.

(Contributor) Albin Zollinger, *Gesammelte Werke,* Volume 1, Atlantis (Zurich), 1961.

Ausgewaehlte Prosa, edited by Stanley Corngold, Suhrkamp, 1961, Harcourt, 1968.

Stuecke, two volumes, Suhrkamp, 1962.

(Author of texts with Kurt Hirschfeld and Oskar Waelterlin) Teo Otto, *Skizzen eines Buehnenbildners: 33 Zeichnungen,* Tschudy (St. Gallen, Switzerland), 1964.

(Contributor) Alexander J. Seiler, *Siamo italiani/Die Italiener: Gespraeche mit italienischen Arbeitern in der Schweiz,* EVZ Verlag (Zurich), 1965.

(Author of preface) Gody Suter, *Die grossen Staedte: Was sie zerstoert und was sie retten kann,* Luebbe (Bergisch Gladbach, West Germany), 1966.

Oeffentlichkeit als Partner (essays), Suhrkamp, 1967.

Erinnerungen an Brecht, Friedenauer (West Berlin), 1968.

Dramaturgisches: Ein Briefwechsel mit Walter Hoellerer, Literarisches Colloquium (West Berlin), 1969.

(Author of postscript) Andrei Sakharov, *Wie ich mir die Zukunft vorstelle: Gedanken ueber Fortschritt, friedliche Koexistenz und geistige Freiheit,* Diogenes (Zurich), 1969.

(With Rudolf Immig) *Der Mensch zwischen Selbstentfremdung und Selbstverwirklichung,* Calwer (Stuttgart), 1970.

Glueck: Eine Erzaehlung, Brunnenturm-Presse, 1971.

Wilhelm Tell fuer die Schule, Suhrkamp, 1971.

Tagebuch, 1966-71, Suhrkamp, 1972, translation by Skelton published as *Sketchbook, 1966-71,* Harcourt, 1974.

Dienstbuchlein, Suhrkamp, 1974.

Stich-Worte, Suhrkamp, 1975.

(With Hartmut von Hentig) *Zwei Reden zum Friedenspreis des Deutschen Buchhandels 1976,* Suhrkamp, 1976.

Gesammelte Werke in zeitlicher Folge, six volumes, Suhrkamp, 1976.

Frisch: Kritik, Thesen, Analysen, Francke (Bern, Switzerland), 1977.

Erzaehlende Prosa, 1939-1979, Volk und Welt (West Berlin), 1981.

Stuecke, two volumes, Volk und Welt, 1981.

Forderungen des Tages, Suhrkamp, 1983.

Contributor to periodicals in West Germany and Switzerland, including *Neue Schweizer Rundschau, Der Spiegel,* and *Atlantis;* contributor to newspapers, including *Neue Zuercher Zeitung* and *Sueddeutsche Zeitung.*

SIDELIGHTS: Along with fellow Swiss dramatist Friedrich Duerrenmatt, Max Frisch "has been a major force in German drama for the generation since 1945," declares Arrigo Subiotto in *The German Theatre: A Symposium.* Best known for such works as *I'm Not Stiller* and *The Firebugs,* Frisch is esteemed as both a novelist and playwright. Winning numerous literary awards, including the Georg Buechner Prize and Neustadt International Prize, he has been a perennial candidate for the Nobel Prize for several years. His writing, characterized by its surrealistic style, "is a sort of poetry," remarks Joseph McLellan in the *Washington Post Book World,* "but a poetry of the mind rather than the senses—sparse and austere, with every detail chosen for its resonances." Several critics have commented on not only the remarkable consistency of this style, which *Dictionary of Literary Biography* contributor Wulf Koepke avers to be "discernable since the early 1940s," but also on Frisch's inventiveness in expressing "a single theme: the near impossibility of living truthfully," concludes Sven Birkerts in his *New Republic* article.

As a student of German literature at the University of Zurich, Frisch admired such writers as Albin Zollinger and Gottfried Keller. His father's death, however, made it necessary for him to leave school to support himself and his mother. Becoming a free-lance journalist for various German and Swiss newspapers, he traveled widely in Europe throughout the 1930s. During this time, Frisch also wrote fiction; but, as Koepke notes, he "grew increasingly disenchanted with his writing, and in 1937 he burned all his manuscripts." Opting for a more utilitarian career, he temporarily abandoned his writing goals to attend architecture classes at the Federal Institute of Technology in Zurich, where he received his diploma in 1940. However, he was not able to refrain totally from writing, and, while serving as a border guard in the Swiss army, he wrote *Juerg Reinhart: Eine sommerliche Schicksalsfahrt, Antwort aus der Stille: Eine Erzaehlung aus den Bergen, Blaetter aus dem Brotsack,* and *Bin; oder, die Reise nach Peking.*

These lesser-known works, considering they were written during the time of Hitler's Third Reich, "astound the reader by their absolutely apolitical character," observe Mona and Gerhard Knapp in *World Literature Today.* Frisch was by no means unconcerned with the war's effects, however. Characterized by *New York Times Book Review* contributor Richard Gilman as "politically liberal, a pacifist," the author "was very much aware of his own unique position regarding the war; as a Swiss, apparently unaffected by the conflict surrounding his own country, Frisch could only attempt to present the lessons of the war from a bipartisan point of view," observes Manfred Jurgensen in *Perspectives on Max Frisch.* This is precisely what the dramatist attempts to do in his first plays written after the war.

Invited in 1945 by the director of the Zurich Schauspielhaus, Kurt Hirschfeld, to write plays for his theater, the author's *Nun singen sie wieder: Versuch eines Requiems* ("Now They Sing Again: An Attempt at a Requiem") explores prejudice by placing characters from both the Axis and Ally countries into the world of the afterlife, where they become equals. In his next play about the war, *Als der Krieg zu Ende war* ("When the War Was Over"), Frisch writes of a German woman who falls in love with a Russian soldier, demonstrating, as Carol Petersen says in his book, *Max Frisch,* "that by true human feelings all kinds of prejudices can and must be overcome."

However, "Frisch has no real hope that [such social] evils can be remedied," remarks Koepke, and his plays and novels are therefore largely pessimistic. For example, in *The Theater of Protest and Paradox: Developments in the Avant-Garde Drama,* George Wellwarth asserts that "Frisch's two best plays, [*The Chinese Wall*] and [*The Firebugs: A Learning Play without a Lesson*], are consciously foredoomed pleas for a better world. The irony implicit in them no longer sounds like the scornful laughter of the gods we hear in Duerrenmatt; it sounds like the self-reproaching wailing of the damned." Underlying this pessimism is, as Jurgensen remarks, Frisch's frustration with "man's incorrigible selfishness and his inability or unwillingness to learn, to change, to think dynamically." According to Petersen, the lesson of *The Chinese Wall* is therefore that "freedom is only in the realm of the spirit; for, in the real world, the possessors of power end up by doing the same things over and over again."

Approaching this theme from another angle in what *World Literature Today* contributor Adolf Muschg calls Frisch's "most successful play internationally," *The Firebugs* creates a character who, instead of trying to prevent disaster, actually fosters it. In this play, a weak-willed hair lotion manufacturer named Gottlieb Biedermann is unable to admit to himself the true intentions of two arsonists, and knowingly allows them to enter and destroy his home. Several interpretations of the political implications of this play have been proposed, as Subiotto explains: "[The Firebugs] can be seen as a metaphor of Hitler's legitimate 'seizure of power' or of the way in which the nations of the world are playing with nuclear bombs as deterrents. . . . It also offers a 'model' of liberal societies allowing freedom of action, in the name of liberty, to extremist elements in their midst (whether of right or left) whose avowed aim is to destroy those societies." According to Koepke, the author endorses the interpretation that *The Firebugs* is about "the weakness of capitalist society." What is also significant about *The Firebugs* is how it further develops Frisch's "theme of the true identity behind an artificial mask, the destruction of false conventions, and the feeling of the self from deeply ingrained prejudices," writes Alex Natan in his introduction to *German Men of Letters: Twelve Literary Essays*.

One of the main obstacles to living truthfully, in Frisch's view, is the inability of people to accept their true identities. The theme of concealed or lost identity, then, has become the central theme of much of the author's work. Martin Esslin reveals in his *Reflections: Essays on Modern Theatre,* that this human shortcoming is for the author "the ultimate sin, the extinction of [people's] true existence, the origin of all the troubles of our time." And the main obstacle to this discovery of the true self are the images we create for ourselves and others to hide reality. In his diary, *Sketchbook, 1946-49,* Frisch summarizes his beliefs this way: "It is written: thou shalt make no graven images of God. But we can also understand the commandment thus: 'god' as that part of every human being which is intangible and ever-changing. To make graven images of each other is a sin which is committed against us and which we almost continually commit against others—except, that is, when we love." Because of his interest in this theme, the central character in many of Frisch's novels and plays, explicates *New York Times Book Review* critic George Stade, is often "either someone who tries to escape from himself, . . . or who writhes in the nets of definition others cast over him, . . . or who finds out, too late, that he is not what he took himself to be."

One example of such a play is *Andorra: A Play in Twelve Scenes,* which, along with *The Firebugs,* the Knapps say "catapulted [Frisch] to international theatrical prominence." *Andorra* revolves around the theme of anti-semitism to illustrate the imposition of images. The story concerns the deception of a schoolteacher, living in fictional Andorra, who hides the identity of his illegitimate son Andri by telling his neighbors that Andri is a Jewish boy whom he has saved from the oppressive "Blacks." With the increasing strength of the Blacks, the Andorrans begin to impose more and more stereotypes on Andri until he eventually accepts himself as Jewish. Even when he learns the truth about who he really is, however, Andri is unable to shed this false identity; and, when the Blacks invade Andorra, he chooses to die under their persecution.

The struggle for self-truth in a world which prefers the stereotypes and simplicity of the image to an authentic existence is also evident in *Don Juan; or, the Love of Geometry.* Here, in what Petersen calls "an uncommonly clever, wittily pointed play, which offers a broad view of the relativity of all human sentiment," Frisch twists the legend of Don Juan by describing Juan as a lover of geometry who is forced into the role of philanderer by the demands and expectations of society. He actually prefers the logic and precision of geometry to the capricious ways of the women who surround him. Compared to the traditional version of Don Juan, critics like Petersen believe that "the twentieth-century man, inclined to rationalism, can more readily recognize himself in Frisch's Don Juan."

The three novels that deal with the theme of identity on its most introspective, individual level are *I'm Not Stiller, Homo Faber: A Report,* and *A Wilderness of Mirrors.* Along with a number of other critics, Charles Hoffman, a contributor to *The Contemporary Novel in German: A Symposium,* feels that with these books, Frisch "has created three of the most important novels of [the mid-nineteenth century]. Taken together, these books are perhaps the most meaningful [in] recent German writing." The years in which they were written, from 1954 to 1964, were also "of singular importance in establishing Frisch's international reputation," add the Knapps.

Like *Don Juan, Homo Faber* appeals to the modern man, but on a much more serious note. Submerging himself in a love of technology over actual human emotions, Frisch's protagonist, engineer Walter Faber, unwittingly enters into a relationship with a woman whom he later discovers to be his illegitimate daughter. Because he cannot face the emotions that result from this discovery, Faber "is punished for his 'blindness' by her loss" when she dies of a snake bite, explain the Knapps. In this description of a man who becomes alienated from his own identity through his reverence for modern technology, "Frisch has captured that essential anguish of modern man which we find in the best of Camus," asserts Richard Plant in *Spectator.* But *Homo Faber* is also one of Frisch's more optimistic works because, notes Koepke, in the "last period of his life, characterized by a growing awareness of human existence, [Faber] not only comes into contact with his own past failures and their long-term consequences but also begins to see the truth of nontechnological realities."

I'm Not Stiller, which Michael Butler in his *The Novels of Max Frisch* says "established [for Frisch] a claim to major status in the history of the novel in post-war Germany and Switzerland," is his most critically acclaimed novel concerning the theme of escape from the self. Told mostly through the point-of-view of the sculptor Anatol Stiller, *I'm Not Stiller* is the story of a man who assumes the identity of an American named White in an effort to flee his feelings of failure as an artist, husband, and lover. Confronted with his true identity by the Swiss government, which has accused him of having worked with the Communists, Stiller is forced to face his true identity, and the resulting personal struggle that Frisch chronicles in Stiller's journal, "consumes not only all his own moral and artistic energy," say the Knapps, "but also that of his frail wife Julika, who soon dies." The last section of *I'm Not Stiller* is told by Stiller's prosecutor, who moralizes: "As long as a person does not accept himself, he will always have the fear of being misunderstood and misconstrued by his environment." Although some critics like Plant feel that the novel's "provocative idea [has] been spoiled . . . by excessive detail and overdecoration," a number of others think that *I'm Not Stiller* is one of Frisch's best works. Butler opines, for example, that in *I'm Not Stiller* "Frisch suddenly produced a narrative work of unsuspected depth and fascination."

In what Hoffman calls a "brilliant demonstration" of writing, *A Wilderness of Mirrors* also deals with the manipulation of identities in order to deal with emotional relationships. The most experimental of the three loosely related novels about identity, *A Wilderness of Mirrors* explores a multitude of plots while characters are cast and recast in a variety of roles. The extremely complex storyline of this book, however, has caused some critics, like *Observer* reviewer D. J. Enright, to remark that "for all the insights and vividness, the ponderous machinery [of the plot] is out of proportion to the final product." Others, like Butler, however, applaud the novel as "an intensely private exploration of personal dislocation and inadequacy."

Although Frisch's more recent works, *Montauk, Triptych: Three Scenic Panels,* and *Man in the Holocene,* address some of the usual Frisch themes, they "mark a turning point in his writing," claims Barbara Saunders in *Forum for Modern Language Studies. Triptychon* and *Man in the Holocene,* says Saunders, "substantiate Frisch's own assertion that he is 'finished' with the autobiographical form he used in such books as *I'm Not Stiller* and *Homo Faber.*" Saunders continues: "*Montauk* indicates the climax of a progression towards positive self-appraisal and has enabled Frisch to develop beyond the preoccupations of ambivalent personal identity." Frisch has given himself the opportunity to write about his own thoughts and experiences in this thinly veiled autobiographical book concerning an ageing writer's weekend with his American girlfriend. Ironically, though, some critics like *Book Forum* contributor Steven Kellman believe that in this book "it is to flee [his own identity] that the Swiss novelist finds himself in Montauk." The author writes in *Montauk* how this is due to a fear that his image as a writer has begun to obscure the real Max Frisch as if he were one of his own characters. In one chapter of the book, for example, he declares: "I have been serving up stories to some sort of public, and in these stories I have, I know, laid myself bare—to the point of non-recognition."

After *Montauk* the author's books betray his awareness of his advancing years. Koepke explains: "While in *Montauk* numerous quotes from Frisch's earlier works indicate self-acceptance, the past has become threatening in the last works. Old age and death are dominant themes, but even more prevalent may be regret of the past—one's own and that of the human race." For example, Jurgensen states that in *Triptychon* "Frisch shows . . . how all acts, thoughts, and misunderstandings are repeated in death; death becomes the stage for re-enacting our lives. The finality does not lie in death but in our unthinking life, in our inability to do anything other than repeat ourselves." "*Triptychon*'s real subject is a social death," Jurgensen concludes, "in fact: the death of society."

Jurgensen also notes that this pessimistic theme is similar to that in *The Firebugs;* and his next book, *Man in the Holocene,* also resembles *The Firebugs* in its "unsettling notion that some rational, well-meaning force is actually *willing* catastrophe," according to *Nation* reviewer Arthur Sainer. In what McLellan asserts to be "a small book but a major achievement," *Man in the Holocene* relates the last few days in the life of a ageing man named Geiser who becomes trapped in his alpine valley home by a landslide. Battling against his own encroaching senility and a dwindling food supply, Geiser ironically passes up the chance to escape his isolation, eventually suffering from a stroke before he finally dies. *Man in the Holocene,* like *Triptychon,* reiterates Frisch's suspicion of the transience of the human race. McLellan phrases it this way: In *Man in the Holocene* "the old man's life itself is being eroded, as are all men's lives—as is, perhaps, the life of the entire species."

Frisch returns to his more familiar theme of identity in *Bluebeard.* But, avers Sven Birkerts in a *New Republic* review, the author "is not so much returning to earlier themes as he is bringing the preoccupations of a lifetime under a more calculated and intense pressure." As in *I'm Not Stiller,* the story's events are related by the protagonist, Dr. Schaad, through his memories about his trial. This time, the main character is accused of being a wife murderer, like the infamous Bluebeard; and this role is forced upon him to the point where he eventually assimilates it. Marga I. Weigel notes the similarity between Dr. Schaad's identity crisis and that of another Frisch character. Writing in *World Literature Today,* Weigel observes: "[Dr. Schaad] works himself more and more into the role of the murderer. He is now convinced he is the person others consider him to be—an attitude identical to the reaction of Andri in *Andorra.*"

Similarities such as this in Frisch's work have been noted by other critics, but the resemblances of *Bluebeard* to other Frisch works do not detract from their value, according to Butler. In an article in the *Times Literary Supplement,* Butler comments: "Although Max Frisch can no longer avoid producing texts which are resonant of earlier achievements, this latest work demonstrates once again his skill in creating new and fascinating ways of exploring old truths." Birkerts also comments: "The structural and stylistic shifts [in the author's work] mark his maturing, the varying of his concerns, his need for increasingly direct statement. The man grows, but his is the same man." *Bluebeard,* like Frisch's other works, reminds the reader that "there is no simple prescription for truthful living," asserts Birkerts. Frisch, instead, desires to force people to think about what he is writing. As he declares in his *Sketchbook, 1946-49,* "I should consider that I had done my duty if I had put a question in such a way that from then on the members of the audience could not bear to live without the answer. But it must be their answer, their own, which they can provide only in the framework of their own lives."

MEDIA ADAPTATIONS: Homo Faber: A Report has been adapted for the screen by Paramount.

BIOGRAPHICAL/CRITICAL SOURCES:

BOOKS

Butler, Michael, *The Novels of Max Frisch,* Oswald Wolff, 1976.
Contemporary Literary Criticism, Gale, Volume 3, 1975, Volume 9, 1978, Volume 14, 1980, Volume 18, 1981, Volume 32, 1985, Volume 44, 1987.
Daemmrich, Horst S., and Diether H. Haenicke, *The Challenge of German Literature,* Wayne State University Press, 1971.
Dictionary of Literary Biography, Volume 69: *Contemporary German Fiction Writers,* Gale, 1988.
Esslin, Martin, *Reflections: Essays on Modern Theatre,* Doubleday, 1969.
Frisch, Max, *Sketchbook, 1946-49,* Harcourt, 1977.
Garten, Hugh Frederic, *Modern German Drama,* Methuen, 1959.
Hayman, Ronald, *The German Theatre: A Symposium,* Barnes & Noble, 1975.
Heitner, Robert R., editor, *The Contemporary Novel in German: A Symposium,* University of Texas Press, 1967.
Lumley, Frederick, *New Trends in 20th Century Drama,* Oxford University Press, 1967.
Natan, Alex, editor, *German Men of Letters: Twelve Literary Essays,* Volume 3, Oswald Wolff, 1968.

Petersen, Carol, *Max Frisch,* translated by Charlotte La Rue, Ungar, 1972.

Probst, Gerhard F., and Jay F. Bodine, editors, *Perspectives on Max Frisch,* University Press of Kentucky, 1982.

Weber, Brom, editor, *Sense and Sensibility in Twentieth-Century Writing,* Southern Illinois University Press, 1970.

Weisstein, Ulrich, *Max Frisch,* Twayne, 1967.

Wellwarth, George, *The Theater of Protest and Paradox: Developments in the Avant-Garde Drama,* New York University Press, 1964.

PERIODICALS

Biography News, June, 1974.
Books Abroad, winter, 1968.
Chicago Sun-Times, May 5, 1974.
Chicago Tribune Book World, September 28, 1980.
Christian Science Monitor, February 12, 1968.
Forum for Modern Language Studies, July, 1982.
German Life and Letters, October, 1974.
Los Angeles Times Book Review, August 10, 1980.
Modern Drama, December, 1975.
Nation, July 3, 1976, September 20, 1980.
New Republic, July 11, 1983.
New Statesman, August 6, 1982.
New Yorker, May 24, 1976, July 11, 1977.
New York Review of Books, September 24, 1981.
New York Times, July 2, 1968, November 27, 1969, May 17, 1970, May 22, 1980.
New York Times Book Review, February 20, 1966, April 28, 1974, May 16, 1976, May 27, 1976, April 3, 1977, March 19, 1978, May 11, 1980, June 22, 1980, July 10, 1983, September 29, 1983.
Observer, July 25, 1982, March 13, 1983.
Saturday Review, April 12, 1958, May 7, 1960, February 26, 1966.
Spectator, April 11, 1958, May 7, 1960.
Times (London), February 24, 1983.
Times Literary Supplement, November 11, 1965, January 25, 1968, September 29, 1972, September 12, 1980, June 4, 1982, July 30, 1982.
Tulane Drama Review, March, 1962.
Village Voice, July 11, 1968.
Washington Post Book World, July 18, 1976, July 27, 1980, July 17, 1983.
World Literature Today, spring, 1977, spring, 1979, spring 1983, autumn, 1984, autumn, 1986.

—*Sketch by Kevin S. Hile*

*   *   *

FROST, Paul
   See CASTLE, Anthony (Percy)

*   *   *

FUENTES, Carlos   1928-

PERSONAL: Born November 11, 1928, in Panama City, Panama; Mexican citizen; son of Rafael Fuentes Boettiger (a career diplomat) and Berta Macías Rivas; married Rita Macedo (a movie actress), 1959 (divorced, 1969); married Sylvia Lemus (a television journalist), 1973; children: (first marriage) Cecilia; (second marriage) Carlos Rafael, Natasha. *Education:* National University of Mexico, LL.B., 1948; graduate study, Institute des Hautes Etudes, Geneva, Switzerland. *Politics:* Independent leftist.

ADDRESSES: Home—716 Watchung Rd., Bound Brook, N.J. 08805.

CAREER: Writer. International Labor Organization, Geneva, Switzerland, began as member, became secretary of the Mexican delegation, 1950-52; Ministry of Foreign Affairs, Mexico City, Mexico, assistant chief of press section, 1954; National University of Mexico, Mexico City, secretary and assistant director of cultural dissemination, 1955-56; head of department of cultural relations, 1957-59; Mexico's ambassador to France, 1975-77. Fellow at Woodrow Wilson International Center for Scholars, 1974. Norman Maccoll Lecturer, Cambridge University, 1977; Virginia Gildersleeve Professor, Barnard College, 1977; Henry L. Tinker Lecturer, Columbia University, 1978; lecturer or visiting professor at University of Mexico, University of California at San Diego, University of Oklahoma, University of Concepción in Chile, University of Paris, University of Pennsylvania, Harvard University, and George Mason University.

MEMBER: American Academy and Institute of Arts and Letters (honorary).

AWARDS, HONORS: Centro Mexicano de Escritores fellowship, 1956-57; Biblioteca Breve Prize from Seix Barral (publishing house; Barcelona), 1967, for *Cambio de piel;* Xavier Villaurrutia Prize (Mexico), 1975; Rómulo Gallegos Prize (Venezuela), 1977, for *Terra Nostra;* Alfonso Reyes Prize (Mexico), 1979, for body of work; National Award for Literature (Mexico), 1984, for "Orchids in the Moonlight"; nominated for *Los Angeles Times* Book Award in fiction, 1986, for *The Old Gringo;* Miguel de Cervantes Prize from Spanish Ministry of Culture, 1987; Rubén Darío Order of Cultural Independence (Nicaragua) and literary prize of Italo-Latino Americano Institute, both 1988, for *The Old Gringo;* honorary degrees from numerous colleges and universities, including Columbia College, Chicago State University, Harvard University, and Washington University.

WRITINGS:

NOVELS

La región más transparente, Fondo de Cultura Económica, 1958, translation by Sam Hileman published as *Where the Air Is Clear,* Ivan Obolensky, 1960, Hileman's translation published as *Where the Air Is Clear: A Novel,* Farrar, Straus, 1982.

Las buenas consciencias, Fondo de Cultura Económica, 1959, translation published as *The Good Conscience,* Ivan Oblensky, 1961, reprinted, Farrar, Straus, 1981.

La muerte de Artemio Cruz, Fondo de Cultura Económica, 1962, reprinted, 1983, translation by Hileman published as *The Death of Artemio Cruz,* Farrar, Straus, 1964.

Aura (also see below), Era, 1962, reprinted, 1982, translation by Lysander Kemp, Farrar, Straus, 1965.

Zona sagrada, Siglo XXI, 1967, translation by Suzanne Jill Levine published as *Holy Place* (also see below), Dutton, 1972.

Cambio de piel, Mortiz, 1967, translation by Hileman published as *A Change of Skin,* Farrar, Straus, 1968.

Cumpleaños, Mortiz, 1969, translation published as "Birthday" in *Holy Place & Birthday: Two Novellas,* Farrar, Straus, in press.

Terra Nostra (also see below), Seix Barral, 1975, translation by Levine, afterword by Milan Kundera, Farrar, Straus, 1976.

La cabeza de hidra, Mortiz, 1978, translation by Margaret Sayers Peden published as *Hydra Head,* Farrar, Straus, 1978.

Una familia lejana, Era, 1980, translation by Peden published as *Distant Relations,* Farrar, Straus, 1982.

El gringo viejo, Fondo de Cultura Económica, 1985, translation by Peden and Fuentes published as *The Old Gringo,* Farrar, Straus, 1985.

Christopher Unborn (translation of *Cristóbal Nonato*), Farrar, Straus, 1989.

Holy Place & Birthday: Two Novellas, Farrar, Straus, in press.

SHORT STORIES

Los días enmascarados (also see below), Los Presentes, 1954, reprinted, Era, 1982.

Cantar de ciegos (also see below), Mortiz, 1964.

Dos cuentos mexicanos (title means "Two Mexican Stories"; two short stories previously published in *Cantar de ciegos*), Instituto de Cultura Hispánica de Sao Paulo, Universidade de Sao Paulo, 1969.

Poemas de amor: Cuentos del alma, Imp. E. Cruces (Madrid), 1971.

Chac Mool y otros cuentos, Salvat, 1973.

Agua quemada (anthology), Fondo de Cultura Económica, 1981, translation by Peden published as *Burnt Water,* Farrar, Straus, 1980.

Constancia and Other Stories for Virgins, Farrar, Straus, 1989.

PLAYS

Todos los gatos son pardos (also see below), Siglo XXI, 1970.

El tuerto es rey (also see below; first produced [in French], 1970), Mortiz, 1970.

Los reinos originarios (contains "Todos los gatos son pardos" and "El tuerto es rey"), Seix Barral, 1971.

Orquídeas a la luz de la luna (first produced in English as "Orchids in the Moonlight" at American Repertory Theater in Cambridge, Mass., June 9, 1982), Seix Barral, 1982.

NONFICTION

The Argument of Latin America: Words for North Americans, Radical Education Project, 1963.

(Contributor) *Whither Latin America?* (political articles), Monthly Review Press, 1963.

Paris: La revolución de mayo, Era, 1968.

La nueva novela hispanoamericana, Mortiz, 1969.

(Contributor) *El mundo de José Luis Cuevas,* Tudor (Mexico City), 1969.

Casa con dos puertas (title means "House With Two Doors"), Mortiz, 1970.

Tiempo mexicano (title means "Mexican Time"), Mortiz, 1971.

Cervantes; o, La crítica de la lectura, Mortiz, 1976, translation published as *Don Quixote; or, The Critique of Reading,* Institute of Latin American Studies, University of Texas at Austin, 1976.

On Human Rights: A Speech, Somesuch Press (Dallas), 1984.

Latin America: At War With the Past, CBC Enterprises, 1985.

Myself With Others: Selected Essays, Farrar, Straus, 1988.

OTHER

(Editor and author of prologue) Octavio Paz, *Los signos en rotacíon, y otros ensayos,* Alianza, 1971.

Cuerpos y ofrendas (anthology; includes selections from *Los días enmascarados, Cantar de ciegos, Aura,* and *Terra Nostra*), introduction by Octavio Paz, Alianza, 1972.

(Author of introduction to Spanish translation) Milan Kundera, *La vida está en otra parte,* Seix Barral, 1977.

(Author of introduction) Omar Cabezas, *Fire From the Mountain,* Crown, 1988.

Collaborator on several film scripts, including "Pedro Páramo," 1966, "Tiempo de morir," 1966, and "Los caifanes," 1967. Work represented in numerous anthologies, including *Antología de cuentos hispanoamericanos,* Nueva Década (Costa Rica), 1985. Contributor to periodicals in the United States, Mexico, and France, including *New York Times, Washington Post,* and *Los Angeles Times.* Founding editor, *Revista Mexicana de Literatura,* 1954-58; co-editor, *El Espectador,* 1959-61, *Siempre,* 1960, and *Política,* 1960.

WORK IN PROGRESS: A novel about the assassination of Emiliano Zapata; a five-part television series for the Smithsonian Institution, to be called "The Buried Mirror," commemorating the 500th anniversary of Christopher Columbus's voyage, to be broadcast in the fall of 1991.

SIDELIGHTS: "Carlos Fuentes," states Robert Maurer in *Saturday Review,* is "without doubt one of Mexico's two or three greatest novelists." He is part of a group of Latin American writers whose writings, according to Alistair Reid's *New Yorker* essay, "formed the background of the Boom," a literary phenomenon Reid describes as a period in the 1960s when "a sudden surge of hither-to unheard-of writers from Latin America began to be felt among [U.S.] readers." Fuentes, however, is singled out from among the other writers of the Boom in José Donoso's autobiographical account, *The Boom in Spanish American Literature: A Personal History,* in which the Chilean novelist calls Fuentes "the first active and conscious agent of the internationalization of the Spanish American novel." And since the 1960s, Fuentes has continued his international influence in the literary world: his 1985 novel, *The Old Gringo,* for example, was the first written by a Mexican to ever appear on the *New York Times* bestseller list.

Although, as Donoso observes, early worldwide acceptance of Fuentes's novels contributed to the internationalization of Latin American literature, his work is an exploration of the culture and history of one nation, his native Mexico. Critics note the thematic presence of Mexico in nearly all Fuentes's writing. Robert Coover comments in the *New York Times Book Review* that in *The Death of Artemio Cruz,* for instance, Fuentes delineates "in the retrospective details of one man's life the essence of the post-Revolutionary history of all Mexico." Mexico is also present in Fuentes's novel *Terra Nostra,* in which, according to *Washington Post Book World* contributor Larry Rohter, "Fuentes probes more deeply into the origins of Mexico—and what it means to be a Mexican—than ever before." Fuentes's *Old Gringo*—published more than twenty years after *The Death of Artemio Cruz*—returns to the same theme as it explores Mexico's relationship with its northern neighbor, the United States.

Fuentes explains his preoccupation with Mexico, and particularly with Mexican history, in a *Paris Review* interview. "Pablo Neruda used to say," he told Alfred MacAdam and Charles Rúas, "that every Latin American writer goes around dragging a heavy body, the body of his people, of his past, of his national history. We have to assimilate the enormous weight of our past so that we will not forget what gives us life. If you forget your past, you die." Fuentes also notes that the development of the same theme in his novels unifies them so that they may be considered part of the same work. The author observes in the same interview, "In a sense my novels are one book with many chapters: *Where the Air Is Clear* is the biography of Mexico City; *The Death of Artemio Cruz* deals with an individual in that city; [and] *A Change of Skin* is that city, that society, facing the world, coming to grips with the fact that it is part of civilization and that there is a world outside that intrudes into Mexico."

Along with thematic unity, another characteristic of Fuentes's work is his innovative narrative style. In a *New Yorker* review, Anthony West compares the novelist's technique to "a rapid cinematic movement that cuts nervously from one character to another." Evan Connell states in the *New York Times Book Review* that Fuentes's "narrative style—with few exceptions—relies on the interruption and juxtaposition of different kinds of awareness." Reviewers Donald Yates and Karen Hardy also comment on Fuentes's experimental style. In the *Washington Post Book World* Yates calls Fuentes "a tireless experimenter with narrative techniques and points of view," while in *Hispania* Hardy notes that in Fuentes's work "the complexities of a human or national personality are evoked through . . . elaborate narrative devices."

Fuentes's novels *The Death of Artemio Cruz* and *Terra Nostra* are especially good examples of his experimental techniques. The first narrative deals with a corrupt Mexican millionaire who on his deathbed relives his life in a series of flashbacks. In the novel Fuentes uses three separate narrations to tell the story, and for each of these narrations he uses a different narrative person. *New York Review of Books* contributor A. Alvarez explains the three-part narration of the novel: "Cruz's story is told in three persons. 'I' is the old man dying on his bed; 'you' is a slightly vatic, 'experimental' projection of his potentialities into an unspecified future . . . ; 'he' is the real hero, the man whose history emerges bit by bit from incidents shuffled around from his seventy-one years." In John S. Brushwood's *Mexico in Its Novel: A Nation's Search for Identity,* the critic praises Fuentes's technique, commenting: "The changing narrative viewpoint is extremely effective, providing a clarity that could not have been accomplished any other way. I doubt that there is anywhere in fiction a character whose wholeness is more apparent than in the case of Artemio Cruz."

Coover observes that in *Terra Nostra* Fuentes once again uses a variety of narrators to tell his story. Commenting favorably on Fuentes's use of the "you" narrative voice in the novel, Coover writes: "Fuentes's second person [narration] is not one overheard on a stage: the book itself, rather than the author or a character, becomes the speaker, the reader or listener a character, or several characters in succession." Spanish novelist Juan Goytisolo similarly states in *Review:* "One of the most striking and most successful devices [in *Terra Nostra*] is the abrupt shift in narrative point of view (at times without the unwary reader's even noticing), passing from first-person narration to second, . . . and simultaneously rendering objective and subjective reality in one and the same passage with patent scorn for the rules of discourse that ordinarily govern expository prose." In the *Paris Review* Fuentes comments on his use of the second person narrative, calling it "the voice poets have always used and that novelists also have a right to use."

Fuentes's use of the second person narrative and other experimental techniques makes his novels extremely complex. The author's remarks in a *New York Times Book Review* interview with Frank MacShane concerning the structure of *Terra Nostra* describe the intricacy of the work: "My chief stylistic device in 'Terra Nostra' is to follow every statement by a counter statement and every image by its opposite." This deliberate duplicity by the author, along with the extensive scope of the novel, causes some reviewers to criticize *Terra Nostra* for being unaccessible to the average reader. Maurer, for instance, calls the novel "a huge, sprawling, exuberant, mysterious, almost unimaginably dense work of 800 pages, covering events on three continents from the creation of man in Genesis to the dawn of the twenty-first century," and adds that "*Terra Nostra* presents a common reader with enormous problems simply of understanding what is going on." *Newsweek*'s Peter S. Prescott notes: "To talk about [*Terra Nostra*] at all we must return constantly to five words: excess, surreal, baroque, masterpiece, [and] unreadable."

Other critics, however, have written more positive reviews, seeing *Terra Nostra* and other Fuentes works as necessarily complex. *Village Voice* contributor Jonah Raskin finds Fuentes is at his best when the novelist can "plunge readers into the hidden recesses of his characters' minds and at the same time allow language to pile up around their heads in thick drifts, until they feel lost in a blizzard of words that enables them to see, to feel, in a revolutionary way." Fuentes also defends the difficulty of his works in a *Washington Post* interview with Charles Truehart. Recalling the conversation with the Mexican author, Truehart quotes Fuentes as saying: "I believe in books that do not go to a ready-made public. . . . I'm looking for readers I would like to *make*. . . . To *win* them, . . . to *create* readers rather than to give something that readers are expecting. That would bore me to death."

While Fuentes's innovative use of theme and structure has gained the author an international reputation as a novelist, he believes that only since *Terra Nostra* has he perfected his craft. "I feel I'm beginning to write the novels I've always wanted to write and didn't know how to write before," he explains to Philip Bennett in a *Boston Globe Magazine* interview. "There were the novels of youth based on energy, and conceptions derived from energy. Now I have the conceptions I had as a young man, but I can develop them and give them their full value."

MEDIA ADAPTATIONS: Two short stories from *Cantar de ciegos* were made into films in the mid-1960s; *The Old Gringo* was adapted into a film of the same title by Fonda Films, 1989.

AVOCATIONAL INTERESTS: Reading, travel, swimming, visiting art galleries, listening to classical and rock music, motion pictures, the theater.

BIOGRAPHICAL/CRITICAL SOURCES:

BOOKS

Authors in the News, Volume 2, Gale, 1976.
Brushwood, John S., *Mexico in Its Novel: A Nation's Search for Identity,* University of Texas Press, 1966.
Contemporary Literary Criticism, Gale, Volume 3, 1975, Volume 8, 1978, Volume 10, 1979, Volume 13, 1980, Volume 22, 1982, Volume 41, 1987.
Donoso, José, *The Boom in Spanish American Literature: A Personal History,* Columbia University Press, 1977.
Plimpton, George, editor, *Writers at Work: The Paris Review Interviews, Sixth Series,* Penguin Books, 1984.

PERIODICALS

Boston Globe Magazine, September 9, 1984.
Hispania, May, 1978.
Los Angeles Times Book Review, October 27, 1985.
Newsweek, November 1, 1976.
New Yorker, March 4, 1961, January 26, 1981, February 24, 1986.
New York Review of Books, June 11, 1964.
New York Times Book Review, November 7, 1976, October 19, 1980, October 27, 1985, August 20, 1989.
Paris Review, winter, 1981.
Review, winter, 1976.
Saturday Review, October 30, 1976.
Tribune Books (Chicago), March 25, 1990.
Village Voice, January 28, 1981, April 1, 1986.
Washington Post, May 5, 1988.

Washington Post Book World, October 26, 1976, January 14, 1979, August 20, 1989.*

—*Sketch by Marian Gonsior*

*   *   *

FUGARD, (Harold) Athol 1932-

PERSONAL: Born June 11, 1932, in Middelburg, Cape Province, South Africa; son of Harold David (an owner of a general store) and Elizabeth Magdalena (a cafe manager) Fugard; married Sheila Meiring (a novelist, poet, and former actress), 1956; children: Lisa. *Education:* Attended Port Elizabeth Technical College, and University of Cape Town, 1950-53.

ADDRESSES: Home—P.O. Box 5090, Port Elizabeth, South Africa. *Agent*—William Morris Agency, 1350 Avenue of the Americas, New York, N.Y. 10019.

CAREER: Actor, director, and playwright. Crew member of a tramp steamer bound from Port Sudan, Sudan, to the Far East, 1953-55; Fordsburg Native Commissioner's Court, Johannesburg, South Africa, clerk, 1958; worked as actor and director in various theatre productions in New York City, London, and South Africa. Actor in television film "The Blood Knot" for British Broadcasting Corp. (BBC-TV), 1968.

AWARDS, HONORS: Obie Award for distinguished foreign play, *Village Voice,* 1971, for "Boesman and Lena"; *Plays & Players* award for best new play, 1973, for "Sizwe Banzi Is Dead"; New York Critics Circle award for best play, 1982, for "A Lesson from Aloes"; Drama Desk award and Critics Circle award for best play, 1983, and *Evening Standard* award, London, 1984, for " 'Master Harold' . . . And the Boys"; Commonwealth Award, 1984, for contribution to the American theatre; honorary degrees from Yale University, Georgetown University, Natal University, Rhodes University, and Cape Town University.

WRITINGS:

Tsotsi (novel), Collings, 1980, Random House, 1981.
Notebooks, 1960-1977, edited by Mary Benson, Faber, 1983, Knopf, 1984.

PLAYS

"No-Good Friday" (also see below), first produced in Cape Town, South Africa, 1956.
"Nongogo" (also see below), first produced in Cape Town, 1957.
The Blood Knot (first produced in Johannesburg, South Africa, and London, 1961; produced Off-Broadway, 1964; also see below), Simondium, 1963, Odyssey, 1964.
Hello and Goodbye (first produced in Johannesburg, 1965; produced Off-Broadway at Sheridan Square Playhouse, September 18, 1969; also see below), A. A. Balkema, 1966, Samuel French, 1971.
"The Occupation," published in *Ten One-Act Plays,* Heinemann, 1968.
Boesman and Lena (first produced in Grahamstown, South Africa, 1969; produced Off-Broadway at Circle in the Square, June 22, 1970; produced on the West End at Royal Court Theatre Upstairs, July 19, 1971; also see below), Buren, 1969, revised and rewritten edition, Samuel French, 1971 (published with "The Blood Knot," "People Are Living There" [also see below], and "Hello and Goodbye" as *Boesman and Lena, and Other Plays,* Oxford University Press, 1978).
People Are Living There (first produced in Cape Town at Hofmeyr Theatre, June 14, 1969; produced on Broadway at Forum Theatre, Lincoln Center, November 18, 1971), Oxford University Press, 1970, Samuel French, 1976.
(With Don MacLennan) *The Coat* [and] *Third Degree* (the former by Fugard, the latter by MacLennan), A. A. Balkema, 1971.
Statements (contains three one-act plays: [with John Kani and Winston Ntshona] "Sizwe Banzi Is Dead," first produced in Cape Town, 1972, produced in New York City, 1974; [with Kani and Ntshona] "The Island," first produced in South Africa, 1972, produced on the West End at Royal Court Theatre, December, 1973, produced in New York at Edison Theatre, November, 1974; and "Statements After an Arrest under the Immorality Act," first produced in Cape Town, 1972, produced in London, 1974), Oxford University Press, 1974.
"Dimetos," first produced in Edinburgh, 1975, produced in London and New York City, 1976 (published with "No-Good Friday" and "Nongogo" as *Dimetos and Two Early Plays,* Oxford University Press, 1977).
(With Ross Devenish) *The Guest: An Episode in the Life of Eugene Marais,* Donker (Johannesburg), 1977.
A Lesson from Aloes (first produced in Johannesburg, December, 1978, produced in New York, 1980), Oxford University Press, 1981.
"The Drummer," produced in Louisville, 1980.
"Master Harold" . . . And the Boys (first produced in New Haven, Connecticut, March, 1982, produced on Broadway at Lyceum Theatre, May 5, 1982), Oxford University Press, 1983 (published with "The Blood Knot," "Hello and Goodbye," and "Boesman and Lena" as *Selected Plays,* Oxford University Press, 1987).
The Road to Mecca (first produced in New Haven, 1984, produced in London at Lyttelton Theatre, March 1, 1985, produced in New York at Promenade Theatre, April, 1988), Faber, 1985.
"A Place with the Pigs," produced in New Haven, 1987.

OTHER

Author of teleplays "Mille Miglia" and "The Guest at Steenkampskraal." Produced screenplays include "Boesman and Lena" (based on his play), 1972, "The Guest," 1976, "Meetings with Remarkable Men," 1979, "Marigolds in August," 1980, "Gandhi," 1982, and "The Killing Fields," 1984. Plays reprinted in various anthologies.

SIDELIGHTS: "If ever there was a born dramatist," writes Edith Oliver in a *New Yorker* article, "it is the South African Athol Fugard." Besides being the best-known dramatic voice from his native country, Fugard often acts in and directs his own stage works, and is a leading anti-apartheid proponent wherever he travels. Though many critics and playgoers rank Fugard among the political "agitprop" playwrights, he insists that his plays are more humanistic than abstract, and that they merely reflect life in segregated South Africa as it now exists.

In "Boesman and Lena," for instance, the title characters are "coloreds" who have more relative freedom than the South African blacks, but less than the whites; consequently, they cannot relate to either group, and live with constant despair. In this play, as in others, Fugard's tendency to write extended dialogues for two or three characters has caused some critics to label him inaccessible. *New York* magazine's description of "Boesman and Lena" typifies the mixed feelings toward Fugard's works: "Even though short, the play seems slow and long-winded at first. . . . But slowly the language muddles through, the underlying humanity of these dehumanized beings creeps up on us. Against our will, we are drawn into compassionate kinship with them. . . . In the end, it is our sense of solidarity that makes a harsh experience rewarding."

Fugard often earns praise for humanizing the issue of apartheid. One archetypical Fugard work, "The Blood Knot," is "agitprop of the best kind," according to John Corry in a *New York Times* review, adding the play seems "never overt, and always more concerned with people than with politics—but it is a good deal more than that. It is an exploration of the human condition, fairly bursting with soul." The plot centers on two half-brothers, one a dark-skinned black, the other light enough to "pass" for white, and their various political and familial conflicts. (Fugard, who is white, has played the light-skinned brother in a New Haven production. He appeared opposite his longtime collaborator, the actor Zakes Mokae.) In a *New York Times* interview by Samuel G. Freedman, Fugard remembers the 1961 opening of "The Blood Knot," then considered a most controversial work because it mixed a black actor with a white one. What was supposed to be a modest production in a makeshift theatre escalated into a *cause celebre* among South African playgoers. "Words were not sufficient," says Fugard of that time. "I remember people would sit and look at us. They'd either say thank you or they'd cry. It was something so hard to describe. You knew something was happening; you knew something had happened. That's why the Government couldn't stop us."

But the Government has stepped in several times throughout Fugard's career, banning his plays from official South African productions on the grounds that they were subversive. This was also the case with the writer's perhaps best-known play, " 'Master Harold' . . . And the Boys," which opened in New York in 1982. In that year the *New York Times* reported that "South African censors have decreed that it is a criminal offense to import or distribute copies of [this play]." This decree, the article pointed out, did not necessarily apply to performing the play, and a year later "Master Harold" did have its Johannesburg premiere. " 'Master Harold' . . . And the Boys" is acknowledged as Fugard's most autobiographical play to date, focusing as it does on a white South African teenager in 1950, the year Fugard himself would have been eighteen, and set in a tearoom, the likes of which Fugard's mother ran back then in Port Elizabeth. Harold ("Hally") is presented as "an intelligent, witty prep-school student who questions the injustices of his society and already dreams about being an artist," as Frank Rich describes in a *New York Times* review. The other two characters in the play—the "boys"—are middle-aged black employees of the family's restaurant. Sadly for Hally, his relationship with his parents is strained, and in his desperation he turns to the servants, Willie and Sam, for guidance.

The two servants, aware of Hally's personal problems, try to counsel him, but are hampered by the youth's confused hostility toward them, which manifests itself in racial taunts (it is Hally who insists "the boys" call him "Master Harold"). This play "is South Africa to its marrow," according to *Washington Post* reviewer David Richards. "And yet, midway through a drama that never once inflates its humble particulars or indulges in lofty pronouncements, you will realize that Fugard is writing about all of us. His play is about the gulfs that suddenly yawn at our feet and the scapegoats we make to exorcise our pain. It is about the punishment we inflict on others, when we are really inflicting it upon ourselves."

The playwright spoke to *Los Angeles Times* reporter Kevin Kelly about using his own past as the basis for a script. "I am Hallie. . . . Rather, I was Hallie when I was 18, 19, 20," says Fugard. He calls creating "Master Harold" "the most painful writing experience of my life," especially in its attempt "to come to terms with my father and mother. I felt like Eugene O'Neill when he was dealing with his ghosts in 'Long Day's Journey into Night.' The awful fear of revealing myself! And the fear that I was on an ego trip; that the play would turn out to be just too personal." As Kelly points out, Fugard needn't have worried: "Some critics, this writer included, consider 'Master Harold' among the handful of great plays of our time." "Fugard's strength is simplicity," observes *Los Angeles Times* critic Sylvie Drake. "He approaches difficult matters head-on, but with pervasive sensitivity of more than a little depth. Paradoxically, he can also border—and does in 'Master Harold'—on melodrama. Powerful histrionics are very much part of this play. What saves it is Fugard's instinctive sense of when to pull back, when to let silence speak, when to let action make its singular, staggering statement"

Speaking to Kelly, Fugard expresses a hope for the future of both his country and himself. "The government did start . . . to relax itself in terms of theater. Now theaters are open to everyone regardless of color. You can even mix a cast without infringing the law. But that doesn't dictate that the society is changing radically. It's window dressing, really." "When I wrote 'A Lesson from Aloes,' which deals with the absolute necessity of friendship between blacks and whites," he continues, "I found myself trying to discover whether I was an optimist or a pessimist about the country I love so much. I don't know. In 'Master Harold,' Hally says, 'I oscillate between hope and despair.' That remains as true for me as it did when I was 18."

BIOGRAPHICAL/CRITICAL SOURCES:

BOOKS

Contemporary Literary Criticism, Gale, Volume 5, 1976, Volume 9, 1978, Volume 14, 1980, Volume 25, 1983, Volume 40, 1986.
Fugard, Athol, *Notebooks 1960-1977,* Faber, 1983, Knopf, 1984.

PERIODICALS

Los Angeles Times, March 13, 1982, July 17, 1983, July 29, 1983.
New Republic, July 25, 1970, December 21, 1974.
Newsweek, May 28, 1984.
New York, June 6, 1970, December 2, 1974, February 20, 1978, May 17, 1982, January 6, 1986.
New Yorker, December 11, 1978.
New York Review of Books, February 19, 1981.
New York Times, September 19, 1969, May 17, 1970, June 4, 1970, July 6, 1970, December 17, 1974, February 2, 1977, April 1, 1980, April 5, 1980, November 16, 1980, February 1, 1981, June 6, 1981, March 21, 1982, May 5, 1982, November 12, 1982, December 5, 1982, May 15, 1984, December 11, 1985, April 3, 1987, May 28, 1987, April 10, 1988, April 13, 1988, April 24, 1988.
Times Literary Supplement, May 2, 1980, March 1, 1985.
Village Voice, February 20, 1978.
Washington Post, April 13, 1985, September 29, 1987.*

—*Sketch by Susan Salter*

G

GALEANO, Eduardo (Hughes) 1940-

PERSONAL: Born September 3, 1940, in Montevideo, Uruguay; son of Eduardo Hughes and Ester Galeano; married first wife Silvia Brando, 1959; married second wife, Graciela Berro, 1962; married third wife, Helena Villagra, 1976; children: (first marriage) Veronica; (second marriage) Florencia, Claudio. *Education:* Attended school in Uruguay. *Politics:* Socialist. *Religion:* None.

ADDRESSES: c/o Susan Bergholz Literary Services, 340 West 72nd, New York, NY. 10023.

CAREER: Marcha (weekly), Montevideo, Uruguay, editor in chief, 1961-64; *Epoca* (daily), Montevideo, director, 1964-66; University Press, Montevideo, editor in chief, 1965-73; *Crisis* (magazine), Buenos Aires, Argentina, founder, 1973, director, 1973-76; writer.

AWARDS, HONORS: Premio Casa de las Américas, 1975, for *La canción de nosotros,* and 1978, for *Días y noches de amor y de guerra;* American Book Award, 1989, for *Memory of Fire.*

WRITINGS:

Los días siguientes (novel), Alfa, 1962.
China 1964: Crónica de un desafío, Jorge Alvarez, 1964.
Los fantasmas del día del léon, y otros relatos (short stories), Arca, 1967.
Guatemala: Clave de Latinoamérica, Ediciones de la Banda Oriental, 1967, translation by Cedric Belfrage published as *Guatemala: Occupied Country,* Monthly Review Press, 1969.
Reportajes: Tierras de Latinoamérica, otros puntos cardinales, y algo más (also see below), Ediciones Tauro, 1967.
(Compiler and author of prologue) *Su majestad, el fútbol,* Arca, 1968.
Siete imágenes de Bolivia, Fondo Editorial Salvador de la Plaza, 1971.
Las venas abiertas de América Latina, Departamento de Publicaciones, Universidad Nacional de la República, 1971, 2nd edition, 1972, translation by Belfrage published as *The Open Veins of Latin America: Five Centuries of the Pillage of a Continent,* Monthly Review Press, 1973.
Crónicas latinoamericanas, Editorial Girón, 1972.
Vagamundo (short stories), Ediciones de Crisis, 1973.
La canción de nosotros (novel), Editorial Sudamericana, 1975.

Conversaciones con Raimon, Granica, 1977.
Días y noches de amor y de guerra, Editorial Laia, 1978, translation by Judith Brister published as *Days and Nights of Love and War,* Monthly Review Press, 1983.
Voces de nuestro tiempo, Editorial Universitaria Centroamericana, 1981.
Los nacimientos (first book in trilogy "Memoria del fuego"), Siglo XXI, 1982, translation by Cedric Belfrage published as *Memory of Fire: Genesis,* Pantheon, 1985.
La piedra arde, Lóguez Ediciones, 1983.
Las caras y las máscaras (second book in trilogy "Memoria del fuego"), Siglo XXI, 1984, translation by Belfrage published as *Memory of Fire: Faces and Masks,* Pantheon, 1987.
Contraseña, Ediciones del Sol, 1985.
El siglo del viento (third book in trilogy "Memoria del fuego"), Siglo XXI, 1986, translation by Belfrage published as *Memory of Fire: Century of the Wind,* Pantheon, 1988.
Aventuras de los jóvenes dioses, Kapelusz, 1986.
Nosotros decimos no: Crónicas (1963-1988), Siglo XXI, 1989.
El libro de los abrazos, Siglo XXI, 1989.

SIDELIGHTS: Eduardo Galeano has had a long and active career as a journalist, historian, and political activist. At the age of thirteen he began publishing cartoons for the Uruguayan socialist paper *El Sol.* He went on to work for the journal *Marcha* while still in his teens, and became editor in chief of that publication at twenty. When he was still in his early thirties, a right wing military coup imprisoned Galeano and later forced him to flee from Uruguay to Argentina. Still later, another coup and several death threats forced him to leave Argentina for Spain, where he lived in exile until he was permitted to return to Uruguay in 1984. Upon his arrival in Spain, he tells Sam Staggs in *Publishers Weekly,* he felt "broken in pieces. . . . I tried to create a structure from all the broken pieces of myself, like putting together a puzzle. *Days and Nights of Love and War* resulted from this open, free conversation with my own memory, as I tried to understand what had really happened and to guess who I really was."

In his memoir *Days and Nights of Love and War,* Galeano recounts and reflects on the murders, tortures, and disappearances that have become a routine part of Latin American politics. Described by Julie Schumacher in the *Nation* as "the notebook of a wandering 'people's reporter,'" *Days and Nights of Love and War* approaches its subject in an unorthodox manner, in which "the action is presented . . . through semi-related paragraphs that jump back and forth in time, place, person and mood." She maintains that *Days and Nights of Love and War* proves the author is "a magical writer in the best sense of the word," a writer whose nonfiction is able to "match the intensity and appeal of the [South American] continent's best fiction." In short, the reviewer concludes, Galeano shows in *Days and Nights of Love and War* that "the reality of Latin America is more fantastic than the lies we've been told, and that nothing is more horrible or poetic than the truth."

Galeano expands on this fragmentary approach to story in his trilogy "Memoria del fuego" ("Memory of Fire"). In the three books of the trilogy, translated as *Genesis, Faces and Masks,* and *Century of the Wind,* the author relates an anecdotal chronicle of all the Americas—North, South, and Central—from the first native myths to modern times. Drawing on a wide variety of primary sources, Galeano dramatizes some scenes in paragraph-length sketches; how God told President McKinley that the United States should retain the Philippines after the Spanish-American War, for instance, or how, when the Chiriguano Indians first learned of paper, they called it "the skin of God." In others, he reprints historic documents to form a work described by Thulani Davis in the *Voice Literary Supplement* as "historical fact written with a fiction writer's sensibilities." "The result," declares Garry Abrams in the *Los Angeles Times,* "is like a mosaic or an impressionistic painting with each dot contributing to the big picture."

Galeano combines elements of the novel, poetry, and history in "Memory of Fire." Each vignette is based on a documentary source or sources (identified by number in the book's bibliography), but Galeano has recast many of the stories in a poetic form to show the history of the Americas. He states in *Publishers Weekly* that he has reinterpreted the stories to make "the voice of my conscience and the will of my hand coincide. . . . I was looking for little stories that would reveal the great ones, the universe seen through a keyhole. The little things about little people reveal the history of America—the *masked history.*" He tells Staggs, "I'm trying to create a synthesis of all the different ways of expressing life and reality." Talking to Magda Bogin in the *Voice Literary Supplement,* Galeano says, "I remember as a child feeling that history was locked away in a museum, and that she had to be rescued and set free so she could walk the streets and fields again at will. This implies rescuing history by means of a language capable of embracing all its dimensions, the language people on the coast of Colombia call *sentipensante*—a language capable of uniting the reasons of passion with the passions of reason."

"I do not want to write an objective work—neither wanted to nor could," Galeano writes in the preface to *Genesis.* "There is nothing neutral about this historical narration. Unable to distance myself, I take sides: I confess it and I am not sorry. However, each fragment of this huge mosaic is based on a solid documentary foundation." In an interview appearing in the *New Yorker,* Galeano calls the trilogy "highly subjective," and explains, "Back in school, history classes were terrible—boring, lifeless, empty. . . . It was as if the teachers were intentionally trying to rob us of that connection [to reality], so that we would become resigned to our present—not realize that history is something people make, with their lives, in their own present. So, you see, I tried to find a way of recounting history so that the reader would feel that it was happening right now, just around the corner—this immediacy, this intensity, which is the beauty and the *reality* of history."

"Perhaps I write because I know that the people and the things I care about are going to die and I want to preserve them alive," Galeano told *CA.* "I believe in my craft; I believe in my instrument. I can never understand how writers could write while cheerfully declaring that writing has no meaning. Nor can I ever understand those who turn words into a target for fury or an object of fetishism. Words are a weapon: the responsibility for the crime never lies with the knife. Slowly gaining strength and form, there is in Latin America a literature that does not set out to bury our own dead but to perpetuate them; that refuses to clear up the ashes and tries, on the contrary, to light the fire. Perhaps my own words may help a little to preserve for people to come, as the poet put it, 'the true name of each thing.'"

BIOGRAPHICAL/CRITICAL SOURCES:

BOOKS

Galeano, Eduardo, *Memory of Fire: Genesis,* translated by Cedric Belfrage, Pantheon, 1985.

PERIODICALS

Boston Globe, May 1, 1988; December 2, 1988.
Chicago Tribune, May 15, 1988.
Detroit News, April 26, 1987.
El Diario, April, 1986.
Globe and Mail (Toronto), March 22, 1986; May 2, 1987; June 11, 1988.
Guardian, February 5, 1986; June 13, 1986; June 15, 1988.
Los Angeles Times, May 11, 1988.
Los Angeles Times Book Review, December 29, 1985; March 15, 1987; July 17, 1988.
Los Angeles Weekly, May 27, 1988.
Nation, June 25, 1983.
New Yorker, July 28, 1986.
New York Times, May 2, 1988.
New York Times Book Review, October 27, 1985.
Publishers Weekly, January 16, 1987; April 1, 1988; June 3, 1988.
San Francisco Chronicle, May 15, 1988.
Times Literary Supplement, October 20-26, 1989.
Toronto Now, April 21, 1988.
Toronto Star, April 26, 1988.
Tribune Books (Chicago), May 15, 1988.
USA Today, July 14, 1988.
Voice Literary Supplement, March, 1983; April, 1987; May, 1988.
Washington Post Book World, April 5, 1987; May 22, 1988.*

*   *   *

GALVEZ de MONTALVO, Luis
See AVALLE-ARCE, Juan Bautista de

*   *   *

GANS, Roma 1894-

PERSONAL: Born February 22, 1894, in St. Cloud, MN; daughter of Hubert W. (a musician and businessman) and Mary Anne (Ley) Gans. *Education:* Columbia University, B.S., 1926, Ph.D., 1940. *Politics:* Democrat. *Religion:* Roman Catholic.

ADDRESSES: Home and office—Wayside Lane, West Redding, CT 06896.

CAREER: Junior high school mathematics teacher in Clearwater, MN, 1917; high school mathematics teacher in St. Cloud,

MN, 1918-23; director of primary grades at community school in St. Louis, MO, 1924-25; assistant superintendent of schools and research director in Superior, WI, 1925-29; Columbia University, Teachers College, New York City, 1929-59, began as assistant professor, became associate professor, professor of education, 1940-59; writer, 1959—. Co-founder and chairman of New York City's Citizens Committee for Children. Vice-president of New York State Liberal Party. Member of editorial boards, Thomas Y. Crowell Co., and Harper & Row. Lecturer at colleges and universities in Canada, Italy, England, and the United States, including University of Pennsylvania and University of Illinois.

AWARDS, HONORS: Family Life Book Award Child Study Association, and Delta Kappa Gamma Society Educator's Award, 1964, for *Common Sense in Teaching Reading: A Practical Guide;* Child Study Association's "Children's Book of the Year" List, 1968, for *Birds at Night,* 1969, for *Hummingbirds in the Garden,* 1969, for *Bird Talk,* and 1971, for *Oil: The Buried Treasure.*

WRITINGS:

"LET'S READ-AND-FIND-OUT" SERIES

Birds Eat and Eat and Eat, Crowell, 1963.
The Wonder of Stones, Crowell, 1963.
It's Nesting Time, Crowell, 1964.
Icebergs, Crowell, 1964.
Birds at Night, Crowell, 1968.
Hummingbirds in the Garden, Crowell, 1969.
Bird Talk, Crowell, 1971.
Water for Dinosaurs and You, Crowell, 1972.
Millions and Millions of Crystals, Crowell, 1973.
Oil: The Buried Treasure, Crowell, 1975.
Caves, Crowell, 1976.
When Birds Change Their Feathers, Crowell, 1980.
Rock Collecting, Crowell, 1984.
Danger: Icebergs, Crowell, 1986.

OTHER

A Study of Critical Reading Comprehension in the Intermediate Grades, Teachers College, Columbia University, 1940.
Guiding Children's Reading through Experiences: Practical Suggestions for Teaching, Teachers College, Columbia University, 1941.
Reading Is Fun, Teachers College, Columbia University, 1949.
(With Celia Burns Stendler and Millie Almy) *Teaching Young Children in Nursery School, Kindergarten, and the Primary Grades,* World Book Co., 1952.
Common Sense in Teaching Reading: A Practical Guide, Bobbs-Merrill, 1963.
Fact and Fiction about Phonics, Bobbs-Merrill, 1964.

Also contributor of several hundred articles to education journals.

BIOGRAPHICAL/CRITICAL SOURCES:

PERIODICALS

Times Literary Supplement, December 9, 1965; June 26, 1969; March 28, 1980; July 18, 1980.

GEISEL, Theodor Seuss 1904-
(Theo. LeSieg, Dr. Seuss; Rosetta Stone, a joint pseudonym)

PERSONAL: Surname is pronounced *Guy*-zel; born March 2, 1904, in Springfield, Mass.; son of Theodor Robert (superintendent of Springfield public park system) and Henrietta (Seuss) Geisel; married Helen Palmer (an author and vice-president of Beginner Books), November 29, 1927 (died, October 23, 1967); married Audrey Stone Diamond, August 6, 1968. *Education:* Dartmouth College, A.B., 1925; graduate study at Lincoln College, Oxford, 1925-26, and Sorbonne, University of Paris.

ADDRESSES: Home—La Jolla, Calif. *Office*—Random House, Inc., 201 East 50th St., New York, N.Y. 10022. *Agent*—International Creative Management, 40 West 57th St., New York, N.Y. 10019.

CAREER: Author and illustrator. Free-lance cartoonist, beginning 1927; advertising artist, Standard Oil Company of New Jersey, 1928-41; *PM* (magazine), New York, N.Y., editorial cartoonist, 1940-42; publicist, War Production Board of U.S. Treasury Department, 1940-42; Beginner Books, Random House, Inc., New York, N.Y., founder and president, 1957—. Correspondent in Japan, *Life* (magazine), 1954. Trustee, La Jolla (Calif.) Town Council, beginning 1956. One-man art exhibitions at San Diego Arts Museum, 1950, Dartmouth College, 1975, Toledo Museum of Art, 1975, La Jolla Museum of Contemporary Art, 1976, and Baltimore Museum of Art, 1987. *Military service:* U.S. Army Signal Corps, Information and Education Division, 1942-46; became lieutenant colonel; received Legion of Merit.

MEMBER: Authors League of America, American Society of Composers, Authors and Publishers (ASCAP), Sigma Phi Epsilon.

AWARDS, HONORS: Academy Award, 1946, for "Hitler Lives," 1947, for "Design for Death," and 1951, for "Gerald McBoing-Boing"; Randolph Caldecott Honor Award, Association for Library Services for Children, American Library Association, 1948, for *McElligot's Pool,* 1950, for *Bartholomew and the Oobleck,* and 1951, for *If I Ran the Zoo;* Young Reader's Choice Award, Pacific Northwest Library Association, 1950, for *McElligot's Pool;* L.H.D., Dartmouth College, 1956, American International College, 1968, and Lake Forest College, 1977; Lewis Carroll Shelf Award, 1958, for *Horton Hatches the Egg,* and 1961, for *And to Think That I Saw It on Mulberry Street;* Boys' Club Junior Book Award, Boys' Club of America, 1966, for *I Had Trouble in Getting to Solla Sollew.*

Peabody Award, 1971, for animated cartoons "How the Grinch Stole Christmas" and "Horton Hears a Who"; Critics' Award from International Animated Cartoon Festival and Silver Medal from International Film and Television Festival of New York, both 1972, both for "The Lorax"; Los Angeles County Library Association Award, 1974; Southern California Council on Literature for Children and Young People Award, 1974, for special contribution to children's literature; named "Outstanding California Author," California Association of Teachers of English, 1976; Emmy Award, 1977, for "Halloween Is Grinch Night"; Roger Revelle Award, University of California, San Diego, 1978; winner of Children's Choice Election, 1978; grand marshall of Detroit's Thanksgiving Day Parade, 1979.

D.Litt., Whittier College, 1980; Laura Ingalls Wilder Award, Association for Library Services for Children, American Library Association, 1980; "Dr. Seuss Week" proclaimed by State Governors, March 2-7, 1981; Regina Medal, Catholic Library Association, 1982; National Association of Elementary School Principals special award, 1982, for distinguished service to children; Pulitzer Prize, 1984, for his "special contribution over nearly half a century to the education and enjoyment of America's children and their parents"; PEN Los Angeles Center Award for children's literature, 1985, for *The Butter Battle Book;* D.H.L., University of Hartford, 1986; honored with special program by Academy of Motion Picture Arts and Sciences, 1989.

WRITINGS:

UNDER PSEUDONYM DR. SEUSS; SELF-ILLUSTRATED

And to Think That I Saw It on Mulberry Street, Vanguard, 1937.
The 500 Hats of Bartholomew Cubbins, Vanguard, 1938.
The Seven Lady Godivas, Random House, 1939, reprinted, 1987.
The King's Stilts, Random House, 1939.
Horton Hatches the Egg, Random House, 1940.
McElligot's Pool, Random House, 1947.
Thidwick, the Big-Hearted Moose, Random House, 1948.
Bartholomew and the Oobleck, Random House, 1949.
If I Ran the Zoo, Random House, 1950.
Scrambled Eggs Super! (also see below), Random House, 1953.
The Sneetches and Other Stories, Random House, 1953.
Horton Hears a Who! (also see below), Random House, 1954.
On Beyond Zebra, Random House, 1955.
If I Ran the Circus, Random House, 1956.
Signs of Civilization! (booklet), La Jolla Town Council, 1956.
The Cat in the Hat (also see below), Random House, 1957, French/English edition published as *La Chat au chapeau,* Random House, 1967, Spanish/English edition published as *El Gato ensombrerado,* Random House, 1967.
How the Grinch Stole Christmas (also see below), Random House, 1957.
The Cat in the Hat Comes Back!, Beginner Books, 1958.
Yertle the Turtle and Other Stories, Random House, 1958.
Happy Birthday to You!, Random House, 1959.
One Fish, Two Fish, Red Fish, Blue Fish, Random House, 1960.
Green Eggs and Ham, Beginner Books, 1960.
Dr. Seuss' Sleep Book, Random House, 1962.
Hop on Pop, Beginner Books, 1963.
Dr. Seuss' ABC, Beginner Books, 1963.
(With Philip D. Eastman) *The Cat in the Hat Dictionary, by the Cat Himself,* Beginner Books, 1964.
Fox in Socks, Beginner Books, 1965.
I Had Trouble in Getting to Solla Sollew, Random House, 1965.
Dr. Seuss' Lost World Revisited: A Forward-Looking Backward Glance (nonfiction), Award Books, 1967.
The Cat in the Hat Songbook, Random House, 1967.
The Foot Book, Random House, 1968.
I Can Lick 30 Tigers Today! and Other Stories, Random House, 1969.
Mr. Brown Can Moo! Can You?, Random House, 1970.
I Can Draw It Myself, Random House, 1970.
The Lorax, Random House, 1971.
Marvin K. Mooney, Will You Please Go Now?, Random House, 1972.
Did I Ever Tell You How Lucky You Are?, Random House, 1973.
The Shape of Me and Other Stuff, Random House, 1973.
There's a Wocket in My Pocket!, Random House, 1974.
Oh, the Thinks You Can Think!, Random House, 1975.
The Cat's Quizzer, Random House, 1976.
I Can Read with My Eyes Shut, Random House, 1978.
Oh Say Can You Say?, Beginner Books, 1979.
The Dr. Seuss Storybook (includes *Scrambled Eggs Super!*), Collins, 1979.
Hunches in Bunches, Random House, 1982.

The Butter Battle Book (also see below), Random House, 1984.
You're Only Old Once, Random House, 1986.
The Tough Coughs as He Ploughs the Dough: Early Writings and Cartoons by Dr. Seuss, edited by Richard Marschall, Morrow, 1986.
Oh, the Places You'll Go!, Random House, 1990.

UNDER PSEUDONYM THEO. LeSIEG

Ten Apples up on Top!, illustrated by McKie, Beginner Books, 1961.
I Wish That I Had Duck Feet, illustrated by B. Tokey, Beginner Books, 1965.
Come Over to My House, illustrated by Richard Erdoes, Beginner Books, 1966.
The Eye Book, illustrated by McKie, Random House, 1968.
(Self-illustrated) *I Can Write—By Me, Myself,* Random House, 1971.
In a People House, illustrated by McKie, Random House, 1972.
The Many Mice of Mr. Brice, illustrated by McKie, Random House, 1973.
Wacky Wednesday, illustrated by George Booth, Beginner Books, 1974.
Would You Rather Be a Bullfrog?, illustrated by McKie, Random House, 1975.
Hooper Humperdink . . . ? Not Him!, Random House, 1976.
Please Try to Remember the First of Octember!, illustrated by Arthur Cummings, Beginner Books, 1977.
Maybe You Should Fly a Jet! Maybe You Should Be a Vet, illustrated by Michael J. Smullin, Beginner Books, 1980.
The Tooth Book, Random House, 1981.

SCREENPLAYS

"Your Job in Germany" (documentary short subject), U.S. Army, 1946, released under title "Hitler Lives," Warner Bros., 1946.
(With wife, Helen Palmer Geisel) "Design for Death" (documentary feature), RKO Pictures, 1947.
"Gerald McBoing-Boing" (animated cartoon), United Productions of America (UPA)/Columbia, 1951.
(With Allen Scott) "The 5,000 Fingers of Dr. T" (musical), Columbia, 1953.

TELEVISION SCRIPTS

"How the Grinch Stole Christmas," Columbia Broadcasting System, Inc. (CBS-TV), first aired December 18, 1966.
"Horton Hears a Who," CBS-TV, first aired March 19, 1970.
"The Cat in the Hat," CBS-TV, first aired March 10, 1971.
"Dr. Seuss on the Loose," CBS-TV, first aired October 15, 1973.
"Hoober-Bloob Highway," CBS-TV, first aired February 19, 1975.
"Halloween Is Grinch Night," American Broadcasting Companies, Inc. (ABC-TV), first aired October 28, 1977.
"Pontoffel Pock, Where Are You?," ABC-TV, first aired March 2, 1980.
"The Grinch Grinches the Cat in the Hat," ABC-TV, first aired May 20, 1982.
"The Butter Battle Book," Turner Network Television (TNT-TV), first aired November 13, 1989.

OTHER

(Illustrator) *Boners,* Viking, 1931.
(Illustrator) *More Boners,* Viking, 1931.
(Under pseudonym Dr. Seuss) *My Book about Me, by Me, Myself: I Wrote It! I Drew It,* Beginner Books, 1969.

(Under pseudonym, Dr. Seuss) *Great Day for Up!,* illustrated by Quentin Blake, Random House, 1974.

(With Michael Frith, under joint pseudonym Rosetta Stone) *Because a Little Bug Went Ka-Choo!,* illustrated by Frith, Beginner Books, 1975.

Dr. Seuss from Then to Now (museum catalog), Random House, 1987.

(Under pseudonym, Dr. Seuss) *I Am Not Going to Get Up Today!,* illustrated by James Stevenson, Random House, 1987.

Contributor of cartoons and prose to magazines, including *Judge, College Humor, Liberty, Vanity Fair,* and *Life.* Editor, *Jack-o'-Lantern* (Dartmouth College humor magazine), until 1925. The manuscript of *The 500 Hats of Bartholomew Cubbins* is in the collection of Dartmouth College in Hanover, New Hampshire. Other manuscripts are in the Special Collections Department of the University of California Library in Los Angeles.

WORK IN PROGRESS: A musical based on *The Seven Lady Godivas.*

SIDELIGHTS: Theodor Seuss Geisel, better known under his pseudonym "Dr. Seuss," is "probably the best-loved and certainly the best-selling children's book writer of all time," writes Robert Wilson of the *New York Times Book Review.* Seuss has entertained several generations of young readers with his zany nonsense books. Speaking to Herbert Kupferberg of *Parade,* Seuss claims: "Old men on crutches tell me, 'I've been brought up on your books.'" His "rhythmic verse rivals Lewis Carroll's," states Stefan Kanfer of *Time,* "and his freestyle drawing recalls the loony sketches of Edward Lear." Because of his work in publishing books for young readers and for the many innovative children's classics he has himself written, Seuss "has had a tremendous impact," Miles Corwin of the *Los Angeles Times* declares, "on children's reading habits and the way reading is taught and approached in the school system."

Seuss had originally intended to become a professor of English, but soon "became frustrated when he was shunted into a particularly insignificant field of research," reports Myra Kibler in the *Dictionary of Literary Biography.* After leaving graduate school in 1926, Seuss worked for a number of years as a free-lance magazine cartoonist, selling cartoons and humorous prose pieces to the major humor magazines of the 1920s and 1930s. Many of these works are collected in *The Tough Coughs as He Ploughs the Dough.* One of Seuss' cartoons—about "Flit," a spray-can pesticide—attracted the attention of the Standard Oil Company, manufacturers of the product. In 1928 they hired Seuss to draw their magazine advertising art and, for the next fifteen years, Seuss created grotesque, enormous insects to illustrate the famous slogan "Quick, Henry! The Flit!" He also created monsters for the motor oil division of Standard Oil, including the Moto-Raspus, the Moto-Munchus, and the Karbo-Nockus, that, says Kibler, are ancestral to his later fantastic creatures.

It was quite by chance that Seuss began writing by children. Returning from Europe by boat in 1936, Seuss amused himself during the long voyage by putting together a nonsense poem to the rhythm of the ship's engine. Later he drew pictures to illustrate the rhyme and in 1937 published the result as *And to Think That I Saw It on Mulberry Street,* his first children's book. Set in Seuss' home town of Springfield, Massachusetts, *Mulberry Street* is the story of a boy whose imagination transforms a simple horse-drawn wagon into a marvelous and exotic parade of strange creatures and vehicles. Many critics regard it as Seuss' best work.

Mulberry Street, along with *The 500 Hats of Bartholomew Cubbins, Horton Hatches the Egg* and *McElligot's Pool,* introduces many of the elements for which Seuss has become famous. *Mulberry Street* features rollicking anapestic tetrameter verse that compliments Seuss's boisterous illustrations. Jonathan Cott, writing in *Pipers at the Gates of Dawn: The Wisdom of Children's Literature,* declares that "the unflagging momentum, feeling of breathlessness, and swiftness of pace, all together [act] as the motor for Dr. Seuss's pullulating image machine." Whimsical fantasy characterizes *The 500 Hats of Bartholomew Cubbins,* while *Horton Hatches the Egg* introduces an element of morality and *McElligot's Pool* marks the first appearance of the fantasy animal characters for which Seuss has become famous.

The outbreak of World War II forced Seuss to give up writing for children temporarily and to devote his talents to the war effort. Working with the Information and Education Division of the U.S. Army, he made documentary films for American soldiers. One of these Army films—"Hitler Lives"—won an Academy Award, a feat Seuss repeated with his documentary about the Japanese war effort "Design for Death," and the UPA cartoon "Gerald McBoing-Boing," about a little boy who can only speak in sound effects. "The 5,000 Fingers of Dr. T," which Seuss wrote with Allen Scott, achieved cult status during the 1960s among music students on college campuses. Later, Seuss adapted several of his books into animated television specials, the most famous of which—"How the Grinch Stole Christmas"—has become a holiday favorite.

The success of his early books confirmed Seuss as an important new children's writer. However, it was *The Cat in the Hat* that really established his reputation and revolutionized the world of children's book publishing. By using a limited number of different words, all simple enough for very young children to read, and through its wildly iconoclastic plot—when two children are alone at home on a rainy day, the Cat in the Hat arrives to entertain them, wrecking their house in the process—*The Cat* provided an attractive alternative to the simplistic "Dick and Jane" primers then in use in American schools, and critics applauded its appearance. For instance, Helen Adams Masten of *Saturday Review* marveled at the way Seuss, using "only 223 different words, . . . has created a story in rhyme which presents an impelling incentive to read." The enthusiastic reception of *The Cat in the Hat* led Seuss to found Beginner Books, a publishing company specializing in easy-to-read books for children. In 1960, Random House acquired the company and made Seuss president of the Beginner Books division.

In the years since 1960 Seuss and Beginner Books have created many modern classics for children, from *Green Eggs and Ham,* about the need to try new experiences, and *Fox in Socks,* a series of increasingly boisterous tongue-twisters, to *The Lorax,* about environmental preservation, and *The Butter Battle Book,* a fable based on the nuclear arms race. In 1986, at the age of 82, however, Seuss produced *You're Only Old Once,* a book for the "obsolete children" of the world. The story follows an elderly gentleman's examination at "The Golden Age Clinic on Century Square," where he's gone for "Spleen Readjustment and Muffler Repair." The gentleman, who is never named, is subjected to a number of seemingly pointless tests by merciless physicians and grim nurses, ranging from a diet machine that rejects any appealing foods to an enormous eye chart that asks, "Have you any idea how much these tests are costing you?" Finally, however, he is dismissed, the doctors telling him that "You're in pretty good shape/For the shape that you're in!"

In its cheerful conclusion *You're Only Old Once* is typically Seuss; "The other ending is unacceptable," Seuss confides to *New York Times Book Review* contributor David W. Dunlap. In other ways, however, the book is very different. Seuss tells Dunlap that *You're Only Old Once* is much more autobiographical than any of his other stories. Robin Marantz Henig, writing in the *Washington Post Book World*, says *You're Only Old Once* "is lighthearted, silly, but with an undertone of complaint. Being old is sometimes tough, isn't it . . . Seuss seems to be saying." *Los Angeles Times Book Review* contributor Jack Smith declares that in it Seuss "reveals himself as human and old, and full of aches and pains and alarming symptoms, and frightened of the world of geriatric medicine, with its endless tests, overzealous doctors, intimidating nurses, Rube Goldberg machines and demoralizing paperwork." Nonetheless, Henig concludes, "We should all be lucky enough to get old the way this man, and Dr. Seuss himself, has gotten old."

MEDIA ADAPTATIONS: Dr. Seuss' animated cartoon character Gerald McBoing-Boing appeared in several other UPA pictures, including "Gerald McBoing-Boing's Symphony," 1953, "How Now McBoing-Boing," 1954, and "Gerald McBoing-Boing on the Planet Moo," 1956. In December of 1956, Gerald McBoing-Boing appeared in his own animated variety show, "The Gerald McBoing-Boing Show," which aired on CBS-TV on Sunday evenings. The program ran through October of 1958.

BIOGRAPHICAL/CRITICAL SOURCES:

BOOKS

Children's Literature Review, Gale, Volume 1, 1976, Volume 9, 1985.
Cott, Jonathan, *Pipers at the Gates of Dawn: The Wisdom of Children's Literature,* Random House, 1983.
Dictionary of Literary Biography, Volume 61: *American Writers for Children since 1960: Poets, Illustrators, and Nonfiction Authors,* Gale, 1987.
Lanes, Selma G., *Down the Rabbit Hole: Adventures and Misadventures in the Realm of Children's Literature,* Atheneum, 1972.

PERIODICALS

Chicago Tribune, May 12, 1957, April 15, 1982, April 17, 1984, June 29, 1986, January 14, 1987.
Los Angeles Times, November 27, 1983, October 7, 1989.
Los Angeles Times Book Review, March 9, 1986.
New York Times, May 21, 1986, December 26, 1987.
New York Times Book Review, November 11, 1952, May 11, 1958, March 20, 1960, November 11, 1962, November 16, 1975, April 29, 1979, February 26, 1984, March 23, 1986.
Parade, February 26, 1984.
Publishers Weekly, February 10, 1984.
Saturday Review, May 11, 1957, November 16, 1957.
Time, May 7, 1979.
Washington Post, December 30, 1987.
Washington Post Book World, March 9, 1986.

—*Sketch by Kenneth R. Shepherd*

*   *   *

GERASIMOV, Gennadi (Ivanovitch) 1930-

PERSONAL: Born March 3, 1930, in Kazan, U.S.S.R.; son of Ivan (a physician) and Nina (Chernov) Gerasimov; married Margarita Ponomareva (an editor), November 26, 1953. *Educa-*

tion: Attended Institute of Foreign Relations, Moscow, U.S.S.R., 1948-53; graduate study at Moscow University.

CAREER: New Times, Moscow, U.S.S.R., editor, 1955-61; *World Marxist Review,* Prague, Czechoslovakia, editor, 1962-67; Novosti Press Agency, Moscow, diplomatic correspondent, beginning 1967; currently official Soviet government spokesman. Has covered political affairs in the United States and the Soviet Union, as well as the war in Nigeria.

MEMBER: Union of Soviet Journalists.

WRITINGS:

Stanet li tesno na zemmom share?: Problema narodonaseleniia, Znanie (Moscow), 1967, translation published as *Standing Room Only?: When?*
(With Georgi Kuznetsov and Vladimir Morev) *Nabat v nochi,* Novosti Press Agency Publishing House (Moscow), 1968, translation published as *Fire Bell in the Night,* 1968.
Kljuch k miru vo Vietname, Novosti Press Agency Publishing House, translation published as *The Key to Peace in Vietnam,* 1968.
(Contributor) *Problems of War and Peace,* Progress Publishing House (Moscow), 1971.
Za spinol statul Svobody, Znanie, 1978.
Obshchestvo potrebleniia: Mify i real'nost, Znanie, 1980, 2nd edition, 1984.
Disarmament: Who Is for, Who Is Against, translation by Natalia Korolyova, Novosti Press Agency Publishing House, 1982.
Ne dopustit' oruzhie v kosmos!, translation published as *Keep Space Weapon-Free,* Novosti Press Agency Publishing House, 1984.
SOI—astral'nye zabluzhdeniia, translation by Natalia Mazitova published as *SDI, Stellar Delusions: The U.S. Threat of Space Militarization,* Novosti Press Agency Publishing House, 1986.

WORK IN PROGRESS: A book on the United States.

SIDELIGHTS: Gennadi Gerasimov once told *CA* that his interests lie in global issues: population, survival in the nuclear age, energy resources, and ecological balance. He is often seen on U.S. network television in his official capacity as a Soviet government spokesman.*

*   *   *

GIDDINS, Gary 1948-

PERSONAL: Born March 21, 1948, in Brooklyn, N.Y.; son of Leo (a businessman) and Alice (a decorator; maiden name, Gelber) Giddins; married Susan Rogers (a writer and publicist), April 23, 1972 (divorced, 1978); married Deborah Eve Halper (a health care administrator), May 19, 1985; children: (second marriage) Lea Aviva. *Education:* Grinnell College, B.A., 1970. *Religion:* Jewish.

ADDRESSES: Home—145 East 15th St., New York, N.Y. 10003. *Office*— 842 Broadway, New York, N.Y. 10003. *Agent*—Curtis Brown, Ltd., Ten Astor Pl., New York, N.Y. 10003.

CAREER: Hollywood Reporter, Hollywood, Calif., film critic, 1972; *Down Beat,* Chicago, Ill., contributing editor, 1972-73; *Village Voice,* New York City, staff writer and author of column, "Weather Bird," 1973—. Staff writer, *Vanity Fair,* 1983-84. Founder, president, and artistic director, American Jazz Orchestra, 1985—. Radio producer and disc jockey, WBAI-FM, New York City, 1975-80; producer of several jazz albums. Teacher of jazz history at New York University School of Continuing Education, 1977-87; instructor of writing, Columbia University, 1988—; visiting instructor and guest lecturer at numerous colleges, universities, and arts centers. Fellow, Smithsonian Colloquium on jazz criticism, 1974.

MEMBER: National Academy of Jazz (member of board of directors), PEN, Authors Guild, Authors League of America.

AWARDS, HONORS: ASCAP Deems-Taylor Award, 1976, 1977, and 1984, for music criticism, and 1988, for *Celebrating Bird: The Triumph of Charlie Parker;* Grammy nomination for best album notes, 1982, for *Duke Ellington 1941;* Art Directors' Club Merit Award, 1985; Guggenheim fellowship, 1986; Grammy Award for best album notes, 1987, for *Frank Sinatra: The Voice/The Columbia Years;* American Book Award, 1987, for *Celebrating Bird;* AFI Video Conference Award, and VIDEO Magazine Award, both 1988, both for "Celebrating Bird"; honorary degree, Grinnell College, 1988.

WRITINGS:

Riding on a Blue Note: Jazz and American Pop, Oxford University Press, 1981.
(With Carol Friedman) *A Moment's Notice: Portraits of American Jazz Musicians,* Schirmer Books, 1983.
(Contributor) Elizabeth Cowen, editor, *Readings for Writings,* Scott, Foresman, 1983.
Rhythm-a-ning: Jazz Tradition and Innovation in the '80s, Oxford University Press, 1985.
Celebrating Bird: The Triumph of Charlie Parker (also see below), Beech Tree Books, 1986.
(And director with Kendrick Simmons) "Celebrating Bird" (documentary film; adapted from his book; aired on Public Broadcasting System [PBS-TV], 1989), Sony/Pioneer, 1987.
(Contributor) Gay Talese and Robert Atwan, editors, *The Best American Essays of 1987,* Ticknor & Fields, 1987.
Satchmo (also see below), Dolphin Books, 1988.
(And director) "Satchmo" (documentary film; adapted from his book; first aired on PBS-TV, 1989), CBS-Video, 1989.
(Contributor) Ben Sonnenberg, editor, *Performance and Reality,* Rutgers University Press, 1989.

Also author of album notes for over sixty records, including *American Jazz Orchestra: Ellington Masterpieces, The Complete Art Pepper on Galaxy, Duke Ellington 1941,* and *Frank Sinatra: The Voice/The Columbia Years.* Contributor of articles to numerous periodicals, including *Atlantic, Grand Street, New York Times, Esquire, Stereo Review,* and *Boston Globe.* Author of jazz columns for *Hifi/Stereo,* 1975-78, and *New York,* 1975-80.

WORK IN PROGRESS: A history of recorded jazz, for Prentice-Hall; a collection of essays on musical and literary subjects, for Oxford University Press.

SIDELIGHTS: "Gary Giddins is the best jazz critic now at work," asserts *Newsweek* writer Walter Clemons. "The most consistently stimulating of the younger jazz writers," as Robert Palmer terms him in the *New York Times Book Review,* the *Village Voice* columnist is "a careful and knowledgeable listener, and he is particularly scrupulous in his evenhanded appreciation of jazz from every period." In *Riding on a Blue Note: Jazz and American Pop,* one of his two collections of music criticism, Giddins writes "about [jazz's] beauty and pain, its achievements and failures as seen through [its] personalities," Robert Richman observes in *Commentary;* Giddins also "offers a number of fairly astute and adept considerations of jazz styles." While the author declines to trace the rise of jazz's status from a popular to a "serious" musical form, Richman explains that "still, it is possible to

glean from this book an understanding of how the current high valuation of jazz developed." Part of this is due to the author's extensive knowledge and his ability to discuss the music as part of a larger framework, as Palmer notes: "Giddins has learned to write crisp jazz criticism that focuses on the music and its context without resorting to showy word play." "Giddins's loving, encyclopedic knowledge of the past makes one trust him," Clemons concludes, adding that "I read him to correct my ignorance and for his prose. He's an elegant enthusiast."

With *Rhythm-a-ning: Jazz Tradition and Innovation in the '80s,* "Giddins more than fulfills the promise of his 'Riding on a Blue Note'. . . , a work that established him as the most important young jazz essayist to emerge in years," remarks *Los Angeles Times Book Review* contributor Grover Sales. "Combining unusual catholicity of taste with refreshing insight, wit and a readable style much too rare in his field," the critic continues, "Giddins has assembled delightful and instructive pieces that can be returned to again and again." While *Rhythm-a-ning,* like Giddins's previous anthology, is distinguished by the quality of its writing, it also displays a cohesiveness rare to column compilations, as Jack Chambers recounts in the Toronto *Globe and Mail:* "Few jazz journalists find the time between deadlines to winnow, rethink and rewrite their collected columns into more bookish fare, but Gary Giddins . . . seems more than willing. He goes a step further and finds a theme, spells it out at the beginning," the critic elaborates, and "returns to it, directly or indirectly, often enough to keep it alive." This theme, as Amy Duncan describes it in the *Christian Science Monitor,* is that "this is not a time of ground-breaking innovation in jazz—instead, it's a time of refinement and eclecticism, in which up-and-coming jazz musicians are feeding off tradition, refining and redefining it."

Although *New York Times Book Review* contributor Francis Davis does not completely agree with this interpretation, he maintains that "one measure of the book's value is that the issues Mr. Giddins raises are so pertinent. . . . The author's ability to recognize and convey the historical and esthetic subtleties surrounding any given jazz performance makes 'Rhythm-a-ning' (named for a Thelonius Monk composition) an indispensable guidebook to jazz in the 1980's." The critic also comments that "one comes away from this volume impressed with Mr. Giddins's graceful prose and the breadth and depth of his critical understanding." Duncan concurs with this assessment, writing that "anyone with a knowledge of jazz will appreciate Giddins's insightful observations, whether or not they agree with him. His prose is intelligent, probing, and often hilarious. . . . Not only was my curiosity aroused about the records I haven't heard, but I felt inclined to reexamine the ones I have heard," the critic continues, explaining that "I can only attribute this to his descriptive and analytic charisma." "It's not that I always hear in a piece of music what he says he hears," notes *Nation* contributor Evan Eisenberg, "but that I know he does, and I think that is rare in a critic." As Chicago *Tribune Books* reviewer Clarence Peterson concludes, Giddins "is a pleasure to read for his prose, which is, like the best of jazz, lyrical, rhythmic, authoritative and rooted in tradition."

Giddins has also brought his expertise in the field to the biography of famed alto saxophone player Charlie "Bird" Parker, who was one of the founders of the 1940s jazz style known as "bebop." *Celebrating Bird: The Triumph of Charlie Parker* relates the meteoric rise and fall of a largely self-taught musician who transformed himself into one of the age's leading jazz soloists, only to destroy his life with heroin and alcohol by the age of thirty-four. "Until the appearance of Gary Giddins's *Celebrating Bird*—published more than thirty years after Parker's death—it's been difficult to read about the life of one of the most important musicians of the twentieth century with any confidence in the accuracy of the details," contends *Nation* reviewer Peter Watrous. In addition to a wealth of new information, Giddins brings an appreciation of the sax player's work to this biography, as *Los Angeles Times Book Review* writer Art Seidenbaum observes: " 'Celebrating Bird' is a tribute, in photographs and text, to Parker's gift and grief. Giddins knows the music and the sources and as much of the story as the survivors make available. He is at his best when arranging the elements of a short sonic life." "The book is packed with anecdotes from the gamut of modern jazz greats," describes an *Esquire* reviewer, and, "as Parker himself always did, the book shuns the affectations and lingo of its genre and sticks to finding a pure and fast melody to fit the changes of the given song."

Although Parker's short life included many devastating changes, "Giddins, through extensive research and a shrewd reappraisal of the facts, extracts the triumph from Parker's tragedy," *Village Voice* contributor Dean Robbins claims, "making this extended essay . . . a celebration of the highest order. Realizing that his subject has been obscured by myth," the critic explains, the author "presents Parker as a plausible tragic hero. Giddins avoids simplifications while he addresses the most intriguing questions of this peculiar life." While Giddins "isn't breaking any new ground" in his analysis of Parker's music or his anecdotes of Parker's unpredictable behavior, Robbins states that "he also shows another side of Charlie. . . . He succeeds in capturing the spirit that allowed this so-called maniac to make a sound so rich, so ravishing, and so boundlessly alive." "This book does not pretend to be a definitive biography," Jason Berry suggests in the *New York Times Book Review;* "however, it is as penetrating a character study of Bird as any yet written and that is no small accomplishment." As Geoffrey C. Ward remarks in *American Heritage,* "it is Giddins's special achievement that the reader finishes his elegant biographical essay . . . with a fresh appreciation of Parker's demanding music as well as a greater understanding of the troubled individual who made it."

Giddins similarly challenges old perceptions in *Satchmo,* a biography of famed trumpet player Louis Armstrong. "In this elegant and affecting book," comments the *Washington Post Book World*'s Jonathan Yardley, "Gary Giddins has written both a perceptive biography of Louis Armstrong and a sensitive appreciation of his music, yet he has accomplished even more than that. Not merely does Giddins come to praise Armstrong," the critic details; "he insists that we reappraise our received assumptions about the overall character and achievement of Armstrong's career. His is, in the best sense of the term, a 'revisionist' biography; it requires us to look at his subject in new and revealing light, and to grant him even deeper respect than heretofore we had." As *Times Literary Supplement* contributor Charles Fox recounts, many jazz critics believe that Armstrong's greatest work was done early in his career, and that later performances were "mere showmanship, a matter of high notes and high jinks. It is an attitude on which Gary Giddins mounts an impassioned attack," Fox relates. "Armstrong's genius, he asserts, was not confined to what are undoubtedly masterpieces by the purest of jazz standards, but was also reflected in his development as an entertainer, all the skills that made up a complete artistic personality." "As for Armstrong the man," maintains Yardley, "he emerges more fully in Giddins' portrait than in any other." Tom Piazza likewise concludes in the *New York Times Book Review* that Armstrong's "magic jumps off the pages of *Satchmo,*" which he calls "a valuable, jubilant look at a great man and art-

ist, whose ability to fuse exaltation with profundity still inspires awe."

Giddins told *CA:* "It's difficult to write about jazz for very long without developing a siege mentality. *I* know jazz is the most forceful indication of American achievement in the arts in the present century, but confirmation is more easily found in Europe than at home. Perhaps a kind of activism is inevitable. For me it took the form of starting an orchestra, The American Jazz Orchestra, in 1985. John Lewis of the Modern Jazz Quartet is the music director and Roberta Swann, a poet who is also director of the Great Hall at Cooper Union, provides us with a home. Our 18-piece ensemble, formed along the lines of the classic big band (an indigenous American creation if there ever was one), aims to do what a good philharmonic does—keep the classics alive, and occasionally commission new work. Instead of hammering out the classics of 19th-century Europe, however, we are learning to do something rather new—interpret 20th-century American jazz classics by Ellington, Lunceford, Henderson, Basie, Gil Evans, et al. Too many jazz enthusiasts are content to consign jazz to the record shelf. We cherish the great recordings, of course, but we also consider them analogous to scores. Great music ought to be able to withstand interpretation. Ellington's masterpieces will die if they aren't played. I believe that we have already shown that his music can electrify contemporary audiences unfamiliar with his records. But we have yet to receive any national or corporate funding. We limp along gamely. Come hear us."

BIOGRAPHICAL/CRITICAL SOURCES:

PERIODICALS

American Heritage, December, 1988.
Christian Science Monitor, October 2, 1985.
Commentary, October, 1981.
Esquire, May, 1988.
Globe and Mail (Toronto), April 13, 1985.
Los Angeles Times Book Review, March 17, 1985, December 21, 1986.
Nation, May 18, 1985, February 28, 1987.
Newsweek, June 24, 1985.
New York Times Book Review, July 19, 1981, March 7, 1985, January 11, 1987, February 26, 1989.
Times Literary Supplement, November 15, 1985, April 7, 1989.
Tribune Books, March 15, 1987.
Village Voice, May 5, 1987.
Washington Post Book World, December 11, 1988.

—*Sketch by Diane Telgen*

* * *

GILMER, Ann
See ROSS, W(illiam) E(dward) D(aniel)

* * *

GILROY, Frank D(aniel) 1925-

PERSONAL: Born October 13, 1925, in Bronx, N.Y.; son ⸱ Frank B. (a coffee broker) and Bettina (Vasti) Gilroy; marri⸱ Ruth Dorothy Gaydos (a secretary), February 13, 1954; ch⸱ dren: Anthony, Daniel and John (twins). *Education:* Dartmou⸱ College, B.A. (magna cum laude), 1950; graduate study, Y⸱ University, 1967.

ADDRESSES: Home—Monroe, N.Y. *Office*—Drama⸱ Guild, 234 West 44th St., New York, N.Y. 10036.

CAREER: Playwright and author of scripts for television and motion pictures, 1952—; director of motion pictures. Worked as messenger for Young and Rubicam, New York, N.Y.; beach cabana renter in Atlantic City, N.J. *Military service:* U.S. Army, Infantry, 1943-46; fought in Europe.

MEMBER: Writers Guild of America, Dramatists Guild (president, 1969-71), Authors League of America, Directors Guild of America.

AWARDS, HONORS: Obie Award for best play produced Off-Broadway, *Village Voice,* 1962, for *Who'll Save the Plowboy?;* Outer Circle Award for outstanding new playwright, 1964; New York Drama Critics Circle Award, 1964, for *The Subject Was Roses;* New York Theatre Club Award, Antoinette Perry ("Tony") Award from League of New York Theatres and Producers, and Pulitzer Prize for drama, all 1965, all for *The Subject Was Roses;* Dartmouth College, D.Lett., 1966, grant, 1967; Silver Bear Award, Berlin Film Festival, 1971, for "Desperate Characters."

WRITINGS:

About Those Roses; or, How Not to Do a Play and Succeed (journal), Random House, 1965.
Private (novel), Harcourt, 1970.
(With wife, Ruth G. Gilroy) *Little Ego* (juvenile), Simon & Schuster, 1970.
From Noon till Three: The Possibly True and Certainly Tragic Story of an Outlaw and a Lady Whose Love Knew No Bounds (novel; also see below), Doubleday, 1973 (published in England as *For Want of a Horse,* Coronet, 1975).

PLAYS

"The Middle World," first produced in Hanover, N.H., at Dartmouth College, 1949.
Who'll Save the Plowboy? (three-act; first produced Off-Broadway at Phoenix Theater, January 9, 1962), Random House, 1962.
The Subject Was Roses (two-act; first produced on Broadway at Royale Theater, May 26, 1964; also see below), Samuel French, 1962.
That Summer—That Fall; and Far Rockaway (the latter first produced for television, 1965; the former first produced in New York at Helen Hayes Theatre, March 16, 1967), Random House, 1967.
The Only Game in Town (two-act; first produced in New York at Broadhurst Theatre, May 23, 1968; also see below), Samuel French, 1967.
A Matter of Pride (adapted from the story by John Langdon, "The Blue Serge Suit"; first produced for television, 1957), Samuel French, 1970.
Present Tense: Four Plays by Frank D. Gilroy (includes "Come Next Tuesday," "'Twas Brillig," "So Please Be Kind," and "Present Tense"; first produced Off-Broadway at Sheridan Square Playhouse, July 18, 1972), Samuel French, 1973.
The Next Contestant: A Drama in One Act (first produced Off-Broadway at Ensemble Studio Theatre, 1978), Samuel French, 1979.
"Last Licks," first produced on Broadway at Longacre Theatre, October 20, 1979.
Dreams of Glory: A Play in One Act (first produced at Ensemble Studio Theatre), Samuel French, 1980.
"Real to Reel" (one-act), first produced Off-Broadway, 1987.
"Match Point," first produced Off-Broadway, 1990.

Also author of "The Fastest Gun Alive" (also see below).

SCREENPLAYS

(With Russel Rouse) "The Fastest Gun Alive" (adapted from the play and short story by Gilroy), Metro-Goldwyn-Mayer (MGM), 1956.
(With Beirne Lay, Jr.) "The Gallant Hours," United Artists, 1960.
"The Subject Was Roses" (adapted from the play by Gilroy), MGM, 1968.
"The Only Game in Town" (adapted from the play by Gilroy), Twentieth Century-Fox, 1969.
(And director and producer) "Desperate Characters" (adapted from the novel by Paula Fox), Lew Grade/Paramount, 1971.
(And director and producer) "From Noon till Three" (adapted from the novel by Gilroy), United Artists, 1976.
(And director and producer) "Once in Paris," Independent/Atlantic, 1978.
(And director and producer) "The Gig," McLaughlin, Piven, Vogel, 1985.
(And director) "The Luckiest Man in the World," McLaughlin, Piven, Vogel, 1989.

OTHER

Originator of television series "Burke's Law," and contributor of scripts to other series, including "The Rifleman," "Have Gun, Will Travel," and "Gibbsville"; contributor of scripts to television programs, including "U.S. Steel Hour," "Kraft Theatre," "Playhouse 90," "Studio One," "Lux Video Theatre," and "Omnibus."

WORK IN PROGRESS: A play.

SIDELIGHTS: Early in his career, Frank D. Gilroy made a grand entrance as the playwright of the Obie Award-winning *Who'll Save the Plowboy?* and Pulitzer Prize-winning *The Subject Was Roses.* Both plays suggest "an element of autobiography," according to *Dictionary of Literary Biography* contributor Stephen C. Coy, ". . . in the push-pull nature of [two couples'] relationships and in the spirit with which they are observed by the playwright." Coy hypothesizes that the married couples in these plays are reminiscent of the author's parents; the references in both works to World War II (Gilroy is a World War II veteran) also suggests that these productions have an autobiographical element. With the exception of the play "Last Licks," however, the author drifted away from adding elements of his personal life to his writing after *The Subject Was Roses.* He has written a variety of plays and screenplays over the years with some success since then, but critics generally consider *Who'll Save the Plowboy?* and *The Subject Was Roses* to be Gilroy's highest achievements.

Who'll Save the Plowboy? concerns the reunion of two veterans, Albert and Larry, fifteen years after the end of World War II. During the War, Larry saved Albert's life, and in the play Larry, who is dying of a terminal illness, returns to reassure himself that Albert is leading a fulfilling life. Over the years, Albert has been writing Larry about his son and wife, Helen, without revealing that his son is mentally handicapped and his marriage is in trouble. In order not to disappoint Larry, Albert puts up a front that succeeds in fooling his wartime friend until Albert leaves the house and Helen reveals the truth. When Albert returns with a young boy he has hired to act as his son, Larry chooses to accept the ruse, thus saving Albert a second time by sparing his dignity through this act of compassion. Although Coy feels the play suffers from "sometimes awkward manipulation" and a "tone of pathos in the ending," he believes it still "succeeds on its ending, which seems genuinely moving." And John D. Simon actually considers this play to be better than *The Subject Was Roses* because of "its spareness." "In fact," the critic concludes in *New York Magazine,* "this simplest and bitterest work of Gilroy's was modestly but unquestionably art."

The similarity between Gilroy's art and his life is more apparent in *The Subject Was Roses,* in which the conflict between husband and wife is complemented by their son Timmy's return from the European theater of war. The autobiographical element is further enhanced by Timmy's announcement that he "might become a writer . . . someday" and that the father in the play, like Gilroy's, is a coffee merchant. *The Subject Was Roses* involves the awkward relationship between mother, father, and son after Timmy's return, it shows how three people who care for and love one another can hurt each other simply from a lack of mutual understanding. Besides the prestigious Pulitzer Prize, *The Subject Was Roses* also won a New York Drama Critics Circle Award, New York Theatre Club Award, and a Tony Award. Today, however, some reviewers like *New York Times* critic James Atlas believe that the play "seems rather dated," though it remains the author's best-known and most lauded work. "Gilroy," says Coy, "has not since equalled the intensity of perception and feeling in *The Subject Was Roses.*"

Gilroy's later plays, several of which have appeared on Broadway or Off-Broadway, have been less enthusiastically received. The next play to contain a personl touch by the author is Gilroy's 1979 work, "Last Licks." "There are certain strains in 'Last Licks' that are intensely personal," Gilroy tells Leah D. Frank in a *New York Times* interview. "It's my Broadway chance to cleanse myself of some guilt I either didn't deserve or did deserve. It's wrestling with some old ghosts." "Last Licks" is about the reconciliation between a father and son after the mother's death. However, a number of critics have asserted that "Last Licks" is not Gilroy at his best. Character motivation in the play has been considered a problem, and the final reconciliation scene remains unconvincing. "The problem with the resolving actions of the play," remarks Coy, "is that they do not improve upon, or even measure up to, the original model, the end of *The Subject Was Roses.*" Walter Kerr observes in a *New York Times* review that the humorous tone of the first act is discordant with the dramatic and serious tone of the second, thus diminishing the work's overall effectiveness. The tension that results from the son's jealous desire to mourn more than his father does over the loss of his mother "is really the wrong [source of conflict] for the play we'd begun to delight in," writes Kerr.

Gilroy has written screen adaptations of *The Subject Was Roses* and *The Only Game in Town,* as well of as his novel *From Noon till Three: The Possibly True and Certainly Tragic Story of an Outlaw and a Lady Whose Love Knew No Bounds;* but he achieved his greatest success with an independently produced movie adaptation of a novel by Paula Fox, "Desperate Characters." The film marked Gilroy's directorial debut and won a Silver Bear Award at the Berlin Film Festival. Encouraged by the popularity of "Desperate Characters" and the positive criticism of "From Noon till Three," the author attempted to get studio support for his next screenplay. But his low-key approach to movies failed to interest major studios, so Gilroy went on to produce several more low budget films independently, including "Once in Paris," "The Gig," and "The Luckiest Man in the World." These ventures are generally light-hearted, humorous, and, in the case of "Once in Paris," romantic.

Gilroy's interest in these and other projects has distracted him from the theater for years. As he explains to Laermer: "I remem-

ber how I would wait for a play idea. I wasted a tremendous amount of time. I didn't realize that [non-play] ideas could be made into movies or novels. I hope I live long enough to write about all the ideas that have come to me since." The 1987 production of "Real to Reel" is the only work Gilroy has written for the stage since 1980. He tells Laermer, however, that he has plans to return to the theater with a new play.

BIOGRAPHICAL/CRITICAL SOURCES:

BOOKS

Contemporary Literary Criticism, Volume 2, Gale, 1974.
Dictionary of Literary Biography, Volume 7: *Twentieth-Century American Dramatists,* Gale, 1981.

PERIODICALS

Los Angeles Times, April 27, 1983, June 14, 1985, April 17, 1986.
New York Magazine, August 7, 1972.
New York Times, February 13, 1977, November 9, 1978, November 18, 1979 (interview), November 21, 1979, January 18, 1980, November 26, 1985, June 14, 1987, June 17, 1987, February 19, 1989, February 22, 1989.
New York Times Book Review, June 3, 1987.
Saturday Review, November 7, 1970.
Washington Post, October 3, 1986, October 9, 1986.
Variety, August 9, 1972.*

—*Sketch by Kevin S. Hile*

*   *   *

GLUCK, Robert 1947-

PERSONAL: Surname rhymes with "look;" born February 2, 1947, in Cleveland, OH; son of Morris and Dorothy (Philips) Gluck. *Education:* Attended University of California, Los Angeles, 1964-66, and University of Edinburgh, 1966-67; University of California, Berkeley, B.A., 1969; California State University, San Francisco (now San Francisco State University), M.A., 1973. *Politics:* "Left."

ADDRESSES: Home and office—16 Clipper Street, San Francisco, CA 94114.

CAREER: Small Press Traffic (book store and literary center), San Francisco, CA, writer-in-residence, 1977-85; San Francisco State University, Poetry Center, assistant director, 1985-88, director, 1988—.

MEMBER: National Writers Union.

AWARDS, HONORS: Award from Academy of American Poets, 1973, for *Andy;* Monoclonal Antibodies, Inc., Fellowship in Literature, Djerassi Foundation, 1989.

WRITINGS:

Andy (poetry), Panjandrum, 1973.
Metaphysics (poetry and prose), Hoddypoll, 1977.
Family Poems, Black Star Publishing, 1979.
(Translator with Bruce Boone) *La Fontaine,* Black Star Publishing, 1981.
Elements of a Coffee Service (stories), Four Seasons Foundation, 1982.
(Editor) *Saturday Afternoon,* Black Star Series, 1985.
Jack the Modernist (novel), Seahorse Press, 1985.
Reader (poetry and prose), Lapis Press, 1989.

Contributor to anthologies, including *Writing/Talks, Men on Men, High Risk, New Directions Anthology,* and *Personal Dis-*

patches; contributor of stories, poems, and articles to periodicals, including *Social Text, Ironwood, Poetics Journal, New York Native, Zyzzyva, Sulfur,* and *City Lights Review.*

WORK IN PROGRESS: Everyman, a book of stories.

*   *   *

GOLDEMBERG, Isaac   1945-

PERSONAL: Born November 15, 1945, in Chepén, La Libertad, Peru; immigrated to United States, 1964; son of Isaac (a merchant) and Eva (a merchant; maiden name, Bay) Goldemberg; married Mona Stern, December 19, 1963 (separated); children: David, Dina. *Education:* City College of the City University of New York, B.A. (magna cum laude), 1968; New York University, graduate study, 1968.

ADDRESSES: Home—515 West 110th St., Apt. 6A, New York, N.Y. 10025.

CAREER: Writer. Worked in a kibbutz in Israel, 1962-63; insurance salesman in Barcelona, Spain, 1963; New York Public Library, New York City, clerk in Jewish Division, 1965-66; Grolier, Inc., New York City, Spanish editor, 1968-69; American Book Co., New York City, Spanish editor, 1969; New York University, New York City, lecturer in Spanish, 1970—; Latin American Writers Institute at City College, New York City, director, 1987—. Coordinator, New York's Latin American Book Fair, New York City, 1985—. Writer in residence, Center for Inter-American Relations, 1981, Ollantay Center for the Arts, 1988.

MEMBER: Phi Beta Kappa.

WRITINGS:

Tiempo de silencio (poems; title means "Time for Silence"), Colección de Poesía Hispanoamericana, 1969.
(With José Kozer) *De Chepén a la Habana* (poems; title means "From Chepén to Havana"), Editorial Bayu-Menorah, 1973.
The Fragmented Life of Don Jacobo Lerner (novel), translated by Robert Picciotto, Persea Books, 1976.
(And translator with David Unger) *Hombre de paso/Just Passing Through* (poems), bilingual edition, Ediciones del Norte, 1981.
Tiempo al tiempo; o, La conversión (novel), Ediciones del Norte, 1983, translated by Hardie St. Martin, published by Persea Books as *The Conversion,* 1983, and as *Play by Play,* 1985.
La vida al contado (poems; title means "Life Paid in Cash"), Lluvia, 1989.

Contributor to Spanish- and English-language journals, including *Present Tense, Nimrod,* and *Mundo Nuevo.*

WORK IN PROGRESS: An anthology of Latin American fiction by writers living in New York; an anthology of Latin American Jewish writers; a novel.

SIDELIGHTS: Isaac Goldemberg once told *CA:* "I am a Peruvian of Jewish, Russian, English, Italian, Spanish, and Indian descent. I traveled to Israel in 1962. Then I moved to Barcelona, where I spent a year in medical school. I decided (age eighteen) I wanted to be a writer and quit medical school. I settled in New York. Prior to my return to Peru (for the first time in fifteen years) in 1976, I wrote *The Fragmented Life of Don Jacobo Lerner,* an attempt at reconstructing my own past and that of the Peruvian Jewish community at large. Even though my work deals mainly with the Jewish experience in Peru, the burdens of exile and spiritual rootlessness, I am also concerned with Peruvian life as a whole, particularly that of provincial Peru, marked by narrowness and claustrophobia. This is the world depicted in my first novel, where I attempted to draw the life of the Jewish immigrant as a tragic and heroic parody of the legend of the Wandering Jew."

Frank Macshane comments on *The Fragmented Life of Don Jacobo Lerner* in an article for the *New York Times Book Review,* writing that the world depicted by Goldemberg "is a nightmare world of frustrated hopes, of narrowness and claustrophobia where no one can afford to be generous and where people become insane and destructive. Goldemberg allows his characters to tell their own stories and interrupts these private narratives with notices, documents and newspaper headlines to give a sense of the public dimension of the life of these exiles. This technique also insures that the novel remains refreshingly free of the exotic trimmings that are often associated with Latin American fiction: it is a moving exploration of the human condition." In another review of Goldemberg's novel, Margo Jefferson says in *Newsweek* that the author "shows with great perception how history, belief and myth can burden people with more contradictions than they can bear. This insight, joined to well-observed details makes this novel a wonderfully promising debut for a gifted writer."

But Goldemberg's attempt to integrate Peruvian and Jewish concerns in *The Fragmented Life of Don Jacobo Lerner* has caused him to fall under the attack of both sectors of Peru's population. As *Village Voice* contributor Ellen Lesser observes, "When *Jacobo Lerner* appeared in Peru, a self-appointed Jewish community spokesman attacked Goldemberg as an anti-Semite. On the other side, non-Jewish Peruvian critics tended to address themselves to the novel's Jewish aspect alone." The reviewers acted "as if it were about Peruvian Jews only and not about Peru itself," the author tells Lesser. "One critic, whose name I wish to forget, said, 'What does Goldemberg have to do with Peru? Just look at his name. He doesn't represent any of our traditions.' "

In an effort to appease his critics, Goldemberg set out to write a novel that would not offend either the Peruvians or the Jews. The result was a first draft of *Play by Play* that took Goldemberg two years to compose. But, as he says in Lesser's article, "I felt the novel was very dishonest. I burned it. That was like an exorcism, a purification. Then I started writing the second version and I said exactly what the narrator wanted to say." The theme of the problems of racial integration in *Play by Play* is much like that in Goldemberg's first novel; the stories are also similar in that they end in tragedy. In *The Fragmented Life of Don Jacobo Lerner* the protagonist's inability to accept both sides of his mixed racial background results in his son's insanity, while in *Play by Play* the main character, Marcos, ultimately commits suicide. *New York Times Book Review* contributor Ariel Dorfman compares the protagonist in *Play by Play* with the "characters in the work of Proust, Philip Roth and Elias Canetti," adding that Marcos "is a fascinating addition to that group."

After spending over twenty years in New York City writing about his native country, Goldemberg now feels an urge to return to Peru. "I know I have to go back," he tells Lesser. "I had a feeling I was missing something in all my years in New York. The conditions in Peru are very difficult, but people live their lives passionately. You read the newspapers, and when there's an editorial, it is passionate. If you read the newspapers here, everybody tries to be very objective about things, and I hate that. I've had it." Lesser later adds that "while the distance of exile has helped shape Goldemberg's work so far, he's now convinced that going home will stimulate his writing, that he needs to close the circle and reconnect with his source."

BIOGRAPHICAL/CRITICAL SOURCES:

PERIODICALS

Newsweek, May 9, 1977.
New Yorker, April 4, 1977.
New York Times, May 18, 1977.
New York Times Book Review, June 12, 1977.
Times Literary Supplement, March 10, 1978.
Village Voice Literary Supplement, May, 1982.

*   *   *

GOLDIE, Terrence William 1950-
(Terry Goldie)

PERSONAL: Born July 17, 1950, in Regina, Saskatchewan, Canada; son of Angus Maclean (a chartered accountant) and Dorothy Florence (Little) Goldie; married Robyn Louise Salter, August 29, 1970; children: Norah, Alexander. *Education:* University of Saskatchewan, Saskatoon, B.A. (with honors), 1972; Carleton University, Ottawa, Ontario, M.A., 1975; Queen's University, Kingston, Ontario, Ph.D., 1977.

ADDRESSES: Home—460 Beresford Ave., Toronto, Ontario, Canada. *Office*—Department of English, York University, North York, Ontario, Canada M3J 1P3.

CAREER: Memorial University of Newfoundland, St. John's, lecturer, 1976-77, assistant professor, 1977-83, associate professor of English, 1983-88; York University, North York, Ontario, associate professor of English, 1988—. Theatre critic for Canadian Broadcasting Corp. (CBC), 1980-87.

WRITINGS:

UNDER NAME TERRY GOLDIE

Violence in the Canadian Novel since 1960, Memorial University of Newfoundland, 1981.
Louis Dudek and His Works, Longwood Publishing Group, 1985.
Fear and Temptation: The Image of the Indigene in Canadian, Australian and New Zealand Literatures, University of Toronto Press, 1989.

Contributor of articles and reviews to journals, including *Kunapipi, Journal of Commonwealth Literature, Canadian Literature,* and *Books in Canada;* member of editorial boards of *Studies in Canadian Literature* and *English Studies in Canada.*

WORK IN PROGRESS: An anthology of writing by Canadian native peoples, edited with Daniel David Moses; also a study of the way gendered figures of the land shape the process of indigenization in Canada, Australia, and New Zealand.

SIDELIGHTS: Terrence William Goldie told *CA:* "In *Fear and Temptation* indigenous peoples are viewed as only symbols of white interests. As a friend of mine who has studied the image of the Aborigine in contemporary Australia society once said: 'I've never written about Aborigines, just about what white people think are Aborigines.' *Fear and Temptation* shows how these 'white thoughts' have been an important part of indigenization, the attempt by the white cultures to become as though they belong.

"The anthology is thus one half of an extension of *Fear and Temptation. Fear and Temptation* consciously avoids writing by native people but the proposed anthology will celebrate it. Daniel David Moses, a native writer, and I hope to contribute to a very recent but very large explosion of native writing in Canada. It becomes the obvious answer to my latest book.

"If the anthology is 'the answer,' my other project extends the question. It seems to me that there are many parts to that process of indigenization but one of the major ones is to 'embrace the land.' I intend to consider the many ways the land is figured in this process, primarily as female but also at times as male. There is a psychological journey which entire nations must trace to create a community which seems of theirs."

*   *   *

GOLDIE, Terry
See GOLDIE, Terrence William

*   *   *

GOLDSTEIN, Jeffrey H(askell) 1942-

PERSONAL: Born August 11, 1942, in Norwalk, CT; son of Robert and Sylvia (Schwartz) Goldstein; married Helene Feinberg, August 22, 1973 (divorced). *Education:* University of Connecticut, B.A., 1964; Boston University, M.S., 1966; Ohio State University, Ph.D., 1969. *Religion:* Jewish.

ADDRESSES: Home—3C Pier 43, Sea Isle City, NJ 08243. *Office*—Department of Psychology, Temple University, Philadelphia, PA 19122.

CAREER: Temple University, Philadelphia, PA, assistant professor, 1969-72, associate professor, 1972-78, professor of psychology, 1978—. Visiting associate professor, University of Massachusetts, 1973-74; visiting professor, University of London, 1986-87, and University of Utrecht, 1990-91. Member, National Toy Council (Britain). Consultant to National Science Foundation, Canada Council, U.S. Department of Labor, H. F. Guggenheim Foundation, We the People 200, and British Toy and Hobby Association.

MEMBER: International Society for Research on Aggression (fellow), Amnesty International, American Psychological Association (fellow), American Psychological Society (fellow), Society of Experimental Social Psychology, Society for Research on Child Development.

AWARDS, HONORS: Award for "best publication on constructive alternatives to destructive aggression," Foundation for Idiodynamics, 1988, for 2nd edition of *Aggression and Crimes of Violence.*

WRITINGS:

(Editor with Paul E. McGhee) *The Psychology of Humor,* Academic Press, 1972.
Aggression and Crimes of Violence, Oxford University Press, 1975, 2nd edition, 1986.
Sports, Games, and Play, Lawrence Erlbaum, 1979, 2nd edition, 1989.
Social Psychology, Academic Press, 1980.
Sports Violence, Springer-Verlag, 1983.
(Editor with McGhee) *Handbook of Humor Research,* 2 volumes, Springer-Verlag, 1983.
Reporting Science: The Case of Aggression, Lawrence Erlbaum, 1986.
(With Patricia Wallace and Peter Nathan) *Psychology: An Introduction,* W. C. Brown, 1987, 2nd edition, 1990.
(Contributor) W. Fry and W. Salameh, editors, *Handbook of Humor and Psychotherapy,* Professional Resource, 1987.

(Editor with Jo Groebel) *Terrorism: Psychological Perspectives,* University of Seville Press, 1989.

(Contributor) E. Barnouw, W. Schramm, and G. Gerbner, editors, *International Encyclopedia of Communication,* Oxford University Press, 1989.

Also contributor of chapters to books. Contributor of articles to periodicals. Editor, *Current Psychology.*

WORK IN PROGRESS: A critical history of the Seville Statement on Violence, funded by the H. F. Guggenheim Foundation; *Escalation of Aggression,* with Michael Potegal and John Knutson.

SIDELIGHTS: Jeffrey H. Goldstein told *CA:* "Human violence, which it is within our means to curtail, continues to plague the planet. The human and material resources wasted on violence or its anticipation discourages us from facing problems affecting us all: hunger, poverty, the environment. Most of my research and writing are concerned with human violence, especially the justifications for it given by violent individuals, groups, and countries."

Some of Goldstein's books have been translated into Italian, Spanish, and Portuguese.

*   *   *

GOLDSTEIN, Malcolm   1925-

PERSONAL: Born August 18, 1925, in Huntington, WV; son of Jack A. (a businessman) and Lillian (Cohen) Goldstein. *Education:* Princeton University, A.B., 1949, Columbia University, M.A., 1951, Ph.D., 1956. *Avocational interests:* Architectural history, art history.

ADDRESSES: Home—New York, NY. *Office*—Department of English, Queens College of the City University of New York, Flushing, NY 11367.

CAREER: Stanford University, Stanford, CA, instructor, 1953-57, assistant professor of English, 1957-61; Queens College of the City University of New York, Flushing, assistant professor, 1961-65, associate professor, 1965-71, professor of English, 1971—. Adjunct professor, Columbia University, 1977-79, 1980. *Military service:* U.S. Army, Signal Corps, 1944-46; became staff sergeant.

MEMBER: PEN, Modern Language Association of America, American Society for Theater Research, Century Association.

AWARDS, HONORS: Guggenheim fellowship, 1967.

WRITINGS:

Pope and the Augustan Stage, Stanford University Press, 1958.
The Art of Thornton Wilder, University of Nebraska Press, 1965.
(Contributor) *American Drama and Its Critics,* University of Chicago Press, 1965.
(Editor) Nicholas Rowe, *The Fair Penitent,* University of Nebraska Press, 1968.
The Political Stage: American Drama and Theater of the Great Depression, Oxford University Press, 1974.
George S. Kaufman: His Life, His Theater, Oxford University Press, 1979.

WORK IN PROGRESS: A history of art dealing in the United States.

SIDELIGHTS: Commenting on Malcolm Goldstein's *George S. Kaufman: His Life, His Theater,* a biography of the American playwright, *New York Times* contributor John Russell observes

that Goldstein "writes a good plain English, and he tells us everything that we should like to know about George S. Kaufman. . . . This is a good and painstaking book about a remarkable man and a period in the American theater that came to a full close with his death."

BIOGRAPHICAL/CRITICAL SOURCES:

PERIODICALS

New York Times, October 18, 1979.
New York Times Book Review, December 16, 1979.

*   *   *

GOMBRICH, E(rnst) H(ans Josef)   1909-

PERSONAL: Born March 30, 1909, in Vienna, Austria; son of Karl B. (a lawyer) and Leonie (a pianist; maiden name, Hock) Gombrich; married Ilse Heller, 1936; children: Richard. *Education:* Vienna University, Ph.D.

ADDRESSES: Home—19 Briardale Gardens, London NW3 7PN, England.

CAREER: University of London, Warburg Institute, London, England, research assistant, 1936-39, senior research fellow, 1946-48, lecturer, 1948-54, reader, 1954-56, special lecturer, 1956-59, professor of history of classical tradition, 1959-76, director of Institute, 1959-76. Slade Professor of Fine Arts at Oxford University, 1950-53, and at Cambridge University, 1961-63; Durning-Lawrence Professor of the History of Art, University College, University of London, 1956-59; visiting professor, Harvard University, 1959; Lethaby Professor, Royal College of Art, 1967-68; Andrew D. White Professor-at-large, Cornell University, 1970-77. *Wartime service:* Served as translator with British Broadcasting Corp. (BBC) Monitoring Service, 1939-45.

MEMBER: British Academy (fellow), Society of Antiquaries (fellow), Royal Society of Literature (fellow), Royal Institute of British Architects (fellow), American Academy of Arts and Sciences, American Academy and Institute of Arts and Letters, American Philosophical Society, Accademia delle Scienze a Torino (corresponding member), Royal Academy of Arts and Sciences (Uppsala; corresponding member), Royal Netherlands Academy of Arts and Sciences, Bayerische Akademie der Wissenschaften, Accademia de Lincei (Rome), Royal Swedish Academy of Sciences, Royal Belgian Academy of Science, Goettingen Akademie der Wissenschaften (honorary member).

AWARDS, HONORS: Honorary fellow, Royal College of Art, 1961, Jesus College, Cambridge University, 1963; W. H. Smith Literary Award, 1964, for *Meditations on a Hobbyhorse;* Commander, Order of the British Empire, 1966; New York University medal for distinguished visitors, 1970; knighted, 1972; Erasmus Prize, 1975; Austrian Cross of Honour for Science and Art, 1975; Hegel Prize, 1976; member, Order *pour le merite,* 1978; Austrian Ehrenzeichen fur Wissenschaft und Kunst, 1984; International Balzan Prize, 1985; Rosina Viva Prize of the Commune of Anacapri for the Italian translation of *The Sense of Order,* 1985; *Encyclopaedia Britannica* award, 1989, for "excellence in the dissemination of knowledge for the benefit of mankind." Honorary degrees from numerous universities, including University of Belfast, 1963, University of Leeds, 1965, University of St. Andrews, 1965, Oxford University, 1969, Cambridge University, 1970, University of Manchester, 1974, University of Chicago, 1975, University of London, 1976, Harvard University, 1976, University of Essex, 1977, University of Philadelphia, 1977, Royal College of Art (London), 1981, and Brandeis University, 1981.

WRITINGS:

Weltgeschichte fuer Kinder, [Vienna], 1936, [Cologne], 1985.
(With Ernst Kris) *Caricature,* Penguin Books, 1940.
The Story of Art, Phaidon, 1950, 15th revised edition, 1989.
Raphael's Madonna della sedia, Oxford University Press, 1956.
Lessing, Oxford University Press, 1957.
(Editor) *Essays in Honor of Hans Tietze, 1880-1954,* Gazette des Beaux-Arts (Paris), 1958.
Art and Illusion: A Study in the Psychology of Pictorial Representation, Pantheon, 1960, 5th edition, Phaidon, 1977.
The Cartoonist's Armory, Duke University Press, 1963.
Meditation on a Hobby Horse, and Other Essays on the Theory of Art, Phaidon, 1963, 2nd edition, 1971.
Studies in the Art of the Renaissance, Volume 1: *Norm and Form,* Phaidon, 1966, 2nd edition, 1971, Volume 2: *Symbolic Images,* Phaidon, 1972, Volume 3, *The Heritage of Apelles,* Cornell University Press, 1976, Volume 4: *New Light on Old Masters,* Phaidon, 1986, University of Chicago Press, 1988.
In Search of Cultural History, Oxford University Press, 1969.
Aby Warburg: An Intellectual Biography, Warburg Institute, 1970, revised edition, University of Chicago, 1986.
The Ideas of Progress and Their Impact on Art, Cooper Union School of Art and Architecture, 1971.
(With others) *Art, Perception, and Reality,* Johns Hopkins Press, 1972.
(Editor with R. L. Gregory) *Illusion in Nature and Art,* Scribner, 1973.
Art History and the Social Sciences, Clarendon Press, 1975.
Means and Ends: Reflections on the History of Fresco Painting, Thames & Hudson, 1976.
The Sense of Order: A Study in the Psychology of Decorative Art, Phaidon, 1979.
Ideals and Idols, Phaidon, 1979.
The Image and the Eye: Further Studies in the Psychology of Pictorial Representation, Phaidon, 1981.
Tributes, Phaidon, 1984.

Contributor to journals.

SIDELIGHTS: E. H. Gombrich is one of those rare academic writers who has managed to become popular outside academia. His insightful books about art and art history have sold as well as some works of fiction; his *The Story of Art,* for example, has been translated into eighteen languages and sold more than two million copies. Noting the effect the book's publication had on Gombrich, London *Times* contributor Clive Aslet writes: "*The Story of Art* changed Sir Ernst's life. It was reviewed by one of the electors to the Slade Professorship at Oxford, to which Sir Ernst was duly appointed in 1950. The prestige that the professorship carried with it established his reputation in the United States." Forty years after its first appearance, the book is still in demand as a basic survey of the field and Gombrich takes time out from his busy schedule to update each new printing with the newest additional information from the art world.

Gombrich brings his interest in the history of ideas, as well as of art, to each of his works and in them expounds on highly original and stimulating theories. "One of Sir Ernst's more provocative theses," observes Grace Glueck in the *New York Times,* "is that art is not necessarily related to other developments of a particular era, not a product of a Zeitgeist, or spirit of the times. 'We search for one common denominator, which says, for example, that Cubism relates to relativity, or that Mannerism was the result of the deep spiritual crisis of the age,' he said. 'But I don't like those intellectual shortcuts. Culture has no such monolithic

character. Art is the product of individual artists, and sometimes it's even they who influence history.' "

Discussing another one of Gombrich's theories, critic Henri Zerner of the *New York Review of Books* writes that in *Art and Illusion: A Study in the Psychology of Pictorial Representation,* the art historian "once and for all [dispelled] the myth of the 'innocent eye,' the idea that the artist looks at the world and transcribes what he sees as best he can." Discussing yet another one of his ground-breaking works, Mary Ann Tighe notes in the *Washington Post Book World* that Gombrich opens his *The Sense of Order: A Study in the Psychology of Decorative Art* "with the thesis that the human mind is not a *tabula rasa,* but comes equipped with a framework, a 'filing system' that enables man to organize and understand time and space."

Offering an evaluation of Gombrich's work as a whole a *Yale Review* commentator estimates that the author, "almost single-handedly, is releasing the discipline of art history from certain grave difficulties deeply imbedded, on the one hand, in the semantics of Woelfflin, and, on the other, in the increasingly hairy questions surrounding the identification of stylistic categories. Although, he does not produce a needle from each haystack, he is surely on the right track in telling us which haystacks to avoid and which to search more thoroughly." In similarly glowing terms, Donald Posner, deputy field director of the Institute of Fine Arts at New York University, tells Glueck, "Gombrich is certainly one of the giants in our field. . . . His studies of visual perception, whether they're right or wrong, are really the starting point for all our discussions—whether Structuralist, semiotic or post-modern—of what art and seeing art mean."

BIOGRAPHICAL/CRITICAL SOURCES:

PERIODICALS

New York Review of Books, June 28, 1979.
New York Times, February 23, 1989.
Times (London), March 29, 1984.
Washington Post Book World, August 26, 1979.
Yale Review, June, 1967.

*   *   *

GOOR, Nancy (Ruth Miller) 1944-

PERSONAL: Born March 27, 1944, in Washington, D.C.; daughter of Martin H. (a government worker) and Helen (a teacher; maiden name, Zarkower) Miller; married Ronald S. Goor (a health administrator and photographer), March 12, 1967; children: Alexander, Daniel. *Education:* Received B.S. from University of Pennsylvania and M.F.A. from Boston University.

CAREER: Teacher of art at public high school in Bethesda, Md., 1966-70; Smithsonian Institution, Natural History Museum, Washington, D.C., director of Insect Zoo, summer, 1971, scientific illustrator, 1975-78.

MEMBER: Children's Book Guild, Guild of Natural Science Illustrators (corresponding secretary), Phi Beta Kappa.

AWARDS, HONORS: Shadows: Here, There, and Everywhere was named outstanding children's science book by National Science Teacher's Association/Children's Book Council Joint Committee, as notable book by American Library Association, and as one of Library of Congress's best books of the year, all 1981; *In the Driver's Seat* was named one of the best children's books of the year by *New York Times* and *School Library Journal,* both 1982; *Signs* was named one of the Notable Children's

Books for the Language Arts, 1983; *All Kinds of Feet* was named an Outstanding Science Trade Book for Children, 1984; Best Books of 1986 citation, *School Library Journal,* 1986, for *Pompeii,* which was also named on the American Library Association Booklist's Children's Editor's Choices list, the Notable Children's Trade Books in the Field of Social Studies list, and the Notable Children's Trade Books for the Language Arts list, all 1986; *Heads* was named an Oustanding Trade Book for Children, 1988.

WRITINGS:

NONFICTION FOR CHILDREN; ILLUSTRATED WITH PHOTOGRAPHS BY HUSBAND, RON GOOR

(With Ron Goor) *Shadows: Here, There, and Everywhere,* Crowell, 1981.
In the Driver's Seat (Junior Literary Guild selection), Crowell, 1982.
Signs, Crowell, 1983.
All Kinds of Feet, Crowell, 1984.
Pompeii: Exploring a Roman Ghost Town, Crowell, 1984.
Heads, Atheneum, 1988.
Insect Metamorphosis: From Egg to Adult, Atheneum, 1990.

NONFICTION FOR ADULTS; WITH HUSBAND, RON GOOR

Eater's Choice: A Food Lover's Guide to Lower Cholesterol, Houghton, 1987.
The Choose to Lose Diet: A Food Lover's Guide to Permanent Weight Loss, Houghton, 1990.

WORK IN PROGRESS: A teen-age diet book, a survival primer cookbook, a children's book on Williamsburg, all with R. Goor.

SIDELIGHTS: Nancy Goor told *CA:* "I have always considered myself an artist. I majored in art in college, taught art in public high school, did scientific illustrations, and enjoy silkscreening, painting, and drawing. Although I have written and illustrated stories since childhood, it was not until I wrote a newspaper article—'Traveling to Sicily With Children'—that my career took a new direction. I began writing children's books when Harper & Row said they would publish my husband's fictional manuscript on shadows if he would change it to nonfiction. I wrote the new text, and *Shadows: Here, There, and Everywhere* was published by Thomas Y. Crowell in fall, 1981. *In the Driver's Seat,* a children's book using Ron's photographs and my text, was published in fall, 1982. Our third book together, *Signs,* was published by Crowell in fall, 1983.

"Ron and I work well together. When he was special assistant to the director of the National Museum of Natural History, he got the idea to have a live insect zoo in the museum. He needed a volunteer to direct the museum and do the artwork. I eagerly agreed. Creating the insect zoo and directing it that first summer (1971) was a fantastic experience.

"Writing books together has also been exciting and rewarding. Getting the ideas seems to be the easiest part. For example, when my younger son was in the first grade he told me, 'Mommy, I like to read signs.' 'Aha,' said I. Then Ron and I set to work. Ron took hundreds of pictures of signs. I organized, reorganized, and reorganized them again, wrote several texts, and *Signs* was published.

"Niether Ron nor I remember which one of us thought of the idea for *In the Driver's Seat;* however, we were both convinced that driving a tank, a supersonic jet, or front-end loader would be something any kid—or even old kids like us—would love to do. By doing the book I got to ride in an army tank, an electric engine, and an eighteen-wheel truck, on a combine, and to sit in the driver's seat of the Concorde, a front-end loader, and a race car!

"Each book brings new adventures. I got to ride in the cab of an old-time steam engine and pull the horn! To get a picture of a beach umbrella making a shadow for *Shadows,* we went to the beach for the day. We buried our older son up to his neck in the sand. Children kept running over his sand-covered body thinking he was truly only a head. We took pictures of killer guard dogs—a frightening but fascinating experience—to illustrate 'Beware of Dog' sign for *Signs.*

"Writing nonfiction for young children is a challenge. You have to write simply about subjects that are often difficult or complicated. How does a blimp work? What is a shadow? The text must be clear, and, as in all writing, the words must have rhythm and sound right when placed together.

"The aim of our books is to expand a child's awareness and interest in the common, everyday things around him. The advantage of using photography is that photographs capture the real thing—that which can be found in a child's environment.

"Ron and I began writing health books as a result of Ron's professional and our personal life. When Ron was 31 he learned he had dangerously high cholesterol. I began adapting and creating recipes to be low in saturated fat (the culprit in the diet that raises blood cholesterol) and delicious. We love to eat. Ron soon became the National Coordinator of the Coronary Primary Prevention Trial of the National Institutes of Health. This trial determined that if you lower your cholesterol you lower your risk for heart disease. He later became National Coordinator of the Cholesterol Education Program, also at National Heart, Lung, and Blood (NIH). When Ron left NIH to develop health programs, we wrote *Eater's Choice: A Food Lover's Guide to Lower Cholesterol.* Because so many people lost weight following *Eater's Choice,* we just wrote a book called *The Choose to Lose Diet.* The books take a similar approach. Following *The Choose to Lose Diet* the reader determines his own fat budget (*Choose to Lose* focuses on total fat because fat makes fat), and then knowing the fat contents of foods, he can choose any food he wants to eat as long as it fits into his daily fat budget."

*   *   *

GOOR, Ron(ald Stephen) 1940-

PERSONAL: Born May 31, 1940, in Washington, D.C.; son of Charles G. (a statistician) and Jeanette (a statistician; maiden name, Mindel) Goor; married Nancy Ruth Miller (an author and illustrator), March 12, 1967; children: Alexander, Daniel. *Education:* Swarthmore College, B.A. (magna cum laude), 1962; graduate study at University of Chicago, 1962-63; Harvard University, Ph.D., 1967, M.P.H., 1977.

ADDRESSES: Office—National Heart, Lung, and Blood Institute, National Institutes of Health, Bethesda, Md. 20205.

CAREER: National Institutes of Health, Bethesda, Md., laboratory assistant, 1967-70; Smithsonian Institution, Natural History Museum, Washington, D.C., special assistant to director, 1970-72; National Science Foundation, Washington, D.C., program manager, 1972-76; National Institutes of Health, National Heart, Lung, and Blood Institute, Bethesda, clinical trial coordinator, 1976-84, national coordinator of Cholesterol Education Program, 1984—.

MEMBER: American Chemical Society, American Association for the Advancement of Science, Children's Book Guild, Phi Beta Kappa.

AWARDS, HONORS: Shadows: Here, There, and Everywhere was chosen as outstanding children's science book by National Science Teacher's Association/Children's Book Council Joint Committee, as notable book by American Library Association, and as one of Library of Congress's best books of the year, all 1981; *In the Driver's Seat* was chosen as one of the best children's books of the year by *New York Times* and *School Library Journal,* both 1982.

WRITINGS:

(With wife, Nancy Goor) *Eater's Choice: A Food Lover's Guide to Lower Cholesterol,* Houghton, 1987.
(With N. Goor and others) *The Choose to Lose Diet: A Food Lover's Guide to Permanent Weight Loss,* Houghton, 1990.

NONFICTION FOR CHILDREN; ILLUSTRATED WITH OWN PHOTOGRAPHS

(With Millicent Selsam) *Backyard Insects,* Scholastic Book Services, 1981, hardcover edition, Four Winds Press, 1983.
(With N. Goor) *Shadows: Here, There, and Everywhere,* Crowell, 1981.

ILLUSTRATOR WITH PHOTOGRAPHS; ALL WRITTEN BY WIFE, NANCY GOOR

In the Driver's Seat (Junior Literary Guild Selection), Crowell, 1982.
Signs, Crowell, 1983.
All Kinds of Feet, Crowell, 1984.
Pompeii: Exploring a Roman Ghost Town, Crowell, 1984.
Heads, Atheneum, 1988.
Insect Metamorphosis: From Egg to Adult, Atheneum, 1990.

WORK IN PROGRESS: A teen-age diet book, a survival primer cookbook, and a children's book on Williamsburg, all with Nancy Goor.

SIDELIGHTS: Ron Goor once explained that ever since he can remember he has been interested in biology, but it was not until he had a Ph.D. in biochemistry and was doing laboratory research that he found he needed to express himself and teach. He began to take photographs while at the Smithsonian Institution developing biological exhibits for the lay public. He discovered that "photography opened up new avenues of self-expression as well as exploring and documenting the world."

Goor believes that writing books for children has been a natural outgrowth of his interest in photography. As he stated: "Good photography helps us see the world through fresh eyes. In my books I share with the reader a heightened awareness and appreciation of the beautiful and intricate natural world and new ways to see the complex man-made world."

Backyard Insects, Ron Goor's first book, explores the many ways that the shapes and colors of insects protect them from their enemies. He said, "Ever since my wife, Nancy, and I started the nation's first live insect zoo at the Smithsonian's Natural History Museum in 1971, I became aware of the natural interest most children have in insects. These tiny, ubiquitous creatures illustrate many of the most important biological principles and are so easily found, observed, and raised that they make ideal teaching tools for understanding biology."

The enlarged photographs of the insects in the book help the reader see the insects in more detail than is possible with the naked eye. The text explains the variety of ways that color and shape protect the insects. Goor explained: "The lessons learned in the book provide basis for seeing the animal world with fresh eyes. The use of domestic insects, easily found in both city and countryside, as examples in the book encourages readers to go outside to observe first-hand the phenomena described. Armed with this knowledge, the readers can go beyond the examples to understand and appreciate new observations in the field."

In *Shadows: Here, There, and Everywhere,* Ron and Nancy Goor explore the world of shadows, using carefully conceived black-and-white photographs. Set-ups consisting of a child's blocks and hand-held flashlight accompany each environmental scene and show how shadows are formed. As Goor observed: "Shadows are all around us—on the floor, the ground, the walls. They are long, short, bent, folded. They are beautiful, useful, scary. Yet how often do we notice them? The book is designed not only to heighten awareness of shadows but to increase understanding of the interactions of light, objects, and surfaces in the making of shadows."

With *In the Driver's Seat,* the Goors explore what it is like to drive a variety of vehicles—a blimp, a tank, an engine, the Concorde supersonic jet, a race car, a combine, a wrecking crane, a front-end loader, and an eighteen-wheel truck. Wide-angle lens photographs put the reader into the driver's seat of these nine vehicles. The text, by Nancy Goor, explains how to drive each vehicle and what each is like to operate. Additional pictures show the vehicles in action.

Prior to producing their third book, *Signs,* the Goors questioned a number of children and discovered that all either learned to read or practiced their reading on signs. As a result, *Signs* is aimed at reading-ready children or children who are just learning to read. Photographs on every page show signs in settings that help to convey their meanings and reinforce the beginning reader's sense of accomplishment in word-recognition.

Of another collaboration, Ron Goor said: "In *All Kinds of Feet* we focus on how animals' feet have adapted to moving in different environments, getting food, defending themselves, or escaping from enemies, and, in the case of man, making and using tools. The book is designed to make children look at animals analytically and see differences in animal structure as solutions to problems."

The husband-and-wife team have developed a compatible working method when producing their books. Goor told *CA:* "Nancy and I are often asked how we work together on a book. Generally, I begin by exploring the topic photographically. At the same time, Nancy and I begin to develop conceptual approaches to the subject matter. As Nancy develops the text, she suggests specific pictures that I have not yet taken during the early photographic exploration. Likewise, the photographs sometimes suggest changes in the text. Obviously, it is most helpful to have the writer and photographer working so closely together. Also, it is more fun that way!"

BIOGRAPHICAL/CRITICAL SOURCES:

PERIODICALS

Popular Photography, February, 1982.

*   *   *

GOYENECHE, Gabriel
    See AVALLE-ARCE, Juan Bautista de

GOYTISOLO, Juan 1931-

PERSONAL: Born January 5, 1931, in Barcelona, Spain; immigrated to France, 1957. *Education:* Attended University of Barcelona and University of Madrid, 1948-52.

CAREER: Writer. Worked as reporter in Cuba, 1965; associated with Gallimard Publishing Co., France. Visiting professor at universities in the United States.

AWARDS, HONORS: Received numerous awards for *Juegos de manos;* Premio Europalia, 1985.

WRITINGS:

NOVELS

Juegos de manos, Destino, 1954, recent edition, 1975, translation by John Rust published as *The Young Assassins,* Knopf, 1959.

Duelo en el paraíso, Planeta, 1955, Destino, 1981, translation by Christine Brooke-Rose published as *Children of Chaos,* Macgibbon & Kee, 1958.

El circo (title means "The Circus"), Destino, 1957, recent edition, 1982.

Fiestas, Emecé, 1958, Destino, 1981, translation by Herbert Weinstock published as *Fiestas,* Knopf, 1960.

La resaca (title means "The Undertow"), Club del Libro Español, 1958, J. Mortiz, 1977.

La isla, Seix Barral, 1961, reprinted, 1982, translation by José Yglesias published as *Island of Women,* Knopf, 1962 (published in England as *Sands of Torremolinos,* J. Cape, 1962).

Señas de identidad, J. Mortiz, 1966, translation by Gregory Rabassa published as *Marks of Identity,* Grove, 1969.

Reivindicación del Conde don Julián, J. Mortiz, 1970, Cátedra, 1985, translation by Helen R. Lane published as *Count Julian,* Viking, 1974.

Juan sin tierra, Seix Barral, 1975, translation by Lane published as *Juan the Landless,* Viking, 1977.

Makbara, Seix Barral, 1980, translation by Lane published as *Makbara,* Seaver Books, 1981.

Paisajes después de la batalla, Montesinos, 1982, translation by Lane published as *Landscapes After the Battle,* Seaver Books, 1987.

SHORT STORIES

Para vivir aquí (title means "To Live Here"), Sur, 1960, Bruguera, 1983.

Fin de fiesta: Tentativas de interpretación de una historia amorosa, Seix Barral, 1962, translation by Yglesias published as *The Party's Over: Four Attempts to Define a Love Story,* Weidenfeld & Nicolson, 1966, Grove, 1967.

TRAVEL NARRATIVES

Campos de Níjar, Seix Barral, 1960, Grant & Cutler, 1984, translation by Luigi Luccarelli published as *The Countryside of Nijar* in *The Countryside of Nijar* [and] *La chanca,* Alembic Press, 1987.

La chanca, Libreria Española, 1962, Seix Barral, 1983, translation by Luccarelli published in *The Countryside of Nijar* [and] *La chanca,* Alembic Press, 1987.

Pueblo en marcha: Instantáneas de un viaje a Cuba (title means "People on the March: Snapshots of a Trip to Cuba"), Librería Española, 1963.

Crónicas sarracinas (title means "Saracen Chronicles"), Ibérica, 1982.

OTHER

Problemas de la novela (literary criticism; title means "Problems of the Novel"), Seix Barral, 1959.

Las mismas palabras, Seix Barral, 1963.

Plume d'hier: Espagne d'aujourd'hui, compiled by Mariano José de Larra, Editeurs Francais Réunis, 1965.

El furgón de cola (critical essays; title means "The Caboose"), Ruedo Ibérico, 1967, Seix Barral, 1982.

Spanien und die Spanien, M. Bucher, 1969.

(Author of prologue) José María Blanco White, *Obra inglesa,* Formentor, 1972.

Obras completas (title means "Complete Works"), Aguilar, 1977.

Libertad, libertad, libertad (essays and speeches), Anagrama, 1978.

(Author of introduction) Mohamed Chukri, *El pan desnudo* (title means "For Bread Alone"), translation from Arabic by Abdellah Djibilou, Montesinos, 1982.

Coto vedado (autobiography), Seix Barral, 1985, translation by Peter Bush published as *Forbidden Territory: The Memoirs of Juan Goytisolo,* North Point Press, 1989.

En los reinos de taifa (autobiography), Seix Barral, 1986.

(Author of commentary) Omar Khayyam, *Estances,* translation into Catalan by Ramon Vives Pastor, del Mall, 1985.

Contracorrientes, Montesinos, 1985.

Space in Motion (essays), translation by Lane, Lumen Books, 1987.

Work represented in collections and anthologies, including *Juan Goytisolo,* Ministerio de Cultura, Dirección General de Promoción del Libro y la Cinematografía, 1982. Contributor to periodicals.

SIDELIGHTS: "Juan Goytisolo is the best living Spanish novelist," wrote John Butt in the *Times Literary Supplement.* The author, as Butt observed, became renowned as a "pitiless satirist" of Spanish society during the dictatorship of Francisco Franco, who imposed his version of conservative religious values on the country from the late 1930s until his death in 1975. Goytisolo, whose youth coincided with the rise of Franco, had a variety of compelling reasons to feel alienated from his own country. He was a small child when his mother was killed in a bombing raid, a casualty of the civil war that Franco instigated to seize power from a democratically elected government. The author then grew up as a bisexual in a country dominated, in Butt's words, by "frantic machismo." Eventually, said Goytisolo in his memoir *Coto vedado* (*Forbidden Territory*), he became "that strange species of writer claimed by none and alien and hostile to groups and categories." In the late 1950s, when his writing career began to flourish, he left Spain for Paris and remained in self-imposed exile until after Franco died.

The literary world was greatly impressed when Goytisolo's first novel, *Juegos de manos* (*The Young Assassins*), was published in 1954. David Dempsey found that it "begins where the novels of a writer like Jack Kerouac leave off." Goytisolo was identified as a member of the Spanish "restless generation" but his first novel seemed as much akin to Fedor Dostoevski as it did to Kerouac. The plot is similar to Dostoevski's *The Possessed:* a group of students plot the murder of a politician but end up murdering the fellow student chosen to kill the politician. Dempsey wrote, "Apparently, he is concerned with showing us how self-destructive and yet how inevitable this hedonism becomes in a society dominated by the smug and self-righteous."

Duelo en el paraíso (*Children of Chaos*) was seen as a violent extension of *The Young Assassins.* Like Anthony Burgess's *A*

Clockwork Orange and William Golding's *Lord of the Flies, Children of Chaos* focuses on the terror wrought by adolescents. The children have taken over a small town after the end of the Spanish Civil War causes a breakdown of order.

Fiestas begins a trilogy referred to as "The Ephemeral Morrow" (after a famous poem by Antonio Machado). Considered the best volume of the trilogy, it follows four characters as they try to escape life in Spain by chasing their dreams. Each character meets with disappointment in the novel's end. Ramon Sender called *Fiestas* "a brilliant projection of the contrast between Spanish official and real life," and concluded that Goytisolo "is without doubt the best of the young Spanish writers."

El circo, the second book in "The Ephemeral Morrow," was too blatantly ironic to succeed as a follow-up to *Fiestas.* It is the story of a painter who manages a fraud before being punished for a murder he didn't commit. The third book, *La resaca,* was also a disappointment. The novel's style was considered too realistic to function as a fitting conclusion to "The Ephemeral Morrow."

After writing two politically oriented travelogues, *Campos de Níjar* (*The Countryside of Nijar*) and *La chanca,* Goytisolo returned to fiction and the overt realism he'd begun in *La resaca.* Unfortunately, critics implied that both *La isla* (*Island of Women*) and *Fin de Fiesta* (*The Party's Over*) suffered because they ultimately resembled their subject matter. *The Party's Over* contains four stories about the problems of marriage. Although Alexander Coleman found that the "stories are more meditative than the full-length novels," he also observed, "But it is, in the end, a small world, limited by the overwhelming ennui of everything and everyone in it." Similarly, Honor Tracy noted, "Every gesture of theirs reveals the essence of the world, they're absolutely necessary, says another: we intellectuals operate in a vacuum. . . . Everything ends in their all being fed up."

Goytisolo abandoned his realist style after *The Party's Over.* In *Señas de identidad* (*Marks of Identity*), wrote Barbara Probst Solomon, "Goytisolo begins to do a variety of things. Obvious political statement, he feels, is not enough for a novel; he starts to break with form—using a variety of first, second and third persons, he is looking and listening to the breaks in language and . . . he begins to break with form—in the attempt to describe what he is really seeing and feeling, his work becomes less abstract." Robert J. Clements called *Marks of Identity* "probably his most personal novel," but also felt that the "most inevitable theme is of course the police state of Spain." Fusing experimentation with a firm political stance, Goytisolo reminded some critics of James Joyce while others saw him elaborating his realist style to further embellish his own sense of politics.

Reivindicación del Conde don Julián (*Count Julian*), Goytisolo's next novel, is widely considered to be his masterpiece. In it, he uses techniques borrowed from Joyce, Céline, Jean Genet, filmmaker Luis Buñuel, and Pablo Picasso. Solomon remarked that, while some of these techniques proved less than effective in many of the French novels of the 1960s, "in the hands of this Spanish novelist, raging against Spain, the results are explosive." *Count Julian* is named for a legendary Spanish nobleman who betrayed his country to Arab invaders in the Middle Ages. In the shocking fantasies of the novel's narrator, a modern Spaniard living as an outcast in Africa, Julian returns to punish Spain for its cruelty and hypocrisy. Over the course of the narration, the Spanish language itself gradually transforms into Arabic. Writing in the *New York Times Book Review,* Carlos Fuentes called *Count Julian* "an adventure of language, a critical battle against the language appropriated by power in Spain. It is also a search for a new/old language that would offer an alternative for the future."

With the publication of *Juan sin tierra* (*Juan the Landless*), critics began to see Goytisolo's last three novels as a second trilogy. However, reviews were generally less favorable than those for either *Marks of Identity* or *Count Julian.* Anatole Broyard, calling attention to Goytisolo's obsession with sadistic sex and defecation, remarked, "Don Quixote no longer tilts at windmills, but toilets." A writer for *Atlantic* suggested that the uninformed reader begin elsewhere with Goytisolo.

Even after the oppressive Franco regime was dismantled in the late 1970s, Goytisolo continued to write novels that expressed deep alienation by displaying an unconventional, disorienting view of human society. *Makbara,* for example, is named for the cemeteries of North Africa where lovers meet for late-night trysts. "What a poignant central image it is," wrote Paul West in *Washington Post Book World,* "not only as an emblem of life in death . . . but also as a vantage point from which to review the human antic in general, which includes all those who go about their daily chores with their minds below their belts." "The people [Goytisolo] feels at home with," West declared, "are the drop-outs and the ne'er do wells, the outcasts and the misfits." In *Paisajes después de la batalla* (*Landscapes After the Battle*), the author moved his vision of alienation to Paris, where he had long remained in exile. This short novel, made up of seventy-eight nonsequential chapters, displays the chaotic mix of people—from French nationalists to Arab immigrants—who uneasily coexist in the city. "The Paris metro map which the protagonist contemplates . . . for all its innumerable permutations of routes," wrote Abigail Lee in the *Times Literary Supplement,* "provides an apt image for the text itself." *Landscapes* "looked like another repudiation, this time of Paris," Butt wrote. "One wondered what Goytisolo would destroy next."

Accordingly, Butt was surprised to find that the author's memoir of his youth, published in 1985, had a markedly warmer tone than the novels that had preceded it. "Far from being a new repudiation," Butt observed, *Forbidden Territory* "is really an essay in acceptance and understanding. . . . Gone, almost, are the tortuous language, the lurid fantasies, the dreams of violation and abuse. Instead, we are given a moving, confessional account of a difficult childhood and adolescence." Goytisolo's recollections, the reviewer concluded, constitute "a moving and sympathetic story of how one courageous victim of the Franco regime fought his way out of a cultural and intellectual wasteland, educated himself, and went on to inflict a brilliant revenge on the social system which so isolated and insulted him."

BIOGRAPHICAL/CRITICAL SOURCES:

BOOKS

Contemporary Literary Criticism, Gale, Volume 5, 1976, Volume 10, 1979, Volume 23, 1983.
Goytisolo, Juan, *Forbidden Territory,* translation by Peter Bush, North Point Press, 1989.
Schwartz, Kessel, *Juan Goytisolo,* Twayne, 1970.
Schwartz, Ronald, *Spain's New Wave Novelists 1950-1974: Studies in Spanish Realism,* Scarecrow Press, 1976.

PERIODICALS

Atlantic, August, 1977.
Best Sellers, June 15, 1974.
Los Angeles Times Book Review, January 22, 1989.
Nation, March 1, 1975.
New Republic, January 31, 1967.
New York Times Book Review, January 22, 1967, May 5, 1974, September 18, 1977, June 14, 1987, July 3, 1988, February 12, 1989.

Saturday Review, February 14, 1959, June 11, 1960, June 28, 1969.

Texas Quarterly, spring, 1975.

Times Literary Supplement, May 31, 1985, September 9, 1988, May 19, 1989, November 17, 1989.

Washington Post Book World, January 17, 1982, June 14, 1987.*

* * *

GRAY, Simon (James Holliday) 1936-
(Hamish Reade)

PERSONAL: Born October 21, 1936, in Hayling Island, Hampshire, England; son of James Davidson (a pathologist) and Barbara Cecelia Mary (Holliday) Gray; married Beryl Mary Kevern (a picture researcher), August 20, 1964; children: Benjamin, Lucy. *Education:* Dalhousie University, B.A. (honors in English), 1958; Trinity College, Cambridge, B.A. (honors in English), 1962. *Politics:* None. *Religion:* None.

ADDRESSES: Home—London, England. *Agent*—Judy Daish, 83 Eastbourne Mews, London W2 6LQ, England.

CAREER: Author and playwright. Teacher of English in France, 1960-61, and Spain, 1962-63; lecturer, University of British Columbia, 1963-64; supervisor in English, Trinity College, Cambridge University, 1964-66; lecturer in drama and literature, Queen Mary College, University of London, 1966-86.

MEMBER: Dramatists Guild, Societe des Auteurs (France).

AWARDS, HONORS: Writers Guild Award for best play, 1967, for "Death of a Teddy Bear"; *Evening Standard* Award for best play, 1972, for "Butley"; *Evening Standard* Award, *Plays and Players* Award, and New York Drama Critics Circle Award, all for best play, all 1976, for "Otherwise Engaged"; Cheltenham Prize for Literature, 1981, for "Quartermaine's Terms."

WRITINGS:

Colmain (novel), Faber, 1962.

Simple People (novel), Faber, 1964.

Little Portia (novel), Faber, 1966.

(Editor with Keith Walker) *Selected English Prose,* Faber, 1967.

(Under pseudonym Hamish Reade) *A Comeback for Stark,* Putnam, 1968.

An Unnatural Pursuit and Other Pieces (journal), Faber, 1985, St. Martin's, 1986.

How's That for Telling 'Em, Fat Lady? (journal), Faber, 1988.

TELEVISION PLAYS

"The Caramel Crisis," British Broadcasting Corp. (BBC-TV), 1966.

"Death of a Teddy Bear" (also produced as "Molly"; also see below), BBC-TV, 1967.

"A Way with the Ladies," BBC-TV, 1967.

Sleeping Dog (first broadcast on BBC-TV, 1967), Faber, 1968.

"Spoiled" (also see below), BBC-TV, 1968.

"Pig in a Poke" (also see below), BBC-TV, 1969.

"The Dirt on Lucy Lane," BBC-TV, 1969.

"Style of the Countess," BBC-TV, 1970.

"The Princess," BBC-TV, 1970.

"Man in a Side-Car" (also see below), BBC-TV, 1971.

"Plaintiffs and Defendants" (also see below), BBC-TV, 1975.

"Two Sundays" (also see below), BBC-TV, 1975.

"After Pilkington," BBC-TV, 1987.

PLAYS

Wise Child (first produced on the West End at Wyndham's Theatre, October 10, 1967; produced on Broadway at Helen Hayes Theatre, January 27, 1972), Faber, 1968, Samuel French, 1974.

Dutch Uncle (first produced in Brighton, England, at Theatre Royal, March 3, 1969; produced on the West End at National Theatre, 1969, and at Aldwych Theatre, March 26, 1969), Faber, 1969.

Spoiled (first produced in Glasgow, Scotland, at Close Theatre Club, 1970; produced on the West End at Haymarket Theatre, February 24, 1971; produced on Broadway at Morosco Theatre, October 31, 1972), Methuen, 1971.

The Idiot (adapted from the novel by Fyodor Dostoevsky; first produced on the West End at National Theatre, July 15, 1970), Methuen, 1971.

Butley (first produced in Oxford, England, at Oxford Playhouse, July 7, 1971; produced on the West End at Criterion Theatre, July 14, 1971; produced on Broadway at Morosco Theatre, 1972; also see below), Methuen, 1971, Viking, 1972.

"Otherwise Engaged," first produced on the West End at Queen's Theatre, July 30, 1975; published as *Otherwise Engaged, and Other Plays* (also contains *Two Sundays* and *Plaintiffs and Defendants*), Methuen, 1975.

Dog Days (produced in Oxford at Oxford Playhouse, October 26, 1976; produced Off-Broadway at Hudson Guild Theatre [directed by Gray], 1985), Eyre Methuen, 1976.

"The Rear Column," produced on the West End at Globe Theatre, February 23, 1978; produced in New York at Manhattan Theatre Club, November, 1978; published as *The Rear Column, and Other Plays* (also contains *Molly* [also see below] and *Man in a Side-Car*), Eyre Methuen, 1978, Heinemann, 1985.

Molly (produced in Watford, England, at Palace Theatre, November 23, 1977; produced Off-Broadway at Hudson Guild Theatre, January, 1978), Samuel French, 1979.

Stage Struck (produced on the West End at Vaudeville Theatre, November 21, 1979), Eyre Methuen, 1979, Seaver, 1981.

Close of Play (produced on the West End at Lyttleton Theatre, May 24, 1979; produced in New York at Manhattan Theatre Club, 1981), Methuen, 1980, published as *Close of Play* [and] *Pig in a Poke,* Heinemann, 1984.

Quartermaine's Terms (produced on the West End at Queen's Theatre, July 28, 1981; produced in New Haven, Conn., at Long Wharf Theatre, 1982; produced in New York at Playhouse 91, February, 1983), Eyre Methuen, 1981, Heinemann, 1983.

The Common Pursuit: Scenes from the Literary Life (first produced in London at Lyric Hammersmith Theatre, July, 1984; produced in New Haven at Long Wharf Theatre, February, 1985), Methuen, 1984, Heinemann, 1985.

Plays, Methuen, 1986.

Melon (produced on the West End at Royal Haymarket Theatre, 1987), Methuen, 1987.

OTHER

"Butley" (screenplay; adapted from his play), American Film Theatre, 1974.

Also author of play adaptation of *Tartuffe,* produced at Kennedy Center, Washington, D.C., 1982, and of screen adaptation of *A Month in the Country.*

SIDELIGHTS: No one has ever accused Simon Gray of writing plays that are too mainstream. In fact, the Briton's first stage work, "Wise Child," was originally written for television but was "considered too bizarre for home viewing," according to Anthony Stephenson in a *Dictionary of Literary Biography* article on the writer. Gray was a product of Cambridge University during the early 1960s, a place and an era that produced a notable group of creative talent, including novelists Frederick Raphael and Margaret Drabble, satirist Peter Cook, comedian-turned-interviewer David Frost, and actor Derek Jacobi. "Many of these people were already beginning to make their mark in the world at large while still pursuing their studies," observes Stephenson. "Gray was no exception." Though he lived abroad for several years, teaching the English language to natives of France and Spain, Gray returned to his homeland in 1965 to lecture in drama and literature at Queen Mary College, London University, and worked there for twenty years.

Journeyman television writing prepared Gray for his first West End opening. "When Gray began writing ['Wise Child'], he conceived the central character as a woman, but gradually the character evolved into a man dressed as a woman," Stephenson relates. "The character, Mrs. Artminster, . . . is in fact a male criminal wearing women's clothing to evade the police, who want him for a brutal mail robbery. He is staying with his young accomplice, Jerry, who poses as Mrs. Artminster's son, at a shabby provincial hotel run by a homosexual. The curious interdependence of the pair reaches its climax when, after murdering the homosexual landlord, Jerry dresses in the maid's clothes and Mrs. Artminster reverts to his male attire."

Several successful if not so memorable Gray plays followed "Wise Child" until 1971, when "Butley" opened at London's Criterion Theatre. Considered one of the playwright's best works, its title character, says Stephenson, is a "viper-tongued teacher of English at London University," inviting comparisons with the author himself. The play takes place in one day, when Butley's raw wit and skepticism cause problems for virtually everyone in his life, including his wife, his students, his office-mate and another faculty member. As Stephenson notes: "His technique is to put them in the wrong by demonstrating through satire the woolliness of their thinking and the insincerity of their motives. In striking out at everyone around him, [Butley] reveals the emptiness and hollowness of his own life."

To *New York Times* critic Clive Barnes, in "Butley" Gray has "written about this half-baked academic with astonishing compassion. Butley goes around 'spreading futility.' He slouches like a lost soul, and yet uses his wit like a sledgehammer to ward off the world and reality. And despite his glorious and desperate faults, he remains oddly likable and strangely sympathetic. Even his pompousness and mad egoism have been made in some way attractive." In a *Midwest Quarterly* review of the play, Sophia B. Blaydes sees the anti-protagonist in a different light. "[The work] has as much laughter as any comedy could evoke," she writes, "but it is a laughter generated by literary allusions, by wit, and by skilled word play that were used as weapons of defense and attack. Butley's skill is verbal, and for a while his wit captures our sympathies and our admiration, yet he manages to create a distance so that ultimately he is isolated from us, too." Blaydes also notes that "in a perverse manner, Butley demonstrates those qualities we believe essential to the English professor: sensitivity, kindness, perceptiveness, eloquence, but he uses them on this day to annihilate, destroy, or dismiss those around him and to reject and sever his professional ties." "Butley" enjoyed a healthy run both on the West End and on Broadway. It is the only original Gray play yet to have been produced as a film.

A subsequent stage work, "Otherwise Engaged," has met with equal critical and popular success. "Essentially the idea [behind the play] is to present a character preoccupied with a single, simple activity and have the activity delayed by a series of increasingly dramatic interruptions," as Stephenson describes. "Otherwise Engaged" thus presents Hench, a publisher, at home attempting to merely listen to a recording of Richard Wagner's opera *Parsifal*. But, as Stephenson continues, poor Hench is "interrupted by his brother, who is anxious about his prospects of becoming a deputy headmaster; by Jeff, a literary critic, who, like Butley, launches a series of verbal attacks on a variety of targets; by Jeff's mistress, who tries to seduce him; by Wood, a failure, who at one time had attended a private boarding school, reveals Hench's homosexual activities as a schoolboy and accuses Hench of seducing his fiancee; by his wife, who tells him she is pregnant by either Hench or her lover, Ned; by his tenant Dave, who denounces him as a complacent fake liberal and moves squatters [illegal tenants] into Hench's house; and by a telephoned suicide message from Wood, which Hench switches off in mid-sentence."

In "Butley" and "Otherwise Engaged," John Bush Jones sees a shift away from the kind of farce Gray originally presented in plays like "Wise Child." "Gone is the complex plotting and overt stage action of the early pieces in favor of in-depth examinations of character through a drama whose movement comes largely through its dialogue," writes Jones in *West Virginia University Philological Papers*. "It is this dominance of language, especially the incessant exercise of wit by the protagonists [Butley and Hench], that has led to the popular labeling of these plays as comedies of manners. Perhaps to some extent this is accurately descriptive; the witty banter and the occasional exposure of the posturing types that inhabit twentieth-century academia and literary circles do partially admit these plays to that genre. And yet, their underlying structure does not."

Jones goes on to explain that both "Butley" and "Otherwise Engaged" more approach the tragic in tone than the comic. "To begin with, in [both works] Gray has economically compressed the action into one climactic day in the life of the protagonist. The alleged unities of time and place are rigorously adhered to as the unity of action: all events . . . work toward the ultimate overwhelming of the hero. Very little 'happens' in either play, at least in the sense of stage action or permutations of plot. In both, most everything 'has happened' already, largely because of the behavior of the protagonists, and what occurs on stage is the unveiling to the audience of his destructive behavior and the gradual revelation to him himself of the finally disastrous consequences of that mode of conduct." Jones sees everything necessary for tragic implications "is present in the fate of Ben Butley and Simon Hench. Both are permitted to come to that condition not allowed by protagonists of Gray's farces—the moment of recognition that they themselves are the causes of their present state."

As with his other notable plays, Gray drew upon his own early experience as an English-language teacher abroad to create the atmosphere for "Quartermaine's Terms." The title character of "Quartermaine's Terms"—a single, middle-aged teacher of English to foreigners at a British university—"has a tendency to doze off in mid-conversation, to drift away early from his own classes, to miss the punch line of any joke," as Frank Rich puts it in a *New York Times* review. "But he's one of those benign fellows who can be carried on indefinitely by arcane British institutions. Though professionally incompetent, Quartermaine is unfailingly polite, loyal and undemanding." This play takes place over three years, while Quartermaine and his fellow teachers, a singularly disillusioned lot with names like Meadle, Sackling and Windscape, face various crises of career and life. But as the story progresses, it is Quartermaine who gets the sack, fired abruptly for lackluster performance even after he has devoted his entire career to this one school. "Grim as that may sound," says *Washington Post* critic David Richards, "Gray's play manages to be acutely funny. The humor comes not from the particular misfortunes, but from the way one character invariably manages to elbow another's problems aside in favor of his own." Interviewed by Nan Robertson for the *New York Times,* Gray professed a strong affection for his once and future backup career: "It's extremely depressing not to be making progress with writing a play, and I do really deeply love reading poems and plays and the discipline of doing it for and with students. It's stimulating."

John Russell Taylor, in a *Plays & Players* article, has mixed feelings about the play. Though "Quartermaine's Terms" "is very respectable and not actually boring, Gray seems to be holding his characters at a distance, filling out the picturesque details of their mostly horrible out-of-school lives with great ingenuity but never actually persuading us to believe, much less to care." But to *New York* magazine's John Simon, the work "keeps us suspended between laughter and melancholy, [and also melds] primal (almost primitive) emotions with fastidious speculations about the compromises, contradictions, numbing paradoxes of existence, and allows each spectator to enjoy the show according to his intellectual means." Simon concludes that if "Gray's understatedly heartbreaking ending does not get you where you live, either you or I don't know what theater—and art—is."

Gray again visits his alma mater, Cambridge, with "The Common Pursuit," a where-are-they-now comedy centering on the reunion of a handful of 1960s collegiate *artistes* turned 1980s sellouts. The circle of friends includes the editor and staff of a Cambridge literary magazine ("The Common Pursuit"), and what happens when the campus intelligentsia become hack writers, television critics, and professional money-mongerers. "We witness the moral, emotional and spiritual ravages inflicted by the [twenty years] on the editor, his associates and the journal itself," notes Benedict Nightingale in a *New York Times* piece. In another *New York Times* article, Mel Gussow remarks that toward the end of the play, Stuart, the editor who serves as main character, "stands looking at unpublished, perhaps unpublishable poems by a friend, recently deceased, who may have been the best of their misfortunate lot. Stuart's silence touchingly communicates his own despair." The author, Gussow also observes, "has sometimes been criticized for writing undramatic plays about inconsequential people, a charge that could of course also be raised against [famed Russian playwright Anton] Chekhov. One of several differences is that Chekhov's characters often become violent about vaunting their unhappiness; Mr. Gray's characters are more resigned to accept their fate. But in the Chekhovian sense, he writes plays of indirect action; the characters are the action."

In the Robertson interview, Gray tells of his passion for "found" dialogue. "I can't resist listening," he says, citing the time on a London subway when he overheard a woman describing a date to her girlfriend: "And then he put his hand up my skirt—you know the one—the blue dirndl skirt." In such inspiration does Gray begin his plays. He always opens "with a bit of dialogue: a character in a room who says something, and I hope someone else will say something," as Gray explains. Robertson adds that a typical Gray play can go through 35 or 40 revisions: "It is 'grinding' agony until then," but as the author puts it, "the last draft is always effortless, which is how I know it's finished."

BIOGRAPHICAL/CRITICAL SOURCES:

BOOKS

Authors in the News, Volume 1, Gale, 1976.
Contemporary Authors Autobiography Series, Volume 3, Gale, 1980.
Contemporary Literary Criticism, Gale, Volume 9, 1978, Volume 14, 1980, Volume 36, 1986.
Dictionary of Literary Biography, Volume 13: *British Dramatists since World War II,* Gale, 1982.
Kerensky, Oleg, *The New British Drama: Fourteen Playwrights since Osborne and Pinter,* Hamish Hamilton, 1977.
Taylor, John Russell, *The Second Wave: British Drama for the Seventies,* Hill & Wang, 1971.

PERIODICALS

American Theatre, June, 1986.
Drama, winter, 1981.
Los Angeles Times, February 10, 1986.
Midwest Quarterly, summer, 1977.
Newsweek, February 11, 1985.
New York, January 24, 1983.
New York Times, November 1, 1972, February 4, 1977, February 9, 1977, February 25, 1981, January 7, 1983, February 25, 1983, February 28, 1983, March 6, 1983, February 2, 1985, February 22, 1986, September 30, 1986, October 19, 1986, October 20, 1986, November 2, 1982, May 10, 1987.
Plays and Players, October, 1981.
Time, November 3, 1986.
Times Literary Supplement, September 6, 1985, December 11, 1987, April 22, 1988.
Washington Post, April 23, 1982, March 29, 1983.
West Virginia University Philological Papers, Volume 25, 1979.

—*Sketch by Susan Salter*

*   *   *

GREEN, Hannah
   See GREENBERG, Joanne (Goldenberg)

*   *   *

GREENBERG, Joanne (Goldenberg) 1932-
Hannah Green

PERSONAL: Born September 24, 1932, in Brooklyn, NY; daughter of Julius Lester and Rosalie (Bernstein) Goldenberg; married Albert Greenberg, September 4, 1955; children: David, Alan. *Education:* American University, B.A. *Religion:* Jewish.

ADDRESSES: Home—29221 Rainbow Hills Rd., Golden, CO 80401. *Agent*—Lois Wallace, Wallace & Sheil Agency, Inc., 177 East 70th St., New York, NY; William Morris Agency, 1350 Ave. of the Americas, New York, NY 10019.

CAREER: Writer. Adjunct professor of anthropology, Colorado School of Mines, 1983—. Medical officer, Lookout Mountain Fire Department; certified emergency medical technician.

MEMBER: Authors Guild, Authors League of America, PEN, American Civil Liberties Union, National Association of the Deaf, Colorado Authors' League.

AWARDS, HONORS: Harry and Ethel Daroff Memorial Fiction Award, 1963, and William and Janice Epstein Fiction Award, 1964, both from the National Jewish Welfare Board, both for *The King's Persons;* Marcus L. Kenner Award from the

New York Association of the Deaf, 1971; Christopher Book Award, 1971, for *In This Sign;* Frieda Fromm-Reichman Memorial Award from Western Maryland College, 1977, and Gallaudet College, 1979; Rocky Mountain Women's Institute Award, 1983.

WRITINGS:

The King's Persons (novel), Holt, 1963.
(Under pseudonym Hannah Green) *I Never Promised You a Rose Garden* (autobiographical novel), Holt, 1964.
The Monday Voices (novel), Holt, 1965.
Summering (short stories), Holt, 1966.
In This Sign (novel), Holt, 1968.
Rites of Passage (short stories), Holt, 1971.
Founder's Praise (novel), Holt, 1976.
High Crimes and Misdemeanors (short stories), Holt, 1979.
A Season of Delight (novel), Holt, 1981.
The Far Side of Victory (novel), Holt, 1983.
Simple Gifts, Holt, 1986.
Age of Consent, Holt, 1987.
Of Such Small Differences, Holt, 1988.

Contributor of articles, reviews, and short stories to numerous periodicals, including *Hudson Review, Virginia Quarterly, Chatelaine,* and *Saturday Review.*

MEDIA ADAPTATIONS: I Never Promised You a Rose Garden was filmed by New World Pictures in 1977.

SIDELIGHTS: "Joanne Greenberg is a charming writer who writes about our current social problems without being doctrinaire or propagandistic or stuffy," states J. Mitchell Morse in the *Hudson Review.* As a novelist and short-story writer, Greenberg writes on subjects that are, according to Thomas Lask in the *New York Times,* "astonishingly varied: the farm life of a poor white; the world of the deaf, the family circle of great aunts from the old country, suburban academia and much else. She makes them all tangible." And John Nicholson describes Greenberg in this manner in the London *Times:* "Greenberg is a professional storyteller of the old school, who believes in putting plausible characters into interesting situations and letting them get on with it."

Greenberg's first book, *The King's Persons,* is a historical novel set in twelfth-century England. In it, she examines the resentment that existed between the Jewish moneylenders of York and the local Christian barons. Although this bitterness began over financial matters, it soon developed into general feelings of hatred and religious bigotry that spread to others in the community, resulting in the massacre of many Jewish people.

The King's Persons was highly praised for its attention to historical detail and Greenberg's sensitive portrayal of her characters. "Greenberg's first novel recreates a little-known aspect of English history with attention to the nuances of common-place life usually lost amid the panoply of historical romances that are preoccupied with large and glamorous movements," writes G. E. Grauel in *Best Sellers.* Pamela Marsh remarks in the *Christian Science Monitor* that "the special fascination of this book lies in its background." Marsh continues: "Strangely enough the final, inevitable massacre, appalling though it was, touches less closely than all the small tragedies and humiliations that happen along the way to people we have grown to care about." And a reviewer for *Time* notes that "with painstaking care, [Greenberg] has woven each of the skeins of medieval life into a vivid tapestry that shows the loutishness and insensitivity of the baronial landholders, the obtuseness of the peasantry, the twisted fervor of churchmen who found virtue in the wholesale slaughter of here-

tics, and the disturbing contrast between the warmth of Jewish communal life and the demeaning nature of usury."

Greenberg's second—and most popular—novel tackles a completely different subject matter. Written under the pseudonym Hannah Green, *I Never Promised You a Rose Garden* is the story of a young girl's long and difficult battle against schizophrenia. The book is based on Greenberg's own struggle with mental illness and follows the main character, Deborah Blau, as she retreats from reality to her mythical kingdom of Yr, attempts suicide, enters a mental hospital, and undergoes treatment and intensive therapy. R. V. Cassill remarks in the *New York Times Book Review* that Greenberg "has done a marvelous job of dramatizing the internal warfare in a young psychotic. She has anatomized, in full detail, the relationship between a whole, sick human being and the clinical situation—including doctors, other patients and the abstract forces of institutional life." And a reviewer for the *Times Literary Supplement* remarks that in *I Never Promised You a Rose Garden* Greenberg "tries to create the whole world of the mental hospital as the schizophrenic sees it, as the doctor sees it, as the nurses see it, and as the parents, terrified and ignorant see it from outside. . . . [Greenberg] is excellent when conveying relief and delight at the freedom from lies, and most of all the freedom to call mad mad, crazy crazy. She is excellent too on the inventiveness of the insane."

Due to the sensitive and highly personal nature of the book, Greenberg decided to publish *I Never Promised You a Rose Garden* under a pseudonym. She explains her reason for adopting the Hannah Green name in a *Saturday Review* article written by Rollene W. Saal: "I used the pseudonym when I wrote *Rose Garden* because my children were small. I wanted to protect them. Even so, a schoolmate asked my younger son if he was going to go crazy like his mother. It was like being hit in the face."

Greenberg's third novel, *The Monday Voices,* follows the character of Ralph Oakland, an employee of the Department of Rehabilitation, as he tries to help his handicapped and disadvanaged clients. W. G. Rogers describes *The Monday Voices* in the *New York Times Book Review* as "somber, disheartening, grand and gripping." Rogers goes on to remark: "Few books stick so closely to a theme. . . . [Oakland] never lifts his nose from the grindstone, and the reader never does, either. Nor does he want to. The final note is optimistic. . . . There could be no better plea for society's support of the lame, the halt, and the blind."

In This Sign, Greenberg's fourth novel, was praised for its sensitive and enlightening description of a deaf couple's trials and tribulations during their nearly fifty years of marriage. A reviewer for the *Times Literary Supplement* writes that *In This Sign* "usually avoids the excesses of sentimentality expected of a novel about the deaf, while technically Joanne Greenberg has managed to find a way of writing conversations between deaf and hearing with inordinate skill, as well as the less usual situations between deaf and deaf."

"Those who protect their heartstrings at all costs from being tugged at by professional writers would do well to avoid Joanne Greenberg's *In This Sign,*" comments R. R. Davies in the *New Statesman.* "As a stolid family chronicle it resembles the less vigorous works of Zola in its deliberate, almost deterministic progress. Its skill . . . consists in its coming to terms with the problem of deafness, not merely in its readily imaginable practical implications but in the more fundamental sense of what can and cannot be said with the hands. I was surprised by the tact of the book." And Ruth Nadelhaft states in the *Library Journal* that *In This Sign* is an "unsettling, haunting book. . . . The isolation and the often frenzied rage of the deaf couple are unforgettably vivid. . . . Reading this book is not easy; but it ends with hard-earned laughter and is worth the struggle."

The publication of *Founder's Praise* and *A Season of Delight,* both of which revolve around religious themes, followed *In This Sign. Founder's Praise,* for example, explores three generations of an American family and their involvement with the formation of a grass roots religion. J. R. Frakes remarks in the *New York Times Book Review:* "The bulk of [Greenberg's] darkly beautiful and disturbing novel is devoted to the rise and dissolution of [a] new religion. . . . Tough issues [are] dealt with dramatically and persuasively in this gnarled book, which never indulges in cheap mockery or cynical patronizing of the religious impulse."

In *A Season of Delight* the reader is introduced to Grace Dowben, who is trying to cope with her children's rejection of their traditional Jewish background. Norma B. Williamson states in the *National Review* that "Greenberg takes a woman who could fill about half a dozen popular stereotypes and exposes the unique human being beneath. Grace is a middle-aged Jewish homemaker, attempting to deal with the pain and sense of loss engendered by the finality of her children's leaving home. Her son has become a Moonie and her daughter has embraced radical feminism, and both have rejected the traditions that have always been a vital part of Grace's life." And Ellen Sweet explains in *Ms.* that *A Season of Delight* "is about [Dowben's] efforts to come to terms with their choices and with her own feelings. . . . Thanks to Joanne Greenberg's funny/sad, sensitive treatment, we don't have to put up with parody, either."

In *The Far Side of Victory,* Greenberg's more recent novel, young Eric Gordon, after having too much to drink, drives down a snowy Colorado highway and collides with another car. As a result, five passengers in the other car—two men and three children—die; the only survivor, Helen, is the wife of one of the men and the mother of the three children. Gordon receives a sentence of fifteen months probation and proceeds to get his life back in order. Eventually he meets, falls in love with, and marries Helen, the woman who survived the crash he caused. Over the years they have three children. Thirteen years after the original accident another freakish one occurs—this time killing Helen and Gordon's three children.

Greenberg's novel has been compared to a Greek tragedy. Remarks Elaine Kendall in the *Los Angeles Times:* "The spare style, the inexorable progress of events and the rigid symmetry of plot all follow accepted classical principles. The characters are obedient to the capricious whims of the gods, the fundamental lesson of the book more dreadful than ordinary mortals can bear." On the other hand, a reviewer for the *Washington Post Book World* believes that "what Greenberg is writing about in her gentle and perceptive book is how hard it is to know the people you love—and how that knowledge, once gained, must be tenderly held."

In addition to the respect critics have for her ability to write sensitive, heart-warming, and intelligent novels, Greenberg has been praised for her skillful short story writing. While reviewers agree that Greenberg successfully handles the technical transition from writing novels to short stories, they note that her topics do not change, for Greenberg still seeks out and explores the problems of the less fortunate. For example, in a *Los Angeles Times Book Review* article concerning *High Crimes and Misdemeanors,* Leah Fritz explains that "in her short stories, Greenberg rails against the unfairness of life and invokes all sorts of unearthly powers—sublime and absurd—to redress it. She despairs of mundane remedies for mundane ills." Fritz goes on to state: "Greenberg's characters use their [brains] to outwit an assortment of evils running the gamut from the perils of city streets to terminal disease, from the disenfranchisement of mental patients to the problems of an amateur cocaine smuggler from attempted suicide to just plain boredom. . . . Greenberg produced fabrications as layered and light as good strudel." And also writing about *High Crimes and Misdemeanors,* Ellen Carter notes in *Voyager* that this is "an outstanding collection of short stories reminiscent of the late Flannery O'Connor, many concerned with the problems of belief by contemporary man. . . . Beware, these stories will haunt you."

In a review of *Rites of Passage,* Joyce Carol Oates states in *Book World* that "this group of twelve excellent short stories is all the more remarkable for its being not only artistically 'beautiful' but morally and spiritually beautiful as well. . . . In story after story, she sets forth characters populating entirely believable, dense, frightening worlds (or visions of worlds—because her people suffer in their isolation), sometimes establishing contact with another person, sometimes reaching out but failing, sometimes falling back, selfishly, content in failure." And finally, Norma B. Williamson comments in the *National Review* that in all of her writing "Greenberg clearly believes in traditional values, along with such old-fashioned themes as good and evil, but there is humor and compassion in her treatment of both, making her always a joy to read."

Greenberg examines the inner life of a reconstructive surgeon in *Age of Consent.* Daniel Sanborn, himself a survivor of strife in Israel, uses his skills to rebuild the lives of injured people from all over the world. At the time of his death in a sniper's attack, he is regarded as a heroic saint. His sister Vivian, realizing his family actually knew very little about him, begins to search for information about his private life and finds more enigmas than answers. For example, Sanborn has willed most of his estate to a Las Vegas comic named "Jack the Ripper" Ripstein. "Greenberg has spun a story that is as much a mystery as a character study, a picture of Dorian Gray in which the image eerily darkens as the tale progresses. Some of the most stunning revelations come in the final lines of the book," Michael J. Bandler remarks in *Chicago Tribune Book World.* Other reviewers also praise Greenberg's confrontation with the complexities of human personality, communication, and virtue.

The deaf and blind John Moon, main character of the novel *Of Such Small Differences,* grows out of isolation into closer relationships with others. A poet who at first writes verses about the experiences of sighted people, he develops a poetic voice that reflects his unique perspective on the world. He is particularly adept at perceiving the subtle nuances of thought, the various textures and interrelationships of ideas. Though his attempts to reconcile with estranged family members and a former teacher fail, John "is not defeated," Richard Perry observes in the *New York Times Book Review.* "Because he has learned to trust himself and others, he can continue to take . . . risks. . . . He is armed now with an authentic voice and convinced that there is a place for him. . . . He can sing the blues now, which means he can temper his self-destructive rage, acknowledge his condition and celebrate his survival." Suggests James Idema in the *Chicago Tribune Book World,* "That Greenberg, a hearing and sighted writer, manages to show how the world seems to people who can neither see nor hear makes the book a wondrous *tour de force.*"

BIOGRAPHICAL/CRITICAL SOURCES:

BOOKS

Contemporary Literary Criticism, Gale, Volume 7, 1977; Volume 30, 1984.

PERIODICALS

Atlantic, August, 1965; February 3, 1980.
Best Sellers, March 1, 1963; May 1, 1964; July 1, 1965; August 1, 1966; December 1, 1970.
Book Week, May 3, 1964; July 18, 1965; March 19, 1972.
Christian Science Monitor, March 14, 1963; March 16, 1977.
Commentary, May, 1982.
Hudson Review, winter, 1966-67.
Library Journal, February 15, 1964; November 15, 1970; October 1, 1976.
Los Angeles Times, February 9, 1989.
Los Angeles Times Book Review, March 16, 1980; October 27, 1983; December 13, 1987.
Ms., July, 1981; December 13, 1987.
National Review, May 2, 1980.
New Republic, February 13, 1971.
New Statesman, August 14, 1964; September 3, 1971.
New Yorker, April 15, 1972.
New York Review of Books, May 4, 1972.
New York Times, March 18, 1972; October 3, 1988.
New York Times Book Review, May 3, 1964; July 11, 1965; October 31, 1976; February 3, 1980; October 12, 1986; December 27, 1987; October 30, 1988.
Publishers Weekly, September 23, 1988.
Saturday Review, July 18, 1964; September 10, 1966; January 22, 1972.
Time, March 29, 1963; January 21, 1980; January 19, 1984.
Times (London), January 19, 1984.
Times Literary Supplement, August 13, 1964; November 18, 1965; October 15, 1971; May 19, 1978.
Top of the News, April, 1977.
Tribune Books (Chicago), October 12, 1986; November 22, 1987; October 30, 1988.
Voyager, June, 1980.
Washington Post Book World, March 2, 1980; October 2, 1983.

*   *   *

GROSECLOSE, Kel(vin)   1940-

PERSONAL: Born November 14, 1940, in McMinnville, OR; son of Bruce (a minister) and E. Mildred (Ingram) Groseclose; married Ellen Emert (a book store owner), July 20, 1962; children: John, Stephen, Amy, Michael, Sara, David. *Education:* University of Puget Sound, B.A., 1963; Boston University, S.T.B., 1967; doctoral study at San Francisco Theological Seminary, 1982—.

ADDRESSES: Home—1401 Seattle, Wenatchee, WA 98801. *Office*—Cover to Cover Bookstore, 1300 North Miller, Wenatchee, WA 98801.

CAREER: Ordained United Methodist minister, 1968. Fellowship Methodist Church, Lowell, MA, minister, 1964-67; United Methodist Church, Nezperce-Cottonwood, ID, minister, 1967-70; United Methodist Church, Bonners Ferry, ID, minister, 1970-75; United Methodist Church, Wenatchee, WA, minister, 1975-1987; currently owner, Cover to Cover Bookstore, Wenatchee.

WRITINGS:

Three-Speed Dad in a Ten-Speed World, Bethany House, 1983.

Coming up Short in a Tall World, Bethany House, 1984.
Foundations: Basics of Christian Faith for Youth, Graded Press, 1988.

Columnist for *Wenatchee World,* 1989—.

SIDELIGHTS: Kel Groseclose commented: "Writing is a second career for me, squeezed out of bits of time after I have fulfilled my primary responsibilities. It's a delightful chore for me, a frustrating but highly satisfying endeavor. I believe a sense of humor is a required quality for writers. The ability to laugh at oneself is the key to overcoming writer's block."

The author added that "owning and managing a bookstore has deepened my appreciation in the written word and given me renewed appreciation for those with the courage to write it."

*   *   *

GRUB, Phillip D.   1932-

PERSONAL: Born August 8, 1932; son of Carl D. and Barbara (Johnson) Grub. *Education:* Eastern Washington State College (now Eastern Washington University), B.A. in economics and B.A. in education (both with highest honors), 1953; George Washington University, M.B.A., 1960, Ph.D., 1964.

ADDRESSES: Home—Arlington, VA. *Office*—School of Government and Business Administration, George Washington University, Washington, DC 20052.

CAREER: George Washington University, Washington, DC, assistant professor, 1954-67, associate professor, 1967-72, professor of business administration, 1972-74, Aryamehr Professor of Multinational Management, 1974—, chairman of department of business administration, 1968-70, special assistant to the president for International Program Development, 1974-80, founding director of International Business Programs. Visiting lecturer in business administration, Eastern Washington State College (now Eastern Washington University), 1960-62; Distinguished Visiting Professor of International Business, Ecole superiere des Sciences economiques et commerciales, Paris, 1970, and University of International Business and Economics, People's Republic of China, 1981; Distinguished Visiting Professor of International Marketing, Helsinki School of Economics, Finland, 1971; visiting professor of international business administration, Cleveland State University, 1972-73; guest lecturer, Romanian Institute of Management, CEPECA, 1976; Distinguished Visiting Professor and Research Scholar, Alaska Center for International Business, Anchorage, 1988. Honorary professorship, Chung-Ang University, Korea, 1975; distinguished honorary professorship, University of International Business and Economics, People's Republic of China, 1987.

Member of International Relations Committee, American Assembly of Collegiate Schools of Business, 1975-78; chairman of board of governors, African Institute for Economic Development, 1980-84. Member of board of directors and chairman of executive committee, Diplomat National Bank, 1977-80; member of board of directors, OZMA Corp., 1979-80, World Trade Center, Washington, 1980—, and Washington World Trade Institute (and president, 1984-86), 1980—; member of board of directors and executive secretary, United States-Japan Culture Center, 1979—; associate director, CICCO and Associates, 1978—. Member of President's Regional Export Expansion Council, 1968-88; director of Ohio World Trade-Education Center, 1972-73. Member of Ohio Governor's Advisory Committee on World Trade, 1972-73, and International Real Estate Advisory Board, Donaldson, Lufkin and Jennerette, 1981-84. Headed first official U.S. seminar team in marketing and management to Eastern Europe for the U.S. Departments of Commerce and State, 1968; led team to Second Asian International Trade Fair in Tehran, Iran, 1969; led delegation of U.S. industrial research and development specialists to the Autumn International Exposition, Bucharest, Romania, 1970; chairman of international conference on "The Role of Multinational Corporations in Economic Development," Alexandria, Egypt, 1977; co-chairman of International Symposium on Technology Transfer, Seoul, Korea, 1978; has conducted numerous other seminars and conferences. Co-owner and co-manager of 7G Ranch, Medical Lake, Washington, 1962-70.

International public speaker, giving more than thirty major addresses annually to community service organizations, labor and industry groups, colleges and universities, and foreign chambers of commerce; has appeared on television, at press conferences, and on radio interviews concerning international politics and business issues. Management consultant to businesses, governments, and organizations, including General Electric Corp., Federation of Korean Industries, U.S. Civil Service Commission, Central Bank of Malaysia, U.S. Departments of Commerce and State, and governments of Sweden, Iran, Qatar, and Egypt. *Military service:* U.S. Army, 1954-56; served in Japan as public information specialist, acted as assistant director of the Office of Public Information Headquarters.

MEMBER: Academy of International Business (fellow; treasurer, beginning 1969; president, 1975-77), Association of International Executives, Kiwanis International, Academy of Management, American Economic Association, American Management Association, American Marketing Association.

AWARDS, HONORS: Citation, U.S. Department of Commerce, 1968; named one of Outstanding Educators of America, 1970; Distinguished Alumnus Award, Eastern Washington State College (now Eastern Washington University), 1970; one of three delegates named by President Gerald Ford to represent the United States at the Bicentennial Ceremony in Genoa, Italy, 1976; International Founders Award, High-12 International, 1979, for outstanding service to the United States of America; Trustees Award for Distinguished Service to the Youth of America, Wolcott Foundation, 1984.

WRITINGS:

(With Karel Holbik) *American-East European Trade: Controversy, Progress, Prospects,* National Press, 1968.
(With Norma M. Loeser) *Executive Leadership: The Art of Successfully Managing Resources,* MDI Publications, 1969.
(With Mika S. Kaskimies) *International Marketing in Perspective,* Sininen Kirja Oy (Helsinki), 1971.
(With Ashok Kapoor) *The Multinational Enterprise in Transition,* Darwin Press, 1972.
(With Robert F. Dyer and Charles V. Jackson) *A Handbook for Term Papers, Theses and Dissertations,* George Washington University, 1974.
(With Tan Chwee Huat, Kwan Kuen-Chor, and George Rott) *East Asia Dimensions of International Business,* Prentice-Hall, 1982.
(With Fariborz Ghadar and Dara Khambata) *Multinational Corporations in Transition,* Volume II, Darwin Press, 1983, Volume III, 1987.
(With Bryan L. Sudweeks) *Foreign Direct Investment: Country Profiles and Pieces,* Mercury Press, 1986.
(With Robert Moran and Ghadar) *Global Business Management in the 1990s,* Roger Beacham, 1990.

(With Jian Hai Lin) *Foreign Direct Investment in the People's Republic of China,* Quorum Books, 1990.

Also author of monographs. Contributor of case studies to "Harvard University Intercollegiate Case Clearinghouse Series on Multinational Business and Developing Countries." Contributor of numerous articles and reviews to professional journals.

WORK IN PROGRESS: Revision of *The Multinational Enterprise in Transition.*

SIDELIGHTS: Phillip D. Grub told *CA* that he has conducted research in "more than eighty countries, with major work in Japan, Korea, Malaysia, Indonesia, Iran, Egypt, Kuwait, Saudi Arabia, Yugoslavia, Finland, France, Poland, and the People's Republic of China." He continues that his "specific focus has been varied and included development of an industrial trade zone in Egypt, tourism development, the organization and development of a university of Qatar." He adds that he has conducted a considerable amount of research and consulting "on export development for emerging countries, technology transfer, joint-venture negotiation, and developing information and control systems for multinational corporations. On an international scale, major research emphasis has been on the social responsibility of business, economic and business development in emerging countries, and long-range planning."

Many of Grub's writings have been translated into foreign languages.

* * *

GURNEY, A(lbert) R(amsdell), Jr. 1930-
(Peter Gurney)

PERSONAL: Born November 1, 1930, in Buffalo, N.Y.; son of Albert Ramsdell (in real estate) and Marion (Spaulding) Gurney; married Mary Goodyear, 1957; children: George, Amy, Evelyn, Benjamin. *Education:* Willliams College, B.A., 1952; Yale University, M.F.A., 1958.

ADDRESSES: Home—40 Wellers Bridge Rd., Roxbury, Conn. 06783. *Office*—120 West 70th St., New York, N.Y. 10023.

CAREER: Teacher of English and Latin at day school in Belmont, Mass., 1959-60; Massachusetts Institute of Technology, Cambridge, professor of humanities, 1960—.

MEMBER: Dramatists Guild (member of council; secretary), Phi Beta Kappa.

AWARDS, HONORS: Everett Baker Teaching Award, Massachusetts Institute of Technology, 1969; Drama Desk Award, 1971; Rockefeller playwright-in-residence award, 1977; National Education Association playwriting award, 1981-82; McDermott Award for the Arts, Massachusetts Institute of Technology, 1984; award of merit, American Academy and Institute of Arts and Letters, 1987; honorary degree, Williams College, 1984; New England Conference Annual Award for Greater Achievement, 1987; Lucile Locke Award for outstanding production, 1988-89.

WRITINGS:

The Gospel According to Joe (novel), Harper, 1974.
Entertaining Strangers (novel), Doubleday, 1977.
The Snow Ball (novel), Arbor House, 1984.

PLAYS

"Love in Buffalo," produced in New Haven, Conn., 1958.

"Tom Sawyer" (musical), first produced in Kansas City, Mo., at Starlight Theatre, July, 1959.

"The Bridal Dinner," produced in Cambridge, Mass., 1962.

(Under pseudonym Peter Gurney) *Around the World in Eighty Days* (two-act musical; based on the book by Jules Verne), Dramatic Publishing, 1962.

The Rape of Bunny Stuntz (one-act; first produced in New York City at Playwrights Unit, Cherry Lane Theatre, 1962), Samuel French, 1964.

The Comeback (one-act; first produced in Cambridge at Image Theatre, May, 1964), Dramatists Play Service, 1966.

The Golden Fleece (one-act; first produced in Los Angeles at Mark Taper Forum, June, 1968; produced in New York City, 1968; also see below), Samuel French, 1967.

The Problem (one-act; first produced in London at King's Head Theatre, March, 1973; produced in New York City at Soho Repertory Theatre, January, 1978), Samuel French, 1968.

The Open Meeting (one-act; first produced in Boston at The Atma Coffee House Theatre, January, 1965), Samuel French, 1968.

The David Show (one-act; first produced in Tanglewood, Mass., 1966; produced in New York City at Players Theatre, October, 1968; also see below), Samuel French, 1968.

"Tonight in Living Color" (contains "The David Show" and "The Golden Fleece"), first produced in New York City at Actors Playhouse, June 10, 1969.

The Love Course (one-act; first produced in Boston, 1970; produced in London at King's Head Theatre, July, 1974; produced in New York City, 1976), Samuel French, 1969.

Scenes from American Life (two-act; first produced in Tanglewood, 1970; produced in New York City at Lincoln Center, March, 1971; also see below), Samuel French, 1970.

The Old One-Two (one-act; first produced in Waltham, Mass. at Brandeis University, 1973; produced in London at King's Head Theatre, August, 1975), Samuel French, 1971.

Children (two-act; suggested by short story "Goodbye, My Brother," by John Cheever; first produced in London at Mermaid Theatre, April, 1974; produced in New York City at Manhattan Theatre Club, November, 1976; also see below), Samuel French, 1975.

Who Killed Richard Cory? (one-act; first produced in New York City at Circle Repertory Theatre, March, 1976; revision produced as "Richard Cory" in Williamstown, Mass. at Williamstown Theatre Festival, 1986), Samuel French, 1976.

The Middle Ages (first produced in Los Angeles at Mark Taper Forum Laboratory, 1977; produced in New York City at Theatre at St. Peter's, March, 1983; also see below), Dramatists Play Service, 1978.

The Wayside Motor Inn (first produced in New York City at Manhattan Theatre Club, 1977), Dramatists Play Service, 1979.

The Golden Age (first produced in London at Greenwich Theatre, 1981; produced in New York City at Jack Lawrence Theatre, March, 1984), Dramatists Play Service, 1981.

The Dining Room (first produced in New York City at Playwrights Horizon, February, 1982; also see below), Dramatists Play Service, 1982.

What I Did Last Summer (first produced in New York City at Circle Repertory Company, February, 1983), Dramatists Play Service, 1983.

Four Plays (contains "Scenes from American Life," "Children," "The Middle Ages" and "The Dining Room"), Avon, 1985.

The Perfect Party (two-act; first produced in New York City at Playwrights Horizons, April, 1986), Doubleday, 1986.

"Sweet Sue," produced on Broadway at Music Box Theatre, January, 1987.

"Another Antigone," produced in New York at Playwrights Horizon, January, 1988.

"The Cocktail Hour," produced in New York City at Promenade Theatre, October, 1988.

"Love Letters," produced in New York City at Promenade Theatre, 1989.

SCREENPLAYS AND TELEPLAYS

"The Golden Fleece" (teleplay), N.E.T. Playhouse, National Educational Television, November 8, 1969.

"The House of Mirth" (screenplay), 1972.

"O Youth and Beauty" (teleplay; adapted from the John Cheever story), Great Performances, Public Broadcasting Service (PBS-TV), 1979.

"The Dining Room" (teleplay; based on his play), Great Performances, PBS-TV, 1984.

"The Hit List" (teleplay for series "Trying Times"), PBS-TV, 1989.

OTHER

Contributor to anthologies, including *The Best Short Plays, 1955-56,* Beacon Press, 1956; *The Best Short Plays, 1957-58,* Beacon Press, 1958, *The Best Short Plays, 1969,* Chilton, 1970; and *The Best Short Plays, 1970,* Chilton, 1971.

SIDELIGHTS: "In comedies such as 'The Dining Room' and 'The Middle Ages,' the playwright A. R. Gurney has claimed [novelist] John Cheever's territory for the stage," declares the *New York Times*' Frank Rich. Indeed, Gurney's plays are peopled with the kind of upper-class WASP characters not seen on stage for many years beforehand. And yet the Buffalo, New York-born Gurney would be the first to admit he doesn't enjoy being pigeonholed as a "WASP" writer. "I'm not a stereotype," he tells Charlotte Curtis in a *New York Times* interview. "I don't own a suit."

When not writing plays, Gurney taught literature for many years at the Massachusetts Institute of Technology. His dramatic influences seem steeped in the classics. "Of course, all playwrights everywhere have long been used to dancing in various chains," he notes in a *New York Times* article he himself wrote. "Aeschylus was bound by the ritual rule that only two characters on stage at one time were allowed to exchange dialogue. Moliere had to be scrupulously tactful about church and court under the shadow of Louis XIV. Samuel Beckett embraces and makes a virtue of the very spareness which good contemporary drama is asked to impose upon itself." Gurney adds, "I used to tell my students that it is the very pressure of these esthetic restrictions that gives drama so much of its particular power. I would point to the thrilling resonances of offstage events in Greek drama, or the special sense of enclosed space that emerges in Ibsen and Chekhov. 'What's left out lends importance to what's put in,' I'd say, and we'd explore the glories of artistic structure, as in the sonnet, or the sonata form, or a good play."

Gurney brings this sense of structure to his own works. Reviewing "Children," a 1974 play, *Plays and Players* writer Sandy Wilson expresses surprise that this piece, unlike many of its contemporaries, eschewed countercultural theatrical techniques so popular at the time. "Can it be?" Wilson asks rhetorically. "Is this that dear, forgotten, old-fashioned thing, a Good Play? . . . I am not going to be bored, or baffled. I am not going to be preached at or bludgeoned over the head with statistics or propaganda. And I am not going to be shocked, brutalised, outraged or assaulted." In "Children," continues Wilson, Gurney has created "a soundly structured piece, absorbing, amusing, occasionally exciting and finally very moving, about the tensions of a middle-class American family on a July the Fourth week-end." Though *New York Post* critic Martin Gottfried was less enthusiastic about "Children"—he finds the play "an excellent subject but Gurney has explored it only in an illustrative way and even then, he's wandered"—the reviewer adds that Gurney is "a talented writer. [In the past] his 'Scenes from American Life' successfully presented the promise of a dramatic intelligence directed toward the middle class that is too often ignored by our stage. That intelligence and interest are present in ['Children']."

In one of Gurney's best-known plays, "The Dining Room," all the action takes place in the titular room, which "represents not a particular home or family, but a host of such dining rooms peopled by families in varying degrees of stability or disintegration," according to Gerald Weales in a *Commonweal* review. As in his other plays, in "The Dining Room" Gurney takes a satiric look at the mores and manners of WASPy society. One young character, for instance, attends dinner with his camera, intending to make a study of "the eating habits of various vanishing cultures—the WASPs of Northeastern United States," and diligently shoots his aunt's finger bowls.

"The Dining Room" "isn't flawless," notes Rich, "but it's often funny and rueful and, by the end, very moving. [The playwright has] learned some lessons well. If he doesn't share [John Cheever's] gift for subtlety, he does share his compassion and ability to create individual characters within a milieu that might otherwise seem as homogenous as white bread. Though dozens of people whirl in and out of Mr. Gurney's metaphorical dining room, they all come through as clearly and quickly as the voices we hear in a Cheever story like 'The Enormous Radio.' " Though *New Republic* critic Robert Brustein complains that in "The Dining Room" the playwright has offered less a dramatic story than a depiction of a dying class, London *Times* critic Irving Wardle finds that "Gurney has a wonderful ear for the evasive nuances of authoritarian speech: particularly for pre-war parents coaxing their children before exploding into defeated commands, or employers putting in long-suffering requests to the kitchen staff ('Sometimes I think it is almost better if we do things ourselves')."

Traditional values are reflected in the very titles of two other Gurney plays, "The Middle Ages" and "The Golden Age." In the former, the setting is the paneled trophy room of an exclusive men's club, where Gurney "actually makes us mourn for people who, at their worst, use expressions like 'perfectly ghastly' and raise their eyebrows over any proper name that sounds Jewish (whole cities like Harrisburg not excepted)," as Rich puts it. In a *Nation* article Richard Gilman groups "The Middle Ages" with "The Dining Room" as two plays that "display most of Gurney's methods and concerns. They wander around in time—*The Middle Ages* begins in the mid-1940s and ends in the late 1970s—their scenes are connected not by narrative progression but by a ruling idea, and they deal with aspects of WASP life."

"The Golden Age," by contrast, examines the past as seen through the eyes of just one character, an aging woman who was friends with the author F. Scott Fitzgerald during the 1920s and who may have in her possession a lost chapter of Fitzgerald's classic novel "The Great Gatsby." Sparked by the challenge of finding it, a young writer, Tom, ingratiates herself with her, moving into her home, tentatively romancing her reclusive granddaughter, and rummaging through her personal items in search of the lost chapter. Rich found that this formula didn't work for him: The play "fails," he comments in a *New York*

Times piece, "because [the] characters are too pale and unconvincing to turn [the] plot into either drama or high comedy."

Another foray into WASP country sets the scene for "The Perfect Party." In this comedy, the protagonist, a middle-aged professor, Tony, prepares a sumptuous affair for every notable person he knows. "Like past Gurney heroes, Tony is of two minds about his patrician lot and prerogatives," Rich says in another *New York Times* review. The high-born attitudes of the guests and Tony's wife, Sally, do not help him sort out his feelings. Rich adds that "when the party finally gets under way (offstage, in Act II), it proves a Wagnerian social event that is variously likened to everything from 'Gatsby' to 'Citizen Kane' to 'civilization itself.' " To Rich, " 'The Perfect Party' seems a metaphor for the relationship between a playwright, his audience and his critics—with a strong statement about esthetics thrown in." The critic also labels this play as "surely Mr. Gurney's funniest, meanest and most theatrical play yet."

Following a production of "Sweet Sue," a comedy that finds two actors playing every one character onstage, Gurney produced "Another Antigone" and "The Cocktail Hour," each deeply critical of prevailing upper-class attitudes. "Another Antigone" examines modern anti-Semitism as seen through the characters of a middle-aged WASPy professor at odds with his young, strident Jewish student. In "The Cocktail Hour" a genteel couple faces public humiliation when their son writes a stinging play about their society. Rich declares that even after years of skewering the upper classes, Gurney "still has new and witty observations to make about a nearly extinct patrician class that regards psychiatry as an affront to good manners, underpaid hired help as a birthright and the selling of blue-chip stocks as a first step toward Marxism."

"I don't write about rebels or dissenters or gangsters; I write about my own people, the Americans you see haunting [the upscale London department store] Harrods in midsummer," Gurney once told London *Times* reporter Sheridan Morley, "the Americans who call themselves Anglos now because WASP has become such a pejorative term." For his part, Morley finds the playwright perhaps not "everybody's idea of the typical modern Broadway dramatist: I happen to believe that he is [the] most elegant and accomplished theatrical writer to have come out of America since the war."

BIOGRAPHICAL/CRITICAL SOURCES:

BOOKS

Contemporary Literary Criticism, Gale, Volume 32, 1985, Volume 50, 1989.

PERIODICALS

Chicago Tribune, March 6, 1983.
Commonweal, April 23, 1982.
Los Angeles Times, January 3, 1985.
Nation, April 30, 1983.
New Republic, May 12, 1982.
New York, March 8, 1982, February 14, 1983, April 23, 1983.
New Yorker, April 3, 1971, April 4, 1983, January 25, 1988.
New York Post, October 26, 1976.
New York Times, October 26, 1976, November 12, 1977, February 15, 1981, February 15, 1982, March 14, 1982, February 7, 1983, April 5, 1983, April 24, 1983, April 13, 1984, March 27, 1986, April 3, 1986, April 13, 1986, July 27, 1986, September 19, 1986, January 9, 1987, January 10, 1988, January 15, 1988, October 21, 1988.
New York Times Book Review, May 26, 1974, February 10, 1985.

Plays and Players, May, 1974.
Time, February 25, 1985, April 4, 1986, January 19, 1987.
Times (London), June 2, 1983, June 6, 1983, July 1, 1987.
Village Voice, January 26, 1988.

—Sketch by Susan Salter

*   *   *

GURNEY, Peter
  See GURNEY, A(lbert) R(amsdell), Jr.

H

HAGGERTY, Brian A(rthur) 1943-

PERSONAL: Born July 27, 1943, in Grand Rapids, MI; son of Frank J. (a certified public accountant) and Margaret N. (Tucker) Haggerty. Education: Sacred Heart Seminary College, Detroit, MI, B.A. (philosophy), 1965; Catholic University of Louvain, B.A. (theology), 1967, M.A., 1969, S.T.B., 1969; San Diego State University, M.S., 1979.

ADDRESSES: Home—San Diego, CA. Office—6816 Dennison St., San Diego, CA 92122.

CAREER: Free-lance writer and editor, 1969—; University of Southern California, Citizens' Research Foundation, Los Angeles, research associate and editor, 1979-89; San Diego City Schools, San Diego, CA, editor, 1986—.

WRITINGS:

(With Christiane Brusselmans) We Celebrate the Eucharist, Silver Burdett, 1972, 4th edition, 1990.
(With Brusselmans) We Celebrate Reconciliation, Silver Burdett, 1976, 3rd edition, 1990.
(With Joseph M. Champlin) Together in Peace for Children, Ave Maria Press, 1976.
(With Thomas P. Walters) We Receive the Spirit of Jesus, Paulist Press, 1978.
Out of the House of Slavery, Paulist Press, 1978.
(With T. P. Walters and Rita Tyson Walters) We Share New Life, Paulist Press, 1979.
(With Herbert E. Alexander) Political Reform in California: How Has It Worked? (monograph), Citizens' Research Foundation, 1980.
(With Alexander) The Federal Election Campaign Act: After a Decade of Political Reform (monograph), Citizens' Research Foundation, 1981.
(Editor of revisions) Herbert E. Alexander, Financing Politics, Congressional Quarterly, 2nd edition, 1980, 3rd edition, 1984.
(With Alexander) Financing the 1980 Election, Heath, 1983.
Money, Parties, and the Electoral Process (monograph), Edmund E. Brown Institute of Government Affairs, 1984.
(With Alexander) PACs and Parties: Relationships and Interrelationships (monograph), Citizens' Research Foundation, 1984.
(With Alexander) Financing the 1984 Election, Heath, 1987.

Nonviolence and Social Change: A Text for High School Students, Hal Clarke, Inc., in press.

Contributor of articles and reviews to magazines and newspapers, including Commonweal, Christian Century, Public Relations Review, Journal of Negro History, Public Opinion, San Diego, Religious Education, Christian Science Monitor, and Los Angeles Times.

SIDELIGHTS: Brian A. Haggerty told CA: "My interest in writing was spurred by an unpleasant incident during my sophomore year in high school. My English literature teacher returned to me an analysis I had written on Sir Gawain and the Green Knight. A critic-reader he had engaged attached a note to the paper concluding that it must have been plagiarized—that it was too mature in style and content to have been written by a high school sophomore. I was both incensed and flattered. The paper was my own work, and I worked thereafter to prove it by maintaining high standards."

*   *   *

HANMER, Davina
See COURTNEY, Nicholas (Piers)

*   *   *

HARDING, James 1929-

PERSONAL: Born May 30, 1929, in Bath, Somerset, England; married Gillian Russell, January 28, 1956; children: Rupert, Lucy. Education: University of Paris, Diplome de la civilisation francaise, 1948; University of Bristol, B.A. (with honors), 1950; University of London, Ph.D., 1973. Avocational interests: French music, literature, and theatre, and English literature of the 18th, 19th, and 20th centuries; collecting manuscripts of French authors, musicians, and composers.

ADDRESSES: Home—100 Ridgemount Gardens, Torrington Place, London WC1E 7AZ, England. Agent—Tony Peake, Peake Associates, 18, Grafton Crescent, London NW1 8SL, England.

CAREER: Copywriter and advertising executive in advertising agencies and mass-magazine publishing houses, London, England, 1952-64; lecturer, broadcaster, and author in French and

English, 1965—. *Military service:* Royal Air Force, 1950-52; served as flying officer.

MEMBER: Classical Association, Royal Society of Literature (fellow).

WRITINGS:

Saint-Saens and His Circle, Fernhill, 1965.
Sacha Guitry: The Last Boulevardier, Scribner, 1968.
The Duke of Wellington, Morgan Grampian, 1968, published as *Wellington,* A. S. Barnes, 1969.
(Author of introduction) Richard Doddridge Blackmore, *The Maid of Sker,* Anthony Blond, 1968.
Massenet, Dent, 1970, St. Martin's, 1971.
Boulanger, Scribner, 1971 (published in England as *General Boulanger,* W. H. Allen, 1971).
Rossini, Crowell, 1971.
The Ox on the Roof, St. Martin's, 1972.
(Editor and author of preface) *Lord Chesterfield's Letters to His Son,* Folio Society, 1973.
Gounod, Stein & Day, 1973.
Lost Illusions: Paul Leautaud and His World, Allen & Unwin, 1974, Fairleigh Dickinson University Press, 1975.
Eric Satie, Praeger, 1975.
Folies de Paris: The Rise and Fall of French Operetta, Chapell, 1978.
Jacques Offenbach, Riverrun Press, 1980.
Maurice Chevalier: His Life, Secker & Warburg, 1982.
Jacques Tati, Frame by Frame, Secker & Warburg, 1984.
Agate, Methuen, 1986.
Ivor Novello, W. H. Allen, 1987.
The Rocky Horror Show Book, Sidgwick & Jackson, 1988.
Cochran, Methuen, 1988.
Gerald Du Maurier, Hodder & Stoughton, 1989.

Contributor to numerous journals, periodicals, reference works and dictionaries.

WORK IN PROGRESS: A biography of George Robey, the English music-hall comedian, for Hodder & Stoughton, London.

SIDELIGHTS: Reviewing James Harding's biography of the composer Jacques Offenbach, Joseph McLellan writes in the *Washington Post:* "It seems impossible to be bored by James Harding's biography . . . which reads more like a novel about the composer than a scholarly study. Harding has dug out colorful material from all relevant sources and a few that are only marginally relevant. . . . There are detailed pages on Offenbach eating breakfast, Offenbach directing a rehearsal, a soiree at the Offenbachs'. Even the most minor characters are usually introduced with a short, colorful description and often an anecdote or two that may have little to do with Offenbach. It is a very splendidly readable book and very much in the spirit of the subject."

BIOGRAPHICAL/CRITICAL SOURCES:

PERIODICALS

Globe and Mail (Toronto), February 16, 1985.
London Evening Standard, March 5, 1987.
Los Angeles Times, April 26, 1981.
Spectator, April 19, 1986.
Times (London), November 29, 1984; April 3, 1986; November 29, 1986; January 28, 1989.
Times Literary Supplement, January 23, 1983; April 11, 1986; October 20, 1989.
Washington Post, April 9, 1981.

HARDWICK, Elizabeth 1916-

PERSONAL: Born July 27, 1916, in Lexington, Ky.; daughter of Eugene Allen and Mary (Ramsey) Hardwick; married Robert Lowell (a poet), July 28, 1949 (divorced, 1972); children: Harriet. *Education:* University of Kentucky, A.B., 1938, M.A., 1939; Columbia University, additional study.

ADDRESSES: Home—15 West 67th St., New York, N.Y. 10023.

CAREER: Writer; adjunct associate professor of English, Barnard College, New York, N.Y.

MEMBER: American Academy and Institute of Arts and Letters.

AWARDS, HONORS: Guggenheim fellowship in fiction, 1948; George Jean Nathan Award for dramatic criticism (first woman recipient), 1967; National Academy and Institute of Arts and Letters award in literature, 1974; National Book Critics Circle Award nomination, 1980, for *Sleepless Nights.*

WRITINGS:

The Ghostly Lover (novel), Harcourt, 1945.
The Simple Truth (novel), Harcourt, 1955.
(Editor) *The Selected Letters of William James,* Farrar, Straus, 1960.
A View of My Own: Essays on Literature and Society, Farrar, Straus, 1962.
Seduction and Betrayal: Women and Literature (essays), Random House, 1974.
(Editor) *Rediscovered Fiction by American Women: A Personal Selection* (series; 18 volumes), Ayer, 1977.
Sleepless Nights (novel), Random House, 1979.
Bartleby in Manhattan (essays), Random House, 1984.
(Editor) *The Best American Essays 1986,* Ticknor & Fields, 1986.

OTHER

Contributor to periodicals, including *Partisan Review, New Yorker,* and *Harper's.* Founder and advisory editor, *New York Review of Books.*

SIDELIGHTS: An accomplished essayist and novelist, Elizabeth Hardwick is perhaps best known "primarily for brilliant literary and social criticism, which has graced the pages of many of the country's leading liberal journals, most notably the *Partisan Review* and the *New York Review of Books,*" according to Joseph J. Branin, in a *Dictionary of Literary Biography* article on Hardwick. Hardwick was born and raised in Kentucky, but found her way to New York City during her young adult years; she's lived in New York ever since.

Her first novel, *The Ghostly Lover,* mirrors this aspect of the author's life: the protagonist, Marian, grew up in the South and moved to Manhattan. As the story goes on, Marian returns to her hometown to care for her ailing grandmother, but so misses New York that she moves there for good following her grandmother's death. "Throughout the novel, Marian is presented as a profoundly lonely young person," notes Branin. "[She] longs for connection and intimacy with another person but finds it impossible to break through the separateness of the characters in the novel. She is especially disappointed with her mother, whom she adores from a distance."

As Branin reports, *The Ghostly Lover* garnered mixed critical reaction. But soon after its publication, Hardwick was contacted by Philip Rahv, an editor of the avant-garde *Partisan Review,* to become a contributor. "She accepted the offer eagerly and thus began her long and successful career as a social and literary critic," Branin writes. As Hardwick's reputation as a writer grew, so did her fame outside the editorial offices. She married the poet Robert Lowell in 1949, a union that lasted until 1972, when Lowell divorced Hardwick to marry Caroline Blackwood, an Irish writer. "In 1977, the last year of his life, Lowell returned to Hardwick," relates Branin. "They summered together in Castine, Maine, before Lowell died of heart failure in New York." The piece continues with Hardwick telling a *New York Times* reporter at that time that her former husband was "the most extraordinary person I have ever known, like no one else— unplaceable, unaccountable."

Hardwick's published works include a second novel, *The Simple Truth,* a story of speculation and accusation surrounding a sensational murder trial. That novel, like the author's first, was greeted with mixed reviews. Hardwick continued publishing, first a selection of William James' letters, then an collection called *A View of My Own: Essays on Literature and Society.* A 1974 collection, *Seduction and Betrayal: Women and Literature,* caught the attention of several critics, including Rosemary Dinnage, who remarks in a *Times Literary Supplement* article that the book "is so original, so sly and strange, but the pleasure in embedded in the style, in the way [the author] flicks the English language around like a whip." Hardwick's concern in *Seduction and Betrayal,* Dinnage goes on to say, "is to present her own angry and witty view of the sexes, and for this she has more scope with the fictional beings and the companions of writers than with the great creative women, for these less easily align themselves with the victims." Hardwick "is no hand-wringer," says *Books and Bookmen* critic Jean Stubbs. "She is a literary surgeon, admirably equipped to expose the nerves." And in the opinion of Joan Didion, writing in *New York Times Book Review,* "Perhaps no one has written more acutely and poignantly about the ways in which women compensate for their relative physiological inferiority, about the poetic and practical implications of walking around the world deficient in hemoglobin, deficient in respiratory capacity, deficient in muscular strength and deficient in stability of the vascular and autonomic nervous systems."

By the time Hardwick's collection *Bartleby in Manhattan* came out, in 1984, she was almost universally acclaimed as a major essayist, prompting *New York Times* reviewer Christopher Lehmann-Haupt to remark, "One is interested in anything that Elizabeth Hardwick writes. That is a given." For this volume of social and literary musings, however, Lehmann-Haupt does have some reservations: "The subjects . . . give one a moment or two of pause. The atmosphere in the South during the civil rights movement of the 1960's? The significance of Martin Luther King, Jr. and of Lee Harvey Oswald and his family? . . . It isn't so much that we've lost interest in these topics as that they've become as familiar to us by now as our fingers and our toes." Another reviewer finds more to recommend in *Bartleby in Manhattan.* "As these essays of the past 20 years show, Hardwick's [concerns] have two qualities that make her one of our finest critics: a heart that wants to be moved and a critical intelligence that refuses to indulge it," finds *Los Angeles Times Book Review* writer Richard Eder. "Much that she deals with produces more disquiet in her than reward; she looks for values in the fiery writing of the '60s and the distanced writing of the '70s and finds them poor or limited. Our reward is the record of her search." "Whatever her subject," says novelist Anne Tyler, acting as critic for *New Republic,* Hardwick "has a gift for coming up with descriptions so thoughtfully selected, so exactly right, that they strike the reader as inevitable." As Tyler also notes, "Mere aptitude of language, of course, is not sufficient. What makes *Bartleby in Manhattan* memorable is the sense of the author's firm character. 'Pull yourself together,' she says briskly to a racist who tells her he feels sick at the sight of an integrated crowd."

The author's third novel, *Sleepless Nights,* "is a difficult work to classify," comments Branin. One possible definition may be "autobiographical": the fiction centers on a writer named Elizabeth, who grew up in Kentucky and moved to Manhattan. In the course of the story the narrator "remembers certain people and places from her past. . . . [Her] compassion for her old acquaintances and her careful observations as she brings these memories to life give the work its power and unity," Branin states.

Elizabeth Hardwick "is the voice of toughminded gentility," says Joan Joffe Hall in a *New Republic* review from 1974. "She inspires confidence because she seems just like the reader, a shade smarter perhaps, able to turn the commonplace into revelation, talking in someone's living room with an earnest casualness beyond personality. It's the quality most of us aspire to."

BIOGRAPHICAL/CRITICAL SOURCES:

BOOKS

Contemporary Literary Criticism, Volume 13, Gale, 1980.
Dictionary of Literary Biography, Volume 6: *American Novelists since World War II,* Gale, 1980.

PERIODICALS

Books and Bookmen, January, 1976.
Chicago Tribune, November 25, 1986.
Los Angeles Times Book Review, May 29, 1983.
New Republic, May 25, 1974, June 20, 1983.
Newsweek, June 17, 1974, May 30, 1983.
New York Review of Books, January 27, 1974, April 29, 1979.
New York Times, April 2, 1982, May 24, 1983.
New York Times Book Review, May 5, 1974, June 12, 1983.
Times Literary Supplement, November 29, 1974.
Village Voice, May 7, 1979.
Washington Post Book World, May 12, 1974, May 29, 1983.

—*Sketch by Susan Salter*

*   *   *

HARMON, William (Ruth) 1938-

PERSONAL: Born June 10, 1938, in Concord, NC; son of William Richard (a textile executive) and Virginia (Pickerel) Harmon; married Lynn Chadwell, December 20, 1965; married Anne Margretta Wilson, May 7, 1988; children: (first marriage) Sally Frances, William Richard Harmon II; (second marriage) Caroline Ruth. *Education:* University of Chicago, A.B., 1958, A.M., 1968; University of Cincinnati, Ph.D., 1970. *Politics:* Democrat. *Religion:* None.

ADDRESSES: Home—1919 Southwood, Apt. 5, Durham, NC 27707. *Office*—Department of English, University of North Carolina, Chapel Hill, NC 27599-3520.

CAREER: U.S. Navy, active duty as officer, 1960-67; reserve service, 1967-1980, retiring as lieutenant commander; University of North Carolina at Chapel Hill, instructor, 1970-71, assistant professor, 1971-72, associate professor, 1973-77, professor of English, 1977—, department chairman, 1972-77.

MEMBER: Modern Language Association of America, Academy of American Poets, American Anthropological Association, South Atlantic Modern Language Association.

AWARDS, HONORS: Military—Navy Commendation with Combat V; Vietnamese Staff Service Honor Medal, first class. Civilian—Fellowships from Rockefeller Foundation, Ford Foundation, and Elliston Poetry Fund; research grants from Kenan Fund; Lamont Award, Academy of American Poets; William Carlos Williams Award, Poetry Society of America.

WRITINGS:

Treasury Holiday (poetry), Wesleyan University Press, 1970.
Legion: Civic Choruses (poetry), Wesleyan University Press, 1973.
The Intussusception of Miss Mary America (poetry), Kayak Books, 1976.
Time in Ezra Pound's Work (criticism), University of North Carolina Press, 1977.
(Editor) *The Oxford Book of American Light Verse,* Oxford University Press, 1979.
One Long Poem (poetry), Louisiana State University Press, 1982.
Mutatis Mutandis, Wesleyan University Press, 1985.
(Editor) *Handbook to Literature,* 5th edition, Macmillan, 1986.

Contributor to *Quickly Aging Here: Some Poets of the 1970's,* edited by Geof Hewitt, Doubleday, 1969, and to a Pushcart selection. Contributor to journals, including *Antioch Review, Carolina Quarterly,* and *Sewanee Review.*

WORK IN PROGRESS: Two volumes of poetry, *Brass and Percussion: Prose Songs and Other Pieces,* and *What Rhymes* for Columbia University Press; a book of critical pieces entitled *A Scythian Suite;* a volume of essays on T. S. Eliot; editing the *Handbook to Literature,* 6th edition, and the *Concise Columbia Book of Poetry.*

SIDELIGHTS: William Harmon told *CA:* "I try to avoid subjecting what I do to any very agonizing scrutiny. Poetry is so demanding that, certainly, I would not write it if I did not absolutely as a matter of necessity have to. Teaching, criticism, editing, and other such academic or belletristic pastimes make up a much less ulcerating regimen."

Harmon later wrote: "Addendum ('LXXIV): Jubilate agno: My prose grows less mandarin-florist, I hope, wincing now at 'belletristic . . . regimen' [above]. I seem to attend more to rose-colored bats and punctuation than I used to. Is this senility?"

Harmon subsequently added: "Addendum (MXM): Now wince at rose-colored bats."

BIOGRAPHICAL/CRITICAL SOURCES:

PERIODICALS

Antioch Review, fall/winter, 1970-71.
New York Times, August 9, 1979.
Washington Post Book World, August 19, 1979.

*   *   *

HARRIS, Lavinia
    See St. JOHN, Nicole

*   *   *

HASSEL, David John   1923-

PERSONAL: Born July 13, 1923, in Chicago, IL; son of David Julius (a sales manager) and Catherine Elizabeth (Carroll) Hassel. *Education:* Xavier University, Cincinnati, OH, Litt.B., 1946;

Loyola University of Chicago, A.M., 1953, S.T.L., 1956; St. Louis University, Ph.D., 1963.

ADDRESSES: Home—Loyola University of Chicago, Jesuit Community, 6525 North Sheridan Rd., Chicago, IL 60626.

CAREER: Entered Society of Jesus (Jesuits), 1942, ordained Roman Catholic priest, 1955, director of Tertians, 1971-76; teacher at Roman Catholic high schools in Detroit, MI, 1949-52; St. Mary of the Lake Seminary, Mundelein, IL, instructor, 1962-64, assistant professor of philosophy and chairman of department, 1964-67; Xavier University, Cincinnati, OH, visiting professor of philosophy, 1967-68; Loyola University of Chicago, Chicago, IL, associate professor, 1969-89, research professor of philosophy, 1989—.

MEMBER: American Catholic Philosophical Association, Jesuit Philosophical Association (president, 1975-76).

WRITINGS:

(With Frank Yartz and Allan L. Larson) *Progress and the Crisis of Man,* Nelson-Hall, 1976.
Radical Prayer: Creating a Welcome for God, Ourselves, Other People, and the World, Paulist Press, 1983.
City of Wisdom: A Christian Vision of the American University, Loyola University Press, 1983.
Searching the Limits of Love: An Approach to the Secular Transcendent-God, Loyola University Press, 1984.
Dark Intimacy: Hope for Those in Difficult Prayer-Experiences, Paulist Press, 1986.
Healing the Ache of Alienation, Paulist Press, 1990.
The Last Estrangement: The Final Embrace, Paulist Press, 1991.

Contributor to theology and philosophy journals.

WORK IN PROGRESS: Secularizing the Christian College, for Paulist Press; *A Philosophy of Secularization* and *Finding the Secular God,* both for Loyola University Press.

SIDELIGHTS: David John Hassel told *CA:* "The best decision I ever made was to become a Jesuit. Out of my teaching experience in Jesuit high schools and colleges have come my books on secularization and God. Out of experience with giving spiritual direction have come my books on prayer. I have been writing for publication since I was eighteen, so I have an extensive collection of rejection slips, some sad and others hilarious—all of which would make another book.

"I wrote *Radical Prayer* to encourage people who had prayed faithfully for many years seemingly without results. I tried to show them that the basis of all prayer is attitude, out of which comes all our actions, all our feelings, and all our words, and that through their prayer-life they may well have developed deep attitudes of generosity, graciousness, and love that they may have overlooked. These attitudes are a radical welcoming of others and of God into their lives, a magnificent forming of community implicit in all they do.

"*City of Wisdom* describes how our American universities can help people achieve fuller wisdom in their lives so that they can serve others professionally and also personally. It shows how complexly beautiful wisdom is, how long and careful must be its acquirement, how important it is to the building of American life, how enriched it can be by Christian faith, how necessary it is to the survival of world culture. Wisdom contains our deepest knowledges, experiences, loves, and hopes.

"*Searching the Limits of Love* and *Finding the Secular God* are two volumes of a projected three volumes that aim to discover God within interpersonal relationships, heroic decisions, intelligent liberty, evolution, the balance of the individual and the community in daily politics, and the rise of the good out of evil. The secular God is the God we can discover in our daily life in the world, not an esoteric God on some lofty celestial shelf far out of our reach.

"*Secularizing the Christian College* asks: To what is our culture-civilization headed? What are the dynamisms driving our culture? Do we like where we are going? Can we direct our culture to something better, or is it already out of control? Is there a Christian secularization theory, one that has place for God's providence, or are we caught inextricably in secularism (even if God exists, he can't do anything)?"

Hassel adds: "*Dark Intimacy* is an attempt to give hope to those in difficult prayer-experiences. It tries to map the prayerful attitudes which are radically our continual prayer to God—attitudes such as hunger for intimacy with God, gratitude to him for forgiveness of faults, strong hope in him, desire to serve his people, total dependence on him, empathy for and friendship with him, his people, his world.

"The aims of *Healing the Ache of Alienation* are to tentatively explore and describe the intimacy of God to our inmost pains, especially alienation from one's world, work, body, self, dearest friend, and God, and to bridge the gap between the past language of spirituality and the contemporary experience of God in our daily lives."

BIOGRAPHICAL/CRITICAL SOURCES:

BOOKS

Braxton, Edward K., *The Wisdom Community*, Paulist Press, 1980.

PERIODICALS

America, October 29, 1983; March 22, 1986.
American Journal of Education, February, 1984.
Journal of Higher Education, September-October, 1984.
Living Prayer, May-June, 1987.
National Catholic Reporter, September 23, 1983.
Review for Religious, March-April, 1988.
Theological Educator, spring, 1986.

*   *   *

HAYASECA y EIZAGUIRRE, Jorge
   See ECHEGARAY (y EIZAGUIRRE), Jose (Maria Waldo)

*   *   *

HELLER, Peter   1920-

PERSONAL: Born January 11, 1920, in Vienna, Austria; naturalized U.S. citizen; son of John (a businessman) and Margarete (Steiner) Heller; married Katrina Ely Burlingham, 1944 (divorced, 1951); married Christiane Menzel, August 20, 1951; children: (first marriage) Anne; (second marriage) Joan Heller Humphreys, Vivian, Stephen, Eve. *Education:* McGill University, Licentiate of Music and B.A., 1944; Columbia University, M.A., 1945, Ph.D., 1951.

ADDRESSES: Home—280 Brompton Rd., Williamsville, NY 14221. *Office*—Department of Modern Languages, Clemens Hall, State University of New York, Buffalo, NY 14260.

CAREER: Columbia University, New York, NY, instructor in German, 1948-51; Harvard University, Cambridge, MA, in-

structor in German, 1951-54; University of Massachusetts—Amherst, associate professor, 1954-59, professor of German, 1959-61, Commonwealth Professor, 1961-68; State University of New York at Buffalo, professor of German and comparative literature, 1968—, head of German department, 1968-71, acting chair of modern languages department, 1989. Co-founder and director of Institute of Atlantic Studies of University of Massachusetts, Freiburg, West Germany, 1967-68. Director of National Endowment for the Humanities summer seminars for college and secondary school teachers, 1979, 1983, and 1984.

MEMBER: Modern Language Association of America.

AWARDS, HONORS: Fulbright research grants for study in Germany, 1954-56; Guggenheim fellow, 1982.

WRITINGS:

(With F. C. Ellert) *German One*, Heath, 1962.
(Contributor) *Masterpieces of Western Literature*, W. C. Brown, 1966.
Dialectics and Nihilism: Essays on Lessing, Nietzsche, Mann, and Kafka, University of Massachusetts Press, 1966.
(With Edith Ehrlich) *German Fiction and Prose*, Macmillan, 1967.
(With Ehrlich and J. Schaefer) *German Essays and Expository Prose*, Macmillan, 1969.
(Contributor) *Franz Kafka: His Place in World Literature*, Texas Tech University Press, 1971.
(Contributor) *Benn-Wirkung Wider Willen*, Athenaeum (Frankfurt), 1971.
Von den Ersten und Letzten Dingen, De Gruyter (Berlin), 1972.
Prosa in Versen (poetry), Blaeschke, 1974.
Menschentiere (poetry), Lyrik und Prosa, 1975.
Probleme der Zivilisation, Bouvier, 1978.
Emigrantenlitaneien (poetry), Blaeschke, 1978.
Studies on Nietzsche, Bouvier, 1980.
(With Ehrlich) *Dichter, Denker und Erzaehler*, Macmillan, 1982.
(Editor with Ed Dudley) *American Attitudes toward Foreign Languages and Foreign Cultures*, Bouvier, 1983.
(With Guenther Bittner) *Eine Kinderanalyse bei Anna Freud, 1929-1932*, Koenigshausen & Neumann, 1983.
(Contributor) Gerhard Friesen, editor, *Nachrichten aus den Staaten*, Olms (Hildesheim), 1983.
(Contributor) Alan Udoff, editor, *Kafka's Contextuality*, Gordian Press, 1986.
(Contributor) Moshe Lazar, editor *The Dove and the Mole*, Undena, 1987.
(Contributor) Volker Duerr, editor, *Nietzsche: Literature and Values*, Madison, 1988.
(Contributor) S. Cocalis and S. Lennox, editors, *Nietzsche Heute*, Francke (Bern), 1988.
A Child Analysis with Anna Freud, International Universities Press, 1989.

Also contributor to *Encyclopedia Britannica*. Editor, "Modern German Studies" series, Bouvier, 1978—, and "Literature and the Sciences of Man" series, Peter Lang, 1986—; associate editor, "German Literature, Art and Thought" series, University Press of America, 1986—. Contributor of articles and reviews to periodicals, including *German Life and Letters, Lyrica Germanica, Germanic Review, Massachusetts Review, Modern Language Forum, Malahat Review*, and *Contemporary German Arts and Letters*.

WORK IN PROGRESS: A book of fables; a book on the experience of being a refugee; editing *Anna Freud's Letters to Eva Rosenfeld*.

SIDELIGHTS: Peter Heller told *CA:* "Within academia, literary theory has become a menace to the major art of writing as well as to the minor art of literary criticism, and to literary scholarship. Let us regain the courage to appear as what we are or could be if we did not try to hide in the blind reflexivity of opaque mirrors or the shelter of obscure sophistication."

* * *

HENLEY, Beth
See HENLEY, Elizabeth Becker

* * *

HENLEY, Elizabeth Becker   1952-
(Beth Henley)

PERSONAL: Born May 8, 1952, in Jackson, Miss.; daughter of Charles Boyce (an attorney) and Elizabeth Josephine (an actress; maiden name, Becker) Henley. *Education:* Southern Methodist University, B.F.A., 1974; attended University of Illinois, 1975-76.

ADDRESSES: Home—Los Angeles, Calif. *Agent*—Gilbert Parker, William Morris Agency, 1350 Avenue of the Americas, New York, N.Y. 10019.

CAREER: Actress and playwright. Theatre Three, Dallas, Tex., actress, 1972-73; Southern Methodist University, Directors Colloquium, Dallas, member of acting ensemble, 1973; Dallas Minority Repertory Theatre, Dallas, teacher of creative dramatics, 1974-75; University of Illinois, Urbana, teacher of beginning acting, Lessac voice technique, 1975-76. Actress, Great American People Show, summer, 1976.

AWARDS, HONORS: Co-winner of Great American Playwriting Contest, Actor's Theatre of Louisville, 1978, nominee for Susan Smith Blackburn Award, 1979, New York Drama Critics Circle Award for best new American play, 1981, Guggenheim Award from *Newsday,* 1981, Pulitzer Prize for drama, 1981, and Antoinette Perry (Tony) Award nomination for best play, 1981, all for "Crimes of the Heart"; Academy Award nomination for best adapted screenplay, 1986, for movie version of "Crimes of the Heart."

WRITINGS:

ALL UNDER NAME BETH HENLEY

Am I Blue (one-act play; first produced in Dallas, Tex., at Southern Methodist University Margo Jones Theatre, fall, 1973), Dramatists Play Service, 1982.

Crimes of the Heart (three-act play; first produced in Louisville, Ky., at Actors Theatre, February 18, 1979; produced on Broadway at John Golden Theatre, November 4, 1981; also see below), Dramatists Play Service, 1981.

"Morgan's Daughters" (script for television pilot), Paramount, 1979.

The Miss Firecracker Contest (two-act play; first produced in Los Angeles, Calif., at Victory Theatre, spring, 1980; produced Off-Broadway at Manhattan Theatre Club, June, 1980; also see below), Dramatists Play Service, 1985.

The Wake of Jamey Foster (two-act play; first produced in Hartford, Conn., at Hartford Stage Theatre, January 1, 1982; produced on Broadway at Eugene O'Neill Theatre, October 14, 1982), Dramatists Play Service, 1985.

"The Debutante Ball" (play), first produced in Costa Mesa, Calif., at South Coast Repertory, April, 1985.

(With Budge Threlkeld) "Survival Guides" (television script), Public Broadcasting System, 1985.

"Crimes of the Heart" (screenplay; based on author's play of the same title), De Laurentiis Entertainment Group, 1986.

"Nobody's Fool" (screenplay), Island Pictures, 1986.

(With David Byrne and Stephen Tobolowsky) "True Stories" (screenplay), Warner Bros., 1986.

The Lucky Spot (play; first produced in Williamstown, Mass., at Williamstown Theatre Festival, summer, 1986; produced on Broadway at City Center Theatre, April, 1987), Dramatists Play Service, 1987.

"Miss Firecracker" (screenplay), Corsair Pictures, 1988.

SIDELIGHTS: Elizabeth Becker Henley—Beth Henley to theatregoers—is a member of the new breed of American playwrights dedicated to preserving regional voices on the stage. In Henley's case, her Mississippi upbringing provides the background for a host of Southern-accented plays, one of which, the black comedy "Crimes of the Heart," went on to win its author a Pulitzer Prize when she was 29. Like many playwrights before her, Henley originally set her sights on being an actress. She ventured into writing, though, after deciding there weren't many good contemporary roles for Southern women. A product of Southern Methodist University, Henley got her first play produced there, a one-act work called "Am I Blue." In 1976, the playwright moved to Los Angeles to live with actor/director Stephen Tobolowsky (with whom she would later collaborate on the screenplay "True Stories"). Three years later Henley submitted a three-act play to the Great American Play Contest sponsored by Actors Theatre of Louisville, Kentucky. Henley's play— "Crimes of the Heart"—won the contest and there began the first of its many successful stagings.

Set in Hazlehurst, Mississippi, "five years after Hurricane Camille," the story centers on three eccentric sisters who converge in the home of the youngest, Babe, after she has shot her well-to-do husband because, as Babe puts it, "I didn't like his looks." The other sisters include Meg, a would-be singer who has struck out in Hollywood; and Lenny, single and desperate at age 30. These sisters, according to Edith Oliver in a *New Yorker* review, "walking wounded, who are in tears at one moment and giggling and hugging at the next, . . . are very much of the South, of Mississippi, and [novelist] Eudora Welty has prepared us for them." John Simon reviewed the production for *New York* magazine and finds "the play is an essence, *the* essence of provincial living." Simon further calls "Crimes of the Heart" a "loving and teasing look back at deep-southern, small-town life, at the effect of constricted living and confined thinking on three different yet not wholly unalike sisters amid Chekhovian boredom in honeysuckle country, and, above all, at the sorely tried but resilient affection and loyalty of these sisters for one another."

Some critics took exception to Henley's use of ironic black-humor in "Crimes of the Heart." Michael Feingold, writing in *Village Voice,* for instance, thinks the playwright's attitude toward her three main characters, with its "pity and mockery aimed at them in laser-gun bursts," has "no organic connection and no deep roots. The play gives the impression of gossiping about its characters rather than presenting them, and [Henley's] voice, though both individual and skillful, is the voice of a small-town southern spinster yattering away on the phone, oozing pretended sympathy and real malice for her unfortunate subjects, and never at any point coming close to the truth of their lives." And to *New Leader* reviewer Leo Sauvage, "I find nothing enthralling in spending an evening with three badly adjusted, if not mentally retarded sisters, who are given free rein to exhibit their individual eccentricities." Sauvage concludes that he would label Henley's humor as "sick, not black."

But others see great value in Henley's work. "Crimes of the Heart" may be "overlong, occasionally cliched and annoyingly frivolous at moments," notes *Daily News* critic Don Nelson, "but Henley keeps intriguing us with a delightfully wacky humor plus a series of little mysteries played out by characters we can never dismiss as superficial on a set that absorbs us into their lives." "The physical modesty of her play belies the bounty of plot, peculiarity, and comedy within it," concludes *Saturday Review* writer Scot Haller of Henley's effort. "Like Flannery O'Connor [another Southern novelist], Henley creates ridiculous characters but doesn't ridicule them. Like Lanford Wilson [a contemporary playwright], she examines ordinary people with extraordinary compassion. Treating the eccentricities of her characters with empathy, [Henley] manages to render strange turns of events not only believable but affecting."

"Crimes of the Heart" was eventually adapted into movie form, as was another Henley play, "The Miss Firecracker Contest." In the latter story, a ne'er-do-well young woman, Carnelle Scott, seeks to uplift her station in her small Mississippi town. She figures the best way to gain respect would be to win the "Miss Firecracker" beauty contest, a rather cheesy local affair. To that end, Carnelle enlists other outcasts in her town to aid in her quest. As the play opens, Carnelle is seen on a bare stage dressed in a leotard and draped in an American flag, tap-dancing and baton-twirling her way through the "Star-Spangled Banner." "Though [the playwright's] territory looks superficially like the contemporary American South," writes *Time*'s Richard Schickel, "it is really a country of the mind: one of Tennessee Williams' provinces that has surrendered to a Chekhovian raiding party, perhaps. Her strength is a wild anecdotal inventiveness, but her people, lost in the ramshackle dreams and tumble-down ambitions with which she invests them, often seem to be metaphors waywardly adrift. They are blown this way and that by the gales of laughter they provoke, and they frequently fail to find a solid connection with clear and generally relevant meaning." Unfortunately for Henley, "The Miss Firecracker Contest" did not last long on the boards.

"It is not often that a girl from Jackson, Mississippi, can accomplish so much in what might be called a 'big city' world of film and theatre," declares Lucia Tarbox in a *Dictionary of Literary Biography Yearbook: 1986* article on the playwright. "However, Beth Henley has managed to succeed by bringing her southern small-town past with her. [Though she's known both financial success and failure], she does not allow the negative to overcome that which is positive." Quoting Henley, Tarbox concludes with the observation, "Something I'm sure has to do with the South's defeat in the Civil War, which is that you should never take yourself too seriously. You may be beaten and defeated, but your spirit cannot be conquered. The South has the gall to still be able to say we have our pride, but as a human characteristic it is admirable."

BIOGRAPHICAL/CRITICAL SOURCES:

BOOKS

Contemporary Literary Criticism, Gale, Volume 23, 1983.
Dictionary of Literary Biography Yearbook: 1986, Gale, 1987.

PERIODICALS

Daily News (New York), November 5, 1981.
Los Angeles Times, April 16, 1983.
New Leader, November 30, 1981.
Newsweek, December 22, 1986.
New York, November 16, 1981.
New Yorker, January 12, 1981.

New York Times, June 8, 1979, December 22, 1980, February 15, 1981, April 14, 1981, June 10, 1981, June 11, 1981, October 25, 1981, November 5, 1981, December 28, 1981, April 14, 1982, May 28, 1984, November 2, 1986.
New York Times Magazine, May 1, 1983.
Saturday Review, November, 1981, January, 1982.
Time, June 11, 1984, December 22, 1986.
Village Voice, November 18, 1981.
Washington Post, December 12, 1986.*

—*Sketch by Susan Salter*

*   *   *

HERALD, Kathleen
See PEYTON, Kathleen Wendy

*   *   *

HERNDON, Venable 1927-

PERSONAL: Born October 19, 1927, in Philadelphia, PA. *Education:* Alliance Francaise, certificate, 1948; Princeton University, B.A., 1950; Harvard University, M.A., 1951. Married Sharon Anson, 1985.

ADDRESSES: Home—238 West 22nd St., New York, NY 10011.

CAREER: Screenwriter, playwright, and writer. Copywriter, Gimbels, 1951-53, Bamgergers, 1953-56; copywriter and account executive, Hicks & Greist Advertising, 1956-66. Teacher of screenwriting, Dramatic Writing Program, Tisch School of the Arts, New York University, 1975—. Consultant for Films In Progress Inc. on *Hamilton and Burr*, and a documentary on *Big Jim Dandy* (about Alabama governor Big Jim Folsom), both projects of the National Endowment for the Humanities. *Military service:* Army Language School, Monterrey.

AWARDS, HONORS: Stanley Drama Award from Wagner College, 1967, for *Bag of Flies;* CAPS Grant, fiction, 1980-1981, for novel, *Dangerous Species.*

WRITINGS:

James Dean: A Short Life (biography), Doubleday, 1974.

Also author of the novels *Dangerous Species* and *Never Never Land.*

SCREENPLAYS

Too Far to Walk, adaptation of John Hersey's novel, Paramount, 1967.
(With Arthur Penn) *Alice's Restaurant: A Screenplay Based on Arlo Guthrie's Alice's Restaurant Massacree* (United Artists), Doubleday, 1970.
Location, Paramount, 1970.
Uncle Sam's Wild West Show, United Artists, 1971.
Jimmy Shine, Columbia, 1972.
The Diviners, adaptation of Margaret Lawrence novel, Canadian Group, 1981.

Also author of screenplays, "Until the Monkey Comes," and *Snow Gold*. Author of television scripts, *Best of Friends*, a Liberty Mutual Special; *Another Such Victory*, three-hour special for Bert Leonard and Walter Bernstein; *Just Imagine That; The Eighth Day*, Public Broadcasting Systems; *Lollipop Dragon*, a children's animated special, Blair Entertainment.

PLAYS

Independence Night (two-act play), produced in New York at Bond Street Theatre, September, 1970.

Bag of Flies, produced Off-Off Broadway at the Cubiculo, 1968.

Until the Monkey Comes (two-act play; produced Off-Broadway at Martinique Theatre, June 20, 1966; produced at Schauspeilbuhne, Berlin, 1968), published in *New American Plays,* Volume 2, Farrar, Straus, 1968.

Also author of the musicals *Tom Thumb* (with composer Robert Dennis), 1978, and *Sugar Mill* (with composer Ken Guilmartin), 1979.

OTHER

Contributor of articles to periodicals, including *Ms.* Poetry editor, *Quixote,* 1957; co-founder of *Chelsea Review* (literary quarterly), and editor for eighteen issues, 1958-66.

BIOGRAPHICAL/CRITICAL SOURCES:

PERIODICALS

Best Sellers, October 1, 1974.
Chelsea Review (twenty-fifth year commemorative issue), 1973.
New York Times Book Review, September 22, 1974.

*　　*　　*

HESTER, Thomas R(oy) 1946-

PERSONAL: Born April 28, 1946, in Crystal City, TX; son of Jim Tom and Mattie Laura (Umphres) Hester; married Lynda Sue Broadway, July 2, 1966; children: Lesley Elise, Amy Lynne. *Education:* University of Texas at Austin, B.A. (with honors), 1969; University of California, Berkeley, Ph.D., 1972. *Politics:* Democrat. *Religion:* Methodist.

ADDRESSES: Home—1205 Falcon Ledge Dr., Austin, TX 78746. *Office*—Department of Anthropology, University of Texas at Austin, Austin, TX 78712.

CAREER: University of California, Berkeley, acting assistant professor of anthropology, 1972-73; University of Texas at San Antonio, assistant professor, 1973-75, associate professor, 1975-77, professor of anthropology, 1977-87, director of Center for Archaeological Research, 1974-87; University of Texas at Austin, Austin, professor of anthropology, 1987—, director of Texas Archeological Research Laboratory, 1987—. Visiting associate professor at University of California, Berkeley, 1976. Administrator of Colha Project, a joint program of University of Texas at Austin, University of Texas at San Antonio, Centro Studi Ricerche Ligabue in Venice, Italy, and Texas A & M University; member of scientific committee of Centro Studi Ricerche Ligabue, 1979—. Consultant to Southwest Research Institute.

MEMBER: Society for American Archaeology (member of executive committee, 1984-86), Society for Historical Archaeology, Association for Field Archaeology (member of executive committee, 1979-82), American Association for the Advancement of Science, Society for Archaeological Sciences, Texas Archeological Society (fellow; member of board of directors, 1978-81), Sigma Xi (president of Alamo chapter, 1979).

AWARDS, HONORS: Woodrow Wilson fellow, 1969.

WRITINGS:

Chronological Ordering: Great Basin Prehistory, University of California Archaeological Research Facility, 1973.
(With Robert F. Heizer) *Bibliography of Archaeology I,* Addison-Wesley, 1973.
(With Heizer and John A. Graham) *Field Methods in Archaeology,* Mayfield, 1975.

(Editor with Norman Hammond) *Maya Lithic Studies,* University of Texas at San Antonio Center for Archaeological Research, 1976.
Digging into South Texas Prehistory, Corona, 1980.
(With Heizer and Carol Graves) *Archaeology: A Bibliographical Guide to the Basic Literature,* Garland Publishing, 1980.
(Editor with Giancarlo Ligabue, Sandro Salvatori, and Mario Sartor) *Colha e I Maya del Bassipiani,* Erizzo, 1983.
(With Ellen S. Turner) *Guide to Stone Artifacts of Texas Indians,* Texas Monthly Press, 1985.
(With others) *Human Adaptation in Central, South, and Lower Pecos, Texas,* Arkansas Archeological Survey, 1989.

Also contributor to *Science Year* and *Archaeology.* Contributor of more than three hundred articles to periodicals and archaeology and anthropology journals, including *Science.* Editor of Texas Archeological Society, 1974-78, 1985; member of editorial advisory board, *Journal of Field Archaeology,* 1987—.

WORK IN PROGRESS: Texas Archaeology, for Academic Press; *Maya Stone Tool Studies; Primitive Technology Sourcebook;* editing, with Ellen S. Turner, Robert F. Heizer's *Ancient Heavy Transport: Moving the Monuments of Antiquity; Field Methods in Archaeology,* with Harry J. Shafer.

BIOGRAPHICAL/CRITICAL SOURCES:

PERIODICALS

Fortune, October, 1976.

*　　*　　*

HILGARD, Ernest R(opiequet) 1904-

PERSONAL: Born July 25, 1904, in Belleville, IL; son of George E. (a physician) and Laura (Ropiequet) Hilgard; married Josephine Rohrs (a psychiatrist), September 12, 1931; children: Henry R., Elizabeth (Mrs. Jerald W. Jecker). *Education:* University of Illinois, B.S., 1924; Yale University, Ph.D., 1930.

ADDRESSES: Home—850 Webster, Palo Alto, CA 94301.

CAREER: Yale University, New Haven, CT, instructor in psychology, 1928-33; Stanford University, Stanford, CA, assistant professor, 1933-35, associate professor, 1935-38, professor of psychology, 1938-69, professor emeritus, 1969—, executive head of department, 1942-50, dean of Graduate Division, 1951-55. Fellow at Center for Advanced Study in the Behavioral Sciences, Palo Alto, CA, 1956-57. Held civilian positions with the U.S. Department of Agriculture, Office of War Information, and War Production Board, 1942-44. Member of board of directors of Annual Review, Inc., 1950-73, and Stephens College, 1953-68; member of national advisory mental health council of National Institute of Mental Health, 1952-56.

MEMBER: International Society for Hypnosis (president, 1974-77), American Psychological Association (president, 1948-49), American Philosophical Society, National Academy of Education, National Academy of Sciences, American Academy of Arts and Sciences, British Psychological Association (honorary fellow).

AWARDS, HONORS: Warren Medal, Society of Experimental Psychologists, 1940, for research on conditioned reflexes; D.Sc., Kenyon College, 1964, Colgate University, 1988, and Northwestern University, 1988; distinguished contribution award, American Psychological Association, 1968; Wilbur Cross Medal, Yale University, 1971; LL.D., Centre College, 1974; gold medal, American Psychological Foundation, 1978; gold medal,

International Society of Hypnosis, 1979; award from National Academy of Sciences, 1984, for scientific reviewing.

WRITINGS:

Conditioned Eyelid Reactions to a Light Stimulus Based on the Reflex Wink to Sound (monograph), Psychological Review Co., 1931.
(With Donald G. Marquis) *Conditioning and Learning,* Appleton, 1940.
Theories of Learning, Appleton, 1948, 5th edition, Prentice-Hall, 1981.
(Contributor) Eugene Pumpian-Mindlin, editor, *Psychoanalysis as Science: The Hixon Lectures on the Scientific Status of Psychoanalysis,* Stanford University Press, 1952.
Introduction to Psychology, Harcourt, 1953, 9th edition, 1987.
Unconscious Processes and Man's Rationality, Graduate College, University of Illinois, 1958.
(With Lillian W. Lauer and Arlene H. Morgan) *Manual for Stanford Profile Scales of Hypnotic Susceptibility,* Forms 1 and 2, Consulting Psychologists Press, 1963.
(Editor) *Theories of Learning and Instruction,* National Society for the Study of Education, 1964.
Hypnotic Susceptibility, Harcourt, 1965, abridged edition published as *The Experience of Hypnosis,* 1968.
(With wife, Josephine Hilgard) *Hypnosis in the Relief of Pain,* William Kaufmann, 1975, revised edition, 1983.
Divided Consciousness: Multiple Controls in Human Thought and Action, Wiley, 1977.
(Editor) *American Psychology in Historical Perspective: Addresses of the Presidents of the American Psychological Association, 1892-1977,* American Psychological Association, 1978.
Psychology in America: A Historical Survey, Harcourt, 1987.
(Editor) *Fifty Years of Psychology: Essays in Honor of Floyd Ruch,* Scott, Foresman, 1988.

Contributor to psychology journals.

SIDELIGHTS: Ernest R. Hilgard told *CA:* "My recent work in history convinces me that the practitioner of a science has a great deal to learn about history as a craft (historiography) before his personal experiences over a period of years can be written down as acceptable history. At the same time, the familiarity with the persons who have contributed to his own field and with the issues arising our of their scientific work can provide raw materials for the historian who may write from a broader perspective."

BIOGRAPHICAL/CRITICAL SOURCES:

BOOKS

Lindzey, Gardner, editor, *History of Psychology in Autobiography,* Volume 6, Prentice-Hall, 1974.

*   *   *

HILL, Reginald (Charles) 1936-
(Dick Morland, Patrick Ruell, Charles Underhill)

PERSONAL: Born April 3, 1936, in West Hartlepool, England; son of Reginald and Isabel (Dickson) Hill; married Patricia Ruell, August 30, 1960. *Education:* St. Catherine's College, Oxford, B.A. (with honors), 1960. *Politics:* "Agnostic." *Religion:* "Cynic."

ADDRESSES: Home—"Oakbank," Broad Oak, Ravenglass, Cumbria, CA18 1RN, England. *Agent*—A. P. Watt, 20 John St., London WL1N 2DR, England.

CAREER: Worked as a secondary school teacher in England, 1962-67; Doncaster College of Education, Doncaster, England,

lecturer in English literature, 1967-82; full-time writer, 1982—. *Military service:* National Service, 1955-57.

MEMBER: Crime Writers Association, Mystery Writers of America.

AWARDS, HONORS: Edgar Award nomination, Mystery Writers of America, 1981, for *The Spy's Wife.*

WRITINGS:

CRIME NOVELS

A Clubbable Woman, Collins, 1970, Countryman Press, 1984.
Fell of Dark, Collins, 1971.
An Advancement of Learning, Collins, 1971, Countryman Press, 1985.
A Fairly Dangerous Thing, Collins, 1972, Countryman Press, 1983.
Ruling Passion: A Dalziel and Pascoe Novel, Collins, 1973, Harper, 1977.
A Very Good Hater, Collins, 1974, Countryman Press, 1982.
An April Shroud: A Dalziel and Pascoe Novel, Collins, 1975, Countryman Press, 1986.
Another Death in Venice, Collins, 1976.
A Pinch of Snuff: A Dalziel and Pascoe Novel, Harper, 1978.
Pascoe's Ghost, Collins, 1979.
The Spy's Wife, Pantheon, 1980.
A Killing Kindness: A Dalziel and Pascoe Novel, Collins, 1980, Pantheon, 1981.
Who Guards the Prince?, Pantheon, 1982.
Traitor's Blood, Collins, 1983, Countryman's Press, 1986.
Deadheads: A Dalziel and Pascoe Novel, Collins, 1983, Macmillan, 1984.
Exit Lines, Collins, 1984, Macmillan, 1985.
No Man's Land, St. Martin's, 1985.
Child's Play, Macmillan, 1987.
The Collaborators, Collins, 1987, Countryman Press, 1989.
Underworld, Scribner, 1988.
Bones and Silence, Delacorte, 1990.

SCIENCE FICTION NOVELS UNDER PSEUDONYM DICK MORLAND

Heart Clock, Faber, 1973.
Albion! Albion!, Faber, 1976.

ADVENTURE NOVELS UNDER PSEUDONYM PATRICK RUELL

The Castle of the Demon, Hutchinson, 1971, Hawthorne, 1972.
Red Christmas, Hutchinson, 1972, Hawthorne, 1973.
Death Takes the Low Road, Hutchinson, 1974, Mysterious Press, 1987.
Urn Burial, Hutchinson, 1975, Countryman Press, 1987.
The Long Kill, Methuen, 1986, Countryman Press, 1988.
Death of a Dormouse, Myterious Press, 1987.
Dream of Darkness, Methuen, 1989, Countryman Press, 1990.

HISTORICAL ADVENTURE NOVELS UNDER PSEUDONYM CHARLES UNDERHILL

Captain Fantom: Being an Account of Sundry Adventures in the Life of Carlo Fantom, Soldier of Misfortune, Hard Man and Ravisher, Hutchinson, 1978, St. Martin's, 1980.
The Forging of Fantom, Hutchinson, 1979.

OTHER

Crime Writers: Reflections on Crime Fiction (nonfiction), British Broadcasting Corp., 1978.
There Are No Ghosts in the Soviet Union: A Novella and Five Short Stories, Collins, 1987, Countryman Press, 1988.

SIDELIGHTS: Reginald Hill is a former lecturer in English whose passion for writing crime novels has recently become a full-time occupation. Hill told CA: "I became a full-time writer because I realised that's what I was, no matter what other activity I was ostensibly pursuing." With a reputation as a "writer of wit and precision, with a sensitivity for place and atmosphere," as one London Times reviewer remarks, Hill is best-known for the characters Superintendent Dalziel (pronounced Dee-ell) and Detective-Inspector Peter Pascoe, who appear in a number of his procedural novels.

Hill once remarked to CA: "I lead a quiet life punctuated by loud bursts of laughter at its absurdity. I play tennis, badminton, and golf to as low a standard as possible without running out of partners. My wife and I devote ourselves to looking after two Siamese cats who are the only living creatures whose lot I envy."

BIOGRAPHICAL/CRITICAL SOURCES:

PERIODICALS

Globe and Mail (Toronto), November 3, 1984; July 30, 1988.
Los Angeles Times, March 27, 1981.
New York Times Book Review, January 18, 1981; April 5, 1981; June 24, 1984; March 2, 1986; June 1, 1986; November 30, 1986; March 15, 1987.
Spectator, February 11, 1984; September 26, 1987.
Time, November 4, 1985.
Times (London), July 7, 1983; March 31, 1990.
Times Literary Supplement, November 6, 1970; July 9, 1971; February 4, 1972; November 10, 1972; August 15, 1975; March 24, 1978; April 18, 1980; December 26, 1980; July 2, 1982; March 30, 1984; October 30, 1987; August 17, 1990.
Tribune Books (Chicago), August 5, 1990.
Village Voice, July 3, 1984.
Village Voice Literary Supplement, July, 1986.
Washington Post Book World, April 19, 1971; January 15, 1978; March 18, 1979; June 16, 1985; August 11, 1985; August 21, 1988.

* * *

HINTON, S(usan) E(loise) 1950-

PERSONAL: Born in 1950 in Tulsa, Okla.; married David E. Inhofe (a mail order businessman), September, 1970; children: Nicholas David. Education: University of Tulsa, B.S., 1970.

ADDRESSES: Home—Tulsa, Okla. Office—c/o Press Relations, Dell Publishing Co., 666 Fifth Ave., 10th Fl., New York, N.Y. 10103.

CAREER: Began writing at the age of sixteen; author of young adult novels. Has consulted on and appeared in film adaptations of her novels, including "Tex" and "The Outsiders."

AWARDS, HONORS: New York Herald Tribune best teen-age books list, 1967, Chicago Tribune Book World Spring Book Festival Honor Book, 1967, Media & Methods Maxi Award, 1975, and Massachusetts Children's Book Award, 1979, all for The Outsiders; American Library Association (ALA) Best Books for Young Adults list, 1971, Chicago Tribune Book World Spring Book Festival Honor Book, 1971, and Massachusetts Children's Book Award, 1978, all for That Was Then, This Is Now; ALA Best Books for Young Adults list, 1975, School Library Journal Best Books of the Year list, 1975, and Land of Enchantment Award, New Mexico Library Association, 1982, all for Rumble Fish; ALA Best Books for Young Adults list, 1979, School Li-

brary Journal Best Books of the Year list, 1979, New York Public Library Books for the Teen-Age, 1980, American Book Award nomination for children's paperback, 1981, Sue Hefly Honor Book, Louisiana Association of School Libraries, 1982, California Young Reader Medal nomination, California Reading Association, 1982, and Sue Hefly Award, 1983, all for Tex; Golden Archer Award, 1983; ALA Young Adult Services Division/School Library Journal Author Award, 1988, for body of work.

WRITINGS:

The Outsiders (young adult novel), Viking, 1967, reprinted, Dell, 1989.
That Was Then, This Is Now (young adult novel), Viking, 1971, reprinted, Dell, 1989.
Rumble Fish (young adult novel; also see below), Delacorte, 1975.
Tex (young adult novel), Delacorte, 1979.
(With Francis Ford Coppola) "Rumble Fish" (screenplay; adapted from her novel of same title), Universal, 1983.
Taming the Star Runner (young adult novel), Delacorte, 1988.

SIDELIGHTS: As a teenager in Tulsa, Oklahoma, S. E. Hinton enjoyed reading but often found her options limited, as she told Newsweek's Gene Lyons: "A lot of adult literature was older than I was ready for. The kids' books were all Mary Jane-Goes-to-the-Prom junk. I wrote 'The Outsiders' so I'd have something to read." Angered by the random beating of a friend, Hinton was inspired to write a story of an escalating class conflict between "greasers" and "socs" that ends in tragedy. Published in 1967 when Hinton was seventeen, The Outsiders "gave birth to the new realism in adolescent literature" and launched its author toward achieving "almost mythical status as the grand dame of young adult novelists," Patty Campbell relates in the New York Times Book Review. Hinton's frank depiction of the cruelty and violence that teens can perpetrate upon one another was a new development in books for adolescents, and led some adult critics to condemn the novel's realism. Teenagers, however, responded overwhelmingly to the book and Hinton became an overnight success.

The Outsiders opens with a group of "greasers" preparing for one of their habitual fights with their upper-middle-class rivals, the "socs"; with their parents indifferent or absent, the boys, including narrator Ponyboy Curtis, substitute their gang for family. But when one of Ponyboy's friends kills a soc in self-defense, it sets off a chain of events that eventually tears the group apart. "By almost any standard," writes Thomas Fleming in the New York Times Book Review, "Miss Hinton's performance is impressive. . . . She has produced a book alive with the fresh dialogue of her contemporaries, and has wound around it a story that captures, in vivid patches at least, a rather unnerving slice of teen-age America." Saturday Review critic Zena Sutherland similarly observes that The Outsiders is "written with distinctive style by a teen-ager who is sensitive, honest, and observant." A Times Literary Supplement reviewer, however, notes that "the plot creaks and the ending is wholly factitious," and remarks that the language "is both arresting and tiring to read in its repetitiousness." While likewise faulting the author for unlikely plot twists and occasional overwriting, Lillian N. Gerhardt nevertheless comments in School Library Journal that Hinton is a writer "seeing and saying more with greater storytelling ability than many an older hand."

"For all its weaknesses, this young writer's first novel The Outsiders made a considerable impact and offered an uncomfortable glimpse into the world of teenage violence in America," David

L. Rees states in *Children's Book Review*. "We are still in that world, but here," in *That Was Then, This Is Now*, "it is even more strikingly drawn," says Rees. Instead of a conflict between rich and poor teens, *That Was Then, This Is Now* presents two foster brothers, Bryon and Mark, moving apart as one becomes more involved in school and girlfriends while the other moves deeper into a career of crime and drugs. "The phrase 'if only' is perhaps the most bittersweet in the language, and Miss Hinton uses it skillfully to underline her theme: growth can be a dangerous process," Michael Cart summarizes in the *New York Times Book Review*. *Book World* contributor Polly Goodwin also considers Hinton's novel "a powerful story, which pulls no punches in portraying a way of life its protagonists casually accept as normal," although she feels that Bryon's eventual decision to turn his friend in to the police is not very believable. Cart similarly faults the author for portraying Bryon's decisions as "made not intellectually but emotionally," but states that "otherwise she has written a mature, disciplined novel, which excites a response in the reader. Whatever its faults, her book will be hard to forget." "*That Was Then, This Is Now* is a searing and terrible account of what life can be like [for teens]," a *Times Literary Supplement* writer comments, concluding that the novel is "a starkly realistic book, a punch from the shoulder which leaves the reader considerably shaken."

While Hinton's next novel, *Rumble Fish,* demonstrates her usual aptitude for memorable dialogue and fast-paced narrative, many critics feel that this story of a disillusioned young man who gradually loses everything meaningful to him does not match the quality of her previous work. In *Tex,* however, Hinton "has taken a larger canvas on which to group more varied characters," asserts Margery Fisher of *Growing Point*. The author moves her setting from Tulsa to California to explore the relationship of fourteen-year-old Tex and his older brother Mason, who must take the place of the boys' traveling cowboy father. Resentful of his brother's authority at home and having difficulties at school, Tex's problems multiply when he and Mason are kidnapped by a hitchhiker; Tex later gets into a confrontation with a drug pusher. *New York Times Book Review* contributor Paxton Davis believes that the number of unusual events occurring in the story strains credulity: "There's too much going on here. Even by the standards of today's fiction, S. E. Hinton's vision of contemporary teen-age life is riper than warrants belief. . . . [*Tex* is] busier and more melodramatic than the real life it purports to show." Lance Salway agrees that *Tex* is very theatrical, but comments in *Signal* that "a writer as good as Hinton can carry it off effortlessly; one believes implicitly in the characters and cares what happens to them." "In this new book," Fisher concludes, "Susan Hinton has achieved that illusion of reality which any fiction writer aspires to and which few ever completely achieve."

Hinton spent the ten-year interval between *Tex* and her latest novel, *Taming the Star Runner,* advising on the sets of several film adaptations of her books and starting a family. But after just "one paragraph [of *Taming the Star Runner*] the reader is back in familiar Hinton country," notes Campbell. "Once again," a *Kirkus Reviews* writer observes, "Hinton puts a bright, rebellious teen-ager, stubbornly pushing against society's expectations, into a powerful story lashed together with bands of irony." After nearly killing his stepfather in a fight, young Travis is dispatched to his uncle's farm, where he must adjust to a "country" lifestyle unfamiliar to him. While trying to maintain his tough exterior, Travis is also working on a novel and falling in love with Casey, an older girl who is a riding instructor at the horse ranch. *School Library Journal* contributor Charlene Strickland considers the

plot "sparse" and built "around a predominately bleak theme." Campbell, however, states that *Taming the Star Runner* "is remarkable for its drive and the wry sweetness and authenticity of its voice." Because the novel "is also a more mature and difficult work," the critic continues, "it may not be as wildly popular as the other Hinton books have continued to be with succeeding generations. . . . But S. E. Hinton continues to grow in strength as a young adult novelist."

Although Hinton's work has frequently been characterized as representative of teenage life, some critics believe that her novels are more graphic than factual. Michael Malone, for instance, in a *Nation* essay on the author's work, notes that the language used by Hinton's characters is often "heightened" and poetical; in addition, most of the characters are situated outside their families, thus avoiding the problem of parental authority and conflict. "Far from strikingly realistic in literary form, these novels are romances," the critic explains, "mythologizing the tragic beauty of violent youth." Campbell similarly observes that the typical Hinton novel includes "a tough young Galahad in black T-shirt and leather jacket," but the critic maintains that each variation Hinton creates is distinctive in itself: "The pattern is familiar, but [Hinton's] genius lies in that she has been able to give each of the five protagonists she has drawn from this mythic model a unique voice and a unique story." And as Hinton told Jay Scott of *American Film*, it is the people, not the circumstances, of her novels that concern her most: "I don't know what the latest hot trend is. I hate the 'problem' approach. Problems change. Character remains the same. I write character."

Hinton has not been as prolific as other young adult novelists, but that hasn't prevented her from becoming a consistent favorite with her audience; two of the movies adapted from her books, "Tex" and "The Outsiders," were filmed in response to suggestions from adolescent readers. Even though she is no longer a teenager involved in the world about which she writes, Hinton believes that she is suited to writing adolescent fiction: "I don't think I have a masterpiece in me, but I do know I'm writing well in the area I choose to write in," she commented to *Los Angeles Times* writer Dave Smith. "I understand kids and I really like them. And I have a very good memory. I remember exactly what it was like to be a teen-ager that nobody listened to or paid attention to or wanted around. I mean, it wasn't like that with my own family, but I knew a lot of kids like that and hung around with them. . . . Somehow I always understood them. They were my type." And while other young adult novelists have branched out into mainstream fiction, Hinton has no ambitions to write an "adult" best seller, she related to Stephen Farber in the *New York Times:* "If I can ever find any adults who are as interesting as the kids I like, maybe I'll write about adults some day. The reason I keep writing about teen-agers is that it's a real interesting time of life. It's the time of most rapid change, when ideals are clashing against the walls of compromise." "After all," she told Smith, "I was born and raised in Tulsa, never wanted to live anywhere else and still don't, and never wanted to be anything but a writer."

MEDIA ADAPTATIONS: Tex was adapted by Buena Vista/ Walt Disney Productions in 1982; *The Outsiders* inspired the 1983 Warner Brothers adaptation by Francis Ford Coppola, as well as a Fox Television weekly series scheduled to begin in 1990; actor Emilio Estevez adapted and starred in a Paramount production of *That Was Then, This Is Now* in 1985.

BIOGRAPHICAL/CRITICAL SOURCES:

BOOKS

Children's Literature Review, Volume 3, Gale, 1978.
Contemporary Literary Criticism, Volume 30, Gale, 1984.
Daly, Jay, *Presenting S. E. Hinton,* Twayne, 1987.

PERIODICALS

American Film, April, 1983.
Book World, May 9, 1971.
Children's Book Review, December, 1971.
Growing Point, May, 1980.
Kirkus Reviews, August 15, 1988.
Los Angeles Times, July 15, 1982, October 14, 1983.
Nation, March 8, 1986.
Newsweek, October 11, 1982.
New York Times, March 20, 1983, March 23, 1983, October 7, 1983, October 23, 1983.
New York Times Book Review, May 7, 1967, August 8, 1971, December 14, 1975, December 16, 1979, April 2, 1989.
Saturday Review, May 13, 1967, January 27, 1968.
School Library Journal, May, 1967, October, 1988.
Signal, May, 1980.
Times Literary Supplement, October 30, 1970, October 22, 1971, April 2, 1976, March 20, 1980.
Village Voice, April 5, 1983.
Washington Post, October 8, 1982, October 18, 1983.
Washington Post Book World, February 12, 1989.*

—*Sketch by Diane Telgen*

*   *   *

HIRO, Dilip

PERSONAL: Born in Sind, Pakistan. *Education:* Virginia Polytechnic Institute and State University, M.S.

ADDRESSES: Home—31 Waldegrave Rd., Ealing, London W5 3HT, England.

CAREER: Writer.

MEMBER: Royal Institute of International Affairs, Middle East Studies Association of North America, Center for Iranian Research and Analysis.

AWARDS, HONORS: Award from Chicago Film Festival, 1975, for "A Private Enterprise."

WRITINGS:

A Triangular View (novel), Dobson, 1969.
To Anchor a Cloud: A Play in Three Acts (first produced in London, England, at Collegiate Theatre, September 25, 1970), Writers Workshop (Calcutta, India), 1972.
Black British, White British, Eyre & Spotiswoode, 1971, revised edition, Monthly Review Press, 1973.
The Untouchables of India, Minority Rights Group (London), 1975.
Inside India Today, Routledge & Kegan Paul, 1976, revised edition, Monthly Review Press, 1977.
"Apply, Apply, No Reply" (television play; also see below), first broadcast by British Broadcasting Corp. Television, June 12, 1976.
"A Matter of Honor" (television play), first broadcast by Granada Television, 1976.
"A Clean Break: A Play in One Act" (also see below), first produced at Ravi Shankar Hall, London, November 24, 1977.

Apply, Apply, No Reply [and] *A Clean Break* (one-act plays), Writers Workshop, 1978.
Interior, Exchange, Exterior (poems), Writers Workshop, 1980.
Inside the Middle East, McGraw, 1982.
Iran Under the Ayatollahs, Methuen (New York), 1985.
Three Plays, Madison Books, 1987.
Iran: The Revolution Within, Center for Security and Conflict Studies, 1988.
Islamic Fundamentalism, Paladin Books, 1988.
The Longest War: The Iran-Iraq Military Conflict, Grafton Books, 1989.
Holy Way: Rise of Islamic Fundamentalism, Routledge & Kegan Paul, 1989.

Also author of "A Private Enterprise" (a feature film), 1975, and "Video Wicked" (a multi-media show produced at Half Moon Theatre, London, in 1985). Author of scripts for television serial "Parosi," 1977-78. Contributor to magazines and newspapers, including *Wall Street Journal, Washington Post, Los Angeles Times, Middle East Report, Times Literary Supplement,* and many others.

WORK IN PROGRESS: A book on the Lebanese Civil War.

BIOGRAPHICAL/CRITICAL SOURCES:

PERIODICALS

Los Angeles Times, December 20, 1985.
New York Times Book Review, January 29, 1978.
Times (London), January 31, 1985.
Times Literary Supplement, March 21, 1986, August 4, 1989.

*   *   *

HIRSCH, Steven R(ichard)   1937-

PERSONAL: Born March 12, 1937, in Philadelphia, PA; son of Sylvan Hobson and Ruth Butler (Spiegel) Hirsch; married Maureen Mitchel (a social worker), March, 1964 (marriage ended, 1977); married Teresa Mitchell, May, 1979; children: Georgina, Colette, Eleanor, Phineas. *Education:* Amherst College, B.A. (cum laude), 1959; Johns Hopkins University, M.D., 1963; University of London, M.Phil., 1969.

ADDRESSES: Office—Department of Psychiatry, Medical School, Charing Cross Hospital, University of London, Fulham Palace Rd., London W6 8RF, England.

CAREER: Johns Hopkins University, Baltimore, MD, fellow in medicine, 1963-64; Broadgreen Hospital, Liverpool, England, honorary medical registrar, 1964-65; Brompton Hospital for Diseases of the Chest, London, England, house physician, 1965-66; Bolingbroke Hospital, house surgeon, 1966-67; Maudsley Hospital, London, registrar, 1967-69, senior registrar, 1970-71, honorary senior registrar in psychiatry, 1971-73; University of London, Institute of Psychiatry, lecturer, 1972-73; Westminster Hospital, London, senior lecturer in psychiatry and honorary consultant, 1973-74; Queen Mary's Hospital, Roehampton, England, senior lecturer and honorary consultant and chairman of Division of Psychiatry, 1974-75; University of London, Division of Psychiatry, chairman, 1975-79, vice chairman, 1979-83, Charing Cross Hospital, honorary consultant, 1975—, Charing Cross and Westminster Medical School, professor of psychiatry and head of department, 1975—.

Metropolitan Hospital, medical registrar, 1965; West End Hospital for Neurology and Neurosurgery, senior house officer, 1966; Medical Research Council Social Psychiatry Unit, attached research worker, 1971-73; University of London, member of special advisory committee on sociology, 1977-85, Charing Cross Hospital, member of clinical research committee, 1977-82, chairman of psychiatry training committee, 1989—, Charing Cross and Westminster Medical School, member of school council, 1988; St. Bernard's Hospital, honorary consultant, 1981; Horton Hospital, honorary consultant, 1985. South Hammersmith Health District, member of health care planning team on psychiatric services, 1976-78; World Health Organization, temporary adviser on psychopharmacology, 1977; Wellcome Trust, member of Schizophrenia Group, 1977—; Ealing, Hammersmith, and Hounslow Area Health Authority, member of medical committee, 1978-80; South Hammersmith Health Authority, member of unit management group, 1982-86; Northwest Thames Regional Postgraduate Medical Federation, honorary psychiatric tutor. Member of Medical Council on Alcoholism, 1983-86; member of Joint Committee on Higher Psychiatric Training, 1985—.

MEMBER: International Sociological Association (member of research committee on mental health, 1973-79), Collegium International Neuropharmacology, Royal College of Physicians (fellow), Royal College of Psychiatrists (fellow; member of executive standing committees of social and community section, 1976-84, of general psychiatry section, 1989—; member of council, 1979-83; member of court of electors, 1980-83), British Medical Association (member of standing committees, 1986—), British Association of Psychopharmacology (member of council, 1979—), Royal Society of Medicine (fellow; member of council, 1979—; honorary secretary, 1982-84; vice-president, 1984-85; president, 1987-88), Association of University Teachers in Psychiatry (member of standing committee, 1973—), American Psychiatric Association (fellow), Association of University Clinical and Academic Staff, Biological Psychiatry Association, Association of University Professors of Psychiatry.

AWARDS, HONORS: Starkey Memorial Prize, Royal Society of Health, 1976.

WRITINGS:

(Editor with Michael Shepherd) *Themes and Variations in European Psychiatry: An Anthology,* Wright and Sons Ltd., 1974.
(With Julian Leff) *Abnormalities in Parents of Schizophrenics: A Review of the Literature and an Investigation of Communication Defects and Deviances* (monograph), Oxford University Press, 1975.
(Editor with Richard Farmer) *The Suicide Syndrome,* Croom Helm Ltd., 1980.
(With S. Platt and A. Weyman) *Social Behavior Assessment Schedule,* NFER-Nelson, 1983.
(Editor with P. Bradley; also contributor) *The Psychopharmacology and Treatment of Schizophrenia,* Oxford University Press, 1986.
Psychiatric Beds and Resources: Factors Influencing Bed Use and Service Planning, Gaskell Press, 1988.
(Editor with J. Harris) *Consent and the Incompetent Patient: Ethics, Law, and Medicines,* Gaskell Press, 1988.
(With T. E. Sensky and C. Thompson) *Learning Psychiatry through MCQ: A Comprehensive Text,* Wiley and Sons Ltd., 1988.

Contributor of articles to nearly twenty books, including *Psychopathology and Psychopharmacology,* edited by Jonathan O. Cole, Alfred M. Freedman, and Arnold J. Friedhoff, Johns Hopkins University Press, 1973; *On the Origin of Schizophrenic Psychoses,* edited by H. M. Van Praag, De Erven Bohn, 1975; *New Methods of Mental Health Care,* edited by Molly Meacher, Pergamon, 1979; *Neuroleptics and Schizophrenia,* edited by J. M. Simister,

Lundbeck, 1979; *Handbook of Psychiatry,* Volume 3, edited by J. Wing, Oxford University Press, 1983; *Psychosocial Treatment of Schizophrenia,* edited by J. S. Strauss, W. Boker, and H. Brenner, Hans Huber Publishers, Toronto, 1987; and *Depression in Schizophrenia,* edited by L. de Lisi, American Psychiatric Press, 1990. Contributor of over eighty articles to medical journals. Member of editorial boards of *Human Psychopharmacology, Mental Health Advisor,* and *Schizophrenia Research.*

SIDELIGHTS: Steven R. Hirsch told *CA:* "I approach psychiatric research from the combined point of view of English social psychiatry and psychopharmacology. My special interest is the interaction of social and biological factors as they affect schizophrenia and its treatment."

*   *   *

HOBEL, Phil
See FANTHORPE, R(obert) Lionel

*   *   *

HOLT, John (Caldwell)   1923-1985

PERSONAL: Born April 14, 1923, in New York, N.Y.; died September 14, 1985, in Boston, Mass., of cancer; son of Henry (an insurance broker) and Elizabeth (Crocker) Holt. *Education:* "I have come to believe that a person's schooling is as much a part of his private business as his politics or religion, and that no one should be required to answer questions about it. May I say instead that most of what I know I did not learn in school, or even in what most people would call 'learning situations.' "

CAREER: American Movement for World Government, New York, N.Y., held various posts, 1946-52; executive director of New York state branch, United World Federalists (now World Federalists U.S.A.), 1951-52; traveled in Europe, 1952-53; Colorado Rocky Mountain School, Carbondale, Colo., teacher of high school English, French, and mathematics, 1953-57; Shady Hill School, Cambridge, Mass., teacher, 1957-59; Lesley Ellis School, Cambridge, secondary school English teacher in Boston, Mass., 1959-63; Commonwealth School, Boston, Mass., teacher, 1965-67; Harvard University, Cambridge, visiting lecturer in education, 1968; University of California, Berkeley, visiting lecturer, 1969; "writing, reading, lecturing, playing the cello, working on large issues confronting society," 1969-85; Holt Associates, Inc., Boston, Mass., president, 1969-85; publisher of magazine *Growing without Schooling,* 1977-85. Lecturer in Canada, France, Great Britain, Denmark, Sweden, Mexico, and other countries. *Military service:* U.S. Navy, 1943-46; received submarine combat insignia and Pacific theatre ribbon.

WRITINGS:

How Children Fail (Book-of-the-Month Club selection), Pitman, 1964, revised edition, Delacorte, 1982.
How Children Learn (Book-of-the-Month Club selection), Pitman, 1967, revised edition, Delacorte, 1983.
The Underachieving School, Pitman, 1969.
What Do I Do Monday? (Book-of-the-Month Club selection), Dutton, 1970.
Freedom and Beyond, Dutton, 1972.
Escape from Childhood, Dutton, 1974.
Instead of Education: Ways to Help People Do Things Better, Dutton, 1976.
Never Too Late: A Musical Autobiography, Delacorte, 1978.
Teach Your Own: A Hopeful Path for Education, Delacorte, 1981.

OTHER

Contributor to *Life, Atlantic, Redbook, Saturday Evening Post, Parents' Magazine, Look, Progressive, Time, Mother Earth News, Wall Street Journal, Harper's, Ms., Psychology Today,* and other publications.

SIDELIGHTS: After a career teaching elementary and high school students, John Holt came to the conclusion that today's educational system simply did not work. In fact, he believed that schools stunted the natural desire to learn. As he once explained in *USA Today,* "Children come into the world . . . 'biologically driven' to learn. . . . Our attempts to coerce, control and measure this natural and powerful process turn it off for all but a few children." What schools care most about, Holt claimed, is the appearance of knowledge, not true understanding. "What would happen at Harvard or Yale," he once asked, "if a prof gave a surprise test in March on work covered in October? Everyone knows what would happen; that's why they don't do it." Holt believed that students should be taught how to learn and then be allowed to explore subjects that fascinate them. By the 1970s, Holt had grown disillusioned with educational reform and was recommending that parents teach their children at home. "Most home-schooled children . . . ," he stated in *USA Today,* "are academically well ahead of their age group. Many have gone to top colleges and done well." To further this movement, Holt published the magazine *Growing without Schooling.*

Holt's first book, *How Children Fail,* was based on his own classroom teaching experience. It recounted his encounters with failing children and presented his observations of why they failed. Much of the blame lay with the schools themselves, according to Holt. He claimed that schools "taught confusion" and trained children to respond to questions with teacher-pleasing answers. "It is a rare child," Holt wrote in *How Children Fail,* "who can come through his schooling with much left of his curiosity, his independence or his sense of his own dignity, competence and worth." The book won critical praise. Eliot Fremont-Smith of the *New York Times* called it "possibly the most penetrating, and probably the most eloquent, book on education to be published in recent years." *How Children Fail* went on to sell over one and half million copies.

In subsequent books, Holt developed his ideas on improving the educational system. In *How Children Learn,* he argued against large classrooms, pointing out that most children learned best alone or in small groups. He also advocated that children decide what they should study for themselves. In later works he went on to call for more flexible school schedules, the abolition of fixed school curriculum, and the use of outside non-teacher adults in the classroom. What Holt wanted, he once told the *Boston Globe,* was a "de-schooled society in which learning is not separated from but is integrated with the rest of life."

With the founding of his magazine *Growing without Schooling,* Holt turned to a new approach. Rather than try to change the existing school system, he now called for parents to teach their children at home. Reform of the system, he believed, was not truly possible. A return to traditional home teaching of children was needed. His 1981 book *Teach Your Own: A Hopeful Path for Education* dealt with the subject in detail, explaining how parents could legally remove their children from public school, how they could establish their own private school, and how they could obtain the necessary certificates and licenses to teach their children at home. His magazine *Growing without Schooling* reached some 5,000 readers and was intended, as Holt explained in the first issue, to cover "ways in which people, young or old, can learn and do things, acquire skills, and find interesting and useful work, without having to go through the process of schooling." By the 1980s, Holt had established himself as one of the nation's leading spokesmen for the home schooling movement.

The criticism Holt leveled against the public education system met with criticism of its own. Samuel McCracken in *Commentary* called *How Children Fail* "ultimately an infuriating book, infuriating because although it contains any number of exceptionally keen insights into the learning process, observations which would entitle their author to some importance in the history of education, it ends by finally marshalling these observations about the methodology of education into an exceptionally dogmatic and imperceptive theory of its content and end." Donald Barr in the *New York Times Book Review* found that, in *How Children Fail,* "Holt was still capable . . . of brilliant insights." But in later works, as his educational theories evolved, "his original suspicions congealed into dogmas. . . . The doubts are gone, and so is the openness."

Holt's call for home schooling was also criticized. Edmund Fuller in the *Wall Street Journal* found Holt's "willingness to scrap the whole system of compulsory public schools" to be "absurd." John Merrow, in his *New Republic* review of *Teach Your Own,* claimed that although the book provided many examples of parents who had taught their children at home, "Holt never explores the less cheerful side of any of the stories he prints, and he never admits the possibility that home schooling could be vexing, boring, or counterproductive." Peter Schrag in the *Saturday Review,* who grouped Holt with several other critics of education, noted a discrepancy between these critics' politics and their actual proposals for reform. Schrag explains with irony that "their tone is often that of the radical left, but the values are conservative, upholding the virtues of honest, meaningful work, of community and family, and of civil human relationships."

Still, many critics praised Holt's insights, while his books helped to raise important questions about the state of American education. Holt, according to Robert Coles in *Book World,* "wrote forcefully and with a kind of old-fashioned sense of indignation that all too many educators shun." Joseph Featherstone in *New Republic* called *How Children Fail* a "brilliant and angry" book, while he declared its sequel, *How Children Learn,* to be "splendid." Together, Featherstone stated, "these two works . . . deserve to become classics, books to reread and think about."

At the time of his death in 1985, Holt was remembered as a forceful advocate of educational reform as well as a leading supporter of home schooling. Following his own advice about education, Holt claimed that he had taught himself far more than he had ever learned in the classroom. He took up French and Italian at the age of 30, skiing at 31, cello for the first time at 40, water skiing at 47, horseback riding at 48, and violin at 60. "The results show that an old dog *can* learn new tricks," he explained.

BIOGRAPHICAL/CRITICAL SOURCES:

BOOKS

Contemporary Issues Criticism, Volume 2, Gale, 1985.
Holt, John, *How Children Fail,* Pitman, 1964, revised edition, Delacorte, 1982.
Holt, John, *Never Too Late: A Musical Autobiography,* Delacorte, 1978.

PERIODICALS

Book World, January 14, 1968.
Commentary, June, 1970.
Growing without Schooling, Number 1, 1977.
New Republic, March 2, 1968, December 23, 1981.

New York Times, December 4, 1967.
New York Times Book Review, September 14, 1969.
Saturday Review, February 18, 1967.
USA Today, December 2, 1983, December 14, 1983.
Wall Street Journal, August 3, 1981.

OBITUARIES:

PERIODICALS

Chicago Tribune, September 17, 1985.
Detroit Free Press, September 16, 1985.
Los Angeles Times, September 18, 1985.
New York Times, September 16, 1985.
Washington Post, September 16, 1985.*

—*Sketch by Thomas Wiloch*

*   *   *

HOOD, Sarah
See KILLOUGH, (Karen) Lee

*   *   *

HOWKINS, John 1945-

PERSONAL: Born August 3, 1945, in Northampton, England; son of Walter and Lesley (Stops) Howkins. *Education:* Keele University, B.A., 1968; Architectural Association, diploma in town planning, 1972.

CAREER: Free-lance journalist. Marketing manager, Lever Brothers, 1968-70; International Institute of Communications, London, England, editor of *InterMedia* magazine, 1975-84, executive director, 1984-89; Whittet Books, London, director, 1976-84; director of ETR Ltd., 1989—. Joint founder, TV-4 Conference, 1971; director, *Time Out* Ltd., 1974; producer, "The People's Television," 1974; programme director for Satellite Broadcasting conference, 1981. Director of executive board, Broadcasting Research Unit, 1981—; member of executive committee of British Standing Conference on Broadcasting, 1975—; secretary of Standing Conference on Broadcasting, 1975-77; member, Interim Action Committee on the Film Industry, 1980-85, and British Screen Advisory Council, 1985—. Consultant, British Broadcasting Corp. (BBC) Broadcasting Centre and Foster Associates, 1982-83; advisor, Committee on European Communities, House of Lords, 1985-86; chief consultant, Competitive Strategies in TV Broadcasting, 1989; European consultant, HBO, Inc., 1989—.

MEMBER: London International Film School (governor, 1976—; chairman, 1979-84), National Union of Journalists, Critics Circle, Guild of Broadcasting Journalists, Association of Independent Producers (vice-chairman for new media, 1984-85).

WRITINGS:

Understanding Television, Sundial, 1976.
(Editor) *Vision and Hindsight: The Future of Communications,* International Institute of Communications, 1976.
The Media in China, Nord Media, 1980.
Mass Communication in China, Nord Media, 1980, Longman, 1982.
(Editor) *TV: A New Beginning?,* Royal Television Society, 1981.
New Technologies, New Policies?, New York Zoetrope, 1982.
(Co-author) *Satellite Broadcasting in Western Europe,* International Institute of Communications, 1982.

Also contributor to *Encyclopaedia Britannica Yearbook,* 1976-86; also editorial consultant, *1992 Now,* IBM/Omnific,

1988—. Television columnist, *Illustrated London News,* 1981-83. Contributor to periodicals, including *Sunday Times* (London). Editor, *Vision,* 1977-79; executive editor, *National Electronics Review,* 1981—; TV/radio editor and books editor, *Time Out,* 1971-74.

*   *   *

HOWORTH, M. K.
See BLACK, Margaret K(atherine)

*   *   *

HUNT, Peter (Leonard) 1945-

PERSONAL: Born September 2, 1945, in Rugby, England; son of Walter Henry (an engineer) and Lillian (McPherson) Hunt; married Angela Sarah Theodora Wilkinson (a researcher), October 24, 1981; children: Felicity Sarah Eve, Amy Harriet Mary, Abigail Celestine Rose, Chloe Amaryllis Verity. *Education:* University College of Wales, Aberystwyth, B.A., 1966; University of Wales, Cardiff, M.A., 1969, Ph.D., 1981.

ADDRESSES: Office—University of Wales, College of Cardiff, Colum Dr., Cardiff CF1 3EU, Wales, United Kingdom.

CAREER: University of Wales, Cardiff, lecturer, 1969-88, senior lecturer in English, 1988—. Lecturer at University of Michigan, Ann Arbor, 1978. Joint examiner of Engineering Council, 1978—. Principal associate at John Kirkman Communication Consultancy, 1981—.

WRITINGS:

Children's Book Research in Britain, Institute of Science and Technology, University of Wales, 1977, 2nd edition, 1982.
(Editor) *Further Approaches to Research in Children's Literature,* Institute of Science and Technology, University of Wales, 1977, 2nd edition, 1982.
The Maps of Time (fiction), Julia MacRae, 1983.
A Step off the Path (fiction), Julia MacRae, 1985.
Backtrack (fiction), Julia MacRae, 1986.
Going Up (fiction), Julia MacRae, 1989.
Fay Cow and the Missing Milk (fiction), Julia MacRae, 1989.
Sue and the Money Machine (fiction), Julia MacRae, 1989.
(Editor) Richard Jefferies, *Bevis,* Oxford University Press, 1989.
Children's Literature: The Development of Criticism, Routledge & Kegan Paul, 1990.

Contributor of articles and reviews to periodicals, including *Times Literary Supplement, Signal, Children's Literature in Education, Advocate,* and *Social Work Today.*

WORK IN PROGRESS: Researching narratology and children's books.

SIDELIGHTS: According to Dominic Hibberd in the *Times Literary Supplement,* Peter Hunt presents a "fascinating time puzzle" in *The Maps of Time.* The story follows a curate, four teenagers, and an eleven-year-old boy as they travel through their imaginations back in time, courtesy of magical Victorian maps found in an old bookstore. The worlds in which the characters travel "allow the novelist to enjoy himself," comments Hibberd. "One narrative splits into four (now, then, and two versions of imagined now). . . . Plenty can happen—four times as much, in fact—and there are nice touches of irony and ambiguity. . . . The time machinery is too ingenious, but it does make us think twice—four times—about the art of narrative."

Peter Hunt told *CA,* "During my sabbatical from 1982 to 1983, I visited nearly one hundred universities and colleges in the

United States, Canada, Australia, New Zealand, and India, and lectured at sixty-five of them on children's literature."

He adds: "I believe in the serious (but not solemn) application of the highest and most sophisticated theories to children's literature; I think children are capable of a very sophisticated level of literary appreciation. Contrary to popular thought, I think this appreciation is different in *kind*, rather than degree, from adult appreciation of literature. A new discipline of what might be called 'childist' criticism must be developed to account for it. My writing for children adheres to these principles: that only the best—by which I mean writing that is as sophisticated as any other—will do. The only possible differentiation (if any) is in the *timbre* of the subject matter."

BIOGRAPHICAL/CRITICAL SOURCES:

BOOKS

Chevalier, Tracy, editor, *Twentieth-Century Children's Writers*, St. James Press, 1989.

PERIODICALS

Times Literary Supplement, February 25, 1983; November 29, 1985; November 28, 1986.

* * *

HUNTER, E. Waldo
  See STURGEON, Theodore (Hamilton)

* * *

HUTCHINS, Pat 1942-

PERSONAL: Born June 18, 1942, in Yorkshire, England; daughter of Edward (a soldier) and Lilian (Crawford) Goundry; married Laurence Hutchins (a film director), July 21, 1965; children: Morgan, Sam. *Education:* Attended Darlington School of Art, 1958-60, and Leeds College of Art, 1960-62.

ADDRESSES: Home—75 Flask Walk, London NW3, England.

CAREER: J. Walter Thompson (advertising agency), London, England, assistant art director, 1963-65; free-lance writer and illustrator, 1965—.

AWARDS, HONORS: Kate Greenaway Award, Library Association (England), 1974, for *The Wind Blew*.

WRITINGS:

JUVENILES; SELF-ILLUSTRATED

Rosie's Walk, Macmillan, 1968.
Tom and Sam, Macmillan, 1968.
The Surprise Party, Macmillan, 1969.
Clocks and More Clocks, Macmillan, 1970.
Changes, Changes, Macmillan, 1971.
Titch, Macmillan, 1971.
Goodnight, Owl, Macmillan, 1972.
The Wind Blew, Macmillan, 1974.
The Silver Christmas Tree, Macmillan, 1974.
Don't Forget the Bacon, Greenwillow, 1976.
The Best Train Set Ever, Greenwillow, 1978.
Happy Birthday, Sam, Greenwillow, 1978.
One-Eyed Jake, Greenwillow, 1979.
The Tale of Thomas Mead, Greenwillow, 1980.
One Hunter, Greenwillow, 1982.
You'll Soon Grow into Them, Titch, Greenwillow, 1983.
King Henry's Palace, Greenwillow, 1983.

The Very Worst Monster, Greenwillow, 1985.
The Doorbell Rang, Greenwillow, 1986.
Where's the Baby?, Greenwillow, 1988.
Which Witch Is Which?, Greenwillow, 1989.
What Game Shall We Play?, Greenwillow, 1990.

JUVENILES; ILLUSTRATED BY HUSBAND, LAURENCE HUTCHINS

The House That Sailed Away, Greenwillow, 1975.
Follow That Bus, Greenwillow, 1977.
The Mona Lisa Mystery, Greenwillow, 1981.
The Curse of the Egyptian Mummy, Greenwillow, 1983.
Rats, Greenwillow, 1989.

MEDIA ADAPTATIONS: Clocks and More Clocks, Rosie's Walk, The Surprise Party, and *Changes, Changes* have all been made into filmstrips by Weston Woods.

SIDELIGHTS: Pat Hutchins is noted for children's books that use humor in presenting sometimes complex situations. *The Mona Lisa Mystery*, for example, is "superior children's fare . . . with enough humorous episodes to make readers of all ages laugh," Laurel Graeber states in the *Christian Science Monitor*. While the critic believes that the mystery may present some vocabulary problems for younger readers, she nevertheless encourages the reading of the book: "It's just too good to miss." Called "a major British illustrator/author" by *Chicago Tribune Book World* contributor Zena Sutherland, Hutchins presents a "convincing" blend of "fanciful and realistic elements" in *The Very Worst Monster*, a story of monster sibling rivalry. Calling the book "witty and whimsical," Toronto *Globe and Mail* writer Sandra Martin praises the author for "us[ing] the monster theme exquisitely and to gruesome advantage in dealing with the ultimate wicked sibling fantasy. [Hutchins] has a keen respect for children and an understanding for how they respond to situations." As Nancy Schmidtmann concludes in *School Library Journal*, "Hutchins is completely original in her treatment. . . . [*The Very Worst Monster* is] a monstrously wonderful addition to any picture book collection."

Hutchins told *CA:* "To me, the most important thing about a children's picture book is that it should be logical, not only the story, but the layout, too. To a very small child, an opened book is one page, not two—he doesn't see the gutter as a dividing line.

"I like to build my stories up, so the reader can understand what is happening and, in some cases, anticipate what is likely to happen on the next page. I think one can get quite complicated ideas across to small children as long as they are presented in a simple, satisfying way."

BIOGRAPHICAL/CRITICAL SOURCES:

BOOKS

Bader, Barbara, *A History of American Picture Books: From Noah's Ark to the Beast Within*, Macmillan, 1976.

PERIODICALS

Chicago Tribune Book World, June 9, 1985.
Christian Science Monitor, October 14, 1981.
Globe and Mail (Toronto), March 30, 1985.
New York Times Book Review, April 17, 1977; April 25, 1982.
School Library Journal, May, 1985.
Times Literary Supplement, March 27, 1981; May 24, 1985.

HYNES, Samuel (Lynn) 1924-

PERSONAL: Born August 29, 1924, in Chicago, Ill.; son of Samuel Lynn and Margaret (Turner) Hynes; married Elizabeth Igleheart, July 28, 1944; children: Miranda, Joanna. *Education:* University of Minnesota, B.A., 1947; Columbia University, M.A., 1948, Ph.D., 1956.

ADDRESSES: Office—Department of English, Princeton University, Princeton, N.J. 08540.

CAREER: Swarthmore College, Swarthmore, Pa., 1949-68, began as instructor, professor of English literature, 1965-68; Northwestern University, Evanston, Ill., professor of English, 1968-76; Princeton University, Princeton, N.J., professor of English, 1976—, Woodrow Wilson Professor of Literature, 1977—. *Military service:* U.S. Marine Corps Reserve, active duty, 1943-46 and 1952-53; became major; received Air Medal and Distinguished Flying Cross.

MEMBER: English Institute, Phi Beta Kappa.

AWARDS, HONORS: Fulbright fellow, 1953-54; Guggenheim fellow, 1959-60, 1981-82; Explicator Award, Explicator Literary Foundation, 1962, for *The Pattern of Hardy's Poetry;* Bollingen Foundation fellow, 1964-65; American Council of Learned Societies fellow, 1969, 1985-86; National Endowment for the Humanities senior fellow, 1973-74, 1977-78.

WRITINGS:

The Pattern of Hardy's Poetry, University of North Carolina Press, 1961.
William Golding, Columbia University Press, 1964.
The Edwardian Turn of Mind, Princeton University Press, 1968.
Edwardian Occasions: Essays on English Writing in the Early Twentieth Century, Oxford University Press, 1972.
The Auden Generation: Literature and Politics in England in the 1930's, Bodley Head, 1976, Viking, 1977.
(Author of introduction) *Rebecca West, A Celebration: A Selection of Her Writings Chosen by Her Publisher and Rebecca West,* Viking, 1977.
Thomas Hardy, Oxford University Press, 1984.
Flights of Passage: Reflections of a World War II Aviator (memoir), Frederic Beil/Naval Institute Press, 1988.

EDITOR

Further Speculations by T. E. Hulme, University of Minnesota Press, 1955.
English Literary Criticism: Restoration and Eighteenth Century, Appleton, 1963.
(With Daniel G. Hoffman) *English Literary Criticism: Romantic and Victorian,* Appleton, 1963.
Great Short Works of Thomas Hardy, Harper, 1967.
Arnold Bennett, *The Author's Craft and Other Critical Writings of Arnold Bennett,* University of Nebraska Press, 1968.
Christopher Caudwell, *Romance and Realism: A Study in English Bourgeois Literature by Christopher Caudwell,* Princeton University Press, 1970.
(And author of introduction) *Twentieth-Century Interpretations of 1984: A Collection of Critical Essays,* Prentice-Hall, 1971.
Graham Greene: A Collection of Critical Essays, Prentice-Hall, 1973.
Complete Poetical Works of Thomas Hardy, Oxford University Press, Volume 1, 1982, Volume 2, 1984, Volume 3, 1985.

SIDELIGHTS: A long-time scholar of late nineteenth- and early twentieth-century literature, Samuel Hynes attempts "to describe, by drawing upon a wide variety of firsthand sources, the cultural temper of the [Edwardian] age," writes Steven Marcus in his *Atlantic* review of *The Edwardian Turn of Mind.* Covering the period from about 1895 to 1914, Hynes's study "is not concerned with the Edwardian mental temper as a whole, but with, as he puts it, the examples and individuals that have interested him most," relates *Saturday Review* contributor Marghanita Laski, "although, as it develops, these are some aspects of the Edwardian intellectual climate which were, in today's light, most seminally influential." The result, as Michael Holroyd terms it in the *New York Times Book Review,* is "a study of Edwardianism that retains much of the glow of real life. [Hynes] has done this by refusing, so far as possible, to simplify the issues. Throughout his book, he preserves an excellent balance between sentiment and shrewd common sense." Although Hynes examines specific works of literature, his book "is largely literary biography," the critic explains. "He approaches reality, therefore, not through statistics, but through the individual. His method of recapturing the intellectual climate of the times is to explore those areas of Edwardian conflict that seem to him most crucial—'politics, science, the arts, the relations between men and women.' "

Laski, however, while finding *The Edwardian Turn of Mind* "a delightful book to read, often witty in its turn of phrase," faults the author for "concentrat[ing] on popular and partial responses at the expense of the full picture. . . . So long as we have done our background homework we can fairly give ourselves up to enjoyment of Professor Hynes's merry-melancholy interpretations." Gertrude Himmelfarb similarly criticizes the author for the lack of a "systematic attempt to explain" the movements of the age; "the job of finding out what *did* happen is all the more challenging if [Hynes] does not presume to know what *should* have happened," the critic comments in the *New Republic.* But Holroyd observes that Hynes's work "is not intended as a definitive work of reference," and adds that while "there will be many more studies of the age . . . few of them are likely to be so well-constructed as [his]." " 'The Edwardian Turn of Mind' is entirely satisfactory in almost every respect," concludes William E. Buckler in the *Virginia Quarterly Review.* "Professor Hynes treats with urbanity and genuine illumination a very diverse list of topics . . . [with a] style [that] is always clear and usually graceful."

"There is no more accomplished literary historian, writer and 'researcher' than Samuel Hynes," William H. Pritchard claims in his *New Republic* review of *The Auden Generation: Literature and Politics in England in the 1930's,* "and his year-by-year tour through the 1930's in England is full of good things." "Hynes's excellent book," relates *Newsweek* writer Walter Clemons, "traces the commitment of [W. H.] Auden and his close contemporaries during the '30s to the idea that poetry could be an agent in history and might even change its course." In *The Auden Generation,* "Hynes, a careful, meticulous scholar, patiently sorts through the novels, poems, reviews, periodicals, and literary fads of the period," John R. Boly summarizes in the *National Review.* "The result is a masterly account of the contradictions surrounding the generation whose creativity had to contend with the tragic circus of the Thirties." Including such writers as Auden, Christopher Isherwood, Stephen Spender, and C. Day Lewis, the "Auden generation" consisted of several authors and critics who had similar theories and politics, and who "grew up together, read the same books, and put one another in their own [works]," as *Washington Post Book World* contributor John Breslin describes them. Hynes "documents the intellectual incest," the reviewer continues, "but he is too good a literary critic and historian to reduce the achievement of this extraordinary group to these compulsive cross-references."

Other critics, however, believe Hynes does not provide enough background information on his subjects; Ronald Berman, for instance, remarks in *Commentary* that *The Auden Generation* "is about political writing, but it does not have an adequate sense of intellectual history. Its characters seem to respond instantaneously to [world] events." *New York Times Book Review* contributor Diana Trilling likewise asserts that Hynes "supplies a pitifully meager background to the political ardor even of his gifted few." And Karl Miller, while deeming Hynes's work "enviably lucid and judicious," states in the *New York Review of Books* that the author "is rather sparing in his attention to biography, pushing on with his chronological critical accounts." "*The Auden Generation* is nonetheless a superb account of the writer's dilemma in times of crisis," maintains Boly, countering criticisms of incompleteness by noting that Hynes "has the highly defensible bias of a literary historian. As a portrait of its age," he declares, "*The Auden Generation* is a clear, thorough, and important book that merits serious attention."

New York Times reviewer Christopher Lehmann-Haupt also has praise for Hynes's study, which he calls written "with exemplary grace and clarity. . . . His book is a useful blueprint to a literary culture that, whether we know it or not, continues to inform our own even on the most vulgar level." The critic elaborates: "What is most arresting about 'The Auden Generation' is the degree to which it speaks to our own most recent period of political ferment, the 1960's. . . . And that is finally what makes Professor Hynes's study most valuable: It teaches us more about our times than our times have taught us about themselves." Breslin likewise suggests that the author's "discussion of the tension between art and politics casts light on our own recent past as well as on England's troubled decade." "Hynes, in *The Auden Generation,* his extremely lucid, readable and intelligent study of the literary history in England of the Thirties, greatly enlarges the reader's view of the generation," Auden contemporary Stephen Spender writes in the *New Statesman.* "Hynes makes clearer than anyone before has done the most puzzling aspect of Auden's career, his retraction of some of the best poems of his youth," says Clemons. "Still better, the straightforward year-by-year placement of poems and novels in historical context produces striking juxtapositions." Although the survey may be selective to the point of exclusivity, the critic concludes, Hynes's work "is opinionated literary history of the most desirable kind."

Hynes departs from his literary studies to present a memoir of his years as a marine pilot during World War II in *Flights of Passage: Reflections of a World War II Aviator.* Hynes's work differs from the numerous wartime accounts of military brass and heroes, *Washington Post Book World* contributor James Salter reports: "Trailing along modestly, some years after [other war stories], is an unusual and moving book, *Flights of Passage,* which draws its considerable strength not from the scale of events but from its truth and clarity. . . . It convinces one that it is an authentic fragment, poignant and real, of a great and tumultuous past." "Touching, bawdy, at times very funny," Diane Ackerman remarks in the *New York Times Book Review, Flights of Passage* is "about coming of age as a Marine aviator during World War II. Looking at old photographs of himself and his squadron-mates, Mr. Hynes tries to remember how it felt, on the pulse, to be young in that era." The author succeeds in re-creating a young man's experience of the war; as *Time*'s Paul Gray observes, a "paradox shimmers throughout *Flights of Passage:* the war makes men out of Hynes and his comrades but also allows them to remain boys, irresponsible, as free as the birds when they climb into their cockpits."

In order to create an accurate portrait of the time, "Hynes tells the story from the point of view of the young man, with very little distancing," Ackerman notes. "In each of his units, soldiers fuse into a family, and he remembers their mannerisms and habits in vivid detail," with the "brief, quirky sketches" of his roguish comrades making "this book at times a cross between [James Michener's] 'Tales of the South Pacific' and [Joseph Heller's] 'Catch-22.' " While Hynes "makes good on his promise to tell his story as he remembers it," states Gray, nevertheless "his prose betrays a mature intelligence. It is deceptively simple and consistently enchanting." Salter, who also compares *Flights of Passage* to Michener's work, elaborates: "Although his story is told as much through the eyes of youth as possible, there is a certain maturity about it. The vision has not changed," the critic explains, "but the ability to describe that vision is greater and more assured."

While much of Hynes's account concerns his aviator's training and the escapades of his fellow airmen, it also recounts the squadron in combat at Okinawa; "It is this final third of the book," writes Salter, "with its unexpected incidents, candid observation, and almost saintly dispassion which grips the reader in an embrace that leaves its mark. The detail is exact, imperishable." *National Review* contributor Jeffrey Hart concurs, asserting that Hynes's "memoir of his experiences as a Marine pilot in the Pacific is extraordinarily moving. . . . His prose catches the exact mood of World War II," the critic continues, adding that "this book is so good I was sorry to finish it." "In part, one's pleasure is derived from its use of language," comments Christopher Thorne in the *Times Literary Supplement;* "in part, from the sensitivity of its observation." With events "beautifully captured in these pages," the critic concludes that "quite simply, [*Flights of Passage*] is a joy to read."

BIOGRAPHICAL/CRITICAL SOURCES:

BOOKS

Hynes, Samuel, *Flights of Passage: Reflections of a World War II Aviator,* Frederic Beil/Naval Institute Press, 1988.

PERIODICALS

Atlantic, October, 1968.
Commentary, September, 1977.
National Review, May 26, 1978, June 24, 1988.
New Republic, July 20, 1968, April 16, 1977, December 3, 1977.
New Statesman, July 2, 1976.
Newsweek, May 23, 1977.
New York Review of Books, June 9, 1977.
New York Times, May 16, 1977.
New York Times Book Review, February 16, 1969, May 22, 1977, April 24, 1988.
Saturday Review, July 6, 1968, May 14, 1977.
Time, March 7, 1988.
Times Literary Supplement, February 27, 1969, November 10, 1972, March 7, 1986, April 7, 1989.
Virginia Quarterly Review, autumn, 1968.
Washington Post Book World, May 22, 1977, April 3, 1988.*

—*Sketch by Diane Telgen*

I-J

ISRAELOWITZ, Oscar 1949-

PERSONAL: Surname is pronounced *Iz*-ray-lowitz; born July 22, 1949, in Brussels, Belgium; came to the United States, 1950; naturalized U.S. citizen, 1956; son of Jacob Baruch and Helen (Domb) Israelowitz. *Education:* Brooklyn College of the City University of New York, B.S., 1972; attended Cooper Union School of Architecture, 1972-75; Pratt Institute, B.Arch., 1978.

ADDRESSES: Office—P.O. Box 228, Brooklyn, NY 11229.

CAREER: Project director, researcher, photographer, graphic designer, and guest curator for museum exhibitions, 1973—. Architect; free-lance architectural consultant in New York City and Israel, 1979—; publisher, Israelowitz Publishing, Brooklyn, NY. Director of photography for television program "Israel through Music and Dance," WNYC-TV, 1979. Organizer of walking, bus, and boat tours; lecturer. Has appeared on television and radio programs, 1982-86; has exhibited photographs in museums.

WRITINGS:

(Photographer) Jeffrey Gurock, *When Harlem Was Jewish,* Columbia University Press, 1979.

Synagogues of New York City: A Pictorial Survey in 150 Photographs, Dover, 1981.

The Complete Guide to Jewish New York, Israelowitz Publishing, 1983.

Asher Israelowitz's Guide to Jewish Europe, Israelowitz Publishing, 1985.

Shopper's Guide to Borough Park, Israelowitz Publishing, 1986.

Oscar Israelowitz's Guide to the Lower East Side, Israelowitz Publishing, 1986.

Oscar Israelowitz's Guide to Jewish U.S.A., Israelowitz Publishing, 1987.

WORK IN PROGRESS: Synagogues of the World, a large-format color volume.

SIDELIGHTS: Oscar Israelowitz's pictorial survey, *Synagogues of New York City,* features 123 photographs. His own architectural projects include the Synagogue and Holocaust Center of the Bobover Chassidim and the Yeshiva Rabbi Chaim Berlin Elementary School, both in New York City. He has also designed several homes and villas around the world.

BIOGRAPHICAL/CRITICAL SOURCES:

PERIODICALS

New York Times Book Review, December 26, 1982.

* * *

JAFFE, Dennis T(heodore) 1946-

PERSONAL: Born September 20, 1946, in New York City; son of Sidney (a teacher) and Rhoda (a teacher; maiden name, Oltarsh) Jaffe; married Cynthia Scott (a management consultant), August, 1975; children: Oren, Kai. *Education:* Yale University, B.A., 1967, M.A., 1969, Ph.D., 1974. *Religion:* Jewish.

ADDRESSES: Home—764 Ashbury St., San Francisco, CA 94117. *Office*—Heartwork Group, 764 Ashbury St., San Francisco, CA 94117. *Agent*—Sandra Dijkjtra, P.O. Box 2287, Del Mar, CA 92138.

CAREER: University of Southern California, Los Angeles, adjunct assistant professor of sociology and psychology, 1975-77; Learning for Health, Los Angeles, director of psychosomatic medicine clinic, beginning 1977; Saybrook Institute, San Francisco, CA, professor, 1980—; Heartwork Group, San Francisco, owner, 1984—.

MEMBER: Association for Humanistic Psychology (president).

WRITINGS:

(With Ted Clark) *Worlds Apart: Young People and Drug Programs,* Vintage, 1974.

(With Harold Bloomfield, Michael Cain, and Robert Kory) *TM: Discovering Inner Energy and Overcoming Stress,* Delacorte, 1975.

(Editor) *In Search of a Therapy,* Harper, 1975.

(With Clark) *Number Nine: Autobiography of an Alternative Counseling Service,* Harper, 1976.

(With Lawrence Allman) *Abnormal Psychology in the Life Cycle,* Harper, 1978.

Healing from Within, Knopf, 1979.

(Editor with James S. Gordon and David Bresler) *Body, Mind, and Health: Toward an Integral Medicine,* Human Sciences, 1984.

(With wife, Cynthia D. Scott) *From Burnout to Balance: A Workbook for Personal Self-Renewal,* McGraw, 1985.

Take This Job and Love It, Simon & Shuster, 1988.

Self-Renewal, Simon & Shuster, 1989.
Managing Organizational Change, Crisp Publications, 1989.

Also author of *Working with the Ones You Love,* 1990.

WORK IN PROGRESS: The Visionary Manager, a book on new dimensions in management.

SIDELIGHTS: "I became a writer almost by accident," Dennis T. Jaffe told *CA.* "In graduate school I became involved in a number of new mental health experiments, and I traveled to visit some around the world. I kept a journal, which I continued when I began my own street clinic in New Haven, Connecticut. I wrote some of my experiences and sent them to journals and magazines, without thinking, and they were published. Exciting events were set in motion, as I found people contacted me and visited, sharing their experiences. I began to feel that the best service I could offer as a mental health practitioner was to help people, especially the recipients of services, to describe their needs and feelings to the public and professionals. I feel that such descriptions are an extension of my role as a service professional, therapist, and professor.

"My work has been concerned in many ways with self-help, with individual attempts to help one another. I have found that writing is a form of direct service. In my work, I have tried to steer clear of promising incredible results, and of hucksterism, and to provide instead clear, simple, and useful accounts of self-help methods and projects. I have also worked with UCLA to create some self-learning packages for health professionals.

"I feel that therapists have increasingly chosen to be social prophets, guides, and public helpers, and that there is a need for a code of ethics, individual restraint, and professionalism in that area. My activity as a writer is to create a bridge between writing and other forms of professional activities.

"My purpose in writing is always to educate, and to serve the public. I write when I feel an issue is important, and I address my writing to a specific public, whether in a book, professional journal or popular magazine. I feel that all audiences can benefit from clear psychological information, and in the future I expect that more and more therapists will pursue this direction."

* * *

JAY, Mel
See FANTHORPE, R(obert) Lionel

* * *

JEFFREY, William
See PRONZINI, Bill

* * *

JENSEN, Michael C(ole) 1939-

PERSONAL: Born November 30, 1939, in Rochester, Minn.; son of Harold J. and Gertrude M. Jensen; married second wife, Toni S. Walcott, June 30, 1984; children: (first marriage) Natalie Ann, Stephanie Katherine. *Education:* Macalester College, A.B., 1962; University of Chicago, M.B.A., 1964, Ph.D., 1968.

ADDRESSES: Office—Harvard Business School, Soldiers Field, Boston, Mass. 02163.

CAREER: Chicago Junior College System, Chicago, Ill., instructor in business administration, 1966; Northwestern Univer-

sity, Evanston, Ill., instructor in business administration, 1967; University of Rochester, Rochester, N.Y., assistant professor, 1967-71, associate professor of finance, 1971-79, professor of business administration, 1979-84, LaClare Professor, 1984-88, director of managerial economics research center, Graduate School of Management, 1977-88; Harvard University, Boston, Mass., professor of business administration, 1985-89, Edsel Bryant Ford professor, 1989—. Visiting professor of business administration, Harvard University, 1984-85. Member of board of advisers, Pacific Institute, 1983—; member of Eller Center advisory board, University of Arizona, 1984—; member of advisory commission, Institute for the Study of Regulation, 1985—, and Manhattan Institute, 1986—; advisory director, LaClare Management, Inc., 1986; member of board, Analysis Group, Inc., 1989—. Consulting editor, Quorum Books, 1979.

MEMBER: American Economic Association, American Finance Association (member of board of directors, 1983-85; vice president, 1990—), Econometric Society, Western Economic Association (member of executive committee, 1981-83), Beta Gamma Sigma, Pi Gamma Mu, Omicron Delta Gamma.

AWARDS, HONORS: Security Trust Co. fellowships, 1968-69, 1970-71, 1971-72; Ford Foundation fellowship, 1970; National Science Foundation fellowship, 1970-71; Graduate School of Management Superior Teaching Award, University of Rochester, 1974; co-recipient, Graham and Dodd Plaque, 1978; Leo Melamed prize, 1978; Joseph Coolidge Shaw medal, 1984; University of Chicago fellowship; United States Steel Foundation fellowship; Harold Stonier Fellowship in Banking.

WRITINGS:

(Editor) *Studies in the Theory of Capital Markets,* Praeger, 1972.
(With Clifford W. Smith, Jr.) *The Modern Theory of Corporate Finance,* McGraw-Hill, 1984.

CONTRIBUTOR

Henry Manne, editor, *Economic Policy and the Regulation of Corporate Securities,* American Enterprise Institute for Public Policy Research (Washington, D.C.), 1969.
Empirical Research in Accounting: Selected Studies, Institute of Professional Accounting, University of Chicago, 1970.
E. Bruce Frederikson, editor, *Frontiers of Investment Analysis,* International Textbook Company, 1971.
G. P. Szego and Karl Shell, editors, *Mathematical Methods in Finance,* North-Holland, 1972.
E. Elton and M. Gruber, editors, *Security Evaluation and Portfolio Analysis,* Prentice-Hall, 1972.
J. Lorie and R. Brealey, editors, *Investment Management: Some Readings,* Praeger, 1972.
Is Financial Analysis Useless?, Financial Analysis Research Foundation, 1975.
Stanford Lectures in Accounting, Stanford University, 1976.
The World Capital Shortage, Bobbs-Merrill, 1977.
Karl Brunner, editor, *Economics and Social Institutions,* Martinus Nijhoff, 1979.
(With William H. Meckling) *Controlling the Giant Corporation: A Symposium,* Center for Research in Government Policy and Business, University of Rochester, 1982.
Proceedings of Conference on Corporate Capital Structures in the United States, University of Chicago Press, 1984.
(With Smith) E. Altman and M. Subrahmanyam, editors, *Recent Advances in Corporate Finance,* Dow Jones-Irwin, 1985.
Proceedings of the William G. Karnes Symposium on Mergers and Acquisitions, Bureau of Economic and Business Research, University of Illinois, 1986.

John Thackay, editor, *Chief Financial Officer U.S.A.,* Sterling Publications, 1988.

Yakov Amihud, editor, *Leveraged Management Buyouts: Causes and Consequences,* Dow Jones-Irwin, 1989.

Also contributor, with Meckling, to *Corporate Governance: A Definite Exploration of the Issues,* edited by C. J. Huizenga, 1983.

OTHER

Author, with Meckling, of unpublished book, *Democracy in Crisis,* 1977. Contributor to professional journals. Associate editor, *Journal of Financial and Quantitative Analysis,* 1969-73; founding editor, *Journal of Financial Economics,* 1973—; advisory editor, *Economic Letters,* 1978—; associate editor, *Journal of Accounting Economics,* 1978-87; member of editorial advisory board, *Journal of Applied Corporate Finance,* 1988—.

WORK IN PROGRESS: Economics, Information, Coordination Costs, and Control in Large Organizations.

*   *   *

JOHNS, Marston
   See FANTHORPE, R(obert) Lionel

*   *   *

JOHNSTON, Norma
   See St. JOHN, Nicole

*   *   *

JONAS, George   1935-

PERSONAL: Born June 15, 1935, in Budapest, Hungary; emigrated to Canada, 1956; son of George Maurice (a lawyer and composer) and Magda (Klug) Hubsch; married Sylvia Nemes (an assistant industrial psychologist), September, 1960 (divorced, 1974); married Barbara Amiel (a journalist); children: (first marriage) Alexander. *Education:* Attended Lutheran Gymnasium, Budapest, Hungary, eight years, and Institute of Art and Folklore, Budapest, two years.

ADDRESSES: Office—c/o The Colbert Agency, 303 Davenport Rd., Toronto, Ont., Canada.

CAREER: Radio Budapest, Budapest, Hungary, editor, 1955-56; Canadian Broadcasting Corp., Toronto, Ontario, script editor, 1962-67, chief story editor, 1968-70, television drama producer, 1970—.

MEMBER: League of Canadian Poets (treasurer, 1969-70), Composers, Authors and Publishers Association of Canada, Poets and Writers, New York State Council on the Arts.

AWARDS, HONORS: Canada Council short term grant, 1968, 1971, and 1974; Edgar Allan Poe Award, 1977, for *By Persons Unknown.*

WRITINGS:

The Absolute Smile (poetry), House of Anansi, 1967.
The Happy Hungry Man (poetry), House of Anansi, 1970.
Cities, (poetry), House of Anansi, 1973.
(With Barbara Amiel) *The Strange Death of Christine Demeter,* Macmillan, 1983.
(Editor) *The Scales of Justice,* Lester & Orpen Dennys, Volume 1: *Seven Famous Criminal Cases Recreated* (based on Ed-

ward Greenspan's CBC radio broadcasts), 1983, Volume 2: *Ten Famous Criminal Cases Recreated,* 1986.
Vengeance, Collins, 1984, published as *Vengeance: The True Story of an Israeli Counter-Terrorist Mission* (nonfiction; Book-of-the-Month Club alternate), Simon & Schuster, 1985.
Final Decree, Totem Books, 1985.
Crocodiles in the Bathtub and Other Perils, Collins, 1987.
(With Edward C. Greenspan) *Greenspan: The Case for the Defense,* Macmillan, 1987.

PLAYS

(Adaptor) "Of Mice and Men" (radio; from John Steinbeck's novel), produced on "CBC Stage," 1963.
"To Cross a Bridge" (original radio script), produced on "CBC Matinee Theatre," 1964.
"The Major" (television; based on story by Milovan Djilas), produced on "CBC Shoestring Theatre," 1964.
The European Lover (libretto for comic opera), produced by Jason Ensemble for tour in Canada, 1966.
"The Redl Affair" (original radio script), produced on "CBC Summer Stage," 1966.
"The Agent Provocateur" (original radio script), produced on "CBC Summer Stage," 1966.
"Fasting Friar" (based on a novel by Edward McCourt), produced on "CBC Summer Stage," 1967.
"Master and Man" (radio; based on a story by Tolstoy), produced on "CBC FM Theatre," 1967.
(Adaptor) "Mr. Pym Passes By" (radio; from the play by A. A. Milne), produced on "CBC Summer Stage," 1967.
"First and Vital Candle" (radio; based on a novel by Rudy Wiebe), produced on "CBC Stage," 1967.
"Catullus" (original radio script), produced by CBC, 1967.
"Tell His Majesty . . . ' (original radio script), produced on "CBC Summer Stage," 1968.
(Translator and adaptor) "Ave Luna, Morituri Te Salutant" (from a poem by George Faludy), produced on "CBC Anthology," 1970.
"The Glove" (libretto), first produced by the Canadian Opera Company, 1975, produced by CBC, 1975.

OTHER

Contributor of poems, articles, and reviews to *Saturday Review, Prism International, Canadian Forum, Quarry, Toronto Star, Maclean's, Books in Canada,* and other periodicals.

WORK IN PROGRESS: Peaceville North, a novel; *Pushkin,* a stage play; *New and Selected Poems,* a fourth collection of poems.

SIDELIGHTS: George Jonas is known in Canada as a poet and the producer of radio documentaries. He is also a crime writer who is known throughout the world as the author of *Vengeance: The True Story of an Israeli Counter-Terrorist Mission.* Writing by Jonas in nearly all these genre sustains a particularly Canadian flavor. Reviewing the poetry of Jonas and three other Canadians in *Poetry* magazine, Margaret Atwood points out their differing techniques but unmistakable Canadian imprint, "something to do with space, sensed as vast open, unconfining, and oppressive." About *Absolute Smile,* she notes, "The spaces are between people. George Jonas's usual subject is himself, but he moves from an individual self with private histories to the self as representative urbanite . . . to the self as the very society under attack."

The Scales of Justice, a two-volume set of nonfiction crime studies by Jonas and Toronto lawyer Edward Greenspan "are treated not only for their sensationalism but also for their impact on and explication of Canadian justice," Margaret Cannon comments in the *Globe and Mail*. They introduce lay readers to the workings of the justice system in Canada, showing both its strengths and weaknesses. The cases included in Volume 1: *Seven Famous Criminal Cases Recreated* are present "because of the precedents they set in Canadian law," Marina Dowsley notes in *Quill and Quire*. In addition, Cannon finds the volumes exemplary "in retaining accuracy while enhancing interest when adapting factual materials."

The issue of factual accuracy often appeared in reviews of *Vengeance,* the 1984 book in which Jonas retells the story of assassinations carried out by the Mossad, an Israeli terrorist group formed to avenge the 1972 massacre of Israeli athletes in Munich. Controversy centered on two questions: the credibility of his source (a Mossad agent who calls himself Avner), and the extent of the publisher's responsibility, if any, to verify information. While some argued that verification is necessary before one can assess the ultimate value of the book, others stressed that gaining verification in such cases is limited if not impossible due to the nature of covert operations. "Even if Avner's story were true, observers of the intelligence field say, it would doubtless be officially denied, given the volatility of the material," Philip Taubman explains in the *New York Times*. In the case of *Vengeance,* the fact that Avner claims he was not paid for his work, together with the possible motive of providing disinformation to fend off counter-counter terrorism, place the whole story in doubt. In his introduction, Jonas expresses regrets that he was unable to corroborate Avner's story, but felt it was worth telling, nevertheless. Publishers in twenty-one countries agreed. After publication, Avner told interviewers, "If you don't believe me, don't buy the book," Gene Lyons reports in *Newsweek*.

Jeff Sallot of the Toronto *Globe and Mail* writes, "What sets *Vengeance* apart [from other books on terrorism] is that the story is told by a gifted writer from the point of view of a key participant. On that basis alone, *Vengeance* is a literary success. Jonas' fast-paced narrative is compelling. The story seems to sag a bit only when the writer adds unnecessary details about street scenes and the layouts of hotel lobbies." Some feel that, more importantly, the book exposes the ironies involved in such actions, as when a counter-terrorist squad finds it must collaborate with other terrorists in order to fulfill its anti-terrorist mission. Despite doubts about the ultimate success of counter-terrorism, Sallot appreciates the book's final effect; he concludes, "*Vengeance* should serve to stimulate timely debate about the nature of terrorism and the morality of the steps a Government might take to counter the threat."

In Canada, Jonas has been the subject of two educational television films, "Robert Fulford in Conversation with George Jonas," 1968, and "Dennis Lee in Conversation with George Jonas," 1970, and a Canadian Broadcasting Corp. film, "Adrianne Clarkson Talks with George Jonas," 1970. His background as a Hungarian Jew who emigrated to Canada in 1956 enhances his perceptions of both Canadian and international politics. Jonas told *CA:* "Politically, I've always felt that most of our problems in the West are nothing that a month in the Gulag wouldn't cure. The trick is not to conclude from this that we need the Gulag, but that we can only avoid it by seeing our problems in perspective."

BIOGRAPHICAL/CRITICAL SOURCES:

PERIODICALS

Canadian Literature, summer, 1969.

Globe and Mail, May 12, 1984.
Newsweek, June 18, 1984, August 2, 1986, May 30, 1987, October 10, 1987.
New York Times, May 2, 1984.
New York Times Book Review, June 3, 1984.
Poetry, June, 1969.
Quill and Quire, May, 1984.
University of Toronto Quarterly, January, 1968.*

*   *   *

JUST, Ward (Swift) 1935-

PERSONAL: Born September 5, 1935, in Michigan City, Ind.; son of Franklin Ward (a newspaper publisher) and Elizabeth (Swift) Just; married Jean Ramsay; married Anne Burling; married Sarah Catchpole, 1983; children: (first marriage) Jennifer Ramsay, Julia Barnett, (second marriage) Ian Ward. *Education:* Attended Trinity College, 1953-57.

ADDRESSES: Home—5 Rue des Saints Peres, Paris 75006, France; Box 342 R.F.D., Vineyard Haven, Mass. 02568.

CAREER: Waukegan News-Sun, Waukegan, Ill., reporter, 1957-59; *Newsweek* magazine, New York, N.Y., reporter in Chicago and Washington, D.C. bureaus, 1959-62; *Reporter* magazine, political reporter, 1962-63; *Newsweek,* New York City, London correspondent, 1963-65; *Washington Post,* Washington, D.C., correspondent in Saigon, South Vietnam, 1965-67, and in Washington, D.C., 1968-70; writer, 1970—. Writer in residence, Phillips Academy, Andover, Mass., 1982-84.

AWARDS, HONORS: National Magazine awards for nonfiction, 1970, and for fiction, 1980; *Washington Monthly* political book award, 1973, for *The Congressman Who Loved Flaubert and Other Washington Stories; Chicago Tribune* Heartland award for fiction, 1989.

WRITINGS:

FICTION

A Soldier of the Revolution, Knopf, 1970.
The Congressman Who Loved Flaubert and Other Washington Stories, Little, Brown, 1973.
Stringer, Little, Brown, 1974.
Nicholson at Large, Little, Brown, 1975.
A Family Trust, Little, Brown, 1978.
Honor, Power, Riches, Fame and the Love of Women, Dutton, 1979.
In the City of Fear, Viking, 1983.
The American Blues, Viking, 1984.
The American Ambassador, Houghton, 1987.
Jack Gance, Houghton, 1989.
Twenty-One Selected Stories, Houghton, 1990.

Contributor to *The Best American Short Stories,* Houghton, 1972, 1973, and 1976.

NONFICTION

To What End: Report from Vietnam, Houghton, 1968.
Military Men, Knopf, 1970.

OTHER

Contributing editor, *Atlantic,* 1972-84.

WORK IN PROGRESS: A novel.

SIDELIGHTS: Ward Just draws upon his experiences as a war and government correspondent to create fiction about the political dilemmas of the modern era. Just is fascinated by those people who have public as well as private lives; he is the rare fiction writer who chooses to tackle the complicated web of professional intrigue in Washington, D.C. *New York Times Book Review* contributor Judith Martin writes of Just: "He is not only the most literary chronicler of the daily lives and moral dilemmas of contemporary politicians, bureaucrats, intelligence agents, military officers, diplomats, lawyers and journalists, but one of the few novelists even interested in depicting such people realistically." Likewise, *Los Angeles Times Book Review* correspondent Gary Dretzka notes that the author "makes politics a substantially more colorful calling than it actually is. . . . His contribution to our understanding of the political game in [his] novels is enormous, and he deserves a broad and enthusiastic readership."

Just's own career has been decidedly more colorful than average. He was born and raised in a small Midwestern town near Chicago, the son and grandson of newspaper publishers. Rather than taking his turn with the family newspaper, he moved to Chicago and joined the *Newsweek* magazine bureau there. From Chicago he moved to Washington, D.C., where he covered politics for *Newsweek,* and then he became a foreign correspondent for the *Washington Post.* In 1965 he was posted to Saigon, where he covered the Vietnam War for two years. He returned to the United States in 1967, after having been seriously wounded in a jungle skirmish. The *Washington Post* gave Just a sabbatical to write his first book, a nonfiction work called *To What End: Report from Vietnam.* In a *Newsweek* review of the book, Saul Maloff notes that it "records and describes, evokes and portrays, with the fine eye of a good, skeptical but feeling journalist trying to make sense out of his experience."

Just continued to cover national politics for the *Washington Post* for several years after returning from Vietnam. Gradually, however, he began to find fiction writing more compelling than journalism. He began to write novels based on the events he observed in Vietnam and about the people he encountered in the American capital. Just told the *New York Times Book Review* that his experiences as a correspondent "were burned into my mind. The milieu I knew as a reporter is the milieu I write about—the world of journalists, politicians, diplomats and soldiers." In the *New York Times Book Review,* Jonathan Yardley maintains that the prevailing subjects in Just's fiction "are politics, war, and, more recently, the Middle West. His view of all three is bleak and ironic, yet it is tempered by affection: Mr. Just genuinely likes politicians, understands the appeal of warfare and loves his native Middle West . . . even as he despairs of what has happened to it. Thus his fiction has an ambiguous quality that is most effective, providing as it does an underlying tension and an appreciation of complexity."

"The city where the former journalist first made his mark as a reporter nearly 30 years ago refuses to leave him alone," writes Elizabeth Mehren in the *Los Angeles Times.* "Washington provides a significant backdrop for all of Just's . . . novels and . . . collections of short stories. His characters play politics, practice diplomacy. They ponder patriotism and debate moral dilemmas. Certainly moral dilemmas exist equally in Ithaca or Indianapolis, Just would willingly concede, but somehow they seem more at home in Washington, where private quandaries are magnified through massive public lenses." Yardley notes: "Mr. Just hands out no victories, offers no moral judgments. He understands that people respond to stress in different ways, and he is content merely to observe them, sketching their twists and turns for our consideration." In the *Washington Post Book World,* C. D. B. Bryan concludes that Just "writes subtly, has that knack for precise detail, and tends to concentrate upon the ambiguous feelings

men have about their careers, their women and the past in these changing times. He places his characters into confrontations that demand choices. His people hurt and get hurt; hearts break; and although there is surprisingly little blood, there are always ugly scars which do not fade."

Now a full time fiction writer, Just lives in Paris most of the year. He is far from a disillusioned expatriate, however—American issues continue to inspire him from abroad. "Having seen it all," writes Julian Moynahan in the *New York Times Book Review,* "Mr. Just bids to be considered the political novelist of his generation. He may even be considered for a rarer title, that of national novelist . . . provided one believes that the capital and the nation are still in touch with each other these days for any essential purposes." *Chicago Tribune Books* reviewer Douglas E. Kneeland praises Just for his portraits of politicians and their various satellites, adding: "How do you properly celebrate a Ward Just? He writes books for grownups who like to read. No screenplays palpitate indecently close to the surface of his novels. No miniseries. No sitcoms. Only real people whose almost ordinary lives are enriched by his prose and by the depth of his understanding of, and compassion for, the human condition. . . . He writes of the mind and of the heart and of the soul, although he does not mention these things. He writes of choices made, of decisions deferred, of acceptance, of the large gray spaces between the easy blacks and whites of life." Judith Martin concludes of Just's books: "Readers who are willing to listen without prejudice, are going to learn a great deal about how our society works."

CA INTERVIEW

CA interviewed Ward Just on June 22, 1989, at his summer residence in Vineyard Haven, Massachusetts.

CA: You were born in the Midwest, grew up there, and then lived for some years in the East. Recently you've gone even farther from home. How did you decide to move to Paris?

JUST: I had been teaching at Andover Academy on one of those finite contracts; it ended after three years, but I really bailed out after two. As much as I enjoyed teaching, I couldn't get any work done. My son, who had been living with us, graduated from Andover High School at that point and went off. My wife was working for WGBH Television Station in Boston, and she had one of those finite contracts. All of a sudden, in June of 1986, we found ourselves with no place we had to be, and it was she who suggested that we move to Paris. I said, "That's impossible." She said, "Why is that impossible?" I looked at it and realized that it wasn't impossible if you're not employed; you can go where your typewriter goes. So we went to Paris, intending to stay for a year. We'll be going into our fourth year come September, and it's proven to be very successful.

CA: Are you're planning to stay there?

JUST: I think we'll stay for awhile, as long as we can afford it and life continues agreeably. My wife has been doing radio pieces for a French production company in Paris, and I seem to be getting some work done on my books. France—Paris particularly—treats Americans extremely well and agreeably.

CA: Yes. You were saying that when you appeared on television's "Today" show after the publication of Jack Gance.

JUST: The French have got a terrible rap of being rude. I have not found that at all. My friends maintain that the reason I have not found that at all is that my French is so poor I don't understand the people. But I don't think so. I think the French are extremely jolly. If you're jolly with them, they're jolly back.

CA: You said in an interview for Publishers Weekly *that "Paris is an easy city not to work in." What did you mean?*

JUST: The French are terrific with their pleasures. Fortunately or unfortunately, their pleasures happen to be my pleasures; they center around food and drink. It's such a pretty city, obviously, and a good city just to get around in. Even though we've been there for about three years, there are a number of places in the city which we haven't even begun to explore. It's very simple to walk out your door at nine o'clock, take a long march to wherever, have a nice lunch, take another long march, and get home about six o'clock, in time to think about the evening meal. But you settle down after a while. I think I work as hard there as I used to work in Andover—well, maybe not quite as hard, but I've gotten older too. In any case, I'm happy with my production there, and it's a very, very agreeable place to live. And if you don't have to live in New York or Boston, why would you!

CA: Do you think you're getting a better understanding of this country by living in France?

JUST: Yes, and it's hard to explain why. In part, just so far as the media are concerned, you are seeing it without the benefit of American television. Dan Rather shows up at 7:30 in the morning on French TV. And if you want to, you can watch the previous night's "CBS Evening News." I think we've done that twice or maybe three times, right around the time of the election—otherwise we don't bother. So you come at America from a particularly European point of view. I've gotten very interested in the last eight or nine years in Germany. In Germany specifically, but also living in France, in a certain sense you're just off-center of the continent and you tend to see the United States through those lenses. I tend to look at America not so much with a focus on the domestic politics but in terms of foreign policy vis-a-vis Europe, trade policy, NATO, and that kind of thing.

If you asked me what shattering insights I've gathered from all this, I would not be able to say. I only know that my last novel was written mostly in France, and it had to do entirely with Chicago and Washington—primarily Chicago. I have a feeling that it would have been a different novel, and not so good a novel, if I had been writing it in the United States. It's very hard for me to explain why that is. But there is a quality of distance that you get from abroad; you see it through the wrong end of the telescope, maybe, and that provides some illumination that you wouldn't otherwise have. Then too, I lived for fifty years in the United States. It doesn't go away. All you're doing is stepping back a bit.

CA: After you graduated from college, you worked for a while at the Waukegan News-Sun. *That was your family's paper, I believe.*

JUST: Yes. It was founded by my grandfather in the 1920s. He died in the early fifties, and my father took it over. I went to work for the paper when I was fifteen as a cub reporter during the summers. Apart from that I worked for it only briefly, for a year and a half or two years.

CA: Had you chosen, couldn't you have taken over the paper yourself?

JUST: I could have, and I think in all candor it's what the family wanted me to do. Alas, whatever talents I have were never in the direction of being a newspaper publisher, especially on a paper that size—it had a circulation then of around thirty thousand, and I think it's around thirty-five thousand now. I couldn't spend the rest of my life writing for a paper, and I didn't enjoy editing much either. And you cannot sit atop an institution of that kind without certain talents for publishing, which I did not possess. So it was inevitable, since Waukegan, Illinois, didn't provide much range for maneuver, that I would leave sooner or later. It ended up being sooner rather than later.

CA: Do you think it was a disappointment for your father?

JUST: I think so. I think it was also a disappointment for my mother and for the rest of the family. But, as I've pointed out to them repeatedly since then, it would have been a disaster if I had stayed. I would have become an exemplar of the Peter Principle. When my father died, in 1970, I became chairman of the board of directors, and remained until we sold the paper in 1983. But I was really doing that from a remove, and it's no way to run a newspaper.

CA: You and I knew each other very briefly at Lake Forest Academy. Did any of the teachers there have a serious influence on your decision to become a writer?

JUST: There was only one. He was then the chairman of the English department, Kendall Pennypacker. My grades were dismal at Lake Forest Academy, and I was no better in English than I was in any of the other subjects. In fact, I only lasted there for two years and then I went on. I had to take a course in remedial English from Mr. Pennypacker, and I was his despair. But at one point he said to me, "You know, you probably are a writer. It's hard for me to support this with the evidence, but you probably ought to keep on with it." It was paradoxical, because my grades went from bad to worse. But sometimes you want to do something so damned badly, you end up doing it.

CA: I remember Pennypacker, now that you mention him. I liked him too.

JUST: He was a kind of bird-like gent. He did not have an enormous amount of charm, as my recollection goes. But he was a subtle man, and of the people at Lake Forest Academy, he certainly is the one I remember the best.

CA: In reading about you I've come across over and over again the comment that Hemingway was a big influence on you. When you were at the Washington Post, *Ben Bradlee even nicknamed you "Ernie." How much is there to this?*

JUST: I don't think there's much to it. There are two people who've been influences on me from the early days. F. Scott Fitzgerald was my great literary hero when I was a teenager. I would pore over his stories and *The Great Gatsby* and *Tender is the Night* to try to find out if there was some secret. I was convinced there was one, and if I could learn it, I thought, maybe then I could write like that too. I didn't get interested in Ernest Hemingway until my early twenties. I think the thing that prompts the comments about me and Hemingway is that certain surface comparisons can be made. The two principal ones are that I went to work as a journalist, as he did, and we were both particularly attracted to wars. To the extent that I have a reputation in journalism, it rests on my war coverage. People have to put a writer in some pocket, so they see those two things and put me in that one. It's not a bad pocket, but I don't think I fit it in the way they assume.

Of course, if one is talking about stylistic influence or moral influence, you cannot have started to write seriously after, say, 1935 (the year I was born, by the way) without having been influenced by Hemingway. I suppose there are American writers who were not, but I think most, in one way or another, were, and I certainly was. He is part of the atmosphere. It's as if you look up at the sky and you see the Big Dipper, the Little Dipper, the North Star. He's in the sky along with Fitzgerald and Henry James, who was the second big influence on me as I got older.

CA: You went to Vietnam early in the war, in December of 1965. Did you have your mind pretty well made up as to how you felt about it when you went?

JUST: I didn't know anything about the war. I'd never been to Asia before. I had covered the rebellion in Cyprus in '63 and '64, and I'd been down to the Dominican Republic during the troubles there in February of '65. I knew about Vietnam only what I had read in the papers. I don't think I even read David Halberstam's book *The Making of the Quagmire,* which was published in 1963, until I actually got over there myself. I remember climbing on the plane at Dulles with my clothes and a book bag: I had Bob Shaplen and Halberstam and Bernard Fall and the rest of those writers with me, and I said, "I'd really better get into this." I applied for the job in October of 1985, and I was gone by December. I had talked to a few people before I left, but there wasn't time to do much work in advance. And I am of such a temperament that I can never make up my mind about anything until I see it firsthand.

CA: Weren't you injured in Vietnam?

JUST: Yes. I went out on a reconnaissance patrol in June 1966 that was "inserted," as they called it, up in the Highlands. There were forty people, and I was along because I'd never seen one of these operations and wanted to see how it was done. There was what the army types like to call a "meeting engagement," which is to say that we stumbled into a base camp, making for a long afternoon. I got some grenade fragments here and there.

CA: Does it still bother you?

JUST: It bothers me to the extent that the damned stuff still leaches out of my skin here and there. From time to time there'll be an abscess, and I'll have to have that taken out. It was a hand grenade of Chinese manufacture; they call it a potato masher. There were big fragments, but there were also a lot of small ones, because I was pretty well peppered, and these things enter the body and tend to stay there. But other than that, it's no problem. I don't have a stiff knee if it rains, or anything like that.

CA: So many veterans of that war, even all these years later, are still haunted by it. Do you have any of that feeling?

JUST: There's no question that it was a formative experience, that following by a couple of years the two tours that I did in Cyprus. I believe it affected me maybe more than I like to think about for the first ten or fifteen years after I was out. I assume that's true, because I'm looking over some of my early stories in the process of putting together a short story collection, and I had forgotten how many of them had to do with the war; I'd forgotten the themes of them. My first four or five novels are all about the war, and I'd forgotten that. You tend to forget what you write until you sit down and read it again. But today, twenty years later, it's not much of a presence in my life.

CA: Something that does seem to be a presence in your life, or at least it was for a long time, is Washington. Your latest book, Jack

Gance, *is partly about Washington. Howard Means said in the* Washingtonian *that "Washington is a place for journalists, not novelists." Why would Washington be considered a bad place for novelists?*

JUST: It's terribly hard, I think, to get inside the city in any real way unless you've lived there as part of it. I lived there as part of it as a journalist. If you're trying to write about it seriously, non-schematically—that is to say, you're not writing a political thriller, but using the city as a setting the way Henry James used London, where you have the city itself a character in a novel and the characters very much a part of the city—this seems extremely difficult to do in Washington. I think the reason is that there's so much publicity; the city is so overwhelmed with television journalists and magazine writers that it's almost too familiar to us. In order to bring it to life, you've got to back way away from it somehow on the one hand and have a truly intimate knowledge of it on the other. There are not very many writers who have that. I don't think Washington's a hospitable place for a novelist to live in, because in Washington, more than any city than I've ever lived in, you must be part of the game to have any fun at it. You go out to some party and everybody's invited; it's like a commodities exchange, in which everybody will tell you what they heard today if you'll tell them what you heard. You've got to be part of it. People will go down there for a while and be taken up as a pet—a pet novelist, a pet filmmaker, or whatever—but it can't last very long. And to understand that city, you can't stay there for two months and then leave with a few place names and some argot. You've got to get further into the warp of it, and that isn't available to very many people. It's very difficult to do.

I have written a lot about Washington. All of my novels have a little bit of a Washington edge somewhere, and the reason is that I arrived in that city in 1961, working for *Newsweek,* when I was twenty-six years old. It was the time of the Kennedys, of Camelot. The month after I arrived in town, the Bay of Pigs happened; the year after that there was the Cuban missile crisis. By the time Kennedy died, I was over in London working for the magazine. But these were two extremely tense years for me at a very impressionable age, and I've never forgotten it. It's sort of like Melville's whaling ship or Philip Roth's mom—or better yet, Philip Roth's dad! The atmosphere of Washington at that time has never left me. I haven't lived in Washington for seventeen years, but I still think I have some understanding of the ambience and the way of the place, as one does almost for any kind of childhood home. I could say the same thing about Waukegan, Illinois.

CA: But there seems to be another side of you too. You liked Washington, you like Paris, but there's another part of you that may be related to your character in American Blues *who withdrew from the cities and lived in the woods for a while.*

JUST: That's right. I lived up in Vermont for six years. I did feel for a while that the world got a little bit too much with me. There was a time, in 1973, when I just found it useless to live in Washington. I think in part that was because I'd been writing fiction for three years, and I felt that Washington wasn't the place for a fiction writer who wanted to reach as far as he could with the craft. You're just surrounded by too many facts all the time.

CA: That seems like a dramatic change.

JUST: It was a huge change, and it was a very, very productive period in terms of novels and stories. I did nothing but work for six years—and, I think, wrote myself out. I did what I consider good work up there, but I'm not a reclusive type. I tend to be convivial, maybe a little too convivial for my own good. From that standpoint it was no kind of long-term solution; it was too remote there. And I went from a world I knew all too well to a world in which I knew nothing. I might as well have been living in Siberia. I couldn't connect with the people. I loved the landscape, but it was not my kind of place to live.

CA: Are you writing a novel now?

JUST: Yes. I'm a quarter or a third of the way done with one, and I'd like to have it finished some time next year.

CA: You've hinted elsewhere that Jack Gance *may have gotten Washington out of your system. Will the next book signal a change of direction that you can talk about at this point?*

JUST: A change of direction, definitely. And beyond that, it's not wise to go.

BIOGRAPHICAL/CRITICAL SOURCES:

BOOKS

Contemporary Literary Criticism, Gale, Volume 4, 1975, Volume 27, 1984.

PERIODICALS

Atlantic, October, 1970.
Best Sellers, July 15, 1970.

Chicago Tribune, March 15, 1987, January 25, 1989.
Chicago Tribune Books, January 1, 1989.
Chicago Tribune Book World, July 19, 1970.
Christian Science Monitor, February 11, 1971.
Los Angeles Times, July 24, 1984, January 29, 1989.
Los Angeles Times Book Review, January 15, 1989.
National Review, April 26, 1974, October 26, 1979.
New Republic, April 6, 1974, October 4, 1975, October 25, 1982.
Newsweek, April 8, 1968, December 28, 1970, March 11, 1974, October 13, 1975, September 17, 1979, January 16, 1989.
New York Times, January 1, 1971, March 31, 1978, December 23, 1982, March 9, 1987, December 26, 1988.
New York Times Book Review, August 26, 1973, April 16, 1978, September 9, 1979, October 17, 1982, July 8, 1984, March 15, 1987, January 1, 1989.
Publishers Weekly, March 13, 1987.
Saturday Review, April 15, 1978.
Time, February 8, 1971, July 8, 1974.
Washingtonian, September, 1988.
Washington Post Book World, April 7, 1968, July 22, 1973, March 10, 1974, April 2, 1978, September 2, 1979, September 26, 1982, June 17, 1984, March 22, 1987, January 29, 1989.

—*Sketch by Anne Janette Johnson*

—*Interview by Walter W. Ross*

K

KAHN, Alfred J. 1919-

PERSONAL: Born February 8, 1919, in New York City; son of Meyer and Sophie (Levine) Kahn; married Miriam Kadin, September 3, 1949 (divorced, 1980); children: Nancy. *Education:* College of the City of New York (now City College of the City University of New York), B.S.S., 1939; Seminary College of Jewish Studies, Bachelor of Hebrew Literature, 1940; Columbia University, New York School of Social Work, M.S., 1946, Doctor of Social Welfare, 1952. *Religion:* Jewish.

ADDRESSES: Home—250 Gorge Rd., Cliffside Park, NJ 07010. *Office*—School of Social Work, Columbia University, 622 West 13th St., New York, NY 10025.

CAREER: Jewish Board of Guardians, New York City, psychiatric social worker, 1946-47; Columbia University, School of Social Work, New York City, 1947—, began as instructor, professor of social policy and planning, 1952-89, professor emeritus and senior lecturer, 1989—. Smith College School of Social Work, Northhampton, MA, member of summer faculty, 1949-54; member and chairman of committee on child development research and public policy, National Research Council/ National Academy of Sciences, 1971-83. Consultant to Citizen's Committee for children of New York City, Inc., 1948-73, and to several foundations, United Nations Units, and to federal, state, and local voluntary social welfare programs in child welfare, social policy, social services, and planning. *Military service:* U.S. Army Air Forces, 1942-46; served as psychiatric social worker; became staff sergeant.

MEMBER: American Association of University Professors, National Association of Social Workers, American Sociological Association (fellow), American Planning Association, American Orthopsychiatry Association, Policy Studies Organization, Association for Public Policy Analysis and Management, Phi Beta Kappa.

AWARDS, HONORS: Various foundation and Fulbright grants to study social welfare programs in Europe; distinguished scholar medal, State University of New York, 1983; D.H.L., Adelphi University, 1984; D.S., University of Maryland, 1989.

WRITINGS:

WITH SHEILA B. KAMERMAN

Not for the Poor Alone: European Social Services, Temple University Press, 1975.
Social Services in the United States: Policies and Programs, Temple University Press, 1976.
Social Services in International Perspective: The Emergence of the Sixth System, U.S. Department of Health, Education, and Welfare, 1977, reprinted with a new introduction, Transaction Books, 1980.
(Editor) *Family Policy: Government and Families in Fourteen Countries,* Columbia University Press, 1978.
Child Care, Family Benefits, and Working Parents: A Study in Comparative Policy, Columbia University Press, 1981.
(And with Paul Kingston) *Maternity Policies and Working Women,* Columbia University Press, 1983.
Income Transfers for Families and Children, Temple University Press, 1983.
Child Care: Facing the Hard Choices, Auburn House, 1987.
The Responsive Workplace: Employers and a Changing Labor Force, Columbia University Press, 1987.
(Editor) *Child Support: From Debt Collection to Social Policy,* Russell Sage, 1987.
Mothers Alone: Strategies for a Time of Change, Auburn House, 1988.
(Editor) *Privitization and the Welfare State,* Princeton University Press, 1989.

Also editor, with Kamerman, of *Essays on Income Transfers and Related Programs,* 1983.

EDITOR

Issues in American Social Work, Columbia University Press, 1959.
The Planning and Coordination of Services for Children and Youth in New York City, Citizens' Committee for Children of New York City, Inc., 1959.
Shaping the New Social Work, Columbia University Press, 1973.

OTHER

(With T. Lash) *Children Absent from School: A Report and a Program,* Citizens' Committee for Children of New York City, Inc., 1949.

Police and Children: A Study of the Juvenile Aid Bureau of the New York City Police Department, Citizens' Committee for Children of New York City, Inc., 1951.

A Court for Children: A Study of the New York City Children's Court, Columbia University Press, 1953.

For Children in Trouble, Citizens' Committee for Children of New York City, Inc., 1957.

The Crisis in the New York City Police Program for Youth, Citizens' Committee for Children of New York City, Inc., 1959.

When Children Must Be Committed, Citizens' Committee for Children of New York City, Inc., 1960.

New York City Boys Committed to New York State Training Schools in 1957 and 1958, New York State Department of Social Welfare, 1960.

Protecting New York City's Children, Citizens' Committee for Children of New York City, Inc., 1961.

New York City Schools and Children Who Need Help, Citizens' Committee for Children of New York City, Inc., 1962.

Planning Community Services for Children in Trouble, Columbia University Press, 1963.

(With Anne Mayer) *Day Care as a Social Instrument,* Columbia University School of Social Work, 1965.

(With others) *Neighborhood Information Centers: A Study and Some Proposals,* Columbia University School of Social Work, 1966.

Studies in Social Policy and Planning, Russell Sage, 1969.

Theory and Practice of Social Planning, Russell Sage, 1969.

(With others) *Child Advocacy: Report of a National Baseline Study,* Child Advocacy Research Project, Columbia University, 1972.

Social Policy and Social Service, Random House, 1973, 2nd edition, 1979.

BIOGRAPHICAL/CRITICAL SOURCES:

PERIODICALS

Time, June 22, 1987.

*   *   *

KAIRYS, Anatolijus 1914-

PERSONAL: Surname is accented on second syllable; given name is accented on third syllable; born August 28, 1914, in St. Petersburg (now Leningrad), Russia (now U.S.S.R.); came to the United States in 1947, naturalized citizen, 1953; son of Justinas (a farmer) and Monike (Juodvalkyte) Kairys. *Education:* Attended University of Kaunas, 1938-40; University of Vilnius, M.A., 1942. *Politics:* None.

ADDRESSES: Home—3142 West 61st St., Chicago, IL 60629.

CAREER: High school principal and teacher of psychology and logic in Siauliai, Lithuania, 1942-44; high school teacher of psychology and logic in Germany, 1946-47; writer. *Military service:* Lithuanian Army, 1935-36.

MEMBER: International PEN, National Writers Club, Lithuanian Writers Association in Exile (chairman, 1983-86).

AWARDS, HONORS: First prize for satirical comedy, Lithuanian Theatre Association (Chicago, IL), 1964, for *Visciuku ukis;* Lithuanian Scouts of Chicago, first prize, 1965, for *Sviesa, kuri uzsidege,* and second prize, 1965, for "Eldorado"; Los Angeles Drama Association, second prize, 1970, for "Ku-Ku," and prize in play contest, 1982, for *Sventasis Princas;* second prize, Lithuanian Regeneration Association, 1971, for *Istikimoji zole;* prize from *Draugas* novel contest, 1978, for *Po Damoklo kardu,* and

1982, for *Kelione i Vilniu;* prize in book-of-the-year contest, Lithuanian Writers Association in Exile, 1982, for *Pazadu dvaras;* prize in short story contest, *Dirva* weekly newspaper, 1982, for "Vaidilute," and 1986, for "Liptai i save"; prize in juvenile novel contest, Lithuanian World Community, 1985, for *Viena sirdis;* prize in drama contest, Adelaide/Australia/ Lithuanian Theatre Group, 1986, for "Paskutine valia;" prize in drama contest, Lithuanian Christianity Jubilee Committee, for "*Kriksto vanduo.*"

WRITINGS:

Blaskomi lapai (poems; title means "Scattered Leaves"), [Germany], 1946.

Auksine seja (poems; title means "The Golden Sowing"), Nemunas, 1954.

Istikimoji zole (novel; title means "Faithful Grass"), Lithuanian Rejuvenation Association, 1971.

Po Damoklo kardu (novel), Draugas Lithuanian Book Club, 1978, revised translation by Nijole Grazulis published as *Under the Sword of Damocles,* Lithuanian Literary Associates, 1980, Part II, Lithuanian National Guard in Exile, 1981.

Laisves sonata (poems; title means "Sonata of Freedom"), Dialogas, 1979.

Lotofagu saly (poems; title means "In the Land of Lotus-Eaters"), Lithuanian Literary Association, 1982.

Pazadu dvaras (folktale novel; title means "The Manor of Promises"), Draugas Lithuanian Book Club, 1982.

Kelione i Vilniu (novel; title means "The Journey to Vilnius"), Draugas Lithuanian Book Club, 1983.

Dulkiu atspindziai (short stories; title means "Reflections of Dust"), Lithuanian Literary Associates, 1985.

Aukurai ir altoriai (poems; title means "Sanctuaries and Altars"), Lithuanian Literary Associates, 1987.

Viena sirdis (novel; title means "One Heart"), Lithuanian American Community Educational Council, 1988.

Zalcio sapnas (short stories; title means "Serpent's Dreams"), Lithuanian Literary Associates, 1988.

Nemarioji Giesme (historical novel; title means "The Immortal Hymn"), Lithuanian Historical Society, 1988.

PLAYS

Diagnoze (three-act comedy; title means "Diagnosis"; first produced in Detroit, MI, 1959; produced in New York, 1964), Terra, 1956.

Visciuku ukis (three-act satire; title means "The Chicken Farm"; first produced in Chicago, IL, May 15, 1965), Terra, 1965.

Curriculum vitae (two-act; first produced in Chicago, May 18, 1968), published in *Pradalge* (magazine), 1966, translation by Anthony Mikulas published under same title in *Lithuanian Days* (magazine), 1971.

Sviesa, kuri uzsidege (three-act; title means "The Light Which Kindled"; first produced in Chicago, December 1, 1968), Terra, 1968.

Palikimas (one-act; title means "The Legacy"; first produced in Australia, May 17, 1970), Laiskai Lietuviams, 1969.

Du broliukai (three-act; title means "Two Little Brothers"; first produced in Chicago, March 23, 1969), Amerikos Lietuviu Vaiko Ugdymo Draugija, 1970.

Sidabrine diena (libretto for three-act operetta; title means "Silvery Day"; first produced in Chicago, December 11, 1971), Lietuviu Meno Ansamblis Dainava, 1972.

Karuna (nine-act; title means "The Crown"), Dialogas, 1974.

Trys komedijos (title means "Three Comedies"; contains "Ku-Ku" [three-act; first produced in Los Angeles, CA,

December 19, 1970], "The Good Friday" [five-act; first produced in Chicago, February 3, 1974], and "Boys and Girls" [three-act]), Dialogas, 1975.

Gintaro saly (libretto for one-act opera; title means "In the Land of Amber"; first produced in Chicago, May 8, 1976), Chicago Lithuanian Opera, 1976.

"Eldorado" (three-act), first produced in Sao Paolo, Brazil, August 6, 1978.

Trys dramos (title means "Three Plays"; contains "Rutele" [four-act; title means "The Flower"], "Saules rumai" [title means "The Palace of the Sun"], and "Zmogus ir tiltas" [three-act; title means "The Man and the Bridge"; first produced in Cleveland, OH, May 4, 1974]), Dialogas, 1978.

"Emilija plateryte" (libretto for three-act opera; title means "Emilia Plateris"), first produced in Chicago, 1979.

"Cicinskas" (libretto for three-act opera), first produced in Chicago, November 8, 1980.

Vyskupo sodas (three-act; title means "The Garden of the Bishop"), Lithuanian Literary Associates, 1980.

Kryzkele (three-act; title means "Crossroad"), Lithuanian Literary Associates, 1980.

Sventasis Princas (five-act drama-poem; title means "The Holy Prince"; first produced in Daytona Beach, FL, November 17, 1984), Committee for the 500th Anniversary of the St. Casimir Death, 1984.

Dvylika (twelve one-act plays for Youth Theatre; title means "The Twelve"), Lithuanian Literary Associates, 1985.

Ugnies daina (three-act; title means "The Song of Fire"), Lithuanian National Guard in Exile, 1986.

Kriksto vanduo (historical drama trilogy; title means "Baptismal Water"), Lithuanian Historical Society, 1989.

OTHER

Also author of political novel *Epigonai* (title means "Epigoni"), 1989; also author of drama "Paskutine valia"; also author of short stories.

WORK IN PROGRESS: Pusbroliai (title means "Cousins"), an historical novel about Lithuania at the end of the fourteenth century.

SIDELIGHTS: Anatolijus Kairys told *CA:* "This question is really unnecessary. There is nothing new under lights in front, rear, or sides. Many noted writers give their views, reviews, and interviews on this subject without revealing anything of importance. As for me, my fate as a writer will be even worse than that of Sisyphus because forty years ago 'red marauders' stole my mountain, and I have no way to roll my stone up. So I'm fighting with pen and paper to get it back. Or maybe I'm sick of hearing the broken 'Human Rights' record, and writing is only medicine to stay alive."

BIOGRAPHICAL/CRITICAL SOURCES:

BOOKS

Bradunas, Kazys, editor, *Lithuanian Literature Abroad, 1945-1967*, Freedom Fund for Lithuanian Culture, 1968.
Naujokaitis, Pranas, editor, *Lithuanian Literature*, Volume 4, Council of Lithuanian Culture, 1976.

*   *   *

KAMARCK, Lawrence   1927-

PERSONAL: Surname is pronounced *Kay*-mark; born June 6, 1927, in Canton, N.Y.; son of Martin and Frances (Earle) Kamarck; married Caroline Langmaid, June 18, 1949 (divorced,

1970); married Mary Catherine Rich (an economist), November 5, 1970; children: Jonathan, Matthew, Mitchell, Valerie. *Education:* Harvard University, A.B., 1950; Yale University, M.F.A., 1983. *Politics:* Democrat.

ADDRESSES: Home—P.O. Box 304, Woodstown, N.J. 08098. *Agent*—Helen Merrill, 435 West 23rd, Suite 1A, New York, N.Y. 10011.

CAREER: Worked as a reporter for *Newsweek* and *Forbes* and as swingman for *New Yorker* during the 1950s; Crotched Mountain Foundation, Greensfield, N.H., director of public information, 1960-66; New Hampshire Governor's Committee on Education for the Handicapped, Concord, chairman, 1967-68; writer. Member, Governor's Committee on Vocational Rehabilitation, 1969; director, New Hampshire Easter Seals, 1969-71. *Military service:* U.S. Army, 1945-47.

MEMBER: Authors Guild, Dramatists Guild, Authors League of America.

AWARDS, HONORS: Edgar Allan Poe Special Award, Mystery Writers of America, 1968, for *The Dinosaur;* FDG-CBS prize, 1984, for "The Keeping of Phillip."

WRITINGS:

The Dinosaur, Random House, 1968.
The Bellringer, Random House, 1969.
The Zinsser Implant, Dial, 1978.
Informed Sources, Dial, 1979.
"The Keeping of Phillip," first produced in Minneapolis, Minn., at Cricket Theatre, 1984.

WORK IN PROGRESS: A novel; a play.

SIDELIGHTS: "I am primarily interested in storytelling," Lawrence Kamarck once told *CA.* "Having produced what the *New York Times* chose as one of the ten best chillers in 1968 and in 1969, I'm probably well conditioned to do what it seems I do well. However, I feel that *chilling* books are central to the chilling experience of life today."

Lawrence later added: "Having dealt successfully with the relationship of a quadriplegic and his attendant in 'Phillip' in the play form, I intend to continue to write plays. Writing is difficult and time-consuming as I am also a quadriplegic."

BIOGRAPHICAL/CRITICAL SOURCES:

PERIODICALS

Library Journal, June 1, 1968.
New York Times Book Review, August 11, 1968, October 19, 1969, May 13, 1979, September 30, 1979.

*   *   *

KANFER, Frederick H.   1925-

PERSONAL: Born December 6, 1925, in Vienna, Austria; naturalized U.S. citizen; son of Oscar and Ann (Schneier) Kanfer; married Ruby Weber, January 20, 1952; children: Ruth, Lawrence P. *Education:* Engineering student, Cooper Union, 1942-44; Long Island University, B.S. (cum laude), 1948; Indiana University, M.A., 1952, Ph.D., 1953.

ADDRESSES: Home—Champaign, IL. *Office*—Department of Psychology, University of Illinois, 603 East Daniel St., Champaign, IL 61820.

CAREER: Diplomate in clinical psychology, American Board of Examiners in Professional Psychology, 1969. Intern at Veterans

Administration hospital, 1951-52; Washington University, St. Louis, MO, assistant professor of psychology and director of psychoeducational clinic, 1953-57; Purdue University, Lafayette, IN, associate professor, 1957-62; University of Oregon, Medical School, Portland, professor of psychiatry, 1962-69, visiting professor of psychology on main campus, Eugene, 1963, 1967-68; University of Cincinnati, Cincinnati, OH, professor of psychology, 1969-73; University of Illinois at Urbana-Champaign, professor of psychology, 1973—, director of clinical psychology, 1984-90. Visiting professor, Louisiana State University, 1961; Fulbright lecturer, Ruhr University, 1968; senior lecturer, University of Bern, 1980—. Member of clinical and personality sciences fellowship review committee, National Institute of Mental Health, 1971-74. Advisory editor, Research Press, 1978—. *Military service:* U.S. Army, 1944-46.

MEMBER: American Psychological Association (fellow), American Association for the Advancement of Science, Association for Advancement of the Behavioral Therapies (former member of board of directors), Midwestern Psychological Association, Sigma Xi.

AWARDS, HONORS: Research grants, U.S. Public Health Service, 1955-81; A. V. Humboldt Senior Scientist Prize, 1987-88; Golden Honor Medal, Vienna, Austria, 1989; University Scholar, University of Illinois, 1990-93.

WRITINGS:

(With J. S. Phillips) *Learning Foundations of Behavior Therapy,* Wiley, 1970.

(With A. P. Goldstein) *Helping People Change: A Textbook of Methods,* Pergamon, 1975, 4th edition, 1991.

(Editor with Goldstein) *Maximizing Treatment Gains: Transfer Enhancement in Psychotherapy,* Academic Press, 1979.

(Editor with P. Karoly, and contributor) *Self-Management and Behavior Change: From Theory to Practice,* Pergamon, 1982.

(With B. K. Schefft) *Guiding the Process of Therapeutic Change,* Research Press, 1988.

(With H. Reinecker and D. Schmelzer) *Selbstmanagement therapie als Aenderungsprozess,* Springer-Verlag, 1990.

Contributor to psychology texts, including *Behavior Therapy: Appraisal and Status,* 1969, *The Future of Psychotherapy,* 1969, *Behavior Modification in Education,* 1973, *Behavioral Self-Management,* 1977, *Contemporary Behavioral Therapy,* 1982, and *Theoretical Issues in Behavior Therapy,* 1985. Contributor of over 130 articles to professional journals, including *Journal of Clinical Psychology, Journal of Abnormal and Social Psychology, Contemporary Psychology, Psychological Reports,* and *Journal of Experimental Psychology.* Associate editor, *Psychological Reports,* 1961—, and *Journal of Addictive Behaviors,* 1974-80; member of editorial boards, *Behavior Therapy,* 1969-76, *Cognitive Therapy and Research,* 1976-80, 1984—, *Journal of Behavioral Assessment,* 1979-81, *Clinical Psychology Review,* 1980—, and *Journal of Social and Clinical Psychology,* 1982—; consulting editor, *Journal of Abnormal Psychology,* 1970-75.

WORK IN PROGRESS: Research on self-control, and on motivation and emotion in therapy.

*   *   *

KAZAN, Elia 1909-

PERSONAL: Born Elia Kazanjoglous, September 7, 1909, in Constantinople (now Istanbul), Turkey; son of George (a rug dealer) and Athena (Sismanoglou) Kazan; married Molly Day Thacher (a playwright), December 2, 1932 (died December 14, 1963); married Barbara Loden (an actress), June 5, 1967 (died September 5, 1980); married Frances Rudge, June 28, 1982; children: (first marriage) Judy, Chris, Nick, Katharine; (second marriage) Leo. *Education:* Williams College, A.B., 1930; Yale University School of Drama, graduate study, 1930-32; Group Theatre, apprentice to Lee Strasberg and Harold Clurman, 1932-33.

ADDRESSES: Home—Connecticut.

CAREER: Theatrical director, film director, actor, and author. Co-founder of Actor's Studio. Actor, 1932-41; made his Broadway debut as Louis in "Chrysalis" (also assistant stage manager), Martin Beck Theatre, November 15, 1932; went on to appear in and/or act as stage manager for such Broadway productions as "Men in White," "Gold-Eagle Guy," "Till the Day I Die," "Waiting for Lefty," "Paradise Lost," and "Case of Clyde Griffiths." Member of Group Theatre, New York City, 1936-41; productions included "Johnny Johnson" and "Golden Boy." Made London debut in "Golden Boy," 1938. Returned to New York City to appear in "The Gentle People," "Night Music," "Liliom," and "Five Alarm Waltz." Actor in movies "City for Conquest," 1941, and "Blues in the Night," 1941. Radio performer on "The Philip Morris Hour," "The Kate Smith Hour," and "The Group Theatre Radio Program."

Director of stage plays, 1935-64, including (with Alfred Saxe) "The Young Go First," "Casey Jones," "Thunder Rock," "Cafe Crown," "The Strings, My Lord, Are False," "The Skin of Our Teeth," "Harriet," "One Touch of Venus," "It's up to You," "Jacobowsky and the Colonel," "Deep Are the Roots," "Dunnigan's Daughter," "All My Sons," "Truck-line Cafe," "A Streetcar Named Desire," "Sundown Beach," "Love Life," (and producer) "Death of a Salesman," "Camino Real," "Tea and Sympathy," "Cat on a Hot Tin Roof," (and producer) "The Dark at the Top of the Stairs," "J.B.," "Sweet Bird of Youth," "After the Fall," "But for Whom Charlie," and "The Changeling." Also involved with, but not director of, "Marco Millions" and "Incident at Vichy."

Director of screenplays, 1944-76, including "A Tree Grows in Brooklyn," "Sea of Grass," "Boomerang," "Gentleman's Agreement," "Pinky," "Panic in the Streets," "A Streetcar Named Desire," "Viva Zapata!," "Man on a Tightrope," "On the Waterfront," "East of Eden," "Baby Doll," "A Face in the Crowd," "Wild River," "Splendor in the Grass," (and producer) "The Arrangement," "The Visitors," and "The Last Tycoon."

MEMBER: Screen Directors Guild of America, Screen Writers Guild, Phi Beta Kappa.

AWARDS, HONORS: Variety-New York Drama Critics Poll, 1943, for direction of "The Skin of Our Teeth," 1947, for "All My Sons," 1949, for "Death of a Salesman," and 1959, for "Sweet Bird of Youth"; Academy Award (Oscar) for direction, 1947, for "Gentleman's Agreement," and 1954, for "On the Waterfront"; Donaldson Award and Antoinette Perry (Tony) Award for direction, 1948, for "A Streetcar Named Desire," 1954, for "Tea and Sympathy," and 1955, for "Cat on a Hot Tin Roof"; National Board of Review, Venice Film Festival Award, 1951, for "A Streetcar Named Desire"; D.Litt., Wesleyan University, 1954; Tony Award, 1959, for "J.B."; D.Litt., Carnegie Institute of Technology (now Carnegie-Mellon University), 1962; Oscar Award nominations for best picture, best writing, and best direction, all 1963, all for "America, America"; Handel Medallion, New York City's Cultural Award, 1972, for forty-year contribution to the arts; D. W. Griffith Award, Directors

Guild of America, 1987, for the body of his work; honored by American Museum of the Moving Image, 1987.

WRITINGS:

America, America (autobiography; also see below), Stein & Day, 1962, reprinted, 1984.

(And director and co-producer) "America, America" (screenplay based on autobiography; released in Great Britain as "The Anatolian Smile"), Warner Bros., 1963.

The Arrangement (novel), Stein & Day, 1966.

The Assassins (novel), Stein & Day, 1972.

The Understudy (novel), Stein & Day, 1974.

Acts of Love (novel), Knopf, 1978.

The Anatolian (novel), Knopf, 1982.

A Life (autobiography), Knopf, 1988.

Also author of stage play, with Cheryl Crawford, "The Chain."

SIDELIGHTS: The name of Elia Kazan has long been synonymous with some of the greatest productions of theatre and film in this century. As director, he has overseen such stage classics as "Death of a Salesman," "A Streetcar Named Desire," and "After the Fall"; for the movies, he has brought "On the Waterfront," "Gentleman's Agreement," and "East of Eden" to the screen. Born in Istanbul at the turn of the century, the young Kazan emigrated with his parents to the United States as part of a great wave of newcomers to this country. The family settled in New York City, where the elder Kazan was a rug merchant. Elia Kazan was to put these early experiences on film years later with "America, America," the only movie he wrote as well as directed.

After graduation from Williams College, Kazan enrolled at the Yale School of Drama. He later served an apprenticeship with the renowned acting coaches Lee Strasberg and Harold Clurman when he became involved with the avant-garde Group Theatre, a socially conscious company of actors whose political loyalties leaned firmly to the left. Kazan, in fact, joined the Communist Party during this period, though he was to resign a few years later in a now-famous conflict. During the Party years in the company of fellow travelers, the Group Theatre produced some of its most memorable plays. "It was the young Kazan who, in the original Group Theatre production of Clifford Odets's *Waiting for Lefty,* incited a stunned opening-night audience to yell 'Strike! Strike! Strike!' and moved [the journal] *New Masses* to dub him 'Proletariat Thunderbolt,' " notes J. Hoberman in a *Village Voice* article. Thus, few who have studied Kazan's early career could have predicted that, years later, the director would become, in Hoberman's words, "the most distinguished American artist to sing before the House Un-American Activities Committee."

Kazan brought the same sense of social responsibility to his screen works, beginning in the mid-1940s with adaptations of "A Tree Grows in Brooklyn," about how one young girl faces the reality of her father's alcoholism, and "Gentleman's Agreement," a 1948 Academy Award winner. This movie examined the way anti-Semitism thrives in an obligingly oblivious postwar America. Gregory Peck played the lead as a writer who poses as Jewish in order to expose the constant slights and subtle discrimination prevalent in both big cities and small towns. Kazan tackled the subject of discrimination again in the film "Pinky," in which a light-skinned black woman "passes" for white in order to better her chances in life. "It is a film about principles; but principles conveyed by emotional means," wrote Dilys Powell in an article reprinted in the book *Shots in the Dark: A Collection of Reviewers' Opinions of Some of the Leading Films Re-*

leased between January 1949 and February 1951. In the same volume, C. A. Lejune found "Pinky" "not really a 'daring' film, except in so far as it admits that there is a colour question at all. It seems to me a fair film."

Two other Kazan movies take a sharp look at social and political mores in the 1950s. "Baby Doll," a highly controversial 1956 release because of its steamy sexual nature, took a Tennessee Williams story of one man's obsession with a half-witted Southern nymphet and turned it into an "uneasy blend of surface realism and theatrical exaggeration," in the words of *Film Culture* critic Andrew Sarris, who goes on to find the film a career setback for its director: "It is misleading to condemn *Baby Doll* for its divergence from its original source or for its failure to say more about race relations in the South. These are not the crucial issues. The absence of a consistent rationale for the characters is a more serious flaw." To the late director Francois Truffaut, in his book *The Films in My Life,* the movie's appeal outweighs its flaws. "We know . . . that Elia Kazan has nothing more to say to us than what his screenplay writers have written for him, and at the same time that he [knows] best of all how to reveal actors to themselves. The second time we see *Baby Doll,* we discover a second film which is still richer. Whether it is a work of genius or mere talent, whether decadent or generous, profound or brilliant, *Baby Doll* is fascinating."

A 1957 release, "A Face in the Crowd," covers a topic still debated today: whether television plays too important a role in politics. A variation on the "Frankenstein" myth, the story shows how a media-created monster, the itinerant hillbilly singer "Lonesome" Rhodes, overdoses on political power and runs amok through the American consciousness. Though criticized in its time for its often over-the-top pacing and imagery, "A Face in the Crowd" has since achieved cult status as a satiric cautionary tale.

But perhaps the two films most often associated with Kazan are "East of Eden" and "On the Waterfront," two seminal works of the 1950s, each featuring Method actors and memorable plots. Though both films are widely regarded as classics, they actually received mixed reviews on their first runs. Bosley Crowther, for instance, regarded "East of Eden" as a work full of "energy and intensity but little clarity and emotion. It is like a great, green iceberg," Crowther concluded in his *New York Times* review, "mammoth and imposing but very cold." And Sarris, in a *Film Culture* piece, said the work was "the deepest film Kazan has ever made and, in many respects, the best," though he also warns that the movie "has serious structural flaws. . . . Puzzling shifts in feeling in the main characters are unexplained."

"On the Waterfront," a tale of corruption and conscience, was named best picture of 1955 by the motion picture Academy. According to Pauline Kael in her book *I Lost It at the Movies,* "The subject matter of *On the Waterfront* is alienation at the lowest social level." Protagonist Terry Malloy, played by Marlon Brando, is a dockside stevedore who uncovers union corruption, then agonizes over the decision whether or not to expose the wrongdoers. A "political allegory cast in the form of a morality play," as Peter Biskind describes it in *Film Quarterly,* "On the Waterfront" presents a quandary "in which informing on criminal associates is the only honorable course of action for a just man. The injunction against informing on friends and colleagues is axiomatic in most societies where the state does not exercise overwhelming moral authority, but the film's dialogue repeatedly defines squealing not as an absolute but a relative matter. It depends on where you stand."

Lindsay Anderson, in a *Sight and Sound* review, finds grounds for contention in "On the Waterfront." It "may be objected," he writes, "that the makers of [this film] have purposely chosen to dramatise the problem [of corruption] through one particular case: the moral awakening of Terry Malloy. There is nothing to be said against such an approach, so long as its limits are clearly defined. The vital question then arises: what exactly does Terry awake to?" Anderson goes on to state that "On the Waterfront" is "essentially an extremely artful conjuring trick; underneath its brilliant technical surface, essential conclusions are evaded and replaced by a personal drama whose implications are entirely different." Such mixed feelings about the movie did not prevent "On the Waterfront" from gaining the reputation as one of the most important American movies ever made. In the words of *New York Times* critic A. H. Weiler, "Despite its happy ending, its preachments and a somewhat slick approach to some of the facets of dockside strife and tribulations, 'On the Waterfront' is moviemaking of a rare and high order."

With all his reputation as a social critic of the left, it must have been a surprise to many of Kazan's followers when the "Proletariat Thunderbolt" joined Schulberg in testifying before the House Un-American Activities Committee during the Communist "witchhunt" era of the early 1950s. Kazan provided some answers in his 1988 autobiography, *A Life*. In these pages the author tells of conflict with the Group Theatre and its Communist Party members. Kazan "had resisted an attempt by V. J. Jerome, the party's cultural commissar, to dictate an artistic line for the company; when pressure was applied, he had handed in his party card," says Bruce Cook in a *Washington Post Book World* review of *A Life*. Schulberg sided with Kazan. At that time, the recriminations against Kazan (and, indeed, any HUAC informant) were tantamount to professional suicide. The director, however, "never surrendered his social zeal," as Schulberg wrote in an *American Film* article on Kazan. "The identification with the oppressed that brought him into the Communist Party during the depths of the Depression was to stay with him all his life, and would inspire and inform much of his best work."

To this day, Kazan has publicly stated that he never regretted his political actions. "If I had my life to live over," he says in an interview with Alvin P. Sanoff published in *U.S. News and World Report*, "I wouldn't do anything differently. I did exactly what I wanted. It doesn't bother me that I testified . . . and provided [the HUAC] with names. New York intellectuals who had not been in the Communist Party, who only had been to a meeting or two, had no goddamn business making judgments of the actions of people who had been in the party, as I had. How can you say anything unless you've been there?" And yet, as a passage from his autobiography attests, Kazan indeed has let his testimony affect his life. "No one who did what I did, whatever his reasons, came out of it unchanged," he writes in *A Life*. "Here I am, thirty-five years later, still worrying over it."

Another aspect of *A Life* that caught critics' attention was the author's uninhibited testimony to his private love life. He describes details of his three marriages and numerous liaisons with a zeal that surprised some. "No serious writer has made such free use of the now widely accepted (even expected) tell-all confessional mode in an autobiography," remarks Cook. "It's not simply a matter of kiss-and-tell, but rather of spilling everything. He has fed off women—love, sex—drawing nourishment for his ego and art, regretting only the inconvenient duplicity made necessary by his marriages." In a *New York Review of Books* piece on the autobiography, David Denby sees Kazan's work this way: "Absurdly garrulous, and often coarse to the point of moral unconsciousness, [the author] tells so much—airing other people's critical opinions of his behavior as well as his own self-explanations and doubts—that he almost asks us to catch him fibbing, evading. He may be an egotist, but he is not vain, and his autobiography, for all its loutish demand on our patience, is also a soulful portrait of a man flailing about in a thicket of desire and guilt. Admitting his weaknesses and miseries, Kazan can be touching—a man longing to be a hero but uneasily aware that he may be a clown."

"The last 100 pages or so [of *A Life*] are descriptions of other people's deaths," notes *Los Angeles Times Book Review* critic Richard Eder, adding that Kazan writes as someone "obsessed with the details, he cannot seem to stop; as if stopping meant dying. The resilience that gave energy to the darker passages of the memoir disappears; Kazan's turbulent stream sinks into a morass." In the opinion of Arthur Schlesinger, Jr., in a *New York Times Book Review* article, Kazan ultimately manages "to take of the mask of affability, . . . not to deny his violent feelings but to respect them. He may overdo his claims of a lifelong silence in the face of intolerable provocation. His own narrative suggests a sufficient capacity for anger throughout his life. Nor does one get the impression that [the author] has entered into tranquillity at last. Self-revelation does not necessarily equal self-knowledge."

BIOGRAPHICAL/CRITICAL SOURCES:

BOOKS

Contemporary Literary Criticism, Gale, Volume 6, 1976, Volume 16, 1981.
Guernsey, Otis L., Jr., editor, *Broadway Song and Story: Playwrights/Lyricists/Composers Discuss Their Hits,* Dodd, Mead, 1986.
Jones, D. R., *Great Directors at Work,* University of California Press, 1986.
Kael, Pauline, *I Lost It at the Movies,* Little, Brown, 1965.
Kazan, Elia, *A Life,* Knopf, 1988.
Kazan, Elia, *America, America,* Stein & Day, 1962, reprinted, 1984.
Kazan Reader, Stein & Day, 1977.
Michaels, L., *Elia Kazan,* G. K. Hall, 1985.
Shots in the Dark: A Collection of Reviewers' Opinions of Some of the Leading Films Released between January 1949 and February 1951, Allen Wingate Ltd., 1951.
Truffaut, Francois, *The Films in My Life,* Simon & Schuster, 1978.

PERIODICALS

American Film, July/August, 1988.
Chicago Tribune, April 24, 1988.
Chicago Tribune Book World, April 24, 1988.
Film Comment, summer, 1972, May/June, 1988.
Film Culture, May-June, 1955, Volume 3, number 1, 1957.
Film Quarterly, fall, 1975.
Los Angeles Times, March 9, 1987.
Los Angeles Times Book Review, April 10, 1988.
New York Review of Books, May, 1988.
New York Times, July 29, 1954, March 10, 1955, July 14, 1982, April 28, 1988.
New York Times Book Review, March 5, 1982, May 1, 1988, May 3, 1988.
Sight and Sound, July-September, 1953, December, 1954, January-March 1955, summer, 1955.
Times Literary Supplement, July 15, 1988.
U.S. News and World Report, June 6, 1988.
Village Voice, May 17, 1988.

Washington Post Book World, May 8, 1988.

—*Sketch by Susan Salter*

*   *   *

KEEGAN, Marcia 1943-

PERSONAL: Born May 23, 1943, in Tulsa, Okla.; daughter of Otis Claire and Mary Elizabeth (Collar) Keegan; married Harmon Houghton, 1975. *Education:* University of New Mexico, B.A., 1963.

ADDRESSES: Office—140 East 46th St., New York, N.Y. 10017.

CAREER: Albuquerque Journal, Albuquerque, N.M., editor and photographer, 1961-65; free-lance writer and photographer, 1965—.

MEMBER: American Society of Magazine Photographers.

AWARDS, HONORS: New Mexico Press Award, 1963.

WRITINGS:

(Illustrator) Richard Margolis, *Only the Moon and Me,* Lippincott, 1968.
(And photographer) *The Taos Indians and Their Sacred Blue Lake,* Messner, 1971.
(And photographer) *Mother Earth, Father Sky: Ancient Chants by Pueblo and Navaho Indians of the Southwest,* Grossman, 1974.
(And photographer) *We Can Still Hear Them Clapping,* Avon, 1975.
Pueblo and Navajo Cookery, Morgan & Morgan, 1978.
Oklahoma, Abbeville, 1979.
(Editor and photographer) *Teachings of His Holiness the Dalai Lama,* Clear Light, 1981.
(Photographer) Jamake Highwater, *Moonsong Lullaby,* Lothrop, 1981.
New Mexico, Skyline Press, 1984.

*   *   *

KENNEDY, Marilyn Moats 1943-

PERSONAL: Born April 15, 1943, in Kansas City, KS; daughter of Orin L. (a lawyer) and Georgia (a secretary; maiden name, Jeffries) Moats; married Daniel Joseph Kennedy, Jr. (a banker), June 3, 1967; children: Anne Evelyn. *Education:* Attended Baker University, 1961-62; Northwestern University, B.S.J., 1965, M.S.J., 1966. *Politics:* Republican. *Religion:* Presbyterian.

ADDRESSES: Home—714 Sheridan Rd., Wilmette, IL 60091. *Office*—1153 Wilmette Ave., Wilmette, IL 60091. *Agent*—Jane Jordan Browne Multimedia Product Development, Inc., 410 South Michigan Ave., Room 828, Chicago, IL.

CAREER: DePaul University, Chicago, IL, assistant professor of journalism and director of student publications, 1966-77, assistant dean of students, 1969-76, associate dean of students, 1976-77; Career Strategies (consultants), founder, 1975, managing partner and consultant in career planning and management, 1977—.

MEMBER: Women in Management (president of North Shore chapter, 1978-79; national secretary, 1981; national first vice-president, 1982), Chicago Headline Club (president, 1976-77), Chicago Women in Communications (president, 1980).

WRITINGS:

Office Politics: Seizing Power, Wielding Clout, Follett, 1980.

Career Knockouts: How to Battle Back, Follett, 1980.
Salary Strategies: Everything You Need to Know to Get the Salary You Want, Rawson, Wade, 1982.
Powerbase: How to Build It, How to Keep It, Macmillan, 1984.
Office Warfare: Getting Ahead in the Aggressive 80's, Macmillan, 1985.
Glamour Guide to Office Smarts, Fawcett Ballantine, 1986.

Also author of monthly newsletter on career planning, *Kennedy's Career Strategist,* 1986—. Author of monthly column "Job Strategies," published in *Glamour.* Contributor of articles to periodicals, including *Mademoiselle, Graduating Engineer, Self,* and *Savvy.*

SIDELIGHTS: While researching material for *Office Politics: Seizing Power, Wielding Clout,* Marilyn Moats Kennedy interviewed 1,000 people who had been fired from their jobs, discovering that only twenty-four percent were dismissed for incompetence, whereas conflicts with employers and co-workers accounted for most other firings. Her advice for preventing such conflict situations includes tips on developing skills in office politics and practicing "personal distancing" from the workplace in order to be better able to assess the situation from an objective stance. "She talks concretely—and not for women only—about how to assess what's going on within the organization, how to develop informal information networks, and cope with unforeseen change," Susan McHenry wrote in *Ms.*

On another book Kennedy wrote on the topic of office behavior and politics, *Office Warfare: Getting Ahead in the Aggressive 80's,* a reviewer for the *New York Times* stated that Kennedy's book "offers strategies for not only surviving but triumphing in what she calls the 'Aggressive 80's.'. . . The book tells how to recognize the signs of impending battle, how to stake out and defend one's turf—even how to accept defeat in order to live to fight another day."

Kennedy told *CA:* "I have been intensely interested in office politics for years. My consulting fits very nicely with writing because I usually consult with companies about employee-related problems and/or employees having work-related problems. This provides an unending source of ideas, information, and problems to write about. I have always been strongly research oriented and find focus group research especially valuable in trying to find out people's work-related attitudes.

"I think I'd find it very difficult to write as much as I do about careers and job-related problems if I weren't 'on the stump' so much. What audiences ask about is exactly what career articles will deal with six to eighteen months from now. By hearing the questions people ask and watching their work-related concerns change, I have an enormous advantage in timing my writing to appear when a trend is on the up side. Individual career counseling also helps direct my research.

"Office political problems are especially difficult to write about unless one is constantly in contact with people who have problems. If you would try to make up a problem you thought most people had, you'd find out most didn't. This is one kind of writing in which imagination doesn't enter into writing until the problem has been verified."

BIOGRAPHICAL/CRITICAL SOURCES:

PERIODICALS

Ms., November, 1980.
New York Times, April 28, 1985.

KERCKHOFF, Alan C(hester) 1924-

PERSONAL: Born March 14, 1924, in Lakewood, OH; son of August E. (a purchasing agent) and Mary Helen (Heacock) Kerckhoff; married Sylvia Stansbury, June 11, 1949; children: Steven, Sharon Connery. *Education:* Oberlin College, A.B., 1949; attended Kent State University, 1942-43; University of Wisconsin—Madison, M.A., 1951, Ph.D., 1953.

ADDRESSES: Home—1511 Pinecrest Rd., Durham, NC 27705. *Office*—Department of Sociology, 268 Sociology-Psychology, Duke University, Durham, NC 27706.

CAREER: Vanderbilt University, Nashville, TN, assistant professor of sociology, 1953-55; Air Force Personnel and Training Research Center, San Antonio, TX, civilian assistant to director of Office of Social Science Programs, 1955-57; Vanderbilt University, assistant professor of sociology, 1957-58; Duke University, Durham, NC, associate professor, 1958-64, professor of sociology, 1964—, chairman of department, 1972-76, 1981-86, director of graduate studies, 1964-67. Visiting scholar, University of Stockholm, 1979, and Nuffield College, Oxford, 1980. Member of advisory panel of Social Science Division of National Science Foundation, 1964-66; National Institutes of Health, member of developmental behavioral sciences study section, 1976-78, and chairman of human development study section, 1978-80. *Military service:* U.S. Navy, 1943-46.

MEMBER: International Sociological Association, American Sociological Association, Sociological Research Association, Southern Sociological Society (member of executive committee, 1961-63 and 1974-79; president, 1975-76), Phi Beta Kappa.

AWARDS, HONORS: Senior postdoctoral fellow, National Science Foundation, at Stanford University, 1965-66, and University of London, 1971-72; grants from Spencer Foundation, 1973, U.S. Department of Labor, 1976 and 1977, National Science Foundation, 1979, 1982, 1985, and 1987, and National Center for Education Statistics, 1982.

WRITINGS:

(With Kurt W. Back) *The June Bug: A Study of Hysterical Contagion,* Appleton-Century-Crofts, 1968.
Socialization and Social Class, Prentice-Hall, 1972.
Ambition and Attainment: A Study of Four Samples of American Boys (monograph), American Sociological Association, 1974.
Getting Started: Entering the Adult World in Great Britain, Westview, 1990.

CONTRIBUTOR

Julius Gould and William L. Kolb, editors, *A Dictionary of the Social Sciences,* Free Press, 1964.
Ethel Shanas and Gordon Streib, editors, *The Family, Intergenerational Relationships, and Social Structure,* Prentice-Hall, 1965.
Ida Harper Simpson and John C. McKinney, editors, *Social Aspects of Aging,* Duke University Press, 1966.
Tamotsu Shibutani, editor, *Human Nature and Collective Behavior: Papers in Honor of Herbert Blumer,* Prentice-Hall, 1970.
M. Sussman and B. Cogswell, editors, *Cross-National Family Research,* E. J. Brill, 1972.
Ted L. Huston, editor, *Foundations of Interpersonal Attraction,* Academic Press (New York City), 1974.
William H. Sewell, Robert M. Hauser, and David L. Featherman, editors, *Schooling and Achievement in American Society,* Academic Press (New York City), 1976.

Benjamin B. Wolman, editor, *International Encyclopedia of Neurology, Psychiatry, Psychoanalysis and Psychology,* Van Nostrand, 1977.
M. J. Colligan, J. W. Pennebacker, and L. R. Murphy, editors, *Mass Psychogenic Illness: A Social Psychological Analysis,* Lawrence Erlbaum, 1982.
Richard F. Tomasson, editor, *Comparative Social Research,* Volume 5, JAI Press, 1982.
John G. Richardson, editor, *Handbook of Theory and Research in the Sociology of Education,* Greenwood Press, 1986.
Abraham Yogev, editor, *Schooling and Status Attainment: Social Origins and Institutional Determinants,* Volume 2: *International Perspectives on Education and Society,* JAI Press, 1990.
Arne L. Kalleberg, editor, *Research in Social Stratification and Mobility,* Volume 9, JAI Press, 1990.

OTHER

Also editor and contributor, *Research in Sociology of Education and Socialization: An Annual Compilation of Research,* 1977-86. Contributor to periodicals, including *Journal of Gerontology, Sociometry, Journal of Marriage and the Family, Contemporary Psychology, Public Opinion Quarterly, Sociological Inquiry,* and *American Journal of Sociology.* Editor, *Sociology of Education,* 1978-81; associate editor, *American Sociological Review,* 1976-78, and *Contemporary Sociology,* 1986-88; advisory editor, *Social Forces,* 1969-71, and *Sociological Quarterly,* 1982-86.

WORK IN PROGRESS: A chapter in a book.

SIDELIGHTS: Alan C. Kerckhoff told *CA:* "All of my writing and editing is related to reporting or summarizing sociological and social psychological research. The core topics of most of my work are the processes of social influence that effect the positioning of individuals in society; the effects of family influences and school experiences are of primary interest.

"The one exception is *The June Bug,* a report on an epidemic of what purported to be insect bites in a clothing manufacturing plant. The analysis noted the importance of stress, personal qualities, and social relations in the generation and spread of physical symptoms that were interpreted as having been caused by a poisonous insect."

*   *   *

KESSLER-HARRIS, Alice 1941-

PERSONAL: Born June 2, 1941, in Leicester, England; daughter of Zoltan and Ilona (Elefant) Kessler; married Jay Evans Harris, August 28, 1960 (divorced, 1974); married Bertram Silverman, January 22, 1982; children: (first marriage) Ilona Kay. *Education:* Goucher College, B.A. (cum laude), 1961; Rutgers University, M.A., 1963, Ph.D., 1968.

ADDRESSES: Home—141 East 88th St., New York, NY 10128. *Office*—Department of History, Rutgers University, New Brunswick, NJ 08903.

CAREER: Baltimore City Public Schools, Baltimore, MD, teacher, 1961-66; assistant instructor, Douglass College, 1964-65; Hofstra University, Hempstead, NY, assistant professor of history, 1968-73; Sarah Lawrence College, Bronxville, NY, professor of history and women's studies and director of Women's Studies Program, 1974-76; Hofstra University, associate professor, 1977-81, professor of history, 1981-88, co-director of Center for the Study of Work and Leisure, 1976-88; Temple University, Philadelphia, PA, professor of history,

1988-90; Rutgers University, New Brunswick, NJ, professor of history and director of Women's Studies Program, 1990—. Visiting professor, State University of New York at Binghamton, 1985; visiting senior lecturer, University of Warwick, 1979-80. Columbia University Seminar on Women in Society, member, 1975—, chair, 1983-84; member, Columbia University Seminar in American Civilization, 1971—; member of nominating jury, Pulitzer Prize in History, 1987. Has given numerous papers and presentations. Consultant to numerous organizations and projects.

MEMBER: American Association of University Professors (treasurer of Hofstra University chapter, 1969-71), American Historical Association (committee on women historians, member, 1983-86, chair, 1984-86; member of nominating committee, 1988-90), Organization of American Historians (member of program committee, 1982; member of lectureship program, 1987—), Women in the Historical Profession (member of coordinating committee), American Studies Association (member of program committee, 1972-75; member of executive council, 1973-78; International Committee, member, 1981-83, 1988-92, chair, 1982-83; member of nominating committee, 1984-86), American Civil Liberties Union (member of academic freedom committee, 1971-77), American Council of Learned Societies (reader in fellowship program, 1988), Berkshire Conference of Women Historians (member of program committee, 1972-76, 1982-84, 1988-90; member of prize committee, 1977-78), New York State Council for the Humanities (member of Speakers' Bureau, 1982—).

AWARDS, HONORS: Danforth Foundation Auxiliary grant, 1962-63; Louis M. Rabinowitz Foundation grant, 1973-74; American Philosophical Society grant, 1973-74; National Endowment for the Humanities fellowship, 1976-77, 1985-86; Radcliffe Institute fellowship, 1977; Philip Taft Prize for the best book in labor history, 1982, for *Out to Work: A History of Wage-Earning Women in the U.S.;* Dean's Award for Excellence, Hofstra University, 1983; University Faculty Development and Research grant, 1983-84, 1984-85; American Council of Learned Societies travel grant, 1986; Rockefeller Foundation fellowship, 1988-89; John Simon Guggenheim Memorial Foundation fellowship, 1989-90.

WRITINGS:

(Editor with Blanche Cook and Ronald Radosh) *Past Imperfect: Alternative Essays in American History,* Random House, 1972.

(Author of introduction) William Ladd, *On the Duty of Females to Promote the Cause of Peace,* Garland Publishing, 1972.

(Author of introduction) George Cone Beckwith, *The Peace Manual; or, War and Its Remedies,* Garland Publishing, 1972.

(Author of introduction) Theodore Parker, *Sermon of War,* Garland Publishing, 1973.

(Author of introduction) Ronald Grele, editor, *Envelopes of Sound: Six Practitioners Discuss the Theory and Method of Oral History,* Precedent Publishing, 1975, revised edition, 1985.

(Author of introduction) Anzia Yezierska, *Bread Givers,* Braziller, 1975.

(Editor) Yezierska, *The Open Cage: An Anzia Yezierska Collection,* Persea Books, 1979.

Women Have Always Worked, Feminist Press and McGraw, 1980.

Out to Work: A History of Wage-Earning Women in the U.S., Oxford University Press, 1982.

(Author of introduction with others) Joan Kelly, *Women, History and Theory,* University of Chicago Press, 1984.

(Editor with Judith Friedlander, Cook, and Carroll Smith-Rosenberg) *Women in Culture and Politics: A Century of Change,* Indiana University Press, 1986.

(Editor with William McBrien) *Faith of a Woman Writer: Essays in Twentieth-Century Literature,* Greenwood Press, 1988.

(Editor with Carroll Moody) *Perspectives on American Labor History: Conceptual Dilemmas and the Problem of Synthesis,* Northern Illinois University Press, 1989.

A Woman's Wage: Historical Meanings and Social Consequences, [Kentucky], 1990.

CONTRIBUTOR

Ernest Hohlnitz, editors, *The Study of American History,* Volume 2, Dushkin, 1974.

Cooperative History of the United States, Dushkin, 1974.

Richard Edwards and others, editors, *Labor Market Segmentation,* Lexington Books, 1975.

Berenice Carroll, editor, *Liberating Women's History: Theoretical and Critical Essays,* University of Illinois Press, 1976.

Milton Cantor and Bruce Laurie, editors, *Class, Sex and the Woman Worker,* Greenwood Press, 1977.

(With Virginia Yans-McLaughlin) Thomas Sowell, editor, *American Ethnic Groups,* Urban Institute, 1978.

John Hague, editor, *American Character and Culture,* revised edition, Greenwood Press, 1979.

Nancy Cott and Elizabeth Pleck, editors, *A Heritage of Her Own,* Simon & Schuster, 1979.

Barbara Sicherman, editor, *Notable American Women,* supplement, Harvard University Press, 1979.

Wendy Chavkin, editor, *Report from the Front Lines,* Monthly Review Press, 1984.

Ruth Milkman, editor, *Women, Work and Protest: A Century of Women's Labor History,* Routledge & Kegan Paul, 1985.

Laurie Larwood and others, editors, *Woman and Work: An Annual Review,* Sage Publications, 1985.

Joyce Kornbluh and Mary Frederickson, editors, *Sisters and Solidarity: Workers Education for Women, 1914-1980,* Temple University Press, 1985.

(With Karen Brodkin Sacks) Lourdes Beneria and Catharine R. Stimpson, *Women, Households and the Economy,* Rutgers University Press, 1987.

Melvyn Dubovsky and Warren Van Tine, *Labor Leaders in America,* University of Illinois Press, 1987.

Karen Hansen and Ilene Philipson, editors, *Class and the Feminist Imagination,* Temple University Press, 1989.

OTHER

Editor with David Brody, David Montgomery, and Sean Wilentz, "Working Class in American History" series, University of Illinois Press, 1985—. Contributor to numerous periodicals, including *Science and Society, Signs, Ms., Reviews in American History, Women's Review of Books, Nation,* and *New York Times Book Review.* Member of editorial board, *Labor History,* 1983-88, *Journal of American History,* 1985-88, *Feminist Studies, Women and History,* and *Women and Work.*

WORK IN PROGRESS: Gender Ideology in Social Policy: 1920-1980, for Oxford University Press; *Gender and Culture: Reviewing the Historical Paradigm,* for University of North Carolina Press; contributing a chapter to N. S. Dye and Noralee Frankel, editors, *Women in the Progressive Period.*

KILLOUGH, (Karen) Lee 1942-
(Sarah Hood)

PERSONAL: Born May 5, 1942, in Syracuse, KS; daughter of Rex Ledonald and Esther Margaret (Reed) Schwein; married Howard Patrick Killough, Jr. (an attorney and business manager), August 27, 1966. *Education:* Attended Fort Hayes State College, 1960-62, and Hadley Memorial Hospital School of Radiologic Technology, 1962-64. *Politics:* Independent. *Religion:* Independent.

ADDRESSES: Home—P.O. Box 422, Manhattan, KS 66502. *Office*—Kansas State University Veterinary Medical Teaching Hospital, Manhattan, KS 66506.

CAREER: St. Joseph Hospital, Concordia, KS, radiologic technician, 1964-65; St. Mary Hospital, Manhattan, KS, radiologic technician, 1965-67; Morris Cafritz Memorial Hospital, Washington, DC, radiologic technician, 1968-69; St. Mary Hospital, radiologic technician, 1969-71; Kansas State University, Veterinary Hospital, Manhattan, radiologic technician, 1971—. Member of advisory council for Kansas Center for the Book, 1988—.

MEMBER: World Science Fiction, Science Fiction Writers of America, Mystery Writers of America, Sisters in Crime, Novelists, Inc.

AWARDS, HONORS: Hugo Award nominee, 1985, for short story "Symphony for a Lost Traveler."

WRITINGS:

A Voice out of Ramah (science fiction novel), Del Rey, 1979.
The Doppelganger Gambit (science fiction novel), Del Rey, 1979.
The Monitor, the Miners, and the Shree (science fiction adventure novel), Del Rey, 1980.
Deadly Silents (science fiction novel), Del Rey, 1981.
Aventine (short stories), Del Rey, 1982.
Liberty's World, DAW Books, 1985.
Spider Play (science fiction mystery), Popular Library, 1986.
Blood Hunt (vampire novel), Tor Books, 1987.
The Leopard's Daughter (fantasy novel), Popular Library, 1987.
Bloodlinks (vampire novel), Tor Books, 1988.
Dragon's Teeth (science fiction mystery), Popular Library, 1990.

Contributor to several anthologies, including *The Best from Fantasy and Science Fiction,* edited by Edward Ferman, Mercury Press, 1980; *1981 World's Best SF,* edited by Donald A. Wollheim, DAW Books, 1981. Also contributor, sometimes under pseudonyms, of articles to technical journals and stories to magazines, including *Sol Plus* and *American Girl.*

WORK IN PROGRESS: Armageddon Summer, a science fiction mystery novel.

SIDELIGHTS: Lee Killough told *CA:* "I write science fiction. Although more difficult than mainstream fiction, for science fiction requires me to build a new world and explain it to the reader in each book, I consider that science fiction offers me more artistic scope, more possibilities, than mainstream fiction. Also, I believe science fiction can serve a vital function in today's world by exploring future possibilities and helping condition readers for change.

"Mystery themes keep appearing in what I write. I became hooked on mysteries and science fiction in junior high school, and I suppose I've never outgrown the love of either. Fortunately, I don't have to choose between the two. The genres combine well and even enhance each other, science fiction expanding what is possible in the mystery.

"I find myself writing two kinds of stories. Most of my short fiction is psychological or surrealistic, bordering on fantasy. For my novels, however, I work out extrapolations of today's softer sciences: sociology, anthropology, psychology.

"I take some pains to make the novels as realistic as I can, but without being too pessimistic. In spite of a somewhat cynical view of humanity as a whole, I tend to have faith in its individual members and believe my general outlook is optimistic. If I didn't believe there was a future for Man, I don't believe I could write science fiction. But I do believe that some of Mankind will survive, perhaps be able to deal with the destructiveness and greed in our nature. I embrace science fiction as a delightful, hopeful genre and make full use of its open-end anything-is-possible outlook to play with ideas about the future and alternate realities."

*   *   *

KING, John N. 1945-

PERSONAL: Born February 2, 1945, in New York, NY; son of Luther (a minister) and Alba (an educator; maiden name, Iregui) King. *Education:* Randolph-Macon College, B.A., 1965; University of Chicago, M.A., 1966, Ph.D., 1973.

ADDRESSES: Home—1811 Coventry Rd., Upper Arlington, OH 43212. *Office*—Department of English, Ohio State University, 164 West 17th Ave., Columbus, OH 43210.

CAREER: Abdullahi Bayero University, Kano, Nigeria, lecturer in English, 1967-69; Bates College, Lewiston, ME, 1971-1989, began as instructor, became professor of English; Ohio State University, Columbus, professor of English, 1989—. Fellow of Southeastern Institute of Medieval and Renaissance Studies, 1976; visiting lecturer at Oxford University, 1978-79; visiting fellow at Brown University, 1981-82; visiting scholar at University of California, Los Angeles, Center for Medieval and Renaissance Studies, 1984; NEH senior fellow at the Huntington Library, 1984; NEH senior resident fellow at the Folger Shakespeare Library, 1986-87.

MEMBER: Modern Language Association, Renaissance Society of America, Milton Society, Spenser Society.

AWARDS, HONORS: Fellowships from Newberry Library, 1981, National Endowment for the Humanities, 1981-82, American Council of Learned Societies, 1983, American Philosophical Society, 1983, and Huntington Library, 1984.

WRITINGS:

English Reformation Literature: The Tudor Origins of The Protestant Tradition, Princeton University Press, 1982.
Tudor Royal Iconography: Literature and Art in the Age of Religious Crisis, Princeton University Press, 1989.
Spenser's Poetry and the Reformation Tradition, Princeton University Press, 1989.
(Editor with Peter Happe) *The Vocacyon of John Bale,* Renaissance English Text Society, 1990.

Contributor of articles to library and literature journals, including *Renaissance Quarterly, English Literary Renaissance, Modern Philology, Huntington Library Quarterly,* and *Studies in Literary Imagination.* Contributor to *Yearbook of English Studies,* 1978. Assistant editor, *British Studies Monitor,* 1979-82.

WORK IN PROGRESS: Preparing books and articles on the poetry of Edmund Spenser, and on Renaissance English literature and art.

SIDELIGHTS: John N. King told *CA* that his work "considers the interrelationship of literature, history, politics, and religion.

Much of it considers the iconographical component of sixteenth- and seventeenth-century literature and art."

English Reformation Literature: the Tudor Origins of the Protestant Tradition, for example, "offers the first assessment of the origins and early development of the literary and aesthetic movement that would eventually produce the great English authors Spenser and Milton." The author added: *"Spenser's Poetry and the Reformation Tradition* is the sequel to this study." A third and final volume "will consider literary developments between the time of Spenser and Milton."

BIOGRAPHICAL/CRITICAL SOURCES:

PERIODICALS

Times Literary Supplement, March 4, 1983.

*   *   *

KING-HELE, Desmond (George) 1927-

PERSONAL: Surname is pronounced King-Heeley; born November 3, 1927, in Seaford, England; son of Sydney George (in government service) and Bessie (Sayer) King-Hele; married Marie Therese Newman, August 31, 1954; children: Carole, Sonia. *Education:* Trinity College, Cambridge, B.A. (with first-class honors), 1948, M.A., 1952.

ADDRESSES: Home—3 Tor Rd., Farnham, Surrey, England. *Office*—Royal Society, 6 Carlton House Terrace, London SW1Y 5AG, England.

CAREER: Royal Aircraft Establishment, Farnborough, England, member of scientific research staff, 1948-88, researcher concentrating on space, 1955-88, deputy chief scientific officer in space department, 1968-88; Royal Society, London, England, editor of *Notes and Records of the Royal Society,* 1989—. Bakerian Lecturer, Royal Society, 1974; Halley Lecturer, Oxford University, 1974; Milne Lecturer, Oxford University, 1984.

MEMBER: International Academy of Astronautics, Royal Society (London; fellow), Royal Astronomical Society (fellow), Institute of Mathematics and Its Application (fellow).

AWARDS, HONORS: Bronze Medal, Royal Aeronautical Society, 1959, for work on the theory of satellite orbits; Eddington Gold Medal, Royal Astronomical Society, 1971; Charles Chree Medal and Prize, Institute of Physics, 1971; D.Sc., University of Aston, 1979; D.Univ., University of Surrey, 1986.

WRITINGS:

Shelley: The Man and the Poet, Yoseloff, 1960, 3rd edition, Macmillan, 1984 (published in England as *Shelley: His Thought and His Work,* Macmillan, 1960).
Satellites and Scientific Research, Routledge & Kegan Paul, 1960, 2nd revised edition, Dover, 1962.
Erasmus Darwin, Macmillan, 1963, Scribner, 1964.
Theory of Satellite Orbits in an Atmosphere, Butterworth & Co., 1964.
(Editor) *Space Research V,* North-Holland Publishing, 1965.
Observing Earth Satellites, Macmillan, 1966, revised edition, 1983.
(Editor and author of linking commentary) *The Essential Writings of Erasmus Darwin,* MacGibbon & Kee, 1968, Hillary, 1969.
The End of the Twentieth Century?, St. Martin's, 1970.
Poems and Trixies, Mitre Press, 1972.
Doctor of Revolution: The Life and Genius of Erasmus Darwin, Faber, 1977.

(Editor) *The Letters of Erasmus Darwin,* Cambridge University Press, 1981.
The RAE Table of Earth Satellites, Facts on File, 1981, 3rd edition, 1987.
Erasmus Darwin and the Romantic Poets, Macmillan, 1986.
Satellite Orbits in an Atmosphere, Blackie & Son, 1987.

Also author of *Animal Spirits* (poems), 1983; also author of technical reports for Royal Aircraft Establishment, including *Average Rotational Speed of the Upper Atmosphere from Changes in Satellite Orbits,* 1970, and *The Shape of the Earth,* 1970. Also contributor to *Proceedings of the Royal Society.* Contributor of more than 250 scientific and literary papers to periodicals, including *Nature, Keats-Shelley Memorial Bulletin,* and *Planetary and Space Science.*

WORK IN PROGRESS: A book reviewing thirty years' research on analysis of satellite orbits.

SIDELIGHTS: Desmond King-Hele told *CA* that his first book "was begun in the 1950s because I thought that previous books on Shelley failed to bring out his keenly analytical and scientific mind. Today, things are quite different: Shelley is well appreciated and, when revising my book for its third edition, I found that I had to review 85 new books about Shelley published between 1971 and 1982.

"From Shelley," continued King-Hele, "I was led to Erasmus Darwin, the eighteenth-century physician, who achieved more in a wider variety of subjects than anyone since, as a scientist, an inventor, a poet, and a doctor. He has proved endlessly fascinating."

In his books on Darwin, King-Hele explores the physician's foresight in predicting later developments in areas such as botany, physics, and psychology. In the *Times Literary Supplement,* David Porter outlines the breadth of Darwin's achievements as described by King-Hele: "In countless fields—meteorology, photosynthesis, rocket motors, sewage farms, steam turbines, and submarines, to name a few—Darwin foreshadowed scientific hypotheses indicated a century or more later, and anticipated futuristic technology." In a *Times Literary Supplement* review of *The Letters of Erasmus Darwin,* critic Redmond O'Hanlon lauds King-Hele's efforts in his varied books on Darwin, asserting that "Darwin's range of interests certainly seem to have inspired his editor toward feats of similar virtuosity. [He] has succeeded in his two biographies and now in this magnificent (and first) edition of the letters, in dragging . . . Darwin's large and various planet, highly supportive of all kinds of life, back into full view."

In addition to his works on Shelley and Darwin, King-Hele has also authored a number of technical volumes on satellites. Describing his motivation for writing, he states: "I have a bad memory, and a prime incentive for writing books is to record my ideas and findings on a subject before I forget them. That also means including notes and references—how else can I remember where I found the information? I rarely write articles (apart from scientific papers) because they are often mangled by editors, so that (a) I am ashamed at what appears, (b) it does not say what I want to say, and (c) I do not have the incentive to bring the writing to the standard I like. I enjoy writing poems and constantly strive for perfection of style—in vain, of course. But the striving is beneficial and provides an excellent target, carried over to the other books, which are usually revised many times before reaching their final form."

AVOCATIONAL INTERESTS: Tennis, cross-country running, "savouring the beauties of nature."

BIOGRAPHICAL/CRITICAL SOURCES:

PERIODICALS

Spectator, December 3, 1977.
Times Literary Supplement, December 24, 1971, December 30, 1977, March 19, 1982, September 19, 1986.

* * *

KIYOTA, Minoru 1923-

PERSONAL: Born October 12, 1923, in Seattle, WA; son of Ishisaku and Ine (Aoyagi) Kiyota; married Noriko Motoyoshi; children: Noreen, Eileen. *Education:* University of California, Berkeley, B.A., 1950; Tokyo University, M.A., Ph.D., 1963. *Politics:* "No preference." *Religion:* "No preference."

ADDRESSES: Home—2422 Chamberlain Ave., Madison, WI 53705. *Office*—Department of South Asian Studies, University of Wisconsin—Madison, Madison, WI 53706.

CAREER: University of Wisconsin—Madison, assistant professor, 1962-68, associate professor, 1968-78, professor of East Asian languages and literature and South Asian studies, 1978—, chairman of Buddhist studies program, 1978—.

WRITINGS:

(Editor) *Mahayana Buddhist Meditation: Theory and Practice,* University Press of Hawaii, 1978.
Shingon Buddhism: Theory and Practice, Buddhist Books International, 1978.
Tantric Concepts of Bodhicitta: A Buddhist Experiential Philosophy, Center of South Asian Studies, University of Wisconsin—Madison, 1982.
Gedatsukai: Its Theory and Practice; a Study of a Shinto-Buddhist Syncretic School in Contemporary Japan, Buddhist Books International, 1982.
(Editor) *Japanese Buddhism: Its Tradition, New Religions and Interaction with Christianity,* Buddhist Books International, 1987.
(Editor with Hideaki Kinoshita) *Japanese Martial Arts and American Sports: Cross-Cultural Perspectives on Means to Personal Growth,* Nihon University Press, 1990.
Nikkei hangyakuji: minken jurin to hakugai no kiroku (title means "A Japanese-American Rebel: A Record of Oppression and the Suppression of Civil Liberties"), Nihon Hanbaisha (Tokyo), 1990.

* * *

KOCH, Joanne 1940-
(Joanna Z. Adams)

PERSONAL: Born March 28, 1940, in Chicago, IL; daughter of Isadore (a pediatrician) and Ceil (Eidelsheim) Schapiro; married Lewis Koch (a writer), May 30, 1964; children: Lisa, Rachel, Joshua. *Education:* Cornell University, B.A., 1962; Columbia University, M.A., 1962. *Religion:* Jewish.

ADDRESSES: Home and office—343 Dodge Ave., Evanston, IL 60202. *Agent*—Timothy Seldes, Russell & Volkening, 551 Fifth Ave., New York, NY 10017.

CAREER: Writer and playwright. Roosevelt University, Chicago, IL, director of educational information, 1964-65; Educational Methods, Inc., Chicago, director of advertising, 1966-69; Newspaper Enterprise Association, New York City, columnist, 1972-76. Chairman, "Women in Film" screenwriter's program.

MEMBER: Society of Midland Authors (president, 1978-80), American Society of Journalists and Authors, Dramatists Guild, Alliance of Chicago Playwrights (director), Phi Beta Kappa, Phi Kappa Phi.

AWARDS, HONORS: Family Services Association Media award, 1973, for *Family Lib;* Harris Media Award, American Psychoanalysts Association, 1977; Illinois Art Council grant, 1983; National Angel Award, 1983, for *Today I Am a Person;* Emmy Award nomination, 1984, for *The Final Interview;* Evanston Cable Commission grant, 1984; Women in Theatre Award, Illinois Theatre Association, for *XX-XY;* Patron's award, Chicago Cultural Center, for *Haymarket: Footnote to a Bombing;* first prize, International Playwriting contest, Southern Illinois University and the Pischtor Foundation.

WRITINGS:

(With husband, Lewis Koch) *The Marriage Savers,* Coward, 1976.
(With Alison Clarke Stewart) *Children: Development through Adolescence,* Wiley, 1983.
(With L. Koch and Diane Levande) *Marriage and the Family,* Houghton, 1983.
(With Clarke Stewart and Susan Friedman) *Child Psychology,* Wiley, 1985.
(Under pseudonym Joanna Z. Adams) *Makeovers,* Pocket Books, 1987.
(Under pseudonym Joanna Z. Adams) *Rushes,* Pocket Books, 1988.

Also co-author of the "Families InTouch" Series, Parents InTouch Project, 1989.

PLAYS

XX-XY, produced as a reading at Northwestern University, Evanston, IL, 1981.
Haymarkey: Footnote to a Bombing, produced at Southern Illinois University, 1986.
Teeth, produced in Chicago, IL, 1988.
Nesting Dolls, produced in Chicago, IL, 1989.
(With S. Cohen) *Sophie, Totie and Belle,* produced in Albany, NY, 1990.

Also author of *Coming Out, The Mentor, Socks, Car Pool,* and *Danceland.*

FILM AND TELEVISION SCRIPTS

Today I Am a Person, WLS-TV (Chicago), 1982.
Baby, You're Okay, State of Illinois, 1983.
The Final Interview, WLS-TV, 1984.

Also author of *The Price of Daffodils, Mr. Macivor Steals a Million, The Team,* and *High Top Tower,* a children's television series.

WORK IN PROGRESS: Child Development, with Clarke Stewart and Susan Friedman, for Wiley.

SIDELIGHTS: Joanne Koch told *CA* that she and her husband Lewis created the six-book "Families InTouch" series "to help parents and children understand and cope with problems related to alcohol, drugs and sexually transmitted diseases including AIDS. These issues are best approached in a family context, with both parents and children having ample information. These books are . . . designed for families to be able to read the materials together. Over one million of the InTouch books are being used in homes and schools around the country. This has been one of the most gratifying projects we've ever had the pleasure of working on."

Koch has also written novels under the name Joanna Z. Adams. She once commented: "I write novels rich in relationships, rooted in a world of particular appeal—such as the film business of *Rushes* or the magazine business and plastic surgery profession of *Makeovers*. I like to follow characters who are struggling to overcome personal or professional conflicts."

BIOGRAPHICAL/CRITICAL SOURCES:

PERIODICALS

Library Journal, October 1, 1987.

* * *

KOENIG, Laird

PERSONAL: Born in Seattle, Wash.; son of Rowland Hill and Betty (Roeder) Koenig. *Education:* University of Washington, Seattle, B.A., 1950; additional study at University of California, Los Angeles, and New York University. *Politics:* "More or less liberal." *Religion:* None.

CAREER: Full-time writer. *Military service:* U.S. Army.

MEMBER: Authors Guild, Dramatists Guild, Writers Guild of America West, Beta Theta Pi.

WRITINGS:

NOVELS

(With Peter L. Dixon) *The Children Are Watching* (also see below), Ballantine, 1970.
The Little Girl Who Lives down the Lane (also see below), Coward, 1973.
The Neighbor (also see below), Avon, 1978.
Rockabye, St. Martin's, 1981.
The Disciple, Bantam, 1983.
The Sea Wife, Warner Books, 1986.

OTHER

(With William Redlin) "The Cat" (screenplay), Embassy, 1966.
"The Dozens" (play), produced on Broadway, 1968.
"California Wine" (comedy), produced on Broadway, 1969.
(With D. B. Petitclerc, W. Roberts, and L. Roman) "Red Sun" (screenplay; based on a story by Laird), National General, 1972.
"Turn On" (play), produced in London, 1974.
"The Little Girl Who Lives down the Lane" (screenplay; based on his novel of the same title), American International Pictures, 1977.
"The Week the War Was Over" (play), produced in Los Angeles, 1978.
"Bloodline" (screenplay; based on Sidney Sheldon's novel), Paramount, 1979.
(With Robin Moore) "Inchon" (screenplay), M-G-M/United Artists, 1982.

Also author of play, "The Rubaiyat of Sophie Klein"; writer of television plays and screenplays, including "The Children Are Watching" and "The Neighbor," both based on his novels, and "The Amityville Horror."

WORK IN PROGRESS: Stage and screen plays.

MEDIA ADAPTATIONS: United Artists released "Attention, the Kids Are Watching," based on Laird and Peter L. Dixon's novel *The Children Are Watching,* in 1978.

BIOGRAPHICAL/CRITICAL SOURCES:

PERIODICALS

New Yorker, March 22, 1969.
New York Times Book Review, February 24, 1974, December 20, 1981.*

* * *

KONSTAN, David 1940-

PERSONAL: Born November 1, 1940, in New York City; son of Harry (a store manager) and Edythe (a school board president; maiden name, Wahrman) Konstan; children: Eve Anna, Geoffrey. *Education:* Columbia University, B.A. (cum laude), 1961, M.A., 1963, Ph.D., 1967.

ADDRESSES: Home—92 Ivy St., Providence, RI 02906. *Office*—Department of Classics, Brown University, Providence, RI 02912.

CAREER: Hunter College of the City University of New York, New York City, lecturer in classics, 1964-65; Brooklyn College of the City University of New York, Brooklyn, NY, instructor in classics, 1965-67; Wesleyan University, Middletown, CT, assistant professor, 1967-72, associate professor, 1972-77, John A. Seney Professor of Greek, 1977-87, chairman of department of classics, 1975-77, 1978-80, director of humanities program, 1972-74; Brown University, Providence, RI, professor, 1987—, chairman of department of classics, 1989-92. American University in Cairo, visiting professor, 1981-83; University of California, Los Angeles, visiting professor, 1987.

MEMBER: American Philological Association, Classical Association of New England (Connecticut president, 1979), Phi Beta Kappa.

AWARDS, HONORS: National Endowment for the Humanities summer fellowship, 1978; Fulbright senior lecturer at Monash University, 1988; National Endowment for the Humanities fellowship, 1990; American Council of Learned Societies fellowship, 1991; award for outstanding academic book, *Choice,* 1989-90, for his translation of Simplicius' *On Aristotle's Physics Six.*

WRITINGS:

Some Aspects of Epicurean Psychology, E. J. Brill, 1973.
Catullus' Indictment of Rome: The Meaning of Catullus 64, Hakkert, 1977.
Roman Comedy, Cornell University Press, 1983.
(Editor) Menander, *Dyskolos,* Bryn Mawr Commentaries, 1983.
(Editor with Michael Roberts) *Apollonius of Tyre,* Bryn Mawr Commentaries, 1985.
(Translator) Simplicius, *On Aristotle's Physics Six,* Cornell University Press, 1989.

Contributor to books, including, *Essays in Ancient Greek Philosophy,* Volume 2, edited by John P. Anton and Anthony Preus, State University of New York Press, 1983; *What Is Art?,* edited by Hugh Curtler, Haven Publishing, 1983; *The Death of Art: Critical Essays in Philosophy,* edited by Berel Lang, Haven Publishing, 1984; *The Left Academy,* Volume 2, edited by Bertell Ollman and Edward Vernoff, Praeger, 1984; contributor of over one hundred articles and reviews to scholarly journals. Guest editor of *Arethusa,* 1980.

WORK IN PROGRESS: Greek Comedy, publication expected in 1991; *Love in the Ancient Novel,* 1992; editor, Xenophon's *Apology of Socrates* for Bryn Mawr Commentaries.

SIDELIGHTS: David Konstan told *CA:* "Among my original motives for pursuing the classics were these: that one could study a few texts lovingly, and that all disciplines, it seemed, lay open to one who commanded the languages. I have been fortunate: I have had the chance to spend months with a few dozen verses of Catullus, to meditate on why atoms fall and how slavery transformed the Roman world. I approach the ancient world as an anthropologist. True, I cannot ask direct questions of the Greeks and Romans, but they have left us a marvelous set of documents.

"The classical world was not all glory and grandeur. It marginalized women, foreigners, slaves, the dependant poor. Part of our task is [to] demystify the past, and understand it in a critical way."

* * *

KOTZ, Nick 1932-

PERSONAL: Born September 16, 1932, in San Antonio, Tex.; son of Jacob (a physician) and Tybe (Kallison) Kotz; married Mary Lynn Booth (a free-lance writer), August 12, 1960; children: Jack Mitchell. *Education:* Dartmouth College, A.B., 1955; attended London School of Economics, 1955-56.

ADDRESSES: Home—5508 Montgomery St., Chevy Chase, Md. 20015.

CAREER: Des Moines Register, Des Moines, Iowa, reporter, 1958-64, Washington correspondent, 1964-70; *Washington Post,* Washington, D.C., reporter, beginning 1970. Distinguished adjunct professor, American University School of Communications. *Military service:* U.S. Marine Corps Reserve, 1956-58; became first lieutenant.

MEMBER: National Press Club, Sigma Delta Chi.

AWARDS, HONORS: Raymond Clapper Awards, 1966, 1968; Pulitzer Prize for national reporting, 1968; the first Robert Kennedy Memorial Award in journalism, 1969; Olive Branch Award, Editors' Organizing Committee, 1989, for *Wild Blue Yonder: Money, Politics and the B-1 Bomber.*

WRITINGS:

Let Them Eat Promises: The Politics of Hunger in America, introduction by George S. McGovern, Prentice-Hall, 1969.
The Unions, Simon & Schuster, 1972.
(With wife, Mary Lynn Kotz) *A Passion for Equality: George A. Wiley and the Movement,* Norton, 1977.
Wild Blue Yonder: Money, Politics, and the B-1 Bomber, Pantheon, 1988.

Contributor to *Look, Harper's, Nation, Progressive, Washington Monthly,* and other publications.

SIDELIGHTS: In *Let Them Eat Promises: The Politics of Hunger,* Pulitzer Prize-winning journalist Nick Kotz "paints an appalling picture of political persiflage, bureaucratic ineptitude and moral obtuseness," states John Leonard of the *New York Times.* "His is investigative reportage of the highest order, telling us what we need to know" about how the government has allowed hunger to become widespread in the United States. As *Atlantic* contributor Edward Weeks observes, Kotz's "well-written, firmly documented, coolly indignant book is too disturbing and too factual to be brushed off as another troublemaker. It strikes at the most persistent mismanagement in our federal system." "There isn't an aspect of this 'dismal story' that Mr. Kotz neglects," remarks Leonard, and as a result "his conclusions are compelling."

Kotz conducts a similar investigation in *Wild Blue Yonder: Money, Politics, and the B-1 Bomber.* In this book, which *Washington Post Book World* contributor Arthur T. Hadley calls "well-researched and superbly documented," Kotz "describes the 20-year gestation of the B-1 bomber, from President Eisenhower's first 'no,' through endless crass political maneuvering, to President Reagan's final 'yes.' " "Apart from its scope and detail," writes Sheila Tobias in the *New York Times Book Review,* "the book's strength lies in the subtlety of its argument. By rooting the story of the B-1 in that of its predecessor," the critic continues, the author "gives himself three decades of bomber politics to discuss." And, as Harry G. Summers, Jr., explains in his *Los Angeles Times Book Review* critique, "Kotz found the fundamental flaw" of the B-1 program "in the very concept of strategic bombing itself." As a result, Summers notes, "in one sense, Kotz's 'Wild Blue Yonder' is a history of that campaign [for strategic bombing], a campaign that spanned 30 years and seven Presidents. But in a broader sense, it is an indictment of our entire process for the conception, design, production and deployment of those weapons systems upon which our national security and our survival itself depends." *Wild Blue Yonder,* concludes Tobias, "is not just another tale of waste, fraud and abuse. Nor does the author merely rail against the military-industrial complex. Mr. Kotz makes clear that bomber politics . . . is the result of a skew in our economy that has given one sector of the aerospace industry, in collaboration with its military partners, an unhealthy power."

BIOGRAPHICAL/CRITICAL SOURCES:

PERIODICALS

Atlantic, February, 1970.
Best Sellers, February 1, 1970.
Christian Science Monitor, July 21, 1988.
Los Angeles Times Book Review, April 17, 1988.
Nation, May 25, 1970.
New York Times, January 15, 1970.
New York Times Book Review, March 6, 1988.
Washington Post Book World, March 13, 1988.*

* * *

KOUSSER, J(oseph) Morgan 1943-

PERSONAL: Born October 7, 1943, in Lewisburg, TN; son of Joseph Maximillian and Alice (a teacher and television coordinator; maiden name, Morgan) Kousser; married Sally Ward, June 1, 1968; children: Rachel Meredith, Thaddeus Benjamin. *Education:* Princeton University, A.B. (summa cum laude), 1965; Yale University, M.Phil., 1968, Ph.D., 1971; Oxford University, M.A., 1984. *Politics:* "Left." *Religion:* "Puritan-Atheist." *Avocational interests:* Marathon running.

ADDRESSES: Home—1818 North Craig Ave., Altadena, CA 91001. *Office*—Department of Humanities and Social Sciences, California Institute of Technology, Pasadena, CA 91125.

CAREER: California Institute of Technology, Pasadena, instructor, 1969-71, assistant professor, 1971-74, associate professor, 1974-79, professor of history, 1979-80, professor of history and social science, 1980—. University of Michigan, visiting instructor, 1980; Harvard University, visiting professor, 1981-82; Oxford University, Harmsworth visiting professor, 1984-85.

MEMBER: American Historical Association, Organization of American Historians, Social Science History Association, Southern Historical Association, American Political Science Association, ACT, F.D.R. Democratic Club (Pasadena; past president), Phi Beta Kappa.

AWARDS, HONORS: Grants from National Endowment for the Humanities, 1974-75, 1981-83; Graves Foundation Award, 1976; fellowships from Woodrow Wilson Center, 1984-85, Howard Foundation, 1979-80, Guggenheim Foundation, 1984-85, and Haynes Foundation, 1989-90.

WRITINGS:

The Shaping of Southern Politics: Suffrage Restriction and the Establishment of the One-Party South, 1880-1910, Yale University Press, 1974.
(Editor with James M. McPherson) *Region, Race, and Reconstruction: Essays in Honor of C. Vann Woodward,* Oxford University Press, 1982.
Dead End: The Development of Nineteenth Century Litigation on Racial Discrimination in Schools, Oxford University Press, 1986.

Contributor to *Encyclopedia of Southern History, Encyclopedia of American Political History,* and *Encyclopedia of Southern Culture.* Contributor to periodicals and journals, including *Journal of Interdisciplinary History, Social Science History, Journal of Southern History, Reviews in American History, Historical Methods, American Journal of Political Science, Political Science Quarterly, Public Historian,* and *Los Angeles Times.*

WORK IN PROGRESS: Two collections of essays, titled *Toward "Total Political History" and Other Essays in the Philosophy and Methodology of History* and *"The Supremacy of Equal Rights": The Law and School Segregation in the Nineteenth Century.*

SIDELIGHTS: J. Morgan Kousser told *CA:* "My prime scholarly goal is to change the way history is done. Until about 20 years ago, historians lacked good methods for studying large numbers of people, as well as for systematically forming and attempting hypotheses. Since then, Quantitative Social Scientific History (QUASSH) has developed considerably, but most historians are still insufficiently trained in its techniques and theories to use it most efficiently. I hope through setting an example in my writings, through propagandizing and book reviewing, and through teaching to convince historians that QUASSH is the best way to determine what the past masses did.

"I've also testified as an expert witness in federal court cases on black voting rights, and before Congress regarding the 1982 renewal of the Voting Rights Act. History can be useful in the study of current policy, especially where, as in Southern voting rights, the past is very much present. Besides, it is delicious for a historian of disfranchisement to believe that he might be able to help overturn the fag-ends of a set of 1901 laws which disfranchised blacks in Alabama. If one cannot prevent the Trojan War from taking place, one can at least bury the dead properly."

*   *   *

KOVEL, Joel S. 1936-

PERSONAL: Born August 27, 1936, in Brooklyn, NY; son of Louis and Rose (Farber) Kovel; married Dee Dee Halleck; children: (previous marriage) Jonathan, Erin, Molly. *Education:* Yale University, B.S. (summa cum laude), 1957; Columbia University, M.D., 1961.

ADDRESSES: Home—Box 50, Willow, NY 12495. *Office*—Bard College, Annandale on Hudson, NY 12504.

CAREER: Bronx Municipal Hospital Center, Bronx, NY, intern in medical service, 1961-62; Yeshiva University, Albert Einstein College of Medicine, New York, NY, and Bronx Municipal Hospital Center, assistant resident, then resident in psychiatry, 1962-64, chief resident in psychiatry at both institutions, 1964-65; Yeshiva University, Albert Einstein College of Medicine, instructor, 1967-69, assistant professor, 1969-74, associate professor, 1974-79, professor of psychiatry, 1979-86; Bard College, Annandale on Hudson, NY, Alger Hiss Professor of Social Studies, 1988—. Psychoanalyst and psychiatrist in private practice, 1967-86. Visiting professor of anthropology, New School for Social Research, 1980-85; visiting professor, University of California, San Diego, 1986-87.

AWARDS, HONORS: Nomination for National Book Award in philosophy and religion, 1970, for *White Racism: A Psychohistory;* Guggenheim fellowship, 1987.

WRITINGS:

White Racism: A Psychohistory, Pantheon, 1970, 2nd edition, Columbia University Press, 1984.
(Contributor) Jean Strouse, editor, *Women in Analysis: Dialogues on Psychoanalytic Views of Femininity,* Grossman, 1974.
A Complete Guide to Therapy: From Psychoanalysis to Behavior Modification, Pantheon, 1976.
The Age of Desire: Case Histories of a Radical Psychoanalyst, Pantheon, 1981.
Against the State of Nuclear War, Pan Books, 1983, South End Press, 1984.
In Nicaragua, Free Association Books, 1988.
The Radical Spirit: Essays in Psychoanalysis and Society, Free Association Books, 1988.
History and Spirit, Beacon Press, 1990.

Contributor of articles and reviews to periodicals, including *Social Research, Social Policy, Telos, New York Times Book Review,* and *Psychoanalytic Review.*

WORK IN PROGRESS: The Anticommunist Society, for Basic Books.

SIDELIGHTS: "Psychoanalysts of the world, unite: put Joel Kovel back on the couch before he has you up against the wall," challenges Harvey Mindess in the *Los Angeles Times.* In *The Age of Desire: Case Histories of a Radical Psychoanalyst,* Kovel criticizes his profession, labeling the majority of its practitioners "certifiably out-and-out hacks." John Leonard explains in the *New York Times,* "When we feel so rotten that we can't function, psychoanalysis purports to be a form of help. It isn't, according to Joel Kovel, . . . nor is any other adjunct of the 'mental health' industry in the Western world. Why not? Because, says Dr. Kovel, 'bourgeois psychology' is in business to abet capitalism. . . . The object of most therapies is not to make us feel worthy, but to get us back to work."

Joel S. Kovel describes himself as a Marxist psychoanalyst, "and in a sense *The Age of Desire* is a book-length attempt to define that unlikely hybrid," notes Walter Kendrick in *Nation.* Finally, Kendrick concludes, "Kovel acknowledges that there can be no such thing as Marxist psychotherapy, but he maintains that there can be a therapy compatible with Marxism—'a transcendent therapy, one predicated on the movement toward universality.' "

Kovel supports his argument with partially fictionalized case histories; Seymour Kleinberg observes in the *Village Voice* that when Kovel is discussing "the people he has known so intimately, the book is alive." Kendrick similarly believes the histories "read like tales of real life: Curtis the investment banker, Sarah the spoiled Jewish princess, and Hector the Puerto Rican 'vigilante' are firmly placed in the contexts of race, family, and work, so that we seem to know them—though, as Kovel admits, it's impossible even after years of analysis for an analyst to 'know' his patient."

The fictional aspects of the book, however, bother some reviewers. While admitting there may be some professional validity in altering some of the actual details, Leonard claims "it injures my credulity and Dr. Kovel seems to enjoy it too much." Kleinberg, moreover, suggests that Kovel fictionalizes because "he wants his evidence to conform to his theories, so that one case can symbolize 'the family under capitalism,' and another can invite him to dwell for a bit on the economic and psychological history of women. . . . When he begins to theorize, the prose shifts, in a matter of sentences, into the oracular, thickening, bogging the reader down under the weight of the labor to be profound."

Benjamin DeMott concedes in *Psychology Today* that Kovel's generalizations and use of jargon weaken *The Age of Desire,* but ultimately maintains that each case history "lights up the interdependencies that [Kovel] claims his profession as a whole neglects—the linkups between the state of individual psyches and the terms of individual participation in history and the public world." Describing the book "as strong and flexible an argument on the side of the party of hope as I've heard in years from within a working professional elite," DeMott concludes that *The Age of Desire* "begins as a probe of the ills of a single sector of American professional life but emerges, before it's done, as a powerful address to a central problem of our time—how to preserve and nourish moral ambition in an immoral society. . . . Refusing to wrestle with [this book] would be an act of self-impoverishment."

BIOGRAPHICAL/CRITICAL SOURCES:

BOOKS

Kovel, Joel S., *The Age of Desire: Case Histories of a Radical Psychoanalyst,* Pantheon, 1981.

PERIODICALS

Los Angeles Times, March 19, 1982.
Nation, January 30, 1982.
New Leader, October 25, 1976.
New York Times, June 24, 1976, January 14, 1982.
New York Times Book Review, July 18, 1976.
Psychology Today, January, 1982.
Times Literary Supplement, July 15, 1977.
Village Voice, January 20-26, 1982.

*   *   *

KRIPPNER, Stanley (Curtis) 1932-

PERSONAL: Born October 4, 1932, in Edgerton, WI; son of Carroll Porter (a farmer) and Ruth (Volenberg) Krippner; married Lelie Harris, June 25, 1966; children: (stepchildren) Caron Harris, Robert Harris. *Education:* University of Wisconsin—Madison, B.S., 1954; Northwestern University, M.A., 1958, Ph.D., 1961. *Politics:* Independent. *Religion:* Presbyterian, Taoist. *Avocational interests:* Cinema, theater, jogging.

ADDRESSES: Home—79 Woodland Rd., Fairfax, CA 94930. *Office*—Saybrook Institute, 1772 Vallejo St., San Francisco, CA 94123.

CAREER: Speech therapist for city of Warren, IL, 1954-55, and for public schools of Richmond, VA, 1955-56; Kent State University, Kent, OH, director of Child Study Center, 1961-64; Maimonides Medical Center, Brooklyn, NY, director of dream laboratory, 1964-73; Saybrook Institute, San Francisco, CA, professor of psychology, 1973—. Director of Center for Consciousness Studies. Lecturer at universities and academies, including University of California, Los Angeles, 1968, and U.S.S.R. Academy of Pedagogical Sciences, 1971; adjunct professor at universities, including West Georgia College, 1976—; visiting professor at universities in the United States and South America. Member of board of directors, Academy of Religion and Psychical Research; trustee, National Foundation for Gifted and Creative Children; member of advisory boards of foundations, schools, and health centers, including Foundation for Mind Research, Center for Attitudinal Healing, National Research Institute for Self-Understanding, and Student Association for the Study of Hallucinogens; member of Menninger Foundation.

MEMBER: International Association for Psychotronic Research (vice-president, 1973-77), International Reading Association, International Society for General Semantics, Inter-American Psychological Association, National Society for the Study of Education, National Association for Gifted Children (vice-president, 1968-74), American Society for Clinical Hypnosis (fellow), American Psychological Association (fellow; division president, 1980-81), American Psychological Society (fellow), American Society for Psychical Research, American Association for the Advancement of Science, American Academy of Social and Political Science, American Educational Research Association, American Personnel and Guidance Association, American Psychosomatic Society, Association for Humanistic Psychology (president, 1974-75), Association for the Psychophysiological Study of Sleep, Biofeedback Research Society, Council for Exceptional Children, College Reading Association, Parapsychological Association (president, 1983), Psychologists for Social Action, Society for Clinical and Experimental Hypnosis, Society for the Scientific Study of Sex, Society for the Scientific Study of Religion, Albert Schweitzer Cultural Association (honorary vice-president), New York Speech and Hearing Association, New York Society of Clinical Psychologists.

AWARDS, HONORS: Service to Youth Award, Young Men's Christian Association, 1959; citations of merit, National Association for Gifted Children, 1972, and National Association for Creative Children and Adults, 1975; certificate of recognition, U.S. Office of the Gifted and Talented, 1976; Maurice Volker Award, 1980, for contributions to parapsychology; honorary doctorate, University for Humanistic Studies, 1982.

WRITINGS:

(With Montague Ullman) *Dream Studies and Telepathy* (monograph), Parapsychological Foundation, 1970.
Shamlet, Exposition, 1971.
(Editor with Daniel Rubin) *Galaxies of Life: The Human Aura in Acupuncture and Kirlian Photography,* Gordon & Breach, 1973.
(With Ullman and Alan Vaughan) *Dream Telepathy: Experiments in Nocturnal E.S.P.,* Macmillan, 1973, 2nd edition, McFarland & Co., 1989.
(Editor with Rubin) *The Kirlian Aura,* Doubleday, 1974.
(Editor with Rubin) *The Energies of Consciousness: Explorations in Acupuncture, Auras, and Kirlian Photography,* Gordon & Breach, 1975.
Song of the Siren: A Parapsychological Odyssey, Harper, 1975.

(With Alberto Villoldo) *The Realms of Healing,* Celestial Arts, 1976.

(With Roy Dreistadt) *The Psychology of Societies* (monograph), Kishkam Press, 1976.

(With Eleanor Criswell) *Physiology of Consciousness* (monograph), Kishkam Press, 1976.

(Editor) *Advances in Parapsychological Research,* Volume 1: *Psychokinesis,* Plenum, 1977, Volume 2: *Extrasensory Perception,* Plenum, 1978, Volume 3, Plenum, 1982, Volume 4, McFarland & Co., 1984, Volume 5, McFarland & Co., 1987, Volume 6, McFarland & Co., 1990.

(Editor with John White) *Future Science: Life Energies and the Physics of Paranormal Phenomena,* Doubleday-Anchor, 1977.

(With Dreistadt and Judith Malamud) *The Measurement of Behavior* (monograph), Kishkam Press, 1977.

(With Dreistadt) *Cognitive Functions of Human Intentionality* (monograph), Kishkam Press, 1977.

(With Brian Leibovitz) *Drug-Related Altered States of Consciousness* (monograph), Kishkam Press, 1978.

Psychoenergetic Systems: The Interaction of Consciousness, Energy and Matter, Gordon & Breach, 1979.

Human Possibilities, Anchor Press, 1980.

(With David Feinstein) *Personal Mythology: The Psychology of Your Evolving Self,* Tarcher, 1988.

(With Joseph Dillard) *Dreamworking: How to Use Your Dreams for Creative Problem Solving,* Bearly, 1988.

(With Richard Noll) *The Psychology of Shamanism* (includes cassette), Irvington, 1990.

(Editor) *Dreamtime,* Tarcher, 1990.

(Editor) *Dreamworking,* Tarcher, 1990.

Co-editor of *LSD into the Eighties,* Orenda/Unity; also editor of "Psychic Studies" series, Gordon & Breach. Contributor to psychology texts and other books, including *Issues in Urban Education and Mental Health,* 1971, and *The Emotional Stress of War, Violence, and Peace,* 1972. Contributor of more than 500 articles to journals in psychology, education, psychiatry, and parapsychology. Editor in chief, *Advances in Parapsychological Research: A Biennial Review;* member of editorial or advisory boards, *Gifted Child Quarterly, International Journal of Psychophysical Systems, Journal of Holistic Medicine, Journal of Indian Psychology, Journal of Creative Children and Adults, Psi Research, ReVision, Revista/Review, International Journal of Paraphysics, Journal of Humanistic Psychology,* and *Journal of Transpersonal Psychology.*

SIDELIGHTS: In 1971 Stanley Krippner gave the first lecture on parapsychology ever presented at the U.S.S.R. Academy of Pedagogical Sciences in Moscow, and in 1972 in Tokyo he read the first paper on parapsychology ever accepted by the International Congress of Psychology. In 1981 he gave an invited lecture on parapsychology before the Chinese Academy of Sciences in Peking, the first such presentation. His main research interest has been the understanding of psychic ability and the function of psychic ability in different altered states of consciousness. He has also studied gifted and exceptional children, with an interest in the relationship between creativity and human consciousness.

*   *   *

KROEBER, Clifton B(rown) 1921-

PERSONAL: Surname is pronounced *Crow*-burr; birth-given name, Brown, name legally changed, 1942; born September 7, 1921, in Berkeley, Calif.; son of Clifton Spencer and Theodora (an anthropologist and writer; maiden name, Kracaw) Brown;

married Elizabeth MacSwain Jones, April 29, 1944; children: Jeffrey, Alan, Keith, Scott. *Education:* University of California-Berkeley, A.B., 1943, M.A., 1947, Ph.D., 1951.

ADDRESSES: Home—1701 Linda Rosa Ave., Los Angeles, CA 90041. *Office*—Department of History, Occidental College, 1600 Campus Rd., Los Angeles, CA 90041.

CAREER: University of Wisconsin-Madison, assistant professor of history, 1951-55; Occidental College, Los Angeles, Calif., assistant professor, 1955-59, associate professor, 1959-64, professor of history, 1964, Norman Bridge Professor of Hispanic American History, 1964—. Fellow, Social Science Research Council, 1949. Consultant. *Military service:* U.S. Naval Reserve, active duty, 1943-46; became lieutenant.

AWARDS, HONORS: Grants from Haynes Foundation, 1959, 1980, American Philosophical Society, 1966, 1986, and Wenner-Gren Foundation for Anthropological Research, 1970; Sterling Memorial award from Occidental College, 1984.

MEMBER: American Historical Association, Latin American Studies Association, Pacific Coast Council on Latin American Studies.

WRITINGS:

(Editor with Walker D. Wyman) *The Frontier in Perspective,* University of Wisconsin Press, 1957.

The Growth of the Shipping Industry in the Rio de la Plata Region, 1794-1860, University of Wisconsin Press, 1957.

Rosas y la revision de la historia Argentina (title means "The Revision of Argentine History Concerning the Dictator Rosas"), translated into Spanish by J. L. Munoz Azpiri, Fondo Editor Argentino, 1964.

(With stepfather, Alfred L. Kroeber) *A Mohave War Reminiscence, 1854-1880,* University of California Press, 1973.

Man, Land, and Water: Mexico's Farmlands Irrigation Policies, 1885-1911, University of California Press, 1983.

(With Bernard L. Fontana) *Massacre on the Gila,* University of Arizona Press, 1987.

Contributor of articles and reviews to history journals.

WORK IN PROGRESS: A book on Mexican irrigation policies, 1911-1926; continuing research on twentieth-century revolutions.

SIDELIGHTS: Clifton Kroeber once told *CA:* "I am fluent in Spanish, less so in German and French. My research arises from problems encountered and found to be unsolved while teaching. I try to publish when I can as a kind of recompense to others who have published informative books and articles. I'm also interested in the research itself (how to do it well) and in writing (how to write briefly and clearly)."

Kroeber also commented on his work concerning Mexico's irrigation practices: "The study of Mexico's irrigation policy may be important in two ways. It shows how long ago Mexico's government undertook modern methods of providing for the nation's agricultural needs and how hard they worked at that. The study also shows how long ago the Mexicans began to favor large-scale, capital-intensive agriculture (while neglecting medium and small-scale farming). That emphasis still hampers their agricultural effort seriously today."

Kroeber's work with Bernard L. Fontana, *Massacre on the Gila,* "describes an attack by Quechan and Mohave warriors on a Maricopa village in southern Arizona in 1857—the last intertribal fight in the Southwest," describes Evan S. Connell in the *Los Angeles Times Book Review.* Connell adds, "Despite the rousing battle scene with which [*Massacre on the Gila*] opens, [the book] is an exploration of a much larger phenomenon. The narrative style is dulled by academic locution, but Kroeber and Fontana are meticulous professionals." Connell concludes that the authors' study "of this neglected slice of Southwestern history deserves applause."

BIOGRAPHICAL/CRITICAL SOURCES:

PERIODICALS

Los Angeles Times Book Review, March 15, 1987.

* * *

KROEBER, Karl 1926-

PERSONAL: Surname is pronounced *Crow*-burr; born November 24, 1926, in Oakland, CA; son of Alfred L. (a teacher) and Theodora Quinn (an anthropologist and writer; maiden name, Kracaw) Kroeber; married Jean Taylor, March 21, 1953; children: Paul Demarest, Arthur Romeyn, Katharine. *Education:* College of the Pacific, A.A., 1945; University of California, Berkeley, B.A., 1947; Columbia University, M.A., 1951, Ph.D., 1956.

ADDRESSES: Home—226 St. Johns Place, Brooklyn, NY 10027. *Office*—Department of English and Comparative Literature, Columbia University, New York, NY 10027.

CAREER: University of Wisconsin-Madison, assistant professor, 1956-61, associate professor, 1961-63, professor of English, 1963-70, associate dean of Graduate School, 1963-65; Columbia University, New York City, professor of English and comparative literature, 1970—, Mellon Professor in the Humanities, 1986—, chairman of department, 1973-76. *Military service:* U.S. Navy, 1944-46.

MEMBER: International Association of University Professors of English, Academy of Literary Studies, American Comparative Literature Association, Modern Language Association of America, Modern Humanities Research Association.

AWARDS, HONORS: Fulbright research grant to Italy, 1960-61; grant from U.S. Office of Educational Research, 1965-66; Guggenheim fellow, 1966-67; Distinguished Career Scholar Award, Keats-Shelley Association, 1990.

WRITINGS:

Romantic Narrative Art, University of Wisconsin Press, 1960.
The Artifice of Reality, University of Wisconsin Press, 1964.
(With John L. Lyons) *Studying Poetry,* Harper, 1965.
Backgrounds to British Romantic Literature, Chandler (San Francisco), 1968.
Styles of Fictional Structure, Princeton University Press, 1970.
Romantic Landscape Vision: Constable and Wordsworth, University of Wisconsin Press, 1974.
(Editor with William Walling) *Images of Romanticism: Verbal and Visual Affinities,* Yale University Press, 1978.
(Editor) *Traditional Literatures of the American Indian: Texts and Interpretations,* University of Nebraska Press, 1981.
British Romantic Art, University of California Press, 1986.
Wordsworthian Scholarship and Criticism, 1973-84, Garland, 1986.
Romantic Fantasy and Science Fiction, Yale University Press, 1988.

Emeritus editor of *Studies in American Indian Literatures;* member of editorial board, *The Wordsworth Circle, Native American Bibliography Series, Studies in English Literature,* and *Boundary 2.*

KROEBER, Theodora (Kracaw) 1897-1979
(Theodora K. Quinn)

PERSONAL: Surname is pronounced *Crow*-burr; born March 24, 1897, in Denver, CO; died July 4, 1979, in Berkeley, CA, of cancer; daughter of Charles Emmett (a merchant) and Phebe (Johnston) Kracaw; married Clifton Spencer Brown, July 6, 1920 (died October, 1923); married Alfred L. Kroeber (an anthropologist), March 26, 1926 (died, 1961); married John Harrison Quinn (a psychologist); children: Clifton, Theodore, Karl, Ursula Le Guin. *Education:* University of California, B.A., 1919, M.A., 1920. *Politics:* Democrat. *Avocational interests:* Cooking and gardening (Pacific Coast style), reading, discussing books and music, the opera and string quartets, and exploring strange cities.

ADDRESSES: Home—1325 Arch St., Berkeley, CA 94708. *Agent*—Scott Meredith, 845 Third Ave., New York, NY 10022.

CAREER: Anthropologist and writer. Member of University of California board of regents, 1978, and charter member of University Art Museum Council, University of California-Berkeley.

MEMBER: Society of Women Geographers, Women's Faculty Club (University of California).

AWARDS, HONORS: Silver Medal, Commonwealth Club of San Francisco, 1961, and California Literature Medal Award, 1962, both for *Ishi in Two Worlds: A Biography of the Last Wild Indian in North America;* Distinguished Woman, City of San Francisco, 1966.

WRITINGS:

The Inland Whale, Indiana University Press, 1959, published as *The Inland Whale: Nine Stories Retold from California Indian Legends,* University of California Press, 1959.
Ishi in Two Worlds: A Biography of the Last Wild Indian in North America, University of California Press, 1961, Cresset Library, 1987.
(Editor) Alfred L. Kroeber, *An Anthropologist Looks at History,* University of California Press, 1963.
Ishi: Last of His Tribe (juvenile), Parnassus, 1964.
A Green Christmas (juvenile), Parnassus, 1967.
(With Robert F. Heizer) *Almost Ancestors: The First Californians,* edited by F. David Hales, Sierra Club, 1968.
Alfred Kroeber: A Personal Configuration, University of California Press, 1970.
Carrousel (juvenile novel), Atheneum, 1977.
(Compiler with others) *Drawn from Life: California Indians in Pen and Brush,* Ballena, 1977.
(Editor with Heizer) *Ishi: A Documentary History,* University of California Press, 1979.
Theodora, [Berkeley, CA], 1979.
Poem for the Living, [Berkeley, CA], 1979.
(Editor with Heizer) *Ishi the Last Yahi: A Documentary History,* University of California Press, 1979.
(With daughter, Ursula K. Le Guin) *Tillai and Tylissos,* Red Bull, 1979.

Contributor of articles and book reviews to anthropology journals, and to *American Scholar.*

WORK IN PROGRESS: More writing similar to that of *The Inland Whale;* writings for children; novellas.

SIDELIGHTS: Of *Ishi in Two Worlds: A Biography of the Last Wild Indian in North America,* Phoebe Adams writes in the *Atlantic:* "In writing Ishi's story, Mrs. Kroeber has drawn on her husband's experiences with him and on a vast knowledge of California Indian history in general. She skillfully interweaves the dreadful story of the extermination of Ishi's people with what he confided of his own past life and with his character as it was revealed to his white friends. [The] book is remarkably lively and interesting anthropology." Kimmis Hendrick notes in the *Christian Science Monitor* that *Ishi in Two Worlds* has "a poetic, moving quality" and adds, "Perhaps [Theodora Kroeber's] subject accounts for her book's special poignancy, but the way in which she handles it is undoubtedly a factor also."

A few years before her death, Theodora Kroeber told *CA:* "I began seriously to write only in 1955. My homily to young writers, particularly young women writers, is not to worry over what you will do when the children are grown. They may need you as much then as now. In any case, you do not know who you will be in that far time. Live your life with total commitment to that piece of it which is yours now; live it, whatever it is, creatively."

BIOGRAPHICAL/CRITICAL SOURCES:

PERIODICALS

Atlantic, November, 1961.
Christian Science Monitor, October 12, 1961.
New Statesman, April 27, 1962.
Saturday Review, December 16, 1961.*

* * *

KRUEGER, Anne O. 1934-

PERSONAL: Born in 1934 in Endicott, NY; daughter of Leslie A. (a physician) and Dora (Wright) Osbom; married William R. Krueger, 1953 (divorced, 1957); married James M. Henderson, 1981; children: (first marriage) Kathleen Suzanne. *Education:* Oberlin College, B.A., 1953; University of Wisconsin, M.S., 1956, Ph.D., 1958.

ADDRESSES: Home—30 Sedgewood Dr., Chapel Hill, NC 27514. *Office*—Department of Economics, 227 Social Sciences Building, Duke University, Durham, NC 27706; and World Bank, 1818 "H" St. N.W., Washington, DC 20433.

CAREER: University of Wisconsin Madison, instructor in economics, 1958-59; University of Minnesota, Minneapolis, assistant professor, 1959-63, associate professor, 1963-66, professor of economics, 1966-82, research associate of Upper Midwest Economic Study, 1962-64; World Bank, Washington, DC, vice-president of economics and research, 1982-86; Duke University, Durham, NC, arts and sciences professor of economics, 1986—. Visiting professor, Monash University, Melbourne, Australia, 1973, 1976, 1978, and 1981; Massacusetts Institute of Technology, Cambridge, MA, 1973-74; Northwestern University, 1976; Australian National University, Canberra, 1977; University of Aarhus, 1979; University of Paris, 1980; Institute for International Economic Studies and Industrial Institute for Economic and Social Research, Stockholm, 1982; and University of Maryland, College Park, 1983.

International economist, Bankers' Trust Co., 1961-62; National Bureau of Economic Research, research associate, 1969-76, member of senior research staff, 1977—. Consultant to U.S. Agency for International Development, 1965-72, Upper Midwest Research and Development Council, 1966, and National Science Foundation, 1971—, and Brookings Institution, 1988—.

MEMBER: American Economic Association (vice-president, 1977-78), American Academy of Arts and Sciences (fellow, 1983—), Econometric Society (1961—; fellow, 1981—), Royal Economic Society (1965—), Midwest Economic Association (president, 1974-75), Minnesota Economic Association (president, 1971-72).

AWARDS, HONORS: National Science Foundation grant, 1966-69; Robertson Award, National Academy of Sciences, 1984; Ph.D. Honoris Causis, Hacettepe University (Ankara, Turkey), 1990; Bernhard-Harms prize, Kiel Institute of World Economics, 1990.

WRITINGS:

(With James M. Henderson) *National Growth and Economic Change in the Upper Midwest,* University of Minnesota Press, 1965.

(With Henderson) *Economic Growth and Adjustment in the Upper Midwest, 1960-75: A Supplement to the Upper Midwest Economic Study,* Upper Midwest Research and Development Council, 1967.

(Editor with Wontack Hong) *Trade and Development in Korea,* Korea Development Institute (Seoul), 1975.

Benefits and Costs of Import-Substitution: A Micro-Economic Study, University of Minnesota Press, 1975.

Foreign Trade Regimes and Economic Development: Turkey, Columbia University Press, 1975.

Foreign Trade Regimes and Economic Development: Liberalization Attempts and Consequences, Ballinger, 1978.

The Developmental Role of the Foreign Trade Sector and Aid: Studies in the Modernization of the Republic of Korea, 1945-1975, Harvard University Press, 1979.

(Editor with Hal B. Lary, Terry Monson, and Narongchai Akrasanee and contributor) *Trade and Employment in Developing Countries,* University of Chicago Press for National Bureau of Economic Research, Volume 1: *Individual Studies,* 1981; (sole author) Volume 2: *Factor Supply and Substitution,* 1982; (sole author) Volume 3: *Synthesis and Conclusions,* 1983, 2nd edition, 1988.

Exchange Rate Determination, Cambridge University Press, 1983.

(Editor with R. Baldwin and contributor with H. Hughes) *American Trade Relations,* University of Chicago Press, 1984.

(Editor with Vittorio Corbo and Fernando Osso) *Export-Oriented Development Strategies: The Success of Five Newly Industrialized Countries,* Westview Press, 1985.

(Editor) *Development with Trade: LDCs and the International Economy,* ICS Press, 1988.

(Editor with Vernon Ruttan and Constantine Michalopoulos) *Aid and Development,* Johns Hopkins University Press, 1989.

(Editor with Ronald W. Jones) *The Political Economy of International Trade: Essays in Honor of Robert E. Baldwin,* Basil Blackwell, 1990.

Perspectives on Trade and Development, University of Chicago Press/Harvester Wheatsheaf (Oxford), 1990.

CONTRIBUTOR

John Black and Brian Hindley, editors, *Current Issues in Commercial Policy and Diplomacy,* St. Martin's, 1980.

William R. Cline and Sidney Weintraub, editors, *Economic Stabilization in Developing Countries,* Brookings Institution, 1981.

Lars Matthiessen and Steiner Stroem, editors, *Unemployment: Macro-and Micro-Economic Explanations,* Macmillan (London), 1981.

R. W. Jones and P. B. Kenen, editors, *Handbook of International Economics,* Volume 1, North-Holland, 1983.

(With M. G. Porter) L. H. Cook and Porter, editors, *The Minerals Sector and the Australian Economy,* Allen & Unwin (Australia), 1984.

Jacob A. Frenkel and Michael Mussa, editors, *The World Economic System: Performance and Prospects* (M.I.T. Key Issues lecture series), Auburn House, 1984.

M. Syrquin and others, editors, *Ecomonic Structure and Performance: Essays in Honor of Hollis B. Chenery,* Acdemic Press, 1984.

Klaus-Detlev Groethusen, editor, *Handbook on Southeastern Europe,* Vendenhoeck & Ruprecht, 1985.

V. Corbo and others, editors, *Export-Oriented Development Strategies: The Success of Five Newly Industrialized Countries,* Westview Press, 1985.

Henryk Kierzkowski, editor, *Protection and Competition in International Trade,* Basil Blackwell, 1987.

Silvio Borner, editor, *International Finance and trade in a Polycentric World,* Macmillan, 1988.

Martin Feldstein, editor, *The U.S. in the World Economy,* University of Chicago Press for the National Bureau of Economic Research, 1988.

Rudiger Dornbusch, editor, *International Money and Debt,* in press.

C. Schultze, editor, *Alternative Trade Strategies for the U.S.,* Brookings Institute, in press.

Also contributor to more than thirty other books on trade and economics since 1963.

OTHER

Co-Editor of Development Series, Johns Hopkins Press, 1981-82. Board of editors, *Journal of Economic Literature,* 1973-76, and *Economics and Finance,* 1988—; *Journal of International Economics,* book review editor, 1973-76, associate editor, 1980-84; consulting editor, *Portfolio,* 1974-82, *Economics Letters,* 1979—, and *Revista de Economia Politica,* 1988—; editorial board member, *Pakistan Development Review,* 1979—, and *American Economic Review,* 1980-83; associate editor, *Economics and Politics,* 1988-90.

*   *   *

KURZMAN, Dan 1927-

PERSONAL: Born March 27, 1927, in San Francisco, CA; son of Joseph (a businessman) and Lillian (a writer; maiden name, Halperin) Kurzman; married Florence Knopf (a writer), February 27, 1977. *Education:* University of California, Berkeley, B.A., 1946; Sorbonne, University of Paris, certificate, 1947.

ADDRESSES: Office—c/o H. Knopf, 187 Boulevard, Apt. 9-H, Passaic, NJ 07055. *Agent*—Julian Bach, 747 3rd Ave., New York, NY 10017.

CAREER: Writer. International News Service, Paris, France, correspondent, 1946-48; Marshall Plan Information Division, Paris, feature writer, 1949; National Broadcasting Co. (NBC), New York City, Middle East correspondent, 1950-53; McGraw-Hill World News Service, New York City, Tokyo bureau cheif, 1954-60; *Washington Post,* Washington, DC, foreign correspondent, 1962-68.

MEMBER: Overseas Press Club, PEN, National Press Club, Tokyo Foreign Correspondents Club, Overseas Writers Club, State Department Correspondents Club, Authors League of America.

AWARDS, HONORS: Overseas Press Club award for best book on foreign affairs (named the Cornelius Ryan Award in 1978), 1963, for *Subversion of the Innocents,* and 1980, for *Miracle of November: Madrid's Epic Stand, 1936;* Front Page Award, 1964; George Polk Award for international reporting, 1965, from Long Island University; Dr. Moses Leo Gitelson award for biography, Jewish Book Council on the Jewish Welfare Board, 1984, for *Ben-Gurion: Prophet of Fire.*

WRITINGS:

Kishi and Japan: The Search for the Sun, Obolensky, 1960.
Subversion of the Innocents, Random House, 1963.
Santo Domingo: Revolt of the Damned, Putnam, 1965.
Genesis 1948: The First Arab-Israeli War, World Publications, 1970.
The Race for Rome, Doubleday, 1975.
The Bravest Battle: The Twenty-Eight days of the Warsaw Ghetto Uprising, Putnam, 1976.
Miracle of November: Madrid's Epic Stand, 1936, Putnam, 1976.
Ben-Gurion: Prophet of Fire, Simon & Schuster, 1983.
Day of the Bomb: Countdown to Hiroshima, McGraw-Hill, 1985.
A Killing Wind: Inside Union Carbide and the Bhopal Catastrophe, McGraw-Hill, 1987.
Fatal Voyage: The Sinking of the U.S.S. Indianapolis, Atheneum, 1990.

Contributor to several periodicals, including *Washington Star* and *Independent News Alliance.*

MEDIA ADAPTATIONS: Otto Preminger acquired the rights to *Genesis 1948: The First Arab-Israeli War* in 1970; CBS-TV is preparing a television adaptation of *Day of the Bomb.*

SIDELIGHTS: A former foreign correspondent in Europe, the Middle east, and Asia, Dan Kurzman has become a practitioner of a form of history writing closely related to journalism. This "new history," as it is often described, is a synthesis of scholarly research, investigative reporting, and a form of creative writing, which, as Kurzman told *CA* is creative "not in the fictional sense, but in the sense of creating images with facts." Thus, more factually detailed than historical fiction and more dramatic than traditional histories, Kurzman's books appeal to a wide range of readers. Quoted in a *Times Literary Supplement* article, Kurzman explains, "Using the techniques of the novelist and the biographer, I have tried to bring history alive."

As John S. Carroll notes in the *Saturday Review,* Kurzman uses the tools of various trades to compose a picture of history that captures the complexity of the original events. From the historian, he borrows a concern for the events, their chronology and significance. He engages in extensive research of his subject, drawing information from official documents, books, magazines, and newspapers to provide the backdrop for his story.

Acting as a journalist, Kurzman focuses his picture by emphasizing the people involved and their individual experiences. He interviews thousands of participants from major contributors to minor players and makes use of diaries, memoirs, and letters to supplement and substantiate the interviews. Then, to clarify complicated or conflicting information, Kurzman examines key witnesses.

Finally, Kurzman introduces elements of the novel to enhance his picture, exploiting the natural tension of the events to build drama, intertwining the experiences of several individuals to simulate characterization, and finally, adding dialogue quoted from first-hand writings and interviews. Larry Collins, in a *New York Times Book Review* article, writes that Kurzman's technique creates a "whole that conveys the feel, color and emotion of the event as well as its historical significance."

Kurzman's early books—accounts of Japanese prime minister Nobusuke Kishi, Soviet influence in Africa and Asia, and the mid-nineteen-sixties revolt in Santo Domingo—drew some favorable reviews, but *Genesis 1948: The First Arab-Israeli War* was his first work to receive wide attention. Phil Freshman in a *Los Angeles Times Book Review* article calls *Genesis 1948* "the best book I've read on the first Arab-Israeli war." Some reviewers find factual errors in Kurzman's account; others, however, commend his objectivity in handling an issue as volatile as the struggle to reestablish a Jewish state in Palestine. Roderick Mac-Leish writes in the *Washington Post,* "[Kurzman] declines to reduce Israelis and Arabs to the stereotypes of invincible heroes at war with sleazy rat finks."

In *Miracle of November: Madrid's Epic Stand, 1936,* Kurzman recreates Franco's seige of Madrid during the Spanish Civil War. Writes Robert Kirsch in the *Los Angeles Times,* "This is no romanticized or whitewashed version of events, no facile portrayal of propaganda heroes." In a *New York Review of Books* article, Bernard Knox faults Kurzman's incomplete notation of sources, which he feels makes the book "of no use to the historian." Knox also writes that Kurzman's image of this conflict "fails to give the reader a sense of the unique atmosphere of Madrid in November." On the other hand, *New York Times* writer Richard F. Shepard feels that "Mr. Kurzman has chronicled this epic with the attention and detail and the sense of the human spirit that it requires."

Ben-Gurion: Prophet of Fire, Dan Kurzman's biography of David Ben-Gurion, is the story of Israel's founding father and first prime minister. Phil Freshman points out that Kurzman's research has uncovered new information about Ben-Gurion, especially concerning his private life. In assessing the biography, however, Freshman contends that Kurzman "seems to excuse some of [Ben-Gurion's] formidable faults." Yet, Alden Whitman writes in the *Chicago Tribune Book World* that Kurzman's "reportorial biography is at once coherent and informative. From it, Ben-Gurion emerges as a titan of our times."

BIOGRAPHICAL/CRITICAL SOURCES:

PERIODICALS

Chicago Tribune Book World, March 4, 1984.
Christian Science Monitor, December 4, 1970; November 9, 1983.
Detroit News, December 10, 1983.
Los Angeles Times, October 14, 1976; February 20, 1980.
Los Angeles Times Book Review, November 20, 1983.
New York Review of Books, November 6, 1980.
New York Times, March 7, 1975; November 26, 1976; April 7, 1980; January 5, 1986.
New York Times Book Review, December 13, 1970; February 23, 1975; November 28, 1976; February 24, 1980; December 25, 1983; January 12, 1986; November 29, 1987.
Saturday Review, November 27, 1965; June 27, 1970.
Time, September 28, 1987.
Times Literary Supplement, October 13, 1972.
Washington Post, September 3, 1970.
Washington Post Book World, March 20, 1980; January 8, 1984.

L

LABIN, Suzanne (Devoyon) 1913-

PERSONAL: Born May 6, 1913, in Paris, France; daughter of Louis Leon (a metal worker) and Marie-Eugenie (Leplatre) Devoyon; married Edouard Labin (an electronic engineer), April 4, 1935. *Education:* Ecole des hautes etudes internationales et de journalisme, diplomee, 1935; Sorbonne, University of Paris, licenciee es sciences, 1936. *Religion:* Roman Catholic. *Avocational interests:* Collecting unusual sculpture, riding horseback, swimming, skiing.

ADDRESSES: Home and office—3 rue Thiers, Paris 75116, France.

CAREER: Journalist, author, and lecturer. Founder and president of International Conference on Political Warfare, with headquarters in Paris, 1960—. Has launched campaigns in support of the Hungarian Revolution, in support of the Tibetan uprising against the Chinese invasion, in support of the South Vietnamese and their U.S. allies, and against the Ceaucescu tyranny. Lecturer in (French, English, and Spanish) in most countries of Asia, Africa, Latin America, and North America. Member of the Asian Speakers Bureau (United States) and of the Church League of America Speakers Bureau. Producer of film, "Freedom Is at Stake in Berlin," for French television, 1962.

MEMBER: World Anti-Communist League (chairman of French chapter), League of Freedom (president), Societe des gens de lettres, European Freedom Council (president of Committee for Information), Federacion Argentina Entidades Democraticas Anti-Communistas (honorary member), Association for the Study of the Problems of Public Opinion (honorary board member).

AWARDS, HONORS: Freedom Prize for *Les Entretiens de Saint-Germain: Liberte aux liberticides?;* Golden Cross of European Merit; Golden Cross of Cultural and Philanthropic Merit; Freedom Award, Assembly of Captive Nations; Freedom Award, Freedoms Foundation of Valley Forge; Prix Henri Malherbe, Association des Ecrivains Combattants, 1980; Officer of Bernardo O'Higgins Order (Chile), 1982; Grand Officer of European Merit, 1983.

WRITINGS:

Staline le terrible: Panorama de la Russie sovietique, Editions Self, 1948, translation by Edward Fitzgerald published as *Stalin's Russia,* Gollancz, 1950.

Le Drame de la democratie, Horay, 1954, translation by Otto E. Albrecht published as *The Secret of Democracy,* Vanguard, 1955.

La Conspiration communiste, l'Hydre totalitaire: Comment la museler, Spartacus, 1957.

Les Entretiens de Saint-Germain: Liberte aux liberticides?, Spartacus, 1957.

La Condition humaine en Chine communiste, La Table Ronde, 1959, translation by Fitzgerald published as *The Anthill: The Human Condition in Communist China,* Stevens & Sons, 1960, Praeger, 1961.

The Technique of Soviet Propaganda (pamphlet; originally written in French as a report for the tenth anniversary of the North Atlantic Treaty Organization), [London], 1959, expanded version prepared for U.S. Senate published as *The Techniques of Soviet Propaganda,* U.S. Government Printing Office, 1960, revised, 1965, also published as *The Unrelenting War: A Study of the Strategy and Techniques of Communist Propaganda and Infiltration,* American-Asian Educational Exchange, 1960, further expanded version published as *Il est moins cinq: Propagande et infiltration sovietiques,* Berger-Levrault, 1960.

(Editor) *Vie ou mort de monde libre* (principal speeches at International Conference on Political Warfare, 1960), La Table Ronde, 1961.

Competition U.S.S.R.—U.S.A.: Economique, militaire, culturelle, La Table Ronde, 1962.

Counter Attack: A Plan to Win the Political Warfare of the Soviets, American-Asian Educational Exchange, 1963.

Reconnaissance Chine communiste, Ambassades pour subversions, Editions de la Ligue de la Liberte, 1963, translation published with an introduction by Senator Thomas J. Dodd as *Embassies of Subversion,* American Afro-Asian Education Exchange, 1965.

Le Tiers Monde entre l'est et l'ouest: Vivre en dollars, voter en roubles, La Table Ronde, 1964, translation published as *Red Foxes in the Chicken Coop,* Crestwood, 1966.

Vietnam: An Eye-Witness Account, Crestwood, 1964, revised and enlarged edition published as *Sellout in Vietnam?,* Crestwood, 1966.

(Contributor) *Trouble Abroad,* Crestwood, 1965.

La Liberte se joue a Saigon, Editions de la Ligue de la Liberte, 1965.

Les Colonialistes chinois en Afrique, Editions de la Ligue de la Liberte, 1965.

DeGaulle ou la France enchainee, Editions de la Ligue de la Liberte, 1965.

Menaces chinoises sur l'Asie, La Table Ronde, 1966.

50 Annees de communisme, Berger-Levrault, 1967, translation published as *Promise and Reality: 50 Years of Soviet "Achievements,"* John Graham, 1967.

Goliath and David: Justice pour la Chine libre, Editions de la Ligue de la Liberte, 1967.

Le Petit Livre rouge: Arme de guerre, La Table Ronde, 1969.

Hippies, drogues et sexe, La Table ronde, 1970, translation published as *Hippies, Drugs and Promiscuity,* Arlington House, 1970.

Le Monde des drogues, France Empire, 1975.

La Violence politique, France Empire, 1977.

Chili: Le Crime de Resister, Nouvelles Editions Debresse, 1980, translation published as *Chile: The Crime of Resistance,* Foreign Affairs Publishing Co. Ltd., 1982.

Israel: Le Crime de Vivre, Nouvelles Editions Debresse, 1981.

Socialisme: La Demagogie du changement, Nouvelles Editions Debresse, 1983.

Les Colombes Rouges: Les Mouvements pacifistes et la guerre des Etoiles, [France], 1985.

Les Requins Rouges et leurs Poissons Pilotes, [France], 1987.

Les Etats terroristes, la guerre des laches, [France], 1987.

Vivre en dollars et voter en roubles: L'Occident cocu et payant, le scandale doit cesser, [France], 1989.

Contributor of articles to magazines and newspapers in many countries.

SIDELIGHTS: Many of Suzanne Labin's books have been translated into English, Spanish, Portuguese, and other languages.

BIOGRAPHICAL/CRITICAL SOURCES:

PERIODICALS

American Legion Magazine, December, 1962.

*   *   *

LAFFERTY, R(aphael) A(loysius) 1914-

PERSONAL: Born November 7, 1914, in Neola, Iowa; son of Hugh David (an oil-lease broker) and Julia Mary (a teacher; maiden name, Burke) Lafferty. *Education:* Attended University of Tulsa, 1932-33; further study with International Correspondence Schools, 1939-42. *Politics:* Independent. *Religion:* Roman Catholic.

ADDRESSES: Home—1715 South Trenton Ave., Tulsa, Okla. 74120. *Agent*—Virginia Kidd, Box 278, Milford, Pa. 18337.

CAREER: Clark Electrical Supply Co., Tulsa, Okla., buyer, 1935-42, 1946-50, and 1952-71; free-lance writer, 1971—. *Military service:* U.S. Army, 1942-46; became staff sergeant; received New Guinea Campaign Star.

MEMBER: Science Fiction Writers of America.

AWARDS, HONORS: Nebula Award nomination, Science Fiction Writers of America, 1968, for *Past Master,* 1970, for *Fourth Mansions,* and 1971, for *The Devil Is Dead;* Hugo Award nomination, World Science Fiction Convention, 1968, for *Past Master;* Phoenix Award, 1971; Hugo Award, World Science Fiction Convention, 1973, for story "Eurema's Dam"; E. E. Smith Memorial Award, 1973.

WRITINGS:

SCIENCE FICTION NOVELS

Past Master, Ace Books, 1968.

The Reefs of Earth, Berkley Publishing, 1968.

Space Chantey, Ace Books, 1968.

Fourth Mansions, Ace Books, 1969, reprinted, Bart Books, 1988.

The Devil Is Dead, Avon, 1971, reprinted, Bart Books, 1988.

Arrive at Easterwine: The Autobiography of a Ktistec Machine, Scribner, 1971.

Not to Mention Camels, Bobbs-Merrill, 1976.

Apocalypses, Pinnacle Books, 1977.

Archipelago, Manuscript Press (New Orleans), 1979.

Aurelia, Donning, 1982.

The Annals of Klepsis, Ace Books, 1983.

My Heart Leaps Up, Chris Drumm Books, *Chapters 1 and 2,* 1986, *Chapters 3 and 4,* 1987, *Chapters 5 and 6,* 1987.

Serpent's Egg, Morrigan Publications, 1987.

East of Laughter, Morrigan Publications, 1988.

The Elliptical Grave, United Mythologies Press, 1989.

Mantis, Corroboree, in press.

Dotty, United Mythologies Press, in press.

STORY COLLECTIONS

Nine Hundred Grandmothers, Ace Books, 1970.

Strange Doings, Scribner, 1971.

Does Anyone Else Have Something Further to Add?: Stories about Secret Places and Mean Men, Scribner, 1974.

Funnyfingers, and Cabrito, Pendragon Press (Oregon), 1976.

Horns on Their Heads, Pendragon Press, 1976.

Golden Gate and Other Stories, edited by Ira M. Thornhill, Corroboree, 1983.

Four Stories, Chris Drumm Books, 1983.

Heart of Stone, Dear, and Other Stories, Chris Drumm Books, 1983.

Snake in His Bosom and Other Stories, Chris Drumm Books, 1983.

Through Elegant Eyes: Stories of Austro and the Men Who Knew Everything, edited by Thornhill, Corroboree, 1983.

Ringing Changes, Ace Books, 1984.

The Man Who Made Models and Other Stories, Chris Drumm Books, 1984.

Slippery and Other Stories, Chris Drumm Books, 1985.

OTHER

The Fall of Rome (historical novel), Doubleday, 1971.

The Flame Is Green (historical novel), Walker & Co., 1971.

Okla Hannali (historical novel), Doubleday, 1972.

(Contributor) Fred Saberhagen, editor, *A Spadeful of Spacetime,* Ace Books, 1981.

(Contributor) Martin H. Greenberg, editor, *Fantastic Lives: Autobiographical Essays by Notable Science Fiction Writers,* Southern Illinois University Press, 1981.

(Contributor) Alan Ryan, editor, *Perpetual Light,* Warner Books, 1982.

(Contributor) Isaac Asimov and Alice Laurance, editors, *Speculations,* Houghton, 1982.

Laughing Kelly and Other Verses, Chris Drumm Books, 1983.

Half a Sky (historical novel), edited by Thornhill, Corroboree, 1984.

It's Down the Slippery Cellar Stairs (essays), Chris Drumm Books, 1984.

Sindbad (historical fantasy novel), Broken Mirrors Press, 1989.

Also author of chapbooks *The Early Lafferty, Promontory Goats, Strange Skies, The Back Door of History, True Believers,* and

How Many Miles to Babylon, all published by United Mythologies Press. Contributor to *Chrysalis, Universe, Shadows, Whispers, Orbit,* and *The Year's Best Fantasy Stories* anthology series. Contributor of over 200 stories to *Magazine of Fantasy and Science Fiction, Literary Review, New Mexico Quarterly Review,* and other publications. Author of column, *Alien.*

SIDELIGHTS: R. A. Lafferty is one of those writers "who usually [publishes] under a science fiction label but whose stories stretch the definitions of 'reasonableness' to the breaking point," Gerald Jonas writes in the *New York Times Book Review.* Jonas calls Lafferty "a teller of tall tales" rather than a science fiction writer. Lafferty's stories are often based on absurd or satirical situations and then develop logically, following their unlikely premises to their natural conclusion. Writing in *A Reader's Guide to Fantasy,* Baird Searles, Beth Meacham and Michael Franklin claim: "Lafferty doesn't see the world in quite the same way that most people do; his logic is rigorous, but his premises are deadpan insanity." He has written stories about a speeded-up world in which fads last only a few hours, about a child's shoebox camera that makes things disappear, and about a group of archaeologists who unearth an old chimney which not only tells them of the past, but of the present and future as well. Writing in *Fantasy Review,* Paul Feeny allows that Lafferty's "writing suggests at its best a collaboration of [Jorge Luis] Borges, Mark Twain, and [Arthur] Rimbaud." "Lafferty's stories," Mary Weinkauf states in *Science Fiction and Fantasy Book Review,* "represent the best in science fiction—whimsical examinations of the notions and obsessions of the most exotic animal [man]." In his introduction to his *Ringing Changes* collection, Lafferty modestly comments: "These stories are intended to be entertainments, even the several of them that leak a little blood out of them. They are amusements."

Lafferty's novels display the same freewheeling inventiveness as do his stories. Speaking of the novel *Aurelia,* Thom Gunn of *Science Fiction and Fantasy Book Review* describes what makes this book different from more conventional works of science fiction. It is, he writes, "decidedly not in the 'hard' SF tradition of gadgetry and physics; this book is rather a whimsical Magical Mystery Tour. [It features] a shifting kaleidoscope of cartoon characters . . . all bopping about a daffy Dali-esque canvas of comic surrealism, a big glittering junkyard of linguistic effects, literalized puns, and overstated symbolism. . . . At its best it is a firework celebration of imagination."

More often, Lafferty combines this comic exuberance with a concern for the eternal struggle between good and evil, approaching this subject from a surprisingly traditional Roman Catholic perspective. But, as Patricia Ower of the *Dictionary of Literary Biography* points out, Lafferty's "vision, despite his Roman Catholicism, does not incline to the positive. It is at best ironic and comic in a black vein." In an article for *Extrapolation,* Dena C. Bain sees Lafferty as "a shaper of myth who . . . bases his mythological pictures on the mystical tradition of the West, and on the attempt of man to transcend the rational and expand his perception of the cosmos." Bain further sees Lafferty as primarily concerned with a theological struggle. "To Lafferty," Bain writes, "the mystical Christian archetypes of good and evil represent the eternal struggle between forces of darkness and light in a dualistic universe, and he creates out of his own beliefs an ethic as well as a cosmology."

In *The Devil Is Dead,* for example, Lafferty chronicles the struggle between two "archetypal groups of dark forces" for control of humanity, Bain writes. These two groups—the Demons, who are descended from aliens, and the Elder Race, an ancient group

of prehumans—have been battling for centuries and, even though the climactic battle at novel's end is certain to destroy them both, they are destined to rise once again and renew the struggle. Told in a rambunctious style heavily influenced by Irish folktales, the battle features a menagerie of characters, including a mermaid, a king, and various devils and aliens. The "convoluted plot," Ower writes, "[makes] it difficult for the narrator, Finnegan, and therefore for the reader, to tell exactly who the devil is, who is on which side of the fight, and who is really dead." Ower sees the "strange logic and metamorphoses of the novel" as "most strongly rooted in the world of dreams."

Another Lafferty novel concerned with theological struggle is *Fourth Mansions,* a novel about " 'returnees,' people who reincarnate themselves in order to prevent mankind's breakthrough to a higher plane of existence," as Ower explains. The struggle between the returnees and the "Harvesters," a rival group seeking to push mankind to a higher evolutionary level, is chronicled by Freddy Foley, a reporter investigating the failures of human history. As James Blish writes in the *Magazine of Fantasy and Science Fiction,* the novel's "genre is rare but well known: Heraldic fantasy with a religious intent." Despite its serious intentions, the novel manages to be "a light, entertaining book," Ower states. Blish finds that Lafferty's style is "cadenced without being pseudo-bardic, he relies heavily on extravagant metaphors, and he often bursts into verse, much of it original and all of it good."

In *Past Master,* Lafferty treats the question of religion in another manner, creating the society of Astrobe, a utopian world which has denied man's religious nature and in so doing has destroyed his essence. Designed in accordance with the ideas of Sir Thomas More, Astrobe finds itself being abandoned by its citizens. They leave the cities, where all of man's traditional fears and wants have been conquered, to live in Cathead, "Astrobe's largest city," explains Harold L. Berger in *Science Fiction and the New Dark Age,* "a monstrous, festering cancer of a city, a sprawl of twenty million ground down by hunger, plague, poisonous stench, and breaking labor, an infernal place of short life and bodies rotting in the streets." The leaders of Astrobe bring Thomas More forward in time to examine their society and suggest a solution to this perplexing situation.

What More finds is that Astrobe has cut man off from his unconscious mind and made all nonmaterial ideas illegal. Religion, superstition, and psychic phenomena, for example, are suppressed. Because of mechanical thought-police who can literally read minds and instantly kill those who think "incorrectly," the cities of Astrobe have become inhuman and sterile places to live. As the leaders of Astrobe seek to deny the human unconscious, "the archetypes of the collective unconscious are able to assume physical reality," Bain writes. More finally "allies himself with the rebels of the slums and the group of archetypal figures," Bain relates, ". . . and his death at the end of the novel triggers the revolution that will destroy the world and bring about the birth of a new order."

"Though prolific," writes Ower, "[Lafferty] has been neglected, and his lot has been relative obscurity perhaps traceable to the limited appeal of his religious themes." Much of Lafferty's work, too, has been published in scattered magazines or by relatively small presses. But Ower sees this situation changing. Because he has been praised by other science fiction writers for his "virtues of vitality, absurd vision, and underground humor," Ower believes that "these qualities may yet lead to a broad readership for R. A. Lafferty."

In summarizing Lafferty's career, Jack Dann writes in the *Washington Post Book World:* "Writing as he does from a conservative Catholic teleological point-of-view, his major themes are transformation, resurrection, and redemption. His preoccupation with the nature of reality and a sort of Heisenbergian notion of history is evident . . . , as is his celebration of mythic, pythonic wacky creation." The best of Lafferty's stories, Dann believes, "convey a real joy coupled with a comic lamentation; they are wrestlings with life and all its forces." Feeny also finds much to praise in the author's work. "Lafferty," he writes, "is one of the finest contemporary writers of science fiction and fantasy. His work is an unprecedented combination of allegory, tall tale, myth, dream, and comic strip, written in one of the most unique styles in current letters."

BIOGRAPHICAL/CRITICAL SOURCES:

BOOKS

Berger, Harold L., *Science Fiction and the New Dark Age,* Bowling Green University, 1976.
Dictionary of Literary Biography, Volume 8: *Twentieth Century American Science Fiction Writers,* Gale, 1981.
Drumm, Chris, *R. A. Lafferty Checklist: A Bibliographical Chronology with Notes and Index,* Chris Drumm Books, 1983.
Greenberg, Martin H., editor, *Fantastic Lives: Autobiographical Essays by Notable Science Fiction Writers,* Southern Illinois University Press, 1981.
Searles, Baird, Beth Meacham, and Michael Franklin, *A Reader's Guide to Fantasy,* Avon, 1982.
Walker, Paul, *Speaking of Science Fiction,* Luna Publications, 1978.

PERIODICALS

Amazing Stories, September, 1983.
Extrapolation, summer, 1982.
Fantasy Review, February, 1985, April, 1987.
Foundation, October, 1980.
Magazine of Fantasy and Science Fiction, May, 1968, May, 1971, January, 1972, January, 1976.
New York Times Book Review, August 8, 1971, October 3, 1976.
Science Fiction and Fantasy Book Review, December, 1982, June, 1983.
Science Fiction Review, fall, 1986.
Washington Post Book World, May 27, 1984.

*   *   *

LAINEZ, Manuel Mujica
 See MUJICA LAINEZ, Manuel

*   *   *

LALLY, Michael (David) 1942-

PERSONAL: Born May 25, 1942, in Orange, NJ; son of James A. and Irene I. (Dempsey) Lally; married Carol Lee Fisher, August 8, 1964 (divorced, 1978); married Penelope Dale Milford, February 14, 1982 (divorced, 1985); children: (first marriage) Caitlin Maeve, Miles Aaron. *Education:* University of Iowa, B.A., 1968, M.F.A., 1969.

ADDRESSES: Home—711 10th St., Santa Monica, CA 90402.

CAREER: Free-lance writer, poet, actor, musician, and screenwriter, 1975—. Trinity College, Washington, DC, instructor, 1969-74; Franklin Library, New York City, editor, 1976-78. Member of board of directors, Print Center, Brooklyn, 1972-77,

and Washington Film Classroom, 1972. Founder and president, Some of Us Press, 1972-75; founder and publisher, O Press, 1975-79; founder and director, Mass Transit Poetry Project, 1972-76; co-founder and co-director, Poetry in Motion Poetry Project, 1988-90. *Military service:* U.S. Air Force, 1962-66.

MEMBER: PEN, Screen Actors Guild, Writers Guild of America.

AWARDS, HONORS: Discovery Award, New York Poetry Center, 1972; National Endowment for the Humanities fellow, 1974, 1981; award from New York Poets Foundation, 1974.

WRITINGS:

POETRY

What Withers, Doones Press, 1970.
The Lines Are Drawn, Asphalt Press, 1970.
Stupid Rabbits, Morgan Press, 1971.
MCMLXVI Poem, Nomad Press, 1971.
The South Orange Sonnets, Some of Us Press, 1972.
Late Sleepers, Pellet Press, 1973.
My Life, Wyrd Press, 1975.
Rocky Dies Yellow, Blue Wind Press, 1975.
Dues, Stonewall Press, 1975.
Sex: The Swing Era, Lucy & Ethel Press, 1975.
Mentally, He's a Sick Man, Salt Lick Press, 1975.
Oomaloom, Dry Imager, 1975.
Charisma, O Press, 1976.
(Editor) *None of the Above,* Crossing Press, 1976.
Catch My Breath (prose and poems), Salt Lick Press, 1978.
In the Mood, Titanic Books, 1978.
Just Let Me Do It, Vehicle Editions, 1978.
White Life, Jordan Davies, 1980.
Attitude, Hanging Loose Press, 1982.
Hollywood Magic, Little Caesar Press, 1982.

PLAYS

(And director) "Four Grown Men" (one-act), first produced in New York City, 1982.
(And director and starring actor) "Hollywood Magic" (performance play), first produced in Los Angeles, CA, 1983.
(Co-author and co-star) "The Rhythm of Torn Stars" (two-act), first produced in Los Angeles in 1988.

OTHER

Reviewer, *Washington Post,* 1975-80, and *Village Voice,* 1978-80. Contributor to more than two hundred periodicals. Editor of periodicals, including *Iowa Defender, Daily Iowan, Campus Underground,* and *Washington Review of the Arts.*

WORK IN PROGRESS: A novel; a volume of selected poems; a two-act play; a screenplay.

SIDELIGHTS: Michael Lally told *CA,* "I started out as a musician (piano and bass), mostly jazz, so music, especially American music, has been a great source of inspiration for my work and the generating force behind my ideas on structure and movement, both in poetry and prose."

Some of Lally's work has appeared in foreign editions.

BIOGRAPHICAL/CRITICAL SOURCES:

BOOKS

The Language Book, Southern Illinois University Press, 1984.
Thompson, Toby, *The Sixties Report,* Rawson Wade Publishers, 1979.

PERIODICALS

Sun and Moon Quarterly, spring, 1976.

*   *   *

LAMONT-BROWN, Raymond 1939-

PERSONAL: Some biographical and bibliographical sources index under name Brown; born September 20, 1939, in Leeds, England; son of James (a civil engineer) and Margaret Isabella (Johnston) Lamont-Brown; married Jean Elizabeth Adamson, April 14, 1973 (died December 11, 1979); married Dr. Elizabeth Moira McGregor, September 6, 1985. *Education:* Attended British Institute of Technology, 1958-59, and School of Oriental and African Studies, 1959-60; Nihon Daigaku, Tokyo, M.A., 1961; Institute of Engineering Technology, M.A., 1963; also attended Bradford Technical College. *Religion:* Anglican.

ADDRESSES: Home—3 Crawford House, 132 North St., St. Andrews, Fife KY 16 9AF, Scotland.

CAREER: Yorkshire Electricity Board, Bradford, England, staff member in commercial and accounting departments, 1963-65; free-lance writer, 1965—. Adult education lecturer at University of St. Andrews, 1978—; extra-mural lecturer at University of Dundee, 1982—. Founder of Japan Research Projects, 1965. Editor of M. B. Publications, Ltd., 1967-69.

MEMBER: Japan Society, Society of Authors in Scotland (honorary secretary), Royal Society of Antiquaries of Scotland, St. Andrews Rotary Club (past president).

WRITINGS:

History of St. Mark's Church, Dewsbury, 1865-1965, Birkdale Books, 1965.
A Book of Epitaphs, Taplinger, 1967.
Doncaster Rural District Official Guide, Directory Publications, 1967.
Clarinda: The Intimate Story of Robert Burns and Agnes MacLehose, M. B. Publications, 1968.
Sir Walter Scott's Letters on Demonology and Witchcraft, Citadel, 1968.
Robert Burns's Commonplace Book, S. R. Publishers, 1969.
A Book of Superstitions, Taplinger, 1970.
A Book of Proverbs, Taplinger, 1970.
A Book of Witchcraft, Taplinger, 1971.
General Trade in Berwick-on-Tweed, 1894, Bell, 1972.
Charles Kirkpatrick Sharpe's Historical Account of the Belief of Witchcraft in Scotland, S. R. Publishers, 1972.
Phantoms of the Sea, Taplinger, 1972.
Robert Burns's Tour of the Borders, Boydell Press, 1972.
Phantoms, Legends, Customs, and Superstitions of the Sea, Taplinger, 1972.
The Magic Oracles of Japan, Fowler, 1972.
Robert Burns's Tour of the Highlands and Stirlingshire, Boydell Press, 1973.
A New Book of Epitaphs, Frank Graham, 1973.
A Casebook of Military Mystery, Drake, 1974.
Phantoms of the Theatre, Thomas Nelson, 1977.
Epitaphs Hunting, Thornhill Press, 1977.
Scottish Epitaphs, Thornhill Press, 1977.
Growing Up with the Highland Clans, Wayland, 1978.
Walks for Motorists: Lothian and the Southeast Borders, Warne, 1980.
(With Peter Adamson) *Victorian and Edwardian Fife from Old Photographs,* Ramsey Head Press, 1980.
(With Adamson) *The Victorian and Edwardian Borderland from Rare Photographs,* Alvie, 1980.

East Anglian Epitaphs, Acorn, 1980.
My Fun Book of Scotland, Holmes McDougall, 1981.
(With Adamson) *Victorian and Edwardian Dundee and Broughty Ferry,* Alvie, 1981.
Mary Queen of Scots, Spurbooks, 1982.
Mysteries and Legends, Spurbooks, 1982.
(With Adamson) *Fife, 1910-50,* Alvie, 1982.
Drives around Edinburgh, Macdonald, 1983.
Drives around Glasgow, Macdonald, 1983.
Visitor's Guide to St. Andrews, Alvie, 1983.
Mothers-in-Law, Alvie, 1983.
A Book of British Eccentrics, David & Charles, 1984.
(With Adamson) *St. Andrews: City of Change,* Alvie, 1984.
Irish Grave Humour, Dufour, 1987.
Discovering Fife, J. Donald, 1988.
The Life and Times of Berwick-on-Tweed, J. Donald, 1989.
The Life and Times of St. Andrews, J. Donald, 1989.
Royal Murder Mysteries, Alvie, 1990.

Contributor of about two hundred fifty articles to magazines all over the world. Managing editor, *Writers' Monthly,* 1984-86.

WORK IN PROGRESS: Royal Murder Mysteries; general dictionaries and reference books on literature and history; researching a photographic history of Scotland from Victorian times; books on Scottish culture.

SIDELIGHTS: Raymond Lamont-Brown writes *CA:* "I strive, through the written word, to bring a greater understanding of the motivation of the 'Oriental mind' to the West. I have travelled widely in the Far East, and promoted English literature in the Orient. To this may be added a wish to promote the writing of humour and the dissemination of the culture of Scotland."

Lamont-Brown's work has been translated into French, German, Spanish, Japanese, and Hebrew.

*   *   *

LANGFORD, Gerald 1911-

PERSONAL: Born October 20, 1911, in Montgomery, AL; son of Samuel Martin and Mary Selma (Jackson) Langford; married Anne Crenshaw Phelps, 1938; children: Mary Jackson, Ann Phelps. *Education:* University of Virginia, B.A., 1933, M.A., 1934, Ph.D., 1940. *Religion:* Episcopalian.

ADDRESSES: Home—1711 Pearl St., Austin, TX 78701. *Office*—Department of English, University of Texas, Austin, TX 78712. *Agent*—McIntosh & Otis, Inc., 475 Fifth Ave., New York, NY 10017.

CAREER: University of Kentucky, Lexington, instructor, 1936-38; North Carolina State College (now North Carolina State University at Raleigh), instructor, 1938-40; Winthrop College, Rock Hill, SC, associate professor of English, 1940-43; University of Texas at Austin, assistant professor, 1946-50, associate professor, 1950-62, professor of English, 1962-83, professor emeritus, 1983—. *Military service:* U.S. Marine Corps, 1943-46.

MEMBER: Texas Institute of Letters.

WRITINGS:

Alias O. Henry, Macmillan, 1957, reprinted, Greenwood Press, 1983.
The Richard Harding Davis Years, Holt, 1961.
The Murder of Stanford White, Bobbs-Merrill, 1962.
(Editor) *Ingenue among the Lions: The Letters of Emily Clark to Joseph Hergesheimer,* University of Texas Press, 1965.

(Editor) *Faulkner's Revision of "Absalom, Absalom": A Collation of the Manuscript and the Published Book,* University of Texas Press, 1971.

(Editor) *Faulkner's Revision of "Sanctuary": A Collation of the Unrevised Galleys and the Published Book,* University of Texas Press, 1972.

Destination (novel), Stonehenge, 1981.

Contributor of short stories to various literary quarterlies such as *Prairie Schooner, Perspective, Epoch,* and *Georgia Review.*

* * *

LANSDALE, Joe R(ichard)   1951-

PERSONAL: Born October 28, 1951, in Gladewater, TX; son of Alcee Bee (a mechanic) and Reta (in sales; maiden name, Wood) Lansdale; married Cassie Ellis, June 25, 1970 (divorced, 1972); married Karen Ann Morton, August 25, 1973; children: (second marriage) Keith Jordan, Kasey JoAnn. *Education:* Attended Tyler Junior College, 1970-71, University of Texas at Austin, 1971-72, and Stephen F. Austin State University, 1973, 1975, 1976.

ADDRESSES: Home and office—113 Timber Ridge, Nacogdoches, TX 75961. *Agent*—Barbara Puechner, 3121 Portage Rd., Bethlehem, PA 18017.

CAREER: Worked variously as a bouncer, bodyguard, transportation manager, custodian, and karate instructor; free-lance writer, 1981—.

MEMBER: Horror Writers of America, Western Writers of America (treasurer, 1987).

AWARDS, HONORS: Bram Stoker Award, Horror Writers of America, 1989, for "Night They Missed the Horror Show."

WRITINGS:

FICTION

Act of Love, Zebra Books, 1981.
Dead in the West, Space & Time Books, 1986.
The Magic Wagon, Doubleday, 1986.
The Nightrunners, Dark Harvest, 1987.
The Drive In, Bantam, 1988.
Cold in July, Bantam, 1989.
The Drive In 2, Bantam, 1989.
By Bizarre Hands, Ziesing, 1989.

EDITOR

Best of the West, Doubleday, 1986.
The New Frontier: Best of the West 2, Doubleday, 1989.
(With Pat Lo Brutto) *Razored Saddles,* Dark Harvest, 1989.

OTHER

Contributor to several anthologies, including *Fears,* 1984, and *Book of the Dead,* Bantam, 1989. Contributor of articles, stories, and reviews to magazines, including *Horror Show, Modern Stories, Espionage,* and *Mike Shayne.*

WORK IN PROGRESS: Short stories.

SIDELIGHTS: Joe R. Lansdale told *CA:* "If I am known at all, I am best known for my short stories. The Martian series by Edgar Rice Burroughs got me started, and I've been writing my own stories ever since. My work ranges from popular to literary. I believe the purpose of fiction is to entertain. Enlightening the reader is nice, but secondary. If you don't have a good tale to tell, no one is listening anyway.

"My preferred genre is the fantastic, but suspense runs a close second, followed by mystery, westerns, and the mainstream. Actually, much of my work and intended work is a combination of these things. I am also interested in screenplays, and hope to work in that medium on occasion. All of my western material has been nothing more than entertainment. However, I do have ambition to do better work that not only entertains but also gives the reader my own peculiar, possibly even warped, vision of those times.

"I like all kinds of horror and fantasy writing, especially the contemporary horror tale. I am not too fond, though, of the vague ending that seems so popular in many publications today. Much of what I write, although it is called horror, is really just oddball or weird fantasy, perhaps never becoming scary, but certainly striking a note of the unusual.

"I am also interested in writing stories about East Texas—mainstream tales that deal with my part of the country."

He later added: "My writing is done to entertain and to please me. And to put bread on the table. I like to think my work has something going for it besides momentum. That there is some thematic depth that will ring in the reader's head afterwards like an echo. I'm attempting to blend the pacing and color of genre fiction with the character and style of the mainstream. And maybe doing a damn bad job of it. But I'm trying."

BIOGRAPHICAL/CRITICAL SOURCES:

PERIODICALS

Horror Show, January, 1987.
Mystery Scene, August, 1987.

* * *

La SALLE, Victor
See FANTHORPE, R(obert) Lionel

* * *

LAURENCE, Dan H.   1920-

PERSONAL: Born March 28, 1920, in New York, NY. *Education:* Hofstra University, B.A., 1946; New York University, M.A., 1950.

ADDRESSES: Office—The Shaw Festival, Box 774, Niagara-On-The-Lake, Ontario, L0S 1J0 Canada.

CAREER: Hofstra University, Hempstead, NY, instructor in English, 1953-58; New York University, New York City, associate professor, 1962-67, professor of English, 1967-70; literary and dramatic advisor, estate of Bernard Shaw, 1973—. The Shaw Festival, literary advisor, 1982—, associate director, 1988. Adjunct professor of drama, University of Guelph, 1985—. Visiting professor, University of Texas at Austin, 1974-75; visiting fellow, Institute for the Arts and Humanistic Studies, Pennsylvania State University, 1976; Mellon Professor, Tulane University, and Mitchell Distinguished Lecturer in Literature, Trinity University, both 1981; visiting distinguished professor of drama, University of Georgia, 1983; visiting professor of English, University of British Columbia, 1984. *Military service:* U.S. Army Air Forces, 1942-45.

MEMBER: Royal Academy of Dramatic Art.

AWARDS, HONORS: Guggenheim fellow, 1960, 1961, 1972; Montgomery fellow, Dartmouth College, 1982.

WRITINGS:

(With Leon Edel) *A Bibliography of Henry James,* Hart-Davis, 1957, third revised edition, 1982.

Robert Nathan: A Bibliography, Yale University Library, 1960.

(Editor) *Uncollected Writings of Bernard Shaw,* Hill & Wang, Volume 1: *How to Become a Musical Critic,* 1961, Volume 2: *Platform and Pulpit,* 1961, Volume 3: (with David Greene) *The Matter with Ireland,* 1962.

(Editor) *Collected Letters of Bernard Shaw,* Dodd, Volume 1, 1965, Volume 2, 1972, Viking, Volume 3, 1985, Volume 4, 1988.

(Editor) *Bodley Head Shaw: Collected Plays,* seven volumes, Reinhardt, 1970-74.

Shaw, Books and Libraries (lecture), Humanities Research Center, University of Texas, 1976.

Shaw: An Exhibit, Humanities Research Center, University of Texas, 1977.

(Editor with Daniel J. Leary) *Flyleaves,* W. Thomas Taylor, 1977.

The Fifth Gospel of Bernard Shaw (lecture), Tulane University, 1981.

(Editor) *Shaw's Music: The Complete Musical Criticism,* three volumes, Dodd, 1981.

(General editor) Bernard Shaw, *Early Texts: Play Manuscripts in Facsimile,* twelve volumes, Garland, 1981.

Bernard Shaw: A Bibliography, two volumes, Oxford University Press, 1982.

(Editor with Martin Quinn) *Shaw on Dickens,* Ungar, 1982.

(Editor with James Rambeau) *Agitations: Shaw's Letters to the Press, 1875-1950,* Ungar, 1983.

(Editor with Nicholas Grene) *Shaw, Lady Gregory, and The Abbey: A Correspondence,* Colin Smythe, 1989.

WORK IN PROGRESS: A study of Shaw and the American theater; an edition of Shaw's theater letters.

SIDELIGHTS: In compiling an editing the vast body of writing that constitutes *Shaw's Music: The Complete Musical Criticism,* Dan H. Laurence, says Edward Rothstein of the *New York Review of Books,* "has performed a service both to [George Bernard] Shaw and the contemporary reader." Included in the three-volume series are "not only reviews," Rothstein continues, "but *The Perfect Wagnerite,* the essay 'How to Become a Musical Critic,' a page from Shaw's musical setting of verses by [Percy Bysshe] Shelley, Shaw's critical showdowns with [fellow British music critic] Ernest Newman in 1910 and 1914, a report he wrote on Salvation Army bands in 1906, and an index that refers to [German poet Johann Wolfgang] Goethe, [German composer Hermann] Goetz, and the Royal College of Music."

While best known for his plays and essays, Shaw took pride in his career as a music critic; according to Donal Henahan's *New York Times Book Review* article, Shaw once bragged that he "could make deaf stockbrokers read [his] two pages on music." Indeed, says Henahan, the renowned author "turns out to have been an amazingly solid critic. He . . . offended many readers, since he made his points with more wit and force than the English musical community of his day considered in good taste. And long after he had retired from music criticism, he was still making enemies by attacking the estimable Ernest Newman for not liking Richard Strauss's later works. The fact that Shaw had not heard some of the works in question mattered little to a man of such powerful convictions."

BIOGRAPHICAL/CRITICAL SOURCES:

PERIODICALS

American Scholar, autumn, 1984.
Globe and Mail (Toronto), September 10, 1988.
Los Angeles Times Book Review, January 3, 1982, July 7, 1985, June 16, 1988.
Newsweek, November 30, 1981.
New York Review of Books, April 1, 1982.
New York Times, June 18, 1985, May 27, 1988.
New York Times Book Review, November 15, 1981, June 30, 1985, June 19, 1988.
Time, July 15, 1985.
Times (London), May 30, 1985.
Times Literary Supplement, July 16, 1982, May 4, 1984, May 31, 1985, February 21, 1986, June 24, 1988.
Tribune Books (Chicago), May 15, 1988.
Washington Post Book World, June 23, 1985, June 5, 1988.

*   *   *

LAWRENCE, D. Baloti 1950-

PERSONAL: Born March 6, 1950, in Washington, DC; son of Eugene (a counselor) and Doris (in sales) Lawrence; children: Sharnell, Zantia, Baloti, Michelle. *Education:* Montgomery Community College, A.A., 1970; Antioch College, B.A., 1978; Columbia Pacific University, received M.A., Ph.D., 1984.

ADDRESSES: *Home*—1900 Broadway, Box 1206, New York, NY 10023. *Office*—Box 116, Ansonia Station, New York, NY 10023. *Agent*—Sam Mitnick, 91 Henry St., San Francisco, CA 94114.

CAREER: Served as assistant professor at Antioch College, Yellow Springs, OH; Fontana Associates, New York City, consultant, 1979-81; Lawrence/Harrison Institute, New York City, co-founder and president, 1980—. U.S. Department of Health, Education, and Welfare, staff educator, 1977—; guest lecturer at Columbia and Georgetown Universities; faculty member at Morgan State College and Upsala College. Guest on radio and television shows in the United States, Europe, and the Virgin Islands; producer of "Point Me to Tomorrow," a film released by the Department of Health, Education, and Welfare; producer of radio program "Good Vibrations" for National Public Radio. Chief operating officer of Holden International; consultant to the Veterans Administration.

MEMBER: American Center for Homeopathy, American Association of Nutritional Consultants, National Academy of Dietary Consultants, American Massage and Therapy Association, Biofeedback Society of America, New York Academy of Sciences.

WRITINGS:

(With Lewis Harrison) *Massageworks: A Practical Encyclopedia of Massage Techniques,* Putnam, 1982.
The Guide to Total Well-Being, Putnam, 1984.
Guide to Total Beauty And Fitness, Lawrence/Harrison Institute, 1985.
Head to Toe Massage, Putnam, 1986.
Water Works, Putnam, 1989.

Inventor of videogame, "Imagination."

SIDELIGHTS: D. Baloti Lawrence told *CA:* "*Massageworks* has been described as the most complete book ever written on massage and total fitness. When writing this book we thought to provide a text for professional health practitioners and those who simply want to know how to relieve their own aches and pains. While it provides a road map to fitness, it also covers important factors such as exercise, nutrition, the use of hydrotherapy, and recipes for beauty.

"World harmony is a concept that is very close to my heart. As the world increases its population, activity increases and the human lifestyle becomes more complicated. Along with this intensity comes a general feeling of overwork, stress, and tension. Healing the individual body and creating harmony between the mind and body seem also to heal the environment. Providing fitness to individuals causes those individuals to feel better about themselves and their fellow human beings. World harmony starts at the root of each person. My contribution to this process is through total well-being. Creating a feeling of well-being—or, bringing the world together—involves the efforts of many people bringing together many issues and projects.

"I have had the opportunity to travel the globe on numerous occasions, and the international experience is interesting to me. The lifestyles and nuances of cultures and the people who comprise them offer the individuality that sparks the creative process. I seek, through the means of communication, to guide people toward mental, physical, and emotional harmony."

*   *   *

LEGEZA, (Ireneus) Laszlo 1934-

PERSONAL: Born June 25, 1934, in Debrecen, Hungary; son of Ireneus (a doctor of political science) and Gizella (Kovesi) Legeza; married Ilona Iren Levai, February 18, 1957. *Education:* Eoetvoes Lorand Tudomanyegyetem, B.A. (honors), 1956; University of London, B.A. (honors), 1960. *Religion:* Taoist.

ADDRESSES: Home—Taal Cottage, Maharlika, Tagaytay City 4120, Philippines.

CAREER: University of Durham, Durham, England, assistant librarian and Chinese cataloger, 1963-67, deputy curator of Gulbenkian Museum of Oriental Art and Archaeology, beginning 1967.

MEMBER: Oriental Ceramic Society (London; member of council, 1973—).

AWARDS, HONORS: Ford scholar at University of London, 1960-63.

WRITINGS:

Guide to Transliterated Chinese in the Modern Peking Dialect, two volumes, E. J. Brill, 1968-69.
A Descriptive and Illustrated Catalogue of the Malcolm MacDonald Collection of Chinese Ceramics, Oxford University Press, 1972.
(With Philip Rawson) *Tao: The Chinese Philosophy of Time and Change,* Avon, 1973.
Tantra: The Indian Cult of Ecstasy, Thames & Hudson, 1973.
(With Ajitcoomar Mookerjee) *Yoga Art,* New York Graphic Society, 1975.
Tao Magic: The Chinese Art of the Occult, Pantheon, 1975 (published in England as *Tao Magic: The Secret Language of Diagrams and Calligraphy,* Thames & Hudson, 1975).
Erotic Art of India, Thames & Hudson, 1977.
Art of Tantra, Thames & Hudson, 1978.
Oriental Erotic Art, Quartet Books, 1981.

General editor of "Oxford in Asia in Ceramics" series, Oxford University Press, 1973—. Contributor to art magazines. Laszlo

Legeza's books on Tao have been published in French, German, and Dutch.

AVOCATIONAL INTERESTS: Foreign travel, languages, cooking.

*   *   *

Le GUIN, Ursula K(roeber) 1929-

PERSONAL: Surname pronounced "Luh-Gwin"; born October 21, 1929, in Berkeley, Calif.; daughter of Alfred L. (an anthropologist) and Theodora Covel Brown (a writer; maiden name, Kracaw) Kroeber; married Charles Alfred Le Guin (a historian), December 22, 1953; children: Elisabeth, Caroline, Theodore. *Education:* Radcliffe College, A.B., 1951; Columbia University, A.M., 1952.

ADDRESSES: Agent—Virginia Kidd, P.O. Box 278, Milford, PA 18337; and Ilse Lahn, Paul Kohner Inc., 9169 Sunset Blvd., Los Angeles, CA 90069.

CAREER: Writer. Department secretary, Emory University, Atlanta, GA. Part-time instructor in French at Mercer University, Macon, GA, 1954-55, and University of Idaho, Moscow, 1956. Visiting lecturer and writer in residence at various locations, including Portland State University, University of California, San Diego, University of Reading, England, Kenyon College, Tulane University, and First Australian Workshop in Speculative Fiction. Creative consultant for Public Broadcasting Service, for television production of *The Lathe of Heaven,* 1979.

MEMBER: Authors League of America, Writers Guild, PEN, Science Fiction Research Association, Science Fiction Writers Association, Science Fiction Poetry Association, Writers Guild West, Planned Parenthood Federation of America, Amnesty International of the USA, Nature Conservancy, National Organization for Women, National Abortion Rights Action League, Women's International League for Peace and Freedom, Phi Beta Kappa.

AWARDS, HONORS: Fulbright fellowship 1953; *Boston Globe-Horn Book* Award, 1968, Lewis Carroll Shelf Award, 1979, *Horn Book* honor list citation, and American Library Association Notable Book citation, all for *A Wizard of Earthsea;* Nebula Award, Science Fiction Writers Association, and Hugo Award, International Science Fiction Association, both for best novel, both 1970, both for *The Left Hand of Darkness;* Nebula Award nomination, novelette category, 1969, for "Nine Lives"; Newbery Silver Medal Award, and National Book Award for Children's Literature finalist, both 1972, and American Library Association Notable Book citation, all for *The Tombs of Atuan;* Child Study Association of America's Children's Books of the Year citation, 1972, and National Book Award for Children's Books, 1973, both for *The Farthest Shore;* Hugo Award for best novella, 1973, for *The Word for World Is Forest;* Hugo Award nomination, Nebula Award nomination, and *Locus* Award, all 1973, all for *The Lathe of Heaven;* Hugo Award for best short story, 1974, for "The Ones Who Walk Away from Omelas"; American Library Association's Best Young Adult Books citation, 1974, for *The Dispossessed: An Ambiguous Utopia;* Hugo Award, Nebula Award, Jupiter Award, all for best novel, and Jules Verne Award, all 1975, all for *The Dispossessed: An Ambiguous Utopia;* Nebula Award, and Jupiter Award, both for best short story, both 1975, both for "The Day Before the Revolution"; Nebula Award nomination and Jupiter Award, both 1976, both for short story "The Diary of the Rose"; National Book Award finalist, American Library Association's Best Young

Adult Books citation, Child Study Association of America's Children's Books of the Year citation, and *Horn Book* honor list citation, all 1976, and Prix Lectures-Jeunesse, 1987, all for *Very Far Away from Anywhere Else;* Gandalf Award nomination, 1978; D.Litt., Bucknell University, 1978; Gandalf Award (Grand Master of Fantasy), 1979; Balrog Award nomination for best poet, 1979; Locus Award, 1984, for *The Compass Rose;* American Book Award nomination, 1985, and Janet Heidinger Kafka Prize for Fiction, University of Rochester English Department and Writer's Workshop, 1986, both for *Always Coming Home.*

WRITINGS:

NOVELS

Rocannon's World (bound with *The Kar-Chee Reign* by Avram Davidson; also see below), Ace Books, 1966.

Planet of Exile (bound with *Mankind Under the Lease* by Thomas M. Disch; also see below), Ace Books, 1966.

City of Illusions (also see below), Ace Books, 1967.

A Wizard of Earthsea (illustrations by Ruth Robbins; also see below), Houghton, 1968.

The Left Hand of Darkness, Ace Books, 1969, reprinted, Chelsea House, 1987.

The Tombs of Atuan (sequel to *A Wizard of Earthsea;* illustrations by Gail Garraty; also see below), Athenaeum, 1970.

The Lathe of Heaven, Scribner, 1971.

The Farthest Shore (sequel to *The Tombs of Atuan;* illustrations by Garraty; Junior Literary Guild selection; also see below), Athenaeum, 1972.

The Dispossessed: An Ambiguous Utopia, Harper, 1974.

Orsinian Tales, Harper, 1976.

Very Far Away from Anywhere Else, Athenaeum, 1976 (published in England as *A Very Long Way from Anywhere Else,* Gollancz, 1976).

The Earthsea Trilogy (includes *The Wizard of Earthsea, The Tombs of Atuan,* and *The Furthest Shore*), Gollancz, 1977.

Three Hainish Novels (contains *Rocannon's World, Planet of Exile,* and *City of Illusions*), Doubleday, 1978.

Malafrena, Putnam, 1979.

The Beginning Place, Harper, 1980 (published in England as *Threshold,* Gollancz, 1980).

The Eye of the Heron and Other Stories (novella; originally published in collection *Millennial Women;* also see below), Panther, 1980, Harper, 1983.

The Visionary (bound with *Wonders Hidden,* by Scott R. Sanders), McGraw, 1984.

Always Coming Home (includes tape cassette of "Music and Poetry of the Kesh," with music by Todd Barton [also see below]; illustrations by Margaret Chodos; diagrams by George Hersh), Harper, 1985, published without cassette, Bantam, 1987.

Tehanu: The Last Book of Earthsea (sequel to *The Farthest Shore*), Atheneum, 1990.

JUVENILES

Solomon Leviathan's Nine Hundred Thirty-First Trip around the World (originally published in collection *Puffin's Pleasures;* also see below), illustrations by Alicia Austin, Puffin, 1976, Cheap Street, 1983.

Leese Webster, illustrations by James Brunsman, Athenaeum, 1979.

The Adventures of Cobbler's Rune, illustrations by Austin, Cheap Street, 1982.

Adventures in Kroy, Cheap Street, 1982.

A Visit from Dr. Katz (picture book), illustrations by Ann Barrow, Atheneum, 1988.

Catwings, illustrations by S. D. Schindler, Orchard, 1988.

Catwings Return, illustrations by Schindler, Orchard, 1989.

POEMS

Wild Angels (collection of early works), Capra, 1974.

(With mother, Theodora K. Quinn) *Tillai and Tylissos,* Red Bull, 1979.

Torrey Pines Reserve (broadsheet), Lord John, 1980.

Hard Words and Other Poems, Harper, 1981.

(With artist Henk Pander) *In the Red Zone,* Lord John, 1983.

Buffalo Gals and Other Animal Presences (short stories and poems), Capra, 1987.

Wild Oats and Fireweed, Harper, 1988.

OTHER

From Elfland to Poughkeepsie (lecture), Pendragon Press, 1973.

The Wind's Twelve Quarters (short stories), Harper, 1975.

Dreams Must Explain Themselves (critical essays), Algol Press, 1975.

Orsinian Tales (short stories), Harper, 1976.

The Water Is Wide (short story), Pendragon Press, 1976.

The Word for World Is Forest (novella; originally published in collection *Again, Dangerous Visions;* also see below), Berkley, 1976.

(Editor) *Nebula Award Stories 11,* Gollancz, 1976, Harper, 1977.

The Language of the Night: Essays on Fantasy and Science Fiction, (critical essays), edited by Susan Wood, Putnam, 1978.

(Editor with Virginia Kidd) *Interfaces: An Anthology of Speculative Fiction,* Ace, 1980.

(Editor with Kidd) *Edges: Thirteen New Tales from the Borderlands of the Imagination,* Pocket Books, 1980.

The Compass Rose (short stories), Harper, 1982.

King Dog: A Screenplay (bound with *Dostoevsky: A Screenplay,* by Raymond Carver and Tess Gallagher), Capra, 1985.

(With Barton) *Music and Poetry of the Kesh* (cassette), Valley Productions, 1985.

(With David Bedford) *Rigel Nine: An Audio Opera,* Charisma, 1985.

(With composer Elinor Armer) *Uses of Music in Uttermost Parts* (music and text), first performed in part in San Francisco, CA, and Seattle, WA, 1986, 1987, and 1988.

Dancing at the Edge of the World: Thoughts on Words, Women, Places (essays), Grove, 1989.

Contributor to anthologies, including *Orbit 5,* 1969, *Orbit 6,* 1970, *Orbit 14,* 1974, *Best SF: 1969,* 1970, *World's Best Science Fiction,* 1970, *Those Who Can,* 1970, *Nebula Award Stories 5,* 1970, *Nebula Award Stories 10,* 1975, *Quark #1,* 1970, *The Dead Astronaut,* 1971, *New Dimensions I,* 1972, *New Dimensions III,* 1973, *Clarion II,* 1972, *Clarion III,* 1973, *Again, Dangerous Visions,* Volume 1, 1972, *The Best from Playboy,* number 7, 1973, *The New Atlantis and Novellas of Science Fiction,* 1975, *Universe 5,* 1974, *The Best from Galaxy,* Volume 2, 1974, *The Best from Galaxy,* Volume 3, 1975, *Dream Trips,* 1974, *Epoch,* 1975, *The New Atlantis and Other Novellas of Science Fiction,* 1975, *The Thorny Paradise,* 1975, *Bitches and Sad Ladies,* 1975, *More Women of Wonder,* 1976, *The Best Science Fiction of the Year #5,* 1976, *Science Fiction at Large,* 1976, 1977, *Future Power,* 1976, *The Altered I: An Encounter with Science Fiction,* 1978, *Puffin's Pleasure,* 1976, *Best Science Fiction Stories of the Year,* Sixth Annual Collection, 1977, *Psy Fi One,* 1977, *The Norton Anthology of Short Fiction,* 1978, *Millennial Women,* 1978, *Cassandra Rising,* 1978, *Dark Imaginings,* 1978. Author of postcard short story, *Post Card Partnership,* 1975, and *Sword & Sorcery*

Annual, 1975. Contributor of short stories, novellas, essays, and reviews to numerous science fiction, scholarly, and popular periodicals, including *Science-Fiction Studies, New Yorker, Antaeus, Parabola, New Republic, Redbook, Playgirl, Playboy, New Yorker, Yale Review,* and *Omni.* Author of abridged version of *The Left Hand of Darkness,* for Warner Audio, 1985. Le Guin recorded *Gwilan's Harp and Intracom,* for Caedmon, 1977, *The Ones Who Walk Away from Omelas and Other Stories, and The Lathe of Heaven,* for Alternate World, 1976, and *The Left Hand of Darkness* for Warner Audio.

MEDIA ADAPTATIONS: The Word for World Is Forest was made into a sound recording by Book of the Road, 1968; *The Tombs of Atuan* became a filmstrip with record or cassette by Newbery Award Records, 1980; an abridged version of *The Earthsea Trilogy* was made into a sound recording by Colophone, 1981; *The Lathe of Heaven* was televised by the Public Broadcasting Service in 1979; "The Ones Who Walk Away from Omelas" was performed as a drama with dance and music at the Portland Civic Theatre in 1981.

SIDELIGHTS: Critics have often found it difficult to classify Ursula Le Guin: while some consider her writing science fiction fantasy, Le Guin herself discounts any narrow genre categorizations. She wrote *CA* that "some of my fiction is 'science fiction,' some of it is 'fantasy,' some of it is 'realist,' [and] some of it is 'magical realism.' " Le Guin has also written several volumes of poetry and essays. "A significant amount of science fiction has been profoundly thoughtful about the situation of contemporary humanity in the light of its possible futures and its imaginable alternatives. In recent years, no [writer] inside the field of science fiction or outside of it [has] done more to create a modern conscience than . . . Ursula K. Le Guin," writes Derek de Solla Price in the *New Republic.* Le Guin, however, "is not competing with Orwell or Hemingway," according to George Edgar Slusser in his book *The Furthest Shores of Ursula Le Guin.* "Her social analysis is acute, but its purpose is not indignation or reform. She has no social program, offers no panaceas." And a *Cambridge Review: Fantasy in Literature* contributor finds Le Guin "an elegant, but not a light writer: not to be trifled with. Superficially, her work charms because it has all the glitter of high intelligence and efficiency."

In his essay on Le Guin in the *Dictionary of Literary Biography,* Brian Attebery writes that the author "has brought to science fiction a new sensitivity to language, a powerful set of symbols and images, and a number of striking and sympathetic characters. She has purposely avoided most technical details in order to concentrate on human problems and relationships. . . . Le Guin's fiction is extraordinarily risky: it is full of hypotheses about morality, love, society, and ways of enriching life expressed in the symbolic language found in myth, dream, or poetry. However, the greater the risk, the greater the reward, and for the reader . . . the reward is a glimpse of something glowing, something very much like truth." Similarly, Joseph D. Olander and Martin Harry Greenberg say in their introduction to *Ursula K. Le Guin* that, while "Le Guin's fiction may be filled with wizards, aliens, and clones, . . . the vision contained in her stories and novels is, above all, concerned with what is most permanent about the human condition." *Modern Fiction Studies* contributor Keith N. Hull notes: "Certainly one of the most important lessons in Le Guin's novels is that humanity is a broader, deeper entity than we ordinarily think and that the definition of humanity requires constant expansion as our experience broadens. Because of this theme, Le Guin's work risks being polemical and sentimental, but her best work exploits it beautifully."

Le Guin first began to receive critical and popular attention with her Earthsea novels, the first being *A Wizard of Earthsea.* The Earthsea trilogy, considered by Le Guin to be among her best work, exemplifies her holistic perspective of the universe, a perspective shaped by Taoist philosophy. As Robert Scholes suggests in a *Hollins Critic* article, "What Earthsea represents, through its world of islands and waterways, is the universe as a dynamic, balanced system . . . which include[s] a role for magic and for powers other than human, but only as aspects of the great Balance or Equilibrium, which is the order of this cosmos. Whereas C. S. Lewis worked out of a specifically Christian set of values, Ursula Le Guin works not with a theology but with an ecology, a cosmology, a reverence for the universe as a self-regulating structure." The theme of equilibrium between opposing forces works on several levels within the trilogy. On the most immediate and recognizable level is the integration of man with himself. In *The Wizard of Earthsea,* the young mage, or wizard, Ged undertakes the journey to maturity and self-knowledge; in *The Tombs of Atuan,* it is the girl-priestess, Tenar; and in *The Furthest Shore,* it is Ged's apprentice Arren. Writing in *Ursula K. Le Guin,* Margaret P. Esmonde suggests that "all of these journeys symbolize the journey every human being must make, one through pain and fear, aided only by trust in the goodness of man, hand holding hand, to the acceptance of mortality." A *Times Literary Supplement* contributor praises the trilogy's depth, and concludes: "After Earthsea-lore, with its weight and substance, most other modern fantasies must ring thin."

"Two Le Guin novels of unquestionably high standing, even among readers who generally do not care for science fiction, are *The Left Hand of Darkness* and *The Dispossessed,*" writes Hull. "In these novels Le Guin . . . describes herself as writing science fiction based on 'social science, psychology, anthropology [and] history,'. . . [The result] is an emphasis on culture." *The Left Hand of Darkness* explores the themes of sexual identity, incest, xenophobia, fidelity and betrayal in a tale of an Earth ambassador, Genly Ai, who is sent to the planet of Gethen, which is peopled by an androgynous culture. Through Genly Ai's relationship with a native, Estraven, he learns to question his sexual orientation. As in many of her works, Le Guin successfully combines a social message with an engrossing story. Scholes feels that "the great power of the book comes from the way it interweaves all its levels and combines all its voices and values into an ordered, balanced, whole." In *The Dispossessed,* another character is an alien in a strange culture; the physicist Shevek, however, is also at odds with his home planet's values. He is devoted to the spread of knowledge, but the development of his theories will inevitably bring his isolated colonial planet and its mother-planet into contact, although the two cultures bitterly oppose one another. Attebery describes the novel's form as "slow, sober, down-to-earth. The writing verges on pure naturalistic reporting, except that the places being written about do not exist on Earth." He adds that *The Dispossessed* "is fuller than any other of [Le Guin's] stories in character and in social and political interplay."

Le Guin has invented many beings to inhabit the alien worlds of her fiction and has endowed them with equally diverse physical and mental characteristics. The Athsheans of *A Word for World Is Forest,* for instance, are an intelligent, hominid species covered with green fur and capable of perceiving reality through daydreams. Several different species live on the planet called Rocannon's World, including a large winged creature much like an angelic robot; the Liuar, a feudal society of very tall, lordly people with yellow hair and dark skin; the Clayfolk, short, pale, intelligent troglodytes; and the Fiia, simple-minded, elfish humanoids. And while Le Guin's societies are sometimes utopian in concept, the inhabitants are capable of very and imperfect human actions. According to the *Cambridge Review* critic, "The satisfaction of [Le Guin's] stories is that her heroes and heroines are constantly on the brink of doing the wrong thing, and sometimes do: a reader holds his breath at every turn."

Le Guin's characters and settings vary widely, and her books take place on many different planets and in varying time spans. Some, like the books of the Earthsea trilogy, take place wholly outside of our defined universe, much as do J.R.R. Tolkien's *Lord of the Rings* and C. S. Lewis's "Chronicles of Narnia." Some of Le Guin's other novels adhere to somewhat more familiar spatial and temporal structures, or are at least set within the parameters of human history. The works which form Le Guin's Hainish Cycle, example (including *Rocannon's World, Planet of Exile, City of Illusions, The Left Hand of Darkness, The Dispossessed: An Ambiguous Utopia,* and many of her short stories), are bound by a common historical context—their characters and cultures originated with a race called the Hain, whose history encompasses Earth.

The unusual work, *Always Coming Home,* concerns a people known as the Kesh, who reside in northern California after a nuclear war. The format moves between poetry and prose, and includes stories, legends, and "autobiography"; along with the book comes a tape of Kesh music. Brian D. Johnson in *Maclean's Magazine* describes *Always Coming Home* as "an 'archaeological dig' into the distant future—a search for 'shards of the broken pot at the end of the rainbow.'" Samuel R. Delaney in the *New York Times Book Review* praises the work: "With high invention and deep intelligence, *Always Coming Home* presents, in alternating narratives, poems and expositions, Ursula K. Le Guin's most consistently lyric and luminous book in a career adorned with some of the most precise and passionate prose in the service of a major imaginative vision." H. J. Kirchhoff in the Toronto *Globe & Mail* expresses the belief that Le Guin "has created an entire culture, not just a cast of characters—an impressive achievement from an impressive writer." And Delaney concludes: "This is her most satisfying text among a set of texts that have provided much imaginative pleasure."

Le Guin's excursions into the world of children's fiction have included *Solomon Leviathan's 931st Trip Around the World, Catwings,* and *Catwings Return.* In *Catwings,* four flying cats, Harriet, James, Thelma and Roger, escape city dangers to live in the country, where they are adopted by two children. *New York Times Book Review* contributor Crescent Dragonwagon finds Le Guin's "dialogue, humor, skill as a storyteller and emotional veracity combine near-flawlessly in a story that is both contemporary and timeless." She continues: "One of the book's weaknesses is that, other than for their wings, the kittens are not so remarkable, at least as individuals. . . . Still, their collective winged adventures, their looking after one another, and the understated charm of Ms. Le Guin's writing keeps us captivated. . . . [When Susan] whispers to her brother, 'Oh, Hank . . . their wings are furry,' as kitten Harriet whispers to her brother, 'Oh, James . . . their hands are kind'—well, who could fail to recognize the enduring, healing power of love?"

Dancing at the Edge of the World: Thoughts on Words, Women, Places is a collection of essays, addresses and reviews. *Los Angeles Times Book Review* critic Nancy Mairs finds the collection "unpredictable and uneven but, for those very reasons, a trove of delights: insightful, impassioned, sometimes lyrical, often funny. . . . Those who appreciate Le Guin's novels will find the pieces in [*Dancing at the Edge of the World*] no substitute for

their intricacies of vision and language. But this volume makes a fine companion, and on occasion a guide, to her fiction, offering insight into the writer at work." And Elizabeth Hand in the *Washington Post Book World* thinks the grouping shows "Ursula Le Guin at her best: insightful, funny, sharp, occasionally tendentious and nearly always provocative."

Eighteen years after the publication of *The Farthest Shore,* Le Guin came out with *Tehanu: The Last Book of Earthsea.* Michael Dirda writes in the *Washington Post Book World* that *Tehanu* "unexpectedly turns the trilogy into a tetralogy." The story concerns both Ged and Tenar, who are now old. Ged abandoned his power at the end of *The Farthest Shore;* Tenar has lived a "normal" life, and is a farmer's widow. Their lives become enmeshed with a little girl's, Therru, who has been raped and burned, but survives. Although Dirda sees the novel as "meditative, somber, even talky," it "builds to a climax of almost pornographic horror, nearly too shocking for its supposedly young adult pages." But, he adds, that while "less sheerly exciting," than the Earthsea Trilogy, *Tehanu* "may be the most moving of them all."

"Can one find a common denominator in the work and thought of Ursula K. Le Guin?" asks author Theodore Sturgeon in a *Los Angeles Times* article. "Probably not; but there are some notes in her orchestrations that come out repeatedly and with power. A cautionary fear of the development of democracy into dictatorship. Celebrations of courage, endurance, risk. Language, not only loved and shaped, but investigated in all its aspects; call that, perhaps, communication. But above all, in almost unearthly terms Ursula Le Guin examines, attacks, unbuttons, takes down and exposes our notions of reality."

CA INTERVIEW

CA interviewed Ursula K. Le Guin by telephone on May 30, 1989, at her home in Portland, Oregon.

CA: In the 1985 book Always Coming Home, *there was a tape cassette of "Music and Poetry of the Kesh," a collaboration between you and the composer Todd Barton. There was also the 1985 audio opera "Rigel Nine," with David Bedford; and there's your later collaboration with Elinor Armer, "Uses of Music in Uttermost Parts." Would you say something about the importance of music as an inspiration in your writing, and its increasing prominence in your work?*

LE GUIN: I think this started with doing a film of *The Lathe of Heaven* and a little stage performance of a short story. I got interested in collaborating with artists who weren't writers, artists in different media. Also last year I worked very hard with a dance troupe here in Portland to do some Kesh dances from *Always Coming Home.* I was one of the musicians on that; I was shaking rattles and beating drums. I got definitely involved in the piece. I do love music, and it has always been an inspiration to me, but I think what's going on is that I feel a delight in working with these other kinds of artists. Collaborating has become a real pleasure in my life. A novelist isn't a performance artist. You send the book out and other people perform it, as it were, by reading it. Sometimes it's really fun to be a ham and get on the stage with performance artists, and to do something which exists as a performance only. That's exciting.

CA: That's so different from sitting in your room writing, although some of that goes into it, of course.

LE GUIN: Yes. With a performance art you collaborate first with your fellow artists—your musicians, dancers, players—and then with the live audience during the performance. Every performance is a collaboration between the artist and the audience. It's new in my life, and I like it.

CA: You've also become increasingly vocal as a feminist, though you've always been a feminist in the deepest sense. What's prompted you to speak up more, and to address specific issues such as abortion, which you did so movingly in "So Much for Prince Charming," collected in Dancing at the Edge of the World?

LE GUIN: In that case, it was an appeal from the local chapter of the National Abortion Rights Action League. There comes a point when you've got to stand up and be counted on issues on which relentless pressure is exerted from the other side. It's not always that I've wanted to do it, but sometimes I've had to if I wanted to keep my own conscience healthy. It's more or less the same with feminism. Partly it was just a learning process: I learned to be a better feminist by reading all the wonderful stuff that's been written in the last fifteen years, both in literary scholarship and from people generally thinking about why things go wrong between men and women. What's wrong with our society as a whole seems to be partly what's wrong between men and women. All of this interests me to the core; I think some tremendously important work is going on. When feminism comes under attack, usually, quite wrongly, it's being called man-hating and nonsense like that. In this case too I want to stand up and be counted. I want to say, Listen to what we say, and don't misjudge us.

CA: Unlike many feminists, you came from a family in which you were not treated differently because you were a girl.

LE GUIN: That's right. I didn't come to feminism from a position of personal injustice or being put down or mistreated. I have no personal anger to work off, which puts me in a kind of strange position but I think a good one to speak from. I don't have to suppress the personal anger, as many women do; they have to clear that out of the way before they can get anywhere. But I would say that in general feminism has become much less angry because we know better where we stand. Bra-burning may have had to be done in the seventies, but that's a long time ago.

CA: Do you feel women have any advantages over men in writing science fiction and fantasy? Might women have more insight, for example, more sensitivity in some areas?

LE GUIN: We really don't know how differently men and women see the world, because it's so culturally ingrained. So I would be cautious about saying anything on that. Certainly as science fiction existed when I came into the field, in the sixties, women had a tremendous lot to bring to it. It had been pretty much a little boys' game. It was full of heroes running around with guns and scientists who knew everything. A lot of it was fairly boyishly childish. We women came sort of stumping in saying, Hey! There are grown-ups out there! And some of them are female! We got the whole field off the simple adventure story and made real novels. It wasn't just the women—some of the men were doing that too—but it needed a little lifting up like that, and I think it's been a much more interesting literature since.

As to the matter of women getting published, by the time I came into science fiction there were several women editors working. There had been a prejudice against women, so women writers either used their initials or took men's pen names right up to around 1960. Then the doors opened. I really don't know why;

maybe there were enough of us leaning up against them. But it's hard to point to a real case of sex prejudice in science fiction publishing. I think there may be some, but I don't know any for sure. My generation certainly found it pretty open, and there are lots of young women writing now. I think some of the best science fiction writers are some of these new women just coming into the field. It seems to be pretty open.

CA: You've spoken and written about "discovering" the worlds of your fiction, about the impossibility of saying where they come from. Are there ways that you consciously try to create a frame of mind in which these gifts can come to you?

LE GUIN: I think what you're talking about is what I call waiting. It seems me that most of an artist's job anyway—not just a writer's—is to be ready, to have the skills perfected. You should have done a lot of practicing in whatever your art is, and then you have to just hang around. I guess this is what the old artists meant when they talked about inspiration, but that sounds so fancy. If you're ready and you've got your skills ready, there's a kind of frame of mind you can cultivate. I try not to clog my mind up too much. I try to be a little bit empty-minded, literally. I would probably avoid reading novels, for instance, because they would fill my mind with the same kind of stuff that I'm waiting for. If I listen to music, I might not listen to very good music; I might turn on the country station and let it ripple by. If you overload, you drive yourself past the point where you're going to receive anything. And that's what it is: there's a reception going on. It's almost like tuning in to a station. You're just wandering around the wavelengths until something comes through.

CA: How much a part do dreams play in the germination and development of your fiction?

LE GUIN: With some writers they're apparently very important. My dreams seem to be more parallel to the creative work, and when I'm working I don't dream very much. The good time for me is not sleep, it's coming out of sleep, in the morning when I'm half awake. I think you're still receiving a lot of unconscious material then; you haven't gone into a full daylight, conscious mode yet, so the stuff comes through. That's when I do my best thinking when I'm writing.

CA: Do you usually begin writing early in the morning?

LE GUIN: Yes. And there again, to keep the channels clear I'll read only the silly parts of the newspaper so that I don't get all upset about what's happening in Israel or something.

CA: How does your poetry begin, and how does writing poetry fit into the pattern of your writing overall?

LE GUIN: Poetry came first. I was writing it when I was five. I tend to write poems in batches. Virginia Woolf said that the whole thing in writing is the rhythm; once you get the rhythm, "the words will follow of themselves." That's an amazing thing to say, and I think it's true. A poem tends to begin with a sort of beat in the mind to which words fit themselves. I don't mean that it has to be a regular beat, but you get this sense of a shape or rhythm. If it's a certain kind of shape or rhythm, you know it's a poem, not a prose piece. A prose piece has its own rhythm, but it is much longer and subtler and more mixed up with ideas. But I do not feel that there's a total, radical, essential difference between prose and poetry. They come from the same root, to me.

A lot of people think that you ought to do one or the other and you can't do both well. That is disproved by so many writers in the past.

CA: And you mix prose and poetry nicely in books.

LE GUIN: In *Always Coming Home* I was trying to do a very, very unformidable kind of poetry that wouldn't frighten a prose reader. Our poetry has been so difficult and so intense in this century, an awful lot of people don't read it because they're scared off by it.

CA: And people are no longer taught to read it in school.

LE GUIN: That's true, and it's a pity, because poetry is such lovely stuff. I think where a lot of young people get their poetry is in rock lyrics. They're mostly pretty low-grade poetry, but you put them with the music, and at least they have some of the impact.

CA: More and more critical essays are being written about what's called the magical realism of the South American writers. Do you have any thoughts about magical realism and how it should be read?

LE GUIN: I think magical realism is one of the better names not only for what Garcia-Marquez and other South American writers do, but for what a lot of us are doing. I think of Italo Calvino in Italy, who died a couple of years ago. A lot of his stuff is a kind of magical realism. I think some of what I write and some of what other science fiction and fantasy writers in America and England write is magical realism. I think it's a worldwide movement, a way of trying to write about the modern world using literary devices that are shifty and tricky and surprising enough that they can catch how very complicated our world really is.

CA: Many people resent the judgmental implications that have always been inherent in the labels "science fiction," "fantasy," and "mainstream." Do you think the classifications serve some useful purposes, on the other hand?

LE GUIN: Oh yes. For one thing, they're useful for booksellers, and therefore for publishers. People like to know where to go to find their author. The trouble with these genre labels comes with university teaching and with criticism. What started, I take it, as a market device becomes a label that means second-class. That's a real pity. It's very hard for an English professor with the best will in the world to teach a science fiction book in an American literature class. They have to have a special course called "Fantastic Literatures." It's not included. This I fight against very hard. People keep accusing me of deserting science fiction and saying I'm not a science fiction writer. Nothing of the kind. I do write science fiction, among other things, and I hope to continue to. I love the stuff. But when the label is stuck on your forehead, then you begin to have to fight, not only for yourself but for the other science fiction and fantasy writers. And look: some of this stuff is some of the best writing that's being done in the United States. You can't sweep it under the carpet and make it go away just by sticking the genre label on it. It's here.

CA: The worst thing may be that such labeling sometimes closes a door to readers.

LE GUIN: Yes. It penalizes both readers and writers. For writers, it says that what you're doing is second-rate. Here again my feminism helps me figure out how to fight the problem. Women have often been told that whatever we do is second-rate because women do it. Science fiction writers are told that whatever they do, no matter how good it is, it's second-rate because it's science fiction. This is simply a prejudice, and usually ignorance, on the part of teachers and critics. They just don't know what they're talking about. They haven't read it.

CA: You've said before in your critical writing and said recently to Kenneth R. Sibley for Book Report, *March/April 1989, that science fiction must be read critically if it is to continue growing. How do you feel science fiction has been affected by its acceptance among academics, by being examined and taught on the high school and college levels when it's done well?*

LE GUIN: I'm absolutely in favor of it. The more teaching and acceptance, the better. The more we're taken seriously, the more seriously we'll take ourselves. If writers know they're going to be seriously read by a lot of little beady-eyed graduate students, it keeps them on their mettle. There is a great deal of critical writing on writers now, and I think that's great. The only problem is that we're still herded together. For instance, Philip K. Dick is one of the science fiction writers who I think is a really good American novelist. They never compare him to Fitzgerald; they compare him to other science fiction writers. There is where there's a barrier that needs to be crossed.

CA: You've called yourself "an unconsistent Taoist and a consistent unChristian." Would you comment on what you find to live by and write by in Taoism and what you reject in Christianity?

LE GUIN: To take the question hind-end first, I was brought up in an anthropologist's household. My father was a cultural relativist. He had been brought up in the Ethical Culture movement in New York in the late nineteenth century, which was a nonreligious but, as the title implies, highly moral system of thought. I was brought up in an unreligious household; there was no religious practice of any kind. There was also no feeling that any religion was better than another, or worse; they just weren't part of our life. They were something other people did. This is a little unusual for an American. Most of us are brought up with at least some sort of brush with an established religion, and it's usually either Judaism or some form of Christianity, most often Christianity. Not having been brought up with a religion gives me a slightly different viewpoint, I realize, from a great many people. I look at Christianity not in any way as belonging to it, not in any way against it. That's why I don't say I'm anti-Christian; I say "unChristian." It puts me in a lot of trouble, believe me, with the fundamentalists. Often, even though they don't know that I made that statement, they see what's going on. They say, This woman is advocating foreign religions. I've had that alleged against my books several times. It's funny, but also a little frightening.

With the Taoism, it's simply that I came on the *Tao te ching*, Lao Tse's little book that is the center of Taoism, and began reading it. It was one of the books in our house when I was a kid. And it answered my need. It's a very quiet way of looking at the world which was developed at a time of great trouble and stress in China, rather like the twentieth century here. It was a time of wars and misery. Taoism was developed to take you through the hard times. Without being a religion, it has a lot of feeling in it, and it allows for being very much in tune with nature, which is very important to me. It seemed to fill my bill, and I love the poetry in it too; it's paradoxical and ironic.

CA: You've presided over writers' workshops as far away as Australia, and have likened the good workshop exchange to group mu-

sical performance. You've obviously contributed a lot to the success of many workshops. What do they and other public functions such as readings give back to you?

LE GUIN: Oh, lots. Energy. The energy of the participants in the workshops, the energy and goodwill of an audience. It's like floating on a river. You get carried along on what other people give you. People are incredibly generous towards artists. They feel they've got something from you and they want to give it back, and they give it back in warmth. All actors know that marvelous lift you get from an audience. With a workshop, of course, it's often working with young writers who are terrifically serious about what they're doing. You get their energy; you see the kind of work they want to do. It's very exciting.

CA: I must say how much I've enjoyed the recent cat books. Catwings *is a lovely story, and so is* A Visit from Dr. Katz. *I gather that cats are still a part of your life.*

LE GUIN: Oh yes, very much so. I was delighted with those books too. I was so lucky in my illustrators. *A Visit from Dr. Katz* is just what I hoped it would be. Ann Barrow used her niece as the model for the little girl, and her neighbor's cats. There's a sequel to *Catwings;* it's called *Catwings Return.* It just came out, with almost equally wonderful pictures, again by S. D. Schindler. I don't know the artist—we'd never met—but I asked the editor please to tell him that the cats' wings should be furry, tabby, like the cats, though of course they have to have a feather structure. I thought he did that splendidly. I've had a lovely letter from a little boy, my first fan letter for *Catwings,* and he said, "I keep looking at my cats and telling them, 'Fly! Fly!'"

CA: Do you see new directions in fiction or in publishing fiction that you consider important?

LE GUIN: I don't think publishing is in great shape at the moment. The publishers keep merging and conglomerating; it's a little worrisome. There seems to be much less adventure in publishing now; they don't seem to be willing to take on a book that they aren't sure will do well. What are young people with really queer new ideas going to do? On the other hand, it's never been easy. It took me twelve years to get published, because I wasn't doing the expectable thing. I suppose new writers will break in somewhere along the margins the way I did, but I do find it depressing when it seems as if most of the publishers are playing it so safe. Many of these bestsellers really aren't books at all, they're products. But it'll work itself out—if need be, by some of the small publishers around the country becoming stronger. Or by writers lowering their sights, realizing that they don't have to have a million-dollar advance, and publishing with smaller presses, the way poets do.

CA: Any new ideas or directions you can talk about in your own work?

LE GUIN: I hope I have some short stories coming on; I love writing short stories. But I never know what's next. I do have to wait and see, and sometimes I'm quite surprised.

BIOGRAPHICAL/CRITICAL SOURCES:

BOOKS

Authors in the News, Volume 1, Gale, 1976.
Children's Literature Review, Volume 3, Gale, 1978.
Contemporary Literary Criticism, Gale, Volume 8, 1978, Volume 13, 1980, Volume 22, 1982, Volume 45, 1987.
Dictionary of Literary Biography, Gale, Volume 8: *Twentieth-Century-American Science Fiction Writers,* Part 1, 1981,

Volume 52: *American Writers for Children since 1960: Fiction,* 1986.
Olander, Joseph D., and Greenberg, Martin Harry, editors, *Ursula K. Le Guin,* Taplinger, 1979.
Scholes, Robert, *Structural Fabulation: An Essay on Fiction of the Future,* University of Notre Dame Press, 1975.
Slusser, George Edgar, *The Farthest Shores of Ursula Le Guin,* Borgo, 1976.

PERIODICALS

Book Report, March/April, 1989.
Cambridge Review: Fantasy in Literature, November 23, 1973.
Globe & Mail (Toronto), December 7, 1985.
Hollins Critic, April, 1974.
Los Angeles Times, September 5, 1982.
Los Angeles Times Book Review, September 5, 1982, March 5, 1989.
Maclean's Magazine, November 4, 1985.
Modern Fiction Studies, spring, 1986.
New Republic, February 7, 1976, October 30, 1976.
New York Times Book Review, September 29, 1985, November 13, 1988.
Times Literary Supplement, April 6, 1973, June 3-9, 1988.
Village Voice, February 25, 1986.
Washington Post Book World, October 6, 1985, January 29, 1989, February 25, 1990.

—*Sketch by Jani Prescott*
—*Interview by Jean W. Ross*

*   *   *

LEM, Stanislaw 1921-

PERSONAL: Born September 12, 1921, in Lvov, Poland; son of Samuel (a physician); married wife, Barbara (a roentgenologist), August, 1953; children: Tomek (son). *Education:* Studied medicine in Lvov, Poland, 1939-41, 1944-46, and in Krakow, Poland, 1946-48.

ADDRESSES: Home—ul. Narwik 66, 30'436 Krakow, Poland. *Agent*—Franz Rottensteiner, Marchettigasse 9/17, A-1060 Vienna, Austria.

CAREER: Worked as garage mechanic during World War II; Jagellonian University, Krakow, Poland, assistant in "Science Circle," 1947-49; *Zycie Nauki* (monthly magazine; title means "The Life of Science"), editor, 1947-49; writer, 1949—. Teacher at University of Krakow.

MEMBER: PEN.

AWARDS, HONORS: Citations from Polish Ministry of Culture, 1965 and 1973; Polish State Prize for literature, 1976; Austrian State Prize for foreign literature, 1985; Alfred Jurzykowski Foundation award, 1987.

WRITINGS:

IN ENGLISH TRANSLATION

Dzienniki gwiazdowe (also see below; portions translated in *Mortal Engines*), Iskry, 1957, translation by Michael Kandel published as *The Star Diaries,* illustrated by the author, Seabury, 1976, translation by Joel Stern and Maria Swiecicka-Ziemianek published as *Memoirs of a Space Traveler: Further Reminiscences of Ijon Tichy,* Harcourt, 1982.
Czas nieutracony (novel; title means "Time Not Lost"), Volume 1: *Szpital przemienienia,* Wydawnictwo Literackie, 1957,

translation by William Brand published as *Hospital of the Transfiguration,* Harcourt, 1988, Volume 2: *Wsrod umarlych* (title means "Among the Dead"), Volume III: *Powrot* (title means "Return"), 1957.

Eden, Iskry, 1959, translation by Marc E. Heine published as *Eden,* Harcourt, 1989.

Sledztwo, Ministerstwa Obrony Narodowej, 1959, translation by Adele Milch published as *The Investigation,* Seabury, 1974.

Solaris, Ministerstwa Obrony Narodowej, 1961, French translation by Jean-Michel Jasiensko published as *Solaris,* Denoel, 1966, translation from the French edition by Joanna Kilmartin and Steve Cox published as *Solaris,* Walker & Co., 1970, reprinted, Harcourt, 1987.

Pamietnik znaleziony w wannie, Wydawnictwo Literackie, 1961, translation by Kandel and Christine Rose published as *Memoirs Found in a Bathtub,* Seabury, 1973.

Powrot z gwiazd, Czytelnik, 1961, translation by Barbara Marszal and Frank Simpson published as *Return from the Stars,* Harcourt, 1980.

Niezwyciezony i inne opowiadania, Ministerstwa Obrony Narodowej, 1964, German translation by Roswitha Dietrich published as *Der Unbesiegbare,* Verlag Volk und Welt, 1967, translation from the German edition by Wendayne Ackerman published as *The Invincible,* Seabury, 1973.

Bajki robotow (also see below; translation published in *Mortal Engines;* title means "Fables for Robots"), Wydawnictwo Literackie, 1964.

Cyberiada, Wydawnictwo Literackie, 1965, translation by Kandel published as *The Cyberiad: Fables for the Cybernetic Age,* Seabury, 1974.

Opowiesci o pilocie Pirxie, Wydawnictwo Literackie, 1968, translations by Louis Iribarne published as *Tales of Pirx the Pilot,* Harcourt, 1979, and *More Tales of Pirx the Pilot,* Harcourt, 1981.

Glos pana, Czytelnik, 1968, translation published as *His Master's Voice,* Harcourt, 1984.

Bezsennosc (title means "Insomnia"), Wydawnictwo Literackie, 1971, portions translated by Kandel and published as *The Futurological Congress (From the Memoirs of Ijon Tichy),* Seabury, 1974.

Doskonala proznia, Czytelnik, 1971, translation by Kandel published as *A Perfect Vacuum,* Harcourt, 1979.

Wielkosc urojona, Czytelnik, 1973, translation by Marc E. Heine published as *Imaginary Magnitude* (also see below), Harcourt, 1985.

Katar, Wydawnictwo Literackie, 1976, translation by Iribarne published as *The Chain of Chance,* Harcourt, 1978.

Maska (also see below; portions translated in *Mortal Engines;* title means "The Mask"), Wydawnictwo Literackie, 1976.

Mortal Engines, translated by Kandel, Seabury, 1977.

The Cosmic Carnival of Stanislaw Lem: An Anthology of Entertaining Stories by the Modern Master of Science Fiction, edited by Kandel, Continuum, 1981.

Golem XIV, Wydawnictwo Literackie, 1981, translation published in *Imaginary Magnitude,* Harcourt, 1985.

Microworlds: Writings on Science Fiction and Fantasy, edited by Franz Rottensteiner, Harcourt, 1984.

Biblioteka XXI Wieka, Wydawnictwo Literackie, 1986, translation by Catherine S. Leach published as *One Human Minute,* Harcourt, 1986.

Fiasko, Wydawnictwo Literackie, 1987, translation by Kandel, Harcourt, 1987.

IN POLISH

Astronauci (title means "The Astronauts"), Czytelnik, 1951.

(With Roman Hussarski) *Jacht Paradise* (play), Czytelnik, 1951.

Sezam i inne opowiadania (title means "Sesame and Other Stories"), Iskry, 1954.

Oblok Magellana (title means "The Magellan Nebula"), Iskry, 1955.

Dialogi (nonfiction; title means "Dialogues"), Wydawnictwo Literackie, 1957.

Inwazja z Aldebarana (title means "Invasion from Aldebaran"), Wydawnictwo Literackie, 1959.

Ksiega robotow (title means "Book of Robots"), Iskry, 1961.

Wejscie na orbite (nonfiction; title means "Getting into Orbit"), Wydawnictwo Literackie, 1962.

Noc ksiezycowa (title means "Lunar Night"), Wydawnictwo Literackie, 1963.

Summa technologiae (nonfiction), Wydawnictwo Literackie, 1964.

Wysoki zamek (title means "The High Castle"), Ministerstwa Obrony Narodowej, 1966.

Ratujmy kosmos i inne opowiadania (title means "Let Us Save the Cosmos and Other Stories"), Wydawnictwo Literackie, 1966.

Filozofia prypadku: Literatura w swietle empirii (nonfiction; title means "The Philosophy of Chance: Literature Considered Empirically"), Wydawnictwo Literackie, 1968.

Opowiadania (title means "Stories"), Wydawnictwo Literackie, 1969.

Fantastyka i futurologia (nonfiction; title means "Science Fiction and Futurology"), Wydawnictwo Literackie, 1970.

Opowiadania wybrane (title means "Selected Stories"), Wydawnictwo Literackie, 1973.

Rozprawy i szkice (title means "Essays and Sketches"), Wydawnictwo Literackie, 1975.

Suplement (title means "Supplement"), Wydawnictwo Literackie, 1976.

Powtorka (title means "Repetition"), Iskry, 1979.

Wizja lokalna (title means "The Scene of the Crime"), Wydawnictwo Literackie, 1982.

Prowokacja (title means "Provocation"), Wydawnictwo Literackie, 1984.

Pokoj na Ziemi (title means "Peace on Earth"), Wydawnictwo Literackie, 1987.

(With Stanislaw Beres) *Rozmowy ze Stanislawem Lemem* (title means "Conversations with Stanislaw Lem"), Wydawnictwo Literackie, 1987.

Ciemnosc i plesn (title means "Darkness and Mildew"), Wydawnictwo Literackie, 1988.

Also author of screenplay, "Przekledaniec" (title means "Roly Poly"), Film Polski.

OTHER

(Contributor) *Science Fiction: A Collection of Critical Essays,* Prentice-Hall, 1976.

(Contributor) *The Mind's Eye: Fantasies and Reflections on Self and Soul,* Basic Books, 1981.

Contributor to magazines in Europe and America, including *New Yorker.*

MEDIA ADAPTATIONS: Solaris was filmed in the Soviet Union.

SIDELIGHTS: Polish author Stanislaw Lem is the best known, most widely translated science fiction writer outside the English-speaking world. With more than twenty million books sold in some thirty-six languages, Lem has earned international recognition; he is especially popular in both Germany and the Soviet

Union, where he is regarded as a leading contemporary philosopher of science. As George Zebrowski notes in the *Magazine of Fantasy and Science Fiction,* however, Lem's stature as a deep thinker transcends the science fiction genre. "Lem has now reached an all but unattainable position for an SF writer," claims Zebrowski. "He is recognized as one of the world's finest writers." *New York Times* columnist John Leonard calls Lem "a Jorge Luis Borges for the Space Age, who plays in earnest with every concept of philosophy and physics, from free will to probability theory."

The circumstances of Lem's life have predisposed him to a philosophical frame of mind. Before he was born, his father narrowly escaped execution by firing squad—marching to his death, the elder Lem was recognized by a friend passing in the street who persuaded the commander to rescind the order. Later, during the Second World War, Lem himself came within inches of capture by the Nazis when a soldier brushed him as he carried a concealed weapon for the Resistance. These moments of chance salvation affected Lem profoundly; they have found their way into both his fiction and his nonfiction. To quote Paul Delany in the *New York Times Book Review,* Lem's books "are haunted by the whims of chance, the insignificance of individual fate in the perspective of the species, the ease with which a thoughtless move—but, just as well, a thoughtful one—can lead to disaster."

Lem was raised in Lvov, Poland, the son of a prosperous doctor. As he grew he indulged in flights of fancy, creating entire fictitious worlds and then outfitting himself with "papers"—passports, diplomas, and certificates—that gave him the highest honors in his imaginary kingdom. Lem decided to study medicine as his father had, and he was in medical school when World War II began. Jewish by descent, he and his family used forged documents to escape internment in the ghetto, and he continued his studies when he could. When rule by the Soviet Union replaced Nazi occupation after the war, Lem decided not to practice medicine—he would have had to serve as an army doctor. He deliberately flunked his last examination and went to work helping to support his aging parents. The work to which he committed himself was writing, and soon he was selling stories and essays to periodicals in Poland.

"In postwar Poland," writes Delany, "science fiction appealed to Mr. Lem as a genre in which an original mind could still express itself with relative freedom. . . . When he writes allegories of the Cold War, his viewpoint is that of a spectator rather than a partisan; and his books . . . are probably more popular in the Soviet Union than in the United States." Lem's artistic freedom has developed slowly; not surprisingly, his earliest fiction was "fashioned more or less along the obligatory ideological lines of its time," according to Stanislaw Baranczak in the *New Republic.* Having lived through the horrors of a World War, Lem wrote several novels depicting a rosy future of one-world government, free of the nuclear threat. "My first two books—which I now never release for reprinting—there's nothing Communist Party about them, but there is this wonderful world that could evoke in a certain sense the communist utopia," Lem told the *Washington Post.* "Now I won't allow them to be republished because I simply stopped believing in the utopia." Although he became dissatisfied with them in time, Lem's early novels helped to establish his reputation, thereby assuring an audience—and a Polish publisher—for his subsequent work.

Lem first reached a number of Western readers with the novel *Solaris,* a book that explores a favorite Lem theme—man's inadequacies in an alien environment. The account of a scientific expedition sent to study a huge, thinking ocean on the planet So-

laris, the novel describes the paranoia and fear of the unknown to which the researchers succumb. Frustrated by their inability to communicate with the inscrutable liquid mass, the researchers bombard it with radiation. In response the being somehow creates physical manifestations based on the humans' most submerged psychological traumas. Hence the novel becomes a study of humanity's inability to comprehend the nature of vastly different intelligences. A similar theme appears in Lem's novels *The Invincible* and *Fiasco,* both of which concern confrontation between humans and phenomena they cannot comprehend.

"Books such as *Solaris* and *Fiasco* do more than present intellectual arguments about the universe in an unmistakably Central European voice," writes John Clute in the *Times Literary Supplement.* "As science fiction of the highest order, and as examples of surreally barbed wit, they are very threatening texts indeed. They demand attentive reading, and they show contempt for those too lazy to pay heed." Zebrowski concludes that Lem "realistically shows us what it would be like to come face to face with genuine 'differentness'—an alien non-human system or being which is beyond our understanding. . . . We go out into the universe only to meet ourselves and fight with ourselves."

Lem's forays into future worlds include not only alien life forms but also advanced technology—cyborgs and computers with vast capabilities that nevertheless reflect the foibles of their creators. *New York Times Book Review* contributor Philip Jose Farmer believes that Lem "has no equal in his literary explorations of machines and their physical and philosophical potentialities. . . . The theme he stresses in most of his work is that machines will someday be as human as Homo sapiens and perhaps superior to him. Mr. Lem has an almost Dickensian genius for vividly realizing the tragedy and comedy of future machines; the death of one of his androids or computers actually wrings sorrow from the reader." Lem's tales suggest that humanity and technology are locked into a symbiotic relationship that can amplify the consequences of good and evil. According to *Voice Literary Supplement* reviewer David Berreby, the author "doesn't believe technology can change human nature, but he's far too subtle to conclude that technology makes no difference. It extends the reach of human folly and restricts the human imagination to those things that mechanisms make possible." Berreby concludes: "The new tools of relentlessly advancing science change what people can do, but they don't change people."

Very few of Lem's numerous stories, then, depict improvements in the human condition. His characters are almost always victims of clumsiness, psychological vulnerability, crackpot ambition, or incompetence. As Adam Mars-Jones puts it in the *Times Literary Supplement,* however far Lem extrapolates into the future, and however far into the universe he extends his speculations, "he is exploring recognisable human possibilities. The settings may be cosmic, but the morals are terrestrial." Critics find Lem's outlook bleak—in *The Nation,* Kurt Vonnegut called the author "a master of utterly terminal pessimism, appalled by all that an insane humanity may yet survive to do."

Pessimistic or hopeful, darkly comic or ironic, Lem's works abound in subtle philosophy and sociology. *Washington Post* correspondent Jackson Diehl observes that Lem advances a view of man "as a creature unable to find a stable place in the universe or control the consequences of accelerating technological advances." Baranczak concludes: "Lem is one of those writers who is interested more in the essential immutability of human existence than in any superficial evolution that history may provide. Paradoxically, he visualizes the future only to find more proof of his suspicion that human fate has remained, will remain, bound by the same laws of pain, love, and death, no matter what space suits we wear or what utopias we build."

Literary critics have noted that Lem's work resembles that favorite European genre, the fable or fairy tale. Lem is by training a scientist, however, and his books reveal an up-to-date knowledge of medicine, engineering, and cybernetics. The author also enjoys experimenting with form; several of his works offer "book reviews" or "introductions" to books that will be written in the future, and many of his conventional stories offer philosophical speculation and technical data. "In spite of the scientific authority that informs even the lightest of these near-parables, their immediate appeal grows out of the sensibility behind them," writes Peter S. Beagle in the *New York Times Book Review*. "Every Lem story is haunted by a passionate, prophetic understanding of what the human being is going to have to learn and become merely to survive, coupled with an unblinded realism about the nature of the species."

Lem is therefore a philosopher concerned with the moral and ethical consequences of advancing technology, a storyteller who feels that *science* fiction implies an obligation to verisimilitude, and a literary practitioner who is compelled to craft high-quality work. Delany writes: "Starting at the very edge of current theories of artificial intelligence, communications, cosmology and nuclear strategy, [Lem] soars out into dizzy flights of speculation, grafting one field onto another to populate whole new realms of possibility." As the author himself put it in an essay for the *Contemporary Authors Autobiography Series*, "I am trying not to limit the meaning of the name of this category of writing but rather to expand it."

That expansion of science fiction into literary and philosophical terrain has become a Lem trademark. His works have appeared in the *New Yorker*, and his books are widely reviewed for discerning mainstream audiences. "Those who have read any of . . . Lem's numerous books know that even the most timeworn subject can be the occasion for fresh surprises," observes Paul Gray in *Time*. "Lem's international reputation rests on two qualities rarely found together in one mortal: he is both a superb literary fantasist, . . . and a knowledgeable philosopher of the means and meanings of technology. Lem . . . not only builds castles in the air, he also provides meticulous blueprints and rationales for their construction." *Bloomsbury Review* contributor J. Madison Davis declares that with his romantic attitude towards art, Lem "challenges himself constantly in search of the new. . . . If the reader takes the active role Lem demands, reading can take on the quality of conversation with a unique character whose writings should be more appreciated."

Washington Post correspondent Jackson Diehl notes that the author "has avoided confrontation with Polish governments, yet he retains the respect of both dissident writers and western critics, who acknowledge him as a major artist. . . . He seems to be regarded by Polish authorities as a kind of international cultural showpiece, exempted from the normal constraints of East Bloc life in tacit exchange for his retention of citizenship." Lem does not see himself as apolitical; rather, he feels that his work confronts the human condition on a global basis—the human race as a species, not a body politic. "I have always resisted the label of science fiction," he told the *Washington Post*. "I've always believed in science, but I write about the real world. . . . I write about what is happening, only in my own way, in my own terms."

BIOGRAPHICAL/CRITICAL SOURCES:

BOOKS

Contemporary Authors Autobiography Series, Volume 1, Gale, 1984.
Contemporary Literary Criticism, Gale, Volume 8, 1978, Volume 15, 1980, Volume 40, 1986.
Updike, John, *Hugging the Shore: Essays and Criticism,* Vintage Books, 1984.

PERIODICALS

Bloomsbury Review, October, 1985.
Books Abroad, spring, 1975.
Chicago Tribune Books, July 12, 1987, October 23, 1988.
Chicago Tribune Book World, June 8, 1980, February 10, 1985.
Detroit News, April 8, 1979.
Discover, December, 1986.
Los Angeles Times Book Review, March 7, 1982, December 5, 1982, November 11, 1984, September 8, 1985, July 6, 1986, July 13, 1986.
Magazine of Fantasy and Science Fiction, May, 1971, July, 1974, July, 1979, April, 1981.
Nation, May 13, 1978.
New Republic, November 26, 1977, February 7, 1983, November 7, 1988.
New Statesman, June 1, 1979.
Newsweek, February 26, 1979, June 30, 1980.
New Yorker, February 26, 1979, September 8, 1980, January 30, 1984.
New York Review of Books, May 12, 1977.
New York Times, February 9, 1979, January 22, 1982.
New York Times Book Review, August 29, 1976, February 11, 1979, February 17, 1980, May 25, 1982, September 19, 1982, March 20, 1983, September 2, 1984, March 24, 1985, February 9, 1986, June 7, 1987, October 30, 1988.
Partisan Review, summer, 1976.
Science Fiction and Fantasy Book Review, June 5, 1979, June, 1983.
Science-Fiction Studies, July, 1977, November, 1986.
Time, January 29, 1979, September 17, 1984, June 1, 1987.
Times Literary Supplement, November 17, 1978, November 7, 1980, March 19, 1982, March 11, 1983, April 8, 1983, February 8, 1985, December 27, 1985, December 4, 1987, March 3, 1989.
Village Voice, May 16, 1989.
Voice Literary Supplement, June, 1987.
Washington Post, July 11, 1987.
Washington Post Book World, February 28, 1982, February 27, 1983, April 24, 1983, February 24, 1985, October 30, 1988.
World Literature Today, autumn, 1977, summer, 1978, winter, 1980.

—*Sketch by Anne Janette Johnson*

* * *

LEON-PORTILLA, Miguel 1926-

PERSONAL: Born February 22, 1926, in Mexico City, Mexico; son of Miguel León-Ortiz and Luisa Portilla; married Ascensión Hernández Trivino (a historian), May 2, 1965. *Education:* Loyola University of Los Angeles (now Loyola Marymount University), B.A., 1948, M.A., 1952; National University of Mexico, Ph.D., 1956.

ADDRESSES: Home—Alberto Zamora 103, Coyoacán, Mexico City, District Federal 21, Mexico.

CAREER: Mexico City College (now University of the Americas), Mexico City, Mexico, professor of ancient Mexican history, 1954-57; National University of Mexico, Mexico City, professor of ancient Mexican history, 1957—, director of Institute of Historical Research, 1963—. Lecturer at universities in the United States, Israel, and Europe; distinguished lecturer at the seventy-fourth meeting of the American Anthropological Association, 1974. Member of council, Institute of Different Civilizations, Brussels, 1959—; Inter-American Indian Institute, secretary general, 1955-60, director, 1960-66; secretary general of thirty-fifth International Congress of Americanists, 1962.

MEMBER: Royal Spanish Academy of History, Royal Spanish Academy of the Language, Societe des Americanistes de Paris.

AWARDS, HONORS: Prize Elias Sourazky, bestowed by Mexican Secretary of Education, 1966; Guggenheim fellow, 1970; Fulbright fellow, 1976-77; Commendatore de la Republica Italiana, 1977; Serra Award, 1978; D.H.L. honoris causa, Southern Methodist University, 1980; Mexican National Prize in history and the social sciences, 1981.

WRITINGS:

(Compiler) *Indices de América indígena y Boletín indigenista,* fourteen volumes, Inter-American Indian Institute, 1954.

La filosofía náhuatl: Estudiada en sus fuentes, Inter-American Indian Institute, 1956, 4th edition, Institute of Historical Research, National University of Mexico, 1974, translation by Jack Emory Davis published as *Aztec Thought and Culture: A Study of the Ancient Nahuatl Mind,* University of Oklahoma Press, 1963.

(With Salvador Matéo) *Catálogo de los códices indígenas del México antiguo,* [Mexico City], 1957.

Siete ensayos sobre cultura náhuatl, National University of Mexico, 1958.

(Translator and author of introduction) Bernardino de Sahagún, *Ritos, sacerdotes y atavios de los dioses,* Institute of Historical Research, National University of Mexico, 1958.

(Editor and author of introduction and notes) *Visión de los vencidos: Relaciones indígenas de la conquista,* National University of Mexico, 1959, 5th edition, 1971, translation by Lysander Kemp published as *The Broken Spears: The Aztec Account of the Conquest of Mexico,* Beacon Press, 1962.

Los antiguos mexicanos a través de sus crónicas y cantares, Fondo de Cultura Económica, 1961, 3rd edition, 1970, translation published as *The Ancient Mexicans,* Rutgers University Press, 1968.

(Contributor) *Estudios de historia de la filosofía en México,* National University of Mexico, 1963, 2nd edition, 1973, translation by A. Robert Caponigri published as *Major Trends in Mexican Philosophy,* University of Notre Dame Press, 1966.

Imagen del México antiguo, University of Buenos Aires Press, 1963.

Las literaturas precolombinas de México, Editorial Pormaca, 1964, translation by León-Portilla and Grace Lobanov published as *Pre-Columbian Literatures of Mexico,* University of Oklahoma Press, 1969.

Historia documental de México, Institute of Historical Research, National University of Mexico, 1964, 2nd edition, 1974.

El reverso de la conquista: Relaciones aztecas, mayas e incas, Editorial J. Mortiz, 1964, 2nd edition, 1970.

Trece poetas del mundo azteca, Institute of Historical Research, National University of Mexico, 1968, 2nd edition, 1975.

Quetzalcoatl, Fondo de Cultura Económica, 1968.

(Editor and author of introduction and notes) Jaime Bravo, Juan de Ugarte, and Clemente Guillen, *Nueva entra tablecimiento en el puerto de La Paz, 1720,* National University of Mexico, 1970.

(Compiler) *De Teotihuacan a los aztecas: Antología de fuentes e interpretaciones históricas,* Institute of Historical Research, National University of Mexico, 1971.

(Author of introduction) Andrés de Olmos, *Arte para aprender la lengua mexicana,* Levy, 1972.

Nezahualcoyotl: Poésia y pensamiento, 1402-1472, Gobierno del Estado de México, 1972.

Religión de los nicaraos: Análisis y comparación de tradicionos culturales nahuas, Institute of Historical Research, National University of Mexico, 1972.

Tiempo y realidad en el pensamiento maya: Ensayo de acercamiento, foreword by Eric S. Thompson, Institute of Historical Research, University of Mexico, 1973, 2nd edition published as *Time and Reality in the Thought of the Maya,* translated by Charles L. Boiles and Fernando Horcasitas, University of Oklahoma Press, 1988.

Voyages of Francisco de Ortega: California 1632-1636, Dawson's Book Shop, 1973.

(Editor and author of introductory essay, notes, and appendices) Miguel del Barco, *Historia natural y crónica de la antigua California,* Institute of Historical Research, University of Mexico, 1973.

Microhistoria de la Ciudad de México, Secretary of Works and Services, Department of the Federal District (Mexico City), 1974.

(With Edward H. Spicer) *Aztecs and Navajos: A Reflection on the Right of Not Being Engulfed* [and] *Indian Identity versus Assimilation* (the former by León-Portilla, the latter by Spicer), Weatherhead Foundation, 1975.

Culturas en peligro, Alianza Editorial, 1976.

(With Fernando Pereznieto Castro) *Presencia azteca en la Ciudad de México: Presentación de Miguel León-Portilla,* J. Mortiz, 1977.

La minería en México: Estudios sobre su desarrollo histórico, National University of Mexico, 1978.

México-Tenochtitlán: Su espacio y tiempo sagrados, National Institute of Anthropology and History, 1978.

Los manifesto en náhuatl de Emiliano Zapata, Institute of Historical Research, National University of Mexico, 1978.

(Editor, translator, and author of introduction) *Literatura del México antiguo: Los textos en lengua náhuatl,* Biblioteca Ayacucho, 1978.

Datos para la historia demográfica de Baja California, Centro de Investigaciones Históricas, 1978.

Un catecismo náhuatl en imágenes, Edición Privada de Cartón y Papel de México, 1979.

(Editor and author of foreword, introduction, and notes) *Native Mesoamerican Spirituality: Ancient Myths, Discourses, Stories, Doctrines, Hymns, Poems from the Aztec, Yucatec, Quiche-Maya, and Other Sacred Traditions,* Paulist Press, 1980.

Los olmecas en Chalco-Amaquemecan: Un testimonio de Sahagún aprovechado por Chimalpahin, Centro de Estudios Bernardino de Sahagún, 1980.

Literatura maya, Biblioteca Ayacucho, 1980.

(Author of introductory essay) Horacio Carochi, *Arte de la lengua mexicana: Con la de declaración de los adverbios della; Edición facsimilar de la publicada por Juan Ruyz en la Ciudad de México,* Instituto de Investigaciones Filológicas, Universidad Nacional Autónoma de México, 1983.

Literatura de Mesoamérica, Secretaria de Educación Pública, 1984.

(Editor) Bernal Díaz del Castillo, *Historia verdadera de la conquista de la Nueva España,* 2 volumes, Historia 16 (Madrid), 1984.

(Editor with S. L. Cline) *The Testaments of Culhuacan,* UCLA Latin American Center Publications, 1984.

Los franciscanos vistos por el hombre náhuatl, Centro de Estudios Bernardino de Sahagún, 1985.

Hernán Cortés y la mar del sur, Ediciones Cultura Hispánica, 1985.

(With Clementina Díaz y de Ovando) *Vicente Riva Palacio y la identidad nacional: Discurso,* Dirección General de Publicaciones, Universidad Nacional Autonóma de México, 1985.

Also author of *El templo mayor de México,* 1982. Contributor to periodicals in Mexico, Belgium, France, and the United States, including *Evergreen Review, Current Anthropology, Américas,* and *América Indígena.*

WORK IN PROGRESS: A study "that includes indigenous testimonies on the sixteenth-century Spanish-Aztec confrontation; a work on the lives and productions of twenty pre-Columbian Aztec poets."

SIDELIGHTS: Miguel León-Portilla writes that his "main concern has been to present in a humanistic way the rich heritage of the history, art, and literature of ancient Mexico." *La filosofía náhuatl* was published in Moscow in 1961, and *Visión de los vencidos* has appeared in German, French, and Italian. León-Portilla is fluent in English, French, German, Italian, and Nahuatl; his travels cover most countries of the Americas, and many in Europe and the Far East.

BIOGRAPHICAL/CRITICAL SOURCES:

PERIODICALS

Américan Indígena, October, 1966.
Saturday Review, August 30, 1969.*

*   *   *

LERTETH, Oban
    See FANTHORPE, R(obert) Lionel

*   *   *

LeSIEG, Theo.
    See GEISEL, Theodor Seuss

*   *   *

LESLIE, Anita   1914-1985
    (Anne Leslie)

PERSONAL: Born November 21, 1914, in London, England; died November 5, 1985, in County Galway, Ireland; daughter of Shane (a poet and author) and Marjorie (Ide) Leslie; married William King (submarine commander in the British Navy), 1949; children: Richard Tarka Bourke, Leonie Rose. *Education:* "Seven unfortunate governesses, five day schools, four boarding schools." *Politics:* "We don't mention that in Ireland!" *Religion:* "We don't mention that in Ireland!"

ADDRESSES: Home—Oranmore Castle, County Galway, Ireland.

CAREER: Writer. Trainer of Connemara ponies and horses, beginning 1960. *Wartime service:* Ambulance driver attached to the British Army in the Western Desert, 1941-42, with the British Red Cross in Syria and Italy, 1943, and with the French Army in France and Germany, 1944-45; twice awarded the French croix de guerre for bravery in action.

WRITINGS:

(As Anne Leslie) *Rodin: Immortal Peasant,* Prentice-Hall, 1937.
Train to Nowhere (autobiographical), Hutchinson, 1948.
Love in a Nutshell (travel), Greenberg, 1952.
The Remarkable Mr. Jerome (biography), Holt, 1954 (published in England as *The Fabulous Leonard Jerome,* Hutchinson, 1954).
Mrs. Fitzherbert (biography), Scribner, 1960.
Mr. Frewen of England: A Victorian Adventurer (biography), Hutchinson, 1966.
Jennie: The Life of Lady Randolph Churchill (biography), Hutchinson, 1969, published as *Lady Randolph Churchill: The Story of Jennie Jerome,* Scribner, 1970.
Edwardians in Love, Hutchinson, 1972, published as *The Marlborough House Set,* Doubleday, 1973.
Francis Chichester, Hutchinson, 1975.
Cousin Clare: The Tempestuous Career of Clare Sheridan, Hutchinson, 1976, published as *Clare Sheridan: Jennie's Niece,* Doubleday, 1977.
(With Pauline Chapman) *Madame Tussaud: Waxworker Extraordinary,* Hutchinson, 1978.
The Gilt and the Gingerbread: An Autobiography, Hutchinson, 1981.
A Story Half Told: A Wartime Autobiography, Hutchinson, 1983.
Randolph: The Biography of Winston Churchill's Son, Beaufort Books (New York, NY), 1985 (published in England as *Cousin Randolph: The Life of Randolph Churchill,* Hutchinson, 1985).

SIDELIGHTS: "Anita Leslie always wrote from the inside," noted a London *Times* contributor, "both as a member of the vanishing aristocratic world she so affectionately chronicled, and as a deeply intuitive judge of character." Many of her most important books were about famous members of her family, including her great-aunt Jennie Jerome Churchill profiled in *Lady Randolph Churchill: The Story of Jennie Jerome,* and her cousin Randolph whose life she described in *Randolph: The Biography of Winston Churchill's Son.* Leslie's memories also filled the pages of two volumes detailing her own life story: *The Gilt and the Gingerbread* and *A Story Half Told.*

Lady Randolph Churchill: The Story of Jennie Jerome was perhaps the author's best received work. "Leslie has gracefully filled a gap in the Churchill archives," wrote an *Esquire* reviewer, "bringing into true perspective the Jerome contribution to the makeup of a character often taken to be quintessentially English." As a member of the family, Leslie had access to family documents and personal reminiscences of family members, material that was not generally available (as is the case with her biographies of Leonard Jerome and Maria Fitzherbert, and the story of the Marlborough House). Often praised as a "delightful biography" and a "highly readable and sympathetic book," *Lady Randolph Churchill* was also seen as the story of a whole political and social era. V. G. Kiernan wrote that "the book's real worth lies in the cumulative impression it conveys, trivial or boring as most of the detail may be, of the private life of the class by which [England] has allowed itself in modern times to be ruled."

Critics were not as pleased with Leslie's *Randolph: The Biography of Winston Churchill's Son.* Some reviewers, for instance, questioned if the book actually contributed any new details to what was already known about the younger Churchill. "What we are not told is anything of striking biographical consequence," observed *Washington Post Book World* contributor Edwin M. Yoder, Jr.; while John Jolliffe claimed in the *Times Literary Supplement*, "Leslie's problem is that nearly all the information that anyone could want about her subject is already available." On the other hand, Toronto *Globe and Mail* contributor John Lownsbrough saw some merit in the volume, noting that Leslie had "put together, with a welcome lack of pretension, a collection of anecdotes and reminiscences which tries, and at times succeeds, in delineating the more sympathetic aspects of her bombastic subject."

Of her own writing, Leslie once stated: "I have always been determined to keep writing a pleasure and I manage to drape the rest of my life around the job. . . . Probably few writers are lucky enough to have a secondary occupation which contrasts so nicely with their studies as I have. Horses go very well with writing. They keep me out of doors during the best hours of the day and send me indoors, mentally hungry towards sundown. After a bath I forget stable dramas and return with renewed interest to that unfinished paragraph."

BIOGRAPHICAL/CRITICAL SOURCES:

BOOKS

Leslie, Anita, *The Gilt and the Gingerbread: An Autobiography*, Hutchinson, 1981.
Leslie, Anita, *A Story Half Told: A Wartime Autobiography*, Hutchinson, 1983.

PERIODICALS

Globe and Mail, August 3, 1985.
Times Literary Supplement, August 9, 1985.
Washington Post Book World, July 12, 1985.

OBITUARIES:

PERIODICALS

Esquire, May, 1970.
Los Angeles Times, November 9, 1985.
Times (London), November 8, 1985.*

*   *   *

LESLIE, Anne
See LESLIE, Anita

*   *   *

LEVI-STRAUSS, Claude 1908-

PERSONAL: Born November 28, 1908, in Brussels, Belgium; son of Raymond (a painter) and Emma (Levy) Levi-Strauss; married Dina Dreyfus, 1932 (divorced); married Rosemarie Ullmo, 1946 (divorced); married Monique Roman, April 5, 1954; children: (second marriage) Laurent; (third marriage) Matthieu. *Education:* Universite de Paris, licence, 1929, Agregation, 1931, Doctorat es Lettres, 1948.

ADDRESSES: Home—2 rue des Marronniers, Paris 75016, France. *Office*—Laboratoire d'Anthropologie sociale, 52 rue du Cardinal-Lemoine, Paris 75005, France.

CAREER: Universidade de Sao Paulo, Sao Paulo, Brazil, professor of sociology, 1935-39; New School for Social Research, New York, N.Y., visiting professor, 1942-45; French Embassy, Washington, D.C., cultural counselor, 1946-47; Musee de l'Homme, Paris, France, associate curator, 1948-49; Sorbonne, Ecole Pratique des Hautes Etudes, Paris, director of research, 1950—, College de France, Paris, professor of social anthropology, 1959—.

MEMBER: Academie francaise, National Academy of Sciences, American Academy and Institute of Arts and Letters, British Academy, Royal Academy of the Netherlands (foreign member), Academy of Norway (foreign member), Royal Anthropological Institute of Great Britain (honorary fellow), American Academy of Arts and Sciences, American Philosophical Society, Norwegian Academy of Letters and Sciences, New York Academy of Sciences.

AWARDS, HONORS: Honorary doctorates from University of Brussels, Oxford University, Yale University, University of Chicago, Columbia University, Stirling University, Universite Nationale du Zaire, University of Uppsala, Laval University, Universidad Nacional Autonoma de Mexico, Johns Hopkins University, and Harvard University; Viking Fund Medal, Wenner-Gren Foundation, 1966; Erasmus Prize, 1975; Grand-Officier de la Legion d'Honneur; Commandeur de l'Ordre Nationale du Merite; Commandeur de l'Ordre des Palmes Academiques; Commandeur des Arts et des Lettres; Commandeur de la Coronne de Belgique; Cruzeiro do Sul.

WRITINGS:

La Vie familiale et sociale des Indiens Nambikwara, Societe de Americanistes, 1948.
Les Structures elementaires de la parente, Presses Universitaires de France, 1949, translation by J. H. Bell and J. R. von Strumer published as *The Elementary Structures of Kinship*, Beacon, 1969.
Race et histoire, Gonthier, 1952.
Tristes Tropiques, Plon, 1955, revised edition, Adler, 1968, partial translation by John Russell published as *Tristes Tropiques*, Criterion, 1961 (published in England as *A World on the Wane*, Hutchinson, 1961), complete translation by John Weightman and Doreen Weightman, J. Cape, 1973, Atheneum, 1974.
Anthropologie structurale, Volume 1, Plon, 1958, translation by Claire Jacobson and Brooke Grundfest Schoepf published as *Structural Anthropology*, Basic Books, 1964, Volume 2, Plon, 1973, translation by Monica Layton, Basic Books, 1977.
Entretiens avec Claude Levi-Strauss, edited by Georges Charbonnier, Plon-Julliard, 1961, translation published as *Conversations with Claude Levi-Strauss*, J. Cape, 1969.
La Pensee sauvage, Plon, 1962, translation published as *The Savage Mind*, University of Chicago Press, 1966, revised edition, Adlers Foreign Books, 1985.
Le Totemisme aujourd'hui, Presses Universitaires de France, 1962, translation by Rodney Needham published as *Totemism*, Beacon, 1963, revised edition, Penguin, 1969.
Mythologiques, Plon, Volume 1: *Le Cru et le cuit*, 1964, Volume 2: *Du Miel aux cendres*, 1967, Volume 3: *L'Origine des manieres de table*, 1968, Volume 4: *L'Homme nu*, 1971, translation by J. Weightman and D. Weightman published as *Introduction to a Science of Mythology*, Volume 1: *The Raw and the Cooked*, Harper, 1969, Volume 2: *From Honey to Ashes*, J. Cape, 1973, harper, 1974, Volume 3: *The Origin of Table Manners*, Harper, 1978, Volume 4: *The Naked Man*, Harper, 1981.
The Scope of Anthropology, J. Cape, 1968.
Discours de reception a l'Academie francaise, Institut de France (Paris), 1974.

La Voie des masques, two volumes, Skira, 1975, enlarged edition, Plon, 1979, translation by S. Modelski published as *The Way of the Masks,* University of Washington Press, 1982.

Myth and Meaning: Five Talks for Radio, University of Toronto Press, 1978, Schocken, 1979.

Le Regard eloigne, Plon, 1983, translation by J. Neugroschel and P. Hoss published as *The View from Afar,* Basic Books, 1985.

Paroles donnees, Plon, 1984, translation by Roy Willis published as *Anthropology and Myth: Lectures, 1957-1982,* Blackwell, 1987.

La Potiere jalouse, Plon, 1985, translation by Benedicte Chorier published as *The Jealous Potter,* University of Chicago Press, 1988.

Introduction to the Work of Marcel Mauss, Routledge & Kegan Paul, 1987.

(With Didier Eribon) *De pres et de loin,* Jacobs, 1988.

Comparative Mythology, Johns Hopkins University Press, 1988.

SIDELIGHTS: Often ranked with Jean-Paul Sartre and Andre Malraux as one of France's greatest modern intellectuals, Claude Levi-Strauss is "the last uncontested giant of French letters," as James M. Markham describes him in the *New York Times.* Acclaimed for his studies of primitive mythology and for his autobiographical book *A World on the Wane (Tristes Tropiques),* Levi-Strauss is also credited with founding the movement known as structural anthropology, "the search for underlying patterns of thought in all forms of human activity," as Markham defines it. So pervasive is Levi-Strauss's influence in such diverse fields as language theory, history, and psychology that George Steiner claims in his *Language and Silence: Essays on Language* that "an awareness of Levi-Strauss's thought is a part of current literacy." Marshall D. Sahlins believes the professional attention accorded Levi-Strauss is almost "unparalleled in the history of anthropology."

Tristes Tropiques, Levi-Strauss's study of Brazilian Indians, is "one of the great books of our century," according to Susan Sontag in her *Against Interpretation and Other Essays.* As much a rationale for anthropology as it is a study of a primitive people, the book asks why Western culture is the first to study other cultures and it explores the role of the anthropologist. Sontag finds the book to be "rigorous, subtle, and bold in thought. It is beautifully written. And, like all great books, it bears an absolutely personal stamp; it speaks with a human voice." This personal dimension is noted by Richard A. Shweder in the *New York Times Book Review,* who describes *Tristes Tropiques* as the book in which Levi-Strauss "transformed an expedition to the virgin interiors of the Amazon into a vision quest, and turned anthropology into a spiritual mission to defend mankind against itself."

In his *Introduction to a Science of Mythology,* Levi-Strauss attempts to systematize myths, discover their underlying structures, and expose the process of their creation. James Redfield in *Thinkers of the Twentieth Century* sees the massive four-volume work as "a book about human nature—if we understand that 'nature' here means the mind, which is to say, the sense that things make." "Levi-Strauss was intrigued by the way that languages as well as myths of different cultures resembled each other and appeared to be structured in a similar fashion," Edith Kurzweil explains in *The Age of Structuralism: Levi-Strauss to Foucault.* Steiner credits Levi-Strauss with "seeking a science of mythology, a grammar of symbolic constructs and associations allowing the anthropologist to relate different myths as the structural linguist relates phonemes and language systems. Once the code of myths is deciphered and is seen to have its own logic and translatability, its own grid of values and interchangable signifi-

cants, the anthropologist will have a tool of great power with which to attack problems of human ecology, of ethnic and linguistic groupings, of cultural diffusion. Above all, he may gain insight into mental processes and strata of consciousness which preserve indices . . . of the supreme event in man's history—the transition from a primarily instinctual, perhaps pre-linguistic condition to the life of consciousness and individualized self-awareness." Although Kurzweil admits that Levi-Strauss's structuralist approach has not been wholly successful in studying mythology, "his theory of the elusive, unconscious structures did lead to the creation of various new subjects of inquiry such as the relationships between the structures of all signs in language, their function within messages, and their rapport with other sign systems, such as music, gestures, [and] body language."

Several observers find that how Levi-Strauss expresses his ideas is as important as what he says. He often presents an intellectual position only to tear it down, uses irony and digression, and ranges over a number of seemingly unrelated subjects—all while displaying a mastery of such diverse fields as linguistics, psychiatry, genetics, and neuroscience. "Levi-Strauss once described his own rather cultivated, but sometimes savage, mind as the intellectual equivalent of slash-and-burn agriculture," Shweder reports. "The prose of Levi-Strauss," Steiner writes, "is a very special instrument, and one which many are trying to imitate. It has an austere, dry detachment. . . . It uses a careful alternance of long sentences, usually organized in ascending rhythm, and of abrupt Latinate phrases. While seeming to observe the conventions of neutral, learned presentation, it allows for brusque personal interventions and asides." "There is more to understanding Levi-Strauss than knowing what he himself has written," adds Godfrey Lienhardt. "Perhaps beyond any other living anthropologist he has established a dialogue with part of the intellectual public, appearing to speak personally to educated general readers and engaging them in his own processes of analysis and reflection." "The outstanding characteristic of his writing . . . ," Edmund Leach maintains in his study *Claude Levi-Strauss,* "is that it is difficult to understand; his sociological theories combine baffling complexity with overwhelming erudition." Leach goes so far as to say that "Levi-Strauss is admired not so much for the novelty of his ideas as for the bold originality with which he seeks to apply them. He has suggested new ways of looking at familiar facts; it is the method that is interesting rather than the practical consequences of the use to which it has been put." But Lienhardt identifies Levi-Strauss's writing as "an exhortation to wonder at the complex creativity of mankind, to revere it and finally to see through it."

Levi-Strauss cheerfully admits that his books "are hard to understand" and that he "stands outside of the anthropological mainstream," notes a writer for *Newsweek.* " 'I think,' he says, 'I'm a school by myself.' " With Sartre and Malraux dead, and their leftist politics increasingly discredited, Levi-Strauss now holds a unique and powerful position in the French intelligensia. But though he is widely respected, he refuses to accept the role of "prophet," a role long common among French philosophers. Markham quotes Pierre Bourdieu explaining that "one of [Levi-Strauss's] effects has been to change the nature of the French intellectual, to propose something more modest." David Pace, writing in *Claude Levi-Strauss: The Bearer of Ashes,* reports that Levi-Strauss "has made no real effort to disseminate his ideas of cultural progress to a large popular audience or to translate them into any political movement. On the contrary, he has taken every opportunity to deny the importance of his own speculations on these topics and to focus attention upon his technical achievements in structural anthropology."

Speaking to Markham, Levi-Strauss identified his deep concern for "a certain number of values which are those of my society and which I consider to be threatened. They are threatened by the Soviet Union, by Islamic fundamentalism, and by the demographic growth of the Third World." Among these values are the importance of a national culture over a world "monoculture" and the ideal of the traditional peasant who lives close to nature. Yet Pace finds "something fundamentally nihilistic about Levi-Strauss's world-view. . . . There is neither a serious effort to protect the things which he sees as threatened nor an attempt to abandon his attachment to them. He himself has described his own position as a 'serene pessimism.' "

"For 25 years," Shweder notes, "[Levi-Strauss] has been the object of adoration and scorn in the English-speaking world." Redfield reports that "it is possible that . . . later ages will speak of our time as the age of Levi-Strauss. . . . He is a maker of the modern mind, and has influenced many who have never read him, and some who have quite mistaken ideas about what he says." As Joan Bamberger writes: "Whatever the future impact of [Levi-Strauss's] work, certainly the anthropological study of myth will never be the same."

BIOGRAPHICAL/CRITICAL SOURCES:

BOOKS

Contemporary Literary Criticism, Volume 38, Gale, 1986.

Girard, Rene, *"To Double Business Bound": Essays on Literature, Mimesis, and Anthropology,* Johns Hopkins University Press, 1978.

Kurzweil, Edith, *The Age of Structuralism: Levi-Strauss to Foucault,* Columbia University Press, 1980.

LaPointe, Francois Y. and Claire C. LaPointe, *Claude Levi-Strauss and His Critics: An International Bibliography of Criticism (1950-1976) Followed by a Bibliography of the Writings of Claude Levi-Strauss,* Garland Publishing, 1977.

Leach, Edmund, *Claude Levi-Strauss,* Viking Press, revised edition, 1974.

Pace, David, *Claude Levi-Strauss: The Bearer of Ashes,* Routledge & Kegan Paul, 1983.

Rossi, Ino, editor, *The Logic of Culture: Advances in Structural Theory and Methods,* J. F. Bergin Publishers, 1982.

Sontag, Susan, *Against Interpretation and Other Essays,* Farrar, Straus, 1966.

Steiner, George, *Language and Silence: Essays on Language, Literature, and the Inhuman,* Atheneum, 1967.

Thinkers of the Twentieth Century, St. James, 2nd edition, 1987.

PERIODICALS

Atlantic, July, 1969.
Book Week, February 9, 1964.
Book World, November 9, 1969.
Commentary, May, 1968.
Globe & Mail (Toronto), May 14, 1988.
Hudson Review, winter, 1967.
Kenyon Review, March, 1967.
Listener, May 23, 1968.
Nation, March 16, 1970.
Natural History, June/July, 1973.
New Republic, July 22, 1969, May 18, 1974.
Newsweek, February 23, 1967.
New York Review of Books, November 28, 1963, October 12, 1967.
New York Times, December 31, 1969, December 21, 1987.
New York Times Book Review, June 3, 1973, April 14, 1985.
Reporter, April 6, 1967.

Saturday Review, December 31, 1966, May 17, 1969.
Spectator, May 12, 1961, March 21, 1969.
Time, June 30, 1967.
Times Literary Supplement, May 12, 1961, June 15, 1967, September 12, 1968.

—Sketch by Thomas Wiloch

*   *   *

LEVITIN, Sonia (Wolff) 1934-
(Sonia Wolff)

PERSONAL: Born August 18, 1934, in Berlin, Germany; brought to United States in 1938; daughter of Max (a manufacturer) and Helene (Goldstein) Wolff; married Lloyd Levitin (a business executive), December 27, 1953; children: Daniel Joseph, Shari Diane. *Education:* Attended University of California, Berkeley, 1952-54; University of Pennsylvania, B.S., 1956; San Francisco State College (now University), graduate study, 1957-60.

ADDRESSES: Home—Southern California. *Agent*—Toni Mendez, Inc., 141 East 56th St., New York, NY 10022.

CAREER: Writer and lecturer. Junior high school teacher in Mill Valley, CA, 1956-57; adult education teacher in Daly City, CA, 1962-64; Acalanes Adult Center, Lafayette, CA, teacher, 1965-72; teacher of creative writing, Palos Verdes Peninsula, CA, and University of California, Los Angeles Extension. Founder of STEP (adult education corporation) in Palos Verdes Peninsula.

MEMBER: Authors League of America, Authors Guild, PEN, Society of Children's Book Writers, California Writer's Guild, Moraga Historical Society (founder and former president).

AWARDS, HONORS: Journey to America received the Charles and Bertie G. Schwartz Award for Juvenile Fiction from the Jewish Book Council of America, 1971, and American Library Association Notable Book honors; *Roanoke: A Novel of the Lost Colony* was nominated for the Dorothy Canfield Fisher Award, Georgia Children's Book Award, and Mark Twain Award; *Who Owns the Moon?* received American Library Association Notable Book honors; *The Mark of Conte* received the Southern California Council on Literature for Children and Young People Award for fiction, 1976, and was nominated for California Young Reader Medal award in the junior high category, 1982; Golden Spur Award from Western Writers of America, 1978, and Lewis Carroll Shelf Award, for *The No-Return Trail;* Southern California Council on Literature for Children and Young People award for a distinguished contribution to the field of children's literature, 1981; National Jewish Book Award in Children's Literature, PEN Los Angeles Award for Young Adult Fiction, Association of Jewish Libraries Sydney Taylor Award, Austrian Youth Prize, Catholic Children's Book Prize (Germany), Dorothy Canfield Fisher Award nomination, Parent's Choice Honor Book citation, and American Library Association best Book for Young Adults award, all 1988, for *The Return;* Edgar Allen Poe Award from Mystery Writers of America, Dorothy Canfield Fisher Award nomination, and Nevada State Award nomination, all 1989, for *Incident at Loring Groves.*

WRITINGS:

JUVENILES

Journey to America (Junior Literary Guild selection), Atheneum, 1970.
Rita the Weekend Rat, Atheneum, 1971.
Who Owns the Moon?, Parnassus, 1973.

Roanoke: A Novel of the Lost Colony, Atheneum, 1973.
Jason and the Money Tree, Harcourt, 1974.
A Single Speckled Egg, Parnassus, 1975.
The Mark of Conte, Atheneum, 1976.
Beyond Another Door, Atheneum, 1977.
The No-Return Trail (Junior Literary Guild selection), Harcourt, 1978.
A Sound to Remember (Jewish Book Club selection), Harcourt, 1979.
Nobody Stole the Pie, Harcourt, 1980.
The Fisherman and the Bird, Houghton, 1982.
All the Cats in the World, Harcourt, 1982.
The Year of Sweet Senior Insanity, Harcourt, 1982.
Smile Like a Plastic Daisy, Atheneum, 1983.
A Season for Unicorns, Atheneum, 1986.
The Return, Atheneum, 1987.
Incident at Loring Groves, Dial, 1988.
Silver Days, Atheneum, 1989.
The Man Who Kept His Heart in a Bucket, Dial, in press.

OTHER

Reigning Cats and Dogs, Atheneum, 1978.
(Under name Sonia Wolff) *What They Did to Miss Lily,* Harper, 1981.

Feature columnist for Sun Newspapers, Contra Costa, CA, and *Jewish Observer of the East Bay,* Oakland, CA. Contributor to periodicals, including *Smithsonian, Parent's magazine, The Writer, Woman's World,* and *San Francisco Magazine.*

WORK IN PROGRESS: *Connections,* an adult novel set in Southern California and Israel.

SIDELIGHTS: Based upon the author's childhood experiences, Sonia Levitin's *Journey to America* is the story of a Jewish family's escape from Nazi Germany. In a review in the *School Library Journal,* Terry M. Cole describes Levitin's first book as "a very moving though never maudlin story with good characterization and a fast pace." Commenting on the author's realistic portrayal of people and events, Zena Sutherland writes in the *Bulletin of the Center for Children's Books* that *Journey to America* is "well-written and perceptive in describing the tensions and reactions of people in a situation of stress." Concludes Elizabeth Minot Graves in *Commonweal,* "[This is] one of the best books of the year, indeed, any year."

Levitin's other books feature characters who confront the harsh environment of the unexplored New World as well as such complex contemporary issues as wealth, ESP, and feminism. Levitin told *CA:* "In each book I try to do something quite different from the previous work. Themes and characters might repeat themselves, but I believe that my growth as a writer and as a person depends on accepting new challenges, deepening my experience and my efforts."

BIOGRAPHICAL/CRITICAL SOURCES:

BOOKS

Contemporary Literary Criticism, Volume 17, Gale, 1981.
Something about the Author Autobiography Series, Volume 2, Gale, 1986.

PERIODICALS

Bulletin of the Center for Children's Books, February, 1971.
Commonweal, May 22, 1970.
Los Angeles Times, August 15, 1987.
New York Times Book Review, May 24, 1970; May 15, 1987.
School Library Journal, May, 1970.

Wilson Library Bulletin, May, 1984.
Writer, August, 1972.

*   *   *

LIFSON, David S. 1908-

PERSONAL: Born December 29, 1908, in New York, N.Y.; son of Louis (a merchant) and Sarah (Saffro) Lifson; married Dorothy Marburger (a librarian), November 27, 1932; children: Hugh A. *Education:* New York University, B.S., 1931, M.A., 1957, Ph.D., 1962.

ADDRESSES: *Home*—40 East 10th St., New York, N.Y. 10003. *Agent*—Bertha Klausner, Writers International Agency, 71 Park Ave., New York, N.Y. 10016. *Office*—Department of English, Monmouth College, West Long Branch, N.J. 07764.

CAREER: Playwright and director; 20th Century Paint and Varnish Manufacturing Corp., New York, N.Y., founder and president, 1937-57; Maryland State College (now University of Maryland Eastern Shore), Princess Anne, Md., professor and director of drama, 1957-58; Pratt Institute, Brooklyn, N.Y., assistant professor and director of drama, 1957-63; Jersey City State College, Jersey City, N.J., assistant professor, 1963-64; Monmouth College, West Long Branch, N.J., associate professor, 1964-65, professor of English, 1965—. Visiting professor, Oxford University, 1989. Member of board of directors, Brooklyn Heights Youth Center.

MEMBER: PEN, Drama Desk, Actors Equity Association, Outer Critics Circle, Players Club.

AWARDS, HONORS: Otto Kahn Award, Metropolitan Opera, 1930; Founders Day Award, New York University, 1963; Fulbright-Hays scholar, 1970-71.

WRITINGS:

"Familiar Pattern" (play), first produced Off-Broadway at Provincetown Playhouse, 1943.
"Mummers and Men" (play), first produced at Provincetown Playhouse, 1962.
The Yiddish Theatre in America, Yoseloff, 1965.
(Contributor) George Freedley and J. A. Reeves, editors, *A History of the Theatre,* 3rd edition (Lifson was not associated with earlier editions), Crown, 1968.
"Le Poseur" (play), first produced in New York at Italian Drama Festival, 1974.
Epic and Folk Plays from the Yiddish Theatre, Associated University Press, 1975.
"How to Rob a Bank" (play), first produced in New York at PAF Playhouse, 1976.
Headless Victory (suspense novel), A. S. Barnes, 1978.
Best Evidence, Macmillan, 1981.
Sholem Aleichem's Wandering Star & Other Plays of Jewish Life, Associated University Press, 1988.

Also author of plays "Greet Tomorrow," "Buffoons," "News Item," "At the Gate," "The Troubador," "Gift of the Magi," "Children at the White House," "Gimpy," "Farvorfen Vinkel," "Hirsch Lekert," "Yankel Boyla," "Hurrah for Us," "Oh, Careless Love!," "Ivory Tower," "Eye of the Storm," "Masquerade," "The Flatbush Football Golem," "Emeritus," and *Recruits,* Fairleigh-Dickinson Press. Contributor to *Encyclopaedia Britannica, Encyclopaedia Judaica, Jewish Quarterly,* and *Jewish Currents.* Drama critic and drama editor, Jewish Telegraph Agency.

WORK IN PROGRESS: *The Closing Door,* a novel; "Banco," a play.

SIDELIGHTS: "As an authority on Yiddish Theatre, critic for the New York Theatre, and a voter in the Tony Awards, I travel the country and England as a lecturer," David S. Lifson tells *CA.* "Starting in the mid-1940s, I've been a theatre director in the professional theatre." He later added: "I am about to launch a fringe theatre in London: the Anglo Jewish Theatre."

* * *

LIHN, Enrique 1929-1988

PERSONAL: Born September 3, 1929, in Santiago, Chile; died July 10, 1988, in Santiago; son of Enrique Lihn Döll and María Carrasco; married Yvette Mingram, November 10, 1957 (divorced January 14, 1960); children: Andrea. *Education:* Attended Liceo de los Padres Alemanes, Institute of Fine Arts (Santiago), and University of Chile.

ADDRESSES: Office—c/o Andrea Lihn, Marcel Duhaut 2935, Santiago, Chile.

CAREER: Poet and novelist, beginning 1949; University of Chile, Santiago, professor and researcher of literature, beginning 1973.

AWARDS, HONORS: Atenea Prize from Universidad de Concepcion, 1964; municipal prize for narrative, 1965, for *Agua de arroz: Cuentos;* Casa de las Américas prize for poetry, 1966, for "Poesía de paso"; Pedro de Oña prize and municipal prize for poetry, both for "La musiquilla de las pobres esferas"; fellowships from UNESCO and Guggenheim.

WRITINGS:

Poemas de este tiempo y de otro, 1949-1954, Ediciones Renovación (Santiago), 1955.
La pieza oscura (title means "Dark Room"; also see below), Editorial Universitaria (Santiago), 1963.
Poesía de paso, Casa de las Américas (Havana), 1966.
Escrito en Cuba, Era (Mexico), 1969.
Agua de arroz: Cuentos (title means "Rice Water"; fiction), Centro Editor (Buenos Aires), 1969.
The Endless Malice: Twenty-five Poems of Enrique Lihn, translated by William Witherup and Serge Echeverria, Lillabulero, 1969.
La musiquilla de las pobres esferas, Editorial Universitaria (Santiago), 1969.
Algunos poemas, Ocnos (Barcelona), 1972.
La Chambre noire/La pieza oscura (bilingual edition), translated and presented by Michele Cohen and Jean-Michel Fossey, Pierre Jean Oswald Editeur, 1972.
(Editor and author of prologue) *Diez cuentos de bandidos* (fiction), Quimantu (Santiago), 1972.
Batman en Chile; o, El ocaso de un ídolo; o, Solo contra el desierto rojo (fiction), Ediciones de la Flor (Buenos Aires), 1973.
Por fuerza mayor, Ocnos, Barral Editores (Barcelona), 1975.
La orquesta de cristal (title means "The Crystal Orchestra"; novel), Editorial Sudamerica (Buenos Aires), 1976.
París, situación irregular, Ediciones Aconcagua (Santiago), 1977.
If Poetry Is to Be Written Right, translated by Dave Oliphant, Texas Portfolio, 1977.
The Dark Room and Other Poems (selections from *La pieza oscura*), edited and with an introduction by Patricio Lerzundi, translated by Jonathan Cohen, John Felstiner, and David Unger, New Directions, 1978.
A partir de Manhattan, Ediciones Ganymedes (Santiago), 1979.
El arte de la palabra (title means "The Art of Speaking"; novel), Pomaire (Barcelona), 1980.

Antología al azar (poetry), Ruray, 1981.
Derechos de autor, 1981/72, 69, etc., The Author, 1981.
Estación de los desamparados (poetry), Premià Editora, 1982.
Al bello aparecer de este lucero (title means "At the Beautiful Arising of This Star"; poetry), Ediciones del Norte, 1983.
El paseo ahumada: Poema, Ediciones Minga, 1983.
(With Carmen Foxley, Cristián Huneeus, and Adriana Valdés) *Paradiso, Lectura de conjunto,* Coordinación de Humanidades, Universidad Nacional Autónoma de México, 1984.
Pena de extrañamiento, Sinfronteras (Santiago), 1986.
Mester de juglaría (poetry), Hiperión (Madrid), 1987.
(With Pedro Lastra) *Señales de ruta de Juan Luis Martínez,* Ediciones Archivo (Santiago), 1987.
La aparición de la Virgen (poem), [Santiago], 1987.
Eugenio Téllez, descubridor de invenciones, [Santiago], 1988.
La república independiente de Miranda (fiction), Editorial Sudamericana (Buenos Aires), 1988.
Diario de muerte (poetry), edited by Lastra and Valdés, Editorial Universitaria (Santiago), 1988.
(And author of prologue) *Album de toda especie de poemas* (poetry anthology), Editorial Lumen (Barcelona), 1989.

Also author of *Nada se escurre,* 1949.

SIDELIGHTS: Enrique Lihn was a popular poet in Chile for many years and is gaining recognition in the United States as his works are translated into English. His poetry often expresses sadness about death, loss of love, and other tragedies in life. Reviewing *La musiquilla de las pobres esferas,* F. A. Butler of *Books Abroad* writes, "This is poetry to be read with care and disquiet, for its beauty lies in its aberration." Hayden Carruth of *Nation* predicts, "Lihn's poems are certain to become better known in this country before long."

BIOGRAPHICAL/CRITICAL SOURCES:

BOOKS

Lastra, Pedro, *Conversaciones con Enrique Lihn,* Centro de Investigaciones Lingüistico-Literarias, Instituto de Investigaciones Humanisticas, Universidad Veracruzana. 1980.
Lihn, Enrique, *Derechos de autor, 1981/72, 69, etc.,* The Author, 1981.

PERIODICALS

Books Abroad, winter, 1971.
Nation, December 23, 1978.
World Literature Today, winter, 1985.

[Sketch reviewed by Andrea Lihn, Professor Felipe Alliende, and Adriana Valdés]

* * *

LIONEL, Robert
See FANTHORPE, R(obert) Lionel

* * *

LIPMAN, Matthew 1923-

PERSONAL: Born August 24, 1923, in Vineland, NJ; son of William Leo (a manufacturer) and Sophie (Kenin) Lipman; children: Karen, Will. *Education:* Attended Stanford University, 1943-44; Columbia University, B.S., 1948, Ph.D., 1953.

ADDRESSES: Home—40 Park St., Montclair, NJ 07042. *Office*—Department of Philosophy and Religion, Montclair State College, Upper Montclair, NJ 07043.

CAREER: Columbia University, New York City, instructor in philosophy, and instructor in contemporary civilization at Columbia College, 1954-62, assistant professor, 1957-61, associate professor, 1961-66, professor of philosophy, 1966-72, research associate in department of philosophy, 1971-72, chairman of department of general education at College of Pharmaceutical Sciences, 1962-72; Montclair State College, Upper Montclair, NJ, professor of philosophy, 1972—, director of Institute for the Advancement of Philosophy for Children, 1974—. Adjunct associate professor of philosophy, City College of the City University of New York, 1953-75; lecturer in contemporary civilization, Mannes College of Music, 1955-63. Visiting professor, Sarah Lawrence College, 1963-64. *Military service:* U.S. Army, Infantry, 1943-46; received two Bronze Star Medals.

MEMBER: American Philosophical Association, American Society for Aesthetics, Society for the Advancement of American Philosophy, Philosophy of Education Society (fellow), John Dewey Society.

AWARDS, HONORS: Fulbright scholar at Sorbonne, University of Paris, 1950-51; Matchette Prize for Aesthetics, 1956; American Council of Learned Societies grant, 1967; National Endowment for the Humanities grants, 1970-71 and 1971-72; New Jersey Council for the Humanities grant, 1975; Rockefeller Foundation grant, 1978-81; Schumann Foundation grant, 1982-84; honorary doctor of letters, Quincy College, 1988.

WRITINGS:

(Contributor) Kurt Wolff, editor, *Georg Simmel, 1858-1958,* Ohio State University Press, 1961.
What Happens in Art, Appleton, 1967.
Discovering Philosophy, Appleton, 1969, 2nd edition, Prentice-Hall, 1977.
Contemporary Aesthetics, Allyn & Bacon, 1973.
(Editor with Terrell Ward Bynum) *Philosophy for Children,* Basil Blackwell, 1976.
(Editor with Ann Margaret Sharp) *Growing up with Philosophy,* Temple University Press, 1978.
(Contributor) Judith Segal, Susan Chipman, and Robert Glaser, editors, *Thinking and Learning Skills: Relating Instruction to Basic Research,* Lawrence Erlbaum Associates, 1984.
Philosophy Goes to School, Temple University Press, 1988.

PUBLISHED BY INSTITUTE FOR THE ADVANCEMENT OF PHILOSOPHY FOR CHILDREN

Harry Stottlemeir's Discovery, 1974, revised edition, 1975.
(With Sharp) *Instructional Manual to Accompany Harry Stottlemeir's Discovery,* 1975, 2nd edition (with Sharp and Frederick S. Oscanyan) published as *Philosophical Inquiry: An Instructional Manual,* 1979.
Lisa, 1976, 2nd edition, 1983.
(With Sharp) *Instructional Manual to Accompany Lisa,* 1977.
(With Sharp and Oscanyan) *Philosophy in the Classroom,* 1977, 2nd edition, Temple University Press, 1980.
Suki, 1978.
Mark, 1980.
Writing: How and When, 1980.
Social Inquiry, 1980.
Pixie, 1981.
(With Sharp) *Looking for Meaning,* 1982.
Kio and Gus, 1982.
(With Sharp) *Wondering at the World,* 1983.
Elfie, 1987.
Harry Prime, 1987.
(With Ann Gazzard) *Getting Our Thoughts Together,* 1988.

OTHER

Editor, *Thinking: The Journal of Philosophy for Children,* 1979—; member of advisory board, *Teaching Philosophy,* 1975—.

WORK IN PROGRESS: Critical Thinking and the Improvement of Judgment.

BIOGRAPHICAL/CRITICAL SOURCES:

PERIODICALS

Newsweek, September 20, 1976.
New York Times, October 20, 1974.
Time, November 18, 1974.

*   *   *

LIPSITZ, George R(aymond)   1947-

PERSONAL: Born November 10, 1947, in Paterson, NJ; son of Herbert (a teacher) and Paulette (a teacher; maiden name, Politinsky) Lipsitz. *Education:* Washington University, St. Louis, MO, A.B., 1968; University of Missouri—St. Louis, M.A., 1975; University of Wisconsin—Madison, Ph.D., 1979.

ADDRESSES: Office—203 Scott Hall, 72 Pleasant St. S.E., Minneapolis, MN 55455-0225.

CAREER: University of Houston at Clear Lake City, Houston, TX, assistant professor of history, 1979-81; University of Missouri—St. Louis, visiting assistant professor of history, 1981-82; University of Houston at Clear Lake City, assistant professor of history, 1982-86; University of Minnesota—Minneapolis, assistant professor, 1986-88, associate professor of American studies, 1988—. Visiting assistant professor of history, Mount Holyoke College, 1985-86. Director of St. Louis History Project, 1981-82. Has presented papers at conferences. Consultant to numerous organizations.

MEMBER: American Historical Association, American Culture Association, Association for the Study of Afro-American Life and History, Southwest Social Science Organization.

AWARDS, HONORS: Anisfield-Wolf Book Award in Race Relations, and Gustavus Meyers Center Outstanding Book Award, both 1988, both for *A Life in the Struggle: Ivory Perry and the Culture of Opposition.*

WRITINGS:

Class and Culture in Cold War America: A Rainbow at Midnight, Praeger, 1981.
(Contributor) Paul Buhle and Alan Dawley, editors, *Working for Democracy,* University of Illinois Press, 1985.
(Contributor) Donald Lazere, editor, *American Media and Mass Culture: Left Perspectives,* University of California Press, 1987.
(Contributor) Buhle, editor, *Popular Culture in America,* University of Minnesota Press, 1987.
A Life in the Struggle: Ivory Perry and the Culture of Opposition, Temple University Press, 1988.
(Contributor) Rob Kroes, editor, *The American West: As Seen by Europeans and Americans,* Free University Press, 1989.
(Contributor) Adam Sorkin, editor, *Politics and the Muse: Studies in the Politics of Recent American Literature,* Popular Press, 1989.
(Contributor) Lary May, editor, *Recasting America: Culture and Politics in the Age of Cold War,* University of Chicago Press, 1989.

Time Passages: Collective Memory and Popular Culture in the U.S. since 1945, University of Minnesota Press, 1990.

Also author of art exhibit catalogue. General editor of "American Culture" series, University of Minnesota Press, 1989—. Also creator of film, "Beyond a Boundary: The Emancipatory Vision of Edgar Ulmer," Goethe Institute (Houston), 1984. Contributor to periodicals, including *Humanities in the South, Telos, Journal of American History, Cultural Anthropology,* and *Knowledge and Society.* Editor, *Southwest Media Review,* 1982-85; contributing editor, *St. Louis Magazine,* 1982-85; member of editorial board, *Journal of Sport and Social Issues,* 1986—.

SIDELIGHTS: George R. Lipsitz told *CA:* "My work concerns the way in which ordinary people make history and are made by it. The history of public institutions—governments, economic systems, and armies—makes most sense when viewed in the light of the ways in which it intersects the hopes and aspirations of ordinary people.

"My book *Class and Culture in Cold War America: A Rainbow at Midnight* explores the greatest strike wave in American history in the years after World War II from the perspective of the everyday shop floor and community experiences of American workers. The 'rainbow at midnight' in the subtitle refers to the lyrics of a popular country and western song from 1946, but it also expresses the utopian visions of the postwar world that propelled the general and mass strikes of that era."

*   *   *

LIVINGOOD, James W(eston) 1910-

PERSONAL: Born July 5, 1910, in Birdsboro, Pa.; son of Howard Manwiller and Minnie (Potts) Livingood; married Alma Lawshe, June 19, 1937; children: James Weston, Jr.; Richard Shafto. *Education:* Gettysburg College, B.S., 1932; Princeton University, M.A., 1934, Ph.D., 1937. *Religion:* Episcopalian.

ADDRESSES: Home—395 Shallowford Rd., Chattanooga, Tenn. 37411.

CAREER: Princeton University, Princeton, N.J., instructor in history, 1935-36; University of Tennessee at Chattanooga, 1937—, professor of history, 1951-75, Guerry Professor of History, 1962-75, distinguished research professor of history, 1969-75, distinguished professor emeritus, 1975—, chairman of Division of Social Sciences, 1951-52, dean of College of Arts and Sciences, 1957-66, dean of the university, 1966-69. Official Hamilton County historian, 1975—; member of history advisory committee of Moccasin Bend Task Force.

MEMBER: American Historical Association, Southern Historical Association, Tennessee Historical Society, East Tennessee Historical Society, Tennessee College Association (president, 1967-68), Chattanooga Area Historical Society (charter member; past president), Chattanooga Civil War Roundtable (president, 1979-80), Phi Beta Kappa, Pi Gamma Mu, Phi Delta Theta.

AWARDS, HONORS: American Spirit Award.

WRITINGS:

Philadelphia-Baltimore Trade Rivalry, 1780-1860, Pennsylvania Historical and Museum Commission, 1947, reprinted, Arno, 1970.

(With Gilbert E. Govan) *The University of Chattanooga: Sixty Years,* University of Chattanooga Press, 1947.

(With Govan) *The Chattanooga Country: From Tomähawks to T.V.A.,* Dutton, 1952, revised edition, University of Tennessee Press, 1977.

(With Govan) *A Different Valor: The Story of General Joseph E. Johnston, C.S.A.,* Bobbs-Merrill, 1956, reprinted, Greenwood Press, 1974.

(Editor with Govan) *The Haskell Memoirs,* Putnam, 1960.

(Contributor) *Landmarks of Tennessee History,* Tennessee Historical Society and Tennessee Historical Commission, 1965.

(With J. Leonard Raulston) *Sequatchie: A Story of the Southern Cumberlands,* University of Tennessee Press, 1974.

Chattanooga: An Illustrated History, Windsor Publication, 1981.

Hamilton County, University Press of Memphis State University, 1981.

Chattanooga and Hamilton County Medical Society, Centennial History, 1983.

A Department's Story: A Centennial History of the Chemistry's Department of the University of Tennessee at Chattanooga, 1886-1986, Centennial History, 1987.

Also author with Govan, of *Chronology: University of Chattanooga, 1872-1961,* University of Chattanooga Press. Contributor to *Collier's Encyclopedia, Encyclopedia Americana,* and *Enyclopaedia Britannica.* Book reviewer for *Chattanooga Times;* contributor of articles and reviews to *Saturday Review, Tennessee Valley Perspective, Civil War Times Illustrates,* and numerous history journals.

SIDELIGHTS: James W. Livingood told *CA:* "I am a committed believer in scholarly-researched local history, which has too long been prepared [only] for patriotic speeches and chamber of commerce messages. It is the fundamental base for all state, regional, and national history. It's where the roots dig in."

*   *   *

LOBKOWICZ, Nicholas 1931-

PERSONAL: Last syllable of surname rhymes with "blitz"; born July 9, 1931, in Prague, Czechoslovakia; son of Jan (a landowner) and Maria (Czernin) Lobkowicz; married Josephine Waldburg-Zeil, August 22, 1953; children: John, Eric, Franz, Monika, Joseph (deceased), Miriam. *Education:* Kollegium Maria Hilf, Schwyz, Switzerland, B.A., 1950; University of Erlangen, graduate study, 1950; University of Fribourg, Ph.D., 1958. *Politics:* None. *Religion:* Roman Catholic.

ADDRESSES: Home—Ensfeld 2, 8831 Moernsheim, West Germany. *Office*—Katholische Universitaet, 8078 Eichstaett, West Germany.

CAREER: University of Notre Dame, Notre Dame, IN, associate professor of philosophy, 1960-67; University of Munich, Munich, West Germany, professor of political philosophy, 1967-70, 1982-84, dean of School of Arts and Letters, 1971, university rector, 1971-75, president, 1975-82; Katholische Universitaet (Catholic University), Eichstaett, West Germany, president, 1984—. Member of board of directors, Federal Institute for International and East European Studies, 1972-75; president, Freier Deutscher Autorenverband, 1984—; member of permanent committee, 1979-84, of European Rectors' Conference.

MEMBER: International Association for Metaphysics (founding member), International Federation of Catholic Universities (member of council, 1984—), American Association for Metaphysics, Association for Symbolic Logic, Association for the Advancement of Slavic Studies, Deutsch Osteuropagesellschaft, Central Committee of German Catholics, Ukrainian Academy of Arts and Sciences (honorary member, New York chapter), Association for the United Nations (president of Bavarian section, 1980—).

AWARDS, HONORS: National Endowment for the Humanities senior fellowship to complete second volume of *Theory and Practice*, 1967-68; D.H.L., Wayne State University, 1978; Ludwig Thoma Medal, Munich, 1978; Order of Merit, Bavaria, 1978, and Republic of Senegal, 1979; Knight of Order of the Toison d'Or, 1980; D.L.L., University of Notre Dame, 1981; Dr.phil. honoris causa, Sung Kyun Kwan University, Seoul, 1981, and Free Ukrainian University, Munich, 1984; Award of Deutschlandstiflung for scholarship, 1985.

WRITINGS:

Das Widerspruchsprinzip in der neuren sowjetischen Philosophie, D. Reidel (Dordrecht, Netherlands), 1959.
Marxismus-Leninismus in der CSR: Die tschechoslowakische Philosophie seit 1945, D. Reidel, 1961.
Theory and Practice, Volume 1: *From Aristotle to Marx*, University of Notre Dame Press, 1967.
(Editor and contributor) *Marx and the Western World*, University of Notre Dame Press, 1967.
(Editor for philosophy content and contributor) *Sowjetsystem und demokratische Gesellschaft* (title means "The Soviet System and Democratic Society"), five volumes, Herder (Freiburg, Germany), 1967.
(Editor and contributor) *Philosophie und Ideologie*, three volumes, Herder, 1973.
(With A. Hertz) *Ende aller Religion?*, Fromm Verlag, 1976.
Marxismus und Machtergreifung, Fromm Verlag, 1978.
Die Tschechoslowakei 1945-1970, Oldenbourg, 1978.
Die Politische Herausforderung der Wissenschaft, Hoffmann & Campe, 1978.
Geisteswissenschaft als Aufgabe, deGruyter, 1978.
Die Schicksalsjahre der Tschechoslowakei, 1945-1948, Oldenbourg, 1981.
Wortmeldung zu Staat, Styria Verlag, 1981.
Was brachte uns das konsil?, Naumann, 1986.
(Translator) Jan Zahradnicek, *Der Haeftling Gottes*, Naumann, 1986.

CONTRIBUTOR

E. McMullin, editor, *The Concept of Matter*, University of Notre Dame Press, 1963.
J. Gebhardt, editor, *Die Revolution des Geistes*, Paul List (Munich), 1968.
W. Dallmayr, editor, *Materialien zu Habermas' "Erkenntnis und Interesse,"* Suhrkamp (Frankfurt), 1974.
D. Dahm, editor, *Die Technik der Macht*, Walter-Verlag (Olten, Switzerland), 1974.
H. Laufer, editor, *Freichert und Gleichheit*, C. H. Beck, 1974.

OTHER

Also co-editor of *Studies in Soviet Thought* (Netherlands), *Zeitschrift fuer Politik*, and *Geisteswissenschaftliche Riehe der Goerresgesellschaft* (both Germany). Co-editor of "Herfunft und Zukunft" monograph series.

WORK IN PROGRESS: History of the Notion of Virtues, for Styria Verlag.

* * *

LOCK, Dennis (Laurence) 1929-

PERSONAL: Born September 15, 1929, in London, England; son of Douglas Leonard and Marjorie (Rouledge) Lock; married Gladys Nancie (Shilling) Purves, July 11, 1953. *Education:* Acton Technical College, Higher National Certificate in applied physics, 1955. *Politics:* Conservative. *Religion:* Church of England. *Avocational interests:* Music, opera, mountain walking.

ADDRESSES: Home—29 Burston Dr., Park St., St. Albans, Hertfordshire AL2 2HR, England. *Office*—Seltrust Engineering Ltd., 57/61 Clerkenwell Rd., London EC1M 5SP, England.

CAREER: General Electric Co., Wembley and Stanmore, England, physicist, 1945-48 and 1950-62; Honeywell Controls Ltd., Hemel Hempstead, England, contracts control manager, 1963-68; Herbert-Ingersoll Ltd., Daventry, England, manager of engineering administrative services, 1968-71; Seltrust Engineering Ltd., London, England, office services manager, 1971-86; free-lance management writer, 1987—. Consultant. *Military service:* Royal Air Force, 1948-50.

MEMBER: British Institute of Management, Institute of Industrial Managers, Institute of Management Services (fellow), Physical Society (fellow).

WRITINGS:

Project Management, Canner, 1968, 4th edition, Gower Press, 1988.
(Editor) *Director's Guide to Management Techniques*, Gower Press, 1970, 2nd edition, 1972.
Industrial Scheduling Techniques, Gower Press, 1971.
(Editor) *Engineer's Handbook of Management Techniques*, Gower Press, 1973.
(Editor) *Financial Management of Production*, Gower Press, 1975.
Factory Administration Handbook, Gower Press, 1976.
(Editor) *Gower Handbook of Management*, Gower Press, 1983, 2nd edition, 1988.
(Editor) *The Complete Manager*, Wildwood House, 1986.
(Editor) *Handbook of Engineering Management*, Heinemann/Newnes, 1989.
Project Planner, Gower Press, 1990.
(Editor) *Handbook of Quality Management*, Gower Press, 1990.

Also editor of *Project Management Handbook*, Gower Press.

* * *

LOCKLIN, Gerald (Ivan) 1941-

PERSONAL: Born February 17, 1941, in Rochester, NY; son of Ivan Ward and Esther (Kindelen) Locklin; married Mary Alice Keefe; married second wife, Maureen McNicholas; married third wife, Barbara Curry; children: (first marriage) James, Heidi, Rebecca; (second marriage) Blake, John; (third marriage) Vanessa, Zachary. *Education:* St. John Fisher College, B.A., 1961; University of Arizona, M.A., 1963, Ph.D., 1964.

ADDRESSES: Office—Department of English, California State University, Long Beach, CA 90840.

CAREER: California State College at Los Angeles (now California State University, Los Angeles), instructor in English, 1964-65; California State University, Long Beach, 1965—, began as associate professor, currently professor of English. Has given readings of his works.

MEMBER: Phi Beta Kappa.

WRITINGS:

Sunset Beach, Hors Commerce Press, 1967.
The Toad Poems, Runcible Spoon Press, 1970, new edition, Venice Poetry Co., 1975.

Poop, and Other Poems, Mag Press, 1973.
Toad's Europe, Venice Poetry Co., 1973.
Locked In, True Gripp Press, 1973.
Son of Poop, Maelstrom Press, 1974.
(With Koertge and Stetler) *Tarzan and Shane Meet the Toad,* Russ Haas Press, 1975.
The Chase: A Novel, Duck Down Press, 1976.
The Criminal Mentality, Red Hill Press, 1976.
The Four-Day Work Week and Other Stories, Russ Haas Press, 1977.
Pronouncing Borges, Wormwood Review Press, 1977.
A Weekend in Canada, Rumba Train Press, 1979.
The Cure, Applezaba Press, 1979.
Two Summer Sequences, Maelstrom Press, 1979.
Stanford's Farm, Rumba Train Press, 1980.
The Last of Toad, Venice Poetry Co., 1980.
Two for the Seesaw and One for the Road, Northwoods Press, 1980.
Poop: Gedichte und stories, Maro Verlag (West Germany), 1980.
Scenes from a Second Adolescence, Applezaba Press, 1981.
A Clear and Present Danger to Society, Four Zoas Night House Press, 1981.
By Land, Sea, and Air, Maelstrom Press, 1982.
Why Turn a Perfectly Good Toad into a Prince?, Mt. Alverno Press, 1983.
Fear and Paternity in the Pauma Valley, Planet Detroit Press, 1984.
(With Ray Zepeda) *The Ensenada Poems,* Truly Fine Press, 1984.
The Case of the Missing Blue Volkswagen (novel), Applezaba Press, 1984.
The Phantom of the Johnny Carson Show, Illuminati, 1984.
(With Zepeda) *We Love L.A.,* 22 Press, 1985.
The English Mini-Tour, Vergin' Press, 1987.
Gringo and Other Poems, Vergin' Press, 1987.
A Constituency of Dunces, Slipstream Press, 1988.
Children of a Lesser Demagogue, Wormwood Review Press, 1988.
On the Rack, Trout Creek Press, 1988.
Lost and Found, Zerx Press, 1989.
The Treasure of the Sierra Faulkner, Zerx Press, 1989.
The Gold Rush and Other Stories, Applezaba Press, 1989.
Die Rosskuere, Maro Verlag, 1989.

Also author of *Frisco Epic,* Russ Haas Press, *Toad's Sabbatical,* Venice Poetry Co., and *The Death of Jean-Paul Sartre and Other Poems,* Ghost Pony Press; also author of play "The Dentist." Contributor to numerous periodicals, including *Wormwood Review, Poetry, Los Angeles Times, Coast,* and *Long Beach Independent Press-Telegram.*

WORK IN PROGRESS: Poems, stories, novels, plays, and literary criticism.

SIDELIGHTS: Some of Gerald Locklin's books and stories have been translated into German and Dutch.

BIOGRAPHICAL/CRITICAL SOURCES:

PERIODICALS

Los Angeles Times Book Review, October 31, 1982; August 18, 1985.

*   *   *

LOSONCY, Lawrence J.   1941-

PERSONAL: Surname is accented on second syllable; born September 12, 1941, in Detroit, MI; son of Joseph Michael (a busi-

nessman) and Rose (Laus) Losoncy; married Mary Jan Sibley (a teacher and researcher), August 16, 1965; children: David Lawrence, John Michael, Kristen Mary. *Education:* Sacred Heart Seminary College, B.A., 1963; attended St. John's Seminary, 1963-65; University of Detroit, M.A., 1968; Wayne State University, Ph.D., 1971. *Politics:* Democrat. *Religion:* Roman Catholic.

ADDRESSES: Home—1701 West Virgin Ave., Tulsa, OK 74127. *Office*—Hope Associates, 2512 East 71st, Suite G, Tulsa, OK 74136.

CAREER: School music teacher and church organist in Lincoln Park, MI, 1965-68; University of Detroit, Detroit, MI, instructor in philosophy, 1968; high school religion teacher in Southgate, MI, 1968-69; Wayne State University, Detroit, instructor in philosophy of education, 1969; Hi-Time Publisher, Elm Grove, WI, editor, 1969; U.S. Catholic Conference, Washington, DC, director of Adult Education Division and project director for national study "The Church's Expanding Role in Adult Education," 1970-72; became professional marriage and family counselor; Oral Roberts University, Tulsa, OK, associate professor, 1979-82; currently marriage and family therapist with own firm, Hope (Handling Our Problems Effectively) Associates, Tulsa. Holds clinical certification with American Association of Marriage and Family Therapists. Adjunct professor, Phillips Seminary, Tulsa campus. Member of board and on staff, St. Anne Institute, Tulsa. Former national consultant, U.S. Catholic Conference; religious education consultant, Diocese of Trenton and Immaculate Conception Parish, both NJ, 1972-76; currently does extensive consulting work in religious education.

WRITINGS:

Common Sense Vision: A Philosophy of Religious Education, privately printed, 1968.
For Parents: Teaching Religion at Home, privately printed, 1969.
(With wife, Mary Jan Losoncy) *Love,* Ave Maria Press, 1970.
(With M. J. Losoncy) *Sex and the Adolescent,* Ave Maria Press, 1971.
The ABCs of Adult Education, Volume 1, U.S. Catholic Conference, 1971.
Land of Promise, Dimension, 1972.
Religious Education and the Life Cycle, Catechetical Communications, 1977.
When Your Child Needs a Hug, Abbey Press, 1978.
(With Dan MacNeil) *Heart Attacks: The Answer Book,* Fleming Revell, 1983.
(Contributor) *The Whole Book of Health,* Fleming Revell, 1984.
What God Has Joined Together, Hensley, 1986.

Also author of cassette tapes, "History and Practice of Adult Religious Education," Abbey Press, 1975, "When Your Child Needs a Hug" (based on his book of the same title), Abbey Press, 1979, and "Grieving through Divorce," "Children of Divorce," "The Art of Successful Worrying," "The World's Worst Salesman," and "Overcoming Discouragement in Sales," all Modern Education Corp., 1987. Author of monthly column in *Marriage and Family;* author of weekly column in *South Grand Laker;* author of column "Less Than Perfect" in *Eastern Oklahoma Catholic;* guest columnist in *Baculus* (Tulsa University student law review), 1988-90. Editor and publisher of newsletter, *HOPE-NOTES,* in conjunction with his counseling practice; co-editor of monthly newsletter, *Fingerprints,* St. Anne Institute.

SIDELIGHTS: Lawrence J. Losoncy told *CA:* "I began writing as a challenge, something I wished to master. I still have not mastered the craft, 25 years later, but I have grown to appreciate the power of the pen and the demands of the craft. Now I write to convey a message. That's the main advice I can give: only write when you have something important to convey and you might pop if you do not convey it. I made myself write one hour per day for years, just to learn how. That made me much more appreciative of the good work other writers did. I began reading with a deeper appreciation of their style, always with two questions: what is the writer communicating, and how well is the writer communicating? Those are the standards by which I judge myself: if it does not convey a message and convey it well, it goes in the trash.

"Although I now write a wide variety of newsletters, columns, essays, and self-help material, what I do reflects my personal convictions. That is still, I think, what makes the written piece interesting and valuable. In this aspect Andrew Greeley and Mitchener have been my writing heroes. Gabriel Marcel's comment that modern entertainment media should reflect what humans can be rather than mirror their worst nightmares has served as a challenge all these years. I am convinced our world must work harder at community in all sizes and shapes or die because of alienation and hatred. Writers are, therefore, challenged more than ever to use the power of the pen to uphold individual dignity and rights while describing the higher ground to which we can yet rise as people, together. I have also let show the growing conviction in my life that human life must be ordered around God as our Creator and source of meaning, in which respect relating to one another and our environment and working for community are key challenges."

*   *   *

LOVINS, Amory B(loch)   1947-

PERSONAL: Born November 13, 1947, in Washington, D.C.; son of Gerald Hershel (an engineer) and Miriam (a social service administrator; maiden name, Bloch) Lovins; married L. Hunter Sheldon (an attorney, environmentalist, and author), September 6, 1979. *Education:* Attended Harvard University, 1964-65, 1966-67, and Magdalen College, Oxford, 1967-69; Merton College, Oxford, M.A., 1971. *Politics:* Jeffersonian. *Religion:* "Thoreauvian."

ADDRESSES: Home and office—1739 Snowmass Creek Rd., Old Snowmass, Colo. 81654-9199.

CAREER: International consultant physicist, 1963-68; Merton College, Oxford, England, junior research fellow, 1969-71; Friends of the Earth, San Francisco, Calif., and London, England, British representative and policy advisor, 1971-84; Rocky Mountain Institute, Old Snowmass, Colo., vice president and director of research, 1982—. Regents' Lecturer, University of California, 1978, 1981; Luce Visiting Professor, Dartmouth College, 1982; distinguished visiting professor, University of Colorado, 1982; Grauer Lecturer, University of British Columbia. Mountain guide at Camp Winona, summers, 1966-81. Government and private-sector energy consultant, 1971—; member of advisory board, U.S. Department of Energy, 1980-81; technical advisor, National Association of Regulatory Utility Commissioners.

MEMBER: World Academy of Art and Science (fellow), International Association of Energy Economists, American Association for the Advancement of Science (fellow), Federation of American Scientists, Association of Energy Engineers, Lindisfarne Association.

AWARDS, HONORS: Sprout Award, International Studies Association, 1977; Public Education award, National Energy Resources Organization, 1978; D.Sc., Bates College, 1979, Williams College, 1981, Kalamazoo College, 1983, University of Maine, 1985; Public Service Award, National Association for Environmental Education, 1980; Mitchell prize, Mitchell Energy Foundation, 1982; Right Livelihood Award, Right Livelihood Foundation, 1983; LL.D., Ball State University, 1983; Delphi Prize, Onassis Foundation, 1989.

WRITINGS:

Eryri, the Mountains of Longing, edited and introduced by David R. Brower, Friends of the Earth, 1971.
The Stockholm Conference: Only One Earth, Earth Island, 1972.
Openpit Mining, Earth Island, 1973.
World Energy Strategies: Facts, Issues, and Options, Friends of the Earth/Ballinger, 1975.
(With John Price) *Non-Nuclear Futures: The Case for an Ethical Energy Strategy,* Friends of the Earth/Ballinger, 1975.
Soft Energy Paths: Toward a Durable Peace, Friends of the Earth/Ballinger, 1977, Harper, 1979.
(With others) *The Energy Controversy: Soft Path Questions and Answers,* edited by Hugh Nash, Friends of the Earth, 1979.
(With wife, L. Hunter Lovins) *Energy/War: Breaking the Nuclear Link,* Friends of the Earth, 1980, Harper, 1981.
(With others) *Least-cost Energy: Solving the Carbon Dioxide Problem,* Brick House, 1981.
(With L. H. Lovins) *Brittle Power: Energy Strategy for National Security,* Brick House, 1982.
(With Patrick O'Heffernan and L. H. Lovins) *The First Nuclear World War: A Strategy for Preventing Nuclear Wars and the Spread of Nuclear Weapons,* Morrow, 1983.
(With L. H. Lovins) *Energy Unbound: A Fable for America's Future,* Sierra Books, 1986.

Author of several hundred monographs, technical papers, and articles about energy issues.

WORK IN PROGRESS: Directing research of forty-four staff and consultants on energy, water, agriculture, security, and local economic development issues, and their interconnections; personal research in advanced techniques for resource (especially electrical) efficiency.

SIDELIGHTS: "Amory Lovins is the real thing: an antinuclear-power polemicist whose arguments are so well organized, clearly expressed and documented that even the most enthusiastic partisans on the other side will have to take notice," claims Gerald Jonas of the *New York Times Book Review.* Advocating what he calls the "soft" technology approach to energy, Lovins believes that more efficient use of energy, as well as implementation of renewable sources such as solar, wind, and hydro power, is cheaper and more appropriate for most energy purposes than "hard" technologies like nuclear and coal-fired plants, which tend to produce power of higher quality at a larger scale than necessary for simple tasks like heating and lighting. But if Lovins "were just antinuclear, he would be one-eighth as effective," energy and environmental researcher Deborah Bleviss told Brad Lemley in the *Chicago Tribune Magazine.* Instead, Lovins espouses the idea "that there is an alternative that is superior in terms of finances, the environment and public safety," Bleviss explained. Through his ideas "he has helped to change the whole frame of reference" of the energy debate.

Lovins's expertise in physics contributes to the effectiveness of his arguments against hard technologies; as he commented to Ellen Frank in the *New Times,* "I have used the hard technologists' language, numbers and intellectual framework in a complete rebuttal of the values and conclusions." A student at Harvard University at sixteen, Lovins soon transferred to Oxford, where he studied experimental physics and became the youngest research don at the university in at least 400 years. But he was becoming disenchanted with the rigidity of the academic life, and left Oxford to pursue his new interest in energy systems. "They wanted me to specialize" in one discipline, Lovins told *People*, "but I thought the world needed more people who could make connections that had not been made before." This led to "my main professional role," Lovins told *CA*, "as a synthesist and as a translator between technical specialties: I circulate on the international energy grapevine, cross-pollinating and moving ideas and papers around faster than they might otherwise go." In 1976 Lovins published his first major article in the influential journal *Foreign Affairs;* "Energy Strategy: The Road Not Taken?," which explored the ideas of "soft" and "hard" technologies, set a record for reprint requests and led *Newsweek* to call Lovins "one of the Western world's most influential energy thinkers."

Lovins soon expanded "Energy Strategy" into an entire book on the advantages of conservative energy technologies, *Soft Energy Paths: Toward a Durable Peace.* "A comprehensive rationale for conservation that is political as well as economic," as *Nation* contributor Fred D. Baldwin describes it, *Soft Energy Paths* manages "to define a pattern against which a jumble of technical choices can be compared and evaluated." Lovins's key reforms focus on increasing the energy effiency of machines by reducing the amount of power they need to operate, and promoting the concept of appropriate use. "Where we want to only create temperature differences of tens of degrees," Lovins explained to Frank, "we should meet the need with sources whose potential is tens or hundreds of degrees [such as passive solar heating], not with a flame temperature of thousands or a nuclear reaction temperature equivalent to trillions. That is like cutting butter with a chainsaw." The author continued: "If we applied energy in the right scale, we'd largely eliminate the costs and losses of conversion and distribution of energy."

While Lovins's theories have been praised for their novel, broad approach to energy strategies, they have also come under criticism for over-simplification of the issues they consider. Samuel McCracken, for example, writes in the *National Review* that *Soft Energy Paths* "is plagued by inaccuracy, uncalled-for generosity, and misleading treatments of its subjects," sometimes substituting "promise for reality." Lemley similarly reports than even some of Lovins's supporters "agree that some of [his] contentions are difficult or even impossible to back up to everyone's satisfaction." But, as former Solar Energy Research Institute director Dennis Hayes explained to Lemley, Lovins "has taken a huge body of information and has had to simplify it to make it fit. It's a necessary and essential part of the process. . . . He is conveying a truth—that we have seen a significant change in how America" is looking at energy sources. "If it all sounds too good to be true," Jonas similarly notes, "Lovins has at least won the right to be heard; his contribution both enlivens and deepens the Great Energy Debate."

However, with the establishment of the Rocky Mountain Institute, a nonprofit foundation fostering resource efficiency and global security, Lovins's analyses have become "painfully respectable," the theorist noted to *CA*. Most of the Institute's $1 million annual budget comes from consultant services "to about ninety utilities, governments, and related organizations in twenty countries." As he told Frank, he also hopes to see his theories gain acceptance among the general population: "Every alternative energy project generates enough enthusiasm to spawn about seven more. The spiraling impact is tremendous. . . . You don't have to agree about why you [use soft energy], or

about price versus regulation, capitalism versus socialism. We can continue to reflect our own pluralism in the way our energy system evolves."

"Though my formal education added to its main strand (physics and related sciences) parallel strands in math, classics, music, linguistics, some law, a little medicine, and mountain photography, I wish it had been broader still," Lovins once told *CA.* "My main avocations are music (piano and composition), mountaineering (about 100 days a year [until 1981]), landscape photography, writing, a few sports, and, most of all, people. I regard writing not as my profession, but rather as one of the crafts essential to my main function as an energy and resource strategist. Wordsmithing is also, however, a worthy and exacting discipline."

BIOGRAPHICAL/CRITICAL SOURCES:

PERIODICALS

Atlantic, November, 1980.
Chicago Tribune Magazine, August 3, 1986.
Los Angeles Times Book Review, December 18, 1983, April 20, 1986.
Nation, November 12, 1977.
National Review, February 2, 1979.
Newsweek, November 14, 1977.
New Times, August 21, 1978.
New York Times Book Review, January 8, 1978.
People, October 19, 1987.
Times Literary Supplement, December 22, 1972, October 19, 1973, January 25, 1974, January 25, 1985.

—*Sketch by Diane Telgen*

*   *   *

LUCAS, John   1937-

PERSONAL: Born June 26, 1937, in Devon, England; married Pauline van Meeteren; children: Ben, Emma. *Education:* University of Reading, B.A., 1959, Ph.D., 1965. *Politics:* Socialist. *Religion:* None. *Avocational interests:* Jazz, sports, beer.

ADDRESSES: Home—19 Devonshire Ave., Beeston, Nottinghamshire, England. *Office*—Department of English, University of Loughborough, Leicestershire LE11 3TU, England.

CAREER: University of Reading, Reading, England, lecturer in English, 1961-64; University of Nottingham, Nottingham, England, lecturer, 1964, senior lecturer, 1971-75, reader in English, 1975-77; University of Loughborough, Leicestershire, England, professor of English and drama, 1977—. Visiting professor at University of Maryland and University of Indiana, 1967-68; Lord Byron Professor of English Literature, University of Athens, 1984-85.

WRITINGS:

(With John Goode and David Howard) *Tradition and Tolerance in Nineteenth-Century Fiction,* Barnes & Noble, 1966.
(Editor and author of introduction and notes) *A Selection from George Crabbe,* Longmans, Green, 1967.
The Melancholy Man: A Study of Dickens's Novels, Barnes & Noble, 1970.
(Editor and author of introduction) *Literature and Politics in the Nineteenth Century* (essays), Barnes & Noble, 1971.
About Nottingham, Byron Press, 1971.
A Brief Bestiary (poems), Pecten Press, 1972.
Chinese Sequence (poems), Sceptre Press, 1972.
Arnold Bennett: A Study of His Fiction, Methuen, 1975.
Egillssaga: The Poems, Dent, 1975.

(Editor) W. H. Mallock, *The New Republic,* Leicester University Press, 1975.

The Literature of Change, Barnes & Noble, 1977.

The 1930s: A Challenge to Orthodoxy, Harvester Press, 1978.

(Editor with Ian Fletcher) *Poems of G. S. Fraser,* Leicester University Press, 1981.

Romantic to Modern Literature: Essays and Ideas of Culture, 1750-1900, Harvester Press, 1982.

The Days of the Week: A Poem Sequence, Dodman Press, 1983.

(With Basil Haynes) *The Trent Bridge Battery: The Story of the Sporting Gunns,* Collins, 1985.

Moderns and Contemporaries: Essays, Barnes & Noble, 1985.

Modern English Poetry from Hardy to Hughes, Batsford, 1986.

Oliver Goldsmith: A Selection, Fyfield Books, 1988.

Studying Grosz on the Bus (poems), Peterloo Poets, 1989.

D. H. Lawrence: Poems and Non-Fictional Prose, a Selection, Routledge & Kegan Paul, 1990.

England and Englishness: Ideas of Nationhood in Poetry, 1688-1900, Chatto & Windus, 1990.

WORK IN PROGRESS: A volume of poems; a study of Dickens, for Penguin; a study of the 1920s.

SIDELIGHTS: "The time may soon be coming when a book of literary essays will seem the appurtenance of a vanished cult, like volumes of Victorian sermons," writes Graham Hough in his *Times Literary Supplement* review of John Lucas's *Romantic to Modern Literature: Essays and Ideas of Culture, 1750-1900.* "Hence perhaps the slightly defiant air with which [the author] introduces his collection." Hough continues that Lucas's various pieces "range from Wordsworth to Forster, and they do not suffer from the essay's habitual defect—that of being a mere exhibition of opinion. They have a ballast of history; and it is to history, character and society that [the author's] study of literature naturally leads. He has no particular axe to grind, but he has a point of view."

Lucas told *CA:* "I find myself increasingly out of sympathy with contemporary literary and critical theory, which seeks—often barbarously—to supplant works of literature with and by works of criticism. I think I know the dangers lurking in William Carlos Williams's remark that 'men die miserably every day' for lack of what can be found in poems. Nevertheless, the spirit of that remark rings true, while the letter of criticism killeth the spirit. Or would do, were literature less tough. As it is, it is heartening to reflect that this year's critical trend is next year's forgotten fad. Meanwhile, the poems and the novels and the plays go on and on and on."

BIOGRAPHICAL/CRITICAL SOURCES:

PERIODICALS

Times Literary Supplement, October 2, 1981; March 4, 1983; May 9, 1986; August 23, 1985; December 1, 1989; February 23, 1990.

*   *   *

LUMPKIN, Angela 1950-

PERSONAL: Born May 17, 1950, in Helena, AR; daughter of Carol Ray (a preacher) and Audrey Janice (Ward) Lumpkin. *Education:* University of Arkansas, B.S.E., 1971; Ohio State University, M.A., 1972, Ph.D., 1974; University of North Carolina, M.B.A., 1989.

ADDRESSES: Home—4200 Crisfield Ct., Raleigh, NC 27613. *Office*—Department of Physical Education, Box 8111, North Carolina State University, Raleigh, NC 27695-8111.

CAREER: Ohio State University, Columbus, assistant basketball coach, 1971-74; University of North Carolina, Chapel Hill, assistant professor, 1974-80, associate professor of physical education, 1980-88, basketball coach, 1974-77, assistant tennis coach, 1974-75, director of physical education activities program, 1977-86, coordinator of undergraduate physical education majors program, 1983-88, coordinator of physical education graduate admissions, 1985-88; North Carolina State University, Raleigh, professor and head of department, 1988—. President of National Association for Sport and Physical Education History Council, 1978-79; member of North Carolina Governor's Council on Physical Fitness and Health, 1986-93. Has given over sixty presentations at state, regional, national, and international conferences and workshops.

MEMBER: North American Society for Sport History (chairperson of membership committee, 1982-84; member of publications board, 1987-89), American Alliance for Health, Physical Education, Recreation, and Dance, North Carolina Alliance for Health, Physical Education, Recreation, and Dance (Physical Education Association president, 1983-84; president, 1988-89).

WRITINGS:

(Editor with W. T. Ladd, and contributor) *Sport in American Education: History and Perspective,* American Alliance for Health, Physical Education, Recreation, and Dance, 1979.

Women's Tennis: A Historical Documentary of the Players and Their Game, Whitston Publishing, 1981.

History and Principles of Physical Education, Alpha Editions, 1981, 2nd edition, 1983.

(Contributor) Reet Howell, editor, *Her Story in Sport: A Historical Anthology of Women in Sports,* Leisure Press, 1982.

Tennis: A Bibliography Guide, Greenwood Press, 1984.

(Contributor) Don Morrow, editor, *Directory of Scholars Identifying with the History of Sport,* North American Society for Sport History, 1984.

(Contributor) *Biographical Dictionary of American Sport,* Greenwood Press, 1984.

A Guide to the Literature of Tennis, Greenwood Press, 1985.

Physical Education: A Contemporary Introduction, Mosby, 1986, 2nd edition published as *Physical Education and Sport: A Contemporary Introduction,* 1990.

(With others) *Racquetball Everyone,* Hunter Textbooks, 1984, 2nd edition, 1988.

Also contributor to *Sports Encyclopedia North American* and *Book of Days 1987.* Contributor to periodicals, including *Journal of Teaching in Physical Education, Journal of Popular Culture, Journal of Physical Education, Recreation, and Dance, British Journal of Physical Education, North Carolina Journal,* and *Quest.*

WORK IN PROGRESS: A history of sportswomen in North Carolina and Arkansas; a sport management book; a sport ethics book; coverage of blacks and women in *Sports Illustrated.*

SIDELIGHTS: Angela Lumpkin told *CA:* "I believe that physical educators must serve as role models of healthy, physically-active lifestyles. I love to jog and to play all racquet sports. I enjoy serving my university, faculty, and students by administering a program that is of the highest quality. My research interests include sharing knowledge learned in the areas of sport history and sport management."

LYMAN, Stanford M(orris) 1933-

PERSONAL: Born June 10, 1933, in San Francisco, Calif.; son of Arthur H. (a grocer) and Gertrude (Kramer) Lyman. *Education:* University of California, Berkeley, A.B., 1955, M.A., 1957, Ph.D., 1961. *Politics:* Independent. *Religion:* Jewish.

ADDRESSES: Home—2668 Northwest 39th St., Boca Raton, Fla. 33434. *Office*—College of Social Science, Florida Atlantic University, 500 Northwest 20th St., Boca Raton, Fla. 33431.

CAREER: University of British Columbia, Vancouver, instructor, 1960-62, assistant professor of sociology, 1962-63; University of California Extension, Berkeley, associate professor and head of liberal arts department, 1963-64; Sonoma State College (now University), Rohnert Park, Calif., associate professor of sociology and chairman of department, 1964-68; University of Nevada at Reno, 1968-70, began as associate professor, became professor of sociology; University of California, San Diego, associate professor of sociology, 1970-72; New School for Social Research, Graduate Faculty of Political and Social Research, New York, N.Y., professor of sociology, 1972-81, professor of sociology and Asian studies, 1981-85, chairman of department of sociology, 1972-75; Florida Atlantic University, Boca Raton, Fla., Robert J. Morrow Eminent Scholar and Professor of Social Science, 1985—. Lecturer in Southeast Asia for United States Information Service, 1975; senior member, Linacre College, Oxford University, 1975; Fulbright lecturer, Doshisha University and Ryukoku University, Kyoto, Japan, 1981-82. Visiting distinguished professor, University of Tulsa, fall, 1985; visiting foreign expert, Beijing Foreign Studies University, fall, 1986.

MEMBER: American Sociological Association, Chinese American Historical Society, Center for Japanese American Studies, Society for the Study of Symbolic Interaction, Fulbright Alumni Association, Japanese American Historical Society, Southern Sociological Society, Eastern Sociological Society, Mid-South Sociological Society, Phi Beta Kappa, Phi Kappa Phi.

WRITINGS:

The Oriental in North America, University of British Columbia Extension Service, 1962.

(Contributor) Marcello Truzzi, editor, *The Sociology of Everyday Life,* Prentice-Hall, 1968.

(Contributor) Jack Douglas, editor, *Deviance and Respectability,* Basic Books, 1970.

(With Marvin B. Scott) *Sociology of the Absurd,* Appleton, 1970, revised edition, General Hall, 1989.

(With Scott) *The Revolt of the Students,* C. E. Merrill, 1970.

The Asian in the West, Desert Research Institute, University of Nevada, 1970.

The Black American in Sociological Thought: A Failure of Perspective, Putnam, 1972.

Chinese Americans, Random House, 1974.

(With Scott) *The Drama of Social Reality,* Oxford University Press, 1975.

The Asian in North America, American Bibliographic Center-Clio Press, 1977.

(Contributor) Richard Sennett, editor, *The Psychology of Society,* Vintage Press, 1977.

(Editor with Richard Harvey Brown) *Structure, Consciousness, and History,* Cambridge University Press, 1977.

The Seven Deadly Sins: Society and Evil, St. Martin's, 1978, revised edition, 1989.

(Contributor) Ronald M. Glassman and Vatro Murvar, editors, *Weber's Political Sociology: A Pessimistic Vision of the Rationalized World,* Greenwood Press, 1984.

(With Arthur J. Vidich) *Amercian Sociology: Worldly Rejections of Religion and Their Directions,* Yale University Press, 1984.

Selected Writings of Henry Hughes: Antebellum Southerner, Slavocrat, Sociologist, University Press of Mississippi, 1985.

(Contributor) Mark L. Warde and Stephen P. Turner, editors, *Sociological Theory in Transition,* Allen & Unwin, 1986.

(With Vidich) *Social Order and the Public Philosophy: An Analysis and Interpretation of the Work of Herbert Blumer,* University of Arkansas Press, 1988.

M

MAAS, Jeremy (Stephen) 1928-

PERSONAL: Born August 31, 1928, in Penang, Malaya; son of Henry Oscar (a businessman) and Marjorie (Pope) Maas; married Antonia Armstrong Willis, November 10, 1956; children: Athena, Rupert, Jonathan. *Education:* Pembroke College, Oxford, M.A. (honors), 1952. *Religion:* Church of England.

ADDRESSES: Home—Hook Farm House, Itchingfield, Horsham, West Sussex, England. *Office*—15A Clifford St., London W.1, England.

CAREER: Advertising and printing executive in London, England, 1952-58; art auctioneer, London, 1958-60; Maas Gallery, London, owner/director, 1960—. *Military service:* British Army, national service; became second lieutenant.

MEMBER: Society of Authors, Society of Antiquaries (fellow), Society of London Art Dealers, Garrick Club.

WRITINGS:

Victorian Painters, Putnam, 1969, reprinted, Abbeville Press, 1984.
Gambart: Prince of the Victorian Art World, Barrie & Jenkins, 1976.
The Prince of Wales's Wedding: The Story of a Picture, Cameron & Tayleur, 1977.
"This Brilliant Year": Queen Victoria's Jubilee, 1887, Royal Academy of Arts, 1977.
Victorian Painters, Barrie & Jenkins, 1978.
The Victorian Art World in Photographs, Universe Books, 1984.
Holman Hunt and the Light of the World, Scholar, 1984.
(Contributor) Vivien Noakes, *Edward Lear, 1812-1888,* Royal Academy of Arts in association with Weidenfeld & Nicolson, 1985.

Contributor to *Times Literary Supplement, Punch, Arts Review, Connoisseur, Queen,* and other publications.

WORK IN PROGRESS: Research on aspects of Victorian painting for several books.

BIOGRAPHICAL/CRITICAL SOURCES:

PERIODICALS

Art at Auction, December, 1988.
British Book Notes, August, 1984.
Choice, October, 1984.

Encounter, June, 1984.
Harper's, April, 1970.
New Yorker, August 27, 1984.
Spectator, September 6, 1969.
Times Literary Supplement, March 30, 1984, April 12, 1984.
Vogue, March 1, 1970.

* * *

MacLAINE, Shirley 1934-
(Shirley MacLean Beaty)

PERSONAL: Born Shirley MacLean Beaty, April 24, 1934, in Richmond, Va.; daughter of Ira O. (a real estate agent) and Kathlyn (MacLean) Beaty; married Steve Parker (a businessman), September 17, 1954 (divorced, 1977); children: Stephanie Sachiko. *Education:* Attended high school in Washington, D.C. *Politics:* Democrat.

ADDRESSES: Home—Los Angeles, Calif., and New York, N.Y. *Agent*—c/o International Creative Management, 8899 Beverly Blvd., Los Angeles, Calif. 90048.

CAREER: Chorus dancer and singer, 1950-53; stage actress in Broadway plays and revues including "Me and Juliet," 1953, "Pajama Game," 1954, "A Gypsy in My Soul," 1976, and "Shirley MacLaine on Broadway," 1984. Made screen debut in "The Trouble with Harry," 1954; subsequent films include "Around the World in 80 Days," "Some Came Running," "Ask Any Girl," "Can-Can," "The Apartment," "My Geisha," "Children's Hour," "Two for the Seesaw," "Irma la douce," "What a Way to Go," "Two Mules for Sister Sara," "The Yellow Rolls-Royce," "John Goldfarb Please Come Home," "Sweet Charity," "The Bliss of Mrs. Blossom," "Desperate Characters," "The Turning Point," "Being There," "Loving Couples," "A Change of Seasons," "Terms of Endearment," "Cannonball Run II," "Madame Sousatzka," and "Steel Magnolias." Starred in television series "Shirley's World," 1971; also appeared in television productions of "Amelia," "If They Could See Me Now," "Gypsy in My Soul," and in movie adaptation of her book "Out on a Limb." Delegate to Democratic National Convention, 1968, 1972; member of platform committee, 1972, co-chairperson of McGovern-Shriver National Advisory Committee, 1972. Proprietor of "Higher Self" spiritual seminars, 1987.

AWARDS, HONORS: International Stardom Award, Hollywood Foreign Press Association, 1954; Academy Award nomination for best actress, American Academy of Motion Picture Arts and Sciences, 1958, for "Some Came Running," 1960, for "The Apartment," 1963, for "Irma la douce," and 1977, for "The Turning Point"; Foreign Press award for best actress, 1958, 1961, 1963, 1988; Silver Bear award for best actress, International Berlin Film Festival, 1959, for "Ask Any Girl," and 1971, for "Desperate Characters"; best actress award from Venice Film Festival and British Film Academy, both 1960, both for "The Apartment," and 1988, for "Madame Sousatzka"; Golden Globe Award, Foreign Press Association, 1964, for "Irma la douce," and 1988, for "Madame Sousatzka"; best actress award, Italian Film Festival, 1964; Star of the Year Award from Theater Owners of America, 1967; recipient of Emmy awards from Academy of Television Arts and Sciences, including 1974, for "If They Could See Me Now"; named female musical star of the year from Las Vegas Entertainment Awards, 1976; Academy Award for best actress, American Academy of Motion Picture Arts and Sciences, 1984, for "Terms of Endearment."

WRITINGS:

Don't Fall off the Mountain (autobiography), Norton, 1970.
(Editor) *McGovern: The Man and His Beliefs,* Norton, 1972.
(Editor and author of introduction) *The New Celebrity Cookbook,* Price, Stern, 1973.
You Can Get There from Here (memoirs), Norton, 1975.
Out on a Limb (memoirs), Bantam, 1983.
Dancing in the Light (memoirs), Bantam, 1987.
It's All in the Playing (memoirs), Bantam, 1987.
Going Within: A Guide for Inner Transformation, Bantam, 1989.

OTHER

Author of narration for "The Other Half of the Sky: A China Memoir," a film documentary for Public Broadcasting Service, 1975. Also author of video "Shirley MacLaine's Inner Workout."

WORK IN PROGRESS: A novel.

SIDELIGHTS: An actress who has moved audiences to laughter and tears, an entertainer who has amazed fans with her seemingly nonstop energy, an author who has outraged critics with tales of New Age spiritualism—Shirley MacLaine wears so many hats that she is all but undefinable. As she enters her fourth decade in the public eye, MacLaine continues to draw attention to herself while steadfastly protecting her personal privacy.

Born Shirley MacLean Beaty in Richmond, Va. (her younger brother would also alter his name and achieve fame as Warren Beatty), the young girl knew early on that she was meant for the stage and screen, taking ballet lessons and preparing for her debut. Her first opportunity came in 1950 when, while still in high school, MacLaine won a place in the chorus of a revival of "Oklahoma!" A variety of stage work followed. The 1954 Broadway musical "Pajama Game" introduced MacLaine to the public in the manner from which legends are made. When the second lead Carol Haney broke her ankle, the 19-year-old chorus girl went on as Haney's understudy and was declared an overnight sensation. A Hollywood producer was in the "Pajama Game" audience one night and immediately signed MacLaine to her first movie role, in the Alfred Hitchcock black comedy "The Trouble with Harry." The raft of subsequent film roles displayed a range of characterizations—a princess in "Around the World in 80 Days," a prostitute in "Irma la douce," a nun in "Two Mules for Sister Sara," a naive dance-hall girl in "Sweet Charity." To some critics, MacLaine's best acting in the earlier years came in

her role as a frustrated urban wife in a little-seen film called "Desperate Characters."

As she was establishing her career on the screen, MacLaine also took time to pursue her political interests. MacLaine "frolicked at the fringe of President Kennedy's Camelot," relates William A. Henry III in a *Time* cover story on the actress. "Then the civil rights movement confronted the racism that she remembered from her Southern girlhood, and she shipped off to Issaquena County, Miss., to stay with black families, facing insults and threats on the street. She joined in the Viet Nam War protest, and noisily campaigned for Robert Kennedy in 1968, and, full time for 18 months, for George McGovern four years later."

After a relatively long absence from the big screen, MacLaine re-emerged in films in 1977 as an ex-ballet dancer fighting her old rival for the soul of her daughter in "The Turning Point." MacLaine earned her fourth Academy Award nomination for that role, but the Oscar would again elude her. MacLaine followed "The Turning Point" with the critically acclaimed satire "Being There." Then there was another lengthy absence from the screen ("Every four years or so, I find a script," she tells *Parade* magazine's James Brady in 1988), until, in 1983, MacLaine signed on to play the lead in James Brooks' film of the Larry McMurtry novel *Terms of Endearment.*

As Aurora Greenway, described by the actress as "an impossible, demanding, smothering, self-indulgent woman who made me laugh a lot," MacLaine shared scenes with Jack Nicholson and Debra Winger in this contemporary tear-jerker. MacLaine received raves for her portrayal of one woman's life of heartbreak and humor. "To many people the character was unsympathetic—monstrous or, worse, ridiculous," notes Henry. "[Winger's] cancer-ridden daughter . . . would get most of the sympathy, and [Nicholson's] breezy, boozy ex-astronaut would get most of the laughs. Even more perilous for an actress past 40, Aurora had to age, painfully, gracelessly. Unlike stars who demand that the camera flatter them, the vibrant MacLaine made herself look ravaged, the neglected ruin of a beauty."

While "Terms of Endearment" was widely publicized for its quality and audience appeal, almost as much publicity resulted from the rumors of unrest on the set, particularly in the pairing of the outspoken MacLaine and the equally feisty Winger. Director Brooks quickly dispelled such gossip, telling *People* reporter Scot Haller that following one emotional scene, the two performers "didn't do 20 minutes on how wonderful each other was. It's easy to do dear-darling-hug-hug, but they weren't like that. They were real with each other." Both MacLaine and Winger were nominated for the Academy Award in the best actress category for "Terms of Endearment." This time, MacLaine did take home the statuette.

The Oscar was just one triumph for MacLaine in 1984, though. That same year she opened on Broadway in a song-and-dance tour de force, garnered a *Time* cover story, and saw one of her books, *Out on a Limb,* reach the top of the bestseller lists. It was also the year MacLaine turned 50, prompting her to tell Haller that she considers age just a number to ignore. "When I saw the invitations for my [birthday] party . . . I realized how dissociated I am from the meaning of time," she says. "To me, the moment is the only time there is now. The present." While MacLaine professes her loyalty to the present, many of her fans (and most of her critics) associate her with the past. To hear the actress tell it, she goes back far beyond the "Pajama Game" days. As MacLaine details to Henry in the *Time* story, she had spent past lives as "a former prostitute, my own daughter's daughter, and a male court jester who was beheaded by Louis XV of France."

Reincarnation, trance channeling, and other spiritual matters of the New Age sciences make up the bulk of MacLaine's successful nonfiction books. Autobiographical in nature, such works as *Don't Fall off the Mountain, You Can Get There from Here, Out on a Limb, Dancing in the Light, It's All in the Playing* and *Going Within: A Guide for Inner Transformation* have divided readers, who make these books hot properties, and critics, who almost unanimously dismiss MacLaine's claims as naive and unproven. In a *Playboy* interview, the actress/author explains to David Rensin that "you never really die. If you really read Martin Luther King's writing—and I went to his library in Atlanta and did, the handwritten stuff—you'd see he was quoting Thoreau, Gandhi. And I've read Gandhi and Sadat, and all they talk about is that they don't die. So their knowledge makes them fearless and makes them contribute in an altruistic way. That's real leadership."

She adds she also believes "the world is in a transitional period. We're slowly gliding into a new dimension, actually vibrating on a higher frequency. . . . I've been checking out these things that have been happening to other people—for example, flashes of intense heat that bathed me in perspiration at the most incongruous moments in the middle of cold weather; a sense of clairvoyant imagery that turns out to be true the next day; ESP, knowing someone who just walked into a room somewhere is trying to reach you and you pick up the phone and call and he was." Those, says MacLaine, "are the little clues that you get along the way. Those who are not going with this harmonious flow of the body's subatomic structure vibrating to a higher frequency are getting sick. Dis-eased." Expounding on the realities of healing crystals, *deja vu*, and Eastern philosophy, MacLaine declares in a *People* interview with Frank Deford: "I don't believe in accidents anymore. I don't mean there's a grand design, with our lives all planned for us. But I've seen too many coincidences, and I'm sure that people who float in and out of our lives are there for reasons."

By 1987, after the string of bestseller books (one of which, *Out on a Limb,* was adapted into a television miniseries, supposedly on the advice of one of the souls trance-channeled through the author), MacLaine embarked on yet another career. She began a series of spiritual consciousness-raising seminars in which, according to Barbara Kantrowitz in a *Newsweek* story, "the message is always the same: tune into your higher self *or else.*" The "Higher Self" seminar Kantrowitz attended in Florida was "part cosmic pep rally, part seance-in-a-circus tent. Posted on bulletin boards outside the ballroom in Orlando were business cards of psychic counseling services, a brochure describing a cosmic Japanese barley diet and ads for healing crystals." At one point, "MacLaine told the group to climb into an imaginary crystal tank filled with a golden liquid. There, they were to 'blend' with their perfect soul mate."

MacLaine used her brand of motivation for her 1988 book *Going Within.* The volume covers meditation and visualization for the novice soul-seeker. As the book's spokesman says in a *Publishers Weekly* article, "It's not just for New Age junkies, but for everyday people who want to reduce stress and understand the contrary forces around them. [MacLaine's] reaching for a much broader audience." *Newsweek* critic David Gates finds *Going Within* amusing, if rather hard wading at times. "But the stories are worth the wade—especially the one about the man whose speciality is channeling famous artists. 'I am Toulouse,' he announces in a French accent. 'Toulouse-Lautrec?' MacLaine asks.

'But of course,' he says. (He doesn't actually speak French because simply doing accents 'doesn't tax the medium's energies as much as forcing through a foreign language.')"

"Talent," says MacLaine in the *Time* cover story, "is sweat and knowing yourself, and I feel that mine is increasing with the years." To William A. Henry, the performer's core identity has changed over those same years, from actress, to spiritualist, to writer. MacLaine's style, he says, "is chatty and at times endearingly naive; her theme is that of the wide-eyed innocent discovering the wonders of the world. She never sounds jaded." MacLaine offers her own description in James Brady's *Parade* interview. "An actor has many lives and many people within him. I *know* there are lots of people inside me." MacLaine concludes with the observation: "No one ever said I'm dull."

BIOGRAPHICAL/CRITICAL SOURCES:

BOOKS

MacLaine, Shirley, *Dancing in the Light,* Bantam, 1986.
MacLaine, Shirley, *Don't Fall off the Mountain,* Norton, 1970.
MacLaine, Shirley, *It's All in the Playing,* Bantam, 1987.
MacLaine, Shirley, *Out on a Limb,* Bantam, 1983.
Spada, James, *Shirley and Warren,* Collier, 1985.

PERIODICALS

Chicago Tribune, June 26, 1983, April 23, 1984, March 26, 1989.
Esquire, June, 1975, September, 1975.
Los Angeles Times, July 19, 1987, October 20, 1988.
Los Angeles Times Book Review, August 24, 1983.
Ms., December, 1985, July-August, 1987.
Newsweek, July 27, 1987, April 24, 1989.
New York Times, April 1, 1984.
New York Times Book Review, September 18, 1983.
Parade, December 18, 1988.
People, July 18, 1983, January 26, 1984, February 6, 1984, April 30, 1984.
Playboy, September, 1984.
Publishers Weekly, March 18, 1983, February 3, 1989.
Time, March 7, 1977, May 14, 1984, October 14, 1985.
Washington Post, June 21, 1983.

—*Sketch by Susan Salter*

*   *   *

MACRO, Eric 1920-

PERSONAL: Surname is pronounced *Mac*-ro; born March 5, 1920, in London, England; son of Harvey Lancelot (a pilot, Royal Air Force) and Margaret (Parkins) Macro; married Joan Bulmer, June 17, 1944; children: Howard, Jane. *Education:* Attended Lancing College, Sussex, 1933-37, Royal Air Force College, Cranwell, 1938-39, and Royal Air Force Staff College, Bracknell, 1949. *Religion:* Church of England. *Avocational interests:* Arabian Peninsula, Albania, Soviet Central Asia, Yugoslavia, Spanish Civil War, Siena and Tuscany.

ADDRESSES: Home—26 Marketa Crescent, Kitchener, Ontario N2B 3B7, Canada.

CAREER: Commissioned in the Royal Air Force, 1939, and served in Europe, Africa, Asia, and North America, until 1969; became wing commander. Lectured in Arabian Studies at Oxford University, Cambridge University, and London University, beginning 1980.

MEMBER: Royal Canadian Military Institute, Royal Society for Asian Affairs.

AWARDS, HONORS: Military: Officer of the Order of the British Empire; medals for various wartime operations.

WRITINGS:

Bibliography of the Arabian Peninsula, University of Miami Press, 1960.
Bibliography of Yemen and Notes on Mocha, University of Miami Press, 1962.
Yemen and the Western World, Praeger, 1968.
Al Yaman, [Damascus], 1979.

Contributor to *Middle East Journal, Middle East, Asian Affairs, Geographical Journal, Arabian Studies, Sudan Notes and Records, New Middle East, Arab World,* and *Port of Aden Annual.* Contributor to *Proceedings of the Seminar for Arabian Studies.*

WORK IN PROGRESS: George Wyman Bury, Arabian Explorer; Arabia and Austria, 1714-1900; research on the overland route to India, 1760-1800; the topography of early Mocha; biographical studies of Arabian explorers; a book on European penetration of the East.

*   *   *

MADARIAGA (y ROJO), Salvador de   1886-1978

PERSONAL: Born July 23, 1886, in La Coruña, Galicia, Spain; died December 14, 1978, in Locarno, Switzerland; son of José (a colonel) and Ascensión (Rojo) de Madariaga; married Constance Helen Margaret Archibald, October 10, 1912 (died, 1970); married Emilie Szekely Rauman, November 18, 1970; children: (first marriage) Nieves and Isabel (daughters). *Education:* Graduated from College Chaptal, Paris, France, 1906; attended Ecole Polytechnique, Paris, 1906-08; graduated from Ecole Nationale Superieure des Mines, Paris, 1911. *Politics:* Liberal.

ADDRESSES: Home—L'Esplanade, 6600 Locamo, Switzerland.

CAREER: Employed by Railway Company of Northern Spain, Madrid, 1911-16, simultaneously wrote political articles for newspapers under a pseudonym; became a writer; spent 1916-21 in London as a journalist and critic; entered Secretariat of League of Nations, Geneva, Switzerland, 1921, member of press section, 1921-22, head of disarmament section, 1922-27; first occupant of King Alfonso XIII Chair of Spanish Studies at Oxford University, Oxford, England, 1927-30; Spanish Ambassador to United States, 1931, to France, 1932-34, and Spain's permanent delegate to League of Nations Assembly, 1931-36; served briefly as Spain's Minister of Education, 1934, then as Minister of Justice. Broadcaster to Latin America for British Broadcasting Corp. during war; broadcaster in Spanish, French, and German to European countries. Associated with various international organizations in postwar years, first president of Liberal International (became president of honor) and honorary president of Congress for Cultural Freedom. Honorary co-chairman of Spanish Refugee Aid, Inc.; Emory L. Ford Professor of Spanish at Princeton University, 1954; lecturer and speaker in many countries.

MEMBER: Spanish Academy of Letters and of Moral and Political Sciences, French Academy of Moral and Political Sciences, Academy of History of Caracas, and many other Spanish American learned societies; Reform Club (London), Ateneo (Madrid).

AWARDS, HONORS: M.A., Oxford University, 1928; gold medalist, Yale University; fellow, Exeter College, University of Pavia; honorary doctor of the Universities of Arequipa, Lima, Poitiers, Liege, and Lille, and of Oxford and Princeton Universities; Ere Nouvelle Prize, for *Englishmen, Frenchmen, Spaniards;* Knight Grand Cross of Order of the Republic (Spain), White Lion (Czechoslovakia), Order of Merit (Chile), Order of Jade in Gold (China), Order of Merit (Hungary), Boyaca (Colombia), Order of the White Rose (Finland), Grand Cross of Legion d'Honneur (France), Aztec Eagle (Mexico), and Order of the Sun (Peru); Europa Prize, Hans Deutsch Foundation, Bern University, 1963; Hanseatic Goethe Prize, 1967.

WRITINGS:

BIOGRAPHY AND HISTORY

Quatre Espagnols a Londres, Plon, 1928.
Spain (also see below), Scribner, 1930, 3rd edition, J. Cape, 1942, Creative Age, 1943.
Christopher Columbus: Being the Life of the Very Magnificent Lord Don Cristóbal Colón (first of the "New World" trilogy), Hodder & Stoughton, 1939, Macmillan, 1940, new edition, Hollis & Carter, 1949, Ungar, 1967.
Hernán Cortés: Conqueror of Mexico (second in the trilogy), Macmillan, 1941, 2nd edition, Regnery, 1955, reprinted, Greenwood Press, 1979.
Spain, two volumes (first volume based on previous book of same title), J. Cape, 1942, Creative Age, 1943.
Cuadro histórico de las Indias, Editorial Sudamericana, Volume 1: *El auge del Imperio Español en América,* 1945, 2nd edition, 1959, reprinted, Espasa-Calpe, 1977, translation published as *The Rise of the Spanish-American Empire,* Macmillan, 1947, reprinted, Greenwood Press, 1975, Volume 2: *El ocaso del Imperio Español en América,* 1945, 2nd edition, 1959, translation published as *The Fall of the Spanish-American Empire,* Hollis & Carter, 1947, Macmillan, 1948, revised edition, Collier, 1963, reprinted, Greenwood Press, 1975.
Bolívar (third in the trilogy), two volumes, Editorial Hermes (Mexico), 1951, 3rd edition, Editorial Sudamericana, 1959, translation by the author published in abridged edition with the same title, Hollis & Carter, 1951, reprinted, Greenwood Press, 1979.
De Colón a Bolívar, E.D.H.A.S.A. (Editorial y Distribuidora Hispano Americana, S.A.) (Barcelona), 1956.
El ciclo hispánico, two volumes, Editorial Sudamericana, 1958.
Spain: A Modern History, Praeger, 1958.
Españoles de mi tiempo, Editorial Planeta, 1974, 5th edition, 1976.
Memorias, 1921-1936: Amanecer sin mediodía, Espasa-Calpe, 1974.

POLITICAL BOOKS

La guerra desde Londres, Editorial Monclús (Tortosa), 1918.
Disarmament, Coward, 1929, reprinted, Kennikat Press, 1967.
Discursos internacionales, M. Aguilar (Madrid), 1934.
Anarquía o jerarquía, M. Aguilar, 1935, 3rd edition, 1970, translation by the author published as *Anarchy or Hierarchy,* Allen & Unwin, 1937, reprinted, 1970.
Theory and Practice in International Relations: William J. Cooper Foundation Lectures, 1937, Swarthmore College, University of Pennsylvania Press, 1937.
The World's Design, Allen & Unwin, 1938.
(With Edward Hallett Carr) *Future of International Government,* Universal Distributors, 1941.
(With others) *The British Commonwealth and the U.S.A. in the Postwar World,* National Peace Council, 1942.
¡Ojo, vencedores!, Editorial Sudamericana, 1945, translation by the author published as *Victors, Beware,* J. Cape, 1946.

De l'Angoisse a la liberte, Calmann-Levy (Paris), 1954, translation of second part by M. Marx published in England as *Democracy Versus Liberty?,* Pall Mall Press, 1958.

Rettet die Freiheit! (selected articles originally published in *Neue Zuercher Zeitung,* 1948-57), Francke (Bern), 1958.

¡General, márchese usted! (collection of lectures broadcast for the Spanish Service of the Radiodiffusion Francaise, 1954-57), Ediciones Ibérica, 1959.

The Blowing Up of the Parthenon; or, How to Lose the Cold War, Praeger, 1960, revised edition, 1961.

Latin America Between the Eagle and the Bear, Praeger, 1962.

Weltpolitisches Kaleidoskop (second collection of articles originally published in *Neue Zuercher Zeitung),* Fretz & Wasmuth Verlag (Zurich), 1965.

ESSAYS

Shelley and Calderón, and Other Essays on English and Spanish Poetry, Constable, 1920, reprinted, Kennikat Press, 1965.

The Genius of Spain, and Other Essays on Spanish Contemporary Literature, Clarendon Press, 1923, reprinted, Books for Libraries Press, 1968.

Arceval y los ingleses, Espasa-Calpe (Madrid), 1925, reprinted, 1973.

Guía del lector del "Quijote," Espasa-Calpe, 1926, reprinted, 1976, translation by the author published as *Don Quixote: An Introductory Essay in Psychology,* Gregynogg Press (Wales), 1934, revised edition, Oxford University Press, 1961, reprinted, Greenwood Press, 1980.

Englishmen, Frenchmen, Spaniards: An Essay in Comparative Psychology, Oxford University Press, 1928, 2nd edition, Hill & Wang, 1969.

Americans, Oxford University Press, 1930, reprinted, Books for Libraries Press, 1968.

On Hamlet, Hollis & Carter, 1948, 2nd edition, Barnes & Noble, 1964.

Bosquejo de Europa (also see below), Editorial Hermes, 1951, reprinted, Editorial Sudamericana, 1969, translation by the author published as *Portrait of Europe,* Hollis & Carter, 1952, Roy, 1955, revised edition, University of Alabama Press, 1967.

Essays with a Purpose, Hollis & Carter, 1954.

Presente y porvenir de Hispanoamérica, y otros ensayos, Editorial Sudamericana, 1959, 2nd edition, 1974.

De Galdós a Lorca, Editorial Sudamericana, 1960.

El Quijote de Cervantes, Editorial Sudamericana, 1962.

Retrato de un hombre de pie, E.D.H.A.S.A., 1965, translation by the author published as *Portrait of a Man Standing,* University of Alabama Press, 1968.

Memorias de un federalista, Editorial Sudamericana, 1967.

(Contributor) Ivar Ivask and Juan Marichal, editors, *Luminous Reality: The Poetry of Jorge Guillén,* University of Oklahoma Press, 1969.

Selecciones de Madariaga (includes selections from *Bosquejo de Europa* [and] *El enemigo de Dios*), edited by Frank Sedwick and Elizabeth Van Orman, Prentice-Hall, 1969.

Mujeres españolas, Espasa-Calpe, 1972.

Obras escogidas: Ensayos, Editorial Sudamericana, 1972.

Mi respuesta: Artículos publicados en la revista Ibérica (1954-1974), selected with prologue by Victoria Kent, Espasa-Calpe, 1982.

NOVELS

The Sacred Giraffe: Being the Second Volume of the Posthumous Works of Julio Arceval (satire), Hopkinson, 1925.

Sir Bob (juvenile), Harcourt, 1930.

El enemigo de Dios (also see above), M. Aguilar, 1926, 2nd edition, Editorial Sudamericana, 1965.

Ramo de errores, Editorial Hermes, 1952, translation by the author published as *A Bunch of Errors,* J. Cape, 1954.

La camarada Ana, Editorial Hermes, 1954, 2nd edition, Editorial Sudamericana, 1956.

Sanco Panco, Latino-Americana (Mexico), 1963.

POETRY

Romances de ciego, Publicaciones Atenea (Madrid), 1922.

La fuente serena, Editorial Cervantes, 1927.

Elegía en la muerte de Unamuno, Oxford University Press, 1937.

Elegía en la muerte de Federico García Lorca, Oxford University Press, 1938.

The Home of Man (18 sonnets), privately printed, 1938.

Rosa de cieno y ceniza, Editorial Sudamericana, 1942.

El sol, la luna y las estrellas: Romances a Beatriz, Editorial Juventud (Barcelona), 1954, 3rd edition, 1974.

La que huele a tomillo y a romero, Editorial Sudamericana, 1959.

Poppy, bilingual Spanish and English edition, Imprenta Bernasconi (Lugano), 1965.

Obra poética, Plaza y Janés (Barcelona), 1977.

DRAMATIC WORKS

Elysian Fields, Allen & Unwin, 1937.

El toisón de oro, y tres obras más: La muerte de Carmen, Don Carlos y Mío Cid (the first a lyrical fantasy in three acts; the following three dramatic poems), Editorial Sudamericana, 1940, 2nd edition, 1945.

Don Juan y la Don-Juania (one-act verse play), Editorial Sudamericana, 1950.

Los tres estudiantes de Salamanca (includes "Los tres estudiantes de Salamanca," a three-act tragicomedy; "Viva la muerte," a three-act modern tragedy, produced in the Piccola Scala, Milan, Italy, 1966; and "El doce de octubre de Cervantes," a one-act historical fantasy), Editorial Sudamericana, 1962.

La Mappe-monde et le Pape-monde (three-act French verse play; broadcast by Radiodiffusion Francaise, 1948), Editions d'Art Jacques O'Hana (London), 1966.

La cruz y la bandera [y] Las tres carabelas (romances), Editorial Sudamericana, 1966.

Numance: Tragedie lyrique en un acte (opera; first produced in Paris, 1954), libretto by Henri Barraud, Boosey & Hawkes, 1970.

Diálogos famosos: Campos eliseos—Adán y Eva, Editorial Sudamericana, 1970.

RADIO PLAYS

"Campos eliseos" (Spanish version of "Elysian Fields"), broadcast by the British Broadcasting Corp. (BBC) for Spain, Radio Varsovia, c. 1937, updated version broadcast in German by Radio Berna, 1966.

"Cristóbal Colón," BBC, 1941.

"Las tres carabelas," BBC, 1942.

"Numancia" (English verse translation of Cervantes's tragedy), BBC, 1947.

"Christophe Colomb" (dramatization of the discovery of America in French), Radiodiffusion Francaise, 1954.

OTHER

(Author of introduction) Miguel de Unamuno, *The Tragic Sense of Life,* Macmillan, 1921.

(Contributor) *A League of Minds* (letters), International Institute of Intellectual Cooperation, League of Nations, 1933.

Europe: A Unit of Human Culture, European Movement, [Brussels], 1952.

Sobre mi Bolívar, Editorial Sudamericana, 1953.

Critique de l'Europe (originally published as preface to *European Annual*), Council of Europe, 1959.

(Author of introduction) *Echo de monde,* Metz Verlag (Zurich), 1960.

(Contributor) *Dauer im Wandel,* Verlag Georg D. W. Callwey (Munich), 1961.

(Editor) *Miguel de Cervantes, El ingenioso hidalgo don Quijote de la Mancha,* Editorial Sudamericana, 1962.

(Contributor) *Die Kraft zu leben,* Bertelsmann Verlag (Guetersloh), 1963.

Yo-yo y yo-el, Editorial Sudamericana, 1967.

(Compiler) *Charles Quint,* A. Michel, 1969.

(With others) *Freiheitliche Politik fuer eine freie Welt,* M. Hoch (Ludwigsburg), 1969.

(With others) *Ist die Marktwirtschaft noch gesichert?,* M. Hoch, 1971.

Morgen ohne Mittag (memoirs), Ullstein (Berlin), 1973, translation published as *Morning Without Noon,* Saxon House, 1974.

A la orilla del río de los sucesos, Ediciones Destino, 1975.

Dios y los españoles, Editorial Planeta, 1975.

"Esquiveles y Manriques" series; published by Editorial Sudamericana, except as indicated: *El corazón de piedra verde,* 1943, reprinted, Espasa-Calpe, 1975, translation by the author published as *The Heart of Jade,* Creative Age, 1944, reprinted, Hamilton, 1964, published in Spanish in three volumes, 1952, Volume 1: *Los fantasmas,* Volume 2: *Los dioses sanguinarios,* Volume 3: *Fe sin blasfemia.*

Guerra en la sangre, 1956, 4th edition, 1971, bound with *Una gota de tiempo,* Espasa-Calpe, 1977, translation by the author published as *War in the Blood,* Collins, 1957.

Una gota de tiempo, 1958, 3rd edition, 1971, bound with *Guerra en la sangre,* Espasa-Calpe, 1977.

El semental negro, 1961, 2nd edition, 1967, bound with *Satanael,* Espasa-Calpe, 1977.

Satanael, 1966, bound with *El semental negro,* Espasa-Calpe, 1977.

TRANSLATOR

Manojo de poesías ingleses puestas en verso castellano, William Lewis (Cardiff), 1919.

(And compiler) *Spanish Folk Songs,* Constable, 1922.

(And editor) William Shakespeare, *Hamlet,* bilingual edition, Editorial Sudamericana, 1949.

Assisted L. Araquistain in translating Rudyard Kipling's "The Fringes of the Fleet" and "Tales of 'The Trade'" (stories) into Spanish. Also author of numerous essays, studies, and commentaries on current affairs. Contributor to periodicals.

SIDELIGHTS: A European liberal, scholar, and statesman, Salvador de Madariaga was one of Spain's outstanding intellectuals. Aristide Briand described him as one of the ten best conversationalists in Europe. "Man's most precious possession is the gift of thinking freely," Madariaga once stated, "of adventuring in the realms of the mind and of nature, thus to discover his own existence and remain master of his fate."

In addition to his native Spanish, Madariaga wrote in English, German, and French. He occasionally prepared some of his books in all four languages. Many of Madariaga's writings, of both literary and political content, have stimulated heated discussion. The third book in the "New World" trilogy, *Bolívar,* proved to be "a literary bombshell that caused Spain and Latin America to go to war again, with plenty of ink spilled on both sides," said Marcelle Michelin of *Books Abroad.* Highly revered in Latin America as a key figure in the struggle for independence from Spain, Simón Bolívar, according to Madariaga, was "nothing but a vulgar imitator of Napoleon with dreams of reigning over a South American empire." Although very well received in North America and England, the book generated shock and outrage in Latin America and was banned in Argentina.

A severe critic of Francisco Franco's regime, Madariaga traveled to England in self-imposed exile at the outbreak of the Spanish Civil War in 1936 and did not return to Spain until after the country's military leader, Generalissimo Francisco Franco, died in 1975. Although he bore a passionate love for his homeland, he believed that Spain was caught in the grip of a totally destructive dictatorship. "Fascism hardly counts in Spain," he wrote. "It is the Army that keeps its boot on the neck of the Spanish people." In an August, 1969, article in the *New York Times,* he made the statement that Franco, "once an intelligent colonel, [has] turned insane by decades of unchecked power. We are told by his friends that he gave Spain thirty years of peace and ten of prosperity. Neither of these assertions is true. Outward quiet is not peace. Before it explodes, a bomb is quiet enough."

BIOGRAPHICAL/CRITICAL SOURCES:

PERIODICALS

Books Abroad, autumn, 1953.
Newsweek, June 9, 1958.
New York Herald Tribune Book Review, October 12, 1952.
New York Times, August 9, 1969.
Saturday Review, July 2, 1960.
Times Literary Supplement, February 22, 1968, February 8, 1974.
Washington Post, May 26, 1961.

OBITUARIES:

PERIODICALS

Chicago Tribune, December 15, 1978.
Time, December 25, 1978.
Washington Post, December 15, 1978.*

* * *

MAGUIRE, Daniel Charles 1931-

PERSONAL: Uses original spelling of surname; born April 4, 1931, in Philadelphia, Pa.; son of Bernard and Catherine (Gallagher) McGuire; married Marjorie Reiley (an author), August 10, 1971; children: Daniel Charles, Jr. (deceased), Thomas Edmond Reiley. *Education:* St. Charles Borromeo Seminary, B.A., 1953; Gregorian University of Rome, S.T.B., 1955, S.T.L., 1957, S.T.D., 1969. *Politics:* Democrat. *Religion:* Liberal Roman Catholic.

ADDRESSES: Home—2712 East Bradford Ave., Milwaukee, Wis. 53211. *Office*—Department of Theology, Marquette University, Coughlin Hall, Milwaukee, Wis. 53233.

CAREER: Roman Catholic priest, 1956-71. Villanova University, Villanova, Pa., lecturer in religious studies, 1960-64; St. Mary's University and Seminary, Baltimore, Md., extraordinary professor of ethics, 1964-66; Catholic University of America, Washington, D.C., interim assistant professor, 1966-67, assistant professor, 1967-69, associate professor of ethics, 1969-71; Marquette University, Milwaukee, Wis., associate professor,

1971-76, professor of ethics, 1977—. Member of board of directors, Catholics for a Free Choice, 1983-89.

MEMBER: American Society of Christian Ethics (member of board of directors, 1970-73, 1975-78; vice president/president elect, 1980; president, 1981-82), College Theology Society (member of board of directors, 1973-75), Catholic Theological Society of America.

AWARDS, HONORS: Best Book of the Year Award, College Theology Society, and Best Scholarly Book of the Year, Wisconsin Authors Association, both 1979, both for *The Moral Choice.*

WRITINGS:

The Gifts of the Holy Spirit in John of St. Thomas, Gregorian University Press, 1969.
Death by Choice, Doubleday, 1974.
The Moral Choice, Doubleday, 1978.
A New American Justice: Ending the White Male Monopolies, Doubleday, 1980, paperback edition published as *A New American Justice: A Moral Proposal for the Reconciliation of Personal Freedom and Social Justice,* Harper, 1982.
The New Subversives: Anti-Americanism of the Religious Right, Continuum, 1982.
The Moral Revolution: A Christian Humanist Vision, Harper, 1986.

CONTRIBUTOR

Katherine T. Hargrove, editor, *The Paradox of Religious Secularity,* Prentice-Hall, 1968.
Charles Curran, editor, *Absolutes in Moral Theology?,* Corpus Publications, 1968.
Mary P. Ryan, editor, *Toward Moral Maturity: Religious Education and the Formation of Conscience,* Paulist-Newman, 1968.
Thomas Quigley, editor, *American Catholics and Vietnam,* Eerdmans, 1968.
Daniel Callahan, editor, *God, Jesus, Spirit,* Herder & Herder, 1969.
Curran, editor, *Contraception: Authority and Dissent,* Herder & Herder, 1969.
Martin Marty and Dean Peerman, editors, *New Theology,* Volume 10, Macmillan, 1973.
Marvin Kohl, editor, *Beneficent Euthanasia,* Prometheus Books, 1975.
Thomas M. McFadden, editor, *America in Theological Perspective,* Seabury, 1976.

OTHER

Contributor to *Encyclopedic Dictionary of Christian Doctrine.* Contributor of articles and reviews to popular magazines and theology journals, including *Cosmopolitan, Theological Review, Humanist, Commonweal, Atlantic, Christianity and Crisis,* and *New York Times.*

WORK IN PROGRESS: A book on a moral creed for all Christians.

BIOGRAPHICAL/CRITICAL SOURCES:

PERIODICALS

Washington Post Book World, August 1, 1982.

* * *

MAIR, Victor H(enry) 1943-

PERSONAL: Born March 25, 1943, in Canton, Ohio; son of Joseph Charles (a lathe operator) and Esther Frieda Louise Mair; married Li-ching Chang (a college instructor), December 15, 1969; children: Thomas Krishna. *Education:* Dartmouth College, B.A., 1965; University of London, B.A. (with honors), 1972, M.Phil., 1984; Harvard University, Ph.D., 1976. *Politics:* None. *Religion:* None.

ADDRESSES: Home—Swarthmore, Pa. *Office*—Department of Oriental Studies, University of Pennsylvania, Philadelphia, Pa. 19104-6305.

CAREER: U.S. Peace Corps, Washington, D.C., volunteer worker in Nepal, 1965-67; Tunghai University, Taichung, Taiwan, lecturer in English literature and language, 1970-72; Harvard University, Cambridge, Mass., assistant professor of Chinese religion and literature, 1976-79; University of Pennsylvania, Philadelphia, assistant professor, 1979-84, associate professor, 1984-88, professor of Oriental studies, 1989.

MEMBER: Association for Asian Studies, American Association of University Professors, Oriental Club of Philadelphia (president, 1989-90).

AWARDS, HONORS: Woodrow Wilson fellow, 1967-68; Marshall Fund scholar in England, 1968-69; grants from American Council of Learned Societies, 1981-82, 1986-87, and National Endowment for the Humanities, 1984.

WRITINGS:

(Editor) *Experimental Essays on Chuang-tzu,* University Press of Hawaii, 1983.
Tun-huang Popular Narratives, Cambridge University Press, 1983.
Four Introspective Poets: A Concordance to Selected Poems by Roan Jyi, Lii Bor, Chern Tzyy-arng, and Jang Jeouling, Arizona State University Center for Asian Studies, 1987.
Mei Cherng's "Seven Stimuli" and Wang Bor's "Pavilion of King Terng": Chinese Poems for Princes, Edwin Mellin, 1988.
Painting and Performance: Chinese Picture Recitation and Its Indian Genesis, University of Hawaii Press, 1988.
T'ang Transformation Texts: A Study of the Buddhist Contribution to the Rise of Vernacular Fiction in China, Harvard University Council on East Asian Studies, 1989.
Tao Te Ching: The Classic Book of Integrity and the Way, Bantam, 1990.

Contributor to Asian studies, linguistics, and philosophy journals. Editor of *Sino-Platonic Papers* and *Xin Tang* (the world's only journal of romanized Mandarin).

WORK IN PROGRESS: Translation of P'u Sung-ling's *Liaochai chih i* [*Tales from Recourse Studio*], a massive collection of over 400 late 17th-, early 18th-century stories about marvelous happenings; a monograph on the origins of the Chinese script, including its Eurasian connections; and a comparison of Sinitic and Indo-European languages.

SIDELIGHTS: Victor H. Mair commented: "My primary research focuses on Sino-Indian cultural relations and China's dealings throughout history with all her neighbors. The impact of Buddhism on Chinese civilization has been enormous and was operative in almost every area of human endeavor (art, architecture, literature, astronomy, medicine, mathematics, etc.). It is my hope that by trying to understand the mechanics of the relationships between China and surrounding countries in the past we today will better understand how to relate to the self-styled 'Central Kingdom.'

"I have also become increasingly interested in the effect of China's extremely difficult and unwieldy writing system on the course of her development. There is presently being waged in China a momentous struggle to romanize the written language. The Chinese, already in 1919, took the huge step of rejecting the dead classical written language in favor of the vernacular (Mandarin) written characters. The next logical and, it seems to me, inevitable step is to phoneticize the vernacular through romanization. This would have enormously positive influence on China's ability to make intellectual and technological progress.

"You may wonder what popular Buddhist narrative of one thousand and more years ago has to do with current script reform. Actually, quite a lot! The manuscripts I have been studying for the past fifteen years were the first attempts at writing extended vernacular texts. As I worked on these texts, I came to sympathize deeply with the individuals who were attempting to express their thoughts and ideas through the medium of an intractable writing system. Full literacy in old China was enjoyed only by about 2 percent of the population—those who were professional scholars.

"It is likely that I will spend the next ten years doing research and writing on the sociopolitical history of the Sinitic language. This may sound like a rather stuffy topic for some readers of *Contemporary Authors,* but I am excited by it and think that it is important for assessing China's probable future. Unless China can devise effective ways to deal with the massive illiteracy and societal fragmentation that results from having dozens of Sinitic and non-Sinitic languages, many of which have never been written down, I fear that the horrors of June 4, 1989 will tragically recur.

"I have written an unpublished novel entitled *China Babel* about China's serious linguistic problems. It has a futuristic setting and shows how advances in language policy can lead to better living conditions for all humanity."

        *   *   *

MALONE, Michael (Christopher) 1942-

PERSONAL: Born November, 1942, in North Carolina; son of Thomas Patrick (a psychiatrist) and Faylene (Jones) Malone; married Maureen Quilligan (a professor of English), May 17, 1975; children: Margaret Elizabeth. *Education:* Attended Syracuse University; University of North Carolina, A.B., M.A., 1963-66; Harvard University, M.A., A.B.D., 1967-73. *Politics:* Democrat. *Religion:* Episcopalian.

ADDRESSES: Home—32 Commerce St., Clinton, CT 06413. *Agent*—Peter Matson, Sterling Lord, Literistic, Inc., One Madison Ave., New York, NY 10001.

CAREER: Writer. Instructor at various colleges, including Yale University, Connecticut College, University of Pennsylvania, and Swarthmore College, 1967—. Lecturer, reader, and panel member. Board member for several arts organizations, including Connecticut Opera Company.

MEMBER: International Association of Crime Writers, PEN America, Writers Guild of America, Dramatists Guild, Authors Guild, Authors League of America, Dramatists Guild, National Book Critics Circle, Writers and Publishers Alliance.

WRITINGS:

NOVELS

Painting the Roses Red, Random House, 1975.
The Delectable Mountains, Random House, 1977.
Dingley Falls, Harcourt, 1980.
Uncivil Seasons, Delacorte, 1983.

Handling Sin, Little, Brown, 1986.
Time's Witness (mystery), Little, Brown, 1989.
The Passionate Pilgrim, Little, Brown, 1991.

PLAYS

Defender of the Faith (play), produced at Yale Divinity School, 1981.
Washington Slept Here (screenplay), Metro-Goldwyn-Mayer, 1986.
Handling Sin (screenplay adapted from his own novel), Twentieth-Century Fox, 1987.
The Rich Brother (television script), VISN Cable Network, 1989.

NONFICTION

Psychetypes, Dutton, 1977.
Heroes of Eros: Male Sexuality in the Movies, Dutton, 1979.
Fiction's Map: A Writer's Pilgrimage through America, in press.

Contributor of articles and reviews to magazines, including *Viva, Nation, Human Behavior, Harper's, Playboy, Mademoiselle,* and *New York Times Book Review.*

OTHER

Contributor of stories to literary journals and magazines. Stories represented in anthologies, including *Fast Forward, Incarnation,* and *O'Henry Prize Stories.*

MEDIA ADAPTATIONS: Film rights to *Uncivil Seasons* were bought by Warner Bros.

WORK IN PROGRESS: Fiction's Map: A Writer's Pilgrimage through America; Take Over, a musical.

SIDELIGHTS: New York Times Book Review critic Alan Cheuse describes the setting of *Dingley Falls* as a town "inhabited by more homey, colorful characters than all of Winesburg, Ohio, Raintree County and Batavia, N.Y., put together." He adds, "There are scores of [characters], all neatly listed in a cast sheet preceding the first chapter—and they stroll, stalk, hitchhike, jog, or drive police cars, motorcycles, bicycles, jalopies, sports cars or fire engines along the town's simple streets and bordering highways. Each is convinced that life in Dingley Falls, U.S.A., is neither comic nor tragic but merely life."

Calling *Dingley Falls* "a wonderful novel, impressive in every way, and constantly absorbing and entertaining," Susan Fromberg Schaeffer goes on to note in the *Chicago Tribune Book World* that the book "takes its structure from a metaphor Malone uses early in the [novel]: that of the spider and his web. Just as each person is at the center of his own web, so each web is entangled in larger webs, and the plot of 'Dingley Falls' is to uncover the two largest webs in which the townspeople are entangled. First they are entangled in the web of government, which has built a secret army base on the outskirts of town (the base's personnel test out their poisons on Dingleyan guinea pigs), and lastly, they are entangled in God's web. So beautifully is this novel rendered, scene by scene, character by character, sentence by sentence, that the end of the journey is much less important than the journey itself—as indeed it should be. Everything in this book sparkles and rings true."

While *Washington Post* reviewer Pat McNees doesn't agree that every word in *Dingley Falls* rings true—the critic labels the book "schizophrenic in tone and concept"—McNees ultimately finds that this "imperfect novel [is] so full of energy and gems of characterization, so successful at creating a sense of place and people, that you forgive it its excesses and awkwardness, are sorry when it's finished, and look forward to the author's next book. There's talent there, and life. One senses Malone will grow."

Malone takes another look at the American south in the comic novel *Handling Sin*. A minister leaves his church for life on the road with a black woman who is old enough to be his grand-daughter, and the novel's hero combs the southland trying to find him. Along the way, the son is mugged by Satan-worshippers and rescued by nuns. He learns, says Laszlo J. Buhasz of the Toronto *Globe and Mail*, "that there is more to life than membership in the Chamber of Commerce, a comfort-able retirement plan and smug entrenchment in the middle class." Critics recommend the book for its striking a balance be-tween serious moral issues and rollicking humor. A *New York Times Book World* reviewer claims that in this "irreverent, un-afraid comedy," the author's "twists and turns and surprises are downright phenomenal, verging on genius." A *Washington Post Book World* reviewer explains: "*Handling Sin* is a larky tale that asks us to take its merry adventures at face value. We do gladly. It's somewhat later . . . that we realize it's something wiser and deeper. . . . It's a parable of love and reconciliation. It's also a celebration of plain old fun as one of God's great pedagogical de-vices. . . . It's a delightful book." Concludes Buhasz, "Malone has written a winner that deserves to become a humor classic."

Uncivil Seasons—a mystery novel—also "bears Malone's im-print," a *Washington Post Book World* reviewer observes. The Malone hallmarks include "the vividly drawn ambience," "a stylish gift for language," and "a tender and believable ro-mance," as well as lively characters. While a team of detectives unravel a murky mystery in a small Southern town, Malone raises questions about the human condition. Rising above the mystery genre in the manner of Umberto Eco's *The Name of the Rose* and Italian novelist Leonardo Sciascia, *Uncivil Seasons* with its vivid scenes and wry humor invites rereading.

Reviewers of *Time's Witness* remark that Malone's depictions of life in Piedmont are as fully drawn as the novels of William Faulkner and more fun to read. In this mystery-thriller Malone puts prejudice and the death penalty on trial. Reviewers are unanimous in their praise for the novel. For example, "There's a lot to savor in *Time's Witness*" in addition to "an unusually fine sense of reality in a place and time," says a writer in the *Chi-cago Tribune;* the novel's "thoroughly satisfactory ending . . . send[s] the reader to the shelves for Malone's earlier work." A *New York Times Book Review* critic concludes, "Malone is the most generous of writers. . . . Malone peoples his fiction with large, quirky casts, and his readers come to know not only what these characters eat, drink, chew, whistle, sing, listen to, read . . . and dream, but—most important, most especially in 'Time's Witness'—what they believe." He also provides "a complex and satisfying plot, a rich panorama," and "a moral vision," all "re-minders that beliefs need not be separated from character, that beliefs are character. . . . He should be congratulated . . . and thanked once again for his generosity."

BIOGRAPHICAL/CRITICAL SOURCES:

PERIODICALS

Chicago Tribune, April 24, 1989.
Chicago Tribune Book World, June 15, 1980, November 28, 1983, April 20, 1986.
Globe and Mail (Toronto), June 21, 1986.
Los Angeles Times Book Review, August 10, 1980, April 6, 1986.
Nation, August 30, 1980.
Newsweek, June 2, 1986.

New York Times Book Review, May 11, 1980, November 13, 1983, April 13, 1986, April 5, 1987, April 23, 1989.
Times Literary Supplement, January 9, 1987.
Washington Post, May 26, 1980.
Washington Post Book World, November 20, 1983, April 13, 1986.

*   *   *

MALZ, Betty 1929-

PERSONAL: Born November 6, 1929, in Terre Haute, IN; daughter of Perkins G. (a minister) and Fern (a writer; maiden name, Burns) Glenn; married John W. Upchurch, November 24, 1948 (died July 15, 1965); married Carl Malz (a college vice-president), June 3, 1971; children: Connie, Brenda, April. *Edu-cation:* Graduated high school in North Terre Haute, IN, 1947.

ADDRESSES: Home—Box 564, Crystal Beach, FL 34681. *Of-fice*—Dunedin, FL 34697.

CAREER: Writer, 1971—; Trinity College, Ellendale, ND, guid-ance counselor, beginning 1973. Church organist; public speaker.

WRITINGS:

My Glimpse of Eternity, Zondervan, 1976.
Prayers That Are Answered, Chosen Books, 1979.
Super-Natural-Living, Chosen Books, 1982.
Angels Watching over You, Chosen Books, 1985.
Women in Tune, Fleming Revell, 1988.
Heaven: A Bright and Glorious Place, Fleming Revell, 1990.

Author of column "Betty's Bits" in *Leader,* 1971-76. Contribu-tor of about thirty articles to magazines.

WORK IN PROGRESS: Touching the Unseen World, for Flem-ing Revell; *How to Make Your Husband Feel Loved,* for Creation House.

SIDELIGHTS: Betty Malz told *CA,* "Most of the material in my first four books is true, and concerns my life and my family," ad-ding, "Success is finding a need and filling it."

My Glimpse of Eternity has been published in eighteen languages.

*   *   *

MANLOVE, Colin Nicholas 1942-

PERSONAL: Born May 4, 1942, in Falkirk, Scotland; son of Denis (a chemical engineer) and Winifred Ann (Wardrop) Man-love; married Evelyn Mary Schuftan (a research assistant), Sep-tember 2, 1967; children: John Derek, David Francis. *Education:* University of Edinburgh, M.A. (with first class honors), 1964; Pembroke College, Oxford, B.Litt., 1968. *Avocational interests:* Model-making (including radio-controlled models), do-it-yourself projects, walking.

ADDRESSES: Home—92 Polwarth Terr., Edinburgh EH11 1NN, Scotland. *Office*—Department of English Literature, Uni-versity of Edinburgh, David Hume Tower, George Sq., Edin-burgh EH8 9JX, Scotland.

CAREER: University of Edinburgh, Edinburgh, Scotland, lec-turer, 1967-84, reader in English literature, 1984—.

AWARDS, HONORS: Distinguished Scholarship Award, Inter-national Association for the Fantastic in the Arts, 1989.

WRITINGS:

Modern Fantasy: Five Studies, Cambridge University Press, 1975.

Literature and Reality, 1600-1800, Macmillan (London), 1978, St. Martin's, 1979.

The Gap in Shakespeare: The Motif of Division from "Richard II" to "The Tempest," Barnes & Noble, 1981.

The Impulse of Fantasy Literature, Kent State University Press, 1983.

Science Fiction: Ten Explorations, Kent State University Press, 1986.

C. S. Lewis: His Literary Achievement, St. Martin's, 1987.

Critical Thinking: A Guide to Interpreting Literary Texts, St. Martin's, 1989.

CONTRIBUTOR

Faith Pullin, editor, *New Perspectives on Melville,* Edinburgh University Press, 1978.

Ian Campbell, editor, *Nineteenth-Century Fiction: Critical Essays,* Carcanet New Press, 1979.

Dictionary of National Biography Supplement, 1961-1970, Oxford University Press, 1981.

Roger Schlobin, editor, *The Aesthetics of Fantasy Literature and Art,* University of Notre Dame Press, 1982.

Colin Nicholson, editor, *Alexander Pope, 1688-1988: Essays for the Tercentenary,* Aberdeen University Press, 1988.

OTHER

Also contributor to *Dickens Studies Annual.* Contributor to periodicals, including *Studies in Scottish Literature, Swansea Review, Essays in Criticism, Journal of Narrative Technique, Kansas Quarterly, Durham University Journal,* and *Journal of the Fantastic in the Arts.*

WORK IN PROGRESS: *Christian Fantasy: From 1200 to the Present.*

SIDELIGHTS: Colin Nicholas Manlove told *CA:* "The impulse behind my writing (and teaching) has always been the pleasure of intellectual adventure. In literary criticism this happens at the moment when penetration into one aspect of a work begins to make the whole seem to open out. To achieve this I have always tried to set aside other people's views on a given topic before I have worked out my own. I find that, whatever novelty this may produce, it also leads to a measure of dogmatism in the end, whereby I do not often change my views about a text. To find further adventures I then have to find new texts; failing which, as increasingly now, I am thinking of writing some form of fiction, a different and possibly less limiting form of stimulative exploration. I have the feeling that, were I ever to tire of such travels in fiction, I would, like a megalomaniac, have to start trying to impose them on real life. I hope someone may be instructed by these bourgeois and middle-aged struggles to keep living intensely. I have a liking for originality in literature and life generally; I think that some of it stems from a sense of the multiple possibilities of life and a frustration at being tied to only one of them."

BIOGRAPHICAL/CRITICAL SOURCES:

PERIODICALS

Times (London), October 30, 1986.
Times Literary Supplement, October 31, 1986.

*   *   *

MARA, Sally
See QUENEAU, Raymond

MARSTON, Elsa 1933-

PERSONAL: Born March 18, 1933, in Newton, MA; daughter of Everett Carter (a professor of English) and Harriet (Peirce) Marston; married Iliya Harik (a professor of political science), July 25, 1959; children: Ramsay, Amahl, Raif. *Education:* Attended Vassar College, 1950-52; University of Iowa, B.A., 1954; Radcliffe College, M.A., 1957; attended American University of Beirut, 1957-59; Indiana University, M.S., 1980. *Politics:* Democrat.

ADDRESSES: *Home*—1926 Dexter St., Bloomington, IN 47401.

CAREER: American University of Beirut, Beirut, Lebanon, instructor in English, 1959; Pig Industry Development Authority, London, England, secretary, 1959-60; American Society for Public Administration, Chicago, IL, editor and liaison, 1960-63; free-lance writer, 1983—; instructor, Institute of Children's Literature, 1985—. Artist, with exhibitions in Tunisia, 1975, and New York, 1979. President of cooperative nursery school, 1976-77; coordinator of local jail improvement committee and director of local art gallery, both 1980-81.

MEMBER: National Society of Arts and Letters, Authors Guild, Society of Children's Book Writers, Nature Conservancy, New England Antiquities Research Association.

WRITINGS:

The Cliffs of Cairo (juvenile novel), Beaufort Book Co., 1981.
How to Be a Helper (juvenile short stories), Doubleday, 1982.
Art in Your Home Town, Cambridge Book Co., 1983.
Some Artists: Their Lives, Loves, and Luck, Cambridge Book Co., 1983.
The Politics of Education in Colonial Algeria and Kenya, Ohio University Press, 1984.
The Phoenix and the Carpet (juvenile play), first produced in Bloomington, IN, 1984.
Mysteries in American Archaeology, Walker, 1986.
The Lebanese in America, Lerner Publications, 1987.

Contributor to periodicals, including *Highlights for Children* and *Odyssey.*

WORK IN PROGRESS: Several novels, including *The Shadow of the Sphinx,* and picture books; a musical play, "The Boy from the Forest."

SIDELIGHTS: Elsa Marston told *CA:* "I write the sorts of stories I loved as a child—stories that stimulated my curiosity about our amazing world, its far corners, and past wonders. I can't imagine that children today, despite the lure of instant entertainment and obsession with personal and broader problems, do not still feel this desire to know the world and experience romantic (in the best sense of the word) adventures. In my books I try to combine the present with the past, the contemporary American character with the foreign. Their settings are places where I have lived or visited: Cairo, Carthage, Lebanon, the Greek islands, a historic seacoast town in Massachusetts. Currently I'm working on a sequel to my first novel, which reflected the fabulous 'Arabian Nights' time in Egypt's history. The new story, *The Shadow of the Sphinx,* gives a picture of present-day Cairo and Sinai, Egyptian character, and the problems of alienation that a child of two cultures may feel.

"Along with history, art, and archaeology, my literary interests lie in fantasy and myth and their effect in stretching the minds and sensibilities of young people. I feel strongly that more attention in fiction (and education!) should be given to the 'wrong-side-of-the-tracks' kids: young people who are *not* from comfortable mainstream American backgrounds; and this is another of my concerns in writing. At the same time, I'm enormously impressed by the diversity, quality, and beauty of books for young people today—far superior, in my opinion, to the majority of books published for the adult trade market.

"Recently I've been involved in efforts to improve children's literature in Egypt. Greater availability of good reading for young people in the Arab world is a long-range concern I share with my husband. I enjoy the teaching of writing and feel that although the field of writing for publication is crowded and competitive, anyone can grow as a unique person by bringing out what's inside via the written word."

*   *   *

MARTIN, Ann M(atthews) 1955-

PERSONAL: Born August 12, 1955, in Princeton, NJ; daughter of Henry R. (a cartoonist) and Edith M. (a teacher; maiden name, Matthews) Martin. *Education:* Smith College, A.B. (cum laude), 1977.

ADDRESSES: Agent—Amy Berkower, Writers House, Inc., 21 West 26th St., New York, NY 10010.

CAREER: Elementary school teacher in Noroton, Conn., 1977-78; Pocket Books, Inc., New York City, editorial assistant for Archway Paperbacks, 1978-80; Scholastic Book Services, New York City, copywriter for Teen Age Book Club, 1980-81, associate editor, 1981-83, editor, 1983; Bantam Books, Inc., New York City, senior editor of Books for Young Readers, 1983-85; writer and free-lance editor, 1985—.

MEMBER: PEN, Authors Guild, Society of Children's Book Writers, Psi Chi.

WRITINGS:

Bummer Summer, Holiday House, 1983.
Just You and Me, Scholastic Book Services, 1983.
(With Betsy Ryan) *My Puppy Scrapbook,* Scholastic Book Services, 1983.
Inside Out, Holiday House, 1984.
Stage Fright, Holiday House, 1984.
Me and Katie (the Pest), Holiday House, 1985.
With You and Without You, Holiday House, 1986.
Missing Since Monday, Holiday House, 1986.
Just a Summer Romance, Holiday House, 1987.
Slam Book, Holiday House, 1987.
Yours Turly, Shirley, Holiday House, 1988.
Ten Kids, No Pets, Holiday House, 1988.
Fancy Dance in Feather Town, Western Publishing, 1988.
Ma and Pa Dracula, Holiday House, 1989.
Moving Day in Feather Town, Western Publishing, 1989.
Eleven Kids, One Summer, Holiday House, 1991.
The Million Dollar Kid, Holiday House, in press.

"BABY-SITTERS CLUB" SERIES

Kristy's Great Idea, Scholastic Book Services, 1986.
Claudia and the Phantom Phone Calls, Scholastic Book Services, 1986.
The Truth about Stacey, Scholastic Book Services, 1986.
Mary Anne Saves the Day, Scholastic Book Services, 1987.
Dawn and the Impossible Three, Scholastic Book Services, 1987.
Kristy's Big Day, Scholastic Book Services, 1987.
Claudia and Mean Janine, Scholastic Book Services, 1987.
Boy-Crazy Stacey, Scholastic Book Services, 1987.
The Ghost at Dawn's House, Scholastic Book Services, 1988.

Logan Likes Mary Anne!, Scholastic Book Services, 1988.
Kristy and the Snobs, Scholastic Book Services, 1988.
Claudia and the New Girl, Scholastic Book Services, 1988.
Good-bye Stacey, Good-bye, Scholastic Book Services, 1988.
Hello, Mallory, Scholastic Book Services, 1988.
Little Miss Stoneybrook . . . and Dawn, Scholastic Book Services, 1988.
Jessi's Secret Language, Scholastic Book Services, 1988.
Mary Anne's Bad-Luck Mystery, Scholastic Book Services, 1988.
Stacey's Mistake, Scholastic Book Services, 1988.
Claudia and the Bad Joke, Scholastic Book Services, 1988.
Kristy and the Walking Disaster, Scholastic Book Services, 1989.
Mallory and the Trouble with the Twins, Scholastic Book Services, 1989.
Jessi Ramsey, Pet-sitter, Scholastic Book Services, 1989.
Dawn on the Coast, Scholastic Book Services, 1989.
Kristy and the Mother's Day Surprise, Scholastic Book Services, 1989.
Mary Anne and the Search for Tigger, Scholastic Book Services, 1989.
Claudia and the Sad Good-bye, Scholastic Book Services, 1989.
Jessi and the Superbrat, Scholastic Book Services, 1989.
Welcome Back, Stacey!, Scholastic Book Services, 1989.
Mallory and the Mystery Diary, Scholastic Book Services, 1989.
Mary Anne and the Great Romance, Scholastic Book Services, 1990.
Dawn's Wicked Stepsister, Scholastic Book Services, 1990.
Kristy and the Secret of Susan, Scholastic Book Services, 1990.
Claudia and the Great Search, Scholastic Book Services, 1990.
Mary Anne and Too Many Boys, Scholastic Book Services, 1990.
Stacey and the Mystery of Stoneybrook, Scholastic Book Services, 1990.
Jessi's Baby-sitter, Scholastic Book Services, 1990.
Dawn and the Older Boy, Scholastic Book Services, 1990.

"BABY-SITTERS CLUB SUPER SPECIALS" SERIES

Baby-sitters on Board!, Scholastic Book Services, 1988.
Baby-sitters Summer Vacation, Scholastic Book Services, 1989.
Baby-sitters Winter Vacation, Scholastic Book Services, 1989.
Baby-sitters Island Adventure, Scholastic Book Services, 1990.

"BABY-SITTERS LITTLE SISTER" SERIES

Karen's Witch, Scholastic Book Services, 1988.
Karen's Roller Skates, Scholastic Book Services, 1988.
Karen's Worst Day, Scholastic Book Services, 1989.
Karen's Kittycat Club, Scholastic Book Services, 1989.
Karen's School Picture, Scholastic Book Services, 1989.
Karen's Little Sister, Scholastic Book Services, 1989.
Karen's Birthday, Scholastic Book Services, 1990.
Karen's Haircut, Scholastic Book Services, 1990.
Karen's Sleepover, Scholastic Book Services, 1990.
Karen's Grandmothers, Scholastic Book Services, 1990.
Karen's Prize, Scholastic Book Services, 1990.

WORK IN PROGRESS: Other volumes in the "Baby-Sitter's Club" and "Baby-Sitter's Little Sister" series.

CA INTERVIEW

CA interviewed Ann M. Martin by telephone on May 16, 1989, at her home.

CA: If writing is an indulgence for you, as you told Contemporary Authors *a few years ago, it's certainly one that has brought pleasure to a lot of other people too. How early did you start?*

MARTIN: Seriously writing, not until after college. But I had always enjoyed writing, even as a child. Before I could write, I dictated stories to my mother. I took creative writing classes and that sort of thing as a kid, but I wanted desperately to be a teacher, so that was what I prepared for. I did teach for one year after college, and I enjoyed it, but I was beginning to realize then that I wanted to do something with children's books, though not necessarily with writing. I entered the publishing field and started writing seriously not long after that. That was around 1979 when I'd been out of college for a couple of years. My first book was published in 1983.

CA: When you began writing your books, did the teaching and editing experience turn out to be helpful?

MARTIN: Very helpful, both of them. In fact, I'd have to give them equal weight. I picked up so much from working with the kids, but I also learned a lot about writing from reading other people's manuscripts. I wasn't actually editing by the time I began my first book, but I had read enough of other people's manuscripts and been in publishing just long enough for it to be a lot of help. As I developed both my writing and my editing skills, they built on each other and helped each other along.

CA: You told Something about the Author *that your memory of events from your own childhood is very clear, and that writing from that memory gives you a chance to play out the "if onlys." Does a book often begin with a remembered event?*

MARTIN: Some of my books have been based on past experiences, although very few of them have been based on actual events in my childhood. But I would say that while I write any book, I'm remembering how I felt when I was a kid. Those feelings definitely go into the books. *Inside Out* was based on my work as a therapist for autistic children; it wasn't really something that happened in my childhood. *Stage Fright* is probably the most autobiographical of my books. I had terrible stage fright when I was a kid, though I don't anymore, and that was the inspiration for that book.

CA: Was there a real-life inspiration for the Rosso family in Ten Kids, No Pets?

MARTIN: Not really; I just love big families. Although, when my sister and I were growing up in Princeton, there was one family with six kids that we knew fairly well, and there was another family in town with fourteen children to whom my sister was close. I've always been fascinated by large families, and I love pets. So it seemed like a good combination: a big family and the idea of wanting to have a pet.

CA: It's obvious that you love cats, at least, because you're often photographed with one and there are cats in your books. So many of your characters love horses, I suspect that's also a touch from your own life. In fact, you've written a whole book about horseback riding.

MARTIN: Yes, *Me and Katie (the Pest).* That was definitely from my own life. That was a story about horseback riding, but the real thrust of the story was sibling rivalry. My sister and I had our problems getting along, although I would say that our roles were reversed in terms of the characters in the book. I was the older child who was more successful at certain things; Jane was the younger child who was more successful in other areas. But the backdrop for *Me and Katie (the Pest)* is horseback riding,

which certainly is something that I was very fond of when I was in grade school.

CA: How did the Baby-sitters Club series come about?

MARTIN: I can't take any credit for the original idea. That came from Jean Feiwel, the editor-in-chief of books for young readers at Scholastic. She had noticed five years or so ago that books about clubs were selling very well in Scholastic's book clubs, and books about baby-sitting were selling very well in the clubs. So she had the idea for a great series title, the Baby-Sitters Club. At that time I was leaving Bantam, where I'd been the editor of books for young readers, to begin writing full-time, and Jean came to me because some of my novels had already been published at that point. She told me about the idea for the series, and I developed the characters and the situations for the first four books. That's all we thought the series was going to be, a nice little miniseries that would do well. We very cautiously signed up two more books after the first four had done moderately well—nothing to shout about—and by the time the sixth book came out it suddenly shot to the top of the B. Dalton best-seller list. Then all the other books that had been published before began to climb on the B. Dalton list, and subsequently almost every book published after that has gone to the top. Of the twenty books on the B. Dalton paperback juvenile list, it's not unusual for there to be anywhere from seven to nine books from the Baby-sitters Club series. It's incredible.

CA: Some of your books deal with tremendous problems. In Inside Out, *which you mentioned earlier, James Peterson is autistic; in* Yours Turly, Shirley *a child has to cope with dyslexia and an adopted Vietnamese sister who's doing better in school than she is; in* With You and Without You, *Liza O'Hara's father dies of heart disease. Have you heard from young people who have been comforted by these books?*

MARTIN: Not on *Yours Turly, Shirley* yet, because it hasn't been out long enough, but I have heard from a number of kids about *With You and Without You,* kids who write to me and say things like, "I understand exactly how Liza felt in the book, because my mother died a year ago. I had to explain to my younger sister that Mommy isn't coming back," or, "My brother died two years ago, so I understand how Liza felt." When *Inside Out* first came out, I got a lot of letters about the book. Those letters weren't necessarily from kids who had autistic brothers and sisters, but from kids who lived with a handicapped child—it could be any kind of handicap. I heard from a number of children about that, and about how living with a handicapped child affected their family or their friendships.

CA: Your dialogue really sounds like kids talking, or at least the ones I hear. Do you have a lot of contact with young people?

MARTIN: I have some contact with young people, but I think quite a bit of the dialogue results just from remembering what it was like to be a kid talking with my friends. I go on a lot of school visits and autographings now. And I'm connected with a school in New York, P.S. 2, so I see the kids down there a lot. In terms of keeping up with younger children—for instance, kids who are the age that the baby-sitters would be baby-sitting for in the series—most of my friends have children who are now nine and under. So I do have a lot of contact with young children.

CA: What's your connection with the public school in New York?

MARTIN: It's through the Adopt-a-School Program with the National Dance Institute. Jacques D'Amboise, who used to dance with the New York City Ballet, decided about ten years ago that dance would be a wonderful program for inner-city school kids. He thought it would be a great outlet for their energy, and would bring them discipline, because it takes great discipline to be a dancer. So he started the National Dance Institute, which initially received government and local funding. The way it works is that dance teachers go into schools in September and hold auditions for any students interested in becoming part of a special dance program, so special that they're taken out of their classes during the day—it's not held at lunchtime or after school. The students have to keep up their grades to remain in the program. It's been great for them in terms of building up their self-esteem. These kids don't necessarily want to be dancers when they grow up, but after they've been in the program for a while, they begin saying things like, "I want to be a doctor when I grow up," or "I want to be a lawyer." The teachers say that some of the quietest kids have become more vocal and some of the restless ones have become more attentive. At the end of the year, every kid in the program city-wide (and this is now about a thousand kids) has the opportunity to participate in a dance that's performed at the Felt Forum in New York, or at the Brooklyn Academy of Music. At times, all one thousand of them are on the stage at once. It really is terrific.

I became involved with the NDI because the government funding for it recently ran out, and the organization needed private funding. They developed the Adopt-a-School Program, in which an individual or corporation "adopts" a school for a period of five years and helps with forty or fifty percent of the funding. I happened to get a wonderful school in Chinatown, and it turned out that there was an Ann Martin fan club in the school, so I feel as adopted by the kids as the school does by me. I go down there and watch the rehearsals, and I've spoken to the fan club. It's turned into a neat experience. Each year I wait with bated breath for the beginning of June and the big performance (the Event of the Year), so that I can see my kids dance.

CA: Your books fall into several of the age-group categories that seem to be a necessary evil of publishing and selling books and organizing libraries. Do you approach them differently in any way as you're writing?

MARTIN: In terms of content, yes; I won't address certain subjects if I'm writing for younger kids. The spin-off series of the Baby-sitters Club, Baby-sitters Little Sister, is for readers about seven to nine—there's always a broader range than that, but that's the target group. The Baby-sitters Club is for eight- to twelve-year-olds. In the Baby-Sitters Club, I will talk about the death of a pet or the death of a grandparent, but my editors and I decided we would not deal with the death of a parent or a sibling. In Baby-sitters Little Sister, we may sometime touch on the death of a pet, although we haven't done it yet. The problems that are encountered in the Little Sister books are younger and more kid-oriented, such as falling down and breaking a bone or having a fight with a friend or wanting to get a pet. So the difference for me is in the issues being discussed. The voice seems to change on its own for the two series. For the younger kids it's definitely a younger voice, more playful, but I'm not consciously saying to myself, All right, there are seven-year-olds who are going to be reading this book; I can't use this word. I don't do that. In fact, I like to make kids stretch a little when they're reading my books. I've gotten letters from kids who have said, "I really love your books, but I had to look up this word and that word to understand it." But they did it, and that's what I like.

CA: Do you think there are special challenges in writing for children, over and above the ever-present difficulties of any kind of writing?

MARTIN: I think one has to keep in mind exactly what kids are going to be getting out of the books. Children, no matter what anybody thinks, are very vulnerable. Anyone in the baby boom generation, which is my generation, grew up in a society of guns and violence on television, a much more fast-paced, open society in which you hear on the news every night about rape, murder, incest. If you're going to touch on a subject like incest or murder or missing children or death, you have to do it with great sensitivity. I spent an hour on the phone recently with a daughter of a friend of mine; she was not quite eight at the time, and the first half-hour of our conversation was on the crash of Pan-Am Flight 103 and terrorism and how you could sneak a weapon on board, how you could hijack a plane, how you could bomb a plane. And we talked about death. She had known the son of the copilot, so she had been touched by the tragedy more personally than most kids her age would have been; it was very much on her mind. But I'm sure that in 1925 no seven-year-old would have been sitting around having a conversation like that about death and violence. However, it's all around us today. I think you have to be very clear about how kids are going to be affected by what you write.

CA: How do you feel generally about books currently being written for children? Any particular peeves or praise?

MARTIN: When I was an editor, I used to read voraciously because it was part of my job, and I needed to know what was being published. Now I'm so busy writing that I don't have as much time to read the newer material, and I feel sort of out of touch. I am in favor of non-censorship of books, although I think that libraries and schools and teachers and parents have to be involved and make their own decisions about what books they'll have in their libraries or allow their kids to read. In a way that is a kind of censorship, but I'm very much in favor of writers being able to write what they want to write about. I just think that they have to keep in mind what kids are going to be getting out of the books. I'm not in love with books that are full of four-letter words, but I think some kids have a need to read about certain sensitive subjects. I can only hope that such subjects are handled with foresight and a knowledge of kids today. Writers need to keep their audience in mind.

CA: Are there advantages to a series besides the fact that series seem to sell especially well?

MARTIN: I think series, and especially paperback series, have been looked down upon for a long time. I never thought I would become a series writer; I accepted the challenge when Jean Feiwel offered it to me because it seemed interesting and it was only going to be four books. As it snowballed, I became more and more involved in it, more tied to my characters. Now I can't foresee ever letting go of it. I receive about twelve thousand letters a year from kids, and I'm beginning to see the true advantages to series books. I think they attract kids who are reluctant readers, if not children with definite learning problems such as dyslexia, and turn them into readers. And for kids who are already readers, I don't think there's anything wrong with picking up a series and reading it. I write the books as pure entertainment for myself as well as for the kids, but I am hoping that avid readers who are reading series are reading other things as well, and I also hope that reluctant readers who get hooked on reading through series reading, whether it's the Baby-sitters Club or another series, will then "graduate" to other kinds of books.

CA: According to a survey done by Waldenbooks on their reading club members and reported in the July 15, 1988, issue of Publishers Weekly, seventy-five percent of the five-to-thirteen-year-old readers prefer reading to watching television. You were included as a favorite author of the Kids' Club in that survey. What's your perception of the popularity of television compared to books among young readers?

MARTIN: Occasionally a child will write and say what his favorite TV show is, but often kids write to me for a school assignment, so all they're talking about is books. But I have to admit that when kids list their favorite hobbies or what they do after school apart from homework, they rarely list television. I know they're watching it, so it may be that they're just not apt to list it. They're more likely to list sports, even the girls—most of the letters I get are from girls. Also, shopping apparently is a favorite hobby, and so is talking on the phone, and art. When kids do mention television, though, they mention pretty much what you might expect: the sitcoms that come on between about eight and ten, mostly on weekday evenings, and especially the ones revolving around teenagers. I'm surprised at the report you quoted. But I hope it's true, because I can't think of anything better than kids reading instead of watching TV. I *can* say that the last time I baby-sat, I sat for an eight-year-old and she had no interest whatsoever in television. And it was at a time near Christmas, when a lot of specials were on as well as the regular programming. She wanted to read, she wanted to play games, she wanted to teach me cheerleading drills, and the one time *I* suggested TV, she said no, she was tired of it.

CA: What's coming up for your readers to look forward to?

MARTIN: Definitely more of the Baby-sitters Club, probably sixty or more. There will be more Little Sister books as well, perhaps as many as thirty. I hope to be able to continue writing one hardcover a year. Last fall *Ma and Pa Dracula* was published. That's about a boy who discovers that he's the adopted son of vampires. It was a fun one to write. And in the fall of 1991 there'll be a sequel to *Ten Kids, No Pets* called *Eleven Kids, One Summer.* We even have a book signed up for 1992, although I haven't begun writing it yet. It's about a girl who wins the lottery in New York, and it will be called *The Million Dollar Kid.*

BIOGRAPHICAL/CRITICAL SOURCES:

BOOKS

Contemporary Authors, Volume 111, Gale, 1984.
Something about the Author, Volume 44, Gale, 1986.

PERIODICALS

New York Times Book Review, April 30, 1989.
Publishers Weekly, July 15, 1988.

—*Interview by Jean W. Ross*

*   *   *

MARX, Gary T. 1938-

PERSONAL: Born October 1, 1938, in Hanford, CA; son of Donald and Ruth Marx; married Phyllis A. Rakita. *Education:* University of California, Los Angeles, B.A., 1960; University of California, Berkeley, M.A., 1962, Ph.D., 1966.

ADDRESSES: Office—Department of Urban Studies and Planning, Massachusetts Institute of Technology, 77 Massachusetts Ave., Cambridge, MA 02139.

CAREER: Traveled around the world, preparing for the study of comparative race and ethnic relations, 1963-64; University of California, Berkeley, research associate at Survey Research Center, 1965-67, lecturer in sociology, 1966-67; Harvard University, Cambridge, MA, assistant professor of social relations, 1967-69, lecturer, 1969-73, research associate, Harvard-Massachusetts Institute of Technology Joint Center for Urban Studies, 1967-73; Massachusetts Institute of Technology, Cambridge, associate professor, beginning 1973, professor, 1979—. Visiting associate professor or lecturer, Boston College, spring, 1973, fall, 1974, University of California, Santa Barbara, summer, 1974, Wellesley College, fall, 1975, Boston University, spring, 1976, University of California, San Diego, 1977-78, and State University of New York at Albany, 1980-81; Jensen Lecturer, American Sociological Association, 1988-89. Has presented papers at professional meetings. Consultant to several national commissions and federal agencies, including the House Committee on the Judiciary, General Accounting Office, Office of Technology Assessment, and Justice Department; consultant to state and local governments, interest groups and foundations; consultant to the National Academy of Sciences and the Social Science Research Council.

MEMBER: American Sociological Association (member of executive council, 1973-76), Society for the Study of Social Problems, Society for the Psychological Study of Social Issues, Eastern Sociological Society.

AWARDS, HONORS: Guggenheim fellow in England and France, 1970-71; recipient of research grants, 1970-72, 1973-75, 1981-85; fellow, Center for Advanced Study in the Behavioral Sciences, 1987-88.

WRITINGS:

The Social Basis of the Support of a Depression Era Extremist: Father Coughlin, Survey Research Center, University of California, Berkeley, 1962.
Protest and Prejudice, Harper, 1967, edition with postscript, Torchbooks, 1969.
(Editor with others) *Confrontation: Psychology and the Problems of Today,* Scott, Foresman, 1970.
(Editor) *Radical Conflict: Tension and Change in American Society,* Little, Brown, 1971.
(With others) *Inquiries in Sociology,* Allyn & Bacon, 1972.
(Editor) *Muckraking Sociology: Research as Social Criticism,* Transaction Books, 1972.
(Reviser with N. Goodman) *Society Today,* 4th edition, Random House, 1982.
(Editor with Goodman) *Sociology: Classic and Popular Approaches,* Random House, 1980.
Undercover: Police Surveillance in America, University of California Press, 1988.

CONTRIBUTOR

A. Mier and E. Rudwick, editors, *Readings in Negro Life and History,* Atheneum, 1967.
C. E. Lincoln, editor, *Is Anybody Listening to Black America?,* Seabury, 1968.
M. Minnis and W. Cartwright, editors, *Sociological Perspectives: Readings in Deviant Behavior and Social Problems,* W. C. Brown, 1968.
T. Moran and R. Roth, editors, *Law and Order: A Panacea?,* Proceedings of the Fifth Annual Police Seminar of Northeastern University, 1968.
C. Bonjean and N. Glenn, editors, *Blacks in America: An Anthology,* Chandler Publishing, 1969.
P. Washburn and C. Larson, editors, *Power, Participation and Ideology,* McKay, 1969.

M. Goldschmid, editor, *The Negro American and White Racism,* Holt, 1970.

C. Anderson, editor, *Sociological Essays and Research: Introductory Readings,* Dorsey, 1970.

J. F. Szwed, editor, *Black Americans: A Second Look,* Basic Books, 1970.

P. Rose, editor, *Study of Society,* Random House, 1970.

H. Nelsen and others, editors, *The Black Church in America,* Basic Books, 1971.

G. Gavligio and D. Raye, editors, *Society as It Is,* Macmillan, 1971.

D. Boesel and P. Rossi, editors, *Cities under Siege,* Basic Books, 1971.

D. A. Wilkinson, editor, *Black Revolt: Strategies of Protest,* McCuchan Publishing, 1972.

G. Thielbar and S. Feldman, editors, *Issues in Social Inequality,* Little, Brown, 1972.

E. Greer, editor, *Black Political Power: A Reader,* Allyn & Bacon, 1972.

M. Wolfgang and J. Short, editors, *Collective Violence,* Aldine, 1972.

S. Guterman, editor, *The Personality Patterns of Black Americans,* Glendessary, 1972.

Guterman, editor, *Black Psyche,* Glendessary, 1972.

C. Glock, editor, *Religion in Sociological Perspective,* Wadsworth, 1973.

S. McNall, editor, *The Sociological Perspective,* Little, Brown, 1973.

B. Franklin and F. Kohout, editors, *Social Psychology and Everyday Life,* McKay, 1973.

S. Wasby, editor, *American Government and Politics,* Scribner, 1973.

B. Beit-Hallahmi, editor, *Research in Religious Behavior,* Brooks/Cole, 1974.

W. Newman, editor, *The Social Meanings of Religion,* Rand McNally, 1974.

Privacy in a Free Society, Roscoe Pound American Trial Lawyers' Association, 1974.

C. Reasons, editor, *Criminology: A Radical Perspective,* Goodyear, 1974.

R. Evans, editor, *Social Movements,* Rand McNally, 1974.

J. Rosenbaum and C. Sederberg, editors, *Vigilantism,* University of Pennsylvania, 1975.

E. Viano, editor, *Criminal Justice Research,* Heath, 1976.

(With M. Useem) J. Rothman, editor, *Issues in Race and Ethnic Relations,* Peacock, 1977.

J. Douglas, editor, *Official Deviance,* Lippincott, 1977.

D. Larsen, editor, *Performance Measures and Analytical Tools,* Heath, 1978.

J. McCarthy and M. Zald, editors, *The Dynamics of Social Movements,* Winthrop, 1979.

H. Blalock, editor, *Social Theory and Research: A Critical Appraisal,* Free Press, 1981.

M. Jackson and J. Wood, editors, *Social Movements,* Brooks/Cole, 1982.

P. Manning and R. Smith, editors, *An Introduction to Social Research,* Ballinger, 1982.

J. Johnson and L. Savitz, editors, *Legal Processes and Corrections,* Wiley, 1982.

S. Kadish, editor, *Encyclopedia of Crime and Justice,* Macmillan, 1983.

C. Klockars, editor, *Police Issues,* McGraw-Hill, 1983.

J. Kitsuse and J. Schneider, editors, *Studies in the Sociology of Social Problems,* Albex, 1984.

D. Kelly, *Deviant Behavior: Readings in the Sociology of Deviance,* St. Martin's, 1984.

W. Hefferman and T. Stroup, editors, *Police Ethics: Hard Choices in Law Enforcement,* John Jay, 1985.

Short, *The Social Fabric,* Sage Publications, 1986.

R. Rist, editor, *Policy Studies Review Annual,* Transaction Books, 1986.

R. Menzies and others, *Essays in the Sociology of Social Control,* Gower, 1988.

D. Altheide and others, *New Directions in the Study of Law and Social Control,* Plenum, 1989.

B. Berger, editor, *Authors of Their Own Lives: Intellectual Autobiographies by Twenty American Sociologists,* University of California Press, 1990.

OTHER

Also contributor to *World Book Encyclopedia* and *Encyclopaedia Britannica.* Contributor of articles to numerous periodicals, including *Nation, Dissent, Harvard Business Review, Contemporary Sociology, Yale Law Journal, Wall Street Journal,* and *Washington Post.* Associate editor, *Social Problems,* 1969-75, and *American Sociological Review,* 1972-75; advisory editor, *Politics and Society,* 1970-73; member of editorial board, *Annual Review of Sociology,* 1978-84, *Journal of Conflict Resolution,* 1984—, *Qualitative Sociology,* 1987—, *Contemporary Crisis,* 1987—, and *Studies in Law, Politics and Society,* 1988—.

WORK IN PROGRESS: Collective Behavior and Collective Behavior Process, for Prentice-Hall.

*   *   *

MASON, Alpheus Thomas 1899-

PERSONAL: Born September 18, 1899, in Snow Hill, MD; son of Herbert William and Emma Leslie (Hancock) Mason; married Christine Este Gibbons, June 12, 1934; children: Louise Este (Mrs. Joseph Bachelder III). *Education:* Dickinson College, A.B., 1920; Princeton University, M.A., 1921, Ph.D., 1923.

ADDRESSES: Home—8 Edgehill St., Princeton, NJ 08540.

CAREER: Duke University, Durham, NC, assistant professor of political science, 1923-25; Princeton University, Princeton, NJ, assistant professor 1925-30, associate professor, 1930-36, professor of politics, 1936-47, McCormick Professor of Jurisprudence, 1947-68, McCormick Professor of Jurisprudence emeritus, 1968—. Lecturer or visiting professor at over twenty universities and law schools in the United States, and at Liberal Summer School, Cambridge, England. Member, Institute for Advanced Study, Princeton University, 1938, and American Studies Seminars, Tokyo University, Japan, 1953. *Military service:* U.S. Army, Infantry, 1918.

MEMBER: American Political Science Association (vice-president, 1959-60), PEN, American Academy of Arts and Sciences (fellow), Phi Beta Kappa, Sigma Alpha Epsilon, Nassau Club (Princeton), London Author's Club.

AWARDS, HONORS: Guggenheim fellowship, 1952; American Library Association Liberty and Justice Award, 1957, for *Harlan Fiske Stone: Pillar of the Law;* American Society of Historians prize, 1957; Rockefeller Foundation grants, 1959, 1963, for three-year study of office and powers of Chief Justice of the United States; honorary doctorates awarded from numerous colleges and universities, including Dickinson College, 1947, Princeton University, 1974, and Franklin and Marshall College, 1981.

WRITINGS:

Organized Labor and the Law, Duke University Press, 1925.

Brandeis: Lawyer and Judge in the Modern State, Princeton University Press, 1933.

The Brandeis Way, Princeton University Press, 1938.

Bureaucracy Convicts Itself, Viking, 1941.

Brandeis: A Free Man's Life, Viking, 1946.

Fall of a Railroad Empire, Syracuse University Press, 1947.

(With Gordon E. Baker) *Free Government in the Making: Readings in American Political Thought,* Oxford University Press, 1949, 4th edition, 1985.

The Supreme Court: Instrument of Power or of Revealed Truth?, Princeton University Press, 1953.

The Supreme Court: Vehicle of Revealed Truth or Power Group, 1930-37, Boston University Press, 1953.

(With William M. Beaney) *American Constitutional Law: Introductory Essays and Selected Cases,* Prentice-Hall, 1954, 8th edition, 1987.

Security through Freedom: American political Thought and Practice, Cornell University Press, 1955.

Harlan Fiske Stone: Pillar of Law, Viking, 1956.

The Supreme Court from Taft to Warren, Louisiana State University Press, 1958, 3rd edition published as *The Supreme Court from Taft to Burger,* 1979.

(With Richard H. Leach) *In Quest of Freedom: American Political Thought and Practice,* Prentice-Hall, 1959, 2nd edition, University Press of America, 1981.

(With Beaney) *The Supreme Court in a Free Society,* Prentice-Hall, 1959.

The Supreme Court: Palladium of Freedom, University of Michigan Press, 1962.

The States Rights Debate: Antifederalism and the Constitution, Prentice-Hall, 1964.

William Howard Taft: Chief Justice, Simon & Shuster, 1965.

(Editor with D. Grier Stephenson) *American Constitutional Development,* AHM, 1977.

Contributor to law journals, including *Harvard Law Review* and *American Political Science Review.* Member of editorial boards, *American Political Science Review,* 1936-40, and *Political Science Quarterly,* 1972—.

*   *   *

MAZER, Harry 1925-

PERSONAL: Born May 31, 1925, in New York, N.Y.; son of Sam (a dressmaker) and Rose (a dressmaker; maiden name, Lazeunick) Mazer; married Norma Fox (a novelist), February 12, 1950; children: Anne, Joseph, Susan, Gina. *Education:* Union College, B.A., 1948; Syracuse University, M.A., 1960.

ADDRESSES: Home and office—Brown Gulf Rd., Jamesville, N.Y. 13078. *Agent*—Marilyn Marlow, Curtis Brown Ltd., Ten Astor Pl., New York, N.Y. 10003.

CAREER: Railroad brake man and switchtender for New York Central, 1950-55; New York Construction, Syracuse, N.Y., sheet metal worker, 1957-59; Central Square School, Central Square, N.Y., teacher of English, 1959-60; Aerofin Corp., Syracuse, welder, 1960-63; full-time writer, 1963—. *Military service:* U.S. Army Air Forces, 1943-45; became sergeant; received Purple Heart and Air Medal.

MEMBER: Authors Guild, Society of Children's Book Writers, American Civil Liberties Union.

AWARDS, HONORS: Kirkus Choice list, 1974, for *The Dollar Man;* Children's Choice list, International Reading Association, 1977, for *The Solid Gold Kid;* Best Books for Young Adults list, American Library Association (ALA), 1977 (with Norma Fox Mazer), for *The Solid Gold Kid,* 1978, for *The War on Villa Street,* 1979, for *The Last Mission,* 1981, for *I Love You, Stupid!,* 1986, for *When the Phone Rang,* and 1987, for *The Girl of His Dreams;* Dorothy Canfield Fisher Children's Book Award nomination, 1979, for *The War on Villa Street; New York Times* Best Books of the Year list, 1979, New York Public Library Books for the Teen Age list, 1980, and ALA Best of the Best Books list, 1970-83, all for *The Last Mission; Booklist* Contemporary Classics list, 1984, and German "Preis der Lesseratten," both for *Snowbound;* Arizona Young Readers Award nomination, 1985, for *The Island Keeper;* Iowa Teen Award Master list, 1988, for *When the Phone Rang.*

WRITINGS:

JUVENILE NOVELS

Guy Lenny, Delacorte, 1971, reprinted, Avon, 1988.

Snow Bound, Delacorte, 1973.

The Dollar Man, Delacorte, 1974.

(With wife, Norma Fox Mazer) *The Solid Gold Kid,* Delacorte, 1977.

The War on Villa Street, Delacorte, 1978.

The Last Mission, Delacorte, 1979.

The Island Keeper: A Tale of Courage and Survival, Delacorte, 1981.

I Love You, Stupid!, Crowell Junior Books, 1981.

When the Phone Rang, Scholastic, Inc., 1985.

Hey Kid! Does She Love Me?, Crowell Junior Books, 1985.

Cave under the City, Crowell Junior Books, 1986.

The Girl of His Dreams, Crowell Junior Books, 1987.

City Lights, Scholastic, Inc., 1988.

(With N. F. Mazer) *Heartbeat,* Bantam, 1989.

SIDELIGHTS: "Harry Mazer writes about young people caught in the midst of moral crises, often of their own making," asserts Kenneth L. Donelson in *Voice of Youth Advocates.* "Searching for a way out, they discover themselves, or rather they learn that the first step in extricating themselves from their physical and moral dilemmas is self-discovery. Intensely moral as Mazer's books are," the critic continues, "they present young people thinking and talking and acting believably," a characteristic which accounts for Mazer's popularity. In the recent *The Girl of His Dreams,* for example, Mazer relates the romance of two ordinary young adults with "a credibility apart from its fairy-tale ending," comments Marianne Gingher in the *Los Angeles Times,* a credibility due to the "dimensional characters." Although "contrivances abound," the critic believes that "the happy ending feels earned. Harry Mazer writes deftly about the nature of adolescent yearning, both from a boy's and girl's perspective." And *Snow Bound,* the tale of two mismatched teens who are caught unprepared in a New York blizzard and must cooperate to survive, has a similar appeal. *New York Times Book Review* contributor Cathleen Burns Elmer notes that "occasionally a plot turn seems contrived," but she admits that the book has a "capacity to enthrall [that] lies in the *mature* reader's willingness to suspend disbelief. 'Snow Bound' is a crackling tale; Mazer tells it with vigor and authority."

The Dollar Man presents another "average" youth in uncommon circumstances; Marcus Rosenbloom is overweight, prone to daydreaming, and obsessed with finding out the identity of his father, about whom his single mother refuses to speak. "The idea is not novel, or even presented with extraordinary subtlety or style," observes Tobi Tobias in the *New York Times Book Review,* "but there is such charged energy in Mazer's work and

Marcus is such an authentic person that you care, very much, what happens." "Not incidentally," a *Kirkus Reviewer* writer remarks, "this is an outstandingly empathetic and realistic study of . . . a food addict and, moreover, a sensitive interior view— undistorted by the self-discounting sarcasm that has become a narrative cliche—of the kind of kid who is usually shoved into the background . . . but who in this case deserves the front and center attention Mazer accords him." The result, concludes the critic, is "a rare combination—uncompromising yet ever so easy to connect with."

The Last Mission, based in part on Mazer's own experiences in World War II, "represents an amazing leap in writing, far surpassing anything [the author] had written before," claims Donelson. Fifteen-year-old Jack Raab is Jewish and so desperate to fight against Hitler that he borrows his older brother's identification to enlist in the Army Air Forces. Jack is trained as a gunner, and he and his fellow crew members fly out of England on over twenty missions before being hit by enemy fire; Jack bails out and is the only one to survive—but he ends up a German prisoner of war. While war stories form a much-explored genre, Paxton Davis feels *The Last Mission* stands out; as he details in the *New York Times Book Review,* the force of Mazer's novel "lies less with details of Air Force training and service . . . than with the emotional substance upon which the experience depends. For Jack Raab is no mere author's pawn," the critic explains. "The reader feels his shock and grief at losing his friends, suffers with him the doubts and apprehensions that being a Jewish prisoner inevitably raise, and especially, experiences with him the bewildering mixture of relief and repugnance that comes with returning to civilian life."

A *Kirkus Reviews* writer, however, believes that "despite Mazer's evident and convincing first-hand acquaintance with the material," the novel is a "reduction of a genre that is best met at full strength." Donelson, on the other hand, asserts that *The Last Mission* "conveys better than any other young adult novel, and better than most adult novels, the feeling of war and the desolation it leaves behind. . . . This book is a remarkable achievement, both for its theme and its portrait of a young man who searches and acts and finds the search futile and the actions incoherent." As Davis concludes, "Harry Mazer is a prize-winning writer for young people. No wonder."

Mazer told *CA:* "I felt—I've always felt—that I write and even speak with difficulty. I think I am a writer not because this was something I did well—an inborn talent—but for the opposite reason, because I did it so poorly. I was like the child suffering from polio who determines to become a runner.

"Everything I've done as a writer I've done despite the feeling that I have no natural talent. I've never felt articulate or fluent, rarely felt that flow of language. When I think of the origins of these feelings, I wonder if this may be physical, some form of dyslexia. My mother, despite strenuous efforts, never learned to read or write with fluency and my brother seemed to have the same problem in school."

The author added: "When I started writing I had no idea I would find myself writing for young readers. My agent suggested I do something in this area, and I discovered that I liked writing about this time of life. Adolescence for me was so intense, so filled with joy, pain, expectations, hope, despair, energy, that though those years are far behind me they remain real to me, and have a vividness and clarity that events much closer to me in time do not have. To my surprise I discovered a 13-year-old voice inside me."

"In writing for the young you can't allow yourself the diversions, the long descriptions, philosophical ruminations, endless dialogues of other fictions. You have to rivet the interest of your reader rapidly. I don't expect my reader to be any more patient than I am.

"A greater danger, though, is to oversimplify, to write down, to fudge on emotion, and development, and the realistic working out of the story. Good children's fiction is finally no different than good adult fiction. It needs fully shaped characters, conflict, and development. It has form, a beginning, middle and end.

"I'm interested in character, in those parts of people that are hidden, misunderstood, areas of deprivation, longing, separation and isolation. I write out of the memory of those feelings in myself. When I feel the conflict in the character, the disparate feelings, then I begin to feel the truth of the character, the inner tension, the opposing emotions, that inform the book as well."

For an earlier published interview, see entry in *Contemporary Authors,* Volume 97-100.

MEDIA ADAPTATIONS: Snowbound was produced as an NBC After School Special in 1978.

BIOGRAPHICAL/CRITICAL SOURCES:

BOOKS

Children's Literature Review, Volume 16, Gale, 1989.
Nilsen, Alleen Pace and Kenneth L. Donelson, *Literature for Today's Young Adults,* Scott, Foresman, 1985.

PERIODICALS

English Journal, April, 1982.
Kirkus Reviews, August 15, 1974, January 1, 1980, May 15, 1985, September 15, 1985.
Los Angeles Times, March 12, 1988.
New York Times Book Review, August 12, 1973, November 17, 1974, December 2, 1979, September 13, 1981.
School Library Journal, September, 1980.
Voice of Youth Advocates, February, 1983, October, 1984.
Washington Post Book World, July 10, 1977.

*   *   *

MAZER, Norma Fox   1931-

PERSONAL: Born May 15, 1931, in New York, N.Y.; daughter of Michael and Jean (Garlen) Fox; married Harry Mazer (a novelist), February 12, 1950; children: Anne, Joseph, Susan, Gina. *Education:* Attended Antioch College and Syracuse University. *Politics:* "I believe in people—despise institutions while accepting their necessity." *Religion:* "Jewish by birth, pantheistic by nature."

ADDRESSES: Home and office—Brown Gulf Rd., Jamesville, N.Y. 13078.

CAREER: Writer, 1964—.

AWARDS, HONORS: National Book Award nomination, 1973, for *A Figure of Speech;* Lewis Carroll Shelf Award, University of Wisconsin, 1975, for *Saturday the Twelfth of October;* Christopher Award, *New York Times* Outstanding Books of the Year list, *School Library Journal* Best Books of the Year list, American Library Association (ALA) Best Books for Young Adults list, ALA Notable Book, all 1976, all for *Dear Bill, Remember Me? and Other Stories;* (with Harry Mazer) ALA Best Books for Young Adults list, 1977, and International Reading Association-Children's Book Council Children's Choice, 1978, both for *The*

Solid Gold Kid; ALA Best Books for Young Adults list, 1979, *School Library Journal* Best Books of the Year list, 1979, and ALA Best of the Best Books 1970-83 list, all for *Up in Seth's Room;* Austrian Children's Books list of honor, and German Children's Literature prize, both 1982, both for *Mrs. Fish, Ape, and Me, the Dump Queen;* Edgar Award, Mystery Writers of America, 1982, and California Young Readers Medal, 1985, both for *Taking Terri Mueller;* ALA Best Books for Young Adults list, 1983, for *Someone to Love;* ALA Best Books for Young Adults list, and *New York Times* Outstanding Books of the Year list, both 1984, both for *Downtown;* Iowa Teen Award, 1985-86, for *When We First Met;* International Reading Association Children's Choice, 1986, for *A, My Name Is Ami;* Newbery Honor Book, *School Library Journal* Best Books of the Year list, ALA Notable Book, ALA Best Books for Young Adults list, Canadian Children's Books Council Choice, *Horn Book* Fanfare Book, and Association of Booksellers for Children Choice, all 1988, all for *After the Rain;* ALA Best Books for Young Adults list, 1989, for *Silver.*

WRITINGS:

JUVENILE FICTION

I, Trissy, Delacorte, 1971, reprinted, Dell, 1986.
A Figure of Speech, Delacorte, 1973.
Saturday the Twelfth of October, Delacorte, 1975.
Dear Bill, Remember Me? and Other Stories, Delacorte, 1976.
(With husband, Harry Mazer) *The Sold Gold Kid,* Delacorte, 1977.
Up in Seth's Room, Delacorte, 1979.
Mrs. Fish, Ape, and Me, the Dump Queen, Dutton, 1980.
Taking Terri Mueller, Avon/Morrow, 1981.
When We First Met, Four Winds, 1982.
Summer Girls, Love Boys, and Other Short Stories, Delacorte, 1982.
Someone to Love, Delacorte, 1983.
Downtown, Avon/Morrow, 1983.
Supergirl (screenplay novelization), Warner Books, 1984.
(Contributor) Donald R. Gallo, editor, *Sixteen. . . Short Stories by Outstanding Writers for Young Adults,* Delacorte, 1984.
A, My Name Is Ami, Scholastic, Inc., 1986.
Three Sisters, Scholastic, Inc., 1986.
(Contributor) Elizabeth Segal, *Short Takes,* Lothrop, 1986.
B, My Name Is Bunny, Scholastic, Inc., 1987.
(Contributor) Gallo, editor, *Visions,* Delacorte, 1987.
After the Rain, Morrow, 1987.
Silver, Morrow, 1988.
(With H. Mazer) *Heartbeat,* Bantam, 1989.

OTHER

(With Margery Lewis) *Waltzing on Water: Poetry by Women,* Dell, 1989.

Contributor of stories and articles to magazines, including *Jack and Jill, Ingenue, Calling All Girls, Child Life, Boys and Girls, Redbook, English Journal, Voice of Youth Advocates, Signal, T.O.N.,* and *ALAN Review.*

WORK IN PROGRESS: Several novels; a short story.

SIDELIGHTS: "It's not hard to see why Norma Fox Mazer has found a place among the most popular writers for young adults these days," observes Suzanne Freeman in the *Washington Post Book World.* "At her best, Mazer can cut right to the bone of teenage troubles and then show us how the wounds will heal. She can set down the everyday scenes of her characters' lives in images that are scalpel sharp," the critic continues, adding that

"what's apparent throughout all of this is that Mazer has taken great care to get to know the world she writes about. She delves into the very heart of it with a sure and practiced hand." Part of this is due to her writing ability; as *New York Times Book Review* contributor Barbara Wersba describes her, "Mazer is a dazzling writer and brings to her work a literacy that would be admirable in any type of fiction." For example, in *A Figure of Speech,* Mazer's story of an elderly man neglected by all of his family except his granddaughter, "the fine definition of all characters, the plausibility of the situations and the variety of insights into motivation make [the novel] almost too good to be true," Tom Heffernan asserts in *Children's Literature: Annual of the Modern Language Association Seminar on Children's Literature and the Children's Literature Association.* "There is no point at which it passes into an area of depiction or explanation that would exceed the experience of a young adolescent. But there is also no point at which the psychological perceptiveness and narrative control would disappoint an adult reader."

Mazer's short story collections also have a broad appeal, as reviewers have commented about *Summer Girls, Love Boys and Other Short Stories.* Bruce Bennett, for instance, notes in the *Nation* that the collection "is accessible to teen-agers as well as adults. Most of the characters are young people," the critic elaborates, "but Mazer writes about them with an affectionate irony that older readers will appreciate." Because Mazer "has the skill to reveal the human qualities in both ordinary and extraordinary situations as young people mature," states *New York Times Book Review* contributor Ruth I. Gordon, ". . .it would be a shame to limit their reading to young people, since they can show an adult reader much about the sometimes painful rite of adolescent passage into adulthood." Strengthening the effect of Mazer's collections is that they are "written specifically as a book, a fact which gives the stories an unusual unity and connectedness," relates Bennett. "Clearly, Mazer appreciates the short story form, with its narrow focus and spotlit moments," comments a *Kirkus Reviews* writer about *Dear, Bill, Remember Me? and Other Stories,* "where others might do up the same material as diluted novels."

While she has earned praise for her forays into the short story form, it is Mazer's novels that have brought her the most recognition, both with critics and readers. *Taking Terri Mueller,* for example, earned Mazer an Edgar Award from the Mystery Writers of America although she had not intended it as a mystery. The book follows Terri Mueller and her father as they wander from town to town, never staying in one place for more than a year. Although Terri is happy with her father, she is old enough to wonder why he will never talk about her mother, who supposedly died ten years ago; an overheard discussion leads her to discover that she had been kidnapped by her father after a bitter custody battle. "The unfolding and the solution of the mystery [of the truth about Terri's mother] are effectively worked," remarks a *Horn Book* reviewer; "filled with tension and with strong characterization, the book makes compelling reading." Freeman similarly observes that despite the potential for simplifying Terri's conflict, "Mazer does not take the easy way out in this book. There are no good guys or bad guys. There are no easy answers." The critic concludes: "We believe in just about everything Terri does, because Mazer's writing makes us willing to believe. She wins us completely with this finely wrought and moving book."

In her Newbery Honor Book *After the Rain,* Mazer returns to the subject of a elderly man dying; but in this instance, grandfather Izzy rebuffs his loving family, and granddaughter Rachel must exert herself to build a relationship with him. As it becomes clear to her that Izzy is dying and needs companionship, Rachel decides to regularly spend her free time with him. "It's surprising that she should make such a decision," claims *Washington Post Book World* contributor Cynthia Samuels, "but once the reader accepts her choice and begins to join her on her daily visits with the crotchety old man, the story becomes both moving and wise." The result, continues the critic, is a book that "deals with death and loss in an original and sensitive way." Carolyn Meyer, however, feels that there is a lack of tension in the story; "you never really worry that Rachel won't do the right thing," she writes in the *Los Angeles Times Book Review*. In contrast, a *Kirkus Reviews* critic suggests that "what distinguishes this book, making it linger in the heart, are the realistic portrayals of the tensions, guilt, and sudden, painfully moving moments involved in Rachel's and Izzy's situations." As a *Horn Book* reviewer concludes, Izzy's "harsh, rough personality [is] so realistic and recognizable that we feel we have known him and can understand the sorrow that overcomes Rachel. [*After the Rain* is] a powerful book, dealing with death and dying and the strength of family affection."

Mazer told *CA:* "I seem to deal in the ordinary, the everyday, the real. I should like in my writing to give meaning and emotion to ordinary moments. In my books and stories I want people to eat chocolate pudding, break a dish, yawn, look in a store window, wear socks with holes in them. . . ."

AVOCATIONAL INTERESTS: Reading, racquetball in winter, "living in summer on our land in Canada with sun, rain, wind, and water, and without electricity, telephone, newspaper, radio, indoor plumbing, stove, refrigerator, lights, etc., etc., etc."

BIOGRAPHICAL/CRITICAL SOURCES:

BOOKS

Butler, Francelia, editor, *Children's Literature: Annual of the Modern Language Association Seminar on Children's Literature and the Children's Literature Association,* Volume 4, Temple University Press, 1975.
Contemporary Literary Criticism, Volume 26, Gale, 1983.
Something about the Author Autobiography Series, Volume 1, Gale, 1986.

PERIODICALS

Horn Book, April, 1983, September, 1987.
Kirkus Reviews, October 1, 1976, May 1, 1987.
Los Angeles Times, September 12, 1987.
Los Angeles Times Book Review, July 5, 1987.
Nation, March 12, 1983.
New York Times Book Review, March 17, 1974, October 19, 1975, January 20, 1980, March 13, 1983, November 25, 1984.
School Library Journal, September, 1980.
Washington Post Book World, July 10, 1977, April 10, 1983, October 14, 1984, March 9, 1986, May 10, 1987.

—*Sketch by Diane Telgen*

*   *   *

McCARTHY, Barry (Wayne) 1943-

PERSONAL: Born September 7, 1943, in Chicago, IL; son of Edward J. (a contractor) and Dorothy (Small) McCarthy; married Emily Jeannette McCabe (a writer), November 19, 1966; children: Mark, Kara Dawn, Paul T. *Education:* Loyola University at Chicago, B.A., 1965; Southern Illinois University at Car-

bondale, Ph.D., 1969. *Politics:* Democrat. *Religion:* Roman Catholic.

ADDRESSES: Office—4201 Connecticut Ave. N.W., Suite 602, Washington, DC 20008. *Agent*—Ellen Levine Literary Agency, Inc., 432 Park Ave. S., Suite 1205, New York, NY 10016.

CAREER: American University, Washington, DC, instructor, 1969-70, assistant professor, 1970-74, associate professor, 1974-78, professor of psychology, 1978—, counselor at Counseling Center, 1969-76, associate director of training for Peer Counseling Program, 1973-76. Private practice of psychology, 1971—; partner of Washington Psychological Center, 1977—.

MEMBER: American Psychological Association, American Association of Sex Educators, Counselors, and Therapists, Association for the Advancement of Behavior Therapy, Behavior Research and Therapy Association (clinical fellow), American Association for Marriage and Family Therapy (clinical member), Society for Sex Therapy and Research.

WRITINGS:

(With Mary Ryan and Fred Johnson) *Sexual Awareness: A Practical Approach,* Boyd & Fraser, 1975.
What You (Still) Don't Know about Male Sexuality, Crowell, 1977.
(With wife, Emily J. McCarthy) *Sex and Satisfaction after Thirty,* Prentice-Hall, 1981.
(With E. J. McCarthy) *Sexual Awareness: Sharing Sexual Intimacy,* Carroll & Graf, 1984.
Male Sexual Awareness: Increasing Sexual Pleasure, Carroll & Graf, 1988.
(With E. J. McCarthy) *Female Sexual Awareness: Achieving Sexual Fulfillment,* Carroll & Graf, 1989.
(With E. J. McCarthy) *Couple Sexual Awareness,* Carroll & Graf, in press.

SIDELIGHTS: Barry McCarthy told *CA:* "I am a clinical psychologist and sex therapist. Most of my time is spent doing clinical work with some teaching and presenting professional workshops.

"For me, writing is a way to inform the public of new findings in the human sexuality field and hopefully to prevent sexual problems. For too many people, sex is seen as a performance where you have to prove yourself to your partner. In my opinion, sexuality is best perceived as a cooperative, sharing experience in giving and receiving pleasure.

"Writing books with my wife is particularly enjoyable, and we are trying to decide if the next project will be on sexuality or focus more broadly on psychological well-being."

*   *   *

McCARTHY, Emily J(eannette) 1945-

PERSONAL: Born July 19, 1945, in Peoria, IL; daughter of Ralph Jennings (a maintenance foreman) and Jeannette (a psychiatric aide; maiden name, Rhodes) McCabe; married Barry Wayne McCarthy (a psychologist and writer), November 19, 1966; children: Mark, Kara Dawn, Paul T. *Education:* Attended Western Illinois University, 1963-64; Southern Illinois University at Carbondale, B.S., 1967. *Politics:* Democrat. *Religion:* Roman Catholic.

ADDRESSES: Office—126 Gills Neck Rd., Lewes, DE 19958. *Agent*—Ellen Levine Literary Agency, Inc., 432 Park Ave. S., Suite 1205, New York, NY 10016.

CAREER: Christopher/Zeigler School Districts, IL, speech correctionist, 1967-68; writer.

WRITINGS:

(With husband, Barry McCarthy) *Sex and Satisfaction after Thirty,* Prentice-Hall, 1981.
(With B. McCarthy) *Sexual Awareness: Sharing Sexual Intimacy,* Carroll & Graf, 1984.
(With B. McCarthy) *Female Sexual Awareness: Achieving Sexual Fulfillment,* Carroll & Graf, 1989.
(With B. McCarthy) *Couple Sexual Awareness,* Carroll & Graf, in press.

*   *   *

McCORMICK, (George) Donald (King) 1911-
(Richard Deacon)

PERSONAL: Born December 9, 1911, in Rhyl, Flintshire, Wales; son of Thomas Burnside (a journalist) and Lillie Louise (King) McCormick; married Rosalind Deirdre Buchanan Scott, 1934 (divorced); married Sylvia Doreen Cade, 1947 (deceased); married Eileen Dee Challinor James, October 4, 1963; children: Anthony Stuart. *Education:* Attended Oswestry School. *Politics:* Non-party.

ADDRESSES: Home—8 Barry Court, 36 Southend Rd., Beckenham, Kent, BR3 2AD England.

CAREER: Worked a variety of jobs on numerous provincial and British national newspapers, 1931-39; *Gibraltar Chronicle,* Gibraltar, Spain, managing editor, 1946; Kemsley Newspapers, London, England, foreign correspondent in Northwest Africa, 1946-49, Commonwealth correspondent, 1949-55; *Sunday Times,* London, with foreign department, 1949-65, foreign manager, 1963-73; writer. *Military service:* Royal Navy Volunteer Reserve, 1941-46; served in Combined Operations; became lieutenant commander.

WRITINGS:

The Talkative Muse, Lincoln Williams, 1934.
Islands for Sale, Garnett, 1949.
Mr. France, Jarrolds, 1955.
The Wicked City: An Algerian Adventure, Jarrolds, 1956.
The Hell-Fire Club: The Story of the Amorous Knights of Wycombe, Jarrolds, 1958.
The Mystery of Lord Kitchener's Death, Putnam, 1959.
The Identity of Jack the Ripper, Jarrolds, 1959, revised edition, John Long, 1970.
The Incredible Mr. Kavanagh, Putnam, 1960.
The Wicked Village, Jarrolds, 1960.
The Temple of Love, Jarrolds, 1962, Citadel, 1965.
Blood on the Sea: The Terrible Story of the Yawl "Migonette," Muller, 1962.
The Mask of Merlin: A Critical Study of David Lloyd George, Macdonald, 1963, published as *The Mask of Merlin: A Critical Biography of David Lloyd George,* Holt, 1964.
The Unseen Killer: A Study of Suicide, Its History, Causes and Cures, Muller, 1964.
Peddler of Death: The Life and Times of Sir Basil Zaharoff, Holt, 1965 (published in England as *Pedlar of Death: The Life of Sir Basil Zaharoff,* Macdonald, 1965).
The Red Barn Mystery: Some New Evidence on an Old Murder, John Long, 1967, A. S. Barnes, 1968.
Murder by Witchcraft: A Study of Lower Quinton and Hagley Wood Murders, John Long, 1968.

Murder by Perfection: Maundy Gregory, the Man Behind Two Unsolved Murders, John Long, 1970.
One Man's Wars: The Story of Charles Sweeney, Soldier of Fortune, Arthur Barker, 1972.
How to Buy an Island, David & Charles, 1973.
The Master Book of Spies (young adult), Watts, 1974.
Islands of England & Wales: A Guide to 138 English & Welsh Islands, Osprey, 1974.
Islands of Scotland: A Guide to 247 Scottish Islands, Osprey, 1974.
Islands of Ireland: A Guide to 110 Irish Islands, Osprey, 1974.
The Master Book of Escapades (young adult), Watts, 1975.
Taken for a Ride: The History of Cons & Conmen, Harwood-Smart, 1976.
Who's Who in Spy Fiction, Taplinger, 1977.
Approaching 1984, David & Charles, 1980.
Love in Code, Methuen, 1980.
(With Katy Fletcher) *Spy Fiction: A Connoiseur's Guide,* Facts on File, 1990.

UNDER PSEUDONYM RICHARD DEACON; NONFICTION, EXCEPT AS INDICATED

The Private Life of Mr. Gladstone, Muller, 1966.
Madoc and the Discovery of America, Muller, 1967, Braziller, 1968.
John Dee, Muller, 1968.
A History of the British Secret Service, Muller, 1969, Taplinger, 1970.
A History of the Russian Secret Service, Taplinger, 1972.
The Chinese Secret Service, Taplinger, 1974 (published in England as *A History of the Chinese Secret Service,* Muller, 1974).
William Caxton: The First English Editor, Muller, 1976.
Matthew Hopkins: Witchfinder-General, Muller, 1976.
The Book of Fate: Its Origins and Uses, Muller, 1976.
The Israeli Secret Service, Hamish Hamilton, 1977, Taplinger, 1978.
The British Connection, Hamish Hamilton, 1977.
Spy!, B.B.C. Publications, 1979.
Escape, B.B.C. Publications, 1980.
A History of the Japanese Secret Service, Muller, 1982, published as *Kempei Tai: A History of the Japanese Secret Service,* Beaufort, 1983.
With My Little Eye, Muller, 1982.
Zita: A Do-It-yourself Romance (novel), Muller, 1983.
"C": A Biography of Sir Maurice Oldfield, Macdonald, 1985.
The Cambridge Apostles: A History of Cambridge University's Elite Intellectual Secret Society, Farrar, Straus, 1986.
The Truth Twisters, Macdonald, 1987.
Spyclopaedia, Morrow, 1988.
Super-Spy, Macdonald, 1989.
The Greatest Treason, Century Hutchinson, 1989.

SIDELIGHTS: Donald McCormick's *The Cambridge Apostles: A History of Cambridge University's Elite Intellectual Secret Society,* written under the pseudonym Richard Deacon, covers the society founded as the Cambridge Conversazione Society, and its twelve members, who designated themselves the "apostles." Through the years, the group came to include such luminaries as Alfred Tennyson, Bertrand Russell, E. M. Forster, John Maynard Keynes, and Ludwig Wittgenstein. Christopher Lehmann-Haupt writes in the *New York Times* that "the apostles came to represent the cream of the cream of British civilization, or at least a portion of it; so its interests and activities were bound to become known to a degree and to be newsworthy." Lehmann-Haupt continues that McCormick's sometimes unfavorable assessments of the group are "always evenhanded, which is to say he hits just as hard with either fist. Indeed he can be staggering in his evenhandedness." He concludes that *The Cambridge Apostles* "is always arresting." An *Economist* contributor, however, finds the history "disjointed," and claims that McCormick "veers too much to the view that the best minds in Cambridge were in love with Stalin at the height of his murderous purges. Actually, Keynes was lecturing to the apostles on 'Why Marxist economics is an insult to the intelligence.'" But Helle Bering-Jensen in the *National Review* judges *The Cambridge Apostles* a "chatty and entertaining account," and believes "the Society itself [is] a worthwhile object of study."

McCormick once told *CA:* "I have—on the principle that it helps to save one from getting stale—switched from one type of nonfiction to another in my books. My first book, *The Talkative Muse,* was a youthfully pretentious dialogue between two friends in the form of essays on a wide range of subjects. A passion for islands has led me to write *Islands for Sale, How to Buy an Island,* and three books on the islands surrounding England, Wales, Scotland and Ireland, large and small. I have also become fascinated in studying the histories of the secret services of the world. I was prompted to tackle the British Secret Service first as a result of doing a biography of John Dee, astrologer to Queen Elizabeth I, who was also a secret agent. Then I found that down the ages there were frequent links between the British and Russian secret services. Not just the notorious Philby link, but that of the quadruple agent, Sidney Reilly, and the fact that Catherine the Great stayed up late at night to decipher messages for the British Ambassador. I then switched to the Chinese secret service largely as a challenge because everybody said it was an impossible subject. I found they had a text book on espionage way back in the fourth century B.C. Finally, I got down to the subject of the Israeli secret service because it seemed to me to be the youngest, smallest and yet most efficient in the whole world and very much part and parcel of the gallant little nation's fight for survival—perhaps a lesson for all of us.

"In the end espionage becomes something of an inescapable obsession. One escapes from it for a time to do another type of book and then, out of one's network of contacts all over the world, a new slant on it presents itself. Lo and behold, there is another book! What fascinated me most about working on *Who's Who in Spy Fiction* was the constantly recurring links between fact and fiction. This is so much more marked in modern times when almost every intelligence service studies the spy fiction of its rivals just in case somebody let leak a little truth. So often the spy fiction books reveal more fact than the spymasters get from their agents! This has been markedly the case with some fiction concerning the CIA."

BIOGRAPHICAL/CRITICAL SOURCES:

PERIODICALS

Economist, October 25, 1985.
National Review, May 22, 1987.
New York Times, June 2, 1986.

* * *

McFARLAND, Ron(ald Earl) 1942-

PERSONAL: Born September 22, 1942, in Bellaire, OH; son of Earl A. (a salesman) and Maxine (a homemaker; maiden name, Stullenburger) McFarland; married Elsie Watson (a homemaker), January 29, 1966; children: Kimberley, Jennifer, Jonathan. *Education:* Brevard Junior College, A.A., 1962; Florida State University, B.A., 1963, M.A., 1965; University of Illinois at Urbana-Champaign, Ph.D., 1970.

ADDRESSES: Office—Department of English, FOC 122, University of Idaho, Moscow, ID 83843.

CAREER: Sam Houston State College (now University), Huntsville, TX, instructor in English, 1965-67; University of Idaho, Moscow, assistant professor, 1970-74, associate professor, 1974-79, professor of English, 1979—. Chairman of Moscow Arts Commission, 1980-81. Gives poetry readings and conducts workshops. Consultant to Idaho Commission on the Arts.

MEMBER: Western Literature Association.

AWARDS, HONORS: Grant from Association for the Humanities in Idaho, 1983; named Idaho State Writer-in-Residence, 1984.

WRITINGS:

(Editor with Paul K. Dempsey) *American Controversy,* Scott, Foresman, 1968.
Certain Women (poetry chapbook), Confluence, 1977.
(Editor and contributor) *Eight Idaho Poets,* University Press of Idaho, 1979.
Composting at Forty (poems), Confluence, 1984.
The Villanelle (monograph), Confluence, 1984.
(Author of introduction) Dixie Lee Partridge, *Deer in the Haystacks* (poems), Ahsahta, 1984.
(Editor) *James Welch,* Confluence, 1986.
(Editor with Hugh Nichols) *Norman Maclean,* Confluence, 1988.
(Editor with William Studebaker) *Idaho Poetry: A Centennial Anthology,* University of Idaho Press, 1988.
David Wagoner (monograph), Boise State University, 1989.

Also contributor to anthologies, including *Anthology of Magazine Verse and Yearbook of American Poetry,* 1981, 1985, 1986, 1987, and 1989. Contributor of numerous stories, articles, poems, and reviews to periodicals, including *Poetry Now, Samisdat Review, Poetry Northwest, New Voices, Journal of Human Relations, Southern Humanities Review,* and *Gray's Sporting Journal.* Literary editor, *Snapdragon,* 1977-87; *Slackwater Review,* poetry editor, 1979-80, general editor, 1981-82.

WORK IN PROGRESS: A novel; a collection of poems; short stories; research on the poems of Tess Gallagher and others.

SIDELIGHTS: Ron McFarland told *CA:* "As a writer I suppose I'm a 'jack of all trades, master of none,' the going euphemism for which is 'eclectic.' In poems I generally try to catch a small dramatic moment, usually centering on a character with a distinct voice, often touched with whimsy. Lacking the wit of John Donne, I've resorted to what I hope is my own brand of whimsy (poor man's wit). I've written about everything in my poems from hotdogs to hide-and-seek, but women tend to frequent my poems as characters (though I claim to have no special wisdom about them, God knows), and images, events, and characters from the northwest are common.

"I admire the obvious aural jubilee of Wallace Stevens, but my own manipulations of ear come closer to the subtleties of William Stafford, Richard Hugo, or David Wagoner. My poems and stories generally reflect a comic vision of life, one that is not exceptionally intellectual, despite my academic background and vocation. When I give a reading I like to think that most of the audience has heard, understood, and enjoyed my poems and stories. Generally, I want them to recognize that poetry can be fun and that it doesn't have to be arcane or esoteric to be good. I'm also pleased to hear some laughter from time to time, though I don't pretend to be a comedian. I admire Ezra Pound's dictum early in the *ABC of Reading:* 'Gloom and solemnity are entirely out of place in even the most rigorous study of an art originally intended to make glad the heart of man.'

"So when it comes to my scholarly dabblings, I give full vent to my own meandering interests. What seems curious to me about a poem or story or book is what I write about, neglecting blithely what the supposed needs of scholarship might be. I'm not very concerned whether I make a 'worthwhile contribution to scholarship.' I am concerned to use good scholarly techniques, to conduct responsible and mature research, and to offer honest and (I hope) interesting observations or insights. Aside from that, I follow whatever spoor I discover.

"For example, if Elizabeth Bishop's 'The Fish' intrigues me so much that I want to make an account of it, I follow through, even though my supposed area of expertise is seventeenth-century English poetry. I try not to neglect the seventeenth century, which is my first literary love, but there, too, I've been whimsical. The interrelationships between science and poetry have provided subjects for a number of my investigations (Jonson and magnetism, Edward Herbert of Cherbury and optics, poems dealing with tobacco), but I've also dealt with mythological references and with close textual studies (repetition in Donne's poems, for example). Since I teach both modern and seventeenth-century poetry it has been easy for me to encounter a wide range of subjects of interest to me—the villanelle, for example, and the work of David Wagoner.

"Recognizing that mine would not likely be a major voice in criticism and that I am possessed of middling talents, I decided to indulge myself and to check out the various types of literary criticism. Wellek and Warren's *Theory of Literature* has probably influenced me somewhat here. Why limit myself simply to a single 'extrinsic' or 'intrinsic' approach? Some works are well approached from the outside, so to speak, while others virtually demand emphasis on the text. Most, of course, require something of each. At any rate, that's how I've proceeded. I've always told myself that if scholarship got in the way or ceased being fun, I'd give it up, but I still enjoy it, and it sometimes offers welcome relief from the poems and stories I'm struggling with in a very different way. I told a friend once that it's like the difference between hunting squirrels and hunting unicorns."

McFarland added: "Although I have always written some journalistic prose, essays, and stories, I've turned increasingly to prose, especially to fiction and to what some call 'creative nonfiction,' in recent years. I write some stories that I would characterize as modestly experimental, but my most representative story would be a first-person narration in which I exaggerate and outright prevaricate on details and episodes of my life or that of family members. My teenaged daughter is a co-protagonist in a number of these stories. Most of my essays, excluding literary scholarship and criticism, have a narrative line and pertain to hunting and fishing. I have also had some success and considerable pleasure with what some editors call 'sudden fiction,' the very condensed one- or two-page story."

*   *   *

McHUGH, (Berit) Elisabet 1941-

PERSONAL: Born January 26, 1941, in Stoede, Sweden; came to the United States in 1971; naturalized U.S. citizen, 1982; daughter of Nils G. O. (a journalist) and Rut E. (a homemaker; maiden name, Gradin) Oejerhag; married Richard G. McHugh (a commander in the U.S. Navy), February 14, 1972 (divorced March, 1982); children: (adopted) Fred R., Lee Ann, Erin V., Jan M., Ryan C., Karen E. *Education:* Royal Naval College, Stockholm, Sweden, diploma, 1961. *Avocational interests:* Reading, walking, classical music, cross-country skiing, travel.

ADDRESSES: Home—2131 Robinson Park Rd., Moscow, ID 83843. *Agent*—Barbara S. Kouts, 788 Ninth Ave., New York, NY 10019.

CAREER: Writer, 1979—. Has worked as a radio officer in Sweden.

WRITINGS:

JUVENILE

Raising a Mother Isn't Easy, Greenwillow, 1983.
Karen's Sister, Greenwillow, 1983.
Karen and Vicki, Greenwillow, 1984.
Beethoven's Cat, Atheneum/Macmillan, 1988.
Wiggie Wins the West, Atheneum/Macmillan, 1989.

Contributor of articles to periodicals.

WORK IN PROGRESS: A young adult book for Bantam.

SIDELIGHTS: Elisabet McHugh told *CA:* "With my six children all grown up and gone, I have more time to write than before. In addition to books, I now also do a lot of magazine articles. As always, the biggest bonus of being a writer is not having to get in the car every morning and go off somewhere to work. I can get up at 5 a.m. (which I frequently do), turn on the computer, and start writing. Or I can spend the afternoon doing other things and write until midnight.

"I share my large rambling country home with my own dog and cats, as well as a varying number of other people's dogs. My dog boarding service is unique and rather exclusive insofar that I only accept four or five animals at a time, and all of them live and sleep in the house. You can find them napping on the living-room sofa, playing in the yard, or chewing on a bone by my desk while I am working. The majority of my boarders are local or from neighboring states, but some come from as far as California, Arizona, and Texas.

"I easily get distracted from my writing by people, but never by animals. Thus the dog boarding meshes perfectly with my occupation as a writer. It also gets me out of the house at regular intervals during the day.

"There are no kennels here, not even a fenced yard. The dogs are free to go outside whenever they want to. With ten acres of land and no close neighbors there is plenty of room, and during our regular walks across the fields they can run to their heart's content. Despite differences in size and temperament they all get along. Most are only dogs whose owners are gone all day. Here they enjoy complete freedom, there is always someone to play with, and everyone gets a lot of attention since I'm around most of the time. I guess this accounts for the fact that no one ever strays from the immediate area of the house.

"On and off, mainly during the summer months, I also accept would-be or beginning writers as my paying guests. To them I give advice, critique, and encouragement. I have met many wonderful and interesting people this way, and it's always exciting to get a letter or phone call when someone has sold an article or a story."

BIOGRAPHICAL/CRITICAL SOURCES:

PERIODICALS

New York Times Book Review, September 4, 1988.

*　　*　　*

McNAB, Oliver
See FREDE, Richard

*　　*　　*

MEAD, William B(owmar) 1934-

PERSONAL: Born April 1, 1934, in St. Louis, MO; stepson of Beelis O. (a manufacturer) and Charlotte (Bowmar) Burkitt; married Jennifer Hilton (an artist), June 9, 1956; children: Christopher, Andrew, Meagan. *Education:* Northwestern University, B.A., 1955.

ADDRESSES: Home and office—7520 Radnor Rd., Bethesda, MD 20817. *Agent*—Arnold Goodman, Goodman Assos., 500 West End Ave., New York, NY 10024.

CAREER: United Press International, Richmond, VA, newswriter, 1958-60; Reynolds Metals Co., Richmond, in public relations, 1960-64; United Press International, newswriter in Chicago, IL, 1964-65, Michigan news manager in Detroit, MI, 1965-67, correspondent in Washington, D.C., 1968-72; *Money,* New York City, correspondent in Washington, D.C., 1972-76; free-lance writer, 1976—. *Military service:* U.S. Army, 1955-57.

MEMBER: Washington Independent Writers.

AWARDS, HONORS: American Political Science Association Congressional fellow, 1967-68; John Hancock award for excellence, 1973, for article on how to deal with inflation; award from J. C. Penny Co. and University of Missouri School of Journalism, 1975, for article on how to compare store brand and nationally advertised grocery products.

WRITINGS:

Even the Browns: The Zany, True Story of Baseball in the Early Forties, Contemporary Books, 1978.
(With Mike Feinsilber) *American Averages: Amazing Facts of Everyday Life,* Doubleday, 1980.
The Official New York Yankees Hater's Handbook, Putnam, 1983.
(With Paul N. Strassels) *Strassels' Tax Savers,* Times Books, 1985.
(With Strassels) *Money Matters: The Hassle-Free, Month-by-Month Guide to Money Management,* Addison-Wesley, 1986.
The Explosive Sixties: Baseball's Decade of Expansion, Redefinition, 1989.
Low and Outside: Baseball in the Depression, 1930-39, Redefinition, 1990.
Two Spectacular Seasons. 1930: The Year the Hitters Ran Wild; 1968: The Year the Pitchers Took Revenge, Macmillan, 1990.

SIDELIGHTS: Reviewing *Even the Browns: The Zany, True Story of Baseball in the Early Forties,* a critic for *Sports Illustrated* comments that the book is "a thoroughly diverting and occasionally surprising exploration of a slice of baseball history heretofore largely ignored," adding that it is "marvelously informative and fun to read." "Mr. Mead describes the Browns and baseball's war years with wit and irony," writes a *New York Times* reviewer. "The tone is chatty, informal and humorous." Mead's more recent book on baseball, *Two Spectacular Seasons. 1930: The Year the Hitters Ran Wild; 1968: The Year the Pitchers Took Revenge,* has also been favorably reviewed. For example, *New York Times Book Review* critic Allen Barra calls it a "genial, well-researched barroom argument—or, rather, discussion—about hitting versus pitching, old-timers versus new(er)-timers."

BIOGRAPHICAL/CRITICAL SOURCES:

PERIODICALS

Chicago Tribune, May 21, 1978.
Boston Globe, April 28, 1978.
Minneapolis Tribune, May 7, 1978.
New York Times, April 23, 1978.
New York Times Book Review, April 1, 1990.
Philadelphia Inquirer, March 26, 1978.
Sporting News, May 27, 1978.
Sports Illustrated, April 3, 1978.
Time, July 23, 1978.
Washington Post, September 9, 1978.

*　　*　　*

MELFI, Mary 1951-

PERSONAL: Born June 10, 1951, in Casacalenda, Italy; daughter of Joseph and Jovanna Melfi; married George Nemeth (a psychologist), May 17, 1975; children: Julian, Stephen. *Education:* Concordia University, Loyola Campus, B.A. (cum laude), 1973; McGill University, M.L.S. (with first class honors), 1976.

ADDRESSES: Home—5040 Grand Blvd., Montreal, Quebec, Canada H3X 3S2.

CAREER: Canadian Trend Report, Montreal, Quebec, research assistant, 1978-88. Gives poetry readings; guest on radio programs.

AWARDS, HONORS: Grants from Ontario Arts Council, 1974, 1976, and Canada Council, 1980-81, 1981-82.

WRITINGS:

POETRY

The Dance, the Cage, and the Horse, D Press, 1976.
A Queen Is Holding a Mummified Cat, Guernica Editions, 1982.
A Bride in Three Acts, Guernica Editions, 1983.
The O Canada Poems, Dollarpoems, 1986.
A Season in Beware, Black Moss Press, 1989.

OTHER

Equation: Sex Plus Death (three-act play), first produced in Toronto, Ontario, at Factory Theatre Lab, April 12, 1980.
A Dialogue with Masks (fiction), Mosaic Press, 1985.

Contributor to anthologies, including *Anthology of Magazine Verse & Yearbook of American Poetry for 1984,* edited by Alan F. Pater, Monitor Book Company, 1984; *Italian Canadian Voices,* edited by Caroline Morgan Di Giovanni, Mosaic Press, 1984; *Dix poetes anglophones du Quebec (Voix-off),* edited by Antonio D'Alfonso, Guernica Editions, 1985; *The Other Language,* edited by Endre Farkas, The Muses' Co., 1989. Contributor of hundreds of poems and stories to magazines, including *Antigonish Review, Descant, Canadian Forum, Toronto Life, Prism International,* and *Exile.*

WORK IN PROGRESS: The Bodycage, a novel, expected in 1991; *Umff and Grandma Moses,* a fantasy; *The Thumb and Other Tales,* stories.

SIDELIGHTS: Mary Melfi commented: "Having been born into a working class family (where there was little or no need for 'art'), I became motivated to write for no particular reason but that I was compelled to do it. I was pressured by an internal drive. Even now I find myself writing, even though I often question its value (or rather its absurdity in our electronic age). I do it because I need to, not necessarily because I want to, though admittedly I love (and hate) every minute of it. Through writing I become 'myself.'

"A great deal of my work seems to focus on the relationship between men and women. My perspective on this relationship is doubtlessly a 'feminine and/or feminist' one, and because of it my adult prose may lend itself more to an audience made up of my own sex. However, both my poetry and my writings for children focus on many different aspects of human life with all its possibilities (rather than its limitations). My juvenile works are either in the form of fairy tales and/or fantasy. My poetry is characterized by a 'surreal' imagination and a certain intensity that may surprise pleasantly or unpleasantly (depending on how one likes one's poetry). I hope my poetry goes beyond the limits of all decency."

BIOGRAPHICAL/CRITICAL SOURCES:

PERIODICALS

Books in Canada, May, 1986.
Globe and Mail (Toronto), June 21, 1986.

*   *   *

MEMMI, Albert   1920-

PERSONAL: Born December 15, 1920, in Tunis, Tunisia; son of Francois (an artisan) and Marguerite (Sarfati) Memmi; married Germaine Dubach; children: Daniel, Dominique, Nicolas. *Education:* University of Algiers, licence es philosophie, 1943; Sorbonne, University of Paris, Dr. es lettres, 1970.

ADDRESSES: Home—5 rue St. Merri, 75004 Paris, France. *Office*—University of Paris, 92 Nanterre, France.

CAREER: High school teacher of philosophy in Tunis, Tunisia, 1953-56; Center of Educational Research, Tunis, director, 1953-57; National Center of Scientific Research, Paris, France, researcher, 1958-60; University of Paris, Sorbonne, Ecole pratique des hautes etudes, Paris, France, assistant professor, 1959-66, professor of social psychology, 1966-70; University of Paris, Nanterre, France, professor of sociology, 1970—. School of Higher Studies in Social Sciences, conference director, 1958, director of department of social sciences, 1975-78; Walker Ames Professor, University of Seattle, 1972.

MEMBER: Societe des Gens de Lettres, PEN Club (France; vice-president), Academie des Sciences d'Outremer.

AWARDS, HONORS: Commander of Ordre de Nichan Iftikhar (Tunisia); Chevalier de la Legion d'Honneur; Officier of Tunisian Republic; Officier des Arts et des Lettres; Officier des Palmes Academiques; Prix Carthage (Tunis), 1953; Prix Feneon (Paris), 1954; Prix Simba (Rome).

WRITINGS:

La Statue du sel (novel), introduction by Albert Camus, Correa, 1953, translation by Edouard Roditi published as *Pillar of Salt,* Criterion, 1955, reprinted, O'Hara, 1975.
Agar (novel), Correa, 1955, translation by Brian Rhys published as *Strangers,* 1958, Orion Press, 1960.
Portrait du colonise precede du portrait du colinisateur, introduction by Jean-Paul Sartre, Buchet/Chastel, 1957, translation by Howard Greenfield published as *The Colonizer and the Colonized,* Orion Press, 1956, reprinted, Beacon Press, 1984.
Portrait d'un Juif, Gallimard, 1962, translation by Elisabeth Abbott published as *Portrait of a Jew,* Orion Press, 1962.
La Liberation d'un Juif, Gallimard, 1962, translation by Judy Hyun published as *The Liberation of a Jew,* Orion Press, 1966.
La Poesie algerienne de 1830 a nos jours: approches socio-historiques, Mouton, 1963.
(Editor) *Anthologie des ecrivains maghrebins d'expression francaise,* two volumes, Presence africaine, 1964, revised and updated edition, 1965.
(With Paul Hassan Maucorps) *Les Francais et le racisme,* Payot, 1965.
Ecole pratique des hautes etudes, Mouton, 1965.
L'Homme domine, Gallimard, 1968, new edition, Payot, 1973, translation published as *Dominated Man: Notes Towards a Portrait* (collection of essays), Orion Press, 1968.
Le Scorpion ou la confession imaginaire (novel), Gallimard, 1969, translation by Eleanor Levieux published as *The Scorpion or the Imaginary Confession,* Grossman, 1971, 2nd edition, J. Philip O'Hara, 1975.
Juifs et Arabes, Gallimard, 1974, translation by Levieux published as *Jews and Arabs,* J. Philip O'Hara, 1975.
Albert Memmi: un entretien avec Robert Davies suivi d'itineraire de l'experience vecue a la theorie de la domination, Reedition Quebec, 1975.
La Terre interieure entretiens avec Victor Malka, Gallimard, 1976.
Le Desert: ou, La vie et les aventures de Jubair Ouali El-Mammi (novel), Gallimard, 1977.
La dependance: esquisse pour un portrait du dependant, Gallimard, 1979, translation published as *Dependence,* Beacon Press, 1983.
La Racisme, Gallimard, 1982.
L'Ecriture coloree, Periple, 1986.
Le Pharaoh (novel), Julliard, 1988.
Le Mirliton du ciel (poems), Julliard, 1989.

Also contributor to textbooks and numerous anthologies.

SIDELIGHTS: The English translations of Albert Memmi's works have been well-received in the United States. In his autobiographical novels *Pillar of Salt* and *Strangers,* Memmi, who grew up in a traditional Jewish household in Tunisia, vividly describes life in North Africa. "But these novels are far more than exotic Durrellian travel guides," writes a *New York Times* critic, "for Memmi, like a Tunisian Balzac graced with Hemingway's radical simplicity and sadness, gave us this world through the voice of a quiet, well-behaved, quite charmingly sad but earnest young man who was slowly disintegrating before our eyes." These novels "today remain two of the best works to appear in Europe after the war," concludes the critic, comparing them to Albert Camus's *The Stranger* and *The Plague.*

Memmi, in *The Scorpion,* treats man's alienation from himself and from others as a major theme. In the story, the protagonist, Emile Memmi, expresses the self-doubts that the author sees as an integral part of the human condition. While the *New York Times* critic does not consider *The Scorpion* completely successful as a novel, he does however observe that "the audacious form and technique of the book are totally unprecedented in Memmi: a richly interwoven net of autobiography, diary, commentary, aphorism, parable, *faux memoire* and novel-within-the-novel."

In *Portrait d'un colonise, Portrait d'un Juif,* and some of his other books, Memmi explores the theories of colonization and the rule and the exploitation of minorities, concluding that once the exploited gain their freedom, they then become like those who ruled them. He details the Jews' complicity in this scenario in *The Liberation of a Jew,* as *Nation* reviewer David Joravsky notes: "The Enlightenment and the democratic revolutions have undermined the belief of Jews that they are chosen to hold a spiritual fortress against gentile assault until the true Messiah comes. The overwhelming majority of Jews leave the besieged life as soon as the gentiles offer a way out. They prefer peace in their own time, on almost any terms the gentiles offer. Memmi calls this 'self-rejection.' He doesn't bother with superficial things like beards, clothes or diet. He goes straight to such fundamentals as name, language, characteristic ideas and national allegiance. In all these essentials Jews come close to complete 'self-rejection,' but hold back at the very end, indulging in curiously ambiguous or whimsical acts of 'self-acceptance'—like changing the name from Silverstein to Silvers, or arguing that Jewishness is an advantage because it is a burden."

Translations of Memmi's books have been published in many countries, including Israel, Italy, Germany, England, Spain, Argentina, Yugoslavia, and Japan.

BIOGRAPHICAL/CRITICAL SOURCES:

PERIODICALS

Best Sellers, July 1, 1971.
Los Angeles Times, August 17, 1984.
Nation, May 22, 1967.
New York Times, May 22, 1971.
Research in African Literatures, Volume I, number 1, 1970.

* * *

METHOLD, Kenneth (Walter) 1931-
(Alexander Cade)

PERSONAL: Born December 23, 1931, in Sussex, England; son of Walter Herbert and Winifred (Elliot) Methold; married Chuntana Chulasathira (a physician), July 8, 1962. *Education:* University of London, teacher's certificate. *Politics:* "Floating voter."

ADDRESSES: c/o Longman-Cheshire, Longman House, Kings Gardens, 95 Coventry St., South Melbourne, Victoria 3205, Australia.

CAREER: Speech and drama specialist in United Kingdom schools; advisor overseas on teaching English as a foreign or second language, including various official positions in Thailand, Hong Kong, Australia, and Indonesia; marketing director, Longman Group (F.E.) Ltd., 1970-74; full-time writer, 1974—.

MEMBER: Amnesty International (vice president, Queensland Branch, 1979-82), Australian Society of Authors (chairman, 1982-85, deputy chairman, 1986-88), National Book Council (executive, 1984-88), Australian Writers Guild.

AWARDS, HONORS: Awgie Award for best radio play, Australian Writers Guild, 1980, for "Stardance."

WRITINGS:

(Compiler) *Modern Tales of Mystery and Detection* (for young people), Hamish Hamilton, 1960.
All Suspect (also see below; novel), Macdonald, 1960.
The Man on His Shoulder (novel), Macdonald, 1962.

(Under pseudonym Alexander Cade) *Turn Up a Stone* (novel), Bles, 1969.
The World Tomorrow (short stories), Eichosha (Tokyo), 1985.
Story One (short stories), Longman Cheshire, 1986.
Moonlight over the Estuary (also see below; comic novel), Penguin (Australia), 1989.

RADIO PLAYS

"Flanagans Family Feeling," Radio Eireann, 1958.
"Sweet Singing the Choir," British Broadcasting Radio (BBC-Radio), 1960.
"All Suspect," BBC-Radio, 1961.
"Queen's Pawn Gambit," BBC-Radio and American Broadcasting Companies, (ABC-Radio), 1971.
"An Item on the Agenda," BBC-Radio, ABC-Radio, and New Zealand Broadcasting Corporation (NZBC-Radio), 1975.
"Any Fool Can," ABC-Radio, 1976.
"The Headhunters," ABC-Radio and NZBC-Radio, 1977.
"Stardance," ABC-Radio, 1979.
"The Force," ABC-Radio and NZBC-Radio, 1980.
"For Services to the Community," ABC-Radio and NZBC-Radio, 1980.
"Song for Lya," ABC-Radio, 1982.
"All Our Realities," ABC-Radio, 1985.
"Moonlight over the Estuary" (comedy serial), ABC-Radio, 1987.
"Tourist Attraction," ABC-Radio, 1988.

OTHER

"The Room Next Door" (television movie), Vision TV, 1986.
"Jackson's Crew" (television movie), Portman Productions, 1987.
"Contagion" (feature film), Broadstar International, Inc., 1988.

Also author of stage plays, "Any Fool Can," South Australian Theatre Company, and "Here Comes Pansy Trotter," Queensland Arts Council; also author of treatment for feature film, "Skeletons"; also author of over one hundred educational books for University of London Press, Hulton Educational Publications, and Longman Group and associated companies, mostly on English as a first, second, or foreign language, but also on history and economics. Contributor to periodicals of articles on the book trade and writing profession. Science fiction reviewer, *The Australian* and *Omega Science Digest,* 1980-85.

WORK IN PROGRESS: "Animal Park," a 16 by 24 children's series; "Death Adder Dreaming," a feature film; *Death by Defamation,* a novel for Bantam; "The Widow Mahler" a play for ABC; *How to Write and Produce a Feature Film,* for Longman-Cheshire; further texts on English as a second language.

SIDELIGHTS: Kenneth Methold told *CA:* "Although I now work in film and television as well as in radio and the printed word, I remain unconvinced that television has contributed significantly to any improvement in the quality of most people's lives, and I have a nagging suspicion that it is not only the greatest time-waster yet devised by man, but also dangerous in that it trivialises everything and encourages people to lead their lives as if they are one long soap opera."

AVOCATIONAL INTERESTS: "Finding a cause to believe in"; music; broadcasting.

* * *

MEYER, Doris (L.) 1942-

PERSONAL: Born January 2, 1942, in Summit, NJ; daughter of Hans J. (an importer-exporter) and Maria L. (an editor and translator) Meyer. *Education:* Radcliffe College, B.A., (magna cum laude), 1963; University of Virginia, M.A., 1964, Ph.D., 1967.

ADDRESSES: Office—Department of Modern Languages, Brooklyn College of the City University of New York, Bedford Ave. and Ave. H., Brooklyn, NY 11210. *Agent*—Sanford J. Greenburger Associates, Inc., 825 Third Ave., New York, NY 10022.

CAREER: University of North Carolina, Wilmington, assistant professor of Spanish, 1967-69; Brooklyn College of the City University of New York, Brooklyn, NY, assistant professor, 1972-75, associate professor, 1976-79, professor of Spanish, 1980—.

MEMBER: Modern Language Association of America, American Association of Teachers of Spanish and Portuguese, PEN, Latin American Studies Association, American Literary Translators Association, National Women's Studies Association, Phi Beta Kappa.

AWARDS, HONORS: Woodrow Wilson fellowship, 1964-66; American Philosophical Society grant, 1976; National Endowment for the Humanities fellowship, 1977-78.

WRITINGS:

Traditionalism in the Works of Francisco de Quevedo, University of North Carolina Press, 1970.
Victoria Ocampo: Against the Wind and Tide, Braziller, 1979.
(Editor with Margarite Fernández Olmos) *Contemporary Women Authors of Latin America,* two volumes, Brooklyn College Press, Volume 1: *New Translations,* Volume 2: *Introductory Essays,* both 1983.
(Editor) *Lives on the Line: The Testimony of Contemporary Latin American Authors,* University of California Press, 1988.

Contributor of articles and translations to history and Spanish studies journals; contributor to *Nimrod.*

SIDELIGHTS: Regarding her 1979 work *Victoria Ocampo: Against the Wind and Tide,* Doris Meyer told *CA:* "I was motivated to write the book . . . through a combination of an Argentine background on my mother's side and an intense concern with bringing to the attention of North American readers the remarkable contributions of a much-overlooked South American woman, a legend in her own country, a social rebel and a feminist." Meyer knew Ocampo personally for nearly twenty years and, according to John Russell in the *New York Times,* provides an "unremittingly earnest" view of her life. "Books and the men who wrote them were what [Ocampo] most cared for in life," notes Russell. "She had the looks, the means and the gall to chase the writers of her choice, and for much of her life she did just that." The founder in 1931 of the influential literary review *Sur,* Ocampo also ran a publishing company that provided Spanish translations of such literary giants as James Joyce, Andre Malraux, William Faulkner, and Vladimir Nabokov. Russell praises Meyer's book as a "decent, serious, well-researched survey, and it is graced by a discretion now rare among biographers."

Since her book on Ocampo, Meyer has provided English-speaking readers with access to other Latin American authors, in particular women writers. In 1983, she co-edited the two-volume *Contemporary Women Authors of Latin America,* which collects previously unpublished translations by forty female writers and provides in-depth profiles of the lives and work of over a dozen. According to Sonja Karsen in *World Literature Today,* the volumes, which cover both established and little-known writ-

ers, "fill an important gap that has existed in our knowledge of Latin American literature." In 1988, Meyer edited *Lives on the Line: The Testimony of Contemporary Latin American Writers,* a collection of first-hand accounts by writers which, according to Alberto Ciria in the Toronto *Globe and Mail,* show "the artists' involvement (or lack of it) in social and political issues together with considerations about their literary experiences." Ciria comments that *Lives on the Line* is "helpful in suggesting some of the roots of [Latin American] literature, some of the problems faced by those writers in their lives as well as in their crafts, and some of the painful consequences of repression, exile and 'interior exile' for Latin American intellectuals."

BIOGRAPHICAL/CRITICAL SOURCES:

PERIODICALS

Globe and Mail (Toronto), June 25, 1988.
Los Angeles Times Book Review, July 17, 1988.
New York Times, August 9, 1979.
World Literature Today, winter, 1985.

* * *

MEYERS, Carol L(yons) 1942-

PERSONAL: Born November 26, 1942, in Wilkes-Barre, Pa.; daughter of Harry J. (a dentist) and Irene (a dental assistant; maiden name, Winkler) Lyons; married Eric M. Meyers; children: Julie Kaete, Dina Elisa. *Education:* Wellesley College, B.A. (with honors), 1964; attended Hebrew Union College, Jerusalem, Israel, 1964, and Hebrew University of Jerusalem, 1964-65; Brandeis University, M.A., 1966, Ph.D., 1975.

ADDRESSES: Home—3202 Waterbury Dr., Durham, N.C. 27707. *Office*—Department of Religion, Duke University, P.O. Box 4735, Durham, N.C. 27706.

CAREER: Duke University, Durham, N.C., visiting lecturer, 1976-77, assistant professor, 1977-84, associate professor, 1984-89, professor of religion, 1990—, associate director of women's studies, 1985-90; instructor in continuing education, 1978-79. Oxford University, visiting scholar at Centre for Postgraduate Hebrew Studies and visiting research fellow at Queen Elizabeth House, both 1982-83. Lecturer at Hebrew Union College, Jerusalem, Israel, summers, 1973-74; instructor at Academy for Jewish Studies without Walls, 1974-78; University of North Carolina at Chapel Hill, lecturer, spring, 1975 and 1976-77, visiting assistant professor, autumn, 1979; vice-president of Albright Institute of Archaeological Research, 1982—.

Member of staff of Harvard University/Peabody Museum of Archaeology and Ethnology expedition to Hell Gap, Wyo., 1962, and University of Chicago excavations at Beit Yerah, Israel, 1963; volunteer worker at Tell Arad Excavations, 1964, and Masada Excavations, 1964-65; area supervisor of joint expedition to Meiron, 1972; Meiron Excavation Project, field archaeologist, 1974-78, associate editor, 1978—. Director, Joint Sepphoris Project, 1985—. American delegate to International Conference on Christians and Jews, 1976. Member of academic committee of World Jewish Congress Heritage Commission, 1978—. Consultant to WNET-TV, Near Eastern Pictorial Archives, National Geographic, Thames Television, The Jewish Museum, and the North Carolina Museum of Art. Member of board of directors of Triangle Jewish Federation, 1980-82, and Bethel Community.

MEMBER: American Academy of Religion, American Schools of Oriental Research (member of board of trustees, 1976-78), Archaeological Institute of America (state vice-president, 1976; state secretary-treasurer, 1984-85), Association of Jewish Studies, Catholic Biblical Association, National Women's Studies Association, Harvard Semitic Museum, Society of Biblical Literature, Society for Values in Higher Education, British School of Archaeology in Jerusalem, Israel Exploration Society, Palestine Explorations Society, Hadassah (member of regional board of directors, 1970-72).

AWARDS, HONORS: Thayer fellow at Albright Institute of Archaeological Research, 1975-76; Myrtle Wreath Award from Hadassah, 1981; fellow of National Endowment for the Humanities, 1982-83, 1990-91; Howard Foundation fellowship, 1985-86.

WRITINGS:

The Tabernacle Menorah: A Synthetic Study of a Symbol from the Biblical Cult, Scholars Press (Missoula, Mont.), 1976.
(With J. F. Strange and E. M. Meyers) *Excavations at Ancient Meiron, Upper Galilee, Israel, 1971-1972, 1974-1975, 1977,* American Schools of Oriental Research, 1981.
(Editor with M. O'Connor, and contributor) *The Word of the Lord Shall Go Forth,* American Schools of Oriental Research, 1983.
Jerusalem, Palestine, and the Jewish World, 200 B.C. to A.D. 200, Religion and Ethics Institute, 1983.
(With E. M. Meyers and Strange) *Ancient Synagogue at Gush Halav,* American Schools of Oriental Research, 1990.
(With E. M. Meyers) *Haggai, Zechariah, and Malachi,* Doubleday, 1987.
Discovering Eve: Ancient Israelite Women in Context, Oxford University Press, 1988.
(With E. M. Meyers and E. Netzer) *Sepphoris and its Mosaics,* Israel Exploration Society and Israel Museum, in press.

CONTRIBUTOR

Meyers and others, *Ancient Synagogue Excavations at Khirbet Shema', Upper Galilee, Israel, 1970-1972,* Duke University Press, 1976.
Norman K. Gottwald, editor, *The Bible and Liberation: Political and Social Hermeneutics,* Orbis, 1983.
Truman G. Madsen, editor, *The Temple in Antiquity,* Brigham Young University Press, 1984.
P. D. Miller and others, editors, *Ancient Israelite Religion,* Fortress Press, 1987.
Jean O'Barr, editor, *Women and a New Academy,* University of Wisconsin Press, 1989.
Barbara Lesko, editor, *Women's Earliest Records,* Scholars Press, 1989.

Contributor to *World Book Encyclopedia, Anchor Bible Dictionary, Harper's Bible Dictionary, Theological Dictionary of the Old Testament, Oxford Study Bible,* and *Interpreter's Dictionary of the Bible.* Contributor of articles and reviews to archaeology and biblical studies journals. Member of editorial committees of *Biblical Archaeology,* 1982—, American Schools of Oriental Research *Discussion* Series, 1978—, *Social World of Biblical Antiquity* series, 1983—, *Hebrew Annual Review,* 1987—, and *Semeia,* 1990; section editor for Oxford's *Encyclopedia of Archaeology in the Biblical World,* 1989.

WORK IN PROGRESS: Research on gender roles in the biblical world; archaeology of Nabratein, of Sapphoris; commentary on *Second Zechariah and Malachi.*

SIDELIGHTS: Carol L. Meyers told *CA:* "Archaeology for me is experimental investigation of the human past. I got hooked in college when I took part in a summer field project. I love the combined intellectual and physical challenge. I thrive on the strange mixture of mystery and tedium. I am absorbed by the enterprise of organizing the ordinary scraps of daily life into a pattern that helps reveal the roots of our Western culture, and I cherish the sense of continuity I feel with the ancients when I handle the artifacts of their existence. It is rare for a humanist to be able to pursue his discipline with both head and hand. In archaeology I can do that; I can absorb myself totally in the search for understanding. And one thing more, archaeology is a group effort. The excavation part, at least, brings people together in intense and difficult labors, striving towards a common goal. The social rewards of this shared quest contribute mightily to my passion for archaeological research and balance the solitude of the analytical and writing stages that must follow the field work."

*   *   *

MILLER, Charles D(avid)   1942-

PERSONAL: Born December 25, 1942, in Monroe, LA; son of Estelle (a clerk) Clegg; married Mary Sullivan (a pharmacist), December 19, 1971. *Education:* Fresno State College, B.A., 1964, M.A., 1965.

ADDRESSES: Home—Sacramento, CA. *Office*—Department of Mathematics, American River College, 4700 College Oak Dr., Sacramento, CA 95841.

CAREER: American River College, Sacramento, CA, professor of mathematics, 1966—.

MEMBER: Mathematical Association of America, American Mathematical Association of Two-Year Colleges, National Council of Teachers of Mathematics.

AWARDS, HONORS: First annual president's award, American Mathematical Association of Two-Year Colleges, 1976.

WRITINGS:

PUBLISHED BY SCOTT, FORESMAN

(With Vern E. Heeren) *Mathematical Ideas,* 1969, 5th edition, 1986.
(With Margaret L. Lial) *Beginning Algebra,* 1971, 5th edition, 1988.
(With Lial) *Intermediate Algebra: A Text Work-Book,* 1972, 5th edition, 1988.
College Algebra, 1973, 5th edition with Lial, 1989.
(With Stanley A. Salzman) *Business Mathematics,* 1973, 4th edition, 1987.
(With Lial) *Mathematics with Applications in the Management, Natural, and Social Sciences,* 1974, 4th edition, 1987.
(With Lial) *Essential Calculus,* 1975, 2nd edition published as *Essential Calculus: With Applications,* 1980, 4th edition published as *Calculus with Applications,* 1989, abridged version published as *Calculus with Applications: Brief Version,* 4th edition, 1989.
College Algebra and Precalculus Mathematics: Study Guide, 1975.
(With Heeren) *Mathematics: An Everyday Experience,* 1976, 2nd edition, 1980.
(With Lial) *Trigonometry,* 1976, 4th edition, 1989.
(With Salzman) *Mathematics for Business,* 1977, 3rd edition, 1986.
(With Lial) *Finite Mathematics: With Applications in Business, Biology, and Behavioral Sciences,* 1977, 4th edition, 1989.

(With Lial) *Algebra and Trigonometry,* 1978, 2nd edition, 1980, 4th edition published as *Algebra and Trigonometry: An Alternate Approach,* 1986.
(With Salzman) *Mathematics for Business in a Consumer Age,* 1978.
(With Lial) *Introductory Algebra: A Worktext,* 1979, 3rd edition published as *Introductory Algebra: A Text-Workbook,* 1987.
(With Salzman) *Business Mathematics: A Programmed Approach,* Book 1, 1980, Book 2, 1981.
(With Lial) *Intermediate Algebra: A Text-Workbook,* 1980, 3rd edition, 1987.
(With Lial) *Mathematics and Calculus with Applications,* 1980, 2nd edition, 1985.
(With Salzman) *Arithmetic: A Text-Workbook,* 1981.
(With Lial) *Fundamentals of College Algebra,* 1982, 2nd edition, 1986.
(With Lial) *Fundamentals of Trigonometry,* 1987.
(With Salzman) *Basic College Mathematics: A Text-Workbook,* 2nd edition, 1987.
(With Lial) *Algebra for College Students,* 1988.
(With Lial) *Finite Mathematics and Calculus with Applications,* 3rd edition, 1989.
(With Lial) *Precalculus,* 1989.*

* * *

MILLETT, Kate 1934-

PERSONAL: Given name Katherine Murray Millett; born September 14, 1934, in St. Paul, Minn.; daughter of James Albert (an engineer) and Helen (a teacher; maiden name, Feely) Millett; married Fumio Yoshimura (a sculptor), 1965 (divorced, 1985). *Education:* University of Minnesota, B.A. (magna cum laude), 1956; St. Hilda's College, Oxford University, M.A. (first class honors), 1958; Columbia University, Ph.D. (with distinction), 1970. *Politics:* "Left, feminist, liberationist."

ADDRESSES: Home—295 Bowery St., New York, N.Y. 10003. *Agent*—Georges Borchardt, 136 East 57th St., New York, N.Y.

CAREER: Sculptor, photographer, and painter, 1959—, with numerous exhibitions, including Minami Gallery, Tokyo, Japan, 1963, Judson Gallery, Greenwich Village, N.Y., 1967, and Los Angeles Women's Building, Los Angeles, Calif., 1977; writer, 1970—. Professor of English at University of North Carolina at Greensboro, 1958; kindergarten teacher in Harlem, N.Y., 1960-61; English teacher at Waseda University, Tokyo, 1961-63; professor of English and philosophy at Barnard College, New York, N.Y., 1964-69; professor of sociology, Bryn Mawr College, 1971; distinguished visiting professor at State College of Sacramento, 1973—.

MEMBER: National Organization of Women (chairperson of education committee, 1965-68), Congress of Racial Equality, Phi Beta Kappa.

WRITINGS:

Sexual Politics, Doubleday, 1970.
Prostitution Papers, Banc Books, 1971.
(And director) "Three Lives" (documentary film strip), released by Impact Films, 1971.
Flying (autobiography), Knopf, 1974.
Sita (autobiography), Farrar, Straus, 1977.
(Contributor) *Caterpillars: Journal Entries by 11 Women,* Epona, 1977.
The Basement, Simon & Schuster, 1980.
Going to Iran, Coward, McCann, 1981.
The Loony-Bin Trip, Simon & Schuster, 1990.

Contributor of essays to numerous magazines, including *Ms.*

SIDELIGHTS: Author-artist Kate Millett has been an acknowledged leader of the women's liberation movement since 1970, when her book *Sexual Politics* became a manifesto on the inequity of gender distinctions in Western culture. Millett, who has described herself as an "unknown sculptor" who was transformed into a "media nut in a matter of weeks," has approached the topics of feminism and homosexuality from scholarly, personal, and artistic perspectives. Her books, including *Flying, Sita,* and *The Basement,* explore the dilemmas and dangers of growing up female in America. According to Susan Paynter in the *Seattle Post-Intelligencer,* "National Leader" is a label that has stuck with Millett since *Sexual Politics* "won her a Ph.D. at Columbia University and the wrath of much of the nation." Paynter adds, however, that "overall social, not just sexual, change is Millett's concern, and she uses her teaching, writing and speaking talents to make her contribution."

Millett was born Katherine Murray Millett in St. Paul, Minnesota in 1934. When she was fourteen, her father left the family, and her mother was forced to look for work in order to support the household. Millett recalled in the New York *Post* that despite a college degree, her mother faced nearly insurmountable odds in the postwar job market, eventually finding only commission work selling insurance. "We went hungry," Millett said. "We lived on fear largely." Her family's difficult circumstances notwithstanding, Millett was able to attend the University of Minnesota, where she graduated in 1956 with *magna cum laude* and Phi Beta Kappa distinctions. She then went to Oxford University for two years of graduate study, earning honors grades there as well. A rebellious young woman who enjoyed flouting convention, Millett decided in 1959 that she wanted to pursue painting and sculpting. Supporting herself by teaching kindergarten in Harlem, New York, she went to work crafting art in a Bowery studio. In 1961 she went to Japan, where she taught English at Waseda University and studied sculpting. Her first show was in Tokyo at the Minami Gallery in 1963. While in Japan she met her future husband, Fumio Yoshimura, also a sculptor.

Returning to the United States in 1963, Millett became a lecturer in English at Barnard College, a division of Columbia University. She also became passionately involved with the burgeoning civil rights movement. First she joined the Congress of Racial Equality; then, in 1965, the National Organization for Women, where she served as chairman of the education committee. Her fiery speeches on women's liberation, abortion reform, and other progressive causes did not endear her to the administration of Barnard, and she was relieved of her duties in 1968. When she returned to teaching in 1969, she was hard at work on a doctoral thesis aimed at dissecting the way literature and political philosophy subtly conspire against sexual equality. The thesis, *Sexual Politics,* won her a Ph.D. "with distinction" from Columbia in 1970.

Few doctoral dissertations see publication outside of the academic community. Fewer still become bestsellers. Millett's *Sexual Politics* was just such a success, going through seven printings and selling 80,000 copies in its first year on the market. *New York Times Book Review* correspondent Jane Wilson describes the work as "an original and useful book . . . that imposed a moratorium on reiterated, dead-end feminist complaint against the male chauvinist pig in the street. Millett's oblique approach to the problem of women's liberation—concentrating on the incidence of sexism in literature, as opposed to life—made cooler and somewhat more productive discussion possible." The critic explains that *Sexual Politics* "also dramatically increased the number of potential participants in the ongoing seminar. Where once personal experience of sexist discrimination had been the paramount credential, it was now possible to enter the fray armed only with a working knowledge of the perfidy of D. H. Lawrence or Norman Mailer." Although some reviews of *Sexual Politics* have been decidedly hostile, most critics have found the book a reasonable and scholarly political analysis of the sex war. In the *Saturday Review,* Muriel Haynes writes: "[*Sexual Politics*] is an impressively informed, controlled polemic against the patriarchal order, launched in dead seriousness and high spirits, the expression of a young radical sensibility, nurtured by intellectual and social developments that could barely be glimpsed even twenty years ago. . . . *Sexual Politics* speaks in the newly emerging voice of the modern temper: self-realization lies in the embrace of process, the constant testing of creeds and social structures for their logic and their spiritually liberating content. Beyond patriarchy we can glimpse a world where the richness of human variety and choice among genuine alternatives will replace confinement by cultural stereotypes and institutions already put in question by the manifest problems and promise of the future. If men can read Kate Millett's book without prejudice, and it won't be easy, they will understand she is offering deliverance for them no less than for women."

Sexual Politics lifted Millett from the anonymity of the New York art world and ensconced her as a widely-interviewed spokesperson for the women's movement. Within months, Wilson observes, the author "came up hard against the fact that she could not control the image of herself that was projected by the press and on television. This being the case, and finding herself constitutionally unsuited to life as a talk-show exhibit, . . . why did she not simply quit the scene? Once recognized as an articulate member of the movement, she somehow ceased to be a free agent. In her uncomfortable new spokeswoman status she was urged on by her sisters to do her duty in speaking out on their behalf, while also being browbeaten and harassed for her arrogance and 'elitism' in presuming to do so." Millett's book *Flying,* published in 1974, details her struggle to remain self-aware, personally happy, and productive in the face of all the publicity. The central theme of that work, as well as that of her 1977 memoir *Sita,* is her avowed lesbianism and the effect her forthright admission had on her public and private roles. "The publicity that has attached to figures such as Kate Millett in America is unimaginable," notes Emma Tennant in the *Times Literary Supplement.* "Her greatest desire . . . was to reconstruct some sort of personality for herself after the glare of the cameras had begun to fade."

With the two biographical works behind her, Millett turned to a topic that had haunted her for over ten years—the brutal torture-death of an Indianapolis teenager named Sylvia Likens. *The Basement,* released in 1980, offers a chilling chronology of Sylvia's last months, from her point of view as well as her killers'. A *Ms.* reviewer contends that the book combines reporting, the various consciousnesses of those involved in the crime, and a feminist analysis of power "to follow human realities wherever they might lead." What emerges is "not just a story of an isolated incident, but of the powerlessness of children, the imposition of sexual shame on adolescent girls, [and] the ways in which a woman is used to break the spirit and the body of younger women." In the *New Republic,* Anne Tyler suggests that the fourteen years Millett spent pondering Sylvia's fate and how to write about it clearly enhance the book's value. "The writing is fully ripened, rich and dense, sometimes spilling out in torrents," Tyler states. "[*The Basement*] can stand alone, quite apart from

any feminist polemics. It is an important study of the problems of cruelty and submission, intensely felt and movingly written."

Millett now divides her time between her art studio in New York City and a seventy-five acre Christmas tree farm she owns north of Poughkeepsie. The farm also serves as a summer retreat for artists—Millett has described it in *Ms.* as "26,000 trees and the company of good women." Millett and her guests farm the land in the morning and spend the afternoon hours making prints, paintings, and sculptures, and writing. "For three years now," she writes, "the plan has worked splendidly. At last we are artists from one in the afternoon until dinner, seven solid hours to do our own work. I adore this arrangement because I have seven hours to print my silkscreen pictures every day. And these prints are, like the trees, a way to support the colony." Reflecting on her hectic years as a crusader for women's rights, Millett told *Life* magazine: "I hope I pointed out to men how truly inhuman it is for them to think of women the way they do, to treat them that way, to act that way toward them. All I was trying to say was, look, brother, I'm human."

BIOGRAPHICAL/CRITICAL SOURCES:

BOOKS

Authors in the News, Volume 1, Gale, 1976.
Millett, Kate, *Flying,* Knopf, 1974.
Millett, Kate, *Sita,* Farrar, Straus, 1977.
Smith, Sharon, *Women Who Make Movies,* Hopkinson & Blake, 1975.

PERIODICALS

Books and Bookmen, June, 1971.
Book World, November 22, 1970.
Canadian Forum, November/December, 1970.
Kirkus Reviews, March 1, 1977.
Life, September 4, 1970.
Los Angeles Times Book Review, September 16, 1979.
Mademoiselle, February, 1971.
Ms., February, 1981, May, 1988.
Nation, April 17, 1982.
National Review, August 30, 1974.
New Leader, December 14, 1970.
New Republic, August 1, 1970, July 6-13, 1974, July 7-14, 1979.
Newsweek, July 27, 1970, July 15, 1974.
New Yorker, August 9, 1974.
New York Times, July 20, 1970, August 5, 1970, August 6, 1970, August 27, 1970, September 6, 1970, December 18, 1970, November 5, 1971, May 13, 1977.
New York Times Book Review, September 6, 1970, June 23, 1974, May 29, 1977, September 9, 1979, May 16, 1982.
People, April 2, 1979.
Post (New York), August 1, 1970.
Ramparts, November, 1970.
Saturday Review, August 29, 1970, June 15, 1974, May 28, 1977.
Seattle Post-Intelligencer, March 4, 1973.
Time, August 31, 1970, December 14, 1970, July 26, 1971, July 1, 1974, May 9, 1977.
Times Literary Supplement, April 9, 1971, October 7, 1977.
Washington Post, July 30, 1970.
Washington Post Book World, January 8, 1978.

—*Sketch by Anne Janette Johnson*

MOHR, Nicholasa 1935-

PERSONAL: Born November 1, 1935, in New York, N.Y.; daughter of Pedro and Nicholasa (Rivera) Golpe; married Irwin Mohr (a clinical child psychologist), October 5, 1957 (deceased); children: David, Jason. *Education:* Attended Art Students League, 1953-56, Brooklyn Museum of Art School, 1959-66, and Pratt Center for Contemporary Printmaking, 1966-69.

ADDRESSES: Home—727 President St., Brooklyn, N.Y. 11215.

CAREER: Fine arts painter in New York, California, Mexico, and Puerto Rico, 1952-62; printmaker in New York, Mexico, and Puerto Rico, 1963—; teacher in art schools in New York and New Jersey, 1967—; art instructor at Art Center of Northern New Jersey, 1971-73; MacDowell Colony, Peterborough, N.H., writer in residence, 1972, 1974, and 1976; artist in residence with New York City public schools, 1973-74; State University of New York at Stony Brook, lecturer in Puerto Rican studies, 1977. Visiting lecturer in creative writing for various educator, librarian, student, and community groups, including University of Illinois Educational Alliance Program (Chicago), 1977, Cedar Rapids community schools (Iowa), 1978, writers in residence seminar, University of Wisconsin—Oshkosh, 1978, and Bridgeport, Connecticut, public schools, 1978. Head creative writer and co-producer of television series "Aqui y Ahora" (title means "Here and Now"). Member of New Jersey State Council on the Arts; member of board of trustees, and consultant, of Young Filmmakers Foundation; consultant on bilingual media training for Young Filmmakers/Video Arts.

MEMBER: Authors Guild, Authors League of America.

AWARDS, HONORS: Outstanding book award in juvenile fiction from *New York Times,* 1973, Jane Addams Children's Book Award from Jane Addams Peace Association, 1974, and citation of merit for book jacket design from Society of Illustrators, 1974, all for *Nilda;* outstanding book award in teenage fiction from *New York Times,* 1975, best book award from *School Library Journal,* 1975, and National Book Award finalist for "most distinguished book in children's literature," 1976, all for *El Bronx Remembered;* best book award from *School Library Journal,* best book award in young adult literature from American Library Association, and Notable Trade Book Award from joint committee of National Council for the Social Studies and Children's Book Council, all 1977, all for *In Nueva York; Nilda* selected as one of *School Library Journal*'s "Best of the Best 1966-78"; Notable Trade Book Award from joint committee of National Council for the Social Studies and Children's Book Council, 1980, and American Book Award from Before Columbus Foundation, 1981, both for *Felita;* commendation from the Legislature of the State of New York, 1986, for *Rituals of Survival: A Woman's Portfolio;* distinguished visiting professor at Queens College of the City University of New York, 1988-90; honorary doctorate of letters from State University of New York at Albany, 1989.

WRITINGS:

JUVENILE

(And illustrator) *Nilda* (novel), Harper, 1973, 2nd edition, Arte Publico, 1986.
(And illustrator) *El Bronx Remembered: A Novella and Stories,* Harper, 1975, 2nd edition, Arte Publico, 1986.
In Nueva York (short story collection), Dial, 1977.
(And illustrator) *Felita* (novel), Dial, 1979.
Going Home (novel; sequel to *Felita*), Dial, 1986.

OTHER

Rituals of Survival: A Women's Portfolio (adult fiction), Arte Publico, 1985.

Also author, with Ray Blanco, of "The Artist," a screenplay. Contributor of stories to textbooks and anthologies, including *The Ethnic American Woman: Problems, Protests, Lifestyles,* edited by Edith Blicksilver. Contributor of short stories to *Children's Digest, Scholastic Magazine,* and *Nuestro.* Member of board of contributing editors of *Nuestro.*

WORK IN PROGRESS: A novel; a screenplay.

SIDELIGHTS: Nicholasa Mohr is the author of young adult novels and short stories that offer what reviewers consider realistic and uncompromising portraits of life in New York's Puerto Rican barrio. In *Nilda,* Mohr's first novel, the author portrays a Puerto Rican girl as she grows from a child to a teenager, posing the question, "what does it feel like being poor and belonging to a despised minority?" according to *New York Times Book Review* contributor Marilyn Sachs, who found that although several books for young people have attempted to explore this condition, "few come up to 'Nilda' in describing the crushing humiliations of poverty and in peeling off the ethnic wrappings so that we can see the human child underneath." Another article in the *New York Times Book Review* notes that *Nilda* "provides a sharp, candid portrayal of what it means to be poor and to be called 'spics,' 'animals,' 'you people'—and worse."

Mohr's subsequent story collections, *El Bronx Remembered* and *In Nueva York,* have afforded similar insight into the lives of Hispanics in New York City. Sachs offers this assessment of *El Bronx Remembered:* "If there is any message . . . in these stories, any underlying theme, it is that life goes on. But Nicholasa Mohr is more interested in people than in messages." The reviewer notes that the stories are without "complicated symbolism . . . , trendy obscurity of meaning . . . hopeless despair or militant ethnicity. Her people endure because they are people." Sachs adds: "Some of them suffer, some of them die, a few of them fail, but most of the time they endure."

BIOGRAPHICAL/CRITICAL SOURCES:

BOOKS

Contemporary Literary Criticism, Volume 12, Gale, 1980.

PERIODICALS

Newsweek, March 4, 1974.
New York Times Book Review, November 4, 1973, November 10, 1974, November 16, 1975, May 22, 1977.

*   *   *

MOREY, Robert A(lbert) 1946-

PERSONAL: Born November 13, 1946, in Orlando, Fla.; son of Charles W., Jr. (in real estate) and Gloria (Salazar) Morey; married Anne V. Smadbeck, June 3, 1972; children: Ruthanne, John. *Education:* Covenant College, B.A., 1969; Westminster Theological Seminary, Philadelphia, Pa., M.Div., 1972, D.Min., 1979. *Politics:* Conservative.

ADDRESSES: Home and office—R.D. 1, Box 989, Shermans Dale, Pa. 17090.

CAREER: Ordained Baptist minister, 1974; Geneva House, New York, N.Y., founder and director, 1969-72; pastoral assistant at Baptist church in Essex Fells, N.J., 1972-74; Community Church, Shermans Dale, Pa., pastor, 1974-78; New Life Bible

Church, Duncannon, Pa., pastor, 1979—. Professor at Perry Bible Institute, 1982—; guest lecturer at colleges, universities, and seminaries; special lecturer in Taiwan, 1983.

MEMBER: Evangelical Theological Society, Spiritual Counterfeits Project, Perry County Christian Coalition (president, 1980—).

AWARDS, HONORS: The Dooyeweerdian Concept of the Word of God was listed among *Christianity Today*'s "best books of the year" in 1974; Best of the Good Books award, for *Worship Is All of Life;* Best Book of the Year nomination, for *Death and the Afterlife.*

WRITINGS:

The Bible and Drug Abuse, Presbyterian & Reformed, 1972, 2nd edition, 1973.
The Dooyeweerdian Concept of the Word of God, Presbyterian & Reformed, 1974.
A Christian Handbook for Defending the Faith, Presbyterian & Reformed, 1979, revised edition, 1981.
Is Sunday the Christian Sabbath?, Baptist Reformation Review, 1979.
An Examination of Exclusive Psalmody, New Life Publishers, 1979.
The Saving Work of Christ, Grace Abounding Ministries, 1979, revised edition, 1984.
The New Life Notebook, New Life Publishers, 1980.
How to Answer a Jehovah's Witness, Bethany House, 1980.
Reincarnation and Christianity, Bethany House, 1981.
Horoscopes and the Christian, Bethany House, 1981.
How to Answer a Mormon, Bethany House, 1984.
Worship Is All of Life, Christian Publications, 1984.
When Is It Right to Fight?, Bethany House, 1985.
The New Atheism and the Erosion of Freedom, Bethany House, 1986.
The Battle of the Gods, Crowne, 1989.
How to Keep Your Faith While at College, Crowne, 1989.
How to Keep Your Kids Drug Free, Crowne, 1989.
Here Is Your God, Crowne, 1989.
Introduction to Defending the Faith, Crowne, 1989.
Studies in the Atonement, Crowne, 1990.
A Discipleship Manual for Christians, two volumes, Crowne, 1990.
The Origin, History and Doctrines of Freemasonry, Crowne, 1990.

WORK IN PROGRESS: Fearing God; The Priesthood of the Believer; Healing in the Bible; Remedies to Satan's Devices; and *The Last Laugh* (a science fiction novel).

SIDELIGHTS: Robert A. Morey told *CA:* "There is a renewed interest in philosophy and theology among many young people today. Evangelical and Reformed seminaries are finding it difficult to accommodate thousands of new students each year. Religious books are outselling secular books two to one in many stores. People have found out that materialism is boring, as well as aesthetically impotent, and they are beginning to deal with the ultimate issues of life and death. As people begin to *think* and not just *feel,* their lives will deepen in richness.

"In the midst of Western decay, historic biblical Christianity is experiencing a renaissance. As a trained theologian, one of my tasks is to apply biblical truths to all areas of life, including contemporary issues such as drug abuse, the occult, death and the afterlife, and parapsychological research. I believe the Gospel of Jesus Christ is capable of holding its own in any philosophical or theological debate. The gates of hell itself cannot prevail against it. The gospel shall triumph in the end."

*   *   *

MORLAND, Dick
See HILL, Reginald (Charles)

*   *   *

MORROW, Bradford 1951-

PERSONAL: Born April 8, 1951, in Baltimore, MD; son of Ernest Dean (an employment manager) and Lois (Hoffman) Morrow; married Kathleen Anderson, April 23, 1975 (divorced, 1984). *Education:* Liceo Scientifico (Turin, Italy), graduated with honors, 1968; University of Colorado at Boulder, B.A. (summa cum laude), 1973; Yale University, M.A., 1974.

ADDRESSES: Home and office—Conjunctions, 33 West Ninth St., New York, NY 10011. *Agent*—Andrew Wylie, Wylie Aitken & Stone, Inc., 250 W. 57th St., 2106, New York, NY 10107.

CAREER: Professional jazz musician and music teacher, 1970-74; self-employed as a rare book archivist in California, 1974-81, and in New York, 1981-82; *Conjunctions* (literary magazine), New York City, editor, 1981—; Bard College, fellow, 1990—. Literary executor for the Kenneth Rexroth Trust, 1982—. Juror, Pennsylvania State Council on the Arts, 1986, and Open Voice awards, 1989. Poetry reader and lecturer at Brown University, Ohio State University, New York University, Bard College, State University of New York at Buffalo, Books & Co., Dixon Place, Simon's Rock of Bard College, Temple University, Manhattan Theatre Club, University of Colorado, Rhode Island School of Design, and Shippensburg University.

AWARDS, HONORS: CCLM Editor's award, 1984, and 1988; General Electric Foundation award, 1985; General Electric Foundation Younger Writer's award, 1988, for editing *Conjunctions;* New York Foundation for the Arts Grant in fiction, 1989.

MEMBER: PEN American Center, Contemporary Council of Literary Magazines, (advisory board, 1986—), New Writing Foundation, Inc. (president, 1985—).

WRITINGS:

(With Bernard Lafourcade) *A Bibliography of the Writings of Wyndham Lewis,* Black Sparrow Press, 1978.
(With Seamus Cooney) *A Bibliography of the Black Sparrow Press,* Black Sparrow Press, 1981.
Passing from the Provinces (poems), Cadmus Editions, 1981.
Posthumes (selected poems, 1977-82), Cadmus Editions, 1982.
Danae's Progress (poems), Cadmus Editions, 1982.
The Preferences (poems), Grenfell Press, 1983.
(Editor and author of introduction) *Selected Poems of Kenneth Rexroth,* New Directions, 1984.
After a Charme (poems), Grenfell Press, 1984.
(Editor and author of foreword) Kenneth Rexroth, *Classics Revisited* (Book-of-the-Month-Club alternate), New Directions, 1986.
(Editor) *Thirty-Six Poems of Tu Fu,* with etching by Brice Marden, Peter Blum Editions, 1987.
(Editor and author of introduction) *World Outside the Window: Selected Essays of Kenneth Rexroth,* New Directions, 1987.
Come Sunday (novel), Weidenfeld & Nicolson, 1988, Collier (New York), 1989.
(Editor and author of introduction) Rexroth, *More Classics Revisited,* New Directions, 1989.

A Bestiary, illustrations by Joel Shapiro, Eric Fischl, Kiki Smith, Richard Tuttle, Louisa Chase, and Gregory Amenoff, Grenfell Press, 1990.

(Editor with Patrick McGrath) *The New Gothic* (textbook anthology of contemporary Gothic fiction), Random House, 1991.

A Conjunctions Reader, Paris Review Editions, 1991.

Contributor of stories, poems, and essays to magazines, including *Sulfur, Sagetreib, Ark, Paris Review,* and *Washington Post.* Contributing editor of *Blast,* 1981.

MEDIA ADAPTATIONS: A musical version of *A Bestiary* was broadcast on WCKR radio, New York.

WORK IN PROGRESS: The Almanac Branch, a novel, 1991; *Quagg, or the Life and Adventures of a Boy* and *Roman's Box,* both novels.

SIDELIGHTS: Bradford Morrow told *CA:* "Since the earliest years of childhood I have experimented—for reasons which still escape me, though I've attributed it to everything from spiritual mandate to sheer ennui—with various art forms. I've been a musician, a painter, and a writer and have tried to be serious about 'perfecting' the craft of each; it has emerged that, of the three, what I handle best is words. I've tried playwriting, poetry, and fiction; it turns out that the latter is the best format for what I seem to know. There is no motivation which I can personally fathom beyond the actual initiating and then completing of a text.

"I am fluent in Italian, less so in French."

BIOGRAPHICAL/CRITICAL SOURCES:

PERIODICALS

Los Angeles Times, August 13, 1987, May 19, 1988.
Los Angeles Times Book Review, March 31, 1985.
New York Times Book Review, February 10, 1985.

*   *   *

MORTON, Carlos 1947-

PERSONAL: Born October 15, 1947, in Chicago, Ill.; son of Ciro (a non-commissioned army officer) and María Elena (López) Morton; married Azalea Marin, 1981; children: Seth Alexander Frack, Miguel Angel, Carlos Xuncú. *Education:* University of Texas, El Paso, B.A., 1975; University of California, San Diego, M.F.A., 1979; University of Texas at Austin, Ph.D., 1987.

ADDRESSES: Home—7931 Parral, El Paso, Tex. 79915. *Office*—Theatre Arts Department, University of California, Riverside, Calif. 92525.

CAREER: Essayist, poet, playwright, and actor, 1971—; *La Luz* magazine, Denver, Colo., associate editor, beginning 1975; University of California, Berkeley, lecturer, 1979-81; University of Texas at Austin, assistant instructor, 1981-85; University of California, Riverside, associate professor of theatre arts, 1990—. Instructor, Laredo Junior College, 1985-88. Playwright, San Francisco Mime Troupe, 1979-80. Artist-in-residence for California Arts Council and Texas Commission of the Arts.

WRITINGS:

White Heroin Winter (poetry), One Eye Press, 1971.
El Jardín (play), Quinto Sol, 1974.
Pancho Diablo (musical comedy), Tonatiuth International, 1976.
Las Many Muertes de Richard Morales, Tejidos, 1977.
The Many Deaths of Danny Rosales, and Other Plays, Arte Público Press, 1983.

Critical Responses to Zoot Suit and Corridos, University of Texas at El Paso, 1984.

Also author of unpublished plays, including: "The Foundling," "Desolation Car Lot," 1973, "Los Dorados," 1978, "Squash," 1979, "Rancho Hollywood," 1979, "Johnny Tenorio," 1983, "Malinche," 1985, "The Savior," 1986, (with Angel Vigil) "Cuentos," 1989, "The Miser of Mexico," 1989, and "At Risk," 1989. Contributor to *Drama Review, Nuestro, Caracol,* and other periodicals. Contributing editor, *Revista Chicano-Riqueña.*

SIDELIGHTS: Carlos Morton told *CA:* "I am working on recreating a viable reality for the colonized Chicano-Latino in the United States. Much of my work deals with stereotypes, both mythological and sociological, and my words are a mixture of English and Spanish.

"I am questioning stereotypes, especially in regards to the Latino here in the United States. For example, how could we explore the evolution of the infamous 'frito bandido' on stage? We would have to show the historical transition of the defeated soldier (Mexican) of the War of 1848 to that of the social Robin Hood bandits of the late 19th century (Juan Cortina and Jouquin Murieta) in Texas and California who carried on a type of guerrilla warfare against the Anglo colonizers in the Southwest. We would then have to switch to the Mexican Revolution (1910-1921) and the arrival of Pancho Villa and Emiliano Zapata who to the Mexican people are heros and standards of the Revolution, but who to the gringos were nothing more than 'bandits' and 'outlaws.' Throw in a dash of 'machismo' and a bit of the 'sleepy peon' and you got your modern day 'frito bandido.' "

*   *   *

MORTON, Desmond 1937-

PERSONAL: Born September 10, 1937, in Calgary, Alberta, Canada; son of R. E. A. (a brigadier general, Canadian Army) and Sylvia Cuyler (Frink) Morton; married Janet L. Smith (a political organizer), July 5, 1967; children: David, Marion. *Education:* College Militaire Royal de St.-Jean, Cadet, 1954-57; Royal Military College of Canada, B.A. (with honors), 1959; Oxford University, B.A., M.A.; London School of Economics and Political Science, Ph.D., 1969. *Politics:* New Democratic Party.

ADDRESSES: Home—362 Queen St. 5., Streetsville, Ontario, Canada L5M 1M2. *Office*—Erindale College, University of Toronto, Mississauga, Ontario, Canada L5L 1C6.

CAREER: Canadian Army, officer cadet and commissioned officer, 1954-64, rising to captain; New Democratic Party of Ontario, assistant secretary, 1964-68; University of Ottawa, Ottawa, Ontario, assistant professor, 1966-69; University of Toronto, Erindale College, Toronto, Ontario, assistant professor, 1969-71, associate professor, 1971-75, professor, 1975—, academic vice-principal, 1975-79, principal, 1986—. Chairman, Minister of National Defence's committee on service dependents and political activity, 1987; member, federal task force on military museums, 1990—. Consultant to Grolier, Ltd.

MEMBER: Canadian Historical Association, Royal Canadian Military Institute, Canadian Commission on Military History, Ontario Historical Society, Ontario Woodsworth Foundation, Peel Police-Race Relations Committee, Foodpath.

AWARDS, HONORS: Received Killam fellowship, 1983-84, 1984-85; fellow, Royal Society of Canada, 1983.

WRITINGS:

Ministers and Generals: Politics and the Canadian Militia, 1868-1904, University of Toronto Press, 1970.

The Last War Drum: The Northwest Campaign of 1885, Hakkert, 1972.

(Editor with R. H. Roy) *Telegrams of the Northwest Campaign, 1885,* Champlain Society, 1972.

Mayor Howland: The Citizens' Candidate, Hakkert, 1973.

The Canadian General: Sir William Otter, Hakkert, 1974.

N.D.P.: The Dream of Power, Hakkert, 1974.

Canada and War: A Political and Social History, Butterworth, 1981.

A Peculiar Kind of Politics, University of Toronto Press, 1982.

A Short History of Canada, Hurtig, 1983.

(With J. L. Granatstein) *Bloody Victory: Canadians and the D-Day Campaign, 1944,* Lester & Orpen Dennys, 1984.

Working People: An Illustrated History of the Canadian Labour Movement, Deneau, 1984, revised edition, Summerhill Press, 1990.

The Military History of Canada, Hurtig, 1985, revised edition, 1990.

The New Democrats, 1961-1986: The Politics of Change, Copp, Clark, Pitman, 1986.

(Contributor) John C. Anderson, Morley Gunderson and Allen Ponak, *Union-Management Relations in Canada,* Addison-Wesley, 1986.

(Contributor) R. C. Brown, editor, *The Illustrated History of Canada,* Lester & Orpen Dennys, 1986.

(With Glenn Wright) *Winning the Second Battle: Canadian Veterans and the Return to Civilian Life, 1915-1930,* University of Toronto Press, 1987.

(With Granatstein) *Marching to Armageddon: Canadians in the First World War,* Lester & Orpen Dennys, 1988.

(With Granatstein) *A Nation Forged in Fire: Canadians and the Second World War,* Lester & Orpen Dennys, 1989.

Contributor to *Encyclopedia Americana.* Contributor of articles to *Canadian Historical Review, Journal of Canadian Studies, Queen's Quarterly, Saturday Night, Canadian Journal of Higher Education, Revue d'historie de l'Amerique francaise, Ottawa Citizen,* and *Toronto Star.* Member of editorial board, *History and Social Science Teacher.*

WORK IN PROGRESS: Research on social history of Canadian soldiers, 1914-19; nationalism in Canada, 1867 to the present.

SIDELIGHTS: Desmond Morton told *CA:* "History, to me, is another word for experience. It is not a technique of prophecy nor an invitation to glorify or denigrate ancestors but an opportunity to understand more than our own narrow lives can comprehend. That search for experience has led me into unexplored areas like the development of veterans' policies but increasingly it makes me seek broad syntheses of the history of people I know best, in politics, the labour movement and, increasingly, in Canada's armed forces."

BIOGRAPHICAL/CRITICAL SOURCES:

PERIODICALS

Globe and Mail (Toronto), June 16, 1984; September 14, 1985; September 19, 1987; March 25, 1989; September 9, 1989.

*   *   *

MUJICA LAINEZ, Manuel 1910-1984

PERSONAL: Surname is pronounced "Moo-he-ka Ly-ness"; born September 11, 1910, in Buenos Aires, Argentina; died April 21, 1984, in Cruz Chica, Córdoba, Argentina; son of Manuel (a lawyer) and Lucía (Láinez) Mujica Farias; married Ana María de Alvear, November 5, 1936; children: Diego, Ana, Manuel Florencio. *Education:* Escuela Nacional de San Isidro, Buenos Aires, Argentina, B.A., 1928; studied law at University of Buenos Aires, 1928-30. *Politics:* Conservative. *Religion:* Roman Catholic.

ADDRESSES: *Home*—El Paraíso, 5178 Cruz Chica, Córdoba, Argentina; and O'Higgins 2150, Buenos Aires, Argentina.

CAREER: Novelist, short story writer, journalist, biographer, and art critic. *La Nación,* Buenos Aires, Argentina, staff member and critic, 1932-68; National Museum of Decorative Arts, Buenos Aires, secretary, 1935-45; Argentina Ministry of Foreign Relations, Buenos Aires, general director of cultural relations, 1955-58. *Military service:* Served in Argentine Navy; became commander.

MEMBER: Argentine Academy of Letters, National Academy of Fine Arts, Argentine Society of Writers (former vice-president).

AWARDS, HONORS: Argentine Society of Writers Grand Prize of Honor for Literature, 1955; Grand National Prize of Honor for Literature, 1962; First National Prize of Letters, 1963; John Kennedy Prize, 1964, for *Bomarzo;* Alberto Gerchunoff Prize; Forti Glori Prize.

WRITINGS:

NOVELS

Don Galaz de Buenos Aires (also see below), [Buenos Aires], 1938.

Los ídolos (also see below), Sudamericana (Buenos Aires), 1953.

La casa (also see below), Sudamericana, 1954, reprinted, 1984.

Los viajeros (also see below), Sudamericana, 1955, reprinted, 1984.

Invitados en El Paraíso (also see below), Sudamericana, 1957.

Bomarzo (also see below), Sudamericana, 1962, reprinted, 1979, English translation by Gregory Rabassa published under same title, Simon & Schuster, 1969.

El unicornio, Sudamericana, 1965, translation by Mary Fitton published as *The Wandering Unicorn,* Taplinger, 1982.

De milagros y de melancolías, Sudamericana, 1968.

Cecil (autobiographical), Sudamericana, 1972.

El laberinto, Sudamericana, 1974.

Sergio, Sudamericana, 1976.

Los cisnes, Sudamericana, 1977.

El escarabajo, Plaza & Janés, 1982.

Also author of *Hector Basaldúa,* 1956.

OTHER

Glosas castellanas (also see below), Librería y Editorial "La Facultad," Bernabé & Cia (Buenos Aires), 1936.

Miguel Cané (padre), C.E.P.A. (Buenos Aires), 1942.

Canto a Buenos Aires (long poem; also see below), Guillermo Kraft (Buenos Aires), 1943.

(Editor) *Poetas Argentinos en Montevideo,* Emecé (Buenos Aires), 1943.

Vida de Aniceto el Gallo (biography; also see below), Emecé, 1943, reprinted, Kapelusz (Buenos Aires), 1974.

(Author of introduction) Hilario Ascasubi, *Paulino Lucero,* Estrada (Buenos Aires), 1945.

Vida de Anastasio el Pollo (biography; also see below), Emecé, 1948.

(Author of introduction) Margarita Drago, *Figuras,* F. A. Colombo (Buenos Aires), 2nd edition, 1948.

Aquí vivieron: Historias de una quinta de San Isidro, 1583-1924 (short stories; also see below), Sudamericana, 1949, reprinted, 1979.

Misteriosa Buenos Aires (short stories; also see below), Sudamericana, 1951, reprinted, 1980.

(With Córdova Iturburu and Roger Pla) *Gambartes* (bilingual edition in Spanish and English), English translation by Patrick Orpen Dudgeon, Bonino's Gallery (Buenos Aires), 1954.

Victoria, 1884-1955, Bonino's Gallery, 1955.

Argentina, English translation by William McLeod Rivera, Pan American Union, 1961.

Russo (critical study), El Mangrullo (Buenos Aires), 1963.

(Compiler) *Lira romántica sudamericana,* new edition (Mujica Láinez was not associated with 1st edition), Emecé, 1964.

(Author of introduction) Oscar Hermes Villordo, *Oscar Hermes Villordo,* Culturales Argentinas (Buenos Aires), 1966.

Vidas del Gallo y el Pollo (biography), Centro Editor de América Latina, 1966.

"Bomarzo" (two-act opera; adapted by the author from his novel), music by Alberto Ginastera, first produced in Washington, D.C., May 19, 1967, published as *Cantata de Bomarzo: A Libretto,* with etchings by Luciano De Vita, Plain Wrapper Press (Verona), 1981.

Crónicas reales (short stories), Sudamericana, 1967.

(Contributor) *Cuentos recontados,* Tiempo Contemporáneo (Buenos Aires), 1968.

Cuentos de Buenos Aires (anthology), Huemul (Buenos Aires), 1972.

El viaje de los siete demonios, Sudamericana, 1974.

Antología general e introducción a la obra de Manuel Mujica Láinez, Felman (Madrid), 1976.

Letra e imagen de Buenos Aires, photographs by Aldo Sessa, Librería la Ciudad, 1977, reprinted as *Más letras e imágenes de Buenos Aires,* 1980.

Obras completas (title means "Complete Works"; contains *Glosas castellanas, Don Galaz de Buenos Aires, Miguel Cané (padre), Canto a Buenos Aires, Estampas de Buenos Aires, Cuatro poemas franceses, Vida de Aniceto el Gallo, Vida de Anastasio el Pollo, Cincuenta sonetos de Shakespeare, Aquí vivieron: Historias de una quinta de San Isidro, 1583-1924, Misteriosa Buenos Aires, Algunos poemas, 1940-1968, Los ídolos, La casa, Discurso en la Academia, Los viajeros, Miguel Carlos Victórica,* and *Invitados en El Paraíso*), Sudamericana, 1978.

El brazalete y otros cuentos (short stories), Sudamericana, 1978.

Los porteños (addresses, essays, and lectures), Librería la Ciudad, 1979.

El poeta perdido y otros relatos (short stories), edited and with an introduction by Jorge Cruz, Centro Editor de América Latina (Buenos Aires), 1981.

Jockey Club, un siglo, photographs by Sessa, Cosmogonías (Buenos Aires), 1982.

Páginas de Manuel Mujica Láinez, Celtia, 1982.

Nuestra Buenos Aires/Our Buenos Aires (bilingual edition in Spanish and English), photographs by Sessa, La Gaceta de Tucumán, 1982.

Placeres y fatigas de los viajes: Crónicas andariegas, Sudamericana, 1983.

Vida y gloria del Teatro Colón (in Spanish, with English, French, Italian, and German translations), photographs by Sessa, Cosmogonías (Buenos Aires), 1983.

Un novelista en el Museo del Prado, Sudamericana, 1984.

Cartas de Manuel Mujica Láinez (correspondences), collected by Oscar Monesterolo, Sudamericana, 1984.

SIDELIGHTS: During the 1960s and 1970s, a number of South American writers such as Gabriel García Márquez and Jorge Luis Borges came into international prominence. But another South American novelist, Manuel Mujica Láinez, remained a somewhat obscure author, despite his popularity in his native Argentina. Although critics recognized him for his skill as a writer, they also noticed that the works of Mujica Láinez were unique compared to other Hispanic writers of the time. As *New York Times Book Review* contributor David Gallagher remarked, Mujica Láinez's writing is "anachronistic" in that it is more reflective of "the modernist movement that flourished in the 1890's" than of more contemporary literature. John Walker also observed in *Queen's Quarterly* that "by style, temperament and cultural awareness, Mujica Láinez belongs to the Europeanized, cosmopolitan aristocracy of the nineteenth century."

This is not to say, however, that the novelist's works completely ignore the contemporary problems of Argentina. Like García Márquez, one of Mujica Láinez's common themes was that of decay within his country's society. The four novels, *Los ídolos, La casa, Los viajeros,* and *Invitados en El Paraíso,* which together form the "Saga of Buenos Aires" tetralogy, concern the events in Argentina after World War II that led to the decline of the elite sector of the population. Decay is also the theme of *De milagros y de melancolías,* a novel about the deterioration of a fictional city. This novel was compared to García Márquez's *One Hundred Years of Solitude,* since both combine fantasy, reality, and satire to relate the history of a fictional city. Yet *De milagros y de melancolías* "received meager attention," according to George O. Schanzer, a *Latin America Literary Review* critic who surmised that this lack of notice occurred because Mujica Láinez's book was eclipsed by the enormous success of *One Hundred Years of Solitude.* But Schanzer asserted that *De milagros y de melancolías* "deserves to be better known" because it "lampoons both foibles and traditions [of Latin America] . . . in a delightful, intelligently and artistically humorous way."

As Schanzer noted, *De milagros y de melancolías* was a "thematic homecoming" for its author. The novels that proceeded it, *Bomarzo,* Mujica Láinez's best-known work, and *The Wandering Unicorn,* have European settings and concern broader themes such as love, art, and human values. These two novels, the only ones by Mujica Láinez as yet to be translated into English, also share the device of immortal narrators who reflect back on the events of their lives centuries past with a contemporary perspective. In using this technique, the author's narrators have the advantage of employing modern interpretative techniques such as psychoanalysis to comment on the lives they led centuries before.

In *Bomarzo* Mujica Láinez's protagonist is a combination of the few known facts about Prince Pier Francesco Orsini, Duke of Bomarzo, who lived in sixteenth-century Italy, and the novelist's own imagination. Inspired by the bizarre stone statues of goddesses, demonic heads, and men being slain by elephants and giants that Duke Orsini ordered constructed fifty miles north of Rome, Mujica Láinez reconstructed the duke as an immortal, but psychologically tortured hunchback. The story is thus told by a present day Duke Orsini, who tells the reader how, despite his intelligence and otherwise handsome features, he was rejected by his family because of his hunchback. The stigmatization this deformity brings also leads to Duke Orsini's impotency. "Orsini's back is the burden of his genius," interpreted one *Time* critic. "It compels him to refine everything into art, including cruelty and murder." Developing this idea as the explanation for the statues at Bomarzo, Mujica Láinez "conveys not only the well-known creative energies of the Renaissance but its less understood anxieties as well," the *Time* writer concluded.

Once a best-seller in Argentina, *Bomarzo* "is a skillful novel," in Gallagher's opinion. However, the reviewer also felt that the novel was a "slender" achievement because it catered too much to the sensationalist ingredients of a best-seller, such as exotic settings, larger-than-life characters, and sexual themes. David William Foster similarly believed that *Bomarzo* was "unlikely ever to be considered a great novel," although it is "one of the most memorable—and unusual—works of Argentine fiction in recent years."

Some critics also had doubts about the literary merit of Mujica Láinez's *The Wandering Unicorn*. A tale of fantasy, this novel about the Middle Ages is filled with dragons, knights, fairies, and heroic battles woven into a tale told by the immortal fairy Melusine. She regales the reader with her story about the exploits of a knight named Aiol, with whom she is in love. However, because she is an invisible spirit to him her love goes unreturned, and the narration ends tragically when Aiol dies and Melusine is unable to join him in Heaven. Although the novel "appears to be just a brilliant and imaginative exercise in the recreation of places and times of far away and long ago," said Walker, acknowledging the objections of some reviewers, "[the author's] treatment of the eternal themes of life and death, love and hate, mortality and immortality, and the search for values and ideals . . . transcends the geographical and chronological barriers to penetrate to the heart of the human condition."

Despite their merits, a number of critics doubted that *Bomarzo* and *The Wandering Unicorn* aspired to be anything more than popular fiction. *New York Times Book Review* contributor Ronald De Feo, for example, opined that in these works Mujica Láinez "comes across as an author who plays with history and myth rather than one who employs them to make a unique and personal statement. And 'The Wandering Unicorn,' for all of its remarkable scholarship and imagery, seems more an overelaborate entertainment than a serious work of literature." However, Anne Collins held that these books should not be judged harshly, even though they dwell on more fantastic than real subjects. "In Mujica Láinez's case," Collins asserted in *Maclean's*, "wishful thinking is not so much an evasion as a recognition of all those functional things that can make us happy." But because his writing was meant more to entertain than provoke, even when set in contemporary Argentina, *Punch* reviewer Anthony Burgess correctly (and somewhat ironically) predicted before the author's death that "Láinez will never get the Nobel: he writes too well and there is no political protest in him."

BIOGRAPHICAL/CRITICAL SOURCES:

BOOKS

Contemporary Literary Criticism, Volume 31, Gale, 1985.

PERIODICALS

America, February 7, 1970.
Américas, February, 1972.
Books, October, 1970.
Hispania, March, 1974.
Latin American Literary Review, spring, 1973.
Los Angeles Times Book Review, June 26, 1983.
Maclean's, March 29, 1982.
New Republic, June 10, 1967.

New York Times Book Review, January 11, 1970, March 25, 1984.
Punch, April 27, 1983.
Queen's Quarterly, winter, 1983.
Time, December 12, 1969.
Washington Post, December 31, 1969.
World Literature Today, autumn, 1977.*

—*Sketch by Kevin S. Hile*

* * *

MULLER, John E.
　See FANTHORPE, R(obert) Lionel

* * *

MURDOCK, M(elinda) S(eabrooke) 1947-

PERSONAL: Born April 30, 1947, in Omaha, NB; daughter of A. Clark (an attorney) and Virginia (Seabrooke) Murdock. *Education:* William Woods College, B.A. (summa cum laude), 1969; University of Nebraska at Omaha, M.A., 1981.

ADDRESSES: Home and office—10427 North 53rd St., Omaha, NB 68152.

CAREER: Commercial artist, typesetter, layout artist, and copywriter, 1970—; has worked for University of Nebraska at Omaha, University of Nebraska at Lincoln, and Paragon Press, Omaha.

MEMBER: Nebraska Writers Guild, Nebraska Saddlebred Association, Nebraska Dressage Association, Phi Theta Kappa, Alpha Chi.

AWARDS, HONORS: Media award for art, Omicron, 1983; award from Contretemps, 1984, for best pen and ink drawing.

WRITINGS:

Web of the Romulans, Pocket Books, 1983.
Vendetta, Warner Books, 1987.
Dynteryx, Warner Books, 1988.
Arrival, TSR, 1989.
Rebellion 2456 A.D., TSR, 1989.
The Hammer of Mars, TSR, 1989.
Armageddon off Vesta, TSR, 1989.
Prime Squared, TSR, 1990.

WORK IN PROGRESS: A Sea of Troubles.

SIDELIGHTS: M. S. Murdock told *CA:* "My main interest as a writer is in telling a story and developing strong characters. I like action and adventure. I am also interested in theatre and film, and I am a Star Trek fan. My fascination with Star Trek's marvelous characters and Shakespearean breadth of subject matter lured me into writing. I am now firmly addicted to the profession and have enough work in my head to keep my busy until I am at least eighty."

* * *

MUSKE, Carol
　See MUSKE-DUKES, Carol (Anne)

* * *

MUSKE-DUKES, Carol (Anne) 1945-
　(Carol Muske)

PERSONAL: Born December 17, 1945, in St. Paul, MN; daughter of William Howard (in real estate) and Elizabeth (Kuchera)

Muske; married Edward Healton (a neurologist; divorced); married David C. Dukes (an actor), January 31, 1983; children: (second marriage) Annie Cameron, Shawn (stepchild). *Education:* Creighton University, B.A., 1967; San Francisco State College (now University), M.A., 1970. *Avocational interests:* Travel.

ADDRESSES: Home—Los Angeles, CA. *Office*—Department of English, University of Southern California, Los Angeles, CA 90089.

CAREER: Free Space (a creative writing program), Women's House of Detention, Riker's Island, NY, founder and director, 1972-73; Art Without Walls/Free Space (a writing/art program for women prisoners), New York City, director, 1974-82; University of Southern California, Los Angeles, lecturer in creative writing, 1985-89, assistant professor of English, 1989—. Instructor at New School for Social Research, New York University, Columbia University, University of California, Irvine, University of Virginia, University of Iowa. Jenny McKean Moore lecturer, George Washington University; lecturer to women's groups; poetry readings given around the country.

MEMBER: Authors Guild, Authors League of America, Poets and Writers, Poetry Society of America, PEN, National Writers Union, National Organization for Women, Los Angeles Library Association (member of board of advisors).

AWARDS, HONORS: Dylan Thomas Poetry Award, New School for Social Research, 1973, for poem, "Swansong;" Alice Fay Di Castagnola Award, Poetry Society, 1979; fellowships from John Simon Guggenheim Memorial Foundation, 1981, National Endowment for the Arts, 1984, and Ingram Merrill Foundation, 1988.

WRITINGS:

POETRY; UNDER NAME CAROL MUSKE

Camouflage, University of Pittsburgh Press, 1975.
Skylight, Doubleday, 1981.
Wyndmere, University of Pittsburgh Press, 1985.
Applause, University of Pittsburgh Press, 1989.

UNDER NAME CAROL MUSKE-DUKES

Dear Digby (novel), Viking, 1989.

OTHER

Contributor to books, including *Eating the Menu,* edited by B. E. Taylor, W. C. Brown, 1974; *The American Poetry Anthology,* edited by Daniel Halpern, Avon, 1975; also *The Pushcart Prize Anthology, Poet's Choice,* and *Woman Poet.* Contributor to periodicals, including *Ms., Oui, New Yorker, Field, Esquire, American Poetry Review, New York Times, New York Times Book Review, Los Angeles Times Book Review, Yale Review,* and *Village Voice.* Assistant editor of *Antaeus,* 1972—.

MEDIA ADAPTATIONS: The novel *Dear Digby* has been optioned by Orion Pictures for a feature film.

WORK IN PROGRESS: A fifth book of poems, titled *Red Trousseau;* and a second novel, tentatively titled *Mr. Kite.*

SIDELIGHTS: Carol Muske-Dukes has developed a reputation as a careful writer who balances rhetorical precision with her unique style of relating personal experience. Holly Prado, reviewing the poems in *Wyndmere* for the *Los Angeles Times,* terms Muske-Dukes' work "honed and consciously crafted," and points out that "she's discovered a way to work magic within the boundaries of technical achievement." For Prado, one of the ways Muske-Dukes works her "magic" is through a process of

intimation with her audience: "Her contemplation of experience is personal yet moves further, into the spiritual and philosophical; then it belongs not only to the poet but to all of us." In a critique of Muske-Dukes' latest book of poems, *Applause,* Wayne Koestenbaum is equally impressed with her method of identification ("she reaches past anecdote," he writes in the *New York Times Book Review*) and, although Koestenbaum suggests that her wordage gives "too little tonal pleasure," he admits "[Muske-Dukes] tempers glib candor with a recognition that language is inevitably impeded and enriched by all that resists easy saying."

In her first published departure from poetry, the 1989 novel *Dear Digby,* Muske-Dukes examines sexual politics, voyeurism, and neurosis through the cynical eyes of Willis Jane Digby, an editor of reader mail to the feminist magazine, *SIS.* "The social satire gets diluted by some of the more difficult aspects of the plot," claims Stephen McCauley reviewing the book for the *New York Times Book Review.* He does insist, however, that "[Muske-Dukes] has written a novel full of sharp insights and surprising images. . . . She is particularly good at writing amusing hit-and-run portraits." Linsey Abrams, in the *Los Angeles Times Book Review,* writes, "Muske-Dukes is a fine stylist. Her sculpted images and energetic prose make her storytelling vivid and compelling." With the same precision she composes her poetry, Muske-Dukes extracts real meaning from the images that words create. Abrams compares her technique to that found in Nathanael West's *Miss Lonelyhearts,* whose "brilliance . . . lies in its disturbing redefinition of an American vocabulary. What we had called Manifest Destiny, rugged individualism, freedom . . . was by another name, loneliness, alcoholism, and the edge of madness."

Carol Muske-Dukes told *CA:* "I published my first story at eleven years old and I wrote poetry from the time I was six—but I was fairly unconscious about the power of words and what it meant to have the power to use them until I came to New York in 1971. . . . I took poetry workshops and worked on a literary magazine and soon I began to hear the dialogue between craft and sentiment, form and feeling. I'm still at work on perfecting my ear, because by nature I'm an 'eye' poet—images come more easily to me, imagistic phrases litter my poems. I feel very close to painters, our processes are similar. The problem for me is 'hearing' what I write—that's why it was so refreshing for me to write *Dear Digby.* I found a voice, I trusted it, I let it speak. Beyond time and how time happens in a poem or a story, the relationship between eye and ear forms the difference for me between poetry and prose. In prose, the reader listens, the reader is being told a story, she hears, *then* sees—in poems, the reader *sees* aurally, the eye and ear become one.

"I have no answer as to why I write—I know that it makes the world clearer for me. Writing is the same process of enlightenment as reading, except it's more arrogant. A whole lot more arrogant. Because I read and write, I know much more now than I ever did about the nature of good and evil, about the nature of miracles, details, change. Words as used by writers and people who really pay attention to words are the only real order that exists for me in the world, the rest is all imposed by society or political morons, creators of electronic amnesias. I've learned the lessons of life by reading literature. I've learned about myself by writing."

She added: "My advice to aspiring writers is to read—and beyond that, don't take any advice. Especially from writers, they all lie."

BIOGRAPHICAL/CRITICAL SOURCES:

PERIODICALS

Chicago Tribune, May 23, 1989.
Los Angeles Times, April 6, 1989.
Los Angeles Times Book Review, December 1, 1985; May 21, 1989.
New York Times Book Review, November 3, 1985; April 16, 1989; September 24, 1989.
Washington Post, April 24, 1989.

N

NEAL, Marie Augusta 1921-

PERSONAL: Born June 22, 1921, in Brighton, Mass. *Education:* Emmanuel College, Boston, Mass., A.B., 1942; Boston College, A.M., 1953; Harvard University, Ph.D., 1963. *Religion:* Roman Catholic.

ADDRESSES: Office—Department of Sociology, Emmanuel College, 400 The Fenway, Boston, Mass. 02115.

CAREER: Member of Sisters of Notre Dame de Namur. High school teacher in diocese of Boston, Mass., 1946-53; Emmanuel College, Boston, instructor, 1953-63, professor of sociology, 1963—, chairperson of department, 1963-73, 1988-90. Lecturer, Cornell University, 1966, Boston College, summers, 1976-77, La Salle College, summer, 1978; visiting professor, University of California, Berkeley, 1968-69, Harvard University Divinity School, 1973-75, 1982-83. Consultant and research director, Conference of Major Religious Superiors of Women's Institutes in the United States, 1966-72. Area chairperson, Massachusetts Governor's Commission of the Status of Women, 1964-67; member, Archdiocesan Commission of Human Rights, Boston, 1966—, Catholic Commission on Intellectual and Cultural Affairs, 1973-76; director of research, South African Catholic Education Study, 1970-71. Member of advisory board, U.S. Catholic Conference of Bishops, 1969-72.

MEMBER: American Sociological Association, American Catholic Sociological Society (vice president and program chairperson, 1965-66), Association for the Sociology of Religion (member of executive council, 1962-64; vice president, 1965-66; president, 1971-72; member of council, 1979-81), Society for the Scientific Study of Religion (member of executive council, 1975-77; vice president, 1979-81; president, 1982-84), National Liturgical Conference (member of board, 1968-69), Association of Urban Sisters (member of advisory board, 1968-69), Massachusetts Sociological Association (vice president, 1972-73), Phi Beta Kappa, Kappa Gamma Pi.

AWARDS, HONORS: Isaac Haeker Award, Paulist Center (Boston), 1977; honorary degree, Our Lady of the Elms College, 1979; Pope John XXIII Award, College of New Rochelle, 1985; honorary Doctor of Laws degree, Notre Dame University, 1985; Distinguished Teaching Award, American Sociological Association, 1986; D.H.L., St. Michael's College, 1987; Ecumenical Award, Xavier University, 1988.

WRITINGS:

Values and Interests in Social Change, Prentice-Hall, 1965.
Sociotheology of Letting Go: The Role of the First World Church Facing Third World Peoples, Paulist Press, 1977.
Catholic Sisters in Transition: From the 1960s to the 1980s, Michael Glazier, 1984.
The Just Demands for the Poor, Paulist Press, 1987.
From Nuns to Sisters: An Expanding Vocation, Twenty-Third, 1990.

CONTRIBUTOR

Sister Maryellen Muckenhirn, editor, *The Changing Sister,* Fides, 1965.
L. W. Lizbetak, editor, *The Church in the Changing City,* Divine Word Publications, 1966.
Eugene Grollmes, editor, *Vows but No Walls,* B. Herder, 1968.
Muckenhirn, editor, *The New Nuns,* New American Library, 1968.
Robert N. Bellah and William G. McLaughlin, editors, *Religion in America,* Volume 12, Houghton, 1968.
William C. Bier, editor, *Women in Modern Life,* Fordham University Press, 1968.
Thomas M. McFadden, editor, *American Theological Perspective,* Seabury, 1976.
Anne Marie Gargner, editor, *Women and Catholic Priesthood,* Paulist Press/Newman, 1976.
F. Bockle and J. Pohler, editors, *Sexuality in Contemporary Catholicism,* Seabury, 1976.
Harry M. Johnson, editor *Religious Change and Continuity,* Jossey Bass, 1979.
Michael Glazier, editor, *Where We Are: American Catholics in the 1980s,* Michael Glazier, 1985.
D. M. Johnson, editor, *Justice and Peace Education: Models for University Faculty,* Paulist Press, 1986.
David G. Gil and Eva A. Gil, editors, *The Future of Work: A Conference of the Center for Social Change Practice and Theory,* Schenkman, 1987.
Alice E. Evans and Robert A. Evans, *Pedagogies for the Non-Poor,* Orbis Books, 1987.
Marc H. Ellis and Otto Maduro, editors, *The Future of Liberation Theology: Essays in Honor of Gustavo Gutierrez,* Orbis Books, 1989.
Edward L. Cleary, *Born of the Poor,* Notre Dame University Press, 1990.

OTHER

Contributor to *New Catholic Encyclopedia* and to professional journals. Associate editor, *Sociological Analysis,* 1964-74; contributing editor, "Sisters' Forum," in *National Catholic Reporter,* 1964-66.

WORK IN PROGRESS: Research on women's religious institutes.

SIDELIGHTS: Sister Marie Augusta Neal once told *CA:* "Essay writing inserts itself with an urgency into my on-going systematic research on the changing structures of religious orders of women, that is my major monography preoccupation. The essays address the wider issues of the changing structures of modern society in world perspective but especially how the moral quality of American life affects the life chances of third world people."

* * *

NEEF, Elton T.
See FANTHORPE, R(obert) Lionel

* * *

NEWBY, P(ercy) H(oward)　1918-

PERSONAL: Born June 25, 1918, in Crowborough, Sussex, England; son of Percy and Isabel Clutson (Bryant) Newby; married Joan Thompson, 1945; children: Sarah Jane, Katharine Charlotte. *Education:* Attended St. Paul's College, Cheltenham, England, 1936-38.

ADDRESSES: Home—Garsington House, Garsington, Oxford OX9 9AB, England. *Agent*—David Higham Associates, 5-8 Lower John St., London W1R 4HA, England.

CAREER: Fouad I University, Cairo, Egypt, lecturer in English literature, 1942-46; free-lance novelist, 1946-49; British Broadcasting Corp., London, England, producer in Talks Department, 1949-58, chief of Third Programme (now Radio Three), 1958-71, director of programs, 1971-75, managing director of radio, 1975-78. Chairman, English Stage Company, 1978-85. *Military service:* British Army, Royal Army Medical Corps, 1939-42; served in France and Egypt.

MEMBER: Society of Authors, Royal Society of Literature (fellow).

AWARDS, HONORS: Atlantic Award, Rockefeller Foundation, 1946; Somerset Maugham Prize, 1948, for *A Journey to the Interior;* Smith-Mundt fellowship, 1952; Yorkshire Post Fiction Award, 1968; Booker Prize, 1969, for *Something to Answer For;* Commander of the Order of the British Empire, 1972.

WRITINGS:

NOVELS

A Journey to the Interior, J. Cape, 1945, Doubleday, 1946.
Spirit of Jem (juvenile), illustrated by Keith Vaughan, foreword by Maia Wojciechowska, Lehmann, 1947, Delacorte, 1967.
Agents and Witnesses, Doubleday, 1947.
Mariner Dances, J. Cape, 1948.
Snow Pasture, J. Cape, 1949.
The Loot Runners (juvenile), Lehman, 1949, Macdonald, 1951.
The Young May Moon, J. Cape, 1950, Knopf, 1951.
A Season in England, J. Cape, 1951, Knopf, 1952.
A Step to Silence, J. Cape, 1952.
The Retreat, Knopf, 1953.
The Picnic at Sakkara, Knopf, 1955.

Revolution and Roses, Knopf, 1957.
A Guest and His Going, J. Cape, 1959.
The Barbary Light, Faber, 1962, Lippincott, 1964.
One of the Founders, Lippincott, 1965, new edition, Chivers, 1987.
Something to Answer For, Faber, 1968, Lippincott, 1969.
A Lot to Ask, Faber, 1973.
Kith, Little, Brown, 1977.
Feelings Have Changed, Faber, 1981.
Leaning in the Wind, Faber, 1986, Beaufort Books, 1987.

OTHER

(Author of introduction) A. W. Kinglake, *Eothen,* Lehmann, 1948.
Maria Edgeworth (criticism), A. Swallow, 1950, reprinted, Norwood, 1975.
The Novel, 1945-50, Longmans, Green, for British Council, 1951, reprinted, Richard West, 1978.
(Editor) *A Plain and Literal Translation of the Arabian Knight's Entertainments, Now Entitled "The Book of the Thousand and One Knights,"* translated by Richard Francis Burton, illustrated by W. M. Cuthill, Arthur Barker, 1950, published as *Tales from the Arabian Knights,* Pocket Books, c. 1951, reprinted, Washington Square, 1967.
Ten Miles from Anywhere, and Other Stories, J. Cape, 1958.
The Egypt Story: Its Art, Its Monuments, Its People, Its History, photographs by Fred Maroon, Abbeville Press, 1979.
The Warrior Pharaohs: The Rise and Fall of the Egyptian Empire, Faber, 1980.
Saladin in His Times (biography), Faber, 1983.

Former book reviewer for *Listener* and *New Statesman and Nation.*

SIDELIGHTS: When P. H. Newby first won the Booker Prize in 1969 for *Something to Answer For,* it was somewhat of a surprise to the critical community, which expected either Muriel Spark or Iris Murdoch to be awarded Britain's most remunerative literary prize. Newby had already written over a dozen novels at that time, and had been awarded the Atlantic Award in 1946 and the Somerset Maugham Prize in 1948 for his first novel, *A Journey to the Interior;* yet he was then, as he is now, a relatively unknown author. As Stanley Poss explains in *Critique: Studies in Modern Fiction,* "Newby has had neither a popular nor a critical success . . . because he puzzles the expectations of both camps. Enigmatic to the layman, 'traditional' (in his reliance on tangled plots) to the expert, he is truly, as a 1962 [*Times Literary Supplement*] article has it, a 'Novelist On His Own.' " Nevertheless, the author has become one of the most respected writers of his generation. In a *Dictionary of Literary Biography* article, E. C. Bufkin calls Newby "one of the most distinguished of the English novelists who began their careers immediately following World War II. . . . His sizeable body of work is notable for seriousness of themes, mastery of fictional techniques, and a style which—at once precise and suggestive, graceful and powerful—is capable of the subtlest as well as the broadest effects."

A thirty-year veteran producer and director for the British Broadcasting Corp., Newby calls himself a "weekend novelist," according to one *New York Times Book Review* writer; yet he has still managed to produce a steady stream of publications, most of which were written during the 1950s and 1960s. "[But] there is no link between the BBC and my writing really," the novelist tells Bolivar Le Franc in a *Books and Bookmen* interview. What did have a profound influence on Newby's writing was his four-year stay at Fouad I University in Cairo, Egypt, as a lecturer in

English literature during World War II. "The central experience in my life was living in Egypt," Newby told *CA,* "where looking at the world through non-European and non-Christian eyes, my imagination was stimulated in a way it would not have been if I had remained in England." Although he has composed several novels that involve only English subjects, Newby reveals to Le Franc: "It's only when I detach myself from the British scene and in some way bring my Middle East experience into the novel I really think the thing comes alive."

From his first novel, *A Journey to the Interior,* to his more recent *Leaning in the Wind,* Newby has repeatedly returned to the subject of the Third World, its people, and its customs. In addition to his novels, he has written three nonfiction works about Egypt and the Middle East: *The Egypt Story: Its Art, Its Monuments, Its People, Its History, The Warrior Pharaohs: The Rise and Fall of the Egyptian Empire,* and *Saladin in His Time,* a biography about the Crusades-period Moslem leader. Newby's novels deal with the themes of appearance versus reality, misunderstanding and reconciliation, and the relationship between knowledge and innocence. Within these themes is the central idea in the author's work that "we never fully understand either our own behavior or that of other people," says G. S. Fraser in his *P. H. Newby.* Fraser concludes that the novelist's portrayal of this idea "is one of Newby's greatest gifts."

Several critics have divided Newby's fiction into different categories. Fraser classifies them as "early romanticism, comedy, and compassionate realism," while Poss distinguishes only two groups: "political comedies" and "romances." Both Fraser and Poss, however, consider the novelist's earlier works to be romances. The first of these books, *A Journey to the Interior,* is set in a fictional Middle East sultanate. Roger Winter, the recently widowed protagonist, travels to an Arabian country ostensibly to recover from typhoid. Actually, he is going on "a quest for health and life on both the physical and spiritual planes," writes Bufkin. While there, Winter falls in love with a woman named Nellie, who reminds him of his wife. The other half of the novel involves Winter's quest to find two men who have disappeared in the desert. Although the fate of these men remains a mystery by the end of the book, Winter's experiences while searching for them help him to understand himself and accept Nellie for who she is, rather than as a mere reflection of his dead wife.

"The qualities that P. H. Newby demonstrates in his first novel . . . ," asserts Frederick R. Karl in his 1962 book, *A Reader's Guide to the Contemporary English Novel,* "are characteristic of all his serious fiction: the discovery of a man's self through a journey or quest." Earlier novels by Newby also demonstrate what Fraser calls a "hallucinatory vividness," and, according to Poss, reveal the author's interest in the "myth-making part of writing." The central theme of several of these books, *Mariner Dances, The Snow Pasture,* and *The Young May Moon,* is concerned with the alienation and reconciliation between people. In Fraser's view, these works have several redeeming features, such as the "delicacy of natural description" in *The Snow Pasture,* and Newby's "surer hand . . . [in] getting inside a boy's mind" in *The Young May Moon;* but some reviewers like Karl believe they "lack vitality and intensity."

With *A Season in England,* Newby once again explores the theme of self-knowledge, and several reviewers have compared it to *A Journey to the Interior* because of this similarity. One difference, however, is that the protagonist, Tom Passmore, journeys from Egypt to England, rather than the other way around. Poss also notes that the tone of *A Season in England* "suggests that Newby's earlier beliefs in the possibilities of renewal of the

psyche have diminished somewhat, or at least . . . he has come to believe that these possibilities do not always assert themselves in so splendid, perhaps even theatrical, a manner as in *A Journey to the Interior.*" *A Season in England* and the two novels that followed, *A Step to Silence* and *The Retreat,* "mark, though not dramatically, a steady progress in Newby's art," Fraser avers. "They handle tense and unpredictable situations with a new assurance."

Actually two parts of the same work, *A Step to Silence* and *The Retreat* contain a "darkness and exhaustion, madness and humorlessness not found elsewhere in the Newby canon," according to Bufkin. They also "display a firmer sense of moral pattern than Newby had so far achieved" at that time, says Fraser. Using the backdrop of the chaotic years before and during World War II, Newby presents a story of an equally chaotic relationship between an Englishman named Oliver Knight, his irrational Egyptian friend, Hesketh, and the two women they love. *The Retreat* ends tragically with the death of Hesketh's wife. Because Knight was alone with her when she died, Hesketh decides to write a letter confessing to the "murder" so that his friend would not be blamed; and he then commits suicide. Although the death of Hesketh's wife was due to natural causes, Knight decides to let himself be arrested for her murder. Together, writes Fraser, these two books present a recurring riddle in Newby's books in which "the madman protect[s] the almost excessively sane man and . . . the sane man . . . insist[s] on taking his own punishment."

After *The Retreat,* Newby's novels return to a lighter vein, though their subjects are still serious in nature. As Poss explains, the political comedies that followed *The Retreat* "turn on the 'Forsterian' question of how far can you go in getting to know a people whose class, race, religion, or whatever differ radically from your own." Other critics have noticed this influence as well, and Newby acknowledges this in his *Books and Bookmen* interview. "[*The Picnic at Sakkara*] owed a great deal to [E. M.] Forster's *A Passage to India,*" the novelist tells Le Franc. "Indeed," Newby continues, "Forster's attitude to the East is something I suppose has made a deep impression on me." However, one trait of Newby's work that distinguishes him from Forster is his use of humor when describing the clashes between cultures. It is a "sympathetic" type of comedy, though, says Fraser, who notes that Newby "is temperamentally incapable of writing corrective comedy, or satire."

The Picnic at Sakkara, Revolution and Roses, and *A Guest and His Going* comprise a trilogy that critics like Bufkin consider to demonstrate some of "Newby's best work, and most endearing." Setting these books during the last years of Farouk I's reign in Egypt, the Nasser revolution, and the Suez Canal crisis, the author brings together English and Egyptian characters to illuminate the differences in cultures. The two most prominent people in this trilogy, English professor Edgar Perry and his student, Muawiya Khaslat, are central to the first and third books, while *Revolution and Roses* focuses on the relationship between an English journalist and the Egyptian nationalist who courts her. Several critics feel, as Fraser does, that this second volume "is a much slighter work" than the other books in the trilogy. *The Picnic at Sakkara,* however, "is a masterly mixture generously flavored with irony," according to Bufkin, while V. S. Naipaul remarks in a *New Statesman* review that Newby "is wonderfully and intelligently inventive" in *A Guest and His Going.*

Contrasting the comical character of Muawiya, who is reminiscent of Hesketh in *A Step to Silence* and *The Retreat,* with the naive and high-principled Perry, Newby illustrates a fundamental difference in philosophy between East and West. Westerners tend to believe that the universe is unknowable, asserts the novelist, and, therefore, in an attempt to make sense of the world, they invent "little illusions of order," as *Twentieth Century Literature* contributor Francis X. Mathews phrases it. Mathews continues: "The Oriental, on the other hand, thinks he knows [about the world]. . . . His fantasy, which Newby terms 'the supreme Oriental luxury,' is founded on an instinctive acceptance of the improbable and the contradictory." With these contradictory views embodied in his characters, Newby adds a background set in a politically turbulent time to produce a "comic conflict between a fantastic society and fantastic individuals," says Mathews. "But beneath the laughter," the reviewer later adds, "is the same serious theme of the failure to connect," both on the personal and international level. *A Guest and His Going* ends with Perry's ultimate failure to communicate with Muawiya. But despite this defeat, Mathews concludes that "he has at least come to recognize his illusions for what they are."

Something to Answer For, also a political novel that deals with the theme of illusions, has "something of the vivid colour, violence, and mysteriousness of Newby's first two novels," reflects Fraser. A number of critics consider *Something to Answer For* to be the novelist's finest work to date. *New Yorker* contributor Wilfred Sheed calls the book "a first-rate novel about a major political subject." And a *Time* reviewer asserts: "*Something to Answer For* finds Newby at his often brilliant but racking best. If the reader does not mind getting his lumps, he will also come in for a fair share of illumination."

Something to Answer For is set in Egypt during the 1956 Suez Canal crisis. Jack Townrow is a small-time crook who has come to Port Said from Britain in order to take advantage of a widow who has recently received an inheritance. Being English, Townrow is a character who assumes, "as many English people do," according to Newby in a quote from Bufkin's essay, "that by and large the society he lives in is governed by good forces—forces that are operating wisely and well." But the struggle for control of the Suez Canal between the Egyptians, British, and French forces Townrow to realize that he is no more corrupt than his government. This, in turn, convinces him to reconsider his own conduct, and as a result he redefines his sense of morals.

Some critics, like *London Magazine* writer Michael Wilding, find this change of heart "a little unconvincing." Wilding believes that "a certain schematization of the moral positions ultimately limits *Something to Answer For.*" But Sheed feels that the juxtaposition between Townrow's conscience and the political issues at hand is well conceived. "This marshalling of all the resources of the human psyche to produce a universal historical consciousness is an enterprise worthy of Joyce," the reviewer observes. the skill with which the novelist combines issues in the political world with the problems of private morality prompts Bufkin to declare that *Something to Answer For* is "Newby's masterpiece: the richest in conception, the widest in scope, the most technically innovative, and the most assured of his novels."

With the exception of *Something to Answer For* and *A Lot to Ask,* a novel which, according to D. J. Enright in *Listener* "reads like a relatively austere replay" of its predecessor, most of Newby's more recent novels have a more comical tone reminiscent of *The Picnic at Sakkara.* Indeed, *One of the Founders* is "pure farce," attests Fraser. But Newby's other novels written after the 1960s are familiar combinations of serious themes with humorous overtones. For example, *Kith,* the story of a young man who falls in love with his uncle's beautiful Egyptian wife, is a "wise, sad, and very funny novel," according to *New York Times Book Re-*

view contributor Sheldon Frank, who also calls the book "hilariously bleak."

Similarly, *Feelings Have Changed* is described in a *Times Literary Supplement* article by Alan Brownjohn as "a novel which is as carefully woven as it is mordantly witty." In this book, Newby ambitiously addresses the question of the meaning of life in, as *Spectator* contributor James Lasdun phrases it, "an elaborate pattern of coincidences involving [a] radio play, a priest, the two central couples, and the temples at Abu Simbel in Egypt, with the purpose of showing that there is a rightness in the disposition in life, despite all its hardships." Although this blend of elements makes for an "absorbing book," as London *Times* critic Andrew Sinclair labels it, some critics feel that *Feelings Have Changed* is somewhat flawed. Lasdun, for example, asserts that there "is a certain lack of continuity between the very ordinary characters and the very extraordinary moral vision they are made to illuminate."

Leaning in the Wind has also received mixed reviews from critics. Some reviewers have complained that this novel, involving forgery, adultery, and 1970s African politics, has an unfocused plot. "It meanders without apparent purpose through a series of coincidences," claims *Times* contributor Isabel Raphael. In a completely contradictory *Library Journal* review, however, Bryan Aubrey holds that *Leaning in the Wind* has a "skillfully handled, highly ingenious plot." Furthermore, a *Publishers Weekly* writer concludes that the novel is "a story of fundamental human relationships, rendered with humor, sympathy, and feeling."

In taking all of the novelist's fictional works into consideration, Fraser concludes: "The final picture of life that emerges . . . from Newby's novels is that of life as rich, funny, but terrifyingly uncertain." It is this view of life which takes precedence over any other message, political or otherwise, in the author's writing. As Newby explains to Le Franc, "We're terribly vulnerable, weak animals in a cold and hostile universe. I mean, this is my view of life. Life is precarious. Life is hell and this is much more fundamental about a man than any thought about the particular social status he might happen to occupy." But despite life's seriousness, there is still room for levity. "Ever since *Picnic at Sakkara,*" Newby told *CA,* "I have tried to handle potentially tragic material in a light, even comic way. I have been called bleak by some who think they are paying me a compliment. I do not feel at all that bleak; I am just trying to be realistic about the sometimes comfortless world we live in, and doing so, I hope, with charity."

BIOGRAPHICAL/CRITICAL SOURCES:

BOOKS

Bufkin, E. C., *P. H. Newby,* Twayne, 1975.
Contemporary Literary Criticism, Gale, Volume 2, 1974, Volume 13, 1980.
Dictionary of Literary Biography, Volume 15: *British Novelists, 1930-1959,* Gale, 1983.
Fraser, G. S., *P. H. Newby,* Longman, 1974.
Karl, Frederick R., *A Reader's Guide to the Contemporary English Novel,* Farrar, Straus, 1962.
T.L.S. 1962: Essays and Reviews from The Times Literary Supplement, Oxford University Press, 1963.

PERIODICALS

Best Sellers, April 15, 1969.
Books and Bookmen, January, 1969, June, 1969, July, 1969.
Book Week, July 2, 1967.
Book World, June 29, 1969.

British Book News, January, 1987.
Christian Science Monitor, August 3, 1967, June 5, 1969.
Critique: Studies in Modern Fiction, Volume 8, number 1, 1965, Volume 12, number 1, 1970.
Globe and Mail (Toronto), April 18, 1987.
Kirkus Reviews, February 1, 1988.
Library Journal, March 15, 1988.
Listener, November 14, 1968, May 3, 1973, September 25, 1980.
London Magazine, December, 1965, February, 1969.
London Review of Books, April 18, 1985.
Nation, April 28, 1969.
New Statesman, June 20, 1959, April 25, 1969.
Newsweek, August 15, 1977.
New Yorker, September 6, 1969.
New York Review of Books, June 5, 1969.
New York Times, April 19, 1953, August 10, 1977.
New York Times Book Review, April 19, 1953, May 11, 1969, August 7, 1977, August 26, 1984.
Observer, November 2, 1986.
Publishers Weekly, January 22, 1988.
Spectator, November 15, 1968, November 7, 1981, January 7, 1984.
Texas Studies in Literature and Language, spring, 1970.
Time, April 18, 1969.
Times (London), October 8, 1981, November 6, 1986.
Times Literary Supplement, April 6, 1962, December 4, 1969, May 11, 1973, April 8, 1977, October 9, 1981, March 9, 1984, December 12, 1986.
Twentieth Century Literature, April, 1968.
Wilson Library Bulletin, March, 1953.

—*Sketch by Kevin S. Hile*

*   *   *

NIGGLI, Josefina (Maria) 1910-

PERSONAL: Born July 13, 1910, in Monterrey, Neuvo Leon, Mexico; United States citizen; daughter of Frederick Ferdinand (a cement manufacturer) and Goldie (Morgan) Niggli. *Education:* Incarnate World College, B.A., 1931; University of North Carolina, M.A., 1937; attended Old Vic Theatre School, 1955. *Avocational interests* Color photography.

ADDRESSES: Office—Department of Speech and Theatre Arts, Western Carolina University, Cullowhee, NC 28723. *Agent*—Ashley Famous Agency, Inc., 1301 Avenue of the Americas, New York, NY 10019.

CAREER: University of North Carolina, Chapel Hill, instructor in radio, 1942-44; Metro-Goldwyn-Mayer Studios, Culver City, CA, writer, 1951-52; University of North Carolina, Woman's College, Greensboro, assistant professor of drama, 1955-56; Western Carolina University, Cullowhee, NC, associate professor, 1956-76, emeritus professor of speech and theatre arts, 1976—. Broadcaster of Latin American material for U.S. Department of State, 1942; guest instructor in playwriting at Bristol University, 1955-56.

MEMBER: American Theatre Association, American Educational Theatre Association, Dramatists Guild, Authors Guild, Photographic Society of America, Carolina Dramatic Association (past president).

AWARDS, HONORS: Rockefeller fellowships in playwriting, 1935-36 and 1937-38; Theatre Guild Bureau of New Plays fellowship, 1938-39; Rockefeller fellowship in Europe, 1950-51; Mayflower Cup for best work by a North Carolinian, 1946, for *Mexican Village;* Alumnia Award from University of North Carolina for work in drama.

WRITINGS:

Mexican Silhouettes (verse), privately printed, 1928, revised edition, Silhouette Press (San Antonio), 1931.
Tooth or Shave (play), first produced in 1935.
The Cry of Dolores (play), first produced in 1935.
Soladadera (play), first produced in 1936, published in *The Best One-Act Plays of 1937,* edited by Margaret Mayorga, Dodd, 1938.
"Azteca" (play), first produced in 1936.
The Fair God (play), first produced in 1936.
Singing Valley (play), first produced in 1936.
(Editor) *Mexican Folk Plays,* University of North Carolina Press, 1938, reprinted, Arno, 1976.
This Is Villa (one-act play), first produced in 1938, published in *The Best One-Act Plays of 1938,* edited by Mayorga, Dodd, 1939.
Red Velvet Goat (one-act play; first produced in 1936), Samuel French, c. 1938.
Sunday Costs Five Pesos (one-act play; first produced in 1936), Samuel French, 1939.
Miracle at Blaise (play), Samuel French, c. 1940, published in *Non-Royalty One-Act Plays for All-Girl Casts,* edited by Betty Smith, Greenburg, 1942.
The Ring of General Macias (play), published in *Twenty Prize-Winning Non-Royalty One-Act Plays,* edited by Smith, Greenburg, 1943.
This Bull Ate Nutmeg (play), in *Plays Without Footlights,* edited by Esther E. Galbraith, Harcourt, 1945.
Mexican Village (novel), University of North Carolina Press, 1945.
Pointers on Playwriting, The Writer (Boston), 1945, revised and enlarged edition published as *New Pointers on Playwriting,* 1967.
Pointers on Radio Writing, The Writer, 1946.
Step Down, Elder Brother (novel; Book-of-the-Month Club selection), Rinehart, 1947.
(With Norman Foster) *Sombrero* (screenplay), Metro-Goldwyn-Mayer, 1953.
A Miracle for Mexico (juvenile), New York Graphic Society, 1964.

Author of screenplays and television scripts. Work represented in anthologies. Contributor to periodicals, including *Collier's, Mexican Life, Ladies Home Journal, Vogue,* and *Writer.*

WORK IN PROGRESS: Red Amapola, a novel.

SIDELIGHTS: Josefina Niggli has distinguished herself in a variety of media and literary genres. As a playwright she has won particular acclaim for her one-act works, and as a novelist she has been recognized as a formidable colorist. In addition, she has written for film and has published a book offering advise to aspiring playwrights. Altogether, her writings constitute what Paula W. Shirley described in the *Dictionary of Literary Biography Yearbook: 1980* as "a notable contribution to American drama and prose."

Niggli is probably best known for her first novel, *Mexican Village.* In this episodic work Niggli conveys the rich and varied aspects of life in small-town Mexico. Ostensibly, the novel's hero is Bob Webster, a half-Mexican, half-American who arrives in the village of Hidalgo with intentions of only a brief stay. In ensuing episodes, village life is extensively revealed, with Niggli relying on folktales and related lore to enhance the account. Tradition is seen as an immensely important aspect of Hidalgo life, and social customs are emphasized as key elements in day-to-day activities. Webster, skeptical and aloof, initially resists the appeal of village traditions and thus gains respect as a relatively independent thinker. By novel's end, however, he has undergone complete integration into Hidalgo life. He abandons the Anglo surname acquired from his father, who never acknowledged the illegitimate Webster as his own son, and assumes his mother's family name, Ortega.

Upon publication in 1945, *Mexican Village* was hailed as a classic portrait of small-town Mexico. Orville Prescott, in *Yale Review*, declared that Niggli "is steeped in Mexican atmosphere" and added that *Mexican Village* is "an utterly engaging book by a richly gifted writer." Similarly, J. H. Jackson wrote in the *Weekly Book Review* that Niggli's novel is "without a peer in its field." "The American reader," Jackson continued, "will understand this particular Mexico . . . better, after he has read *Mexican Village*, than ever before."

Reviewers of *Mexican Village* also praised Niggli's narrative sensibility and her skill in creating believable characters. *New York Times* critic Mildred Adams noted the work's "pace and charm," while Prescott wrote in *Yale Review* that Niggli "is a strong advocate of the old-fashioned story-telling virtues." And *Book Week* reviewer J. T. Frederick noted that the book's "characters and incidents are warm with human reality."

Step Down, Elder Brother, Niggli's second novel, also features vivid descriptions and memorable characters. In this ambitious work Niggli addresses issues pertinent to both Mexico's upper and lower-middle classes in Monterrey: Domingo Vázquez de Anda, the oldest son in a distinquished family, finds himself torn between adherence to traditional values and pursuit of his own beliefs; Mateo Chapa, a budding businessman from a less prosperous family, aspires to the status of the Vázquez de Anda clan, and eventually marries into the family.

Like *Mexican Village*, Niggli's *Step Down, Elder Brother* impressed reviewers with its vivid, authentic depiction of Mexican life. Mildred Adams wrote in the *New York Times* that "the skill with people, the sense of place and dialogue, the ability to make the reader smell and taste and feel . . . are here," and B. D. Wolfe, in his assessment for the *New York Herald Tribune Weekly Book Review*, noted that "every page of [*Step Down, Elder Brother*] pulses with the pulsing life of Monterrey." For Wolfe, Niggli succeeded in evoking "the sense of being of an entire community." Likewise, *Commonweal* reviewer Bonaventure Schwinn declared that Niggli's "love for [Monterrey's] local color and her sympathetic understanding of the Mexican mind shine on every page."

Aside from her two novels, Niggli has published the children's book *A Miracle for Mexico*, which details a Spanish-Indian boy's adventures during the sixteenth-century. She also produced a how-to volume, *Pointers on Playwriting* (revised as *New Pointers on Playwriting*), that *New York Times* reviewer C. V. Terry hailed as "pure gold for anyone interested in the mysteries of dramaturgy."

Niggli has also written many plays, including various one-act works presented by the Carolina Players while she attended the University of North Carolina in the 1930s. In such plays as *Tooth or Shave*, *The Red Velvet Goat*, and *Sunday Costs Five Pesos*, she presented humorous depictions of Mexican village life. *Tooth or Shave*, for instance, provides a comedic perspective on the importance of possessions in determining status. In this play, one woman plans for her elaborate funeral, while another

woman covets a record player. Ludicrous behavior is also manifest in this work—one character fears that he is too cowardly because he resists having his head removed. The more curious aspects of human nature are also explored in *Sunday Costs Five Pesos*, in which a wood-carver becomes convinced that his lover has jumped down a well.

Among Niggli's other plays are historical works such as *The Fair God*, *The Cry of Dolores*, and *Azteca*, which depicts Mexican life a century before the arrival of Spanish conquistadors. Another historical play, *Soldadera*, is set during the Mexican revolution of 1910, as is *This Is Villa*, which details the exploits of the controversial revolutionary.

Since the 1940s Niggli has published few works. But she is known to be working on another novel, *The Red Amapola*, which is concerned with leftist politics in Mexico in the later nineteenth century. Perhaps this work will lead to further recognition for Niggli as one whose writings afford readers an unmatched perspective on Mexican life.

BIOGRAPHICAL/CRITICAL SOURCES:

BOOKS

Dictionary of Literary Biography Yearbook: 1980, Gale, 1981.
Spearman, Walter, *The Carolina Playmakers: The First Fifty Years*, University of North Carolina Press, 1970.

PERIODICALS

Chicago Sun, January 29, 1948.
Christian Science Monitor, November 3, 1945.
Cleveland Open Shelf, January, 1948.
Commonweal, December 14, 1945; December 19, 1947; May 22, 1964.
MELUS, summer, 1978.
New York Herald Tribune Weekly Book Review, February 22, 1948.
New York Times, December 16, 1945; February 8, 1948.
New York Times Book Review, July 12, 1964.
San Francisco Chronicle, February 9, 1948.
Saturday Review of Literature, October 13, 1945; January 24, 1948.
Times Literary Supplement, September 7, 1967.
Weekly Book Review, October 7, 1945.
Yale Review, winter, 1946; spring, 1948.*

—*Sketch by Les Stone*

*　　*　　*

NOLAN, Dennis 1945-

PERSONAL: Born October 19, 1945, in San Francisco, CA; son of Arthur Thomas (an opera singer) and Helen (Fortier) Nolan; married Susan Christine Ericksen, January 28, 1967; married Lauren Ainsworth Mills, June 1, 1987; children: (first marriage) Andrew William. *Education:* Attended College of San Mateo, 1963-65; San Jose State College (now University), B.A., 1967, M.A., 1968.

ADDRESSES: Home and office—Westhampton, MA 01027.

CAREER: San Mateo County Library, Belmont, CA, graphic artist, 1970-77; Canada Junior College, Redwood City, CA, art instructor, 1979-86; University of Hartford, West Hartford, CT, coordinator of illustration program in Hartford Art School, 1986—. Art instructor at College of San Mateo, 1982-86, and at San Jose State University, 1983-86. Work has been exhibited in six one-man shows and in group shows.

AWARDS, HONORS: John Cotton Dana Public Relations Award, 1973; Annual Report Award, American Library Association, 1975; Outstanding Science Book Award, National Science Teachers Association, 1981, for *The Joy of Chickens,* and 1987, for *Step into the Night;* Pick of the List, *American Bookseller,* 1987, Top Twelve Books, *Christian Science Monitor,* 1987, and Prix de Zephyr, French Librarian Award, 1988, all for *The Castle Builder; Parents Choice Magazine* Top 15 Books, 1988, for *Step into the Night;* Notable Social Studies Books list, 1988, for *Legend of the White Doe.*

WRITINGS:

JUVENILES; SELF-ILLUSTRATED

Big Pig (fiction), Prentice-Hall, 1976.
Monster Bubbles: A Counting Book (fiction; a Junior Literary Guild selection), Prentice-Hall, 1976.
Alphabrutes (fiction), Prentice-Hall, 1977.
Wizard McBean and His Flying Machine (fiction), Prentice-Hall, 1977.
Witch Bazooza (fiction), Prentice-Hall, 1979.
The Joy of Chickens (nonfiction for young adults), Prentice-Hall, 1981.
The Castle Builder, Macmillan, 1987.
Wolf Child, Macmillan, 1989.

ILLUSTRATOR

William Hooks, *Legend of the White Doe,* Macmillan, 1988.
Joanne Ryder, *Step into the Night,* Four Winds, 1988.
Ryder, *Mockingbird Morning,* Four Winds, 1989.
Jane Yolen, *Dove Isabeau,* Harcourt, 1989.
Nancy Carlstrom, *Heather Hiding,* Macmillan, 1990.
Ryder, *Under Your Feet,* Four Winds, 1990.

SIDELIGHTS: Dennis Nolan told *CA:* "My grandparents were artists, as were my parents (my father was an operatic tenor). Art was not only encouraged but always around. Books have always been a large part of my life so the blending of two loves—art and books—seemed natural.

"I enjoy a wide variety of stories, formats, and techniques. Each book calls for something new, either in color, composition, choice of painting or drawing material, or mood. This variation is challenging and exciting and keeps the work fresh."

BIOGRAPHICAL/CRITICAL SOURCES:

PERIODICALS

Washington Post Book World, August 9, 1987.

*   *   *

NOWLAN, Robert Anthony, Jr. 1934-

PERSONAL: Surname is pronounced *No*-lan; born July 23, 1934, in Mount Sterling, IL; son of Robert Anthony and Marian (Shields) Nowlan; married Marilyn Lyons, July 7, 1958 (divorced, 1982); married Gwendolyn Lawson Wright (a professor), June 4, 1983; children: Robert Anthony III, Philip L., Edward S., Jennifer L.; (stepchildren) Evan Wright, Andrew

Wright. *Education:* Illinois State Normal University (now Illinois State University), B.S., 1956; Northern Illinois University, M.S., 1959; University of Notre Dame, Ph.D., 1969. *Avocational interests:* Travel, gardening, collecting movies and movie books, trivia, rereading favorite books, "golf, golf, and golf."

ADDRESSES: Home—111 Whittier Rd., New Haven, CT 06515. *Office*—Southern Connecticut State University, New Haven, CT 06515.

CAREER: High school mathematics teacher in Hennepin and Marengo, IL, 1956-62; St. Mary's College, Notre Dame, IN, assistant professor, 1963-68, associate professor of mathematics, 1968-69; Southern Connecticut State University, New Haven, assistant professor, 1969-73, professor of mathematics, 1973—, vice-president for academic affairs, 1978-87. *Military service:* U.S. Army, 1957.

MEMBER: Mathematical Association of America, American Mathematical Society.

WRITINGS:

(With R. M. Washburn) *Geometry for Teachers,* Harper, 1975.
(With C. E. Lowe) *Lessons in Essential Mathematics,* Books 1 and 2, Harper, 1977.
Lessons in College Algebra with Trigonometry, Harper, 1978.
Lessons in College Algebra, Harper, 1978.
College of Trivial Knowledge, Morrow, Volume 1, 1983, Volume 2, 1985.
(With wife, Gwendolyn W. Nowlan) *An Encyclopedia of Film Festivals,* JAI Press, 1988.
(With G. W. Nowlan) *Cinema Sequels and Remakes, 1903-1987,* McFarland & Co., 1989.
(With G. W. Nowlan) *Movie Characters of the Leading Performers of the Sound Era,* American Library Association, 1990.
(With G. W. Nowlan) *The Name Is Familiar: A Directory of Motion Picture Title Characters, 1910-1988,* Neal-Schuman, 1990.
(With G. W. Nowlan) *Films of the Eighties,* McFarland & Co., 1991.

Contributor to mathematics journals.

WORK IN PROGRESS: A Film Quote Book; Once and Forever Young; Performers in Young Roles.

SIDELIGHTS: Robert Anthony Nowlan told *CA:* "My wife, Gwendolyn W. Nowlan (Wendy), and I have turned our love of movies and facts about movies into a kind of cottage industry of writing light movie reference books—'light' because they contain our highly opinionated comments on the movies and performers that we feature, 'reference' as they contain as complete and accurate information about the movies and performers as we can provide. Our work requires us to review large numbers of movies, some marvelous, some lacking in any redeeming qualities. Although we review movies, we do not consider ourselves professional critics, being still too much fans of the media. Our work is meant to inform and entertain. We are delighted in this way to be a part of the movie industry."

O

OERUM, Poul (Erik) 1919-

PERSONAL: Born December 23, 1919, in Nykoebing, Mors, Denmark; son of Lauritz (a boiler attendant) and Constance (Noerholm) Oerum; married Signe Andersen, May 27, 1944 (died January, 1980), married Anne Jonna Thiesen, August 16, 1986; children: Bente, Jan, Eva. *Education:* High school graduate. *Religion:* Danish Official Church.

ADDRESSES: Home—Svenskervej 9, 6720 Nordby Fanoe, Denmark.

CAREER: Worked as laborer, farmer, sailor, and journalist (during the later years of this period as a crime reporter in Copenhagen), 1944-57; writer, 1957—.

MEMBER: Danish Writers' Association.

AWARDS, HONORS: Danish Writers' Association Award, 1957, for *Slet dine spor;* Danish Literary Critics' Award, 1958, for *Lyksalighedens oe;* "Author of the Year" Golden Laurels, Danish Booktrade, 1963, for *Natten i ventesalen;* Johannes Ewald Award, 1964; Henry Nathansens Award, 1966; Otto Rung Award, 1969; Henrik Pontoppidan Award, 1970; Soeren Gyldendal Prize, 1973; Edgar Allan Poe Award, 1974, for *Kun Sandheden,* and 1975, for *De uforsonlige;* Hans Christian Andersen prize, 1976; LO Culture prize, and Martin Andersen Nexoe Award, both 1985.

WRITINGS:

NOVELS

Dansen med de fire vinde (title means "The Dance with the Four Winds"), E. Wangel, 1953.

Ulveleg (title means "Wolf's Playing"), E. Wangel, 1954.

Sidste flugt (title means "Last Escape"), Forlaget Fremad, 1955.

Slet dine spor (title means "Cover Your Tracks"), Forlaget Fremad, 1956.

Det gyldne rav (title means "The Golden Amber"), Forlaget Fremad, 1957.

Raeven og jomfruen (title means "The Fox and the Virgin"), Forlaget Fremad, 1957.

Lyksalighedens oe (title means "The Island of Happiness"), Forlaget Fremad, 1958.

Skyggen ved din hoejre haand (title means "The Shadow at Your Right Hand"), Forlaget Fremad, 1959.

Komedie i Florens (title means "Comedy in Florence"), Forlaget Fremad, 1960, revised edition published as *Komedie i Firenze,* 1977.

Natten i ventesalen (title means "The Night in the Waiting Room"), Forlaget Fremad, 1962.

Rundt om en enebaerbusk (title means "Round the Mulberry Bush"), Forlaget Fremad, 1963.

Hanegal (title means "Cockcrow"), Gyldendal, 1965.

Romance for Selma, Gyldendal, 1966.

Ukendt offer (title means "Unknown Victim"), Gyldendal, 1967.

Spionen ud af den blaa luft (title means "The Spy out of the Blue Air"), Gyldendal, 1968.

Et andet ansigt (title means "Another Face"), Forlaget Fremad, 1970.

Hjemkomst til drab (title means "Homecoming to Homicide"), Forlaget Fremad, 1970.

Den stjaalne ild (title means "The Stolen Fire"), Forlaget Fremad, 1971.

Det 11. bud (title means "The Eleventh Commandment"), Forlaget Fremad, 1972.

Kun Sandheden (novel; also see below), Gyldendal, 1974, translation by Barclay published as *Nothing But the Truth,* Pantheon, 1976.

Syndebuk (novel), Forlaget Fremad, 1972, translation by Kenneth Barclay published as *Scapegoat: A Mystery,* Pantheon, 1975 (published in England as *The Whipping Boy,* Gollancz, 1975).

De uforsonlige (title means "The Irreconcilables"), Forlaget Fremad, 1975.

Tavse vidner (title means "The Silent Witnesses"), Forlaget Fremad, 1976.

Bristepunktet (title means "The Breaking Point"), Forlaget Fremad, 1978.

Efterforskningen (title means "The Investigation"), Gyldendal, 1986.

Dagens lys (title means "Light of Day"), Gyldendal, 1989.

OTHER

Sommerens genfaerd (poetry; title means "The Ghost of the Summer"), Forlaget Fremad, 1956.

Det lille lys (short stories; title means "The Small Light"), Forlaget Fremad, 1959.

(With Tom Kristensen) *Groenlandsskibet* (poetry; title means "The Greenland Ship"), Thejls bogtryk., 1959.

I vandenes dyb (short stories; title means "In the Depth of the Waters"), Forlaget Fremad, 1961.

Tagdryp (short stories; title means "Dripping from the Eaves"), Forlaget Fremad, 1962.

Uskylds frugt (short stories; title means "Fruit of Innocence"), Forlaget Fremad, 1964.

Et udvalg af Pout Oerums digte (title means "A Selection of Poul Oerum's Poems"), holding Tekniske Skole, 1967.

Nattens gaester (short stories; title means "Guests of the Night"), Gyldendal, 1969.

Tilbagerejsen (autobiography; title means "The Return Journey"), Forlaget Fremad, 1973.

(With wife, Signe Oerum) *Retssikkerhedens illusion: Analyse af et justitsmord,* Gyldendal, 1980.

Ravnen mod aften (autobiography), Gyldendal, 1982.

Strandbilleden (poetry), Gyldendal, 1983.

Sorgens Foelelser (title means "Emotions of the Great"), Gyldendal, 1984.

Also author of radio plays, television plays and motion picture scripts; author of motion picture adaptation of *Kun sandheden,* 1975. Story included in anthology, *Tre danske noveller* (title means "Three Danish Stories"), compiled by Erik Mertz, Gjellerup, 1970.

ADAPTATIONS: De uforsonlige has been filmed by a Swedish movie company; *Nothing But the Truth* has been filmed by a Danish movie company.

SIDELIGHTS: Poul Oerum's poem *Groenlandsskibet* was inspired by the tragic wreck of a Danish ship bound for Greenland. The ship was on its maiden voyage, and the entire crew was lost. The poem, first published in a Danish newspaper, was later published with the work of Tom Kristensen under the name *Groenlandsskibet.* The proceeds of the sale of the book were donated to the bereaved families of the lost crewmen.

Oerum's only two works to appear in English translation, *Scapegoat* and *Nothing But the Truth,* are police procedurals. Set in Denmark, these murder mysteries feature middle-aged Detective Inspector Jonas Morck and his assistant, Einarsen.

*   *   *

O'FLINN, Peter
See FANTHORPE, R(obert) Lionel

*   *   *

O'FLYNN, Peter
See FANTHORPE, R(obert) Lionel

*   *   *

OLIEN, Diana Davids 1943-

PERSONAL: Born February 24, 1943, in Oceanside, NY; daughter of Winston Ford and Beatrice (Clary) Davids; married Roger M. Olien (a professor of history and a writer), 1970; children: Christina. *Education:* Swarthmore College, B.A. (with highest honors), 1964; Yale University, M.A., 1966, M.Phil., 1967, Ph.D., 1969.

ADDRESSES: Home—3208 West Dengar, Midland, TX 79705. *Office*—University of Texas, Permian Basin, Odessa, TX 79762.

CAREER: Yale University Press, New Haven, CT, history editor, 1969; Southern Methodist University, Dallas, TX, assistant

professor of history, 1969-73; University of Texas, Permian Basin, Odessa, senior lecturer in history, 1986—. Midland College, instructor, 1977, 1982, 1985; research fellow at Permian Basin Petroleum Museum, 1979-80, Texas Historical Foundation, 1982-83, and Communities Foundation of Texas, 1986-87, 1988-89.

MEMBER: American Historical Association, Business History Society, Texas State Historical Association, West Texas Historical Association, Permian Historical Society, Phi Beta Kappa.

AWARDS, HONORS: Woodrow Wilson fellow, 1964-65, 1967-68; Lewis-Farmington fellow, 1968-69.

WRITINGS:

(With husband, Roger M. Olien) *Oil Booms: Social Change in Five Texas Towns,* University of Nebraska Press, 1982.

Morpeth: A Victorian Public Career, University Press of America, 1983.

(With R. M. Olien) *Wildcatters: Texas Independent Oil Men,* Texas Monthly, 1984.

(With R. M. Olien) *Life in the Oil Fields,* Texas Monthly, 1986.

(With R. M. Olien) *Easy Money: Oil Promoters and Investors during the Jazz Age,* University of North Carolina Press, 1990.

Co-editor, *Permian Historical Annual,* 1985—.

WORK IN PROGRESS: The Public Perception of the American Petroleum Industry: The Interaction of American Business and Culture, with R. M. Olien, completion projected 1991-1992.

SIDELIGHTS: Diana Davids Oliens told *CA:* "After I moved to Midland, Texas, in 1973, I found myself in an oil field community, and I became very interested in the petroleum industry. Petroleum is a complex and unique industry, and its effect upon community and regional development has been profound. It has, of course, been of tremendous importance in the economy of Texas, and it is vital to the nation. A management center in the middle of the Permian Basin oil fields, Midland is ideal as a base from which to study many features of the petroleum industry. Working with my husband as co-author, I have to published a series of works that cover the social impact of petroleum development, the business methods and role of independent oil men, the conditions of daily work and life in the oil fields, and oil promoters of the 1920's. West Texans and oil community residents have been very helpful and cooperative in our work, and we hope our work will enable them to preserve this part of their history, a long overlooked part of American experience."

The author later added: "Roger and I have now shifted to a national focus, and, using petroleum as our case study, are studying the way in which culture defines and limits business stucture and strategy."

*   *   *

O'NEIL, W(illiam) M(atthew) 1912-

PERSONAL: Born June 15, 1912, in Sydney, Australia; son of James Lambert (a grazier) and Susan (Kennedy) O'Neil; married Kathleen Ferris, December 19, 1936; children: Judith Lyndal O'Neil Ryan, James Lawrence. *Education:* University of Sydney, B.A., 1933, Dip. Ed., 1934, M.A., 1935. *Religion:* None.

ADDRESSES: Home—80 Macquarie St., Roseville, New South Wales 2069, Australia.

CAREER: Vocational Guidance Bureau, Department of Labour and Industry, Sydney, Australia, psychologist in charge,

1936-41; Sydney Technical College, Sydney, guidance and research officer, 1941-45; University of Sydney, Sydney, McCaughey Professor of Psychology, 1945-65, professor emeritus and deputy vice-chancellor, 1965—. Australian Research Grants Committee, member, 1965-68, chairman, 1969-72; member of New South Wales Board of Senior Studies, 1974-81.

MEMBER: International Union of Psychological Science (member of executive committee, 1963-66 and 1969-72), Academy of Social Sciences of Australia (fellow, 1945—; honorary fellow, 1982—), Australian Psychological Society (honorary fellow), British Psychological Society (chairman of Australian branch, 1951).

AWARDS, HONORS: Titled officer of Order of Australia, 1978; D.Litt., University of Sydney, 1979.

WRITINGS:

Guide to Elementary Statistics in Psychology, University Cooperative Book Shop, 1957, revised edition, 1965.
An Introduction to Method in Psychology, Melbourne University Press, 1957, revised edition, 1962.
The Beginnings of Modern Psychology, Penguin, 1968, revised edition, Harvester Press and Sydney University Press, 1982.
Fact and Theory: An Aspect of the Philosophy of Science, Sydney University Press, 1969.
Time and the Calendars, Sydney University Press, 1975.
Early Astronomy, Sydney University Press, 1986.
A Century of Psychology in Australia, Sydney University Press, 1987.

Contributor of articles to philosophy and psychology journals in Australia, England, and the United States.

WORK IN PROGRESS: An historical and critical assessment of American behaviorism.

SIDELIGHTS: W. M. O'Neil's Fact and Theory: An Aspect of the Philosophy of Science uses a case history approach to the relations between fact and theory in science. Included are discussions of the discovery of the movement of blood, the laws of planetary motions, the periodic table, and gene theory. A Times Literary Supplement critic praised O'Neil's prose, describing it "a welcome corrective to over-formal and abstract analysis." The reviewer concluded that "university and school teachers will find this pleasant and well illustrated little book helpful."

BIOGRAPHICAL/CRITICAL SOURCES:

PERIODICALS

Times Literary Supplement, October 23, 1969.

* * *

ONETTI, Juan Carlos 1909-

PERSONAL: Born July 1, 1909, in Montevideo, Uruguay; son of Carlos and Honoria (Borges) Onetti; married Dolly Muhr, November, 1955; children: Jorge, Isabel.

ADDRESSES: Home—Gonzalo Ramfrez 1497, Montevideo, Uruguay.

CAREER: Writer of novels and short stories. Worked as editor for Reuter Agency in Montevideo, Uruguay, 1942-43, and in Buenos Aires, Argentina, 1943-46; manager of advertising firm in Montevideo, 1955-57; director of municipal libraries in Montevideo, beginning 1957.

AWARDS, HONORS: National Literature Prize of Uruguay, 1963; Ibera-American Award from William Faulkner Foundation, 1963; Casa de las Américas Prize, 1965; Italian-Latin American Institute Prize, 1972.

WRITINGS:

El pozo (also see below), Signo, 1939, enlarged and revised edition bound with Origen de un novelista y de una generación literaria by Angel Rama, Editorial Alfa, 1965, 2nd revised edition, Arca, 1973.
Tierra de nadie (novel), Editorial Losada, 1941, reprinted, Editorial Seix Barral, 1979.
Para esta noche, Editorial Poseidon, 1943.
La vida breve (novel), Editorial Sudamericana, 1950, reprinted, Edhasa, 1980, translation by Hortense Carpentier published as A Brief Life, Grossman, 1976.
Un sueño realizado y otros cuentos (also see below), Número, 1951.
Los adioses (novel; also see below), Sur, 1954, reprinted, Bruguera, 1981.
Una tumba sin nombre, Marcha, 1959, published as Para una tumba sin nombre (also see below), Arca, 1959, reprinted, Editorial Seix Barral, 1982.
La cara de la desgracia (novella; also see below), Editorial Alfa, 1960.
El astillero (novel), Compañía General Fabril Editora, 1961, reprinted, Cátedra, 1983, translation by Rachel Caffyn published as The Shipyard, Scribner, 1968.
El infierno tan temido, Editorial Asir, 1962.
Tan triste como ella (also see below), Editorial Alfa, 1963, reprinted, Lumen, 1982.
Juntacadáveres (novel), Editorial Alfa, 1964, revised edition, Arca, 1973.
Jacob y el otro (also see below) [and] Un sueño realizado y otros cuentos, Ediciones de la Banda Oriental, 1965.
Cuentos completos, Centro Editor de América Latina, 1967, revised edition, Corregidor, 1974.
Tres novelas (contains La cara de la desgracia, Tan triste como ella, and Jacob y el otro), Editorial Alfa, 1967.
Novelas cortas completas (contains El pozo, Los adioses, La cara de la desgracia, Tan triste como ella, and Para una tumba sin nombre), Monte Avila Editores, 1968.
La novia robada y otros cuentos (short stories including "La novia robada"; also see below), Centro Editor de América Latina, 1968, reprinted, Siglo Veintiuno Editores, 1983.
Los rostros del amor, Centro Editor de América Latina, 1968.
Obras completas, Aguilar, 1970.
La muerte y la niña (also see below), Corregidor, 1973.
Onetti (collection of articles and interviews), Troisi y Vaccaro, 1974.
Tiempo de abrazar y los cuentos de 1933 a 1950 (short stories), Arca, 1974.
(With Joacquin Torres-García and others) Testamento artístico, Biblioteca de Marcha, 1974.
Réquiem por Faulkner, Arca, 1975.
Tan triste como ella y otros cuentos (short stories), Lumen, 1976.
El pozo [and] Para una tumba sin nombre, Editorial Calicanto/ Arca, 1977, 2nd edition, Seix Barral, 1980.
Dejemos hablar al viento, Bruguera Alfaguara, 1979.
La muerte y la niña [and] La novia robada, Bruguera, 1980.
Cuentos secretos, Biblioteca de Marcha, 1986.
Presencia y otros cuentos, Almarabu, 1986.
Cuando entonces, Editorial Sudamericana, 1988.

Editor of Marcha, 1939-42, and Vea y Lea, 1946-55.

SIDELIGHTS: Although considered by a number of critics to be among the finest and most innovative novelists in South

America, Juan Carlos Onetti is generally not well known outside of his homeland of Latin America. While praised and admired for their richness in imagination, creativity, and unique vision, Onetti's writings have also been described as fundamentally ambiguous, quite fragmentated, and often complex. As M. Ian Adams confirms in his book, *Three Authors of Alienation: Bombal, Onetti, Carpentier,* "Complexity and ambiguity are the major characteristics of Onetti's novels."

"Onetti's art is a strange aggregate of cultural characteristics and personal circumstances (some elusive, many contradictory and a few truly illuminating) none of which would really endear his writings to us were it not for the extraordinary nature of his style," states Luys A. Diez in *Nation.* Diez continues, "His prose has a genuinely hypnotic force, digressive and meandering, but quite without apparent *longueurs,* studded with linguistic quirks and poetic flights, economically terse and playfully serious; he teases the reader with alternate scenarios for a given situation to concentrate afterwards on a passing thought or a seemingly unimportant gesture."

Only two of Onetti's books have been translated into English. *The Shipyard,* though written after *A Brief Life,* was published first. It tells the story of Larsen, a shipyard worker who seeks to improve his social status by attaching himself to the shipyard owner's daughter. But he is unable to see that the society he aspires to has disintegrated, and the novel ends with his death. "Larsen moves through Onetti's pages as a figure virtually doomed to disaster," declares James Nelson Goodsell in the *Christian Science Monitor.* "Onetti is trying to evoke a picture of futility and hopelessness—a task which he performs very ably. . . . Onetti's purpose is to keep the reader absorbed, but to remain enigmatic. He succeeds admirably. [He] is a skillful writer whose prose is absorbing and demanding." And David Gallagher endorses *The Shipyard* in the *New York Times Book Review* as "a book which, for all its portentousness, few Latin American novelists have equaled."

The plot of *A Brief Life* is much more fantastical than that of *The Shipyard.* It concerns Juan Carlos Brausen, referred to as a "sort of Argentine Walter Mitty" by Emir Rodriguez Monegal in the *New York Times Book Review.* Brausen escapes from his many burdens by retreating from reality into a series of complex and often bizarre fantasy adventures. In *Review 75,* Hugo J. Verani calls *A Brief Life* "one of the richest and most complex novelistic expressions in Spanish-American fiction."

In a *Newsweek* review, Margo Jefferson writes that *A Brief Life* "is a virtuosic blend and balance of opposites: melodrama and meditation, eroticism and austerity, naturalism and artifice. . . . In Onetti's hands, the novel becomes an excursion into a labyrinth where the real and the imagined are mirror images. . . . Behind his sleight of hand is a melancholy irony—for all our efforts to escape a single life, we remain prisoners of a pattern, 'condemned to a soul, to a manner of being.' "

Because of its unique unfolding of plot, *A Brief Life* has received inevitable comparisons with the work of William Faulkner. Luys A. Diez notes in the *Nation* that "much of Faulkner's rich, dark sap flows through the meandering narrative." Diez also contends that "Onetti's novelistic magic, like Faulkner's, requires a certain amount of perseverance on the reader's part." And Rodriguez Monegal remarks that "in *A Brief Life,* Onetti's love for Faulknerian narrative is already evident."

Several critics have expressed their high regard for Onetti's skillful use of experimental narration. Zunilda Gertel writes in *Review 75* that "Onetti's narrative does not postulate an ideology or an intellectual analysis of the ontological. Instead, the existential projection of the 'I' is shown as a revelation within the signs imposed on him by literary tradition considered as ritual, not as reconciliation." Also writing in *Review 75,* John Deredita claims that *A Brief Life* "exhaustively tests the power of fantasy and fictional imagination as a counter to the flow of time. . . ." And Verani concludes that "Onetti does not emphasis the mimetic quality of narrative. The aim of his fiction is not to reflect an existent reality, a factual order, but . . . to create an essentially fabulated reality invested with mythic significance."

BIOGRAPHICAL/CRITICAL SOURCES:

BOOKS

Adams, M. Ian, *Three Authors of Alienation: Bombal, Onetti, Carpentier,* University of Texas Press, 1975.
Contemporary Literary Criticism, Gale, Volume 7, 1977, Volume 10, 1979.
Harss, Luis and Barbara Dohmann, *Into the Mainstream: Conversations with Latin-American Writers,* Harper, 1967.
Kadir, Djelal, *Juan Carlos Onetti,* Twayne, 1977.
Milián-Silveira, María C., *El primer Onetti y sus contextos,* Editorial Pliegos, 1986.

PERIODICALS

Christian Science Monitor, October 8, 1968.
Hispania 71, May, 1988.
Library Journal, March 1, 1976.
Nation, April 3, 1976.
Newsweek, February 16, 1976.
New Yorker, February 9, 1976.
New York Times Book Review, June 16, 1968, January 11, 1976.
Review 75, winter, 1975.
Saturday Review, January 24, 1976.*

* * *

ORJUELA, Hector H(ugo) 1930-

PERSONAL: Born July 6, 1930, in Bogotá, Colombia; son of Reynaldo (a broker) and Carmen (Gómez) Orjuela; married Helena Aguirre, June 25, 1965; children: Héctor H., Jr., Luis-Reynaldo, Andres-Felipe, Ximena del Pilar, Rodrigo. *Education:* North Texas State University, B.A., M.A., 1952; Indiana University, graduate study, 1952-53; University of Kansas, Ph.D., 1960; Universidad Central (Madrid), postdoctoral study, 1962.

ADDRESSES: Home—Transv. 31, No. 136-14, Bogotá, Colombia. *Office*—Ediciones El Dorado, Bogotá, Colombia.

CAREER: Virginia Military Institute, Lexington, assistant professor of Spanish, 1957-60; University of Southern California, Los Angeles, associate professor of Spanish, 1960-69; University of California, Irvine, professor of Spanish, 1969-73; Ediciones El Dorado, Bogotá, Colombia, director-editor, 1973—. Visiting professor, Texas Tech University, summer, 1963. Consultant, Instituto Caro y Cuervo (Colombia), 1972—.

MEMBER: Academia Colombiana de la Lengua, Instituto de Literatura Iberoamericana, Sigma Delta Pi (adviser, Eta Chapter, 1960-64).

AWARDS, HONORS: First International Literary Prize, Laureano Carus Pando, 1978, for *La imagen de los Estados Unidos en la poesía de Hispanoamérica;* Légion de Honor Nacional y Academia de Bellas Artes, 1979; Diploma de Honor, Comité Hernandiano de California, 1979.

WRITINGS:

(Author of introduction) José Joaquín Ortega Torres, *Indice del "Papel periódico ilustrado" y de "Colombia ilustrada,"* Instituto Caro y Cuervo, 1961.

(With E. W. Hesse) *Spanish Conversational Review Grammar,* 2nd edition (Orjuela was not associated with earlier edition), American Book Co., 1964, 5th edition published as *Spanish Review,* Van Nostrand, 1980.

Biografía y bibliografía de Raphael Pombo (title means "Biography and Bibliography of Rafael Pombo"), Instituto Caro y Cuervo, 1965.

Las antologías poéticas de Colombia (title means "The Poetic Anthologies of Colombia"), Instituto Caro y Cuervo, 1966.

(Editor) José A. Silva, *Obras completas* (title means "Complete Works"), two volumes, Plus Ultra (Buenos Aires), 1967.

Fuentes generales para el estudio de la literatura colombiana: Guía bibliográfica, (title means "General Sources for the Study of Colombian Literature"), Instituto Caro y Cuervo, 1968.

(Editor) Rafael Pombo, *Poesía inédita y olvidada* (title means "Unpublished and Forgotten Poetry"), two volumes, Instituto Caro y Cuervo, 1970.

Bibliografía de la poesía colombiana (title means "Bibliography of Colombian Poetry"), Instituto Caro y Cuervo, 1971.

Poemas de encrucijada (title means "Crossroads Poems"), Editorial Cosmos (Bogotá), 1972.

(Editor) *José A. Silva: Poesías* (title means "José A. Silva: Poems"), Editorial Cosmos, 1973, critical edition, Instituto Caro y Cuervo, 1979.

(Editor) *Ficciones de "El Carnero,"* Editorial Cosmos, 1974.

Bibliografía del teatro colombiano, Instituto Caro y Cuervo, 1974.

Relatos y ficciones, Ediciones El Dorado, 1975.

(Editor) Pombo, *Antología poética,* Ediciones La Candelaria, 1975.

La obra poética de Raphael Pombo, Instituto Caro y Cuervo, 1975.

"De sobremesa" y otros estudios sobre José Asunción Silva, Instituto Caro y Cuervo, 1976.

(Editor and author of introduction) *José Asunción Silva: Intimidades,* Instituto Caro y Cuervo, 1977, reprint with introduction by Germán Arciniegas published as *Intimidades: José Asunción Silva,* Instituto Caro y Cuervo, 1977.

El primer Silva, Editorial Kelly, 1978.

La imagen de los Estados Unidos en la poesía de Hispanoamérica, Universidad Nacional Autónoma de México, 1980.

Los hijos de la salamandra (novel), Ediciones Tercer Mundo, 1980.

Literatura hispanoamericana, Instituto Caro y Cuervo, 1980.

Yurupary, Instituto Caro y Cuervo, 1983.

"El desierto prodigioso y prodigio del desierto," de Pedro de Solís y Valenzuelá, Instituto Caro y Cuervo, 1984.

Estudios sobre literatura indígena y colonial, Instituto Caro y Cuervo, 1986.

Mitopoemas, Instituto Caro y Cuervo, 1987.

WORK IN PROGRESS: Historia de la poesía hispanoamericana, Volume I: *Poesía indígena de Hispanoamérica: Azteca, maya, quechua.*

BIOGRAPHICAL/CRITICAL SOURCES:

PERIODICALS

Hispaña, March, 1967, September, 1968, September, 1969, September, 1976, May, 1977, December, 1977, March, 1978, May, 1982, December, 1982, March, 1984.

ORLEANS, Leo A(nton) 1924-

PERSONAL: Born June 13, 1924, in Sverdlovsk, U.S.S.R.; came to United States, 1939, naturalized citizen, 1944; son of Anton J. (a furrier) and Susan (Agranovich) Orleans; married Helen Willis, August 20, 1949; children: Nina, David. *Education:* University of Southern California, B.A., 1950; graduate study at George Washington University and American University, 1951-56.

ADDRESSES: Home—655 E St. S.E., Washington, D.C. 20003.

CAREER: Library of Congress, Washington, D.C., research analyst, 1951-65; National Science Foundation, Washington, D.C., associate studies director of Office of Economic and Manpower Studies, 1965-66; Library of Congress, China research specialist, 1966-81; consultant on China, 1981—. *Military service:* U.S. Army Air Forces, 1943-46; served in Pacific Theater.

MEMBER: Society for International Development, Association for Asian Studies.

WRITINGS:

Professional Manpower and Education in Communist China, National Science Foundation, 1961.

Every Fifth Child: The Population of China, Stanford University Press, 1972.

(Editor) *A Bibliography of Chinese Sources on Medicine and Public Health in the People's Republic of China: 1960-1970,* John E. Fogarty International Center for Advanced Study in the Health Sciences, 1973.

(Editor and author of introduction) *Chinese Approaches to Family Planning,* M. E. Sharpe, 1979.

(Editor and contributor) *Science in Contemporary China,* Stanford University Press, 1980.

Chinese Students in America: Policies, Issues, and Numbers, National Academy Press, 1988.

Contributor to numerous books, including *Population Trends in Eastern Europe, the USSR, and Mainland China,* American Academy for the Advancement of Science, 1961; C. T. Hu, editor, *Aspects of Chinese Education,* Teachers College Press, 1969; Charles K. Wilber, editor, *The Political Economy of Development and Underdevelopment,* Random House, 1973; *The National Research Council in 1979: Current Issues and Studies,* National Academy of Sciences, 1979; Ruth Hayhoe and Marianne Bastid, editors, *China's Education and the Industrialized World,* M. E. Sharpe, 1987; Denis Simon and Merle Goldmans, editors, *China's New Technological Revolution,* Harvard University Press, 1989; Kaplan, Sobin, and Andors, editors, *Encyclopedia of China Today,* Eurasia Press, 1990. Also contributor to *Collier's Encyclopedia.* Contributor of articles and reviews to numerous journals, including *China Quarterly, Journal of Asian Studies, Chinese Communist Education, Bulletin of Atomic Scientists, Science, World Affairs, Political Science Quarterly, Foreign Service Journal, Comparative Education Review,* and *Current Scene. Chinese Education,* editor, 1968-69, currently member of editorial board.

WORK IN PROGRESS: Continuing to write on social and economic problems of contemporary China.

SIDELIGHTS: Leo A. Orleans was taken to China as a six-month-old child, and he lived there until 1939. In a note to *CA,* he made the following observation: "Whether because of increased expectations or a decrease in the number of brain cells, writing, unfortunately, does not become easier with experience and age."

ORMOND, John 1923-

PERSONAL: Born April 3, 1923, in Dunvant, Glamorgan, Wales; son of Arthur Thomas (a shoemaker) and Elsie Ormond; married Glenys Roderick, September 21, 1946; children: Eirianedd Evans, Garan Thomas, Branwen. *Education:* University of Wales, B.A., 1945.

ADDRESSES: Home—15 Conway Rd., Cardiff, Wales. *Office*—Broadcasting House, British Broadcasting Corp., Llandaff, Cardiff, Wales.

CAREER: Picture Post, London, England, writer, 1945-49; *South Wales Evening Post,* Swansea, sub-editor, 1949-55; British Broadcasting Corp., Cardiff, Wales, television news editor, 1955-57, producer, director, and documentary filmmaker, 1957—. Lecturer at British and American universities. Chairman of Cardiff's Civic Trust Organization, 1973-77.

AWARDS, HONORS: Literature prizes from Welsh Arts Council, 1970 and 1974; Cholmondeley Award, 1975.

WRITINGS:

POETRY

(With James Kirkup and John Bayliss) *Indications,* Grey Walls Press, 1942.
Requiem and Celebration, Christopher Davies, 1969.
Definition of a Waterfall, Oxford University Press, 1973.
(With Emyr Humphreys and John Tripp) *Penguin Modern Poets 27,* Penguin, 1979.
In Place of Empty Heaven, University College of Swansea, 1984.
Selected Poems, Poetry Wales, 1988.

TELEVISION SCRIPTS

A Sort of Welcome to Spring, British Broadcasting Corp., 1958.
Under a Bright Heaven, BBC, 1966.
A Bronze Mask, BBC, 1968.
The Fragile Universe, BBC, 1969.
R. S. Thomas: Priest and Poet, BBC, 1971.
I Sing to You Strangers, BBC, 1983.

OTHER

Poets of Wales: John Ormond and Raymond Garlick (recording), Argo, 1971.
(Author of text) *Ceri Richards Memorial Exhibition,* National Museum of Wales, 1973.
Graham Sutherland, O.M.: A Memorial Address, National Museum of Wales, 1981.

Contributor to *Planet* and *Poetry Wales.*

SIDELIGHTS: Writing in the *Times Literary Supplement,* Neil Corcoran describes John Ormond's poetry as "a tentative, unshowy art, solidly craftsmanlike, suspicious of rhetoric, but willing to push beyond its usual limits when . . . the material seems to demand it." In poems often concerned with nature and history, Ormond "at once celebrates the joys of ordinary life and mourns their inevitable loss," as Michael J. Collins notes in the *Dictionary of Literary Biography.* His work has gained Ormond a reputation as one of the leading poets of Wales. In a review of the poetry collection *Definition of a Waterfall* for *Poetry Wales,* Cary Archard calls it "one of the best books of English language poetry to appear in the Seventies." Collins concludes that "Ormond is one of the finest poets writing in English today."

BIOGRAPHICAL/CRITICAL SOURCES:

BOOKS

Abse, Dannie, editor, *Corgi Modern Poets in Focus: 5,* Corgi, 1973.
Dictionary of Literary Biography, Volume 27: *Poets of Great Britain and Ireland, 1945-1960,* Gale, 1984.

PERIODICALS

Anglo-Welsh Review, spring, 1974.
Poetry, November, 1970.
Poetry Wales, winter, 1969; summer, 1972; summer, 1973; autumn, 1980.
Times Literary Supplement, August 21, 1943; April 22-28, 1988.
World Literature Today, autumn, 1977.

P

PAIGE, Harry W(orthington) 1922-

PERSONAL: Born September 25, 1922, in Syracuse, NY; son of Montfort S. and Ruth (Converse) Paige; married Ruth Killough (a high school teacher), March 16, 1946; children: Sandra Paige Sorell, Judith Ann Paige McKinnon. *Education:* Union College, Schenectady, NY, A.B., 1946; State University of New York at Albany, M.A., 1953, Ph.D., 1967. *Politics:* Independent. *Religion:* Roman Catholic.

ADDRESSES: Home—Meadow East, Apt. K-6, Potsdam, NY 13676. *Agent*—Norma Lewis Agency, 521 Fifth Ave., New York, NY 10175.

CAREER: Clarkson College of Technology (now Clarkson University), Potsdam, NY, assistant professor of literature and creative writing, 1953-60; Rockland Community College, Suffern, NY, associate professor of literature and creative writing, 1960-62; Clarkson University (formerly Clarkson College of Technology), professor of humanities, 1966-88, professor emeritus, 1988—; freelance writer, 1988—. Visiting professor of creative writing, New Mexico State University, 1973-74. Professional tennis player, summers, 1956-66. *Military service:* U.S. Army Air Forces, 1943-45.

AWARDS, HONORS: National Theatre Conference Award, 1955, for "The Vigil"; *Johnny Stands* was named a notable children's trade book in the field of social studies by the Book Review Subcommittee of the National Council for the Social Studies-Children's Book Council Joint Committee, 1982; Spur Award for Best Juvenile Book, Western Writers of America, 1985, for *Shadow on the Sun; Land of the Spotted Eagle: A Portrait of the Reservation Sioux* was named a "Best Book" by the Catholic Press Association of the United States and Canada, 1987.

WRITINGS:

The Far and Near (one-act play), first produced in Albany, NY, at Albany Arena Theatre, July 29, 1955.
Songs of the Teton Sioux, Westernlore, 1970.
Wade's Place (young adult novel), Scholastic Book Services, 1973.
Night at Red Mesa (young adult novel), McCormick-Mathers, 1975.
The CB Mystery (young adult novel), McCormick-Mathers, 1978.

Johnny Stands (young adult novel), Warne, 1982.
The Summer War (young adult novel), Warne, 1983.
Shadow on the Sun (young adult novel), Warne, 1984.
(With Don Doll) *Land of the Spotted Eagle: A Portrait of the Reservation Sioux* (collection), Loyola University Press, 1987.
The Eye of the Heart (collection), Crossroad Publishing/Continuum, 1990.

Also author of one-act play *The Vigil.* Contributor of poems, articles, and stories to periodicals, including *Saturday Review, America, Catholic Digest, Spirit,* and *New York Times.*

WORK IN PROGRESS: Eagle Rock, an adult novel about a writer's colony in the Adirondack Mountains of New York State.

SIDELIGHTS: Harry W. Paige told *CA:* "When I was in the third grade or so, I won a story writing contest (the prize was a book), and although I didn't know it at the time, it set a pattern. Writing was something I always came back to, whether I was in the service, a tennis professional, or a college professor. In fact, I think I chose college teaching because it gave me the time and the atmosphere in which to write.

"I started sending my work out in the early 1950s. It was mostly poetry then, but over the years I wrote one-act plays, articles, and short stories.

"I didn't attempt a longer work until I was forced to for my doctoral dissertation. I wrote it on the songs of the Teton Sioux because of my long-standing interest in Native Americans and in the West and because I didn't want to go over the usual academic ground. To gather research, I went to the Rosebud and Pine Ridge Sioux reservations in South Dakota, lived among the Sioux, and learned their language, Lakota. The resulting work, the first literary study of the songs of the Plains Indians, was published by Westernlore and was well received.

"After that, I tried my first young adult novel, *Wade's Place.* Since its publication in 1973 it has sold more than two hundred thousand copies. In later works, *Night at Red Mesa* and *Johnny Stands,* I returned to Indian themes.

"I like to write about the West and its people. The time spent on Indian reservations and in Las Cruces, New Mexico, has given me enough material to keep me going. The fact that I know the West as an 'outsider' and an Easterner has, I feel, given me a valuable perspective, helping me to see objectively and avoid confusing the myths with the reality.

"I try not to write down to younger readers, and I try to deal with themes I consider important—the rites of passage, divided loyalties, self-betrayals—the same things I write about in my adult fiction.

"In recent years I have discovered that my paternal grandfather and some other relatives have written stories, poems, and books, and so, in the absence of more logical explanations for my own writing, I can always credit it to heredity. I feel that writing and the other arts contain a good deal of mystery, and I become inarticulate when I try to explain too much.

"My last two books, *Land of the Spotted Eagle* and *The Eye of the Heart* are collections of essays/articles, most previously published. Now that I am retired from college teaching I can concentrate on freelance writing."

*   *   *

PANEK, LeRoy Lad 1943-

PERSONAL: Born January 26, 1943, in Cleveland, OH; son of Lad (an industrial manager) and Alice (a teacher; maiden name, Krejci) Panek; married to Susan Phoebus (a teacher), July 7, 1973; children: Alexander, Claire. *Education:* Marietta College, B.A., 1964; Lehigh University, M.A., 1965; Kent State University, Ph.D., 1968.

ADDRESSES: Home—823 Winchester Dr., Westminster, MD 21157. *Office*—Department of English, Western Maryland College, Westminster, MD 21157.

CAREER: Western Maryland College, Westminster, 1968—, began as assistant professor, currently professor of English. Member of Carroll County Arts Council.

AWARDS, HONORS: Grant from National Endowment for the Humanities, 1980; Edgar Allen Poe Award, Mystery Writers of America, 1981, for *Watteau's Shepherds,* and 1988, for *An Introduction to the Detective Story.*

WRITINGS:

Watteau's Shepherds: The Detective Novel in Britain, 1914-1940, Bowling Green University, 1979.

The Special Branch: The British Spy Novel, 1890-1980, Bowling Green University, 1981.

An Introduction to the Detective Story, Bowling Green University, 1987.

Probable Cause: Crime Fiction in America, Bowling Green University, 1990.

Contributor to magazines, including *American Literature, Poe Studies, Armchair Detective, Clues,* and *Studies in Short Fiction.*

WORK IN PROGRESS: The Hard-Boiled Story.

SIDELIGHTS: LeRoy Lad Panek commented: "Reading sensational fiction changed from a hobby to a mission when I realized how little extant criticism made sense to me. It was either jejune or unnecessarily abstruse. I was the first, I think, to describe detective stories as games or jokes instead of puzzles. More importantly, I have tried to discuss sensational fiction as literature as opposed to seeing it as mere entertainment or a kind of curious cultural artifact."

PARINI, Jay (Lee) 1948-

PERSONAL: Born April 2, 1948, in Pittston, PA; son of Leo Joseph (a minister) and Verna Ruth (Clifford) Parini; married Devon Stacey Jersild, June 21, 1981. *Education:* Lafayette College, A.B., 1970; University of St. Andrews, B.Phil., 1972, Ph.D., 1975. *Politics:* Democrat. *Religion:* Episcopalian. *Avocational interests:* Traveling, skiing, tennis.

ADDRESSES: Home—R.R.1, Box 195, Middlebury, VT 05753. *Office*—Department of English, Middlebury College, Middlebury, VT 05753. *Agent*—Elaine Markson Literary Agency, Inc., 44 Greenwich Ave., New York, NY 10011.

CAREER: Dartmouth College, Hanover, NH, assistant professor of English and director of creative writing, 1975-1982; Middlebury College, Middlebury, VT, professor of English, 1982—. Teaching associate, Bread Loaf Writer's Conference, 1982—. Editor of "North Star" poetry series. Member of Vermont Council on the Humanities and Social Sciences, 1975—; member of Vermont Council of the Arts, 1980-82; editorial committee, University of Massachusetts Press, Juniper Prize for poetry, 1984—.

MEMBER: Modern Language Association of America, Poetry Society of Great Britain.

AWARDS, HONORS: Fellowship, American Council of Learned Societies, 1985—.

WRITINGS:

Singing in Time (poems), J. W. B. Laing, 1972.
Theodore Roethke: An American Romantic, University of Massachusetts Press, 1979.
(Editor with M. Robin Barone and Sydney Lea) *Richard Eberhart: A Celebration,* Kenyon Hill, 1980.
The Love Run (novel), Little, Brown, 1980.
Anthracite Country (poems), Random House, 1982.
(Editor with Robert Pack) *The Bread Loaf Anthology of Contemporary American Poetry,* University Press of New England, 1985.
An Invitation to Poetry (textbook), Prentice-Hall, 1987.
(Editor with Pack) *The Bread Loaf Anthology of Contemporary American Short Stories,* University Press of New England, 1987.
The Patch Boys (novel), Holt, 1988.
Town Life (poems), Holt, 1988.
A Vermont Christmas, Little, Brown, 1988.
(Editor with Pack) *The Bread Loaf Anthology of Contemporary American Essays,* University Press of New England, 1989.
The Last Station (novel), Holt, 1990.

Contributor to language and literature journals. Founder, co-editor of *New England Review,* 1977—.

SIDELIGHTS: "Jay Parini brings to his poetry a calm self-assured tone of voice, a classical sense of balance, and a rare skill at the art of writing verse," asserts Richard Tillinghast in the *Sewanee Review.* Parini's collection of poetry entitled *Anthracite Country* is noted both for its nostalgic yet serious tone and the author's skillful manipulation of language. In the *New York Times Book Review,* Anne Stevenson observes that the book "takes risks. . . . *Anthracite Country* will be read for its honesty, for its emotional commitment to experience and its artistic commitment to a craft." "Direct and deceptively simple, many of these poems speak volumes," added Joseph Parisi of the *Chicago Tribune Book World.* Parini adopted a nostalgic tone again for *Town Life,* an autobiographical poetry compilation. Bruce Bennett in the *New York Times Book Review* describes the cyclical, highly personal nature of the volume as "the stock-taking of a poet at mid-life who wishes to determine both how he has fared so far and how he expects to fare. His philosophical bent inclines him to speculate about, in Frost's phrase, 'our place among the infinities' ". W. C. Hamlin lauds the volume's variety and depth, commenting: "Overall, the poems offer a marvelous diversity of imagery and form and attest greatly to the illusion of artlessness and freedom born of total control."

Parini's skill with language is also evident in his prose. His novel *The Patch Boys* chronicles a young boy's coming of age in Pennsylvania's anthracite country around 1925. In the *New York Times Book Review,* James D. Bloom remarks that "Parini has produced a subtly paced narrative." *Los Angeles Times Book Review* critic Lewis Stone elaborates: "Parini relates Sammy's reminiscences in a down-home first-person idiom that clings to the memory as coal dust to a miner's overalls." Robert Ward likewise emphasizes the author's ability to describe colorful detail in the *Washington Post Book World:* "[Parini] writes with a wonderful sense of place. Not only nature, but the patch itself is fully alive." The critic concludes: "My final impression was that I had visited a lost part of America. . . . It is this vivid rendering of place that is the true success of *The Patch Boys.*" The life of Leo Tolstoy is the emphasis of Parini's novel *The Last Station.* Set in Russia in 1910, the events of the text are told from six different view points. As with his earlier prose, *The Last Station* is noted for its sense of place and the author's attention to detail. A reviewer for the *New York Times Book Review* called the book "one of those rare works of historical fiction that manage to demonstrate both scrupulous historical research and true originality of voice and perception."

Jay Parini's mastery at evoking emotional and visual images is partly the result of his experimentation with different writing forms. Parini once told *CA:* "Although my primary interest is writing poetry, I am now writing a lot of fiction and criticism. . . . I intend to keep writing novels, poems, and critical essays. In a sense, I use writing to pay attention to the world, to explain it to myself. The poems arise out of a strong wish to embody things: objects, emotions, ideas. I celebrate the physical world and my relationship to it. . . . I write criticism because, as T. S. Eliot once said, it is as natural as breathing."

The author later added: "I write every morning and, when I can, in the afternoon and evenings. I have children and a wife, and we like to spend time together, so I find myself having to focus my work as much as possible. There seems to be a natural rhythm for me as I move among new poems, novels, stories, and critical essays or reviews. I write lots of short reviews for papers like the *Washington Post, USA Today, Boston Globe,* and for magazines like *Vanity Fair* and *Horizon, The New Republic,* and *The Saturday Review.* This keeps me in pocket money and more-or-less abreast of current fiction, poetry, and non-fiction. I always have a long essay-review on a serious topic, usually criticism, underway at *The Hudson Review* or *The Sewanee Review.* I love doing these pieces, though nobody ever sees or reads them (so it seems). I'm against typecasting writers who don't want those assignments, so I'd rather be thought of as a 'writer' than a poet, critic, or novelist."

BIOGRAPHICAL/CRITICAL SOURCES:

BOOKS

Contemporary Literary Criticism, Volume 54, Gale, 1989.

PERIODICALS

Chicago Tribune Book World, August 8, 1982.
Choice, May, 1988.

Hudson Review, December 3, 1982.
Library Journal, February 1, 1982; May, 1990.
Los Angeles Times Book Review, October 19, 1986; November 2, 1986.
New York Times, July 17, 1990.
New York Times Book Review, June 8, 1980; December 12, 1986; June 12, 1988; March 12, 1989; July 23, 1990.
Publisher's Weekly, December, 1981; July 20, 1990.
Salmagundi, summer, 1983.
Sewanee Review, winter, 1983; summer, 1983.
Times Literary Supplement, February 6, 1981; July 10, 1981; August 27, 1982; August 14, 1987.
Washington Post Book World, December 13, 1986; August 5, 1990.

*   *   *

PARKER, (James) Stewart   1941-1988

PERSONAL: Born October 20, 1941, in Belfast, Northern Ireland; died of cancer, November 2, 1988; son of George Herbert (a tailor's cutter) and Isabel (Lynas) Parker; married Kate Ireland, August 26, 1964. *Education:* Queen's University of Belfast, B.A., 1964, M.A., 1966. *Politics:* Socialist.

ADDRESSES: Home and office—29 Chelverton Rd., London SW15 1RN, England. *Agent*—London Management, 235/241 Regent St., London W1A 2JT, England.

CAREER: Hamilton College, Clinton, NY, instructor in English, 1964-67; Cornell University, Ithaca, NY, instructor in English, 1967-69; writer, 1969-88.

MEMBER: Writers Guild of Great Britain, Dramatists Guild.

AWARDS, HONORS: Most promising playwright award from London *Evening Standard,* 1976, for "Spokesong"; Thames-Television bursary, 1977; prize from Christopher Ewart-Biggs Memorial Trust, 1979, for "I'm a Dreamer, Montreal"; special commendation from Italia Prize, 1980, and Giles Cooper Award from British Broadcasting Corp., 1981, both for "The Kamikaze Ground Staff Reunion Dinner"; Banff International Television Festival prize, 1985.

WRITINGS:

PLAYS

"Speaking of Red Indians" (radio play), first broadcast on British Broadcasting Corp., (BBC-Radio), 1967.
"Minnie and Maisie and Lily Freed" (radio play), first broadcast on BBC-Radio, 1970.
"The Iceberg" (radio play), first broadcast on BBC-Radio, 1975.
Spokesong (two-act; first produced in Dublin, Ireland, at Dublin Theatre Festival, 1975; produced on Broadway at Circle in the Square, March 15, 1979), Samuel French, 1979.
"The Actress and the Bishop" (one-act), first produced in London at King's Head Theatre, 1976.
Catchpenny Twist (two-act; first produced in Dublin at Peacock Theatre, 1977; produced in Hartford, Conn., 1978), Samuel French, 1980.
"Kingdom Come" (two-act musical), first produced in London at King's Head Theatre, 1978.
"I'm a Dreamer, Montreal," first broadcast on Thames-Television, 1979.
"Tall Girls Have Everything," first produced in Louisville, 1980.

Nightshade (two-act; first produced in Dublin at Peacock Theatre, 1980), Co-Op Books (Dublin), 1980.
"The Kamikaze Ground Staff Reunion Dinner" (radio play; first produced on BBC-Radio, 1980), published in *Best Radio Plays of 1980,* Methuen, 1981.
"Iris in the Traffic, Ruby in the Rain," first produced on BBC-TV, 1981.
"Pratt's Fall," first produced in Glasgow, Scotland, at Glasgow Theatre Club, 1983.
"Blue Money," first produced on London Weekend Television, 1984.
"Northern Star," first produced in Belfast at Lyric Theatre, 1984.
"Radio Pictures," first produced on BBC-TV, 1985.
"Heavenly Bodies," first produced at Birmingham Repertory Theatre, 1986.
"Pentecost," first produced in Londonderry, 1987, produced in New York City, 1987.

Also author of television plays, "Joyce in June," 1982, and "Lost Belongings," 1987, and of radio play, "The Traveller," 1985.

OTHER

The Casualty's Meditation (verse collection), Festival (Belfast), 1967.
Maw (verse collection), Festival, 1968.
(Editor) Sam Thompson, *Over the Bridge,* Gill & Macmillan (Dublin), 1971.

Rock music columnist for *Irish Times.*

SIDELIGHTS: Innovative Irish dramatist Stewart Parker will probably be best remembered for his first play for stage, "Spokesong." Premiered at the 1975 Dublin Theatre Festival, the piece introduced Parker and the clever dialogue which characterizes his work to an international audience. Parker received the London *Evening Standard*'s most promising playwright award for the work, the first of numerous honors bestowed on him during the period of his short, yet prolific, career.

"Spokesong" deals with the conflict between Catholics and Protestants in Northern Ireland as seen through the eyes of Frank, a proprietor of a Belfast bicycle shop, who believes that the world would be a saner place if more people rode the two-wheeled vehicles he markets. The bicycle comes to symbolize freedom and all of the good things in life missing from the war-torn society of Northern Ireland. The playwright's use of the bicycle in "Spokesong" is an example of how, as *Contemporary Dramatists* contributor Paul Lawley wrote, "Parker establishes and develops his themes less by soberly discursive means than by a constant play of symbol and metatheatrical reference operating within a fast-moving, eventful narrative."

Various U.S. productions of the play received favorable comments from critics. Noting in a *New York Times* review that much had already been written about the situation in Northern Ireland, Richard Eder nevertheless declared, "Nothing I know has approached so closely an artistic vision of the subject as a small, undoubtedly flawed and cheerfully instructive play called 'Spokesong.'" In comments published in the same periodical regarding another presentation of the same work, Eder called it "a most funny and piercingly intelligent play." Reviewing "Spokesong" for the *Washington Post,* James Lardner referred to Parker as "an astonishing fount of wit and word-play."

BIOGRAPHICAL/CRITICAL SOURCES:

BOOKS

Contemporary Dramatists, 4th edition, St. James Press, 1988.

PERIODICALS

Los Angeles Times, July 14, 1986.
New York Times, February 11, 1978, March 16, 1979.
Washington Post, August 9, 1979.

OBITUARIES:

PERIODICALS

Chicago Tribune, November 5, 1988.
Los Angeles Times, November 5, 1988.
New York Times, November 4, 1988.
Times (London), November 5, 1988.*

*   *   *

PARRA, Nicanor 1914-

PERSONAL: Born September 5, 1914, in Chillán, Chile; son of Nicanor P. (a teacher) and Clara S. (Navarette) Parra; married Ana Troncoso, 1948 (marriage ended); married Inga Palmen; children: seven. *Education:* University of Chile, degree in mathematics and physics, 1938; attended Brown University, 1943-45; studied cosmology at Oxford University, 1949-51.

ADDRESSES: Home—c/o Julia Bernstein, Parcela 272, Lareina, Santiago, Chile. *Office*—Instituto Pedagógico, Avenida Macul 774, Santiago, Chile.

CAREER: Poet and scientist. Secondary school teacher, 1938-43; University of Chile, Santiago, professor, 1947-52, director of school of engineering, 1948—, professor of theoretical physics, 1952—. Visiting professor at Louisiana State University, 1966-67, and New York University, Columbia University, and Yale University, 1971; has given poetry readings in many countries, including the United States, Russia, Venezuela, Cuba, Peru, and Argentina.

AWARDS, HONORS: Premio municipal de poesía, Santiago, Chile, 1937, for *Cancionero sin nombre,* and 1954, for *Poemas y antipoemas;* Writers Union Prize, 1954; Premio Nacional de Literatura (national prize for literature), Chile, 1969, for *Obra gruesa;* Guggenheim fellowship, 1972; first Richard Wilbur prize for poetry, American Literary Translators Association and University of Missouri Press, 1984, for *Sermons and Homilies of the Christ of Elqui.*

WRITINGS:

IN ENGLISH TRANSLATION

Poemas y antipoemas, Nascimento, 1954, Cátedra (Madrid), 1988, translation of selected poems by Jorge Elliot published as *Anti-poems,* City Lights, 1960.
Poems and Antipoems (bilingual selection of poems from other works), edited by Miller Williams, New Directions, 1967.
Obra gruesa, Editorial Universitaria, 1969, Editorial Andrés Bello, 1983, translation by Williams of selected poems published as *Emergency Poems,* New Directions, 1972.
Sermones y prédicas del Cristo de Elqui, Universidad de Chile Estudios Humanísticos, 1977, translation by Sandra Reyes published as *Sermons and Homilies of the Christ of Elqui* (bilingual edition; also see below), University of Missouri Press, 1984.
Nuevos sermones y prédicas del Cristo de Elqui, Ganymedes, 1979, translation by Reyes published in *Sermons and Homi-*

lies of the Christ of Elqui, University of Missouri Press, 1984.

Antipoems: New and Selected, edited by David Unger, translation by Lawrence Ferlinghetti and others, New Directions, 1985.

OTHER

Cancionero sin nombre (title means "Untitled Book of Ballads"), Nascimento, 1937.

La cueca larga (also see below), Editorial Universitaria, 1958, 2nd edition, 1966.

Versos de salón, Nascimento, 1962.

(With Pablo Neruda) *Discursos,* Nascimento, 1962.

La cueca larga y otros poemas, edited by Margarita Aguirre, Editorial Universitaria de Buenos Aires, 1964.

(Editor) *Poesía soviética rusa,* Editorial Progreso, 1965.

Canciones rusa, Editorial Universitaria, 1967.

Poemas, Casa de las Américas, 1969.

Poesía rusa contemporánea, Ediciones Nueva Universidad, Universidad Católica de Chile, 1971.

Los profesores, Antiediciones Villa Miseria (New York), 1971.

Antipoemas: Antología (1944-1969), Seix Barral, 1972.

Artefactos/Nicanor Parra, Ediciones Nueva Universidad, Universidad Católica de Chile, 1972, enlarged edition, 1972.

Poema y antipoema a Eduardo Frei, Editorial América del Sur, 1982.

Coplas de Navidad, Ediciones del Camaleón, 1983.

Poesía política, Bruguera, 1983.

Nicanor Parra: Biografía emotiva (selected poems), compiled by Efrain Szmulewicz, Ediciones Rumbos, 1988.

Also author of *La evolución del concepto·de masa,* 1958; *Deux poemas,* 1964; *Tres poemas,* 1965; *Defensa de Violeta Parra,* 1967; (translator from the English) R. D. Lindsay and Henry Margenau, *Fundamentos de la física* (title means "Foundations of Physics"), 1967; *Muyeres,* 1969; and *Ejercicios respiratorios.*

SIDELIGHTS: Chilean poet Nicanor Parra, a contemporary of Pablo Neruda, inherited a poetic tradition that ensconced lofty themes in grandiose language. "Parra," declared *New York Times Book Review* contributor Alexander Coleman, "is an antipoet. Antipoets . . . dread the very idea of Poetry and its attendant metaphors, inflated diction, romantic yearning, obscurity and empty nobility." Poetry is not an elite pastime, but belongs to the less-privileged majority, he believes. Its proper subject matter is not truth and beauty, but the vulgar surprises of life that more often than not amount to a bad joke. His antipoems relate the ironies of life in ordinary speech made colorful by witty insights into the unpretentious characters he presents. Coleman describes Parra's tools as "irony, burlesque, an astringent barrage of cliches and found phrases, all juxtaposed in a welter of dictions that come out in a wholly original way, laying open everybody's despair." With these methods, says a *Publishers Weekly* reviewer, "Parra bids to break the barrier between the poem and the public." As a champion of accessible poetry, Parra has exerted a major influence on Hispanic literature.

Parra was born in southern Chile near the small town of Chillán in 1914. Having an interest in science and an aptitude for mathematics, he studied mathematics and physics at the University of Chile, advanced mechanics at Brown University in Rhode Island, and, with the aid of a British Council grant, cosmology at Oxford. Since 1948, he has been a professor of theoretical physics at the University of Chile. In addition to his professional activities, he has maintained an interest in American and British poetry, both of which have influenced his work. The factor which perhaps shaped his personal aesthetic the most, however, was

having to write in the shadow of the Nobel Prize winner Neruda. Parra became an antipoet, says Emir Rodríguez Monegal in *The Borzoi Anthology of Latin American Literature,* "in order to negate the exalted conception of the poet that Neruda represented so grandly. The fact that he finally succeeded in creating a viable alternative confirms his unique gifts." Parra's antipoetry "is a prime example of a generational reaction to the styles and concerns of earlier poets: it negates the highly metaphorical, surrealistic style of the 1930s," Edith Grossman suggests in *Contemporary Foreign Language Writers.*

Though Parra's early books contain some surreal imagery, later books rely on manipulation of narrative structure to achieve their effects. "Using narrative devices but deflecting the normal expectations of the reader by interrupting and even cutting short the anecdotal flow, Parra 'deconstructs' the poem and finally achieves an almost epigrammatic structure that moves from one intense fragment of verbal reality to the next," Rodríguez Monegal suggests. In addition, the antipoet feels that poetry need not be musical to be good. He maintains that since man talks more than he sings, man should leave the singing to the birds. Another feature the antipoems borrow from prose is the presence of characters found in contemporary urban settings. Mobsters and nymphomaniacs, ragged and rough-talking bag ladies, pugilistic youth and frustrated office workers alike have their say in Parra's antipoems.

Another character that caught Parra's sustained attention was Domingo Zarate Vega, a construction worker who became a self-styled prophet in the 1920s. Parra borrows the folk legend's voice for all the poems in *Sermons and Homilies of the Christ of Elqui.* The result, says a *Georgia Review* contributor, "makes for a powerful, entertaining, and often quirky reading experience." Doing for the figure of Christ what he has always done for Hispanic poetry, Parra demythologizes the Chilean prophet (and, by implication, other religious figures) by describing the profane conditions of their lives. Parra's Christ matter-of-factly jokes about his sackcloth robe and his breakfast of hot water. Later, he chides followers for giving the pages of the Bible and the Chilean flag a reverence that is inappropriate and impractical. Here, as in his other books, Parra shows the humor (and fury) to be gained from recognizing that people or objects traditionally considered sacred are not.

Parra's iconoclasm is so thoroughgoing that after poetry readings, he says "Me retracto de todo lo dicho" ("I take back everything I told you"). He also refuses to formulate a firm definition of antipoetry. He turns interviews into anti-interviews, frustrating most inquiries into his personal life and writing process, which he calls "a professional secret," Grossman reports. He has written that the thanks he gets for his freedom from tradition is to be declared *persona non grata* in literary circles. Yet many critics offer generally favorable impressions of Parra's work. In his *New York Times Book Review* piece about *Poems and Antipoems,* Mark Strand comments: "Parra's poems are hallucinatory and violent, and at the same time factual. The well-timed disclosure of events—personal or political—gives his poems a cumulative, mounting energy and power that we have come to expect from only the best fiction." In a *Poetry* review, Hayden Carruth adds: "Free, witty, satirical, intelligent, often unexpected (without quite being surrealistic), mordant and comic by turns, always rebellious, always irreverent—it is all these and an ingratiating poetry too."

Partisan Review contributor G. S. Fraser observes that among Hispanic writers, Parra possesses the liveliest wit. "I think that being a professor of mathematics may have given him the logical quickness which lies at the essence of wit," Fraser suggests. Grossman concurs that Parra "has brought to Hispanic literature a new vision of the expressive possibilities of colloquial Spanish." Strand points out, "It is the difference between Parra's antipoems and anybody else's that is significant. . . . To many readers Parra will be a new poet, but a poet with all the authority of a master."

BIOGRAPHICAL/CRITICAL SOURCES:

BOOKS

Contemporary Foreign Language Writers, St. Martin's, 1984.
Contemporary Literary Criticism, Volume 2, Gale, 1974.
Gottlieb, Marlene, *No se termina nunca de nacer: La poesía de Parra,* Playor, 1977.
Grossman, Edith, *The Antipoetry of Parra,* New York University Press, 1975.
Montes, Hugo, *Parra y la poesía de lo cotidiano,* Pacifico, 2nd edition, 1974.
Rodríguez Monegal, Emir, editor, *The Borzoi Anthology of Latin American Literature,* Volume 2: *The Twentieth Century—From Borges and Paz to Guimaraes Rosa and Donoso,* Knopf, 1986.

PERIODICALS

Arizona Quarterly, summer, 1967.
Books Abroad, summer, 1968.
Carleton Miscellany, spring, 1968.
Hudson Review, autumn, 1968, winter, 1972-73.
Nation, August 7, 1972.
National Observer, March 24, 1973.
New Statesman, November 8, 1968.
New York Times Book Review, December 10, 1967, May 7, 1972.
Partisan Review, summer, 1974.
Poetry, September, 1968.
Review, winter, 1971, spring, 1972.*

—*Sketch by Marilyn K. Basel*

* * *

PAZ, Octavio 1914-

PERSONAL: Born March 31, 1914, in Mexico City, Mexico; son of Octavio Paz (a lawyer) and Josephina Lozano; married Marie José Tramini, 1964; children: one daughter. *Education:* Attended National Autonomous University of Mexico, 1932-37. *Politics:* "Disillusioned leftist." *Religion:* Atheist.

ADDRESSES: Home—Lerma 143-601, México 5, DF, México. *Office*—c/o *Vuelta,* Avenida Contreras 516, Tercer Piso, San Jerónimo 10200 DF, México City, México.

CAREER: Writer. Government of Mexico, Mexican Foreign Service, posted to San Francisco, CA, and New York, NY, secretary at Mexican Embassy in Paris, beginning 1945, charge d'affaires at Mexican Embassy in Japan, beginning 1951, posted to Mexican Secretariat for External Affairs, 1953-58, Extraordinary and Plenipotentiary Minister to Mexican embassy, 1959-62, ambassador to India, 1962-68. Visiting professor of Spanish American literature, University of Texas at Austin and Pittsburgh University, 1968-70; Simón Bolívar Professor of Latin American Studies, 1970, and fellow of Churchill College, Cambridge University, 1970-71; Charles Eliot Norton Professor of Poetry, Harvard University, 1971-72. Regent's fellow at University of California, San Diego.

MEMBER: American Academy and Institute of Arts and Letters (honorary).

AWARDS, HONORS: Guggenheim fellowship, 1944; Grand Prix International de Poésie (Belgium), 1963; Jerusalem Prize, Critics Prize (Spain), and National Prize for Letters (Mexico), all 1977; Grand Aigle d'Or (Nice), 1979; Premio Ollin Yoliztli (Mexico), 1980; Miguel de Cervantes Prize (Spain), 1982; Neustadt International Prize for Literature, 1982; Wilhelm Heinse Medal (West Germany), 1984; T. S. Eliot Award for Creative Writing, Ingersoll Foundation, 1987; Tocqueville Prize, 1989; Nobel Prize in Literature, 1990.

WRITINGS:

POETRY

Luna silvestre (title means "Sylvan Moon"), Fábula (Mexico City), 1933.
¡No pasarán!, Simbad (Mexico City), 1936.
Raíz del hombre (title means "Root of Man"; also see below), Simbad, 1937.
Bajo tu clara sombra y otros poemas sobre España (title means "Under Your Clear Shadow and Other Poems about Spain"; also see below), Españolas (Valencia), 1937, revised edition, Tierra Nueva (Valencia), 1941.
Entre la piedra y la flor (title means "Between the Stone and the Flower"; Nueva Voz (Mexico City), 1938, 2nd edition, Asociación Cívica Yucatán (Mexico City), 1956.
A la orilla del mundo y Primer día; Bajo tu clara sombra; Raíz del hombre; Noche de resurrecciones, Ars (Mexico City), 1942.
Libertad bajo palabra (title means "Freedom on Parole"), Tezontle (Mexico City), 1949.
¿Aguila o sol? (prose poems), Tezontle, 1951, 2nd edition, 1973, translation by Eliot Weinberger published as *¿Aguila o sol?/ Eagle or Sun?* (bilingual edition), October House, 1970, revised translation by Weinberger published under same title, New Directions, 1976.
Semillas para un himno, Tezontle, 1954.
Piedra de sol, Tezontle, 1957, translation by Muriel Rukeyser published as *Sun Stone/Piedra de sol* (bilingual edition; also see below), New Directions, 1963, translation by Peter Miller published as *Sun-Stone,* Contact (Toronto), 1963, translation by Donald Gardner published as *Sun Stone,* Cosmos (New York), 1969.
La estación violenta, Fondo de Cultura Económica (Mexico City), 1958, reprinted, 1978.
Agua y viento, Ediciones Mito (Bogotá), 1959.
Libertad bajo palabra: Obra poética, 1935-1958, Fondo de Cultura Económica, 1960, revised edition, 1968.
Salamandra (1958-1961) (also see below), J. Mortiz (Mexico City), 1962, 3rd edition, 1975.
Selected Poems of Octavio Paz (bilingual edition), translation by Rukeyser, Indiana University Press, 1963.
Viento entero, Caxton (Delhi), 1965.
Blanco (also see below) J. Mortiz, 1967, 2nd edition, 1972, translation by Weinberger published under same title, The Press (New York), 1974.
Disco visuales (four spatial poems), Era (Mexico City), 1968.
Ladera este (1962-1968) (title means "Eastern Slope (1962-1968)"; also see below) J. Mortiz, 1969, 3rd edition, 1975.
La centena (Poemas: 1935-1968), Seix Barral (Barcelona), 1969, 2nd edition, 1972.
Topoemas (six spatial poems), Era, 1971.
Vuelta (long poem), El Mendrugo (Mexico City), 1971.
Configurations (contains *Piedra de sol/Sun Stone, Blanco,* and selections from *Salamandra* and *Ladera este*), translations by G. Aroul and others, New Directions, 1971.

(With Jacques Roubaud, Edoardo Sanguinetti, and Charles Tomlinson; also author of prologue) *Renga* (collective poem written in French, Italian, English, and Spanish), J. Mortiz, 1972, translation by Tomlinson published as *Renga: A Chain of Poems,* Braziller, 1972.

Early Poems: 1935-1955, translations by Rukeyser and others, New Directions, 1973.

3 Notations/3 Rotations (contains fragments of poems by Paz), Carpenter Center for the Visual Arts, Harvard University, 1974.

Pasado en claro (long poem), Fondo de Cultura Económica, 1975, revised edition, 1978, tranlation included as title poem in *A Draft of Shadows and Other Poems* (also see below), New Directions, 1979.

Vuelta, Seix Barral, 1976.

(With Tomlinson; sonnets written by Paz and Tomlinson in Spanish and English) *Air Born/Hijos del aire,* Pescador (Mexico City), 1979.

Poemas (1935-1975), Seix Barral, 1979.

A Draft of Shadows and Other Poems, edited and translated by Weinberger, with additional translations by Elizabeth Bishop and Mark Strand, New Directions, 1979.

Selected Poems (biligual edition), translations by Tomlinson and others, Penguin, 1979.

Octavio Paz: Poemas recientes, Institución Cultural de Cantabria de la Diputación Provincial de Santander, 1981.

Selected Poems, edited by Weinberger, translations by G. Aroul and others, New Directions, 1984.

Cuatro chopos/The Four Poplars (bilingual edition), translation by Weinberger, Center for Edition Works (New York), 1985.

The Collected Poems, 1957-1987: Bilingual Edition, New Editions, 1987.

PROSE

El laberinto de la soledad (also see below), Cuadernos Americanos, 1950, revised edition, Fondo de Cultura Económica, 1959, reprinted, 1980, translation by Lysander Kemp published as *The Labyrinth of Solitude: Life and Thought in Mexico,* Grove, 1961.

El arco y la lira: El poema; La revelación poética; Poesía e historia, Fondo de Cultura Económica, 1956, 2nd edition includes text of *Los signos en rotación* (also see below), 1967, 3rd edition, 1972, translation by Ruth L. C. Simms published as *The Bow and the Lyre: The Poem, the Poetic Revelation, Poetry and History,* University of Texas Press, 1973, reprinted, 1977, 2nd edition, McGraw-Hill, 1975.

Las peras del olmo, Universidad Nacional Autónoma de México, 1957, revised edition, Seix Barral, 1971, 3rd edition, 1978.

Tamayo en la pintura mexicana, Universidad Nacional Autónoma de México, 1959.

Cuadrivio: Darío, López Velarde, Pessoa, Cernuda, J. Mortiz, 1965.

Los signos en rotación, Sur (Buenos Aires), 1965.

Puertas al campo (also see below), Universidad Nacional Autónoma de México, 1966.

Claude Lévi-Strauss; o, El nuevo festín de Esopo, J. Mortiz, 1967, translation by J. S. Bernstein and Maxine Bernstein published as *Claude Lévi-Strauss: An Introduction,* Cornell University Press, 1970 (published in England as *On Lévi-Strauss,* Cape, 1970).

Corriente alterna, Siglo Veintiuno Editores (Mexico City), 1967, reprinted, 1980, translation by Helen R. Lane published as *Alternating Current,* Viking, 1973.

Marcel Duchamp; o, El castillo de la pureza, Era, 1968, translation by Gardner published as *Marcel Duchamp; or, The Castle of Purity,* Grossman, 1970.

Conjunciones y disyunciones, J. Mortiz, 1969, 2nd edition, 1978, translation by Lane published as *Conjunctions and Disjunctions,* Viking, 1974.

México: La última década, Institute of Latin American Studies, University of Texas, 1969.

Posdata (also see below) Siglo Veintiuno, 1970, translation by Kemp published as *The Other Mexico: Critique of the Pyramid,* Grove, 1972.

(With Juan Marichal) *Las cosas en su sitio: Sobre la literatura española del siglo XX,* Finisterre (Mexico City), 1971.

Los signos en rotación y otros ensayos, edited and with a prologue by Carlos Fuentes, Alianza (Madrid), 1971.

Traducción: Literatura y literalidad, Tusquets (Barcelona), 1971.

Aparencia desnuda: La obra de Marcel Duchamp, Era, 1973, new enlarged edition, 1979, translation by Rachel Phillips and Gardner published as *Marcel Duchamp: Appearance Stripped Bare,* Viking, 1978.

El signo y el garabato (contains *Puertas al campo*), J. Mortiz, 1973.

(With Julián Ríos) *Solo a dos voces,* Lumen (Barcelona), 1973.

Teatro de signos/Transparencias, selection and montage by Ríos, Fundamentos (Madrid), 1974.

La búsqueda del comienzo: Escritos sobre el surrealismo, Fundamentos, 1974, 2nd edition, 1980.

El mono gramático, Seix Barral, 1974, translation from the original Spanish manuscript published as *Le singe grammarien,* Skira (Geneva), 1972, translation by Lane of Spanish original published as *The Monkey Grammarian,* Seaver, 1981.

Los hijos del limo: Del romanticismo a la vanguardia, Seix Barral, 1974, translation by Phillips published as *Children of the Mire: Modern Poetry from Romanticism to the Avant-Garde,* Harvard University Press, 1974.

The Siren and the Seashell, and Other Essays on Poets and Poetry, translations by Kemp and Margaret Sayers Peden, University of Texas Press, 1976.

Xavier Villaurrutia en persona y en obra, Fondo de Cultura Económica, 1978.

El ogro filantrópico: Historia y política, 1971-1978 (also see below), J. Mortiz, 1979.

In/mediaciones, Seix Barral, 1979.

México en la obra de Octavio Paz, edited by Luis Mario Schneider, Promexa (Mexico City), 1979.

El laberinto de la soledad; Posdata; Vuelta a El laberinto de la soledad, Fondo de Cultura Económica, 1981.

Sor Juana Inés de la Cruz; o, Las trampas de la fe, Seix Barral, 1982, translation by Peden published as *Sor Juana; or, The Traps of Faith,* Harvard University Press, 1988.

(With Jacques Lassaigne) *Rufino Tamayo,* Ediciones Poligrafia (Barcelona), 1982, translation by Kenneth Lyons published under same title, Rizzoli, 1982.

(With John Golding) *Guenther Gerzo* (Spanish, English and French texts), Editions du Griffon (Switzerland), 1983.

Sombras de obras: Arte y literatura, Seix Barral, 1983.

Hombres en su siglo y otros ensayos, Seix Barral, 1984, translation by Michael Schmidt published as *On Poets and Others,* Seaver Books, 1987.

Tiempo nublado, Seix Barral, 1984, translation by Lane with three additional essays published as *On Earth, Four or Five Worlds: Reflections on Contemporary History,* Harcourt, 1985.

The Labyrinth of Solitude, The Other Mexico, Return to the Labyrinth of Solitude, Mexico and the United States, The Philanthropic Ogre, translated by Kemp, Yara Milos, and Rachel Phillips Belash, Grove, 1985.

Arbol adentro, Seix Barral, 1987, translation published as *A Tree Within,* New Directions, 1988.

Convergences: Essays on Art and Literature, translation by Lane, Harcourt, 1987.

EDITOR

Voces de España, Letras de México (Mexico City), 1938.

(With others) *Laurel: Antología de la poesía moderna en lengua española,* Séneca, 1941.

Antologie de la poesie mexicaine, Nagel, 1952.

Antología poética, Revista Panoramas (Mexico City), 1956.

(And translator with Eikichi Hayashiya) Matsuo Basho, *Sendas de Oku,* Universidad Nacional Autónoma de México, 1957, 2nd edition, Seix Barral, 1970.

Anthology of Mexican Poetry, translation of Spanish manuscript by Samuel Beckett, Indiana University Press, 1958, reprinted as *Mexican Poetry: An Anthology,* Grove, 1985.

Tamayo en la pintura mexicana, Imprenta Universitaria (Mexico City), 1958.

Magia de la risa, Universidad Veracruzana, 1962.

Fernando Pessoa, *Antología,* Universidad Nacional Autónoma de México, 1962.

(With Pedro Zekeli) *Cuatro poetas contemporáneos de Suecia: Martinson, Lundkvist, Ekeloef, y Lindegren,* Universidad Nacional Autónoma de México, 1963.

(With others and author of prologue) *Poesía en movimiento: México, 1915-1966,* Siglo Veintiuno, 1966, translation edited by Mark Strand and published as *New Poetry of Mexico,* Dutton, 1970.

(With Roger Caillois) *Remedios Varo,* Era, 1966.

(And author of prologue) Xavier Villaurrutia, *Antología,* Fondo de Cultura Económica, 1980.

CONTRIBUTOR

In Praise of Hands: Contemporary Crafts of the World, New York Graphic Society, 1974.

Avances, Fundamentos, 1978.

Democracy and Dictatorship in Latin America: A Special Publication Devoted Entirely to the Voices and Opinions of Writers from Latin America, Foundation for the Independent Study of Social Ideas (New York), 1982.

Instante y revelación, Fondo Nacional para Actividades Sociales, 1982.

Frustraciones de un destino: La democracia en América Latina, Libro Libre, 1985.

Weinberger, editor, *Nineteen Ways of Looking at Wang Wei: How a Chinese Poem Is Translated,* Moyer Bell, 1987.

TRANSLATOR

(And author of introduction) William Carlos Williams, *Veinte Poemas,* Era, 1973.

Versiones y diversiones (translations of poems from English, French, Portuguese, Swedish, Chinese, and Japanese), J. Mortiz, 1974.

Apollinaire, *15 Poemas,* Latitudes (Mexico City), 1979.

OTHER

"La hija de Rappaccini" (one-act play; based on a short story by Nathaniel Hawthorne; first produced in Mexico, 1956), translation by Harry Haskell published as "Rappaccini's Daughter" in *Octavio Paz: Homage to the Poet,* Kosmos (San Francisco), 1980.

(Author of introduction) Carlos Fuentes, *Cuerpos y ofrendas,* Alianza, 1972.

(Author of introduction) *Antonio Paláez: Pintor,* Secretaría de Educación Pública (Mexico), 1975.

(Author of foreword) *A Sor Juana Anthology,* translation by Alan S. Trueblood, Harvard University Press, 1988.

One Word to the Other, Latitudes, 1989.

Contributor to numerous anthologies. Founder of literary review, *Barandal,* 1931; member of editorial board and columnist, *El Popular,* late 1930s; co-founder of *Taller,* 1938; co-founder and editor, *El Hijo Pródigo,* 1943-46; editor of *Plural,* 1971-75; founder and editor, *Vuelta,* 1976—.

SIDELIGHTS: Winner of the 1990 Nobel Prize, Mexican author Octavio Paz has a world-wide reputation as a master poet and essayist. Although Mexico figures prominently in Paz's work—one of his best-known books, *The Labyrinth of Solitude,* for example, is an comprehensive portrait of Mexican society—*Los Angeles Times* contributor Jascha Kessler calls Paz "truly international." *World Literature Today*'s Manuel Durán feels that Paz's "exploration of Mexican existential values permits him to open a door to an understanding of other countries and other cultures" and thus appeal to readers of diverse backgrounds. "What began as a slow, almost microscopic examination of self and of a single cultural tradition widens unexpectedly," Durán continues, "becoming universal without sacrificing its unique characteristic."

One aspect of Paz's work often mentioned by critics is his tendency to maintain elements of prose—most commonly philosophical thought—in his poetry and poetic elements in his prose. Perhaps the best example to support this claim can be found in Paz's exploration of India entitled *The Monkey Grammarian,* a work which *New York Times Book Review* contributor Keith Botsford calls "exceedingly curious" and describes as "an extended meditation on the nature of language." In separate *World Literature Today* essays critics Jaime Alazraki and José Miguel Oviedo discuss the difficulty they would have assigning the book to a literary genre. "It is apparent," Alazraki notes, "that *The Monkey Grammarian* is not an essay. It is also apparent that it is not a poem, at least not in the conventional sense. It is both an essay and a poem, or perhaps neither." Oviedo similarly states that the book "does not belong to any specific genre—although it has a bit of all of them—because it is deliberately written at the edge of genres."

According to Oviedo, *The Monkey Grammarian* is the product of Paz's long-stated quest "to produce a text which would be an intersection of poetry, narrative and essay." The fusion of opposites found in this work is an important element in nearly all Paz's literary production. In many instances both the work's structure and its content represent a blending of contradictory forces: *Renga,* for example, is written in four languages, while *Air Born/Hijos del Aire,* is written in two. According to *World Literature Today* contributor Frances Chiles, Paz strives to create in his writing "a sense of community or communion" which he finds lacking in contemporary society. In his Neustadt Prize acceptance speech reprinted in *World Literature Today,* Paz attempts to explain his emphasis on contrasting thoughts: "Plurality is Universality, and Universality is the acknowledging of the admirable diversity of man and his works. . . . To acknowledge the variety of visions and sensibilities is to preserve the richness of life and thus to ensure its continuity."

Through juxtaposition of contrasting thoughts or objects Paz creates a more harmonious world, one based on complementary association of opposites found in the Eastern concept of yin and yang. This aspect of Paz's thinking reveals the influence of his six-year stay in India as Mexican ambassador to that country. Grace Schulman explains Paz's proclivity for Eastern philosophy in her *Hudson Review* essay: "Although he had embraced contraries from the beginning of his writing career, [as] Mexican ambassador to India [he] found in Tantric thought and in Hindu religious life dualities that enforced his conviction that history turns on reciprocal rhythms. In *Alternating Current,* he writes that the Hindu gods, creators or destroyers according to their names and region, manifest contradiction. 'Duality,' he says, 'a basic feature of Tantrism, permeates all Hindu religious life: male and female, pure and impure, left and right. . . . In Eastern thought, these opposites can co-exist; in Western philosophy, they disappear for the worst reasons: far from being resolved into a higher synthesis, they cancel each other out.' "

Critics point to several repeated contrasting images that dramatically capture the essence of Paz's work. Ronald Christ, for example, comments in his *Nation* review of *¿Aguila o sol?/Eagle or Sun?* (the Spanish portion of which is the equivalent of the English expression "heads or tails?"): "The dual image of the Mexican coin which gives *Eagle or Sun?* its title epitomizes Paz's technique and credo, for we see that there is no question of eagle *or* sun rather than eagle *and* sun which together in their oppositeness are the same coin." Another of the poet's images which reviewers frequently mention is "burnt water," an ancient Mexican concept which appears in Paz's work in both Spanish and in the Aztec original, "atl tlachinolli." Schulman maintains that "burnt water" is "the dominant image of [Paz's] poetry" and finds that the image fulfills a role similar to that of the two sides of the coin in *Eagle and Sun?* She notes: "Paz sees the world burning, and knows with visionary clarity that opposites are resolved in a place beyond contraries, in a moment of pure vision: in that place, there are no frontiers between men and women, life and death." Chiles calls the Aztec combination of fire and water "particularly apt in its multiple connotations as a symbol of the union of all warring contraries."

Critics agree that Paz's great theme of a blended reality situates his work in the forefront of modern literature. As Christ notes: "By contraries then, by polarities and divergences converging in a rhetoric of opposites, Paz [has] established himself as a brilliant stylist balancing the tension of East and West, art and criticism, the many and the one in the figures of his writing. Paz is thus not only a great writer: he is also an indispensable corrective to our cultural tradition and a critic in the highest sense in which he himself uses the word." Enrique Fernández similarly sees Octavio Paz as a writer of enormous influence. "Not only has he left his mark on world poetry, with a multilingual cortege of acolytes," Fernández writes in a *Village Voice* essay, "he is a force to be reckoned with by anyone who chooses that modernist *imitatio Christi,* the Life of the Mind."

BIOGRAPHICAL/CRITICAL SOURCES:

BOOKS

Contemporary Literary Criticism, Gale, Volume 3, 1975; Volume 4, 1975; Volume 6, 1976; Volume 10, 1979; Volume 19, 1981; Volume 51, 1989.
Wilson, Jason, *Octavio Paz,* Twayne, 1986.

PERIODICALS

Hudson Review, autumn, 1974.

Interview, October, 1989.
Los Angeles Times, November 28, 1971.
Nation, August 2, 1975.
New York Times Book Review, December 27, 1981; December 25, 1988.
Times (London), June 8, 1989.
Village Voice, March 19, 1985.
World Literature Today, autumn, 1982.*

—*Sketch by Marian Gonsior*

*   *   *

PEPPER, Stephen C(oburn)   1891-1972

PERSONAL: Born April 29, 1891, in Newark, N.J.; died May 1, 1972; son of Charles Hovey and Frances (Coburn) Pepper; married Ellen Hoar, February 12, 1914; children: Sherman Hoar (deceased), Elizabeth Hoar Wood, Frances Tarson. *Education:* Harvard University, A.B., 1913, M.A., 1914, Ph.D., 1916.

ADDRESSES: Home—2718 Buena Vista Way, Berkeley, Calif. *Office*—Department of Philosophy, University of California, Berkeley, Calif.

CAREER: Wellesley College, Wellesley, Mass., instructor in philosophy and psychology, 1916-17; University of California, Berkeley, assistant, 1919-20, instructor, 1920-23, assistant professor, 1923-27, associate professor, 1927-30, professor of philosophy, 1930-58, professor emeritus, 1958-72, chairman of department, 1953-58. Visiting professor at seven other universities and colleges. *Military service:* U.S. Army, Artillery, 1918.

MEMBER: International Institute of Philosophy, American Philosophical Association, College Art Association, American Society for Aesthetics, American Association of University Professors, American Academy of Arts and Sciences, Americans for Democratic Action, Faculty Club (Berkeley), Harvard Club (San Francisco).

AWARDS, HONORS: L.H.D. from Colby College, 1950, and Tulane University, 1961; L.L.D. from University of California, 1960.

WRITINGS:

Aesthetic Quality: A Contextualistic Theory of Beauty, Scribner, 1938, reprinted, Greenwood Press, 1979.
World Hypotheses: A Study in Evidence, University of California Press, 1942, reprinted, 1970.
The Basis of Criticism in the Arts, Harvard University Press, 1945.
A Digest of Purposive Values, University of California Press, 1947.
Principles of Art Appreciation, Harcourt, 1950, reprinted, Greenwood Press, 1970.
The Work of Art, Indiana University Press, 1956.
The Sources of Value, University of California Press, 1958.
Ethics, Appleton, 1960.
Concept and Quality: A World Hypothesis, Open Court, 1966.

Also author of *Modern Color,* 1919, and *Knowledge and Society,* 1938. Contributor to *Psychological Review, Journal of Philosophy, Philosophical Review,* and *Journal of Aesthetics.*

OBITUARIES:

PERIODICALS

New York Times, May 6, 1972.*

PEYTON, K. M.
See PEYTON, Kathleen Wendy

*　　*　　*

PEYTON, Kathleen Wendy 1929-
(Kathleen Herald, K. M. Peyton)

PERSONAL: Born in 1929, in Birmingham, England; married Michael Peyton (a commercial artist and cartoonist), 1950; children: Hilary, Veronica. *Education:* Attended Kingston School of Art; Manchester Art School, A.T.D.

ADDRESSES: Home—Rookery Cottage, North Fambridge, Essex, England.

CAREER: Art teacher at high school in Northampton, England, 1952-56; writer, 1956—.

MEMBER: Society of Authors.

AWARDS, HONORS: American Library Association Notable Book listing, 1963, for *Sea Fever,* 1969, for *Flambards in Summer,* 1971, for *Pennington's Last Term* and *The Beethoven Medal,* and 1972, for *A Pattern of Roses; New York Herald Tribune* award, 1965, for *The Maplin Bird;* Carnegie Medal, 1969, for *The Edge of the Cloud; Guardian* award, 1970, for *Flambards, The Edge of the Cloud,* and *Flambards in Summer; Prove Yourself a Hero* was named to the "Best Books for Young Adults 1979" list.

WRITINGS:

JUVENILE; UNDER NAME KATHLEEN HERALD

Sabre: The Horse from the Sea, A. & C. Black, 1947, reprinted, Macmillan, 1963.
The Mandrake: A Pony, illustrated by Lionel Edwards, A. & C. Black, 1949.
Crab the Roan, A. & C. Black, 1953.

JUVENILE; UNDER NAME K. M. PEYTON

North to Adventure, Collins, 1959, Platt, 1965.
Stormcock Meets Trouble, Collins, 1961.
The Hard Way Home, Collins, 1962, revised edition, Goodchild, 1986, published as *Sing a Song of Ambush,* Platt, 1964.
Sea Fever, illustrated by Victor G. Ambrus, World Publishing, 1963 (published in England as *Windfall,* Oxford University Press, 1963).
Brownsea Silver, Collins, 1964.
The Maplin Bird, illustrated by Ambrus, Oxford University Press, 1964, World Publishing, 1965, reprinted with a new introduction by Peyton, Gregg Press, 1980.
The Plan for Birdsmarsh, illustrated by Ambrus, Oxford University Press, 1965, World Publishing, 1966.
Thunder in the Sky, illustrated by Ambrus, Oxford University Press, 1966, World Publishing, 1967, reprinted, Bodley Head, 1985.
Flambards (first book in a trilogy; also see below), illustrated by Ambrus, Oxford University Press, 1967, World Publishing, 1968.
(And illustrator) *Fly-by-Night,* Oxford University Press, 1968, World Publishing, 1969.
The Edge of the Cloud (second book in a trilogy; also see below), illustrated by Ambrus, World Publishing, 1969.
Flambards in Summer (third book in a trilogy; also see below), illustrated by Ambrus, Oxford University Press, 1969, World Publishing, 1970.

(And illustrator) *Pennington's Seventeenth Summer* (also see below), Oxford University Press, 1969, World Publishing, 1970, published as *Pennington's Last Term,* Crowell, 1971.
(And illustrator) *The Beethoven Medal* (also see below), Oxford University Press, 1971, Crowell, 1972.
(And illustrator) *A Pattern of Roses,* Oxford University Press, 1972, Crowell, 1973.
(And illustrator) *Pennington's Heir* (also see below), Oxford University Press, 1973, Crowell, 1974.
(And illustrator) *The Team,* Oxford University Press, 1975, Crowell, 1976.
The Right-Hand Man, Oxford University Press, 1977.
Prove Yourself a Hero, Oxford University Press, 1977, Philomel Books, 1978.
A Midsummer Night's Death: With an Afterword by the Author, Oxford University Press, 1978, Philomel Books, 1979.
Marion's Angels, Oxford University Press, 1979.
The Flambards Trilogy (contains *Flambards, The Edge of the Cloud,* and *Flambards in Summer*), Puffin Books, 1980.
Flambards Divided, Oxford University Press, 1981, Philomel Books, 1982.
Dear Fred, Bodley Head, 1981.
Going Home, illustrated by Chris Molan, Philomel Books, 1982.
Who, Sir? Me, Sir?, Philomel Books, 1983.
Free Rein, Philomel Books, 1983.
The Last Ditch, Oxford University Press, 1983.
Pennington: A Trilogy (contains *Pennington's Seventeenth Summer, The Beethoven Medal,* and *Pennington's Heir*), Oxford University Press, 1984.
Frogett's Revenge, illustrated by Leslie Smith, Oxford University Press, 1985, U.S. edition illustrated by Maureen Bradley, Puffin Books, 1987.
The Sound of Distant Cheering, Bodley Head, 1986.
Downhill All the Way, Oxford University Press, 1988.
(And illustrator) *Plain Jack,* Hamish Hamilton, 1988.
Skylark, Oxford University Press, 1989.

WORK IN PROGRESS: Darkling, for Delacorte.

SIDELIGHTS: "I became a children's writer because I started writing as a child and naturally wrote children's books," explains Kathleen Wendy Peyton in *The Thorny Paradise: Writers on Writing for Children.* "Since then," she continues, "I must have suffered some sort of mental retardation, for I still write, as I did then, the sort of stories I like writing best and my audience is still young." Peyton's stories deal with the problems children face as they become adults, with a skill that prompts a *Junior Bookshelf* reviewer to declare that "few writers deal more convincingly with the exquisite agony of growing up than Mrs. Peyton." She has earned praises from critics like Dennis Butts, who remarks in *The Use of English:* "It is clear that Kathleen Peyton's books deal with themes and interests of a rather wider and deeper kind than one finds in most children's books. The presence of death, the awareness of sexual love, the importance of money, give her novels an unusual texture for which their romantic structures provide a successful and accessible framework."

Peyton's love of horseback riding, sailing, music, and flying is reflected in many of her books, and several reviewers have felt that the author's descriptions of these activities are one of the best features of her work. For example, in his book *A Sense of Story: Essays on Contemporary Writing for Children,* John Rowe Townsend comments that Peyton "has, among many other gifts, the unusual one of writing extremely well about *movement:* about the way people move with and through and against the elements, in boats, on horseback, and—in the *Flambards* novels—in those frail, wind-buffeted early aircraft." Living on an estuary in

Essex, England, Peyton regularly "sails the tricky waters of that deeply indented coast," according to *Junior Bookshelf* contributor Marcus S. Crouch. "She knows the sea," Crouch continues, "the creeks and the saltings, as well as the villages and the ports." Several of her stories, such as *The Maplin Bird, The Plan for Birdsmarsh, Thunder in the Sky,* and *Sea Fever,* take advantage of this background. One contributor to *School Librarian and School Library Review,* Margaret Meek, writes in a review of *The Maplin Bird* that "the estuary scenery and details of seafaring are skillfully woven into the texture of the relationships" in the story.

In *The Plan for Birdsmarsh,* the tale of a boy who tries to save his family's farm from being turned into a marina, social issues come into play as well. As Crouch notes, "the social awareness of the book is agonizingly sharp." And the introduction of this element of awareness in the author's work leads Crouch to consider *The Plan for Birdsmarsh* to be a "major turning-point in Mrs. Peyton's career." But just as her stories about sailing are not solely limited to descriptions of boating, critics have noted that Peyton's books about horses are balanced by their attention to the personal problems of her young protagonists. In a review of *Fly-by-Night,* a story about a young girl who raises a horse in her lower middle-class home, Crouch comments in his book, *The Nesbit Tradition: The Children's Novel in England, 1945-70,* that "when Mrs. Peyton turned again to examine the fortunes of her young heroine, ponies quickly disappeared and she wrote a serious social novel." The story's protagonist, Ruth, a *Young Readers' Review* critic further asserts, "is a fine creation. She is a likeable, intense girl whose heart is in the right place. The way she meets her problems is completely realistic." The reviewer concludes that *Fly-by-Night* is a "beautifully written horse story."

The *Flambards* trilogy, Peyton's "most impressive achievement" in Butts opinion, won the Guardian award in 1970 for all three books, *The Edge of the Cloud, Flambards,* and *Flambards in Summer,* and the Carnegie Medal for its second novel. These books follow the life of Christina, an orphan who lives in the crumbling English mansion Flambards with her uncle Russell, a crippled yet domineering man whose only concerns are hunting, horses, and making certain his two sons carry on his Edwardian lifestyle. However, Will, the younger son, loves airplanes more than horses, and has no desire to be part of a class which believes that horses should be treated better than servants. Christina, who, as one *Times Literary Supplement* reviewer describes, "loves hunting but hates the mindless world of the hunters," marries Will after discovering that they have similar beliefs.

Becoming an army pilot, Will later dies during World War I, and the last book of the trilogy relates how Christina attempts to restore new life to Flambards. She marries Dick, a former stable hand at the mansion, and their life together represents the rise of a new social class to replace the old gentry. "It is the triumph of Mrs. Peyton's art that she evokes this sense of social transformation by means of a few richly-actualised symbols in a historical romance of highly popular elements," concludes Butts. Part of this transformation is portrayed by Peyton through the generation gap between Will and Christina and her uncle. It is this element which makes *Flambards* an "important novel," in *Washington Post Book World* contributor Madeline L'Engle's view. A *Young Readers' Review* critic adds: "Young readers will recognize that Will, today, would talk astrophysics and Christina would join the Peace Corps. They are timeless creations."

Another of Peyton's well-known characters is Patrick Pennington, who first appears in *Pennington's Last Term.* Pamela T. Cleaver's article in *Children's Book Review* describes this work

as "a rare, marvelous book." The reviewer continues, "Penn[ington], the seventeen-year-old rebel, hating his last year at school, arrogant and surly, butting his head against authority, . . . [is] a totally believable teenager." Pennington has a talent for playing the piano, and it is this ability which eventually redeems him in the eyes of his elders. In the next two books, *The Beethoven Medal* and *Pennington's Heir,* Pennington marries Ruth, the protagonist from *Fly-by-Night,* and they have a baby. Although Ruth and Pennington suffer some setbacks, such as Pennington's brief term in jail for striking a policeman, their ability to grow as people helps them overcome many obstacles successfully.

Objecting to Peyton's penchant for happy conclusions like the one in *Pennington's Heir,* critic D. L. Rees complains in *Children's Book News* that the complications in these books are "too easily resolved." In a *Junior Bookshelf* article, however, one writer more generously reflects that "it is not in plot but in depth of characterization and in the evocation of society that [Peyton] excels." In some of the author's other books, similar criticisms about plot structure have been offered. For example, Dominic Hibberd remarks in a *Children's Literature in Education* article that having the character of Will die between the second and third *Flambards* books is "the greatest single weakness of the trilogy." And in a *Times Literary Supplement* review, one critic opines that "the chief weakness [in the plot of Peyton's *The Plan for Birdsmarsh*] lies in her conception of villainy." Crouch also notes certain problems with the earlier Peyton villains, remarking that they are not well developed characters; but he adds that "Mrs. Peyton does better now. There are no villains in *Flambards,* only people."

Despite what some reviewers see as flaws in the author's work, Townsend attests, "Mrs. Peyton can deal with large themes, and construct excellent plots if she is so minded. She can tell a story with great pace and certainty. In her historical, or semi-historical, novels her research appears impeccable, but she never gives the impression of bookishness." As for Peyton's depiction of adolescents, John W. Conner uses the Pennington books as proof that the author "understands the emotional turbulence of adolescents and portrays this. An adolescent reader of *The Beethoven Medal* will appreciate Mrs. Peyton's skill at portraying young people as they really are." In general, Peyton has been characterized by critics like *New Statesman* contributor Naomi Lewis as "a strong, trenchant, curiously unsentimental novelist." But because of her books' optimistic conclusions, the author has also been said to have a "strong but romantic heart," according to one *Times Literary Supplement* critic.

Today, Peyton continues to write stories about horses for young adults, as in *Free Rein,* as well as other favorite subjects. In 1981, she also returned to the characters of the *Flambards* trilogy with her novel, *Flambards Divided.* The purpose of all her writing, Peyton asserts in *The Thorny Paradise,* is solely to entertain, and not to convey any particular moral message. "When a writer knows he has a juvenile audience," she explains, "a certain responsibility is inevitably felt, but to think that he can 'con' his audience into what might be called correct attitudes [is an effort that] must be doomed to failure."

MEDIA ADAPTATIONS: The Right Hand Man was adapted as a film in 1987.

AVOCATIONAL INTERESTS: Riding, walking in the mountains, airplanes, sailing, horseback riding, music.

BIOGRAPHICAL/CRITICAL SOURCES:

BOOKS

Blishen, Edward, *The Thorny Paradise: Writers on Writing for Children,* Kestrel Books, 1975.
Children's Literature Review, Volume 3, Gale, 1978.
Crouch, Marcus S., *The Nesbit Tradition: The Children's Novel in England, 1945-70,* Benn, 1972.
Townsend, John Rowe, *A Sense of Story: Essays on Contemporary Writing for Children,* Longmans, 1971.

PERIODICALS

Chicago Tribune Book World, December 29, 1968, May 9, 1971.
Children's Book News, March-April, 1969, September-October, 1970.
Children's Book Review, October, 1971, February, 1973, spring, 1974.
Children's Literature in Education, July, 1972, November, 1972.
English Journal, November, 1971, November, 1972.
Junior Bookshelf, November, 1964, December, 1966, June, 1969, October, 1971, February, 1974.
New Statesman, November 3, 1967.
New York Times Book Review, July 10, 1966.
School Librarian and School Library Review, March, 1965.
Spectator, November 1, 1969, November 13, 1971.
Times Literary Supplement, December 9, 1965, November 30, 1967, October 3, 1968, April 3, 1969, October 16, 1969, November 30, 1970, November 3, 1972, December 5, 1975, September 29, 1978, September, 17, 1982, March 29, 1985, August 16, 1985.
Use of English, spring, 1972.
Washington Post Book World, November 11, 1979, February 12, 1984.
Young Readers' Review, December, 1968, May, 1969.

—*Sketch by Kevin S. Hile*

*   *   *

PIETRI, Pedro (Juan) 1943-

PERSONAL: Born March 21, 1943, in Ponce, Puerto Rico; immigrated to United States, 1945; son of Francisco and Petra (Aponte) Pietri; married Phyllis Nancy Wallach (a teacher and translator), March 3, 1978. *Education:* Attended public schools in New York, N.Y.

ADDRESSES: Home—New York, N.Y. *Office*—Cultural Council Foundation, 175 Fifth Ave., New York, N.Y. 10010; and 400 West 43rd St., 38E, New York, N.Y. 10036.

CAREER: State University of New York at Buffalo, instructor in creative writing, 1969-70; poet and playwright, 1970-78; Cultural Council Foundation, New York, N.Y., literary artist, 1978—. Conducted children's poetry workshops, 1970-72; member of bilingual and bicultural early childhood project of Puerto Rican Association for Community Affairs, 1974; consultant to El Museo del Barrio. *Military service:* U.S. Army, 1966-68.

MEMBER: Latin Insomniacs Motorcycle Club.

AWARDS, HONORS: New York State Creative Arts in Public Service Grant, 1974-75.

WRITINGS:

Puerto Rican Obituary (poems), c. 1971, reprinted, Monthly Review Press, 1974.
The Blue and the Gray, Cherry Valley, 1975.
Invisible Poetry, Downtown Train Publishers, 1979.

Loose Joints (sound recording), Folkways Records, 1979.
Lost in the Museum of Natural History (short story), Ediciones Huracán, 1980.
Out of Order (poems), Downtown Train Publishers, 1980.
Uptown Train (poems), Downtown Train Publishers, 1980.
An Alternate, Hayden Book, 1980.
Traffic Violations (poems), Waterfront Press (Maplewood, N.J.), 1983.
Missing Out of Action, Waterfront Press, in press.

Work represented in *Inventing a Word: An Anthology of Twentieth-Century Puerto Rican Poetry,* edited by Julio Marzán, Columbia University Press, in association with the Center for Inter-American Relations, 1980.

PLAYS

"Lewlulu" (one-act), first produced in New York City at Harlem Performance Center, April 23, 1976.
"What Goes Up Must Come Down" (one-act), first produced in New York City at El Porton, May 7, 1976.
"The Living-room" (one-act), first produced in New York City at H. B. Studio, March 15, 1978.
"Dead Heroes Have No Feelings" (one-act), first produced in New York City at Manhattan Plaza, October 8, 1978.
"Appearing in Person Tonight—Your Mother" (one-act), first produced in New York City at La Mama, November 8, 1978.
"Jesus Is Leaving" (one-act), first produced in New York City at Nuyorican Poets' Cafe, December 13, 1978.
(Translator) Luis Rochani Agrait, "The Company" (one-act), first produced in New York City by Puerto Rican Traveling Theater, 1978.
The Masses Are Asses (produced by Puerto Rican Traveling Theater, 1984), Waterfront Press, 1984.

Also author of the plays "No More Bingo at the Wake," "Eat Rocks!," and an unproduced play, "I Dare You to Resist Me."*

*   *   *

PLIMPTON, George (Ames) 1927-

PERSONAL: Born March 18, 1927, in New York, N.Y.; son of Francis T. P. (a lawyer and former U.S. deputy representative to the United Nations) and Pauline (Ames) Plimpton; married Freddy Medora Espy (a photography studio assistant), March 28, 1968; children: Medora Ames, Taylor Ames. *Education:* Harvard University, A.B., 1950; King's College, Cambridge, B.A., 1952, M.A., 1954. *Politics:* Democrat. *Religion:* Unitarian Universalist.

ADDRESSES: Home—541 East 72nd St., New York, N.Y. 10021. *Office*—Paris Review, Inc., 45-39 171st Pl., Flushing, N.Y. 11358. *Agent*—Russell & Volkening, 50 West 29th St., New York, N.Y. 10001.

CAREER: Writer and editor. Editor of the *Lampoon* while at Harvard. Principal editor, *Paris Review,* 1953—, publisher, with Doubleday & Co., of Paris Review Editions (books), 1965—. Associate editor, *Horizon,* 1959-61; contributing editor, *Sports Illustrated,* 1967—; associate editor, *Harper's,* 1972—; contributing editor, *Food and Wine,* 1978; member of editorial advisory board, *Realities,* 1978. Director, American Literature Anthology program, 1967—; chief editor of annual anthology of work from literary magazines for the National Foundation on the Arts and Humanities; adviser on John F. Kennedy Oral History Project. Instructor at Barnard College, 1956-58; associate fellow, Trumbull College, Yale, 1967. Occasional actor in films; journalistic participant in sporting and musical events. Honorary commissioner of fireworks, New York City, 1973—. Trustee, National Art Museum of Sport, 1967—, WNET-TV, 1973—, Police Athletic League, 1976—, African Wildlife Leadership Foundation, 1980—, Guild Hall, East Hampton, 1980—. *Military service:* U.S. Army, 1945-48; became second lieutenant.

MEMBER: Pyrotechnics Guild International, American Pyrotechniques Association, Explorers Club, NFL Alumni Association; clubs include Century Association, Racquet and Tennis, Brooks, Piping Rock, Dutch Treat, Coffee House, Devon Yacht, Travelers (Paris).

AWARDS, HONORS: Distinguished achievement award, University of Southern California, 1967; D.H.L., Franklin Pierce College, 1968.

WRITINGS:

The Rabbit's Umbrella (juvenile), Viking, 1955.
(Editor) *Writers at Work: The Paris Review Interviews,* Viking, Volume 1, 1957, Volume 2, 1963, Volume 3, 1967, Volume 4, 1976, Volume 5, 1981, Volume 6, 1984, Volume 7, 1986, Volume 8, 1988.
(Editor with Peter Ardery) *The American Literary Anthology,* Number 1, Farrar, Straus, 1968, Number 2, Random House, 1969, Number 3, Viking, 1970.
(Editor) Jean Stein, *American Journey: The Times of Robert Kennedy* (interviews), Harcourt, 1970.
(Editor) Stein, *Edie: An American Biography,* Knopf, 1982.
(Editor with Christopher Hemphill) Diana Vreeland, *D.V.,* Random House, 1984.
Fireworks: A History and Celebration, Doubleday, 1984.
(Editor) *Poets at Work,* Viking, 1989.
(Editor) *Women Writers at Work,* Viking, 1989.
(Editor) *Paris Review Anthology,* Norton, 1990.
(Editor) *The Writer's Chapbook: A Compendium of Fact, Opinion, Wit, and Advice from the 20th-Century's Preeminent Writers,* Viking, 1990.

SPORTS WRITING

Out of My League (baseball anecdotes), Harper, 1961, reprinted, Penguin, 1983.
Paper Lion (football anecdotes), Harper, 1966.
The Bogey Man (golf anecdotes), Harper, 1968, reprinted, Penguin, 1983.
(Editor and author of introduction) Pierre Etchebaster, *Pierre's Book: The Game of Court Tennis,* Barre Publishers, 1971.
(With Alex Karras and John Gordy) *Mad Ducks and Bears: Football Revisited* (football anecdotes), Random House, 1973.
One for the Record: The Inside Story of Hank Aaron's Chase for the Home Run Record, Harper, 1974.
Shadow Box (boxing anecdotes), Putnam, 1977.
One More July: A Football Dialogue with Bill Curry, Harper, 1977.
(Author of text) *Sports!,* photographs by Neil Leifer, H. N. Abrams, 1978.
A Sports Bestiary (cartoons), illustrated by Arnold Roth, McGraw-Hill, 1982.
Open Net (hockey anecdotes), Norton, 1985.
The Curious Case of Sidd Finch (baseball novel), Macmillan, 1987.

OTHER

(With William Kronick) "Plimpton! Shoot-out at Rio Lobo" (script), American Broadcasting Companies, Inc. (ABC-TV), 1970.
"Plimpton! The Man on the Flying Trapeze" (script), ABC-TV, 1970.
(With Kronick) "Plimpton! Did You Hear the One About . . . ?" (script), ABC-TV, 1971.
(With Kronick) "Plimpton! The Great Quarterback Sneak" (script), ABC-TV, 1971.
(With Kronick) "Plimpton! Adventure in Africa" (script), ABC-TV, 1972.
(Author of introduction) Bill Plympton, *Medium Rare: Cartoons,* Holt, 1978.
(Author of introduction) *Oakes Ames: Jottings of a Harvard Botanist, 1874-1950,* edited by Pauline Ames Plimpton, Harvard University Press, 1980.

SIDELIGHTS: The "career" section cited above does not do justice to George Plimpton's life. Authorities call Plimpton a "professional amateur," for, although writing is his primary occupation, he has also pitched in a post-season All-Star game in Yankee Stadium, held the position of third-string rookie quarterback for the Detroit Lions in 1963, taking the field in one exhibition game (and later playing with the Baltimore Colts against the Lions), golfed in several Pro-Am tournaments, briefly appeared in a basketball game for the Boston Celtics, boxed with former light heavyweight champion Archie Moore, and served as a goalie for the Boston Bruins hockey team in 1977 and the Edmonton Oilers in 1985. He also fought in a bullfight staged by Ernest Hemingway in 1954, and worked as a trapeze artist, lion-tamer, and clown for the Clyde Beatty-Cole Brothers Circus.

In less athletic activities, Plimpton developed a stand-up comedy routine and performed it in Las Vegas. He served as a percussionist with the New York Philharmonic and as a guest conductor of the Cincinnati Symphony. He has also been seen in films, including "Rio Lobo," where he played a bad guy shot by John Wayne, Norman Mailer's "Beyond the Law," and the film version of "Paper Lion." On television he has hosted specials and appeared in commercials, and since 1973 he has exercised his interest in pyrotechnics as honorary commissioner of fireworks for New York City.

Reviewers consider *Paper Lion,* Plimpton's book about his football adventures with the Detroit Lions, a classic of sports writing. It "is the best book written about pro football—maybe about any sport—because he captured with absolute fidelity how the average fan might feel given the opportunity to try out for a professional football team," explains Hal Higdon in the *Saturday Review.* The book attracted sports fans not only through its innovative concept—a writer actually taking the field with a professional team—but also through the author's command over language. "Practically everybody loves George's stuff because George writes with an affection for his fellow man, has a rare eye for the bizarre, and a nice sense of his own ineptitude," declares Trent Frayne in the Toronto *Globe and Mail.* "[Ernest] Hemingway . . . [once] said, 'Plimpton is the dark side of the moon of Walter Mitty.' "

Many writers echo Hemingway's statement. However, although Plimpton's adventures superficially resemble those of James Thurber's famous character, there are many differences between the two. "In his participatory journalism [Plimpton] has been described wrongly as a Walter Mitty, and he is nothing of the sort. This is no daydreaming nebbish," declares Joe Flaherty in the *New York Times Book Review.* Plimpton's adventures are tangible rather than imaginary. Yet, while Mitty in his dreams is a fantastic success at everything he undertakes, Plimpton's efforts almost invariably result in failure and humiliation. "Plimpton has stock in setting himself up as a naif . . . many of us are familiar with his gangling, tweedy demeanor and Oxford accent. He plays the 'fancy pants' to our outhouse Americana," Flaherty asserts. "George Plimpton doesn't want to be known as an athlete," explains Cal Reynard in the *Arizona Daily Star*. "He figures his role in sports is that of the spectator, but he wants to get closer to the game than the stands."

After more than twenty years of writing non fiction about sports, Plimpton published his first sports novel, *The Curious Case of Sidd Finch*, in 1987. Plimpton based the story on a *Sports Illustrated* article he had written for the 1985 April Fools Day issue about a former Harvard man-cum-Buddhist-monk, Siddhartha (Sidd) Finch, who can pitch a baseball half again as fast as any other pitcher in the history of the game—about 150 MPH. Plimpton's article claimed that Finch was about to sign with the New York Mets, and speculated about the impact an unhittable pitcher would have on the game of baseball. *The Curious Case of Sidd Finch* expands on the article, telling how Finch, after much self-doubt, is persuaded to play for the Mets and, on his return to Shea Stadium, pitches what former major league pitcher Jim Brosnan, writing in the *Washington Post Book World*, calls "THE perfect game"; he strikes out the entire batting lineup of the St. Louis Cardinals in perfect order.

Plimpton's reviewers have read *The Curious Case of Sidd Finch* with mixed feelings. Although Brosnan finds the novel "sort of like a shaggy-dog tale that once was a crisp one-liner," he continues, "*The Curious Case of Sidd Finch* is not the rollicking farce I'd hoped for, but it's worth a reading." Lee Green, writing in the *Los Angeles Times Book Review*, calls the book a "wonderfully wry and whimsical debut novel," while National League president and *New York Times Book Review* contributor A. Bartlett Giamatti states, "Mr. Plimpton's control is masterly," and adds, "[The baseball] culture is splendidly rendered with an experienced insider's knowledge, and the whole saga of Finch's brief, astonishing passage through big-league baseball is at once a parody of every player's as-told-to biography, a satire on professional sports, an extended (and intriguing) meditation on our national pastime and a touching variant on the novel of education as Sidd learns of the world."

Although his sports writing remains his best-known work, Plimpton's own interest centers on the small literary magazine he has edited since 1953. James Warren explains in the *Chicago Tribune*, "It's the Paris Review, not the chronicles of his own sporting foibles . . . that constitutes the soul—and takes up much of the time—of Plimpton's life." The *Paris Review*, unlike many other literary magazines, focuses on creative writing rather than criticism. Many famous American writers—including Jack Kerouac, Philip Roth, Henry Miller, and John Updike—have published first efforts or complete works in its pages.

Plimpton's interviews with writers about the craft of writing are a major attraction of the journal. It was the *Paris Review*, explains Nona Balakian in the *New York Times*, that first "developed a new kind of extended and articulate interview that combined the Boswellian aim with an exploration of the ideas of major contemporary writers on the art of fiction and poetry." "The thing that makes these interviews different from most interviews," writes Mark Harris in the *Chicago Tribune Book World*, "is that they go on long enough to get somewhere. If they do not arrive at the point I dreamily hoped for—creativity totally clarified with a supplementary manual on How To Write—they

supply very good instruction nevertheless." The result, Balakian concludes, is "a heightened awareness of a writer's overall purpose and meaning."

MEDIA ADAPTATIONS: "Paper Lion," the story of Plimpton's experiences as a short-term member of the Detroit Lions football team, was filmed by United Artists in 1968. Alan Alda portrayed Plimpton, but the author himself also had a role—he played Bill Ford.

BIOGRAPHICAL/CRITICAL SOURCES:

BOOKS

Authors in the News, Volume 1, Gale, 1976.
Contemporary Literary Criticism, Volume 36, Gale, 1986.
Talese, Gay, *The Overreachers,* Harper, 1965.

PERIODICALS

Arizona Daily Star, March 24, 1974.
Book Week, October 23, 1966.
Chicago Tribune, December 22, 1986, June 15-June 16, 1987.
Chicago Tribune Book World, May 3, 1981, September 2, 1984, October 14, 1984, November 24, 1985.
Christian Science Monitor, December 5, 1968.
Commentary, October, 1967.
Detroit News, March 16, 1986.
Globe and Mail (Toronto), July 7, 1984, February 8, 1986, June 14, 1986.
Los Angeles Times, July 22, 1982, March 20, 1987.
Los Angeles Times Book Review, September 30, 1984, June 21, 1987.
Milwaukee Journal, November 12, 1974.
New Yorker, November 12, 1966.
New York Herald Tribune, April 23, 1961.
New York Review of Books, February 23, 1967, February 7, 1974.
New York Times, November 12, 1973, July 29, 1977, November 16, 1977, March 28, 1981, June 14, 1984, November 14, 1985, July 30, 1987.
New York Times Book Review, April 23, 1961, November 10, 1968, January 6, 1974, July 31, 1977, November 6, 1977, June 17, 1984, September 23, 1984, November 24, 1985, July 5, 1987.
Saturday Review, December 10, 1966, August 14, 1971.
Spectator, October 14, 1978.
Time, December 19, 1977, September 10, 1984, December 8, 1986, June 8, 1987.
Times Literary Supplement, December 1, 1978, January 21, 1983, December 21, 1984, August 2, 1985, September 5, 1986, March 20, 1987.
Tribune Books (Chicago), July 5, 1987.
Wall Street Journal, August 28, 1984.
Washington Post, January 7, 1986.
Washington Post Book World, May 27, 1984, September 2, 1984, June 21, 1987.*

—*Sketch by Kenneth R. Shepherd*

*   *   *

POMEROY, Elizabeth W(right)   1938-

PERSONAL: Born July 31, 1938, in San Francisco, CA; daughter of Fulton W. (a business executive) and Margaret (Baker) Wright; married June 25, 1966; children: Margaret, John. *Education:* Stanford University, B.A. (with distinction), 1960; Harvard University, M.A.T., 1961; University of California, Berkeley, M.A., 1964; University of California, Los Angeles, Ph.D. (with distinction), 1970.

ADDRESSES: Home—420 South Parkwood Ave., Pasadena, CA 91107. *Office*—W. M. Keck Foundation, 555 South Flower St., Suite 3230, Los Angeles, CA 90071.

CAREER: High school English teacher in San Mateo, CA, 1964-66; University of California, Los Angeles, instructor in English, 1966-67; California State College (now University), Dominguez Hills, lecturer in English, 1971; University of California, Berkeley, lecturer in English and program coordinator in Arts and Humanities Division of extensions at University of California, Los Angeles, and University of California, Irvine, 1972-74; Claremont Colleges (consortium), Claremont, CA, intern in academic administration, 1974-75; Henry E. Huntington Library and Art Gallery, San Marino, CA, special projects coordinator, 1975-77, head of development, 1977-85; University of California, Los Angeles, lecturer, 1985-87; W. M. Keck Foundation, Los Angeles, program screening officer, 1987—.

MEMBER: Modern Language Association of America, Renaissance Society of America, National Organization for Women (founding member of Long Beach chapter; president, 1973-74), Philological Association of the Pacific Coast, Pacific Coast Conference on British Studies, Phi Beta Kappa, Pi Lambda Theta.

WRITINGS:

The Elizabethan Miscellanies: Development and Conventions, University of California Press, 1973.
The Huntington Library, Art Gallery, and Botanical Gardens, Harper, 1983.
Reading the Portraits of Queen Elizabeth I, Shoe String, 1989.

Also author of articles on literature, art, and gardens.

WORK IN PROGRESS: A book on Southern California gardens.

SIDELIGHTS: Elizabeth W. Pomeroy told *CA:* "I like to bring the idea of 'reading' into my writing, in the sense of 'interpreting.' The landscape and works of art can be 'read,' as can literary texts. I hope I have tied together my lifetime interests in literature, art, and gardens by letting them overlap in my thinking, by crossing formal lines of disciplines, by stirring up new questions. Also, I enjoy carrying academic ideas out of their specialized departments to reach a wider audience—as I intended in writing about Queen Elizabeth's portraits.

"My current project is a book on Southern California gardens—seven in particular—which will tell their history as works of art and as part of the social fabric, tracing what has become of these once carefully-created spaces up to the present day."

* * *

PONIATOWSKA, Elena 1933-

PERSONAL: Born May 19, 1933, in Paris, France; daughter of John E. and Paula (Amor) Poniatowska; married Guillermo Haro (an astronomer); children: Emmanuel, Felipe, Paula. *Education:* Educated in Philadelphia, Pa. *Religion:* Roman Catholic.

ADDRESSES: Home—Cerrada del Pedregal 79, Coyoacán, Z.P. 21, Mexico City, Mexico. *Office*—*Novedades,* Balderras 87, Mexico City 1, Mexico.

CAREER: Member of writing staff of *Excelsior,* 1954-55; *Novedades,* Mexico City, Mexico, staff member, 1955—. Instructor at Injuve. Founder of Editorial Siglo Veinto Uno, Cineteca Na-

cional, and Taller Literario. Speaker at schools and conferences; guest on radio and television programs.

MEMBER: International PEN.

AWARDS, HONORS: D.H.C. from University of Sinaloa; fellowship from Centro de Escritores, 1957; Premio de Periodismo from Turismo Frances, 1965; Premio Mazatlan, 1970, for *Hasta no verte Jesús mío;* Premio Villaurrutia, 1970, for *La noche de Tlatelolco: Testimonios de historia oral;* Premio de Periodismo from *Revista Siempre,* 1973; Premio Nacional de Periodismo, 1978.

WRITINGS:

IN ENGLISH TRANSLATION

La noche de Tlatelolco: Testimonios de historia oral, Ediciones Era, 1971, translation by Helen R. Lane published as *Massacre in Mexico,* introduction by Octavio Paz, Viking, 1975.
Querido Diego, te abraza Quiela, Ediciones Era, 1978, translation by Katherine Silver published as *Dear Diego,* Pantheon, 1986.
Until We Meet Again, translation by Magda Bogin, Pantheon, 1987.

IN SPANISH

Lilus Kikus, Los Presentes, 1954.
Melés y teleo: A puntes para una comedia, Panoramas, 1956.
Palabras cruzadas: Crónicas, Ediciones Era, 1961.
Todo empezó el domingo, Fondo de Cultura Económica, 1963.
Los cuentos de Lilus Kikus (title means "The Stories of Lilus Kikus"), Universidad Veracruzana, 1967.
Hasta no verte, Jesús mío (novel; title means "See You Never, Sweet Jesus"), Ediciones Era, 1969, reprinted, 1983.
(Contributor) *El Primer Primero de Mayo,* Centro de Estudios Históricos del Movimiento Obrero Mexicano, 1976.
Gaby brimmer, Grijalbo, 1979.
De noche vienes (stories), Grijalbo, 1979.
Fuerte es el silencio, Eras Crónicas, 1980.
Domingo 7, Océano, 1982.
El último guajolote, Cultura, 1982.
¡Ay vida, no me mereces!, J. Mortiz, 1985.
Serena y alta figura, Océano, 1986.

Author of screenplay "Hasta no verte, Jesús mío," released by Producciones Barbachano Ponce.

OTHER

Work represented in anthologies, including *Antología de cuentistas mexicanos,* Emmanuel Carballo, 1956; *Rojo de vida, y negro de muerte,* edited by Carlos Coccoli. Contributor to magazines, including *Revista Mexicana de Literatura, Siempre!, Estaciones, Abside,* and *Evergreen Review.*

SIDELIGHTS: Elena Poniatowska is a respected and well-known journalist contributing to several of Mexico's finest newspapers and periodicals as well as an author of many books of fiction and nonfiction. Born in Paris, the daughter of a Polish father and Mexican mother, Poniatowska immigrated with her family to Mexico when she was ten years old. A few years later, Poniatowska was sent to Philadelphia to attend the Convent of the Sacred Heart.

Poniatowska writes almost exclusively in Spanish—to date only a few of her books have been translated into English. *La noche de Tlatelolco: Testimonios de historia oral* later translated as *Massacre in Mexico* recounts Poniatowska's experiences in Mexico City during the 1968 student riots. J. A. Ellis explains in the

Library Journal that Poniatowska's *Massacre in Mexico* is "the story of the continuing tragedy of Mexico. . . . The mood ranges from the early heady optimism of the students . . . to shock and despair. In a *Commonweal* review, Ronald Christ states that *Massacre in Mexico* is a "shatteringly beautiful book. . . . Recording everything she could about the incident and the events that led up to it, Poniatowska has assembled what she calls 'a collage of voices,' a brilliantly edited text whose texture is the weaving of anecdote, official history, gossip, placards, graffiti, journalism, eye-witness accounts, agonized interpretation."

Dear Diego, the translation of Poniatowska's *Querido Diego, te abraza Quiela,* is a fictionalized reconstruction of the correspondence between the internationally famed artist, Diego Rivera, and his common-law wife of seven years, Russian painter Angelina Beloff. Written in the voice of Beloff, *Dear Diego* is a series of twelve imaginary letters describing the emotions and thoughts the young woman must have experienced after her lover leaves their home in Paris to return to his native Mexico. Although hopeful at first that Rivera will send for her and they will be reunited, Beloff eventually realizes that they will never be together again.

Barbara Probst Solomon explains the premise of this book in the *Nation:* "Elena Poniatowska's *Dear Diego* . . . is about a heated *ménage á trois* between Diego Rivera, his Russian émigré common-law wife, Angelina Beloff, and the jealous third lover, art itself. Poniatowska's narrative . . . blends real documents with her own imaginative reconstruction of Angelina Beloff's relation to Diego Rivera. Exactly how much of this is Poniatowska and how much is drawn from actual documents is not made clear, and since Rivera was a real person, the reader can't help filling the gaps in this impressionistic novella with what is already known about him."

"The novella's subject is longing," writes Hayden Herrera in the *New York Times Book Review.* Herrera continues: "Angelina tries to span the ocean separating her from Diego with a bridge of words. Her mood shifts from despair to anger to nostalgic affection. We feel her growing apprehension that his absence is permanent. As we share her struggle with loneliness, poverty, and illness, we come to admire her determination to survive. . . . Although she was abandoned, she was not a loser. To be able to love as she did was a gift."

BIOGRAPHICAL/CRITICAL SOURCES:

PERIODICALS

Best Sellers, November, 1975.
Commonweal, January 16, 1976.
Library Journal, June 1, 1975.
Nation, August 2-9, 1986.
New York Times Book Review, July 20, 1986.*

*   *   *

PORTILLO, Estela
   See PORTILLO TRAMBLEY, Estela

*   *   *

PORTILLO TRAMBLEY, Estela   1936-
   (Estela Portillo)

PERSONAL: Born January 16, 1936, in El Paso, Tex.; daughter of Frank (a diesel mechanic) and Delfina (Fierro) Portillo; mar-

ried Robert D. Trambley (in the automobile business), 1953; children: Naurene (Mrs. Karl Klements), Joyce, Tina, Robbie, Tracey (Mrs. Kenneth Nance). *Education:* University of Texas, El Paso, B.A., 1957, M.A., 1977.

ADDRESSES: Home—131 Clairemont, El Paso, Tex. 79912. *Office*—Department of Drama, Community College, 6601 Dyer, El Paso, Tex. 79904.

CAREER: High School English teacher in El Paso, Tex., 1957-64; El Paso Technical Institute, El Paso, chairman of department, 1965-69; Community College, El Paso, resident dramatist, 1970-75; affiliated with Department of Special Services, El Paso Public Schools, 1979—. Hostess of "Estela Sezs," a talk show on Radio KIZZ, 1969-70, and "Cumbres," a cultural show on KROD-TV, 1971-72.

AWARDS, HONORS: Quinto Sol Award from Quinto Sol Publications Bilingual League of the San Francisco Bay Area, 1973.

WRITINGS:

Impressions (haiku poetry), El Espejo Quinto Sol, 1971.
(Editor) *Chicanas en literatura y Arte* (title means "Chicana Women in Literature and Art"), Quinto Sol, 1974.
Rain of Scorpions and Other Writings (short stories), Tonatiuh International, 1976.
Trini, Bilingual Press, 1986.

PLAYS

The Day of the Swallows (also see below), El Espejo Quinto Sol, 1971.
"Morality Play" (three-act musical), first produced in El Paso, Tex., at Chamizal National Theatre, 1974.
(Contributor) *We Are Chicano,* Washington Square Press, 1974.
"Black Light" (three-act), first produced in El Paso at Chamizal National Theatre, 1975.
"El hombre cósmico" (title means "The Cosmic Man"), first produced at Chamizal National Theatre, 1975.
"Sun Images" (musical), first produced at Chamizal National Theatre, 1976.
(Contributor) Roberto Garza, editor, *Chicano Theatre* (includes "the Day of the Swallows"), Notre Dame University Press, 1976.
"Isabel and the Dancing Bear" (three-act), first produced at Chamizal National Theatre, 1977.
Sor Juana and Other Plays, Bilingual Press, 1983.

Also author of "Autumn Gold" (three-act comedy), "Broken Moon" (three-act play), and "Los amores de Don Estafa" (three-act comedy in English).

OTHER

Author of unpublished novel, *Women of the Earth.* Contributor of poems and plays to *El Grito* and *Grito del Sol.*

WORK IN PROGRESS: Perla, a novel; producing and directing a video film, "Por la Calle" (title means "Along the Street").

SIDELIGHTS: Estela Portillo Trambley is the first Chicana to publish a book of short stories and first to write a musical comedy. Her work examines the quest for self-determination of women and Chicanos in societies that assign them to subservient roles. Critics relate that her acclaimed work tends to use powerful images. For example, in *Rain of Scorpions and Other Stories,* young boys trapped in a smelting town barrio enter a cave looking for a mythical underground paradise; meanwhile, a rainstorm starts an avalanche of mud above them. "The thousands of scorpions unearthed by the avalanche rumble down the main street of Smeltertown like a sea of filth and death, a symbol of the Anglo city's dumping its waste and poison into the ghetto," Vernon E. Lattin observes in *Studies in American Literature.* Some readers find these images overwhelming, while others appreciate her ability to give topics familiar to Chicano literature new life.

While other fiction cries out against the destructive forces of the ghetto, Portillo Trambley's stories present the barrio as the site of spiritual growth and comfort despite its squalor. The triumph of the human spirit over oppression and natural catastrophe makes the ghetto a place that, her characters decide, finally, is difficult to leave behind. In "Duende," Lattin notes, "although [Portillo] Trambley realistically represents the poverty and suffering of the ghetto, the final impression is of a spirit which transcends this misery. It is the spirit of [the young man] Triano, a mountain freedom brought from Duende, that the author sees as more powerful. The reader is left with the expectation that even Marusha [a woman who longs to escape the ghetto] will find warmth and freedom in the barrio."

Portillo Trambley found these qualities in her childhood home. As she told Juan Bruce-Novoa for an interview collected in *Chicano Authors: Inquiry by Interview,* "I would watch sunlight continuing itself on adobe walls; the silences in early afternoon had a mysterious splendor. We were poor. I am still poor, pero la pobreza nunca derriba el espíritu [but poverty never defeats the spirit]. When I was a child, poverty was a common suffering for everybody around me. A common suffering is a richness in itself." Her view that the human spirit is more powerful than its environment is rooted in ancient Náhuatl cosmology, notes Thomas Vallejos in *Frontiers: A Journal of Women Studies.*

Portillo Trambley's plays express feminist, ethnic, and nonpolitical themes. *The Day of the Swallows,* considered her best work in this genre, follows the lesbian protagonist Josefa through stages of secrecy, violence against a boy who accidentally discovers her secret, despair when her affair ends, and suicide by drowning while dressed in a wedding gown. Phyllis Mael, writing in *Frontiers,* suggests that Josefa's desperate actions are not actions of free choice, but reactions against a male-dominated society. Portillo Trambley's other plays carry images from the past forward to express the reality of life for Chicanos in the United States, the conflict between traditional values and contemporary institutions. "Black Light" includes a Mayan dance as one of many contrasts between the Chicano past and the urban present. "Morality Play," also unpublished, borrows the fifteenth-century drama form to show the victory of human faith, hope, and charity over the dehumanizing influences of power-brokers. Perhaps the least political of her plays is "Sun Images," a musical comedy in which viewers are allowed to draw their own conclusions about the long-standing conflict between Chicanos and immigration officers.

Portillo Trambley appreciates Chicano literature that stresses what it means to be human anywhere in the world. She told Bruce-Novoa, "There are so many features of the Chicano experience that are 100 percent eternal, that any people in the world can identify with. The strengths, our hopes, our family structure, our capacity to love, all the results of the closure of our society and what it has made of us. This vital and human experience could actually find readers, aside from the Americans, readers in Italy, Spain and . . . because it is a universal one. They have all been through the same thing historically."

When asked if her work has a political focus, she told Bruce-Novoa, "I separate politics from literature because I believe that when you inject politics into it you limit its life, as I said before.

All good literature is based on the human experience which is nonpolitical. Use literature as a political tool and it becomes provincial, time-bound. . . . There is a place for the powerful force literature can be; it's needed in our Movement to give it cohesion. But literature itself is very impersonal, nonpolitical. There is a tenacity about it, to stay alive, to believe in love, to cope, to pick ourselves up, to fly. Political literature, no matter how clever it might be, tends to make stereotypes of the evil exploiter and the poor, innocent victim. That is not life. The exploiter is a human being too. He might be violent and selfish and greedy and mean, but down deep, despite having mutated into a Machiavellian oddity, he is still human. Once you take this away from your character in literature, you've taken away his life. Political literature assassinates characters."

The former resident dramatist of Community College in El Paso once told *CA:* "I would like to write and produce plays that are structured in traditional form. It is another direction from the 'acto' and the socio-political products which, innovative though they may be, still fail to meet the standards of good theatre. My own work in drama must undergo a lot of rewriting and change to meet those standards too. Having the opportunity to experiment with live productions of my own work focuses the flaws and the strong points in my work.

"The writing of the novel is another kind of challenge, lonely, retrospective, an inward drama of evolutionary growth and change. A novel is 'all up to me' if it has any worth or success. Drama involves the players, the audience outside of myself. It is a more precarious challenge, more joyous than the writing of a novel because one works with people—energy outside of oneself as a writer. But the 'power of myself,' the lonely and creative elation of novel-writing is winning over. The energy is from within."

BIOGRAPHICAL/CRITICAL SOURCES:

BOOKS

Bruce-Novoa, Juan, *Chicano Authors: Inquiry by Interview,* University of Texas Press, 1980.
Meier, Matt S., *Mexican American Biographies: A Historical Dictionary, 1836-1987,* Greenwood Press, 1988.

PERIODICALS

Belles Lettres, May, 1988.
Critique, Volume 21, number 1, 1979.
De Colores, Volume 3, number 3, 1977.
Drama, winter, 1983.
Frontiers: A Journal of Women Studies, summer, 1980.
MELUS, Volume 7, number 4, 1980, Volume 9, winter, 1981.
Revista Chicano-Riqueña, summer, 1977, winter, 1979.
Studies in American Fiction, spring, 1978.*

*   *   *

POULIN, A(lfred A.), Jr. 1938-

PERSONAL: Born March 14, 1938, in Lisbon, ME; son of Alfred A. (a laborer) and Alice (Michaud) Poulin; married Basilike H. Parkas; children: Daphne. *Education:* St. Francis College, Biddeford, ME, B.A. (cum laude), 1960; Loyola University, Chicago, IL, M.A., 1962; University of Iowa, M.F.A., 1968.

ADDRESSES: Home—92 Park Ave., Brockport, NY 14420. *Office*—Department of English, State University of New York College at Brockport, Brockport, NY 14420.

CAREER: St. Francis College, Biddeford, ME, instructor in humanities, 1962-64; University of Maryland, European Division,

Heidelberg, Federal Republic of Germany, instructor in English, 1965; University of New Hampshire, Durham, instructor in English, 1965-66; St. Francis College, assistant professor of English, 1968-71, chairman of humanities department, 1969-71, assistant to president, 1971; State University of New York College at Brockport, Brockport, 1971—, began as assistant professor, became professor of English. Resident at Corporation of Yaddo, 1977, 1980; visiting professor at University of Athens, December, 1980, May, 1981, May, 1982. Founding editor and publisher, BOA Editions, 1976—; founding executive director and chairman of board of New York State Literary Center, Inc., 1978-81. Director of Brockport Writers Forum, 1971-78; New York State Council on the Arts, panelist on literature program, 1977-80, member of task force on the individual writer, 1980-81. Consultant to publishing companies and literary organizations.

AWARDS, HONORS: Danforth Foundation associate, 1970-74; Research Foundation of the State University of New York fellowships and grants, 1972-74, 1977, 1979; National Endowment for the Arts creative writing fellowship, 1974, grant, 1982; translation awards, Translation Center, Columbia University, 1976, for *The Sonnets to Orpheus,* and 1987, for *Anne Hebert: Selected Poems.*

WRITINGS:

TRANSLATOR

Rainer Maria Rilke, *Duino Elegies* [and] *The Sonnets to Orpheus,* Houghton, 1977.
Rilke, *Saltimbanques,* Graywolf Press, 1979.
Rilke, *The Roses and the Windows,* Graywolf Press, 1979.
Anne Hebert, *Poems,* Quarterly Review of Literature, 1980.
Rilke, *The Astonishment of Origins,* Graywolf Press, 1982.
Rilke, *Orchards,* Graywolf Press, 1982.
Rilke, *The Migration of Powers,* Graywolf Press, 1983.
Rilke, *The Complete French Poems of Rainer Maria Rilke,* Graywolf Press, 1986.
Anne Hebert, *Anne Hebert: Selected Poems,* BOA Editions, 1987.

OTHER

(Editor, with David DeTurk, and contributor) *The American Folk Scene: Dimensions of the Folksong Revival,* Dell, 1967.
(Editor) *Contemporary American Poetry,* Houghton, 1971, 4th edition, 1985.
(Editor) *Making in All Its Forms: Contemporary American Poetics and Criticism,* Dutton, 1972.
In Advent: Poems, Dutton, 1972.
Catawba: Omens, Prayers and Songs, Graywolf Press, 1977.
The Widow's Taboo: Poems after the Catawba, Mushinsha, 1977.
The Nameless Garden: Poems, (chapbook), Ohio Review, 1981.
(Editor) *A Ballet for the Ear: Interviews, Reviews and Essays by John Logan,* University of Michigan Press, 1983.
A Nest of Sonnets (pamphlet), BOA Editions, 1986.
A Momentary Order, Graywolf Press, 1987.

Contributor of poems and translations to numerous anthologies; contributor of poems, translations, essays, and reviews to magazines and journals, including *Atlantic, Esquire, Ms., Journal of Modern Literature, Modern Poetry Studies,* and *New England Review.* Contributing editor, *American Poetry Review,* 1972—.

WORK IN PROGRESS: Writing *Begin Again: Poems, Cave Dwellers: Poems,* and *The Dangerous Widows and Other Eskimo Tales;* translating *Ode to the Saint Lawrence: The Poems of Gatien Lapointe;* editing *I Sing the Body Electric: Sexuality in American Poetry, Contemporary American Poetry,* Volume 2, *Modern American Poetry,* and *The Figure of Experience: An Introduction to Poetry;* translating and editing *Like a Singing Tree: Contemporary French Poetry of Canada.*

SIDELIGHTS: A. Poulin, Jr. once told *CA:* "For good or ill, I have chosen not to be exclusively a poet. I have not isolated my work as a poet from my interest in the popular arts, especially songwriting, from my critical interest in the poetry and criticism of others, from the challenge of editing, or from my activities as a teacher. I am convinced that each of these feeds on the other, is strengthened by such interchange. Besides, a man—at least this man—survives on a number of levels, each with its own stress of energy and identity."

*   *   *

POWELL, Anthony (Dymoke) 1905-

PERSONAL: Surname rhymes with "Noel"; born December 21, 1905, in London, England; son of Philip Lionel William (an army officer) and Maude Mary (Wells-Dymoke) Powell; married Lady Violet Pakenham, daughter of fifth Earl of Longford, December 1, 1934; children: Tristram, John. *Education:* Balliol College, Oxford, B.A., 1926, M.A., 1944.

ADDRESSES: Home—The Chantry, near Frome, Somerset, England.

CAREER: Writer, 1930—. Affiliated with Duckworth & Co., Ltd. (publishing house), London, England, 1926-35; scriptwriter for Warner Brothers of Great Britain, 1936. Trustee of National Portrait Gallery, London, 1962-76. *Military service:* Welch Regiment, Infantry, 1939-41, Intelligence Corps, 1941-45; served as liaison officer at War Office; became major; received Order of the White Lion (Czechoslovakia), Order of Leopold II (Belgium), Oaken Crown and Croix de Guerre (both Luxembourg).

MEMBER: American Academy of Arts and Letters (honorary member), Travellers' Club (London), Modern Language Society (honorary member).

AWARDS, HONORS: Named Commander of Order of the British Empire, 1956, named Companion of Honor, 1988; James Tait Black Memorial Prize, 1958, for *At Lady Molly's;* W. H. Smith Fiction Award, 1974, for *Temporary Kings;* Bennett Award from *Hudson Review* and T. S. Eliot Award from Ingersoll Foundation, both 1984, both for body of work. D.Litt., University of Sussex, 1971, University of Leicester and University of Kent, 1976, Oxford University, 1980, and Bristol University, 1982.

WRITINGS:

(Editor) *Barnard Letters, 1778-1884,* Duckworth, 1928.
Afternoon Men (novel), Duckworth, 1931, Holt, 1932, reprinted, Popular Library, 1978.
Venusberg (novel; also see below), Duckworth, 1932, Popular Library, 1978.
From a View to a Death (novel), Duckworth, 1933, reprinted, Popular Library, 1978, published as *Mr. Zouch, Superman: From a View to a Death,* Vanguard, 1934.
Agents and Patients (novel; also see below), Duckworth, 1936, Popular Library, 1978.
What's Become of Waring? (novel), Cassell, 1939, Little, Brown, 1963, reprinted, Popular Library, 1978.
(Editor and author of introduction) *Novels of High Society from the Victorian Age,* Pilot Press, 1947.
John Aubrey and His Friends, Scribner, 1948, revised edition, Barnes & Noble, 1963, reprinted, Chatto & Windus, 1988.

(Editor and author of introduction) John Aubrey, *Brief Lives and Other Selected Writings,* Scribner, 1949.

(Author of introduction) E. W. Hornung, *Raffles,* Eyre & Spottiswoode, 1950.

Two Novels: Venusberg [and] *Agents and Patients,* Periscope-Holliday, 1952.

(Author of preface) *The Complete Ronald Firbank,* Duckworth, 1961.

(Contributor) *Burke's Landed Gentry,* Burke's Peerage Publications, 1965.

Two Plays: The Garden God [and] *The Rest I'll Whistle,* Heinemann, 1971, Little, Brown, 1972.

(Contributor) Richard Shead, *Constant Lambert,* Simon Publications, 1973.

To Keep the Ball Rolling: The Memoirs of Anthony Powell, Volume 1: *Infants of the Spring,* Heinemann, 1976, published as *Infants of the Spring: The Memoirs of Anthony Powell,* Holt, 1977, reprinted, Penguin, 1984, Volume 2: *Messengers of Day,* Holt, 1978, Volume 3: *Faces in My Time,* Heinemann, 1980, Holt, 1981, Volume 4: *The Strangers Are All Gone,* Heinemann, 1982, Holt, 1983, abridged edition of all four volumes published as *To Keep the Ball Rolling,* Penguin, 1983.

(Author of introduction) Jocelyn Brooke, *The Orchid Trilogy,* Secker & Warburg, 1981.

O, How the Wheel Becomes It! (novella), New American Library, 1985.

The Fisher King (novel), Norton, 1986.

Miscellaneous Verdicts (criticism), Heinemann, 1990.

"A DANCE TO THE MUSIC OF TIME" SERIES; NOVELS; ALSO SEE BELOW

A Question of Upbringing, Scribner, 1951, reprinted, Warner Books, 1985.

A Buyer's Market, Heinemann, 1952, Scribner, 1953, reprinted, Warner Books, 1985.

The Acceptance World, Heinemann, 1955, Farrar, Straus, 1956, reprinted, Warner Books, 1985.

At Lady Molly's, Heinemann, 1957, Little, Brown, 1958, reprinted, Warner Books, 1985.

Casanova's Chinese Restaurant, Little, Brown, 1960, reprinted, Warner Books, 1985.

The Kindly Ones, Little, Brown, 1962, reprinted, Warner Books, 1985.

The Valley of Bones, Little, Brown, 1964, reprinted, Warner Books, 1985.

The Soldier's Art, Little, Brown, 1966, reprinted, Warner Books, 1985.

The Military Philosophers, Heinemann, 1968, Little, Brown, 1969, reprinted, Warner Books, 1985.

Books Do Furnish a Room, Little, Brown, 1971, reprinted, Warner Books, 1986.

Temporary Kings, Little, Brown, 1973, reprinted, Warner Books, 1986.

Hearing Secret Harmonies, Heinemann, 1975, Little, Brown, 1976, reprinted, Warner Books, 1986.

"A DANCE TO THE MUSIC OF TIME" OMNIBUS VOLUMES

A Dance to the Music of Time: First Movement (contains *A Question of Upbringing, A Buyer's Market,* and *The Acceptance World*), Little, Brown, 1963.

A Dance to the Music of Time: Second Movement (contains *At Lady Molly's, Casanova's Chinese Restaurant,* and *The Kindly Ones*), Little, Brown, 1964.

A Dance to the Music of Time: Third Movement (contains *The Valley of Bones, The Soldier's Art,* and *The Military Philosophers*), Little, Brown, 1971.

A Dance to the Music of Time: Fourth Movement (contains *Books Do Furnish a Room, Temporary Kings,* and *Hearing Secret Harmonies*), Little, Brown, 1976.

WORK IN PROGRESS: Miscellaneous Verdicts, a collection of criticism.

SIDELIGHTS: Novelist Anthony Powell has spent more than forty years chronicling the changing fortunes of Great Britain's upper class in the twentieth century. He is best known for his twelve-volume series "A Dance to the Music of Time," the longest fictional work in the English language. Published in installments over almost twenty-five years, "A Dance to the Music of Time" follows a number of characters from adolescence in 1914 to old age and death in the late 1960s. *New Yorker* contributor Naomi Bliven calls the series "one of the most important works of fiction since the Second World War," and *New Republic* reviewer C. David Benson describes the novels as "the most sophisticated chronicle of modern life we have." In the Toronto *Globe and Mail,* Douglas Hill observes that Powell "has had the good fortune to be in the right place at the right time and among the right people, and to be able to watch all this passing scene and transform the most apparently insignificant moments into the fabric of his fiction."

Newsweek correspondent Gene Lyons notes that Powell is "entirely provincial, yet not at all a snob, . . . an aristocratic man of letters in the best British tradition." Lyons continues: "He is a contemporary of that extraordinary group of English writers who were born during the first decade of this century." Indeed, Powell enjoyed close friendships with Evelyn Waugh, Cyril Connolly, and George Orwell, and he knew numerous other important writers, including Dylan Thomas and F. Scott Fitzgerald. Powell grew up in comfortable circumstances—he is a descendent of nobility—and was educated at Eton and Oxford. As Benson notes, however, the author's entire generation "was marked by having experienced the extinction of the privileged England of their childhoods which was replaced by a completely different post-war world." In his fiction Powell explores the extinction, or rather the metamorphosis, of the British upper class.

Powell graduated from Oxford in 1926 and took a job with Duckworth, a major publishing house in London. While he served as an editor at Duckworth, Powell began to write fiction of his own; eventually, Duckworth published four of his five early novels. *Dictionary of Literary Biography* contributor James Tucker describes Powell's first few books as "entertaining, light, but not lightweight." Tucker also observes that in his early works Powell "appears to be interested in societies under threat, either from their own languor and foolishness or from huge political reverses or from calculated infiltration by arrivistes." Powell's first novel, *Afternoon Men,* has become his best known pre-war work. A satire of the upper-middle-class penchant for aimlessness, *Afternoon Men* begins and ends with party invitations. Tucker contends that, in the novel, Powell "expertly depicts the banality of the lives under scrutiny by having characters talk with a remorseless, plodding simplicity, as if half-baked, half-drunk, or half-asleep after too many nights on the town."

Even though Powell's first five novels sold only several thousand copies apiece, by the 1930s the author "had come to be recognized as one of several significant novelists who had emerged in Britain since World War I," to quote Tucker. Like most Englishmen his age, however, Powell faced a cessation of his career when the Second World War began. He enlisted in the Welsh

Regiment and then served four years with the Intelligence Corps as liaison to the War Office. When the war ended, Powell still did not return to fiction for some time. Instead, he wrote a comprehensive biography on John Aubrey, a seventeenth century writer and antiquary of Welsh descent. Only when *John Aubrey and His Friends* was completed did Powell return to fiction—but he did so in a grand way. Tucker writes: "Believing that many authors went on producing what were virtually the same characters in book after book, though with different names and in fresh circumstances, [Powell] wanted to break out from the confines of the 80,000 word novel. The *roman-fleuve* would allow him to recognize the problem openly and continue with established characters through successive volumes. During the late 1940s, while visiting the Wallace Collection in London, he saw Nicolas Poussin's painting *A Dance to the Music of Time* and felt he had at last found the theme and title of his work."

The Poussin painting depicts the four seasons as buxom young maidens, dancing under a threatening sky to music provided by a wizened, bearded man—Father Time. Powell's work, too, involves "dancers," a coterie of interrelated men and women living in modern Britain, whose lives intersect on the whims of fate. As Tucker notes, "scores of major characters dance their way in and out of one another's lives—and especially one another's beds—often in seemingly random style; yet when the whole sequence is seen together there is some sort of order. To put it more strongly than that would be wrong; but music and dance do imply a system, harmony, pattern."

Kerry McSweeney describes "A Dance to the Music of Time" in a *South Atlantic Quarterly* essay. According to McSweeney, the book's subject "is a densely populated swathe of upper-class, upper-middle-class, artistic, and Bohemian life in England from the twenties to the seventies. The vehicle of presentation is the comedy of manners. Attention is consistently focused on the nuances of social behavior, the idiosyncrasies of personal style, and the intricacies of sexual preference. All of the characters in the series . . . are seen strictly from the outside—that is, in terms of how they choose to present themselves to the world." In the early volumes, the characters leave school to establish careers which are often less important than the whirl of social obligations. The middle volumes concern the years of the Second World War, and the later volumes send many of the characters to their deaths. In *The Situation of the Novel*, Bernard Bergonzi notes that "A Dance to the Music of Time" is "a great work of social comedy in a central English tradition" that "also conveys the cumulative sense of a shabby and dispirited society." A *Washington Post Book World* reviewer calls the series "an addictive social fantasy, strictly controlled by the author's sense of the ambiguity of human relationships and an indispensable literary style."

The action in "A Dance to the Music of Time" is revealed by Nicholas Jenkins, a non-participant observer who is happily married, urbane, and loyal to his values. From his vantage point in society, Jenkins describes the ascent of several power-hungry men—chief among them Kenneth Widmerpool—who become consumed by the perfection of their public images. Bliven contends that the series "subtly but ever more insistently contrasts the quest for power with the urge to create. The power seekers are killers and lovers of death, and the defenses against them are disinterestedness, playfulness, and, above all, artistic dedication." Tucker sees the tension between Jenkins and Widmerpool as "the difference between a man who is nothing but ambition, a sort of burlesque Faust, and another who represents enduring standards of humaneness, creativity, and artistic appreciation in a shoddy world."

"A Dance to the Music of Time" does not provide a continuous narrative; rather, it presents a series of minutely-observed vignettes, described with an understated prose. "What strikes one first about [the series]," Tucker writes in *The Novels of Anthony Powell*, "is its elaborate texture and seemingly cast-iron poise, qualities suiting the narrator's wisdom, favoured status, knowledge and assurance. . . . The prose is largely appositional: to borrow the mode, plain statement followed by commentary or modification or conjecture, so that the reader feels himself presented with a very wide choice of possible responses; the uncertainties of real life are caught. . . . This modulated dignity, mandarin with the skids under it, gives Powell's style its distinction." In the *New York Review of Books,* Michael Wood concludes that the most "persistent pleasure" to be gained from Powell's masterwork "is that of having your expectations skillfully and elegantly cheated: the musician plays a strange chord, or an old chord you haven't heard for a long time, even a wrong note now and then." Lyons makes the observation that "A Dance to the Music of Time" provides a remarkable steadfastness of vision—"the novel's closing pages, written 25 years after the opening, make so perfect a fit they might have been the product of a single morning's work."

Powell's series has found numerous champions in both Great Britain and the United States. *Chicago Tribune Books* reviewer Larry Kart, for one, calls "A Dance to the Music of Time" the "century's finest English-language work of fiction." In *The Sense of Life in the Modern Novel,* Arthur Mizener writes that the effect of the work "is a very remarkable one for the mid-twentieth century. It is as if we had come suddenly on an enormously intelligent but completely undogmatic mind with a vision of experience that is deeply penetrating and yet wholly recognizable, beautifully subtle in ordination and yet quite unostentatious in technique, and in every respect undistorted by doctrine." *Commonweal* contributor Arnold Beichman praises Powell's novels for their "great cosmic sadness about our lives," adding: "It is Powell's skill and power in depicting man's helplessness that makes [his] novels so unforgettable, so wonderfully sad." Speaking to the universality of "A Dance to the Music of Time," *National Review* correspondent Anthony Lejeune concludes that Powell "makes us see not only his world, but ours, through his eyes. Not only his characters, but our own lives and the lives which are constantly weaving and unweaving themselves around us, become part of the pattern, part of the inexplicable dance."

Powell has not been idle since the completion of "A Dance to the Music of Time." Since 1975 he has written a four-volume memoir, a novella entitled *O, How the Wheel Becomes It!,* and a novel, *The Fisher King.* In *The Novels of Anthony Powell,* Tucker suggests that one feels "a plea throughout Powell's books for the natural warmth and vitality of life to be allowed their expression. . . . The distinction of Powell's novels is that they engagingly look at surfaces and, at the same time, suggest that this is by no means enough. They will continually disturb the surface to show us much more. In their quiet way they direct us towards a good, practical, unextreme general philosophy of life." *Voice Literary Supplement* contributor Ann Snitow observes that Powell can be recommended "for his long, honorable battle with language, his unavoidable anxieties, his preference for kindness over gaudier virtues. If he's brittle, it's because he knows things break; he's never complacent in either his playfulness or his hauteur." Snitow concludes: "Powell's a writer who values humility—antique word—a virtue now so necessary, and even more rare and obscure, perhaps, than Powell himself."

BIOGRAPHICAL/CRITICAL SOURCES:

BOOKS

Allen, Walter, *The Modern Novel,* Dutton, 1965.

Bergonzi, Bernard, *The Situation of the Novel,* University of Pittsburgh Press, 1970.

Bergonzi, Bernard, *Anthony Powell,* Longman, 1971.

Contemporary Literary Criticism, Gale, Volume 1, 1973, Volume 3, 1975, Volume 7, 1977, Volume 9, 1978, Volume 10, 1979, Volume 31, 1985.

Dictionary of Literary Biography, Volume 15: *British Novelists, 1930-1959,* Gale, 1983.

Hall, James, *The Tragic Comedians,* Indiana University Press, 1963.

Karl, Frederick R., *A Reader's Guide to the Contemporary English Novel,* Farrar, Straus, 1962.

Mizener, Arthur, *The Sense of Life in the Modern Novel,* Houghton, 1964.

Morris, Robert K., *The Novels of Anthony Powell,* University of Pittsburgh Press, 1968.

Ries, Lawrence R., *Wolf Masks: Violence in Contemporary Poetry,* Kennikat, 1977.

Russell, John, *Anthony Powell, A Quintet, Sextet and War,* Indiana University Press, 1970.

Shapiro, Charles, *Contemporary British Novelists,* Southern Illinois University Press, 1965.

Spurling, Hilary, *Invitation to the Dance: A Guide to Anthony Powell's "Dance to the Music of Time,"* Little, Brown, 1978.

Symons, Julian, *Critical Occasions,* Hamish Hamilton, 1966.

Tucker, James, *The Novels of Anthony Powell,* Columbia University Press, 1976.

PERIODICALS

Atlantic, March, 1962.
Best Sellers, March 15, 1969.
Books and Bookmen, April, 1971, March, 1976, January, 1977.
Book Week, April 9, 1967.
Chicago Tribune Books, September 28, 1986.
Chicago Tribune Book World, July 19, 1981.
Christian Science Monitor, October 6, 1960, January 25, 1967, March 16, 1967, March 9, 1981.
Commonweal, July 31, 1959, May 12, 1967, May 30, 1969.
Contemporary Literature, spring, 1976.
Critique, spring, 1964.
Encounter, February, 1976.
Globe and Mail (Toronto), March 31, 1984.
Hudson Review, summer, 1967, spring, 1976, winter, 1981-82, autumn, 1984.
Kenyon Review, winter, 1960.
Listener, October 14, 1968, September 11, 1975, May 11, 1978.
London Magazine, January, 1969.
London Review of Books, May 18, 1983.
Los Angeles Times Book Review, May 22, 1983, November 6, 1983.
Nation, May 29, 1967, December 10, 1973, June 19, 1976.
National Review, December 7, 1973, June 11, 1976, January 11, 1985.
New Leader, November 26, 1973.
New Republic, September 24, 1962, April 22, 1967, October 27, 1973, June 11, 1977.
New Review, September, 1974.
New Statesman, June 25, 1960, July 6, 1962, May 19, 1980, May 21, 1982.
Newsweek, March 24, 1969, October 29, 1973, April 5, 1976, April 25, 1983, September 2, 1985.

New Yorker, July 3, 1965, June 3, 1967, May 10, 1976.
New York Herald Tribune Books, February 11, 1962.
New York Review of Books, May 18, 1967, November 1, 1973.
New York Times, March 14, 1968, March 13, 1969, September 8, 1971, February 17, 1972, February 4, 1981, November 16, 1984, September 23, 1986.
New York Times Book Review, January 21, 1962, September 30, 1962, March 19, 1967, March 9, 1969, October 14, 1973, November 1, 1973, April 11, 1976, February 8, 1981, June 26, 1983, January 22, 1984, October 19, 1986, February 21, 1988.
Observer Review, October 10, 1967, October 13, 1968, February 14, 1971.
Publishers Weekly, April 5, 1976.
Saturday Review, March 18, 1967, March 8, 1969, November 11, 1973, April 17, 1976.
Sewanee Review, spring, 1974.
South Atlantic Quarterly, winter, 1977.
Spectator, June 24, 1960, September 16, 1966, October 18, 1968, September 13, 1975, October 9, 1976, June 5, 1982.
Time, August 11, 1958, March 3, 1967, March 28, 1969, March 9, 1981.
Times (London), April 3, 1980, May 13, 1982, June 16, 1983, April 3, 1986.
Times Literary Supplement, October 17, 1968, March 28, 1980, June 24, 1983, September 21, 1984, April 4, 1986.
Twentieth Century, July, 1961.
Virginia Quarterly Review, summer, 1976, spring, 1978, autumn, 1985.
Voice Literary Supplement, February, 1984.
Washington Post Book World, April 4, 1976, May 30, 1976, October 9, 1977, September 17, 1978, January 18, 1981, October 12, 1986, December 13, 1987.
World Literature Today, summer, 1979.

—*Sketch by Anne Janette Johnson*

* * *

PRADA OROPEZA, Renato 1937-

PERSONAL: Born October 17, 1937, in Potosí, Bolivia; son of Augusto (an advocate) and Bertha (Oropeza) Prada; married Elda Rojas, December 17, 1956; children: Ingmar, Fabrizio. *Education:* Calatayud High School, bachelor of humanities, 1961; Normal Superior Católica, high school teacher certification, 1964; Universita degli Studi di Roma, Ph.D. (philosophy), 1972. *Religion:* Roman Catholic.

ADDRESSES: Home—Fochplein 19, Louvain, Belgium 3000. *Agent*—Carmen Ballcels, Urgel 241, Barcelona 11, Spain.

CAREER: High school teacher of Spanish and philosophy in Cochabamba, Bolivia, 1965-67; Normal Superior Católica, Cochabamba, professor of philosophy, 1967-70. Subdirector and professor of philosophy, Maryknoll Institute, 1963-67; professor of philosophy, Universidad Católica, 1969-70. *Military service:* Bolivian Army, 1956.

AWARDS, HONORS: Premio Municipal de Cuento, 1967, for *Argal;* Premio Nacional de Cuento, 1968, for short story "El combate"; Concurso Nacional del Novela Erich Guttentag, Los Amigos del Libro, and Premio de Novela, Casa de las Américas (Cuba), both 1969, both for *Los fundadores del alba.*

WRITINGS:

Argal (short stories), Los Amigos del Libro, 1967.
Ya nadie espera al hombre (short stories), Don Bosco, 1969.
Al borde del silencio (short stories), ALFA, 1969.

Los fundadores del alba (novel), Los Amigos del Libro, 1969, translation by Walter Redmond published as *The Breach,* Doubleday, 1971.

El último filo, Planeta (Barcelona), 1975.

La autonomía literaria: sistema y función, Los Amigos del Libro, 1976.

La autonomía literaria: formalismo ruso y Círculo de Praga, Centro de Investigaciones Lingüístico-Literarias, Universidad Veracruzana (Jalapa, Mexico), 1977.

(Editor and author of prologue) Roland Barthes and others, *Lingüística y literatura,* Centro de Investigaciones Lingüísticas-Literarias, Instituto de Investigaciones Humanísticas, Universidad Veracruzana, 1978.

El lenguaje narrativo: prolegómenos para una semiótica narrativa, EDUCA (Costa Rica), 1979.

Larga hora, la vigilia, Premia Editora (Mexico), 1979.

La ofrenda y otros relatos, Premia Editora, 1981.

Los nombres del infierno, Universidad Autónoma de Chiapas (Mexico), 1985.

SIDELIGHTS: Renato Prada Oropeza's award-winning short novel, *Los fundadores del alba* (*The Breach*), helped to introduce the theme of the guerrilla to literature by telling the story of a group of rebels who are exterminated by the Bolivian Army. Prada Oropeza does not take sides in this narrative, however, and offers a sympathetic eye to both factions while attempting to show the need for compassion for all of humanity.

The author's short stories address the themes of the isolation of modern man and his inability to affect changes in his life.

BIOGRAPHICAL/CRITICAL SOURCES:

PERIODICALS

Times Literary Supplement, July 3, 1969.

*   *   *

PRONZINI, Bill 1943-
(Jack Foxx, Alex Saxon; William Jeffrey, a joint pseudonym)

PERSONAL: Born April 13, 1943, in Petaluma, CA; son of Joseph (a farm worker) and Helene (Guder) Pronzini; married Laura Patricia Adolphson, May 15, 1965 (divorced, 1967); married Brunhilde Schier, July 28, 1972. *Politics:* Liberal Democrat. *Avocational interests:* Sports, old movies and radio shows, book collecting.

ADDRESSES: Home—P.O. Box 1349, Sonoma, CA 95476. *Agent*—Clyde Taylor, Curtis Brown Ltd., 10 Astor Place, New York, NY 10003.

CAREER: Petaluma Argus-Courier, Petaluma, CA, reporter, 1957-60; writer, 1969—.

WRITINGS:

CRIME NOVELS

The Stalker, Random House, 1971.

Panic!, Random House, 1972.

(Under pseudonym Alex Saxon) *A Run in Diamonds,* Pocket Books, 1973.

Snowbound, Putnam, 1974.

Games, Putnam, 1976.

(With Barry N. Malzberg) *The Running of Beasts,* Putnam, 1976.

(With Malzberg) *Acts of Mercy,* Putnam, 1977.

(With Malzberg) *Night Screams,* Playboy Press, 1979.

A Killing in Xanadu, Waves Press, 1980.

Masques, Arbor House, 1981.

(With John Lutz) *The Eye,* Mysterious Press, 1984.

Quincannon, Walker & Co., 1985.

(With Marcia Muller) *Beyond the Grave,* Walker & Co., 1986.

(With Muller) *The Lighthouse,* St. Martin's, 1987.

"NAMELESS DETECTIVE" SERIES NOVELS

The Snatch, Random House, 1971.

The Vanished, Random House, 1973.

Undercurrent, Random House, 1973.

Blowback, Random House, 1977.

(With Collin Wilcox) *Twospot,* Putnam, 1978.

Labyrinth, St. Martin's, 1980.

Hoodwink, St. Martin's, 1981.

Scattershot, St. Martin's, 1982.

Dragonfire, St. Martin's, 1982.

Bindlestiff, St. Martin's, 1983.

Quicksilver, St. Martin's, 1984.

Nightshades, St. Martin's, 1984.

Bones, St. Martin's, 1985.

Deadfall, St. Martin's, 1986.

Shackles, St. Martin's, 1988.

Jackpot, Delacorte, 1990.

NOVELS UNDER PSEUDONYM JACK FOXX; PUBLISHED BY BOBBS-MERRILL

The Jade Figurine, 1972.

Dead Run, 1975.

Freebooty, 1976.

Wildfire, 1978.

NOVELS WITH JEFFREY M. WALLMANN; UNDER JOINT PSEUDONYM WILLIAM JEFFREY

Duel at Gold Buttes, Leisure Books, 1982.

Border Fever, Leisure Books, 1983.

Day of the Moon, R. Hale, 1983.

OTHER NOVELS

(With Malzberg) *Prose Bowl,* St. Martin's, 1980.

(With Jack Anderson) *The Cambodia File,* Doubleday, 1981.

The Gallows Land, Walker & Co., 1983.

Starvation Camp, Doubleday, 1984.

(With Muller) *Double,* St. Martin's, 1984.

The Last Days of Horse-Shy Halloran, M. Evans, 1987.

The Hangings, Walker, 1989.

Firewind, M. Evans, 1989.

SHORT STORIES

Casefile: The Best of the "Nameless Detective" Stories, St. Martin's, 1983.

Graveyard Plots, St. Martin's, 1985.

Small Felonies: Fifty Mystery Short Stories, St. Martin's, 1988.

The Best Western Stories of Bill Pronzini, Swallow Press, 1990.

NONFICTION

Gun in Cheek: A Study of "Alternative" Crime Fiction, Coward, McCann, 1982.

(With Muller) *1001 Midnights: The Aficionado's Guide to Mystery and Detective Fiction,* Arbor House, 1986.

Son of Gun in Cheek, Mysterious Press, 1987.

EDITOR

(With Joe Gores) *Tricks and Treats,* Doubleday, 1976.

Midnight Specials: An Anthology for Train Buffs and Suspense Aficionados, Bobbs-Merrill, 1977.
Werewolf!: A Connoisseur's Collection of Werewolfiana, Arbor House, 1979.
The Edgar Winners: Thirty-third Annual Anthology of the Mystery Writers in America, Random House, 1980.
Voodoo!: A Chrestomathy of Necromacy, Arbor House, 1980.
Mummy!: A Chrestomathy of Crypt-ology, Arbor House, 1980.
The Arbor House Necropolis, Arbor House, 1981.
(With Malzberg and Martin H. Greenberg) *The Arbor House Treasury of Mystery and Suspense,* Arbor House, 1981.
(With Malzberg and Greenberg) *The Arbor House Treasury of Horror and the Supernatural,* Arbor House, 1981.
Creature!: A Chrestomathy of "Monstery," Arbor House, 1981.
Specter!: A Chrestomathy of "Spookery," Arbor House, 1982.
The Arbor House Treasury of Detective and Mystery Stories from the Great Pulps, Arbor House, 1983.
Wild Westerns, Walker & Co., 1986.
(With Malzberg and Greenberg) *Mystery in the Mainstream,* Morrow, 1986.
(With Greenberg and Muller) *Lady on the Case,* Bonanza, 1988.
More Wild Westerns, Walker & Co., 1989.

EDITOR WITH BARRY N. MALZBERG

Dark Sins, Dark Dreams: Crime in Science Fiction, Doubleday, 1978.
The End of Summer: Science Fiction of the Fifties, Ace Books, 1979.
Shared Tomorrows: Science Fiction Is Collaboration, St. Martin's, 1979.
Bug-Eyed Monsters, Harcourt, 1980.

EDITOR WITH MARTIN H. GREENBERG

The Arbor House Treasury of Great Western Stories, Arbor House, 1982.
The Lawmen, Fawcett, 1984.
The Outlaws, Fawcett, 1984.
The Reel West, Doubleday, 1984.
The Western Hall of Fame: An Anthology of Classic Western Stories Selected by the Western Writers of America, Morrow, 1984.
The Mystery Hall of Fame: An Anthology of Classic Mystery and Suspense Stories, Selected by the Mystery Writers of America, Morrow, 1984.
The Best Western Stories of Steve Frazee, Southern Illinois University Press, 1984.
The Best Western Stories of Wayne D. Overholser, Southern Illinois University Press, 1984.
13 Short Mystery Novels, Greenwich House, 1985.
13 Short Espionage Novels, Bonanza, 1985.
Women Sleuths, Academy Chicago, 1985.
Ethnic Detectives, Dodd, 1985.
Police Procedurals, Academy Chicago, 1985.
(And Charles G. Waugh) *Murder in the First Reel,* Avon, 1985.
The Cowboys, Fawcett, 1985.
The Warriors, Fawcett, 1985.
The Second Reel West, Doubleday, 1985.
A Treasury of Civil War Stories, Bonanza, 1985.
A Treasury of World War II Stories, Bonanza, 1985.
The Railroaders, Fawcett, 1986.
The Third Reel West, Doubleday, 1986.
The Steamboaters, Fawcett, 1986.
Great Modern Police Stories, Walker & Co., 1986.
101 Mystery Stories, Avenal, 1986.
Locked Room Puzzles, Academy Chicago, 1986.

Prime Suspects, Ivy, 1987.
(And Carol-Lynn Rossel Waugh) *Manhattan Mysteries,* Avenal, 1987.
Uncollected Crimes, Walker & Co., 1987.
Suspicious Characters, Ivy, 1987.
The Horse Soldiers, Fawcett, 1987.
The Best Western Stories of Lewis B. Patten, Southern Illinois University Press, 1987.
The Cattlemen, Fawcett, 1987.
The Gunfighters, Fawcett, 1988.
The Texans, Fawcett, 1988.
Criminal Elements, Ivy, 1988.
13 Short Detective Novels, Bonanza, 1988.
Cloak and Dagger, Avenal, 1988.
The Mammoth Book of Private Eye Stories, Carroll & Graf, 1988.
Homicidal Acts, Ivy, 1989.
Felonious Assaults, Ivy, 1989.
The Californians, Fawcett, 1989.
The Best Western Stories of Loren D. Estleman, Swallow Press, 1989.
The Best Western Stories of Frank Bonham, Swallow Press, 1989.
The Arizonans, Fawcett, 1989.
New Frontiers, Volume 1, Tor Books, 1990.
New Frontiers, Volume 2, Tor Books, 1990.
The Northerners, Fawcett, 1990.
The Northwesterners, Fawcett, 1990.
The Best Western Stories of Ryerson Johnson, Swallow Press, 1990.

EDITOR WITH MARCIA MULLER

The Web She Weaves, Morrow, 1983.
Child's Ploy, Macmillan, 1984.
Witches' Brew, Macmillan, 1984.
Chapter and Hearse, Morrow, 1985.
Dark Lessons, Macmillan, 1985.
Kill or Cure, Macmillan, 1985.
The Wickedest Show on Earth, Morrow, 1985.
The Deadly Arts, Arbor House, 1985.
She Won the West, Morrow, 1985.

OTHER

Contributor to anthologies; also contributor of over three hundred short stories and articles to magazines, including *Argosy, Ellery Queen's Mystery Magazine,* and *Magazine of Fantasy and Science Fiction.* Books translated into eighteen languages and published in more than thirty countries.

MEDIA ADAPTATIONS: Several of Pronzini's books have been adapted to film, including *The Jade Figurine, Snowbound* (Columbia Pictures), *Panic!* (Hal Wallis Productions), *Games* (Sara Films), *Night Screams* (Soge Films), and *The Lighthouse.*

SIDELIGHTS: "Pronzini . . . is a master of suspense who here has turned confusing political history into taut adventure." Thus Jeff Gillenkirk describes Bill Pronzini's part in *The Cambodia File,* a novel written in collaboration with columnist Jack Anderson. Drawn from Anderson's reports of American involvement in Cambodia during the Vietnam War, Pronzini creates a dramatic story set during the U.S. withdrawal from Cambodia and the revolution that followed. Gillenkirk credits Pronzini for "movingly portraying the human consequences of the Nixon/ Kissinger Cambodian 'incursion.'"

In addition to *The Cambodia File* Pronzini's work includes writings of the western and horror varieties, but he primarily concentrates on crime fiction. While he has gained popular recognition for his "Nameless Detective" series crime novels, Pronzini has garnered critical respect for the numerous anthologies he compiles each year, works which display his extensive knowledge of the crime fiction genre. Margaret Cannon has termed Pronzini the "ultimate enthusiast" of crime fiction. In a review for the *Globe and Mail* she writes, "[Pronzini is] one of the genre's most astute editor-critics, known for his witty introductions to more than two dozen collections of criminous short stories ranging from pulp classics to the best of the Mystery Writers of America." Two of his more notable anthologies are *Gun in Cheek* and *Son of Gun in Cheek*, "[works] in which Bill Pronzini surveys the worst of crime fiction," notes John Gross in a review for the *New York Times*. "Not just the average inferior product, but the junk classics, works that achieve a heroic degree of badness."

BIOGRAPHICAL/CRITICAL SOURCES:

PERIODICALS

Globe and Mail (Toronto), April 7, 1984; August 3, 1985; December 7, 1985; April 11, 1987.
Los Angeles Times, March 12, 1981; August 14, 1985; October 24, 1985.
Los Angeles Times Book Review, October 20, 1985.
New York Times, April 24, 1987.
New York Times Book Review, March 2, 1980; September 13, 1987.
Times (London), July 29, 1989.
Village Voice Literary Supplement, February, 1984.
Washington Post Book World, January 18, 1981; April 18, 1982.

*   *   *

PUIG, Manuel   1932-1990

PERSONAL: Born December 28, 1932, in General Villegas, Argentina; died of a heart attack following surgery, July 15, 1990, in Cuernavaca, Mexico; son of Baldomero (a businessman) and Maria Elena (a chemist; maiden name, Delledonne) Puig. *Education:* Attended University of Buenos Aires, beginning 1950, and Centro Sperimentale di Cinematografia, beginning 1955; studied languages and literature at private institutes. *Religion:* None.

ADDRESSES: c/o Erroll McDonald, Vintage Books, 201 East 50th St., New York, N.Y. 10022.

CAREER: Translator and Spanish and Italian teacher in London, England, and Rome, Italy, 1956-57; assistant film director in Rome and Paris, France, 1957-58; worked as a dishwasher in London and in Stockholm, Sweden, 1958-59; assistant film director in Buenos Aires, Argentina, 1960; translator of film subtitles in Rome, 1961-62; Air France, New York, N.Y., clerk, 1963-67; writer, 1967-90. *Military service:* Argentina Air Force, 1953; served as translator.

AWARDS, HONORS: La traición de Rita Hayworth was named one of the best foreign novels of 1968-69 by *Le Monde* (France); best script award, 1974, for "Boquitas pintadas," and jury prize, 1978, for "El lugar sin límites," both from San Sebastian Festival; American Library Association (ALA) Notable Book, 1979, for *The Kiss of the Spider Woman; Plays & Players* Award for most promising playwright, 1985, for "Kiss of the Spider Woman."

WRITINGS:

La traición de Rita Hayworth, Sudamericana (Buenos Aires), 1968, reprinted, Casa de las Américas, 1983, translation by Suzanne Jill Levine published as *Betrayed by Rita Hayworth,* Dutton, 1971, reprinted, 1987.

Boquitas pintadas (also see below), Sudamericana, 1969, translation by Levine published as *Heartbreak Tango: A Serial,* Dutton, 1973.
The Buenos Aires Affair: Novela policial, Sudamericana, 1973, translation by Levine published as *The Buenos Aires Affair: A Detective Novel,* Dutton, 1976.
El beso de la mujer araña (also see below), Seix-Barral (Barcelona), 1976, translation by Thomas Colchie published as *The Kiss of the Spider Woman,* Knopf, 1979.
Pubis angelical (also see below), Seix-Barral, 1979, translation by Elena Brunet published under same title, Vintage, 1986.
"El beso de la mujer araña" (play; adapted from his novel; also see below), first produced in Spain, 1981, translation by Allan Baker titled "Kiss of the Spider Woman," first produced in London at the Bush Theatre, 1985, produced in Los Angeles at the Cast Theatre, 1987.
Eternal Curse upon the Reader of These Pages, Random House, 1982, Spanish translation by the author published as *Maldición eterna a quien lea estas páginas,* Seix Barral, 1982.
Sangre de amor correspondido, Seix Barral, 1982, translation by Jan L. Grayson published as *Blood of Requited Love,* Vintage, 1984.
Bajo un manto de estrellas: Pieza en dos actos [and] *El beso de la mujer araña: Adaptación escénica realizada por el autor* (plays; also see below), Seix Barral, 1983.
Under a Mantle of Stars: A Play in Two Acts, translation by Ronald Christ, Lumen Books, 1985 (produced in the original Spanish as "Bajo un manto de estrellas").
(Contributor) G. W. Woodyard and Marion P. Holt, editors, *Drama Contemporary: Latin America,* PAJ Publications, 1986.
Mystery of the Rose Bouquet (play; produced at the Bush Theatre, 1987, produced in Los Angeles, Calif., at Mark Taper Forum, November 16, 1989), translation by Baker, Faber, 1988 (produced in the original Spanish as "Misterio del ramo de rosas").

Also author of screenplays for "Boquitas Pintadas," adapted from his novel, 1974, "El lugar sin límites," adapted from José Donoso's novel, 1978, and "Pubis angelical." Contributor to various periodicals, including *Omni.*

WORK IN PROGRESS: Production of his screenplay "Seven Tropical Sins" by David Weisman's Sugarloaf Films company; developing a musical comedy with Weisman, "Chica Boom!"; the book for a musical version of *The Kiss of the Spider Woman.*

SIDELIGHTS: As a boy growing up in rural Argentina, novelist Manuel Puig spent countless hours in the local movie house viewing screen classics from the United States and Europe. His enchantment with films led him to spend several years pursuing a career as a director and screenwriter until he discovered that what he wanted to write was better suited to fiction; nevertheless, Puig's work is saturated with references to films and other popular phenomena. "[But] if Puig's novels are 'pop,' " observes Jonathan Tittler in his *Narrative Irony in the Contemporary Spanish-American Novel,* it is because "he incorporates into his fiction elements of mass culture—radionovelas, comic books, glamour magazines, and in *Betrayed by Rita Hayworth,* commercial movies—in order to unveil their delightfully insidious role in shaping contemporary life." Puig echoes the design of these media, "us[ing] those forms as molds to cast his corny, bathetic material in a form displaying a witty, ironic attitude toward that material," notes Ronald Christ in *Commonweal.* Ronald Schwartz concurs with this assessment; writing in his study *Nomads, Exiles, and Emigres: The Rebirth of the Latin American Narrative, 1960-80,* the critic contends that Puig employs "the techniques of pop art to communicate a complex vision of his own world. It is [the] cinematic influence that makes *Betrayed by Rita Hayworth* and Puig's subsequent novels some of the most original contemporary Latin American narratives."

In *Betrayed by Rita Hayworth,* "the idea of the novel is simple: the drama and pathos of moviegoing as a way of life in the provinces, where often people get to respond to life itself with gestures and mock programs taken over from film," describes *New York Times Book Review* contributor Alexander Coleman. The story is narrated primarily through the eyes of Toto, a young boy born in the Argentinian pampas, and recounts the everyday life of his family and friends. "The novel's charm," claims *Newsweek* writer Walter Clemons, "is in the tender gravity with which Puig records the chatter of Toto's family and neighbors. Kitchen conversations, awkwardly written letters and flowery schoolgirl diary entries . . . combine to evoke lives of humblest possibility and uncomplaining disappointment."

While this description may sound gloomy, states Coleman, nevertheless *Betrayed by Rita Hayworth* "is a screamingly funny book, with scenes of such utter bathos that only a student of final reels such as Puig could possibly have verbally re-created [it] for us." "Above all, Puig has captured the language of his characters," D. P. Gallagher reports in his *Modern Latin American Literature,* and explains: "There is no distance separating him from the voices he records, moreover, for they are the voices that he was brought up with himself, and he is able to reproduce them with perfect naturalness, and without distortion or parodic exaggeration. That is not to say that his novels are not very polished and very professional," the critic continues. "Like all the best Latin American novels . . . , they are structured deliberately as fictions. But the authenticity with which they reflect a very real environment cannot be questioned."

Puig's next novel, *Heartbreak Tango,* "in addition to doing everything that *Rita Hayworth* did (and doing it better, too) actually proclaims Puig not only a major writer but a major stylist whose medium brings you both the heartbreak *and* the tango," Christ declares in *Review 73.* Bringing together letters, diaries, newspapers, conversations, and other literary artifices, *Heartbreak Tango,* as *New York Times* reviewer Christopher Lehmann-Haupt relates, "reconstructs the lives of several Argentine women, most of whom have in common the experience of having once passionately loved a handsome, ne'er-do-well and doomed young man who died of tuberculosis." Mark Jay Mirsky comments in the *Washington Post Book World* that at first "I missed the bustle, noise and grotesque power of *Betrayed by Rita Hayworth.* The narrative of *Heartbreak Tango* seemed much thinner, picking out the objects and voices of its hero [and] heroines with too obvious a precision." Nevertheless, the critic admits, "as we are caught up in the story, this taut line begins to spin us around."

Michael Wood, however, believes that it is this "precision" which makes *Heartbreak Tango* the better novel, as he details in a *New York Review of Books* article: "*Heartbreak Tango* seems to me even better than Puig's earlier *Betrayed by Rita Hayworth* because its characters' moments are clearer, and because the general implication of the montage of cliché and cheap romance and gossip is firmer." The critic adds that "the balance of the new book," between irony and sentimentalism, "is virtually perfect." Gallagher presents a similar opinion in the *New York Times Book Review,* noting that "it has been said that [*Heartbreak Tango*] is a parody, but that underestimates the balance between distance and compassion that Puig achieves. His characters are camp, but they are not camped up, and their fundamental hu-

manity cannot be denied." Despite this serious aspect, the critic remarks that *Heartbreak Tango* "is a more accessible book than its predecessor without being less significant. It is compelling, moving, instructive and very funny." "At the same time," concludes David William Foster in *Latin American Literary Review,* "no matter how 'popular' or 'proletarian' the novel may appear to be on the surface, the essential and significant inner complexity of [*Heartbreak Tango*], like that of *Betrayed by Rita Hayworth,* bespeaks the true artistic dimensions of Puig's novel."

"The appearance of Manuel Puig's new novel, *The Buenos Aires Affair,* is especial cause for celebration," Ronald De Feo asserts in the *National Review,* "not only because the book makes for fascinating reading, but also because it demonstrates that its already highly accomplished author continues to take chances and to grow as an artist." Subtitled *A Detective Novel,* the story takes place in the city and investigates a kidnapping involving two sexually deviant people. "It is not devoid of the lucid and witty observation of absurd behaviour that characterized" *Heartbreak Tango,* maintains a *Times Literary Supplement,* "but it is altogether more anguished." As Toby Moore elaborates in another *Times Literary Supplement* review, "Puig's subject is the tangle made up of love and sexual desire. . . . In *The Buenos Aires Affair* the anxieties and inhibitions of the two characters are so great that they never get to a point of love; all they have is the dream of sex which obsesses and torments them."

The author sets this psychological drama within the framework of a traditional thriller; "what makes Puig so fascinating," writes *New York Times Book Review* contributor Robert Alter, is "the extraordinary inventiveness he exhibits in devising new ways to render familiar material." De Feo, however, faults the author for being "a shade too inventive, [for] we are not always convinced that [these methods] are necessary. But," the critic adds, "the book is more intense, serious, and disturbing than the other novels, and it is a welcome departure for this searching, gifted writer." And the *Times Literary Supplement* writer claims that *The Buenos Aires Affair* "is technically even more accomplished than the previous novels, and Sr Puig is able to handle a wide variety of narrative devices in it without ever making them seem gratuitous."

Shortly after the publication of *The Buenos Aires Affair* in 1973, Puig found it more difficult to remain in Argentina; *Affair* had been banned (presumably because of its sexual content), and the political situation was becoming more restrictive. This increasingly antagonistic climate led Puig to a self-imposed exile, and is reflected in what is probably his best-known work, *The Kiss of the Spider Woman.* Set almost entirely in an Argentinian jail cell, the novel focuses on Valentín, a radical student imprisoned for political reasons, and Molina, a gay window dresser in on a "morals" charge, who recounts his favorite 1930s and '40s movies as a means of passing time. "In telling the story of two cellmates, Puig strips down the narrative to a nearly filmic level—dialogue unbroken even to identify the speakers, assuming we can project them onto our own interior screens," relates Carol Anshaw in the *Voice Literary Supplement.* "If this insistent use of unedited dialogue tends to make the book read a bit like a radio script, however," observes *New York Times Book Review* contributor Robert Coover, "it is Mr. Puig's fascination with old movies that largely provides [the novel's] substance and ultimately defines its plot, its shape. What we hear," the critic continues, "are the voices of two suffering men, alone and often in the dark, but what we see . . . [is] all the iconographic imagery, magic and romance of the movies." The contrast between the two men, who gradually build a friendship "makes this Argentinian odd couple both funny and affecting," Larry Rohter states in the *Washington Post Book World*. But when Molina is released in hopes that he will lead officials to Valentín's confederates, "the plot turns from comedy to farce and Puig's wit turns mordant."

In addition to the continuous dialogue of the jail cell and surveillance report after Molina's release, *The Kiss of the Spider Woman* contains several footnotes on homosexuality whose "clumsy academic style serves to emphasize by contrast that the two prisoners' dialogue is a highly contrived storytelling device, and not the simulation of reality you may take it to be at first," comments Lehmann-Haupt. Because of this, the critic explains, the book becomes "a little too tricky, like a well-made, 19th-century play." Other reviewers, however, find *The Kiss of the Spider Woman* "far and away [Puig's] most impressive book," as Anshaw says. "It is not easy to write a book which says something hopeful about human nature and yet remains precise and unsentimental," Maggie Gee remarks in the *Times Literary Supplement.* "Puig succeeds, partly because his bleak vision of the outside world throws into relief the small private moments of hope and dignifies them, partly through his deft manipulation of form." Schwartz similarly concludes that *The Kiss of the Spider Woman* "is not the usual jumble of truncated structures from which a plot emerges but, rather, a beautifully controlled narrative that skillfully conveys basic human values, a vivid demonstration of the continuing of the genre itself."

Inspired by a stay in New York, *Eternal Curse on the Reader of These Pages* was written directly in English and, similar to *The Kiss of the Spider Woman,* is mainly comprised of an extended dialogue. Juan José Ramírez is an elderly Argentinian living in exile in New York and Lawrence John is the irritable, taciturn American who works part-time caring for him. But as their dialogues progress, Lehmann-Haupt notes, "it becomes increasingly difficult to tell how much is real and how much the two characters have become objects of each other's fantasy life." *Los Angeles Times Book Review* critic Charles Champlin, although he believes these dialogues constitute a technical "tour de force," questions "whether a technical exercise, however clever, [is] the best way to get at this study of conflicting cultures and the ambiguities in the relationship."

Gilbert Sorrentino similarly feels that *Eternal Curse* is "a structural failure, . . . for the conclusion, disastrously, comments on and 'explains' an otherwise richly ambivalent and mysterious text." The critic continues in the *Washington Post Book World:* "It's too bad, because Puig *has* something, most obviously a sense that the essential elements of life, life's serious 'things,' are precisely the elements of soap opera, sit-coms, and B-movies." But Lehmann-Haupt thinks *Eternal Curse* is "more austere and intellectually brittle than any of [Puig's] previous books, [and] less playful and dependent on the artifacts of American pop culture," and calls the novel a "fascinating tour de force." "Puig is an artist, . . . and his portrait of two men grappling with their suffering is exceedingly moving and brilliantly done," declares William Herrick in the *New Leader.* "Strangely, the more space I put between the book and myself, the more tragic I find it. It sticks to the mind. Like one cursed, I cannot find peace, cannot escape from its pain."

Echoing themes of Puig's previous work, maintains *Nation* contributor Jean Franco, "politics and sexuality are inseparable in *Pubis Angelical,*" the latest of Puig's novels to be published in the United States. Alternating the story of Ana, an Argentinian exile dying of cancer in Mexico, with her fantasies of a 1930s movie star and a futuristic "sexual soldier," *Pubis Angelical* speaks "of the political nightmares of exile, disappearance, tor-

ture and persecution," describes Franco, "though as always in Puig's novels, the horror is tempered by the humor of his crazy plots and kitsch stage props." "Puig is both ruthless and touching in his presentation of Ana's muddled but sincere life," states Jason Wilson in the *Times Literary Supplement;* "and if he is sometimes too camp, he can also be very funny." The critic elaborates: "His humour works because he refuses to settle for any single definition of woman; Ana is all feeling and intuition . . . although she is also calculating, and unfeeling about her daughter." But while Ana's advancing cancer and the problems of her dream counterparts are severe, "however seriously Puig is questioning gender assumptions and behavior his voice is never a solemn one," Nick Caistor claims in the *New Statesman.* "The work as a whole fairly bristles with ingenuity and energy," Robert Towers writes in the *New York Review of Books;* "the thematic parallels between the three texts seem almost inexhaustible, and one finishes the novel with a sense of having grasped only a portion of them." Nevertheless, the critic faults *Pubis Angelical* for being "an impressive artifact rather than a fully engrossing work of fictional art."

Steve Erickson likewise criticizes the novel, commenting in the *New York Times Book Review* that "what's amazing about 'Pubis Angelical' is how utterly in love it is with its own artificiality." The critic adds that "the novel fails most devastatingly" in the portrayals of Ana's fantasies: "There's nothing about their lives to suggest that . . . they have a reality for her." While Jay Cantor similarly believes that "it isn't till the last quarter of the book that the fantasies have sufficient, involving interest," he acknowledges in the *Los Angeles Times Book Review* that "there is an audacity to Puig's method, and an intellectual fire to Puig's marshaling of motifs that did then engage me." "In any case, whatever the whole [of the novel] amounts to, each individual part of 'Pubis Angelical' develops its own irresistible drama," counters Lehmann-Haupt. "Though it takes an exercise of the intellect to add them together, they finally contribute to what is the most richly textured and extravagant fiction [Puig] has produced so far."

"Less interested in depicting things as they might be, and concerned with things as they are, Puig does not resort to make-believe," Alfred J. MacAdam asserts in *Modern Latin American Narratives: The Dreams of Reason.* "His characters are all too plausible, . . . [and their lives] simply unfold over days and years until they run their meaningless course." It is this ordinary, commonplace quality of life, however, that the author prefers to investigate, as he told the *Washington Post*'s Desson Howe: "I find literature the ideal medium to tell certain stories that are of special interest to me. Everyday stories with no heroics, the everyday life of the gray people." And films play such a large role in his work because of the contrast they provide to this mundane world: "I think I can understand the reality of the 1930s by means of the unreality of their films," Puig remarked in a *Los Angeles Times* interview with Ann Marie Cunningham. "The films reflect exactly what people dreamed life could be. The relationships between people in these films are like the negative of a photograph of real life." "I can only understand realism," the author further explained to *New York Times* writer Samuel G. Freedman. "I can only approach my writing with an analytical sense. . . . I can write dreams, but I use them as part of the accumulation of detail, as counterpoint." Because of his realistic yet inventive portrayals, contends Schwartz, "Manuel Puig is a novelist moving in the direction of political commitment in his depiction of the provincial and urban middle class of Argentina, something that has never before been attempted so successfully in Latin American letters." The critic concludes: "Clearly, Puig, thriving self-exiled from his native country, is an eclectic stylist, a consummate artist."

MEDIA ADAPTATIONS: The Kiss of the Spider Woman was made into a film by Brazilian director Hector Babenco in 1985 and starred Raul Julia, William Hurt (in an Oscar-winning performance), and Sonia Braga.

BIOGRAPHICAL/CRITICAL SOURCES:

BOOKS

Contemporary Literary Criticism, Gale, Volume 3, 1975, Volume 5, 1976, Volume 10, 1979, Volume 28, 1984.

Gallagher, D. P., *Modern Latin American Literature,* Oxford University Press, 1973.

MacAdam, Alfred J., *Modern Latin American Narratives: The Dreams of Reason,* University of Chicago Press, 1977.

Schwartz, Ronald, *Nomads, Exiles, and Emigres: The Rebirth of the Latin American Narrative, 1960-80,* Scarecrow, 1980.

Tittler, Jonathan, *Narrative Irony in the Contemporary Spanish-American Novel,* Cornell University Press, 1984.

PERIODICALS

Chicago Tribune Book World, April 15, 1979.

Commonweal, June 24, 1977.

Latin American Literary Review, fall, 1972.

Los Angeles Times, January 30, 1987, February 3, 1987, November 16, 1989, November 17, 1989.

Los Angeles Times Book Review, June 20, 1982, December 28, 1986.

Nation, April 18, 1987.

National Review, October 29, 1976.

New Leader, June 28, 1982.

New Statesman, October 2, 1987.

Newsweek, October 25, 1971, June 28, 1982.

New York Review of Books, December 13, 1973, January 24, 1980, December 18, 1986.

New York Times, November 28, 1973, April 23, 1979, June 4, 1982, September 25, 1984, August 5, 1985, December 22, 1986, October 25, 1988.

New York Times Book Review, September 26, 1971, December 16, 1973, September 5, 1976, April 22, 1979, July 4, 1982, September 23, 1984, December 28, 1986.

Review 73, fall, 1973.

Times (London), August 23, 1985.

Times Literary Supplement, November 6, 1970, August 31, 1973, September 21, 1984, October 16, 1987, August 11-17, 1989.

Voice Literary Supplement, April, 1989.

Washington Post, November 16, 1985.

Washington Post Book World, November 25, 1973, April 22, 1979, August 1, 1982.

World Literature Today, winter, 1981.*

—*Sketch by Diane Telgen*

Q

QUEEN, Ellery
   See STURGEON, Theodore (Hamilton)

*   *   *

QUENEAU, Raymond   1903-1976
   (Sally Mara)

PERSONAL: Born February 21, 1903, in Le Havre, France; died October 25, 1976, in Paris, France; son of Auguste (a businessman) and Josephine (Mignot) Queneau; married Janine Kahn, 1934; children: Jean-Marie. *Education:* University of Paris, licence es lettres, 1926.

ADDRESSES: Office—Gallimard, 5 rue Sebastien-Bottin, 75007 Paris, France.

CAREER: Comptoir national d'escompte (bank), Paris, France, employee, beginning 1927; Gallimard (publishing house), Paris, reader, 1938-39, secretary general, beginning 1941, director of *Encyclopedie de la Pleiade,* 1955-75. Member of l'Academie Goncourt (literary jury), 1951-76. Founder, with Francois Le Lionnais, of Ouvroir de litterature potentielle ("Oulipo"). *Military service:* Served in Algeria and Morocco as a Zouave, 1926-27, and in French army, 1939-40; became corporal.

MEMBER: Academie de l'humour, American Mathematical Society, College of 'pataphysique.

AWARDS, HONORS: Prix de l'Humour Noir for *Zazie dans le metro.*

WRITINGS:

IN ENGLISH TRANSLATION

Le Chiendent (novel), Gallimard, 1933, reprinted, 1974, enlarged edition with an article by Jean Queval and notes by Nicole Onfroy, Bordas, 1975, translation by Barbara Wright of first French edition published as *The Bark Tree,* Calder & Boyars, 1968, New Directions, 1971.

Un Rude hiver (novel), Gallimard, 1939, translation by Betty Askwith published as *A Hard Winter,* Lehmann, 1948.

Pierrot mon ami (novel), Gallimard, 1943, reprinted, 1965, translation by J. McLaren Ross published as *Pierrot,* Lehmann, 1950.

Loin de Rueil (novel), Gallimard, 1944, reprinted, 1967, translation by H. J. Kaplan published as *The Skin of Dreams,* New Directions, 1948, reprinted, H. Fertig, 1979.

Exercises de style, Gallimard, 1947, revised edition, 1973, translation by Wright published as *Exercises in Style,* Gabberbocchus, 1958, reprinted, New Directions, 1981.

(Compiler) Alexandre Kojeve, editor, *Introduction a la lecture de Hegel,* Gallimard, 1947, abridged translation by James H. Nichols, Jr. published as *Introduction to the Reading of Hegel,* Basic Books, 1969.

(Under pseudonym Sally Mara) *On est toujours trop bon avec les femmes* (also see below), Editions du Scorpion, 1947, translation by Wright published under author's real name as *We Always Treat Women Too Well: A Novel,* New Directions, 1981.

Le Dimanche de la vie (novel; also see below), Gallimard, 1951, reprinted, 1973, translation by Wright published as *The Sunday of Life,* Calder, 1976, New Directions, 1977.

Zazie dans le metro (novel), Gallimard, 1959, reprinted, 1977, translation by Wright published as *Zazie,* Harper, 1960.

Cent mille milliards de poemes (novel), Gallimard, 1961, reprinted, 1981, translation published as *One Hundred Million Million Poems* (bilingual edition), Kickshaws (Paris), 1983.

Les Fleurs bleues (novel), Gallimard, 1965, enlarged edition with introduction and notes in English edited by Wright, Methuen, 1971, translation by Wright published as *The Blue Flowers,* Atheneum, 1967 (published in England as *Between Blue and Blue,* Bodley Head, 1967), reprinted, New Directions, 1985.

Le Vol d'Icare, Gallimard, 1968, translation by Wright published as *The Flight of Icarus,* New Directions, 1973.

Raymond Queneau: Poems, translated by Teo Savory, Unicorn Press, 1971.

Pounding the Pavement, Beating the Bushes, and Other Pataphysical Poems (bilingual edition), translation by Savory of poems from *Courir les rues, Battre le campagne,* and other volumes (also see below), Unicorn Press, 1986 (published in England as *Pataphysical Poems,* 1986).

NOVELS

Gueule de Pierre (also see below), Gallimard, 1934.

Chene et chien (title means "Oak and Dog"; novel in verse; also see below), Denoel, 1937.

Odile, Gallimard, 1937, reprinted, 1969.

Les Enfants du limon (title means "Children of the Earth"), Gallimard, 1938.

Les Temps meles (title means "Mixed-up Times"; also see below), Gallimard, 1941.

Saint Glinglin (revision of *Gueule de Pierre* and *Les Temps meles*), Gallimard, 1948.

(Under pseudonym Sally Mara) *Journal intime* (also see below), Editions du Scorpion, 1950.

Also author of *A la limite de la foret,* 1947, *Le Cheval troyen,* 1948, and *Un conte a votre facon,* 1968.

POETRY

Les Ziaux (also see below), Gallimard, 1943.

Une Trouille verte, Editions de Minuit, 1947.

L'Instant fatal (also see below), Gallimard, 1948.

Petite cosmogonie portative (title means "A Portable Little Cosmogony"; also see below), Gallimard, 1950.

Si tu t'imagines, 1920-1951 (title means "If You Imagine"), Gallimard, 1952, revised edition published as *Si tu t'imagines, 1920-1948,* 1968.

Le Chien a la mandoline (title means "The Dog on the Mandolin"), Verviers, 1958, enlarged edition, 1965.

Sonnets, Editions Hautefeuille, 1958.

Variations typographiques sur deux poemes de Raymond Queneau (title means "Typographic Variations of Two Poems by Raymond Queneau"), [Paris], 1964.

L'Instant fatal, precede de Les Ziaux, Gallimard, 1966.

Courir les rues, Gallimard, 1967.

Battre le campagne, Gallimard, 1968.

Chene et chien (includes *Chene et chien,* revised version of *Petite cosmogonie portative,* and *Le Chant de Styrene*), Gallimard, 1968.

Fendre les flots (title means "Parting the Waters"), Gallimard, 1969.

Bonjour Monsieur Prassionos, G. A. Parisod, 1972.

OTHER

Les derniers jours (title means "The Last Days"), Gallimard, 1936, reprinted with a preface by Olivier de Magny, Societe Cooperative (Lausanne), 1965.

Bucoliques, Gallimard, 1947.

Joan Miro; ou, Le poete prehistorique (title means "Joan Miro; or, The Prehistoric Poet"), A. Skira, 1949.

(With Queval) *Rendez-vouz de juillet* (title means "Rendezvous in July"), Chavane, 1949.

Batons, chiffres, et lettres (title means "Sticks, Figures, and Letters"), Gallimard, 1950, revised and enlarged edition, 1965.

(Editor with A. J. Arberry and others) *Les Ecrivains celebres* (title means "Famous Writers"), three volumes, L. Mazenod, 1951-53, 3rd edition, 1966.

(Editor) *Anthologie des jeunes auteurs* (title means "Anthology of Young Authors"), Editions J.A.R., 1955.

(Editor) *Histoire des litteratures* (title means "History of Literatures"), three volumes, Gallimard, 1955-58.

(Compiler) *Pour une bibliotheque ideale* (title means "For an Ideal Library"), Gallimard, 1956.

Lorsque l'espirit (title means "When the Spirit"), Collection Q., 1956.

(Contributor) *Le Declin du romantisme: Edgar Poe* (title means "The Decline of Romanticism: Edgar Poe"), L. Mazenod, 1957.

Les Oeuvres completes de Sally Mara (title means "The Complete Works of Sally Mara"; contains *On est toujours trop bon avec les femmes, Journal intime,* and "Sally plus intime" [title means "More Intimate Sally"]), Gallimard, 1962.

Entretiens avec Georges Charbonnier (title means "Interviews with Georges Charbonnier"), Gallimard, 1962.

Bords: Mathematiciens, precurseurs, encyclopedistes, Hermann, 1963.

Une Histoire modele (title means "A Model History"), Gallimard, 1966.

Texticules, Galerie Louise Leiris, 1968.

Raymond Queneau en verve (title means "Raymond Queneau at His Best"), P. Horay, 1970.

De quelques langages animaux imaginaires et notamment du langage chien dans "Sylvie et Bruno" (title means "Of Several Imaginary Animal Languages, Notably the Dog Language in 'Sylvie and Bruno' "), L'Herne, 1971.

Le Voyage en Grece (title means "Voyage to Greece"), Gallimard, 1973.

Morale elementaire (title means "Elementary Ethics"), Gallimard, 1975.

(With Elie Lascaux) *Correspondance Raymond Queneau-Elie Lascaux,* Gallimard, 1979.

Contes et propos (fiction), Gallimard, 1981.

Une Correspondance: Raymond Queneau-Boris Vian, Association des Amis de Valentin Bru, 1982.

Journal, 1939-1940, suivi de Philosophes et voyous, edited by A. I. Queneau and J.-J. Marchand, Gallimard, 1986.

Also author of "En passant" (play), 1944, and *La Litterature potentielle,* 1973; author of screenplays, including, "Monsieur Ripois," 1954, "La Mort en ce jardin," 1956, (with others) "Un Couple," 1960, and "La Dimanche de la vie" (adapted from his novel of the same title), 1967. Also translator of works by Maurice O'Sullivan, Sinclair Lewis, George du Maurier, and Amos Tutuola. Author of column, "Connaissez-vous Paris?," for *L'Intransigeant,* 1936-38, and of weekly column for *Front National,* 1940-45.

SIDELIGHTS: French novelist and poet Raymond Queneau blended the complex linguistic and narrative patterns of James Joyce, the use of colloquial language of Louis-Ferdinand Celine, and the inane humor of Alfred Jarry to produce a unique brand of writing. The roots of Queneau's style can be traced to the beginning of his career in the 1920s and his involvement with Andre Breton and the Surrealist movement which so influenced the Parisian literary milieu of the era. Queneau's work reflects the Surrealist rebellion against established societal values and emphasis on the irrational forces of the subconscious mind. His novels and poems reveal a deep preoccupation with the problem of language, a concern that often came to be the most important feature of his writing.

Queneau believed that written French had become completely disassociated from the spoken form of the language and, therefore, strove to reproduce spoken rather than written French in his work. He described this new form of language as "le neo francais." "In Queneau's hands," noted Tom Bishop in the *Saturday Review,* "language—vocabulary, spelling, syntax—is manipulated, squeezed, and pulled until it fairly explodes and becomes a 'neo-language' of slang and colloquialisms." Not only did Queneau use language usually heard in the streets of Paris in his books, but he also delighted in stretching language to its utmost limits. Germaine Bree and Margaret Otis Guiton concluded in their assessment of Queneau appearing in *An Age of Fiction: The French Novel from Gide to Camus* that the author wrote in "Queneau-ese" and noted that his readers would find his works so "full of puns, coined words, polysyllables, alliterations and phonetic ornaments" that saying that he wrote in French would be inaccurate. According to *French Studies* contributor Christopher Shorley, "Queneau's commitment to language in all its manifestations is perhaps the most consistent single element in his works."

Queneau also experimented with the printed word and the structure of the novel. Some examples of his innovations include changing typefaces throughout the course of a novel, illustrating a debate going on within a character's mind by dividing a page into two columns, using a short poetic line to represent the rhythm of dialogue, and employing made-up punctuation marks. In *Exercises de style* he recounts a brief anecdote about an ordinary encounter on a bus in ninety-nine different ways, changing styles as well as genres as he tells the incident in prose, in free verse, as a sonnet, and as a play. *The Flight of Icarus* is another example of his experimentation with the novel. The text includes a spoof of mystery stories and a play with seventy-four scenes. In *French Review,* Robert Henkels, Jr. called the work "neither fish nor fowl, . . . it explores several topics, and dabbles with several genres all at once." *Listener* contributor Ronald Bryden observed that it was "less novel than intellectual comic-strip: a daisy-chain of dialogue 'frames' ballooned with puns and in-jokes." Vivian Kogan observes in her *Dictionary of Literary Biography* essay that Queneau's probing of the novelistic form "invites the reader to view all of literature as a series of permutations that have no ultimate or 'authentic' text as their origin. . . . His intentions are therapeutic rather than destructive of literature; his purpose is to rid literature of its rusty, crusty conventions."

It was not until 1959 with publication in France of his *Zazie dans le metro* (published in English translation in 1960 as *Zazie*) that Queneau attained international fame as a novelist. This novel—the story of eleven-year-old Zazie who visits her uncle in Paris and surprises him with her use of foul language—included the experimentation in language and zany comedy that readers had come to expect from Queneau. Although *Zazie* was popularly acclaimed, it was unevenly reviewed by U.S. critics. In his *Critical Essays,* Roland Barthes discussed the confusion surrounding the book as well as his own admiration for it: "*Zazie dans le metro* is really an exemplary work: by vocation, it dismisses both . . . the serious and the comic," Barthes noted. "Which accounts for the confusion of our critics: some have taken it seriously as a serious work of art, suited to exegetical decipherment; others, judging the first group grotesque, have called the novel absolutely frivolous . . . ; still others, seeing neither comedy nor seriousness in the work, have declared they did not understand. But this was precisely the work's intention—to wreck any dialogue about it, representing by the absurd the elusive nature of language." In *Zazie,* Vernon Hall, Jr. observed in *Lively Arts and Book Review,* Queneau appears "intoxicated with a vocabulary partially picked up from the streets, partially invented, [and] he passes on this intoxication to his . . . readers."

Queneau's inimitable use of language is also found in his poetry, most of which has been overlooked by the English-speaking world. In 1986 Teo Savory, one of Queneau's translators, brought out an English-language edition of a selection of his poems written from 1943 to 1969; *Pounding the Pavements, Beating the Bushes, and Other Pataphysical Poems* appeared with Savory's hopes of correcting this situation. These poems reveal the similarities between Queneau the novelist and Queneau the poet. As a poet he used features also found in his fiction: colloquial language, phonetic spelling, and invented words; but in his poetry he was able to add another comic dimension with his playful use of rhyme. *Times Literary Supplement* contributor Peter Reading quoted a portion of one of the translated poems: "Ah when I was young/ how happy I was! Like/ a lizard in the sun/ looking at my toenails." Reading pointed out another similarity between Queneau's poetry and the fiction in "the existence of a number of different possible readings" in many of the poems.

This is reminiscent of Queneau's *Exercises in Style* with its multiple retellings of the same incident and also of the writer's *Morale elementaire* (title means "Elementary Ethics"), a collection containing both prose and verse poems set in columns across the page which can be read in several directions either individually within a column or across all the columns on the page. Reading pointed out that in Queneau's poetry "often the starting-point is purposely minimal and the real subject-matter becomes the language"—a statement which also could be made about Queneau's fiction, in which critics observed characters and content taking a subordinate position to linguistic experimentation.

Queneau's playful use of language has made translation of his work difficult. A *Times Literary Supplement* reviewer commented: "Translation is, in a sense, the whole of Raymond Queneau's art. The task of translating him in turn into an alien language and cultural context is virtually impossible." Reviewers, however, have generally praised Barbara Wright for her attempts to capture in English the spirit of the slang and puns which dominated his work. Those critics, such as Hall and Laurent LeSage, who found the translations lacking the same impact as the original works still seemed to agree that even in English translation Queneau was worth reading. LeSage, for example, noted in his *Saturday Review* essay on *Zazie* that "for French readers, recognition of the familiar under Queneau's distortions made the charm of the book. This, alas, is not for us. But the exotic can have its charm, too, and if Queneau's caricatures are for us bereft of living models, we may find them none the less fascinating for it. Freed of all contingencies, they become pure figures of fun and their story a fantasy taking place on the moon."

MEDIA ADAPTATIONS: Zazie was made into a film by Louis Malle in 1960.

BIOGRAPHICAL/CRITICAL SOURCES:

BOOKS

Barthes, Roland, *Critical Essays,* Northwestern University Press, 1972.
Bree, Germaine, and Margaret Otis Guiton, *An Age of Fiction: The French Novel from Gide to Camus,* Rutgers University Press, 1957.
Contemporary Literary Criticism, Gale, Volume 2, 1974, Volume 5, 1976, Volume 10, 1979, Volume 42, 1987.
Dictionary of Literary Biography, Volume 72: *French Novelists, 1930-1960,* Gale, 1988.

PERIODICALS

French Review, October, 1975.
French Studies, October, 1981.
Listener, July 5, 1973.
Lively Arts and Book Review, December 11, 1960.
Saturday Review, October 15, 1960.
Times Literary Supplement, May 25, 1967, September 19, 1968, March 7, 1986.

OBITUARIES:

PERIODICALS

AB Bookman's Weekly, January 3, 1977.
New York Times, October 26, 1976.*

—*Sketch by Marian Gonsior*

*   *   *

**QUINN, Theodora K.
See KROEBER, Theodora (Kracaw)**

QUIRARTE, Jacinto 1931-

PERSONAL: Surname is pronounced Key-*ar*-tay; born August 17, 1931, in Jerome, Ariz.; son of Francisco (a teamster) and Frutosa (Jimenez) Quirarte; married Sara Bel Farmer, December 18, 1954; children: Sabrina Pilar. *Education:* San Francisco State College (now San Francisco State University), B.A., 1954, M.A., 1958; National University of Mexico, Ph.D., 1964. *Politics:* Democrat. *Religion:* Roman Catholic.

ADDRESSES: Home—10902 Bar X Trail, San Antonio, Tex. 78228. *Office*—Research Center for the Arts, University of Texas at San Antonio, San Antonio, Tex. 78285.

CAREER: Colegio Americano, Mexico City, Mexico, art teacher, 1959-61; National University of Mexico, Mexico City, assistant to Alberto Ruz Lhuillier, 1961-62; University of the Americas, Mexico City, Mexico, professor of art history and dean of men, 1962-64; Centro Venezolano-Americano, Caracas, Venezuela, director of Asuntos Culturales, 1964-66; University of Texas at Austin, Austin, professor of art history, 1967-72; University of Texas at San Antonio, San Antonio, professor of art history and dean of College of Fine and Applied Arts, 1972-1978, director of Research Center for the Arts, 1979—. Visiting professor at Universidad Central de Venezuela, spring, 1966, Yale University, spring, 1967, and University of New Mexico, spring, 1971. *Military service:* U.S. Air Force, flight office, navigator, and radar-bombardier for Strategic Air Command (SAC), 1954-57; became captain. U.S. Air Force Reserve, 1957-62.

MEMBER: International Congress of Anthropology and Ethnology, International Congress of the History of Art, International Congress of Americanists, Society for American Archaeology, Mid-America College Art Association, Texas Council of the Arts in Education (member of visual arts and humanities panel), San Antonio Arts Council (vice president and member of board, 1973-77).

WRITINGS:

(Translator) Alfonso Caso, *El Códice Selden* (title means "The Selden Codex"), Sociedad Mexicana de Antropología, 1964.

Mexican American Artists, University of Texas Press, 1973.

Izapan Style Art: A Study of Its Form and Meaning (monograph), Harvard University Press, 1973.

(Contributor) Philip D. Ortego, editor, *We Are Chicanos: An Anthology of Mexican American Literature,* Washington Square Press, 1973.

(Contributor) Henry Nicholson, editor, *Origins of Religious Art and Iconography in Preclassic Mesoamerica,* Latin American Center, University of California, Los Angeles, 1976.

(Contributor) David L. Browman, editor, *Cultural Continuity in Mesoamerica,* Mouton, 1978.

(Contributor) Gordon Willey and R. E. W. Adams, editors, *Origins of Maya Civilization,* University of New Mexico Press, 1977.

(Contributor) Norman Hammond and Willey, editors, *Maya Archaeology and Ethnohistory,* University of Texas Press, 1979.

(Contributor) Merle Greene Robertson and Connan Call Jeffers, *Tercera Mesa Redonda de Palenque,* Pre-Columbian Art Research, 1979.

(Editor with Maria Elena Gonzalez-Rich) *Directory of Hispanic American Arts Organizations,* Research Center for the Arts and Humanities, University of Texas at San Antonio, 1982.

(Editor) *The Hispanic American Aesthetic,* Research Center for the Arts and Humanities, University of Texas at San Antonio, 1983.

(Editor and author of introductory notes) *Chicano Art History: A Book of Selected Readings,* Research Center for the Arts and Humanities, University of Texas at San Antonio, 1984.

Contributor to proceedings and to journals.

R

RAKOSI, Carl
See RAWLEY, Callman

*   *   *

RAMIREZ de ARELLANO, Diana (T. Clotilde) 1919-

PERSONAL: Born June 3, 1919, in New York, N.Y.; daughter of Enrique Ramírez Brau (a writer and journalist) and Maria Teresa (Rechani) Ramírez de Arellano. *Education:* University of Puerto Rico, B.A., 1941; Columbia University, M.A., 1946; University of Madrid, Ph.D., 1952, licenciada en filosofía y letras, 1959, doctora en filosofía y letras, 1962. *Religion:* Roman Catholic.

ADDRESSES: Home—23 Harbour Circle, Centerport, Long Island, N.Y. 11721; and, de la Marina Española, 22 Benidorm Ave., Alicante, Spain. *Office*—Department of Romance Languages, City College of the City University of New York, 138th St. and Convent Ave., New York, N.Y. 10031.

CAREER: University of North Carolina, Greensboro, instructor in Spanish, 1946-48; Douglass College, Rutgers University, New Brunswick, N.J., instructor, 1948-52, assistant professor of Romance languages, 1953-58; City College of the City University of New York, New York City, assistant professor, 1958-68, associate professor, 1968-71, professor of Romance languages, 1971-84, professor emeritus, 1984——. Lecturer at colleges and organizations in Spain, Puerto Rico, and the United States. Consultant to Ford Foundation, Canadian Council of the Arts.

MEMBER: International PEN, American Association of Teachers of Spanish and Portuguese, American Association of University Professors, Modern Language Association of America, Hispanic Society of America, Puerto Rican Writers' Association, Society of Puerto Rican Authors (San Juan), Ateneo Puertorriqueño de Nueva York (honorary president), Academy of Doctors of Madrid.

AWARDS, HONORS: Poet laureate of Puerto Rico, 1958; first prize in literature from University of Puerto Rico Institute of Puerto Rican Literature, citation from Club Civico de Damas (San Juan), and diploma de honor from Ateneo Puertorriqueño de San Juan, all in 1958, all for *Angeles de ceniza;* award for literary criticism from University of Puerto Rico, and honorary diploma from Ateneo Puertorriqueño de San Juan, both 1961, both for *Poesía contemporánea en lengua española;* poetry prize, Ministry of Bolivia, 1961; citation from Puerto Rican Writers Society of New York, 1963, for contribution to Puerto Rican literature and to the Spanish community of New York; Silver Medal for literature from Republic of Bolivia, 1963; Gold Medal for poetry from Institute of Ecuadorian Culture (New York), 1966; Gold Trophy from Riveroeste Club of Ecuador, 1966; Order of Merit, Ecuador, 1967; literature prize from Instituto de Puerto Rico en Nueva York, 1969; Laurel Clara Lair, APE Poets and Writers Association, 1985; poetry prize Lola Rodriguez de Tió, 1985; Rev Al Marger Agosto, 1985; Medal Dr. Gregorio Marañón, 1985; certificate of honor, Soc. Autores Puerto Rico; Medal Beaux Arts, Institute of Puerto Rican Culture.

WRITINGS:

Yo soy Ariel (poetry; title means "I Am Ariel"), Casa Unida de Publicaciones (Mexico), 1947.

Los Ramírez de Arellano de Lope de Vega (title means "Lope de Vega's Comedy, The Ramírez de Arellano"), Consejo Superior de Investigaciones Cientificas (Madrid), 1954.

Albatros sobre el alma (poetry; title means "Albatross Over the Soul"), Colección de Poesía para Bibliofilos (Madrid), 1955.

Angeles de ceniza (poetry; title means "Angels of Ashes"), Colección de Poesía para Bibliofilos, 1958.

Un vuelo casi humano (poetry; title means "An Almost Human Flight"), Colección de Poesía para Bibliofilos, 1960.

Caminos de la creación poética en Pedro Salinas (title means "Roads to Pedro Salinas' Poetic Creation"), Biblioteca Aristarco de Erudición y Crítica, 1961.

Poesía contemporánea en lengua española (title means "Contemporary Poetry in the Spanish Language"), Biblioteca Aristarco de Erudición y Crítica, 1961.

La cultura en el panorama puertorriqueño de Nueva York, El Ateneo, 1964.

Privilegio (poetry; title means "Privilege"), Colección Ateneo de Poetas Hispánicos (New York), 1965.

Del señalado oficio de la muerte (title means "Of the Assigned Task of Death"), Ateneo Puertorriqueño de Nueva York, 1974.

El himno deseado (title means "The Desired Hymn"), Editorial Romo (Madrid), 1979.

(Contributor) Josefina Romo Arregui, *Poetas románticos desconocidos: Concepción de Estevarena, 1854-1876,* Librería Internacional de Romo, 1979.

Arbol en vísperas (title means "Tree in Vespers"), Torremozas, 1987.

AUTHOR OF INTRODUCTION

Vicente Geigel Polanco, *Canto de la tierra adentro,* Ateneo Puertorriqueño de Nueva York, 1965.

Moises Ledesma, *Ensayos y fábulas,* Ateneo Puertorriqueño de Nueva York, 1966.

Isabel Hernandez de Norman, *La novela romántica en las Antillas,* Ateneo Puertorriqueño de Nueva York, 1969.

Jaime Montesinos, *Viaje al punto de partida,* [Ecuador], 1969.

Taller de poesía diacunista (anthology), Academia de la Lengua en Nueva York, 1973.

OTHER

Also author of *Josefina Romo-Arregui: Homenaje,* 1988. Poetry is represented in anthologies, including *Aguinaldo lírico de la poesía,* edited by Hernandez Aquino, Instituto de Cultura Puertorriquena, 1967. Contributor of articles, poetry, and reviews to Spanish-language journals in Spain, Mexico, Puerto Rico, and the United States.

WORK IN PROGRESS: A book of poems, critical edition and catalogue of Lope de Vega's genealogical comedies; a book of criticism.

BIOGRAPHICAL/CRITICAL SOURCES:

BOOKS

Arce, Margot, *Poesía de Puerto Rico,* Troutman Press, 1969.

López, Julio César, *Pasión de poesía,* Ediciones Rumbos (Barcelona), 1968.

Rosa-Nievos, Cesareo, *Biografías puertorriqueñas,* [Puerto Rico], 1970.

Revilla, Andres, *Estudios segovianos,* Consejo Superior de Investigaciones Científicas, 1962.

Rivera-Alverez, Josefina, *Historia de la literatura puertorriqueña,* Volume 3, University of Puerto Rico, 1971.

PERIODICALS

Bulletin of Hispanic Studies (Liverpool University), Volume 35, number 2, 1958.

El Mundo (San Juan), October 28, 1954, October 22, 1955, January 23, 1957, May 21, 1959.

Modern Language Notes, February, 1959.

Ya (Madrid), December 5, 1954, March 20, 1955, September 7, 1956.

* * *

RANDALL, Diane
  See ROSS, W(illiam) E(dward) D(aniel)

* * *

RANDOLPH, Ellen
  See ROSS, W(illiam) E(dward) D(aniel)

* * *

RAWLEY, Callman 1903-
  (Carl Rakosi)

PERSONAL: Original name, Carl Rakosi; name legally changed; born November 6, 1903, in Berlin, Germany; came to the United States in 1910; son of Hungarian nationals, Leopold and Flora (Steiner) Rakosi; married Leah Jaffe, May 6, 1939; children: Barbara, George. *Education:* University of Wisconsin, B.A., 1924, M.A., 1926; University of Pennsylvania, Master of Social Work, 1940. *Religion:* Jewish.

ADDRESSES: Home—126 Irving St., San Francisco, Calif. 94122.

CAREER: University of Texas at Austin, instructor, 1928-29; Cook County Bureau of Public Welfare, Chicago, Ill., social worker, 1932-33; Federal Transit Bureau, New Orleans, La., supervisor, 1933-34; Tulane University of Louisiana (now Tulane University), Graduate School of Social Work, New Orleans, field work supervisor, 1934-35; Jewish Family Welfare Society, Brooklyn, N.Y., caseworker, 1935-40; Jewish Social Service Bureau, St. Louis, Mo., case supervisor, 1940-43; assistant director of Jewish Children's Bureau and Bellefaire (residential treatment center for disturbed children), both Cleveland, Ohio, 1943-45; Jewish Family and Children's Service, Minneapolis, Minn., executive director, 1945-68; private practice in psychotherapy and marriage counseling, 1958-68; Yaddo, Saratoga Springs, N.Y., resident writer, 1968-75. Writer-in-residence, University of Wisconsin, 1969-70; member of faculty, National Poetry Festival, 1973; poet-in-residence, Michigan State University, 1974.

MEMBER: National Association of Social Workers (president of South Minnesota chapter, 1959-61), National Conference of Jewish Communal Service (vice-president, 1957-58), Family Service Association of America (chairman of Midwest regional committee, 1961-64) chairman of committee on long-range planning, 1964-66).

AWARDS, HONORS: National Endowment for the Arts award, 1969, fellowship, 1972 and 1979; Distinguished Service award, National Poetry Association, 1988.

WRITINGS:

UNDER NAME CARL RAKOSI

Two Poems, Modern Editions Press, 1933.
Selected Poems, New Directions, 1941.
Amulet, New Directions, 1967.
Two Poems, Modern Editions Press, 1971.
Ere-Voice, New Directions, 1971.
Ex-Cranium, Night, Black Sparrow Press, 1975.
My Experiences in Parnassus, Black Sparrow Press, 1977.
History, Oasis Books (London), 1981.
Droles de Journal, Toothpaste Press, 1981.
Carl Rakosi: Collected Prose, National Poetry Foundation, 1983.
Spiritus I, Pig Press (England), 1983.
Carl Rakosi: Collected Poems, National Poetry Foundation, 1986.

Contributor to ten anthologies, including *The American Literary Anthology,* No. 3, edited by Plimpton and Ardery, *Heartland II,* edited by Lucien Stryk, *Modern Things,* edited by Parker Tyler, *An Introduction to Poetry,* edited by Louis Simpson, *The Treasury of American Poetry,* edited by Nancy Sullivan, *A Geography of Poets,* edited by Edward Field, and *Inside Outer Space,* edited by Robert Vas Dias. Contributor of poetry to journals, including *Paris Review, Poetry, Massachusetts Review, Transition, Exile, Sulfur,* and *Conjunctions.*

SIDELIGHTS: Callman Rawley, known in the literary world as poet Carl Rakosi, is a member of the older Objectivist group of poets, "reflecting the influence" of Ezra Pound and William Carlos Williams, a *Choice* reviewer relates. Objectivist writing is characterized by the presentation of concrete images; direct treatment of the subject without ornamental verbiage; and insistence on a high degree of craftsmanship, such that the poem itself is an object deliberately constructed in a form appropriate to its content. In *Contemporary Authors Autobiography Series,* Rakosi explains how he came to be associated with the group: "I received an invitation from Louis Zukofsky to rush him my best poems for a special issue of *Poetry* which he was editing under the sponsorship of Ezra Pound. Here began my association with him and with two of the others in that issue and, later, in *An 'Objectivist' Anthology,* George Oppen and Charles Reznikoff. Zukofsky called us Objectivists. We are still known by that name." Less prolific than others in that school, "Rakosi turns out the carefully disciplined and distinguished work of a mature poet," a *New York Herald Tribune Books* reviewer states.

"Between the years 1939 and 1965 I wrote no poetry," Rakosi once told *CA.* Jim Harrison, writing in *The New York Times Book Review,* explains that the poet had stopped writing because he had come to feel "in the wake of the Depression and World War II, his intensely individual lyricism was irrelevant and impossible to continue." Geoffrey O'Brien reports in *Village Voice* that of Pound's *Cantos,* Rakosi remarked, "All that pretense and double-dealing are nauseating to me. And irrelevant. People today are not heroes, and modern human nature is not epic. It's just human, and anything else is just playing games." Poetry, he felt, would not accomplish much to alleviate the desperation of the people he wanted to help. He devoted himself to his career in social work and to his family.

A letter from Andrew Crozier, a young British poet, moved Rakosi to begin writing again. The letter, written in 1965, explained how Crozier had admired Rakosi's early poems, and had searched out nearly eighty of them in various journals. When he saw that Rakosi must have stopped writing, he politely inquired why and encouraged the elder poet to begin again. "I almost wept when I received this," he said in *Contemporary Authors Autobiography Series.* Of his work since then, O'Brien comments, "Rakosi's late phase is not so much a resumption as a rebirth. The 'Ancient image' which he prays will 'restore / my ancient relation / to words / in which I have set / my hope' seems to have answered him generously." In the poems of this second period, Harrison observes, "The positive effect of Rakosi's social concerns are direct and evident. . . . It is a tremendously engaged poetry, humane, attentive to the ordinary until the ordinary ceases to be so, but scarcely ever committing the usual objectivist sin of mere attitude, that of expecting dumb, unequal objects to stand by themselves as poems. These poems are 'made' things and throughout the book we sense the intelligence that directed the craft." Other critics agree with Harrison that Rakosi "should be read and saluted by those who care for the life of the poem." Poems in *Amulet* "will, I believe, come as something of an unexpected pleasure to those readers who have been so bullied by academic theorists, and anti-academic academic theorists, that they approach objectivist poetry with the foolish solemnity of society matrons attending a light-show," *Prairie Schooner* contributor Stanley Cooperman comments. Cooperman especially enjoys "the ease and comfort and wit of [Rakosi's] work."

Negative responses to Rakosi's work focus on his techniques. *Poetry* contributor Laurence Lieberman feels that "the line weave"—a form made of lines alternately aligned to the right, then the left sides of the page—"dominate all other quantities in the poems" in *Amulet.* As a result, he feels, it is more difficult to appreciate the variety of themes and objects Rakosi presents. Other reviewers feel that his sudden shifts between theme, sound patterns, and levels of diction diffuse the lyric energy of the poems. Cooperman, however, responds more favorably. "It is

the casual leap into serious thought and back again, that keeps us balancing on the points of our mind, doing a verbal and intellectual jig to a fiddle that sometimes—and unexpectedly—becomes an orchestration. Quickness is needed: the ability to shift tones both on the linguistic and intellectual level. For Rakosi's work is at once irreverent and serious; highly intellectual and simplistic," Cooperman suggests.

This "leaping" between various registers of language is closely related to Rakosi's major theme, "the irreducible tension between a perceiving human and physical reality. . . . His most serious poems try to capture the knowledge of the shifty, duplicitous nature" of the human relationship to the physical world, Heller writes in the *New York Times Book Review.* Accordingly, in *Conviction's Net of Branches: Essays on the Objectivist Poets and Poetry,* Heller defines Rakosi as a poet "profoundly in between" his imaginative, emotional life and the objects in his world. Through poetry, he establishes more than a simple link bewteen these two planes of reference; in his variety, he suggests that poetry provides "an infinity of linkages," Heller observes. Therefore, he says, "the substantive quality of [Rakosi's] work lies not in the things it renders but in this arrested quality, the shapely contour of interacting thought and emotion, thought and object." Heller adds, "It is because of this tracing, this linguistic interconnecting, that Rakosi strikes one as, above all, the poet of the lived world, the phenomenal world radiating out from us, the world under the double sign of self and otherness."

"Like Williams's [poetry]," writes *New York Times Book Review* Critic R. W. Flint, "his writing has obviously been nourished every step of the way by the rigors and rewards of exacting work well outside the literary orbit." Heller, writing in *Conviction's Net of Branches,* concurs: "Rakosi's work is among the most compassionate bodies of poetry, . . . because so much seems to be transformed for the express purposes of communication and seems to have been given over to directness of statement and the recognition that another human is reading it."

BIOGRAPHICAL/CRITICAL SOURCES:

BOOKS

Contemporary Authors Autobiography Series, Volume 5, Gale, 1987.
Contemporary Literary Criticism, Volume 47, Gale, 1988.
Heller, Michael, *Conviction's Net of Branches: Essays on the Objectivist Poets and Poetry,* Southern Illinois University Press, 1985.

PERIODICALS

American Book Review, May-June, 1982.
Chicago Review, winter, 1979.
Choice, July-August, 1972.
Contemporary Literature, spring, 1969.
Iowa Review, winter, 1971.
New York Times Book Review, May 17, 1942, January 28, 1968, November 16, 1975, March 8, 1987.
Poetry, August, 1968.
Poetry Flash, March, 1987.
Prairie Schooner, fall, 1968, spring, 1972.
Preview, June, 1975.
Threepenny Review, summer, 1988.
Village Voice, June 13, 1987.

—*Sketch by Marilyn K. Basel*

READ, Jan
See READ, John Hinton

*   *   *

READ, John Hinton 1917-
(Jan Read)

PERSONAL: Born November 18, 1917, in Sydney, Australia; son of John (a scientist) and Ida (an inspector of schools; maiden name, Suddards) Read; married Maria Teresa (Maite) Manjon-Alonso (a writer under name Maite Manjon), November 21, 1956; children: John Carlos. *Education:* Attended Emmanuel College, Cambridge, 1932-33; St. Andrews University, B.Sc. (with honors), 1935.

ADDRESSES: Home—One Donaldson Gardens, St. Andrews, Fife KY16 9DH, Scotland. *Agent*—Curtis Brown Ltd., 162-168 Regent St., London W1R 5TA, England.

CAREER: Armament Research Department, Sheffield, England, experimental officer, 1939-44; Sheffield University, Sheffield, lecturer in chemistry, 1943-44; Birmingham University, Birmingham, England, research fellow, 1944-45; scriptwriter for motion pictures and television, 1947—; Gainsborough Pictures, London, England, scenario editor, 1947-49; Rank Organisation, London, assistant to the executive producer, 1950-52; Triangle Film Productions, London, director, 1952-73; free-lance writer. Consultant to Scientific Exhibitions, Festival of Britain, 1949-50.

MEMBER: Writers Guild, Circle of Wine Writers (honorary secretary, 1981-84), Gran Orden de Caballeros del Vino (founding member).

AWARDS, HONORS: Commonwealth Fund fellow in cinematography, 1946-47; chevalier of Spanish wine order of San Miguel, 1977; Writers Guild award for best television series, for "Dr. Finlay's Casebook."

WRITINGS:

UNDER NAME JAN READ

The Blue Lamp (screenplay), Eagle Lion, 1951.
White Corridors (screenplay), Rank Organisation, 1953.
(With Beverly Cross) *Jason and the Argonauts* (screenplay), Paramount, 1959.
(With Antonio Mingote) *History for Beginners,* Thomas Nelson, 1960.
(With Nigel Kneale) *First Men in the Moon* (screenplay), Columbia, 1964.
The Wines of Spain and Portugal, Faber, 1973, Hippocrene, 1974.
The Moors in Spain and Portugal, Faber, 1974, Rowman & Littlefield, 1975.
War in the Peninsula, Faber, 1977.
Lord Cochrane, Plata Press (Lima), 1977.
(With wife, Maite Manjon) *The Paradores of Spain,* Mason Charter, 1977.
Guide to Wines in Spain and Portugal, Pitman Publishing, 1977.
(With Manjon) *Flavours of Spain,* Cassell, 1978.
The Catalans, Faber, 1978.
(With Manjon) *Visitors' Scotland,* Macmillan, 1979.
The New Conquistadors, Evans Brothers, 1980.
(With Manjon) *The Great British Breakfast,* Michael Joseph, 1981.
The Wines of Spain, Faber, 1982, new edition, 1986.
The Wines of Portugal, Faber, 1982, new edition, 1987.
Pocket Guide to Spanish Wines, Simon & Schuster, 1983, new edition, 1988.

Companion to the Wines of Spain and Portugal, Century, 1983.
Wines of the Rioja, Sotheby, 1984.
(With Manjon and Hugh Johnson) *The Wine and Food of Spain,* Little, Brown, 1987.
Chilean Wines, Sotheby, 1988.
Sherry and the Sherry Bodegas, Sotheby, 1988.

Also author of screenplays *The Haunted Strangler,* 1958, *Blood Orange, The Secret Tent, George Bernard Shaw, The Flying Scot,* and *Street Corner;* author of teleplays for television series, including "Dr. Finlay's Casebook," "Robin Hood," "Sherlock Holmes," and "Danger Man."

Contributor to wine and travel guides, including *Andre Simon's Wines of the World,* 1981, and *Insight Guide to Catalonia* and *Insight Guide to Andalucia,* both 1990. Contributor of articles to periodicals, including *Hollywood Quarterly, History Today, Harper's and Queen, House and Garden, Quarterly Review of Wines,* and London *Times.*

WORK IN PROGRESS: An autobiography, *Young Man in Movieland,* "about my first year in movies when working in the U.S. for Louis de Rochemont and Fritz Lang."

SIDELIGHTS: In *The Catalans,* writes Raymond Carr in *Spectator,* Jan Read "is tantalizingly brief on the re-emergence of Catalanism in the nineteenth century and its fate in the twentieth," but instead "spends most of this book describing the glories of medieval Catalonia which haunted the national revivalists of the nineteenth century." According to Carr, *The Catalans* is "an admirable compression of the immensely confusing . . . history of medieval Catalonia and lively accounts of her epic resistance to the Castilian centralizers."

Read told *CA:* "My first interests were in photography and cinema, but, unable to obtain a union ticket in Hollywood, I turned to writing when working as an assistant, first to Louis de Rochemont at Twentieth Century-Fox and then to Fritz Lang at Universal Pictures Corp. I have travelled widely in Spain and Portugal since 1951, my particular interests being their history and wines. My wife (Maite Manjon) is an accomplished cook and in recent years we have collaborated on a series of books on gastronomy. . . . I take most of the photographs to illustrate my books. Having as a child in St. Andrews a nanny who was the daughter of an Open Champion, I naturally play golf!"

The author later added: "I like to write about subjects which have not previously been tackled—or not, at any rate, for a very long time. It was because there was nothing in any detail in English about the wines of Spain and Portugal that I began writing about them; again the books on the Moors, the Catalans, Lord Cochrane and the role of the British freebooters in the War of Independence in South America, and the Spanish Paradors were firsts. This is not the easiest sort of book to sell to publishers, who are always looking over their shoulder at what has made most money before (for example a book on all the world's wines or food—on which nobody has intimate knowledge); and if the book is successful it immediately attracts copyists. Nevertheless, I see little point in regurgitating something which has been done before. What motivates me is sharing what I enjoy or have discovered with readers."

BIOGRAPHICAL/CRITICAL SOURCES:

PERIODICALS

Spectator, February 3, 1979.
Times Literary Supplement, February 24, 1978; July 3, 1981.

READE, Hamish
   See GRAY, Simon (James Holliday)

*   *   *

RECHY, John (Francisco) 1934-

PERSONAL: Born in 1934, in El Paso, Tex.; son of Roberto Sixto and Guadalupe (Flores) Rechy. *Education:* Texas Western College (now University of Texas at El Paso), B.A.; attended New School for Social Research.

ADDRESSES: Home—Los Angeles, Calif.; and New York, N.Y. *Office*—c/o Georges Borchardt Inc., 136 East 57th St., New York, N.Y. 10022.

CAREER: Writer. Conducted writing seminars at Occidental College and University of California; presently teaches in the graduate school of the University of Southern California. *Military service:* U.S. Army; served in Germany.

MEMBER: Authors Guild, Authors League of America, PEN, Texas Institute of Letters.

AWARDS, HONORS: Longview Foundation fiction prize, 1961, for short story "The Fabulous Wedding of Miss Destiny"; International Prix Formentor nominee, for *City of Night;* National Endowment for the Arts grant, 1976; *Los Angeles Times* Book Award nomination, 1984, for body of work.

WRITINGS:

City of Night (novel), Grove, 1963.
Numbers (novel), Grove, 1967.
This Day's Death (novel), Grove, 1969.
The Vampires (novel), Grove, 1971.
The Fourth Angel (novel), Viking, 1973.
The Sexual Outlaw: A Documentary (nonfiction), Grove, 1977.
"Momma as She Was—Not as She Became" (play), produced in New York, N.Y., 1978.
Rushes (novel), Grove, 1979.
Bodies and Souls (novel), Carroll & Graf, 1983.
"Tigers Wild" (play), first produced in New York, N.Y., at Playhouse 91, October 21, 1986.
Marilyn's Daughter (novel), Carroll & Graf, 1988.

Also author of a screenplay based on his novel *City of Night* and a play based on *Rushes.*

CONTRIBUTOR

LeRoi Jones, editor, *The Moderns,* Corinth, 1963.
Robert Rubens, editor, *Voices,* M. Joseph, 1963.
Bruce Jay Friedman, editor, *Black Humor,* Bantam, 1965.
Donald M. Allen and Robert Creeley, editors, *New American Story,* Grove, 1965.
Collision Course, Random House, 1968.
Floren Harper, editor, *Scripts,* Houghton, 1973.
W. Burns Taylor, Richard Santelli, and Kathleen McGary, editors, *Passing Through,* Santay Publishers, 1974.
Susan Cahill and Michele F. Couper, editors, *Urban Reader,* Prentice-Hall, 1979.
David Madden and Peggy Bach, editors, *Rediscoveries II,* Carroll & Graf, 1988.

Also contributor to Edmundo García Girón, editor, *Literatura Chicana,* Prentice-Hall, and to Carlota Cardeneste Dwyer, editor, *Chicano Voices,* 1975. Contributor of short stories, articles, and reviews to periodicals, including *Evergreen Review, Nugget, Big Table, Mother Jones, London Magazine, Los Angeles Times Book Review, New York Times Book Review, Saturday Review, Washington Post Book World, Village Voice,* and *Nation;* contributor of translations from Spanish to periodicals.

WORK IN PROGRESS: Three novels, *The Miraculous Day of Amalia Gómez, Our Lady of Babylon,* and "Autobiography: A Novel."

SIDELIGHTS: John Rechy's first book, *City of Night,* was "hailed as the advent of a unique voice by critics and writers as diverse as Larry McMurtry, James Baldwin, Herbert Gold, and Christopher Isherwood," declares Gregg Barrios in *Newsday.* It became a best seller in 1963, a rare accomplishment for a first novel, and it is now regarded as a modern classic and is taught in modern literature courses. However, the book's controversial subject matter—it traced the journey of a sexual adventurer through the night life of urban America—has drawn attention away from what Rechy considers a more important aspect of his work: the structure of the novel and the craftsmanship of Rechy's art, aspects the author continues to emphasize in his more recent fiction.

Rechy draws on many aspects of his Mexican-American heritage, as well as his past, to create his own vision of art. His novels, declare Julio A. Martínez and Francisco A. Lomelí in *Chicano Literature: A Reference Guide,* "reveal the underlying power that Chicano culture can exert even on those Mexican-American writers generally considered outside the mainstream of Chicano literature." One recurring symbol Rechy uses in his novel *Rushes* is drawn from the Catholic faith he practiced in childhood; as the protagonist advances further into despair, his trip reflects the stations of the cross, the route that Jesus took through Jerusalem on his way to Calvary. "Whether Chicano literature is defined as literary work produced about Mexican-Americans or by them," state Martínez and Lomelí, "his works can be included in that category, especially since their plots usually contain some Mexican details and their themes frequently derive, at least in part, from Chicano culture." "Still, beyond these restrictive labels," Rechy told *CA,* "I am and always have been a LITERARY WRITER, a novelist, a creative writer who has experimented with various forms."

Much of Rechy's work concerns finding patterns in life, and reflecting those patterns in his fiction. His first novel, he tells John Farrell in the University of Southern California's faculty newsletter *Transcript,* grew out of his "desperate need to try to give order to the anarchy I had experienced." In later books, such as *Numbers, The Vampires, The Fourth Angel, The Sexual Outlaw,* and *Bodies and Souls,* Rechy has experimented not only with content, but also with the form of storytelling itself. *The Sexual Outlaw,* he told *CA,* is an experiment "with a form I called a 'documentary,' " while *Bodies and Souls* "is, I believe," writes Rechy in his *Contemporary Authors Autobiography Series* entry, "a daring novel in content and form; a grand and lasting artistic achievement."

Bodies and Souls relates the story of three runaways who have come to Los Angeles looking for answers and the realization of their dreams. However, Rechy intersperses their tale with vignettes of Los Angeles residents whose lives are as empty as those of the three young people. "The all-pervading isolation and loneliness that Mr. Rechy dramatized so effectively in his novels about homosexual night life," declares Alan Cheuse in the *New York Times Book Review,* "becomes in this . . . book a commonplace about daily life in California." Rechy tells Jean Ross in *Dictionary of Literary Biography Yearbook: 1982,* "I think of it as an epic novel of Los Angeles today—an 'apocalyptic' novel. In it, through the many lives I depict, I explore what I call 'the perfection of what is called accident'—the seemingly random components that come together perfectly to create what in retrospect we name 'fate.' "

Rechy told *CA* that he considers *Marilyn's Daughter* his "most complex and literary novel, dealing with artifice as art, the power of legend over truth." Richard Hall, writing in the *San Francisco Chronicle,* terms the novel "a marvel of literary engineering," praising its "complex plot . . . which loops and doubles back in time." Normalyn Morgan, who may or may not be Marilyn Monroe's daughter by Robert Kennedy, travels to Los Angeles after her foster mother's suicide to find out if Monroe was, in fact, her mother. Normalyn's journey of discovery leads her through a many-layered maze of deception and ambiguity— some of it laid down by Monroe herself, other parts hidden or forgotten by people whose lives intersected at one time with hers. "In her search for Monroe," explains Hall, "Normalyn comes up against one of the great, overarching symbols of American confusion." "Rechy notes that, whether [the book] succeeds on its own terms or not," states Farrell, "what the novelist intended was a truly innovative approach to narrative and a serious exploration into the origin of legends and their power over truth."

Marilyn's Daughter, says its author in *Newsday,* is "an extravagant literary creation. It deals with how one finally cannot run away from one's self." "Marilyn Monroe was a monument to self-creation, to self-consciousness," Rechy explains to Farrell. "She was artifice as art." Farrell continues: "Art, he insists, signifies only secondarily. Primarily and permanently—in all its potency to move us to exquisite vicarious experience—art *is.*"

For an interview with this author, see *Contemporary Authors New Revisions Series,* Volume 6.

BIOGRAPHICAL/CRITICAL SOURCES:

BOOKS

Contemporary Authors Autobiography Series, Volume 4, Gale, 1986.
Contemporary Literary Criticism, Gale, Volume 1, 1973, Volume 7, 1977, Volume 14, 1980, Volume 18, 1981.
Dictionary of Literary Biography Yearbook: 1982, Gale, 1983.
Gilman, Richard, *The Confusion of Realms,* Random House, 1963, 5th edition, 1969.
Martínez, Julio A., and Francisco A. Lomelí, editors, *Chicano Literature: A Reference Guide,* Greenwood Press, 1985.

PERIODICALS

Chicago Review, 1973.
Library Journal, February 1, 1963.
London Magazine, June, 1968.
Los Angeles Times, September 7, 1988.
Los Angeles Times Book Review, July 17, 1982, January 27, 1985, October 2, 1988.
Nation, January 5, 1974.
Newsday, September 10, 1988.
New York Times Book Review, June 30, 1963, January 14, 1968, April 3, 1977, July 17, 1977, February 17, 1980, July 10, 1983.
New York Times, December 27, 1967.
People, May 22, 1978.
Prairie Schooner, fall, 1971.
San Francisco Chronicle, August 7, 1988.
Saturday Review, June 8, 1963.
Times Literary Supplement, September 11, 1970.
Transcript, November 28, 1988.
Village Voice, August 22, 1977, October 3, 1977, March 3, 1980.

Washington Post Book World, August 12, 1973.

—*Sketch by Kenneth R. Shepherd*

* * *

REICH, Bernard 1941-

PERSONAL: Born December 5, 1941, in Brooklyn, N.Y.; son of Moe and Rosalyn (Hartglass) Reich; married Madelyn Sue Ingber, June 16, 1963; children: Barry, Norman, Michael, Jennifer. *Education:* City College of the City University of New York, B.A. (cum laude), 1961; University of Virginia, M.A., 1963, Ph.D., 1964. *Religion:* Jewish.

ADDRESSES: Home—13800 Turnmore Rd., Wheaton, Md. 20906. *Office*—Department of Political Science, George Washington University, Washington, D.C. 20052.

CAREER: George Washington University, Washington, D.C., assistant professor, 1964-67, 1968-70, associate professor, 1970-76, professor of political science and international affairs, 1976—, head of department of political science, 1976-82, 1988—. Visiting assistant professor at University of Virginia, spring, 1969; visiting professor at Baltimore Hebrew College, 1975-78. Member of adjunct faculty at U.S. Defense Intelligence School, 1975—; professional lecturer at Johns Hopkins University, 1978-80; chairperson of Middle East studies at Foreign Service Institute, U.S. Department of State, 1979—; adjunct professor at Defense Institute of Security Assistance Management, 1983—; lecturer at National War College, Foreign Service Institute, U.S. Military Academy, U.S. Naval Academy, Inter-American Defense College, and foreign colleges and universities. Visiting research associate at Tel Aviv University, 1971-72. Participant in international seminars; testified before U.S. Congress; member of advisory council, International Security Studies Program, Woodrow Wilson International Center for Scholars, 1982—; senior advisor, Frost and Sullivan Country Consultation Service, 1983—; consultant to U.S. Department of State and Research Analysis Corp.

MEMBER: International Institute for Strategic Studies (London), Middle East Institute (board of governors, 1980-86; executive committee, 1983-86), Middle East Studies Association (fellow), International Studies Association, Association for Diplomatic Studies, Inter-University Seminar on Armed Forces and Society (fellow), District of Columbia Political Science Association (secretary-treasurer, 1966-67; executive committee, 1967-71), Phi Beta Kappa, Delta Phi Epsilon (honorary member), Pi Sigma Alpha.

AWARDS, HONORS: Fulbright grant for study in Egypt, summer, 1965; National Science Foundation fellowship for study in Israel, 1971-72; American specialist grant, U.S. Department of State, 1978; American participant grants, U.S. International Communication Agency, 1978-79, 1980-84; German Marshal Fund grant, 1981; special travel grants, International Research and Exchanges Board, 1984 and 1990; American participant grants, United States Information Agency, 1985-89.

WRITINGS:

Crisis in the Middle East, 1967: Implications for U.S. Policy, Research Analysis Corp., 1968, revised edition published as *Background on the June War,* 1968.
(Co-author) *A Strategic Appraisal of the Middle East: Eastern Arab States and Israel,* Research Analysis Corp., 1968, revised edition published as *Israel and the Eastern Arab States: A Strategic Source Book,* 1968.
The Cyprus Problem, Research Analysis Corp., 1969.

(Co-author) *The Persian Gulf: Implications for U.S. Security Policy,* Research Analysis Corp., 1970, revised edition published as *Persian Gulf,* 1971.

The United States and the Northern Tier: Some Problems of Security and Defense Policy in Turkey and Iran, Research Analysis Corp., 1971.

Israel in Paperback (bibliography), Middle East Studies Association, 1971.

Israel and the Occupied Territories, U.S. Department of State, 1974.

(With Arnon Gutfeld) *Arzot Habrit Vehasechsuch Yisraeli-Aravi* (title means "The United States and the Israeli-Arab Conflict"), Maarachot (Tel Aviv), 1977.

Quest for Peace: United States-Israel Relations and the Arab-Israeli Conflict, Transaction Books, 1977.

(Editor with David Long, author of introduction, and contributor) *The Government and Politics of the Middle East and North Africa,* Westview, 1980, 2nd edition, revised and enlarged, 1986.

United States Middle East Policy in the Carter and Reagan Administrations, Graduate School of International Studies, University of Miami, 1984.

The United States and Israel: Influence in the Special Relationship, Praeger, 1984.

Israel: Land of Tradition and Conflict, Westview Press, 1985.

(Editor with Gershon R. Kieval) *Israel Faces the Future,* Praeger, 1986.

(Editor with Kieval) *Israeli National Security Policy: Political Actors and Perspectives,* Greenwood Press, 1988.

(Editor) *Political Leaders of the Contemporary Middle East and North Africa: A Biographical Dictionary,* Greenwood Press, 1990.

Historical Dictionary of Israel, Scarecrow Press, 1990.

(With Sanford R. Silverburg) *United States Foreign Policy and the Middle East/North Africa: A Bibliography of Twentieth-Century Research,* Garland Publishing, 1990.

Also author of technical reports.

CONTRIBUTOR

Tareq Ismael, editor, *Governments and Politics of the Contemporary Middle East,* Dorsey, 1970.

Howard R. Penniman, editor, *Israel at the Polls: The Knesset Elections of 1977,* American Enterprise Institute for Public Policy Research, 1979.

Robert O. Freedman, editor, *World Politics and the Arab-Israeli Conflict,* Pergamon, 1979.

Economic Consequences of the Revolution in Iran, Joint Economic Committee, U.S. Congress, 1980.

The Political Economy of the Middle East: 1973-1978, Joint Economic Committee, U.S. Congress, 1980.

The Middle East and the United States: Perceptions and Policies, Transaction Books, 1980.

Edward A. Kolodziej and Robert E. Harkavy, editors, *Security Policies of Developing Countries,* Lexington Book, 1982.

Richard Dean Burns, editor, *Guide to American Foreign Relations since 1700,* American Bibliographical Center-Clio Press, 1983.

George E. Delury, editor, *World Encyclopedia of Political Systems and Parties,* two volumes, Facts on File, 1983.

G. R. Berridge and A. Jennings, editors, *The United Nations, Power Politics and Diplomacy,* Macmillan (London), 1984.

Paul Maranz and Janice Gross Stein, editors, *Peacemaking in the Middle East: Problems and Perspectives,* Croom Helm, 1984.

Penniman and Daniel Elazar, editors, *Israel at the Polls, 1981,* Indiana University Press, 1984.

S. F. Wells, Jr. and M. A. Bruzonsky, editors, *Security in the Middle East: Regional Change and Great Power Strategies,* Westview Press, 1987.

Moshe Efrat and Jacob Berkovitch, editors, *Superpowers and Small States: The Imbalance of Influence,* [London], 1988.

Chitra K. Tiwari, *Security in South Asia: Internal and External Dimensions,* University Press of America, 1989.

Contributor to *Yearbook on International Communist Affairs, Concise Encyclopedia of the Middle East,* and *Collier's Year Book.* Contributor of numerous articles to political science and international affairs journals, including *The Weiner Library Bulletin, Current History, International Insight, The Korean Journal of the Middle East Studies, Australian Outlook, International Correspondent Banker,* and *The Journal of Peace Studies.* Contributor of reviews to *Near East Report, Middle East Journal, Military Affairs, World Affairs, Journal of Palestine Studies,* and other journals.

OTHER

Editor, "Nations of the Contemporary Middle East" series, Westview. Member of board of advisory editors of *Middle East Journal,* 1977—. Consulting editor of *New Middle East,* 1971-73. Member of board of editors, *Terrorism: An International Journal,* 1987—. Member of international advisory board, University Microfilms International terrorism documents collection, 1987—.

WORK IN PROGRESS: Articles and chapters for several books on United States-Middle East policy and on Israeli politics.

SIDELIGHTS: Bernard Reich has toured the Middle East and North Africa as a guest of the governments of Saudi Arabia, Egypt, and Morocco, and the Soviet Union as a guest of the U.S.S.R. Academy of Sciences. Reich's writing has been translated into Hebrew, Arabic, Japanese, Korean, Russian, Chinese, and French.

*   *   *

RENDELL, Ruth (Barbara) 1930-
(Barbara Vine)

PERSONAL: Born February 17, 1930, in London, England; daughter of Arthur Grasemann (a teacher) and Ebba (a teacher) Kruse; married Donald Rendell, 1950 (divorced, 1975; remarried, 1977); children: Simon. *Education:* Educated in Essex, England.

ADDRESSES: Home—Nussteads, Polstead, Colchester, Suffolk CO6 5DN, England. *Agent*—Sterling Lord Agency, 660 Madison Ave., New York, N.Y. 10021.

CAREER: Writer. Express and Independent Newspapers, West Essex, England, reporter and subeditor for the Chigwell *Times,* 1948-52.

AWARDS, HONORS: Edgar Allan Poe Award, Mystery Writers of America, 1974, for story "The Fallen Curtain," 1976, for collection *The Fallen Curtain and Other Stories,* 1984, for story "The New Girlfriend," and 1986, for novel *A Dark-Adapted Eye;* Gold Dagger Award, Crime Writers Association, 1977, for *A Demon in My View,* 1986, for *Live Flesh,* and 1987, for *A Fatal Inversion;* British Arts Council bursary, 1981; British National Book Award, 1981, for *The Lake of Darkness;* Popular Culture Association Award, 1983; Silver Dagger Award, Crime Writers Association, 1984, for *The Tree of Hands.*

WRITINGS:

MYSTERY NOVELS

From Doon with Death (also see below), John Long, 1964, Doubleday, 1965.

To Fear a Painted Devil, Doubleday, 1965.

Vanity Dies Hard, John Long, 1965, reprinted, Beagle, 1970, published as *In Sickness and in Health,* Doubleday, 1966.

A New Lease of Death (also see below), Doubleday, 1967, published as *Sins of the Fathers,* Ballantine, 1970.

Wolf to the Slaughter, John Long, 1967, Doubleday, 1968.

The Secret House of Death, John Long, 1968, Doubleday, 1969.

The Best Man to Die (also see below), John Long, 1969, Doubleday, 1970.

A Guilty Thing Surprised, Doubleday, 1970.

No More Dying Then, Hutchinson, 1971, Doubleday, 1972.

One Across, Two Down, Doubleday, 1971.

Murder Being Once Done, Doubleday, 1972.

Some Lie and Some Die, Doubleday, 1973.

The Face of Trespass, Doubleday, 1974.

Shake Hands Forever, Doubleday, 1975.

A Demon in My View, Hutchinson, 1976, Doubleday, 1977.

A Judgment in Stone, Hutchinson, 1977, Doubleday, 1978.

A Sleeping Life, Doubleday, 1978.

Make Death Love Me, Doubleday, 1979.

The Lake of Darkness, Doubleday, 1980.

Put on by Cunning, Hutchinson, 1981, published as *Death Notes,* Pantheon, 1981.

Master of the Moor, Pantheon, 1982.

The Speaker of Mandarin, Pantheon, 1983.

The Killing Doll, Pantheon, 1984.

The Tree of Hands, Hutchinson, 1984, Pantheon, 1985.

An Unkindness of Ravens, Pantheon, 1985.

Live Flesh, Hutchinson, 1986.

Heartstones, Harper, 1987.

Talking to Strange Men, Pantheon, 1987.

The Veiled One, Hutchinson, 1988.

The Bridesmaid, Mysterious Press, 1989.

STORY COLLECTIONS

The Fallen Curtain: Eleven Mystery Stories by an Edgar Award-Winning Writer, Doubleday, 1976 (published in England as *The Fallen Curtain and Other Stories,* Hutchinson, 1976).

Means of Evil and Other Stories, Hutchinson, 1979, published as *Five Mystery Stories by an Edgar Award-Winning Writer,* Doubleday, 1980.

The Fever Tree and Other Stories, Hutchinson, 1982, Pantheon, 1983, published as *The Fever Tree and Other Stories of Suspense,* Ballantine, 1984.

The New Girlfriend and Other Stories, Pantheon, 1985.

Collected Short Stories, Hutchinson, 1987, published as *Collected Stories,* Pantheon, 1988.

OTHER

(Editor) *A Warning to the Curious: The Ghost Stories of M. R. James,* Hutchinson, 1986.

Wexford: An Omnibus (contains *From Doon with Death, A New Lease of Death,* and *The Best Man to Die*), Hutchinson, 1988.

Contributor of short stories to *Ellery Queen's Mystery Magazine.*

UNDER PSEUDONYM BARBARA VINE

A Dark-Adapted Eye, Viking, 1985.

A Fatal Inversion, Viking, 1987.

(With others) *Yes, Prime Minister: The Diaries of the Right Honorable James Hacker,* Salem House Publishers, 1988.

The House of Stairs, Harmony Books, 1989.

Gallowglass, Harmony Books, 1990.

MEDIA ADAPTATIONS: A Judgment in Stone was filmed as "The Housekeeper," Rawfilm/Schulz Productions, 1987; several of Rendell's Wexford mysteries have been adapted for British television and subsequently aired on Arts and Entertainment network's "Masters of Mystery" series.

SIDELIGHTS: "It's infuriating to see Ruth Rendell consistently referred to as the new Agatha Christie," writes Cryptus in the *Detroit News.* "The fact is that Rendell . . . is incomparably better, attempting more and achieving more." Indeed, since issuing her first novel, *From Doon with Death,* in which she introduced her popular sleuth Chief Inspector Reginald Wexford of murder-plagued Kingsmarkham, Sussex, England, Rendell has been applauded by critics for her deftness of characterization, ingenious plots, and surprising conclusions. Francis Wyndham of the *Times Literary Supplement* praises Rendell's "masterly grasp of plot construction [and] highly developed faculty for social observation." David Lehman of *Newsweek* reports that "few detective writers are as good at pulling such last-second rabbits out of their top hats—the last page making us see everything before it in a strange, new glare."

Rendell writes two different kinds of mystery novels. In her Wexford books, she creates traditional "police procedural" stories, while her non-series books are psychological thrillers, "energized by the startling, disturbing, seductive notion that all psychology is abnormal psychology and that the criminal mind isn't all that different from our own," as Lehman notes. Wyndham remarks on Rendell's agility in both areas of mystery fiction: "Ruth Rendell's remarkable talent has been able to accommodate the rigid rules of the reassuring mystery story (where a superficial logic conceals a basic fantasy) as well as the wider range of the disturbing psychological thriller (where an appearance of nightmare overlays a scrupulous realism)."

Rendell's popular character Chief Inspector Wexford is middle-aged, married, and the father of two grown daughters. His extensive reading allows him to quote from a wide range of literature during his murder investigations. "Wexford is quite witty, I think," Rendell tells Marilyn Stasio of the *New York Times.* "He is also a big, solid type, very cool and calm. He also likes women very much and always has time for them. What more could you want in a man?" Along with his assistant, Michael Burden, Wexford solves mysterious murders in the town of Kingsmarkham in rural Sussex, a gritty and rather glum setting. "I don't want people to see Kings Markham as a pretty village," Rendell explains to Stasio.

Rendell's adroitness at building suspense in all her mystery books is admired by reviewers. In a *New York Times Book Review* critique of *A Demon in My View,* Newgate Callender writes: "Nothing much seems to happen, but a bit here, a bit there, a telling thrust, and suddenly we are in a sustained mood of horror. Rendell is awfully good at this kind of psycho-suspense." Writing in the *Los Angeles Times Book Review* about *The Lake of Darkness,* Charles Champlin calls the book "a cleverly plotted story whose several strands, seemingly only tentatively connected at the start, move toward a last, violent knotting (the sort of construction Alfred Hitchcock, who preferred suspense to the classic timetable mystery, might well have enjoyed)." Commenting on *Master of the Moor,* T. J. Binyon of the *Times Literary Supplement* finds it "immaculately written and constructed, . . . another of Ruth Rendell's skillful studies in abnormal psychol-

ogy; a powerful, intriguing, if ultimately depressing novel."
Speaking of *The Bridesmaid,* Carol Kleiman of the *Chicago Tribune* remarks that "it is a fine, psychological novel that holds its own as good literature." Similarly, John Gross of the *New York Times* claims that "Rendell's work . . . is equally notable for subtle psychological tension and sharp social observation."

CA INTERVIEW

CA interviewed Ruth Rendell by telephone on June 14, 1989, at her home in Colchester, England.

CA: You began professionally as a newspaper reporter and subeditor. Were you also writing fiction during the years you worked as a journalist?

RENDELL: No, I wasn't. I worked only on quite small local papers, and I don't think that what I did had very much effect on my later life as a writer. I don't think it was something that really suited me. I was quite glad to give it up and start writing fiction, even though my fiction was unsuccessful for a long time.

CA: Did crime always hold a fascination for you?

RENDELL: Not really. I wrote several novels at the time when I was starting out, and a lot of short stories. The short stories I sent to magazines and they were rejected, all of them. I think they were quite bad, so it was a good idea that they were rejected! I also wrote several novels of various kinds—I wrote an historical novel, and straight fiction, and then a detective story to see if I could do it, because I enjoyed reading them. People said to me, "You can't keep on writing all this stuff and not trying it on anybody," so I finally wrote what was a sort of light comedy of manners and sent it to a publisher. They kept it a long time and eventually said they couldn't publish it unless I rewrote it, and had I anything else? What I had was a detective story, which I had written to see if I could do it. It was the first Chief Inspector Wexford, *From Doon with Death.* They did publish it, and that was how it began.

CA: So when you created Wexford and Burden for From Doon with Death, *you didn't plan them as series characters?*

RENDELL: I had no idea. If I had, I'm sure I would have done many different things. I based Wexford at that time on other people's detectives, notably Georges Simenon's Maigret, but others too; he was quite an amalgam of classic detectives. Later, when I realized that this was going to be an ongoing character, I began to change him. I thought, I have got this man whom I'm going to write about in several books (I didn't know how many then), and I realized that I was going to have to make somebody who was more acceptable to me. So I began to make him more sensitive, more literate, more interesting, more of a family man and less of a tough cop. He continued to develop and change through the subsequent fiction. I had conceived Wexford as being rather over-liberal, not so much liberal as broadminded in the sense of not having really thought about his attitudes to life, so I made Burden precise and prim and priggish. As Wexford developed into somebody who was very much a thinking person, Burden remained quite rigid. Then I was told by a police officer that, although he and the policemen with whom he was associated liked the books, they felt that Burden was unreal because he was too priggish, too reserved. I tried to change him, and I did, for one book, *No More Dying Then,* in which he has a love affair. But I'm afraid he reverted to what he was; he took over

and I wasn't able to control him. So I ended up with the characters as they now are, with Wexford being very liberal, literate, rather too understanding, tolerant, and sensitive; and Burden awfully prim, rigid, and reactionary. That's the way it is, and I think I'm stuck with the personalities they now have.

CA: There's long been the natural division in your work between the Wexford series and the non-Wexford books, the more complex, unrelated novels. In 1986, with the publication of A Dark-Adapted Eye *under the pseudonym Barbara Vine, there seemed to be yet another direction taking shape. What prompted you to begin writing some books as Barbara Vine?*

RENDELL: I'd had an idea for this novel for about ten years, basically an idea of writing a novel not about someone who didn't know who his father was, which is quite a common theme, but about someone who didn't know the identity of his mother. I began to think about how to do this, and I saw that it necessitated somebody being pregnant and having a child, to the shock of her friends, neighbors, and relatives. I had to set it in a distant time because having a child out of wedlock is quite common today. I originally thought of the First World War, but then I realized that if I was going to do it in the first person, as I had planned, the narrator would be almost too old to have these recollections. So I thought of the Second World War.

By this time I understood that what I was going to do would be a semi-historical novel with a great deal of research in that period, and that my readers would find this quite straight. They might find it acceptable, but I thought they would want to know what was going on. So I chose a pseudonym, but at the same time deciding not to keep my own identity a secret. This has worked for readers, but I think that critics continue even now, after three Barbara Vines and a fourth one just completed, continue to say, "Why did she do this? Who is she trying to deceive?" I'm not trying to deceive anybody. I constantly get letters from my readers saying that they understand why I do this. And I do have three sets of readers who like the different kinds of books; they fall into distinct categories.

CA: I wondered whether readers crossed the lines between the types of books you write.

RENDELL: Some do and some don't. There is a group of people who only want the Wexfords. They write to me and say, "Why do you write anything else?" Then I get the people who like the Ruth Rendell books, the psychological suspense novels and want only those. Then I get the Barbara Vine people, who are specific and a special group, who want the sort of searching examination that takes place in the Barbara Vine books. These are the people who are themselves very sensitive and rather apprehensive. They find my Ruth Rendell psychological novels too frightening. They find that frightening element is missing from Barbara Vine, and that's what they like.

CA: Character is very important in your writing. How do you go about developing a character for a story?

RENDELL: I give it a lot of thought before I start writing, and when I am writing I think myself into the character; I become that character. So that I think, I am this person, and what would I do next in these circumstances? That is all I think I can say about doing the characters, because it is quite a complex, subliminal process.

CA: You said in an article in the Writer *that looking at portraits sometimes helps you in character development. Is it important for you to be able to "see" the character?*

RENDELL: Yes, but it's important for me to be able to see the character in a realistic, plastic sense. My imagination is not one that can conjure pictures in my mind; the pictures would be in words. Since I'm very fond of looking at painting anyway and do spend quite a lot of time looking at pictures, I enjoy portraits. To see a face in a painting often can be a way of starting me with a character, or filling out a character that I'd already had an idea of. Say I had a young woman character that I was thinking of for a book. I would then go to an art gallery somewhere and I would see a painting, either one that I'd seen before or not, a famous painting or not, and I might look at it and say, Yes, that's the face of my person. That would somehow help me a lot. And I might then mention the portrait when I'm describing the character in the book.

CA: You often deal with the sexuality of your characters, which is important to their action in the story. Are their any taboos that you impose on yourself in this area?

RENDELL: Yes, I think there are, but they would be concerned with children. I have written a couple of books about incestuous relationships, but I have never written about the sexual abuse of children and I don't think I would. I have never written about the murder of children except very much offstage, in a sort of peripheral way, not as a central motif.

CA: You've written many short stories, and in 1987 there was the lovely book Heartstones, *which runs eighty pages in the Harper Short Novel Series edition. That's a very nice length to read if one is in a certain mood and has just the right length of time. How do you feel about it from the writer's point of view?*

RENDELL: I wrote that because someone I knew was running a delightful magazine in this country called the *Fiction Magazine,* which looked beautiful, had wonderful people writing for it, and was not very successful. She asked me if I would write her a three-part serial, not quite as a gift, but almost, and I did; I wrote three-times-8000 words. Later on my British publishers, Hutchinson, found it and wanted it for their novella series, and then Harper's did too. That's how it came about. I think I enjoyed writing *Heartstones.* I felt about it much as I do about writing short stories. But if it is a short story, it's the longest one I have ever written. I have written short stories of 10,000 words, and that was 24,000. I don't think I will ever do that length again, because I rather think that I prefer a 6,000-word length or a 12,000-word length. I tend to write short stories because I think they're a good discipline for me. I write too much. I can go on and on and on, and I think you have to restrain yourself.

CA: Is there a greater market for short stories in England now than there has been in the past?

RENDELL: This is a difficult question for somebody like me to answer, because for years and years nobody wanted to publish my short stories. Now, because I'm very well-known, they do. If I wasn't quite so famous, would they? My short stories may be quite good or they may not, but I don't know if it makes much difference. I can sell a short story immediately, and I couldn't twenty years ago, but whether that is because my short stories are much better than they were or because the market is better, I don't know. I suspect the market is the same.

CA: Houses figure prominently in your work, as was noted in the Publishers Weekly *interview published on May 26, 1989. They can be as different as the part-fifteenth-century house in* Heart-stones *is from the clean-lined "box with lots of glass" in* Death Notes.

RENDELL: That one in *Death Notes* is a real house that I knew, near where I'm living now. Some friends of mine lived in it and I simply used it for my book. I love houses. I've lived in a great many different types of houses—about fourteen, I think—and I'm very interested in them. I always want to look at people's new houses. I find it very hard to write a novel or a short story which isn't set in a specific house that means something to me, that really is bricks and mortar, that really is somewhere. It's very important to me to be able to have this solid setting, to be able to imagine the rooms and have some kind of firm layout in my mind. I find it awfully hard to create in my mind, from scratch, a house that I don't really know. I find that if I start thinking of the rooms, I have my house or somebody's in mind. My imagination doesn't work in a very visual way; it's got to have some reality to base on. Of course, one usually has a sufficient knowledge of a number of interiors to be able to call on, and I think I know enough houses to have a supply.

CA: Foreign countries sometimes come into your stories. Are you usually taking notes for a book, or perhaps actually writing a book, when you travel?

RENDELL: I've only once done that, and that was for the Wexford book *The Speaker of Mandarin,* which was set in the People's Republic of China. When I went to China, which was in 1980, I knew that I would write a book about that country, though I didn't know which kind. So I read several books about China before I went. I took notes all the time while I was there, and I read more when I got back. I started to write immediately so that it would be fresh in my mind. Otherwise I have set books or short stories partly in Europe, and one of the Wexford books is set partly in the United States. I felt I did know that area fairly well, and I had a friend who was a teacher at Indiana State University at Terre Haute who passed the relevant six chapters round the faculty there so that we could check it out and be sure I hadn't made any awful howlers. I think we should feel very inhibited about writing about the United States, just as Americans should be about us. We do have the language in common, but frankly not much else. People make horrible mistakes, and I was very anxious not to do that. I'm not sure I would write about the United States again. I do have a son living there, and I go there a lot. But I feel that it's almost more dangerous to write about that than to write about some completely different culture like India.

CA: As H. R. F. Keating did—several books before he ever visited that country.

RENDELL: Yes, that was wonderful. You couldn't see any real difference between the books that came after his true-life acquaintance with India and the earlier ones that came from his acquaintance just from reading. But that's a special gift, and I don't have it.

CA: You mentioned earlier that you did a lot of research for A Dark-Adapted Eye. *Do your books often involve a lot of research?*

RENDELL: Some do and some don't; it depends. *A Dark-Adapted Eye* did necessitate reading a lot of books about the Second World War. *A Fatal Inversion,* the second Barbara Vine, involved no research of that sort at all; it was a question of weather for that book because it was set mostly in the summer of 1976, which was in this country a phenomenally hot summer, about the hottest of this century. Since the book proceeds day by day with precise climatic descriptions, I got onto our meteorological office and got them to give me a run-down of temperatures and rainfall every day for the relevant months. I did very intense research for that book to get it right, because I know that when you make a mistake you get floods of letters. The third Barbara Vine, *The House of Stairs,* didn't take much research. It was writing about a period I knew in a place in London which I knew very well. Some of the Wexfords have taken practically none; others have taken a lot. It depends on the particular theme I'm choosing at the time.

CA: You told Michele Field for the Publishers Weekly *interview that you "write too many books," that your life is "all writing and publicity." And you said to me earlier that you write too much.*

RENDELL: I think I do. Besides the fiction, I do a lot of journalism and a lot of reviewing and nonfiction. I've done too much lately. It must stop, because I don't have any other life, and I must.

CA: Is it difficult just to balance the writing and the publicity, or does one provide a sort of welcome relief from the other?

RENDELL: I don't like publicity; I would rather do none. I don't want to go and speak to people and do book signings. But I think if you write these days, you have to do some. If I just sat at home and wrote, I would manage quite well, but it doesn't seem possible any more to do that. It was once.

CA: I suppose once you become well-known, the privacy is all over.

RENDELL: Yes. I would say that every day of my life I get an invitation to speak or appear at something, and ninety percent of those invitations have to be turned down. In a way you like doing that, but in another way you don't, because it seems very unkind and you know that people don't understand: they think you're being standoffish or difficult or arrogant. But you're not. You cannot do it. Not only do you not have the time for it, nor the inclination, but you know that you will simply dissipate yourself, squander yourself. There will be nothing left. You cannot keep on doing that.

CA: How much of a hand have you had in the television and movie adaptations of your work?

RENDELL: Of the television and movie adaptations, the only ones that I have liked are the Wexford adaptations. I think they're very good. The others, on the whole, are less so. I'm very bad at writing scripts. I have done some, but I will never do any more; it isn't something that interests me. I'm asked for my approval all the way, though. I do go and watch the shooting and read the scripts and change them and give my advice. People have been awfully good about this. I have had a good say.

CA: Do the television and movie versions seem to attract new readers to the books?

RENDELL: I think so. People write to me about them and ask why I had this happen, why I allowed that, why I wrote something a certain way. The attitude of readers, although they must know it not to be so, is that I write the script, do the casting, direct, produce, and indeed probably do the camera work myself. Readers blame me for everything.

CA: Do you ever finish a book, get the last corrections made to the galleys, and think, That was just right?

RENDELL: Never, oh, never. The best I ever feel is, I think that's probably OK. But mostly I feel it's terrible; I can't bear it. I don't ever feel pleased with anything, ever.

CA: What keeps the challenge fresh for you?

RENDELL: I like writing. I think I get a bit better, that I write English a bit better, but I never feel satisfied. And now I feel less satisfied than I used to. I find it quite a difficult area to talk about. I do find it rather troubling.

CA: What's coming up that you'd like to talk about?

RENDELL: I've written a new Barbara Vine; I've just finished it. I have done various things in nonfiction that are intensely British. And I will be starting a new Ruth Rendell in July.

BIOGRAPHICAL/CRITICAL SOURCES:

BOOKS

Bestsellers 90, Issue 4, Gale, 1991.
Contemporary Literary Criticism, Gale, Volume 28, 1984; Volume 48, 1988; Volume 50, 1988.

PERIODICALS

Chicago Tribune, August 29, 1989.
Chicago Tribune Book World, December 19, 1982.
Detroit News, August 12, 1979.
Globe and Mail (Toronto), May 31, 1986; September 16, 1989.
Los Angeles Times Book Review, August 3, 1980; May 8, 1983.
Maclean's, May 19, 1986.
Newsweek, September 21, 1987.
New York Times, September 9, 1988; February 4, 1990.
New York Times Book Review, June 25, 1967; June 23, 1968; August 24, 1969; February 26, 1974; June 2, 1974; December 1, 1974; April 27, 1975; November 23, 1975; February 27, 1977; January 23, 1979; October 14, 1979; February 24, 1980.
Saturday Review, January 30, 1971.
Times (London), December 11, 1987.
Times Literary Supplement, February 23, 1967; December 21, 1967; April 23, 1970; October 1, 1976; June 5, 1981; July 23, 1982.
Washington Post Book World, September 20, 1981.

—*Interview by Jean W. Ross*

*　　*　　*

REYNOLDS, Anne
See STEINKE, Ann E(lizabeth)

*　　*　　*

REYNOLDS, Elizabeth
See STEINKE, Ann E(lizabeth)

*　　*　　*

RICKMAN, H(ans) P(eter) 1918-

PERSONAL: Born November 11, 1918, in Prague, Czechoslovakia; son of Ernst (a lawyer) and Grete (Wollin) Weisskopf; adopted by stepfather, 1929; married Muriel Edith Taylor, May 5, 1947 (died May 28, 1981). *Education:* Educated in Chechoslovakia, 1924-38 (with one year at a university); University of

London, B.A. (with honors), 1941, M.A., 1948; New College, Oxford, D.Phil., 1943.

ADDRESSES: Home—12 Fitzroy Ct., 57 Shepherds Hill, London N.6, England. *Office*—Department of Social Sciences and Humanities, City University, London, England.

CAREER: University of Hull, Hull, England, staff tutor in philosophy and psychology, 1949-61; City University (formerly Northampton College of Advanced Technology), London, England, senior lecturer, 1961-67, reader, 1967-82, visiting professor of philosophy, 1982—. Life governor, Imperial Cancer Research Fund. *Military service:* British Army, intelligence and education posts, 1944-47.

MEMBER: Aristotelian Society, Royal Institute of Philosophy, Oxford Union, Association of University Teachers, PEN, Society of Authors.

WRITINGS:

Meaning in History: Dilthey's Thought on History and Society, Allen & Unwin, 1961, published as *Pattern and Meaning in History,* Harper, 1962.
Preface to Philosophy, Schenkman, 1964, published as *The Use of Philosophy,* Routledge & Kegan Paul, 1973.
Living with Technology, Zenith, 1966.
Understanding and the Human Studies, Heinemann, 1967.
(Editor) Wilhelm Dilthey, *Selected Writings,* Cambridge University Press, 1976.
Wilhelm Dilthey: Pioneer of the Human Studies, University of California, 1979.
The Adventure of Reason: The Uses of Philosophy in Sociology, Greenwood Press, 1983.
Change, Nan-Un-Do, 1985.
British Universities, Nan-Un-Do, 1987.
Dilthey Today, Greenwood, 1988.

Contributor to *Encyclopedia of Philosophy,* 1967, *Symposium Volume on VICO,* 1969, 1981, and *The Hero in Transition,* 1983. Also contributor of about fifty articles to *Fortnightly, Hibbert Journal, German Life and Letters, International Studies in Philosophy,* and other periodicals.

WORK IN PROGRESS: A book on the philosophy of literature.

SIDELIGHTS: H. P. Rickman told *CA:* "One of the major concerns of my research and writing is how philosophy can help the social sciences to become more relevant and rigorous without aping the physical sciences."

*　　*　　*

RIELY, John (Cabell) 1945-

PERSONAL: Born August 27, 1945, in Philadelphia, PA; son of James Evans and Marianne (Gateson) Riely; married Elizabeth Dumesnil Gawthrop (a free-lance food writer), August 23, 1969; children: Christopher Cabell, Andrew Carrington. *Education:* Harvard University, A.B. (cum laude), 1967; Exeter College, Oxford, diploma, 1967; University of Pennsylvania, M.A., 1968, Ph.D., 1971.

ADDRESSES: Home—39 Parker Ave., Newton Centre, MA 02159. *Office*—Department of English, Boston University, 236 Bay State Rd., Boston, MA 02215.

CAREER: Yale University, New Haven, CT, lecturer in English, 1973-79; Columbia University, New York City, assistant professor of English and comparative literature, 1979-80; University of Minnesota, Minneapolis, visiting assistant professor of En-

glish, 1980-81; Boston University, Boston, MA, assistant professor, 1981-85, associate professor of English, 1985—.

Organizer of exhibitions, seminars, and symposia. Lecturer on various subjects, including Horace Walpole, eighteenth century art, and caricature.

MEMBER: American Association of University Professors, Modern Language Association, American Society for Eighteenth-Century Studies, British Society for Eighteenth-Century Studies, Modern Humanities Research Association, Bibliographical Society of America, College Art Association of America, The Johnsonians (USA), Johnson Society of Lichfield (England), Johnson Society of Southern California, The Johnson Club (England), Walpole Society (United Kingdom), Irish Georgian Society, Northeast Modern Language Association, Northeast Society for Eighteenth-Century Studies, Club of Odd Volumes (Boston).

AWARDS, HONORS: English-Speaking Union Scholar in England, 1967; B. Hubert Cooper Memorial Scholar of Society of the Sons of St. George of Philadelphia in England, 1970; grants from American Council of Learned Societies, 1972, Swann Foundation for Caricature and Cartoon, 1982-83, and Boston University, 1982, 1985; fellowships from Huntington Library, 1973, Yale Center for British Art, 1983, and National Endowment for the Humanities, 1988-89.

WRITINGS:

The Age of Horace Walpole in Caricature, Library, Yale University, 1973.
Rowlandson Drawings from the Paul Melon Collection, Center for British Art, Yale University, 1977.
(Editor with W. S. Lewis) *Horace Walpole's Miscellaneous Correspondence,* three volumes, Yale University Press, 1980.
(With Richard Godfrey) *English Caricature, 1620 to the Present: Caricaturists and Satirists, Their Art, Their Purpose and Influence,* Victoria and Albert Museum, 1984.
(Co-author) *Town and Country: Gainsborough and Rowlandson,* Birmingham Museum and Art Gallery, 1990.

Contributor to books, including *Evidence in Literary Scholarship: Essays in Memory of James Marshall Osborn,* edited by Rene Welleck and Alvaro Ribeiro, Clarendon Press, 1979; and *Johnson and His Age,* edited by James Engell, Harvard University Press, 1984. Also contributor to professional journals, including *Eighteenth-Century Studies, Yale University Library Gazette,* and *Apollo.* Yale University, "Horace Walpole's Correspondence," assistant research editor, 1971-72, associate research editor, 1973-79.

WORK IN PROGRESS: Mr. Bunbury the Caricaturist, with a Catalogue Raisonne of Prints by Him and after His Designs, Oxford University Press; *Sir Joshua Reynolds: A Critical Biography,* two volumes.

SIDELIGHTS: John Riely told *CA:* "We live in an age of narrow scholarly specialization, but I believe that this narrowness must be resisted if the humanities are to survive as a field of academic study and research—and if the rest of the world is to find the humanities worth supporting. Much lip service is paid to interdisciplinary study as the way of the future, but in practice few liberal arts colleges and universities offer many opportunities of this kind. We must work to increase and broaden these opportunities.

"My research and writing concerning literature and the visual arts, especially British art and caricature, has been an attempt to integrate the study of these disciplines. Each field has much to contribute to the other, but the insights to be gained are likely to be valid and worthwhile only if they are the result of conscientious and rigorous training in both fields. Interdisciplinary study is valuable because it broadens, rather than narrows, one's interests and awareness."

BIOGRAPHICAL/CRITICAL SOURCES:

PERIODICALS

New York Times, November 27, 1977.

* * *

RIVERA, Geraldo (Miguel) 1943-

PERSONAL: First name pronounced Hare-*al*-doe; born July 4 (some sources say July 3), 1942, in New York, N.Y.; son of Cruz Allen (a cab driver and restaurant worker) and Lillian (a waitress; maiden name, Friedman) Rivera; married first wife, Linda (divorced after one year); married Edith Bucket Vonnegut (an artist and fashion designer), December 14, 1971 (divorced); married Sherryl Raymond (a television producer), December 31, 1976 (divorced); married C. C. Dyer (a television producer), 1987; children: (third marriage) Gabriel Miguel. *Education:* Attended New York City Community College of Applied Arts and Sciences and State University of New York Maritime College; University of Arizona, B.S., 1965; Brooklyn Law School, J.D., 1969; graduate study at University of Pennsylvania, 1969, and Graduate School of Journalism, Columbia University, 1970. *Religion:* Jewish.

ADDRESSES: Home—New York, N.Y.; and Cape Cod, Mass. *Office*—Investigative News Group, 311 West 43rd St., New York, N.Y. 10036. *Agent*—William Morris Agency, 1350 Avenue of the Americas, New York, N.Y. 10019.

CAREER: Broadcast journalist. Worked as a salesman and merchant seaman before attending college; Harlem Assertion of Rights and Community Action for Legal Services (anti-poverty neighborhood law firms), New York City, clerk, 1968-70; admitted to the Bar of New York State, 1970; American Broadcasting Co. (ABC), New York City, member of "Eye Witness News" team for WABC-TV, 1970-75, host of late-night program, "Good Night America," 1974-78, contributor to "Good Morning America," 1974-78, special correspondent and producer for "20/20," 1978-85, special correspondent for "Entertainment Tonight," 1985-87; host of syndicated program, "Geraldo," 1987—. Founder and owner of production company, Investigative News Group, 1985—. Host of documentaries and specials aired on network television, including "Willowbrook: The Last Disgrace," "The Littlest Junkie: A Children's Story," "Migrants: Dirt Cheap," "Tell Me Where I Can Go," "Marching Home Again," "Barriers: The View from a Wheelchair," "Working Class Heroes," "Devil Worship: Exposing Satan's Underground," "Whatta Year . . . '86," and "Our Kids and the Best of Everything." Host and executive producer of documentaries and specials aired on network television, including "The Opening of Al Capone's Vault," "American Vice: The Doping of America," "Innocence Lost: The Erosion of American Childhood," "Modern Love," "Sons of Scarface: The New Mafia," and "Murder: Live from Death Row." *Military service:* Served in the U.S. Merchant Marine Corps for two years.

MEMBER: One-to-One (chairman of board).

AWARDS, HONORS: Award from New York State Associated Press Broadcasters Association, 1971, for "Drug Crisis in East Harlem," and named Broadcaster of the Year, 1971, 1972, and 1974; George Foster Peabody Award for distinguished achievement in broadcast journalism, 1972, for "Willowbrook: The Last Disgrace"; Robert F. Kennedy Journalism awards, 1973 and 1975; two Alfred I. du Pont-Columbia University citations; ten Emmy awards for local and national broadcast journalism from the National Academy of Television Arts and Sciences; three honorary doctorates; and has received more than 150 additional awards for achievement in broadcast journalism.

WRITINGS:

Willowbrook: A Report on How It Is and Why It Doesn't Have to Be That Way (based on his television special of the same title), Random House, 1972.

BOOKS FOR YOUNG PEOPLE

(With second wife, Edith Rivera) *Miguel Robles—So Far,* illustrated by E. Rivera, Harcourt, 1973.
Puerto Rico: Island of Contrasts, illustrated by William Negron, Parents Magazine Press, 1973.
A Special Kind of Courage: Profiles of Young Americans, illustrated by E. Rivera, Simon & Schuster, 1976.

TELEVISION SPECIALS

"The Opening of Al Capone's Vault," broadcast on ABC-TV, 1986.
"American Vice: The Doping of America," broadcast on ABC-TV, 1986.

SIDELIGHTS: Geraldo Rivera has become a phenomenon in modern broadcasting journalism. Born the son of working class parents he is now considered by many to be one of the most controversial television journalists in history. Rivera currently hosts the enormously popular program "Geraldo," the third most popular syndicated talk show produced in the United States. While reviewers such as Jeff Jarvis of *People* have described Rivera as "the Robin Leach of TV news," others such as the New York State Associated Press Broadcasters Association have given him a number of awards, hailing him as "a special kind of individualist in a medium which too often breeds the plastic newsman."

Rivera grew up in the Williamsburg section of Brooklyn, N.Y., the son of a Puerto Rican father and a Jewish mother. Well-aware that ethnic prejudices would adversely affect their children the family often used the surname, "Riviera." In a *Christian Science Monitor* interview Rivera spoke of his mixed ethnic background in this manner: "If you add them together, I'm actually a one man majority . . . in New York. But, there are two distinctive identities and it was very difficult for me as a kid to handle them both. So, I guess I compromised by being one or the other at various times in my life."

His ethnicity was especially difficult for Rivera to deal with during his years as an undergraduate at the University of Arizona. As he explains in the *New York Sunday News:* "Here I was, this little hood from New York with the Brooklyn Spanish-American accent. I wanted to be like them, to belong. So I said my name was Jerry Rivers and I did everything I could to please them. But they never accepted me."

A less than model student in high school (he was more interested in sports and street gangs), Rivera completed a two-year stint in the U.S. Merchant Marine Corps before attending the New York City Community College of Applied Arts and Sciences and New York Maritime College. He earned a B.S. from University of Arizona, and a law degree from Brooklyn Law School. And in 1970, Rivera was admitted to the Bar of New York State.

Poverty law was the focus of Rivera's legal career. He was a law clerk for the Harlem Assertion of Rights and for the Community Action for Legal Services before receiving his J.D. After completing graduate work, Rivera worked as a lawyer for the Legal Service Program of the Office of Economic Opportunity. For a short while he represented a gang of Spanish-speaking youths called the Young Lords, whose energies with Rivera's help were eventually redirected from revolutionary action to such things as organizing day care centers. However, Rivera grew restless with his law career. "I couldn't change the world defending gangs and poverty cases," he explained to a writer for *Esquire*. "Besides, all I ever earned in law was maybe three months' rent."

Around the time Rivera was rethinking his career in law, the Federal Communications Commission (FCC) expressed their intent to increase the number of opportunities for minorities in broadcasting. Despite his lack of journalistic experience, Rivera applied for a job as newscaster with WABC-TV in New York City and was hired. In September of 1970, after three months of intensive study at Columbia University's Graduate School of Journalism, Rivera made his debut on the station's "Eyewitness News" program. As a rookie reporter, Rivera was assigned to report such features as fashion shows, charity functions, parties, and conduct celebrity interviews. One day, while en route to cover a story, he encountered a junkie who was threatening to jump from a rooftop. Rivera tape-recorded a dramatic and emotional plea for help from the junkie's brother—also a drug addict—while the camera crew filmed the entire event. This story was shown on the evening news and Rivera was allowed to enlarge the story into a three-part series entitled "Drug Crisis in East Harlem."

Impressed with his aggressive search for a good story, energetic approach to reporting, and flair for dramatically presenting a news item, the "Eyewitness News" management people assigned Rivera more and more hard news stories to cover. Rivera's popularity grew quickly, especially among younger viewers, and his work was being rewarded with honors such as the New York State Associated Press Broadcasters Association Award.

In a 1971 *New York Times* article, John J. O'Connor attempts to sum up Rivera's appeal: "The secret of Rivera's rapid success? He knows what he is talking about. Unlike many newsmen who have difficulty telling the difference between a drunk and a heroin mainliner, he is knowledgeable about all aspects of the city jungle. He is not an outsider relying on 'official sources' for a story; he sees the story 'at the level that it happens.'. . . He is convinced that the television viewer has become immune to statistics—on drug addicts or welfare rolls or moon shots. The people count, he says, and it is the people who must be shown, be given access, on television."

Although well-known locally, Rivera gained extraordinary national publicity after his story "Willowbrook: A Report on How It Is and Why It Doesn't Have To Be That Way" aired. With the help of an employee recently fired from the Willowbrook State School for the Mentally Retarded on Staten Island, Rivera smuggled a camera crew into the school to film the vile conditions in which the patients lived. During the taping, an emotional Rivera declared: "This is what it looked like, this is what it sounded like. But how can I tell you how it smelled? It smelled of filth, it smelled of disease, and it smelled of death." The airing of the heartrending story catapulted Rivera to celebrity status and earned him additional awards. Scores of television and movie offers poured in.

In 1972, Rivera wrote *Willowbrook: A Report on How It Is and Why It Doesn't Have to Be That Way,* revealing the details behind the making of the news series. The book did not meet with the same enthusiasm as the television documentary. I. S. Land remarks in *Library Journal* that "On the air Rivera was obviously touched, upset, and outraged at what he found. And he was able to move the public to action. . . . The written words are as cold and as empty as the tile floors and unlived lives of the children of Willowbrook."

Due in part to the public reaction, support, and donations that poured in following his television report on Willowbrook, Rivera and actress Geraldine Fitzgerald created "One-to-One," a fundraising project to benefit mentally disabled people. As cochairperson, Rivera volunteered many hours working for the group—organizing festivals, participating in telethons and concerts, and anything else to aid the charity. Today he is chairman of the board of the association. Rivera also initiated a consumer action bureau called "Help 7," which is staffed by Fordham University law students and trained volunteers who answer hundred of calls for assistance daily.

Rivera explains his reasons for donating his time and effort to helping others in an article he wrote for *Esquire:* "I love being a newsman. Given enormous power and responsibility by the network, I have tried to use my position to make the world a slightly better place. Questions of style aside, this is where I differ substantively from conventional news-industry wisdom. Sometimes the reporter has to become involved in helping society change the thing he is complaining about."

Along with his meteoric rise in popularity among television viewers, criticism of Rivera's unorthodox reporting methods also rose significantly. A number of reviewers questioned his objectivity, disapproved of his tendency to sensationalize facts, and wondered if some of the truth might be sacrificed in favor of high drama. Alan Richman writes in *People:* "Almost from his beginning in 1970 as a local news reporter, Rivera has been unable to shake unrelenting criticism that he either exaggerates or distorts the news. Years ago he punched out a colleague who spread rumors that footage of Rivera dodging bullets in the Middle East had been faked."

Answering these critics, Rivera remarked to Richman: "Perhaps some critics are sincerely offended by me. Maybe there is professional jealousy involved. Maybe they are judging me by their own inner cynicism. Maybe there is a racial component."

While some critics have questioned his sincerity on some of the issues that he has reported on, Rivera has frequently stood up against convention and the establishment for his convictions, as in the 1972 president campaign. Disregarding WABC-TV's policy of station reporters being neutral, Rivera very vocally and openly supported Senator George S. McGovern for president that year. Eventually, Rivera took a leave of absence without pay from his reporting duties at the station until after the election. Rivera has also been known to refuse assignments he did not believe in and fight for others that he felt were important and needed coverage.

Despite the criticism of some but with the loyal support of fans, Rivera continue to develop and host a number of intriguing and discussion-provoking documentaries that continued to grab a huge share of the television viewers in its time slot. Huge audiences watched such documentary-styled specials as "The Littlest Junkie: A Children's Story," "Migrants: Dirt Cheap," "Tell Me Where I Can Go," "Marching Home, Again," and other extremely popular investigative reports exploring such social problems as drug addition, exploitation of migrant workers, the plight of Vietnam veterans, and discrimination against the physical handicapped.

In 1973, ABC developed "Good Night, America," a ninety-minute news magazine and signed Rivera to host the program. The format of the show, designed by the network with a great deal of input from Rivera, consisted of various entertainment segments mixed carefully with controversial news reports into which Rivera injected his own opinions. According to a reviewer for *Time,* on his late-night programs Rivera took "stands in favor of decriminalization of marijuana, granting amnesty for draft evaders, and setting up quasi-legal redlight districts as a solution to the prostitution problems." For four years this program drew in a very large share of the audience in the large cities in which it aired—such as New York and Los Angeles.

From 1978 to 1985, Rivera worked as a special correspondent and producer for ABC's successful program, "20/20." During this time Rivera traveled the world aggressively and relentlessly covering many of the political and social events that have forever shaped our world. After a brief respite during which he concentrated on "20/20" duties, Rivera returned to the documentary/investigative format to produce and host another series of specials, including "The Opening of Al Capone's Vault," "American Vice: The Doping of America," "Innocence Lost: The Erosion of American Childhood," "Modern Love," "Sons of Scarface: The New Mafia," and "Murder: Live from Death Row." As usual, while all of these shows proved extremely popular and well-watched by the general public, they continued to draw criticism from reviewers for their sensationalized and exploitive treatment of the chosen subject matter.

In 1987, Rivera's syndicated, hour-long talk show, "Geraldo" premiered, establishing the host as a true celebrity in his own right and making his first name a household word. Competing against the great talk show hosts, Phil Donahue, Oprah Winfrey, and Sally Jessy Raphael, Rivera's "Geraldo" is carried daily by over 170 stations, representing about 96 percent of the nation. Rivera takes pride in the fact that he continues to apply as much energy, action, preparation, and dedication to presenting the social and political news of the day on his show as he did when he first started in television. "Take the last twelve months," he told a writer for *Playgirl* in September, 1988. "I've been threatened by the mob. . . . I've had an AIDS-infected needle stuck at me by junkies in a shooting gallery. I've put my ass on the line probably a half a dozen times in the last year. And I bet if you went through the core of network newspeople, you wouldn't find that."

One very public example of Rivera's tendency to find himself in the center of volatile situations is the event that took place during the taping of a "Geraldo" show entitled "Teen Hatemongers." A violent brawl broke out between the guests—white supremacists and black activist, Roy Innis. Fists, bodies, and chairs flew across the stage after Innis, provoked by a racial slur, attacked a member of the White Aryan Resistance Youth Group. Members of the audience jumped on stage and bedlam reigned. Rivera's attempts to calm the group met with more violence. A chair hurled toward him, broke his nose, and a bloody Rivera called for a commercial break. Police were brought in and they got the situation under control. A bandaged Rivera concluded the segment and went on to tape two more episodes of "Geraldo."

As Rivera explains to Charles Leerhsen in *Newsweek:* "It happens. In the course of doing stories in Missouri, Montana, the shooting galleries of New York and Central America, my style of street-level journalism is up close and personal, and people tend to act in a very negative way."

Many television critics have called shows such as these "tabloid tv" or even "trash tv." A writer for *Newsweek* remarks: "Battered by dwindling audience shares and the encroachments of cable and home video, the television industry is fervently embracing a radical survival tactic: anything goes as long as it gets an audience. Shock'em to attention. Hammer their ideological hot buttons. Inflame their libidos. Deliver a visceral rush by playing to their most primitive fascinations." "Shows like 'Geraldo,' " comments Richard Salant, former president of CBS-TV News, are "supermarket checkout-counter journalism." He continues in *Newsweek:* "Nothing on television surprises me anymore. . . . There would be none of this stuff if it did not have an audience."

MEDIA ADAPTATIONS: Miguel Robles—So Far and *Puerto Rico: Island of Contrasts* have been produced on audio cassette.

BIOGRAPHICAL/CRITICAL SOURCES:

PERIODICALS

Best Sellers, June, 1976.
Business Week, November 21, 1988.
Christian Science Monitor, April 3, 1974.
Esquire, April, 1975, April, 1986.
Harper's Bazaar, November, 1972, August, 1974.
Library Journal, June 15, 1972.
Life, June 9, 1972.
Mademoiselle, August, 1974.
Nation, July 19, 1975.
Newsday, March 31, 1974.
Newsweek, July 17, 1972, November 6, 1972, November 14, 1988.
New York Daily News, November 4, 1988.
New York Magazine, August 7, 1972.
New York Post, November 5, 1988.
New York Times, November 21, 1971, October 27, 1988.
New York Sunday News, September 10, 1972.
People, December 7, 1987, May 2, 1988, September 19, 1988, November 21, 1988.
Playgirl, September, 1988.
Time, May 13, 1974, December 22, 1986, October 31, 1988.
Vogue, May, 1988.

—Sketch by Margaret Mazurkiewicz

*   *   *

RIVERA, Tomas 1935-1984

PERSONAL: Born December 22, 1935, in Crystal City, Tex.; died in Fontana, Calif., May 16, 1984; son of Florencio M. (a laborer and cook) and Josefa (Hernández) Rivera; married Concepción Garza, November 27, 1958; children: Ileana, Irasema, Florencio Javier. *Education:* Southwest Texas Junior College, A.A., 1956; Southwest Texas State College (now University), B.A., 1958, M.Ed., 1964; University of Oklahoma, M.A., 1969, Ph.D., 1969.

ADDRESSES: Home—5912 Trone Tr., San Antonio, Tex. 78238. *Office*—College of Multidisciplinary Studies, University of Texas at San Antonio, 4242 Piedras Dr., San Antonio, Tex. 78284.

CAREER: Teacher of English and Spanish in public schools of San Antonio, Tex., 1957-58, Crystal City, Tex., 1958-60, and League City, Tex., 1960-65; Southwest Texas Junior College, Uvalde, instructor in English, French, and Spanish, 1965-66; University of Oklahoma, Norman, instructor in Spanish,

1968-69; Sam Houston State University, Huntsville, Tex., associate professor, 1969-71; University of Texas at San Antonio, professor of Spanish, beginning 1971, associate dean of College of Multidisciplinary Studies, beginning 1973, became vice-president for administration; University of Texas at El Paso, executive vice-president. Chancellor, University of California, Riverside. Visiting professor at Trinity University, San Antonio, Tex., 1973. Member, American Council on Teaching of Foreign Languages.

MEMBER: Pan American Student Forum (member of board of directors, 1965); American Association of Teachers of Spanish and Portuguese; National Association of Bilingual Educators; South Central Modern Language Association; Texas Foreign Language Association; San Antonio Bilingual Educators/Texas Association of Bilingual Educators; Phi Theta Kappa, Sigma Delta Pi (president of University of Oklahoma chapter, 1968).

AWARDS, HONORS: Premio Quinto Sol National Literary Award, 1970, for *. . .y no se lo tragó la tierra/And the Earth Did Not Part;* appointed chancellor, University of California at Riverside, 1979.

WRITINGS:

. . .y no se lo tragó la tierra/And the Earth Did Not Part (bilingual edition of short stories), Quinto Sol Publications, 1971, reprinted, Arte Público Press, 1987, English-language edition published as *The Earth Did Not Part,* Quinto Sol Publications, 1971, English-language edition published as *This Migrant Earth,* Arte Público Press, 1985.

(Contributor) Joseph Flores, editor, *Songs and Dreams,* Pendulum Press, 1972.

(With Ed Simmen) *New Voices in Literature: The Mexican Americans,* Pan American University, 1972.

Always and Other Poems, Sisterdale Press, 1973.

(Author of preface) Ron Arias, *The Road to Tamanzuchale,* West Coast Poetry Review, 1975.

(Contributor of poems) Leonardo Anguiano and Cecilio Garcia, editors, *El Quetzal Emplumece,* Carmela Notalvo, Mexican American Cultural Center, 1976.

(Contributor) Francisco Jiménez, editor, *The Identification and Analysis of Chicano Literature,* Bilingual Press, 1979.

The Harvest-La Cosecha, Arte Público, 1989.

Also author of *Chicano Literature: A Dynamic Intimacy* (nomograph), Pan American University, and *La Casa Grande* (novel). Also contributor to *Proceedings; Conference on Challenge of the Spanish Speaking American,* Brigham Young University, and to *Café Solo,* edited by Ernest Padilla, 1974. Contributor to journals, including *Southwestern American Literature Journal,* and *Foreign Language Quarterly.* Work represented in anthologies, including *Aztlan: An Anthology of La Raza Literature,* Knopf, 1972; *El Espejo/The Mirror: Selected Mexican-American Literature,* Quinto Sol Publications, revised edition, 1972; *Chicano Literature: An Anthology,* Simon & Schuster, 1973; *We Are Chicanos: An Anthology of Mexican-American Literature,* Washington Square Press, 1973; *Anthology of Texas Poets,* Prickly Pear, 1974; *The Chicano Short Story,* University of Indiana Press, 1974; *Cuento: Revista de Imaginación,* Verano, 1975; *Voices of Aztlan,* New American Library, 1974; *The New Breed: Anthology of Texas Poets,* Prickly Pear, 1974; *An Anthology of Mexican Literature,* Mexican American Cultural Center; and *Floricanto II,* Aztlan Publications. Member of editorial board of MICTLA Publications, beginning 1971, and *El Magazin,* beginning 1972; contributing editor of *El Grito,* beginning 1971, and *Revista Chicano-Riqueña,* beginning 1973.

WORK IN PROGRESS: A large volume of poetry.

SIDELIGHTS: Poet and novelist Tomás Rivera's "prose style is concise, even pithy . . . , held carefully within the world of the migrant worker which Rivera has chosen as his subject," writes Juan Bruce-Novoa in *Chicano Authors: Inquiry by Interview.* Rivera once told *Contemporary Authors:* "Up to the time I started teaching, I was part of the migrant labor stream that went from Texas to the Midwest. I lived and worked in Iowa, Minnesota, Wisconsin, Michigan, and North Dakota." Despite the constant travelling required by the migrant's life, Rivera managed to attend school and eventually attended Southwest Texas State College in San Marcos, where he studied English. When Bruce-Novoa asked him how his formal education has affected him as a writer, Rivera responded: "I think it has helped me in several ways. First of all, it allowed me to see better the context of what I write and of the literature emerging from the Chicano Movement within the whole idea of literature itself. Because of the training I have a more total picture. . . . I prefer to see Chicano literature within the context of all these other literatures."

Rivera's collection *. . .y no se lo tragó la tierra,* which *Modern Chicano Writers* contributor Daniel P. Testa calls "a fascinating composite of stories and anecdotes of personal and collective true-to-life situations," parallels Rivera's childhood in that it is a family of migrant workers and their son. According to Testa, "With a free and flexible narrative technique, the author blends abrupt exchanges of dialogue, shifts of perspective, and internal monologue into the account of an external action or series of actions. . . . [Rivera] is at his very best in those well-sustained individual perspectives in which the language expresses the character's intimate thoughts and feelings with true-to-life naturalness and vitality. He has also discovered, in evoking the events of his Chicano past, a joyful cohesiveness." Bruce-Novoa continues: "Though narrative, [his work] is not expository, but, rather, strangely impressionistic. It is a measure of Rivera's talent that the reader thinks that s/he has read a detailed depiction of reality, so much so that many have used the book as an accurate sociological statement of the migrants condition. What Rivera achieves is the evocation of an environment with a minimum of words, and within that environment the migratory farmworkers move with dignity, strength, and resilience."

Ralph F. Grajeda notes in the same book how different generations in the community portrayed in *. . .y no se lo tragó la tierra* respond to their difficult lives: "Throughout the book tension is created between the opposing values of resignation and rebellion as the people are shown enduring the repetitive hardships of the present, and as they anticipate their future." Grajeda also praises Rivera's portrayals of the migrant's existence: "Rivera has a clear eye for the cruel ironies of life. In the world his characters inhabit, people are often victimized by the very hopes they nurture, hopes that spring from the positions in life which they endure." But Rivera does not see his work as political. He told Bruce-Novoa: "I have no distinct political purpose when I write. I do not write a creative piece to prove a political point." He added: "I just feel that there is a separation. I want to have in literature that one point where I can really be creative and totally human, where I can really try to see things apart from any gain or loss aspects, as you must in politics. . . . Literature is a much more complete game than politics, which is kind of mundane and of this world."

BIOGRAPHICAL/CRITICAL SOURCES:

BOOKS

Bruce-Novoa, Juan, *Chicano Authors: Inquiry by Interview,* University of Texas Press, 1980.
Davila, Luis, editor, *Chicano Literature and Tomás Rivera,* University of Indiana Press, 1974.
Sommers, Joseph and Tomás Ybarra-Frausto, editors, *Modern Chicano Writers: A Collection of Critical Essays,* Prentice-Hall, 1979.

*   *   *

ROBERT, Adrian
   See St. JOHN, Nicole

*   *   *

ROBERTS, Dan
   See ROSS, W(illiam) E(dward) D(aniel)

*   *   *

ROBERTS, Len
   See ROBERTS, Leonard

*   *   *

ROBERTS, Leonard   1947-
   (Len Roberts)

PERSONAL: Born March 13, 1947, in Cohoes, N.Y.; son of Raymond R. (a bread deliverer) and Margery (a textiles worker; maiden name, Trudeau) Roberts; married Nancy Crane (a nurse clinician), December 31, 1981; children: three. *Education:* Siena College, B.A., 1970; University of Dayton, M.A., 1971; Lehigh University, Ph.D., 1976.

ADDRESSES: Home—1791 Wassergass Rd., Hellerstown, Pa. 18055.

CAREER: University of Dayton, Dayton, Ohio, lecturer in English, 1972; Northampton County Area Community College, Bethlehem, Pa., assistant professor, 1974-78, associate professor of English, 1978-83, professor of English, 1985-88; Lafayette College, Easton, Pa., visiting assistant professor of English, 1983-85; Janus Pannonius University, Pecs, Hungary, Fulbright lecturer in American literature, 1988-89. Public information specialist for New York State Narcotic Addiction Control Commission, summers, 1967-69. Gives poetry readings and workshops at colleges, universities, and poetry centers. *Military service:* U.S. Coast Guard Reserve, 1968-74, active duty, 1968.

AWARDS, HONORS: Elliston Award from University of Cincinnati, 1981, for *Cohoes Theater;* poetry prize from *Dark Horse,* 1981, for the poem "Grandfather"; Mary Roberts Rinehart Foundation grant, 1981; Pennsylvania state poetry fellowship from Pennsylvania Council on the Arts, 1981; grant from National Endowment for the Arts, 1984; National Faculty award (Fine Arts Category), American Association of Community and Junior Colleges, 1987; Pennsylvania Council on the Arts Writing awards in poetry, 1987 and 1989; National Poetry Series Award for poetry, 1988, for *Black Wings;* National Endowment for the Arts Writing award in poetry, 1989; International Award for Teaching Excellence, College Leadership Program, Austin, Texas, 1989; Guggenheim foundation award in poetry, 1990-91.

WRITINGS:

UNDER NAME LEN ROBERTS

"Nutcracker" (one-act play), first produced in Bethlehem, Pa., at Northampton Community College Theater, March 16, 1978.
Cohoes Theatre (poems), Momentum, 1980.
From the Dark (poems), State University of New York Press, 1984.
Sweet Ones (poems), Milkweed Editions, 1988.
Black Wings (poems), Persea Books, 1989.
Call to Me in My Mother Tongue (translations; chapbook), Mid-American Review, 1990.

Work represented in anthologies, including *Anthology of Magazine Verse and Yearbook of American Poetry,* 1983-89. Contributor of more than one hundred poems to magazines, including *Partisan Review, California Quarterly, Poetry Australia, Poetry Now, Missouri Review, Virginia Quarterly Review,* and others. Translations represented in many magazines, including *American Poetry Review, Translation, Delos, Visions International, Denver Quarterly, Northwest Review, Prism International,* and others.

WORK IN PROGRESS: A volume of translations of Hungarian poems into English; tentatively scheduled to be published by Katydid Books, 1991; a volume of original poetry which should be completed by 1991.

SIDELIGHTS: Len Roberts told *CA:* "I began writing very long-lined poems (I thought they were paragraphs at first, until I started to see the rhythms that each line had set up) in 1976 in order to 'jot down' some feelings about my father, who had died in 1969. Since then most of my poems are still 'about' my first family (mother, father, two brothers), but in the past few years they have been gradually moving toward my second family (wife and three children); the lines have grown gradually shorter, also.

"All four of my books deal with the ghosts of my past as well as the loves and worries of my present. One theme which has become increasingly evident to me is an attempt to come to terms with the randomness of our lives and the final act, death. *Black Wings* deals most directly with these concerns. Presently I'm trying to expand my topics, trying to break into a more diverse subject matter as well as a more varied line. Time will tell if I meet with any success."

AVOCATIONAL INTERESTS: Camping, basketball, rebuilding and remodeling old houses, travel.

*   *   *

ROBERTS, Lionel
   See FANTHORPE, R(obert) Lionel

*   *   *

ROBERTS, William P(utnam)   1931-

PERSONAL: Born April 25, 1931, in New York, NY; son of Clarence and Ruth (Dowd) Roberts; married Challon O'Hearn; children: Carolyn, Laura, Kathryn. *Education:* Fordham University, B.A., 1955, M.A.T., 1957; Loyola Seminary, Shrub Oak, NY, Ph.L. (cum laude), 1956; Weston School of Theology, S.T.L. (magna cum laude), 1963; Marquette University, Ph.D., 1968. *Religion:* Roman Catholic.

ADDRESSES: Home—125 Mahrt Ave., Dayton, OH 45409. *Office*—Department of Religious Studies, University of Dayton, Dayton, OH 45469.

CAREER: Gonzaga High School, Washington, DC, teacher, 1956-59; Wheeling College, Wheeling, WV, assistant professor, 1967-71, became chair of department; Precious Blood Parish, Dayton, OH, director of religious education, 1971-75; Edgecliff College, Cincinnati, OH, associate professor, 1975-78, professor, 1978-80, became chair of department; University of Dayton, Dayton, associate professor, 1980-84, professor of theology, 1984—.

MEMBER: Catholic Theological Society of America, College Theology Society.

WRITINGS:

Teach Us to Pray, Liguori Publications, 1972.
The Quakers as Type of a Spirit-Centered Community: A Roman Catholic View, Catholic and Quaker Studies (Manasquan, NJ), 1972.
At the Door Knocking, Pflaum Press, 1975.
(Co-author) *Adult Participation: Answering the Call to Minister,* Archdiocesan Office of Religious Education (Cincinnati), 1977.
The Prophets Speak Today, St. Anthony Messenger Press, 1981.
Marriage: Sacrament of Hope and Challenge, St. Anthony Messenger Press, 1983, revised and expanded edition, 1988.
Touchstones for Prayer, St. Anthony Messenger Press, 1983.
Encounters with Christ: An Introduction to the Sacraments, Paulist Press, 1985.
(Co-author) *Alternative Futures for Worship,* Volume 5: *Christian Marriage,* Liturgical Press, 1987.
(Editor) *Commitment to Partnership: Explorations of the Theology of Marriage,* Paulist Press, 1987.
(With wife, Challon O'Hearn Roberts) *Partners in Intimacy: Living Christian Marriage Today,* Paulist Press, 1988.
(Editor) *Divorce and Remarriage,* Sheed & Ward, 1990.

Contributor of articles and reviews to magazines.

*   *   *

ROCKLAND, Michael Aaron   1935-

PERSONAL: Born July 14, 1935, in New York, NY; son of Milton (a high school teacher) and Bess (Sherry) Rockland; married Patricia Ard (an attorney), July 16, 1978; children: David, Jeffrey, Keren, Kate, Joshua. *Education:* Hunter College (now Hunter College of the City University of New York), B.A., 1955; University of Minnesota, M.A., 1960, Ph.D., 1968. *Politics:* Democrat. *Religion:* Jewish.

ADDRESSES: Home—11 Farragut Place, Morristown, NJ 07960. *Office*—American Studies Department, Douglass Campus, Rutgers University, New Brunswick, NJ 08903.

CAREER: U.S. Foreign Service, assistant cultural attache in Spain and Argentina, 1961-68; State of New Jersey, Trenton, executive assistant to Chancellor of Higher Education, 1968-69; Rutgers University, Douglass College, New Brunswick, NJ, associate professor and chairman of American Studies department, 1972-81, professor and chairman of American Studies department, 1981—, assistant dean, 1969-72. Director of Casa Americana Cultural Center, Madrid, 1965-67. *Military service:* U.S. Navy, medic, 1955-57; served in Japan.

MEMBER: PEN, American Studies Association.

AWARDS, HONORS: Sarmiento's Travels in the United States in 1847 was selected by the *Washington Post Book World* as one of the Fifty Best Books of 1970; *A Bliss Case* was listed as a Notable Book of 1989 by the *New York Times.*

WRITINGS:

Sarmiento's Travels in the United States in 1847 (History Book Club selection), Princeton University Press, 1970.
(Editor) Julian Marias Aguilera, *America in the Fifties and Sixties: Julian Marias on the United States,* Pennsylvania State University Press, 1972.
Three Days on Big City Waters (filmscript), National Educational Television, 1974.
The American Jewish Experience in Literature, University of Haifa, 1975.
Homes on Wheels, Rutgers University Press, 1980.
(With Angus Kress Gillespie) *Looking for America on the New Jersey Turnpike,* illustrations by Ruth Strohl-Palmer, Rutgers University Press, 1989.
A Bliss Case (novel), Coffee House Press, 1989.

Contributing editor, *New Jersey Monthly,* 1977-82.

WORK IN PROGRESS: Urban Adventure and *Energy Crisis.*

SIDELIGHTS: Michael Aaron Rockland and Angus Kress Gillespie's study, *Looking for America on the New Jersey Turnpike* is "a lively, informative, thoroughly entertaining examination of this most American of highways," writes Edward Allen in the *New York Times Book Review.* Allen continues, "In its examination of both the glory and the squalor of its subject, [*Looking for America*] remains admirably fair-minded. . . . Mr. Gillespie and Mr. Rockland deserve recognition for writing an original and substantial work."

BIOGRAPHICAL/CRITICAL SOURCES:

PERIODICALS

New York Times Book Review, November 19, 1989.

*   *   *

ROEMER, Kenneth Morrison   1945-

PERSONAL: Born June 6, 1945, in East Rockaway, NY; son of Arthur Kenneth (a senior publications engineer) and Mildred Hebert (an artist and teacher) Roemer; married Claire Marie O'Keefe (an educator and administrator), 1968; children: Yvonne, Michael. *Education:* Harvard University, B.A. (cum laude), 1967; University of Pennsylvania, M.A., 1968, Ph.D., 1971.

ADDRESSES: Home—3409 Halifax Dr., Arlington, TX 76013. *Office*—Department of English, Box 19035, University of Texas at Arlington, Arlington, TX 76019.

CAREER: University of Texas at Arlington, assistant professor, 1971-74, associate professor, 1974-82, professor of English, 1982—, assistant dean of graduate school, 1975-77. Visiting professor, Shimane University, Japan, 1982-83, and at International Christian University, Tokyo, 1988; lectured in Austria, Portugal, and Turkey as part of U.S.I.A. Ampart Program, 1988. Public speaker and lecturer. Director of University Catholic Community Choir, 1979-82. Member of numerous community organizations.

MEMBER: Modern Language Association of America (chairman of Late Nineteenth- and Early Twentieth-Century American Literature Division and Native American Literatures Discussion Group, both 1981; member of Publications Committee, 1989-91), American Studies Association, American Historical Association, Melville Society, Association for the Study of American Indian Literatures, Society for Utopian Studies (member of Steering Committee, 1986—; chairman of Publications Committee, 1984-85), American Studies Association of Texas.

AWARDS, HONORS: Research grants and summer stipends, University of Texas at Arlington, 1972, 1974, 1976, 1978, 1984, and 1986; nomination for Pulitzer Prize for American history, 1976, for *The Obsolete Necessity: America in Utopian Writings, 1888-1900;* National Endowment for the Humanities grant, 1977; Exxon Educational Foundation grant, 1977-78; ACLS travel grant, 1986; Senior Scientist Fellowship, Japan Society for the Promotion of Science, 1988; Chancellor's Outstanding Teaching Award, University of Texas at Arlington, 1988.

WRITINGS:

The Obsolete Necessity: America in Utopian Writings, 1888-1900, Kent State University Press, 1976.
(Author of introduction to reprint) King Camp Gillette, *The Human Drift,* Scholars' Facsimiles & Reprints, 1976.
(Editor and contributor) *America as Utopia,* B. Franklin, 1981.
Build Your Own Utopia: An Interdisciplinary Course in Utopian Speculation (textbook), University Press of America, 1981.
(Editor) *Approaches to Teaching Momaday's "The Way to Rainy Mountain,"* Modern Language Association of America, 1988.

CONTRIBUTOR

Paula Gunn Allen, editor, *Studies in American Indian Literature,* Modern Language Association of America, 1983.
Brian Swann, editor, *Smoothing the Ground: Essays on Native American Oral Literature,* University of California Press, 1983.
Eric Rabkin, Martin Greenberg, and Joseph Olander, editors, *No Place Else: Explorations in Utopian and Dystopian Fiction,* Southern Illinois University Press, 1983.
Klaus L. Berghahn and Ulrich Seeber, editors, *Literarisch Utopien von Morus bis zur Gegenwart* (title means "Utopian Literature from More to the Present"), Athenaum (Konigstein), 1983.
Paul Lauter, editor, *Reconstructing American Literature: Courses, Syllabi, Issues,* Feminist Press, 1983.
Clarence Gohdes and Sanford E. Marovitz, editors, *Bibliographical Guide to the Study of the Literature of the U.S.A.,* 5th edition, Duke University Press, 1984.
Arno Heller, editor, *Utopian Thought in American Literature,* Gunter Narr Verlag, 1988.
Daphne Patai, editor, *Looking Backward: 1988-1888,* University of Massachusetts Press, 1988.
Patai, editor, *Essays on Edward Bellamy,* University of Massachusetts Press, 1988.
Giuseppa Saccaro Del Buffa, editor, *Teorie e prassi utopiche nell'eta moderna e postmoderna,* Casa del Libro (Rome), in press.
Alfred Bendixen, editor, *Encyclopedia of American Literature,* Ungar, in press.
Andrew Wiget, editor, *The Dictionary of Native American Literature,* Greenwood Press, in press.

OTHER

Also contributor to *Prospects: An Annual of American Culture Studies,* 1979. Contributor of numerous articles, poems, and reviews to periodicals, including *American Literary Realism, Alternative Futures, American Historical Review, American Indian Culture and Research Journal, Studies in American Indian Literatures,* and *Southwest Review.* Editor, *Utopus Discovered: A Most Informal Newsletter,* 1975-88; *American Quarterly,* assistant editor, 1969-70, managing editor, 1972-78, book review editor, 1978-86; member of editorial board, *SAIL* (publication of the Association for the Study of American Indian Literatures), 1989—.

WORK IN PROGRESS: Utopian Audiences: How Readers Locate Nowhere; Reading the Streets of Matsue and Other Impressions of Japan; A Liberated Father's Survival Manual: A Light-Hearted, Anti-Manual Manual; a collection of Momaday interviews for *Great Plains Quarterly.*

SIDELIGHTS: Kenneth Morrison Roemer told *CA:* "There are obvious drawbacks to writing about such 'unusual' topics as utopian and Indian literatures. People are always asking me to define what I mean and to justify what I do. But these disadvantages are actually advantages. If I were working in more conventional areas, I might be lulled into believing that grappling with fundamental questions of definition and value was unnecessary. My attitude about my writing is closely related to my decision to take my family to a very traditional area of Japan for a year. Living in Matsue, where our family of four accounted for approximately fifty percent of the American population in a city of 130,000, forced us to redefine and reevaluate ourselves. Too many voyages to utopias, Indian visions, and Matsue might lead to acute cases of dislocation, but without periodic, constructive dislocations we really do not know where we are."

BIOGRAPHICAL/CRITICAL SOURCES:

PERIODICALS

American Literature, November, 1976, October, 1982.
Japan Times, October 12, 1983.
Times Literary Supplement, September 10, 1976.
Village Voice Literary Supplement, February, 1982.

*　　*　　*

ROHNER, Ronald P(reston) 1935-

PERSONAL: Born April 17, 1935, in Crescent City, CA; son of Preston Eugene (a U.S. Army colonel) and Leta Chandler (Dorsey) Rohner; married Evelyn Constance Parker, March 27, 1957 (divorced August 26, 1983), married Nancy Diane Carter, June 9, 1984; children: (first marriage) Preston Clark, Ashley Chandler (daughter). *Education:* University of Oregon, B.S., 1958; Stanford University, M.A., 1960, Ph.D., 1964.

ADDRESSES: Home—52 Westgate Lane, Storrs, CT 06268. *Office*—Center for the Study of Parental Acceptance and Rejection, University of Connecticut, Storrs, CT 06268.

CAREER: American School of Tangier, Tangier, Morocco, teacher and resident dormitory director, 1958-59; University of Connecticut, Storrs, assistant professor, 1964-67, associate professor of anthropology, 1967-75, professor of anthropology and human development, 1975—. Rejection-Acceptance Project, director, 1964—; Center for the Study of Parental Acceptance and Rejection, director, 1981—. University of Connecticut, Social Science and Health Service Training Program, member of program faculty, 1970-75, Human Development Studies Group, member of executive committee, 1971-75, NIMH Post Doctoral Training Program in Community Mental Health, member of steering committee, 1980-83; University of Washington, visiting scholar, 1971; Catholic University of America, Boys Town Center for the Study of Youth Development, visiting professor of anthropology and human development, senior research scientist, 1975-77. Field researcher in an Oregon mental hospital, summers, 1955, 1957, among Kwakiutl Indians of British Colombia, 1962-63, 1964, 1971, in Turkish villages, 1970-74, and in India, 1979-84; State of Connecticut, Parent-Child Resources System, research consultant, 1974-75. Natchaug Hospital, Inc., member of board of directors, 1977—, secretary of the board, 1980—, chairman of By-Laws Revision Committee, 1979—, chairman of Planning Committee, 1980—; American Institute of Indian Studies, trustee, 1980-84. *Military service:* U.S. Army, 1953-55.

MEMBER: American Anthropological Association (fellow), Current Anthropology (associate member), Northeastern Anthropological Association, Society for Psychological Anthropology, American Psychological Association (fellow), International Society for the Study of Behavioral Development, Society for Cross-Cultural Research (co-founder; member of executive council, 1972-76; president, 1983-84), International Association for Cross-Cultural Psychology (member of executive council, 1976-78), Transcultural Psychiatry Section of World Psychiatric Association, American Ethnological Society, International Society for the Prevention of Child Abuse and Neglect, Connecticut Association for the Prevention of Child Abuse and Neglect (board of directors, 1983—), Child Protection Council of Northeastern Connecticut.

AWARDS, HONORS: Fellowships from Ford Foundation, 1961-62, National Science Foundation, 1961-64, 1966, University of Connecticut, 1967, 1980, and American Psychological Association, 1980; grants from American Philosophical Society, 1965-67, University of Connecticut Research Foundation, 1965-80, Smithsonian Institution, 1979, National Science Foundation, 1979, 1980-84.

WRITINGS:

The People of Gilford: A Contemporary Kwakiutl Village, National Museum of Canada, 1967.
(Editor) *The Ethnography of Franz Boas: Letters and Diaries of Franz Boas Written on the Northwest Coast from 1886 to 1931,* University of Chicago Press, 1969.
(With former wife, Evelyn C. Rohner) *The Kwakiutl: Indians of British Columbia,* Holt, 1970.
They Love Me, They Love Me Not: A Worldwide Study of the Effects of Parental Acceptance and Rejection, Human Relations Area Files Press, 1975.
International Directory of Scholars Interested in Human Development in Cross-Cultural Perspective, Boys Town Center, 1976.
Parental Acceptance and Rejection: A Critical Review of Research and Theory (monograph), Human Relations Area Files Press, 1978.
Handbook for the Study of Parental Acceptance and Rejection, Center for the Study of Parental Acceptance and Rejection, University of Connecticut, 1980.
The Warmth Dimension: Foundations of Parental Acceptance-Rejection Theory (Volume 5 in "New Perspectives on the Family" series), Sage Publications, 1986.
(With Manjusri Chaki-Sircar) *Women and Children in a Bengali Village,* University Press of New England, 1988.

Also contributor to books, including *Cross-Cultural Perspectives on Learning,* edited by W. J. Lonner and S. Bochner, Sage Publications, 1975; *Issues in Cross-Cultural Research,* edited by L. L. Adler, New York Academy of Sciences, 1977; and *Native North Americans,* edited by G. D. Spindler, Holt, 1977. Contributor of more than 40 articles to anthropology and psychology journals. Contributor of reviews and abstracts to numerous periodicals,

including *American Anthropologist, Current Anthropology,* and *Resources in Education.* Member of editorial board, *Reviews in Anthropology,* 1973-79, *Child Abuse and Neglect: The International Journal,* 1977-81, *Journal of Cross-Cultural Psychology,* 1978—, *Psycho-lingua* (India), 1980—, *Children and Parents* (India), 1983—; advisory editor, *Behavior Science Research,* 1974—; editor, Society for Cross-Cultural Research *Newsletter,* 1976-79.

WORK IN PROGRESS: Research relating to the ongoing Rejection-Acceptance Project.

*   *   *

ROLANT, Rene
    See FANTHORPE, R(obert) Lionel

*   *   *

ROLFE, Bari   1916-

PERSONAL: Born July 20, 1916, in Chicago, IL; daughter of Max (a chiropractor) and Doris (a dress designer; maiden name, Fellin) Wicks. *Education:* Attended Jacques Lecoq School of Mime, Movement, and Theatre, 1963-66, and Etienne Decroux School for Mime, 1963. *Avocational interests:* Folk dancing.

ADDRESSES: Home—434 66th St., Oakland, CA 94609.

CAREER: Mime, dancer, choreographer, teacher, and consultant. Performer in theatres, cabarets, and revues, on television and with dance companies and community theatre programs. Member or past member of faculty at University of Washington, Seattle, University of California, Los Angeles, California State University at Northridge, and Chabot College Conservatory of Mime. Has conducted workshops for colleges, universities, theatre groups, and other organizations throughout the world, including International Festival of Clowning, Sacramento State College, Pomona College, Colorado Mountain College, Stanford University, Tufts University, University of Puerto Rico, Oranim Teachers College (Tivon, Israel), Israel Museum (Jerusalem), Federation Nationale des Theatres Universitaires, Maison de la Culture, French Ministry of Education, Roos Ballet School (Amsterdam), Canadian Mime School, and Spokane Civic Theatre. Director of plays in California and Washington; program coordinator of first American International Mime Institute and Festival, 1974.

MEMBER: American Theatre Association, Association for Theatre in Higher Education.

WRITINGS:

Behind the Mask, Personabooks, 1977.
Commedia dell'Arte: A Scene Study Book, Personabooks, 1977.
(Editor) *Mime Directory Bibliography,* International Mimes and Pantomimists, 1978.
(Editor and translator) *Farces: Italian Style,* Personabooks, 1978.
(Editor and author of notes) *Mimes on Miming: An Anthology of Writings on the Art of Mime,* Panjandrum, 1980.
Movement for Period Plays, Personabooks, 1985.
History and Mystery of Mime, Personabooks, 1990.

Contributor to theatre and dance journals and newspapers. Member of editorial board, *Gestes* (France), 1990.

WORK IN PROGRESS: Workbook for Period Movement; Mimespeak, a collection of articles; *Mime Everywhere; Mask-MimePuppet.*

SIDELIGHTS: Bari Rolfe told *CA:* "My change from professional dancer to professional mime came about when I realized that I had been choreographing dance stories, sometimes with narration. I had no name for it, but when I saw Marcel Marceau in 1955 I knew. I went to study mime to be a better dancer, but the school opened so many doors to a deeper recognition of reality, to tremendous vistas of imagination, that the experience demanded a shift from performer to teacher. I simply had to proselytize. Then writing was the next logical step and has become my prime interest. To my surprise, many mimes call me 'the mime scholar'—surprise, because I've never been to college.

"From Marceau I learned the beauty and poetics of mime; from Lecoq I learned that the world is full of it. Mime is meaningful movement, and that kind of movement informs our thoughts, skills, passions, sciences, arts, rituals, poetry, and daily lives. Recently I have begun to write about these links and interweavings.

"My love for the theatre also includes theatre of social relevance—agit-prop, seniors, children, ethnic, community, reabled—and I frequently volunteer with groups involved in these kinds of theatre.

"I make masks in all languages, masks for my own work and for other teachers and performers."

*   *   *

ROLSTON, Holmes III   1932-

PERSONAL: Born November 19, 1932, in Staunton, VA; son of Holmes (an educator and author) and Mary (Long) Rolston; married Jane Wilson (a teacher), June 1, 1956; children: Shonny Hunter, Giles Campbell. *Education:* Davidson College, B.S. (cum laude), 1953; Union Theological Seminary in Virginia, B.D., 1956; University of Edinburgh, Ph.D., 1958; University of Pittsburgh, M.A., 1968. *Avocational interests:* Backpacking, bryology.

ADDRESSES: Office—Department of Philosophy, Colorado State University, Fort Collins, CO 80523.

CAREER: Ordained Presbyterian minister, 1956; Hampden-Sydney College, Hampden-Sydney, VA, instructor in philosophy, 1958; pastor of Presbyterian church in Bristol, VA, 1958-67; Colorado State University, Fort Collins, assistant professor, 1968-71, associate professor, 1971-76, professor of philosophy, 1976—, overseer of religious studies program and graduate program in environmental ethics. Visiting scholar at Harvard University's Center for the Study of World Religions, 1974-75. Distinguished lecturer at various institutions, including Georgetown University, 1989, and Yale University, 1989. Consultant with two dozen conservation and policy groups, including Congress and a Presidential Commission. Presents seminars. Member of advisory board for various publications and organizations, including Environmental Philosophy, Inc.

MEMBER: American Philosophical Association, American Association of University Professors (president of local chapter, 1979-80), American Academy of Religion (president, Rocky Mountain-Great Plains region, 1987-88), American Association for the Advancement of Science, Philosophy of Science Association, Phi Beta Kappa (president of local chapter, 1979-80).

AWARDS, HONORS: Pennock Medal, Colorado State University, 1983, for distinguished service to the university and for teaching excellence; award recipient, National Endowment for the Humanities, University of Georgia, 1987; award from National Science Foundation.

WRITINGS:

The Cosmic Christ (young adult), John Knox, 1966.
John Calvin Versus the Westminster Confession, John Knox, 1972.
Religious Inquiry: Participation and Detachment, Philosophical Library, 1984.
Philosophy Gone Wild, Prometheus, 1986.
Science and Religion: A Critical Survey, Random House, 1987.
Environmental Ethics, Temple University Press, 1988.

Contributor to books, including *Beyond Spaceship Earth,* edited by Eugene C. Hargrove, Sierra Books, 1986; *Conservation for the Twentieth Century,* edited by David Western and Mary Pearl, Oxford, 1989; and *Ethics of Environment and Development,* edited by J. Ronald Engel and Joan Gibb Engel, University of Arizona Press, 1990. Also contributor of over one hundred articles, reviews, and stories to magazines, including *BioScience, Garden, Conservation Biology,* and *Ethics.* Founder and associate editor of *Environmental Ethics.* Member of advisory board for *Zygon: Journal of Science and Religion.*

SIDELIGHTS: Holmes Rolston III commented to *CA:* "I am best known for my essays on environmental ethics, and I am an active defender of intrinsic value in nature and of the moral considerability of all living things. My work has been cited hundreds of times in philosophical journals. I believe that science and religion cannot adequately be joined until one understands how nature has a history and how the 'way of nature is the way of the cross.' "

BIOGRAPHICAL/CRITICAL SOURCES:

BOOKS

Goodpaster, K. E., and K. M. Sayre, *Ethics and Problems of the Twenty-first Century,* University of Notre Dame Press, 1980.

PERIODICALS

Between the Species, winter, 1989.
Biology and Philosophy, number 2, 1987.
BioScience, April, 1977.
Canadian Philosophical Review, September, 1986; September, 1987.
Conservation Biology, December, 1988.
Environmental Ethics, spring, 1984; summer, 1984; summer, 1986; fall, 1989.
Fides and Historia, autumn, 1973.
Journal of Religion, July, 1988.
Presbyterian Outlook, March 20, 1972.
Reformed Journal, September, 1973.
Scottish Journal of Theology, number 2, 1986,
Theological Studies, June, 1988.
Zygon, June, 1988.

*   *   *

ROREM, Ned   1923-

PERSONAL: Born October 23, 1923, in Richmond, Ind.; son of Clarence R. (a medical economist) and Gladys (Miller) Rorem (a political activist). *Education:* Attended Northwestern University, 1940-42, and Curtis Institute of Music, 1943; Julliard School of Music, B.S., 1946, M.S., 1948. *Religion:* Society of Friends (Quaker).

ADDRESSES: Home—Nantucket, Mass., and New York, N.Y. *Agent*—Boosey & Hawkes, Inc., 24 East 21st St., New York, N.Y. 10010-7200.

CAREER: Composer. Composer in residence, University of Utah, Salt Lake City, 1965-67; professor of composition, Curtis Institute, Philadelphia, Penn., 1980—. Musical copyist to Virgil Thomson, New York City, in the 1940s. Compositions have been performed by major conductors, including Eugene Normandy, Leopold Stokowski, Zubin Mehta, and William Steinberg.

MEMBER: American Society of Composers, Authors, and Performers (ASCAP), PEN, American Academy and Institute of Arts and Letters.

AWARDS, HONORS: Music Library Association award for the best published song of the year, 1948, for "The Lordly Hudson"; George Gershwin Memorial Award, 1949, for "Overture in C"; Lili Boulanger Award, 1950; Fulbright fellowship for study with Honegger in Paris, 1951-52; Prix de Biarritz, 1951, for ballet, "Melos"; Eurydice Choral Award, 1954; Guggenheim fellowships, 1957, 1979; National Institute of Arts and Letters award, 1968; Deems Taylor Award, ASCAP, 1971, for *Critical Affairs: A Composer's Journal,* and 1975, for *The Final Diary: 1961-1972;* Pulitzer Prize in music, 1976, for "Air Music"; honorary D.F.A., Northwestern University, 1977; the Atlanta Symphony Orchestra's recording of his "String Symphony," "Sunday Morning," and "Eagles" was awarded the 1989 Grammy Award for outstanding orchestral recording; grants from the Ford Foundation, Lincoln Center Foundation, and Koussevitzky Foundation.

WRITINGS:

The Paris Diary of Ned Rorem (also see below), Braziller, 1966.
Music from Inside Out, Braziller, 1967.
(Author of introduction) Jean Cocteau, *The Difficulty of Being,* Coward, 1967.
The New York Diary (also see below), Braziller, 1967.
Music and People, Braziller, 1968.
(Contributor) *The Artistic Legacy of Walt Whitman: A Tribute to Gay Wilson Allen,* New York University Press, 1969.
Critical Affairs: A Composer's Journal, Braziller, 1970.
Pure Contraption: A Composer's Essays, Holt, 1974.
The Final Diary: 1961-1972, Holt, 1974, published as *The Later Diaries,* North Point Press, 1983.
An Absolute Gift: A New Diary, Simon & Shuster, 1977.
Setting the Tone: Essays and a Diary, Coward-McCann, 1983.
The Paris and New York Diaries: 1951-1961, North Point Press, 1983.
Paul's Blues, Red Ayier Press, 1984.
The Nantucket Diary of Ned Rorem, 1973-1985, North Point Press, 1987.
(Author of foreword) Arthur K. Peters, *Jean Cocteau and His World: An Illustrated Biography,* Thames & Hudson, 1987.
Settling the Score: Essays on Music (anthology of previously published pieces), Harcourt, 1988.

Author of two one-act plays, "The Pastry Shop," and "The Young among Themselves," produced off-Broadway at The Extension, New York City, June 5, 1970. Also composer and librettist of *The Robbers,* Boosey & Hawkes, 1956. Contributor to *New York Times Review of Books.*

SIDELIGHTS: Washington Post Book World contributor John Malcolm Brinnin describes Ned Rorem as "a composer never far from a keyboard who is also a writer seldom out of range of a mirror. The keyboard has been the source of symphonies, operas, and scores of the most literate songs of the century. From the mirror have come reflections of the writer's passage from the days in Paris . . . to nowadays Nantucket where . . . he casts

a sage cool eye on the musical scene and endures the Daumier-like pleasures of domesticity."

U.S. composer, diarist and essayist Rorem was well-known for his music before his first volume of reminiscences, *The Paris Diary of Ned Rorem,* was published in 1966. The diary shocked critics and general readers alike—but the music world in particular—with its candid revelations of the private lives of important members of Paris cultural set of the 1950s, including such figures as French poet and film writer Jean Cocteau and the French composers Francis Poulenc and Georges Auric. Since then, Rorem has interrupted his work as a composer (he won the Pulitzer prize for music in 1976) on a regular basis to publish a series of diaries that have made him nearly as famous as his musical compositions.

The eighties saw publication of two new volumes of Rorem's diaries, *Setting the Tone: Essays and A Diary* and *The Nantucket Diary of Ned Rorem, 1973-1985,* as well as *The Paris and New York Diaries, 1951-1961.* Reviewing Rorem's recent and older writings at the same time, several critics comment on his development as a writer. Referring to *Setting the Tone* in a *New York Times* review, Time Page observes, "The tone . . . Rorem has chosen in this new book is markedly less lachrymose than in some earlier volumes and, despite a philosophic commitment to artifice, his sights have grown steadily more cohesive and convincing." *Los Angeles Times Book Review* contributor Elaine Kendall writes, "The prose of the older, new Ned Rorem is tranquil, disciplined and analytical where the younger, old Rorem was passionate, feverish and arbitrary, but the flashing insights, the brutal honesty and the felicitous phrasing remain constant."

Some critics seem to prefer Rorem's work as an essayist over that he has produced as a diarist. *New York Times Book Review* contributor Barbara Shulgasser states, "Why . . . Rorem, with his considerable gift as an essayist, continues to publish the diaries is a puzzle." Commenting on the reviews and essays included in *Setting the Tone* Brinnin notes, "In these thoroughly professional discourses, the self-indulgence and logorrheic flow of the diaries is curbed. Perceptions that evade the author when he talks about himself are at his fingertips when he discusses his forebears and contemporaries." In his *New York Times* assessment of *An Absolute Gift: A New Diary,* Thomas Lask downgrades the diary portion of the work calling it "a tired document, marked by petty carpings, weary aphorisms and futile resentments." However, Lask's remarks on the essays about music and musicians included in the last section of the book are much more positive. Rorem's "comments in these essays," Lask observes, "are of the kind that turn a listener back to the music. They convey the strengths and characteristic qualities of these musicians. They tell not only what to listen for, but also those things one will listen for in vain."

While *The Paris Diary of Ned Rorem* details episodes from the composer's youth, the latest installment in his diaries, *The Nantucket Diary,* tells of his confronting and coping with old age. "Does all this matter?," asks Alan Rich in his *Newsweek* review of the book. "It does," Rich continues, "because the author of these intense if effulgent diary lines *is* someone who matters, a composer reckoned among this country's best, a concerned observer of contemporary culture." The *Chicago Tribune's* John von Rhein compares this latest diary to the other autobiographical volumes published by Rorem and concludes: "The Rorem who emerges from these pages is more thoughtful, fretful, more acute in his observations; not so self-conscious or neurotic, however, as to surrender his wit, perspective or fineness of mind. With 'The Nantucket Diaries' the composer finally has reconciled his private and public personae; both make for stimulating company." Michael Dirda of the *Washington Post Book World* finds the book "a delight to read."

BIOGRAPHICAL/CRITICAL SOURCES:

PERIODICALS

Chicago Tribune, December 17, 1987.
Los Angeles Times Book Review, August 7, 1983.
Newsweek, October 12, 1987.
New York Times, July 26, 1978, December 28, 1983.
New York Times Book Review, July 17, 1983.
Washington Post Book World, July 24, 1983, October 25, 1987.

* * *

ROSEN, Michael 1946-

PERSONAL: Born May 7, 1946, in England. *Education:* Attended Middlesex Hospital Medical School, 1964-65, and Wadham College, Oxford, 1965-69. *Politics:* Socialist. *Religion:* Atheist.

ADDRESSES: Home—49 Parkholme Rd., London E83 AQ, England. *Agent*—Charles Walker, Peters Fraser Dunlop, 5th Floor, The Chambers, Chelsea Harbour, London SW10 OXF, England.

CAREER: Writer.

AWARDS, HONORS: Sunday Times National Union of Students Drama Festival Award for best original full-length play, 1968, for *Backbone;* Signal Poetry Award, 1981, for *You Can't Catch Me;* The Other Award, 1983, for *Everybody Here;* Smarties Best Children's Book of the Year, 1989, for *We're Going on a Bear Hunt.*

WRITINGS:

PLAYS

Stewed Figs, first produced at University of Durham, 1968.
Backbone (first produced at Oxford University, 1968; produced on the West End at Royal Court Theatre, February, 1968), Faber, 1968.

CHILDREN'S LITERATURE

Mind Your Own Business, Deutsch, 1974.
Wouldn't You Like to Know, Deutsch, 1977.
(With Roger McGough) *You Tell Me,* Kestrel, 1979.
The Bakerloo Flea, Longmans, 1979.
I See a Voice, Hutchinson, 1981.
You Can't Catch Me and Other Poems, Deutsch, 1981.
Nasty!, Longmans, 1982, revised edition, Puffin, 1984.
The Cat and Mouse Story, Deutsch, 1983.
Quick, Let's Get Out of Here, Deutsch, 1984.
(With David Jackson) *Speaking to You,* Macmillan, 1984.
How to Get Out of the Bath and Other Problems, Scholastic, 1984.
Hairy Tales and Nursery Crimes, Deutsch, 1985.
Don't Put Mustard in the Custard, Deutsch, 1985.
(Editor) *Kingfisher Book of Children's Poetry,* Kingfisher, 1985.
When Did You Last Wash Your Feet?, Deutsch, 1986.
(With Joan Griffiths) *That'd Be Telling,* Cambridge University Press, 1986.
Under the Bed, Walker, 1986.
Smelly Jelly, Smelly Fish, Walker, 1986.
You're Thinking about Doughnuts, Deutsch, 1987.
Spollyollydiddlyfiddlyitis, Walker, 1987.
Hard Boiled Legs, Walker, 1987.
A Spider Bought a Bicycle and Other Poems, Kingfisher, 1987.

The Horribles, Walker, 1988.
The Hypnotiser, Deutsch, 1988.
We're Going on a Bear Hunt, Walker, 1988.
Silly Stories, Kingfisher, 1988.
(Editor) *Kingfisher Book of Funny Stories,* Kingfisher, 1988.
Did I Hear You Write?, Deutsch, 1989.
Rude Rhymes, Deutsch, 1989.

Also author of *Inky Pinky Ponky,* with Susanna Steele and Dan Jones, Granada, *Everybody Here,* Bodley Head, *The Wicked Tricks of Till Owlyglass,* Walker, *The Deadman Tapes,* Deutsch, *Culture Shock,* Penguin, *Dirty Ditties,* Deutsch, *Freckly Feet and Itchy Knees,* Collins, *The Class 2 Monsters,* Heinemann, and *The Golem of Old Prague,* Deutsch.

WORK IN PROGRESS: Children's television programs, poems, and stories.

SIDELIGHTS: "In recent years Michael Rosen has probably contributed more than most contemporary poets to popularizing—in the real sense—poetry amongst school-children [in England]," Roy Blatchford comments in a *Times Educational Supplement* review of Rosen's anthology *I See a Voice.* Describing Rosen as "chirpy, relaxed and good-humoured," *Times Literary Supplement* critic John Fuller states that, in his collection *Wouldn't You Like to Know,* "Rosen satisfies most of the demands that children make of poems, playing for family sentiment, inventing silly phrases, insulting authority."

Michael Rosen told *CA,* "To write children's books is to be part of a popular culture. It means I can go out anytime into schools and libraries and meet the audience and try to entertain them with what I've got to say. In my poems I either try to have fun with the sound of words, or, quite differently, I try to explore the ironies of small happenings in such a way as to leave the audience to deduce the irony. In stories, I either try to adapt folk stories I like, or deal with how certain kinds of ignorance and oppression can be overcome.

"Children's literature is as neglected as children. Writers of children's books are frequently regarded as less important than adult writers, except when we're dead. Society's attitude to children is that they are innocents, nuisances, or victims. As innocents we can imprint training and conditioning on them, as nuisances we can tame and control them, as victims we can abuse them (actively or vicariously). Children's writers try to approach children with ideas, fantasies, intrigues, hopes, failings—which, because they are in book form, can be put down, picked up, enjoyed or thrown away at will. Because we tend to be both democratic and serious with children, we are regarded with patronizing amusement by society except at moments of outrage when we are deemed to have overstepped bounds of decency, order and control."

BIOGRAPHICAL/CRITICAL SOURCES:

PERIODICALS

Christian Science Monitor, February 21, 1968.
Prompt, Number 12, 1968.
Punch, May 15, 1968.
Times Educational Supplement, January 1, 1982.
Times Literary Supplement, March 29, 1974; October 28, 1977; November 25, 1983; March 8, 1985.

* * *

ROSEN, Winifred 1943-

PERSONAL: Born October 16, 1943, in Columbia, SC; daughter of Victor H. (a psychoanalyst) and Elizabeth (a modern dancer and dance therapist; maiden name, Ruskay) Rosen. *Education:* New York University, B.A. (with honors), 1964, M.A., 1966. *Religion:* Jewish. *Avocational interests:* Fabric design, embroidery, music, yoga, silver-smithing.

ADDRESSES: Home—259 East 2nd Ave., Eugene, OR 97401. *Agent*—Betty Ann Clarke, International Famous Agency, Inc., 1301 Avenue of the Americas, New York, NY 10019.

CAREER: High school teacher of English and composition in New York City, 1965-68; Dial Press, New York City, editorial assistant, 1969; writer.

MEMBER: Authors Guild, Authors League of America, Phi Beta Kappa.

AWARDS, HONORS: Newbery Award nomination, American Library Association, for *Henrietta: The Wild Woman of Borneo.*

WRITINGS:

JUVENILE

Marvin's Manhole, Dial, 1970.
Ralph Proves the Pudding, Doubleday, 1972.
Hiram Makes Friends, illustrated by J. Winslow Higginbottom, Four Winds Press, 1974.
The Hippopotamus Book, Golden Press, 1975.
Henrietta: The Wild Woman of Borneo, Four Winds Press, 1975.
Cruisin' for a Bruisin' (novel), Knopf, 1976.
Dragons Hate to be Discrete, pictures by Edward Koren, Knopf, 1978.
Henrietta and the Day of the Iguana, illustrated by Kay Chorao, Four Winds Press, 1978.
Henrietta and the Gong from Hong Kong, Macmillan, 1981.
Three Romances: Love Stories from Camelot Retold, illustrated by Paul O. Zelinsky, Knopf, 1981.

Also author of *A Sand Story.*

OTHER

(With Andrew Weil) *Chocolate to Morphine: Understanding Mind-active Drugs,* Houghton, 1983.

Contributor of reviews to *Washington Post.* Member of editorial staff, *Harper's.*

BIOGRAPHICAL/CRITICAL SOURCES:

PERIODICALS

New York Times Book Review, February 7, 1982.*

*   *   *

ROSNER, Fred   1935-

PERSONAL: Born October 3, 1935, in Berlin, Germany; came to the United states in 1949, naturalized citizen, 1955; son of Sidney and Sara (Feingold) Rosner; married Saranne Eskolsky, February 24, 1959; children: Mitchel, Miriam, Aviva, Shalom. *Education:* Yeshiva University, B.A. (cum laude), 1955, M.D., 1959.

ADDRESSES: Home—750 Elvira Ave., West Lawrence, NY 11691. *Office*—Queens Hospital Center Affiliation, Long Island Jewish Medical Center, 82-86 164th St., Jamaica, NY 11432.

CAREER: Licensed to practice medicine in California and New York; certified by the National Board of Medical Examiners, 1960, and the American Board of Internal Medicine, 1969; Maimonides Medical Center, Brooklyn, NY, rotating intern, 1959-60, junior assistant resident in medicine, 1960-61, assistant

resident, 1961-62; Children's Hospital of the District of Columbia, Washington, DC, research associate in hematology, 1963-65; Maimonides Medical Center, assistant physician and research associate in hematology, 1965-67, assistant attending physician and assistant director of Division of Hematology, 1967-70, assistant visiting physician at Coney Island Hospital, 1965-67, associate visiting physician, 1967-70, assistant chief of Division of Hematology, 1965-70; Long Island Jewish Medical Center, New Hyde Park, NY, attending hematologist, 1970—, director of Division of Hematology at Queens Hospital Center Affiliation in Jamaica, NY, 1970-78, director of department of medicine at Queens Hospital Center, 1978—, coordinator of Supervised Clinical Clerkship Program, 1977-88, editor-in-chief of *Cancer Bulletin,* 1976-78, president of Medical Board, 1980-82.

State University of New York Downstate Medical Center, instructor, 1968-70, assistant professor, 1970-72, lecturer, 1972—; State University of New York at Stony Brook, associate professor, 1972-78, professor, 1978-89; professor at Albert Einstein College of Medicine, Yeshiva University, 1989—; lecturer at hospitals, medical centers, and universities. Kings County Hospital Center, assistant visiting physician, 1968-72, associate visiting physician, 1972—. Member of New York State Genetic Diseases Program Advisory Committee, 1980—; member of advisory board of Israeli Institute of Medical History. Consultant to Medical Research Council of Canada. *Military service:* U.S. Public Health Service, epidemiologist, 1963-65; became lieutenant commander. U.S. Public Health Service Inactive Reserve, 1965—.

MEMBER: International Society of Hematology (fellow), American College of Physicians (fellow), American Medical Association, American Society of Hematology, American Association for the History of Medicine, American Federation for Clinical Research, American Physicians Fellowship for Medicine in Israel, American Association for Cancer Research, American Society of Clinical Oncology, New York Academy of Medicine (fellow), New York Society for the Study of Blood, Queens County Medical Society.

AWARDS, HONORS: Research fellow in hematology, U.S. Public Health Service, 1962-63; award from Maimonides Hospital Research Society, 1965 and 1967, both for excellence in medical research; Maimonides Award, Michael Reese Hospital and College of Jewish Studies, 1969, for notable contributions to the field of medicine and Judaica; Bernard Revel Memorial Award, Yeshiva University Alumni Association, 1971, for distinguished achievement in the arts and sciences; Maimonides Award of Wisconsin, 1977, for distinguished and extraordinary service to learning and science.

WRITINGS:

Modern Medicine and Jewish Law: Studies in Torah Judaism, Yeshiva University Press, 1972.
Sex Ethics in the Medical Writings of Moses Maimonides, Bloch Publishing, 1974.
(Editor) *Proceedings of the Association of Orthodox Jewish Scientists,* Feldheim, Volumes 3-4, 1976, Volume 5, 1979, Volume 6, 1980.
Medicine in the Bible and the Talmud, Ktav, 1977.
(With J. D. Bleich) *Jewish Bioethics,* Sanhedrin Press, 1979.
(With M. D. Tendler) *Practical Medical Halachah,* Feldheim, 1980.
(Editor with D. M. Feldman) *Compendium of Medical Ethics,* 6th edition, Federation of Jewish Philanthropies, 1984.
Medicine in the Mishnah Torah of Maimonides, Ktav, 1984.

EDITOR AND TRANSLATOR

(With Sussman Muntner) *The Medical Writings of Moses Maimonides: Treatise on Hemorrhoids and Responsa,* Lippincott, 1969.

(With Muntner) *The Medical Aphorisms of Moses Maimonides,* Yeshiva University Press, Volume 1, 1970, Volume 2, 1971.

Maimonides, *Commentary on the Mishnah: Introduction to the Mishnah and Commentary on Tractate Berachoth,* Feldheim, 1975.

Julius Preuss, *Biblical-Talmudic Medicine,* Sanhedrin Press, 1978.

Maimonides, *Glossary of Drug Names,* American Philosophical Society, 1979.

Maimonides, *Commentary on the Mishnah: Tractate Sanhedrin,* Sepher-Hermon Press, 1981.

Maimonides, *Treatise on Resurrection,* Ktav, 1982.

Maimonides, *Treatises on Poisons, Hemorrhoids, and Cohabitation,* Maimonides Research Institute, 1984.

Maimonides, *Commentary on the Aphorisms of Hippocrates,* Maimonides Research Institute, 1988.

Maimonides, *Medical Aphorisms,* Maimonides Research Institute, 1990.

CONTRIBUTOR

Bernard Schoenberg, A. C. Carr, and others, editors, *Psychosocial Aspects of Terminal Care,* Columbia University Press, 1972.

Stuart Kornfeld and others, editors, *Transferrin Biology,* Mss Information, 1973.

Chester R. Burns, editor, *Legacies in Ethics and Medicine,* Science History Publications, 1977.

R. Weltsch, editor, *Year Book XXII of the Leo Baeck Institute,* Secker & Warburg, 1977.

Tina Levitan, editor, *Viewpoints on Science and Judaism,* Board of Jewish Education of Greater New York, 1978.

Menachem M. Kellner, editor, *Contemporary Jewish Ethics,* Sanhedrin Press, 1978.

Frederick Gunz and Edward Henderson, editors, *Leukemia,* 4th edition, Grune, 1984.

J. O. Leibowitz, editor, *Memorial Volume in Honor of Professor S. Muntner,* Israel Institute for the History of Medicine, 1983.

OTHER

Also contributor to *Jewish Directory and Almanac, Encyclopedia Judaica,* and *Encyclopedia of Bioethics.* Contributor of over six hundred articles and reviews to medicine and religion journals. Editor of hemato-oncology section of *Cancer Investigation,* 1981—; member of editorial board of *Medica Judaica,* 1970—.

WORK IN PROGRESS: Jewish Biomedical Ethics; Nonlegal Topics in Maimonides's Mishnah Commentary; Maimonides's Treatise on the Unity of God.

*   *   *

ROSS, Clarissa
  See ROSS, W(illiam) E(dward) D(aniel)

*   *   *

ROSS, Dan
  See ROSS, W(illiam) E(dward) D(aniel)

ROSS, Dana
  See ROSS, W(illiam) E(dward) D(aniel)

*   *   *

ROSS, Marilyn
  See ROSS, W(illiam) E(dward) D(aniel)

*   *   *

ROSS, W(illiam) E(dward) D(aniel) 1912-
  (Dan Ross; Leslie Ames, Marilyn Carter, Rose Dana, Ruth Dorset, Ann Gilmer, Diane Randall, Ellen Randolph, Dan Roberts, Clarissa Ross, Dana Ross, Marilyn Ross, Jane Rossiter, Tex Steel, Rose Williams, pseudonyms)

PERSONAL: Born November 16, 1912, in Saint John, New Brunswick, Canada; son of William Edward (a military man) and Laura Frances (an actress; maiden name, Brooks) Ross; married Charlotte Edith MacCormack (died, 1958); married Marilyn Ann Clark (an editor), July 2, 1960. *Education:* Attended Provincetown Theatre School, New York, NY, 1934; further study at University of Chicago, University of Oklahoma, Columbia University, and University of Michigan. *Politics:* None. *Religion:* Anglican.

ADDRESSES: Home—80 Horton Rd., East Riverside, Saint John, New Brunswick, Canada E2H IP8. *Agent*—Richard Curtis, Inc., 164 East 64th St. New York, NY 10021.

CAREER: Worked as traveling actor and actor manager with own company, 1930-48; film distributor for own company, for Paramount, and for Monogram Films, 1948-57; writer, 1957—. Reader at annual convention of "Dark Shadows" series fans, 1985. Member of panel of judges for Gibson National Literary Award, given yearly for best first novel in Canada. *Wartime service:* Served with British Entertainment Services during World War II.

MEMBER: Canadian Authors Association (former president), Playwrights Canada, Mystery Writers of America, Authors Guild, Authors League of America, Western Writers of America, Society of Authors (United Kingdom), Christian Press, Riverside Country Club, Lotus Club, Union Club of Boston, Union Club of Saint John, Boston University Friends of the Library (former president).

AWARDS, HONORS: Dominion Drama Festival Prize for Playwrighting, 1934; Queen Elizabeth Silver Jubilee Medal, 1978, for contributions to popular fiction; honorary B.A., University of New Brunswick, 1988.

WRITINGS:

Alice in Love, Popular Library, 1965.
Fog Island, Paperback Library, 1965, published under pseudonym Marilyn Ross, Popular Library, 1977.
Journey to Love, Bouregy, 1967.
Love Must Not Waver, R. Hale, 1967.
Winslow's Daughter, Bouregy, 1967.
Our Share of Love, R. Hale, 1967.
The Ghost of Oaklands, Arcadia House, 1967.
The Third Spectre, Arcadia House, 1967, published under name Dan Ross, Macfadden-Baftell, 1969.
Dark Villa of Capri, Arcadia House, 1968.
The Twilight Web, Arcadia House, 1968.
Behind Locked Shutters, Arcadia House, 1968, published under name Dan Ross, Manor, 1975.

Dark of the Moon, Arcadia House, 1968.
Let Your Heart Answer, Bouregy, 1968.
Christopher's Mansion, Bouregy, 1969.
Luxury Liner Nurse, R. Hale, 1969.
The Need to Love, Avalon, 1969.
Sable in the Rain, Lenox Hill, 1970.
The Web of Love, R. Hale, 1970.
An Act of Love, Bouregy, 1970.
Magic Valley, R. Hale, 1970.
This Man I Love, R. Hale, 1970.
The Whispering Gallery, Lenox Hill, 1970, published under name Dan Ross, Manor, 1977.
Beauty Doctor's Nurse, Lenox Hill, 1970.
The Yesteryear Phenomenon, Lenox Hill, 1971.
King of Romance, R. Hale, 1971.
The Room without a Key, Lenox Hill, 1971.
Music Room, Dell, 1971.
Wind over the Citadel, Lenox Hill, 1971.
Rothhaven, Avalon, 1972.
The House on Mount Vernon Street, Lenox Hill, 1972.
Dark Mansion, Avalon, 1973.
Mansion on the Moors, Dell, 1974.
An End of Summer, R. Hale, 1974.
Nightmare Abbey, Berkeley, 1975.
One Louisburg Square, Belmont-Tower, 1975.
Witch of Goblin's Acres, Belmont-Tower, 1975.
Dark Is My Shadow, Manor, 1976.
Summer's End, Fawcett World, 1976.
House on Lime Street, Bouregy, 1976.
Pattern of Love, Bouregy, 1977.
Shadows over Garden, Belmont-Tower, 1978.
Return to Barton, Avalon, 1978.
Queen's Stairway, Arcadia House, 1978.
The Dark Lane, Arcadia House, 1979.
Magic of Love, Arcadia House, 1980.
Phantom of Edgewater Hall, Arcadia House, 1980.
Nurse Ann's Secret, Arcadia House, 1980.
Onstage for Love, Arcadia House, 1981.
Nurse Grace's Dilemma, Arcadia House, 1982.
This Uncertain Love, Arcadia House, 1982.
Flight to Romance, Arcadia House, 1983.
The Ghostly Jewels, Arcadia House, 1983.
Rehearsal for Love, Arcadia House, 1984.
A Love Discovered, Arcadia House, 1984.
Nurse Janice's Dream, Arcadia House, 1984.
Dangerous Heart, Bouregy, 1985.
Summer Playhouse, Avalon, 1986.
Dangerous Holiday, Avalon, 1987.

UNDER NAME DAN ROSS

The Castle on the Cliff, Bouregy, 1967.
Nurse in Love, Avalon, 1972.
Murder Game (play; produced in 1984), Playwrights Press, 1982.
Moscow Maze, Dorchester, 1983.
This Frightened Lady (play; produced in 1987), Marginal, 1984.

UNDER PSEUDONYM LESLIE AMES

Bride of Donnybrook, Arcadia House, 1966.
The Hungry Sea, Arcadia House, 1967.
The Hidden Chapel, Arcadia House, 1967.
The Hill of Ashes, Arcadia House, 1968.
King's Castle, Lenox Hill, 1970.

UNDER PSEUDONYM ROSE DANA

Citadel of Love, Arcadia House, 1965.
Down East Nurse, Arcadia House, 1967.
Nurse in Jeopardy, Arcadia House, 1967.
Labrador Nurse, Arcadia House, 1968.
Network Nurse, Arcadia House, 1968.
Whitebridge Nurse, Arcadia House, 1969.
Department Store Nurse, Lenox Hill, 1970.

UNDER PSEUDONYM RUTH DORSET

Front Office Nurse, Arcadia House, 1966.
Hotel Nurse, Arcadia House, 1967.
Nurse in Waiting, Arcadia House, 1967.

UNDER PSEUDONYM ANN GILMER

The Fog and the Stars, Avalon, 1963.
Winds of Change, Bouregy, 1965.
Private Nurse, Bouregy, 1969.
Nurse on Emergency, Bouregy, 1970.
Skyscraper Nurse, Bouregy, 1976.
Nurse at Breakwater Hotel, Arcadia House, 1982.

UNDER PSEUDONYM DIANE RANDALL

Dragon Lover, Jove, 1981.

UNDER PSEUDONYM MARILYN CARTER

The Reluctant Debutante, Warner, 1987.

UNDER PSEUDONYM ELLEN RANDOLPH

Personal Secretary, Avalon, 1963.
The Castle on the Hill, Avalon, 1964.
Nurse Martha's Wish, Arcadia House, 1983.
The Rushden Legacy, Warner, 1987.

UNDER PSEUDONYM DAN ROBERTS

The Wells Fargo Brand, Arcadia House, 1964.
The Cheyenne Kid, Arcadia House, 1965.
Durez City Bonanza, Arcadia House, 1965.
Outlaw's Gold, Arcadia House, 1965.
Stage to Link City, Arcadia House, 1966.
Vengeance Ride, Arcadia House, 1966.
Wyoming Range War, Arcadia House, 1967.
Yuma Brand, Arcadia House, 1967.
Lawman of Blue Rock, Arcadia House, 1967.
The Dawn Riders, Arcadia House, 1968.
Sheriff of Mad River, Leisure Press, 1980.
Wyoming Showdown, J. Curley, 1989.

UNDER PSEUDONYM CLARISSA ROSS

Mistress of Ravenswood, Arcadia House, 1966.
The Secret of Mallet Castle, Arcadia House, 1966.
Fogbound, Arcadia House, 1967, published under name Dan Ross, Manor, 1976.
Secret of the Pale Lover, Magnum, 1969.
Beware the Kindly Stranger, Lancer, 1970.
Gemini in Darkness, Magnum, 1970.
Glimpse into Terror, Magnum, 1971.
The Spectral Mist, Magnum, 1972.
Phantom of Glencourt, Magnum, 1972.
Whispers in the Night, Bantam, 1972.
China Shadow, Avon, 1974.
Drafthaven, Avon, 1974.
Ghost of Dark Harbor, Avon, 1974.
A Hearse for Dark Harbor, Avon, 1974.
Dark Harbor Hunting, Avon, 1975.

Evil of Dark Harbor, Avon, 1975.
Terror at Dark Harbor, Avon, 1975.
Durrell Towers, Pyramid, 1976.
Jade Princess, Pyramid, 1977.
Moscow Mists, Avon, 1977.
A Scandalous Affair, Belmont-Tower, 1978.
Kashmiri Passions, Warner, 1978.
Istanbul Nights, Jove, 1978.
Flame of Love, Belmont-Tower, 1978.
Wine of Passion, Belmont-Tower, 1978.
Casablanca Intrique, Warner, 1979.
So Perilous My Love, Leisure Press, 1979.
Eternal Desire, Jove, 1979.
Fan the Wanton Flame, Pocket Books, 1980.
Only Make Believe, Leisure Press, 1980.
Masquerade, Pocket Books, 1980.
Venetian Affair, Jove, 1980.
Beloved Scoundrel, Belmont-Tower, 1980.
Fortune's Mistress, Popular Library, 1981.
Satan Whispers, Leisure Press, 1981.
Summer of the Shaman, Warner Brothers, 1982.
The Dancing Years, Pinnacle, 1982.
Denver's Lady, Warner, 1985.

UNDER PSEUDONYM DANA ROSS

Demon of Darkness, Paperback Library, 1975.
Lodge Sinister, Paperback Library, 1975.
This Shrouded Night, Paperback Library, 1975.
The Raven and the Phantom, Paperback Library, 1976.

UNDER PSEUDONYM MARILYN ROSS

The Locked Corridor, Paperback Library, 1965.
Beware My Love!, Paperback Library, 1965.
Dark Shadows, Paperback Library, 1968.
The Foe of Barnabas Collins, Paperback Library, 1969.
Barnabas, Quentin and Dr. Jeckyll's Son, Paperback Library, 1971.
Phantom of Fog Island, Warner, 1971.
Dark Stars over Seacrest, Paperback Library, 1972.
Phantom of the Swamp, Paperback Library, 1972.
The Long Night of Fear, Warner, 1972.
Mistress of Moorwood Manor, Warner, 1972.
Night of the Phantom, Warner, 1972.
The Sinister Garden, Warner, 1972.
Witch of Braihaven, Warner, 1972.
Behind the Purple Veil, Warner, 1973.
Face in the Shadows, Warner, 1973.
House of Ghosts, Warner, 1973.
Don't Look Behind You, Warner, 1973.
Marta, Warner, 1973.
Step into Terror, Warner, 1973.
A Garden of Ghosts, Popular Library, 1974.
Loch Sinister, Popular Library, 1974.
The Amethyst Tears, Ballantine, 1974.
The Vampire Contessa, Pinnacle, 1974.
Witches Cove, Warner, 1974.
Dark Towers of Fog Island, Popular Library, 1975.
Fog Island Secret, Popular Library, 1975.
Ghost Ship of Fog Island, Popular Library, 1975.
Phantom of the Thirteenth Floor, Popular Library, 1975.
Ravenhurst, Popular Library, 1975.
Cameron Castle, Warner, 1975.
The Ghostland and the Garnet: Birthstone No. One, Ballantine, 1975.
Satan's Island, Warner, 1975.

Shadow over Emerald Castle, Ballantine, 1975.
The Widow of Westwood, Popular Library, 1976.
The Curse of Black Charlie, Popular Library, 1976.
Haiti Circle, Popular Library, 1976.
Shadow over Denby, Popular Library, 1976.
Stewards of Stormhaven: Cellars of the Dead, Popular Library, 1976.
Brides of Saturn, Berkeley, 1976.
Temple of Darkness, Ballantine, 1976.
Cauldron of Evil, Popular Library, 1977.
Death's Dark Music, Popular Library, 1977.
Mask of Evil, Popular Library, 1977.
Phantom of the Snow, Popular Library, 1977.
This Evil Village, Popular Library, 1977.
Delta Flame, Popular Library, 1978.
Rothby, Popular Library, 1978.
Horror of Fog Island, Popular Library, 1978.
The Twice Dead, Fawcett, 1978.
Beloved Adversary, Popular Library, 1981.
Forbidden Flame, Popular Library, 1982.
Castle Malice, Harlequin, 1986.
Shadows over Briarcliff, Harlequin, 1986.

Also author of books in the "Dark Shadows" series: *Barnabas, Quentin and the Hidden Tomb, . . . and the Mad Magician, . . . and the Sea Ghost, . . . and the Grave Robbers, . . .and the Body Snatchers, . . . and the Magic Potion, . . . and the Serpent, . . . and the Scorpio Curse, . . . and the Frightened Bride, . . . and the Haunted Cave, . . . and the Witch's Curse, . . . and the Crystal Coffin, . . . and the Nightmare Assassin, . . . and the Avenging Ghost, . . . and the Mummy's Curse, . . . and the Gypsy Witch, . . . and Quentin's Demon, . . .and the Mysterious Ghost, The Peril of Barnabas Collins, Barnabas Collins Versus the Warlock, The Phantom and Barnabas Collins, The Secret of Barnabas Collins, The Demon of Barnabas Collins, The Curse of Collinwood, Victoria Winters, Barnabas Collins,* and *House of Dark Shadows.*

UNDER PSEUDONYM JANE ROSSITER

Backstage Nurse, Avalon, 1963.
Love Is Forever, Avalon, 1963.
Summer Star, Avalon, 1964.

UNDER PSEUDONYM TEX STEEL

Vengeance Spur, Curly Press, 1989.

UNDER PSEUDONYM ROSE WILLIAMS

Five Nurses, Arcadia House, 1964.
Nurse in Doubt, Arcadia House, 1965.
Nurse Diane, Arcadia House, 1966.
Nurse in Spain, R. Hale, 1967.
Nurse in Nassau, Arcadia House, 1967.
Nurse in the Tropics, Arcadia House, 1967.
Airport Nurse, Arcadia House, 1968.

OTHER

Author of the play *Phantom Wedding,* 1989. Contributor of short stories to *Saint Mystery Magazine, Mike Shayne Mystery Magazine,* and other periodicals.

WORK IN PROGRESS: Several novels, including *Stormy Crossing, Summer Returns,* and a novel version of the author's play *Murder Game.*

SIDELIGHTS: While he has produced dozens of popular gothic thrillers, nurse romances, and western adventures, W. E. D. Ross stresses the literary value in his works. "I honestly don't consider myself a hack," he tells David Dee in a *Chicago Tribune Book World* interview. "A hack is motivated entirely by money, and I'm not. I'm making money. I do well. But every word I write is sincere.

"Some of the academics," Ross continues, "have a jaundiced view of my writing. I don't mind that. I'm dealing in another area of writing. I'm an entertainer. I'm here to give my readers a good read." The author concludes to Dee: "I can't imagine ever not writing. When I get letters from fans, some of whom have been reading my books for years now, I get a special joy. People can call me a hack or anything they like, but I enjoy what I'm doing and the readers enjoy what they're reading. That's what matters really, isn't it?"

Ross's output to date, he reports, is 323 novels and 600 short stories. His novels have been published in many foreign languages. The author's papers are being collected by Boston University.

BIOGRAPHICAL/CRITICAL SOURCES:

PERIODICALS

Chicago Tribune Book World, October 16, 1983.
Wall Street Journal, February 12, 1987.

*   *   *

ROSSITER, Jane
    See ROSS, W(illiam) E(dward) D(aniel)

*   *   *

ROUCEK, Joseph S(labey)   1902-

PERSONAL: Born 1902, in Slany, Czechoslovakia; immigrated to the United States, 1921; son of Joseph (a merchant) and Pavla (Nebeska) Roucek; married Bozena Slabey, January 10, 1928. *Education:* Attended Prague Commercial Academy and University of Prague; Occidental College, B.A., 1925; New York University, Ph.D., 1928, M.A., 1937. *Politics:* Republican. *Religion:* Roman Catholic.

ADDRESSES: Home—395 Lakeside Dr., Bridgeport, CT 06606.

CAREER: After immigrating to the United States, supported himself by working as a concert pianist, lecturer, vaudeville entertainer, and actor in silent films; Centenary Junior College (now Centenary College for Women), Hackettstown, NJ, instructor, 1929-33; Pennsylvania State College (now Pennsylvania State University), University Park, PA, member of faculty, 1933-35; New York University, New York City, member of faculty, 1935-39; Hofstra College (now Hofstra University), member of faculty, Hempstead, NY, 1939-48; University of Bridgeport, Bridgeport, CT, member of faculty, 1948-67, became professor and chairman of departments of political science and sociology; Queensborough Community College, Bayside, NY, professor of social science, 1969-72. Visiting professor of sociology, political science, or education at other colleges and universities in the United States, Canada, and Puerto Rico, 1940-54; lecturer at European universities, 1955, 1958.

MEMBER: American Sociological Association, American Political Science Association, American Association of University Professors, Delta Tau Kappa (president).

AWARDS, HONORS: Knight, Order of the Star, Rumania; Knight Commander, Order of the Crown, Yugoslavia.

WRITINGS:

The Minority Principle as a Problem of Political Science, Orbis (Prague), 1928.

The Working of the Minorities System under the League of Nations, Orbis, 1929.
Contemporary Roumania and Her Problems: A Study in Modern Nationalism, Stanford University Press, 1932, reprinted, Arno, 1972.
The Poles in the United States of America, Baltic Institute (Gdynia, Poland), 1937.
The Politics of the Balkans, McGraw, 1939, revised edition published as *Balkan Politics: International Relations in No Man's Land,* Stanford University Press, 1948, reprinted, Greenwood Press, 1971.
American Lithuanians, Lithuanian Alliance of America, 1940.
Foreign Politics and Our Minority Groups, privately printed, 1941.
Methods of Meeting Domination: The Czecho-Slovaks, privately printed, 1941.
(With Yaroslav J. Chyz) *Ukrainian Sociology: Its Development to 1914,* privately printed, 1941.
World War II: A Survey of Recent Literature, privately printed, 1941.
Axis Psychological Strategy against the United States, privately printed, 1942.
American Japanese: Pearl Harbor and World War II, privately printed, 1943.
Die Tschechen und Slowaken in der Vereinigten Staaten, Publikatiensstelle (Stuttgart), 1943, translation published as *The Czechs and Slovaks in America,* Lerner, 1967.
Aspirations for a Greater Democracy, privately printed, 1943.
Free Movements of Horthy's Eckhardt and Austria's Otto, privately printed, 1943.
(With Patricia S. Pinkham) *American Slavs: A Bibliography,* New York City Bureau for Intercultural Education, 1944.
Group Tensions in the Modern World, privately printed, 1945.
Recent Literature on Central-eastern Europe, privately printed, 1945.
Geopolitics of the Balkans, privately printed, 1946.
War as a Symptom of Social Crisis, privately printed, 1946.
American Bulgarians, privately printed, 1947.
Sociological Foundations of Education, privately printed, c. 1950.
Regionalism and Separation, edited by Feliks Gross, privately printed, c. 1950.
(With Roland L. Warren) *Sociology: An Introduction,* Littlefield, 1951, 2nd edition, 1965.
Development of Educational Sociology: History and Trends in America and Abroad, privately printed, 1956.
School, Society and Sociology: A Survey of the Social and Sociological Aspects of Education Theories and Experiments, [Bridgeport, CT], 1956.
American Ethnic and Religious Minorities in American Politics (originally published in *Il Politico,* University of Pavia, 1959), A. Giuffre (Milan), 1959.
Some Sociological Aspects of Diplomacy, [Bridgeport], 1960.
The Vote of the American Minorities in President Kennedy's 1960 Election, privately printed, 1961.
(With Kenneth V. Lottich and Theodore H. E. Chen) *Behind the Iron Curtain: The Soviet Satellite States—East European Nationalism and Education,* Caxton, 1964.
United States and the Persian Gulf, Robert E. Krieger, 1985.

Also author of *Political Sociology and Public Administration in the U.S.A.,* c. 1957, and *The Status and Role of American and Continental Professors: A Comparison of Two Educational Traditions,* published in *Journal of Higher Education,* May, 1959.

EDITOR

(With Francis J. Brown) *Our Racial and National Minorities: Their History, Contributions, and Present Problems*, Prentice-Hall, 1937, revised edition published as *One America: The History, Contributions, and Present Problems of Our Racial and National Minorities*, 1945, 3rd edition, 1952.

(With Brown and Charles Hodges) *Contemporary World Politics: An Introduction to the Problems of International Relations*, Wiley, 1939, revised edition, 1940.

Contemporary Europe: A Study of National, International, Economic, and Cultural Trends, Van Nostrand, 1941, 2nd edition, 1947.

(With Roy V. Peel) *Introduction to Politics*, Crowell, 1941.

(And contributor) *Sociological Foundations of Education: A Textbook in Educational Sociology*, Crowell, 1942.

A Challenge to Peacemakers, American Academy of Political and Social Science, 1944.

(With Alice Hero and Jean Downey) *The Immigrant in Fiction and Biography*, Bureau for Intercultural Education, 1945.

(And contributor) *Central-eastern Europe: Crucible of World Wars*, Prentice-Hall, 1946.

(With others) *Governments and Politics Abroad*, Funk, 1947, 2nd edition, 1948.

(And contributor) *Social Control*, Van Nostrand, 1947, 2nd edition, 1956.

Slavonic Encyclopaedia, four volumes, Philosophical Library, 1949.

Moscow's European Satellites, American Academy of Political and Social Science, 1950.

(With George B. Huszar, and contributor) *Introduction to Political Science*, Crowell, 1950.

(With Arthur Henry Moehlman) *Comparative Education*, Dryden Press, 1951.

(And contributor) *Contemporary Social Science*, two volumes, Stackpole, 1953.

Soviet and Russian Educational Imperialism, [Wilberforce], 1955-56.

Contemporary Sociology, Philosophical Library, 1958, abridged edition published as *Readings in American Sociology*, Littlefield, 1961.

Juvenile Delinquency, Philosophical Library, 1958.

(With Howard Boone Jacobson) *Automation and Society*, Philosophical Library, 1959.

The Challenge of Science Education, Philosophical Library, 1959, reprinted, Books for Libraries, 1971.

Contemporary Political Ideologies, Philosophical Library, 1961.

(Contributing editor) Jacobson, editor, *A Mass Communications Dictionary: A Reference Work of Common Terminologies for Press, Print, Broadcast, Film, Advertising, and Communications Research*, Philosophical Library, 1961.

Sociology of Crime, Philosophical Library, 1961.

The Unusual Child, Philosophical Library, 1962.

Classics in Political Science, Philosophical Library, 1963.

The Difficult Child, Philosophical Library, 1964.

Programmed Teaching: A Symposium on Automation Education, Philosophical Library, 1965, revised edition, 1968.

The Teaching of History, Philosophical Library, 1967.

The Study of Foreign Language, Philosophical Library, 1968.

The Slow Learner, Philosophical Library, 1969.

(With Thomas P. Kiernan) *The Negro Impact on Western Civilization*, Philosophical Library, 1970.

Social Control for the 1980s: A Handbook for Order in a Democratic Society, Greenwood Press, 1978.

(With Bernard Eisenberg) *America's Ethnic Politics*, Greenwood Press, 1982.

OTHER

Contributor to books, including *Contemporary Social Theory*, edited by Harry Elmer Barnes, Howard Becker, and Frances Bennett, Appleton, 1940; *Czechoslovakia: Twenty Years of Independence*, edited by Robert H. Kerner, University of California Press, 1940, reprinted as *Czechoslovakia*, 1948; *Modern World Politics*, edited by Thorsten Kalijarvi and others, Crowell, 1942, 3rd edition, 1954; *Global Geography*, edited by George T. Renner, Crowell, 1944; *Twentieth Century Sociology*, edited by Georges Gurvitch and Wilbert E. Moore, Philosophical Library, 1945; *European Ideologies: A Survey of Twentieth Century Political Ideas*, edited by F. Gross, 1948; *World Political Geography*, Crowell, 1948, 2nd edition, 1954; *Yugoslavia*, edited by Kerner, University of California Press, 1949; *Introduction to Sociology*, edited by James H. S. Bossard and others, Stackpole, 1952; *The Development of Historiography*, edited by Matthew A. Fitzsimons, Alfred G. Pundt, and Charles E. Nowell, Stackpole, 1954; *Social Problems*, Crowell, 1955; *Making of Modern America*, edited by Howard R. Anderson and others, Houghton, 1956, 3rd edition, 1968; *Educating Citizens for Democracy: Curriculum and Instruction in Secondary Social Studies*, edited by Richard Edmund Gross and L. D. Zeleny, Oxford University Press, 1958; *Perspectives on World Education*, edited by Carlton E. Beck, W. C. Brown, 1960; *The Heritage of American Education*, edited by R. E. Gross, Allyn & Bacon, 1962; *La Prensa*, edited by Jorge Zifra Heras, Internacional de Prensa (Barcelona), 1963; *The Czechoslovakian Contribution to World Culture*, edited by Miloslav Rechcigl, Jr., Mouton & Co. (The Hague), 1964; *Prensa convivencia internacional*, edited by Heras, Institute de Ciencias Sociales, 1964; *Historia y elementas de la sociologia del conocimiento*, Volume 2, edited by Irving Louis Horwitz, Editorial Universitaria del Buenos Aires, 1964; *Readings in Cultural Anthropology*, edited by Michael O'Leary, Jr., Selected Academic Readings, Inc., 1965; *The World Book of Education, 1965-1966*, edited by George Z. F. Bereday and Joseph A. Lauwerys, Harcourt, 1965-66; *Anuario de la academia de doctores del distrito universitario de Barcelona*, [Barcelona], 1966; *Social Foundations of Education: Current Readings from the Behavioral Sciences*, edited by Jonathon C. McLendon, Macmillan, 1966; *Controversy in American Education: An Anthology of Crucial Issues*, edited by Harold Full, Macmillan, 1967; *A Critique of Empiricism in Sociology*, edited by Kewal Motwani, Allied Publishers Private Ltd. (Bombay), 1967; *Czechoslovakia: Past and Present*, edited by Rechcigl, Mouton & Co., 1968; *The Home of the Learned Man: A Symposium on the Immigrant Scholar in America*, edited by John Kosa, College & University Press, 1968; *Violence: Causes and Solutions*, edited by Renatus Hartogs and Eric Artzt, Dell, 1970.

Contributor to *Encyclopedia Americana, Collier's Encyclopedia, People's Encyclopedia, Encyclopaedia International*, and to *The Annals of the American Academy of Political and Social Science*. Author of articles and book reviews appearing in more than a hundred journals and newspapers. Member of editorial board, *American Journal of Economics and Sociology* and *United Asia;* American editor of *Indian Sociological Bulletin, Indian Journal of Social Research*, and *Journal of Education*, all published in India, and *Il Politico*, published in Italy.

WORK IN PROGRESS: Geopolitics and International Relations, for Greenwood Press.

BIOGRAPHICAL/CRITICAL SOURCES:

PERIODICALS

American Historical Review, April, 1933; October, 1946; January, 1949; January, 1950.
American Political Science Review, April, 1933; December, 1939; October, 1946; December, 1946; October, 1947; September, 1961.
American Sociological Review, December, 1942; April, 1948; December, 1961; February, 1962.
Annals of the American Academy of Political and Social Science, March, 1933; September, 1939; September, 1946; September, 1948; March, 1950.
Books, October 2, 1932.
Book Week, May 26, 1942; June 2, 1946.
Choice, July, 1966; January, 1968; May, 1970.
Christian Century, August 24, 1949; December 10, 1958; June 28, 1961; October 4, 1961.
Christian Science Monitor, July 15, 1939.
Commonweal, November 3, 1939; December 20, 1946; August 12, 1949.
Current History, September, 1946.
Foreign Affairs, October, 1932.
Library Journal, July, 1949; September 1, 1958; November 15, 1958; February 1, 1966; July, 1967; January 15, 1970.
New Statesman, October 1, 1949.
New Yorker, May 18, 1946.
Political Science Quarterly, September, 1946; December, 1948.
Saturday Review of Literature, July 15, 1939.
Social Education, October, 1946.
Social Forces, December, 1942; December, 1959; October, 1962.
Social Studies, January, 1948; November, 1959.
Spectator, April 24, 1959.
Times Literary Supplement, September 1, 1932; October 23, 1959; May 2, 1968; February 12, 1971.*

* * *

RUBENSTEIN, Richard E(dward) 1938-

PERSONAL: Born February 24, 1938, in New York, N.Y.; son of Harold S. (in textiles) and Jo (Feldman) Rubenstein; married Elizabeth Marsh, August 26, 1962 (divorced); married Brenda Libman, September 21, 1975; children: (first marriage) Alec Louis, Matthew Robert. *Education:* Harvard University, B.A., 1959, J.D., 1963; Oxford University, M.A.Juris., 1961. *Politics:* Radical. *Religion:* Jewish.

CAREER: Steptoe & Johnson (law firm), Washington, D.C., attorney, 1963-67; Adlai Stevenson Institute, Chicago, Ill., assistant director, 1967-70; Roosevelt University, Chicago, associate professor of political science, beginning 1969; currently a professor at Antioch University, School of Law, Washington, D.C. Fulbright visiting professor, Universite de Provence, France, 1976-77. Professorial lecturer, Malcolm X Community College, Chicago, 1969-70. Consultant, National Advisory Commission on Causes and Prevention of Violence, 1968-69.

MEMBER: Phi Beta Kappa.

AWARDS, HONORS: Rhodes Scholar at Oxford University, 1959-61.

WRITINGS:

(Editor with Robert M. Fogelson) *Mass Violence in America,* Arno, 1969.
(Contributor) Jerome H. Skolnick, *The Politics of Protest,* Ballantine, 1969.

Rebels in Eden: Mass Political Violence in the United States, Little, Brown, 1970.
(Contributor) Martin Meyerson, editor, *The Conscience of the City,* Braziller, 1970.
(Contributor) R. Aya and N. Miller, editors, *The New American Revolution,* Free Press, 1971.
Left Turn: Origins of the Next American Revolution, Little, Brown, 1973.
(Editor) *Great Courtroom Battles,* Playboy Press, 1973.
The Cunning of History: The Holocaust and the American Future, Harper, 1978.
Reflections on Religion and Public Policy, Paragon House, 1984.
Alchemists of Revolution: Terrorism in the Modern World, Basic Books, 1987.

Series editor with Dan C. McCurry, "American Farmers and the Rise of Agribusiness," Ayer Co., 1975.

BIOGRAPHICAL/CRITICAL SOURCES:

PERIODICALS

Christian Science Monitor, July 3, 1970.
Nation, April 6, 1970.
New York Review of Books, September 24, 1987.
New York Times Book Review, March 12, 1970, June 28, 1987.
Saturday Review, July 11, 1970.
Time, April 20, 1970.
Washington Post, April 24, 1987.*

* * *

RUBIN, Barry (M.) 1950-

PERSONAL: Born January 28, 1950, in Washington, D.C. *Education:* Richmond College of the City University of New York (now College of Staten Island of the City University of New York), B.A. (magna cum laude), 1972; Rutgers University, M.A., 1974; Georgetown University, Ph.D., 1977.

ADDRESSES: Home and office—Orkland Corporation, 8484 Georgia Ave., Silver Spring, MD 20910.

CAREER: Georgetown University, Washington, D.C., research fellow in Middle East studies at Center for Strategic and International Studies, 1978—, professorial lecturer in School of Foreign Service, 1978—. Instructor in history at Frederick Community College, fall, 1976, and at Anne Arundel Community College, spring, 1977. Visiting professor, Johns Hopkins School of Advanced International Studies, 1983.

MEMBER: Society for Iranian Studies, American Historical Association, Society of Historians of American Foreign Relations, Middle East Studies Association, Middle East Institute, Israel Studies Association (vice-president).

AWARDS, HONORS: National Defense Foreign Language fellow, 1977; World Press Freedom Committee grant, 1978-79; writers' grant for research in Africa from German Marshall Fund, 1980; state department grant, 1982; defense department grant, 1982.

WRITINGS:

International News and the American Media, Sage Publications, 1977.
How Others Report Us: America in the Foreign Press, Sage Publications, 1979.
(Editor with Elizabeth P. Spiro) *Human Rights and U.S. Foreign Policy,* foreword by Muriel S. Humphrey, Westview, 1979.
(Editor with Walter Laqueur) *The Human Rights Reader,* New American Library, 1979.

The Great Powers in the Middle East, 1941-1947: The Road to Cold War, Cass & Co., 1980.

Paved with Good Intentions: Iran and the American Experience, Oxford University Press, 1980.

The Arab States and the Palestinian Conflict, Syracuse University Press, 1981.

Secrets of State: The State Department and the Struggle Over U.S. Foreign Policy, Oxford University Press, 1985.

Modern Dictators, McGraw-Hill, 1987.

(With Robert S. Leiken) *The Central American Crisis Reader,* Summit, 1987.

Istanbul Intrigues, McGraw-Hill, 1988.

Co-author of "Unconventional Wisdom," a weekly international affairs column. Associate editor of *Washington Quarterly;* contributing editor and columnist for *World Press Review.* Contributor of more than fifty articles to magazines and scholarly journals, including *Newsday, New Republic, Middle East Journal,* and *Journal of Contemporary History.*

WORK IN PROGRESS: Innocents in the Bazaar: America and the Middle East, for McGraw-Hill.

SIDELIGHTS: Barry M. Rubin's *Paved with Good Intentions: Iran and the American Experience* provides a summary of the role of the United States in Iran from 1947 to 1980. The first half of the book details U.S. relations with the regime of Mohammed Riza Pahlevi, the Shah of Iran, and centers around the issue of Iranian military spending. American involvement with the Shah began in 1947, when the leader requested funds for the establishment of a large independent Iranian army to discourage Soviet advances in the area. The United States supplied $1.8 billion in military aid to Iran over the next twenty years, simultaneously pressuring the Shah to cut back on military expenditures and to make necessary economic and social reforms in his country. The turning point in the relationship, Rubin contends, came in 1969, when the Nixon administration announced that Iran was "the key pillar of support for American interests in the Persian Gulf" and stopped American demands for reform. In his *New York Times Book Review* critique, Daniel Pipes noted, "Mr. Rubin argues that by allowing the Shah to make Iran into a major regional power, the United States lost control over him; quite the opposite of what his domestic foes claim, the Shah's enormous military expenditures gave him wide economic and strategic leverage over the United States." The consequences of the Nixon policy shift were extremely important to American-Iranian relations over the next decade; the Shah's 1971 push for increased oil prices to fund further expansion of his arsenal was unopposed by the United States and resulted in both economic hardship for Iranian citizens and the oil price spiral we acknowledge to this day, says Rubin.

The second half of the work focuses on American-Iranian relations since 1978 and offers, in Pipes's estimation, "the finest analysis of the Islamic revolution yet in print." He adds, "No summary can do justice to Mr. Rubin's skillful and subtle interpretation of the extraordinary events of the past two-and-a-half years in Iran." Rubin suggests that for years "*all* sides have tended to exaggerate the importance of American actions and decisions on events in Iran." He maintains that Islamic radicals, convinced beyond all doubt that American interests would be forever tied to the Shah, viewed all conciliation attempts on the part of the U.S. as posturing meant to cover a counterrevolutionary plot. The Iranians took American hostages to prevent the loss of national independence they feared might occur after a normalization of relations between the two countries.

Scott Armstrong judged *Paved with Good Intentions* "an extremely readable, up-to-date, and balanced study which is also a unique combination of scholarship and reporting," in his *Washington Post Book World* review. In a *South Atlantic Quarterly* article, Bruce R. Kuniholm stated, "no one up to now has delineated the recent history of U.S.-Iranian relations with much clarity, insight, and . . . fair-minded judgment." A *Critic* reviewer assessed, "In what is probably the most objective and comprehensive study yet published, Barry Rubin shows how American ignorance of Iranian culture and politics . . . led to disaster."

BIOGRAPHICAL/CRITICAL SOURCES:

BOOKS

PERIODICALS

Critic, February 1, 1981.
Globe and Mail (Toronto), March 12, 1988.
Los Angeles Times Book Review, September 13, 1987, August 13, 1989.
New York Times Book Review, November 2, 1980, May 26, 1985, April 5, 1987, October 22, 1989.
South Atlantic Quarterly, summer, 1981.
Times Literary Supplement, August 28, 1981.
Washington Post Book World, November 23, 1980, May 19, 1985, May 3, 1987, July 24, 1989.

*　　*　　*

RUELL, Patrick
   See HILL, Reginald (Charles)

S

SABATO, Ernesto (R.) 1911-

PERSONAL: Born June 24, 1911, in Rojas, Argentina; son of Francisco Sábato (a mill owner) and Juana Ferrari; married Matilde Kusminsky-Richter, 1934; children: Jorge Federico, Mario. *Education:* National University of La Plata, Ph.D., 1937; additional study at Joliot-Curie Laboratory (Paris), 1938, and Massachusetts Institute of Technology, 1939.

ADDRESSES: Home—1676 Santos Lugares, Buenos Aires, Argentina.

CAREER: National University of La Plata, La Plata, Argentina, professor of theoretical physics, 1940-43; novelist and essayist, 1943—. Guest lecturer at universities throughout the United States and Europe. Chairman of National Commission on the Disappearance of Persons (Argentina), 1983.

AWARDS, HONORS: Argentine Association for the Progress of Science fellowship in Paris, 1937; sash of honor from Argentine Writers Society and Municipal Prose prize from the City of Buenos Aires, both 1945, both for *Uno y el universo;* prize from the Institute of Foreign Relations (West Germany), 1973; Grand Prize of Honor from the Argentine Writers Society, Premio Consagración Nacional (Argentina), and Chevalier des Arts et des Lettres (France), all 1974; Prix au Meilleur Livre Etranger (Paris), 1977, for *Abaddón, el Exterminador;* Gran Cruz al Mérito Civil (Spain) and Chevalier de la Legion D'Honneur (France), both 1979; Gabriela Mistral Prize from Organization of American States, 1984; Miguel de Cervantes Prize from the Spanish Ministry of Culture, 1985; Commandeur de la Legion d'Honneur (France), 1987; Jerusalem Prize, 1989.

WRITINGS:

NOVELS

El túnel, Sur, 1948, translation by Harriet de Onis published as *The Outsider,* Knopf, 1950, translation by Margaret Sayers Peden published as *The Tunnel,* Ballantine, 1988.
Sobre héroes y tumbas, Fabril, 1961, reprinted, Seix Barral, 1981, excerpt published as *Un dios desconocido: Romance de la muerte de Juan Lavalle (de "Sobre héroes y tumbas"),* A. S. Dabini, 1980, translation by Stuart M. Gross of another excerpt published as "Report on the Blind" in *TriQuarterly,* fall-winter, 1968-69, translation by Helen Lane of entire novel published as *On Heroes and Tombs,* David Godine, 1981.

Abaddón, el Exterminador (title means "Abaddón: The Exterminator"; novel), Sudamericana, 1974.

ESSAYS

Uno y el universo (title means "One and the Universe"), Sudamericana, 1945.
Hombres y engranajes (title means "Men and Gears"), Emecé, 1951, reprinted, 1985.
Heterodoxia (title means "Heterodoxy"), Emecé, 1953.
El otro rostro del peronismo: Carta abierta a Mario Amadeo (title means "The Other Face of Peronism: Open Letter to Mario Amadeo"), López, 1956.
El caso Sábato: Torturas y libertad de prensa—Carta abierta al Gral. Aramburu (title means "Sábato's Case: Torture and Freedom of the Press—Open Letter to General Aramburu"), privately printed, 1956.
Tango: Discusión y clave (title means "Tango: Discussion and Key"), Losada, 1963.
El escritor y sus fantasmas (title means "The Writer and His Ghosts"), Aguilar, 1963.
Tres aproximaciones a la literatura de nuestro tiempo: Robbe-Grillet, Borges, Sartre (title means "Approaches to the Literature of Our Time . . ."; essays), Universitaria (Chile), 1968.
La convulsión política y social de nuestro tiempo (title means "The Political and Social Upheaval of Our Time"), Edicom, 1969.
Ernesto Sábato: Claves políticas (title means "Ernesto Sábato: Political Clues"), Alonso, 1971.
La cultura en la encrucijada nacional (title means "Culture in the National Crossroads"), Ediciones de Crisis, 1973.
(With Jorge Luis Borges) *Diálogos* (title means "Dialogues"), Emecé, 1976.
Apologías y rechazos (title means "Apologies and Rejections"), Seix Barral, 1979.
La robotización del hombre y otras páginas de ficción y reflexión (title means "The Robotization of Man and Other Pages of Fiction and Reflection"), Centro Editorial del América Latina, 1981.

COLLECTIONS

Obras de ficción (title means "Works of Fiction"; contains *El túnel* and *Sobre héroes y tumbas*), Losada, 1966.

Itinerario (title means "Itinerary"; selections from Sábato's novels and essays), Sur, 1969.

Obras: Ensayos (title means "Works: Essays"), Losada, 1970.

Páginas vivas (title means "Living Pages"), Kapelusz, 1974.

Antología (title means "Anthology"), Librería del Colegio, 1975.

Narrativa completa (title means "Complete Narrative"), Seix Barral, 1982.

Páginas de Ernesto Sábato (title means "Pages from Ernesto Sábato"), Celtia (Buenos Aires), 1983.

OTHER

(Editor) *Mitomagia: Los temas del misterio* (title means "Mitomagia: Themes of the Mysterious"), Ediciones Latinoamericanas, 1969.

(Author of introduction) *Testimonios: Chile, septiembre, 1973* (title means "Eyewitness Accounts: Chile, September, 1973"), Jus, 1973.

(With Antonio Berni) *Cuatro hombres de pueblo,* Librería de la Ciudad, 1979.

(Editor with Anneliese von der Lipper) *Viaje a los mundos imaginarios,* Legasa, 1983.

Contributor to *Sur* and other periodicals.

SIDELIGHTS: When one considers that Argentine novelist and essayist Ernesto Sábato has published only three novels, the impact he has had on Hispanic literature is remarkable: His first novel, *The Tunnel,* was a best-seller in his native land; his second work of fiction, *On Heroes and Tombs,* according to Emir Rodríguez Monegal in the *Borzoi Anthology of Latin American Literature,* "is one of the most popular contemporary novels in Latin America." *Abaddón, the Exterminator,* his third novel, was similarly acclaimed and was granted France's highest literary award—the Prix au Meilleur Livre Etranger. Sábato's importance was officially recognized in 1985 when he received the first Miguel de Cervantes Prize (considered the equivalent of the Nobel in the Hispanic world) from Spain's King Juan Carlos. Harley Dean Oberhelman, in his study of the author titled *Ernest Sábato,* calls Sábato "Argentina's most discussed contemporary novelist." His appeal rests largely in his portrayals of Argentine society under the domination of military strongmen such as Juan Perón and others, with his recurrent themes of incest, blindness, insanity, and abnormal psychology reflecting the distress of the Argentine people.

Born into a large, prosperous family of Italian origin, at age thirteen Sábato left the rural community where he had grown up to attend school in the city of La Plata. The transition from familial life to life alone in a unfamiliar urban area was a disturbing one for the future writer, and Sábato found order in his otherwise turbulent world in the study of mathematics. His academic studies were briefly interrupted for a five year period, however, when he became involved in the Argentine communist movement. Soon, upon learning of Stalinist atrocities, he lost faith in the communist cause and decided to retreat again to his academic work.

Sábato's success as a student earned him a research fellowship for study in Paris, and, while there his interest in writing was born. Deeply impressed by the surrealist movement, he secretly began writing a novel. Although his writing started to play an increasingly important role in his life, Sábato continued his scientific research and accepted a teaching position upon his return to Argentina. Nonetheless, his literary efforts continued and he became a regular contributor to the popular Argentine magazine, *Sur.* Teaching was to remain his livelihood until 1943 when

a conflict with the Juan Perón government resulted in his dismissal from his posts.

Commenting on his departure from the scientific world, Sábato wrote in an autobiographical essay appearing in English translation in *Salmagundi,* "The open, public transition from physics to literature was not an easy one for me; on the contrary, it was painfully complicated. I wrestled with my demons a long time before I came to a decision in 1943—when I resolved to sequester myself, with wife and son, in a cabin in the sierras of Córdoba, far from the civilized world. It was not a rational decision. . . . But in crucial moments of my existence I have always trusted more in instinct than in ideas and have constantly been tempted to venture where reasonable people fear to tread."

While living in the cabin for a year Sábato wrote an award-winning book of essays, *Uno y el universo,* in which he condemned the moral neutrality of science. Two years later his first novel, *The Tunnel,* appeared. Profoundly influenced by psychological thought and existential in tone, the work evoked comparison to the writings of French authors Albert Camus and Jean-Paul Sartre. It is the story of an Argentine painter who recounts the events leading up to his murder of his mistress. As an exercise in self-analysis for the lonely painter, unable to communicate his thoughts and feelings, *The Tunnel* contains many of the themes found in Sábato's later work. "The almost total isolation of a man in a world dominated by science and reason," notes Oberhelman, "is the most important of these themes, but at the same time the reader sees the inability of man to communicate with others, an almost pathological obsession with blindness, and a great concern for Oedipal involvement as important secondary themes."

The landmark of Sábato's work stands to be his 1961 novel, *On Heroes and Tombs,* which appeared in an English edition in 1982. It tells the story of Martín del Castillo and his love for Alejandra Vidal Olmos. Alejandra's father, Fernando Vidal Olmos, apparently involved in an incestuous relationship with his daughter, is another important figure in the book along with Bruno Bassán, a childhood friend of Fernando. The work is lengthy and complex and has spawned numerous critical interpretations. "When it first appeared twenty years ago," writes *Newsweek* contributor Jim Miller, "Ernesto Sábato's Argentine epic was widely praised. This belated translation finally lets Americans see why. Bewitched, baroque, monumental, his novel is a stunning symphony of dissonant themes—a Gothic dirge, a hymn to hope, a tango in hell." Commenting on the novel's intricacy, John Butt observes in the *Times Literary Supplement,* "This monster novel . . . works on so many levels, leads down so many strange paths to worlds of madness, surrealistic self-analysis and self-repudiation, and overloads language so magnificently and outrageously, that the reader comes out of it with his critical nerve shot, tempted to judge it as 'great' without knowing why." Also noting the novel's multi-faceted contents, Ronald Christ in his *Commonweal* review referred to it as "wild, hypnotizing, and disturbing."

On Heroes and Tombs is divided into four parts, the third being a novel-within-a-novel called "Report on the Blind." *Review* contributor William Kennedy characterizes this portion of the novel—a first person exploration of Fernando's theories about a conspiracy of blind people who rule the world—as "a tour de force, a document which is brilliant in its excesses, a surreal journey into the depths of Fernando's personal, Boschian hells, which in their ultimate landscapes are the provinces of a 'terrible nocturnal divinity, a demoniacal specter that surely held supreme power over life and death.' " In his *Washington Post Book*

World review Salman Rushdie calls the section "the book's magnificent high point and its metaphysical heart." In Sábato's hands Fernando's paranoidal ravings fuse with the rest of the novel making the work at once a cultural, philosophical, theological, and sociological study of man and his struggle with the dark side of his being. According to Oberhelman, *On Heroes and Tombs* "without a doubt is the most representative national novel of Argentina written in the twentieth century." Kennedy describes the impact of the work when he concludes: "We read Sábato and we shudder, we are endlessly surprised, we exult, we are bewildered, fearful, mesmerized. He is a writer of great talent and imagination."

BIOGRAPHICAL/CRITICAL SOURCES:

BOOKS

Contemporary Literary Criticism, Gale, Volume 10, 1979, Volume 23, 1983.
Oberhelman, Harley Dean, *Ernesto Sábato,* Twayne, 1970.
Rodríguez Monegal, Emir, *The Borzoi Anthology of Latin American Literature,* Knopf, 1986.

PERIODICALS

Commonweal, June 18, 1982.
Newsweek, September 21, 1981.
Review, May-August, 1981.
Salmagundi, spring-summer, 1989.
Times Literary Supplement, August 13, 1982.
Washington Post Book World, August 16, 1981.

—*Sketch by Marian Gonsior*

*   *   *

SAFRAN, William   1930-

PERSONAL: Born July 8, 1930, in Dresden, Germany (now East Germany); came to the United States in 1946; naturalized citizen, 1953; son of Abraham Joshua (a rabbi) and Golda (Chajes) Safran; married Marian Celia Folk (a teacher), March 25, 1961; children: Gabriella Sarah, Joshua Abraham. *Education:* City College (now of the City University of New York), B.A. (with honors), 1953, M.A., 1955; Columbia University, Ph.D., 1964. *Politics:* Democrat. *Religion:* Jewish.

ADDRESSES: Home—2360 Balsam Dr., Boulder, Colo. 80304. *Office*—Department of Political Science, KTCH 135, University of Colorado at Boulder, Boulder, Colo. 80309-0333.

CAREER: Brooklyn College of the City University of New York, Brooklyn, N.Y., lecturer, 1960-62, instructor in political science, 1962-65; University of Colorado at Boulder, assistant professor, 1965-68, associate professor, 1968-73, professor of political science, 1973—, director of program in international affairs, 1966-69, 1979, 1981, spring 1986, and 1987-88, co-director, Center for Comparative Politics, 1989—. Instructor at Hunter College of the City University of New York, 1962; visiting professor at the University of Nice and Hebrew University of Jerusalem. *Military service:* U.S. Army, 1955-57.

MEMBER: International Studies Association (Comparative Interdisciplinary Studies), International Political Science Association (vice-president and editor of newsletter, research group on politics and ethnicity, 1988—), American Political Science Association, American Academy of Political and Social Science, Tocqueville Society, Conference Group on French Politics and Society (national program organizer, 1988—), Conference Group on German Politics, Association Francaise de Science Politique, Western Political Science Association.

AWARDS, HONORS: Fellowships from the Social Science Foundation, 1966, University of Colorado Council on Research and Creative Work, summer, 1966, and 1969-70, National Endowment for the Humanities, 1980-81, American Council of Learned Societies, 1988-89, University of Colorado Graduate School, Committee of Arts and Humanities, 1989.

WRITINGS:

Veto-Group Politics, Chandler, 1967.
The French Polity, McKay, 1977, updated edition, Longman, 1979, 3rd edition, Longman, 1990.
(With George A. Codding, Jr.) *Ideology and Politics: The Socialist Party of France,* Westview, 1979.
(With Dan N. Jacobs, David P. Conradt, and B. Guy Peters), *Comparative Politics: An Introduction to the Politics of the United Kingdom, France, Germany, and the Soviet Union,* Chatham House, 1983.
(With M. D. Hancock, Conradt, Peters, and R. Zariski) *Politics in Western Europe,* Chatham House, 1990.

CONTRIBUTOR

Ronald A. Fracisco and R. D. Laird, editors, *The Political Economy of Collectivized Agriculture,* Pergamon, 1979.
V. P. Nanda, J. R. Scarritt, and G. W. Shepherd, Jr., editors, *Global Human Rights: Public Policies, Comparative Measures, and NGO Strategies,* Westview, 1981.
William G. Andrews and Stanley Hoffmann, editors, *The Fifth Republic at Twenty,* State University of New York Press, 1981.
Fred Eidlin, editor, *Constitutional Democracy: Essays in Honor of Henry W. Ehrmann,* Westview, 1983.
N. J. Vig and S. E. Schier, editors, *Political Economy in Advanced Industrial Societies,* Holmes & Maier, 1983.
S. Bethlen and I. Volgyes, editors, *Europe and the Superpowers,* Westview, 1983.
M. Curtis, editor, *Antisemitism in the Contemporary World,* Westview, 1983.
J. R. Rudolph and R. J. Thompson, editor, *Ethnoterritorial Politics, Policy, and the Western World,* Lynne Reinner, 1989.
Paul Godt, editor, *Policy-making in France from de Gaulle to Mitterand,* Pinter and Columbia University Press, 1989.
George Billias, editor, *American Constitutionalism and the World,* Greenwood, 1990.
Anthony Messina, et al., editors, *Ethnic and Racial Minorities in Advanced Industrial Democracies,* Greenwood, 1990.

Contributor of articles and reviews to political science journals.

WORK IN PROGRESS: Writing on French politics, especially interest groups and public policy; on ethnopolitics, immigration, citizenship, and nationality.

SIDELIGHTS: William Safran told *CA* that his interests include comparative politics and policies, mainly in Western Europe. He is particularly concerned with political parties, interest groups, economic, social and ethnic policies. He is also interested in the politics of Israel and in Western Europe's place in world affairs. Safran has spent extended periods of time in France, West Germany, and Israel, and he has traveled widely throughout Western and Eastern Europe.

St. JOHN, Nicole
(Elizabeth Bolton, Catherine E. Chambers, Kate Chambers, Pamela Dryden, Lavinia Harris, Norma Johnston, Adrian Robert)

PERSONAL: Born in Ridgewood, NJ; daughter of Charles Eugene Chambers (an engineer) and Marjorie (a teacher; maiden name, Pierce) Johnston. *Education:* Montclair College, B.A. *Politics:* None. *Religion:* Reformed Church in America.

ADDRESSES: Home—Wyckoff, NJ. *Office*—Dryden Harris St. John, Inc., Box 299, 103 Godwin Ave., Midland Park, NJ 07432. *Agent*—McIntosh & Otis, Inc., 310 Madison Ave., New York, NY 10017.

CAREER: Writer and editor. President, St. John Enterprises (editorial services), Dryden Harris St. John, Inc., and St. John Institute of Arts and Letters. Former teacher of English in Glen Rock, NJ, public schools; member, Rutgers University Council on Children's Literature. Has also worked in the theatre, fashion publishing and retailing, religious publishing, and has done freelance editing for Prentice-Hall and others. Founder, president, and director of Geneva Players, Inc. (religious drama group).

MEMBER: Authors Guild, Authors League of America, Mystery Writers of America, Sisters in Crime.

AWARDS, HONORS: Several of St. John's books have been included on the New York Public Library's Best Books for Young Readers lists.

WRITINGS:

FOR YOUNGER READERS; AS ELIZABETH BOLTON

The Case of the Wacky Cat, Troll, 1985.
Ghost in the House, Troll, 1985.
The Secret of the Ghost Piano, Troll, 1985.
The Secret of the Magic Potion, Troll, 1985.
The Tree House Detective Club, Troll, 1985.

"ADVENTURES IN FRONTIER AMERICA" SERIES; FOR YOUNGER READERS; AS CATHERINE E. CHAMBERS

California Gold Rush: Search for Treasure, Troll, 1984.
Daniel Boone and the Wilderness Road, Troll, 1984.
Flatboats on the Ohio: Westward Bound, Troll, 1984.
Frontier Dream: Life on the Great Plains, Troll, 1984.
Frontier Farmer: Kansas Adventures, Troll, 1984.
Frontier Village: A Town Is Born, Troll, 1984.
Indiana Days: Life in a Frontier Town, Troll, 1984.
Log-Cabin Home: Pioneers in the Wilderness, Troll, 1984.
Texas Roundup: Life on the Range, Troll, 1984.
Wagons West: Off to Oregon, Troll, 1984.

"DIANA WINTHROP" SERIES; FOR YOUNG ADULTS; AS KATE CHAMBERS

The Case of the Dog Lover's Legacy, New American Library, 1983.
Danger in the Old Fort, New American Library, 1983.
The Secret of the Singing Strings, New American Library, 1983.
The Legacy of Lucian Van Zandt, New American Library, 1984.
The Secrets of Beacon Hill, New American Library, 1984.
The Threat of the Pirate Ship, New American Library, 1984.

FOR YOUNG ADULTS; AS LAVINIA HARRIS

Dreams and Memories, Scholastic, Inc., 1982.
The Great Rip-Off ("Computer Detectives" series), Scholastic, Inc., 1984.
Soaps in the Afternoon ("Computer Detectives" series), Scholastic, Inc., 1985.
A Touch of Madness ("Computer Detectives" series), Scholastic, Inc., 1985.
Cover Up! ("Computer Detectives" series), Scholastic, Inc., 1986.

FOR YOUNG ADULTS; AS NORMA JOHNSTON

The Wishing Star, Funk, 1963.
The Wider Heart, Funk 1964.
Ready or Not, Funk, 1965.
The Bridge Between, Funk, 1966.
The Keeping Days ("Keeping Days" series), Atheneum, 1973.
Glory in the Flower ("Keeping Days" series), Atheneum, 1974.
Of Time and of Seasons, Atheneum, 1975.
Strangers Dark and Gold, Atheneum, 1975.
A Striving after Wind (sequel to *Of Time and of Seasons*), Atheneum, 1976.
A Mustard Seed of Magic, ("Keeping Days" series), Atheneum, 1977.
The Sanctuary Tree ("Keeping Days" series), Atheneum, 1977.
If You Love Me, Let Me Go, Atheneum, 1978.
The Swallow's Song, Atheneum, 1978.
The Crucible Year, Atheneum, 1979.
Pride of Lions: The Story of the House of Atreus (myth), Atheneum, 1979.
A Nice Girl Like You ("Keeping Days" series), Atheneum, 1980.
Myself and I ("Keeping Days" series), Atheneum, 1981.
The Days of the Dragon's Seed, Atheneum, 1982.
Timewarp Summer, Atheneum, 1982.
Gabriel's Girl, Atheneum, 1983.
Carlisles All ("Carlisle Chronicles" series), Bantam, 1986.
Carlisle's Hope ("Carlisle Chronicles" series), Bantam, 1986.
To Jess, with Love and Memories ("Carlisle Chronicles" series), Bantam, 1986.
The Watcher in the Mist, Bantam, 1986.
Shadow of a Unicorn, Bantam, 1987.
Whisper of the Cat, Bantam, 1988.
The Potter's Wheel, Morrow, 1988.
Return to Morocco, Four Winds, 1988.
Such Stuff as Dreams Are Made Of, Morrow, 1989.
The Five Magpies, Four Winds, 1989.
The Delphic Choice, Four Winds, 1989.
Summer of the Citadel, Bantam, 1989.
A Small Rain, Four Winds, 1990.

FOR YOUNGER READERS; AS ADRIAN ROBERT

The Awful Mess Mystery, Troll, 1985.
Ellen Ross, Private Detective, Troll, 1985.
My Grandma, the Witch, Troll, 1985.
The Secret of the Haunted Chimney, Troll, 1985.
The Secret of the Old Barn, Troll, 1985.

OTHER

The Medici Ring (gothic novel), Random House, 1975.
Wychwood (gothic novel), Random House, 1976.
Guinever's Gift (gothic novel), Random House, 1977.
(As Pamela Dryden) *Mask for My Heart* (young adult), New American Library, 1982.
(As Pamela Dryden) *Riding Home* (for younger readers), Bantam, 1988.

Also author of several books ghostwritten for publication under other names. Author of columns on cooking and entertaining, *Keeping Days Cooking,* and on writing.

SIDELIGHTS: Nicole St. John told *CA* that she writes "because all my life I have learned through vicarious empathy of literature, and I believe, with Tennessee Williams, that as a writer of fiction 'I give you truth in the pleasant disguise of illusion.' " St. John wanted to be a writer since she was very young. "I have things that I must say, and I can no more hold back from saying them than I can cease to breathe."

St. John's books are concerned with the "verities I believe to be unchanging in a changing world." Her books are set in the past because "the future can learn of the past. Because people in the past have gone through the same inner and outer struggles that we do now. There are lessons to be learned in the things that they did wrong, and messages for us in the truths they found." Most important, said the author, she writes "to disturb the status quo and draw people into a closer understanding of themselves, their neighbors, and their God."

St. John has traveled extensively in the Caribbean, Europe, and the Mediterranean, and has spent summers in England and Europe doing historical research.

BIOGRAPHICAL/CRITICAL SOURCES:

BOOKS

Something about the Author Autobiography Series, Volume 7, Gale, 1989.

* * *

SALVATORE, Nicholas 1943-
(Nick Salvatore)

PERSONAL: Born November 14, 1943, in Brooklyn, N.Y.; son of Nicholas Anthony (a lawyer) and Katherine (a secretary; maiden name, McManus) Salvatore; married Ann H. Sullivan (a librarian), September 20, 1974; children: Gabriella, Nora. *Education:* Hunter College of the City University of New York, B.A., 1968; University of California, Berkeley, M.A., 1969, Ph.D., 1977.

ADDRESSES: Home—109 Irving Pl., Ithaca, N.Y. 14850. *Office*—School of Industrial and Labor Relations, Cornell University, Ithaca, N.Y. 14850.

CAREER: College of the Holy Cross, Worcester, Mass., assistant professor of U.S. history, 1976-81; Cornell University, Ithaca, N.Y., assistant professor, 1981-83, associate professor of U.S. history, 1984—.

MEMBER: American Historical Association, Organization of American Historians, Society of American Historians.

AWARDS, HONORS: Bancroft Prize, Columbia University, 1983, and John H. Dunning Prize, American Historical Association, 1984, both for *Eugene V. Debs: Citizen and Socialist.*

WRITINGS:

(Under name Nick Salvatore) *Eugene V. Debs: Citizen and Socialist,* University of Illinois Press, 1982.
(Editor and author of introduction) Samuel Gompers, *Seventy Years of Life and Labor: An Autobiography by Samuel Gompers,* ILR Press, 1984.

Contributor to history and labor journals.

WORK IN PROGRESS: A social history of late nineteenth-century northern urban blacks, to be published by Random House.

SIDELIGHTS: In a *Washington Post Book World* review of Salvatore's *Eugene V. Debs: Citizen and Socialist,* Reid Beddow writes that "this sober, well-researched life of Debs . . . will be the standard biography for many years to come."

BIOGRAPHICAL/CRITICAL SOURCES:

PERIODICALS

New York Review of Books, November 10, 1983.
New York Times Book Review, May 22, 1983, August 31, 1986.
Washington Post Book World, February 13, 1983.

* * *

SALVATORE, Nick
See SALVATORE, Nicholas

* * *

SANCHEZ, Ricardo 1941-

PERSONAL: Born March 29, 1941, in El Paso, Tex.; son of Pedro Lucero (a dealer in scrap metals) and Adelina (Gallegos) Sánchez; married Maria Teresa Silva, November 28, 1964; children: Rikard-Sergei, Libertad-Yvonne, Pedro-Cuauhtémoc (deceased), Jacinto-Temilotzín. *Education:* Took extension courses from Alvin Junior College, 1965-69; Union Graduate School, Ph.D., 1975. *Politics:* "AnarchoHumanist." *Religion:* "Indigenist-non-sectarian."

CAREER: Incarcerated in California state prisons, c. early 1960s, and Texas Department of Corrections in Huntsville, Tex., 1965-69; Vista community worker, El Paso, Tex., 1969; research director of Project MACHOS, Inc., 1969; *Richmond Afro-American Newspaper,* Richmond, Va., correspondent, 1969; University of Massachusetts, School of Education, Amherst, staff writer, research assistant, and instructor, 1970; Colorado Migrant Council, Denver, director of Itinerant Migrant Health Project, 1970-71; University of Texas, El Paso, consultant, writer, and lecturer for Chicano Affairs Program and Teacher Corps & TTT Program, 1971-72; New Mexico State University, Las Cruces, community staff consultant and lecturer for Social Welfare Teaching Center, 1972-73; El Paso Community College, El Paso, professor of poetry, literature, and critical theory, 1975, National Endowment for the Arts poet in residence, 1975-76; University of Wisconsin, Milwaukee, visiting professor and lecturer for Spanish-Speaking Outreach Institute, 1977; University of Utah, Salt Lake City, assistant professor of humanities and Chicano studies, 1977-80; deputy director of Project SER, 1980-81; Noel Theraputic, Austin, Tex., associate director, 1981-82; Brown Schools, Austin, psychiatric trainer, 1982; Poets of Tejas Reading Series, San Antonio, Tex., founder and manager, 1982—; Paperbacks y mas, San Antonio, owner and manager, 1983—; Poetry Tejas International, San Antonio, director, 1983—. Free lance writer, poet, and consultant; developer of television programs and cassette recordings on Chicano culture and literature; lecturer and participant in symposia, colloquia, and seminars throughout the United States.

Training consultant, writer, and lecturer for American Program Bureau, Boston, Mass., 1970-72, and La Academia de la Nueva Raza, Dixon, N.M., 1971-72; co-founder and counseling supervisor of Trinity-Opportunities Industrialization Center, El Paso, 1972. Board member of Southwest Poets' Conference, 1970—, Father Rahm Health Clinic, El Paso, 1971-73, Trinity Chicano Coalition, El Paso, 1971-73, Texas Council on Alcoholism, El Paso, 1972-73, and La Luz Mexican American Cultural Center of the El Paso diocese, 1974-76. Chairman of Project TREND, El Paso, 1972-73; co-founder and associate of Chicano Barrio Associates (CHIBAS), El Paso, 1972—; founder and board member of Chicano Light and Power, Inc., El Paso, 1974—. National Endowment for the Arts literary panel member, 1979-82; member of Texas Commission for the Arts, 1982-85; trustee of San Antonio Library System, 1985-87.

MEMBER: International P.E.N., Poets and Writers, Inc. (New York City).

AWARDS, HONORS: Frederick Douglass fellowship in journalism, 1969; Ford Foundation graduate fellow, Union Graduate School, 1973-75; outstanding professor award from the Chicano Student Association, University of Utah, 1979.

WRITINGS:

Canto y grito mi liberación/The Liberation of a Chicano Mind, Mictla, 1971, Doubleday-Anchor, 1973.
(Editor) *Los cuatro* (title means "The Four"), Barrio Press, 1971.
Obras (title means "Works"), Quetzal-Vihio Press, 1971.
Mano a mano (title means "Hand to Hand"), Conference of Unity & Action, 1971.
Hechizospells, Chicano Studies Center, University of California, 1976.
Milhuas blues y gritos norteños (title means "Milwaukee Blues and Northern Cries"), Spanish-Speaking Outreach Institute, University of Wisconsin, 1980.
Brown Bear Honey Madness: Alaskan Cruising Poems, Slough Press, 1982.
Amsterdam cantos y poemas pistos (title means "Amsterdam Songs and Drinking Poems"), Place of Herons, 1983.
Selected Poems, Arte Público Press, 1985.

Also author of *Perdido: A Barrio Story,* 1985, unpublished manuscripts, including "In and Out," "Mexi-Coloured Moods," "With Love & Protest," and "Florimoquiando," and screenplay *Entelequía.* Work represented in several anthologies, including *Points of Departure,* edited by Ernece B. Kelly, Wiley, 1972; *We Are Chicanos,* edited by Philip D. Ortego, Washington Square Press, 1973; *Festival de flor y canto,* University of Southern California Press, 1976; and *Canto al Pueblo: An Anthology of Experiences,* edited by Leonard Carillo and others, Penca Books, 1978.

Contributor to *Publishers Weekly, De Colores, El Diario, Greenfield Review* and numerous other magazines, reviews, newspapers, and journals. Co-founder and editor of Mictla Publications, 1970-75; special issues editor, *De Colores: Journal of Emerging Raza Philosophies,* 1975; arts columnist for *Express-News,* San Antonio, 1985-86.

SIDELIGHTS: A trenchant critic of the rascist, conformist, and materialistic aspects of contemporary American society, author Ricardo Sánchez believes Chicano literature must participate in the political emancipation of the Chicano people by heightening awareness of their identity and distinctive culture and traditions. "I feel that the survival of our *raza* [race] is indeed important," the author told John David Bruce-Novoa in *Chicano Authors: Inquiry by Interview,* "thus I sense that only a politicizing poetics can be of value." Sánchez regularly flays his literary colleagues for what he perceives as their accommodationism, lack of critical rigor, and "moral and social cowardice" before the bitter realities of Chicano *barrio* life. The author is particularly acerbic about a romanticizing strain of *indigenismo* (indigenism) in Chicano literature, which he bluntly described in the *Chicano Authors* interview as a perpetuating source of "quasimystical idiocies."

Sánchez's own literary works reflect a life shaped by the rough urban *barrio,* including childhood years spent in a poor El Paso slum, stints in prison in Texas and California, and community organizing work in Chicano neighborhoods in several ern cities. The author co-founded Mictla Publications to publish his first book, *Canto y grito mi liberación/The Liberation of a Chicano Mind,* in 1971. Sánchez's pungent descriptions of *barrio* life are written in a distinctive stream-of-consciousness style that mixes free verse and prose in English, Spanish, and various Chicano *barrio* and prison slangs. According to Sánchez in *Chicano Authors,* this language "is created out of linguistic fusion, not from a demarcated/fragmentary chaos, but . . . out of synthesis." A deep anger over the Chicano's social lot suffuses the book, but critics have also remarked on the exuberant spirit of creative vigor generated by the author's original word combinations and juxtapositions.

Sánchez's preference for verbal spontaneity and loose aural textures over more formal stylistic structures is also evident in *Hechizospells,* a major collection of poems, essays, and other writings published in 1976. The overriding theme is again the plight of the Chicano endeavoring to build a coherent identity out of his dual roots in the Spanish-Mexican and North American cultures. True to his iconoclastic form, Sánchez lambastes social scientists, politicians, educators, prison officials and myriad other "dehumanizing" agents in both the contemporary Anglo and Chicano societies. Although his language is occasionally "direct" and "incisive," most of Sánchez's writing "is impressionistic and visceral, filled with phantasmagoric images and deeply personal symbolism," remarked critic Charles M. Tatum in *World Literature Today.* Dubbing *Hechizospells* "a literary happening," Tatum added, "Sánchez's panoply of images, shocking statements, feints, attacks and glimpses of personal anguish are sometimes self-indulgent but never dull."

Sánchez told *CA:* "I write in order to liberate myself from past inculcations and to enjoin myself with all who want to create a more sanguine society. As a Chicano I realize the privation that those who are different must suffer. Writing becomes the vehicle for self expression and the means toward one's humanization. My writings are trilingual, i.e., Spanish, English, or an admixture of both—flowing in and out of the linguistic worlds I am able to inhabit simultaneously—creating thus a new world view that contains both. In quest of humanizing liberation do I write, in order to distill from the sordidness of societal oppressiveness a view of beingness which sings and shouts out love, dignity, and the peacefulness of freedom."

AVOCATIONAL INTERESTS: Chess, art, dance, dramatics, readings in history, philosophy, folklore, political theory.

BIOGRAPHICAL/CRITICAL SOURCES:

BOOKS

Bruce-Novoa, John David, *Chicano Authors: Inquiry by Interview,* University of Texas Press, 1980.

PERIODICALS

Hispano, January 24, 1977, May 9, 1977.
Revista Chicano-Riqueña, December, 1977.
Tiempo, December 27, 1976.
World Literature Today, summer, 1977.

*   *   *

SANCHEZ, Thomas 1944-

PERSONAL: Born February 26, 1944, in Oakland, Calif.; son of Thomas and Geraldine (Brown) Sanchez; married Stephanie Spielberger (a landscape painter); children: Dante (daughter). *Education:* San Francisco State College (now University), B.A., 1966, M.A., 1967.

ADDRESSES: Home—Key West, Fla.; and Los Angeles, Calif. *Agent*—Jett Rink Associates, Box 1493, Venice, Calif. 90291.

CAREER: Writer. Active in human rights organizations such as Congress for Racial Equality (CORE) and the United Farm Workers during the 1960s; covered 1973 takeover at Wounded Knee for Pacifica Radio. Author and host of a five-part ABC-TV special on the California Hispanic community. Lecturer at San Francisco State University, University of California, Pennsylvania State University, and other organizations. Awards judge, National Endowment for the Arts.

MEMBER: Southwestern Humanities Council (member of board of directors), California Council for the Humanities in Public Policy (member of board of directors).

AWARDS, HONORS: National Endowment for the Arts fellowship in fiction; Guggenheim fellowship.

WRITINGS:

Rabbit Boss (novel), Knopf, 1973, reprinted, Vintage, 1989.
(Contributor) *Four Visions of America: Henry Miller, Thomas Sanchez, Erica Jong, Kay Boyle,* Capra, 1977.
Zoot-Suit Murders (novel), Dutton, 1978.
Native Notes from the Land of Earthquake and Fire (nonfiction), Sandpiper Press, 1979.
(With Lawrence C. Powell) *Angels Burning; "Ocian" in View,* Capra, 1987.
Mile Zero (novel), Knopf, 1989.

Contributor to anthologies; contributor of articles to *Esquire, Los Angeles Times, San Francisco Chronicle,* and other periodicals. Member of editorial board, *Minority Voices: An Inter-Disciplinary Journal of Literature and the Arts;* contributing editor, *Santa Barbara Magazine.*

SIDELIGHTS: Thomas Sanchez's historical novel *Rabbit Boss* traces four generations of a small tribe of Indians, the Washo, who lived in an area around the California-Nevada border. The novel opens with an encounter between Gayabuc, a descendant of the tribe's powerful elder, the Rabbit Boss, and the ill-fated Donner party who, lost in the Sierras in winter, were forced into cannibalism. The first of his people to see white men, Gayabuc is repelled by their cannibalism and warns the rest of his tribe, beginning the Washo legend that all white men are cannibals. This theme of white cannibalism continues throughout the novel, as H. L. Van Brunt comments in the *Christian Science Monitor:* "Cannibalism at the Donner Pass is becoming the symbol of greedy dreams turned to madness by an indifferent wilderness. To an Indian the image of the white man as cannibal must be irresistible. There are scenes as powerful as the opening one throughout this novel, as well as sharply focused character studies." Calling *Rabbit Boss* "a rare and wonderful book," *Washington Post Book World* contributor Patrick Bernuth likewise observes that the author "has managed to weave this country [the Sierras] and its ancient people deep into his first novel. It is a remarkable achievement," the critic continues. "[Sanchez] has vividly brought the life the Indian's ironic vision of the white man as a savage, as a waster, earth-tourist and thief."

Van Brunt, who finds the novel "abundant and imaginative" in its descriptions, nevertheless faults it as "overlong and diffuse. Long 'mystical' passages throughout the book impede a willing reader's progress." *New York Times Book Review* contributor Gordon Burnside, however, believes that these elaborate sections

make the novel "powerful": "As Sanchez tells it, the safely familiar exaggeration of American frontier humor turns itself inside-out and reappears as the secret language of demons." "Re-creating frontier life with authority and immediacy," Patrick Fanning states in *Library Journal,* Sanchez's work is "illuminated by the author's personal, searing vision . . . [and is] impressive as literature, history, and sociology." A *National Observer* critic similarly asserts that "*Rabbit Boss* deserves to become an American classic. [It is] a great novel, spanning a century in the life and death of an Indian tribe, told with epic perspective and infinite compassion." As a *Times Literary Supplement* reviewer concludes, "*Rabbit Boss* is beautiful, poetic, powerful. Thomas Sanchez has a dominating talent."

Zoot-Suit Murders, Sanchez's second novel, is a mystery set against the riots which took place in Los Angeles in the early 1940s, when the Chicano community was terrorized by truckloads of sailors. Mexican-American women and children were brutalized and their "zoot-suited" men were hunted, beaten, stripped, and shaved. Sanchez's story involves the murder of two FBI agents and its possible connections to the barrio and to fascist and communist groups. John Thomas Stovall writes in the *Chicago Tribune:* "By juxtaposing fiction and fact, Sanchez has created a vivid tale of political intrigue and romance. Sanchez, a master of pictorial detail, accurately describes the energies and squalor of the barrio to reveal one of the novel's recurrent themes: the vulnerability of its inhabitants, a condition fueled by racial prejudice and exploited by almost every character in *Zoot-Suit Murders.*" This novel, maintains a *Publishers Weekly* reviewer, "surpasses a simple mystery story," especially in its "unexpected and shocking climax." As Stovall explains, in *Zoot-Suit Murders* Sanchez "has created a powerful fiction based upon fact—not just upon historical fact, but upon subtler truths about human nature."

"There are a handful of writers who dare to wrestle larger-than-life themes, pursue extremes and transcend the normal limitations of prose to reach for a personal vision of The Great American Novel," *Playboy* critic Digby Diehl observes. "Thomas Pynchon, Norman Mailer and Robert Stone come to mind. With *Mile Zero,* Thomas Sanchez joins them." The author spent ten years preparing the novel, during which time he lost his home and his previous novels went out of print. Nevertheless, his effort has been worthwhile, note critics like *New York Times Book Review* contributor Erica Abeel: "[Sanchez' previous work], it is now clear, was only a warm-up for the dazzling achievement of 'Mile Zero.' Mr. Sanchez' new novel is marked by the same commanding sense of place, the same mix of politics and poetry. But," the critic continues, *Mile Zero* "is more shapely, leaner and free of 'Rabbit Boss's' diffuseness and *longueurs.* Its brilliantly contrived plot uncoils with the suspense of a thriller. Nothing is gratuitous," Abeel relates; "characters and actions are linked in a hidden web, sometimes with devastating irony. And it is funny, a comic masterpiece crackling with back-handed wit and laugh-out-loud humor."

Taking place on Key West, Florida—"Mile Zero" of U.S. Highway 1—the novel follows a series of varied characters whose lives have intertwined: St. Cloud, a former antiwar activist drowning his self-doubt in alcohol; Lila, a complex young Southern woman who becomes focus of St. Cloud's passion; and Justo Tamarindo, a Cuban-American police detective confronted with a series of bizarre crimes on the island. Although Justo's pursuit of Zobop, the mysterious figure who leaves strange messages at the crime scenes, "forms the main action of the novel," states Alan Cheuse in Chicago *Tribune Books,* along the way "Sanchez manages to create the little world of Key West, with its natives, the so-called 'conchs,' its drifters and tourists and illegals and everyone in between." Allen H. Peacock concurs with this assessment, asserting in the *Detroit News* that *Mile Zero* "succeeds more often than not as fiction and magnificently as a spooky, troubling paean to the furtive and flagrant microcosm of America that is Key West in the '80s. . . . *Mile Zero* is above all a novel about Key West itself—its history, colors, smells, tropical allure and deadly menace."

Some critics, however, find the author's detours into the history of Key West and its inhabitants distracting. *Los Angeles Times Book Review* contributor Alejandro Morales, for instance, although he thinks the book is "an accomplished novel" that is "rich in the cultural and literary intertextuality of Steinbeck and Cervantes, Joyce and Shakespeare," writes that "Sanchez falters: He has created truly interesting characters but placed them in a meandering story. Their stories are individualized," the critic elaborates, "rather than united in a clear and concise plot." Ron Hansen likewise remarks in the *Washington Post Book World* that "word drunkenness gets in the way in some passages here, and from first to last Sanchez gives free rein to a kind of flamboyant and torrid writing." Nevertheless, the critic admits that "the immense power and passion of *Mile Zero* owes a great deal to just that willingness to risk foolishness and excess on behalf of his chilling vision of a grotesque American future."

"Sanchez's range is broad—from the lyrical wash of language that opens the novel to the jangly-nerved sequences in which 'Zobop' speaks," comments Cheuse. The result, adds the critic, is "prose that's as agile and pulsating as the blend of American blues and Caribbean rhythms that comes from the region." Abeel similarly praises the author for the variety of his writing: "Sanchez avoids the predictable. He describes his own stylistic practice in St. Cloud's professed liking for 'sentences that slipped off one another with strikingly misguided purpose.' The book's ending," Abeel continues, "is itself a marvel or ambiguity—tragic, funny and hopeful all at once. 'Mile Zero' is a novel of uncommon richness and resonance." As Diehl concludes, *Mile Zero* "is a rare and exhilarating experience, a brilliant wide-angle metaphorical treatise on modern American life."

MEDIA ADAPTATIONS: A film documentary on Sanchez and the writing of *Rabbit Boss* was produced by the University of California.

BIOGRAPHICAL/CRITICAL SOURCES:

BOOKS

Bestsellers 90, Issue 1, Gale, 1990.

PERIODICALS

Chicago Tribune, December 10, 1978.
Christian Science Monitor, July 18, 1973.
Detroit News, November 5, 1989.
Library Journal, May 1, 1973.
Los Angeles Times, October 18, 1989.
Los Angeles Times Book Review, September 17, 1989.
National Observer, June 16, 1973.
New York Times Book Review, March 10, 1974, October 1, 1989.
People, October 16, 1989.
Playboy, September, 1989.
Publishers Weekly, April 2, 1973, September 4, 1978, August 4, 1989.
Time, July 30, 1973.
Times Literary Supplement, March 1, 1974.
Tribune Books (Chicago), September 24, 1989.

Washington Post Book World, June 3, 1973, July 29, 1973, October 8, 1989.

—*Sketch by Diane Telgen*

* * *

SANDFORD, Cedric Thomas 1924-

PERSONAL: Born November 21, 1924, in Basingstoke, Hampshire, England; son of Thomas (a Methodist minister) and Louisa (Hodge) Sandford; married Evelyn Belch (a teacher), December 1, 1945 (died March 19, 1982); married Christina Katarin Privett (a registered nurse), July 21, 1984; children: (first marriage) John, Gillian. *Education:* Victoria University of Manchester, B.A. (economics), 1948, M.A., 1949; University of London, B.A. (history), 1955. *Religion:* Methodist.

ADDRESSES: Home and office—Old Ceach House, Fersfield, Perrymead, Bath BA2 5AR, England.

CAREER: Burnley Municipal College, Burnley, Lancashire, England, assistant lecturer, 1949-51, lecturer in economics and history, 1951-59; Bristol College of Science and Technology, Bristol, Gloucestershire, England, senior lecturer in general and social studies, 1959-60, head of department, 1960-65; University of Bath, Bath, Avon, England, professor of political economy, 1965-87, professor emeritus, 1987—, head of School of Humanities and Social Sciences, 1965-68, 1971-74, and 1977-79, director of Centre for Fiscal Studies, 1974-86. Visiting professor, University of Delaware, 1969; visiting fellow, Australian National University, 1981 and 1985, and Victoria University, Wellington, New Zealand, 1987. Member of Meade Committee on Reform of the Direct Tax System, 1975-78; member of South West Electricity Consultative Council, 1981-90; member of Bath District Health Authority, 1984—. Consultant to International Monetary Fund, World Bank, Organization for Economic Co-operation and Development, National Federation of the Self-Employed and Small Businesses, Irish Tax Commission, and United Nations Organization. *Military service:* Royal Air Force, pilot, 1943-45; became flight sergeant.

MEMBER: Liberal International, Economic Association (past president), Sonnenberg Association.

WRITINGS:

Taxing Inheritance and Capital Gains, Institute of Economic Affairs, 1965, 2nd edition, 1967.
Economics of Public Finance, Pergamon, 1969, 3rd edition, 1984.
(Editor with M. S. Bradbury, and contributor) *Case Studies in Economics,* three volumes, Macmillan, 1970-71.
Realistic Tax Reform, Chatto & Windus, 1971.
Taxing Personal Wealth, Allen & Unwin, 1971.
National Economic Planning, Heinemann Educational, 1972, 2nd edition, 1976.
Hidden Costs of Taxation, Institute for Fiscal Studies, 1973.
(With J. R. M. Willis and D. J. Ironside) *An Accessions Tax,* Institute for Fiscal Studies, 1973.
(With Willis and Ironside) *An Annual Wealth Tax,* Heinemann Educational, 1975.
Social Economics, Heinemann Educational, 1977.
(With Willis) *The Taxation of Net Wealth, Capital Transfers, and Capital Gains of Individuals,* Organization for Economic Co-operation and Development, 1979, new edition, 1988.
(With Alan Lewis and Norman Thomson) *Grants or Loans?,* Institute for Economic Affairs, 1980.
(Editor with Chris Pond and Robert Walker, and contributor) *Taxation and Social Policy,* Heinemann Educational, 1981.

(With M. R. Godwin, P. J. W. Hardwick, and M. I. Butterworth) *Costs and Benefits of VAT,* Heinemann Educational, 1981.

The Case for the Abolition of Non-Domestic Rates, National Federation of the Self-Employed and Small Businesses, 1981.

Wealth Tax: The European Experience; Lessons for Australia, Centre for Research in Federal Financial Relations, Australian National University, 1981.

Value-Added Tax: The UK Experience; Lessons for Australia, Centre for Research in Federal Financial Relations, Australian National University, 1981.

The Economic Structure, Longman, 1982.

(With Ann Robinson) *Tax Policy-Making in the United Kingdom,* Heinemann Educational, 1983.

(With Oliver Morrissey) *The Irish Wealth Tax: A Study in Economics and Politics,* Economic and Social Research Institute, 1985.

Taxing Wealth in New Zealand, Institute of Policy Studies, Victoria University, 1987.

(With Godwin and Hardwick) *Administrative and Compliance Costs of Taxation,* Fiscal Publications, 1989.

Contributor to accounting and tax journals.

SIDELIGHTS: Cedric Thomas Sandford told *CA:* "I had nothing published before the age of forty. It was then that a threat to my job and my self-respect led me to be bold and try my hand at writing. May others have the courage without the provocation."

BIOGRAPHICAL/CRITICAL SOURCES:

PERIODICALS

Spectator, September 18, 1971.

*   *   *

SAVITZ, Harriet May   1933-

PERSONAL: Born May 19, 1933, in Newark, NJ; daughter of Samuel and Susan (Trulick) Blatstein; married Ephraim Savitz (a pharmacist); children: Beth, Steven. *Education:* Attended evening classes at Upsala College, one year, and Rutgers University, one year. *Religion:* Jewish.

ADDRESSES: Agent—Curtis Brown Ltd., 10 Astor Pl., New York, NY 10003.

CAREER: Writer. Teacher of writing, Philadelphia Writer's Conference; guest lecturer in English literature, University of Pennsylvania. Holds workshops in novel-writing; helped organize workshop at Philadelphia's Free Library for the Blind to sensitize the media to the needs of the disabled.

MEMBER: National League of American Pen Women, National Wheelchair Athletic Association, Disabled in Action, VEEP (Very Exciting Education Program), Pennsylvania Wheelchair Athletic Association, Children's Reading Roundtable (Philadelphia; co-founder, 1965; member of steering committee, 1966—).

AWARDS, HONORS: Dorothy Canfield Fisher Memorial Children's Book Award nomination, 1971, for *Fly, Wheels, Fly!; The Lionhearted* was listed in University of Iowa's Books for Young Adults, 1975-76, among the most popular books read by teenagers; Outstanding Author Award, Pennsylvania School Library Association, 1981; California Young Reader Medal nomination, high school category, 1983-84, for *Run, Don't Walk;* received recognition for *Wheelchair Champions,* in celebration of the International Year of Disabled Persons.

WRITINGS:

(With M. Caporale Shecktor) *The Moon Is Mine* (short stories for children), John Day, 1968.

(With Shecktor) *Peter and Other Stories* (juvenile), John Day, 1969.

Fly, Wheels, Fly! (juvenile novel), John Day, 1970.

On the Move (juvenile novel), John Day, 1973.

The Lionhearted, John Day, 1975.

Wheelchair Champions: A History of Wheelchair Sports, John Day, 1978.

Run, Don't Walk (juvenile novel), F. Watts, 1979.

Wait until Tomorrow (juvenile novel), New American Library, 1981.

If You Can't Be the Sun, Be a Star, New American Library, 1982.

Come Back, Mr. Magic, New American Library, 1983.

Summer's End, New American Library, 1984.

The Sweat and the Gold (research project on the history of regional wheelchair sports competitions in the United States), VEEP, 1984.

Swimmer, Scholastic Inc., 1986.

The Cats Nobody Wanted, Scholastic Inc., 1989.

The Pail of Nails, Abingdon, 1989.

Also author of works for Science Research Associates reading program and Lyons & Carnahan readers. Contributor of short stories to collections, including *Short Story Scene;* contributor to *Encyclopaedia Britannica.* Contributor to magazines and newspapers, including *Philadelphia Inquirer, Denver Post, Scholastic, Boys' Life, Children's Friend,* and *Ranger Rick.*

WORK IN PROGRESS: A nonfiction work with Linda Tessler and Judy Baca, *Dyslexia: What You Need to Know;* a children's fiction book about a boy and his emotional attachment to a carousel, *Flame.*

MEDIA ADAPTATIONS: Run, Don't Walk was adapted and produced as an American Broadcasting Co. "Afterschool Special" by Henry Winkler's production company.

SIDELIGHTS: Harriet May Savitz told *CA:* "I find the books walk into my life. My father had a laryngectomy. A young boy at the shore wants to commit suicide. The two join together for *Wait until Tomorrow.*

"A gifted young man I know becomes injured in a hit-and-run and is left in a coma. An artist friend travels about the world seeking adventure. They come together in *Come Back, Mr. Magic.*

"I belong to a neighborhood watch program and am stunned by the crimes against the elderly. I speak at schools where there is no dress code. The two come together in *If You Can't Be the Sun, Be a Star.*

"I walk down the boardwalk and talk to a fellow stroller. He tells me he is a second-generation survivor. I ask, 'What is that?' There is a devastating flood in a mountain town nearby. Someone gives me the news clippings. I move the flood to the shore and include the second-generation survivor of the Holocaust, and we have *Summer's End.*

"For five years I research *The Sweat and the Gold,* bringing the real people into the story. All the disabled who have inspired me in fiction take their places in this nonfiction book.

"Sometimes I just stand somewhere, sit somewhere, walk somewhere, and I feel it. The book. It's around me, and if I look carefully, listen intently, and let myself feel its presence, the book introduces itself. 'How do you do,' I say. 'Let's get on with it,' it answers. From that moment on, there is no other world."

Savitz based her book *Fly, Wheels, Fly!* on factual material drawn from her association with the Central Penn Wheelers, a group of paraplegics in the Norristown, Pa., area. Members of the organization play basketball and compete in other sports, all from their wheelchairs.

*   *   *

SAXON, Alex
See PRONZINI, Bill

*   *   *

SCHLUETER, June 1942-

PERSONAL: Born November 4, 1942, in Passaic, N.J.; daughter of Alex and Erna (Schwedler) Mayer; married Paul Schlueter (a professor and writer), November 9, 1974. *Education:* Fairleigh Dickinson University, B.A. (magna cum laude), 1970; Hunter College of the City University of New York, M.A., 1973; Columbia University, Ph.D., 1977.

ADDRESSES: Home—123 High St., Easton, Pa. 18042. *Office*—Department of English, Lafayette College, Easton, Pa. 18042.

CAREER: Hoffmann-La Roche, Nutley, N.J., affiliated with Fine Chemicals Division, 1960-66; Schlanger, Blumenthal & Lynne, New York City, legal assistant, 1967-69; Stamer & Haft, New York City, legal and administrative assistant, 1969-72; Schlanger, Blumenthal & Lynne, legal assistant, 1972-73; Upsala College, East Orange, N.J., adjunct faculty member, 1973-74; Kean College of New Jersey, Union, adjunct professor of English, 1973-76; Kenneth P. Newman, New York City, legal and administrative assistant, 1976-77; Lafayette College, Easton, Pa., assistant professor, 1977-84, associate professor of English, 1984—. Fulbright professor of Gesamthochschule Kassel, West Germany, 1978-79. Has presented papers and sat on panels at numerous conferences and meetings throughout the U. S., Europe, and Canada.

MEMBER: Modern Language Association of America, Shakespeare Association of America, Beckett Society, New York Shakespeare Society.

AWARDS, HONORS: Summer research grant, Lafayette College, 1978; attended summer seminar of modern drama at Princeton University, National Endowment for the Humanities, 1981.

WRITINGS:

Metafictional Characters in Modern Drama, Columbia University Press, 1979.
(Contributor) Patricia De La Fuente, editor, *Edward Albee,* Pan American University, 1980.
The Plays and Novels of Peter Handke, University of Pittsburgh Press, 1981.
(Editor with husband, Paul Schlueter) *The English Novel: Twentieth-Century Criticism,* Volume II: *Twentieth-Century Novelists,* Ohio University Press, 1982.
(Editor with P. Schlueter) *Modern American Literature,* Supplement II, Ungar, 1985.
(With James K. Flanagan) *Arthur Miller,* Ungar, 1987.
(Editor with P. Schlueter) *Encyclopedia of British Women Writers,* Garland Publishing, 1988.
(Editor) *Feminist Re-Readings of Modern American Drama,* Fairleigh Dickinson University, 1989.

(With Enoch Brater) *Approaches to Teaching Beckett's Waiting for Godot,* Modern Language Association, 1989.

Contributor of articles and reviews to literature and theatre journals, including *Modern Drama, Studies in Twentieth-Century Literature, Thoth,* and *Comparative Drama.*

WORK IN PROGRESS: Reading Shakespeare in Performance: King Lear, with James P. Lusardi; *Reading Shakespeare in Performance: Hamlet,* with Lusardi; editing *Modern American Drama: The Female Canon.*

*   *   *

SCHLUETER, Paul (George) 1933-

PERSONAL: Surname pronounced "Shlooter"; born May 10, 1933, in Chicago, IL; son of Paul George and Ruby (Browning) Schlueter; married Rosetta Van Diggelen, July 14, 1956 (divorced, 1971); married June Mayer (a college professor of English and writer), November 9, 1974; children: (first marriage) Paul George III, Greta Renee, Laurie Ann. *Education:* Atended Bethel College, 1954-57; University of Minnesota, B.A., 1958; University of Denver, M.A., 1963; Southern Illinois University, Ph.D., 1968.

ADDRESSES: Home—123 High St., Easton, PA 18042.

CAREER: College of St. Thomas, St. Paul, MN, lecturer in English, 1959-60; Moorhead State College (now University), Moorhead, MN, instructor in English and director of public relations, 1960-62; University of Denver, Denver, CO, teaching assistant in English, 1962-63; Adrian College, Adrian, MI, assistant professor of English, 1966-68; University of Evansville, Evansville, IN, assistant professor of English, 1968-72; Kean College of New Jersey, Union, assistant professor of English, 1973-76, director of composition, 1974-76; independent scholar, research and consultant, 1976—. Visiting professor, Midwestern University, summer, 1964; guest professor, University of Hamburg, 1973, and University of Giessen and University of Kassel, 1978-79, all West Germany; speaker at colleges and universities in United States and West Germany. Director, Bicentennial Conference on New Jersey's Literary Heritage, 1975-76; member of selection committee, German Academic Exchange Service (DAAD), 1979. Participant, panelist, speaker, and seminar leader at professional conferences.

MEMBER: Doris Lessing Society (member of executive council), Modern Language Association of America (Religious Approaches to Literature Division, member of executive committee, 1975-78), College English Association, Conference on Christianity and Literature (secretary, 1971-73), North East Modern Language Association, Midwest Modern Language Association, Pennsylvania College English Association (member of executive board), Canadian Studies Conference of New Jersey (member of executive committee, 1975-77), Lambda Iota Tau (secretary, 1966-68), Phi Delta Epsilon (honorary member).

WRITINGS:

(Editor) *Literature and Religion: Thorton Wilder's "The Eighth Day,"* Modern Language Association of America, 1970.
(Editor) *The Fiction of Doris Lessing,* Modern Language Association of America, 1971.
The Novels of Doris Lessing, Southern Illinois University Press, 1973.
(Editor) *A Small Personal Voice: Essays, Reviews, Interviews by Doris Lessing,* Knopf, 1974.
Shirley Ann Grau, Twayne, 1981.

(Editor with wife, June Schlueter) *The English Novel: Twentieth-Century Criticism,* Volume 2: *Twentieth-Century Novelists,* Ohio University Press, 1982.

(Editor with Joseph Grau) *Shirley Ann Grau: An Annotated Bibliography,* Garland Publishing, 1983.

(Editor with J. Schlueter) *Modern American Literature,* Supplement 2, Ungar, 1985.

(Editor with J. Schlueter) *Encylopedia of British Women Writers,* Garland Publishing, 1988.

Contributor to numerous books, including *Contemporary American Novelists,* Southern Illinois University Press, 1964; *Dictionary of Literary Biography,* Gale, Volume 15: *British Novelists, 1930-1959,* Volume 27: *Poets of Great Britain and Ireland, 1945-60,* 1984, Volume 40: *Poets of Great Brain and Ireland Since 1960,* 1985; *Critical Survey of Long Fiction,* Salem Press, 1983; *Doris Lessing: Modern Critical Views,* Chelsea House, 1986 and *The Modernists: Studies in a Literary Phenomenon,* Fairleigh Dickinson University Press, 1987. Editor of *Proceedings of the Sixteenth National Conference on the Administration of Research,* Denver Research Institute, 1963. Contributor of articles to *Micropaedia* volumes of *Encyclopaedia Britannica,* 1974; also contributor of more than 1,500 book reviews to newspapers and magazines, including *Chicago Daily News, Chicago Sun-Times, Denver Post, St. Louis Post-Dispatch, Milwaukee Journal, Studies in Short Fiction, Motive, Christianity and Literature, Journal of Religion, Saturday Review,* and *Christian Century.* Editor of *Lambda Iota Tau Newsletter,* 1966-68. *Christianity and Literature,* editor, 1971-72, "Personalia" editor, 1975-77; member of advisory board, *Virginia Woolf Quarterly,* 1976-79. *Doris Lessing Newsletter,* member of advisory board, 1978-88, editor, 1980-82, associate editor, 1982-88; co-editor, *Pennsylvania English,* 1981-88.

SIDELIGHTS: Paul Schlueter once told *CA,* "[I am] particularly interested in relationships between the arts (especially literature) and religious faith (especially Christianity)."

SIDELIGHTS:

PERIODICALS

Christian Century, May 9, 1973.
Christianity and Literature, summer, 1974.
Journal of Modern Literature, November, 1974.
Modern Fiction Studies 19, 1973.
Psychology Today, August, 1973.
Research in African Literatures, fall, 1974.

*   *   *

SCHWARZ, Fred(erick) Charles 1913-

PERSONAL: Born January 15, 1913, in Brisbane, Queensland, Australia; son of Paulus Friedrich and Phoebe (Smith) Schwarz; married Lillian May Morton, 1939; children: John Charles Morton, Rosemary Gai, David Frederick. *Education:* University of Queensland, B.Sc., 1933, B.A., 1939, Bachelor Medicine, Bachelor Surgery, both 1944. *Religion:* Baptist.

ADDRESSES: Home—142 Concord Rd., Concord, New South Wales, Australia. *Office*—Christian Anti-Communism Crusade, P.O. Box 890, 227 East Sixth St., Long Beach, Calif. 90801.

CAREER: Teacher and college professor in Brisbane, Queensland, Australia; practiced medicine in Sydney, New South Wales, Australia, 1944-55; Christian Anti-Communism Crusade, Long Beach, Calif., co-founder and president, 1953—.

WRITINGS:

The Heart, Mind, and Soul of Communism, Christian Anti-Communism Crusade, 1953.
Communism: Diagnosis and Treatment, Christian Anti-Communism Crusade, 1954.
The Christian Answer to Communism, Christian Anti-Communism Crusade, 1954.
You Can Trust the Communists (to Be Communists), Prentice-Hall, 1961, published as *Communism, the Deceitful Tyranny: You Can Trust the Communists to Be Communists,* Chantico Publishing, 1966.
The Three Faces of Revolution, Capitol Hill Press, 1972.
Sidelights on Christology: Did Jesus Die on the Cross?, Exposition, 1977.*

*   *   *

SCOTT, Alastair
   See ALLEN, Kenneth S.

*   *   *

SEGAL, Robert M(ilton) 1925-

PERSONAL: Born August 29, 1925, in Newark, NJ; son of Sol and Pauline (Fishman) Segal; married Beverly E. Gechman (a speech pathologist), June 21, 1953; children: Alicia, Paula, Beth. *Education:* University of Wisconsin, B.A., 1950; University of Pittsburgh, M.S.W., 1952; Brandeis University, Ph.D., 1969.

ADDRESSES: Office—Graduate School of Social Work, University of Houston, 4800 Calhoun, Houston, TX 77004.

CAREER: Family Service Bureau, Chicago, IL, caseworker, 1952-55; Veterans Administration Mental Hygiene Clinic, San Diego, CA, psychiatric social worker, 1955-57; Child and Family Service, New Brunswick, NJ, casework supervisor, 1957-58; Jewish Family and Children Service, Miami, FL, caseworker, 1959-62; Welfare Planning Council of Dade County, Miami, planning consultant, 1962-66; University of Michigan, Ann Arbor, associate professor in School of Social Work, program director for social work, Institute for the Study of Mental Retardation and Related Disabilities, and associate of University Hospital, 1969-78; University of Houston, Graduate School of Social Work, Houston, TX, professor, 1978—. Director of project on serving the aging and aged developmentally disabled, U.S. Department of Health, Education, and Welfare. Member of board of directors, Washtenaw Association for Retarded Children, 1969-71. Provider of expressive art therapies to numerous workshops on grief, death, and dying. Consultant to various government agencies and schools. *Military service:* U.S. Army, 1946-48.

MEMBER: National Association of Social Workers, American Association on Mental Deficiency.

WRITINGS:

Mental Retardation and Social Action: A Study of the Associations for Retarded Children as a Force for Social Change, C. C Thomas, 1970.
(Editor) *Advocacy for the Legal and Human Rights of the Mentally Retarded,* University of Michigan, 1973.
(Editor with Jane Hamilton) *Gerontological Aspects of Mental Retardation,* Institute of Gerontology, University of Michigan, 1975.
(Contributor) William Cruickshank, editor, *Cerebral Palsy: A Developmental Disability,* 3rd edition, Syracuse University Press, 1976.

Hypnotism Fundamentals, Stranon Educational, 1982.

Writer and producer of television films, "The Emotionally Disturbed Child" and "Mental Retardation: A National Problem." Contributor of articles to professional journals.

SIDELIGHTS: Robert M. Segal once wrote *CA:* "The reason I began writing was the pressure I began to feel from the University. 'Perish or publish' was a real message so I began to share my ideas with my collegues and soon found I enjoyed the writing experience as it forced me to pull together many of my scattered thoughts in the field of mental retardation."*

* * *

SEUSS, Dr.
See GEISEL, Theodor Seuss

* * *

SHIPMAN, Harry L(ongfellow) 1948-

PERSONAL: Born February 20, 1948, in Hartford, Conn.; son of Arthur (a lawyer) and Mary (a painter; maiden name, Dana) Shipman; married Editha Davidson (a cellist), April 10, 1970; children: Alice Elizabeth, Thomas Nathaniel. *Education:* Harvard University, B.A. (summa cum laude), 1969; California Institute of Technology, M.S., 1970, Ph.D., 1971.

ADDRESSES: Home—346 Old Paper Mill Rd., Newark, Del. 19711. *Office*—Department of Physics, University of Delaware, Newark, Del. 19716.

CAREER: Yale University, New Haven, Conn., J. Willard Gibbs Instructor in Astronomy, 1971-73; University of Missouri, St. Louis, assistant professor of physics, 1973-74; McDonnell Planetarium, St. Louis, astronomer, 1973-74; University of Delaware, Newark, assistant professor, 1974-77, associate professor, 1977-81, professor of physics, 1981—, fellow of Center for Advanced Study, 1985-86. Co-creator of radio series "Skyhigh"; guest on radio and television programs, including National Public Radio. Harlow Shapley Visiting Lecturer of the American Astronomical Society, 1976—; member of board of trustees, Mt. Cuba Astronomical Observatory, 1978—. Consultant to National Aeronautics and Space Administration (NASA).

MEMBER: International Astronomical Union, American Astronomical Society (education officer, 1979-85), Federation of American Scientists, American Association of University Professors, National Academy of Sciences, American Association of Physics Teachers, American Association for the Advancement of Science (fellow, 1986), Astronomical Society of the Pacific, Sigma Xi (president of Delaware chapter, 1979-80), Harvard Club of Delaware.

AWARDS, HONORS: Grants from the National Science Foundation, 1974—, Research Corp., 1974-76, University of Delaware Research Foundation, 1975-76, and National Aeronautics and Space Administration, 1976-79, 1981—; Guggenheim fellowship, 1980-81; distinguished scientist award, University of Delaware chapter, Sigma Xi, 1981; silver medal, Council for the Advancement and Support of Education, 1985, and honorable mention, AAAS Westinghouse Journalism awards, 1988, both for radio series "Skyhigh."

WRITINGS:

Black Holes, Quasars, and the Universe, Houghton, 1976, 2nd edition, 1980.
The Restless Universe: An Introduction to Astronomy (includes instructor's manual), Houghton, 1978.

(Contributor) Hugh M. Van Horn and V. Weidemann, editors, *White Dwarfs and Variable Degenerate Stars,* University of Rochester Press, 1979.
(Contributor) M. Kafatos, R. S. Harrington, and S. P. Maran, editors, *The Astrophysics of Brown Dwarfs,* Cambridge University Press, 1986.
Space 2000: Meeting the Challenge of a New Era, Plenum, 1987.
Humans in Space: Twenty-first Century Frontiers, Plenum, 1988.

Contributor to proceedings and to *Encyclopedia of Physical Science and Technology.* Contributor of about eighty articles to scientific journals. Associate editor, *American Journal of Physics,* 1981-84.

WORK IN PROGRESS: Analyzing temperatures, masses, and sizes of some of the smallest known stars.

SIDELIGHTS: Harry L. Shipman wrote *CA:* "Is there life on Mars? When will the sun die? How does the universe evolve? Where did it all begin? These are the questions that excite the contemporary scientist. As a science writer, I seek to involve the intelligent reader in the pursuit of the answers to these and other questions of scientific research."

BIOGRAPHICAL/CRITICAL SOURCES:

PERIODICALS

New York Times Book Review, April 9, 1989.
Wilmington News-Journal, July 25, 1976.

* * *

SINFIELD, Alan 1941-

PERSONAL: Born December 17, 1941, in London, England; son of Ernest and Lucy (Seabright) Sinfield. *Education:* University of London, B.A. (with first-class honors), 1964, M.A., 1967. *Politics:* Socialist. *Religion:* Atheist.

ADDRESSES: Home—4 Clifton Pl., Brighton BN1 3FN, England. *Office*—School of Cultural and Community Studies, Arts Building, University of Sussex, Brighton BN1 9QN, England.

CAREER: University of Sussex, Brighton, England, lecturer, 1965-82, reader in English, 1982—. Beckman Professor at University of California, Berkeley, 1989.

AWARDS, HONORS: D.Litt., University of London, 1987.

WRITINGS:

The Language of Tennyson's "In Memoriam," Basil Blackwell, 1971.
Dramatic Monologue, Methuen, 1977.
Literature in Protestant England 1560-1660, Croom Helm, 1983.
(Editor) *Society and Literature 1945-1970,* Methuen, 1983.
(Editor with Jonathan Dollimore) *Selected Plays of John Webster,* Cambridge University Press, 1983.
(Editor with Dollimore) *Political Shakespeare: New Essays in Cultural Materialism,* Manchester University Press, 1985.
Alfred Tennyson, Basil Blackwell, 1986.
Literature, Politics and Culture in Postwar Britain, Basil Blackwell, 1989, published as *Literature, Politics, Culture: Consensus to Conflict in Postwar Britain,* University of California Press, 1989.

WORK IN PROGRESS: A book on Renaissance literature and society from a cultural materialist perspective; a study of theatre and homosexuality since Oscar Wilde.

SIDELIGHTS: Alan Sinfield told *CA:* "My literary criticism began with a formalist study of Tennyson's poetry in which I experimented with the methods of structural linguistics. Then I moved increasingly towards the belief that literature can be properly understood only in its historical context. I explored this approach in relation to the writing of Shakespeare's time and the current disturbing and provocative religious orthodoxy. As this work was progressing, developments in critical theory, especially those deriving from Marxism, helped me to see that the literary text is always interpreted in the specific historical and political conditions in which it is read, and this led me to write again about Tennyson and Shakespeare, and to pursue a study of the conditions and determinants of intellectual life in our own time."

He adds, "In the more repressive atmosphere in Britain since the 1980s, it seems necessary to address the resources of gay history, culture, and politics, as a way of helping to consolidate and defend a beleaguered minority."

BIOGRAPHICAL/CRITICAL SOURCES:

PERIODICALS

Times Literary Supplement, June 22, 1984, November 14, 1986.

*   *   *

SLITOR, Richard Eaton 1911-

PERSONAL: Surname is pronounced "Sly-tor"; born July 1, 1911, in St. Paul, Minn.; son of Ray Francis (a business executive) and Nelle (Eaton) Slitor; married Louise H. Bean, December 24, 1937; children: Prudence (Mrs. William M. Crozier, Jr.), Deborah Slitor Christiana, Nicholas, Christopher. *Education:* Attended University of Wisconsin, 1928-30; Harvard University, S.B. (magna cum laude), 1932, Ph.D., 1940; Colgate University, M.A., 1934. *Religion:* Episcopalian. *Avocational interests:* Travel, golf, gardening.

ADDRESSES: Home and office—9000 Burning Tree Rd., Bethesda, Md. 20034.

CAREER: Harvard University, Cambridge, Mass., instructor in economics, 1934-41; Mount Union College, Alliance, Ohio, associate professor of economics and chairman of department of economics and business administration, 1941-42; U.S. Treasury Department, Office of Tax Analysis, Washington, D.C., economist, 1942-49, assistant director of tax advisory staff, Secretary of Treasury, 1949-51, taxation specialist, 1951-53, fiscal economist, 1953-61, chief of business taxation staff and assistant director of Office of Tax Analysis, 1961-72, member of missions to Europe, 1963, 1965, 1969, 1970, and to Uruguay, 1969; economic consultant, private practice, 1973—. Federal executive fellow, Brookings Institution, 1963-64; professor of economics, University of Massachusetts—Amherst, 1967-68; board of governors, Federal Reserve System. Consultant on economic issues to numerous commissions and organizations, including United Nations, 1971, Department of Housing and Urban Development, Environmental Protection Agency, Rand Corporation, and National Science Foundation.

MEMBER: International Institute of Public Finance, American Economic Association, American Statistical Association, National Tax Association, Academy of Political Science, Royal Economic Society, Phi Beta Kappa, Chi Phi, Phi Eta Sigma, Harvard Club (Washington, D.C.).

WRITINGS:

The Federal Income Tax in Relation to Housing, U.S. Government Printing Office, 1968.
Taxation of Banks in North Carolina, North Carolina State Tax Study Commission, 1973.

Tax Effects of Urban Growth in Three Cities, Rand Corp., 1973.

Also author of *The Value-added Tax as an Alternative to Corporate Income Tax,* 1963, *The Tax Treatment of Research and Innovative Investment,* 1965, *Corporate Tax Incidence: Economic Adjustments to Differentials under a Two-Tier Tax Structure,* 1966, and of research reports. Contributor to numerous texts, including *Alternatives to Present Federal Taxes,* 1964, *Economics of Information and Knowledge,* Chaucer Press, 1971, *Broad-Based Taxes: New Options and Sources,* 1973, and *Anti-Inflation Proposals,* 1978, and to conferences, symposia, and proceedings. Contributor of about fifty articles and reviews to tax and economics journals.

SIDELIGHTS: Richard Eaton Slitor once told *CA:* "Professional writing is both a form of self-expression and a way of earning a living. Productivity in writing calls for working always under a deadline, even though self-imposed. An essential rule of discipline: let no day pass without completing the minimum stint required to meet the goal. Avoid the unspeakable misery of the author who has left needlessly unfinished business."*

*   *   *

SLOATE, Daniel 1931-

PERSONAL: Born January 27, 1931, in Windsor, Ontario, Canada; son of Carl and Jean (Normile) Sloate. *Education:* University of Western Ontario, B.A., 1953; Sorbonne, University of Paris, D.Phil., 1962.

ADDRESSES: Home—4750 Cote des Neiges, Apt. 31, Montreal, Quebec, Canada H3V 1G2.

CAREER: Institut Superieur d'Interpretariat et de Traduction, Paris, France, lecturer in translation, 1955-69; Faculte libre de Paris, associate professor of English literature, 1955-69; University of Montreal, Montreal, Quebec, associate professor, 1969-1984, professor of linguistics and translation, 1985—. Catholic University of Paris, member of faculty, 1969—.

MEMBER: Literary Translators of America, Union des Ecrivains Quebecois.

WRITINGS:

(Translator) Jean Nicholas Arthur Rimbaud, *Illuminations,* Editions Maisonneuve, 1971, revised edition, Guernica Editions, 1990.
Words in Miniature (poems), Editions Maisonneuve, 1972.
A Taste of Earth, a Taste of Flame (poems), Guernica Editions, 1980.
Dead Shadows (poems), Guernica Editions, 1981.
(Translator) Eloi de Grandmont, *First Secrets* (bilingual edition), Guernica Editions, 1984.
(Translator) Andre Roy, *Mister Desire* (poems), Guernica Editions, 1984.
(Translator) Marie Uquay, *Selected Poems,* Guernica Editions, 1990.
Le Cycle des Comtesses (plays), Guernica Editions, 1990.

Contributor to anthologies, including *Cross/Cut: Contemporary English Quebec Poetry,* edited by Peter Van Toorn and Ken Norris, Vehicule Press, 1982. Contributor of poems to magazines, including *Northwood Journal, Moosehead, Antigonish Review,* and *Matrix.* Member of editorial board, *Meta.*

WORK IN PROGRESS: A Critic's Diary; Plays in the Shape of Nought, a collection of twelve one-act plays; translations of poetry volumes by Jean-Paul Daoust and Claude Peloquin, expected in 1991.

SIDELIGHTS: Daniel Sloate commented: "I am interested in the Italian poets (like Ungaretti, Montale, and Gatto) and the French symbolists. I have attempted to use the prose poem in my writings—the form was, of course, well established in French by Rimbaud, but it has never caught on in English.

"My own poetry is meant to be read aloud. This aspect is never lost from sight (or ear) when I write. My training as an actor has helped me in the public readings I give.

"As a translator of poetry, I know that I am marking the translated text with my own stamp. My translations of Rimbaud, for instance, are definitely, in substance, Rimbaud; in style, or form perhaps, the finished text is uniquely mine.

"Most of my experiences, as with any writer, find their way into my writing. Any literary creation is deeply rooted in one's own biography, no matter how transmuted the material may become.

"The *Critic's Diary* is a spoof of the groves of academe. Lydia Thrippe, the 'heroine,' jots down her impressions of friends and colleagues who roam the groves. Excerpts from it have appeared in the magazine *Breches,* and I hope to publish the completed diary soon."

*　　*　　*

SMITH, Julie 1944-

PERSONAL: Born November 25, 1944, in Annapolis, MD; daughter of Malberry (a lawyer) and Claire (a school counselor; maiden name, Tanner) Smith. *Education:* University of Mississippi, B.A., 1965.

ADDRESSES: Home—Santa Barbara, CA. *Agent*—Charlotte Sheedy, 41 King St., New York, NY 10014.

CAREER: Times-Picayune, New Orleans, LA, reporter, 1965-66; *San Francisco Chronicle,* San Francisco, CA, copy editor, 1967-68, reporter, 1968-79; Invisible Ink (editorial consulting firm), San Francisco, partner, 1979—.

MEMBER: Mystery Writers of America, Private Eye Writers of America, Red Headed League.

WRITINGS:

MYSTERY NOVELS

Death Turns a Trick, Walker & Co., 1982.
The Sourdough Wars, Walker & Co., 1984.
True-Life Adventure, Mysterious Press, 1985.
Tourist Trap, Mysterious Press, 1986.
Huckleberry Fiend, Mysterious Press, 1987.
New Orleans Mourning, St. Martin's, in press.

BIOGRAPHICAL/CRITICAL SOURCES:

PERIODICALS

Globe and Mail (Toronto), January 16, 1988.
Washington Post Book World, March 18, 1990.

*　　*　　*

SOLINGER, Dorothy J(ane) 1945-

PERSONAL: Born September 20, 1945, in Cincinnati, OH; daughter of Nathan (an attorney), and Janet (an arts administrator and educator; maiden name, Weiland) Solinger; married Joel

Falk (a professor of engineering), September 2, 1973 (divorced March, 1981). *Education:* University of Chicago, B.A., 1967; Stanford University, M.A., 1970, Ph.D., 1975. *Politics:* Democrat. *Religion:* Jewish. *Avocational interests:* Classical music, playing the piano, biking, swimming.

ADDRESSES: Home—24 Schubert Ct., Irvine, CA 92715. *Office*—School of Social Sciences, University of California, Irvine, Irvine, CA 92717.

CAREER: University of Pittsburgh, Pittsburgh, PA, associate director of Asian Studies program, 1975-86, adjunct associate professor of political science, 1981-86; University of California, Irvine, associate professor of politics and society, 1986—. University of Michigan, Center for Chinese Studies, visiting fellow, 1985; visiting professor at the University of Michigan, 1986, and Stanford University, 1989-90.

MEMBER: Association for Asian Studies.

AWARDS, HONORS: Hoover Institution on War, Revolution, and Peace national fellow, 1981-82; Woodrow Wilson International Center for Scholars fellow, 1984-85.

WRITINGS:

Regional Government and Political Integration in Southwest China, 1949-1954: A Case Study, University of California Press, 1977.
Chinese Business under Socialism: The Politics of Domestic Commerce, 1949-1980, University of California Press, 1984.
(Editor) *Three Visions of Chinese Socialism,* Westview, 1984.
Industrial Policy in China, 1979-1982: Economic Readjustment in Comparative Perspective, Stanford University Press, 1991.

Contributor to Asian studies and political science journals.

WORK IN PROGRESS: A study of the migrant population in China's cities with the onset of economic reform in the 1980's; a collection of articles on the process of economic reform and the transformation from plan to market in China.

SIDELIGHTS: Dorothy J. Solinger wrote: "My work is fired by a love for and fascination with China. I especially enjoy thinking about China in a comparative context, and thinking about how policy making and implementation in China are similar to or different from those processes in other countries and why. I've lived in Taiwan and Hong Kong, studying the Chinese language and doing research. I speak Chinese with some fluency on topics pertinent to my work. I am beginning a project on China's current 'economic readjustment' program in comparative perspective, using the framework of industrial policy. This included four months in China in 1984 to work on the project by gathering material and conducting interviews."

*　　*　　*

SOLOMON, Robert C(harles) 1942-

PERSONAL: Born September 14, 1942, in Detroit, MI; son of Charles M. (an attorney) and Vita (an artist; maiden name, Petrosky) Solomon. *Education:* University of Pennsylvania, B.A., 1963; University of Michigan, M.A., 1965, Ph.D., 1967. *Religion:* "Peter Pantheist." *Avocational interests:* "Travel, food, love, animals, life."

ADDRESSES: Office—Department of Philosophy, University of Texas, Austin, TX 78712.

CAREER: Princeton University, Princeton, NJ, instructor, 1966-68; University of California, Los Angeles, member of faculty, 1968-69; University of Pittsburgh, Pittsburgh, PA, assistant professor, 1969-71; University of Texas at Austin, 1972—, began as associate professor, currently professor of philosophy. Has held visiting positions at University of Pennsylvania, University of Auckland, and La Trobe University. Consultant, Advanced Management Program, IBM.

MEMBER: American Philosophical Association.

AWARDS, HONORS: Standard Oil teaching award, 1973.

WRITINGS:

From Rationalism to Existentialism: The Existentialists and Their Nineteenth-Century Backgrounds, Harper, 1972.
The Passions, Doubleday, 1976.
Introducing Philosophy: Problems and Perspectives, Harcourt, 1977, 2nd edition, 1981.
History and Human Nature: A Philosophical Review of European History and Culture, 1750-1850, Harcourt, 1979.
Love: Emotion, Myth, and Metaphor, Anchor Press, 1981.
Introducing the Existentialists, Hackett, 1981.
Introducing the German Idealists, Hackett, 1981.
The Big Questions: A Short Introduction to Philosophy, Harcourt, 1982.
In the Spirit of Hegel: A Study of G. W. F. Hegel's Phenomenology of Spirit, Oxford University Press, 1983.
(With Kristine R. Hanson) *Above the Bottom Line: An Introduction to Business Ethics,* Harcourt, 1983.
Ethics: A Brief Introduction, McGraw, 1984.
History and Human Nature: A Philosophical Review of European Philosophy and Culture, University Press of America, 1984.
(With Hanson) *It's Good Business,* Atheneum, 1985.
About Love, Simon & Schuster, 1988.
Continental Philosophy since 1750: The Rise and Fall of the Self, Oxford University Press, 1988.
A Passion for Justice, Addison-Wesley, 1990.

Also writer of several published and recorded songs.

EDITOR

Phenomenology and Existentialism, Harper, 1972.
Nietsche: A Collection of Critical Essays, Anchor Press, 1973.
(And author of introduction) *Existentialism,* Modern Library, 1974.
(With Cheshire Calhoun) *What Is an Emotion?: Classical Readings in Philosophical Psychology,* Oxford University Press, 1984.
(With Mark A. Murphy) *What Is Justice?,* Oxford University Press, 1990.
(With Kathleen M. Higgins) *The Philosophy of (Erotic) Love,* Kansas University Press, 1990.

SIDELIGHTS: In his book *Love: Emotion, Myth and Metaphor,* philosopher Robert C. Solomon sketches a history of love in Western civilization, describes the experience and place of love in man's life, and offers a philosophical reconstruction of man's conception of love. According to *New York Times* reviewer Anatole Broyard, "there hasn't been a good, comprehensive survey of love since Denis DeRougemont's 'Love in the Western World,' which was first published in 1940 and revised in 1956. Now there is. If you read Mr. Solomon's book, you'll be in the enviable position of knowing what you mean when you say 'I love you.'"

BIOGRAPHICAL/CRITICAL SOURCES:

PERIODICALS

Los Angeles Times, March 13, 1980.

New York Times, September 19, 1981.
New York Times Book Review, December 30, 1979, June 26, 1988.
Times Literary Supplement, September 21, 1984, May 27-June 2, 1988.

* * *

SPAETH, Harold J(oseph) 1930-

PERSONAL: Born June 8, 1930, in Oak Park, IL; son of Harold C. (an office manager) and Julia (Quinlan) Spaeth; married E. Jean Daulton, August 16, 1952; children: Harold R., Susan J., Catherine J., Esther E. *Education:* Xavier University, Cincinnati, A.B., 1952, M.A., 1953; University of Cincinnati, Ph.D., 1956. *Religion:* Roman Catholic.

ADDRESSES: Home—5400 Blue Haven Dr., East Lansing, MI 48823. *Office*—Department of Political Science, South Kedzie Hall, Michigan State University, East Lansing, MI 48824.

CAREER: American National Red Cross, Cincinnati, OH, administrative assistant and caseworker, 1953-56; University of Detroit, Detroit, MI, instructor, 1956-59, assistant professor, 1959-62, associate professor of political science, 1962-63; Michigan State University, East Lansing, visiting associate professor, 1963-64, associate professor, 1964-66, professor of political science, 1966—. National Institute for Mental Health fellow, Michigan State University, 1968-71; Computer Institute for Social Science Research fellow, 1971. Consultant to numerous groups and organizations, including legal department of Michigan State AFL-CIO, 1962-63, Public Broadcast Laboratory, National Educational Television, 1967-68, and Learning Systems International, 1972—.

MEMBER: American Political Science Association, American Association for the Advancement of Science, Law and Society Association, Psychometric Society, Midwest Political Science Association (member of executive council, 1966-69), Michigan Council for Education in Politics (member of executive board, 1964-65), Michigan Political Science Association (member of executive board, 1969-72).

AWARDS, HONORS: LL.D., Xavier University, 1976.

WRITINGS:

(With Glendon A. Schubert and others) *Judicial Decision Making,* Free Press, 1963.
(Editor) *The Predicament of Modern Politics,* University of Detroit, 1964.
An Introduction to Supreme Court Decision Making: Cases and Commentary, Chandler Publishing, 1965, revised and enlarged edition, Harper, 1972.
The Warren Court, Chandler Publishing, 1966.
(With David W. Rohde) *Supreme Court Decision Making,* W. H. Freeman, 1976.
(Editor) *Classic and Current Decisions of the United States Supreme Court,* W. H. Freeman, 1978.
Supreme Court Policy Making: Explanation and Prediction, W. H. Freeman, 1979.

Contributor to political science, law, psychology, computer science, and statistics journals.

* * *

SPARTACUS, Deutero
See FANTHORPE, R(obert) Lionel

SPENCER, Elizabeth 1921-

PERSONAL: Born July 19, 1921, in Carrollton, Miss.; daughter of James L. (a farmer) and Mary J. (McCain) Spencer; married John Rusher (an educator), September 29, 1956. *Education:* Belhaven College, B.A., 1942, Vanderbilt University, M.A., 1943. *Politics:* Democrat. *Religion:* Episcopalian.

ADDRESSES: Home—402 Longleaf Dr., Chapel Hill, N.C. 27514.

CAREER: Writer, 1948—. Concordia University, Montreal, Canada, professor of creative writing, 1976-86; University of North Carolina—Chapel Hill, professor of creative writing, 1986—.

MEMBER: National Institute of Arts and Letters.

AWARDS, HONORS: Women's Democratic Committee Award, 1949; National Institute of Arts and Letters award, 1952; Guggenheim fellowship, 1953; Rosenthal Foundation award from American Academy of Arts and Letters, 1956; Kenyon College fellow in fiction, 1957; McGraw-Hill fiction award, 1960; Bryn Mawr College Donnelly fellow, 1962; Henry Bellamann Award for creative writing and LL.D., Southwestern University, both 1968; Award of Merit Medal for the Short Story from American Academy and Institute of Arts and Letters, 1983; National Endowment for the Arts, creative award grant, 1983, senior award grant in literature, 1988; D.L., Concordia University, 1988.

WRITINGS:

Fire in the Morning, Dodd, 1948, reprinted, McGraw, 1968.
This Crooked Way, Dodd, 1952, reprinted, McGraw, 1968.
The Voice at the Back Door, McGraw, 1956, reprinted with an introduction by the author, Time-Life, 1982.
The Light in the Piazza, McGraw, 1960, reprinted, Penguin Books, 1986.
Knights and Dragons, McGraw, 1965.
No Place for an Angel, McGraw, 1967.
Ship Island and Other Stories, McGraw, 1968.
The Snare, McGraw, 1972.
(Contributor) *76: New Canadian Stories,* Oberon, 1976.
The Stories of Elizabeth Spencer, Doubleday, 1981.
Marilee, University Press of Mississippi, 1981.
The Salt Line, Doubleday, 1984.
Jack of Diamonds and Other Stories, Viking, 1988.
"For Lease or Sale" (play), first produced by Playmakers Repertory Company, Chapel Hill, N.C., 1989.

Contributor of stories to *Redbook, New Yorker, Southern Review, Texas Quarterly,* and *Atlantic.*

WORK IN PROGRESS: A novel.

SIDELIGHTS: Elizabeth Spencer's many works of fiction draw upon her experiences as a Southerner, a world traveller, and a college-trained educator. Over a period of more than forty years, Spencer "has produced a number of distinguished works marked for their range in subject and style," to quote *Dictionary of Literary Biography* contributor Peggy Whitman Prenshaw. Spencer was born and raised in Mississippi, but she has spent much of her life in Canada and Italy; *Washington Post Book World* reviewer Garrett Epps finds her "a Southern writer . . . whose art has been shaped by exile."

Indeed, though her settings range from Montreal to New Orleans to Italy, Spencer exhibits a recognizably Southern sensibility. She has drawn critical praise for those qualities that distinguish what *Publishers Weekly* correspondent Amanda Smith calls "the grand tradition of Southern writers"—evocative dialogue, spirited narrative, and a well-defined sense of place. Other critics see her work as broader-based, however. In the *Los Angeles Times,* for instance, Elaine Kendall cites Spencer for "a special attention to idiosyncratic idiom, an intense awareness of social distinctions, and a passionate concern with family ties—a literary attitude that can exist without a shred of Spanish moss or a single black-eyed pea." *Saturday Review* essayist Robert Tallant notes that Spencer "writes with clarity and honesty, often with beauty." The critic adds: "Her people live, and her ear for dialogue is fine. She has a magnificent sense of narrative and the gift of sympathy."

Spencer's parents were prosperous farmers, and she grew up in an environment rich in traditional literature. "We were very family and land oriented," she told *Publishers Weekly.* "Both sides of my family had been in [Mississippi] since the Indians. . . . I was fragile when I was a child, and my mother used to pass the time reading to me, mostly fairy stories and myths." Spencer attended Belhaven College and then went to graduate school at Vanderbilt University, the seat of a resurgence of Southern literature. There, as she began her own creative writing about Mississippi, she confronted the powerful legacy of other living Southern writers, including William Faulkner and Eudora Welty. Spencer told *Mississippi Quarterly* that the mid-1940s "was both a very good and a very bad time to be writing, . . . because the giants in literature were people who were dealing with the same people I wanted to deal with. So these were tremendously strong influences for a young writer to shake off. The problem was both to use the same environment and to search your own identity as a writer. This was extremely difficult." At the same time, she told *Publishers Weekly,* the public's revived interest in works by Southerners helped her to find an audience. "Southern literature was in the ascendancy, and people were looking for new Southern writers as a matter of course," she said, "so I seemed to fill that need."

According to Charles Champlin in the *Los Angeles Times,* Spencer quickly "made her reputation as an uncommonly accurate, sensitive and lyrical writer about her Mississippi origins." The author's first three novels, *Fire in the Morning, This Crooked Way,* and *The Voice at the Back Door,* are all set in her native state. *South Atlantic Quarterly* contributor Nash K. Burger suggests that Spencer "ranges widely in time and society within this milieu; and her narratives, in the Southern and nineteenth-century tradition, are rich with happenings and complicating incidents." In the *New Yorker,* Brendan Gill claims that these early works "give off the characteristic ghostly phosphorescence of something (slavery? the plantation system? the War between the States?) that went bad down there a long time ago and that threatens to go on flickering through the swamps and bayous till Kingdom come."

Spencer's early novels cover recognizable terrain—"the rural South during the first half of the twentieth century," to quote Prenshaw—but they also exhibit an independence in both substance and style. *New York* magazine reviewer Anthony West maintains that Spencer's "limpid and attractive prose, accurate and sharp about tastes, smells, appearances, and emotions . . . pleasingly enlarges one's picture of the South." In the *New York Times Book Review,* Reynolds Price praises Spencer for her "distinctive timbre in which to sing familiar scores," adding that the dangers of monotony "are combated by the serene rhythm and salty compassion with which the voice examines its findings." Other critics cite Spencer for her realistic depictions of race relations, especially in her 1956 work *The Voice at the Back Door.* "No other voice so clearly reminded me of a way of life obscured by outrage and oversimplified by headlines," writes John Malcolm Brinnin in the *Washington Post Book World*. ". . . Like other realists before her, Elizabeth Spencer had written of the life she knew with the kind of bare documentary exactitude which time lifts into metaphor—as though, from the mythological murk of Faulkner territory, she had emerged holding up a crisp photograph negative on which black is visible only in relation to white, and vice versa." Tallant puts it more succinctly. Spencer, he concludes, "knows her South, her country, and she draws it with justice."

In 1953 Spencer left the South for what turned out to be a long sojourn abroad. She lived in Italy for five years, and then married a British businessman and settled in Quebec Province, Canada. Spencer told *Publishers Weekly:* "Italy had a lot to do with changing the focus of my work over the years. Before I went to Italy I thought I would always be encased in the Southern social patterns and lineage and tradition, and if the South changed, then I wanted to be part of that change. I didn't see myself as separated from it. Then, especially after I married, I had to come to terms with a life that was going to be quite separate from that. I got to thinking that the Southerner has a certain mentality, especially Southern women—you can no more change a Southern woman than you can a French woman; they're always going to be French no matter what you do. So I thought that really nothing was going to happen to me as far as my essential personality was concerned, that it could broaden and include more scope and maybe get richer. I looked at that from the standpoint of my characters, that the Southern approach was going to be valued no matter where they found themselves. It seemed to me that there wasn't any need in sitting at home in the cottonfield just to be Southern, that you could be Southern elsewhere, in Florence, or Paris, or anywhere you found yourself."

Spencer has written several books set in Italy, including her well-known work *The Light in the Piazza*. She has also crafted a number of short stories set in Europe or Canada, many of which center upon displaced American women who must meet and deal with quiet crises. Champlin notes that the Spencer stories reveal "those moments when the young girls, the young women, the wives and careerists of the stories come to realize the concealed truth of a situation . . . or the inescapable truths about themselves and their lives—where they were, and have arrived at." Critics praise Spencer's sensitivity to the expatriate condition as well as her ability to create compelling characters. Prenshaw observes that the author "shows keen psychological insight into the irrepressible motive for the nonrational, the human need for mystery and awe, the longing for faith." *Saturday Review* contributor John Fludas calls Spencer's male characters "detailed, vivid, and convincing," concluding however that it is "the women of Elizabeth Spencer, in longing childhood and youth, through marriage and divorce, in Canada or Alabama or her beloved Italy, who have inspired her finely hued perceptions."

According to George Core in the *Washington Post,* Spencer "has worked in the shadow of William Faulkner, Eudora Welty and other leading Southern authors. Now, by dint of long persistence and considerable accomplishment, she may be coming into her own so far as critical recognition is concerned." A number of Spencer's early works have been reprinted, and her 1984 novel, *The Salt Line,* received wide review. In 1986 she was invited to a part-time professorship of creative writing at the University of North Carolina—Chapel Hill; after decades of living elsewhere, she has returned to the South. Kendall, for one, feels that Spencer has always retained her ties to the country of her youth. "For her less ambitious and intrepid people," writes the critic, "geography, like biology, will often be destiny. In all cases, it's the enduring power of place to shape lives that supplies these stories with their internal momentum; Spencer's uncanny understanding of the relationship between place and personality that lends them distinction." In the *Washington Post,* Garrett Epps suggests that the author's voice "is deeply feminine; but at a time when many 'women's books' have taken on a kind of hectoring insecurity, she is at her best rendering the ways in which self-confident women stake out a corner of the world—larger or smaller as luck and talent dictate—and claim it for their own." Kendall concludes: "Just off the monotonous freeways and beyond the tacky strip shopping centers, individuality still thrives, revealed and celebrated by a writer whose vision penetrates the blanket of homogeneity that blurs the American landscape."

BIOGRAPHICAL/CRITICAL SOURCES:

BOOKS

Contemporary Literary Criticism, Volume 22, Gale, 1982.
Dictionary of Literary Biography, Volume 6: *American Novelists since World War II,* Gale, 1980.
French, Warren, editor, *The Fifties: Fiction, Poetry, Drama,* Everett/Edwards, 1970.
Prenshaw, Peggy Whitman, *Elizabeth Spencer,* Twayne, 1985.

PERIODICALS

Books in Canada, March, 1981.
Chicago Tribune, August 24, 1988.
Delta Review, autumn, 1964.
Georgia Review, winter, 1974.
Globe & Mail (Toronto), February 11, 1984, March 23, 1985, January 25, 1986.
Los Angeles Times, February 20, 1981, January 12, 1984, September 16, 1988.
Mississippi Quarterly, fall, 1975, fall, 1976.
Nation, September 25, 1948.
National Review, March 30, 1973.
New Republic, June 26, 1965.
New York, March 22, 1952.
New Yorker, December 15, 1956.
New York Times, January 7, 1984.
New York Times Book Review, November 20, 1960, October 26, 1967, March 1, 1981, January 29, 1984, September 4, 1988.
Notes on Mississippi Writers, fall, 1968, fall, 1970, winter, 1974.
Publishers Weekly, September 9, 1988.
Saturday Review, November 6, 1948, October 20, 1956, February, 1981.
South Atlantic Quarterly, summer, 1964, Volume 63, 1964.
Time, February 13, 1984, August 15, 1988.
Times Literary Supplement, July 17, 1969.
Village Voice, September 20, 1988.
Washington Post, August 9, 1988.
Washington Post Book World, March 8, 1981, May 15, 1983.
Weekend Magazine, August 12, 1978.

—*Sketch by Anne Janette Johnson*

*   *   *

SPIELBERG, Steven 1947-

PERSONAL: Born December 18, 1947, in Cincinnati, Ohio; son of Arnold (a computer engineer) and Leah (a restaurateur) Spielberg; married Amy Irving (an actress), November 27, 1985 (divorced); children: Max. *Education:* Attended California State College (now University), Long Beach.

ADDRESSES: Home—Beverly Hills, California. *Office*—Amblin Entertainment, 100 Universal City Plaza, Universal City, Calif. 91608.

CAREER: Writer and director of motion pictures and television shows. Began at Universal City Studios, Inc., Universal City, Calif., directing television series including "Night Gallery," "Marcus Welby, M.D.," "Owen Marshall," "The Name of the Game," and "Columbo"; directed first television movie, "Duel," 1971. Director of "Jaws," 1975, director of "1941," 1979, director of "Raiders of the Lost Ark," 1981, director and co-producer of "E.T. The Extra-Terrestrial," 1982, co-producer of Segment 1 and Prologue, and director of Segment 2 of "Twilight Zone—The Movie," 1983, director of "Indiana Jones and the Temple of Doom," 1984, director, and co-producer of "The Color Purple," 1985, director, and co-producer of "Empire of the Sun," 1987. Executive producer/co-executive producer of films, including "I Wanna Hold Your Hand," "Back to the Future," "Innerspace," "Who Framed Roger Rabbit?," and "The Land before Time." Producer and segment director of television series "Amazing Stories," 1985. Also appeared in a cameo role in "The Blues Brothers," 1980. Founder of Amblin Entertainment, Universal City.

MEMBER: British Academy of Film and Television Arts (fellow).

AWARDS, HONORS: Won film contest for student film, "Escape to Nowhere"; won prizes at Atlanta Film Festival and Venice Film Festival for student film, "Amblin' "; nomination for best director awards from Academy of Motion Picture Arts and Sciences, 1977, for "Close Encounters of the Third Kind," recipient of Irving G. Thalberg Award from the Academy, 1987, for the body of his work; named best director, Directors Guild, 1985, for "The Color Purple," which also received NAACP Image Awards; named best director, National Board of Review, 1987, for "Empire of the Sun," which was also named best picture; guest of honor at Moving Picture Ball, American Cinematheque, 1989.

WRITINGS:

Close Encounters of the Third Kind (novelization of his film of same title), Dell, 1977.
The Goonies Storybook, Simon & Schuster, 1985.

FILMS

(Author of story) "Ace Eli and Rodger of the Skies," Twentieth Century-Fox, 1973.
(Author of story, and director) "The Sugarland Express," Universal, 1974.
(Author of screenplay, and director) "Close Encounters of the Third Kind," Columbia, 1977.
(Author of screenplay with Michael Grais and Mark Victor, and producer with Frank Marshall) "Poltergeist," Metro-Goldwyn-Mayer/United Artists, 1982.
(Author of story, and producer) "The Goonies," Warner Bros., 1985.

Also author and director of amateur films "Escape to Nowhere," "Firelight," and "Amblin'."

WORK IN PROGRESS: A remake of "A Guy Named Joe," a Preston Sturgis film from the 1940s.

SIDELIGHTS: As many film journalists are fond of pointing out, Steven Spielberg's surname translates from the German into "play mountain," an apt image for a writer/director and producer of some of the most popular (and highest-grossing) movies

in cinema history. A Spielberg production has come to gain the reputation as a visually compelling, multilayered mythic tale, as epitomized by the director's most famous offering, "E.T. the Extra-Terrestrial." Even with his success, Spielberg has faced critical wariness throughout his career. On the one hand, some scholars see in him a modern master of film who invokes the great directors of days gone by in his work—witness the pounding tension of Alfred Hitchcock in Spielberg's "Jaws," the sweep of John Ford in "The Color Purple," the folksiness of Frank Capra in "E.T." On the other hand, some critical voices have raised doubt that Spielberg is a true original as opposed to a mere recapitulator of the past with a collection of high-tech tricks up his sleeve.

Certainly the director had an extraordinary childhood. In interviews, Spielberg describes growing up in a world of humor and fantasy. A relentless practical joker whose favorite victims were his three sisters, the young boy discovered an eight-millimeter camera in the family garage and promptly began his career. From the beginning, the youngster had a knack for getting actors and crew to respond: At Steven's request, a *Time* profile relates, his mother, Leah, "boiled cherries jubilee in a pressure cooker until it exploded, and Steven filmed the messy crimson walls and floor." Spielberg has credited his accommodating family partly for his success. Though he did know some bad times—including his parents' divorce when Steven was twelve—the filmmaker remembers events like the time his family's rabbi paid an unexpected visit on a day when "we'd bought three live lobsters for dinner," as he says in another *Time* article, noting that "of course, lobster is not kosher. . . . Mom panicked and threw the live crustaceans at me; I had to hide them under my bed. Then the rabbi came to my room to see how I was doing. You could hear the lobsters clicking and clacking each other with their tails. . . . The minute the rabbi left, my mom and I gleefully threw the lobsters into a pot of boiling water and ate them."

In the same article, Spielberg admits that he had "all the fears that a lot of kids have: of a society of the netherworld living under my bed, of monsters living in the closet waiting to suck me in and do terrible things to me." At school "I felt like a real nerd, the skinny, acne-faced wimp who gets picked on by big football jocks all the way home . . . I hated school. From age twelve or thirteen I knew I wanted to be a movie director, and I didn't think that science or math or foreign languages were going to help me turn out the little 8-mm sagas I was making to avoid homework."

By the time Spielberg was out of high school, he was already winning student awards for his short films. One of them, "Firelight," even had a real premiere at a local movie theatre. But college held little appeal for the young man, who preferred to spend his days on a particular movie lot. "I remember taking a bus tour through Universal Studios," Spielberg tells *Rolling Stone* interviewer Lynn Hirschberg. "I remember getting off the bus; we were all let off to go to the bathroom. Instead, I hid between two soundstages until the bus left, and then I wandered around for three hours. I went back there every day for three months. I walked past the guard every day, waved at him, and he waved back. I always wore a suit and carried a briefcase, and he assumed I was some kid related to some mogul, and that was that."

Persistence finally paid off. At twenty, after an executive viewed some of Spielberg's films, the young director was signed to a seven-year contract for Universal television. Journeyman work in several weekly series led to Spielberg's first television movie, "Duel." The story of a motorist pursued by an unseen driver in a menacing truck, the film gained much critical attention. In fact, according to Hirschberg, "Duel" was released as a feature in Europe and Japan and became a worldwide hit.

After earning a story credit on the 1973 film "Ace Eli and Rodger of the Skies," which failed at the box office, Spielberg embarked on his first feature directorial project, "The Sugarland Express." Goldie Hawn and William Atherton starred in this tale of parents who defy authority to regain custody of their child. In this case, defying authority manifested itself in a number of car chases and other action scenes, prompting critic Pauline Kael of *New Yorker* to note that the movie "is mostly about cars: Spielberg is a choreographic virtuoso with cars. He patterns them; he makes them dance and crash and bounce back. He handles enormous configurations of vehicles; sometimes they move so sweetly you think he must be wooing them." And yet Kael also saw in the novice filmmaker a gift for "very free-and-easy, American" humor, speculating in those early days that Spielberg "could be that rarity among directors, a born entertainer—perhaps a new generation's Howard Hawks." Less impressed was *New York Times* reviewer Stephen Farber, who maintains that in "The Sugarland Express" "everything is underlined; Spielberg sacrifices narrative logic and character consistency for quick thrills and easy laughs."

This kind of polemic critical response, which characterizes virtually every film Spielberg has directed, apparently has had no effect on the commercial success of his projects. That became apparent after Spielberg's second picture was released in the summer of 1975. Based upon a best-selling novel, cast with mostly unknown actors, and filmed with a daunting (for 1975) $8 million budget, "Jaws" exploded into American theatres and instantly became the most talked-about movie of its time—making its 26-year-old director a star in his own right.

In relating the ultimate "fish story"—about how a homicidal great white shark terrorizes an American beachfront community—Spielberg faced unprecedented challenges in filming "Jaws" on Martha's Vineyard in Massachussets. As a *Time* cover story quotes him, the director comments that "nobody thought much about the currents or anything at all about the waves." A strong Atlantic tow "would cause equipment boats to drift away," the article continues. "Water color would change, the rhythm of the waves would fluctuate." What problems Mother Nature neglected, the mechanical shark, nicknamed "Bruce," readily provided. There were, in fact, three mechanical sharks, each created to perform differently, and all "fairly programmed for mishap," as the *Time* article puts it. "Bruce sank when he made his debut. During his second test on water his hydraulic system exploded. . . . A special makeup man in scuba gear would plunge into the ocean to add more blood to Bruce's teeth and gums or administer a touch-up to his tender plastic tissue. Bruce's skin tended to discolor and deteriorate in the salt water."

But any doubt about Bruce's performing abilities—or Spielberg's—faded when "Jaws" became the highest-grossing movie to its date. As the *Time* report points out, this achievement is especially notable considering that it was released during a season full of action/adventure and "disaster" films. "What sets *Jaws* apart from most of the other ceiling busters," says the article, "and makes it a special case, like *The Godfather,* is that it is quite a good movie. For one thing, it is mercifully free of the padding—cosmic, comic, cultural—that so often mars 'big' pictures. In that sense, the movie is very like its subject. If the great white shark that terrorizes the beaches of an island summer colony is one of nature's most efficient killing machines, *Jaws* is an efficient entertainment machine."

"The right things certainly happen in *Jaws,*" remarks Gordon Gow in a *Films and Filming* review. "At given moments, the images before us lead to *frissons* of dread anticipation. The pulses pound. Excitement escalates. And by climax time, when it is impossible to disbelieve that one of the leading actors . . . is actually being swallowed alive by a gigantic shark in an unnerving series of gulps, we are watching movie magic of the highest order. Trickery has mastered the illusion of truth." Though many writers, like Gow, have noted the mythic elements in "Jaws," one critic, Jane E. Caputi, sees the film differently from the rest. To this *Journal of Popular Film* essayist, the shark "actually represents the primordial female and her most dreaded aspects." Noting that "Jaws" was released in France with its title translated as "The Teeth of the Sea," Caputi goes on to say that such an image "can easily lead us, not only to the idea of castration, but to the consideration of two related themes—the mythological motif of the *vagina dentata* (the toothed, i.e. castrating vagina) and the male obsessive fear of abortion."

However popular opinion varied, no one could discount Spielberg's newfound clout within the Hollywood community. He even weathered what he called "a 'Jaws' backlash," the most apparent aspect of which occurred when Spielberg was snubbed by the motion picture academy when the best-director nominations came out. "It hurt me because I felt ['Jaws'] was a director's movie," he continues in a *Newsweek* interview with Jack Kroll. "The same people who had raved about it began to doubt its artistic value as soon as it began to bring in so much money." This would not be the only time Spielberg would be the center of an Oscar controversy.

Many wondered how the young filmmaker could top the commercial appeal of "Jaws." Spielberg answered the challenge in 1977 with another blockbuster, "Close Encounters of the Third Kind." The title was an unfamiliar phrase to American ears, but soon everyone knew that a close encounter of the third kind meant making physical contact with alien life forms. Mainstream films had long portrayed aliens as menacing monsters from beyond; to Spielberg, the thought of interplanetary co-existence held a much more benevolent promise. In a *Film Comment* article by Mitch Tuchman, Spielberg recalls hearing about some women in Georgia "who had a UFO encounter of the first kind, where they saw a lighted vehicle passing low over their heads, and written in lights along the starboard side were the letters 'U,' 'F,' 'O.' Now 99.0 percent of the people who hear this story are going to say here are two very misinformed individuals, who obviously made it up. They were so naive about the phenomena, that that's what they thought. . . . In fact, an otherworldly intelligence has come all this way perhaps to observe growing up in the twentieth century." Spielberg's inspiration resulted in the story of how a series of UFO sightings in Indiana leads to revelation and awe. The sweeping satellites draw in a number of people—a group of scientists, a family man, and a five-year-old boy with his mother. The ultimate landing of the brightly colored "Mother Ship" at Devil's Tower in Wyoming bestows a message of hope and goodwill that helped vault "Close Encounters of the Third Kind" to the top-ten moneymakers and brought further acclaim for the director.

Many people considered "Close Encounters" Spielberg's most personal film. But underlying critics' admiration of the filmmaker's technical gifts was the charge of audience manipulation. In her *New Yorker* column, Kael calls the work "the most innocent of all technological-marvel movies, and one of the most satisfying." And yet she also finds that "Close Encounters" shows "an excess of kindness—an inability (or, perhaps, unwillingness) to perceive the streak of cowardice and ignorance and confusion in the actions of the authorities who balk the efforts of the visionaries to reach their goal." In John Simon's opinion, the technology overpowers the characters. As he tells *Take One*, "In Spielberg's lopsided world, people and their relationships do not begin to make sense. . . . [Humans] have been turned into objects, while objects are accorded maximal importance."

More than one writer has sensed the religious overtones in "Close Encounters." To B. H. Fairchild, in a *Journal of Popular Film* essay, "almost everyone both in and out of [the movie appears] to be waiting for some kind of miraculous salvation, an escape, an awakening, from the bad dream of social stagnation and middle-class malaise which the first half of Spielberg's movie so emphatically reminds us of." Going on, Fairchild notes "three spatial dimensions in *Close Encounters:* not just outer space, but also inner space—mystical and theological consciousness. The face of this consciousness is appropriately innocent, and in this way the film is distinctly Romantic: each vision of the Beyond is a vision of innocence."

"Spielberg sings to innocence," echoes *Rolling Stone* reporter Chris Hodenfield, who interviewed the director. "We see one dazzled face reverberate in three people—a baby boy, a synthesizer musician whose duet with the extraterrestrials is the first dialogue, and finally the Distant Stranger." Hodenfield sees beauty behind the technology that peppers "Close Encounters": Spielberg "draws every scene in intricate detail before shooting. Aided by state-of-the-art cameras with computer memories, he superimposed layers and layers of shots on film, giving the appearance of absolute reality to all manner of weird monkey business. To an Alabama landscape he added a sky full of stars, miniature trees and many Great Beings. The colossal Mother Ship was inspired by an oil refinery in Bombay which he saw all lit up one night." As the director himself tells Hodenfield, his dedication to effects detail stems from his early dissatisfaction with sci-fi epics. "You know, you could go back to class on Monday after everyone's seen a movie over the weekend. 'How'd you like the film?' '*Ah*, that was kind of *fakey*. Those weren't dinosaurs, those were big lizards with things glued on their backs. That wasn't a brontosaur, that was a Gila monster.' "

"Close Encounters" inspired a level of audience loyalty that "Jaws" had merely hinted at. In 1980, Spielberg released a re-edited "Special Edition" of "Close Encounters" that included scenes of Everyman skywatcher Roy Neary entering the Mother Ship to begin a new life among the extraterrestrials, who have taken other earthlings with them in the past. Though many critics suggested that perhaps the original "Close Encounters" was better left untampered with, this new emphasis upon the aliens' characters foretold the theme of Spielberg's biggest film yet, and the number-one box office draw of all time, "E.T. the Extraterrestrial."

The filming of "E.T." was clouded in secrecy; no publicity photos of the alien star were released prior to the movie's opening in 1982. The germ of the story, according to Jim Calio in a *People* article, came to Spielberg in 1980 when he was in the Tunisian desert making "Raiders of the Lost Ark," a homage to old-time adventure serials he made in collaboration with "Star Wars" director George Lucas. "I was kind of lonely at the time," Spielberg tells Calio. "My girlfriend was back in Los Angeles. I remember saying to myself, 'What I really need is a friend I can talk to—somebody who can give me *all* the answers.' " That friend turned out to be a nameless visitor from the heavens who is left stranded on Earth when his spaceship leaves without him. Finding his way into a typical suburban American neighborhood, the little alien—"a squat-looking creature with an expandable neck that sort of looks like an eggplant on a stick," according to *Chicago Tribune* critic Gene Siskel—meets a lonely boy, Elliott. Once the two overcome their mutual apprehension, they become great allies.

Though Elliott initially manages to keep E.T.'s presence a secret from his mother, the alien's existence soon becomes known to a cadre of government scientists and officials who descend upon the family intending to study the visitor at a dangerously intense level. Meanwhile, the boy, his siblings, and their friends attempt to find a way to help E.T. contact his own kind (resulting in the most famous line of the film, "E.T. phone home"). After an inevitably tense chase sequence, E.T. and Elliott triumph. Spielberg felt free to share in the triumph, albeit on a more personal level. "Action is wonderful," he remarks in a *People* interview, "but while I was doing *Raiders* [*of the Lost Ark*] I felt I was losing touch with the reason I became a moviemaker—to make stories about people and relationships. ['E.T.'] is the first movie I ever made for myself."

Gary Arnold, writing in *Washington Post*, recognizes the director's personal contributions. The film, he says, "is essentially a spiritual autobiography, a portrait of the filmmaker as a typical suburban kid set apart by an uncommonly fervent, mystical imagination. It comes out disarmingly funny, spontaneous, big-hearted." In the same article, Arnold sees in "E.T." thematic ties with other famous films. He notes that the screenwriter, Melissa Mathison, also wrote the script for Carroll Ballard's award-winning movie "The Black Stallion," a film that Spielberg admired, and that many details in the boy-and-his-horse epic mirror the relationship between Elliott and the alien in Spielberg's film. The plot for "E.T.," though, says Arnold, "owes more to pictures like 'Whistle down the Wind' and 'Escape from Witch Mountain.' [The alien] enlists the aid of the children concealing him to reestablish contact with the departed spaceship. . . . Despite the devotion of his little helpers, E.T. is threatened in two respects—his physical condition seems to deteriorate the longer he stays on Earth . . . and the hunters continue to close in on his hiding place."

Other works, from "Bambi" to "Peter Pan," have been cited as "E.T." influences but *New York Times* reviewer Vincent Canby offers one more out of the ordinary: Spielberg and Mathison, he writes, "have taken the tale of Dorothy and her frantic search for the unreliable Wizard of Oz and turned it around, to tell it from the point of view of the Scarecrow, the Cowardly Lion and the Tin Woodman. Dorothy has become E.T., Kansas is outer space, and Oz is a modern, middle-class real-estate development in California." Canby joined most other critics and viewers in hailing "E.T. the Extraterrestrial" as a movie that "may become a children's classic of the space age." However, the outpouring of critical and popular acclaim didn't seem to penetrate "the Spielberg jinx," as some called it. Thus when Oscar time came around, both "E.T." and Spielberg were snubbed, to the astonishment of many moviegoers. Insiders speculated that perhaps the Academy was "punishing" the director for producing so many blockbusters. Professional jealousy was also a theory.

Ironically, the same year that brought the gentle, life-affirming extraterrestrial also brought another Spielberg film (one that he wrote and produced, but did not direct) that looks to be the flip side of "E.T." "Poltergeist," directed by Tobe Hooper, dispenses with benign visitors in favor of malicious ghosts tormenting an archetypically Spielbergian American family. As the filmmaker relates to Michiko Kakutani in a *New York Times* piece, " 'Poltergeist' is what I fear and 'E.T.' is what I love. One is about suburban evil and the other is about suburban good. I had different motivations in both instances: in 'Poltergeist,' I wanted to terrify and I also wanted to amuse—I tried to mix the laughs and screams together. 'Poltergeist' is the darker side of my nature—it's me when I was scaring my younger sisters half to death when we were growing up—and 'E.T.' is my optimism about the future and my optimism about what it was like to grow up in Arizona and New Jersey."

Not every Spielberg film has become a classic or even a success—his 1979 comedy "1941" drew critical sneers and failed at the box office. And for all his reputation as a Hollywood *wunderkind,* the director faced charges that he would not, or could not, make a movie specifically for adults. Spielberg answered his critics in 1986 with his most controversial film to date, "The Color Purple." The controversy began when Spielberg announced his involvement with Alice Walker's Pulitzer Prize-winning novel. Some wondered about the appropriateness of a white director at the helm of such a powerful black-consciousness story. (The screenwriter, Menno Meyjes, also is white.) And then there are the charges of tampering with the intent of the novel.

"The Color Purple" tells the story of one woman's coming of age in the rural south in the early years of this century. Celie, with the triple burdens of being black, female and poor in a racist society, endures a brutal marriage and continual heartache until she meets chanteuse Shug Avery, a woman who is everything Celie is not. In the novel, Celie and Shug's friendship takes a physical turn, an aspect Spielberg avoids in his film version. In a *Film Comment* essay, Marcia Pally observes that "in Spielberg's whitewash, Shug's initial dislike of Celie inexplicably changes to charm, and their friendship proceeds without the awakening of passion."

Though the director's vision of "The Color Purple" did win some raves for its sweep and for its fine performances, Pally, for one, notes dissatisfaction with even the setting of the film. "One wonders why Spielberg chose to adapt Walker's novel for his first 'adult' film. Not only was its central relationship unacceptable to him; he renovated the entire setting. A tale about poverty, racism, incest, wife beating, and ceaseless labor became, under his direction, a *Wizard of Oz* for pickaninnies. Most yuppies I know would sell their condos to live in the likes of Celie's house, with its polished wood interiors, rugs, and china. The land around it is lush, fruitful—and dotted with flowers of purple. And no one ever has to tend it." "*The Color Purple* is vintage Spielberg," acknowledges David Blum in a *New York* article that implies "vintage" Spielberg may not be a compliment in this case. "[The work suggests] the conflict between the little people and the big, evil forces of society that has dominated all his movies. The character that Celie, as played by Whoopie Goldberg, most resembles is E.T. Both are outsiders in a strange, cruel world, struggling for freedom." And, Blum concludes, "as with all his movies, Spielberg managed to bring *The Color Purple* to a rousing, uplifting conclusion in the simplest way possible."

The "Color Purple" controversy ignited anew at Academy Awards time, in a rousing upset. The film garnered a record-tying eleven nominations, including best picture. But Spielberg, though he had been voted Best Director of 1985 by the Directors Guild, was not even nominated in that category for the Academy Awards. And then, in another upset, "The Color Purple" failed to win a single Oscar in any of its categories. Popular wisdom held that the Spielberg jinx had surfaced again.

Since 1980, the director has been serving double duty as the head of his own production company, Amblin Entertainment. Under the Amblin banner, Spielberg has been involved with a number of box-office hits and misses. As Blum points out in his article,

such Amblin releases as "Young Sherlock Holmes" and "Gremlins" are nothing if not reworkings of authentic Spielberg epics like "Indiana Jones and the Temple of Doom" and "E.T." But Amblin scored a few genuine, original successes in films like "Back to the Future" and "Who Framed Roger Rabbit?," both of which were directed by Spielberg protege Robert Zemeckis.

The filmmaker returned to the screen in 1987 with "Empire of the Sun." Based on a true story by J. G. Ballard, the movie recounts the adventures of a young British boy serving internment in Shanghai during World War II. The film earned fair reviews and box office attendance, with praise being singled out for Christian Bale, the actor who portrays the boy in the tradition of such Spielbergian child-heroes as Elliott in "E.T." And 1987 also saw the Spielberg jinx lifted, after a fashion, as the Academy chose to bestow one of its highest honors, the Irving J. Thalberg Award, upon the director. The award recognizes a distinguished body of work, and in accepting it Spielberg joined the company of past honorees like Alfred Hitchcock and Walt Disney, two of his childhood idols.

The continuing popularity of Spielberg reflects the tastes of his target audience—young children and their young parents—in the opinion of *Chicago Tribune* writer Dave Kehr. "Spielberg's first hits struck the baby boomers at a precise, very difficult stage in their development. Though cresting into adulthood, the baby boomers of the late '70s—a middle-to-late-20s age group—still wanted to prolong the golden adolescence they had experienced in the prosperous '60s." But the filmmaker's works "also function on a deeper level," says Kehr. "In film after film the same pattern is repeated: A weak, unstable family, burdened with an absent or irresponsible father, is strengthened and saved through the intervention of a supernatural force—a force that can be either sweet and benign ('E.T.,' 'Close Encounters') or evil and destructive ('Jaws,' 'Poltergeist'). There is in these films a yearning for authority, a powerful need to feel protected and watched over (or, in the dark films, a demand for discipline and strength) that has an obvious nostalgic appeal for young adults freshly booted out of the family nest." To his associates, Spielberg represents the new Hollywood, "a regular guy whose detractors, if any, all seem to have been abducted by aliens," as *Newsweek*'s Jack Kroll puts it. A man who believes in loyalty and friendship, Spielberg is often described as a family type even at work. As Robert Zemeckis comments to Kroll, "Sure he drives a Porsche, but he'll still pull into a 7-11 and buy a Slurpie. How much more regular can you get?"

BIOGRAPHICAL/CRITICAL SOURCES

BOOKS

Collins, T., *Steven Spielberg, Creator of E.T.,* Dillon, 1983.
Contemporary Literary Criticism, Volume 20, Gale, 1982.
Farber, S., *Outrageous Conduct,* Arbor House, 1988.
Kael, Pauline, *Reeling,* Little, Brown, 1974.
Kael, Pauline, *When the Lights Go Down,* Holt, 1980.
Leather, M., *The Picture Life of Steven Spielberg,* Watts, 1984.
Mabery, D. L., *Steven Spielberg,* Lerner, 1986.
Monaco, James, *American Film Now: The People, the Power, the Money, the Movies,* Oxford University Press, 1979.
Mott, D. R., *Steven Spielberg,* Twayne, 1982.

PERIODICALS

Chicago Tribune, December 23, 1979, June 4, 1982, June 11, 1982, December 11, 1987, January 10, 1988.
Commonweal, June 20, 1975.
Film Comment, June, 1978, May, 1982, April, 1986.
Films and Filming, January, 1976.

Journal of Popular Film, Volume 6, no. 4, 1978.
Los Angeles Times, June 4, 1982, May 21, 1984, May 23, 1984, December 16, 1986.
Maclean's, June 4, 1984.
Monthly Film Bulletin, July, 1974.
New Republic, December 10, 1977, September 6, 1980.
Newsweek, April 8, 1974, June 23, 1975, November 21, 1977, June 4, 1984.
New York, November 7, 1977, January 7, 1980, June 15, 1981, June 4, 1982, March 24, 1986.
New Yorker, March 18, 1974, November 28, 1977, September 1, 1980.
New York Times, April 28, 1974, November 13, 1977, December 23, 1979, June 7, 1981, May 30, 1982, June 11, 1982, January 10, 1988.
North American Review, fall, 1978.
People, July 29, 1981, August 23, 1982, November 1, 1982, May 5, 1986.
Rolling Stone, January 26, 1978, July 22, 1982, July 19, 1984, October 24, 1985.
Saturday Review, June, 1981.
Sight and Sound, winter, 1972, summer, 1978.
Take One, January, 1978.
Time, June 23, 1975, May 31, 1982, June 4, 1984, July 15, 1985.
Washington Post, May 31, 1975, June 6, 1982, February 9, 1987.*

—*Sketch by Susan Salter*

*   *   *

SPINNER, Stephanie 1943-

PERSONAL: Born November 16, 1943, in Davenport, Iowa; daughter of Ralph (a businessman) and Edna (Lowry) Spinner. *Education:* Bennington College, B.A., 1964.

ADDRESSES: Home—25 Wood Lane, Woodmere, N.Y. 11598.

CAREER: Free-lance editor.

WRITINGS:

First Aid, Golden Press, 1968.
(Adaptor) *Popeye* (juvenile; based on the motion picture of same title), Random House, 1980.
(Adaptor) Bram Stoker, *Dracula,* Random House, 1982.
How Raggedy Ann Was Born (juvenile), Random House, 1982.
(Adaptor) Carlo Collodi (under pseudonym of Carlo Lorenzini) *The Adventures of Pinocchio* (juvenile), Random House, 1983.
The Mummy's Tomb (juvenile), Bantam, 1985.

EDITOR

Rock Is Beautiful: An Anthology of American Lyrics, 1953-1968, Dell, 1969.
Feminine Plural: Stories by Women about Growing Up, Macmillan, 1972.
Live and Learn: Stories about Students and Their Teachers (young adult), Macmillan, 1973.
Motherhood: Stories by Women about Motherhood, Dell, 1978.
Walter Farley, *The Black Stallion Returns,* Random House, 1983.
Bonnie Bogart, *Escape from the Monster Ship* (juvenile), Random House, 1986.
Cathy East-Dubowski, *The Ring, the Witch, and the Crystal* (juvenile), Random House, 1986.
East-Dubowski, *The Shadow Stone* (juvenile), Random House, 1986.

The Red Ghost (juvenile), Random House, 1986.
Lee Martin, *The Invisible Castle* (juvenile), Random House, 1986.
Megan Stine and H. William Stine, *The Spear of Azzurra* (juvenile), Random House, 1986.
Ellen Weiss, *The Pirates of Tarnoonga* (juvenile), Random House, 1986.
Martine Lesly, *Morgan Swift and the Riddle of the Sphinx* (young adult), Random House, in press.
Susan Saunders, *Morgan Swift and the Lake of Diamonds,* Random House, in press.

AVOCATIONAL INTERESTS: Horses, painting, Tai Chi, travel.*

*   *   *

SPITZ, Lewis W(illiam) 1922-

PERSONAL: Born December 14, 1922, in Bertrand, NE; son of Lewis William and Pauline (Griebel) Spitz; married Edna Marie Huttenmaier, August 14, 1948; children: Stephen, Philip. *Education:* Attended St. Paul's College, Concordia, MO, 1940-42, and University of Chicago, summers, 1943-48; Concordia College, A.B., 1944; Concordia Seminary, M.Div., 1947; University of Missouri, M.A., 1948; Harvard University, Ph.D., 1954. *Politics:* Republican. *Religion:* Lutheran.

ADDRESSES: Home—827 Lathrop Dr., Stanford, CA 94305. *Office*—History Department, Stanford University, Stanford, CA 94305.

CAREER: University of Missouri—Columbia, instructor, 1953-54, assistant professor, 1954-56, associate professor, 1957-60; Stanford University, Stanford, CA, associate professor, 1960-64, professor of history, 1964—. Fulbright scholar, University of Vienna, 1952-53; Fulbright professor, Institute for European History, Mainz, Germany, 1960-61; senior fellow, Princeton Institute for Advanced Study, 1979-80.

MEMBER: American Academy of Arts and Sciences (fellow, 1987), American Historical Association, American Society for Reformation Research (president), Renaissance Society of America (member of council), Society for Religion in Higher Education, American Society of Church History (president), Concordia Historical Institute, Luther-Gesellschaft.

AWARDS, HONORS: Guggenheim fellow, 1956-57; Huntington Library fellow, 1959; American Council of learned Societies fellow, 1960-61; Danforth Associates Award for Teaching, 1964-65; National Endowment for the Humanities fellow.

WRITINGS:

Conrad Celtis: The German Arch-Humanist, Harvard University Press, 1957.
(Editor with Helmut T. Lehmann) *Luther's Works: Career of the Reformer IV,* Muhlenberg, 1960.
(Editor) *The Reformation—Material or Spiritual?,* Heath, 1962, 2nd edition published as *The Reformation: Basic Interpretations,* 1972.
The Religious Renaissance of the German Humanists, Harvard University Press, 1963.
(Editor with Richard Lyman) *Major Crises in Western Civilization,* two volumes, Harcourt, 1965.
Life in Two Worlds: William Sihler, Concordia, 1966.
(Editor) *The Protestant Reformation,* Prentice-Hall, 1966.
The Renaissance and the Reformation Movements, two volumes, Rand McNally, 1971.
(Editor) *The Northern Renaissance,* Prentice-Hall, 1972.

(Editor with Wenzel Lohff) *Discord, Dialogue, and Concord: Studies in the Lutheran Reformation's Formula of Concord,* Fortress, 1972.
(Editor) *Humanismus und Reformation in der deutschen Geschichte,* de Gruyter, 1981.
The Protestant Reformation, 1517-1559: The Rise of Modern Europe, Harper, 1984.

Contributor to books, including *Church and State under God,* 1964, and to professional and religious journals. Member of editorial boards, *Journal of Modern History* and *Archive for Reformation History.*

WORK IN PROGRESS: An edition of Johannes Sturm's educational treatises.

SIDELIGHTS: In *The Protestant Reformation, 1517-1559: The Rise of Modern Europe,* Lewis W. Spitz "has combined a fine writing style with exhaustive scholarship in presenting still another account of one of the pivotal events of Western civilization," Harry Trimborn notes in the *Los Angeles Times Book Review.* "The great strength of this book," according to *Choice* reviewer F. J. Baumgartner, "is its presentation of Martin Luther . . . [which] is warmly sympathetic, very well informed, and thoroughly detailed. The section on Lutheranism could stand as a first rate work in its own right." Joachim Whaley similarly praises Spitz's treatment of Luther, stating in the *New York Times Book Review* that "Spitz is most impressive when he writes about ideas. He is often superb when locating the genesis of Luther's ideas in the Sargasso Sea of late medieval philosophy [and] his discussion of Zwingli and Calvin is equally stimulating." As Mark Noll concludes in *Christianity Today, The Protestant Reformation,* "in short, is history at its best—broadly researched, skillfully written, judiciously argued, and also spiritually insightful."

BIOGRAPHICAL/CRITICAL SOURCES:

PERIODICALS

Choice, June, 1985.
Christianity Today, October 4, 1985.
Los Angeles Times Book Review, May 12, 1985.
New York Times Book Review, February 24, 1985.

*   *   *

STANFORD, Ann   1916-1987

PERSONAL: Born November 25, 1916, in La Habra, CA; died July 12, 1987, in Los Angeles, CA; daughter of Bruce (an oil well tools dealer) and Rose (Corrigan) Stanford; married Ronald Arthur White (an architect), September 18, 1942; children: Rosanna Norton, Patricia Jane, Susan Lora, Bruce. *Education:* Stanford University, B.A., 1938; University of California, Los Angeles, M.A. (journalism), 1958, M.A. (English), 1961, Ph.D., 1962. *Politics:* Democrat. *Religion:* Protestant.

CAREER: University of California, Los Angeles, executive secretary for Foreign Press Awards, 1957-58, acting instructor in journalism, 1958-59, extension division instructor in poetry workshop, 1960-61; California State University, Northridge, assistant professor, 1962-66, associate professor, 1966-68, professor of English, 1968-87. Editorial consultant, Los Angeles County council on in-service education, 1958-59; consultant to UCLA department of journalism, 1961-64; poetry consultant, Huntington Library, San Marino, CA, beginning, 1976; poetry critic, Pacific Coast Writers Conference, 1964-66 and 1968; poetry juror, James D. Phelan Awards in Literature, 1966; juror,

Hopwood Awards, 1973, Bush Foundation fellowships, 1977 and 1980, and American Poetry Series, 1979.

MEMBER: Poetry Society of America (former regional vice-president), Modern Language Association of America, Wallace Stevens Society (member of advisory board), PEN, Phi Beta Kappa.

AWARDS, HONORS: James D. Phelan fellowship in literature, 1938-39; Yaddo fellowship, 1957 and 1967; Commonwealth Club of California silver medal in poetry, 1958, for *Magellan: A Poem to Be Read by Several Voices,* 1978, for *In Mediterranean Air,* and 1986, for *The Countess of Forli: A Poem for Voices;* Browning prizes and first award for manuscript of *Magellan,* University of Redlands; Borestone Mountain Poetry Award, 1960, for poem "Pandora"; National Endowment for the Arts grant, 1967 and 1974; Shelley Memorial Award, Poetry Society of America, 1969; National Institute and American Academy award in literature, 1972; Alice Fay di Castagnola Award, Poetry Society of America, 1976, for *In Mediterranean Air.*

WRITINGS:

POEMS

In Narrow Bound, Alan Swallow, 1943.
The White Bird, Alan Swallow, 1949.
The Weathercock, Talisman Press, 1956.
Magellan: A Poem to Be Read by Several Voices, Talisman Press, 1958.
The Descent, Viking, 1970.
Climbing Up to Light: Eleven Poems, Magpie Press, 1973.
In Mediterranean Air, Viking, 1977.
The Countess of Forli: A Poem for Voices, Orirana Press, 1985.

OTHER

(Editor and translator) *The Bhagavad Gita: A New Verse Translation,* Herder, 1970.
(Editor) *The Women Poets in English: An Anthology,* McGraw, 1973.
Anne Bradstreet, the Worldly Puritan: An Introduction to Her Poetry, Burt Franklin, 1974.
(Editor with Pattie Cowell) *Critical Essays on Anne Bradstreet,* G. K. Hall, 1983.

OTHER

Also author of unpublished libretto, "The Lucky Dollar." Co-founder and co-editor, "Renaissance Editions" series, California State University, Northridge, 1968-70. Poetry reviewer, *Los Angeles Times,* 1958-68. Contributor of poetry and articles to *Sewanee Review, Yankee, Poetry, Western Humanities Review, Hudson Review, New Yorker, Southern Review, New York Times Book Review,* and *Atlantic.* Editor, *Uclan Review,* 1961-64; member of editorial board, *Early American Literature,* 1971-73.

SIDELIGHTS: "It is important to know where a poet lives," Ann Stanford once told *CA,* "for the region, the culture surrounds the poetry, gives it a context from which the imagination can move. I live in Southern California, in the chaparral-covered hills that are subject to drenching rains in winter and sudden fires in summer—a dramatic landscape. In such a place it is easy to imagine the myths and tales of the Mediterranean region recreated, for the climate, the kinds of plants, the total landscape are much the same."

Joan Johnstone, writing in *Woman Poet,* Volume 1: *The West,* found that Stanford's poetry accurately reflected her region. Stanford's poems, according to Johnstone, "fill out a landscape of California. It is an environing landscape in which details have meaning and consequence. . . . Reasoned, controlled, Ann Stanford's poetry expresses with subtle articulation historical and moral perceptions grounded in a sense of place and a sense of person."

Maxine Scates of *Northwest Review* believed that regionalism is "significant for all the best poets, and Stanford is one of our best, because everything they know is enhanced by their sense of where they live. Rooted, if you will, in a sense of the land's potential and its failures, the poet creates a sense of place in the poem, a home for feeling to take place in. . . . Stanford's poems are familiar to any reader who recognizes that the poem's emotional impact is dependent upon its being embodied in a context appropriate to its emotion. In fact, a central theme of Stanford's poetry . . . is the vulnerability of the home space, the imminent presence of the intruder on the horizon threatening the inviolability of what we hold most dear, what we recognize as having staked out as our own—and, moreover, what the poem has effectively claimed as its own."

Some critics have seen this "vulnerability of the home space" as indicative of Stanford's traditional poetic themes. She often wrote of love, loneliness, permanence, and change. Johnstone characterized Stanford's early work as "reflective thought consequent upon accurate description and colored by appropriate, usually sober, feeling. The thoughts tend to reflect unavoidable, and thus familiar truths . . . , while the descriptions are sharp and distinctive, pulling truth out of the world itself." Johnstone concluded that Stanford wrote a "conservative poetry" in which she worked "to observe the contradictions, to balance extremes, and to search for those universal truths that reconcile opposites."

Stanford's style was based on classical poetry, and displayed a certain formality, preciseness, and quiet intensity. A *Hudson Review* critic found that Stanford's "poems are classical both in the verbal and passionate meanings of the term: the usual words for unusual situations; a sparing use of simile or the dramatizing adjective; the terrible, structured by dramatic irony from a mind cool in inverse ratio to the warmth of feeling it proposes to reveal." Johnstone compared Stanford to several writers of the sixteenth-century: "Like Gascoigne and Anne Bradstreet, [Stanford] writes with directness, economy, and restraint. Like them she is exact and subtle in diction, yet easy, unself-conscious, serious, and dramatic by turns. . . . At the same time, she has developed her own verse line, accommodating the close, rhymed forms of the earlier lyricists to freer modern forms. . . . In a California that includes 'marvelous Marin' and other approximations of the Land of Cockaigne, her arduous clarity rings like a tuning fork." Writing in the *Dictionary of Literary Biography*, Linwood C. Powers called Stanford "a significant American poet" and "a poet of clarity as well as illusiveness."

Speaking of poetic form, Stanford once wrote: "I like structure in poetry, though not of the rigid kind, rather one that gives a shape to what is being shown within the poem. It is exciting to see the analogies between the syntax of a sentence and what the sentence says. The very landscape gives back to us the concerns and models of our poetry: the layout of a military base of the nineteenth century may resemble the stanzaic structure of a poem. The relationships of sensory images to structure are everywhere. Poetry captures these relationships.

"Such a dynamic, dramatic outer world, the world we can grasp with our senses, gives us the material for describing whatever of our self we choose to reveal; it forms a metaphor for human experiences, a design by which we can best show forth our inner selves."

BIOGRAPHICAL/CRITICAL SOURCES:

BOOKS

Dallman, Elaine and others, editors, *Woman Poet*, Volume 1: *The West*, Women-in-Literature, 1980.
Dictionary of Literary Biography, Volume 5: *American Poets since World War II*, Gale, 1980.

PERIODICALS

Choice, October, 1966; November, 1977.
Commonweal, June 17, 1966.
Fine Arts, December, 1962.
La Habra Review, July 14, 1960.
Hudson Review, winter, 1977-78.
Los Angeles Times, June 16, 1960.
Nation, March 11, 1950.
New Leader, March 27, 1967.
New York Herald Tribune Book Review, August 20, 1950.
New York Times, February 5, 1950.
Northwest Review, Volume XVIII, No. 1, 1979.
Poetry, September, 1950.
Prairie Schooner, winter, 1968-69.
UCLA Alumni Magazine, April, 1962.
Virginia Quarterly Review, winter, 1971.

OBITUARIES:

PERIODICALS

Chicago Tribune, July 20, 1987.
Los Angeles Times, July 18, 1987.
Washington Post, July 20, 1987.

*   *   *

STANLEY, Diane 1943-
(Diane Zuromskis, Diane Stanley Zuromskis)

PERSONAL: Born December 27, 1943, in Abilene, TX; daughter of Onia Burton, Jr. (a U.S. Navy captain) and Fay (a writer; maiden name, Grissom) Stanley; married Peter Zuromskis, May 30, 1970 (divorced, 1979); married Peter Vennema (a corporation president), September 8, 1979; children: (first marriage) Catherine, Tamara; (second marriage) John Leslie. *Education:* Trinity College, San Antonio, TX, B.A., 1965; attended Edinburgh College of Art, 1966-67; Johns Hopkins University, M.A., 1970. *Politics:* Democrat. *Religion:* Episcopal.

ADDRESSES: Home and office—2120 Tangley, Houston, TX 77005.

CAREER: Free-lance medical illustrator, 1970-74; G. P. Putnam's Sons, New York, NY, art director of children's books, 1978-79; illustrator and writer.

AWARDS, HONORS: The Farmer in the Dell was selected a Children's Choice Book by American Reading Association, 1979; "Notable Children's Trade Book in the Field of Social Studies," 1983, for *The Month Brothers* and *The Conversation Club*, 1985, for *A Country Tale*, 1987, for *Peter the Great*, and 1988, for *Shaka: King of the Zulus; The Month Brothers* was named a "best book" by *School Library Journal*, 1984; *All Wet! All Wet!* was selected an "Outstanding Science Trade Book for Children," 1985; Ann Martin Book Mark Award, Catholic Library Association, Bishop Byrne Chapter, 1985, for contribution in the arts; "Pick of the List," American Bookseller, Editor's Choice, *Booklist*, 1986, "Notable Book," American Library Association, 1986, Golden Kite Award Honor Book, Society of

Children's Book Writers, 1987, named to Master List, Texas Bluebonnet Award, 1988-89, named to Master List, William Allen White Children's Book Award, 1988-89, and nominee, South Carolina Children's Book Award, 1988-89, all for *Peter the Great; Captain Whiz-Bang* was selected one of "Best Books of 1987" for children under age five, *Parent's* Magazine, 1987; selection as a "Best Illustrated Book" and "Notable Book," both *New York Times,* 1988, and Editor's Choice, *Booklist,* 1988, all for *Shaka: King of the Zulus.*

WRITINGS:

JUVENILES

The Conversation Club (self-illustrated; a Junior Literary Guild selection), Macmillan, 1983.
A Country Tale (self-illustrated), Four Winds, 1985.
Birdsong Lullaby (self-illustrated), Morrow, 1985.
Peter the Great (self-illustrated), Four Winds, 1986.
The Good Luck Pencil, illustrations by Bruce Degen, Four Winds, 1986.
Captain Whiz-Bang (self-illustrated; a Book-of-the-Month Club selection), Morrow, 1987.
(With husband, Peter Vennema) *Shaka: King of the Zulus* (self-illustrated), Morrow, 1988.
Fortune (self-illustrated), Morrow, 1990.
Good Queen Bess: The Story of Elizabeth I of England (self-illustrated), Four Winds, 1990.

ILLUSTRATOR; JUVENILES

(Under name Diane Stanley Zuromskis) *The Farmer in the Dell,* Little, Brown, 1978.
(Under name Diane Stanley Zuromskis) Verna Aardema, *Half-a-Ball-of-Kenki: An Ashanti Tale Retold,* Warne, 1979.
Tony Johnston, *Little Mouse Nibbling,* Putnam, 1979.
Fiddle-I-Fee: A Traditional American Chant (a Junior Literary Guild selection), Little, Brown, 1979.
M. Jean Craig, *The Man Whose Name Was Not Thomas,* Doubleday, 1981.
Toni Hormann, *Onions, Onions,* Crowell, 1981.
Giambattista Basile, *Petrosinella, a Neopolitan Rapunzel,* translation by John E. Taylor, Warne, 1981.
Jane Yolen, *Sleeping Ugly* (a Junior Literary Guild selection), Coward, 1981.
Joanne Ryder, *Beach Party,* Warne, 1982.
Jean Marzollo and Claudio Marzollo, *Robin of Bray,* Dial, 1982.
James Whitcomb Riley, *Little Orphan Annie,* Putnam, 1983.
Samuel Marshak, reteller, *The Month Brothers,* translation by Thomas P. Whitney, Morrow, 1983.
James Skofield, *All Wet! All Wet!,* Harper, 1984.

SIDELIGHTS: Diane Stanley told *CA:* "I always loved to draw and paint. I remember the awe I felt when I saw my first fine art museum (the National Gallery) when I was sixteen. But I didn't consider art as a career until after college. Looking for a field that was appropriate to my detailed, realistic, miniaturist approach to art, I chose medical illustration. One of my art instructors strongly urged against it. He said it wasn't creative enough, but I saw no place for my skills in the mainstream of fine art.

"My training in Scotland and later at Johns Hopkins was oriented towards classical drawing and painting. At Hopkins we did pen-and-ink work using fine cross-hatching and 'eye-lashing.' We used a delicate dry-brush watercolor technique which I later used in *Petrosinella.* After several years of free-lancing as a medical illustrator, I discovered the world of children's books—through my own baby daughter. I was so impressed by the exciting variety and fine craftsmanship in the field. I remembered my love for books as a child. I knew exactly what I wanted to do and haven't had a doubt since. I spent a year preparing an appropriate portfolio and got my first book contract in 1976, from Little, Brown. I have been busy at books ever since.

"I try to approach each new book in a manner that suits the story; consequently, my books are quite different from one another. This is also because I'm still experimenting with new styles and techniques.

"I often wish I had had a picturesque upbringing, instead of a modern, suburban one. I have to do a lot of research for my books, which invariably have a country, period setting. Whenever I travel I try to observe such things as how thatched roofs are put together, how period houses are furnished, etc. I love beautifully designed books and enjoy such extras as ornaments and initial caps. I basically love my work—though it is lonely at times. I feel lucky to earn a living doing something so full of delight!"

BIOGRAPHICAL/CRITICAL SOURCES:

PERIODICALS

New York Times Book Review, November 9, 1986, November 13, 1988.
Tribune Books, October 16, 1988.

*   *   *

STARN, Randolph 1939-

PERSONAL: Born April 3, 1939, in Modesto, CA; son of Ray Elbearn and Madge (Pedelty) Starn; married Frances Smith, March 23, 1960; children: Orin, Andrea. *Education:* Attended Universitat zu Wien, 1958-59; Stanford University, B.A. (with honors), 1960; University of California, Berkeley, M.A., 1961; Harvard University, Ph.D., 1967.

ADDRESSES: Home—2619 Hillegass Ave., Berkeley, CA 94704. *Office*—Department of History, University of California, Berkeley, CA 94720.

CAREER: University of California, Berkeley, assistant professor, 1966-71, associate professor, 1971-78, professor of history, 1978—. Visiting member, Institute for Advanced Study, Princeton University, 1979-80.

MEMBER: American Historical Association, Renaissance Society of America.

AWARDS, HONORS: Fulbright fellowship to Italy; Social Sciences Research Training fellowship; American Council of Learned Societies fellowship.

WRITINGS:

Donato Giannotti and His Epistolae, Droz, 1968.
(With Loren W. Partridge) *A Renaissance Likeness: Art and Culture in Raphael's Julius II,* University of California Press, 1979.
Contrary Commonwealth: The Theme of Exile in Medieval and Renaissance Italy, University of California Press, 1982.

SIDELIGHTS: Of Randolph Starn's *Contrary Commonwealth: The Theme of Exile in Medieval and Renaissance Italy,* John M. Najemy writes in the *Journal of Modern History:* "This elegant and rewarding book surveys the 'facts,' 'rules,' and 'voices' of Italian exiles from the thirteenth to the sixteenth century with an extraordinary wealth of learning and insight. Indeed, Starn brings to this enterprise a perspective ranging from the Roman law and literature of exile, through three or more centuries of medieval and Renaissance sources, to the 'primitive rebels' of nineteenth-century Tuscany and the still uncertain status of our own century's refugees and exiles." And Julius Kirshner remarks in the *American Historical Review* that *Contrary Commonwealth* "represents an excellent and elegant introduction to [this] subject. Especially valuable is the final chapter, a fine evocation of the voices of exile in the literature of medieval and Renaissance Italy."

BIOGRAPHICAL/CRITICAL SOURCES:

PERIODICALS

American Historical Review, December, 1983.
Journal of Modern History, December, 1984.*

* * *

STEEL, Tex
    See ROSS, W(illiam) E(dward) D(aniel)

* * *

STEIN, Michael B. 1940-

PERSONAL: Born October 20, 1940, in Montreal, Quebec, Canada; son of A. L. (a lawyer) and Eleanor (Speisman) Stein; married Janice Gross (a university professor), September 12, 1965. *Education:* McGill University, B.A., 1961; Princeton University, M.A., 1963, Ph.D., 1967.

ADDRESSES: Office—Department of Political Science, McMaster University, Hamilton, Ontario L8S 4M4, Canada.

CAREER: Carleton University, Ottawa, Ontario, assistant professor of political science, 1965-68; McGill University, Montreal, Quebec, associate professor of political science, 1968-77; McMaster University, Hamilton, Ontario, professor of political science, 1977—, chairman of department, 1980-83. Senior research consultant, Task Force on Canadian Unity, 1978.

MEMBER: Canadian Political Science Association (member at large of executive board, 1968-70).

WRITINGS:

(Editor with Robert J. Jackson) *Issues in Comparative Politics,* St. Martin's, 1971.
The Dynamics of Right-Wing Protest: A Political Analysis of Social Credit on Quebec, University of Toronto Press, 1973.
(Editor with John E. Trent and others) *Aspects of Political Science in Canada: Fifty years in the Development of a Discipline,* McMaster University Press, 1980.

* * *

STEINER, Roger J(acob) 1924-

PERSONAL: Born March 27, 1924, in South Byron, WI; son of Jacob Robert (a printer) and Alice Mildred (Cowles) Steiner; married Kathryn Posey, August 7, 1954; children: David Posey. *Education:* Franklin and Marshall College, A.B. (cum laude), 1945; Union Theological Seminary, New York, NY, M.Div., 1947; University of Pennsylvania, M.A., 1958, Ph.D., 1963.

ADDRESSES: Home—10 Korda Dr., Newark, DE 19713. *Office*—Department of Languages and Literature, University of Delaware, Newark, DE 19711.

CAREER: Ordained minister, United Methodist Church, 1945-61; University of Delaware, Newark, assistant professor,

1963-71, associate professor of French, 1971-80, professor of language and literature, 1980—. Lecturer at University of Bordeaux, 1961-63. *Military service:* U.S. Naval Reserve, active duty, 1942-46.

MEMBER: Modern Language Association of America, American Association of Teachers of French, American Association of Teachers of Spanish and Portuguese, American Association of University Professors, American Dialect Society, International Arthurian Society, Societe Rencesvals, Defense de la Langue Francaise, Newark Twin Towns Association, Phi Beta Kappa.

WRITINGS:

Two Centuries of Spanish and English Bilingual Lexicography: 1590-1800, Mouton & Co., 1970.
A Cardinal Principle of Lexicography: Equivalency, Tijdschrift voor Toegepaste Linguistics, 1971.
(Editor) *Bantam New College French and English Dictionary,* Bantam, 1972.
The New College French and English Dictionary, Amsco School Publications, 1972.
Webster's French and English Dictionary, Castle Books, 1980.

Contributor of articles and reviews to learned journals in the United States and abroad.

WORK IN PROGRESS: The History of Spanish and English Lexicography: 1800 to the Present.

SIDELIGHTS: Roger J. Steiner told *CA,* "My work in bilingual lexicography could be thought of as bridge building between different cultures and civilizations." Steiner has lived or traveled in Canada, Mexico, Spain, and France.

* * *

STEINKE, Ann E(lizabeth) 1946-
    (Beth Christopher, Anne Reynolds, Elizabeth Reynolds, Anne Williams)

PERSONAL: Surname is pronounced *Styn*-kee; born November 5, 1946, in River Falls, WI; daughter of F. Leon and Wilma (Rounds) Reynolds; married William P. Steinke (a teacher of industrial arts), October 28, 1967; children: Christopher, Elizabeth. *Education:* Attended State University of New York College at Buffalo, 1965-66.

ADDRESSES: Home—17 Sutton Park Rd., Poughkeepsie, NY 12603.

CAREER: Writer, 1978—. Worked as a salesperson in Buffalo, NY, Cheektowaga, NY, and with Manpower, Inc., in Buffalo, 1966-69.

MEMBER: Romance Writers of America (charter member).

WRITINGS:

ROMANCE NOVELS

(Under pseudonym Elizabeth Reynolds) *An Ocean of Love,* Silhouette, 1982.
(Under pseudonym Anne Williams) *The Rare Gem,* Bantam, 1982.
(Under pseudonym Beth Christopher) *Love for the Taking,* Avon, 1983.

YOUNG ADULT

(Under pseudonym Anne Reynolds) *Sailboat Summer,* New American Library, 1983.

(Under pseudonym Anne Reynolds) *Jeff's New Girl,* New American Library, 1984.

(Under pseudonym Elizabeth Reynolds) *The Perfect Boy,* Bantam, 1986.

(Under pseudonym Elizabeth Reynolds) *Stolen Kisses,* Bantam, 1986.

Marie Curie and the Discovery of Radium (biography in "Solutions" series), Barron's, 1987.

"CHEERLEADERS" SERIES

(Under pseudonym Anne Reynolds) *Taking Risks* (#17), Scholastic Inc., 1986.

Rivals (#22), Scholastic Inc., 1986.

Stealing Secrets (#25), Scholastic Inc., 1987.

Falling in Love (#29), Scholastic Inc., 1987.

Saying No (#33), Scholastic Inc., 1987.

Having It All (#41), Scholastic Inc., 1988.

WORK IN PROGRESS: Right When I Needed You Most, part of the "Crosswinds Imprint"; a young adult romance novel and a young adult mystery.

SIDELIGHTS: "I began writing ten years ago," Ann E. Steinke told *CA,* "simply by imitating the current style of the adult romance novel, which at that time had no sex or bad language. Since the genre has changed drastically in the last two or three years, I am not at home with it any more. Now I concentrate solely on young adult novels, which I have come to admire very much. I feel the young adult books have a bit more plot, on the whole, and are therefore more likely to hold my attention. It is not easy to find books that can do this.

"I love to travel, and for a time my husband and I owned a hot-air balloon. It has since been sold, but some day it may figure in a new book."

*   *   *

STEPHENS, Lester D(ow) 1933-

PERSONAL: Born February 18, 1933, in Gatesville, Tex.; son of Carl Durwood and Waldine (White) Stephens; married Faye Wilks, 1954 (divorced, 1976); married Marie Ellis, 1976; children: (first marriage) Karen Faye, Janet Kaye. *Education:* University of Corpus Christi, B.S., 1954; University of Texas, M.Ed., 1959; University of Miami, Coral Gables, Ph.D., 1964. *Politics:* Democrat. *Religion:* Unitarian Universalist.

ADDRESSES: Home—1340 Crystal Hills Dr., Athens, Ga. 30606. *Office*—Department of History, University of Georgia, Athens, Ga. 30602.

CAREER: Social studies teacher in public schools of Corpus Christi, Tex., 1954-57; University of Corpus Christi, assistant professor of history and registrar, 1957-61; University of Georgia, Athens, assistant professor of social studies education, 1963-66, associate professor of education and history, 1966-69, associate professor of history, 1969-78, professor of history, 1978—, chair of department, 1981—.

MEMBER: American Historical Association, Organization of American Historians, Society for History Education, History of Science Society, Society for the History of Natural History, Southern Historical Association, Georgia Association of Historians (president, 1974-75), Georgia Historical Society, Phi Theta Kappa, Phi Kappa Phi, Phi Delta Kappa, Phi Alpha Theta.

AWARDS, HONORS: Outstanding Honors Professor Award, University of Georgia, 1971, 1974, 1976, 1978, 1980; Joseph H.

Parks Award, University of Georgia, 1972, for excellence in teaching history; American Philosophical Society grants, 1974, 1978; Sandy Beaver Award for excellence in teaching, 1979; LeConte Medallion, South Carolina Science Council, 1981; Pro Optime Perdocendo Honoratus Medal for excellence in teaching, 1983.

WRITINGS:

(With Oscar T. Jarvis and H. W. Gentry) *Public School Business Administration and Finance,* Parker Publishing, 1967.

Probing the Past: The Study and Teaching of History, Allyn & Bacon, 1974.

(With William C. Merwin and Donald O. Schneider) *Developing Competency in Teaching the Social Studies,* C. E. Merrill, 1974.

Historiography: A Bibliography, Scarecrow, 1975.

Joseph LeConte, Gentle Prophet of Evolution, Louisiana State University Press, 1982.

Ancient Animals and Other Wondrous Things: The Story of Francis Simmons Holmes, Paleontologist and Curator of the Charleston Museum, Charleston Museum (Charleston, S.C.), 1988.

General editor, History of American Science and Technology series, University of Alabama Press. Contributor to *Encyclopedia of Southern History,* 1979, *Dictionary of Georgia Biography,* 1983, *Encyclopedia of Southern Culture,* 1989, and *Science and Medicine in the Old South,* 1989. Contributor to professional journals, including *Agricultural History, Annals of Science, Georgia Historical Quarterly, Georgia Journal of Science, Historian, History Teacher, Journal of the History of the Behavioral Sciences, Journal of the History of Ideas,* and *New England Quarterly.*

*   *   *

STEWART, James Brewer 1940-

PERSONAL: Born August 8, 1940, in Cleveland, Ohio; son of Richard H. (an attorney) and Marian (Brewer) Stewart; married Dorothy Carlson, June 26, 1965; children: Rebecca Ann, Jennifer Lynn. *Education:* Dartmouth College, B.A., 1962; Case Western Reserve University, M.A., 1966, Ph.D., 1968.

ADDRESSES: Home—1924 Princeton Ave., St. Paul, Minn. 55105. *Office*—Department of History, Macalester College, St. Paul, Minn. 55105.

CAREER: Carroll College, Waukesha, Wis., assistant professor of American history, 1968-69; Macalester College, St. Paul, Minn., assistant professor, 1969-72, associate professor, 1972-78, James Wallace Professor of History, 1978—, chairman of department, 1972—, provost, 1987-90. Research and teaching fellow, Newberry Library, 1972-77; visiting professor of history, University of South Carolina, 1978-79.

MEMBER: American Historical Association, Organization of American Historians, American Council of Learned Societies (fellow), Association for the Study of Negro Life and History, Society of Historians of the Early Republic, Southern Historical Association.

WRITINGS:

Joshua R. Giddings and the Tactics of Radical Politics, Press of Case Western Reserve University, 1970.

Holy Wars: The Abolitionists and American Slavery, Hill & Wang, 1976.

(Contributor) Lewis Perry and Michael Fellman, editors, *Antislavery Reconsidered: New Perspectives on the Abolitionists,* Louisiana State University Press, 1979.

(Contributor) Ernest Sandeen, editor, *Bible and Social Reform,* Scholars Press, 1982.

Wendell Phillips: Liberty's Hero, Louisiana State University Press, 1986.

(Editor) Warren E. Burger, *The Constitution, The Law, and Freedom of Expression, 1787-1987,* Southern Illinois University Press, 1987.

Contributor to history journals.*

* * *

STEWIG, John Warren 1937-

PERSONAL: Born January 7, 1937, in Waukesha, WI; son of John G. and Marguerite W. Stewig. *Education:* University of Wisconsin—Madison, B.S., 1958, M.S., 1962, Ph.D., 1967. *Religion:* Episcopalian.

ADDRESSES: Home—941 West Acacia Rd., Glendale, WI 53217. *Office*—University of Wisconsin, 393 Enderis Hall, Milwaukee, WI 53201.

CAREER: Elementary school teacher in Monona Grove, WI, 1958-64; Purdue University, West Lafayette, IN, assistant professor, 1967-72; University of Wisconsin—Milwaukee, associate professor, 1972-77, professor of language arts, 1977—. Faculty member and workshop leader at colleges and universities in the United States and Canada, including Indiana University, School of the Ozarks, Western Montana State University, Northern Montana State University, University of Denver, and University of Victoria; speaker at schools and professional gatherings. Member of Wisconsin Statewide Literacy Assessment Advisory Committee, 1974; member of advisory board of Madison Cooperative Children's Book Center, 1974-78, 1989-92; member of committee to choose Caldecott calendar, American Library Association, 1988. Worked as music teacher at a hospital school for school-age patients.

MEMBER: International Reading Association (member of Children's Book Award Committee, 1984-86), International Visual Literacy Association, Association for Childhood Education International, National Council of Teachers of English (president, 1982-83), Wisconsin Council of Teachers of English (member of board of directors, 1977-79; president, 1980-81), Milwaukee Association for the Education of Young Children, English Association of Greater Milwaukee (member of board of directors, 1973-81).

AWARDS, HONORS: Grant from U.S. Office of Education, 1973; ESEA Title IVC grant from State of Wisconsin, 1981; Creative Drama for Human Awareness Award, American Association of Theatre for Youth, 1987; Distinguished Elementary Education Award, University of Wisconsin—Madison, 1987.

WRITINGS:

Spontaneous Drama: A Language Art, C. E. Merrill, 1973.
Exploring Language with Children, C. E. Merrill, 1974.
Read to Write: Using Literature as a Springboard to Children's Composition, Hawthorn, 1975, 3rd edition, Richard C. Owen Publishers, 1990.
Children's Language Acquisition, Department of Public Instruction (Madison, Wis.), 1976.
Sending Messages (juvenile), Houghton, 1978.

(Editor with Sam L. Sebesta, and contributor) *Using Literature in the Elementary Classroom* (monograph), National Council of Teachers of English, 1978, 2nd edition, 1989.

Children and Literature, Rand McNally, 1980, 2nd edition, Houghton, 1988.

Teaching Language Arts in Early Childhood, Holt, 1982.

Exploring Language Arts in the Elementary Classroom, Holt, 1983.

Informal Drama in the Elementary Language Arts Program, Teachers College Press, 1983.

The Fisherman and His Wife (juvenile), Holiday House, 1988.

Stone Soup (juvenile), Holiday House, in press.

CONTRIBUTOR

Joe L. Frost, editor, *The Elementary School: Principles and Problems,* Houghton, 1969.

Martha King and others, editors, *The Language Arts in the Elementary School: A Forum for Focus,* National Council of Teachers of English, 1973.

Linda Western, editor, *Children's Literature,* Extension, University of Wisconsin—Madison, 1975.

Walter Petty and Patrick Flynn, editors, *Creative Dramatics in the Language Arts Classroom,* State University of New York at Buffalo, 1976.

Bernice Cullinan and others, editors, *Literature for the Young Child,* National Council of Teachers of English, 1977.

Claire Davis Ashby, editor, *The Interrelationships of the Arts in Reading,* Collegium Book, 1979.

Gay Su Pinnell, editor, *Discovering Language with Children,* National Council of Teachers of English, 1980.

Harold E. Mitzel, editor, *Encyclopedia of Educational Research,* American Educational Research Association, 5th edition, 1982, 6th edition (edited by Marvin Alkin), in press.

Carl Personke and Dale Johnson, editors, *Language Arts Instruction and the Beginning Teacher,* Prentice-Hall, 1987.

Roberts Braden and others, editors, *About Visuals,* International Visual Literacy Association, 1989.

OTHER

Also author of series, "Reading Pictures," Child Graphics, 1988, 1989. Contributor of more than sixty articles and reviews to language arts, library, theatre, and children's literature journals. Editor of column, "Instructional Strategies," in *Elementary English,* 1972-73. Associate editor, *Children's Theatre Review,* 1985-86; member of editorial board, *Childhood Education,* 1972-74, *Advocate,* 1983-86, and Children's Literature Association *Quarterly,* 1987—.

SIDELIGHTS: John Warren Stewig told *CA:* "Scholars have shown through research what perceptive teachers have observed for years: children come to school with impressive abilities to use language. The school's task is to help them improve the natural language skills they already possess. This has to be done apart from traditional, analytic/evaluative exercises which have pervaded the curriculum for too long. My writing for teachers is concerned with this common theme: there are imaginative ways to enhance children's language, without forsaking the structure and sequence which creative approaches too often ignore.

"I have written about each of the language arts: listening, speaking, reading, and writing. A particular interest has been showing teachers how to make creative drama integral to all of these language arts. My focus is on providing imaginative activities, set within a framework (rationale) which would help teachers understand why the activities are crucial for children. Too frequently creativity is seen as complete freedom: nothing could be further from the truth. I have written at length about how to use the language of writers for children, and children's own language, to plan curricula that are responsive to children's needs and challenging in ways too often left untapped. One effort was *Sending Messages,* a juvenile title, which helps children understand some ways adults use language in society. To be truly literate, we need to understand the processes involved as adults use language. This book speaks to children on their level about this rather complex activity."

Stewig adds: "More recently, I have been working on the idea of visual literacy, spending a year in the schools studying how children learn to understand visuals. My series, "Reading Pictures" (Child Graphics, 1988, 1989), presents classroom materials developed from the illustrations in children's books."

BIOGRAPHICAL/CRITICAL SOURCES:

BOOKS

Shibles, Wesley, *Metaphor: An Annotated Bibliography and History,* Language Press, 1971.
Leaders in Education, Bowker, 1971.
Men of Achievement, Melrose Press, 1973.

* * *

STONE, Rosetta
See GEISEL, Theodor Seuss

* * *

STURGEON, Theodore (Hamilton) 1918-1985
(Frederick R. Ewing, E. Waldo Hunter, Ellery Queen, E. Hunter Waldo)

PERSONAL: Original name, Edward Hamilton Waldo; name legally changed upon adoption by stepfather; born February 26, 1918, in St. George, Staten Island, N.Y.; died May 8, 1985, of pneumonia, in Eugene, Ore.; son of Edward (a retail paint businessman) and Christine (a teacher and writer; maiden name, Dicker) Waldo; married Dorothy Fillingame, 1940 (divorced, 1945); married Mary Mair (a singer), 1949 (divorced, 1951); married third wife, Marion, 1951; married Wina Bonnie Golden (a television personality), April 16, 1969 (divorced); married Jayne Enelhart; children: Colin, Patricia, Cynthia, Robin, Tandy, Noel, Timothy, Andros. *Education:* Attended Pennsylvania State Nautical School. *Religion:* Episcopal.

CAREER: Science fiction writer, 1938-85. Worked as an engine room wiper in the Merchant Marine, 1935-38; manager of a resort hotel in the West Indies, 1940-41; manager of a tractor lubrication center for the U.S. Army in Puerto Rico, 1941; bulldozer operator in Puerto Rico, 1942-43; copy editor for an advertising agency, 1944; literary agent in New York City, 1946-47; *Fortune* (magazine), New York City, circulation staff member, 1948-49; story editor for *Tales of Tomorrow* (magazine), 1950; *If* (magazine), New York City, feature editor, 1961-64, contributing editor, 1972-74. Teacher at workshops and writing conferences.

MEMBER: Writers Guild of America.

AWARDS, HONORS: Argosy magazine story award, 1947, for "Bianca's Hands"; International Fantasy Award, 1954, for *More Than Human;* guest of honor at Twentieth World Science Fiction Convention, 1962; Nebula Award, 1970, and Hugo Award, 1971, both for "Slow Sculpture"; World Fantasy Award for life achievement, World Fantasy Convention, 1986.

WRITINGS:

NOVELS

The Dreaming Jewels, Greenberg, 1950, published as *The Synthetic Man,* Pyramid, 1961, reprinted, Bluejay, 1984.
More Than Human, Farrar, Straus, 1953, reprinted, Ballantine, 1981.
The King and Four Queens (Western novel; based on a story by Margaret Fitts), Dell, 1956.
(Under pseudonym Frederick R. Ewing) *I, Libertine* (historical novel), Ballantine, 1956.
The Cosmic Rape, Dell, 1958.
Venus Plus X, Pyramid, 1960, reprinted, Carroll & Graf, 1988.
Some of Your Blood (also see below), Ballantine, 1961.
Voyage to the Bottom of the Sea (based on the screenplay by Irwin Allen and Charles Bennet), Pyramid, 1961.
(Under pseudonym Ellery Queen) *The Player on the Other Side,* Random House, 1963.
Two Complete Novels (contains "And My Fear Is Great" and "Baby Is Three"), Galaxy, 1965.
The Rare Breed, Fawcett, 1966.
Amok Time (based on one of his "Star Trek" television scripts), Bantam, 1978.
Godbody, limited edition, Donald I. Fine, 1986, New American Library, 1987.

STORY COLLECTIONS

"It" (single story), Prime Press, 1948.
Without Sorcery, with introduction by Ray Bradbury, Prime Press, 1948, revised edition published as *Not without Sorcery,* Ballantine, 1961.
E Pluribus Unicorn, Abelard, 1953.
Caviar, Ballantine, 1955.
A Way Home, Funk, 1955 (published in England as *Thunder and Roses,* M. Joseph, 1957).
A Touch of Strange, Doubleday, 1958.
Aliens 4, Avon, 1959.
Beyond, Avon, 1960.
The Unexpected, compiled by Leo Margulies, Pyramid, 1961.
Sturgeon in Orbit, Pyramid, 1964.
The Joyous Invasions, Gollancz, 1965.
Starshine, Pyramid, 1966.
(With Ray Bradbury and Oliver Chadwick Symmes) *One Foot and the Grave,* Avon, 1968.
Sturgeon Is Alive and Well, Putnam, 1971.
The Worlds of Theodore Sturgeon, Ace Books, 1972.
To Here and the Easel, Gollancz, 1973.
(With Don Ward) *Sturgeon's West,* Doubleday, 1973.
Case and the Dreamer, New American Library, 1974.
Visions and Venturers, Dell, 1978.
Maturity, Science Fiction Society (Minneapolis), 1979.
The Golden Helix, Doubleday, 1979.
The Stars Are the Styx, Dell, 1979.
Slow Sculpture, Pocket Books, 1982.
Alien Cargo, Bluejay, 1984.
To Marry Medusa, Baen Books, 1987.
A Touch of Sturgeon, Simon & Schuster, 1988.

RADIO AND TELEVISION SCRIPTS

Author of radio scripts, including "Incident at Switchpath," 1950; "The Stars Are the Styx," 1953; "Mr. Costello Here," 1956; "Saucer of Loneliness," 1957; "More Than Human," 1967; "The Girl Had Guts," "The Skills of Xanadu," and "Affair with a Green Monkey." Also author of television scripts for "Beyond Tomorrow," "Star Trek," "Playhouse 90," "CBS Stage

14," "Schlitz Playhouse," "Land of the Lost," "Wild, Wild West," "The Invaders," and other television series. Also author, with Ed MacKillop, of television script "Killdozer!" (based on his short story), 1974.

OTHER

(Contributor) Leo Margulies and O. J. Friend, editors, *My Best Science Fiction Story,* Merlin Press, 1949.

"It Should Be Beautiful" (play), first produced in Woodstock, N.Y., c.1963.

(Contributor) Reginald Bretnor, editor, *Science Fiction: Today and Tomorrow,* Harper, 1974.

(Contributor) Bretnor, editor, *The Craft of Science Fiction,* Harper, 1976.

"Psychosis: Unclassified" (play; based on his novel *Some of Your Blood*), first produced in 1977.

(Editor) *New Soviet Science Fiction,* Macmillan (London), 1980.

Work included in many anthologies. Also author of comic book scripts. Author of column, *National Review,* 1961-73. Contributor of short stories, sometimes under pseudonyms, to *Unknown, Astounding Science Fiction, Omni, Galaxy,* and other magazines. Book reviewer, *Venture,* 1957-58, *Galaxy,* 1972-74, *New York Times,* 1974-75, and *Hustler,* 1983.

SIDELIGHTS: The late Theodore Sturgeon was one of a handful of science fiction writers whose work revolutionized the genre. Beginning as a pulp writer in the late 1930s, Sturgeon became one of science fiction's Golden Age writers of the 1940s, a period when many of the genre's most popular writers came to prominence. Sturgeon published his stories in such influential magazines as *Astounding Science Fiction* and *Unknown.* His stream-of-consciousness technique, concern for humane values, and ability to create unlikely characters and situations, endeared him to readers and influenced a score of other writers. Kurt Vonnegut, Jr., is believed to have modeled his character Kilgore Trout, a prolific and inventive science fiction writer, on Sturgeon.

After dropping out of high school as a teenager, Sturgeon joined the Merchant Marine, worked in the West Indies and Puerto Rico, and finally found himself in the middle 1940s in New York City, working as a writer of science fiction and, for a time, as a literary agent for other writers in the field. His first widely acclaimed book, *More Than Human,* appeared in 1953; it won the International Fantasy Award. Later books, usually collections of short stories, established Sturgeon as one of science fiction's most accomplished and popular writers.

Donald L. Lawler, writing in the *Dictionary of Literary Biography,* credited Sturgeon for his role in "extending the boundaries of the [science fiction] genre into the soft sciences." Sturgeon's stories, Lawler believed, "emphasized the personal and psychological dimensions of human experience with science," while "loneliness and alienation are two persistent themes in his writing." "More than any other figure in Science Fiction's 'Golden Age,' " wrote Bob Collins in *Fantasy Review,* "[Sturgeon] consistently attempted profound themes." Speaking to Charles Platt in *Dream Makers, Volume II: The Uncommon Men and Women Who Write Science Fiction,* Sturgeon explained: "I have my own definition of science, which derives from *scientia,* which is the Latin word that means knowledge. To me, science fiction is *knowledge* fiction, and it's knowledge not only of physical and chemical laws but also the quasi- and soft sciences, and also matters of the human heart and mind. This is all knowledge, and so to me it's all legitimate science fiction."

Among the subjects that Sturgeon made into legitimate science fiction was sex, particularly sex of an unusual or even abberant nature. He was the first writer in science fiction to include homosexual characters in his work, and to portray them as being worthy of tolerance. His story "The World Well Lost" concerns a pair of homosexual lovers from another planet who are aided in their escape from outraged spacemen by an Earthman who empathizes with them. Sturgeon's early story "Bianca's Hands," first written in 1939 but considered too erotically daring by science fiction magazines of the 1940s, was finally published in the British adventure magazine *Argosy* in 1947. It won a $1,000 fiction prize, beating out entries by such writers as Graham Greene. The story tells of the deformed idiot Bianca, who possesses hands which "have a life and will of their own," as Lawler explained. Bianca's friend Ran becomes obsessed with the hands, desiring nothing else but to be strangled by them. Sturgeon's novel *Venus Plus X* features a utopian society of the future whose citizens undergo surgery at birth to render themselves hermaphroditic. This sexual change allows them to transcend the normal conflicts between men and women. In many of Sturgeon's stories, love was seen as the surest method of overcoming the adversities of life. Sturgeon "never abandoned belief in the therapeutic power of love," Collins noted.

An eccentric and outspoken man whose daring ideas made his fiction continually popular, Sturgeon was an iconoclast in his thinking. A long-time columnist for the conservative *National Review,* Sturgeon also wrote book reviews for the explicit men's magazine *Hustler.* He was a nudist, a vegetarian, and a believer in herbal medicines and vitamin cures. "I have a right to my own life-style," he explained to Platt, "and I don't like yahoos coming along to correct me. . . . I like to protect my own way of thinking." Speaking of his political persuasion, Sturgeon told Platt: "Libertarian, at the moment, feels more like home to me than anything else." In private life Sturgeon was also known for his unorthodox attitude toward finances. As Sam Moskowitz observed, "If ever an author epitomized the skittishness and sensitivity attributed to the 'artist,' it is Theodore Sturgeon. While he appreciated the need for money, his primary motivation was not the dollar. Despite the knowledge that he could sell *anything* of a fantastic nature he cared to write . . . , it was typical of him to take a couple of months off to write a three-act play *free* for a small-town theater, with the review in a local weekly his sole reward."

Sturgeon is credited with two observations that have become known not only in science fiction circles but among a wider audience as well. "Sturgeon's Law," so called because he claimed that it applied in every field of endeavor, is stated in polite terms as: "90% of everything is trash." His other abiding observation was the "concept of the 'Prime Directive' " created for the "Star Trek" television program, as Lawler noted. Sturgeon wrote two episodes for the popular series ("Amok Time" and "Shore Leave"). The "Prime Directive," or overriding law of the United Federation of Planets, "prohibits Federation interference with the normal development of alien life and societies," according to Bjo Trimble in *A Star Trek Concordance.*

In his fiction Sturgeon displayed a wide variety of styles, adapting his approach to the story he wanted to tell. Moskowitz, writing in *Seekers of Tomorrow: Masters of Modern Science Fiction,* stated that Sturgeon "strives in *every* story to be as differently and bizarrely off-trail as he is able" and claimed that Sturgeon possessed an "adroitness at altering the rhythm of his writing to conform to the subject [which] gives him as many styles as stories." Lawler agreed. Sturgeon, he wrote, "uses a remarkable variety of styles, points of view, and narrative devices." Lawler also credited the author with having "pointed the way for new developments in the genre by combining the subject matter, themes, and formulas of science fiction with the ideas, modes of treatment, and stylistic features of mainstream literature."

Sturgeon's influence on other science fiction writers, and on the parameters of the genre as a whole, was impressive. Lawler explained that Sturgeon's influence was "great because it is so diffuse. It is not so much an acknowledged influence as it is pervasive, and it tends to be strongest in matters of tone, style, attitudes, and values." Among those writers influenced by Sturgeon were Ray Bradbury, Samuel R. Delaney, Philip K. Dick, Ursula K. LeGuin, and Kurt Vonnegut, Jr.

Vonnegut modeled his character Kilgore Trout on Sturgeon. Trout is a science fiction writer who has authored hundreds of books filled with wildly inventive concepts. But Trout lives in poverty and obscurity because the ridiculous titles he gives his books, and the pornographic magazines in which his stories appear, severely limit his audience. Trout is both homage to Sturgeon for his inventiveness and his ability to confront major themes and a satire of Sturgeon's eccentricity.

At the time of Sturgeon's death in 1985, commentators noted that he had a tremendous reputation both as an individual and as a writer. Reginald Bretnor emphasized in the *Dictionary of Literary Biography Yearbook: 1985* that "*I have never heard anyone—fellow writer or editor or fan—say a bad word about him. I found him to be warm and open, tremendously interested in people and what they did and what made them tick. I felt immediately that he genuinely liked people.*" James Gunn agreed. "Ted loved life, loved people, and loved writing," Gunn recalled in *Fantasy Review*.

Poul Anderson found Sturgeon's work to be among the best in science fiction. Writing in *National Review*, Anderson stated: "One can raise quibbles about Sturgeon, his touches of doctrinaire liberalism (though never, never collectivism), his ungrammatical treatment of 'thou,' his sometimes overly neat plots, nits like that. So what? It's as easy to pick them off Rembrandt and Beethoven, easier off Shakespeare, and none of these are lessened thereby, nor is Sturgeon. He is reliably a joy." In his tribute to Sturgeon for the *Washington Post Book World*, Stephen King noted that as a writer Sturgeon had "entertained, provoked thought, terrified, and occasionally ennobled. He fulfilled, in short, all the qualifications we use to measure artistry in prose."

MEDIA ADAPTATIONS: The film rights to many of Sturgeon's novels and short stories have been sold.

BIOGRAPHICAL/CRITICAL SOURCES:

BOOKS

Contemporary Literary Criticism, Gale, Volume 22, 1982, Volume 39, 1986.
Dictionary of Literary Biography, Volume 8: *Twentieth Century American Science Fiction Writers,* Gale, 1981.
Dictionary of Literary Biography Yearbook: 1985, Gale, 1986.
Ketterer, David, *New Worlds for Old: The Apocalyptic Imagination, Science Fiction, and American Literature,* Anchor Press, 1974.
Moskowitz, Sam, *Explorers of the Infinite,* World Publishing, 1963.
Moskowitz, Sam, *Seekers of Tomorrow: Masters of Modern Science Fiction,* World Publishing, 1965.
Platt, Charles, *Dream Makers, Volume II: The Uncommon Men and Women Who Write Science Fiction,* Berkley, 1983.
Trimble, Bjo, *A Star Trek Concordance,* Ballantine, 1976.

PERIODICALS

Bloomsbury Review, February, 1986.
Books and Bookmen, January, 1969.
Extrapolation, summer, 1979, fall, 1985.
Magazine of Fantasy and Science Fiction, December, 1971.
National Review, May 4, 1971.
Washington Post Book World, May 26, 1985.

OBITUARIES:

PERIODICALS

AB Bookman's Weekly, June 24, 1985.
Fantasy Review, May, 1985.
Los Angeles Times, May 11, 1985.
New York Times, May 11, 1985.
Pittsburgh Post-Gazette, May 10, 1985.
Publishers Weekly, May 31, 1985.
Science Fiction Chronicle, July, 1985.
Washington Post, May 13, 1985.*

—*Sketch by Thomas Wiloch*

* * *

SUKENICK, Ronald 1932-

PERSONAL: Born July 14, 1932, in Brooklyn, N.Y.; son of Louis (a dentist) and Ceceile (Frey) Sukenick; married Lynn Luria, March 19, 1961 (divorced, 1984). *Education:* Cornell University, B.A., 1955; Brandeis University, M.A., 1957, Ph.D., 1962.

ADDRESSES: Home—1505 Bluebell Ave., Boulder, Col. 80302. *Office*—Department of English, Box 226, University of Colorado, Boulder, Col. 80309. *Agent*—Ellen Levine Literary Agency, Suite 1205, 432 Park Ave. South, New York, N.Y. 10016.

CAREER: Brandeis University, Waltham, Mass., instructor, 1956-58, 1959-61; instructor, Hofstra University, 1961-62; toured Europe, wrote, and taught in various schools, 1962-66; City College of the City University of New York, New York City, assistant professor of English, 1966-67; Sarah Lawrence College, Bronxville, N.Y., assistant professor of English and writing, 1968-69; writer in residence, Cornell University, Ithaca, N.Y., 1969, and University of California, Irvine, 1970-72; University of Colorado, Boulder, professor of English, 1975—, director of creative writing, 1975-77, director of Publications Center, 1986—, founder of exchange program and first exchange professor to l'Universite Paul Valery, Montpellier, France, 1979. Lecturer, Brandeis University, 1956-60, Hofstra University, 1961-62. Butler Chair, State University of New York, Buffalo, spring, 1981. Publisher, *American Book Review,* 1977, and *Black Ice,* 1989—. Member of PMLA advisory committee, 1987-90.

MEMBER: PEN, Authors Guild, Authors League of America, National Book Critics Circle, Coordinating Council of Literary Magazines (CCLM; chairman of board of directors, 1975-77), Fiction Collective (founding member; director, 1989—).

AWARDS, HONORS: Fulbright fellowships, 1958 and 1984; Guggenheim Foundation fellowship, 1976; National Edowment for the Arts Fellowships, 1980 and 1989; CCLM Award for Editorial Excellence, 1985; Western Book Award for Publishing, 1985; American Book Award, Before Columbus Foundation, 1988, for *Down and In.*

WRITINGS:

Wallace Stevens: Musing the Obscure, New York University Press, 1967.
Up (novel), Dial, 1968.
The Death of the Novel, and Other Stories, Dial, 1969.
Out (novel), Swallow Press, 1973.
(Contributor) Ray Federman, editor, *Surfiction,* Swallow Press, 1974.
98.6 (novel), Fiction Collective, 1975.
Long Talking Bad Conditions Blues, Fiction Collective, 1979.
In Form, Digressions on the Act of Fiction, Southern Illinois University Press, 1985.
The Endless Short Story, Fiction Collective, 1986.
Blown Away (novel), Sun & Moon, 1987.
Down and In: Life in the Underground (nonfiction narrative), Beech Tree Books, 1987.

Contributing editor, *The Pushcart Prize Anthology,*, Pushcart/Avon. Fiction appears in more than ten anthologies published in the United States and Poland. Contributor of fiction to *New American Review, Partisan Review,* and other periodicals. Contributor of reviews to periodicals, including *New York Times Book Review, Partisan Review,* and *Village Voice.* Contributing editor, *Fiction International,*, 1970-84; guest editor, *Witness,* 1989.

WORK IN PROGRESS: Fiction and criticism.

SIDELIGHTS: In the late 1960s when fiction writer and theorist Ronald Sukenick began his career as a novelist, fiction was at a crucial stage of its development as an art form. Most critics and fictioneers who did not speak of the death of fiction were convinced of its exhaustion. Feeling that writers had followed the novel form to the end of its potential, they were left with an art that was doomed to self-conscious repetition. What could be accomplished in the ancient art of storytelling that had not already been done well, several times over? Clever recombinations of plots and characters, parodies of traditional forms, and emphasis on word play were still possible, and novels that were studies on the process of writing novels became more popular. Apart from these new twists on familiar materials, it appeared to many that it would soon be inaccurate to speak of the novel's progress.

Like other new novelists of the period, Sukenick recognized that the tradition—a standardized way of looking at an art form—had become one of fiction's strongest enemies. "There are all these talented people around trying to write in this form which doesn't suit them at all, so that instead of releasing their energies it blocks them out," Sukenick told interviewer Joe David Bellamy in 1970 (interview collected in *The New Fiction: Interviews with Innovative American Writers*). The tradition was itself a fiction, a result of our selective perception, and needed to be revised. He explains in a *Contemporary Authors Autobiography Series* essay, "By the point some form has become certified Literature it has become a formula useable in prefabricated repetitions. But experience is never prefab. It is immediate, metamorphic, and unpredictable. Writing that tries to package experience can only falsify it. Literature is packaged experience. You can and must learn a lot from the best Literature but you don't learn anything new from it, unless it happens to be new to you. So half the fight when you're writing is to avoid Literature. The other half is to find forms that accommodate, discover, and even create your particular experience."

Sukenick is a major spokesman for the belief that a new tradition can be built to replace the old without rejecting the works upon which the old was built. "It must already be there awaiting only

one final element—that we say it exists," Sukenick writes in "The New Tradition in Fiction," an essay collected in Ray Federman's *Surfiction.* Sukenick elaborates, "It's not modern. . . . The modern behaved as if a new age were due tomorrow, and as if it were it, the final goal of progress. Here in tomorrowland we have a more tragic sense of things. We know there's no such thing as progress, that a new age may be a worse one, and that since the future brings no redemption, we better look to the present. In consequence the new tradition makes itself felt as a presence rather than a development. Instead of a linear sequence of historical influences it seems a network of interconnections revealed to our particular point of view. Like Eliot's view of tradition, it would resemble a reservoir rather than a highway project, a reservoir that is ahistorical, international, and multilingual."

Sukenick's criticism and fiction support the establishment of this new tradition. His first book *Wallace Stevens: Musing the Obscure* studies a poet who was concerned with the complex relation between language, imagination, and reality. Sukenick looks at forty poems separately, taking them as "chapters in the life of the poet's mind," Denis Donoghue relates in the *New York Review of Books.* Condemned for being unconventional by some reviewers, the book was hailed by others as the first study to offer an accurate approach to Stevens's work. *Wallace Stevens* became the first installment of a body of criticism that is esteemed for its clarity and well-defended iconoclasm.

Sukenick's novels are notable for displaying the vitality of fiction amid rumors of its death. More than mere demonstrations of theory, they show Sukenick's attempt "to define a distinct voice while expanding the genre's potential," Frederick R. Karl observes in *American Fictions, 1940-1980: A Comprehensive History and Critical Evaluation.* They show that there is some territory novelists have yet to explore. In addition, notes Jerome Klinkowitz in *Literary Subversions: New American Fiction and the Practice of Criticism,* they present some of "the strongest American innovations" in fiction and fiction theory. Sukenick's innovations are best understood in the context of his thinking about the relation between fiction and reality at this crucial point in the history of the genre.

The turning point fiction had reached in the 1970s was largely a turning away from realism—a turning that followed philosophical challenges to previous views of life. "Realistic fiction presupposed chronological time as the medium of a plotted narrative, an irreducible individual psyche as the subject of its characterization, and, above all, the ultimate, concrete reality of things as the object and rationale of its description. In the world of postrealism, however, all of these absolutes have become absolutely problematic," Sukenick explains in *The Death of the Novel, and Other Stories.* "The contemporary writer—the writer who is acutely in touch with the life of which he is a part—is forced to start from scratch: Reality doesn't exist, time doesn't exist, personality doesn't exist."

Readers and writers alike must stop looking to fiction for pictures of reality, because any novel is an act of the imagination, he says. Sukenick told Bellamy, "People are surrounded by all sorts of information coming in to them through all sorts of media now, and the novel, on that level, doesn't have anything to say to them." Readers know that documentary film and radio broadcasts can represent the real world more accurately than realistic fiction. However, Sukenick argues, the awareness that fiction cannot mirror reality without distorting it need not render fiction obsolete; it presents a challenge to writers to discover new frontiers of content and new forms and techniques for handling them.

Perhaps an inferior vehicle for picturing actual events or conditions of life, the novel can yet provide accurate representations of the imaginative process. "One model for a work of fiction is the jigsaw puzzle," Sukenick explains in "The New Tradition in Fiction." "The picture is filled out but there is no sense of development involved. . . . Situations come about through a cloudburst of fragmented events that fall as they fall and finally can be seen to have assumed some kind of pattern. . . . A novel is both a concrete structure and an imaginative structure—pages, print, binding containing a record of the movements of a mind." The life of the mind, the intricacies of perception, and the interaction between habits of language and how they shape our understanding of the world are the subjects of novels by Sukenick and a number of others who have kept fiction alive.

If there is no absolute reality for the novelist to depict, he can craft a self-consciously imagined one. In Sukenick's novels, this awareness is expressed in changes in form, which is liberated from the conventional obligation to represent chronological time or develop a plot. Instead of progressing through time, the narrative expands only through space; the sequential order follows the author's sense of what is to be revealed at any point in the continuum. In *Out,* the pages count down from Section Nine to Section Zero; the spaces between lines of type increase so that the reader turns pages faster when approaching the end; in Section Zero, words and the author disappear into white space on a blank page.

Out "is a spatial fiction, the idea being to conquer space so as to convey the sense of moving on, fragmentation, things breaking up and never cohering," notes Karl. He suggests, "Sukenick wanted some way to convey the spaced out dimensions of the sixties: spaced out in terms of those who move counterculturally as a consequence of drugs or radical politics; spaced out in the alternative sense of those who move continually. . . . [His] characters belong to a loose organization that blows things up; they carry explosives and move across the country according to certain plans which develop at the last moment. The point is that at any given time, they do not know what they are supposed to do, who their cohorts are, or where their next move will come from. They are lost in space, spaced out, and yet they must move in it."

The novel *Long Talking Bad Conditions Blues* is one long sentence broken into paragraphs. Its style conveys the workings of the narrator's consciousness to connect disparate worlds of "individual and culture," to build bridges of contact between a personal inner world and an alien environment, Karl writes. "At every level, Sukenick's inhabitants are exiled: men from women, each from the other, as individuals or as people seeking, however tentatively, a community. Sukenick tries to wrap these meditations in stylistic equivalents: mainly interior monologue, paragraphs that occupy only a fraction of the page, endlessly run-together sentences which become coils and wraparounds, phrases and sentences interrupted by white space, removal of punctuation so as to approximate consciousness."

98.6 is a record of the search for community as it plays itself out in three different spatial contexts. The landscape of the first section, "Frankenstein," is America, a patchwork of dispossessed remnants. "The land of the living dead," Frankenstein "is a territory the Aztecs would have recognized, death-oriented," observes Karl. The nightmarish lives of "Frankenstein's Children," troubled by experimentation with drugs, group sex, and violent altercations with people from outside their commune, comprise the second section. "Palestine," the third section in which members of a kibbutz achieve the sought-after communal life, seems utopian by contrast. Parallel to the search for new forms of social organization in the novel is Sukenick's quest for a new kind of fiction. "For the unities of realistic fiction—plot, character and causation—Sukenick substitutes the 'discipline of inclusion,' an unceasing energy, and a belief in the primacy of language," Thomas LeClair relates in the *New York Times Book Review.* LeClair credits the novel's success to Sukenick's approach: "Because he sees life as continual invention, he can get at the imaginative bases of the alternative culture with sympathy and humor, without trapping himself in hip cliches." E. M. Potoker, writing in a *Nation* review, comments that Sukenick's work holds together better than the fragmented culture he depicts: "Out of broad humor and a sense of structural irony . . . Sukenick manages to balance the sentimental, the emotional, and the pathetic with the obscene, the trivial and the absurd."

Because personality as it was traditionally perceived also "no longer exists," characters in Sukenick's novels are freed from traditional expectations. The narrator may give a character contradictory traits at different times in the story. He may describe another character first as short, then as tall, then confess he doesn't know what the other looks like. Some characters are Sukenick's actual acquaintances and others merely borrow their names. His fictional people are amorphous, he tells Bellamy, because twentieth-century people are multi-faceted, and because we are in the act of imagining who people are apart from their reality at all times. "You're always making people up, in effect. . . . There you are, and I don't know much about you, but, in a way, I'm making you up. I'm filling up the gaps in my mind, and I create the Joe Bellamy that happens to be there. And probably there's a great gap between my version, which is imaginative, and the real Joe Bellamy. . . . Maybe there isn't a real Joe Bellamy. Maybe there aren't real characters. That's the important thing. Maybe people are much more fluid and amorphous than the realistic novel would have us believe." In *The Life of Fiction,* Klinkowitz comments, "His characters are not so real that they 'walk off the pages.' Instead they stay right there, on the pages, as figures remain on the canvas, so it might be appreciated as art and not life. What the reader reads is an honest account of the artist's work, and what the artist presents is a piece of genuine fabrication and craftsmanship, his *imaginative* response to a world we share. Not the shabby lie that this is the world itself."

Such fiction does not represent reality, "it represents itself," he declares in "The New Tradition of Fiction." It is a real object to be savored and evaluated on the basis of its existence as a work of art. Thus, Sukenick "revalidates our imaginations so that we can look at experience in a new way. For him, fiction is not about experience, it is more experience—at its best, simply a perfection of living, and liable to go afoul only when preconceptions of form step in. Like a sorcerer, Sukenick stops the world, calling a halt to having a culture's provisional view of reality accepted as absolute, and allows the imagination to reinvent according to its needs," Klinkowitz writes in *Literary Subversions.*

Paradoxically, Sukenick's fiction highlights the role of the imagination in order to make readers more, not less, sensitive to reality. Though some of his characters involved in wish-fulfillment activity that some consider pornographic may provide an escape for some readers, he tells Bellamy, "I don't want to present people with illusions, and I don't want to let them off cheaply by releasing their fantasies in an easy way. . . . What that does is allow people to escape, obviously, from reality, and I want to bang them with it." He explains in *Contemporary Authors Autobiography Series* that in *Out* and *98.6,* he "used techniques—very different in each—to break down standard form in fiction in order to reach beyond literary artifice to actual experience (don't think I'm not aware of the contradictions involved)." The same paradox, he feels, is at the heart of post-modern literature; behind new fiction is the urge "to get at the truth of experience beyond our fossilizing formulas of discourse, to get at a new and more inclusive 'reality,' if you will. This is a reality that includes what the conventional novel tends to exclude and that encompasses the vagaries of unofficial experience, the cryptic trivia of the quotidian that help shape our fate, and the tabooed details of life—class, ethnic, sexual—beyond sanctioned descriptions of life." The actual business of writing, he says later, "is to tell it like, to use a cliche, it is. That's not as easy as it looks and you get it only in the greatest, yes, Literature."

In the Bellamy interview, Sukenick comments: "I think that writing styles are very personal things, and it's a mistake to make theories of writing, really. My theories of writing are for two things: mainly, they're to release me into my writing, but also, I suppose, there is a propaganda side. I want people to get off one kind of book and get onto another kind of book which seems to me more appropriate for what's going on now—to get people unstuck from a formulated kind of response and open them up to another thing." Connected to this, Sukenick continues, is his belief that fiction is "a normal, if I may use the word, epistemological procedure; that is, [fiction] is at the very center of everybody all the time at any period, and you don't have to search for psychological reasons [behind it], although they may be there too. But I think the epistemological ones are far more important and anterior. It's a way of making up the world and making sense of it."

The practice of fiction persists also because it is an exercise of freedom against all that tries to regulate experience, as he says in *Lillabulero:* "writers . . . are not thinking of Poetry or The Great Novel or Humanism or even of Experimental Writing or of anything more ponderous than stringing words together in ways that give pleasure and allow one to survive one's particular experience. And in so doing meet the only serious obligations of art in a world that constantly pushes in the direction of the impersonal and systematic and that is to be completely personal and unsystematic thereby saving experience from history from ideology and even from art."

Sukenick's work in the 1980s continues to break new ground for fiction by searching out unconventional subject matter and techniques guided by his awareness of the role of the imagination in making sense of our daily experience. "*Blown Away* explores my idea of the novel as related to suppressed traditions of magic, shamanism, prophecy, and the functions of the holy book, all this based on an interpretation of Prospero, our tradition's most eminent literary wizard. My idea is that narrative is or can be a mediumistic form, rather than the empirical form that positivism has delineated for it. The interconnected pieces in *The Endless Short Story* represent a variety of formal improvisations, reflecting my conviction that improvisation is at the heart of art in the American mode," he relates in *Contemporary Authors Autobiography Series.*

Down and In: Life in the Underground is an autobiographical tour through the New York counterculture of the eighties by way of Manhattan's bars. Included are "the confidences of friends, high times" and "4:00 A.M. despair," Stuart Klawans notes in *Nation.* "The final ingredient, of course, is an argument, which should flare up periodically and be left unsettled when day finally breaks . . . : a debate on the nature of adversary culture, moderated by Sukenick with rare intelligence." The novel also affords the author a retrospective glance at his electronic

novel—an earlier work in which a tape recorder was used as a technique of writing. It was never published because it proved too complex for transcription. Regarding his experimental novels, Robert F. Kiernan observes in *American Writing since 1945: A Critical Survey,* "Sukenick seems determined to open up possibilities of literary play not yet current in our texts."

Like some works of postmodernism and the avant garde, Sukenick's novels and essays are assured of a prominent place in the history of literature. The impact of his technical innovations and his call for a new tradition in literature is radical and far-reaching, with implications for writers within and beyond the American scene. Of Sukenick's contribution to the establishment of a new tradition for fiction, Malcolm Bradbury concludes in *The Modern American Novel,* "the transformation from older realism into new systems of creative notation has been of the largest importance, and has had the deepest implications for the novel internationally, because it has questioned the act of imaginative writing at its heart."

BIOGRAPHICAL/CRITICAL SOURCES:

BOOKS

Bellamy, Joe David, editor, *The New Fiction: Interviews with Innovative American Writers,* University of Illinois Press, 1974.

Bradbury, Malcolm, *The Modern American Novel,* Oxford University Press, 1984.

Contemporary Authors Autobiography Series, Volume 8, Gale, 1988.

Contemporary Literary Criticism, Gale, Volume 3, 1975, Volume 4, 1975, Volume 6, 1976, Volume 48, 1988.

Dictionary of Literary Biography Yearbook: 1981, Gale, 1982.

Federman, Ray, editor, *Surfiction,* Swallow Press, 1974.

Hassan, Ihab, *Liberations,* Wesleyan University Press, 1971.

Karl, Frederick R., *American Fictions, 1940-1980: A Comprehensive History and Critical Evaluation,* Harper, 1983.

Kiernan, Robert F., *American Writing since 1945: A Critical Survey,* Ungar, 1983.

Klinkowitz, Jerome, *Innovative Fiction,* Dell, 1972.

Klinkowitz, Jerome, *Literary Disruptions: The Making of a Post-Contemporary Fiction,* University of Illinois Press, 1975.

Klinkowitz, Jerome, *The Life of Fiction,* University of Illinois Press, 1977.

Klinkowitz, Jerome, *Literary Subversions: New American Fiction and the Practice of Criticism,* Southern Illinois University Press, 1985.

Kutnik, Jerzy, *Fiction as Performance: The Fiction of Ronald Sukenick and Raymond Federman,,* Southern Illinois Press, 1986.

LeClair, Thomas and Larry McCaffery, editors, *Anything Can Happen: Interviews with Contemporary American Novelists,* University of Illinois Press, 1983.

Pearce, Richard, *The Novel in Motion,* Ohio State University Press, 1983.

Sukenick, Ronald, *Wallace Stevens: Musing the Obscure,* New York University Press, 1967.

Sukenick, Ronald, *The Death of the Novel, and Other Stories,* Dial, 1969.

Sukenick, Ronald, *In Form, Digressions on the Act of Fiction,* Southern Illinois University Press, 1985.

PERIODICALS

Best Sellers, July, 1973.

Chicago Review, winter, 1972.

Christian Science Monitor, October 9, 1969.

Esquire, December, 1972.
Fiction International, fall, 1973.
Georgia Review, winter, 1983.
Harpers, May, 1968.
Hudson Review, summer, 1968.
Lillabulero, Number 12, 1973.
Los Angeles Times, February 9, 1987.
Los Angeles Times Book Review, October 18, 1987.
Modern Fiction Studies, winter, 1985.
Nation, July 22, 1968, September 27, 1975, September 19, 1987.
New York Review of Books, February 1, 1968, February 27, 1969.
New York Times, June 22, 1968, September 25, 1969, September 29, 1969.
New York Times Book Review, July 14, 1968, October 21, 1973, May 18, 1975, September 22, 1985, November 16, 1986, March 15, 1987, November 1, 1987.
North American Review, summer, 1973.
Partisan Review, winter, 1974.
Saturday Review, July 6, 1968.
Tribune Books (Chicago), August 30, 1987.
Washington Post Book World, July 21, 1968.*

—*Sketch by Marilyn K. Basel*

* * *

SUTHERLAND, Jon Nicholas 1941-1977

PERSONAL: Born December 8, 1941, in San Diego, CA; died July 6, 1977; son of Verne Nicholas (self-employed) and Margaret (Callard) Sutherland; married; wife's name, Marcia A.. *Education:* San Diego State College (now San Diego State University), A.B., 1963; Harvard University, A.M., 1964; University of California, Los Angeles, Ph.D., 1969.

ADDRESSES: Home—3747 Amaryllis Dr., San Diego, CA 92106. *Office*—Department of History, San Diego State University, San Diego, CA 92182.

CAREER: San Diego State University, San Diego, CA, assistant professor, 1967-71, associate professor, 1971-74, professor of history, 1974-75, professor of history and classics, 1975-77. Fellow in law and history, Harvard University, 1971-72.

MEMBER: American Historical Association, Medieval Academy of America, American Society for Legal History, American Numismatic Society, Classical Alliance of the Western States (vice-president, 1970-73).

WRITINGS:

(With Michael Werthman) *Comparative Concepts of Law and Order,* Scott, Foresman, 1971.
(With Robert Detweiler and Werthman) *Environmental Decay in Its Historical Content,* Scott, Foresman, 1973.
Liudprand of Cremona: Bishop, Diplomat, Historian—Studies of the Man and His Age, Centro Italiano per la Storia Sull Alto Medievalo (Florence), 1977.

Contributor of reviews and articles to periodicals, including *Journal of Medieval History* and *American Historical Review.*

WORK IN PROGRESS: A biography on Paul, the Deacon.*

[Date of death provided by wife, Marcia A. Sutherland]

* * *

SWEDE, George 1940-

PERSONAL: Name originally Juris Purins; name legally changed; born November 20, 1940, in Riga, Latvia (now U.S.S.R.); son of Valdis and Virginia (Seeberg) Purins; adoptive son of Arnold Swede; married Bonnie Lewis, June 20, 1964 (divorced, June, 1969); married Anita Krumins (an educator in business and technical communications), July 23, 1974; children: Juris Krumins, Andris Krumins. *Education:* University of British Columbia, B.A., 1964; Dalhousie University, M.A., 1965.

ADDRESSES: Home—70 London St., Toronto, Ontario, Canada M6G 1N3; P. O. Box 279, Station P, Toronto, Ontario, Canada M6G 1N3 *Office*—Department of Psychology, Ryerson Polytechnical Institute, 350 Victoria St., Toronto, Ontario, Canada M5G 2K3.

CAREER: Vancouver City College, Vancouver, British Columbia, instructor in psychology, 1966-67; Toronto Public Schools, Toronto, Ontario, psychologist, 1967-68; Ryerson Polytechnical Institute, Toronto, instructor, 1968-73, professor of psychology, 1973—, chairman of department, 1974-75. Director of developmental psychology at Open College, Toronto, 1973-75. Director of Poetry and Things, 1969-71. Judge for Japan Air Lines' haiku contest, and for Haiku Society of America's Henderson Award, both 1989.

MEMBER: PEN, Canadian Society of Children's Authors, Illustrators, and Performers (member of executive committee, 1981-84), League of Canadian Poets, Writers Union of Canada, Haiku Society of America, Haiku Canada (co-founder, 1977).

AWARDS, HONORS: Grants from Ontario Arts Council, 1978-80, 1982, 1984-86, 1988-89; honorable mention from Haiku Society of America, 1980, for *Wingbeats;* winner of High/Coo Press mini-chapbook competition, 1982, for *All of Her Shadows;* Museum of Haiku Literature Award from *Frogpond,* 1983, 1985; Children's Book Centre "Our Choice" awards, 1984, for *Tick Bird,* 1985, for *Time Is Flies,* and 1987, for *High Wire Spider; I Throw Stones at the Mountain* was runner-up in Wind Chimes Press minibook competition, 1988.

WRITINGS:

POETRY

Unwinding, Missing Link Press, 1974.
Tell-Tale Feathers, Fiddlehead Poetry Books, 1978.
Endless Jigsaw, Three Tree Press, 1978.
A Snowman, Headless, Fiddlehead Poetry Books, 1979.
Wingbeats, Juniper Press, 1979.
As Far as the Sea Can Eye, York Publishing, 1979.
This Morning's Mockingbird, High/Coo Press, 1980.
Eye to Eye with a Frog, Juniper Press, 1981.
All of Her Shadows, High/Coo Press, 1982.
Flaking Paint, Underwhich Editions, 1983.
Frozen Breaths, Wind Chimes Press, 1983.
Bifids, Curvd H & Z Press, 1984.
Night Tides, South Western Ontario Poetry, 1984.
(With LeRoy Gorman and Eric Amann) *The Space Between,* Wind Chimes Press, 1984.
I Eat a Rose Petal, Haiku Canada, 1987.
Multiple Personality, Silver Bird Press, 1987.
(With John Curry) *Where Even the Factories Have Lawns,* Gesture Press, 1988.
I Throw Stones at the Mountain, Wind Chimes Press, 1988.

JUVENILE

(With wife, Anita Krumins) *Quilby, the Porcupine Who Lost His Quills,* Three Trees Press, 1979.
The Case of the Moonlit Gold Dust, Three Trees Press, 1979.
The Case of the Missing Heirloom, Three Trees Press, 1980.
The Case of the Seaside Burglaries, Three Trees Press, 1981.

The Case of the Downhill Theft, Three Trees Press, 1982.
Undertow, Three Trees Press, 1982.
Tick Bird (poetry), Three Trees Press, 1983.
Time Is Flies, Three Trees Press, 1984.
High Wire Spider, Three Trees Press, 1986.
Leaping Lizard, Three Trees Press, 1988.
Holes in My Cage: Poems for Young Adults, Three Trees Press,
   1989.

OTHER

(Editor) *Canadian Haiku Anthology,* Three Trees Press, 1979.
The Modern English Haiku (essays), Columbine Editions, 1981.
(Editor) *Cicada Voices,* High/Coo Press, 1983.
(Editor) *The Universe Is One Poem* (essays and poems), Simon
   & Pierre, 1990.

Contributor to over fifty anthologies; contributor of poems to over a hundred periodicals, including *Poetry Canada Review, Poetry Nippon, Alchemist, Cicada, Industrial Sabotage, What, University of Toronto Review,* and *Frogpond.* Poetry editor of *Poetry Toronto,* 1980-81; *Writers' Quarterly,* children's book review editor, 1982-84, poetry review editor, 1984—86, and poetry editor, 1986-88; poetry editor of *Writers' Magazine,* 1988-90.

SIDELIGHTS: George Swede told *CA:* "Why do I write? My answer is very behavioristic: for positive reinforcement. Because of a solitary childhood, I learned to value books at companions. Eventually, I tried some writing of my own. When it received modest praise, I wanted to improve my work and, thus, garner more substantial rewards. Now, years later, intermittent reinforcement keeps steadily coming and therefore I keep writing. Of course, I have learned to value most the recognition from a certain group of people—my peers."

T

TATE, (John Orley) Allen   1899-1979

PERSONAL: Born November 19, 1899, in Winchester, Ky.; died February 9, 1979, in Nashville, Tenn.; son of John Orley and Eleanor (Varnell) Tate; married Caroline Gordon (a novelist), November 3, 1924 (divorced, 1959); married Isabella Stewart Gardner, August 27, 1959 (divorced, 1966); married Helen Heinz, July 30, 1966; children: (first marriage) Nancy Meriwether, (third marriage) John Allen, Michael Paul (deceased), Benjamin Lewis Bogan. *Education:* Vanderbilt University, B.A. (magna cum laude), 1922. *Politics:* Democrat. *Religion:* Roman Catholic convert, 1950.

ADDRESSES: Home—113 Groome Dr., Nashville, Tenn. 37205. *Office*—Department of English, 127 Vincent Hall, University of Minnesota, Minneapolis, Minn. *Agent*—Laurence Pollinger Ltd., 18 Maddox St., London W1, England.

CAREER: Writer, 1922-79. *Telling Tales,* New York, N.Y., assistant editor, 1924-25; Southwestern College, Memphis, Tenn., lecturer in English, 1934-36; University of North Carolina, Women's College, Greensboro, professor of English, 1938-39; Princeton University, Princeton, N.J., poet in residence, 1939-42; Library of Congress, Washington, D.C., chair of poetry, 1943-44, fellow in American letters, 1944-50; *Sewanee Review,* Sewanee, Tenn., editor, 1944-46; New York University, New York, N.Y., lecturer, 1947-51; University of Chicago, Chicago, Ill., visiting professor of humanities, 1949; University of Minnesota, Minneapolis, professor of English, 1951-66, Regents' Professor of English, 1966-68. Member of Columbia Broadcasting System (CBS) radio program "Invitation to Learning," 1940-41. Fulbright professor, University of Rome, 1953-54, Oxford University, 1958-59. Member of American delegation to UNESCO Conference on the Arts, and American representative to the International Exposition of the Arts (Congress for Cultural Freedom), both 1952. Lecturer for Department of State in England, France, Italy, and India, 1956. Senior fellow, Indiana School of Letters. Visiting lecturer and poet at numerous universities and public readings.

MEMBER: National Institute of Arts and Letters (president, 1968-69), American Academy of Arts and Letters, American Academy of Arts and Sciences, Society of American Historians, Southern Historical Association, Phi Beta Kappa (senate, 1952-53), Century Association, Princeton Club, Authors Club (London).

AWARDS, HONORS: Guggenheim fellowships, 1928 and 1929; National Institute of Arts and Letters award, 1948; Bollingen Prize for poetry, 1956; Brandeis University Medal for poetry, 1961; gold medal from Dante Society, Florence, Italy, 1962; Academy of American Poets award, 1963; Oscar Williams award, Mark Rothko award, Ingram Merrill award, and National Medal for Literature, all 1976. Numerous honorary degrees, including University of Louisville, 1948, Coe College, 1955, Colgate University, 1956, University of Kentucky, 1960, and Carleton College, 1963.

WRITINGS:

POETRY

(With Ridley Wills) *The Golden Mean, and Other Poems,* privately printed, 1923.
Mr. Pope, and Other Poems, Minton, 1928.
(Contributor) *Fugitives: An Anthology of Verse,* Harcourt, 1928.
Three Poems: Ode to the Confederate Dead, Message from Abroad, [and] The Cross, Minton, 1930.
Poems: 1928-1931, Scribner, 1932.
The Mediterranean and Other Poems, Alcestis, 1936.
Selected Poems, Scribner, 1937.
Sonnets at Christmas, Cummington, 1941.
(Translator) Pervigilium Veneris, *Vigil of Venus,* Cummington, 1943.
The Winter Sea, Cummington, 1944.
Fragment of a Meditation/MCMXXVIII, Cummington, 1947.
Poems, 1920-1945, Eyre, 1948.
Poems: 1922-1947, Scribner, 1948, enlarged edition, 1960.
Two Conceits for the Eye To Sing, If Possible, Cummington, 1950.
Poems, Scribner, 1960.
Christ and the Unicorn, Cummington, 1966.
The Swimmers and Other Selected Poems, Oxford University Press, 1970, Scribner, 1971.
Collected Poems, 1919-1976, Farrar, Straus, 1977.

PROSE

Stonewall Jackson: The Good Soldier, Minton, 1928.
Jefferson Davis: His Rise and Fall, Minton, 1929.
(Contributor) *I'll Take My Stand: The South and the Agrarian Tradition by Twelve Southerners,* Harper, 1930.
(With others) *The Critique of Humanism,* 1930.
(Contributor) *The Best Short Stories, 1934,* Houghton, 1934.

(Editor and contributor) *Who Owns America?: A New Declaration of Independence,* Houghton, 1936.

Reactionary Essays on Poetry and Ideas, Scribner, 1936.

(Contributor) *A Southern Harvest,* Houghton, 1937.

(With A. Theodore Johnson) *America through the Essay,* Oxford University Press, 1938.

The Fathers (novel; also see below), Putnam, 1938, revised edition, A.Swallow, 1960.

Reason in Madness: Critical Essays, Putnam, 1941.

(With Huntington Cairns and Mark Van Doren) *Invitation to Learning,* Random House, 1941.

On the Limits of Poetry: Selected Essays, 1928-1948, A. Swallow, 1948.

The Hovering Fly and Other Essays, Cummington, 1948.

The Forlorn Demon: Didactic and Critical Essays, Regnery, 1953.

The Man of Letters in the Modern World: Selected Essays, 1928-1955, Meridian, 1955.

Collected Essays, A. Swallow, 1959, revised and enlarged edition published as *Essays of Four Decades,* 1968.

Mere Literature and the Lost Traveller, George Peabody College for Teachers, 1969.

The Translation of Poetry, Gertrude Clark Whittall Poetry and Literature Fund, 1972.

John Tyree Fain and Thomas Daniel Young, editors, *The Literary Correspondence of Donald Davidson and Allen Tate,* University of Georgia Press, 1974.

Memoirs and Opinions, 1926-1974, Swallow, 1975 (published in England as *Memoirs & Essays Old and New, 1926-1974,* Carcanet, 1976).

The Fathers and Other Fiction, Louisiana State University Press, 1977.

Thomas Daniel Young and John J. Hindle, editors, *The Republic of Letters in America: The Correspondence of John Peale Bishop and Allen Tate,* University Press of Kentucky, 1981.

Ashley Brown and Frances Neel Cheney, editors, *The Poetry Reviews of Allen Tate,* Louisiana State University Press, 1983.

EDITOR

White Buildings: Poems by Hart Crane, Horace Liveright, 1926.

The Language of Poetry, Princeton University Press, 1942.

Princeton Verse between Two Wars: An Anthology, Princeton University Press, 1942.

(With John Peale Bishop) *American Harvest: Twenty Years of Creative Writing in the United States,* L. B. Fischer, 1942.

Recent American Poetry and Poetic Criticism: A Selected List of References, Library of Congress, 1943.

Sixty American Poets, 1896-1944, Library of Congress, 1945, revised edition, 1954.

A Southern Vanguard: The John Peale Bishop Memorial Volume, Prentice-Hall, 1947.

The Collected Poems of John Peale Bishop, Scribner, 1948.

(With wife, Caroline Gordon) *The House of Fiction: An Anthology of the Short Story, with Commentary,* Scribner, 1950, revised edition, 1960.

(With David Cecil) *Modern Verse in English,* Macmillan, 1958.

(With Ralph Ross and John Berryman) *The Arts of Reading,* Crowell, 1960.

(With Robert Penn Warren) *Selected Poems by Denis Devlin,* Delacorte, 1966.

T. S. Eliot, the Man and His Work: A Critical Evaluation by Twenty-six Distinguished Writers, Delacorte, 1967.

Complete Poetry and Selected Criticism of Edgar Allan Poe, New American Library, 1968.

Six American Poets from Emily Dickinson to the Present: An Introduction, University of Minnesota Press, 1971.

OTHER

Editor, *Kenyon Review,* 1938-42. Contributor of essays and poetry to numerous periodicals, including *Double-Dealer, Hound and Horn, The Fugitive, Literary Review, Nation, New Republic, Minnesota Review, Shenandoah, Kenyon Review, Partisan Review, Yale Review, Criterion, Le Figaro Litteraire,* and *Sewanee Review.* Tate's papers are collected at the Princeton University Library, the Columbia University Library, and the University of Victoria Library, British Columbia.

SIDELIGHTS: The late Allen Tate was a well-known man of letters from the American South, a central figure in the fields of poetry, criticism, and ideas. In the course of a career spanning the middle decades of the twentieth century, Tate authored poems, essays, translations, and fiction; *Dictionary of Literary Biography* contributor James T. Jones claimed that his "influence was prodigious, his circle of acquaintances immense." Tate relished his "man of letters" reputation—he consistently held for the highest standards of literature, feeling that the best creative writing offers the most cogent expressions of human experience. *Sewanee Review* correspondent J. A. Bryant, Jr. called Tate a "sage" who "kept bright the instrument of language in our time and . . . made it illuminate as well as shine."

Tate was born and raised in Kentucky, the youngest of three sons of John Orley and Eleanor Varnell Tate. His family moved frequently when he was young, so his elementary education was erratic. Influenced by his mother's love of literature, however, he did extensive reading on his own; he was admitted to Vanderbilt University in 1918. There Tate proved an excellent student, earning top honors and membership in Phi Beta Kappa. More importantly, while an undergraduate he became aware of the special circumstances of Southern culture and sensibility. *Dictionary of Literary Biography* essayist James A. Hart wrote: "With a Border background [Tate] had to face the question of whether he was a Southerner or an American. Affirming the first, he had to confront the dominant positivist and materialistic Yankee values which were supplanting the older values of the South." Under the influence of his teachers Walter Clyde Curry, Donald Davidson, and John Crowe Ransom, Tate began to analyze his inheritance from a critical, but respectful, perspective.

Tate was the only undergraduate to be admitted to membership in the Fugitives, an informal group of Southern intellectuals that included Ransom, Davidson, Merrill Moore, and Robert Penn Warren. The Fugitives met once a week to discuss poetry—their own and others'—and to mount a defense against the notion that the South did not possess a significant literature of its own. In the periodical *The Fugitive,* and later in an important anthology called *I'll Take My Stand,* Tate argued that the Southern agrarian way of life reflected the artistic beauty, intelligence, and wit of the ancient classic age. Hart explained that Tate and his fellow Fugitives "believed that industrialism had demeaned man and that there was a need to return to the humanism of the Old South." The Agrarian movement, Hart added, "would create or restore something in 'the moral and religious outlook of Western Man.' " Whatever its beliefs, the Fugitive group exerted an enormous influence on American letters in the 1920s and on into the Depression era. A number of its members, including Tate, became the literary spokesmen for their generations.

Although Tate spent several years between 1928 and 1932 in France, he continued to write almost exclusively about the South. While he socialized with Ernest Hemingway, Gertrude

Stein, and the other expatriate American writers in Paris, Tate still explored his own personal philosophical and moral ties to his homeland. He wrote two biographies of Southern Civil War heroes, *Stonewall Jackson: The Good Soldier* and *Jefferson Davis: His Rise and Fall,* he began his most important poem, "Ode to the Confederate Dead," and he worked on his only novel, *The Fathers. Southern Literary Journal* contributor George Core maintained that Tate was aware of the failings of the Old South, but it still remained "his chief model for his whole life. . . . Hence Tate's connections with the South—by inheritance, kinship, custom, and manner—have furnished him with . . . a central allegiance. Out of the tension between Tate's personal allegiance and his awareness of what he has called 'a deep illness of the modern mind' has come the enkindling subject of his work as a whole."

Not surprisingly, Tate's poetry has seemed to come from "a direct sensuous apprehension . . . of the Southern experience—the Southern people, animals, terrain, and climate," to quote Donald E. Stanford in the *Southern Review.* In many of his poems, Tate confronted the relation between an idealized past and a present deficient in both faith and tradition. *New York Times Book Review* correspondent Hilton Kramer found the author "deeply immersed in the materials of history, and there could never be any question of separating *his* literary achievements from their attachment to the historical imagination." Kramer added that the particular history upon which Tate drew was "the history of a lost world carried in the mind of a Southerner, a classicist and an artist exiled to a Northern culture in which the imperatives of industrialism, philistinism and bourgeois capitalism reinforce a sense of irretrievable defeat." Likewise, *Southern Review* essayist Alan Williamson wrote that the stance in Tate's poetry "is that the individual is deeply unworthy, and should desire only to bring himself closer . . . to the destiny and the standards of the ancestors." Williamson concluded, however, that in some of Tate's later work "there is an undercurrent of contrary feeling: a bitter suspicion that the domination of the past, rather than the deficiencies of modern thought, is responsible for the sense of suffocation and unreality in present experience."

The Old South was semifeudal, agrarian, backward-looking, and religious, much like the European communities of the Middle Ages. Some critics have detected in Tate's work a return to somewhat medieval patterns of thought. In *Renascence,* Sister Mary Bernetta wrote: "In the Middle Ages there was one drama which took precedence over all other conflict . . . the Struggle of Everyman to win beatitude and to escape eternal reprobation. Tate recognizes the issue as a subject most significant for literature." Furthermore, like Dante, a poet he admired, Tate employed the most demanding poetic forms, which became "a compelling ritual to which the reader must submit in order to approach this poet's meaning," according to Robert B. Shaw in *Poetry.* As Louise Cowan noted in her book *The Southern Critics,* Tate's "quest throughout all his writing was for the sacramental vision such as Dante's Christianity embodied; for the unity of being, achieved in the philosophy of Thomism; for the classical-Christian synthesis of thought and feeling, formed in the Middle Ages and still underlying, albeit fragmentarily, the Southern sensibility."

One of Tate's preoccupations was indeed "man suffering from unbelief." His modern Everyman, however, faced a more complex situation than the simple medieval morality tale hero. *Michigan Quarterly Review* contributor Cleanth Brooks explained: "In the old Christian synthesis, nature and history were related in a special way. With the break-up of that synthesis, man finds himself caught between a meaningless cycle on the one hand, and on the other, the more extravagant notions of progress—between a nature that is oblivious of man and a man-made 'unnatural' utopia." Even though he had periods of skepticism himself, Tate felt that art could not survive without religion. To quote Pier Francesco Listri in *Allen Tate and His Work: Critical Evaluations,* "In a rather leaden society governed by a myth of science, [Tate's] poetry conducts a fearless campaign against science, producing from that irony a measure both musical and fabulous. In an apathetic, agnostic period he [was] not ashamed to recommend a Christianity to be lived as intellectual anguish."

Tate expounded upon many of the same themes in his criticism. Because he believed in the autonomy of art and the aesthetic formalist basis of critical analysis, he was classified among the "New Critics" of the mid-twentieth century. In *On Native Grounds: An Interpretation of Modern American Prose Literature,* Alfred Kazin observed that, in order to save criticism from the "scientists," Tate "disengaged literature itself from society and men, and held up the inviolate literary experience as the only measure of human knowledge. Literature in this view was not only the supreme end; it was also the only end worthy of man's ambition." Ferman Bishop claimed in his book *Allen Tate* that for the author, "the distinctively literary quality of a poem, play, or novel is the manner of its presentation." *Accent* correspondent Richard Foster contended that Tate was "less a technical literary critic than an essayist using literature as the frame of reference within which he criticizes the mind and life of his time in the light of his convictions about the proper ends of man. He speaks as a twentieth-century humanist intellectual, isolated and virtually unheard in the barbaric society whose larger deformities it is his concern to examine and minister to." *Sewanee Review* essayist Eliseo Vivas concluded: "At the heart of [Tate's] criticism, informing it throughout and giving it remarkable consistency and force, is his protest against the meaning of the present and of the probable future."

Having had a classical education himself, Tate employed numerous classical allusions in his work; he also often wrote intensely personal poetry that would not reveal itself instantly to a reader. In the *Sewanee Review,* Cowan called Tate "the most difficult poet of the twentieth century," and other critics have offered similar assessments. Brooks, for one, noted: "Tate puts a great burden upon his reader. He insists that the reader himself, by an effort of his own imagination, cooperate with the poet to bring the violent metaphors and jarring rhythms into unity." *Georgia Review* contributor M. E. Bradford also contended that Tate, with "his preference for the lyric and for the agonized *persona* in that genre—along with the admiration which his ingenuities in the employment of all manner of strategies have together inspired—have confirmed his reputation for obscurity, allusive privacy, and consequent difficulty. Were it not for his politics, his poetics, and his honesty about them both, he could have become the object of coterie enthusiasms."

Monroe K. Spears offered some reasons why Tate never became merely the "object of coterie enthusiasms." In the *Sewanee Review,* Spears praised Tate for his "independence and common sense and avoidance of cant" as well as for "his stubborn honesty and candor; his ideal of poise, integrity, and intelligence." *New Republic* contributor James Dickey also found Tate to be more than a "Southern writer." Dickey wrote: "[Tate's] situation has certain perhaps profound implications for every man in every place and every time. And they are more than implications; they are the basic questions, the possible solutions to the question of existence. How does each of us wish to live his only life?" Bishop concluded that Tate's place in American letters "is secure," adding: "He is one of a very small number of American writers who have had the ability to present the intellectual as well as the emotional side of the American experience. In a culture which has seemed so often to encourage and even depend on the anti-intellectual, he has emphasized the opposite. Ultimately, . . . he will be proved to have dealt with the truly significant elements in our experience."

BIOGRAPHICAL/CRITICAL SOURCES:

BOOKS

Allen, Walter, *The Modern Novel: In Britain and the United States,* Dutton, 1965.

Arnold, W. B., *Social Ideas of Allen Tate,* Humphries, 1955.

Bishop, Ferman, *Allen Tate,* Twayne, 1967.

Bradbury, John M., *The Fugitives: A Critical Account,* University of North Carolina Press, 1958.

Contemporary Literary Criticism, Gale, Volume 2, 1974, Volume 4, 1975, Volume 6, 1976, Volume 9, 1978, Volume 11, 1979, Volume 14, 1980, Volume 24, 1983.

Cowan, Louise, *The Fugitive Group: A Literary History,* Louisiana State University Press, 1959.

Deutsch, Babette, *Poetry in Our Time,* Holt, 1952.

Dictionary of Literary Biography, Gale, Volume 4: *American Writers in Paris, 1920-1939,* 1980, Volume 45: *American Poets, 1880-1945, Third Series,* 1986, Volume 63: *Modern American Critics, 1920-1955,* 1988.

Dupree, Robert S., *Allen Tate and the Augustinian Imagination: A Study of the Poetry,* Louisiana State University Press, 1983.

Fallwell, Marshall, Jr., *Allen Tate: A Bibliography,* Lewis, 1969.

Foster, Richard, *The New Romantics: A Reappraisal of the New Criticism,* Indiana University Press, 1962.

Frye, Northrop, *Northrop Frye on Culture and Literature: A Collection of Review Essays,* University of Chicago Press, 1978.

Hemphill, George, *Allen Tate,* University of Minnesota Press, 1964.

Kazin, Alfred, *On Native Grounds: An Interpretation of Modern American Prose Literature,* Reynal & Hitchcock, 1942.

Meiners, R. K., *The Last Alternatives: A Study of the Works of Allen Tate,* Swallow, 1963.

Pratt, William, editor, *The Fugitive Poets: Modern Southern Poetry in Perspective,* Dutton, 1965.

Pritchard, John Paul, *Criticism in America,* University of Oklahoma Press, 1956.

Purdy, Rob Roy, editor, *Fugitives Reunion: Conversations at Vanderbilt,* Vanderbilt University Press, 1959.

Ransom, John Crowe, editor, *The Kenyon Critics,* World, 1951.

Rizzardi, Alfredo, *Ode ai Caduti Confederati e Altre Poesie,* Arnoldo Mondadori, 1970.

Rubin, Louis and R. D. Jacobs, editors, *South: Modern Southern Literature in Its Cultural Setting,* Doubleday, 1961.

Spears, Monroe K., *Dionysus and the City: Modernism in Twentieth-Century Poetry,* Oxford University Press, 1970.

Squires, Radcliffe, *Allen Tate: A Literary Biography,* Bobbs-Merrill, 1971.

Squires, Radcliffe, editor, *Allen Tate and His Work: Critical Evaluations,* University of Minnesota Press, 1972.

Stewart, John L., *The Burden of Time: The Fugitives and the Agrarians,* Princeton University Press, 1965.

Stineback, David C., *Shifting World: Social Change and Nostalgia in the American Novel,* Associated University Presses, 1976.

West, Thomas R., *Nature, Community, & Will: A Study in Literary and Social Thought,* University of Missouri Press, 1976.

PERIODICALS

American Scholar, autumn, 1976.
Book World, March 2, 1969.
Commonweal, May 29, 1953.
Critique, spring, 1964.
Georgia Review, spring, 1968, spring, 1971.
Intercollegiate Review, winter, 1973-74.
Michigan Quarterly Review, fall, 1971.
New Republic, April 29, 1936, July 24, 1965, October 1, 1975.
New York Times Book Review, May 4, 1969, December 11, 1977, January 8, 1978, April 8, 1979.
Partisan Review, February, 1949, summer, 1968.
Poetry, May, 1968, April, 1970, January, 1972.
Renascence, spring, 1971.
Sewanee Review, January, 1954, autumn, 1959, summer, 1968, spring, 1972, summer, 1974, spring, 1978, spring, 1979.
Shenandoah, spring, 1961, winter, 1968.
South Atlantic Quarterly, autumn, 1967.
Southern Literary Journal, autumn, 1969.
Southern Review, winter, 1936, winter, 1940, summer, 1971, autumn, 1972, autumn, 1976, April, 1978.
Virginia Quarterly Review, summer, 1969.
Washington Post, May 7, 1969.

OBITUARIES:

PERIODICALS

Chicago Tribune, February 10, 1979.
New York Times, February 10, 1979.
Publishers Weekly, February 26, 1979.
Washington Post, February 10, 1979.*

—*Sketch by Anne Janette Johnson*

* * *

TATE, Robin
See FANTHORPE, R(obert) Lionel

* * *

TAYLOR, A(lan) J(ohn) P(ercivale)   1906-1990

PERSONAL: Born March 25, 1906, in Southport, Birkdale, Lancashire, England; son of Percy Lees and Constance (Thompson) Taylor; married third wife, Eva (a historian), 1976; children: Giles, Sebastian, Amelia, Sophia, Crispin, Daniel. *Education:* Bootham School, student, 1919-24; Oriel College, Oxford, B.A., 1927, M.A., 1932. *Politics:* Labour Party.

ADDRESSES: Home—32 Twisden Rd., London NW5 1DN, England.

CAREER: Rockefeller Fellow in social sciences, 1929-30; Manchester University, Manchester, England, lecturer in history, 1930-38; Oxford University, Oxford, England, fellow of Magdalen College, 1938-76, honorary fellow, 1976—, tutor in modern history, 1938-63, university lecturer in international history, 1953-63, Ford's Lecturer in English History, 1955-56, honorary fellow of Oriel College, 1980—. Leslie Stephen Lecturer, Cambridge University, 1961-62; Creighton Lecturer, London University, 1973; Benjamin Meaker Visiting Professor of History, University of Bristol, 1976-78. In charge of Beaverbrook Library.

MEMBER: British Academy (fellow), American Academy of Arts and Sciences (honorary member), Yugoslav Academy of Sciences (honorary member), Hungarian Academy of Sciences (honorary member), National Union of Journalists, City Music Society (London; president).

AWARDS, HONORS: Honorary degrees include D.C.L. from New Brunswick College, Oxford, 1961, D.Litt. from University of Bristol, 1978, University of Warwick, 1981, and University of Manchester, 1982.

WRITINGS:

The Italian Problem in European Diplomacy, 1847-1849, Manchester University Press, 1934, Barnes & Noble, 1970.

Germany's First Bid for Colonies, 1884-1885: A Move in Bismarck's European Policy, Macmillan, 1938, Archon, 1967.

The Habsburg Monarchy, 1815-1918, Macmillan, 1941, revised edition published as *The Habsburg Monarchy, 1809-1918: A History of the Austrian Empire and Austria-Hungary,* 1949, University of Chicago Press, 1976.

The Course of German History: A Survey of the Development of German History since 1815, Hamish Hamilton, 1945, revised edition, Coward-McCann, 1946, reprinted, Methuen, 1961.

From Napoleon to Stalin: Comments on European History, Hamish Hamilton, 1950.

Rumours of Wars, Hamish Hamilton, 1952.

The Struggle for Mastery in Europe, 1848-1918, Clarendon Press, 1954.

Bismarck: The Man and the Statesman, Knopf, 1955.

Englishmen and Others, Hamish Hamilton, 1956.

The Trouble Makers: Dissent over Foreign Policy, 1792-1939, Hamish Hamilton, 1957, Indiana University Press, 1958.

"The Russian Revolution" (television script), Associated Television, 1959.

Politics in the First World War, [London], 1959.

Lloyd George: Rise and Fall, Cambridge University Press, 1961.

The Origins of the Second World War, Hamish Hamilton, 1961, Atheneum, 1962, 2nd edition, Fawcett, 1966.

The First World War: An Illustrated History, Hamish Hamilton, 1963, published as *An Illustrated History of the First World War,* Putnam, 1964, published as *A History of the First World War,* Berkeley, 1966.

Politics in Wartime and Other Essays, Hamish Hamilton, 1964, Atheneum, 1965.

English History, 1914-1945 (Oxford History of England), Clarendon Press, 1965, reprinted, 1985.

From Sarajevo to Potsdam, Thames & Hudson, 1966, Harcourt, 1967.

From Napoleon to Lenin: Historical Essays, Harper, 1966.

Europe: Grandeur and Decline, Penguin, 1967.

(With Robert Rhodes James, J. H. Plumb, Basil Liddell Hart, and Anthony Storr) *Churchill Revised: A Critical Assessment,* Dial, 1969.

War by Timetable: How the First World War Began, American Heritage Press, 1969.

Beaverbrook, Simon & Schuster, 1972.

(With others) *Churchill: Four Faces and the Man,* Penguin, 1973.

Essays in English History, Hamish Hamilton, 1976.

The Last of Old Europe: A Grand Tour with A. J. P. Taylor, Sidgwick & Jackson, 1976.

The War Lords, Hamish Hamilton, 1977, Atheneum, 1978.

The Russian War, 1941-1945, edited by Daniela Mrazkova and Vladimir Remes, J. Cape, 1978.

How Wars Begin, Atheneum, 1979.

Revolutions and Revolutionaries, Hamish Hamilton, 1980.

Politicians, Socialism and Historians, Hamish Hamilton, 1980, Stein & Day, 1982.

A Personal History (autobiography), Atheneum, 1983.

In Search of C. S. Lewis, Bridge Publications, 1983.

An Old Man's Diary, Hamish Hamilton, 1984.

How Wars End, Hamish Hamilton, 1985.

EDITOR

(And co-translator) Heinrich Friedjung, *The Struggle for Supremacy in Germany, 1859-1866,* Macmillan, 1935.

(With R. Reynolds) *British Pamphleteers,* Volume 2, Wingate, 1948-51.

(With Alan Louis Charles Bullock) *A Select List of Books on European History, 1815-1914,* Clarendon Press, 1949, 2nd edition, 1957.

(With Richard Pares) *Essays Presented to Sir Lewis Namier,* St. Martin's, 1956, reprinted, Books for Libraries Press, 1971.

William Maxwell Aitken and Baron Beaverbrook, *The Abdication of King Edward VIII,* Atheneum, 1966.

(And author of introduction) K. Marx and F. Engels, *The Communist Manifesto,* Penguin, 1967.

(With Mortimer Wheeler and Hugh Trevor-Roper) Winston S. Churchill, *History of English-Speaking Peoples: Based on the Text of "A History of the English-Speaking Peoples,"* twelve volumes, New Caxton Library Service, 1969-74.

Lloyd George: Twelve Essays, Hamish Hamilton, 1971.

Frances Stevenson, *Lloyd George: A Diary,* Hutchinson, 1971.

W. P. Crozier, *Off the Record: Political Interviews, 1933-1943,* Hutchinson, 1973.

The Second World War: An Illustrated History, Putnam, 1975.

My Darling Pussy: The Letters of Lloyd George and Frances Stevenson, 1913-41, Weidenfeld & Nicolson, 1975.

The Illustrated History of the World Wars, Octopus, 1978.

OTHER

(Author of introduction) F. Fertig, editor, *1848: The Opening of an Era,* Howard Fertig, 1967.

(Author of foreword) Arthur Schnitzler, *My Youth in Vienna,* Weidenfeld & Nicolson, 1971.

Also author of *The Russian Revolution of 1917,* 1958. Contributor to *Sunday Express, Observer, New Statesman,* and other publications. Editor in chief, "History of the Twentieth Century," for B.P.C. Publishing. A bibliography of Taylor's writings, articles, and TV lectures has been compiled by A. Wrigley.

SIDELIGHTS: A. J. P. Taylor "must be the most widely read English historian since G. M. Trevelyan, quite possibly since Lord Macaulay, and with good reason," states John Gross in the *New York Times Book Review.* Taylor is familiar to many Britons through his long career as a television commentator, his columns in popular papers such as the *Sunday Express,* and through his television series. Woodrow Wyatt, writing in the London *Times,* calls his television work "the best possible history lesson, combining entertainment with instruction," and adds that "A. J. P. Taylor is the most gifted teacher on television." "My guess," Goss declares, "is that he is relatively better known in Britain than, say, John Kenneth Galbraith or Arthur Schlesinger Jr. is in America."

Taylor's books are also widely acclaimed by critics. London *Times* contributor David Marquand declares that the historian is "capable of a sinewy, apparently effortless prose of bewitching grace." John Kenneth Galbraith, writing in the *Washington Post Book World,* asserts that "when [Taylor] turns to his historical writing, he has been as careful, even meticulous, as the better scholars in his areas of competence, and, in addition, he has shown a phenomenally greater capacity for continuous, committed labor." "He writes," Goss notes, "with a verve which will insure that books like his study of dissent in foreign policy, 'The Trouble Makers,' or 'English History 1914-1945' (in my opinion, his masterpiece) will survive on their literary merits even when they have been overtaken by subsequent research." "Where he excels most of all is in his ability to master a great mass of material, and to weave it into a continuous narrative, of which he is always in control," Marquand maintains. "In . . . *English History 1914-1945,* he did this better than anyone since Macaulay. It is hard to believe that anyone will do it as well again."

BIOGRAPHICAL/CRITICAL SOURCES:

BOOKS

Gilbert, Martin, editor, *A Century of Conflict, 1850-1950: Essays in Honour of A. J. P. Taylor,* Hamish Hamilton, 1966, Atheneum, 1967.

Sked, Alan, and Chris Cook, editors, *Crisis and Controversy: Essays in Honour of A. J. P. Taylor,* Macmillan, 1976.

Taylor, A. J. P., *A Personal History* (autobiography), Hamish Hamilton, 1983.

Taylor, A. J. P., *An Old Man's Diary,* Hamish Hamilton, 1984.

Wrigley, Chris, editor, *Warfare, Diplomacy and Politics: Essays in Honour of A. J. P. Taylor,* Hamish Hamilton, 1986.

PERIODICALS

Los Angeles Times Book Review, February 10, 1985.
New York Times Book Review, September 25, 1983, June 30, 1985.
Times (London), April 11, 1983, June 2, 1983, April 19, 1984, April 4, 1985.
Times Literary Supplement, May 27, 1983, June 15, 1984, July 19, 1985.
Washington Post Book World, September 4, 1983.

[Sketch reviewed by wife, Eva Taylor]

*   *   *

THANET, Neil
    See FANTHORPE, R(obert) Lionel

*   *   *

THESING, William B(arney) 1947-

PERSONAL: Born December 30, 1947, in St. Louis, MO; son of William Victor (an office manager) and Harriett C. (a teacher; maiden name, Barney) Thesing; married Jane Ann Isley (a senior auditor), July 17, 1976; children: Amy Katherine. *Education:* University of Missouri at St. Louis, B.A. (summa cum laude), 1969; Indiana University at Bloomington, M.A., 1970, Ph.D., 1977.

ADDRESSES: Home—5848 Woodvine Rd., Columbia, SC 29206. *Office*—Department of English, University of South Carolina, Columbia, SC 29208.

CAREER: Substitute teacher in public schools in Webster Groves, MO, 1970; Indiana University, Bloomington, associate instructor in English, 1975-77; University of South Carolina, Columbia, instructor, 1977-79, assistant professor, 1979-83, associate professor of English, 1983-89, professor, 1989—, assistant director of freshman English program, 1978-82, associate chairman, 1984-90. Co-host of SCERN (South Carolina Educational Radio Network) Program "South Carolina Poets: New Talents, New Directions," broadcast by WRJA, WNSC, WSCI, WJWJ, WEPR, and WLTR-Radio, January, 1984. *Military service:* U.S.

Army, 1970-73; counter-intelligence agent serving in Baltimore, Md., and Stuttgart, West Germany.

MEMBER: Modern Language Association of America, National Council of Teachers of English, South Atlantic Modern Language Association (SAMLA), Georgia-South Carolina College English Association, South Carolina Council of Teachers of English, University of South Carolina Victorian Studies Club (founding member and executive secretary, 1978-83), Philological Association of the Carolinas, (president, 1985-86).

AWARDS, HONORS: Woodrow Wilson fellow, 1969-70; National Defense Education Act Title IV fellow at Indiana University at Bloomington, 1969-70 and 1973-76; part-time summer research grant from University of South Carolina, 1978; SAMLA Studies award for manuscript "The London Muse: Victorian Poetic Responses to the City," 1980; South Carolina Committee for the Humanities Grant for project "South Carolina Poets: New Talents, New Directions," 1983; American Council of Learned Societies grants, 1984 and 1989; travel grant, Folger Shakespeare Library, 1986; State Service Award, 1988, for ten years of service; South Carolina College research fellow, 1988-89; University of South Carolina Sponsored Programs and Research grants, 1989, 1990, and fellowship, 1990.

WRITINGS:

(Contributor) Donald J. Greiner, editor, *Dictionary of Literary Biography,* Volume 5: *American Poets since World War II,* Gale, 1980.

(Contributor) John MacNicholas, editor, *Dictionary of Literary Biography,* Volume 7: *Twentieth-Century American Dramatists,* Gale, 1981.

(Contributor) David Cowart and Thomas Wymer, editors, *Dictionary of Literary Biography,* Volume 8: *Twentieth-Century American Science Fiction Writers,* Gale, 1981.

The London Muse: Victorian Poetic Responses to the City, University of Georgia Press, 1982.

(With Christopher C. Brown) *English Prose and Criticism, 1900-1950: A Guide to Information Sources,* Gale, 1983.

Conversations with South Carolina Poets, John F. Blair, 1986.

(Editor) *Dictionary of Literary Biography,* Volume 55: *Victorian Prose Writers before 1867,* Gale, 1987.

(Editor) *Dictionary of Literary Biography,* Volume 57: *Victorian Prose Writers after 1867,* Gale, 1987.

Mrs. Humphry Ward (1851-1920): A Bibliography, University of Queensland, 1987.

(Contributor) Alison G. Sulloway, editor, *Critical Essays on Gerard Manley Hopkins,* G. K. Hall, 1990.

(Editor) *Executions and the British Experience: A Collection of Essays,* McFarland, 1990.

Contributor to literary journals, including *Victorian Poetry, Journal of the Eighteen Nineties Society, Tennyson Research Bulletin, Scottish Literary Journal, College Language Association Journal,* and *Victorian Studies.* Editor of volumes 4-10 of *Aspects: Newsletter of the Department of English,* University of South Carolina, Columbia.

WORK IN PROGRESS: Collections of critical essays on Edna St. Vincent Millay and Robinson Jeffers.

SIDELIGHTS: In the *London Muse,* William B. Thesing addresses the role of the city in the nineteenth-century literary imagination, chronologically classifying poetic responses to the city into three main periods. Fred Schwarzbach, reviewing for the *Times Literary Supplement,* deemed Thesing's division "somewhat too neat," but he also pointed out that one of the book's virtues is "that the overall theme does not intrude too much in the discussions of individual poets, where the author shows a firm sense of the outline of each career and the merits and defects of the poetry." Thesing's discussion includes not only such poets as Arthur Hugh Clough and Matthew Arnold, but also such lesser-knowns as Robert Buchanan, Roden Noel, and Alexander Smith.

Thesing told *CA:* "During high school and college, I was influenced and motivated by several fine mentors who expressed unending curiosity about the works they studied. As far as literary criticism is concerned, my writings have been deeply influenced by the many books published by Raymond Williams, especially *The Country and the City.* I also feel that the college teacher has a service obligation that extends beyond his classroom. Thus, I have done administrative service at the University of South Carolina and directed workshops to introduce poetry to the larger public."

BIOGRAPHICAL/CRITICAL SOURCES:

PERIODICALS

Times Literary Supplement, January 14, 1983.

*　　*　　*

THOMPSON, Paul 1943-

PERSONAL: Born November 23, 1943, in Hitchin, England; son of Philip John and Doris (Swann) Thompson; married Janet Catriona (employed by British Broadcasting Corp.), May 8, 1965 (divorced January 10, 1980); married Veronique Bernard (an actress and theatre director), February 14, 1981; children: (first marriage) Karen Nicola; (second marriage) Felix Edward. *Education:* Attended school in Hitchin, England. *Politics:* Socialist.

ADDRESSES: Home—24 Carlton Hill, London NW8, England. *Agent*—Michael Imison, Michael Imison Playwrights, 28 Almeida Street, London N1 1TD, England.

CAREER: Professional actor, 1964-76; theatre director, 1971—; Morley College, London, England, director of Theatre School, 1974-84; National Institute of Dramatic Arts, Sydney, Australia, head of directing, 1984-86; Australian Film, Television, and Radio School, Sydney, head of writing, 1987—. Acting tutor at Royal Academy of Dramatic Arts, 1978-84; playwriting tutor at City Literary Institute and Antioch International, 1978-84. Writer-in-residence, National Theatre, 1977-79, and Royal Shakespeare Co., 1977; chairman, International Festival of Young Playwrights, 1986—.

AWARDS, HONORS: Arts Council bursary, 1976.

WRITINGS:

PLAYS

The Children's Crusade (musical; first produced in London, England, at National Youth Theatre, September, 1973), Heinemann, 1975.
The Motor Show (musical; first produced in Dagenham, England, at Leys Hall, March 1974; produced in London at Half Moon Theatre, April, 1974), Pluto Press, 1975.
By Common Consent (musical; first produced at National Youth Theatre, September 9, 1974; also see below), Heinemann, 1976.
The Lorenzaccio Story (musical; first produced by Royal Shakespeare Co. in Stratford-upon-Avon, England, at The Other Place, July 4, 1977), Pluto Press, 1978.
Future Perfect, first produced by Tricycle Theatre Co., 1980.

Stars, produced in Western Australia, Australia, by SWY Theatre Co., 1986.

OTHER

Author of filmscript, *By Common Consent* (based on his musical play of the same title), British Broadcasting Corp. Television, 1975; contributor to filmscript, *Lion of the Desert,* Falcon Film Productions, 1979. Also author of adaptation, Vampilov, *Last Summer in Chulimsk,* Birmingham Repertory Theatre, 1984.

WORK IN PROGRESS: Research for a play and for a feature film.

SIDELIGHTS: Paul Thompson has directed productions at numerous theatres, including King's Head Theatre, Soho Poly, Almost Free Theatre, Royal Academy of Dramatic Arts, Fallon House Theatre, and Melbourne Theatre Company.

He told *CA:* "I am inspired by Picasso's view that 'art is a lie that enables us to see the truth more clearly.' "

*　　*　　*

THOMSON, James C(laude), Jr. 1931-

PERSONAL: Born September 14, 1931, in Princeton, NJ; son of James Claude (a missionary in China and Japan) and Margaret Seabury (Cook) Thomson; married Diana Dodge Duffy Butler, December 19, 1959; stepchildren: two. *Education:* Attended University of Nanking, 1948-49; Yale University, B.A., 1953; Clare College, Cambridge, B.A. (first class honors in history), 1955, M.A., 1959; Harvard University, Ph.D., 1961. *Religion:* Presbyterian.

ADDRESSES: Home—21 Sibley Ct., Cambridge, MA 02138.

CAREER: Held positions in Washington, D.C., 1959-64, as assistant to Representative Chester Bowles of Connecticut, 1959-60, special assistant to Under Secretary of State, 1961, special assistant to the President's special representative and adviser on African, Asian, and Latin American affairs, 1961-63, special assistant to Assistant Secretary of State for Far Eastern Affairs, 1963-64, and staff member of National Security Council, the White House, 1964-66; Harvard University, Cambridge, MA, assistant professor of history, 1966-70, lecturer, 1970-84, associate, Institute of Politics, 1966-72, associate, Fairbanks Center for East Asia Research, 1984—; Nieman Foundation for Journalism, Cambridge, curator, 1972-84; Boston University, Boston, MA, director of Institute for Democratic Communications, 1984—. Democratic Policy Council, member of international affairs committee, 1969-82; member of board of directors, National Committee on U.S.-China Relations, 1969—, and Council of Foreign Relations, 1969—. Lawrenceville School, trustee, 1971—. *Nieman Reports,* publisher and editor, 1972-84. *Military service:* U.S. Army Reserve, Military Intelligence, 1950-56; became sergeant.

MEMBER: Association for Asian Studies, American Historical Association, China Council of the Asia Society (national co-chairman, 1982-84), Elizabethan Society, Phi Beta Kappa, Zeta Psi, Scroll and Key.

AWARDS, HONORS: Overseas Press Club Award for Magazine Writing on Foreign Affairs, 1968; Council on Foreign Relations international affairs fellowship, 1969-70; Emmy Award, Academy of Television Arts and Sciences, 1972, for co-anchoring ABC-TV coverage of President Nixon's China trip; Honorary scholar of Clare College, Cambridge University.

WRITINGS:

(Editor) *Seventy-five: A Study of a Generation in Transition,* Yale University Press, 1953.

(Contributor) *Papers on China,* Volume 11, Harvard University Press, 1957.

(Contributor) *No More Vietnams?: The War and the Future of American Foreign Policy,* Harper, for Stevenson Institute of International Affairs, 1968.

(Contributor) *Who We Are: An Atlantic Chronicle of the United States and Vietnam, 1966-69,* Little, Brown, 1969.

While China Faced West: American Reformers in Nationalist China, 1928-1937, Harvard University Press, 1969.

(With Ernest R. May) *American-East Asian Relations: A Survey,* Harvard University Press, 1972.

(With Peter W. Stanley and John Curtis Perry) *Sentimental Imperialists: The American Experience in East Asia,* foreword by John King Fairbank, Harper, 1981.

Contributor of articles and reviews to periodicals, including *China Quarterly, Atlantic, New Republic, Washington Post, Boston Globe, New York Times.* Chairman of editorial board, *Yale Daily News,* 1952-53; member of editorial board, *Foreign Policy;* member of advisory board, *Washington Monthly.*

SIDELIGHTS: James C. Thomson, Jr., lived in China and Japan, 1933-40, in China, 1948-49, and traveled in Asia in 1961, 1962, 1966, and 1969. He has also traveled as a government official, scholar, and tourist in Europe, the Middle East, and Africa.

BIOGRAPHICAL/CRITICAL SOURCES:

PERIODICALS

Newsweek, September 14, 1981.
New York Review of Books, December 3, 1970.
New York Times, August 27, 1981.
New York Times Book Review, September 13, 1981.
Washington Post Book World, August 23, 1981.*

*   *   *

THORPE, Trebor
    See FANTHORPE, R(obert) Lionel

*   *   *

THORPE, Trevor
    See FANTHORPE, R(obert) Lionel

*   *   *

THURSTON, Harry   1950-

PERSONAL: Born March 3, 1950, in Yarmouth, Nova Scotia, Canada; son of Kenneth (a carpenter) and Betty (a receptionist) Thurston; married Catherine Rideout (a child psychologist), July 1, 1972; children: Meaghan Ruth. *Education:* Acadia University, B.Sc., 1971.

ADDRESSES: Home and office—R.R. 3, Southampton, Nova Scotia, Canada B0M 1W0.

CAREER: Canada Manpower Centre, Truro, Nova Scotia, youth worker and manpower counselor, 1971-73; farm laborer in Greenfield, Nova Scotia, 1973-75; Ontario Veterinary College, Guelph, Ontario, veterinary research technician, 1975-77; free-lance writer, 1977—. Instructor in writing poetry and writer-in-residence, St. Mary's University, Halifax, Nova Scotia,

1988; writer-in-community, Springhill, Nova Scotia, 1983. Has given numerous poetry readings. Director of Evelyn Richardson Literary Memorial Trust, 1978-80; chairman of Ship's Company Theatre, 1985-87. Reporter for "Farm Focus," 1977-80.

MEMBER: Canadian Periodical Publishers Association, League of Canadian Poets, Canadian Science Writers' Association, Periodical Writers' Association of Canada, Writers' Federation of Nova Scotia (member of executive committee, 1979-81; chairman of writers' council, 1980-81).

AWARDS, HONORS: Dorothy Shoemaker Award for Poetry, Mid-Western Ontario Library System, 1976, for "Professor out of Work"; Foundation for the Advancement of Canadian Letters, 1982, author's award for personality feature, for feature article "Pratt & Pratt, Christopher and Mary: The First Couple of Canadian Contemporary Art," and author's award for public affairs, for magazine feature "The Enemy Above: People versus Pulp in New Brunswick"; National Magazine Award for Science and Technology, National Magazine Awards Foundation (Canada), 1983, for "The Basque Connection"; explorations grant, Canada Council, 1985, for *Tidal Life: A Natural History of the Bay of Fundy;* Science and Society Award, Canadian Science Writers' Association, 1986, for article "Icebound Eden," and 1987, for article "Everlasting Oasis"; author's award, Foundation for the Advancement of Canadian Letters, 1987, for personality profile article.

WRITINGS:

Barefaced Stone (poems), Fiddlehead Poetry Books, 1980.
Clouds Flying before the Eye (poems), Fiddlehead Poetry Books, 1985.
(Contributor) William Van Nest, editor, *Connections: Effective Reading and Writing,* Prentice-Hall, 1988.
(Contributor) Eleanor Goldstein, editor, *SIRS,* Social Science Resources, 1988.
Exploring Change: People and Places (textbook), Douglas & McIntyre, 1989.
(Contributor) Aaron Schneider, editor, *Canada and the Tropics,* University College of Cape Breton, 1989.
Tidal Life: A Natural History of the Bay of Fundy (nonfiction), Camden House, 1990.
Atlantic Outposts (essays), Pottersfield Press, 1990.
Lighthouses of Atlantic Canada, Nimbus Publishing, 1991.

CONTRIBUTOR TO ANTHOLOGIES

Ninety Seasons: Modern Poems from the Maritimes, McClelland & Stewart, 1974.
Nearly an Island: A Nova Scotian Anthology, Breakwater Books, 1978.
Tributaries, an Anthology: Writer to Writer, Mosaic Press, 1978.
1981 Anthology of Magazine Verse and Yearbook of American Poetry, Monitor Publications, 1982.
Easterly: Sixty Atlantic Writers, Academic Press Canada, 1983.
The Atlantic Anthology, Volume 2: *Poetry,* Ragweed Press, 1985.
The Maritimes: Tradition, Challenge, and Change, Maritext, 1987.
1986 Anthology of Magazine Verse and Yearbook of American Poetry, Monitor Publications, 1987.
Till All the Stars Have Fallen, Kids Can Press, 1989.

OTHER

Documentary scriptwriter for CBC-TV series "Land and Sea." Contributor of articles and poems to periodicals, including *Prism International, Audubon, National Geographic, Reader's Digest, Grain, Antigonish Review,* and *Atlantic Insight. Germination,* editor and publisher, 1977-82, publisher, 1982-83; contributing editor, *Equinox,* 1984—.

SIDELIGHTS: Harry Thurston told *CA:* "I live in the oldest part of North America as Westerners know it. To Nova Scotians history is important to their daily lives. People still tell stories here. That oral tradition has led me to speculate that each Nova Scotian has a personal memory that spans one hundred fifty years. The feeling (formed early in childhood) that the past is extant in the present has informed much of my writing. Time—seasonal, historical, and personal—is my natural subject.

"My poetry has a definite quality of rootedness. I describe my first book, *Barefaced Stone,* as agrarian. In it, I explored my farm-boy background, and it reflected the back-to-the-land movement of the 1960s and 1970s. But as one who came from the land, I heed D. H. Lawrence's charge not 'to idealize the soil.' Today, I live on a thirty-acre farmstead, but I do not farm. My writing does not allow time for that. I am a vegetable gardener.

"My science background has proven useful to me, equally as a poet and a free-lance writer. I have not specialized in science writing. In fact, I have found that the best thing about free-lancing—certainly it is not the money—is the opportunity it provides to indulge personal interests that in my case run the gamut of natural history: from art and archaeology through ecology, human community, and primary production.

"I have no journalistic training and consider myself a 'writer' rather than a 'journalist.' I believe that this is a useful distinction only if it leads you to explore your own voice. It seems to me that editors, more than anyone, are looking for writers with a way of saying and seeing things, rather than someone who merely trots out techniques and information. In this sense, my discipline as a poet has helped me in the marketplace. The only trick for me is to allow the free-lancing to nourish me, without, at the same time, having it absorb all my creative juices."

BIOGRAPHICAL/CRITICAL SOURCES:

PERIODICALS

Germination, fall/winter, 1982.
Poetry Canada Review, winter, 1985-86.
Prism International, spring, 1980.

* * *

TIMERMAN, Jacobo 1923-

PERSONAL: Born January 6, 1923, in Bar, Ukraine, U.S.S.R.; immigrated to Argentina, 1928, became citizen, citizenship revoked, 1979, later restored; immigrated to Israel, 1979, became citizen; son of Natan and Eva (a clothing vendor; maiden name, Berman) Timerman; married Risha Mindlin (a pianist), May 20, 1950; children: Daniel, Hector, Javier. *Education:* Attended National University of La Plata.

CAREER: Free-lance writer for literary magazines, Buenos Aires, Argentina, beginning in 1947; reporter for *La Razón* (newspaper), Buenos Aires; broadcast journalist in Buenos Aires; publisher of *Primera Plana* (weekly newsmagazine), Buenos Aires; *Confirmado* (weekly newsmagazine), Buenos Aires, publisher, beginning in 1969; *La Opinión* (newspaper), Buenos Aires, publisher, 1971-77; publisher at Timerman Editores (book publishing company), Buenos Aires; columnist for *Ma'ariv* (newspaper), Tel Aviv, Israel.

AWARDS, HONORS: David Ben-Gurion Award from the United Jewish Appeal, 1979; Hubert H. Humphrey Freedom

Prize from the Anti-Defamation League of B'nai B'rith, 1979; Golden Pen of Freedom from the International Federation of Newspaper Publishers, 1980; *Prisoner Without a Name, Cell Without a Number* was selected one of the twenty best books of 1981 by *Saturday Review; Los Angeles Times* book prize for current interest, 1981, and Kenneth B. Smilen/Present Tense Literary Award for biography and autobiography, both for *Prisoner Without a Name;* Maria Moors Cabot Prize for contributions to inter-American understanding; Arthur Morse Award from Aspen Institute.

WRITINGS:

NONFICTION

Prisoner Without a Name, Cell Without a Number, translated by Toby Talbot from original Spanish manuscript "Preso sin nombre, celda sin número," Knopf, 1981.
The Longest War: Israel in Lebanon, translated by Miguel Acoca, Knopf, 1982.
Chile: Death in the South, translated by Robert Cox, Knopf, 1987.

Contributor to newspapers and magazines, including *New York Times Magazine, New Yorker,* and *Davar* (Israel).

WORK IN PROGRESS: A book on Cuba.

SIDELIGHTS: In the early morning of April 15, 1977, Jacobo Timerman, publisher of an influential daily newspaper that had criticized human rights violations by the Argentine military government, was kidnapped from his Buenos Aires apartment by twenty armed men acting on orders of high army officers. He was subsequently held without charges in prison, sometimes in secret, and subjected to brutal torture despite court orders for his release. Discharged from prison, he spent another thirty months under house arrest. After intense pressure from the U.S. Government under President Jimmy Carter and from international human rights groups, Timerman was finally freed in September, 1979; he was also, however, stripped of his Argentine citizenship and summarily expelled to Israel. He recounted his ordeal in *Prisoner Without a Name, Cell Without a Number,* which won accolades as an acute description of the psychological condition produced by arbitrary imprisonment and torture and as a searing indictment of antidemocratic trends in Argentine society.

During the period of profound social instability that Argentina experienced in the early 1970s, Timerman recalls in *Prisoner Without a Name,* both government authorities and political extremists made repeated attempts to silence his newspaper. In the six years he published the daily *La Opinión,* an equal number of presidents, both military and civilian, sought to govern the country while leftist urban guerrillas battled rightist death squads and members of the armed services violated human rights with impunity. According to *Prisoner Without a Name,* several of these governments sought to censor *La Opinión*'s criticism of economic mismanagement and political repression by withholding state advertising revenue and blocking distribution of some newspaper issues. At the same time, Timerman reports, factions from both the political right and left threatened him with death, and his home and office were bombed because of his newspaper's opposition to political extremes. *La Opinión* also took controversial positions on international issues, strongly supporting Israel while condemning human rights abuses by the military regime in Chile and the Soviet Union's treatment of political dissidents.

In February, 1976, seeing no solution for Argentina's ills under the administration of President Isabel Perón, Timerman printed an article in *La Opinión* urging the country's military leaders to move against the civilian government to restore public order and end the spiral of political violence. "The revolt against the Perón presidency found its principal proponent in *La Opinión,*" Timerman acknowledges in his book, "for we insisted on the need to fill the vacuum in which the country dwelt."

The Argentine armed forces overthrew Perón in a March coup and almost immediately began massive roundups of citizens deemed subversive, which included, according to the author, all opponents or potential opponents of military rule. In his book, Timerman observes how "military leaders hastily organized their personal domains, each one becoming a warlord in the zone under his control, whereupon the chaotic, anarchistic, irrational terrorism of the Left and of Fascist death squads gave way to intrinsic, systemized, rationally planned terrorism." As detentions and kidnappings of Argentinians mounted, Timerman and *La Opinión* passed from initial support of the junta to increasing criticism of the government's human rights record. The newspaper regularly published the names and circumstances of "disappeared" persons, urging the authorities to account for their whereabouts and end illegal imprisonments. Of all the Argentine press, Timerman states that only *La Opinión* and the English-language *Buenos Aires Herald* were bold enough to demand the government's accountability for rights violations.

The consequence, Timerman writes, was his own kidnapping on orders from a far-right sector of the military. In *Prisoner Without a Name,* the author describes his confinement in clandestine prisons, interrogation, and torture at the hands of police and military officials he regards as Nazi-like in their anti-Semitic views and sadistic behavior. Unable to bring a legal case against him, Timerman's captors sought to force him to confess to links with a group of leftist guerrillas and to participation in a supposed Zionist plot to seize the Argentine region of Patagonia as a second Jewish homeland. The author endured solitary confinement, a mock execution, electric shocks to his genitals, and regular beatings; Timerman charges that he received extra punishment as a Jew. According to the author, his psychological survival depended upon a difficult process of divesting himself of all hope and interest in the outside world to reach a condition of absolute passivity, while at the same time avoiding a relationship of dependency with his torturers.

Timerman credits his eventual release into house arrest and final safe passage out of the country in large measure to persistent appeals to the Argentine Government on his behalf by the Carter administration's human rights office and by the Vatican. On the other hand, he is sharply critical in his book of what he sees as a failure by the Argentine Jewish community's leadership to speak out forcefully in his own case and on behalf of the estimated fifteen hundred other Jews who have disappeared in the years of military rule in Argentina. On a U.S. tour to promote *Prisoner Without a Name* after its 1981 publication, Timerman also voiced strong criticism of the Reagan administration's policy of tolerating human rights violations by right-wing nations, such as Argentina, allied to the United States.

Reviewing *Prisoner Without a Name, Cell Without a Number* in the London *Times,* Anthony Holden opined, "Timerman's testimony should prove a lasting work of prison literature." Referring to the author's description of the techniques he discovered to preserve his emotional and psychological strength under torture, the critic termed the book "something of a manual for those who may one day have to attempt to survive such an ordeal." *New York Times Book Review* critic Anthony Lewis remarked, "Timerman writes with passion, but a passion controlled almost to the point of detachment. The effect is devastating." Lewis con-

cluded, "He gives an unforgettable picture of . . . state terrorism."

After settling with his family in Israel, where he authored *Prisoner Without a Name,* Timerman also resumed his career as a journalist. When Israel invaded Lebanon in 1982, he wrote *The Longest War: Israel in Lebanon* to argue that the invasion was militarily unjustified and politically damaging to Israel. In his book, Timerman calls the Lebanese conflict Israel's first aggressive war and the first undertaken without defined security objectives. He takes the view that Israeli Prime Minister Menachem Begin and Defense Minister Ariel Sharon fought the war more to strengthen Israel's geopolitical position vis-a-vis its Arab neighbors than for the declared purpose of removing a Palestinian threat to Israel's northern border. Timerman also accuses Begin and Sharon of harboring a deluded belief that Israel's conflict with the Palestinians can be solved by military means alone. In fact, the author argues, the Israeli-Palestinian dispute is "a conflict over equal rights" requiring political compromise on both sides, and "Israel will have peace only when it can accept living together with a Palestinian state in the same region."

In his London *Times* review of *The Longest War,* Edward Mortimer observed that the author "mercilessly demolishes a number of crucial Israeli myths. Timerman is not taken in by the 'welcome' of the Lebanese to the Israeli invader" and he does not accept that the horrors of the invasion will force acceptance of a political solution. While questioning Timerman's interpretation of Israeli objectives in the war, *New York Times* critic Christopher Lehmann-Haupt credited *The Longest War* with "a powerful argument that the policy of the Begin Government toward the Palestinians has been tantamount to carrying on a blood feud, with the only instrument of justice being acts of revenge."

According to *Los Angeles Times* reporter Kenneth Freed, Timerman's strong opposition to the Lebanese invasion brought him considerable unpopularity in Israel and he subsequently moved to New York. In January, 1984, after the democratic civilian government of Raúl Alfonsín had taken office in Argentina, Timerman returned to Buenos Aires to seek justice against his torturers and the restitution of his newspaper and property. "For an Argentinian, to go back now, is to see his country in a kind of Camelot," Timerman told the *New York Times*'s E. J. Dionne, Jr., shortly before his departure. "After three, four generations of dictatorship, Argentinians are very strongly for democracy. I am amazed, I am impressed and I can't believe it." In Argentina, Timerman filed a civil suit against former Buenos Aires Chief of Police Ramón J. Camps and former President General Jorge Rafael Videla, whom the Alfonsín government also brought to trial on criminal charges for human rights violations. Timerman also met personally with President Alfonsín, who promised to restore his Argentine citizenship and help him win compensation for his newspaper.

Though conditions had improved in Argentina, political oppression continued to plague the neighboring country of Chile. In 1987 Timerman published *Chile: Death in the South,* a book describing life under the military regime of Chile's President General Augusto Pinochet. *New York Times* contributor Lehmann-Haupt called the book "a wrenching portrait of the South American country's suffering. . . . It tells of the torture, rape and murder inflicted on the citizenry as a matter of state policy." The book documents the people's efforts to thwart government-sponsored kidnapping attempts; and the testimony from victims of such crimes supports Timerman's likening of militarist abductors to Nazis.

According to *Washington Post Book World*'s Patrick Breslin, Timerman questions "how Chile, with its proud democratic tradition, its dynamic and urbane people, could succumb for so long [fourteen years] to a dictator who seems a caricature of the Latin American strongman." Timerman blames the political parties and Chilean people for not coming to an agreement about how to combat the abuses of the Pinochet government and suggests that they are avoiding full knowledge of their predicament. Stressing that the people of Chile are deluding themselves in hoping that a dramatic overthrow and return to pre-Pinochet Chile is possible, Timerman argues that "until they . . . accept that the Chile of nostalgia has been utterly vanquished, they will not be able to bring a new Chile out of Pinochet's valley of death," wrote Breslin. As in his other books, Timerman takes a nonviolent position, advocating a gradual transition to democracy within the framework of the current government, rather than a "glorious" coup. While *Los Angeles Times Book Review* contributor Richard Eder declared that "Timerman's style is extreme," the critic added that "his message, on the other hand, is of a moderation, even a benignity, that startles in its contrast. . . . Timerman's prescriptions for a solution are low-keyed, and dramatic only in their avoidance of drama." Timerman advises that the people of Chile need to "find a road to democracy within an antidemocratic context," reported *New York Times* contributor Lehmann-Haupt, and that "the future they must fight for has nothing to do with giving up one's life to recover the past." Breslin was skeptical about some of Timerman's claims, but he characterized Timerman as a prophet who rails against a country's mistakes out of love and concern for its welfare.

BIOGRAPHICAL/CRITICAL SOURCES:

BOOKS

Timerman, Jacobo, *Prisoner Without a Name, Cell Without a Number,* Knopf, 1981.

PERIODICALS

American Poetry Review, November/December, 1981.
Detroit News, June 14, 1981.
Los Angeles Times, January 8, 1984.
Los Angeles Times Book Review, December 20, 1987.
New York Times, September 20, 1979, September 30, 1979, May 7, 1981, December 3, 1982, December 31, 1983, March 11, 1984, November 14, 1987, December 17, 1987.
New York Times Book Review, May 10, 1981, January 10, 1988.
Publishers Weekly, May 29, 1981.
Times (London), July 30, 1981, December 2, 1982.
Tribune Books, December 13, 1987.
Washington Post, September 20, 1979.
Washington Post Book World, January 31, 1988.

*   *   *

TORRES, Jose Acosta 1925-

PERSONAL: Born December 13, 1925, in Martindale, Tex.; married Patricia Resch (an art teacher), August 15, 1970; children: Gregory, Maruca, Angela. *Education:* Southwest Texas State College (now University), B.S., 1950, M.Ed., 1952; Universidad Interamericana, Ph.D., 1965; further study at Spanish Language Institute (National Defense Education Act), Our Lady of the Lake College, San Antonio, 1963, and at University of Texas at Austin, 1967, 1968. *Religion:* Roman Catholic.

CAREER: Elementary school teacher, 1950-58, assistant principal, 1958-60, high school acting assistant principal, 1960-62, coordinator of foreign language department, 1962-65, all in San

Antonio, Tex.; San Antonio College, San Antonio, Tex., instructor, 1965-68, assistant professor of Spanish, 1968-70; Southwest Educational Development Laboratory, Austin, Tex., curriculum development specialist, 1970-72; U.S. Office of Education, project coordinator in Crystal City, Tex., 1972-73; St. Edward's University, Austin, Tex., assistant professor of education, beginning 1973; Texas A&I University, in Kingsville, Kingsville, Tex., formerly assistant professor in migrant and bilingual education. Coordinator of foreign language department, Fort Sam Houston, 1965-66; consultant to HemisFair '68, to Good Samaritan Center education project, 1969, and to *Compton's Encyclopedia* and *Encyclopedia Britannica;* vice-president of Intercontinental Translations; initiator and director of community classes in arts and crafts for disadvantaged children and of citizenship classes for Mexican-American adults. *Military service:* U.S. Army, 1944-45; received Purple Heart.

MEMBER: American Association of Teachers of Spanish and Portuguese, Texans for the Educational Advancement of Mexican-Americans, Kappa Pi (past president), Phi Delta Kappa.

AWARDS, HONORS: Certificate of Commendation from Spanish Government, 1963, for article on Junipero Serra; certificate of commendation from New Braunfels (Tex.) Kiwanis Club, 1969, for services benefiting youth of the community; Literary Award from Spanish Government, 1969, for HemisFair '68 essay.

WRITINGS:

Ortografía comparativa, Southwest Educational Development Laboratory (Austin, Tex.), 1972.
Composición creativa, Southwest Educational Development Laboratory, 1972.
Spanish/English Bilingualism, Southwest Educational Development Laboratory, 1972.
Spanish/English Publications, Southwest Educational Development Laboratory, 1972.
Cachito mío (short stories; title means "My Little One"), Quinto Sol Publications, 1974.
Chicanito Sixty-Nine, Quinto Sol Publications, 1975.

Alamo Messenger (newspaper) columnist, 1955-58, Spanish language editor, 1962-64; *La Voz,* (newspaper), columnist, 1955-58, editor, 1958-62; editor and cofounder, *Hispanavoz* (newspaper), 1964-66. Contributor of about 300 articles, in Spanish and in English, to various publications, including *Texas Outlook* and *El Grito.*

*   *   *

TORRES BODET, Jaime 1902-1974

PERSONAL: Born April 17, 1902, in Mexico City, Mexico; committed suicide by gunshot, May 13, 1974, at his home in Mexico City; son of Alejandro Torres Girbent (a theatrical producer and businessman) and Emilia Bodet de Torres; married Josefina Juárez, March, 1929. *Education:* Studied law at University of Mexico, 1918-1920.

ADDRESSES: Home—Mexico City, Mexico.

CAREER: Diplomat, statesman, writer, orator, and educator. National Preparatory School, Mexico City, Mexico, secretary and teacher of literature, 1921-22; Mexican Ministry of Education, Mexico City, head of libraries department, 1922-24; University of Mexico, Mexico City, professor of French literature, 1924-28; Mexican legation, Madrid, Spain, third secretary, 1929-31; Mexican embassy, Paris, France, second secretary,

1931-32; Mexican embassy, The Hague, Netherlands, acting charge d'affaires, 1932-34; Mexican embassy, Buenos Aires, Argentina, acting charge d'affaires, 1934-35; Mexican embassy, Paris, first secretary, 1935-36; Ministry of Foreign Affairs, Mexico, head of diplomatic department, 1936-37; Mexican embassy, Brussels, Belgium, charge d'affaires, 1937-40; Mexican Under-Secretary for Foreign Affairs, 1940-43; Mexican Minister of Education, 1943-46; Mexican Minister of Foreign Affairs, 1946-48; United Nations Educational, Scientific, and Cultural Organization (UNESCO), Paris, director-general, 1948-52; Mexican ambassador to France, 1954-58; second term as Mexican Minister of Education, 1958-64. Head of Mexican delegation to Ninth International Conference of American States (Bogota), 1948, which drafted the Charter of the Organization of American States; represented Mexico at Conference of Education and Economic and Social Development in Latin America, 1962.

MEMBER: International PEN.

AWARDS, HONORS: Gold medal, Pan American League; gold medal, French Legion of Honor; National Prize for Literature (Mexico), 1966; doctor honoris causa, University of New Mexico and University of Southern California; decorations from Order of the Glittering Stars (China), Order of the Cedar (Lebanon), Order of Polonia Restituta (Poland), Order of the Polar Star (Sweden), Order of Leopold and Order of the Crown (both Belgium), Order of Merit Carlos Manuel de Céspedes (Cuba), Order of Juan Pablo Duarte and Order of Christophe Colomb (both Dominican Republic), Order of Vasco Nuñez de Balboa (Panama), Order of Morazán (Honduras), Knight Commander of Order of Quetzal (Guatemala), Order of the Liberator (Venezuela), Order of the Sun (Peru), Great Officer of Order of the Andean Condor (Bolivia), Order of "Al Mérito" (Ecuador), Order of Boyaca (Colombia), Order of Merit (Chile), Great Cross of the Order of San Martín the Liberator (Argentina).

WRITINGS:

POEMS

Fervor (title means "Fervor"), introduction by E. González Martínez, Ballescá (Mexico), 1918, reprinted, [Mexico], 1968.
Canciones (title means "Songs"), Cultura (Mexico), 1922.
El corazón delirante (title means "The Impassioned Heart"), introduction by Arturo Torres Rioseco, Porrúa (Mexico), 1922.
La casa (title means "The House"), Herrero (Mexico), 1923.
Los días (title means "The Days"), Herrero, 1923.
Nuevas canciones (title means "New Songs"), Calleja (Madrid), 1923.
Poemas (title means "Poems"), Herrero, 1924.
Biombo (title means "Folding Screen"), Herrero, 1925.
Poesías (anthology), Espasa-Calpe (Madrid), 1926.
Destierro (title means "Exile"), Espasa-Calpe (Madrid), 1930.
Cripta (title means "Crypt"), R. Loera y Chávez (Mexico), 1937.
Sonetos (title means "Sonnets"), Gráfica Panamericana (Mexico), 1949.
Selección de poemas, selected by Xavier Villaurrutia, Nueva Voz (Mexico), 1950.
Fronteras (title means "Frontiers"), Fondo de Cultura Económica (Mexico), 1954.
Poesías escogidas (selections from previous works), Espasa-Calpe (Buenos Aires), 1954.
Sin tregua (title means "No Truce"), Fondo de Cultura Económica, 1957.
Trébol de cuatro hojas (title means "Four-Leaf Clover"), privately printed (Paris), 1958, Universidad Veracruzana, 1960.

Poemes (French translations of Torres Bodet's poems), Gallimard (Paris), 1960.
Selected Poems of Jaime Torres Bodet (text in English and Spanish), edited and translated by Sonja Karsen, Indiana University Press, 1964.
Poesía de Jaime Torres Bodet, Finisterre (Mexico), 1965.
Versos y prosas, introduction by Karsen, Ediciones Iberoamericanas (Madrid), 1966.
Obra poética (collected poems, 1916-66), introduction by Rafael Solona, two volumes, Porrúa, 1967.
Viente poemas, Ediciones Sierra Madre (Monterrey, Mexico), 1971.

FICTION

Margarita de niebla (novel; title means "Margaret's Fog"), Cultura, 1927.
La educación sentimental (novel; title means "The Sentimental Education"), Espasa-Calpe (Madrid), 1929.
Proserpina rescatada (novel; title means "Proserpina Rescued"), Espasa-Calpe (Madrid), 1931.
Estrella de día (novel; title means "Movie Star"), Espasa-Calpe (Madrid), 1933.
Primero de enero (novel; title means "First of January"), Ediciones Literatura (Madrid), 1935.
Sombras (novel; title means "Shades"), Cultura, 1937.
Nacimiento de Venus y otros relatos (stories; title means "Birth of Venus and Other Stories"), Nueva Cultura (Mexico), 1941.

CRITICISM

Perspectiva de la literatura mexicana actual 1915-1928 (title means "View of Present-Day Literature 1915-1928"), Contemporáneos, 1928.
Contemporáneos: Notas de crítica (essays; title means "Contemporaries: Notes on Literary Criticism"), Herrero, 1928.
Tres inventores de realidad: Stendhal, Dostoyevski, Pérez Galdós (essays; title means "Three Inventors of Reality: Stendhal, Dostoyevski, Pérez Galdós"), Imprenta Universitaria (Mexico), 1955.
Balzac, Fondo de Cultura Económica, 1959.
Maestros venecianos (essays on painters; title means "Venetian Masters"), Porrúa, 1961.
León Tolstoi: Su vida y su obra (title means "Leo Tolstoy: His Life and Work"), Porrúa, 1965.
Rubén Darío: Abismo y cima (title means "Rubén Darío: Fame and Tragedy"), Universidad Nacional Autónoma de México/Fondo de Cultura Económica, 1966.
Tiempo y memoria en la obra de Proust (title means "Time and Memory in Proust's Work"), Porrúa, 1967.

SPEECHES

Educación mexicana: Discursos, entrevistas, mensajes (main title means "Mexican Education"), Secretaría de Educación Pública (Mexico), 1944.
La escuela mexicana: Exposición de la doctrina educativa, Secretaría de Educación Pública, 1944.
Educación y concordia internacional: Discursos y mensajes (1941-1947) (main title means "Education and International Concord"), El Colegio de México, 1948.
Teachers Hold the Key to UNESCO's Objectives, Naldrett Press, 1949.
Doce mensajes educativos (title means "12 Educational Messages"), Secretaría de Educación Pública, 1960.
Doce mensajes cívicos (title means "Twelve Civic Messages"), Secretaría de Educación Pública, 1961.

La voz de México en Bogotá y Los Angeles (title means "The Voice of Mexico in Bogotá and Los Angeles"), Secretaría de Educación Pública, 1963.

Patria y cultura, Secretaría de Educación Pública, 1964.

Discursos (1941-1964), Porrúa, 1964.

A number of speeches by Torres Bodet have been published individually.

OTHER

(Translator from the French and author of introductory essay) Andre Gide, *Los límites del arte y algunas reflexiones de moral y de literatura,* Cultura, 1920.

(Editor and author of prologue) José Martí, *Nuestra América,* Secretaría de Educación Pública, 1945.

Tiempo de arena (also see below; autobiography; title means "Time of Sand"), Fondo de Cultura Económica, 1955.

Obras escogidas (selected works; contains poems, essays, speeches, and reprint of *Tiempo de arena*), Fondo de Cultura Económica, 1961.

Liberar el alsa de América con la luz de la educación, [Mexico], 1962.

(Editor and author of introduction) Rubén Darío, *Antología de Rubén Darío* (anthology), Universidad Nacional Autónoma de México/Fondo de Cultura Económica, 1967.

Memorias (memoirs), Porrúa, Volume 1: *Años contra el tiempo,* 1969, Volume 2: *La victoria sin alas,* 1970, Volume 3: *El desierto internacional,* 1971, Volume 4: *La tierra prometida,* 1972.

Equinoccio, Porrúa, 1974.

Founder of literary reviews, including *La Falange,* with Ortiz de Montellano, 1922, and *Contemporáneos,* 1928.

WORK IN PROGRESS: Another volume of his autobiography, left unfinished at the time of his death.

SIDELIGHTS: "Quintessentially the intellectual-in-politics," according to *Time,* Mexico's Jaime Torres Bodet was both an accomplished statesman and writer. According to Sonja Karsen in her book *Jaime Torres Bodet,* he "achieved the unusual distinction of successfully combining the qualities of the man of action with the sensitivity of the man of letters." During his long career in government, Torres Bodet was famous as an advocate of literacy and education. As Mexico's Minister of Education in the 1940s, he developed a campaign entitled "Each One Teach One," which in two years increased the literate population in Mexico by more than one million people. Later, as director-general of the United Nations Educational, Scientific, and Cultural Organization (UNESCO), he advocated that world peace and liberty hinged upon people being educated, especially upon their being able to read. From his post at UNESCO, he led the development of specialized educational materials for individual countries, until he resigned in 1952 when his budget was cut by over $2.5 million. Torres Bodet also worked many years in the Mexican diplomatic service and in the late 1940s was Mexican Minister of Foreign Affairs. He represented his country at numerous international conferences, and in 1948 led the Mexican delegation which helped formulate the Charter of the Organization of American States.

As a writer, Torres Bodet authored over twenty books of poetry, six novels, a volume of short stories, and numerous critical studies, ranging from studies of Balzac, Tolstoy, and Rubén Darío, to European painting. He was a leading member of the group called "The Contemporáneos," which sparked a revival of Mexican lyric poetry in the 1920s and 1930s. He was also known for his novels and essays; some scholars, such as Antonio

Castro Leal, have ranked his prose among the finest of Mexican writers. Karsen states that his novels, like those of other "Contemporáneos" writers who produced fiction, were influenced by innovations of European writers of the period such as Kafka, Joyce, and Proust. Like Proust, Torres Bodet especially held the importance of memory to the writer. According to Karsen, poetry and prose represented to him "different ways of approximation and expression of the same poetic substance, from which he trie[d] to lift the opaque veil which hides the secret of life." The main themes of his poetry, also at work in his fiction, include "the haunting . . . search for his own identity and the attempt to establish an identity with his fellow men, . . . one of utter loneliness, of nothingness, of being and not being, . . . [and] a constant preoccupation with the evanescence of time which finally leads us to the theme of death." In his prose, Torres Bodet was "less interested in the nature of the activities to be observed, than in observing all activities in a special way," creating thereby, according to Karsen, "a sensibility hitherto unknown in Mexical letters."

Torres Bodet's contributions as a writer were officially recognized in 1966 when President Díaz Ordaz bestowed him with the Mexican National Prize for Literature. From 1969 to 1972, Torres Bodet published four volumes of an autobiography, *Memorias,* which recounted his years as a statesman within Mexican and world politics. In 1974, he committed suicide at his home in Mexico City. The *New York Times* reported that Torres Bodet, suffering from prostate cancer, wrote in a final note: "I prefer to call on death myself at the right time."

BIOGRAPHICAL/CRITICAL SOURCES:

BOOKS

Carballo, Emmanuel, *Jaime Torres Bodet,* Empresas Editoriales (Mexico), 1968.

Cowart, Billy F., *La obra educativa de Torres Bodet en lo nacional y lo internacional,* El Colegio de México, 1966.

Forster, Merlin H., *Los Contemporáneos 1920-1932,* Ediciones De Andrea, 1964.

Jaime Torres Bodet en quince semblanzas, Ediciones Oasis (Mexico), 1965.

Jarnés, Benjamín, *Ariel disperso,* Stylo (Mexico), 1946.

Karsen, Sonja, *A Poet in a Changing World,* Skidmore College, 1963.

Karsen, Sonja, *Jaime Torres Bodet,* Twayne, 1971.

Kneller, George F., *The Education of the Mexican Nation,* Columbia University Press, 1951.

Laves, Walter L. C., and Charles A. Thomson, *UNESCO: Purpose, Progress, Prospects,* Indiana University Press, 1957.

PERIODICALS

Américas, March, 1949; August, 1969.
Antioch Review, winter, 1968-69.
Books Abroad, spring, 1967; autumn, 1970.
Christian Science Monitor, September 14, 1946.
Nature, December 4, 1948.

OBITUARIES:

PERIODICALS

New York Times, May 14, 1974.
Time, May 27, 1974.

TORRO, Pel
  See FANTHORPE, R(obert) Lionel

*   *   *

TREJO, Arnulfo D(uenes) 1922-

PERSONAL: Born August 15, 1922, in Villa Vicente Guerrero, Durango, Mexico; son of Nicolas F. and Petra (Duenes) Trejo; married Phyllis Bowen, May 21, 1954 (divorced); married Annette Foster Loken, July 1, 1967; children: (first marriage) Rachel, Rebecca, Ruth; stepdaughter: Linda Loken. *Education:* University of Arizona, B.A., 1949; University of the Americas, M.A. (Spanish language and literature), 1951; Kent State University, M.A. (library science), 1953; National University of Mexico, Litt.D. (with honors), 1959.

ADDRESSES: Home—1515 E. First St., Tucson, Ariz. 85719. *Office*—Graduate School of Library Science, College of Education, University of Arizona, Tucson, Ariz. 85721.

CAREER: National University of Mexico, Mexico City, assistant librarian, 1954-55; University of California at Los Angeles, reference librarian, 1955-59; California State University, Long Beach, assistant librarian, 1959-63; University of California at Los Angeles, assistant professor, 1965-66, associate professor of library science, 1966-68; University of Arizona, Tucson, associate professor of library science and English, 1970-75, professor of library science, 1975—. Library director of ESAN (graduate school of business administration), Lima, Peru, 1963-65; American Library Association consultant to United States Agency for International Development (USAID), Caracas, Venezuela, 1968-70. Member of board of directors, Tucson Public Library, 1967-68, and City of Tucson Historical Committee, 1972; president of El Tiradito Foundation, 1972-73. *Military service:* U.S. Army, Infantry, 1943-45; served in South Pacific theater; became sergeant; received Philippine Liberation Ribbon, Purple Heart with oak leaf cluster, and Bronze Star Medal.

MEMBER: American Library Association (council member, 1974—), REFORMA (National Organization of Spanish-Speaking Librarians in the United States; president, 1971-74), American Association of University Professors, Seminar on the Acquisition of Latin American Library Materials, Phi Delta Kappa, Beta Phi Mu, Phi Kappa Phi, Sigma Delta Pi.

AWARDS, HONORS: Simón Bolívar Award, Colegio de Biblioteconomos, Venezuela, 1970; El Tiradito Awards, El Tiradito Foundation, 1973 and 1975; annual award from League of Mexican-American Women, 1973; Rosenzweig Award, Arizona State Library Association, 1976; Distinguished Alumni Award, Kent State University School of Library Science.

WRITINGS:

Bibliografía comentada sobre administración de negocios (title means "Annotated Bibliography on Business Administration"), Addison-Wesley, 1967, 2nd edition published as *Bibliografía comentada sobre administración de negocios y disciplinas conexas,* 1967.
Diccionario etimológico del léxico de la delincuencia (title means "Etymological Dictionary of the Language of the Underworld"), UTEHA, 1969.
(Editor) *Directory of Spanish-Speaking/Spanish Surnamed Librarians in the United States,* Bureau of School Services, College of Education, University of Arizona, 1973, revised edition published as *Quien es Quien: A Who's Who of Hispanic-Heritage Librarians in the United States,* Bureau of

School Services, College of Education, University of Arizona, 1986.
Bibliografía Chicana: A Guide to Information Services, Gale, 1975.
(Editor and contributor) *Proceedings of the April 28-29, 1978, Seminario on Library and Information Services for the Spanish-Speaking: A Contribution to the Arizona Pre-White House Conference,* Graduate Library Institute for Spanish-Speaking Americans (Tucson, Arizona), 1978.
(Editor and contributor) *The Chicanos: As We See Ourselves* (essays by fourteen Chicano scholars), University of Arizona Press, 1979.

Contributor to *American Library, Arizona Highways, Folklore Americas, Wilson Library Bulletin,* and other magazines.

SIDELIGHTS: Arnulfo D. Trejo's reference works on Chicano librarians and scholars are recommended as important contributions to a field previously described only by Anglo observers.*

*   *   *

TRENT, Olaf
  See FANTHORPE, R(obert) Lionel

*   *   *

TRYON, Thomas 1926-
(Tom Tryon)

PERSONAL: Born January 14, 1926, in Hartford, Conn.; son of Arthur Lane (a clothier) and Elizabeth (Lester) Tryon; married Anne Lilienthal, June, 1955 (divorced). *Education:* Yale University, B.A. (with honors), 1949; further study at Art Students League and Neighborhood Playhouse (New York). *Politics:* Democrat.

ADDRESSES: c/o Alfred A. Knopf, Inc., 201 East 50th Street, New York, N.Y. 10022.

CAREER: Actor under name Tom Tryon, 1952-71, writer and producer, 1971—. Set painter and assistant stage manager, Cape Playhouse, Dennis, Cape Cod, Mass., 1950. Production assistant, Columbia Broadcasting System, Inc. (CBS-TV); worked occasionally as an extra on television shows. Appeared in Broadway production of "Wish You Were Here," 1952; joined Jose Ferrer Repertory Co. at New York City Center, 1953, performed in "Cyrano de Bergerac" and "Richard III." Went to California in 1955, appeared in films "The Scarlet Hour," 1956, "Screaming Eagles," 1956, "Three Violent People," 1958, "The Unholy Wife," 1958, "I Married a Monster from Outer Space," 1958, "Texas John Slaughter" for television, 1958, "The Story of Ruth," 1960, "Marines, Let's Go!," 1961, "Moon Pilot," 1962, "The Longest Day," 1962, "Something's Got to Give," 1962, "The Cardinal," 1963, "In Harm's Way," 1965, "The Glory Guys," 1965, "Momento Mori," 1968, "Color Me Dead," 1969, and "The Narco Men," 1971. Also appeared in title role of Walt Disney's television series "Texas John Slaughter," 1958, in television movie "Winchester '73," 1967, and in popular television western series, "The Virginian," "Big Valley," and "Men from Shiloh." *Military service:* U.S. Navy, 1943-46.

AWARDS, HONORS: Prix Femina de Belgique for outstanding male performance, and Laurel Award, Motion Picture Exhibitors, both 1964, both for "The Cardinal"; Ann Radcliffe Award, Count Dracula Society, 1974.

WRITINGS:

The Other (novel; also see below), Knopf, 1971, reprinted, Fawcett, 1987.

(And executive producer) "The Other" (screenplay based upon his novel of same title), Twentieth Century-Fox, 1972.

Harvest Home (novel; Literary Guild selection; also see below), Knopf, 1973.

Lady, Knopf, 1974.

Crowned Heads (novellas; contains "Fedora" [also see below], "Lorna," "Bobbitt," and "Willie"), Knopf, 1976.

All That Glitters: Five Novellas (Literary Guild main selection), Knopf, 1986.

The Night of the Moonbow (novel), Knopf, 1988.

Opal and Cupid (juvenile), Viking, 1990.

The Wings of Morning, Viking, 1990.

Also author of unpublished work, "What Is the Answer, What Was the Question?" Contributor to *Ladies Home Journal* and *Reader's Digest,* 1976.

WORK IN PROGRESS: Kingdom Come, a historical novel.

SIDELIGHTS: Introduced to the theatre after initially preparing for a career in art, Thomas Tryon journeyed to Hollywood in the mid-1950s, appearing in several films before his big career break occurred in 1963 with a memorable performance in the title role of Otto Preminger's "The Cardinal." Described by Larry Swindell in the *Akron Beacon Journal* as an actor with "a reputation for intensity," Tryon remembers the entire filming of "The Cardinal" as an "anguishing" experience, however, adding to John Blades in a Chicago *Tribune Books* interview, "I got to the point where I didn't want to be in front of the camera any more. I lost my actor's nerve." Recalling how he assuaged offscreen anxieties with alcohol and cocaine, he relates in Dennis Wholey's *The Courage to Change: Personal Conversations about Alcoholism,* "If anyone ever picked the wrong profession, I did when I became an actor." Spurning a successfully established acting career in the late 1960s to pursue writing instead, Tryon achieved bestseller status as well as critical plaudits with his first literary attempt.

Tryon's chilling first novel, *The Other,* which remained on the bestseller list for seven months, concerns "the boyhood of a deranged and demonic schizophrenic," notes an *English Journal* contributor. In the *Saturday Review,* I. P. Heldman likens the work to "a Jamesian nightmare of psychological tension in a brooding atmosphere of insidious terror and madness." Calling it "one of the most compelling terror fictions written in this century," Leonard Wolf adds in *Horror: A Connoisseur's Guide to Literature and Film* that the novel is "lucid, luminous and rare, and it gives lovers of terror fiction several fine opportunities to be scared to death." Hailing Tryon for his storytelling mastery in this psychological thriller, several critics perceived in him great promise as a writer of American Gothic. Tryon remained in the genre for his second novel, *Harvest Home,* about a couple who exchange urban tribulations for rural ones when the community they adopt becomes increasingly mysterious and sinister in its practices. Yet, despite acknowledging Tryon's skills as a storyteller, some critics found the story itself implausible and the novel generally disappointing. But even though Pamela March, for instance in the *Christian Science Monitor,* remarks that the novel "reads like a parody," she deems Tryon "a practiced spellbinder." And as Stephen King remarks in the *New York Times Book Review,* "Sentence by sentence, paragraph by paragraph, it is a true book; it says exactly what Tryon wanted it to say."

In *Lady,* however, Tryon moved away from the thriller genre with a novel that explores a young boy's lifelong fascination with a woman. As he once indicated in an interview with Frank Gagnard for the New Orleans *Times-Picayune,* "I wanted to try something different without going totally out of my territory, my proven ground, so to speak. I wanted to try to make strides in another direction." Praising especially the novel's "excellent character sketches," Barton Wimble, in a *Library Journal* review, deems it Tryon's best thus far. Despite the estimation of some critics, such as Martin Levin in the *New York Times Book Review,* that the novel was somewhat overwritten, the general response to it was favorable. As Bruce Cook describes it in the *National Observer*—"evocative and elegiac, full of remembered warmth for times past."

In *Crowned Heads,* the first of what Tryon foresees as a quartet of companion pieces, he draws upon his own film experience and focuses upon the familiar world of Hollywood and its luminaries. Comprised of four novellas in which Tryon depicts the golden days of stardom of four leading actresses. In the opinion of Webster Schott, "Tryon seems to have been born with a silver story in his mouth." Pointing out that "Tryon plays to the senses," and that the book holds something for each reader, Schott adds in the *New York Times Book Review:* "He watches manners, introduces details, covers settings with a Peeping Tom passion. His stories ripple with plots and subplots." A *Virginia Quarterly Review* contributor contends that it "may be the best 'Hollywood novel' you will find" and that "Tryon convincingly depicts what becoming a film star can do to a person." And although *Time*'s Paul Gray suggests that "weaving fiction around such a monstrously self-mythologizing place as Hollywood is like gilding a plastic lily," he calls the book a "loving reconstruction of a fading era."

In a Chicago *Tribune Books* review of Tryon's fifth work, *All That Glitters: Five Novellas,* in which the author returns to the subject of Hollywood and the entertainment industry from the perspective of five actresses whose careers have ebbed, Daniel Fuchs echoes the sentiment that Tryon is "a true fan." Calling it "a study of archetypical Hollywood figures," a *West Coast Review of Books* contributor adds that it is "a ragout of drama and showbiz extravaganza that should more than satisfy the appetites of those who dote on Tinseltown's travails. Most of it is fiction. Guess which parts aren't." Fuchs maintains, though, that "these are amusing stories, nothing to alarm, no malice in them . . . and you can read all day." And although Carolyn See describes the novel in the *Los Angeles Times* as "old news," Bruce VanWyngarden suggests in the *Washington Post* that "Tryon, a former actor, knows his subject, and he knows it for what it is— delicious cotton candy." According to Tom Nolan in the *New York Times Book Review* the novel "is like a great B-movie— irresistible, a little vulgar and once in a while surprisingly moving."

"It is very difficult for people to allow me to be a writer because they have slotted me as an actor," observed Tryon in the New Orleans *Times-Picayune* interview. In the nearly two decades since his decision to abandon acting as a profession, writing has become an obsession with Tryon, who sometimes averages ten to fourteen hour days. Despite the occasional assessment of some critics that his subsequent work fails to fulfill the extraordinary potential they found exhibited in his initial effort, Tryon continues to attract a large and loyal readership with his bestselling work, much of which has been translated into several other languages. And while critical validation of his work might gratify the author, it does not govern his pursuit of a literary career. As he summarizes in *The Courage to Change:* "There is no place for fear as a writer or as an actor. You can't be afraid. . . . I'm not afraid anymore. I'm just not afraid. I was . . . so eager to please, to make the best impression, to be liked. Now I don't care if they don't like me. I like me. I'm a nice guy. I really am."

MEDIA ADAPTATIONS: A television movie based upon Tryon's novel *Harvest Home* was produced in 1973; "Fedora," based upon one of the novellas comprising *Crowned Heads*, was filmed by Gevial Rialto/United Artists in 1978, featuring William Holden, Marthe Keller, and Jose Ferrer.

AVOCATIONAL INTERESTS: Collecting films, painting, antiques.

BIOGRAPHICAL/CRITICAL SOURCES:

BOOKS

Authors in the News, Volume 1, Gale, 1976.
Contemporary Literary Criticism, Gale, Volume 3, 1975, Volume 11, 1979.
Wholey, Dennis, *The Courage to Change: Personal Conversations about Alcoholism*, Houghton, 1984.
Wolf, Leonard, *Horror: A Connoisseur's Guide to Literature and Film*, Facts on File, 1989.

PERIODICALS

Akron Beacon Journal, July 1, 1973.
Christian Science Monitor, June 27, 1973.
English Journal, October, 1973.
Library Journal, October 15, 1974.
Life, May 14, 1971.
Los Angeles Times, November 3, 1986.
National Observer, January 18, 1975.
New York Times Book Review, July 1, 1973, July 11, 1976, October 24, 1976, November 9, 1986.
Philadelphia Inquirer, November 17, 1974.
Saturday Review, June 5, 1971.
Time, June 28, 1976.
Times-Picayune, November 23, 1974.
Tribune Books (Chicago), January 25, 1987.
Virginia Quarterly Review, Volume 53, number 1, 1977.
Washington Post, December 6, 1986.
West Coast Review of Books, April, 1986.

—*Sketch by Sharon Malinowski*

*   *   *

TRYON, Tom
    See TRYON, Thomas

*   *   *

TURNER, Jonathan H.   1942-

PERSONAL: Born September 7, 1942, in Oakland, Calif.; son of John Hugh (a developer) and Maries R. (Rubell) Turner; married Susan Hainge, September 7, 1967 (divorced, 1971); married Sandra Leer, November 24, 1971; children: Patricia, Donna, Kenneth. *Education:* University of California, Santa Barbara, B.A., 1965; Cornell University, M.A., 1966, Ph.D., 1968. *Politics:* Democrat.

ADDRESSES: Home—4260 Quail Rd., Riverside, Calif. 92507. *Office*—Department of Sociology, University of California, Riverside, Calif. 92502.

CAREER: University of Hawaii, Honolulu, assistant professor of sociology, 1968-69; University of California, Riverside, assistant professor, 1969-72, associate professor, 1972-77, professor of sociology, 1977—.

MEMBER: American Sociological Association, Pacific Sociological Association.

WRITINGS:

Patterns of Social Organization, McGraw, 1972.
American Society; Problems of Structure, Harper, 1972.
The Structure of Sociological Theory, Wadsworth, 1974, 5th edition, 1991.
Privilege and Poverty in America, Goodyear Publishing, 1976.
Social Problems in America, Harper, 1977.
Sociology: Studying the Human System, Goodyear Publishing, 1978.
Functionalism, Cummings, 1978.
The Emergence of Sociological Theory, Wadsworth, 1981, 2nd edition, 1988.
Societal Stratification: A Theoretical Analysis, Columbia University Press, 1984.
Oppression: A Socio-History of Black-White Relations, Nelson-Hall, 1984.
American Dilemmas, Columbia University Press, 1985.
Sociology: The Science of Human Organization, Nelson-Hall, 1985.
Herbert Spencer: Toward a Renewed Appreciation, Sage Publications, 1985.
Social Theory Today, Stanford University Press, 1987.
A Theory of Social Interaction, Stanford University Press, 1988.
Theory Building in Sociology, Sage Publications, 1989.
American Sociology, Polish Scientific Publishers, 1990.
The Impossible Science, Sage Publications, 1990.

*   *   *

TURNER, Justin G(eorge)   1898-1976

PERSONAL: Born November 5, 1898, in Chicago, IL; died June 16, 1976; son of Oscar and Bessie (Taxey) Turner; married Gertrude Levin, July 27, 1932; children: Paul S., Linda Barbara (Mrs. Charles Sachs). *Education:* Attended University of Chicago, 1916-18; De Paul University, LL.B., 1920. *Politics:* Democrat. *Religion:* Jewish. *Avocational interests:* Collecting historical manuscripts, golf.

ADDRESSES: Home—1115 South Elm Dr., Los Angeles, CA 90212 *Office*—2389 Westwood Blvd., Los Angeles, CA 90064. *Agent*—Charles B. Block & Associates, 614 North LaPeer Dr., Los Angeles, CA.

CAREER: Admitted to practice before the bar in Illinois; Turner & Turner, Chicago, IL, partner, 1921-43; Town Investments, Chicago, and Los Angeles, CA, partner, 1932-50; Turner Investments, Los Angeles, partner, beginning 1950. Former chairman of board of governors, University of Judaism; former trustee, National Foundation for Jewish Culture; former member of board of directors, Jewish Institute of Religion, California School of Hebrew Union College, and University of Southern California. Fellow, Pierpont Morgan Library, 1959. Consultant to manuscript department, University of California, Los Angeles, beginning 1956. *Military service:* U.S. Army, 1918.

MEMBER: American Historical Association, American Association for State and Local History, American Studies Association, Bibliographical Society of America, Society of American Archivists, Jewish Publication Society (former trustee), Keats-Shelley Society, Renaissance Society of America, Manuscript Society (life member; vice-president), Organization of American Historians, Modern Language Association, Western History Association, Pacific Coast Historical Society, Mississippi Valley Historical Association, Illinois Historical Society, California Historical Commission, Historical Society of Southern California (life member; president, 1962-63; chairman of board of directors, member of editorial board), Southern California Jewish Historical Society (honorary president), Civil War Round Table of Southern California (president, 1955-56), Book Club of California, Chicago Historical Society (life member), Friend of the Library (University of Southern California; member of board of directors), Friends of Jewish Community Library of Los Angeles (president, beginning 1954), Friends of the Library (University of California, Los Angeles; president, 1957-60), Bibliophiles (Brandeis University), B'Nai B'rith (president of Austin branch, 1931-35), Masonic Lodge, Hillcrest Country Club (Los Angeles), Faculty Club (University of California, Los Angeles), Covenant Club (Chicago), Confederate Club (London), Alpha Epsilon Pi.

AWARDS, HONORS: LL.D., Lincoln College, 1955; L.H.D., University of Judaism, 1960; diploma of honor, Lincoln Memorial University, 1962; national award for community service, Jewish Theological Seminary of America, 1964; Friends of Literature Award, 1973, for *Mary Todd Lincoln: Her Life and Letters.*

WRITINGS:

A Note on Solomon Nunes Carvalho and His Portrait of Abraham Lincoln, Plantin Press (Los Angeles), 1960.
(Coauthor) *Lincoln: A Contemporary Portrait,* Doubleday, 1962.
The Thirteenth Amendment and the Emancipation Proclamation, Plantin Press, 1968.
(Editor with Linda L. Turner) *Mary Todd Lincoln: Her Life and Letters* (a History Book Club selection), Knopf, 1972, reprinted, Fromm International, 1987.

Contributor of articles and reviews to history journals. Member of editorial board or publications committee of *America, History and Literature* and *Pacific Historian.*

MEDIA ADAPTATIONS: Mary Todd Lincoln: Her Life and Letters was made into a film entitled "Look Away."

WORK IN PROGRESS: Noah Brooks, a biography; *The Signers of Independence of the State of Israel.*

* * *

TWADDELL, W(illiam) F(reeman)   1906-1982

PERSONAL: Born March 22, 1906, in Rye, NY; died in Providence, RI, March 1, 1982; son of William Powell (a musician) and Emily May (Fawcett) Twaddell; married Helen Treadway Johnson, December 21, 1930; children: Stephen Treadway, James Freeman, William Hartshorne. *Education:* Duke University, A.B., 1926; Harvard University, M.A., 1927, Ph.D., 1930. *Politics:* Independent. *Religion:* None.

ADDRESSES: Home—78 Oriole Ave., Providence, RI 02906.

CAREER: University of Wisconsin, Madison, instructor, 1929-31, assistant professor, 1931-34, associate professor, 1935-37, professor of German, 1937-46; Brown University, Providence, RI, professor of Germanic languages, 1946-71, professor emeritus, 1971-82, chairman of department of linguistics, 1960-68. Fulbright lecturer in Egypt, 1954-55, and the Philippines, 1968; visiting professor at several universities, including University of Hamburg, summer, 1955, and Princeton University, 1957-58. Consultant to U.S. Information Agency.

MEMBER: Modern Language Association of America (member of executive council, 1967-71), Linguistic Society of America (president, 1957), American Academy of Arts and Sciences, Institut fuer deutsche Sprache (member of council), Phi Beta Kappa, Phi Delta Theta.

AWARDS, HONORS: Fellowship from Princeton University's Humanities Council, 1957-58; Litt.D. from Duke University, 1964.

WRITINGS:

On Defining the Phoneme (monograph), Waverly, 1935, reprinted, Norwood Editions, 1978.
(With Helmut Rehder) *Conversational German for Beginning and Refresher Courses,* Holt, 1944.
(With Rehder) *German,* Holt, 1947, 3rd edition, 1960.
The English Verb Auxiliaries, Brown University Press, 1960, 2nd edition, 1963.
Foreign Language Instruction at the Second Level, Holt, 1963.
Linguistics and Foreign Language Teaching (pamphlet), Division of Instruction, State Department of Education (Concord, NH), 1964.
Schriftliche Arbeiten, Holt, c. 1970.
(With Rehder and Ursula Thomas) *Verstehen und Sprechen,* Holt, 1970, revised edition, 1970.
(With Rehder and R.M.S. Heffner) Goethe, *Faust,* student's edition, two volumes, University of Wisconsin Press, 1975.
(With Thomas) *Lesestoff Nach Wahl,* Volume 1: *Einfuhrung,* Volume 2: *Physik und Chemie,* Volume III: *Mensch und Gesellschaft,* Volume IV: *Biologie,* Volume V: *Literatur,* Volume VI: *Teacher's Manual,* University of Wisconsin Press, 1977.
(Translator from the German) Conrad F. Meyer, *The Saint,* Brown University Press, 1977.

Contributor to learned journals.

[Date of death provided by wife, Helen Twaddell]

U

UNDERHILL, Charles
See HILL, Reginald (Charles)

* * *

URISTA, Alberto H. 1947-
(Alurista)

PERSONAL: Born August 8, 1947, in Mexico City, Mexico; immigrated to the United States, 1961; son of Balthazar and Ruth (Heredia) Urista; married Irene Mercado, August 8, 1969 (divorced, 1976); married Xelina Rojas, June 16, 1977; children: (first marriage) Tizoc, Maoxiim; (second marriage) Zamna, Zahi. *Education:* San Diego State University, B.A., 1970, M.A., 1978; University of California, San Diego, Ph.D. (Spanish literature), 1983.

ADDRESSES: Office—Department of Foreign Languages, California Polytechnic State University, San Luis Obispo, Calif. 93407.

CAREER: Friendly Center, Orange, Calif., counsellor, 1963-67; San Diego Children's Home, San Diego, Calif., psychiatric childcare worker, 1967-68; San Diego State University, San Diego, lecturer in Chicano studies, 1968-74, 1976-83, executive director of Chicano Studies Center, 1971-73; University of Texas at Austin, lecturer in Chicano studies, 1974-76; Colorado College, Colorado Springs, assistant professor, beginning 1983; currently a staff member of the foreign language department, California State Polytechnic College, San Luis Obispo. Instructor in psychology, Southwestern Junior College, 1973-74; distinguished visiting lecturer, University of Nebraska, 1979; has lectured and given poetry recitals at numerous colleges and universities and on radio and television programs. San Diego State University, co-founder of MECHA (Movimiento Estudiantil Chicano de Aztlán), 1967, of Chicano studies department, 1968, and of Chicano Studies Center, 1969; co-founder, Centro Cultural de la Raza, 1971. Coordinator and instructor, Volunteers in Service to America (VISTA), San Diego, summer, 1970; teacher corps instructor, San Diego, 1971-72. Member of board of directors and president, Intercultural Council of the Arts, 1978—; member of board of directors, Community Video, 1979—; member of board of directors and executive committee, Combined Arts and Educational Council of San Diego County, 1980. Organizer of Festival Floricanto, an annual literary event.

MEMBER: International Academy of Poets, National Association of Chicano Studies, Association of Mexican-American Educators, Movimiento Estudiantil Chicano de Aztlán, Toltecas en Aztlán.

AWARDS, HONORS: Ford Foundation fellowship, 1976; California Art Council creative writing award, 1978; McArthur Chair of Spanish, McArthur Foundation, 1984.

WRITINGS:

ALL UNDER PSEUDONYM ALURISTA

Floricanto en Aztlán (poems; title means "Flower-song in Aztlán"), Chicano Studies Center, University of California, Los Angeles, 1971, 2nd edition, 1976.
Nationchild Plumaroja, 1969-1972 (poems; title means "Nationchild Redfeather"), Centro Cultural de la Raza, 1972.
Colección Tula y Tonán: Textos generativos (juvenile), nine volumes, Centro Cultural de la Raza, 1973.
Timespace Huracán: Poems, 1972-1975, Pajarito Publications, 1976.
A'nque/Alurista: Acuarelas hechas por Delilah Merriman-Montoya (poems; title means "Even Though/Alurista: Watercolors Done by Delilah Merriman-Montoya"), Maize, 1979.
Spik in Glyph? (poems), Arte Público Press, 1981.
Return: Poems Collected and New, Bilingual Press/Editorial Bilingüe, 1982.
Tremble Purple: Seven Poems, Getting Together, 1986.

EDITOR

(And contributor) *El Ombligo en Aztlán: An Anthology of Chicano Student Poetry,* Chicano Studies Center, San Diego State University, 1971.
Alex Kiraca, *Space Flute and Barrio Paths,* Chicano Studies Center, San Diego State University, 1972.
Gloriamalia Flores, *And Her Children Lived,* Centro Cultural de la Raza, 1974.
Juanfelipe Herrera, *Rebozos of Love,* Centro Cultural de la Raza, 1974.
Lin Romero, *Happy Songs and Bleeding Hearts,* Centro Cultural de la Raza, 1974.
Ricardo Teall, *No Flights Out Tonight,* Pajarito Publications, 1975.

Carmen Tafolla, Cecilio Garcia-Camarillo, and Reyes Cardenas, *Get Your Tortillas Together,* Caracol Publications, 1976.

(And contributor) *Festival Flor y Canto I: An Anthology of Chicano Literature,* University of Southern California Press, 1976.

(And contributor) *Festival Flor y Canto II: An Anthology of Chicano Literature,* Center for Mexican-American Studies, University of Texas at Austin, 1979.

Herberto Espinoza, *Viendo morir a Teresa y otros relatos,* Maize, 1983.

(With wife, Xelina Rojas-Urista) L. J. Griep-Ruiz, *Daily in All the Small,* Maize, 1984.

(With Rojas-Urista) Gary D. Keller, *Tales of El Huitlacoche,* Maize, 1984.

(With Rojas-Urista) Ricardo Cobián, *Para todos los panes no están todos presentes,* Maize, 1985.

(With Rojas-Urista) *Southwest Tales: A Contemporary Collection,* Maize, 1986.

CONTRIBUTOR

Octavio Ignacio Romano-V. and Herminio Ríos C., editors, *El Espejo,* Quinto Sol, 1969.

Castaneda-Shular, Tomás Ybarra-Frausto, and Joseph Sommers, editors, *Literatura Chicana: Texto y Contexto,* Prentice-Hall, 1972.

Stan Steiner and Luis Váldez, editors, *Aztlán: An Anthology of Mexican-American Literature,* Vintage, 1972.

Walter Lowenfals, editor, *From the Belly of the Shark,* Vintage, 1973.

Romano-V. and Rios C., editors, *Chicano Drama,* El Grito Books, 1974.

Lewis M. Baldwin and Dorothy Harth, editors, *Voices of Aztlán: Chicano Literature of Today,* Mentor Books, 1974.

Cárdenas, editor, *Chicano Voices,* Houghton, 1975.

Roberto Garza, editor, *Contemporary Chicano Theater,* University of Notre Dame Press, 1975.

Syquia Mirikitani and others, editors, *Time to Greez,* Glide Urban Center Publications, 1975.

Ishmael Reed, editor, *Calafia: The Calfornia Poetry,* Y'Bird Books, 1979.

OTHER

Author of play, "Dawn," published in the periodical *Grito,* 1974. Contributor to numerous periodicals, including *La Raza, Revista Chicano-Riqueña, El Gallo, Aztlán* and *Hispamerica.* Co-editor and founder, *Maize.*

SIDELIGHTS: Alberto H. Urista, who is best known by his pen name, Alurista, is "considered by many to be the poet laureate of Chicano letters," according to *Dictionary of Literary Biography* contributor Judith Ginsberg. Since his writings were first published in the late 1960s, Alurista has made a number of significant contributions toward making Chicano poetry a vital part of contemporary literature. He is "one of the first to succeed in the creation of interlingual texts," writes Ginsberg, who also adds that "Alurista was perhaps the first to establish the concept of Aztlán at the level of literature and formal ideology as a cultural, political, geographical, and mythical symbol of the aspirations of the Chicano people." Alurista asserts and promotes the value of his people not only through his literature, but also as a teacher and active member of organizations that champion ethnic awareness. He is a co-founder of the Chicano Student Movement of Aztlán (MECHA), the founder and co-editor with his wife Xelina of the Chicano literary magazine *Maize,* the co-founder of the Chicano studies department at San Diego State University, and the chief organizer of the annual literary event,

Festival Floricanto. Both as a writer and as an activist, Alurista has accomplished much for Chicanos in the United States.

An immigrant from Mexico, Alurista arrived in San Diego, Calif., during the 1960s when Chicano activism was beginning to reach its peak. The young Alurista was particularly inspired at the time by the farmworkers' strike led by César Chávez. "It was the farmworkers who brought Chicanos to the forefront of national consciousness," the poet tells Tomás Ybarra-Frausto in *Modern Chicano Writers: A Collection of Critical Essays.* "As I watched the pilgrimage from Delano, I said to myself, that man Chávez is either a fool, a fanatic or a truly wise man. And very soon his genius was apparent." In *Chicano Authors: Inquiry by Interview* Alurista relates to Juan Bruce-Novoa in both Spanish and English (the Spanish has been translated and italicized) that after seeing Chávez, "I made my decision about using my writing skills, my *literature, as a means of communication.* I'm convinced that my *poetry reflects,* or at least I try deliberately to reflect the experience of our people."

Conversant with all the world's major religions and interested in existential philosophy, Alurista is extremely well-read. He can speak fluent Spanish and English (as well as their Chicano and Black dialects), and is familiar with Mayan and the Náhuatl language of the Aztecs. But despite his thorough education, Alurista complains to Bruce-Novoa: "Formal education has attempted, if you will, to hinder my education. Schooling is where you are trained to follow directions, and as a poet, as a writer, as a creative person that is the last thing I wanted."

In keeping with this independent attitude, the poet refused his first editor's request that he write in only one language. An important part of Chicano literature, contends Alurista, is the vitality and diversity of its language use. By employing various forms of Spanish, English, and ancient Amerindian languages in their writing, Alurista attests to Bruce-Novoa that Chicano writers like himself show "our versatility and multidimensional view of the world. That makes us stronger, a broadly based, more universal people. And as writers, that puts us in a completely different category in the history of world literature."

Alurista's first poetry collection, *Floricanto en Aztlán,* ("Flowersong in Aztlán"), is also his best-known and most influential work. The concept of Aztlán that is central to the book refers to the Náhuatl myth of a lost paradise—once the homeland of the Aztecs—located in what is now the southwestern part of the United States. Thus, *Floricanto en Aztlán* extols the virtues of pre-Columbian society as well as that of their Chicano descendants in an effort by the author to exhort "his fellow Chicanos to struggle for their freedom, their values, and their culture," explains Ginsberg. Alurista considers the United States to be an imperialistic power and advocates a nonviolent cultural revolution against Anglo-Saxon domination. This philosophy is further developed in the poet's second collection, *Nationchild Plumaroja, 1969-1972* ("Nationchild Redfeather, 1969-1972"), which is also considered to be an important work. Like its predecessor, *Nationchild Plumaroja* combines a bilingual style with references to ancient Indian culture in a collection of one hundred poems that emphasize the importance of the Chicano identity.

With Alurista's next three collections, *Timespace Huracán: Poems, 1972-1975, A'nque/Alurista,* and *Spik in Glyph?,* the poet began to experiment more with poetic form. Still using references to Mayan and Aztec culture, *Timespace Huracán* is written entirely in Spanish instead of the author's customary bilingual idiom, while *A'nque/Alurista* and *Spik in Glyph?* emphasize a highly "esoteric" style, according to Ginsberg. In *Timespace*

Huracán Alurista also introduces the term "time-space" for the first time in his poetry. Explaining this word to Bruce-Novoa, the poet comments that there are three types of time-space: historical time-space, "which is the collective time-space, one that describes reality as accorded by a consensus of people," a personal time-space "that is very individual, psychological," and a mythological time-space "that unifies the personal and historical time-spaces." Alurista tries to express all three time-spaces in his poetry in order to present a unified picture of reality. This is an essential point in his work, for the poet strongly believes that "given the power to describe reality, we can construct a more human reality beginning with a more human description."

Although his poems have been widely praised by many reviewers, some critics have found fault with what they feel is the poet's romanticization of pre-Columbian history. Even the author of the introduction to Alurista's *Return: Poems Collected and New,* Gary D. Keller, admits that the author "is vulnerable to not representing the past as critically as he has engaged the present." Several critics also believe that Alurista's more recent poetry is not as powerful as his earlier efforts, though this does not detract from his importance. For example, Cordelia Candelaria, author of *Chicano Poetry: A Critical Introduction,* observes: "The fact that the poet has remained a respected figure among Chicano writers despite the dropping off in quality of . . . [his] later volumes reconfirms the greatness of his earlier work." Ginsberg similarly attests that "verbal pyrotechnics . . . threatened to diminish the power of his expression," but she is encouraged by the new poems in *Return: Poems Collected and New.* These new efforts, says Ginsberg, "suggest a reengagement with more accessible language and human themes and a movement away from the often brittle and obscure wordplay of *A'nque/Alurista* and *Spik in Glyph?*"

Even though a number of critics consider Alurista's later works to be less significant and influential than *Floricanto en Aztlán* and *Nationchild Plumaroja,* the ground-breaking impact of these first two collections has been more than enough to establish Alurista's reputation as a major Chicano author. He remains "the best known and most prolific Chicano poet," declares Luis Leal and Pepe Baron in *Three American Literatures.* Predicting the present importance and future potential for Chicano writers, Alurista tells Bruce-Novoa that these authors should create *"a revolution within the literature as much as the literature itself should awaken the desire for liberty in the people. . . . [We] have an opportunity here, and we would be fools to throw it away. That opportunity is to continue to work and work very hard. Write with desire.* This cultivation is going to reap a good *crop. The historical time-space in which we live is going to focus on this terrenal belly-button of consciousness between Hispanic America and Anglo-Saxon North America. Amerindia* is going to bloom. That's inevitable."

Some of Alurista's manuscripts are kept at the Nettie Lee Benson Collection, Latin American Collection, University of Texas at Austin.

BIOGRAPHICAL/CRITICAL SOURCES:

BOOKS

Actas del XVI Congreso del Instituto Internacional de Literatura Iberoamericana, Michigan State University, 1975.
Alurista, *Return: Poems Collected and New,* Bilingual Press/Editorial Bilingüe, 1982.
Baker, Houston A., Jr., *Three American Literatures,* Modern Language Association, 1982.
Bruce-Novoa, Juan, *Chicano Authors: Inquiry by Interview,* translation by Isabel Barraza, University of Texas Press, 1980.
Bruce-Novoa, Juan, *Chicano Poetry: A Response to Chaos,* University of Texas Press, 1982.
Candelaria, Cordelia, *Chicano Poetry: A Critical Introduction,* Greenwood Press, 1986.
Dictionary of Literary Biography, Volume 82: *Chicano Writers,* Gale, 1989.
Jiménez, Francisco, *The Identification and Analysis of Chicano Literature,* Bilingual Press/Editorial Bilingüe, 1979.
Lomelí, Francisco A., and Donald W. Urioste, *Chicano Perspectives in Literature: A Critical and Annotated Bibliography,* Pajarito Publications, 1976.
Maldonado, Jesus, *Poesía Chicana: Alurista, el Mero Chingón,* Centro de Estudios Chicanos (Seattle), 1971.
Ybarra-Frausto, Tomás, and Joseph Sommers, editors, *Modern Chicano Writers: A Collection of Critical Essays,* Prentice-Hall, 1979.

PERIODICALS

Bilingual Review/Revista Bilingüe, January-August, 1978.
De Colores, Volume 3, number 4, 1977.
Palabra, spring, 1981.
Revista Chicano-Riqueña, winter, 1976.
Xalman, spring, 1977.

—Sketch by Kevin S. Hile

*   *   *

URQUHART, Jane 1949-

PERSONAL: Born June 21, 1949, in Geraldton, Ontario, Canada; daughter of W. A. (a professional engineer) and Marianne (a nurse; maiden name, Quinn) Carter; married Paul Brian Keele, January 1, 1969 (deceased); married Tony Urquhart (a professor and visual artist), May 5, 1976; children: (second marriage) Emily Jane. *Education:* University of Guelph, B.A. (English), 1971, B.A. (art history), 1975.

ADDRESSES: Home—24 Water St., Wellesley, Ontario, Canada N0B 2T0.

CAREER: Canada Manpower Center, Trenton, Ontario, student placement officer, 1971-72; Royal Canadian Navy, Halifax, Nova Scotia, civilian information officer, 1972-73; University of Waterloo, Waterloo, Ontario, tutor/coordinator of art history correspondence program, 1973—.

MEMBER: League of Canadian Poets.

AWARDS, HONORS: Grants from Ontario Arts Council, 1980-86, and Canada Council, 1983, 1985.

WRITINGS:

POETRY

False Shuffles, Press Porcepic, 1982.
I Am Walking in the Garden of His Imaginary Palace, Aya Press, 1982.
The Little Flowers of Madame de Montespan, Porcupine's Quill, 1983.

FICTION

The Whirlpool (novel), David Godine, 1986.
Storm Glass (short stories), Porcupine's Quill, 1987.
Changing Heaven (novel), McClelland and Stewart, 1990.

OTHER

Work represented in anthologies, including *Four Square Garden: A Poetry Anthology,* edited by Burnett, MacKinnon, and Thomas, Pas de Loup Press, 1982; *Illusions,* Aya Press, 1983; *Meta Fictions,* Quadrant Editions, 1983; *Views from the North,* Porcupine's Quill, 1983; *Best Canadian Stories,* Oberon Press, 1986; *Magic Realism and Canadian Literature,* University of Waterloo Press, 1986; and *The Oxford Book of Stories by Canadian Women,* Volume 2, 1988. Also contributor to magazines, including *Canadian Fiction Magazine, Descant, Poetry Canada Review,* and *Antigonish Review.*

WORK IN PROGRESS: Away, a novel.

SIDELIGHTS: Jane Urquhart wrote: "I am interested in, and drawn to, subjects that define the relationship between men and women: the roles they play, their effect on their own personal geography, and most importantly, forces and powers that move them and of which they may not be entirely aware. The great amount of time I have spent in Europe . . . has influenced me enormously. Folklore, the supernatural, the effects of the seasons and religion seem to be more accessible, or more easily perceived, in this 'other' world. As a result, the heroes of fairy tales, saints, angels, demons, kings, and counts figure largely in my work, whether they act out their parts in a historical European setting or in a modern North American geography.

"I believe that good writing comes about as the result of a strong inner life—a unique world view fired by imagination and nurtured by intellect and hard work, an eye for detail and the ex-traordinary. But imagination must come first. Without it poetry cannot exist and prose becomes truly prosaic."

With two novels to her credit, Canadian writer Jane Urquhart has been praised for the historical aptitude and poetic insight she brings to her prose. Her first work of fiction, *The Whirlpool,* a gothic novel set in Victorian-era Niagara Falls, has fared well with critics. "Rarely has our history been served so well," writes Nancy Wigston, reviewing the book for the Toronto *Globe and Mail,* "yet this is by no means a 'historical' novel, dishing up yet another helping of gooey romanticism. No, Urquhart's moody, incisive and shimmering prose, her cleverness and wit soar beyond that." Gary Houston, reviewing the same book for the *Chicago Tribune,* points out that although "the sonorous narrative that follows these characters is nearly predictable. . . . Urquhart's prose-poetry is what shines." Her latest book, *Changing Heaven,* a contemporary novel possessed of Victorian overtones via the occasional entrance of nineteenth-century apparitions, has received similar acclaim. "Urquhart's prose is equipped with its own impeccable rhythms," notes William French in the *Globe and Mail.* He also finds favor with her presentation of historical elements within the book, claiming that *Changing Heaven* "verifies her as a kind of neo-Victorian prestidigitator, able to bridge this century and the last with impressive facility."

BIOGRAPHICAL/CRITICAL SOURCES:

PERIODICALS

Chicago Tribune, March 21, 1990.
Globe and Mail (Toronto), December 6, 1986; March 17, 1990.
New York Times Book Review, March 18, 1990.

V

VALDEZ, Luis (Miguel) 1940-

PERSONAL: Born June 26, 1940, in Delano, California; son of Francisco (a farm worker) and Armida Valdez; married wife, Lupe, August 23, 1969; children: Anahuac, Kinan, Lakin. *Education:* San Jose State University, B.A., 1964.

ADDRESSES: Home—53 Franklin St., San Juan Bautista, Calif. 95045. *Office*—P.O. Box 1240, San Juan Bautista, Calif. 95045. *Agent*—Joan Scott, Writers & Artists Agency, 11726 San Vicente Blvd., Suite 300, Los Angeles, Calif. 90049.

CAREER: Actor, director, and writer. Founder and artistic director of El Teatro Campesino, 1965—. Member of San Francisco Mime Troupe, 1964; union organizer for United Farm Workers Organizing Committee in Delano, Calif., 1965-66; lecturer in Chicano history and theatre arts at University of California, Berkeley, 1970-71; lecturer at University of California, Santa Cruz, 1971 and 1977; member of California Arts Council, 1976-81, National Endowment for the Arts Congressional Committee for the State of the Arts, 1978, and board of directors of Theatre Communications Group, 1978-79.

MEMBER: Directors Guild of America, Writers Guild of America, Society of Stage Directors and Choreographers.

AWARDS, HONORS: Prize from playwriting contest, c. 1961, for "The Theft"; Obie Award from *Village Voice*, 1968, for "demonstrating the politics of survival"; awards from Los Angeles Drama Critics, 1969 and 1972, for work with El Teatro Campesino; special Emmy Award for directing from KNBC-TV, 1973; award from Los Angeles Drama Critics Circle, 1978, for play "Zoot Suit"; grant from Rockefeller Foundation, 1978; nomination for Golden Globe for best musical film, 1981, for "Zoot Suit"; award for best musical from San Francisco Bay Critics Circle, 1983, for "Corridos!"; honorary doctorates from Columbia College, San Jose State University, and California Institute of the Arts; also shared other awards for work with El Teatro Campesino.

WRITINGS:

PLAYS

The Shrunken Head of Pancho Villa (first produced in San Jose at San Jose State College, 1964), El Centro Campesino Cultural, 1967.

(And director) "Los vendidos" (one-act; title means "The Sellouts"), first produced in 1967.

"Vietnam Campesino" (one-act), first produced in 1969.

"Soldado Razo" (one-act), first produced in 1969, produced with "The Dark Root of a Scream" (also see below) in New York City in 1985.

Actos (one-act works; first produced in 1969-70), Cucaracha Press, 1971.

(And director) "Bernabé" (one-act), first produced in 1970, published in *Contemporary Chicano Theatre,* edited by Roberto J. Garza, University of Notre Dame Press, 1975.

(And director) "La virgin del Tepeyac" (musical), first produced in San Juan Bautista, Calif., 1971.

"The Dark Root of a Scream" (one-act), first produced in 1971, produced with "Soldado Razo" (also see above) in New York City at Public/Martinson Hall, August, 1985, published in *From the Barrio: A Chicano Anthology,* edited by Lillian Falderman and Luis Omar Salinas, Canfield Press, 1973.

(And director) "La carpa de los Rasquachis," produced in New York City at Chelsea Westside, October, 1974.

(And director) "El fin del mundo" (title means "The End of the World"), first produced in 1976.

(And director) "Zoot Suit," produced in Los Angeles at Mark Taper Forum, April, 1978, produced in New York City at Winter Garden, March, 1979 (also see below).

(And director) "Bandito: The American Melodrama of Tiburcio Vasquez," first produced in 1980.

(And director) "I Don't Have to Show You No Stinking Badges," produced in Los Angeles at the Theatre Center, February, 1986.

Also author of "The Theft" (one-act), 1961. Work represented in anthologies.

SCREENPLAYS

(And director) "I Am Joaquin," El Centro Campesino Cultural, 1969.

(And director) "Zoot Suit" (adapted from his own play), Universal, 1982.

(And director) "La Bamba," Columbia, 1987.

OTHER

(Editor with Stan Steiner) *Aztlan: An Anthology of Mexican American Literature,* Knopf, 1972.

Pensamiento Serpentino: A Chicano Approach to the Theatre of Reality, Cucaracha Press, 1973.

Also writer and director of television productions, including "Corridos! Tales of Passion and Revolution," PBS-TV. Contributor to periodicals, including *Arte Nuevo, Latin American Theatre Review, Performing Arts,* and *Ramparts.*

SIDELIGHTS: Luis Valdez is a distinguished figure in both the stage and film worlds. He began his writing career with "The Theft," a one-act work completed in 1961, and followed that with "The Shrunken Head of Pancho Villa," a full-length production staged in 1964 when he was still a student at San Jose State College. During the mid-1960s, after graduating from college, Valdez worked with a mime troupe, then joined the United Farm Workers, a labor union comprised of migrants. With union members, Valdez staged improvisations designed to address and express problems and issues pertinent to the rank and file. As an outgrowth of these endeavors, Valdez formed El Teatro Campesino, a theatre company that would present his works throughout the United States in the ensuing decades.

During the rest of the 1960s El Teatro Campesino enjoyed steadily increasing prominence in the theatre world. In 1967 the company toured the United States in a production that included both dramatic and musical works, and in 1969 it performed at an international festival in France. By that time, however, the company had broken from the United Farm Workers and established itself as a blue-collar performing group. Among the works that El Teatro Campesino presented during these years was Valdez's early play "The Shrunken Head of Pancho Villa."

In 1970 the company performed Valdez's "Bernabé," which details a simpleton's intellectual development as he realizes a greater tie to his Chicano heritage. Valdez continued exploring the Chicano experience in works such as "Vietnam Campesino," "Soldado Razo," and "The Dark Root of a Scream," each of which addressed aspects of Chicano involvement in the Vietnam War. "Soldado Razo" and "The Dark Root of a Scream" were eventually presented together in New York City, whereupon *New York Times* reviewer D. J. R. Bruckner acknowledged El Teatro Campesino as a company devoted to political and social issues. Bruckner was particularly impressed with "Soldado Razo," which he described as "a simple, brief and very effective piece of political theater." In addition, Bruckner observed that the play's finale, concerning a young soldier's death and his family's subsequent grief, was "profoundly . . . moving."

By the mid-1970s, Valdez and El Teatro Campesino enjoyed substantial popularity in the United States and Europe. Among the company's most successful productions from this period was Valdez's "La carpa de los Rasquachis," a gripping depiction— with music—of a Mexican farmworker's hard life in America. Another work, "El fin del mundo," illuminated the Chicano urban experience. Valdez's most popular work from the 1970s, however, is probably "Zoot Suit," his entertaining account of an actual murder trial that occurred in Los Angeles in the early 1940s. In this play, Valdez offers a jarringly offbeat account— replete with music and dance numbers—of several young Chicanos doomed to life imprisonment for murder despite a disturbing lack of evidence.

Valdez wrote and directed a film version of "Zoot Suit" in 1982, but the adaptation fared poorly with such influential critics as the *New York Times*'s Vincent Canby, who called it "a mess." More appreciative was *Washington Post* writer Richard Harrington, who lamented the film's notoriety. Noting that the work was made within two weeks and for only three million dollars, Har-

rington conceded that "its limitations are apparent," but he nonetheless hailed it as "a powerful film."

After completing the "Zoot Suit" film, Valdez resumed stage work with El Teatro Campesino. Among the company's most celebrated Valdez productions from the 1980s is "I Don't Have to Show You No Stinking Badges," about a middle-class Chicano family and their uneasy assimilation into the American mainstream. The parents are actors specializing in demeaning bit parts such as migrant workers, gardeners, and servants. Their son is a disillusioned law student who resents his parents for making social and artistic compromises. Having returned home after abruptly leaving school, the son becomes increasingly disturbed, and he eventually threatens to kill both his parents and himself.

"I Don't Have to Show You No Stinking Badges" proved extremely popular upon production beginning in 1986. *Newsweek*'s Gerald C. Lubenow hailed the work as evidence that "Valdez has come triumphantly into his own," and reported that the play "has been cheered in Los Angeles and San Diego." For Lubenow, the work was "as much a story of generational conflict as of assimilation." *Los Angeles Times* reviewer Sylvie Drake expressed a mixed appraisal, finding the work "muddled" but added that Valdez was nonetheless an entertaining artist. "His inventiveness is tickling every minute," Drake wrote. "He comes up with more than a few zingers." A more wholeheartedly generous review was supplied by John R. Petrovksky, who wrote in *Hispania* that the play "takes on many themes and manages to treat them all with humor and yet, by the end, depth."

After reaping the rewards of "Badges," Valdez returned to film in 1987 with "La Bamba," which recounts the brief career of Chicano pop musician Ritchie Valens, who enjoyed significant popularity in the late 1950s before perishing in the same airplane crash that killed fellow performers Buddy Holly and the Big Bopper. With "La Bamba" Valdez proved himself a proficient, engaging filmmaker. Among the critics impressed with Valdez's work was the *Washington Post*'s Hal Hinson, who acknowledged the film's "energetic . . . spirit" and its "infectious freshness." Another *Post* writer, Richard Harrington, was at least as enthusiastic, praising "La Bamba" as a "poignant and passionate portrayal" of the ill-fated Valens. Janet Maslin, in her review for the *New York Times,* commended "La Bamba" more for its "warmth" and its "strong feeling for Valens's Chicano roots," while Desson Howe found it "a glorious, drug-free shot in the arm for romantics."

With successes on both the stage and in film, Valdez has established himself as a key figure in the world of performance arts. And though he seems preoccupied with Chicano concerns, critics have noted that his best works transcend ethnic considerations of race or nationality. As *Newsweek*'s Lubenow noted, "He has succeeded by shaping the experience of Chicanos into drama that speaks to all Americans."

BIOGRAPHICAL/CRITICAL SOURCES:

BOOKS

Huerta, Jorge A., *Chicano Theatre: Themes and Forms,* Bilingual Press, 1982.
Meier, Matt S., *Mexican American Biographies: A Historical Dictionary,* Greenwood Press, 1988.

PERIODICALS

American Film, July-August, 1987.
Caracol, April, 1967.
Chicago Tribune, January 25, 1982, July 24, 1987.

Drama Review, December, 1974.
Educational Theatre Journal, March, 1974.
Globe and Mail (Toronto), July 25, 1987.
Hispania, September, 1986.
Los Angeles Times, August 18, 1978, February 7, 1986, July 24, 1987.
Newsweek, May 4, 1987.
New York Review of Books, August 31, 1972.
New York Times, May 4, 1978, March 26, 1979, January 22, 1982, August 10, 1985, July 24, 1987.
Performance, fall, 1973.
Theatre Quarterly, March-May, 1975.
Time, August 17, 1987.
Tulane Drama Review, summer, 1967.
Vista, July 23, 1989.
Washington Post, July 24, 1987, July 27, 1987.

—Sketch by Les Stone

* * *

VALENZUELA, Luisa 1938-

PERSONAL: Born November 26, 1938, in Buenos Aires, Argentina; came to the United States, 1979; daughter of Pablo Francisco Valenzuela (a physician) and Luisa Mercedes Levinson (a writer); married, 1958 (divorced); children: Anna-Lisa. *Education:* University of Buenos Aires, B.A.

ADDRESSES: Home—La Pampa 1202 (SD), 1428 Buenos Aires, Argentina. *Office*—New York Institute for the Humanities, 26 Washington Place, New York, N.Y. 10003.

CAREER: La Nación, Buenos Aires, Argentina, editor of Sunday supplement, 1961-72; free-lance writer for magazines and newspapers in Buenos Aires, 1972-78; Columbia University, New York City, writer-in-residence, 1979-80; New York University, New York City, visiting professor, 1985-90. Fellow of New York Institute for the Humanities.

AWARDS, HONORS: Awards from Fondo Nacional de las Artes, 1966 and 1973, and Instituto Nacional de Cinematografía, 1973, for script based on *Hay que sonreír;* Fulbright fellowship, Iowa International Writers' Program, 1969; Guggenheim fellowship, 1983.

MEMBER: PEN, Fund for Free Expression (member of Freedom to Write Committee).

WRITINGS:

Hay que sonreír (novel; also see below), Américalee, 1966.
Los heréticos (short stories; also see below), Paidós, 1967.
El gato eficaz (novel; portions have appeared in periodicals in English translation under title "Cat-O-Nine-Deaths"), J. Mortiz, 1972.
Aquí pasan cosas raras (short stories; also see below), Ediciones de la Flor, 1975.
Clara: Thirteen Short Stories and a Novel (translations by Hortense Carpentier and J. Jorge Castello; contains translations of *Hay que sonreír,* published as "Clara," and stories from *Los heréticos*), Harcourt, 1976.
Como en la guerra (novel; also see below), Sudamericana, 1977, translation by Helen Lane published as *He Who Searches,* Dalkey Archive Press, 1987.
Strange Things Happen Here: Twenty-Six Short Stories and a Novel (translations by Lane; contains "He Who Searches" and translation of *Aquí pasan cosas raras*), Harcourt, 1979.

Libro que no muerde (title means "Book That Doesn't Bite"; includes stories from *Aquí pasan cosas raras* and *Los heréticos*), Universidad Nacional Autónoma de México, 1980.
Cambio de armas (short stories), Ediciones del Norte, 1982, translation by Deborah Bonner published as *Other Weapons,* Ediciones del Norte/Persea Books, 1986.
Cola de lagartija, Bruguera, 1983, translation by Gregory Rabassa published as *The Lizard's Tail,* Farrar, Straus, 1983.
Donde viven las águilas (short stories), Celtia, 1983, translation published as *Up Among the Eagles,* North Point Press, 1988.
Open Door (short stories), translation by Carpentier and others, North Point Press, 1989.

Also author of script for film adaptation of *Hay que sonreír* and a play, "National Reality from the Bed," 1990. Contributor to *La Nación* and *Crisis;* contributor to U.S. periodicals, including *Vogue* and *Village Voice.*

WORK IN PROGRESS: Novela negro con argentinos, for Plaza y Janés (Spain) and Ediciones del Norte (United States), translation by Asa Zatz to be published as *Black Novel with Argentines,* Simon & Schuster.

SIDELIGHTS: "Luisa Valenzuela's writing belongs to that class of contemporary works Umberto Eco has called 'open works,' " Patricia Rubio observes in *Salmagundi.* "In them the harmonious representation of reality, supported by logic and syllogism, is replaced by a more ample and complex vision in which the laws of causality cease to operate in a linear fashion. The ordered *Weltanschauung* of the standard realist narrative . . . disintegrates in the face of desire, cruelty, the instinctual, the magical, the fantastic, the sickly." Noting the magical and the fantastic elements in the Argentine novelist and short story writer's work, critics often describe her fiction—with its mixture of the fantastic and the real—as belonging to that popular Latin American school of writing called magic realism. Not content with this characterization, Valenzuela is quoted by *Time* magazine's R. Z. Sheppard as saying, "Magical realism was a beautiful resting place, but the thing is to go forward." She has forged into new fictive territory: her work is much more bizarre, erotic and violent than that of magic realism's best-known proponents, such as Gabriel García Márquez and Julio Cortázar. As one of the few Latin American women writers to achieve wide-spread recognition in the United States, Valenzuela also distinguishes herself from other contemporary Latin American writers by bringing a decidedly feminist slant to the male-dominated world of Hispanic literature.

As Rubio points out, Valenzuela's work—with the exception of *Hay que sonreír,* her first novel (published in English translation as "Clara"), and *The Heretics,* her first collection of short stories—is highly experimental. Constantly shifting points of view, extensive use of metaphors, and word-play have become her trademark. In her fiction the form of the work as well as the words used to write it are equal candidates for renewal. *Hispania* contributors Dorothy S. Mull and Elsa B. de Angulo observe that Valenzuela's linguistic experimentations include "efforts to distort language, to 'break open' individual words to examine how they function, to expose their hidden facets as a watchmaker might probe and polish the jewels in a timepiece." In the *Voice Literary Supplement* Brett Harvey notes, "Valenzuela plays with words, turns them inside out, weaves them into sensuous webs. She uses them as weapons, talismans to ward off danger and name the unnameable."

An effort to name the unnameable seems to be a strong motivating force behind Valenzuela's fiction, in this case the unnameable being the surreal reality of Argentine politics. Emily Hicks finds politics such an important facet of Valenzuela's novella, *He Who Searches,* that the critic writes in a *Review of Contemporary Fiction* essay, "The reader of this text will not be able to understand it without considering the current political situation in Argentina." Valenzuela has herself admitted the political content of her work. For example, in an interview with Evelyn Picon Garfield in *Review of Contemporary Fiction,* Valenzuela notes that the reason she wrote her most popular novel, *The Lizard's Tail,* was for "only one purpose: to try to understand." Valenzuela explains that it is almost impossible for her to comprehend how the Argentine people allowed themselves to become victims of the harsh military regimes that dominated their country for such a long time. In a similar conversation with Barbara Case in a *Ms.* interview, Valenzuela reveals that the magic found in her work is paradoxically the result of the reality the writer discovered in her native land. "Everything is so weird now and it becomes more and more strange," Valenzuela explains. "We thought we had this very civilized, integrated, cosmopolitan country, and suddenly we realized we were dealing with magic. It's been discovered that a minister in Isabel Perón's cabinet was in real life a witch doctor and had books published on witchcraft. Argentinians were caught in a trap of believing ourselves to be European while ignoring all our Latin American reality."

The Lizard's Tail has been described as a roman a clef based on the life of the cabinet minister Valenzuela mentions in her interview with Case. José López Rega, Perón's Minister of Social Welfare, appears in the novel as the Sorcerer, a man who has three testicles. He refers to this third testicle as his sister "Estrella" and dreams of having a child with her. "Of course this character," Case observes, "renounces women since he already has one built in—his own 'trinity of the crotch.' But in this unique parody of Latin machismo, his third testicle, Estrella, exists in the Sorcerer to restrain him. When he gets too feisty, Estrella contracts with pain and leaves him doubled up on the floor." Through the use of first-person monologues—described as the Sorcerer's novel or diary—and additional first- and third-person narrations, Valenzuela tells the story of the Sorcerer's rise to power, his fall, his plans to return to power, and his death. Other characters include the Sorcerer's mother (whom he boils and drinks), the Generalissimo, the Dead Woman Eva, and Valenzuela herself.

The work seems to contain everything that readers have come to expect in Valenzuela's fiction: magic, power, political commentary, circular time, female/male conflicts and violence. However, some critics believe Valenzuela tries to cover too much in the work. *New York Times Book Review* contributor Allen Josephs states, "Her attempt at virtuosity tends to undermine the novel. In order to convince the reader of the Sorcerer's madness and narcissistic depravity, she resorts to surrealism, hyperbole and self-indulgent prose. The parody becomes increasingly self-conscious as the novel proceeds." Reviewer Herbert Gold also criticizes the novel, writing in the *Los Angeles Times Book Review,* "She is trying for intelligence and trying for magic; but the novelist here points to herself too much. . . . She broods about making magic too much to be able to make the magic. She wants to be wild; that's not the same as wildness."

Other critics praise the novel, seeing it as an important work of Latin American fiction. In *Review of Contemporary Fiction* Marie-Lise Gazarian Gautier calls *The Lizard's Tail* "one of the most fascinating novels written in recent years by a Latin American." Harvey refers to it as "a gorgeously surreal allegory of Argentine politics." In her *Review* essay on the work, critic and translator Edith Grossman finds the novel "remarkable" and notes that in it "Valenzuela reaffirms the powerful significance

of language and the value of the artful word as legitimate modes of understanding the dark enigmas of brutality and violence."

Valenzuela's criticism of Argentine politics is often coupled with her equally harsh look at the fate of women in such a society. In her *World Literature Today* essay on the writer, Sharon Magnarelli finds Valenzuela "always subtly political and/or feminist." Magnarelli detects a link between Valenzuela's wordplay and her portrayal of women in her fiction, believing that the Argentine's "work is clearly an attempt to free language and women from the shackles of society." Valenzuela's novel, *Hay que sonreír,* deals with Clara, a young woman who comes to Buenos Aires from the provinces and turns to prostitution in order to support herself. In the novel one sees the beginnings of Valenzuela's characteristic experimentation with form: the story is told through first and third person narrations alternating between past and present tenses. The book also contains a clear statement of the writer's feminist concerns. "One of the main themes of the text," Magnarelli notes, "is unquestionably contemporary woman's plight with the social expectations that she will be passive, silent, industrious (but only in areas of minor import), possessed by a male (be he father, husband, or pimp) and that she will continue to smile (*hay que sonreír* ['one has to smile' in English]) in spite of the exploitation or violence perpetrated against her."

Critics also comment on the female protagonists of the stories in Valenzuela's collection, *Other Weapons,* five narratives dealing with male/female relationships. While many Argentine writers have focused attention on the larger social and economic ramifications of their country's continually violent political situation, Valenzuela, as both *Voice Literary Supplement* contributor Brett Harvey and *Review* contributor Mary Lusky Friedman comment, reveals how the stress of living in a repressive society undermines interpersonal ties between individuals in that society. "*Other Weapons* is a book that testifies to the difficulty of forging, in politically distressed times, sustaining personal relationships," Friedman observes. "The failures of intimacy that Valenzuela depicts are the quieter casualties of Argentina's recent crisis." In Valenzuela's work, as Valerie Gladstone points out in the *New York Times Book Review,* "Political absurdity is matched only by the absurdity of human relations."

BIOGRAPHICAL/CRITICAL SOURCES:

BOOKS

Contemporary Literary Criticism, Volume 31, 1985.

PERIODICALS

Hispania, May, 1986.
Los Angeles Times Book Review, September 11, 1983.
Ms., October, 1983.
New York Times Book Review, October 2, 1983, October 30, 1988.
Review, January-May, 1984, July-December, 1985.
Review of Contemporary Fiction, fall, 1986.
Salmagundi, spring-summer, 1989.
Time, March 7, 1983.
Voice Literary Supplement, December, 1985.
World Literature Today, winter, 1984.

—Sketch by Marian Gonsior

*   *   *

van der ZEE, John 1936-

PERSONAL: Born January 30, 1936, in San Francisco, CA; son of Herman A. (a judge) and Mary (McGushin) van der Zee; married Diane Hunt, November 28, 1959; children: Peter John, Katy. *Education:* Stanford University, A.B., 1957.

ADDRESSES: Home—2988 Pacific Ave., San Francisco, CA 94115. *Office*—McCann-Erickson, Inc., 201 California St., San Francisco, CA 94111.

CAREER: Copywriter with Batten, Barton, Durstine & Osborn, San Francisco, CA, 1958-61, Benton & Bowles, Inc., New York, NY, 1961-62, Fletcher Richards, Calkins & Holden, San Francisco, 1962-63, and Batten, Barton, Durstine & Osborn, 1964-66; McCann-Erickson, Inc., San Francisco, copy-writer, 1966-69, associate creative director, beginning 1969, became senior vice-president, senior writer since 1985; Ogilvie & Mather, San Francisco, senior writer, 1984-85. Director, Friends of the San Francisco Library. *Military service:* California National Guard, 1957-61.

MEMBER: Authors League of America, Authors Guild, Phi Gamma Delta.

AWARDS, HONORS: James D. Phelan Award for Literature, 1964, for manuscript of novel (unpublished), "The Hand-Picked Man."

WRITINGS:

The Plum Explosion (novel), Harcourt, 1967.
Blood Brotherhood (novel), Harcourt, 1970.
(With Hugh Wilkerson) *Life in the Peace Zone: An American Company Town,* Macmillan, 1971.
Canyon: The Story of the Last Rustic Community in Metropolitan America, Harcourt, 1972.
The Greatest Men's Party on Earth: Inside the Bohemian Grove, Harcourt, 1974.
Stateline (novel), Harcourt, 1976.
(Editor with Boyd Jacobson) *The Imagined City: San Francisco in the Minds of Its Writers,* California Living, 1980.
While Someone Else Is Eating: American Poets and Novelists on Reaganism, Anchor Books, 1984.
Bound Over: Indentured Servitude and American Conscience, Simon & Schuster 1985.
The Gate: The True Story of the Design and Construction of the Golden Gate Bridge, Simon & Schuster, 1987.

Contributor to *Ramparts, New York Times, Los Angeles Times, Harper's, California Living,* and *Town and Country.*

SIDELIGHTS: In *Canyon: The Story of the Last Rustic Community in Metropolitan America,* John van der Zee offers an account of one community's struggle to maintain its natural relationship with the environment. Once hidden away in the woods fifteen miles from San Francisco, this town has guarded its rustic nature through the efforts of its original settlers and its newer residents, followers of the back-to-nature movement. "Writing with an eye for unobtrusive but telling detail . . . and a sense of fairness," notes Annie Gottlieb in the *New York Times Book Review,* John van der Zee has fashioned "a compact, lucid and loving account of Canyon's history and hassles." Gottlieb concludes, "The readers of this book will determine whether Canyon is an omen that the changes in our minds can really take root [or whether it is a symbol of] what might have been."

"In 1972, by working as a waiter," van der Zee told *CA,* "I penetrated northern California's exclusive Bohemian Grove, and wrote the first on-the-spot account of the nation's largest annual gathering of men of wealth and power." As he explains in the book, "Originally a club for men with talent but no money, the Bohemian Club [has evolved into] the reverse." For two weeks each summer, over a thousand of the richest and most influential

men in the United States, including presidents, oilmen, industrialists, and financiers, gather at this retreat near San Francisco. Peter Barnes comments in the *New Republic,* "Van der Zee, though no theoretician, is a perceptive and fluent writer." And Donald Goddard, contributing to the *New York Times Book Review* writes, "His assessments of character and motive . . . are generally shrewd and often sharp." Goddard adds, "Refraining from any larger judgements on the wider significance of this male chauvinist jamboree, van der Zee amuses at first and then, as the implications sink in, disturbs."

BIOGRAPHICAL/CRITICAL SOURCES:

PERIODICALS

Los Angeles Times Book Review, September 1, 1985, March 29, 1987.
New Republic, April 27, 1974, March 4, 1978.
New Yorker, July 22, 1974.
New York Times, July 30, 1985.
New York Times Book Review, February 27, 1972, March 5, 1974, March 8, 1987.

*   *   *

VARGAS LLOSA, (Jorge) Mario (Pedro) 1936-

PERSONAL: Born March 28, 1936, in Arequipa, Peru; son of Ernesto Vargas Maldonaldo and Dora Llosa Ureta; married Julia Urquidi, 1955 (divorced); married Patricia Llosa, 1965; children: (second marriage) Gonzalo, Alvaro, Morgana. *Education:* Attended University of San Marcos; University of Madrid, Ph.D., 1959. *Politics:* Member of Fredemo, a center-right political party which is part of the Liberty Movement coalition. *Avocational interests:* Tennis, gymnastics, waterskiing, movies.

CAREER: Writer. Journalist with *La Industria,* Piura, Peru, and with La Radio Panamericana and *La Crónica,* both in Lima, Peru, during 1960s; worked in Paris, France, as a journalist with Agence France-Presse, as a broadcaster with the radio-television network URTF, and as a language teacher; University of London, Queen Mary College and Kings College, London, England, faculty member, 1966-68; University of Washington, Seattle, writer in residence, 1968; University of Puerto Rico, Río Piedras, visiting professor, 1969; *Libre,* Paris, co-founder, 1971; Columbia University, New York, NY, Edward Laroque Tinker Visiting Professor, 1975; former fellow, Woodrow Wilson Center, Washington, DC; former host of Peruvian television program "The Tower of Babel"; Peruvian presidential candidate, Liberty Movement, 1990.

AWARDS, HONORS: Premio Leopoldo Alas, 1959, for *Los jefes;* Barral Prix Biblioteca Breve, 1962, for *La ciudad y los perros;* Premio de la Crítica Española, 1963, for *La ciudad y los perros,* and 1967, for *La casa verde;* Premio Nacional de la Novela, 1967, for *La casa verde;* Ritz Paris Hemingway Award, 1985, for *The War of the End of the World;* Premio Internacional Literatura Romulo Gallegos, for *La casa verde.*

WRITINGS:

Los jefes (story collection; title means "The Leaders"), Editorial Roca, 1959.
Los cachorros (novella), Editorial Lumen, 1967, translation by Ronald Christ and Gregory Kolovakos published, with six short stories, as *The Cubs and Other Stories,* Harper, 1979.
La novela, Fundación de Cultura Universitaria, 1968.
Lletra de batalla per "Tirant lo Blanc," Edicions 62, 1969.
Antología mínima de M. Vargas Llosa, Editorial Tiempo Contemporáneo, 1969.

(With Julio Cortázar and Oscar Collazos) *La literatura en la revolución y la revolución en la literatura,* Siglo Vientiuno Editores, 1970.

Día domingo, Ediciones Amadis, 1971.

García Márquez: Historia de un deicidio, Seix Barral, 1971.

La historia secreta de una novela, Tusquets, 1971.

Obras escogidas, Aguilar, 1973.

La orgia perpetua: Flaubert y "Madame Bovary," Seix Barral, 1975, translation by Helen Lane published as *The Perpetual Orgy: Flaubert and Madame Bovary,* Farrar, Straus, 1986.

Art, Authenticity and Latin American Culture, Wilson Center (Washington, DC), 1981.

La señorita de Tacna, Seix Barral, 1982, first produced under title "Señorita from Tacna" in New York at INTAR Hispanic American Arts Center, 1983; produced under title "The Young Lady from Tacna" in Los Angeles at the Bilingual Foundation of the Arts, May, 1985.

Kathie y el hipopótamo: Comedia en dos actos, Seix Barral, 1983, translation by Kerry McKenny and Anthony Oliver-Smith produced as "Kathie and the Hippopotamus" in Edinburgh, Scotland, at the Traverse Theatre, August, 1986.

La cultura de la libertad, la libertad de la cultura, Fundación Eduardo Frei, 1985.

La chunga, Seix Barral, 1986, translation by Joanne Pottlitzer first produced in New York at INTAR Hispanic American Arts Center, February 9, 1986.

Elogio de la madrastra, Tusquets (Barcelona), 1988.

Also author of play "La Huida" (title means "The Escape"), produced in Piura, Peru; contributor to *The Eye of the Heart,* 1973.

NOVELS

La ciudad y los perros, Seix Bartal, 1963, translation by Lysander Kemp published as *The Time of the Hero,* Grove, 1966.

La casa verde, Seix Barral, 1966, translation by Gregory Rabassa published as *The Green House,* Harper, 1968.

Conversación en la catedral, Seix Barral, 1969, translation by Rabassa published as *Conversation in the Cathedral,* Harper, 1975.

Pantaleón y las visitadoras, Seix Barral, 1973, translation by Christ and Kolovakos published as *Captain Pantoja and the Special Service,* Harper, 1978.

Aunt Julia and the Scriptwriter, Farrar, Straus, 1982 (published in the original Spanish as *La tía Julia y el escribidor,* 1977).

The War of the End of the World, translation by Lane, Farrar, Straus, 1984 (published in the original Spanish as *Guerra*).

Historia de Mayta, Seix Barral, 1985, translation by Alfred MacAdam published as *The Real Life of Alejandro Mayta,* Farrar, Straus, 1986.

Who Killed Palomino Molero?, translation by MacAdam, Farrar, Straus, 1987 (published in the original Spanish as *¿Quién mató a Palomino Molero?*).

El hablador, Seix Barral, 1988, translation by Lane published as *The Storyteller,* Farrar, Straus, 1989.

MEDIA ADAPTATIONS: "The Cubs" was filmed in 1971; *Captain Pantoja and the Special Service* was filmed in 1976 (Vargas Llosa directed the film, which was banned in Peru); *Aunt Julia and the Scriptwriter* was adapted as a television series in Peru and as a screenplay written by William Boyd and directed by Jon Amiel in 1989.

SIDELIGHTS: Peruvian writer Mario Vargas Llosa often draws from his personal experiences to write of the injustices and corruption of contemporary Latin America. At one time an admirer of communist Cuba, since the early 1970s Vargas Llosa has been opposed to tyrannies of both the political left and right. He now advocates democracy, a free market, and individual liberty, and he cautions against extreme or violent political action, instead calling for peaceful democratic reforms. In 1989 he was chosen to be the presidential candidate of Fredemo, a political coalition in Peru; he later withdrew from the race. Through his novels—marked by complex structures and an innovative merging of dialogue and description in an attempt to recreate the actual feeling of life—Vargas Llosa has established himself as one of the most important of contemporary writers in the Spanish language. His novels, a London *Times* writer comments, "are among the finest coming out of Latin America."

As a young man, Vargas Llosa spent two years at the Leoncio Prado Military Academy. Sent there by his father, who had discovered that his son wrote poetry and was therefore fearful for the boy's masculinity, Vargas Llosa found the school, with its "restrictions, the military discipline and the brutal, bullying atmosphere, unbearable," he writes in the *New York Times Magazine.* His years at the school inspired his first novel, *The Time of the Hero* (first published in Spanish as *La ciudad y los perros*). The book is, R. Z. Sheppard states in *Time,* "a brutal slab of naturalism about life and violent death." The novel's success was ensured when the school's officials objected to Vargas Llosa's portrayal of their institution. "One thousand copies were ceremoniously burned in the patio of the school and several generals attacked it bitterly. One of them said that the book was the work of a 'degenerate mind,' and another, who was more imaginative, claimed that I had undoubtedly been paid by Ecuador to undermine the prestige of the Peruvian Army," Vargas Llosa recalls in his *New York Times Magazine* article.

In the award-winning *The Green House* (*La casa verde* in the Spanish edition), Vargas Llosa draws upon another period from his childhood for inspiration. For several years his family lived in the Peruvian jungle town of Piura, and his memories of the gaudy local brothel, known to everyone as the Green House, form the basis of his novel. The book's several stories are interwoven in a nonlinear narrative revolving around the brothel and the family that owns it, the military that runs the town, a dealer in stolen rubber in the nearby jungle, and a prostitute who was raised in a convent. "Scenes overlap, different times and places overrun each other . . . echoes precede voices, and disembodied consciences dissolve almost before they can be identified," Luis Harss and Barbara Dohmann write in *Into the Mainstream: Conversations with Latin-American Writers.* Gregory Rabassa, writing in *World Literature Today,* notes that the novel's title "is the connective theme that links the primitive world of the jungle to the primal lusts of 'civilization' which are enclosed by the green walls of the whorehouse." Rabassa sees, too, that Vargas Llosa's narrative style "has not reduced time to a device of measurement or location, a practical tool, but has conjoined it with space, so that the characters carry their space with them too . . . inseparable from their time." Harss and Dohmann find that *The Green House* "is probably the most accomplished work of fiction ever to come out of Latin America. It has sweep, beauty, imaginative scope, and a sustained eruptive power that carries the reader from first page to last like a fish in a bloodstream."

With *Conversation in the Cathedral* (first published in Spanish as *Conversación en la catedral*), Vargas Llosa widened his scope. Whereas in previous novels he had sought to recreate the repression and corruption of a particular place, in *Conversation in the Cathedral* he attempts to provide a panoramic view of his native country. As John M. Kirk states in *International Fiction Review,* this novel "presents a wider, more encompassing view of Peruvian society. [Vargas Llosa's] gaze extends further afield in a determined effort to incorporate as many representative regions of Peru as possible." Set during the dictatorship of Manuel Udria in the late 1940s and 1950s, the society depicted in the novel "is one of corruption in virtually all the shapes and spheres you can imagine," Wolfgang A. Luchting writes in the *Review of the Center for Inter-American Relations.* Penny Leroux, in a review of the book for *Nation,* calls it "one of the most scathing denunciations ever written on the corruption and immorality of Latin America's ruling classes."

The nonlinear writing of *Conversation in the Cathedral* is seen by several critics to be the culmination of Vargas Llosa's narrative experimentation. Writing in the *Review of the Center for Inter-American Relations,* Ronald Christ calls the novel "a masterpiece of montage" and "a massive assault on simultaneity." Christ argues that Vargas Llosa links fragments of prose together to achieve a montage effect that "promotes a linking of actions and words, speech and description, image and image, point of view and point of view." Kirk explains that in *Conversation in the Cathedral,* Vargas Llosa is "attempting the ambitious and obviously impossible plan of conveying to the reader all aspects of the reality of [Peruvian] society, of writing the 'total' novel." By interweaving five different narratives, Vargas Llosa forces the reader to study the text closely, making the reader an "accomplice of the writer [which] undoubtedly helps the reader to a more profound understanding of the work." Kirk concludes that *Conversation in the Cathedral* is "both a perfect showcase for all the structural techniques and thematic obsessions found in [Vargas Llosa's] other work, as well as being the true culmination of his personal anguish for Peru."

Speaking of these early novels in *Modern Latin American Literature,* D. P. Gallagher argues that one intention of their complex nonlinear structures is to "re-enact the complexity of the situations described in them." By juxtaposing unrelated elements, cutting off dialogue at critical moments, and breaking the narration, Vargas Llosa suggests the disparate geological conditions of Peru, recreates the difficulties involved in living in that country, and re-enacts "the very nature of conversation and of communication in general, particularly in a society devoted to the concealment of truth and to the flaunting of deceptive images," Gallagher believes. Ronald de Feo points out in the *New Republic* that these early novels all explore "with a near-savage seriousness and single-mindedness themes of social and political corruption." But in *Captain Pantoja and the Special Service (Pantaleón y las visitadoras* in its Spanish edition), "a new unexpected element entered Vargas Llosa's work: an unrestrained sense of humor," de Feo reports.

A farcical novel involving a military officer's assignment to provide prostitutes for troops in the Peruvian jungle, *Captain Pantoja and the Special Service* is "told through an artful combination of dry military dispatches, juicy personal letters, verbose radio rhetoric, and lurid sensationalist news reports," Gene Bell-Villada writes in *Commonweal.* Vargas Llosa also mixes conversations from different places and times, as he has in previous novels. And like these earlier works, *Captain Pantoja and the Special Service* "sniffs out corruption in high places, but it also presents something of a break, Vargas Llosa here shedding his high seriousness and adopting a humorous ribald tone," Bell-Villada concludes. The novel's satirical attack is aimed not at the military, a *Times Literary Supplement* reviewer writes, but at "any institution which channels instincts into a socially acceptable ritual. The humor of the narrative derives less from this serious underlying motive, however, than from the various linguistic codes into which people channel the darker forces."

The humorous tone of *Captain Pantoja and the Special Service* is also found in *Aunt Julia and the Scriptwriter (La tía Julia y el escribidor* in the original Spanish edition). The novel concerns two characters based on people in Vargas Llosa's own life: his first wife, Julia, who was his aunt by marriage, and a writer of radio soap opera who Vargas Llosa names Pedro Camacho in the novel. The 18-year-old narrator, Mario, has a love affair with the 32-year-old Julia. Their story is interrupted in alternate chapters by Camacho's wildly complicated soap opera scripts. As Camacho goes mad, his daily scripts for ten different soap operas become more and more entangled, with characters from one serial appearing in others and all of his plots converging into a single unlikely story. The scripts display "fissures through which are revealed secret obsessions, aversions and perversions that allow us to view his soap operas as the story of his disturbed mind," Jose Miguel Oviedo writes in *World Literature Today.* "The result," explains Nicholas Shakespeare in the *Times Literary Supplement,* "is that Camacho ends up in an asylum, while Mario concludes his real-life soap opera by running off to marry Aunt Julia."

Although *Aunt Julia and the Scriptwriter* is as humorous as the previous novel, *Captain Pantoja and the Special Service,* "it has a thematic richness and density the other book lacked," de Feo believes. This richness is found in the novel's exploration of the writer's life and of the relationship between a creative work and its inspiration. In the contrasting of soap opera plots with the real-life romance of Mario and Julia, the novel raises questions about the distinctions between fiction and fact. In a review for *New York,* Carolyn Clay calls *Aunt Julia and the Scriptwriter* "a treatise on the art of writing, on the relationship of stimuli to imagination." It is, de Feo observes, "a multilayered, high-spirited, and in the end terribly affecting text about the interplay of fiction and reality, the transformation of life into art, and life seen and sometimes even lived as fiction."

In *The War of the End of the World,* Vargas Llosa for the first time sets his story outside of his native Peru. He turns instead to Brazil of the 19th century and bases his story on an apocalyptic religious movement which gained momentum towards the end of the century. Convinced that the year 1900 marked the end of the world, these zealots, led by a man named the Counselor, set up the community of Canudos. Because of the Counselor's continued denunciations of the Brazilian government, which he called the "antichrist" for its legal separation of church and state, the national government sent in troops to break up this religious community. The first military assault was repulsed, as were the second and third, but the fourth expedition involved a force of some 4,000 soldiers. They laid waste to the entire area and killed nearly 40,000 people.

Vargas Llosa tells Wendy Smith in *Publishers Weekly* that he was drawn to write of this bloody episode because he felt the fanaticism of both sides in this conflict was exemplary of present-day Latin America. "Fanaticism is the root of violence in Latin America," he explains. In the Brazilian war, he believes, is a microcosm of Latin America. "Canudos presents a limited situation in which you can see clearly. Everything is there: a society in which on the one hand people are living a very old-fashioned life and have an archaic way of thinking, and on the other hand progressives want to impose modernism on society with guns. This creates a total lack of communication, of dialogue, and when there is no communication, war or repression or upheaval comes immediately," he tells Smith. In an article for the *Washington Post,* Vargas Llosa explains to Curt Suplee that "in the history of the Canudos war you could really see something that has been happening in Latin American history over the 19th and

20th centuries—the total lack of communication between two sections of a society which kill each other fighting *ghosts,* no? Fighting fictional enemies who are invented out of fanaticism. This kind of reciprocal incapacity of understanding is probably the main problem we have to overcome in Latin America."

Not only is *The War of the End of the World* set in the 19th century, but its length and approach are also of that time. A writer for the London *Times* calls it "a massive novel in the 19th century tradition: massive in content, in its ambitions, in its technical achievement." Gordon Brotherston of the *Times Literary Supplement* describes the book as being "on the grand scale of the nineteenth century," while Salman Rushdie of *New Republic* similarly defines the novel as "a modern tragedy on the grand scale." Richard Locke of the *Washington Post Book World* believes that *The War of the End of the World* "overshadows the majority of novels published here in the past few years. Indeed, it makes most recent American fiction seem very small, very private, very gray, and very timid."

Vargas Llosa's political perspective in *The War of the End of the World* shows a marked change from his earlier works. He does not attack a corrupt society in this novel. Instead he treats both sides in the Canudos war ironically. The novel ends with a character from either side locked in a fight to the death. As Rushdie observes, "this image would seem to crystallize Vargas Llosa's political vision." This condemnation of both sides in the Canudos conflict reflects Vargas Llosa's view of the contemporary Latin American scene, where rightist dictatorships often battle communist guerrillas. Suplee describes Vargas Llosa as "a humanist who reviles with equal vigor tyrannies of the right or left (is there really a difference, he asks, between 'good tortures and bad tortures'?)."

Although his political views have changed during the course of his career, taking him from a leftist supporter of communist Cuba to a strong advocate of democracy, Vargas Llosa's abhorrence of dictatorship, violence, and corruption has remained constant. And he sees Latin American intellectuals as part of a continuing cycle of "repression, chaos, and subversion," he tells Philip Bennett in the *Washington Post.* Many of these intellectuals, Vargas Llosa explains further, "are seduced by rigidly dogmatic stands. Although they are not accustomed to pick up a rifle or throw bombs from their studies, they foment and defend the violence." Speaking of the ongoing conflict in Peru between the military government and a Maoist guerrilla movement, Vargas Llosa clarifies to Suplee that "the struggle between the guerrillas and the armed forces is really a settling of accounts between privileged sectors of society, and the peasant masses are used cynically and brutally by those who say they want to 'liberate' them."

Vargas Llosa believes that a Latin American writer is obligated to speak out on political matters. "If you're a writer in a country like Peru," he tells Suplee, "you're a privileged person because you know how to read and write, you have an audience, you are respected. It is a moral obligation of a writer in Latin America to be involved in civic activities." This belief led Vargas Llosa in 1987 to speak out when the Peruvian government proposed to nationalize the country's banks. His protest quickly led to a mass movement in opposition to the plan, and the government was forced to back down. Vargas Llosa's supporters went on to create Fredemo, a political party calling for democracy, a free market, and individual liberty. Together with two other political parties, Fredemo established a coalition group called the Liberty Movement. In June of 1989, Vargas Llosa was chosen to be the coalition's presidential candidate for Peru's 1990 elections. Visit-

ing small rural towns, the urban strongholds of his Marxist opponents, and the jungle villages of the country's Indians, Vargas Llosa campaigned on what he believes is Peru's foremost problem: "We have to defend democracy against the military and against the extreme Left." Opinion polls in late summer of 1988 showed him to be the leading contender for the presidency, with a 44 to 19 percent lead over his nearest opponent.

"A major figure in contemporary Latin American letters," as Locke explains, and "the man whom many describe as the national conscience of his native Peru," as George de Lama writes in the *Chicago Tribune,* Vargas Llosa is usually ranked with Jorge Luis Borges, Gabriel García Márquez, and other writers of what has been called the Latin American "Boom" of the 1960s. His body of work set in his native Peru, Suzanne Jill Levine writes in the *New York Times Book Review,* is "one of the largest narrative efforts in contemporary Latin American letters. . . . [He] has begun a complete inventory of the political, social, economic and cultural reality of Peru. . . . Very deliberately, Vargas Llosa has chosen to be his country's conscience." But Vargas Llosa warns that a writer's role is limited. "Even great writers can be totally blind on political matters and can put their prestige and their imagination and fantasy at the service of a policy, which, if it materialized, would be destruction of what they do . . . ," Sheppard quotes Vargas Llosa as telling a PEN conference. "To be in the situation of Poland is no better than to be in the situation of Chile. I feel perplexed by these questions. I want to fight for societies where perplexity is still permitted."

BIOGRAPHICAL/CRITICAL SOURCES:

BOOKS

Contemporary Literary Criticism, Gale, Volume 3, 1975; Volume 6, 1976; Volume 9, 1978; Volume 10, 1979; Volume 15, 1980; Volume 31, 1985; Volume 42, 1987.

Feal, Rosemary Geisdorfer, *Novel Lives: The Fictional Autobiographies of Guillermo Cabrera Infante and Mario Vargas Llosa,* University of North Carolina Press, 1986.

Gallagher, D. P., *Modern Latin American Literature,* Oxford University Press, 1973.

Harss, Luis, and Barbara Dohmann, *Into the Mainstream: Conversations with Latin-American Writers,* Harper, 1967.

Rossmann, Charles, and Alan Warren Friedman, editors, *Mario Vargas Llosa: A Collection of Critical Essays,* University of Texas Press, 1978.

Williams, Raymond Leslie, *Mario Vargas Llosa,* Ungar, 1986.

PERIODICALS

Bookletter, April 28, 1975.
Bulletin of Bibliography, December, 1986.
Chicago Tribune, January 3, 1989; June 23, 1989; August 3, 1989.
Chicago Tribune Book World, October 7, 1979; January 12, 1986.
Commonweal, June 8, 1979.
Hispania, March, 1976.
Hudson Review, winter, 1976.
International Fiction Review, January, 1977.
Los Angeles Times, May 20, 1985; December 18, 1988.
Los Angeles Times Book Review, February 2, 1986.
Nation, November 22, 1975.
National Review, December 10, 1982.
New Leader, March 17, 1975; November 15, 1982.
New Republic, August 16-23, 1982; October 8, 1984.
Newsweek, February 10, 1986.
New York, August 23, 1982.

New York Review of Books, March 20, 1975; January 24, 1980.
New York Times, March 30, 1985; January 8, 1986; February 9, 1986; February 12, 1986; September 10, 1989.
New York Times Book Review, March 23, 1975; April 9, 1978; September 23, 1979; August 1, 1982; December 2, 1984; February 2, 1986; October 29, 1989.
New York Times Magazine, November 20, 1983.
Partisan Review, Volume 46, number 4, 1979.
Publishers Weekly, October 5, 1984.
Review of the Center for Inter-American Relations, spring, 1975.
Saturday Review, January 11, 1975.
Spectator, May 14, 1983.
Time, February 17, 1975; August 9, 1982; January 27, 1986; March 10, 1986; September 7, 1987.
Times (London), May 13, 1985; August 5, 1986.
Times Literary Supplement, October 12, 1973; May 20, 1983; March 8, 1985; May 17, 1985; July 1, 1988.
Tribune Books (Chicago), October 29, 1989.
Washington Post, August 29, 1983; October 1, 1984; March 26, 1989.
Washington Post Book World, August 26, 1984; February 9, 1986.
World Literature Today, winter, 1978; spring, 1978.

*   *   *

VERDU, Matilde
See CELA, Camilo Jose

*   *   *

VILLASENOR, Edmund
See VILLASENOR, Victor E(dmundo)

*   *   *

VILLASENOR, Victor
See VILLASENOR, Victor E(dmundo)

*   *   *

VILLASENOR, Victor E(dmundo)   1940-
(Edmund Villasenor, Victor Villasenor)

PERSONAL: Born May 11, 1940, in Carlsbad, Calif.; son of Salvadore (in business) and Lupe (Gómez) Villaseñor; married Barbara Bloch, December 29, 1974; children: David Cuauhtemoc. *Education:* Attended University of San Diego and Santa Clara University.

ADDRESSES: Home—1302 Stewart St., Oceanside, Calif. 92054.

CAREER: Construction worker in California, 1965-70; writer, 1970—. *Military service:* U.S. Army.

WRITINGS:

(Under name Edmund Villaseñor) *Macho!* (novel), Bantam, 1973.
(Under name Víctor Villaseñor) *Jury: The People vs. Juan Corona* (nonfiction), Little, Brown, 1977.
Rio Grande, Putnam, 1989.

Contributor to *Aztlan.*

SIDELIGHTS: Chicano author Víctor E. Villaseñor has attained recognition well beyond the small and somewhat insular Chicano literary community. Villaseñor's first novel, *Macho!,* benefited from being published at the height of a powerful migrant farmworkers' organizing campaign in California in 1973. The novel recounts a year in the life of Roberto García, a young Tarascan Indian from the state of Michoacán, Mexico, who migrates illegally to California in 1963 to work in the fields. Villaseñor describes García's intense culture shock in abandoning his isolated, tradition-bound village for the rich but lonely and frightening land of the north. The victim of exploitation and discrimination in the United States, García finally decides to go back to his village and resume working his family's small farm. But he returns a changed man who can no longer accept without question the traditional Mexican social code, particularly the *machista* demand that he take blood vengeance against the villager who murdered his father. Thus, García's adventure reflects the Chicano's transcultural experience—the melding of features from both the Spanish-Mexican and North American societies.

Villaseñor's second book, *Jury: The People vs. Juan Corona,* is a nonfiction account of the trial of Juan Corona, a California labor contractor who was convicted in 1973 of murdering twenty-five derelicts and drifters. After covering the trial as a journalist, Villaseñor decided to write a book focusing on the jury's agonizing struggle to reach a fair verdict in one of the worst mass murder cases in U.S. history. By exhaustively interviewing all of the jurors over a period of months, Villaseñor was able to reconstruct the details of eight days of emotionally charged deliberations that led the jury from an original majority favoring acquittal to a unanimous verdict of guilty.

Villaseñor's examination of the highly complicated and controversial case offers provocative insights into the workings of the American jury system. The author questions the system, quoting a Corona juror agonizing over whether a man's life should rest in the hands of twelve ordinary people seemingly ill-equipped by education or training to sort out a tangled skein of law and evidence. Based on the Corona trial, Villaseñor determines that the system does indeed work: in the crucible of unrestricted deliberations, a jury will rise to the solemn challenge of judging and render its verdict with integrity and good faith. In light of the Corona jury members' obvious human frailties, Villaseñor nevertheless concludes in *Jury,* "In becoming close to all the jurors and their families, I regained a respect and admiration for my fellow man."

Villaseñor told *CA:* "I was born in the barrio of Carlsbad, California, and raised on a ranch four miles away in Oceanside. Both my parents are from Mexico, and I grew up in a house where there were no books. When I started school, I spoke more Spanish than English. I was a D student and every year of school made me feel more stupid and confused—many of these feelings had to do with being Chicano. In my junior year of high school, I told my parents I had to quit school or I would go crazy. Finally, they allowed me to quit. I was eighteen years old. I felt free, I felt wonderful, but I didn't know what to do with my freedom.

"I worked on the ranch, I worked in the fields—I was making money and it felt great. But then that fall when the other kids went back to school and the illegal workers went back to Mexico, I didn't know what to do with my life. An older cousin got me into college on a temporary basis if I finished high school. It was the University of San Diego and it was just getting started and was not yet accredited. On this campus I found out that books were not punishment, and if I couldn't remember dates I wasn't necessarily stupid. I flunked English of course (because I only had the reading ability of a fifth grader) and every other course except for philosophy and theology.

"The shock of my life came that year when a teacher told me I was very bright. But still I felt like I was going crazy. I was beginning to realize that I was ashamed of being Mexican. So I boxed. I fought with such a rage of confusion that I was undefeated.

"The following summer for the first time in my life I began to drink and discover my sexuality and feel wonderful and yet terrible from guilt. My parents sent me to Mexico where I fell in with some hip people. I was introduced to Mexican art, Mexican history, and I read my first book, Homer's *Iliad*, as well as *Tender Is the Night* by F. Scott Fitzgerald, and *The Little Prince*. I began having all night talks with an older woman. I felt good about myself. I wanted to stay in Mexico and never return to the United States where I felt ashamed of being Mexican. But my parents came for me and after weeks of arguments I agreed to go back home for awhile.

"I found myself feeling like a bombshell—ready to explode, prepared to kill anyone who made me feel ashamed. I was reading a copy of James Joyce's *Portrait of the Artist as a Young Man,* given to me by the woman in Mexico, when it hit me: I would write. Instead of killing or bashing people's brains out, I would change their minds. I would write good books that reach out and touch people and I would influence the world. I got a dictionary and a high school English grammar book and I built a desk and I began to read books eight months out of the year. I'd go to bookstores and buy ten books at a time, read them, dissect them, and then reassemble them. Then for four months of the year I'd support myself in construction.

"Then I began to write. I wrote for ten years, completing nine novels and sixty-five short stories and receiving more than 260 rejections before I sold my first book, *Macho!* Then, while I waited for *Macho!* to be published, I read about Juan Corona being arrested for twenty-five murders. Immediately I thought, Another Mexican being arrested. Hell, no man could kill twenty-five people. He must be innocent. So I talked to my publisher and he told me to look into it and write a short letter about what kind of book I thought I could write. They commissioned me to do the book. I spent the next three years investigating and writing about the Corona case."

BIOGRAPHICAL/CRITICAL SOURCES:

BOOKS

Villaseñor, Víctor, *Jury: The People vs. Juan Corona,* Little, Brown, 1977.

PERIODICALS

Christian Science Monitor, October 13, 1977.
English Journal, January, 1974.
Examiner and Chronicle (San Francisco), November 6, 1973.
New York Times Book Review, May 1, 1977.

*   *   *

VINE, Barbara
   See RENDELL, Ruth (Barbara)

*   *   *

VOIGT, David Quentin 1926-

PERSONAL: Born August 9, 1926, in Reading, PA; son of Henry William (a professor of English) and Ethel Helena (Os-

mond) Voigt; married Virginia Louise Erb (an elementary teacher), December 27, 1951; children: David Jonathan, Mark, William. *Education:* Albright College, B.S., 1948; Columbia University, M.A., 1949; Syracuse University, Ph.D., 1962. *Politics:* Democrat. *Religion:* Protestant. *Avocational interests:* Helping to promote youth baseball teams; golf.

ADDRESSES: Home—112 A Mifflin Blvd., Reading, PA 19607. *Office*—Department of Sociology, Albright College, Reading, PA 19603.

CAREER: Albright College, Reading, PA, associate professor, 1964-72, professor of sociology and anthropology, 1972—. Adjunct professor of anthropology and sociology at Franklin and Marshall College, Kutztown University, Lebanon Valley College, and University of Saskatchewan. Coach, Colt League and Junior League baseball teams, Reading, 1972-77. *Military service:* U.S. Army Air Forces, 1944-46; U.S. Air Force Reserve, beginning 1947; retired as major.

MEMBER: American Sociology Association (fellow), American Anthropological Association (fellow), Society for American Baseball Research (former president), North American Society for Sports History, Northeastern Anthropological Association, Eastern Sociological Association, Pennsylvania Sociology Society (secretary-treasurer, 1966-68; president, 1970-72).

AWARDS, HONORS: Lindback Award for Distinguished Teaching, 1974; Albright College Distinguished Alumnus Award, 1977; named to Baseball's Historical Records Committee by Commissioner Giamatti, 1989.

WRITINGS:

American Baseball (two volumes), foreword by Allan Nevins, University of Oklahoma Press, 1966, 2nd edition published in three volumes as *American Baseball: From Gentleman's Sport to the Commissioner System, American Baseball: From the Commissioners to Continental Expansion,* and *American Baseball: From Postwar Expansion to the Electronic Age,* Pennsylvania State University Press, 1983.
America's Leisure Revolution: Essays in the Sociology of Leisure and Sport, Albright College, 1970, new edition, 1974.
A Little League Journal, Bowling Green University Press, 1974.
America through Baseball, Nelson-Hall, 1976.
Baseball: An Illustrated History, Pennsylvania State University Press, 1987.

CONTRIBUTOR

Play, Games and Sports in Cultural Contexts, edited by Janet C. Harris and Roberta Park, Human Kinetics, 1983.
Total Baseball, edited by John Thorn and Pete Palmer, Warner Books, 1989.
The Baseball Encyclopedia, Macmillan, 1990.
Rituals in American Life, edited by Ray Browne, Bowling Green University Popular Press, 1980.
Fetishisms in American Life, edited by Browne, Bowling Green University Popular Press, 1982.
Forbidden Fruits, Bowling Green University Popular Press, 1984.
American Professional Sports, edited by Paul Staudohar, University of Illinois Press, 1989.
Baseball History, 1989, edited by Peter Levine, Greenville Press, 1989.

Contributor to *Dictionary of American Biography.* Contributor of articles to periodicals, including *New England Quarterly, Journal of Popular Culture, Journal of Leisure Research, National Pastime,* and historical journals.

WORK IN PROGRESS: "Various article assignments, a possible book on the 'big league' game of the 1890s, and continuing research towards a fourth volume of *American Baseball.*"

SIDELIGHTS: David Quentin Voigt told *CA:* "In 1989 I was gratified to read Professor Mel Adelman's review of my ongoing multi-volume study of the history of major league baseball. In his essay entitled 'Captain Voigt and American Baseball History,' published in the *Canadian Journal of the History of Sport,* Adelman reviewed the three volumes published to date and credited me for being a pioneer in making the serious study of baseball academically respectable.

"Likewise Professor Jim Harper's review of my recent *Baseball: An Illustrated History* not only liked the book but credited me as being the foremost narrator of the game's past.

"Such praise is music to this old dog's ears which may have heard enough discordant notes to keep his buttons from popping. But whether my books evoke praise or damnation from critics, I shall continue to monitor this American game. Indeed, a quarter of a century of writing on American baseball has not diminished my fascination with the ways the game mirrors our changing American culture. The reflections one gets of changing American life are limitless and include population shifts, urban transformations, changing ways of transportation and communication, and changes in American values, sexways, race relations and unionism to name but a few. Then there is the humor constantly evoked by the game—that alone is enough to sustain this writer in his continuing work."

W

WALDO, E. Hunter
See STURGEON, Theodore (Hamilton)

* * *

WALDO, Edward Hamilton
See STURGEON, Theodore (Hamilton)

* * *

WATT-EVANS, Lawrence
See EVANS, Lawrence Watt

* * *

WATTS, Alan (Wilson) 1915-1973

PERSONAL: Born January 6, 1915, in Chislehurst, England; came to the United States in 1938, naturalized in 1943; died November 16, 1973, in Mill Valley, Calif.; son of Laurence Wilson and Emily Mary (Buchan) Watts; married Eleanor Everett, April 2, 1938 (divorced, 1950); married Dorothy DeWitt, June 29, 1950 (divorced, 1963); married Mary Jane Yates King, December 4, 1963; children: (first marriage) Joan, Ann; (second marriage) Tia, Mark, Richard, Lila, Diane. *Education:* Seabury-Western Theological Seminary, S.T.M., 1948; University of Vermont, D.D., 1958. *Politics:* "Unclassifiable."

ADDRESSES: Home—Sausalito, Calif. *Agent*—Henry Volkening, 551 Fifth Ave., New York, N.Y. 10017.

CAREER: Ordained Anglican priest, 1944; Northwestern University, Evanston, Ill., religious counselor, 1944-50; University of the Pacific, American Academy of Asian Studies, San Francisco, Calif., professor of comparative philosophy, 1951-57, dean, 1953-56; writer and lecturer, 1956-73. Visiting scholar, San Jose State College (now San Jose State University), 1968; research consultant, Maryland Psychiatric Research Center, 1969. Guest lecturer at numerous universities, colleges, and medical schools in the United States, Canada, Europe, and Asia. Director of "Eastern Wisdom and Modern Life" series on National Educational Television, station KQED, San Francisco, 1959-61; author and presenter of radio lectures in syndication.

MEMBER: World Congress of Faiths (executive committee, 1937-39), American Oriental Society, Society for Comparative Philosophy (president).

AWARDS, HONORS: Bollingen Foundation grant, 1951-53 and 1962-64; Harvard University research fellow, 1962-64.

WRITINGS:

Outline of Zen Buddhism, Golden Vista Press (London), 1933, published as *Zen Buddhism: A New Outline and Introduction,* Buddhist Society (London), 1947, revised and enlarged edition published as *Zen,* James Ladd Delkin, 1948.
Seven Symbols of Life, Buddhist Society, 1936.
The Spirit of Zen: A Way of Life, Work and Art in the Far East, J. Murray, 1936, 3rd edition, 1958, reprinted, Grove, in press.
The Legacy of Asia and Western Man, J. Murray, 1937, University of Chicago Press, 1938.
The Psychology of Acceptance, Analytical Psychology Club of New York, 1939.
The Meaning of Happiness: The Quest for Freedom of the Spirit in Modern Psychology and the Wisdom of the East, Harper, 1940, 2nd edition, James Ladd Delkin, 1953, reprinted, Harper, 1979.
The Theologica Mystica of St. Dionysus, Holy Cross Press, 1944, revised edition, Society of Comparative Philosophy, 1971.
The Meaning of Priesthood, Advent Papers, 1946.
Behold the Spirit, Pantheon, 1947, new edition, 1971.
Easter: Its Story and Meaning, Schuman, 1950.
The Supreme Identity: An Essay on Oriental Metaphysic and the Christian Religion, Pantheon, 1950, new edition, 1972.
The Wisdom of Insecurity: A Message for the Age of Anxiety, Pantheon, 1951.
Myth and Ritual in Christianity, Vanguard, 1953, new edition, Thames & Hudson, 1959.
The Way of Liberation in Zen Buddhism (monograph), American Academy of Asian Studies, 1955, new edition, Society of Comparative Philosophy, 1973.
The Way of Zen (also see below), Pantheon, 1957, reprinted, Random House, 1974.
Nature, Man and Woman (also see below), Pantheon, 1958.
Beat Zen, Square Zen and Zen (pamphlet; first published in *Chicago Review,* summer, 1958), City Lights, 1959, reprinted, Vintage, 1970.
This Is It: And Other Essays on Zen and Spiritual Experience, Pantheon, 1960, reprinted, Rider, 1978.
(Contributor) C. C. Brinton, editor, *The Fate of Man,* Braziller, 1961.

Psychotherapy East and West (also see below), Pantheon, 1961.

The Joyous Cosmology, foreword by Timothy Leary and Richard Alpert, Pantheon, 1962.

The Two Hands of God: The Myths of Polarity, Braziller, 1963.

Beyond Theology: The Art of Godmanship, Pantheon, 1964.

(Editor) John W. Perry, *Lord of the Four Quarters: Myths of the Royal Father,* Braziller, 1965.

The Book: On the Taboo against Knowing Who You Are, Pantheon, 1966.

Nonsense, Stolen Paper Editions, 1967, new edition, Dutton, 1977.

Does It Matter?: Essays on Man's Relation to Materiality, Pantheon, 1970.

Erotic Spirituality: Vision of Konarak, with photographs by Eliot Elisofon, Macmillan, 1971.

In My Own Way: An Autobiography, 1915-1945, Pantheon, 1972.

The Art of Contemplation, Pantheon, 1972.

Cloud Hidden, Whereabouts Unknown: A Mountain Journal, Pantheon, 1973.

(Editor with R. F. Hull) Eugene Herrigel, *Method of Zen,* Random House, 1974.

The Essence of Alan Watts, Celestial Arts, Book I: *God,* 1974, Book II: *Meditation,* 1974, Book III: *Nothingness,* 1974, Book IV: *Death,* 1975, Book V: *The Nature of Man,* 1975, Book VI: *Time,* 1975, Book VII: *Philosophical Fantasies,* 1975, Book VIII: *Ego,* 1975, Book IX: *The Cosmic Drama,* 1975, published in one volume as *The Essential Alan Watts,* 1977.

(With Al Chung-liang Huang) *Tao: The Watercourse Way,* Pantheon, 1975.

Three (contains *The Way of Zen, Nature, Man and Woman,* and *Psychotherapy East and West*), Pantheon, 1977.

Om, Creative Meditations, Celestial Arts, 1980.

Play To Live, And Books, 1982.

The Way of Liberation: Essays and Lectures on the Transformation of the Self, Weatherhill, 1983.

Out of the Trap, And Books, 1985.

(Contributor) *Zen Effects,* Houghton, 1986.

The Early Writings of Alan Watts, Celestial Arts, 1987.

Diamond Web, And Books, 1987.

(With David L. Miller) *Myths, Dreams and Religion,* Spring Publications, 1988.

SOUND RECORDINGS

(With Stanislav Grof and Julian Silverman) *The Science of Madness,* Big Sur Recordings, 1968.

(With others) *The Poetry of Madness,* Big Sur Recordings, 1968.

(With Carl Rogers) *USA 2000,* Big Sur Recordings, 1968.

(With Lynn Townsend White) *Ecological Crisis,* Big Sur Recordings, 1971.

Divine Madness, Superscope Educational Products, 1972.

(Contributor) *The Occult Explosion,* United Artists, 1973.

OTHER

Contributor to *New Republic, New York Times, Playboy, Earth,* and other periodicals. Editor of *The Middle Way* (London), 1934-38. Editor of series "Wisdom of the East," published by Dutton and J. Murray, 1938-41, and "Patterns of Myth," published by Braziller.

SIDELIGHTS: Once called "the brain and Buddha of American Zen," Alan Watts was a leading figure in the popularization of Eastern religious philosophy in the United States. Watts was an ordained Anglican priest, but his eclectic spiritual background included Mahayana Buddhism (Zen), Taoism, and other Eastern practices. His writings on these subjects found an audience among young, disaffected Americans in the 1950s and 1960s, including the writers Jack Kerouac, Gary Snyder, and Allen Ginsberg. *Dictionary of Literary Biography* contributor Dan McLeod contended that Watts "became a near cult figure" in the counterculture, "and those who were attracted by Beat Generation values were likely to be interested in what he had to say about religion." In the *Los Angeles Times Book Review,* Jonathan Kirsch called Watts "an authentic guru, a Zen master with an English accent, a lucid interpreter of Eastern philosophy" whose works "have survived not only the passing of the '60s but his own passing as well."

A native of Kent, England, Watts became fascinated by Eastern ideas in his early adolescence. His first encounter came at the age of twelve through the popular Sax Rohmer "Fu Manchu" novels. While still in his teens, Watts broadened his knowledge of the East considerably through frequent visits to the Buddhist Lodge in London. He joined the World Congress of Faiths and met several spiritual leaders, including Krishnamurti and D. T. Suzuki, who would subsequently inspire him in his own work. Watts's family could not afford to send him to college, even though his secondary school grades were excellent. Instead, he took a job in his father's business and wrote in his spare time. He was only twenty-one when his first full-length book, *The Spirit of Zen,* was published in Great Britain.

"*The Spirit of Zen* is remarkable," wrote McLeod, "not simply because its author was so young, but because it was the first knowledgeable book written on this subject by a Westerner. . . . The clarity of its style and the fact that it requires of its readers no prior knowledge of Buddhism gives it a special distinction. With the writing of this book, Watts had discovered his life's mission: to interpret Asian philosophy for Westerners." McLeod continued: "No one else, before or after Watts, has proven to be so effective as a popularizer of Asian thought or a synthesizer of East-West philosophy."

Watts married in 1938 and moved to America the following year. There, in New York City, he began a career as a "religious entertainer" (his own term), giving lectures and seminars in the private homes of his wife's wealthy friends. His 1940 work, *The Meaning of Happiness,* was based on the information in his seminars. McLeod contended that *The Meaning of Happiness* revealed the themes that Watts addressed throughout his writings, namely, "the necessity of resolving such human oppositions as life-and-death, male-and-female, right-and-wrong, self-and-nonself; and the importance of identifying oneself with the processes of nature if one is to avoid the pain that trails in the wake of too much preoccupation with self." McLeod concluded: "Even though such concerns were a decade or so away from receiving widespread attention, the book enjoyed moderate success with both critics and the reading public."

In 1941 Watts entered the Seabury-Western Theological Seminary, where he studied for the Anglican priesthood. He was ordained in 1944, and for six years thereafter he served as a chaplain at Northwestern University. Watts gradually became disenchanted with certain aspects of Christianity, however; he questioned the "linearity" of Christian thought, its "one-way-street" version of history, its dogmatic chain of commands, and its deceptive expectations of future rewards. Watts returned to Eastern-based thoughts and practices and published *The Wisdom of Insecurity: A Message for the Age of Anxiety.* As its title suggests, *The Wisdom of Insecurity* confronts the specific problems of life in the early 1950s—especially the vain pursuit of material wealth—and urges readers to eliminate self-centered notions and replace them with a sense of the self as part of a much greater All. McLeod noted that, with surprisingly few references to Taoism or Buddhism, Watts managed to write "a splendidly compelling Buddhist sermon" that almost became a motto for the nascent Beat generation.

Watts's interest in Zen led him to become a founding faculty member of the American Academy of Asian Studies in San Francisco in 1951. His tenure lasted until the school folded in 1957, and it was during these years that he became "the Beat generation's local guru," to quote McLeod. Watts gave radio broadcasts, classes at the Academy, and seminars at the Buddhist church in Berkeley; he was an engaging showman with a background in psychotherapy as well as religion, and he attracted enthusiastic attention from the younger generation. Still, Watts never allied himself wholeheartedly with the Beats. He was critical of so-called "Beat Zen," which, he said, used a dissatisfaction with society as an excuse to exploit others.

One of Watts's most important works, *The Way of Zen,* was published while he lived in San Francisco. McLeod stated that the work established Watts as "the most influential spokesman for Zen in the West." *The Way of Zen* sold well and also received favorable reviews from critics—even those who had little respect for Watts's academic credentials. McLeod observed that the book "remains the best as well as the most popular introduction to Zen, the most portable expression of Buddhist life and thought. [It] provides a lucid and coherent introduction to the general rise of Mahayana Buddhism, the nature philosophy of Taoism (which probably comes closest to Watts's personal religious preference), the chance workings of the *I Ching,* and the art and literature inspired by these developments of the Far Eastern spiritual consciousness."

From 1960 until his death in 1973, Watts wrote a number of books and travelled extensively, giving lectures in America, Europe, Canada, and the Far East. Never an ascetic, he experimented with LSD and other drugs and then authored *The Joyous Cosmology,* a work on the spiritual implications of drug use. Many of Watts's works remain in print, and new collections have appeared since he died. "While Asian scholars may still carp about Watts's scholarly credentials and practicing Buddhists his lack of commitment and rigor," McLeod commented, "few can doubt the sincerity of his spiritual quest and the influence of his lectures and writing on the generation of the 1950s and 1960s." Kirsch concluded that all of Watts's teachings provide "ecumenical work endorsing the spiritual value in all expressions of faith."

BIOGRAPHICAL/CRITICAL SOURCES:

BOOKS

Clark, David K., *The Pantheism of Alan Watts,* Inter-Varsity Press, 1978.
The "Deep-In" View: A Conversation with Alan Watts, Dust Magazine Books, 1965.
Dictionary of Literary Biography, Volume 16: *The Beats: Literary Bohemians in Postwar America,* Gale, 1983.
Ellwood, Robert S., Jr., *Alternative Altars: Unconventional and Eastern Spirituality in America,* University of Chicago Press, 1979.
Roszak, Theodore, *The Making of the Counter Culture,* Doubleday, 1969.
Stuart, David, *Alan Watts,* Chilton, 1976.
Watts, Alan, *In My Own Way: An Autobiography, 1915-1945,* Pantheon, 1972.

PERIODICALS

America, August 7, 1976.
Life, April 21, 1961.
Los Angeles Times Book Review, June 19, 1983.
Nation, November 1, 1958.
New Republic, May 1, 1965.
New York Times, December 16, 1972.
New York Times Book Review, November 12, 1972, March 7, 1976.
Redbook, May, 1966.
Sewanee Review, summer, 1953.

OBITUARIES:

PERIODICALS

Newsweek, November 26, 1973.
New York Times, November 17, 1973.
Publishers Weekly, December 10, 1973.
Time, November 26, 1973.*

—*Sketch by Anne Janette Johnson*

* * *

WEBB, Sharon 1936-

PERSONAL: Born February 29, 1936, in Tampa, FL; daughter of William Wesley (a meteorologist) and Eunice (a teacher; maiden name, Tillman) Talbott; married W. Bryan Webb (a tax consultant and writer), February 6, 1956; children: Wendy Webb Nesheim, Jerri Webb Thompson, Tracey Webb Kolbinger. *Education:* Attended Florida Southern College, 1953-56; Miami-Dade Community College, A.D.N., 1972. *Politics:* Democrat. *Religion:* Protestant.

ADDRESSES: Home and office—Route 2, Box 2600, Blairsville, GA 30512. *Agent*—Merrilee Heifetz, Writers House, Inc., 21 West 26th St., New York, NY 10010.

CAREER: Part-time free-lance writer, 1956-72; South Miami Hospital, Miami, FL, cardiac care nurse, 1972-73; Union General Hospital, Blairsville, GA, charge nurse, 1974-81; Towns County Hospital, Hiawassee, GA, registered nurse, 1975-79; Murphy Medical Center, Murphy, NC, registered nurse, 1979-80; writer, 1981—.

MEMBER: Authors Guild, Science Fiction Writers of America (director of South/Central region; member of national board of directors, 1983-86), Horror Writers of America.

WRITINGS:

R.N. (non-fiction), Zebra Books, 1981.
Earthchild (science fiction; first volume of "Earthsong Triad"), Atheneum, 1982.
Earth Song (science fiction; second volume of "Earthsong Triad"), Atheneum, 1983.
Ram Song (science fiction; third volume of "Earthsong Triad"), Atheneum, 1984.
Adventures of Terra Tarkington (science fiction stories), Bantam, 1985.
Pestis 18 (medical/suspense novel), Tor/St. Martin's, 1987.
The Halflife (psychological/suspense novel), Tor/St. Martin's, 1989.

Work represented in anthologies, including *Other Worlds,* edited by Roy Torgeson, *Space Mail 1* and *2,* edited by Isaac Asimov and M. H. Greenberg, *Chrysalis 8,* edited by Torgeson, *Isaac Asimov's Near Futures and Far,* edited by G. Scithers and Asimov, and *1981 Annual World's Best Science Fiction,* edited by Donald Wollheim. Contributor of stories to magazines, including *Isaac Asimov's Science Fiction, Amazing,* and *Parsec.*

WORK IN PROGRESS: "*The Devil's Filament,* a novel set in the Blue Ridge mountains of Georgia, about a child's imaginary playmates, chaos theory, and a kidnapping."

SIDELIGHTS: In Sharon Webb's science fiction novel *Earthchild,* young people under the age of sixteen are given a special drug that makes them immortal. Adults are excluded from the experiment, and a segment of the population goes berserk with jealousy; they riot and attempt to kill the children. The government is eventually forced to protect the immortals by placing them in custody camps. The author complicates her fantasy tale by introducing the premise that this immortality kills human creativity. *Earth Song* is the sequel to *Earthchild,* taking place a century later. By this time immortality is considered the natural state—yet creativity continues to die in those who become immortal. Thus, before their sixteenth birthdays, gifted earth children must decide whether to pursue their artistic dreams during limited life spans or live forever. The author focuses particularly on the life of one fifteen-year-old boy, David Defour, following him to his hard-won decision to fulfill his musical calling.

Creativity is also a factor in *The Halflife,* a medical thriller involving twenty-two year old Tim Monahan, who is invited to participate in a "scientific" study concerning the human mind. *The Halflife's* suspenseful plot eventually connects ongoing murders in Atlanta, Georgia, with Tim's memories of a boy's death at summer camp. The book also brings in medically-induced, artificial personality and psychic research, along with the CIA. *Atlanta Journal/Constitution* contributor Brad Linaweaver thinks that *The Halflife* "is finally a book about fear . . . primarily arising from the idea that one might be the unconscious tool of someone else's designs. The mind is the final battlefield." Webb draws on her nursing background to create "a compelling, chilling tale from the darkest bowels of the subconscious, where madness and mysticism may be the only salvation from a Top Secret experiment gone terribly wrong," writes Elizabeth Shaw in the *Flint Journal.* Shaw continues, "It all adds up to a topnotch medical/spy thriller that is sure to keep readers turning pages to the final, chilling scene."

BIOGRAPHICAL/CRITICAL SOURCES:

PERIODICALS

Atlanta Journal/Constitution, September 17, 1989.
Flint Journal, November 5, 1989.

*   *   *

WELCH, Claude E(merson), Jr. 1939-

PERSONAL: Born June 12, 1939, in Boston, MA; son of Claude Emerson (a surgeon) and Phyllis (Paton) Welch; married Nancy Edwards, June 19, 1961 (died May 9, 1979); married Jeannette Ludwig, June 13, 1981; children: (first marriage) Elisabeth, Sarah Jane, Martha, Christopher. *Education:* Harvard University, B.A., 1961; St. Antony's College, Oxford, D. Phil., 1964. *Politics:* Democratic. *Religion:* Protestant.

ADDRESSES: Home—120 Burroughs Dr., Buffalo, NY 14226. *Office*—417 Park Hall, State University of New York, Buffalo, NY 14260.

CAREER: State University of New York at Buffalo, assistant professor, 1964-68, associate professor, 1968-72, professor of po-

litical science, 1972-89, Distinguished Service Professor, 1989—, chairman of department, 1980-83, dean of Division of Undergraduate Studies, 1967-70, associate vice-president for academic affairs, 1976-80.

MEMBER: African Studies Association (fellow), Inter-University Seminar on Armed Forces and Society, Phi Beta Kappa.

WRITINGS:

Dream of Unity, Cornell University Press, 1966.
(Editor) *Political Modernization,* Duxbury, 1967, revised edition, 1971.
(Editor) *Soldier and State in Africa,* Northwestern University, 1970.
(Editor with Mavis Bunker Taintor) *Revolution and Political Change,* Duxbury, 1972.
(With Arthur Smith) *Military Role and Rule,* Duxbury, 1974.
(Editor) *Civilian Control of the Military,* State University of New York Press, 1976.
(Editor with Alan Smith) *Peasants in Africa,* Crossroads Press, 1978.
Anatomy of Rebellion, State University of New York Press, 1980.
No Farewell to Arms?, Westview, 1987.
(Editor with Virginia Leary) *Asian Perspectives on Human Rights,* Westview, 1990.

Editor, *Armed Forces and Society.*

WORK IN PROGRESS: Editing *International Military and Defense Encyclopedia.*

SIDELIGHTS: Claude E. Welch, Jr., told *CA:* "For over 20 years, my publications focused on the political roles of armed forces, including the causes and consequences of coups d'etat and problems of redemocratization. My interest in civil-military relations continues through my editorship of the quarterly journal *Armed Forces and Society* and the forthcoming *International Military and Defense Encyclopedia.* Increasingly, however, I am writing about human rights—an area in which the United States has contributed much, but which requires continued attention by concerned citizens. Human rights are universal and indivisible; unless writers are active in their defense, freedoms everywhere can be eroded."

*   *   *

WELLS, George A(lbert) 1926-

PERSONAL: Born May 22, 1926, in London, England; son of George John Henry (a textile manufacturers agent) and Lilian (Mand) Wells; married Elisabeth Delhey (a teacher), 1969. *Education:* University of London, B.A., 1947, M.A., 1950, Ph.D., 1954, B.Sc., 1963. *Politics:* "No affiliation." *Religion:* None.

ADDRESSES: Home—St. Albans, England. *Office*—Department of German, Birkbeck College, University of London, Malet St., London WC1, England.

CAREER: University of London, London, England, University College, lecturer, 1949-64, reader in German, 1964-68, Birkbeck College, professor of German and head of department, 1968-88, emeritus professor, 1988—.

MEMBER: Rationalist Press Association (honorary associate), Goethe Society (member of council).

WRITINGS:

Herder and After: A Study in the Development of Sociology, Mouton, 1959.

(With Brian A. Rowley) *Fundamentals of German Grammar*, E. Arnold, 1963.

The Plays of Grillparzer, Pergamon, 1969.

(Editor) Franz Grillparzer, *Die Juedin von Toledo* (title means "The Jewess of Toledo"), Pergamon, 1969.

The Jesus of the Early Christians, Prometheus Books, 1971.

Did Jesus Exist?, Prometheus Books, 1975, 2nd revised and expanded edition, Pemberton, 1986.

(Editor with D. R. Oppenheimer) F. R. H. Englefield, *Language: Its Origin and Its Relation to Thought*, Scribner, 1975.

Goethe and the Development of Science, 1750-1900, Sitjhoff, 1978.

The Historical Evidence for Jesus, Prometheus Books, 1982.

(Editor with Oppenheimer) Englefield, *The Mind at Work and Play*, Prometheus Books, 1985.

The Origin of Language: Aspects of the Discussion from Condillac to Wundt, Open Court, 1987.

(Editor and contributor) *J. M. Robertson (1856-1933): Liberal Rationalist and Scholar—An Assessment by Several Hands*, Pemberton, 1987.

Religious Postures: Essays on Modern Christian Apologists and Religious Problems, Open Court, 1988.

A Resurrection Debate, Rationalist, 1988.

Who Was Jesus? A Critique of the New Testament Record, Open Court, 1989.

(Editor with Oppenheimer) Englefield, *Critique of Pure Verbiage*, Open Court, 1990.

Contributor to language, philology, and philosophy journals, and to *New Humanist*.

WORK IN PROGRESS: Research on German literature.

SIDELIGHTS: In his book *The Historical Evidence for Jesus*, George A. Wells searches the Christian scriptures in an attempt to find the historical Jesus. As J. Duncan M. Derrett observes in the *Times Literary Supplement*, Wells discovers that "critical study of the twenty-seven documents of the New Testament cannot find anything but the vaguest ideas concerning Jesus until about AD 90." Based on his examination, Wells concludes that the events of historical Jesus's life are impossible to reconstruct. Though some theologians have already proposed similar conclusions, Derrett admits that Wells's "exposition is his own, he offers shrewd insights and for what he suggests to an open mind he alone is responsible."

Wells told *CA:* "Of my three books on Jesus, I would claim that [*Did Jesus Exist?*] and [*The Historical Evidence for Jesus*] are the only ones in the field which, while written by a non-theologian, fully assimilate present theological scholarship. My motive in writing them was to inform the public of the very sceptical views on early Christianity advanced by theologians in books and articles seldom consulted except by other theologians; and also to press the implications of these views on the theologians themselves."

Wells added: "[*The Plays of Grillparzer*] and many of my articles on literature are, in part, attempts to combat present-day make-believe, by which I mean writing which purports to be scholarly and informative, but which does not convey clear ideas or consist of coherent argument.

"Concerning [*Goethe and the Development of Science, 1750-1900*], my interest in the natural sciences (particularly geology) began when I was drafted to the coal mines in 1944. Study of the sciences influenced my outlook by convincing me that knowledge can only be reached from slavish dependence on fact and formulation of hypotheses which can be tested by an appeal to fact. In the natural sciences this is not disputed. I have tried to argue the same attitude in theology and in literature—spheres where it is not so universally accepted."

BIOGRAPHICAL/CRITICAL SOURCES:

PERIODICALS

Times (London), December 31, 1987.
Times Literary Supplement, February 18, 1983.

* * *

WELTY, Eudora 1909-

PERSONAL: Born April 13, 1909, in Jackson, MS; daughter of Christian Webb (an insurance company president) and Chestina (Andrews) Welty. *Education:* Attended Mississippi State College for Women (now Mississippi University for Women), 1926-27; University of Wisconsin, B.A., 1929; attended Columbia University Graduate School of Business, 1930-31.

ADDRESSES: *Home*—1119 Pinehurst St., Jackson, MS 39202.

CAREER: Worked for newspapers and a radio station in Mississippi during early depression years, and as a publicity agent for the state office of the Works Progress Administration (WPA). Was briefly a member of the *New York Times Book Review* staff, in New York City. Lecturer and writer in residence at various colleges.

MEMBER: American Academy and Institute of Arts and Letters, National Council on the Arts.

AWARDS, HONORS: Guggenheim fellowship, 1942; O. Henry Award, 1942, 1943, 1968; National Institute of Arts and Letters, 1944, grant in literature, 1972, Gold Medal for fiction writing; William Dean Howells Medal from American Academy of Arts and Letters, 1955, for *The Ponder Heart;* Edward McDowell Medal, 1970; National Book Award nomination for fiction, 1971, for *Losing Battles;* Christopher Book Award, 1972, for *One Time, One Place: Mississippi in the Depression; A Snapshot;* Pulitzer Prize in fiction, 1973, for *The Optimist's Daughter;* National Medal for Literature, 1980; *The Collected Stories of Eudora Welty* was named an American Library Association notable book for 1980; Presidential Medal of Freedom, 1980; American Book Award, 1981, for *The Collected Stories of Eudora Welty*, 1984, for *One Writer's Beginnings;* Common Wealth Award for Distinguished Service in Literature from Modern Language Association of America, 1984; National Book Critics Circle Award and *Los Angeles Times* Book Prize nominations, both 1984, for *One Writer's Beginnings;* National Medal of Arts, 1987.

WRITINGS:

A Curtain of Green (short stories; also see below), with a preface by Katherine Anne Porter, Doubleday, 1941, published as *A Curtain of Green, and Other Stories*, Harcourt, 1964.

The Robber Bridegroom (novella), Doubleday, 1942.

The Wide Net, and Other Stories (also see below), Harcourt, 1943.

Delta Wedding (novel), Harcourt, 1946.

Music from Spain, Levee Press, 1948.

Short Stories (address delivered at University of Washington), Harcourt, 1949.

The Golden Apples (connected stories; also see below), Harcourt, 1949.

Selected Stories (contains all of the short stories in *A Curtain of Green*, and *The Wide Net, and Other Stories*) introduction by Porter, Modern Library, 1953.

The Ponder Heart (novel), Harcourt, 1954.

The Bride of the Innisfallen, and Other Stories, Harcourt, 1955.

Place in Fiction (lectures for Conference on American Studies in Cambridge, England), House of Books, 1957.

Three Papers on Fiction (addresses), Smith College, 1962.

The Shoe Bird (juvenile), Harcourt, 1964.

Thirteen Stories, edited and introduction by Ruth M. Vande Kieft, Harcourt, 1965.

A Sweet Devouring (nonfiction), Albondocani Press, 1969.

Losing Battles (novel), Random House, 1970.

A Flock of Guinea Hens Seen from a Car (poem), Albondocani Press, 1970.

One Time, One Place: Mississippi in the Depression; A Snapshot Album, illustrated with photographs by Welty, Random House, 1971.

The Optimist's Daughter (novel), Random House, 1972.

The Eye of the Story (selected essays and reviews), Random House, 1978.

The Collected Stories of Eudora Welty, Harcourt, 1980.

One Writer's Beginnings (lectures), Harvard University Press, 1984.

Morgana: Two Stories from 'The Golden Apples,' University Press of Mississippi, 1988.

Photographs, University Press of Mississippi, 1989.

Contributor to *Southern Review, Atlantic, Harper's Bazaar, New Yorker, New York Times Book Review,* and other periodicals.

MEDIA ADAPTATIONS: The Ponder House was adapted for the stage and first produced on Broadway in 1956, and was also adapted as an *opera bouffe* with musical score by Alice Parker and produced in Jackson, MS in 1982; *The Robber Bridegroom* was adapted for the stage as a musical and first produced on Broadway in 1978; "The Hitch-hikers" was adapted for television in 1986.

SIDELIGHTS: With the publication of *The Eye of the Story* and *The Collected Stories of Eudora Welty,* Eudora Welty achieved the recognition she has long deserved as an important contemporary American fiction writer. Her position was confirmed in 1984 when her autobiographical *One Writer's Beginnings* made the best-seller lists with sales exceeding 100,000 copies. During the early decades of her career, she was respected by fellow writers but often dismissed by critics as a regionalist, a miniaturist, or an oversensitive "feminine" writer. The late 1970s and 1980s, however, saw a critical reevaluation of her work demonstrating, as Michael Kreyling declares in *Eudora Welty's Achievement of Order,* "that it is not primarily regional writing, or even excellent regional writing, but is the vision of a certain artist who must be considered with her peers—[Virginia] Woolf, [Elizabeth] Bowen, and [E. M.] Forster."

Marked by a subtle, lyrical narrative state, Welty's work typically explores the intricacies of the interior life and the small heroisms of ordinary people. In an article appearing in *Eudora Welty: Critical Essays,* Chester E. Eisinger describes the writer's unique combination of realistic and modernist traditions: "Her work reflects the careful disorder of Chekhovian fiction and the accurate yet spontaneous rendering of detail that belonged to [Anton Checkhov's] slice of life technique. It reflects the modernism, . . . that characterized Woolf's fiction: The door she opened for Welty, she herself had passed through with [James] Joyce, [Franz] Kafka, [Marcel] Proust, [Robert] Musil, and the other twentieth-century makers of experimental, avant-garde fiction." Eisinger has in mind Woolf's rejection of the clear plot structure of the traditional novel, her internalization of experience, her careful rendering of the minutiae of ordinary life, her poetic use of language, and her fragmented point-of-

view. Woolf opened another door for Welty as well, demonstrating in *To the Lighthouse* how to center a serious novel in the experiences of women.

Although Welty has always distanced herself from the women's movement, feminist critical interest in the works of women writers also stimulated renewed attention to her fiction in the 1970s and 1980s. In an article collected in *Eudora Welty: Critical Essays,* Margaret Jones Bolsterli expresses some of the major assumptions of the feminist approach when she argues that "Understanding women's views of themselves and of men is necessary if we are ever going to get at the truth, and the vision Eudora Welty presents of the women's worlds in [her] novels illuminates not only half of the great world which we do not often see, but also touches gently sometimes on the terrible state of affairs on this darkling plain when men and women do not see each other clearly at all." The reading public and the scholarly establishment began to realize that a major body of American fiction had been produced by Southern women writers, as Anne Goodwyn Jones has documented in *Tomorrow Is Another Day: The Woman Writer in the South, 1859-1936.* Moreover, critics perceived that Welty, the most prolific and versatile of these writers, was producing works of an astonishing range: from folktale to historical romance, grotesque farce to novel of manners; from dramatizations of lives contained by sharecropping cabins of the Depression to portraits of relationships in Delta plantations and upper-middle-class suburbs. And all these modes and subject matters are complemented by the distinguished essays, reviews, and reminiscences collected in *The Eye of the Story* and *One Writer's Beginnings.*

The oldest of her family's three children and the only girl, Welty grew up in Jackson, Mississippi. That neither of her parents came from the Deep South may have given her some detachment from her culture and helped her become an astute observer of its manners. Her father, Christian Welty, had been raised on a farm in Ohio and had become a country school teacher in West Virginia. Marrying a fellow teacher, Chestina Andrews, he had moved to Jackson to improve his fortunes by entering business. From bookkeeper in an insurance company, he eventually advanced to president.

Chestina Andrews, the daughter of transplanted Virginians, had grown up on a mountain in West Virginia. At fifteen, she had taken her critically ill father down an icy river on a raft to the railroad and then to a hospital in Baltimore where he died on the operating table of a ruptured appendix. In later years she took her young daughter on memorable summer visits "up home"; Welty's formidable grandmother and five bachelor uncles make a poignant fictional appearance in their mountaintop world as Laurel Hand's grandmother and uncles in *The Optimist's Daughter.*

Welty's reminiscences describe a happy childhood in a close-knit, bookish family. One of her earliest memories was the sound of her parents' voices reading favorite books to one another in the evenings. The Welty children were provided with fairy tales and mythology, dictionaries and encyclopedias, and library cards that allowed young Eudora to practice what she later called, in an essay employing the phrase as a title, "a sweet devouring" of the riches in the Jackson public library. Her delight in the gossip and storytelling that were such a vital part of traditional small-town Southern life was as great as her passion for books. Welty has often said that when her mother's friends would come to visit, she would demand, "Now start talking!" Her experiences of listening established a lifelong pleasure in folktale, mythology, tall tales, humorous anecdote, and comic idiom, which are special marks of her fiction.

Welty's education in the Jackson schools was followed by two years at Mississippi State College for Women between 1925 and 1927, and then by two more years at the University of Wisconsin and a B.A. in 1929. Her father, who believed that she could never earn a living by writing stories, encouraged her to study advertising at the Columbia University Graduate School of Business in New York during 1930-1931. The years in Wisconsin and New York broadened Welty's horizons, and the time she spent in New York City was especially meaningful. The Harlem Renaissance was at its height, and Welty and her friends went to dances in Harlem clubs and to musical and theatrical performances all over the city. "Everybody that was wonderful was then at their peak," the writer told Jan Norby Gretlund in an interview collected in *Conversations with Eudora Welty.* "For somebody who had never, in a sustained manner, been to the theater or to the Metropolitan Museum, where I went every Sunday, it was just a cornucopia."

Her father's sudden death in 1931 brought an end to Welty's northern sojourn. She went home to help her mother and brothers, and she has essentially remained in Jackson ever since. To support herself, Welty first tried various small jobs with local newspapers and with radio station WJDX, which her father had started in the tower of his insurance building. Then, in 1933, she was offered a position as a publicity agent for the Works Progress Administration (WPA). "I did reporting, interviewing," she explained to Jean Todd Freeman in an interview collected in *Conversations with Eudora Welty.* "It took me all over Mississippi, which is the most important thing to me, because I'd never seen it. . . . [The experience] was the real germ of my wanting to become a real writer, a true writer."

In her travels around Mississippi, Welty was learning the art of seeing and capturing significant moments in the lives of ordinary people, an art she first practiced with a camera. She took hundreds of photographs of Mississippians of all social classes, capturing them at work and at leisure with their friends and families. Although her camera was not much better than a Brownie, the results were so effective that she took them to New York and tried to interest a publisher. The majority of the pictures are of blacks, providing a rare documentation that celebrates lives of quiet dignity and joy in the midst of hardship. But publishers felt Welty's photographs would not be able to compete with *Roll, Jordon, Roll,* a sentimental "Old South" collection by Dorothy Peterkin and Doris Ullman, and Welty could only arrange a one-woman show in 1936 in a small gallery on Madison Avenue. In 1971, however, the best of these pictures were published as *One Time, One Place: Mississippi in the Depression; A Snapshot Album.*

Welty's WPA work of the mid-1930s provided her with far more than visual training. Seeing at first hand the Depression-struck lives of rural and small-town people in a state that had always been the poorest in the nation, she was stimulated to capture their struggles and triumphs in stories, beginning with "Death of a Traveling Salesman," which was published in the literary magazine *Manuscript* in 1936. Other stories followed during the next five years, including some of her most famous—"Why I Live at the P.O.," "Powerhouse," "A Worn Path," "Petrified Man," "Lily Daw and the Three Ladies." Six stories were accepted by *Southern Review* between 1937 and 1939 and earned her the friendship and admiration of writers Albert Erskine, Robert Penn Warren, Katherine Anne Porter, and Ford Madox Ford. In a 1944 *Kenyon Review* essay Warren commented on the

contrast between "the sad, or violent, or warped" subjects of the stories and a tone that is "exhilarating, even gay, as though the author were innocently delighted . . . with the variety of things that stories could be and still be stories." These early works established Welty's characteristic comic genius with dialogue and with recording the incongruous developments of everyday life. Here she also developed a way of treating poverty, loss, and pain with a lightness that amounts to exquisite respect and discretion. In 1941 a collection of these stories was published as *A Curtain of Green* with a preface by Katherine Anne Porter. As Ruth Vande Kieft explains in *Eudora Welty,* the stories "are largely concerned with the mysteries of the inner life," "the enigma of man's being—his relation to the universe; what is secret, concealed, inviolable in any human being, resulting in distance or separation between human beings; the puzzles and difficulties we have about our own feelings, our meaning and our identity."

Welty's first sustained experiment with folk materials appeared in 1942 as *The Robber Bridegroom,* a bold fusing of Mississippi history, tall tale, and fairytales of mysterious seducers drawn from British and Germanic sources as well as from the Greek story of Cupid and Psyche. Here, as Carol Manning explains in *With Ears Opening Like Morning Glories: Eudora Welty and the Love of Storytelling,* the innocent tone of the narrative counteracts the dire stuff of robberies, murders, and the depredations of a cruel stepmother. To many early reviewers the result seemed pure magic. Alfred Kazin claimed in a review for the *New York Herald Tribune Books* that Welty had captured "the lost fabulous innocence of our departed frontier, the easy carelessness, the fond bragging and colossal buckskin strut." In the *New York Times Book Review,* Marianne Hauser called it "a modern fairy tale, where irony and humor, outright nonsense, deep wisdom and surrealistic extravaganzas become a poetic unity through the power of a pure, exquisite style." Although some other commentators found it lacking in substance, Kreyling has defended *The Robber Bridegroom* as a valuable addition to the pastoral tradition in American literature: "Welty seems to be saying that the dream of a pastoral paradise on earth is always one step ahead of the dreamers; it is, sadly, only possible in a dream world removed from contact with human flesh and imperfections. But still worth dreaming."

Welty continued to experiment with such materials in her next collection, *The Wide Net, and Other Stories.* Here she explored the interrelationships of everyday Mississippi life with the timeless themes and patterns of myth, creating for her apparently ordinary characters a universality that links them with all times and cultures. The title story, for instance, places a domestic quarrel within the context of fertility tales; the work climaxes with a descent into a watery underworld where the hero encounters "the King of the Snakes" and proves worthy to return to his pregnant wife. In an essay appearing in *Eudora Welty: Critical Essays,* Garvin Davenport sees each of the stories in *The Wide Net* as presenting "at least one character who confronts or encounters a situation which is in some way dark, mysterious or dreamlike. Each such encounter contributes to an awakening or renewal—sometimes only temporarily—of that character's potential for emotional enrichment and experiential meaning. If the nature of the encounter often suggests a kind of regression to a more primitive or fundamental level of consciousness, the overall structures of the stories make clear that it is regression as a phase in problem-solving."

Welty's first novel, *Delta Wedding,* marks a significant change in her focus. Fertility myth still runs as an undercurrent through the daily affairs described in the book, but Welty has shifted from the dreamlike atmosphere of *The Wide Net* to the ordinary milieu of family life in the Mississippi Delta. Many of the circumstances of the Fairchild family in *Delta Wedding* recall those of the Ramsay family in Woolf's *To the Lighthouse.* The center of the Fairchild family is a mother of eight who continually ministers to her husband, her children, and a wider circle of relatives and friends. The novel is organized around domestic imagery of cooking and eating, wedding preparations, and diplomatic maneuvers to avert conflicts and soothe hurt feelings so that the wedding, on which the work centers, can occur. Both Woolf's and Welty's novels admiringly explore the experience and values of women characters and celebrate the community, harmony, and renewal created by mothers for their families.

The narrative technique is similar to Woolf's in its use of multiple perspectives. In Welty's case the observers are all female, from nine-year-old Laura McRaven, a visiting cousin, to the mother, Ellen Fairchild, and her many daughters. In an interview collected in *Conversations with Eudora Welty,* the writer told Jo Brans that the world of *Delta Wedding* is a matriarchy but that it is not at all hostile to men. Men are, instead, the objects of loving attention and perform the occasional acts of heroism that are necessary to protect the charmed and fertile pastoral world of the plantation. Chief among these men is Uncle George Fairchild, who reenacts in modern form the mythic rescue of a maiden from a dragon by St. George. In this case, the dragon is an approaching train, and George Fairchild's rush to pull his niece from the track symbolically expresses his function for the whole Fairchild family.

Welty's allusion to the St. George myth is part of a more complex fabric of myth that bolsters the novel's celebration of human fertility and community. Underlying the story of Dabney Fairchild's wedding to the overseer of the Fairchild family's plantation is the ancient Greek myth of Demeter and Persephone, archetypal mother and daughter.

In the myth, the earth opens up at the feet of the maiden daughter of the goddess Demeter, and Hades (or Pluto) snatches her away to become his bride in his underworld kingdom. In grief, Demeter causes sterility to plague the earth until her daughter is restored, and Persephone's return comes to symbolize the return of vegetation in the spring. In Welty's novel, although the mother loses her daughter to a frightening bridegroom, the loss is only temporary and actually necessary to the initiation of a new cycle of fertility in the family. *Delta Wedding* ends in a picnic feast celebrating the return of bride and groom from their honeymoon and the reunion of the family.

Manning argues that with *Delta Wedding* "the Southern family and community replace the isolated individual and the abnormal one as Welty's favorite focus." Certainly this first novel initiates the period of the writer's creative maturity and her mastery of complex casts of characters. Themes that accompany the emphasis on community include the precariousness of marriage and the intimate suffering it involves, the weight of family tradition and the accompanying tension caused by the need of the young to break out and affirm their individuality, and the stark and hopeless loss that the living must accommodate after the death of parents and mates.

Delta Wedding was followed in 1949 by *The Golden Apples,* a closely related group of stories that functions almost as a novel. *The Golden Apples* depicts several families in the little town of Morgana, Mississippi, during the 1930s or early 1940s, focusing particularly on the defiant and talented Virgie Rainey, who rejects the conventional life of a Southern lady and creates an independent existence for herself while helping her widowed mother run her dairy farm. Fertility myths weave through these stories

with particular attention given to the Pan-like figure of King Maclain, who wanders in and out of town seducing maidens like a mythical satyr and then disappearing in almost a twinkling of cloven hooves. But the main emphasis remains on the lives of the townspeople—the growing pains of children, the tragicomic disappointment of the fierce German music teacher Miss Eckhart, the near-drowning of an orphan girl at summer camp, and then the aging of the community and blighting of the lives of many characters who began as children full of possibility in the early stories.

In a 1984 *PMLA* essay Patricia Yeager emphasizes Welty's subversive exploration to traditional gender distinctions in these stories, arguing that she deliberately transgresses masculine and feminine symbolic boundaries in order to call them into question. For Yeager, "the most interesting and persistent rhetorical strategy Welty employs in *The Golden Apples* is to continually shift the figure and ground of her story, allowing 'male' discourse and female desire to contrast with, to comment on, and to influence each other as each becomes the ground on which the figure of the other begins to interact."

Welty's next book, *The Ponder Heart,* is a comic tour de force that concentrates many of her favorite themes in the dramatic events of an eccentric Southern gentleman's life. Set in the small town of Clay, Mississippi, *The Ponder Heart* is ostensibly an examination of the "heart" or character of Uncle Daniel Ponder, narrated by his spinster niece Edna Earle. Uncle Daniel is one of Welty's typical make heroes who unaccountably marries a selfish and brassy lower-class girl. (George Fairchild of *Delta Wedding* and Judge McKelva of *The Optimist's Daughter* are two more serious versions of the type.) In a tone combining sympathy and outrage, Edna Earle describes her uncle's wooing of seventeen-year-old Bonnie Dee Peacock in a dime store, their elopement, her desertion, return, death and burial, and Uncle Daniel's trial for murder.

Playful use of cliche, giddy inversion of social conventions, and the juxtaposition of kindly motives and silly disasters prevent the story from every moving outside the realm of farce. When Uncle Daniel literally tickles his wife to death in an attempt to distract her from her fear of a thunderstorm, readers can only laugh and recognize the ridiculous dimensions of the most painful human experiences. *The Ponder Heart* can also be seen as a satire on the ideal of the Southern gentleman, a satire which is quite horrifying beneath its humor. The old husband does in fact murder his estranged wife during an attempted reconciliation; family and friends side with him, as does the tone of the novella, so that the death of the young wife is a joke at best and only an inconvenience at worst. Welty received the William Dean Howells Medal of the American Academy of Arts and Letters for *The Ponder Heart* in 1955; and the work was successfully translated into a Broadway play in 1956 and adapted as an *opera bouffe* in 1982.

In 1955, Welty published another collected of short stories, *The Bride of Innisfallen, and Other Stories,* experimenting with a more allusive style. Three of the stories—"Circe," "Going to Naples," and "The Bride of Innisfallen"—are set in Europe and lack the vivid sense of place that gives solidity to most of Welty's fiction. The other four stories operate in familiar Mississippi settings. With the exception of "The Burning," a cryptic account of the burning of a plantation by Yankee soldiers during the Civil War, most continue Welty's comedy of small-town manners: adulterous trysts are foiled by rain and curious children ("Ladies in Spring") or by heat and spiritual fatigue ("No Place for You, My Love"), and a visiting niece offers bemused observations on and childhood memories of her Mississippi relatives' social milieu ("Kin").

In the years between 1955 and 1970, Welty published only a few occasional pieces and a children's story, *The Shoe Bird.* These were years of personal difficulty, as she nursed her mother through a long final illness and lost both of her brothers. She was nevertheless at work on long projects, notably *Losing Battles,* which she continued to shape for a decade. This ambitious, rollicking novel of a family reunion in the Mississippi hill country initiated a second flowering of Welty's career. In an interview collected in *Conversations with Eudora Welty,* she explained to Charles Bunting that a major purpose of the novel was to show indomitability in the tireless though losing battles of a spinster schoolteacher to educate her community, and in the strong ties of the Renfro clan who are celebrating the ninetieth birthday of the family matriarch and awaiting the return from jail of a reckless favorite son. The Renfro family picnic becomes the focal point for the examination of family tensions, the settling of old scores, and the celebration of resulting harmony.

One Time, One Place, the collection of photographs from Welty's 1930s WPA travels, appeared in 1971, followed in 1972 by Pulitzer Prize-winning novel, *The Optimist's Daughter.* The sparest of her novels, it recounts an adult daughter's return to Mississippi to be with her elderly father during an eye operation and then to preside over his funeral a few weeks later. As Laurel Hand confronts her memories of both parents, she comes to understand the pain of her mother's dying years and their effect on her father. Laurel is reconciled to her father's unwise second marriage to a ruthless young woman, and at the same time finally recognizes her own grief for the husband she has lost many years before. Welty's exploration of grief in *The Optimist's Daughter* which was in part a working-out of her own losses during the 1960s, contains many autobiographical elements, particularly in the portrait of Laurel's mother. But the novel is also a close fictional examination of the interdependence of child and parents. In an interview collected in *Conversations with Eudora Welty,* Welty told Martha van Noppen that she "tried to give that feeling of support and dependence that just ran in an endless line among the three of them [mother, father, and daughter]." Finally, Laurel Hand works through her grief to achieve a calmer and more practical accommodation with the past.

Losing Battles and *The Optimist's Daughter* brought renewed attention to Welty's writing and consequently an increasingly heavy burden of requests for interviews and speaking engagements. She continued to protect the essential privacy of her daily life, however, by discouraging biographical inquiries, carefully screening interviews, and devoting most of her energies to her work. During the later 1970s this work consisted largely of collecting her nonfiction writings for publication as *The Eye of the Story* and of assembling her short stories as *The Collected Stories of Eudora Welty.* With these two important collections she rounded out the shape of her life's work in literary commentary and fiction.

An invitation to give a series of lectures at Harvard in 1983 resulted in the three autobiographical pieces published as *One Writer's Beginnings* the next year. Perhaps because she wished to forestall potential biographers or because she came to accept public interest in a writer's early experiences in shaping her vision, Welty provided in *One Writer's Beginnings* a recreation of the world that nourished her own imagination. Characteristically, however, she omitted family difficulties and intimate matters, focusing instead on the family love of books and storytelling, the values and examples her parents provided, and the physi-

cal sensations of life in Jackson that influenced her literary sensitivities.

Welty's fictional chronicle of Mississippi life adds a major comic vision to American literature, a vision that affirms the sustaining power of community and family life and at the same time explores the need for solitude. In his 1944 essay, Robert Penn Warren aptly identified these twin themes in Welty's work as love and separateness. While much of modern American fiction has emphasized alienation and the failure of love, Welty's stories show how tolerance and generosity allow people to adapt to each other's foibles and to painful change. Welty's fiction particularly celebrates the love of men and women, the fleeting joys of childhood, and the many dimensions and stages of women's lives.

BIOGRAPHICAL/CRITICAL SOURCES:

BOOKS

Appel, Alfred, Jr., *A Season of Dreams: The Fiction of Eudora Welty,* Louisiana State University Press, 1965.

Balakian, Nona and Charles Simmons, editors, *The Creative Present,* Doubleday, 1963.

Concise Dictionary of American Literary Biography, Volume 5: *The New Consciousness, 1941-1968,* Gale, 1987.

Contemporary Authors Bibliographical Series, Volume 1, Gale, 1986.

Contemporary Literary Criticism, Gale, Volume 1, 1973, Volume 2, 1974, Volume 5, 1976, Volume 14, 1980, Volume 22, 1982, Volume 33, 1985.

Conversations with Writers II, Gale, 1978.

Cowie, Alexander, *American Writers Today,* Radiojaenst, 1956.

Dictionary of Literary Biography, Volume 2: *American Novelists Since World War II,* Gale, 1978.

Dictionary of Literary Biography Yearbook: 1987, Gale, 1988.

Evans, Elizabeth, *Eudora Welty,* Ungar, 1981.

Jones, Anne Goodwyn, *Tomorrow Is Another Day: The Woman Writer in the South, 1859-1936,* Louisiana State University Press, 1981.

Kreyling, Michael, *Eudora Welty's Achievement of Order,* Louisiana State University Press, 1980.

Manning, Carol, *With Ears Opening Like Morning Glories: Eudora Welty and the Love of Storytelling,* Greenwood Press, 1985.

Prenshaw, Peggy Whitman, editor, *Eudora Welty: Critical Essays,* University Press of Mississippi, 1979.

Prenshaw, Peggy Whitman, editor, *Conversations with Eudora Welty,* University Press of Mississippi, 1984.

Ruas, Charles, *Conversations with American Writers,* Knopf, 1985.

Short Story Criticism, Volume 1, Gale, 1988.

Vande Kieft, Ruth, *Eudora Welty,* Twayne, 1962.

Westling, Louise, *Sacred Groves and Ravaged Gardens: The Fiction of Eudora Welty, Carson McCullers, and Flannery O'Connor,* University of Georgia Press, 1985.

PERIODICALS

American Book Collector, January/February, 1981.

Bulletin of Bibliography, January, 1956; January, 1960; January, 1963; September, 1963.

Chicago Tribune, December 20, 1984.

Chicago Tribune Book World, April 1, 1982.

Critique, winter, 1964-65.

Globe and Mail (Toronto), March 24, 1984.

Kenyon Review, spring, 1944.

Los Angeles Times, November 13, 1987.

Mississippi Quarterly, fall, 1973; fall, 1984.

New York Herald Tribune Books, October 25, 1942.
New York Times, February 18, 1984; March 1, 1985.
New York Times Book Review, November 1, 1942; April 12, 1970; February 19, 1984.
Notes on Mississippi Writers, Number 2, 1985.
PMLA, October, 1984.
Saturday Review, December, 1984.
Sewanee Review, July-September, 1952.
Shenandoah, spring, 1969.
Southern Humanities Review, summer, 1980.
Southern Review, autumn, 1972.
Southwest Review, summer, 1981.
Twentieth Century Literature, winter, 1982.
U.S. News and World Report, August 18, 1986.

—*Sidelights by Louise Westling*

*   *   *

WHALEN, Richard J(ames) 1935-

PERSONAL: Born September 23, 1935, in New York, N.Y.; son of George Carroll (a business executive) and Veronica (Southwick) Whalen; married Joan Marie Guiffre, October 19, 1957; children: Richard Christopher, Laura Anne, Michael James. *Education:* Queens College (now Queens College of the City University of New York), B.A., 1957. *Politics:* Republican. *Religion:* Roman Catholic.

ADDRESSES: Home—Washington, D.C. 20007. *Office*—Suite 304, 1101 30th St. N.W., Washington, D.C. 20007. *Agent*—Owen Laster, William Morris Agency, 1740 Broadway, New York, N.Y. 10019.

CAREER: Richmond News Leader, Richmond, Va., reporter, 1957-58, associate editor, 1958-59; *Time,* New York City, contributing editor, 1959-60; *Wall Street Journal,* New York City, editorial writer, 1960-62; *Fortune,* New York City, associate editor, 1962-65, member of board of editors, 1965-66; Georgetown University, Center for Strategic and International Studies, Washington, D.C., writer in residence, 1966-69; State Department, Washington, D.C., consultant, 1969-72. Advisor to Ronald Reagan, 1975—, senior policy advisor, 1980 campaign. Chairman, Worldwide Information Resources, Ltd. (WIRES), 1971—. Bear, Stearns & Co., advisor, beginning in 1971, limited partner, 1981—. Visiting fellow, American Enterprise Institute. Board of trustees, American Film Institute. Member of board of directors finance committee, Project HOPE.

MEMBER: Cosmos Club (Washington, D.C.).

AWARDS, HONORS: Alumnus of the Year, Queens College, 1973.

WRITINGS:

The Founding Father: The Story of Joseph P. Kennedy, New American Library, 1964.
A City Destroying Itself: An Angry View of New York, Morrow, 1965.
Catch the Falling Flag: A Republican's Challenge to His Party, Houghton, 1972.
Taking Sides: A Personal View of America from Kennedy to Nixon to Kennedy, Houghton, 1974.
(With Ben J. Wattenberg) *The Wealth Weapon: U.S. Foreign Policy and Multinational Corporations,* Transaction Books, 1980.
(With WIRES, Ltd. editors) *Trade Warriors: An Inside Look at Trade Activists in Congress and How to Reach Them,*

Worldwide Information Resources, 1986, 2nd edition published as *Trade Warriors: A Guide to the Politics of Trade and Foreign Investment in the 101st Congress,* EPM Publications, 1989.

Also editor of three presidential commissions, 1970-71. Contributor to *Washington Post, Washington Star,* and *New York Times Magazine.* Contributing editor, *Harper's,* 1973-79; board of editors member, *Public Opinion* magazine.

WORK IN PROGRESS: Research on U.S. political economy since 1969; research in pre-World War II Anglo-American diplomacy.

SIDELIGHTS: Richard J. Whalen's first book, *The Founding Father: The Story of Joseph P. Kennedy,* hit the bestseller list shortly after publication and remained there for some months.

AVOCATIONAL INTERESTS: Thoreau, the Spanish Civil War, hiking, and fishing.

BIOGRAPHICAL/CRITICAL SOURCES:

PERIODICALS

Book Week, March 28, 1965.
Boston Globe Magazine, July 13, 1980.
New York Post, March 22, 1965, June 2, 1972.
Washington Evening Star, May 4, 1972, September 19, 1980.*

*   *   *

WHALING, Frank 1934-

PERSONAL: Born February 5, 1934, in Pontefract, Yorkshire, England; son of Frederick (a civil servant) and Ida (Johnson) Whaling; married Patricia Hill (a college lecturer), August 6, 1960; children: John Prem Francis, Ruth Shanti Patricia. *Education:* Christ's College, Cambridge, B.A. (history), 1957; Wesley House, Cambridge, B.A. (theology), 1959; Cambridge University, M.A., 1961; Harvard University, Th.D., 1973. *Politics:* Liberal Democrat.

ADDRESSES: Home—29 Ormidale Terr., Murrayfield, Edinburgh EH12 6EA, Scotland, U.K. *Office*—New College, University of Edinburgh, The Mound, Edinburgh E.H.1, Scotland, U.K.

CAREER: Ordained Methodist minister, 1962; pastor of Methodist church in Birmingham, England, 1960-62; Methodist minister in Faizabad and Banaras, India, 1962-66; minister of Methodist church in Eastbourne, England, 1966-69; University of Edinburgh, New College, Edinburgh, Scotland, lecturer and coordinator of religious studies, 1973—, senior lecturer and director of religious studies, 1984—. Visiting lecturer, professor, or guest lecturer at numerous colleges and universities, including University of the Witwatersrand, Dartmouth College, University of Aberdeen, Boston University, New York University, London University, Oxford University, and Princeton University. School of the Prophets Lecturer at Indiana University, 1975; British Academy exchange fellow at Chinese Academy of Social Sciences, Beijing, 1982 and 1987; J. N. Pal Lecturer in Religion at Calcutta University, 1985.

Member of council of SHAP Working Party on World Religions in Education, 1973—, of International Center for Integrative Studies, New York City, 1974—, and of Christian Education Movement in Scotland, 1979—. Co-director of Edinburgh/Farmington Project, 1977-82; director of Edinburgh/Cook Project, 1981-84, and of Edinburgh Cancer Help Centre, 1987—. Chairman of Scottish Churches China Group, 1985—, Scottish

Inter-Faith Symposium, 1987—, and Edinburgh Inter-Faith Association, 1987—. Member of numerous boards, including Scottish Education Board, 1982—, and research board of advisers of American Biographical Institute, 1988—; member of Scottish Global Cooperation Council, 1988—.

MEMBER: International Biographical Association (fellow), International Association of Buddhist Studies, International Center for Integrative Studies, International Hall of Leaders, World Institute of Achievement, World Literary Academy (fellow), American Biographical Institute (fellow; associate of Research Academy), Association of Teachers of Religious Education in Scotland, British Association for the History of Religion (member of council, 1980-84), British Fulbright Association, Educational Writers Association, Indian Religion Society, Royal Asiatic Society (fellow), Scottish China Society, Society of Authors, Theology Society, Traditional Cosmology Society, Wesley Historical Society.

AWARDS, HONORS: Peregrine Maitland Fellowship in Comparative Religion, Cambridge University, 1969; John E. Theyer Honor Award, Harvard University, 1970-71; research awards from Farmington Trust, 1977—, Cook Trust, 1981—, Spalding Trust, 1981, British Council, 1981, 1984, and 1988, Fulbright Foundation, 1981-82, Carnegie Foundation, 1982 and 1987, Commonwealth Foundation, 1985, and Moray Trust, 1987.

WRITINGS:

An Approach to Dialogue: Hinduism and Christianity, Lucknow Publishing House, 1966.
The Rise of the Religious Significance of Rama, Motilal Banarsidass, 1980.
John and Charles Wesley, Paulist Press and S.P.C.K., 1981.
Religions of the World, Holmes McDougall, 1984.
The World's Religious Traditions: Current Perspectives in Religious Studies, T. & T. Clark, 1984.
Contemporary Approaches to the Study of Religion, Mouton, Volume 1: *The Humanities,* 1984, Volume 2: *The Social Sciences,* 1985.
Christian Theology and World Religions: A Global Approach, Marshall Pickering, 1986.
Religion in Today's World, T. & T. Clark, 1987.
Compassion through Understanding, Dzalendara, 1990.
The World: How It Came into Being and Our Responsibility towards It, Dzalendara, 1990.
Theory and Practice of Prayer, Paulist Press, 1991.
Essays in Hinduism, E. J. Brill, 1991.
The Raja-Yoga Movement, Penguin Books, 1991.
The Contribution of Non-Western Christian Theology to Global Theology, Marshall Pickering, 1991.
Essays in Comparative Religion, T. & T. Clark, in press.

Also editor of *Festschrift* for Wilfred Cantwell Smith. General editor of series and executive editor of one volume, "Blackwell's Illustrated History of Religion" series, seven volumes, 1990-94; general editor of series and author of one volume, "Global Christian Theology" series, Marshall Pickering, nine volumes, 1990-95. Contributor of more than seventy articles and sixty reviews to philosophy and theology journals.

SIDELIGHTS: Frank Whaling told *CA:* "I am very lucky to have wide academic interests and expertise and to have the opportunity of publishing in all these areas. This is an unusual circumstance in the academic world where specialisation is normally the order of the day. In my case there has been the chance to write in the different areas of my knowledge and across the spectrum of my knowledge so that my books, which are apparently unconnected, actually relate with one another.

"My first book was on dialogue between Hindus and Christians. This arose out of my experience as a missionary in North India. My second book on the Hindu Lord Rama also arose in part from my experience in India. We lived for a short time at Faizabad, near Ayodhya, the birthplace of the Lord Rama.

"Another facet of my life, the fact that I am a Methodist minister, came into play in the volume on John and Charles Wesley. I had spoken often on the Wesleys in the United States and Britain and was able to use these talks and the feedback from them in the writing of this work.

"The two books I edited on contemporary approaches to the study of religion involved the gathering together of a team of scholars from around the world, or at any rate the western world, coming as they did from Edinburgh, Leeds, Los Angeles, Santa Barbara, Wellington, Tuebingen, Leiden, Utrecht, Lancaster, and Massachusetts. It seems to me that in our diminishing global world, collaborative writing exercises of this kind will become increasingly important as writers attempt to overcome the cultural limitations that have been in the past an inevitable part of the human lot. The *Festschrift* I organized for my friend and colleague Wilfred Cantwell Smith of Harvard presented another opportunity to gather into a team thirteen world-class scholars from different centers, and together we wrote on both the content of and the approach to human religiousness in the contemporary world.

"My basic interest in the content of world religions comes out in my books *Religions of the World* and *Religion in Today's World.* I introduce a new model for understanding religion which can be applied in principle to any of the world's religious traditions, and also a new model of the history of religion which brings into one perspective the total religious history of humankind.

"The global situation has become more important in my general thinking and writing in recent years. I reflect on this in a narrow context in *Christian Theology and World Religions: A Global Approach* and far more widely in the gigantic seven-volume "Illustrated History of Religion" that I am editing for Blackwell's of Oxford. This will bring together the histories of past and present religions in order to see them not as side-by-side narratives but as part of an integral connected story.

"The global themes of compassion and understanding and ecology are brought together in two volumes, *Understanding through Compassion* and *The World: How It Came into Being and Our Responsibility for It,* which are the fruit of two important symposia which I chaired in Scotland. Leading figures from the major world religions met for a few days in dialogue and the sharing of papers at a Buddhist temple in the lowlands of Scotland. These books bring together the themes of dialogue and global thought.

"Two of the ongoing motifs of my work are recapitulated in my *Essays on Comparative Religion* and my *Essays on Hinduism.* Three slightly new directions are opened up in my three latest books. *The Raja-Yoga Movement* is the first systematic analysis of a new religious movement which began in Sindh in the 1930s with Hindu roots but has now expanded around the world and is led by women. It is fascinating in many ways and is unique. Spirituality is a keynote of the Raja-Yoga movement, but in my *Theory and Practice of Prayer* I have returned to my own Christian roots. It contains a month's worth of prayers divided for each day into eight sections which are the 'practice' part of the book and are designed for Christians (and others if they want) to deepen their spiritual life, and the long introduction supplies the theory side of prayer to go along with the practice. In my third recent endeavor *The Contribution of Non-Western Christian Theology to Global Theology* I again return to my Christian roots but in order to bring out the great upsurge in non-western Christianity which is taking the balance of power within the Christian tradition from Christendom which is now dead to the non-western part of the globe. This note of the coming importance of non-western Christian theology is picked up by various non-western Christian scholars from Africa, India, China, Japan, Latin America, etc., in the other eight volumes of the series on "Global Christian Theology" that I am editing.

"We are moving into an exciting yet fraught new world, and I see my job as an author to help to understand that coming great world in all its forms—ecological, humane, and spiritual—yet I also see my job as that of helping to change the present world by opening up a global and integral science of love that will create the conditions for the fashioning of a new world of harmony for our children and grandchildren. I see our task as writers to be that of helping a new global world to come into being to integrate the partialities of the old."

* * *

WHEELER, (Robert Eric) Mortimer 1890-1976

PERSONAL: Born September 10, 1890, in Glasgow, Scotland; died July 22, 1976, in Leatherhead, England; son of Robert Mortimer (a university lecturer and newspaper editor) and Emily (Baynes) Wheeler; married Tessa Verney (an archaeologist), 1914 (died, 1936); married Mavis de Vere Cole, 1939 (divorced, 1942); married Margaret Norfolk, October 6, 1945; children: (first marriage) Michael Mortimer. *Education:* University of London, B.A., 1910, M.A., 1912, D.Litt., 1920.

CAREER: National Museum of Wales, Cardiff, keeper of archaeology department, 1920-24, museum director, 1924-26; London Museum, London, England, keeper and secretary, 1926-44; director-general of archaeology for government of India, 1944-48; adviser on archaeological matters, Dominion of Pakistan, 1948-50. University of Wales, University College of South Wales and Monmouthshire, Cardiff, lecturer in archaeology, 1920-24; University of London, London, fellow of University College, 1922-76, honorary director of Institute of Archaeology, 1934-44, professor of the archaeology of the Roman provinces, 1944-45, honorary fellow, School of Oriental and African Studies, 1970, British Academy, London, fellow and lecturer to Royal Academy, 1965-76. Rhys Lecturer, British Academy, 1929; Norman Lockyer Lecturer, British Association, 1937; Dalrymple Lecturer, University of Glasgow, 1937; Lewis Fry Lecturer, University of Bristol, 1937; Rhind Lecturer, Univerity of Edinburgh, 1951; Norton Lecturer, Archaeological Institute of America, 1952; Hobhouse Lecturer, University of London, 1955; Queen's Lecturer in Berlin, 1968. Commissioner, Royal Commission on Historical Monuments, 1939-58; chairman, Ancient Monuments Board for England, 1964-66. Trustee, British Museum, 1963-73. Directed excavations at Colchester, 1917, 1920, Carnarvon, 1921-23, Brecon, 1924-25, Caerleoon, 1926-27, Lydney, 1928-29, St. Albans, 1930-33, Maiden Castle in Dorset, 1934-37, Brittany, 1938, Normandy, 1939, India, 1944-48, Pakistan, 1950, 1958, and Stanwich in York, 1951-52; led government missions from India to Iran and Afghanistan, 1945-46. *Military service:* British Army, 1917-19, served in France, Italy, and germany, mentioned in dispatches, received military cross for valor, 1918, 1939-43, served in Africa and Italy; became brigadier general.

MEMBER: Society of Antiquaries (fellow; president, 1954-59; director, 1940-44, 1949-54), British Association (president of conference of delgates, 1933; president of section H, 1954), Museum Association (president, 1937-38), Royal Society (fellow), Royal Archaeological Institute (president, 1951-53), Cambrian Archaeological Association (president, 1931), Indian Museum Association (president, 1949-50), German Archaeological Institute (corresponding member), Archaeological Institute of America (honorary member), South Eastern Union of Scientific Societies (president, 1931), New York Academy of Sciences (honorary life member).

AWARDS, HONORS: Gold Medal, Society of Antiquaries, 1944; Companion, Order of the Indian Empire, 1947; University of London Petrie Medal, 1950; knighted, 1952; Stara-i-Pakistan, 1964; companion of honor, 1967; Lucy Wharton Drexel Medal from University of Pennsylvania. Honorary degrees include D.Litt. from University of Bristol, University of Delhi, Oxford University, University of Wales, University of Ireland, and University of Liverpool, and D.Sc. from University of Bradford.

WRITINGS:

Prehistoric and Roman Wales, Clarendon Press, 1952.
London and the Saxons, London Museum, 1935.
Twenty-Five Years of the London Museum, Cambridge University Press, 1937.
Maiden Castle, Dorset, Oxford University Press for the Society of Antiquaries, 1943, reprinted, AMS Press, 1989.
Five Thousand Years of Pakistan: An Archaeological Outline, C. Johnson, 1950.
Rome Beyond the Imperial Frontiers, Bell, 1954.
Archaeology from the Earth, Clarendon Press, 1954, Penguin, 1961.
Still Digging: Interleaves from an Antiquary's Notebook (autobiography), M. Joseph, 1955.
(With Katherine M. Richardson) *Hill-Forts of Northern France,* Oxford University Press for Society of Antiquaries, 1957.
Early India and Pakistan: To Akosha, Praeger, 1959, revised edition, 1968.
Charasada, a Metropolis of the North-West Frontier, Oxford University Press for the Government of Pakistan and British Academy, 1962.
Roman Art and Architecture, Praeger, 1964, reprinted, Thames & Hudson, 1985.
(Editor) *Splendors of the East: Temples, Tombs, Palaces and Fortresses of Asia,* Putnam, 1965.
(Author of introduction and commentary) Roger Wood, *Roman Africa in Color,* McGraw, 1966.
Alms for Oblivion: An Antiquary's Scrapbook, Weidenfield & Nicolson, 1966.
Indus Civilization, Cambridge University Press, 1968.
Flames Over Persepolis: Turning-Point in History, Morrow, 1968, reprinted, Greenwood Press, 1979.
(Editor) Sir Winston Leonard Spencer Churchill, *History of the English Speaking Peoples,* B.P.C. Publishing, 1969.
The British Academy, 1949-1968, Oxford University Press, 1970, reprinted, Longwood Publishing Group, 1987.
The Iron Age and Its Hill-Forts, Southhampton University Archaeological Society, 1971.

PAMPHLETS

Wales and Archaeology, H. Milford, 1930.
(With Tessa Verney Wheeler) *The Roman Amphitheatre at Caerleon,* Clowes, 1931.
The Roman Amphitheatre, Caerleon, Monmouthshire, His Majesty's Stainery Office, 1943.

Aspects of the Ascent of a Civilization, Oxford University Press, 1955.

The Virtue of Intolerance, J.W. Ruddock & Sons, 1957.

Roman Archaeology in Wales: A Tribute to V. E. Nash-Williams, British Broadcasting Corp., 1957.

Impact and Imprint: Greeks and Romans Beyond the Himalayas, Kings College, 1959.

(With V. E. Nash-Williams) *Caerleon Roman Amphitheatre and Prysg Field Barrack Buildings,* Her Majesty's Stationery Office, 1970.

Maiden Castle, Dorset, Her Majesty's Stationery Office, 1972.

Frontiers of the Indus Civilization, Books & Books, 1984.

OTHER

Also author of *Stanwick Fortifications,* Society of Antiquaries; *London and the Vikings,* 1927; *London in Roman Times,* 1930; *Parliament and the Premiership,* 1931; and *Verulaminum: A Belgic and Two Roman Cities,* Books On Demand, University of Michigan. Writer of reports and monographs on digs and excavations. Contributor to journals in his field.

SIDELIGHTS: In a review of *Alms for Oblivion: An Antiquary's Scrapbook,* a *Times Literary Supplement* critic credited Mortimer Wheeler with an increase of interest in archaeology: "At a time when archaeology is popular as never before, and when it is increasing our knowledge of the past at an unprecedented rate, it is not easy to recall how recent this all is and how much of it is owed to Sir Mortimer himself, to the excavational techniques which he perfected between the wars on sites such as Verulaminum and Maiden Castle and to the standards of meticulous, imaginative presentation which he set in publishing them."

In this book of essays, "Sir Mortimer does well to remind us with his customary vigour that the purpose of excavation is neither the magpie accumulation of random information about the past nor the enrichment of museums. We dig up objects to learn about the people who made them and used them. People not things. To Sir Mortimer it is above all the humanity of archaeological studies that gives them value today," wrote the *Times Literary Supplement.*

BIOGRAPHICAL/CRITICAL SOURCES:

PERIODICALS

Times Literary Supplement, September 12, 1967.

OBITUARIES:

PERIODICALS

American Bookmen, July 23, 1976.
New York Times, July 23, 1976.
Time, August 2, 1976.*

*   *   *

WHITBURN, Joel (Carver) 1939-

PERSONAL: Born November 29, 1939, in Wauwatosa, WI; son of Russell and Ruth (Bird) Whitburn; married Frances Mudgett, April 25, 1964; children: Kim Marie. *Education:* Attended Elmhurst College, 1957-58, and University of Wisconsin—Milwaukee, 1958-60. *Religion:* Protestant.

ADDRESSES: Home and office—P.O. Box 200, Menomonee Falls, WI 53051.

CAREER: Carnation-Miller Brewing Can Co., Milwaukee, WI, office manager, 1964-68; Taylor Electric Co., Milwaukee, member of sales and record promotion staff, 1968-70; Record Research, Inc., Menomonee Falls, WI, founder and president, 1970—. Producer of "Billboard Top Hits" compilation albums for Rhino Records.

WRITINGS:

Record Research, 1955-1969, Record Research, 1970, supplement, 1971, revised cumulative edition published as *Top Pop Records, 1955-1970,* Gale, 1972, revised cumulative edition published as *Top Pop Records, 1955-1972,* 1973, annual supplements, 1973—, revised cumulative edition published as *Joel Whitburn's Top Pop Artists and Singles, 1955-1978,* Record Research, 1979, revised cumulative edition published as *Top Pop, 1955-1982,* 1983, revised cumulative edition published as *Joel Whitburn's Top Pop Singles, 1955-1986,* 1987.

Top Country and Western Records, 1959-1971, Record Research, 1972, annual supplements, 1973—, revised cumulative edition published as *Joel Whitburn's Top Country Singles, 1944-1988,* 1989.

Top Pop Records, 1940-1955, Record Research, 1973, revised cumulative edition published as *Pop Memories, 1890-1954,* 1986.

Top Rhythm and Blues Records, 1949-1971, Record Research, 1973, annual supplements, 1973—, revised cumulative edition published as *Joel Whitburn's Top R & B Singles, 1942-1988,* 1988.

Joel Whitburn's Top LP's, 1945-1972, Record Research, 1973, annual supplements, 1973—, revised cumulative edition published as *Joel Whitburn's Top Pop Albums, 1955-1985,* 1985.

Joel Whitburn's Top Easy Listening Records, 1961-1974, Record Research, 1975, annual supplements, 1975—.

Joel Whitburn's Pop Annual, 1955-1977, Record Research, 1978, revised cumulative edition published as *Pop Annual, 1955-1982,* 1983, revised cumulative edition published as *Pop Singles Annual, 1955-1986,* 1987.

Bubbling under the Hot 100, 1959-1981, Record Research, 1982.

The Billboard Book of Top Forty Hits: 1955 to Present, Billboard Books, 1983, new editions, 1985, 1987, 1989.

Music Yearbook (annual), Record Research, 1984—.

The Billboard Book of Top Forty Albums, Billboard Books, 1987.

Music and Video Yearbook (annual), Record Research, 1987—.

Top 1000 Singles, 1955-1986, Hal Leonard Books, 1987, revised cumulative edition published as *Billboard Top 1000 Singles, 1955-1987,* 1988.

Joel Whitburn Presents Billboard's Top Ten Charts, 1958-1988, Record Research, 1988.

Joel Whitburn Presents Daily #1 Hits, 1940-1989, Record Research, 1989.

Billboard Songbook Series: Best of 1955-1959, Hal Leonard, 1990.

Billboard's Top 3000 Plus, 1955-1987, Compiled by Joel Whitburn, Record Research, 1990.

Joel Whitburn Presents the Billboard Hot 100 Charts—The Sixties, 1960-1969, Record Research, 1990.

Joel Whitburn Presents the Billboard Hot 100 Charts—The Seventies, 1970-79, Record Research, in press.

Also compiler of other volumes in the "Billboard Songbook Series," Hal Leonard.

WORK IN PROGRESS: New editions of *Top Pop Singles 1955-1990, Top Forty Albums 1955-present,* and *Pop Singles Annual 1955-1990; Top Jazz Albums 1967-1990; Top Dance Hits 1973-1991; Top Videocassette Rentals and Sales 1979-1991.*

SIDELIGHTS: Based on the weekly "Top 100" charts published in *Billboard* magazine, Joel Whitburn has compiled a series of guides that provide a comprehensive look at the popularity of various records and artists. Whitburn began collecting records while in his teens, and uses his collection as a basis for the lists in his books. To date, he has over 120,000 records in his personal collection. As a result, his works are the standard reference for radio stations and record collectors. Referring to *Joel Whitburn's Top Pop Artists and Singles,* Robert Hilburn explains in the *Los Angeles Times:* "Each entry in the 664-page volume notes when the record entered the Top 100, how high it climbed on the chart and how many weeks it remained on the list." Of his success, the author told Stephanie Zimmermann of the *Milwaukee Journal:* "It's amazing the way it worked out. I'm still amazed."

BIOGRAPHICAL/CRITICAL SOURCES:

PERIODICALS

Los Angeles Times, March 4, 1980; July 15, 1989.
Milwaukee Journal, March 14, 1989; July 11, 1990.

* * *

WHITE, Jon (Ewbank) Manchip 1924-

PERSONAL: Born June 22, 1924, in Cardiff, Wales; son of Gwilym Manchip (a shipowner) and Eve Elizabeth (Ewbank) White; married Valerie Leighton, 1946; children: Bronwen, Rhiannon. *Education:* Cambridge University, M.A. (with honors in English literature, prehistoric archaeology, and Egyptology), and University Diploma in Anthropology, 1950. *Avocational interests:* Fishing, music, travel, French, Spanish.

ADDRESSES: Home—96 Cherokee Bluff, Knoxville, TN 37920. *Office*—Department of English, University of Tennessee, Knoxville, TN 37916. *Agent*—Curtis Brown Ltd., 162-168, Regent St., London, England W1R 5TB; 10 Astor Pl., New York NY 10003.

CAREER: British Broadcasting Corp., Television, London, England, story editor, 1950-51; H.M. Foreign Service, London, senior executive officer, 1952-56; Hammer Film Productions Ltd., London, scenario editor, 1956-57; screenwriter in Paris and Madrid, under contract to Samuel Bronston Productions, 1960-64; University of Texas at El Paso, associate professor, 1967-77; University of Tennessee, Knoxville, Lindsay Young Professor of Humanities and professor of English, 1977—. Minsterworth Productions, Ltd., director. *Military service:* Royal Navy and Welsh Guards, 1942-46.

WRITINGS:

NOVELS

Last Race, Mill Books, 1953 (published in England as *Mask of Dust,* Hodder & Stoughton, 1953).
Build Us a Dam, Hodder & Stoughton, 1955.
The Girl from Indiana, Hodder & Stoughton, 1956.
No Home but Heaven, Hodder & Stoughton, 1957.
The Mercenaries, Hutchinson, 1958.
Hour of the Rat, Hutchinson, 1962.
The Rose in the Brandy Glass, Eyre & Spottiswoode, 1965.
Nightclimber, Chatto & Windus, 1968.
The Game of Troy, Chatto & Windus, 1971.
The Garden Game, Bobbs-Merrill, 1974.
Send for Mr. Robinson, Pinnacle Books, 1974.
The Moscow Papers, Major, 1979.
Death by Dreaming, Apple-Wood, 1981.

Fevers and Chills: Three Extravagant Tales; Nightclimber, The Game of Troy, and The Garden Game, Countryman Press, 1983.
The Last Grand Master, Countryman Press, 1985.

SCREENPLAYS

(With Val Guest) *The Camp on Blood Island,* Hammer Film Productions, 1957, produced by Columbia, 1958.
(With Hugh Woodhouse and Bertram Ostrer) *Mystery Submarine,* Universal, 1962.
(With Julian Halevy) *Crack in the World,* Paramount, 1965.

Co-author of *Day of Grace,* 1957, and author of *Man with a Dog,* 1958. Also author of radio and television plays produced in Britain and on *U.S. Steel Hour.*

OTHER

Dragon and Other Poems, Fortune Press, 1943.
Salamander (poems), Fortune Press, 1946.
Rout of San Romano (poems), Hand & Flower Press, 1952.
Ancient Egypt, Wingate, 1952, Crowell, 1953, revised edition, Dover, 1970.
Anthropology, English Universities Press, 1954, Philosophical Library, 1955.
(Translator) Samivel, *The Glory of Egypt,* Thames & Hudson, 1955.
Marshall of France: The Life and Times of Maurice, Comte de Saxe, Rand McNally, 1962.
Everyday Life in Ancient Egypt, Batsford, 1963, Putnam, 1964.
Diego Velazquez: Painter and Courtier, Rand McNally, 1969.
The Land God Made in Anger: Reflections on a Journey through South West Africa, Rand McNally, 1969.
Cortez and the Fall of the Aztec Empire, St. Martin's, 1971.
(Editor) Adolf Erman, *Life in Ancient Egypt,* Dover, 1971.
Mountain Lion (poems), Chatto & Windus, 1971.
(Editor) E. W. Lane, *Manners and Customs of Modern Egyptians,* Dover, 1972.
(Editor) Howard Carter, *The Tomb of Tutankhamen,* Dover, 1972.
A World Elsewhere: One Man's Fascination with the American Southwest, Crowell, 1975 (published in England as *The Great American Desert,* Allen & Unwin, 1977).
Everday Life of the North American Indian, Holmes & Meier, 1979.
(Editor) *Egypt and the Holy Land: 77 Historic Photographs by Francis Frith,* Dover, 1981.
(With Robert Conquest) *What to Do When the Russians Come: A Survivor's Guide,* Stein & Day, 1984.
(Editor) J. H. Breasted, *A History of the Ancient Egyptians,* Bedrick, 1990.

Contributor to *Spectator, Financial Times, Listener,* and other British journals.

* * *

WILHELM, James Jerome 1932-

PERSONAL: Born February 2, 1932, in Youngstown, Ohio; son of James J. and Ruth (Schreckengost) Wilhelm. *Education:* Yale University, B.A., 1954, Ph.D. (comparative literature), 1961; University of Bologna, graduate study, 1954-55; Columbia University, M.A., 1958.

ADDRESSES: Home—165 East 35th St. 3E, New York, N.Y. 10016.

CAREER: Queens College of the City University of New York, Flushing, N.Y., assistant professor of English, 1961-65; Rutgers

University, New Brunswick, N.J., professor of comparative literature, 1965—.

MEMBER: International Comparative Literature Association, American Comparative Literature Association, Modern Language Association of America, Mediaeval Academy of America, Elizabethan Club, Dante Society.

AWARDS, HONORS: Fulbright fellowship, 1955-56.

WRITINGS:

The Cruelest Month: Spring, Nature and Love in Classical and Medieval Lyrics, Yale University Press, 1965.
Seven Troubadours: The Creators of Modern Verse, Pennsylvania State University Press, 1970.
Medieval Song: Anthology of Hymns and Lyrics, Dutton, 1971.
Dante and Pound: The Epic of Judgment, University of Maine Press, 1974.
The Later Cantos of Ezra Pound, Walker & Co., 1977.
(Editor and translator) *The Poetry of Arnaut Daniel,* Garland Publishing, 1981.
Il Miglior Fabbro: The Cult of the Difficult in Daniel, Dante, and Pound, National Poetry Foundation, University of Maine at Orono, 1982.
(Editor with Laila Zamuelis Gross) *The Romance of Arthur: An Anthology,* Garland Publishing, 1984.
The American Roots of Ezra Pound, Garland Publishing, 1985.
(Editor) *The Romance of Arthur II: An Anthology,* Garland Publishing, 1986.
(Editor) *The Romance of Arthur III: An Anthology,* Garland Publishing, 1988.
The Poetry of Sordello, Garland Publishing, 1989.

General editor, Garland Library of Medieval Literature, Garland Publications in Comparative Literature, and Garland Library of World Literature in Transition.

BIOGRAPHICAL/CRITICAL SOURCES:

PERIODICALS

Times Literary Supplement, July 28, 1972, November 8, 1985.

*   *   *

WILL, George F(rederick)   1941-

PERSONAL: Born May 4, 1941, in Champaign, Ill.; son of Frederick L. (a professor emeritus of philosophy at the University of Illinois) and Louise Will. *Education:* Trinity College, B.A., 1962; attended Magdalen College, Oxford, 1962-64; Princeton University, Ph.D., 1967. *Politics:* Conservative.

ADDRESSES: Office—ABC-TV Public Relations, 1330 Avenue of the Americas, New York, N.Y. 10019.

CAREER: Michigan State University, East Lansing, professor of politics, 1967-68; University of Toronto, Toronto, Ontario, professor of politics, 1968-69; U.S. Senate, Washington, D.C., congressional aide to Senator Alcott of Colorado, 1970-72; *National Review,* New York City, Washington editor, 1972-76; writer. Panelist, "Agronsky and Company," Post-Newsweek Stations, 1979-84; participant, "This Week with David Brinkley," American Broadcasting Co. (ABC-TV), 1981—; commentator, "World News Tonight," ABC-TV, 1984—.

AWARDS, HONORS: Named Young Leader of America, *Time* magazine, 1974; Pulitzer Prize, 1977, for distinguished commentary.

WRITINGS:

The Pursuit of Happiness, and Other Sobering Thoughts, Harper, 1978.
The Pursuit of Virtue, and Other Tory Notions, Simon & Schuster, 1982.
Statecraft as Soulcraft: What Government Does, Simon & Schuster, 1983.
The Morning After: American Successes and Excesses, 1981-1986, Free Press, 1986.
The New Season: A Spectator's Guide to the 1988 Election, Simon & Schuster, 1987.
Men at Work, Macmillan, 1990.

Author of a syndicated column for the *Washington Post,* 1974—, and for *Newsweek;* columnist for the *New York Daily News.* Contributor to *London Daily Telegraph* and other periodicals. Contributing editor, *Newsweek,* 1976—.

SIDELIGHTS: George F. Will, author of bi-weekly columns for the *Washington Post* and *Newsweek* and a regular commentator on ABC-TV's "This Week with David Brinkley" and "World News Tonight," is "the most widely read and heard political commentator in America," according to Sally Bedell Smith in the *New York Times.* "Mr. Will's arrival," continues Smith, "has been hailed by conservatives as the first opportunity for a bona fide thinker from among their ranks to have what William F. Buckley calls 'a presence in the room' after years of dominance by what they regard as liberal opinion." A winner of the Pulitzer Prize in 1977 for distinguished commentary, Will writes conservative essays and articles "with a rhythmic cadence that combines logic and literary allusion in concise proportion," says *Christian Science Monitor* contributor Alan L. Miller. These views, however, deviate considerably from what is usually considered to be mainline conservatism. "I trace the pedigree of my philosophy to [Edmund] Burke, [John Henry] Newman, [Benjamin] Disraeli, and others who were more skeptical, even pessimistic, about the modern world than most people who call themselves conservatives," Will tells Miller. Nelson W. Polsby phrases the journalist's beliefs this way in a *Fortune* article: "Will's political philosophy presupposes the primacy of the social order itself and is concerned with the means by which citizens can be encouraged to place civic responsibilities above their own interests."

The Pursuit of Happiness, and Other Sobering Thoughts, Will's first book, is a collection of 138 previously-published essays that express his philosophy while discussing subjects ranging from politics to the author's personal life. Behind this diverse variety of topics lies the consistent opinion in the columnist's essays that American society has degenerated in the last few decades. Will "thinks Americans have become materialistic, selfish, pretentious, and morally flabby, with barely any private, let alone public, sense of what is genuinely important and excellent," writes *New York Review of Books* critic Ronald Dworkin. This is also the attitude that permeates the author's second book, *The Pursuit of Virtue, and Other Tory Notions,* which *New Republic* contributor Charles Krauthammer calls a "textbook of American cultural conservatism" that is "pithy, epigrammatic, and often elegant." "Mr. Will's only noticeable less-than-respectable passion in life appears to be a rock-ribbed loyalty to the Chicago Cubs," notes Neal Johnston in the *New York Times Book Review;* in fact, Will's more recent book, *Men at Work,* is devoted to the subject of baseball, a sport he sometimes alludes to as an example of one of the few virtuous pursuits left in today's society.

Several critics have praised Will for his wit, but Joseph Sobran asserts in the *National Review* that what is important is the journalist's "larger gift of *knowing what needs to be said,* of summoning up a truth whose absence others hadn't even felt." A number of other reviewers, however, have strongly disagreed with Will's views, since, as Dworkin notes, his definition of conservatism "is not . . . how conservative politicians define conservatism. . . . Will thinks they are hopelessly wrong about what conservatism is: he means to define 'true' conservatism, not what passes for political rhetoric." In *Statecraft as Soulcraft: What Government Does,* Will attempts to clarify his beliefs in an extensive treatise on the role of government. The "book has received a mixed, generally unenthusiastic reception," remarks James Nuechterlein in *Commentary.* "The fullest expression of Will's philosophy yet—there is nothing new here for regular readers of his columns—it has encountered far more intellectual resistance than Will's ideas had earlier run into."

Unlike Will's essay collections, which often use specific examples of political cases in order to illustrate his general ideas about society, *Statecraft as Soulcraft* does not deal in particulars. A number of critics complain, therefore, that the book's general thesis that government should instill virtue within its citizens is never fully elucidated. "Will never really tells us 'what government does,' " says *National Review* contributor M. E. Bradford. "We hear of a noble 'ethic of common provision,' meaning, concretely, the welfare state. . . . But we are left to speculate for ourselves" what this entails. However, this lack of a definite outline as to how a government should be run is not a drawback for the book, according to *New York Time Book Review* critic Michael J. Sandel. The "purpose is less to promote particular programs than to change the character and tone of the debate," says Sandel. As the author himself says in *Statecraft as Soulcraft,* "My aim is to recast conservatism."

Discussing *Statecraft as Soulcraft,* Nuechterlein relates that in Will's opinion "what is wrong with American conservatism . . . traces back to flawed philosophic assumptions on the part of the nation's founders." Sobran goes on to explain how the author believes that "America was conceived in coarseness. Its Founders . . . sought to organize American society on the sovereign principle of self-interest," rather than on the promotion of public virtue. This latter view of the proper role of government, which goes back to Aristotle's time, has been called "aristocratic" by reviewers like Sobran, because it is founded on the assumption that there exists in society a natural order in which some people were meant to govern, while others were meant to be governed. Bruce R. Sievers warns in the *Los Angeles Times Book Review* that this Burkeian idea to which Will adheres has a "dark side" in its potential to encourage the "uncritical acceptance of privilege for its own sake under the guise of 'tradition.' "

Despite these reservations about *Statecraft as Soulcraft,* several critics view the book to be a significant commentary on politics. "Will has written a fascinating, and profoundly important, work of contemporary political philosophy," claims Sievers. And Nuechterlein adds that "even those who deplore Will's politics express admiration for the subtlety and sophistication of his arguments as well as the elegance of his prose." Nuechterlein also notes, however, that the author's "columns, taken together, offer a richer and more satisfactory (if less systematic) public philosophy than does his book."

Will's next works, *The Morning After* and *The New Season: A Spectator's Guide to the 1988 Election,* return to his original essay collection format. Like the author's other publications, they have been lauded for their entertaining and skillful style. For example, *Tribune Books* reviewer Clarence Petersen calls Will's essays in *The Morning After* "superbly crafted, witty and skepti-

cal." But although Ronald Steel admits in his *Los Angeles Times Book Review* article that "there is considerable skill at ridicule" in *The Morning After,* he alleges that there is "little effort to understand, much less sympathize" with those who hold different philosophical positions. In *The New Season,* however, Will's steadfast views offer a certain advantage, according to *Washington Post Book World* critic William V. Shannon, because "there is no gross partisanship in Will's comments" about the 1988 election. But there is, Shannon attests, "much good sense and even wisdom."

Even though Will's positions have stirred controversy among mainstream conservatives, he has remained "one of the strongest and most constructive conservative voices addressing contemporary issues, from abortion to impeachment," says Polsby. "His opinions," the reviewer continues, "grounded in serious consideration of basic philosophical questions, are almost always of the greatest interest." With his weekly appearances on television and regularly published columns in widely-read magazines, Will's views reach some twenty million people, estimates Smith in the *New York Times.* The journalist is also "generally credited with exerting influence among policy-makers in Washington," Smith adds. Nevertheless, Will recognizes his limitations. "The idea that multitudes will be driven to their knees by the force of my words is silly," he tells Smith. Yet he also says in a *Newsweek* article that commentaries such as those he offers are indispensable. "There is a scarcity of reasoned, civilized discourses in the world," he insists. "With such discourse we can stand anything. Without it we are doomed."

BIOGRAPHICAL/CRITICAL SOURCES:

BOOKS

Will, George F., *Statecraft as Soulcraft: What Government Does,* Simon & Schuster, 1983.

PERIODICALS

Atlantic, May, 1983.
Chicago Tribune, May 12, 1988.
Christian Science Monitor, April 21, 1982, May 18, 1983, February 13, 1986.
Commentary, October, 1983.
Fortune, July 25, 1983.
Harvard Law Review, January, 1984.
Los Angeles Times, April 6, 1982.
Los Angeles Times Book Review, June 26, 1983, November 30, 1986, December 6, 1987.
Nation, October 14, 1978, March 27, 1982, July 23, 1983.
National Review, June 9, 1978, June 25, 1982, June 10, 1983.
New Republic, June 10, 1978, June 16, 1982.
Newsweek, September 30, 1974.
New York Review of Books, October 12, 1978.
New York Times, May 16, 1983, May 19, 1985.
New York Times Book Review, June 11, 1978, March 28, 1982, July 17, 1983, November 2, 1986, January 3, 1988.
People, September 19, 1983.
Publishers Weekly, March 16, 1990.
Saturday Review, March, 1982.
Time, August 8, 1983, April 1, 1985.
Times Literary Supplement, May 25, 1984.
Tribune Books (Chicago), November 8, 1987.
Washington Post Book World, June 11, 1978, March 21, 1982, June 5, 1983, November 30, 1986, November 29, 1987.

—*Sketch by Kevin S. Hile*

WILLIAMS, Anne
  See STEINKE, Ann E(lizabeth)

* * *

WILLIAMS, Rose
  See ROSS, W(illiam) E(dward) D(aniel)

* * *

WILSON, David Henry 1937-

PERSONAL: Born February 26, 1937, in London, England; son of William Myer (a company director) and Elizabeth (Joseph) Wilson; married Elizabeth Ayo Amaworo (a nursing sister), December 18, 1965; children: Christopher Amaworo, Jennifer Ayo, Jeremy James Amaworo. *Education:* Attended Pembroke College, Cambridge, 1955-58, M.A., 1961.

ADDRESSES: Home—3 Beech Close, Hope Corner Ln., Taunton, Somerset TA2 7NZ, England. *Agent*—(Theatre) ACTAC Ltd., 15 High St., Ramsbury nr. Marlborough, Wiltshire, England; (fiction) Herta Ryder, Toby Eady Associates Ltd., 7 Gledhow Gardens, London SW5 0BL, England.

CAREER: High school teacher in Sekondi. Ghana, 1960-64; University of Cologne, Cologne, West Germany, lecturer in English, 1964-67; University of Konstanz, Konstanz, West Germany, lecturer in English, 1967—.

WRITINGS:

PUBLISHED PLAYS

All the World's a Stage (one-act for children), Dramatists Play Service, 1968.
The Make-up Artist (one-act), Dramatic Publishing, 1973.
On Stage, Mr. Smith (one-act), Dramatic Publishing, 1975.
Monster Man (two-act for children; first produced in Taunton, England, at Taunton School, November 20, 1979), Hope Corner, 1981.
Jones v. Jones (three-act; first produced in Sheffield, England, at Crucible Theatre, August 27, 1975), Hope Corner, 1983.
Professor in Play (two-act; first produced as radio play under title "Spiel oder nicht Spiel" by Radio Bern, Bern, Switzerland, August 22, 1981), Hope Corner, 1983.
Are You Normal, Mr. Norman? (one-act; also see below; first produced in London, England, at Hampstead Theatre Club, February 27, 1966), Hope Corner, 1984.
If Yer Take a Short Cut Yer Might Lose the Way (two-act; also see below; first produced in London at Hampstead Theatre Club, February 27, 1966), Hope Corner, 1984.
Wendlebury Day (one-man one-act; also see below; first produced in Edinburgh, Scotland, at Edinburgh Festival Fringe, August 29, 1977), Hope Corner, 1984.
Gas and Candles (two-act; first produced in Leicester, England, at Leicester Haymarket, September 14, 1979), Dramatic Publishing, 1985.
Shylock's Revenge (five-act; first produced in Hamburg, West Germany, at Hamburg University, June 9, 1989), Hope Corner, 1986.
Are You Normal, Mr. Norman?, and Other Short Plays (also see above; includes *Are You Normal, Mr. Norman?, If Yer Take a Short Cut Yer Might Lose the Way, Wendlebury Day,* and *The Death Artist* [one-act; first produced in England at Theatre Royal Northampton, March 21, 1986]), Samuel French, 1987.
We're Looking for Mary Pickford (three-act; first produced in German in Baden-Baden, West Germany, at Stadttheater,

April 28, 1967; produced in London at King's Head Theatre Club, May 25, 1971), Hope Corner, 1987.
Him a-Layin' Bare (three-act; first produced in London at Collegiate Theatre, March 27, 1971), Hope Corner, 1987.
The Dawn (two-act; first produced in London at Act Inn, June 3, 1975), Hope Corner, 1987.

NOVELS

The Coachman Rat, Krueger/Fischer (West Germany), 1985, Carroll & Graf, 1989.
Der Fluch der Achten Fee, Krueger/Fischer, 1989.

JUVENILES

Elephants Don't Sit on Cars, Chatto & Windus, 1977.
The Fastest Gun Alive, Chatto & Windus, 1978.
Getting Rich with Jeremy James, Chatto & Windus, 1979.
Beside the Sea with Jeremy James, Chatto & Windus, 1980.
How to Stop a Train with One Finger, Dent, 1984.
Superdog, Hodder & Stoughton, 1984.
Do Goldfish Play the Violin?, Dent, 1985.
Superdog the Hero, Hodder & Stoughton, 1986.
There's a Wolf in My Pudding, Dent, 1986.
Yucky Ducky, Dent, 1988.
Superdog in Trouble, Hodder & Stoughton, 1988.
Gander of the Yard, Dent, 1989.

OTHER

"Maxitweet the Cocoa" (two-act play for children), first produced in Taunton at Taunton School, November 27, 1981.
"The Morning Stone" (two-act), first produced as radio play under title "Ein Steinwurf in den Teich" by Radio Bern, Switzerland, August 27, 1983.
"Doves and Smiths," first produced as radio play under title "Taubenflug" by Radio Bern, March 31, 1984.
(Translator) Wolfgang Iser, *Walter Pater: The Aesthetic Moment,* Cambridge University Press, 1988.

* * *

WOLFE, Gene (Rodman) 1931-

PERSONAL: Born May 7, 1931, in Brooklyn, N.Y.; son of Roy Emerson (a salesman) and Mary Olivia (Ayers) Wolfe; married Rosemary Frances Dietsch, November 3, 1956; children: Roy II, Madeleine, Therese, Matthew. *Education:* Attended Texas A & M University, 1949-52; University of Houston, B.S.M.E., 1956. *Religion:* Roman Catholic.

ADDRESSES: Home—P.O. Box 69, Barrington, Ill. 60010. *Agent*—Virginia Kidd, Box 278, Milford, Pa. 18337.

CAREER: Project engineer with Procter & Gamble, 1956-72; *Plant Engineering Magazine,* Barrington, Ill., senior editor, 1972-84; writer. *Military service:* U.S. Army, 1952-54; received Combat Infantry badge.

MEMBER: World S.F., Science Fiction Writers of America, PEN.

AWARDS, HONORS: Nebula Award, Science Fiction Writers of America, 1973, for novella "The Death of Doctor Island"; Chicago Foundation for Literature Award, 1977, for *Peace;* Rhysling Award, 1978, for poem "The Computer Iterates the Greater Trumps"; Nebula Award nomination, 1979, for novella *Seven American Nights;* Illinois Arts Council award, 1981, for short story "In Looking-Glass Castle"; World Fantasy Award, 1981, for *The Shadow of the Torturer;* Nebula Award, and *Locus*

Award, both 1982, both for *The Claw of the Conciliator;* British Science Fiction Award, 1982; British Fantasy Award, 1983; *Locus* Award, 1983, for *The Sword of the Lictor;* John W. Campbell Memorial Award, Science Fiction Research Association, 1984, for *The Citadel of the Autarch;* World Fantasy Award, 1989, for collection *Storeys from the Old Hotel.*

WRITINGS:

SCIENCE FICTION/FANTASY

Operation ARES, Berkley Publishing, 1970.
The Fifth Head of Cerberus (three novellas), Scribner, 1972.
(With Ursula K. LeGuin and James Tiptree, Jr.) *The New Atlantis, and Other Novellas of Science Fiction,* edited by Robert Silverberg, Hawthorn, 1975.
The Devil in a Forest (juvenile), Follett, 1976.
The Island of Doctor Death and Other Stories and Other Stories, Pocket Books, 1980.
The Shadow of the Torturer (first book in "The Book of the New Sun" tetralogy), Simon & Schuster, 1980.
Gene Wolfe's Book of Days (short stories), Doubleday, 1981.
The Claw of the Conciliator (second book in "The Book of the New Sun" tetralogy), Simon & Schuster, 1981.
The Sword of the Lictor (third book in "The Book of the New Sun" tetralogy), Simon & Schuster, 1982.
The Citadel of the Autarch (fourth book in "The Book of the New Sun" tetralogy), Simon & Schuster, 1983.
The Wolfe Archipelago (short stories), Ziesing Brothers, 1983.
Plan(e)t Engineering, New England Science Fiction Association, 1984.
Free Live Free, Ziesing Brothers, 1984, new edition, Tor Books, 1985.
Soldier of the Mist, Tor Books, 1986.
The Urth of the New Sun (sequel to "The Book of the New Sun" tetralogy), Tor Books, 1987.
There Are Doors, Tor Books, 1988.
Storeys from the Old Hotel (short stories), Kerosina, 1988.
Endangered Species (short stories), Tor Books, 1989.
Seven American Nights (bound with *Sailing to Byzantium,* by Silverberg), Tor Books, 1989.
Soldier of Arete (sequel to *Soldier of the Mist*), St. Martin's, 1989.
Castleview, Tor Books, 1990.

OTHER

Peace (novel), Harper, 1975.
The Castle of the Otter (essays), Ziesing Brothers, 1982.
Bibliomen, Cheap Street, 1984.
Empires of Foliage and Flower, Cheap Street, 1987.
For Rosemary (poetry), Kerosina, 1988.

Contributor of stories to anthologies, including awards anthologies *Best SF: 70,* 1970, *Nebula Award Stories 9, The Best SF of the Year #3,* and *Best SF: 73,* all 1974. Contributor of short stories to *Omni, New Yorker, Isaac Asimov's Science Fiction Magazine,* and other publications.

SIDELIGHTS: "With the publication of his tetralogy *The Book of the New Sun,* Gene Wolfe has entered the ranks of the major contemporary writers of science fiction," Pamela Sargent asserts in *Twentieth-Century Science Fiction Writers.* The series is set in a far-future Earth reminiscent of medieval Europe in its social structure and in its forgotten technologies which appear magical. When Severian, an apprentice torturer, is exiled from his guild for aiding the suicide of a prisoner he loves, it inaugurates a journey of discovery that culminates in Severian's elevation to Autarch, ruler of Urth. "The far-future world of Urth through which Wolfe's characters move is a world of beauty and horror,

one in which humanity's great accomplishments are not only past, but also nearly forgotten, and in which the lack of resources makes the knowledge that remains nearly useless," notes Sargent. Severian, however, possesses perfect recall, making his retrospective narration laden with detail and meaning. As Thomas D. Clareson describes it in his *Dictionary of Literary Biography* essay, Severian's account is "a rich tapestry rivaling any imaginary world portrayed in contemporary science fiction," while the series is "one of the high accomplishments of modern science fiction."

In particular, critics have admired Wolfe's realistic presentation of his imaginary society. *London Tribune* contributor Martin Hillman, for instance, declares that "in the evocation of the world, and the unsettling technologies, creatures, and behavioural rules within it," Wolfe's tetralogy "is streets ahead of most tales featuring sword-bearing heroes." "Wolfe is not only deft at creating a whole and strange new world," Tom Hutchinson of the London *Times* claims; "he also, disturbingly, makes us understand a different way of thinking." This vivid depiction of a remote civilization, however, has not prevented the author from creating a comprehensive portrayal of Severian's character. "Although Wolfe has created an epic stage and although he permits his protagonist to travel extensively through the world," Clareson comments in *Extrapolation,* "the emphasis is never upon external action for the sake of action; rather, the four novels become increasingly a study of Severian's reactions and musings. The result," the critic concludes, "is that Gene Wolfe has created one of the richest and most complex characterizations in the field of fantasy and science fiction." Peter Nicholls concurs, stating in a *Washington Post Book World* article that Severian "is perhaps the most extraordinary hero in the history of the heroic epic, and none of his confrontations are without surprises."

While "The Book of the New Sun" has been celebrated for the depth of its descriptions, reviewers have also commended Wolfe's intricate imagery. "In fact, there are two 'Books of the New Sun,' " Nicholls avers. "Out in the open is the wonderfully vivid and inventive story of a brave and lonely hero; below is the sea of allusion and juxtaposition . . . [and] a pungent debate on ontology, eschatology and the metaphysics of time." Contributing to the series' profundity, C. N. Manlove suggests in *Kansas Quarterly,* is Wolfe's literary skill: "The author creates his images with such apparent effortlessness that they seem to have been come upon, to have been always there, rather than to have been invented. Every stage of Severian's journey is accompanied by a startling new image or landscape." "With great urgency, layer after layer," John Clute similarly maintains in the *Washington Post Book World,* Wolfe "has created a world radiant with meaning, a novel that makes sense in the end only if it is read as an attempt to represent the Word of God."

It is this layering of image and meaning that has led critics such as Algis Budrys to praise the overall literary quality of Wolfe's series: "As a piece of literature, the work is simply overwhelming," Budrys relates in the *Magazine of Fantasy and Science Fiction.* "Severian is a character realized in a depth and to a breadth we have never seen in SF before," the critic explains, adding that "as craftsmanship and as literature, what we're talking about are attributes that are world-class as *prose,* not 'just' as SF." As Thomas M. Disch elaborates in the *Washington Post Book World:* "Gene Wolfe has managed to do what no science fantasy author has done heretofore—he's produced a work of art that can satisfy adult appetites and in which even the most fantastical elements register as poetry rather than as penny-whistle whimsy. Furthermore, he's done this without in any way sacrificing the showmanship and splashy colors that auger a popular success."

"In a triumph of imagination, [Wolfe] creates a truly alien social order that the reader comes to experience from within," concludes *New York Times Book Review* critic Gerald Jonas. "The result does not make for easy reading. But once into it, there is no stopping—and you will not quickly forget Severian or his world." Although the author leaves room for future volumes, a *Booklist* reviewer proposes that "it is not necessary that we see any more for this series to loom as a major landmark of contemporary American literature. . . . Wolfe has wrought a genuine marvel here."

While *The Urth of the New Sun* continues Severian's story, it is "neither afterthought nor reprise," *Times Literary Supplement* reviewer Colin Greenland remarks. Nevertheless, Roz Kaveney writes in the *Washington Post Book World,* "this volume makes of the whole work a palimpsest, in which moments from an underlay of earlier versions of reality crop up suddenly, producing seeming inconsistencies. . . . *The Urth of the New Sun* makes of the whole sequence a more perfect work by showing us [these] inconsistencies before ironing them out." The novel traces the journey of Severian, now Autarch, as he travels to a high galactic court to petition for the "new sun" that will renew Urth. While the concept of one person representing his race to a higher authority is a common science fiction convention, a *Washington Post Book World* critic notes that "as usual, Wolfe takes this old [science fiction] chestnut and makes it into something very rich and very strange."

Kaveney likewise claims that "Gene Wolfe's career has thus far been dedicated to making us see in a new light some of what we had thought of as the stock habits of science fiction and fantasy." In *Free Live Free,* for example, "Wolfe extends his freedom in another direction, embracing for his own purposes that problematic mix of nonscientific lore and dreams of power known as the occult," comments Jonas. The result, says the critic, is a series of "characters studies," something "rare in science fiction." *Soldier of the Mist* is also innovative in its account of Latro, a soldier of ancient Greece whose memory is wiped clean every time he sleeps; guided by his journal and various gods, Latro journeys to regain his memory. John Calvin Batchelor observes in the *Washington Post Book World* that "Wolfe displays a happy genius every time Latro must deal with [these] creatures," and adds that *Soldier of the Mist,* while difficult reading, is "a work of consequence." The author "is a master of science fiction," Batchelor concludes, "and for the best of all reasons, vaulting ambition," he explores the various facets of fantasy and science fiction.

Although Wolfe has gained attention as the author of novels and the "Urth" series in particular, his literary reputation also includes short fiction. As Clareson asserts in an *Extrapolation* review of *Gene Wolfe's Book of Days,* the collection "is another cornerstone in emphasizing how important a writer Gene Wolfe has been throughout his surprising brief career. His stature becomes apparent by reading a number of his works. Only in that way does one realize the skill and subtlety with which he brings a fresh perspective to established themes and situations." The critic contends in his *Dictionary of Literary Biography* essay that Wolfe is "a major figure whose stories and novels must be considered among the most important science fiction published in the 1970s. He will undoubtedly become increasingly significant in the 1980s because he skillfully uses the materials of science fiction and fantasy to explore the themes which dominate contemporary fiction." "Gene Wolfe is a writer for the thinking reader," Sargent similarly states; "he will reward anyone searching for intelligence, crafted prose, involving stories, and atmospheric detail. He is the heir of many literary traditions—pulp stories, fan-

tasy, adventurer stories of all kinds, and serious literature—and he makes use of all of them," she continues. "His work can be read with pleasure many times; new discoveries are made with each reading, and the stories linger in one's mind."

Wolfe wrote *CA:* "The books and stories I write are what are usually called escapist, in the pejorative sense. They do not teach the reader how to build a barbecue, or get a better job, or even how to murder his mother and escape detection. I have never understood what was wrong with escape. If I were in prison, or aboard a sinking vessel, I would escape if I could. I would try to escape from East Germany or the U.S.S.R., if I were unfortunate enough to find myself in one of those places. My work is intended to make life—however briefly—more tolerable for my readers, and to give them the feeling that change is possible, that the world need not always be as it is now, that their circumstances may be radically changed at any time, by their own act or God's."

BIOGRAPHICAL/CRITICAL SOURCES:

BOOKS

Contemporary Authors Autobiography Series, Volume 9, Gale, 1989.
Contemporary Literary Criticism, Volume 25, Gale, 1983.
Dictionary of Literary Biography, Volume 8: *Twentieth Century American Science Fiction Writers,* Gale, 1981.
Gordon, Joan, *Gene Wolfe,* Borgo, 1986.
Lane, Daryl, William Vernon, and David Carson, editors, *The Sound of Wonder: Interviews from "The Science Fiction Radio Show,"* Volume 2, Oryx Press, 1985.
Twentieth-Century Science Fiction Writers, St. James Press, 1986.

PERIODICALS

Booklist, July 1, 1975, November 1, 1982.
Chicago Tribune Book World, June 8, 1980, June 14, 1981.
Extrapolation, summer, 1981, fall, 1982.
Kansas Quarterly, summer, 1984.
London Tribune, April 24, 1981.
Los Angeles Times Book Review, April 3, 1983.
Magazine of Fantasy and Science Fiction, April, 1971, May, 1978, June, 1981.
New York Times Book Review, July 13, 1975, September 12, 1976, May 22, 1983, November 24, 1985.
Science Fiction Review, summer, 1981.
Times (London), April 2, 1981.
Times Literary Supplement, May 18, 1973, January 15, 1988.
Washington Post Book World, May 25, 1980, March 22, 1981, July 26, 1981, January 24, 1982, January 30, 1983, November 24, 1985, October 26, 1986, October 27, 1987, August 28, 1988, April 30, 1989.

—*Sketch by Diane Telgen*

*   *   *

WOLFF, Sonia
  See LEVITIN, Sonia (Wolff)

*   *   *

WOLKSTEIN, Diane   1942-

PERSONAL: Born November 11, 1942, in New York City; daughter of Harry W. (a certified public accountant) and Ruth (Barenbaum) Wolkstein; married Benjamin Zucker (a gem merchant), September 7, 1969; children: Rachel. *Education:* Smith College, B.A., 1964; studied pantomime in Paris, 1964-65; Bank Street College of Education, M.A., 1967. *Religion:* Jewish. *Avocational interests:* Travel.

ADDRESSES: Home—10 Patchin Place, New York, NY 10011.

CAREER: Hostess of weekly radio show, "Stories from Many Lands with Diane Wolkstein," WNYC-Radio, New York City, 1967—; featured storyteller at numerous gatherings. Bank Street College, instructor in storytelling and children's literature, 1970—; Sarah Lawrence College, teacher of mythology, 1984; New School for Social Research, teacher of mythology, 1989. Leader of storytelling workshops for librarians and teachers.

AWARDS, HONORS: Honorable mention, New York Academy of Sciences, 1972, for *8,000 Stones;* Lithgow-Osborne fellowship, 1976, 1977; American Institute of Graphic Arts award, 1977, for *The Red Lion: A Persian Sufi Tale;* notable book citation, American Library Association, 1978, for *The Magic Orange Tree and Other Haitian Folk Tales,* and 1979, for *White Wave: A Tao Tale;* recipient of Marshall grant.

WRITINGS:

8,000 Stones, Doubleday, 1972.
The Cool Ride in the Sky: A Black-American Folk Tale (Xerox Book Club selection), Knopf, 1973.
The Visit, Knopf, 1974.
Squirrel's Song: A Hopi-Indian Story, Knopf, 1975.
Lazy Stories, Seabury, 1976.
The Red Lion: A Persian Sufi Tale, Crowell, 1977.
The Magic Orange Tree and Other Haitian Folk Tales, Knopf, 1978.
White Wave: A Tao Tale, Crowell, 1979.
The Banza: A Haitian Folk Tale, Dial, 1980.
(With Samuel Noah Kramer) *Inanna, Queen of Heaven and Earth: Her Stories and Hymns from Sumer,* Harper, 1983.
The Magic Wings, Dutton, 1983.
The Legend of Sleepy Hollow, Morrow, 1987.
The First Love Stories, Harper, 1991.
Oom Razoom, Morrow, 1991.
Little Mouse's Painting, Morrow, 1991.

Also author of audio recordings, "Tales of the Hopi Indians," Spoken Arts, 1972; "California Fairy Tales," Spoken Arts, 1974; "The Cool Ride in the Sky," Miller-Brody, 1975; "Eskimo Stories: Tales of Magic," Spoken Arts, 1976; "Hans Christian Andersen in Central Park," Weston Woods, 1981; "Psyche and Eros," Cloudstone Productions, 1984; "Romping," Cloudstone Productions, 1985; "The Story of Joseph," Cloudstone Productions, 1986; "The Epic of Inanna," Cloudstone Productions, 1987; "Tales from Estonia," Cloudstone Productions, 1988; and a video recording, "Inanna," Cloudstone Productions, 1988. Contributor of articles to periodicals, including *School Library Journal, Wilson Library Bulletin, Parabola, Quadrant,* and *Confrontation.*

SIDELIGHTS: "Diane Wolkstein could be called New York City's official storyteller," remarks Margaret F. O'Connell of the *New York Times Book Review.* The author of children's and young adult books has garnered worldwide attention for her recitations which include performances at the John Masefield Storytelling Festival in Toronto, Canada, the Fifth National Association for the Preservation of Storytelling Festival in Jonesboro, Tennessee, and on two separate occasions, before Queen Margareta of Denmark and Princess Benedikta. She is, notes a critic in the *New York Times Book Review,* "a writer who has made folklore in all parts of the world her specialty."

In her book *Inanna, Queen of Heaven and Earth: Her Stories and Hymns from Sumer,* Wolkstein reanimates an ancient Sumerian poem that describes the fertility goddess Inanna's descent into hell. Wolkstein's efforts to portray Inanna as a role model—sometimes extenuating her less ennobling actions by editorial license—have drawn mixed critical reaction. *Village Voice* reviewer Geoffrey O'Brian suggests that "she wants to restore 'a "grand" story of a woman—as inspiration, guide, and model—for ourselves as well as our children.' " Others, however, like Piotr Michalowski of the *New York Times Book Review,* are less enthusiastic about Wolkstein's liberal reworking of the original manuscript: "She has written [her story] with skill, but it is hers, not the Sumerians', for she has violated the culture that produced the texts in which Inanna appears." O'Brian, though, sees merit in her machinations: "Wolkstein's aim is more than archaeological," he writes, "[Her interpretations] create a hypothetical chronology, filling in gaps, simplifying a confusing system of divine epithets, and alleviating the stylistic feature by which long passages are repeated verbatim many times in the course of an episode."

BIOGRAPHICAL/CRITICAL SOURCES:

PERIODICALS

New York Review of Books, October 13, 1983.
New York Times Book Review, September 30, 1973; March 23, 1980; September 25, 1983.
Village Voice, November 22, 1983.

*   *   *

WORMALD, Jenny 1942-

PERSONAL: Born January 18, 1942, in Glasgow, Scotland; daughter of Thomas (a physician) and Margaret (Dunlop) Tannahill; married Alfred Brown, 1963 (divorced, 1980); married Patrick Wormald (a university lecturer), December 13, 1980; children: (first marriage) Andrew; (second marriage) Tom, Luke. *Education:* University of Glasgow, M.A., 1963, Ph.D., 1974. *Avocational interests:* "Listening to good music, playing the piano inadequately."

ADDRESSES: Home—60 Hilltop Rd., Oxford OX4 1PE, U.K. *Office*—St. Hilda's College, Oxford University, Oxford OX4 1DY, U.K.

CAREER: University of Glasgow, Glasgow, Scotland, lecturer in Scottish history, beginning 1966; currently fellow and tutor in modern history, St. Hilda's College, Oxford University, Oxford, England. British Academy reader in the humanities, 1981-84.

MEMBER: Royal Historical Society, Conference of Scottish Medieval Historical Research, Scottish History Society, Record Society, Text Society, Stair Society, Renaissance Society of America.

AWARDS, HONORS: Award from Scottish Arts Council, 1981, for *Court, Kirk, and Community: Scotland, 1470-1625.*

WRITINGS:

(Editor) *Scottish Society in the Fifteenth Century,* Edward Arnold, 1977.
Court, Kirk, and Community: Scotland, 1470-1625, Edward Arnold, 1981.
Lords and Men in Scotland: Bonds of Manrent, 1442-1603, John Donald, 1985.
Mary Queen of Scots: A Study in Failure, George Philip, 1988.

CONTRIBUTOR

G. Menzies, editor, *The Scottish Nation,* BBC Publications, 1972.

A. G. R. Smith, editor, *The Reign of James VI and I,* Macmillan, 1973.

D. Daiches, editor, *The Companion to Scottish Culture,* Edward Arnold, 1981.

N. Macdougall, editor, *Church, Politics, and Society: Scotland, 1408-1929,* John Donald, 1983.

M. Jones, editor, *Gentry and Lesser Nobility in Late Medieval Europe,* Alan Sutton Publishing, 1986.

A. Maczak, editor, *Klientelsysteme in der Fruehen Neuzeir,* Oldenbourg Verlag, 1988.

P. Contamine, *L'Etat et les Aristocraties XIIe-XVIIe siecle: France, Angleterre, Ecosse,* Presses de l'Ecole Normale Superieure, 1989.

OTHER

Also contributor to *Lexicon des Mittelalters,* Artemis Verlag (Munich). General editor of series "The New History of Scotland," Edward Arnold. Contributor to history journals.

WORK IN PROGRESS: James VI and I: A Study in Dual Monarchy, for Basil Blackwell.

SIDELIGHTS: Jenny Wormald told *CA:* "I was trained in English and European history before turning to research in Scottish history, and I have always perceived my subject in its wider English and European perspectives. Partly because the number of scholars working in Scottish history is small and the country itself not one of the major European powers, the subject has always been overshadowed if not wholly neglected. But a study of Scotland in the medieval and early modern periods has a great deal to offer historians of more 'mainstream' societies: the paradox of a small, remote, and impoverished country whose scholars, politicians, and merchants succeeded in forcing their presence on the universities, courts, and towns of Europe, whose kings were immensely powerful, and whose social controls, based on kinship, created a remarkably stable society, merits far more attention than it has received for the light it casts on major historical themes.

"My own work, on James VI and I, is now taking me into the field of British history. This enigmatic king's historiographical reputation as king of England has been very low and as king of Scotland, high. Scholars working on Jacobean England are now beginning to question this poor reputation. My hope is that my approach, which gives full weight to James's Scottish kingship after he became king of England as well as before, will illumine the problems and tensions inherent in the first experiment in dual monarchy in Britain, laying to rest any lingering idea that he was at best out of his depth as king of England—at worst a buffoon—and contributing to the present stimulating debate on early seventeenth-century England."

BIOGRAPHICAL/CRITICAL SOURCES:

PERIODICALS

Times Literary Supplement, February 21, 1986, July 29, 1988.

*   *   *

WRIGHT, H(arry) Norman 1937-

PERSONAL: Born July 25, 1937, in Hollywood, Calif.; son of Harry N. (a salesman) and Amelia (Cornelius) Wright; married Joycelin Archinal, August 22, 1959; children: Sheryl, Matthew.

Education: Westmont College, B.A., 1959; Fuller Seminary, M.R.E., 1961; Pepperdine University, M.A., 1965. *Religion:* Christian.

ADDRESSES: Home—Long Beach, Calif. *Office*—17821 17th St., Suite 290, Tustin, Calif. 92680.

CAREER: Licensed marriage and family counselor; Biola College, La Mirada, Calif., professor of marriage and family counseling, 1965—. Founder and director, Christian Marriage Enrichment, Family Counseling and Enrichment. Christian education consultant, Gospel Light Publications, 1963—; lecturer at seminars.

MEMBER: American Association for Marriage and Family Therapy, California Association of Marriage Counselors.

WRITINGS:

Help! I'm a Camp Counselor, Regal Books, 1967, revised edition, with Michael Anthony, 1986.

Ways to Help Them Learn: Adults, Regal Books, 1972.

Christian Marriage and Family Relationships, Christian Marriage Enrichment, 1972.

The Christian Use of Emotional Power, Revell, 1974.

Communication: Key to Your Marriage, Regal Books, 1974, revised edition, 1979.

The Living Marriage, Revell, 1975.

The Christian Faces Emotions, Marriage, and Family Relationships: A Curriculum Resource, Christian Marriage Enrichment, 1975.

Pre-Marital Counseling, Moody, 1977, revised edition, 1981.

The Family That Listens, Victor Books, 1978.

(With Rex Johnson) *Characteristics of a Caring Home,* Vision House, 1979.

Into the High Country, Multnomah, 1979.

The Pillars of Marriage, Regal Books, 1979.

(And compiler) *Training Christians to Counsel: A Resource and Training Manual,* edited by Samuel M. Huestis, Christian Marriage Enrichment, 1979.

(And compiler) *Marriage and Family Enrichment Resource Manual,* Christian Marriage Enrichment, 1979.

Preparing for Parenthood, Regal Books, 1980.

Marital Counseling: A Biblically Based Behavioral Cognitive Approach, Christian Marriage Enrichment, 1981.

How to Be a Better-Than-Average In-Law, Victor Books, 1981.

Seasons of a Marriage, Regal Books, 1982.

The Healing of Fears, Harvest House, 1982.

(Compiler) *Celebration of Marriage,* Harvest House, 1983.

Improving Your Self Image, Harvest House, 1983.

Seasons of a Marriage, Regal Books, 1983.

More Communication Keys for Your Marriage, Regal Books, 1983.

Help! We're Having a Baby: Preparing for Parenthood, Regal Books, 1984.

Now I Know Why I'm Depressed and What I Can Do about It, Harvest House, 1984.

Making Peace with Your Past, Revell, 1985.

So You're Getting Married, Regal Books, 1985.

Crisis Counseling: Helping People in Crisis and Stress, Here's Life, 1985.

Energize Your Life through Total Communication, Revell, 1986.

Self-Talk, Imagery, and Prayer in Counseling, Word Books, 1986.

How to Have a Creative Crisis, Word Books, 1986.

Helping Children Handle Stress, Here's Life, 1987.

Romancing Your Marriage, Regal Books, 1987.

Helping Teens Handle Stress, Here's Life, 1987.

Understanding the Man in Your Life, Word Books, 1987.
How to Speak Your Spouse's Language, Revell, 1988.
Making Peace with Your Partner, Word Books, 1988.
Beating the Blues: Overcoming Depression and Stress, Regal Books, 1988.
Before You Remarry: A Guide to Successful Remarriage, Harvest House, 1988.
How to Talk to Your Mate, Tyndale, 1989.
Uncovering Your Hidden Fears, Tyndale, 1989.
Always Daddy's Girl, Regal Books, 1989.

"ANSWER" SERIES; PUBLISHED BY HARVEST HOUSE

An Answer to Worry and Anxiety, 1976.
. . . *the Fulfilled Marriage,* 1976.
. . . *Frustration and Anger,* 1977.
. . . *Divorce,* 1977.
. . . *In-Laws,* 1977.
. . . *Building Your Self-Image,* 1977.
. . . *Parent-Teen Relationships,* 1977.
. . . *Family Communication,* 1977.

Also author of *An Answer to Depression,* . . . *Discipline,* . . . *Loneliness,* and . . . *Submission and Decision Making.*

OTHER

Author of *Communication and Conflict Resolution,* David Cook; also author of *Communication: Key to Your Teens, Building Positive Parent-Teen Relationships, A Guidebook for Dating, Waiting and Choosing a Mate, Preparing Youth for Dating, Courtship and Marriage, Living beyond Worry and Anger, Living with Your Emotions, Self Image and Depression, Before You Say "I Do,"* and *After You Say "I Do,"* all published by Harvest House. Contributor to religious publications and journals in his field.

*   *   *

WRIGHT, L(afayette) Hart   1917-1983

PERSONAL: Born December 3, 1917, in Chickasha, OK; died April 12, 1983, of radiation pneumonitis while undergoing lung cancer treatment, in Baltimore, MD; son of Lafayette Cantrell (a bank president) and Jessie (Hart) Wright; married Phyllis Jeanne Blanchard, July 4, 1938; children: Robin Blanchard, Jana Hart. *Education:* University of Oklahoma, A.B., 1938, J.D., 1941; University of Michigan, LL.M., 1942. *Politics:* Democrat. *Religion:* None.

ADDRESSES: Home—3079 Exmoor, Ann Arbor, MI 48104. *Office*—School of Law, University of Michigan, Ann Arbor, MI 48104.

CAREER: Admitted to the Bar of Oklahoma, 1941, and Michigan, 1952; University of Michigan, Ann Arbor, assistant profes-

sor, 1946-49, associate professor, 1949-53, professor of law, 1953-83; Paul G. Kauper Professor of Law, 1979-83. Visiting associate professor, Stanford University, 1953; visiting distinguished professor of law, University of Oklahoma, 1976. Member of advisory group to Commissioner of Internal Revenue, 1960-61. Member of board of directors, Ann Arbor Family Service, 1954, Americans for Democratic Action (Ann Arbor chapter), 1968; member of advisory board, International Bureau for Fiscal Documentation, Amsterdam, beginning 1970; member of Taxation with Representation Fund, Washington D.C., beginning 1975. Consultant. *Military service:* U.S. Army, 1941-46; became major; received Bronze Star.

MEMBER: International Fiscal Association, American Bar Association, Michigan State Bar Association, Order of Coif, Phi Beta Kappa, Phi Delta Theta.

AWARDS, HONORS: Civilian meritorious service award, U.S. Treasury, 1957; Distinguished Faculty award, University of Michigan, 1968.

WRITINGS:

Income Tax Law, Internal Revenue Service, 1957.
Corporate Tax Affairs, Internal Revenue Service, 1960.
Basic Income Tax Law Course for Internal Revenue Agents and Office Auditors, revised edition, Internal Revenue Service, 1960.
International Tax Affairs, Internal Revenue Service, 1960.
(With William T. Plumb) *Federal Tax Liens,* American Law Institute/American Bar Association, 1961, 2nd edition, 1967.
Advanced Income Tax Law Course for Internal Revenue Agents, Internal Revenue Service Audit Division, 1962.
(With others) *Comparative Conflict Resolution Procedures in Taxation: An Analytic Comparative Study,* University of Michigan, 1968.
Needed Changes in Internal Revenue Service Conflict Resolution Procedures, American Bar Foundation, 1970.

Also author of *Tax Affairs of Individuals,* 1957. Co-author of *American Enterprise in the European Common Market: A Legal Profile,* 1960.

WORK IN PROGRESS: Research on domestic and foreign tax systems.

BIOGRAPHICAL/CRITICAL SOURCES:

OBITUARIES:

PERIODICALS

Chicago Tribune, April 14, 1983.
New York Times, April 14, 1983.

Y

YGLESIAS, Jose 1919-

PERSONAL: Born November 29, 1919, in Tampa, Fla.; son of José and Georgia (Milian) Yglesias; married Helen Bassine (a novelist), August 19, 1950; children: Rafael; stepchildren: Lewis Cole, Tamar Lear. *Education:* Attended Black Mountain College, 1946. *Politics:* "Should like to overthrow capitalism." *Religion:* "What?"

ADDRESSES: Home—North Brooklin, Maine 04661.

CAREER: Writer of nonfiction, novels, and short stories. Held jobs as dishwasher, stock clerk, assembly line worker, and typist-correspondent, 1937-42; *Daily Worker,* New York, N.Y., film critic, 1948-50; assistant to vice-president, Merck, Sharp & Dohme International (pharmaceutical concern), 1953-63. Regents Lecturer at University of California, Santa Barbara, winter, 1973. Occasional reader for publishing companies. *Military service:* U.S. Navy, 1942-45; received Naval Citation of Merit.

MEMBER: PEN.

AWARDS, HONORS: Guggenheim fellowship, 1970, 1976; National Endowment for the Humanities award, 1974.

WRITINGS:

A Wake in Ybor City (novel), Holt, 1963, reprinted, Arno, 1980.
The Goodbye Land (excerpts first published in *New Yorker*), Pantheon, 1967.
In the Fist of the Revolution: Life in a Cuban Country Town, Pantheon, 1968.
An Orderly Life (novel), Pantheon, 1968.
Down There, World Publishing, 1970.
The Truth about Them (novel), World Publishing, 1971.
Double, Double (novel), Viking, 1974.
The Kill Price (novel), Bobbs-Merrill, 1976.
The Franco Years, Bobbs-Merrill, 1977.
Home Again (novel), Arbor House, 1987.
Tristan and the Hispanics (novel), Simon & Schuster, 1989.

TRANSLATOR

Juan Goytisolo, *Island of Women,* Knopf, 1962.
Goytisolo, *Sands of Torremolinos,* Knopf, 1962.
Xavier Domingo, *Villa Milo,* Braziller, 1962.
Goytisolo, *The Party's Over,* Grove, 1966.

OTHER

Contributor of reviews, stories, and articles to *New Yorker, New York Times Magazine, Holiday, Esquire, Nation, New Republic, Venture, New York Review of Books, Massachusetts Review, New York Times Book Review, Book Week,* and other publications.

SIDELIGHTS: A bilingual American of Cuban and Spanish descent, José Yglesias traveled to Galicia, Spain, in 1964 to trace the details of his father's birth and death there and, as a result, wrote *The Goodbye Land.* Accompanied by his wife, Helen, and their then eleven-year-old son, Rafael, Yglesias vividly reacts to the trip as he meets his relatives, visits the land of his father, and experiences life in this quaint, mountainside village. "This book is about the son's journey to the village where his father's last years were spent," wrote a reviewer for the *Times Literary Supplement.* "It has its own quiet suspense and the discovery of facts; more important, it has the very delicately registered sense of self-discovery. . . . The result is as true a picture as one can hope to get of a by-way of modern European history as reflected in the experience of one family."

Written, according to Gerald Brenan of the *New York Review of Books,* in "a deceptively simple style, [it] takes one right into the mysteries of Galician life, as an account by a complete foreigner could never do. . . . The picture it presents of the primitive peasant mind—its warmth and kindness, its reserve and suspicion, its strong family feeling, its obsession about land and money—is the best I have read anywhere." And Clancy Sigal noted in the *New York Times Book Review* that "Yglesias has written a moving and polished book. . . . I was . . . won by his gentleness and control. It is not often that one finds a 'travel book' so affecting, generous and tender."

In most of his books written since *The Goodbye Land,* critics have noted that while avoiding sociological analysis and political moralizing, Yglesias's accounts of life in Cuba and Latin America seek to explore the essence of individual lives, emphasizing personal statements in order to reach the "underlying realities of the revolutionary experience." Yglesias's *In the Fist of the Revolution: Life in a Cuban Country Town* captures many of the emotions of a number of people as they embraced the optimism the Cuban Revolution triggered. *In the Fist of the Revolution* was written from material collected in 1967 during Yglesias's three-month stay in the town of Mayari, Cuba. In Mayari, as well as throughout Cuba, this feeling of hope and renewal seemed to prevail despite the presence of many problems such as government disorganization, food shortages, and the disruption of manufacturing.

Norman Gall remarked in the *New York Times Book Review:* "The dearth of information on the quality of these developments makes José Yglesias's modest book . . . the kind of social reporting on the Cuban Revolution that has long been missing. Mr. Yglesias is an honest and experienced reporter who, though sympathetic, refuses to be drugged by revolutionary rhetoric. He focuses carefully on the character of life in [*In the Fist of the Revolution*] and on the essential quality of the Cuban people that has remained nicely intact through the convulsions of the past decade." In conclusion, Juan de Onis wrote in *New Leader*: "The Cuban Revolution is a strongly emotional experience, and Yglesias does not shield himself from it behind false objectivity. . . . [He] has a writer's ear for dialogue. He speaks fluent, colloquial Spanish, to the point that many of the Cubans with whom he talked remarked, 'you are more like one of us'. . . . Out of their individual stories emerges a sort of collective memory of the pre-revolutionary past, which is full of contradictions, and a picture of the present which does not hide the tensions and psychological contortions of a turbulent period of transition."

Yglesias's narrative study, *Down There,* is written similarly from the personal viewpoints of people in Brazil, Cuba, Chile, and Peru. Yglesias conducted interviews with a number of young revolutionaries and presented their thoughts and philosophies of what life is like for them in these select countries. *Down There* is often cited as being valuable particularly for its disregard of the "official line" on Latin America and for making available to North Americans a more balanced view of these societies. In a review published in the *New Yorker,* a critic remarked: "Yglesias writes not as a spokesman but as a translator or interpreter, so that North Americans can appreciate the sentiments of revolutionary South Americans, who regard Che Guevara as a hemispheric hero and Cuba as the world's best hope, and who believe that the United States is to blame for everything that is—and has been—wrong with their countries." "The ideas and impressions relate deviate from the 'official line,' but they are significant for understanding current Latin America," explained E. S. Johnson in the *Library Journal.*

Yglesias returned to Spain in 1975 and 1976 and was in Spain when the Spanish dictator Francisco Franco died. This experience was the catalyst for *The Franco Years,* a book profiling a number of Yglesias's Spanish acquaintances—detailing their existence during Franco's rule and the effect of his Fascist regime on the lives of the Spanish people. *The Franco Years* is, according to John Leonard in the *New York Times,* "a modest and extremely interesting series of interviews, filtered through a sympathetic intelligence, with Spaniards of various ages, professions and political persuasions who managed to survive Franco's dreary rule." In a *Saturday Review* article on *The Franco Years* Robert Stephen Spitz wrote that "like the sculptor who whittles a graceful swan from a block of ice, José Yglesias has unearthed the spirit of a nation long buried under the shroud of political tyranny. . . . The author spent a great deal of time among dedicated poets, loving infidels, political aspirants, and mine workers whose advanced stages of silicosis forced them to replace toil with courage. This is a powerful work about survivors who found strength in their oppression."

However, Jane Kramer did not find the book entirely satisfactory. She commented in the *New York Times Book Review:* "This is a good book. . . . Yglesias is a fine novelist, and I almost wish that he had tried a novel here, that he had taken a novelist's li-

cense with this research of so many years and shaped it into a more expressive narrative than these sketches offer. His discretion as a journalist seems to go against him. . . . He reaches for drama and then abandons it to some absolute standard of fair-mindedness that, in the end, flattens what he tries to say instead of underlining it. He is obviously a man of decency and compassion—he has many gifts—but he cannot turn understatement onto its cutting edge, and this book, so deliberately, so decently understated, is often bland where it should be powerful."

Leonard was much more accepting of *The Franco Years:* "Mr. Yglesias genuinely likes people. . . . He follows them around—poets, farmers, folklorists, showmen, technocrats, macho waiters, pretty boys of the Madrid homosexual circuit, an old anti-Semite who never leaves home—and he listens. Whether they are going to jail, as most of them have, or starting new political parities, as many of them do, they are allowed their dignity. . . . And always, in a way that I suppose is unintentional and whose manner is impossible to convey, Mr. Yglesias himself comes across as a nice guy. We like him, as much for what he restrains himself from saying—his personal views on property, on rhetoric, on heroism—as for his enthusiasm for the people he meets. He is a kind skeptic."

Yglesias's interest in chronicling the lives and contemporary history of Hispanic people extends also to his novels set in the United States. Yglesias's novels such as *The Truth about Them, The Kill Price, Home Again,* and *Tristan and the Hispanics* deal with the adjustment of working-class Cuban emigre families to American life and seem to reflect Yglesias's intent as a writer. "[I] should like in my work," he told *CA,* "to bring into clear view the moral views and approach to experience of workers, something which seems to me missing from most fiction; [I] should like as well, to do this in the lucid, unpretentious manner of E. M. Forster."

Many reviewers believe that Yglesias is quite successful in his desire to clearly present his subjects and honestly reflect the uniqueness of the emotions, dreams, and disappointments found in people of Hispanic heritage living in America. For example, *The Truth about Them* tells the generational story of a Cuban-American family planting roots in Florida. Yglesias follows the narrator, Pini, as he traces his grandmother's arrival in the United States from Cuba as a young woman to the present witnessing her children and their children as they emerge into America's middle-class. The reader meets the various characters that make up Pini's family as the essence of their lives grow and change over the years and generations.

In his review of *The Truth about Them,* Thomas R. Edwards commented in the *New York Review of Books:* "Yglesias's perspective on America has considerable freshness. These are not the conventional poor people of social protest novels, though they knew poverty well enough in hard times and felt the confused and inept discriminations. . . . As Cubans the family has an identity that for a time remained indifferent to the pressures of their new land. Success, not suffering, dissolves this identity as the third generation begins to prosper, as third generations somehow tend to do." "Blood is thicker than dogma in this book," remarked Martin Levin in the *New York Times Book Review.* Of *The Truth about Them* Levin wrote: "It glows with a respect for human dignity. It delights in the *brio* of a closeknit clan who are broke but not poor. It celebrates those ethnic distinctions that add salt to civilization."

Yglesias continues his study of individual behavior, awareness, and reaction in his next three novels: *The Kill Price, Home Again,* and *Tristan and the Hispanics. The Kill Price* views the relationship between a free-lance journalist of Hispanic descent, Jack Moreno, and his best friend, Wolf, a novelist who is Jewish. The book is set in New York City on a hot, steamy, summer night as Moreno reminiscences while keeping vigil with his dying friend. Various acquaintances arrive on the scene casting additional dimensions to the men's life stories. A *Publishers Weekly* reviewer believed *The Kill Price* is "a splendidly written, sometimes deeply probing story of individuals whose concerns specifice into something approaching universals."

Anatole Broyard felt an aversion for Wolf, the dying protagonist of *The Kill Price.* The critic commented in the *New York Times:* "I was glad to see him die. I was tired of his not very witty pontifications, his unimaginative male chauvinism, his egomania, his sexual braggadocio, and his unkindness." But, recognizing Yglesias's craft, he added: "Mr. Yglesias is an old hand at fiction and he writes well—almost too well for me to believe that the negative impact Wolf had on me was an accident. Perhaps the author wanted to correct the sentimental notion that dying ennobles a man, that powerlessness purifies."

Another study in self-awareness and rediscovery is *Home Again,* Yglesias's story of an aging Cuban-American novelist's return to his home and family in Florida and, as Brunet explained in the *Los Angeles Times Book Review,* his "reacquaintance with his Cuban relatives and heritage and the rediscovery of his powers as a writer." Clay Reynolds wrote in the *New York Times Book Review* that *Home Again* is "built on the promising theme of a frustrated older man's attempt to come to terms with his ethnic background and political commitments. . . . Mr. Yglesias' prose is relaxed and trendy, with sparse dialogue and economical description."

In *Tristan and the Hispanics,* young New Yorker and Yale student Tristan Granados is sent by his family to Tampa, Florida, to arrange for the funeral of his grandfather. Antonio Granados was a once respected leftist novelist who had little contact with Tristan. Tristan is unprepared for the cultural shock he feels when he first meets his grandfather's extended family and assortment of colorful friends who live in a warm, loving emigré Cuban community. However, after several days Tristan discovers the richness of his heritage and begins to look at life and people differently. A reviewer for *Library Journal* noted that *Tristan and the Hispanics* is "a frequently funny and refreshingly down-to-earth novel."

AVOCATIONAL INTERESTS: Vegetable gardening.

BIOGRAPHICAL/CRITICAL SOURCES:

PERIODICALS

Library Journal, October 15, 1970, March 15, 1989.
Los Angeles Times Book Review, September 27, 1987.
New Leader, June 3, 1968.
New Republic, July 20, 1968.
New Yorker, October 17, 1970.
New York Review of Books, March 25, 1971, March 9, 1972.
New York Times, May 28, 1976, October 18, 1977.
New York Times Book Review, July 16, 1967, July 14, 1968, July 25, 1976, October 30, 1977, November 1, 1987.
Publishers Weekly, March 29, 1976, August 22, 1977, January 6, 1989.
Saturday Review, June 8, 1968, November 12, 1977.
Times Literary Supplement, February 22, 1968.*

—*Sketch by Margaret Mazurkiewicz*

Z

ZALLER, Robert 1940-

PERSONAL: Born March 19, 1940, in New York, NY; son of Abraham Morris (an attorney) and Sylvia (Borenstein) Zaller; married Lili Bita (a writer and actress), January 19, 1968; children: Philip Rethis, Kimon Rethis (stepchildren). *Education:* Queens College (now Queens College of the City University of New York), B.A., 1960; graduate study at Brown University, 1960-61; Washington University, St. Louis, MO, M.A., 1963, Ph.D., 1968.

ADDRESSES: Home—326 Bryn Mawr Ave., Bala Cynwyd, PA 19004. *Office*—Department of History and Politics, Drexel University, Philadelphia, PA 19104.

CAREER: Queens College of the City University of New York, Flushing, NY, lecturer in history, 1967-68; University of California, Santa Barbara, visiting assistant professor of history, 1968-69; Nassau Community College, Garden City, NY, visiting assistant professor of sociology, 1970-72; University of Miami, Coral Gables, FL, assistant professor, 1972-75, associate professor, 1975-82, professor, 1982-87; Drexel University, Philadelphia, PA, professor of history, 1987—.

MEMBER: American Historical Association, Conference on British Studies, Phi Beta Kappa, Phi Alpha Theta, Phi Kappa Phi.

AWARDS, HONORS: Phi Alpha Theta prize, 1972, for *The Parliament of 1621;* Tor House Foundation Fellow, 1984; John S. Guggenheim Fellow, 1985-86.

WRITINGS:

The Year One (poems), Blue Oak Press, 1969.
The Parliament of 1621 (nonfiction), University of California Press, 1971.
Lives of the Poet (poems), Barlenmir House, 1974.
(Editor) *A Casebook on Anais Nin* (criticism), New American Library, 1974.
Wind Songs (poetry chapbook), Ragnarok Press, 1976.
(Editor with Richard L. Greaves) *Biographical Dictionary of British Radicals in the Seventeenth Century,* three volumes, Harvester Press, 1982-84.
The Cliffs of Solitude: A Reading of Robinson Jeffers (criticism), Cambridge University Press, 1983.
Europe in Transition 1660-1815, Harper, 1984.
Invisible Music (poems), Mavridis Press, 1988.

(Editor) *The Tribute of His Peers: Elegies for Robinson Jeffers,* Tor House Press, 1989.
(Co-editor and senior author) *Civilizations of the World,* Harper, 1989.

Work anthologized in *For Neruda/For Chile,* edited by Walter Lowenfels, Beacon Press, 1975. Contributor of articles, translations, a play, and reviews to literary and scholarly journals, including *Massachusetts Review, Studies in Romanticism, Critical Inquiry, Michigan Quarterly Review* and *Albion.*

TRANSLATOR OF BOOKS BY WIFE, LILI BITA

Astrapes ste sarka: Lightning in the Flesh, Athens Printing, 1968.
Erotes: Five Love Poems, Guevara Press, 1969.
Furies, Hors Commerce Press, 1969.
Blood Sketches, Guevara Press, 1973.
Sacrifice, Exile, Night, Ragnarok Press, 1976.
Fleshfire: New and Selected Love Poems, Lyra Press, 1980, 2nd augmented edition, 1983.
Firewalkers, Lyra Press, 1984.
Bacchic Odes, Lyra Press, 1986.

ONE-ACT PLAYS

Ampersand, first produced in Miami, FL, at University of Miami, May 19, 1973.
The Elevator, first produced in Miami at Upstage Theatre, February 13, 1976.
The Mayor of Nagasaki, first produced at Upstage Theatre, November 19, 1976, produced on WCKT-TV, October 1, 1977.
The Shrink, first produced at Upstage Theatre, March 11, 1977.

Also author of one-act plays *Pelf,* 1976, *Sauna,* 1976, *Lockup,* 1977, *Crawlspace,* 1978, and full-length play, *Mayakovsky!,* 1986.

SIDELIGHTS: In their three-volume work, *Biographical Dictionary of British Radicals in the Seventeenth Century,* Robert Zaller and Richard L. Greaves include historical figures who "sought fundamental change by striking at the very root of contemporary assumptions and institutions." Unlike those who argue that the English Revolution resulted more from factional squabbles among special interest groups than from opposition to the Stuart monarchy, Zaller and Greaves stress the war's long-term, underlying causes, focusing on "what some have lately ignored, namely the indebtedness of the parliamentary supporters of the 1640s to the legal and political principles worked out in the preceding decades." The Civil War, they argue "was not an accidental aberration into which men unwittingly stumbled in 1642."

According to the *Times Literary Supplement,* "These volumes remind us how many civilized ideas and practices which we now take for granted originated among obscure and often lower or middle-class radicals." Another *Times Literary Supplement* reviewer notes that Zaller and Greaves "are to be congratulated on a worthwhile job well done. . . . A number of fascinating and hitherto obscure characters have been revealed to illuminate our understanding of the English Revolution." The *Biographical Dictionary,* concludes the reviewer, is "a valuable research tool."

BIOGRAPHICAL/CRITICAL SOURCES:

PERIODICALS

Times Literary Supplement, August 6, 1982; October 21, 1983; February 15, 1985.

* * *

ZAVALA, Iris M(ilagros) 1936-

PERSONAL: Born December 27, 1936, in Ponce, Puerto Rico; daughter of Romualdo and Maria M. (Zapata) Zavala. *Education:* University of Puerto Rico, B.A., 1957; University of Salamanca, M.A., 1961, Ph.D. (summa cum laude), 1962. *Politics:* None. *Religion:* None.

ADDRESSES: Home—Keizersgracht 71, 1015 CE Amsterdam, Netherlands. *Office*—Rijksuniversiteit te Utrecht, Faculteit der Letteren, Kromme Nieuwegracht 29, 3512 HD Utrecht, Netherlands.

CAREER: University of Puerto Rico, Río Piedras, assistant professor of Spanish literature, 1962-64; Hunter College of the City University of New York, New York City, assistant professor of Hispanic literature, 1968-69; State University of New York at Stony Brook, associate professor, 1969-71, professor of Hispanic and comparative literature, 1971-83, joint professor of comparative literature, 1976-83, director of graduate studies, 1970-72 and 1975-1981, chair, 1973-74; Rijksuniversiteit Utrecht, Utrecht, Netherlands, chair of Hispanic literatures, 1983—, chair and director of Spanish Institute, 1984—. Visiting lecturer, Queens College, 1966; visiting professor, University of Puerto Rico, 1978 and 1981, and Universitá della Calabria, 1985; visiting scholar, El Colegio de México, 1979. Consultant, Casa de España (Utrecht), 1984—. Has conducted more than 90 lectures throughout Europe, the United States, and Latin America. Consultant to universities and organizations. Member, National Committee, 46th International Congress of Americanists, 1985-86.

MEMBER: Modern Language Association of America (Spanish 5, member of executive committee, 1972-73, chairman, 1974-75; member of commission on minority groups, 1973-74), American Association of Teachers of Spanish and Portuguese (member of committee on bilingual education, 1971-72), Society for Spanish and Portuguese Historical Studies (member of executive council, 1968-72).

AWARDS, HONORS: Grant, University of Puerto Rico, 1963; grant, Instituto de Cultura Puertorriqueña, 1964; research fellow, El Colegio de México, 1964; research fellow, Organization of American States, 1964-65; award from American Philosophical Society, 1966; Guggenheim fellow, 1966-67; grant, Social Science Research Council, 1972; award from American Council of Learned Societies/Social Science Research Council, 1972-73; Premio de Literatura Puertorriqueña (National Literary Prize, Puerto Rico), 1964, 1965, and 1972; grants, State University of New York at Stony Brook, 1969 and 1970; Premio del Instituto de Literatura (New York and Puerto Rico), 1978; Finalista Premio Herralde (novela), 1983; Condecoration from King Juan Carlos of Spain, Encomienda, Lazo de Dama de la Orden de Mérito Civil, 1988, for contributions made to Spanish culture.

WRITINGS:

Unamuno y su teatro de conciencia (title means "Unamuno and His Philosophical Theatre"), Acta Salmanticensia, University of Salamanca (Salamanca, Mexico), 1963.
Barro doliente (poems; title means "Repenting Clay"), La Isla de los Ratones (Santander), 1965.
La angustia y el hombre: Ensayos de literatura española (main title means "Literature of Anguish in the 19th Century"), Universidad Veracruzana (Mexico), 1965.
(Editor with Clara E. Lida) *La Revolución de 1868: Historia, pensamiento, literatura* (title means "Revolution of 1868: History, Thought, and Literature"), Las Américas, 1970.
Masones, comuneros y carbonarios, Siglo Veintiuno (Madrid), 1970.
Ideología y política en la novela española del siglo XIX (title means "Ideology and Politics in the 19th Century Spanish Novel"), Anaya (Madrid), 1971.
Poemas prescindibles (title means "Dispensable Poems"), Anti-Ediciones Villa Miseria, 1972.
Románticos y socialistas: Prensa española del XIX, Siglo Veintiuno, 1972.
(Editor with Rafael Rodríguez; also author of introduction) *Libertad y crítica en el ensayo puertorriqueño,* Puerto, 1973, revised edition translated as *The Intellectual Roots of Independence: An Anthology of Puerto Rican Political Essays,* Monthly Review Press, 1979.
Escritura desatada (poetry), Puerto, 1974.
Fin de siglo: Modernismo, 98 y bohemia, Cuadernos para el Diálogo (Madrid), 1974.
(Editor) Alejandra Sawa, *Iluminaciones en la sombra,* [Madrid], 1977, 2nd edition, Alhambra (Madrid), 1986.
Clandestinidad y libertinaje erudito en los albores del siglo XVIII, Ariel (Barcelona), 1978.
(With Carlos Blanco Aguinaga and Julio Rodríguez Puértolas) *Historia social de la literatura española (en lengua castellana),* three volumes, Castalia (Madrid), 1978-79, 2nd edition, 1983.
El texto en la historia, Nuestra Cultura (Madrid), 1981.
Kiliagonía (novela), Premiá Editora, 1982, translation by Susan Pensak published as *Chiliagony,* Third Woman Press, Indiana University, 1984.
Historia y crítica de la literatura española, Volume 5: *Romanticismo y realismo,* Crítica (Barcelona), 1982.
Que nadie muera sin amar el mar (poetry), Visor (Madrid), 1983.
(Editor with Myriam Díaz-Diocaretz) *Women, Feminist Identity, and Society in the 1980's: Selected Papers,* Benjamins (Amsterdam), 1985.
(Editor with Teun A. van Dijk and Díaz-Diocaretz) *Approaches to Discourse, Poetics, and Psychiatry,* Benjamins, 1987.
Nocturna mas no funesta (novela), Montesinos (Barcelona), 1987.
Lecturas y lectores del discurso narrativo dieciochesco, Rodopi (Amsterdam), 1987.

(With others) *Estelas, laberintos, nuevas sendas: Unamuno, Valle-Inclán, García Lorca, la Guerra Civil,* Anthropos (Barcelona), 1988.

Romanticismo y costumbrismo, Espasa Calpe (Madrid), 1989.

Rubén Darío bajo el signo del cisne, University of Puerto Rico, 1989.

(Editor) *El modernismo y otros ensayos de Rubén Darío,* Alianza (Madrid), 1989.

Modernidad, carnaval político, esperpento: Valle Inclán, Orígenes (Madrid), 1989.

Unamuno y el pensamiento dialógico, Anthropos, 1990.

Teorías de la modernidad, Tuero (Madrid), 1990.

Estudios sobre Bajtin y su círculo, Espasa Calpe, 1990.

Contributor of over 80 articles to publications throughout Europe, the United States, and Latin America. Editor of books series, including "Critical Theory: Interdisciplinary Approaches to Language, Discourse and Ideology," Benjamins, 1984—, "Teoría Literaria: Texto y Teoría," Rodopi, 1986—, and a series for Alianza Editorial/Alianza Teoría, 1989—. Member of editorial or advisory boards to journals in the United States, Latin America, and Europe.

WORK IN PROGRESS: El libro de Apolonia o de las islas (novel); *La concupiscencia de los ojos: Historia apócrifa del bolero* (creative essay); *The Great Narrative: Hispanic Modernism and the Social Imaginary,* for Indiana University Press.

SIDELIGHTS: Iris M. Zavala told *CA:* "I continue to maintain my adolescent goals: that scholarship and creation are the same creative process and that I will try to merge them. Therefore, the reader (if any) will find that my books of poetry and my novella make wide use of history, philosophy, art, literature and foreign languages. Many friends have helped me in writing my books, most are dead and illustrious: Dante, Cervantes, Erasmus, Goethe, Marx. Their peculiar erudition will save me, I hope, from lamentable blunders. Indefatigable research in archives and libraries has given me whatever understanding I have of memories, expectations and disappointments.

"Since in the capitalist age a human being must dutifully put on layers of makeup and dress, Ms. Zavala is a professor of Hispanic and comparative literature, a literary critic and a poet. I earnestly hope that I have been able to slip out of each new fashion, reappraising to my readers the nature of literature, bedfellow of truth."

BIOGRAPHICAL/CRITICAL SOURCES:

PERIODICALS

Choice, January, 1981.*

* * *

ZEIGFREID, Karl
See FANTHORPE, R(obert) Lionel

* * *

ZELL, Hans M(artin) 1940-

PERSONAL: Born January 27, 1940, in Zurich, Switzerland; son of Oskar and Edith (Frey) Zell. *Education:* Received degree from Swiss Institute of Commerce.

ADDRESSES: Home—11 Richmond Rd., Oxford OX1 3EL, England. *Office*—Hans Zell Associates, 11 Richmond Rd., P.O. Box 56, Oxford OX1 3EL, England.

CAREER: Fritz Kellerhals AG (booksellers), Zurich, Switzerland, apprentice bookseller, 1956-59; Haigh & Hochland Ltd.,

Manchester, England, bookshop assistant, 1959-60; Almqvist & Wiksell AB, Stockholm, Sweden, editor for bibliographic and information services, 1960-62; Robert Maxwell & Co. Ltd., Oxford, England, and Maxwell Scientific International, Inc., Long Island, NY, editor for documentation and supply center, 1962-65; Pergamon Press, Oxford, manager of Direct Mail Sales Division, 1963-65; University of Sierra Leone, Fourah Bay College, Freetown, Sierra Leone, manager of university bookstore, 1965-68; Africana Publishing Corp., New York City, editor-in-chief, 1968-71; University of Ife Press, Ile-Ife, Nigeria, director, 1971-73; Hans Zell Publishers, Oxford, director, 1974—; Hans Zell Associates, Oxford, free-lance publishing consultant, 1987—. Secretary of Noma Award Managing Committee, 1979—. Consultant to UNESCO, Ford Foundation, IDRC, African Books Collective Ltd., and Zimbabwe International Book Fair.

MEMBER: African Studies Association (England), African Studies Association (United States).

AWARDS, HONORS: Helen F. Conover-Dorothy Porter Award, African Studies Association, 1984, for *A New Reader's Guide to African Literature.*

WRITINGS:

New Reference Tools for Librarians: 1962-1963, Maxwell, 1964.
New Reference Tools for Librarians: 1964-1965, Maxwell, 1965.
(With Robert J. Machesney) *An International Bibliography of Non-Periodical Literature on Documentation and Information,* Maxwell, 1965.
Freetown Vade Mecum, Fourah Bay College Bookshop, 1966.
Writings by West Africans, Sierra Leone University Press, 1968.
(Editor with Helene Silver) *A Reader's Guide to African Literature,* Heinemann Educational, 1972, 2nd edition (with Carol Bundy and Virginia Coulon) published as *A New Reader's Guide to African Literature,* Africana Publishing, 1983.
(Editor) *African Books in Print: An Index by Author, Subject, and Title/Libres africains disponibles: Index par auteurs, matieres, et titres,* two volumes, International School Book Service, 1975, 4th edition, Mansell Publishing, in press.
(With Edwina Oluwasanmi and Eva McLean) *Publishing in Africa in the Seventies,* University of Ife Press, 1975.
The African Book World and Press: A Directory/Repertoire du livre et de la presse en Afrique, Hans Zell Publishers, 1977, 4th edition, 1989.
Publishing and Book Development in Africa: A Bibliography, UNESCO, 1984.
The African Studies Companion: A Resource Guide and Directory, Hans Zell Publishers/Bowker-K. G. Saur, 1989.

Contributor of articles and reviews to scholarly and professional journals. Contributing specialist to African literature sections of *PMLA Annual Bibliography,* 1973-84. Editor, *Africana Library Journal,* 1969-70, and *African Book Publishing Record,* 1975—.

WORK IN PROGRESS: Research on contemporary African literature and on publishing and book development in Africa.

BIOGRAPHICAL/CRITICAL SOURCES:

PERIODICALS

Times Literary Supplement, April 6, 1984.

ZUROMSKIS, Diane
   See STANLEY, Diane

                    *   *   *

ZUROMSKIS, Diane Stanley
   See STANLEY, Diane